Addictive Behaviors

READINGS ON ETIOLOGY, PREVENTION, AND TREATMENT

EDITED BY

G. Alan Marlatt and Gary R. VandenBos

AMERICAN PSYCHOLOGICAL ASSOCIATION • WASHINGTON, DC

First printing November 1997
Second printing September 1998

Published by
American Psychological Association
750 First Street, NE
Washington, DC 20002

Copies may be ordered from
American Psychological Association
Order Department
P.O. Box 92984
Washington, DC 20090-2984

In the UK and Europe, copies may be ordered from
American Psychological Association
3 Henrietta Street
Covent Garden, London
WC2E 8LU England

Typeset in Goudy by EPS Group Inc., Easton, MD

Printer: Edwards Brothers, Inc., Ann Arbor, MI
Cover designer: Berg Design, Albany, NY
Technical / Production Editor: Olin J. Nettles

Library of Congress Cataloging-in-Publication Data

Addictive behaviors : readings on etiology, prevention, and treatment
    / edited by G. Alan Marlatt, Gary R. VandenBos.—1st ed.
    p.   cm.
    Includes bibliographical references and index.
    ISBN 1-55798-468-9 (acid-free paper)
    1. Substance abuse.   I. Marlatt, G. Alan.   II. VandenBos, Gary R.
RC564.A315   1997
616.86—dc21
                                                                97-37315
                                                                CIP

British Library Cataloguing-in-Publication Data
A CIP record is available from the British Library.

Printed in the United States of America

CONTENTS

114477

CONTRIBUTORS

Robert Abbott
Arthur I. Alterman
James C. Anthony
Raymond F. Anton
Jerald G. Bachman
Gary J. Badger
Martha C. Beattie
Alan S. Bellack
P. M. Bentler
Warren K. Bickel
Jack J. Blanchard
Benjamin P. Bowser
Penny L. Brennan
David Brody
Lawrence Brown
Alan J. Budney
Kathleen M. Carroll
Richard F. Catalano
Laurie Chassin
Craig R. Colder
R. Lorraine Collins
Frances M. Costa
Patrick J. Curran
Frank deGruy
Carlo C. Diclemente
Stewart I. Donaldson
Austin L. Errico
Florian E. Foerg
Mary Gillmore
John W. Graham
Grant R. Grissom
Steven Hahn
William B. Hansen
Philip W. Harden
J. David Hawkins
Stephen T. Higgins

A. Elizabeth Hirky
Gary W. Holden
Andrea M. Hussong
Carl E. Isenhart
Tiffany A. Ito
Richard Jessor
Jeffrey G. Johnson
Lloyd D. Johnston
Ronald C. Kessler
Henry R. Kranzler
Claudia Krenz
Kurt Kroenke
Mark Linzer
Richard Longabaugh
Lester Luborsky
Paul A. McDermott
James R. McKay
A. Thomas McLellan
Grace McNamara
David S. Metzger
Norman Miller
William R. Miller
Michael S. Moncher
Rudolf H. Moos
Diane Morrison
Kim T. Mueser
Peter E. Nathan
Michael D. Newcomb
David B. Newlin
Sara J. Nixon
Nora Noel
John C. Norcross
Charles P. O'Brien
Doris Ogden
Patrick M. O'Malley

Oscar A. Parsons
Andrea M. Piccinin
Robert O. Pihl
Jerome J. Platt
Vicki E. Pollock
James O. Prochaska
Michele M. Pukish
Harold Rosenberg
Lawrence M. Scheier
John Schulenberg
Daniel J. Silversmith
Edward C. Snider
Robert L. Spitzer
Robert Stout
Ralph E. Tarter
John Tassey
James B. Thomson
J. Scott Tonigan
Joseph E. Trimble
Jalie A. Tucker
Mark S. Turbin
Donato Vaccaro
Jill Van Den Bos
Judith Vanderryn
Michael Vanyukov
Rudy E. Vuchinich
Katherine N. Wadsworth
Lynn A. Warner
Elizabeth Wells
Janet B. W. Williams
Thomas Ashby Wills
Philip W. Wirtz
George E. Woody
Carl O. Word
Arturo Zaballero

INTRODUCTION

G. ALAN MARLATT

Psychologists are becoming more involved in the etiology, prevention, and treatment of addictive behaviors. Research shows that behavioral habits such as smoking, drinking, and other substance use are associated with a wide variety of problems both for individuals who engage in addictive behaviors and for the larger society in which we live. Addictive behavior problems may appear in a variety of contexts, from harmful health effects and social and family problems to economic and legal difficulties. Psychologists play critical roles in this agenda, including undertaking basic research studies on mechanisms of drug action, studying the epidemiology and etiology of drug and alcohol use and problems, developing and evaluating effective prevention and treatment programs, and studying the effects of drug policy on human behavior.

The addictive behaviors field in psychology is growing in leaps and bounds. Consider, for example, the following recent developments, all of which have occurred in the mid-1990s:

- The APA established a new Division on Addictions (Division 50) for members interested in research and practice in the field of substance abuse and addictive behaviors. The journal *Psychology of Addictive Behaviors* is published by this division.
- The APA's College of Professional Psychology is now providing a Certificate of Proficiency in the assessment and treatment of alcohol and other psychoactive drug problems for psychologists who have expertise in this area of specialty.
- The managed care revolution has led to the development of

the concept of "behavioral health"—an umbrella term that subsumes the previously disparate fields of mental health and substance abuse into an integrated treatment approach to "dual-disorder" or "comorbidity" problems (e.g., integration of treatment for alcohol and depression problems in the same client).

■ Federal funding and grant support for psychologists working in the addictive behaviors field has increased dramatically in the last few years. Two recent examples are the following: "Project Match," the largest study of psychosocial and behavioral treatment matching in the alcoholism field, is funded by the National Institute for Alcohol Abuse and Alcoholism (NIAAA); and the National Institute of Drug Abuse (NIDA) has also greatly increased funding for the development of new behavior therapies for substance abuse. Both the NIAAA and the NIDA provide significant research and training funding for psychologists.

A BIOPSYCHOSOCIAL APPROACH TO ADDICTIVE BEHAVIORS

Psychologists have made significant contributions to the study of addictive behavior, from basic research on the etiology and development of these disorders to new and exciting advances in prevention and treatment. New concepts and ground-breaking initiatives in the treatment arena have recently emerged, including the stages of change model, treatment matching, motivational interviewing, relapse prevention, cue exposure, community reinforcement, and brief intervention approaches—all of which have been primarily developed by psychologists.

Most psychologists working in this field embrace a "biopsychosocial" model of addictive behavior. As the term implies, addiction problems have multiple etiological determinants. Attempts to prevent and treat these behaviors also fall into multiple categories. What types of variables are included in a biopsychosocial model of addictive behavior?

Biological factors play a significant role in the etiology and development of addictive behavior problems, including the impact of genetic predisposition, possible intrauterine exposure to maternal substance use, physiological and neurological effects of different substances on brain activity and behavior, and the role of biological mechanisms in the development of drug tolerance and withdrawal. Recent advances in the pharmacotherapy of addictive disorders are also based on biological mechanisms of action—examples include methadone maintenance in the treatment of opiate dependency, nicotine replacement therapy in smoking cessation, and naltrexone pharmacotherapy for both alcohol and opiate dependency. Most pharmacotherapies are administered in conjunction with structured behavior therapy programs to maximize overall effectiveness.

Psychological issues are also of primary significance in the development and modification of addictive behavior problems. Behavioral psychologists have made seminal contributions to the theory of how addictive problems develop and have enhanced our understanding of the basic learning and reinforcement mechanisms involved. Addictive behaviors are viewed as learned habits that are reinforced by powerful contingencies. Mechanisms of reward range from positive reinforcement (e.g., the euphoric and energy-enhancing effects of cocaine administration) to negative reinforcement (e.g., alcohol's effects on reduction of tension or anxiety).

Research based on cognitive psychology has demonstrated that learned expectancies about the positive and negative consequences of alcohol or other drug use ("outcome expectancies") may lead to psychological dependency on these substances. Other cognitive variables, such as self-efficacy (e.g., confidence in one's ability to resist drug use), motivation or readiness to change drug use, and attributional processes (personal beliefs about the nature of addiction and the process of behavior change) have also been found to impact the initiation, maintenance, and modification of alcohol and other drug use.

Religious beliefs and spiritual practices (e.g., meditation) are also significant psychological factors, particularly in the prevention and treatment of addictive behavior.

Social and cultural variables also contribute considerable influence in the biopsychosocial model. Early childhood experiences have been found to be associated with a range of both protective (e.g., strong family and community social support) and predisposing (e.g, experience of childhood trauma) factors for subsequent addiction problems. Starting with early school experiences, exposure to peer influence and social norms about drug and alcohol have increased influence on an individual's tendency to use or not use substances. Membership in particular cultural groups may also serve to increase or decrease vulnerability to substance problems, along with demographic factors such as gender, age, and socioeconomic status.

Why do many psychologists prefer the term "addictive behavior" to such alternatives as "addiction," "alcoholism," "substance abuse," or "chemical dependency"? First, because psychology is often defined as the study of behavior, psychologists working in this field usually prefer to focus on what people do (drinking, smoking, or ingesting various substances) rather than placing people in fixed diagnostic categories. By focusing on the determinants of how addictive behavior is acquired and how it can be modified through prevention and treatment procedures, the focus shifts to an optimistic potential for behavior change rather than defining "addiction" as a progressive, chronic disease. Choice of terminology is an important one for both therapists and clients, given the stigma and shame often associated with these "taboo" behaviors.

Second, many psychologists are interested in studying certain addictive behaviors that do not directly involve substance use or abuse. The growing interest in defining compulsive gambling as an addictive behavior represents one such counterexample. Other investigators have expressed an interest in studying commonalities among various addictive behaviors (e.g., parallels and differences among binge drinking, binge eating, and excessive sexual behaviors). Such commonalities appear to exist at both micro and macro levels of examination. An example at the molecular level is recent interest on dopamine, a neurotransmitter thought to mediate brain mechanisms associated with the pleasurable consequences of a variety of potentially addictive behaviors, from drugs to sex. At the macro level, to take another example, commonalities are studied in the process of how addictive behaviors are acquired, are maintained over time, and can be modified— as in the stages of change model that has been applied across a variety of addictive habits. Research has also documented commonalities in the process of relapse for individuals treated for various addictive behaviors.

AN OVERVIEW OF THE CHAPTERS

The articles reprinted in this collection of readings were all selected from APA journals published since 1990. The intent here is to highlight articles published by psychologists and their colleagues in the psychological literature. Selection of representative articles was also determined in part by topic coverage. Key articles in 11 topic areas were selected (each represented in a different section of the book): (a) an epidemiological overview, (b) perspectives on etiology, (c) initiation and progression in adolescence, (d) maintenance and course of abuse, (e) prevention and harm reduction, (f) screening and assessment, (g) diagnosis and comorbidity, (h) family dynamics and family impact, (i) treatment approaches and models, (j) planning and managing treatment and recovery, and (k) issues in specific populations. From a list of 67 selected articles published since 1990 in APA journals, a final selection of 33 articles was chosen for publication in this volume. Because of space limitations and to avoid overlap of topic areas, many excellent articles were left out of the final selection.

In the following introductory commentary, each topic area is addressed briefly.

Epidemiological Overview

The first section of the book contains one article that provides an epidemiological overview of the prevalence of drug use in the United

States. Based on data gathered as part of the National Comorbidity Survey, Anthony, Warner, and Kessler (1994) provide an overview of the prevalence of drug dependence among Americans in the 15–54 age group. It is important to note that dependence on legal substances is higher than that for illegal or controlled substances: One out of four Americans report a history of tobacco dependence, and one out of seven have experienced alcohol dependency, whereas only 1 out of 13 report a dependence problem with controlled substances or inhalants. The report also shows that many individuals report the use of multiple substances (combined use of alcohol and tobacco, or polydrug use among substance abusers). The authors conclude that more Americans ages 15–54 suffer from psychoactive drug dependency than from other psychiatric or mental health conditions that now receive priority in health delivery systems.

Perspectives on Etiology

The second section is devoted to perspectives on etiology and contains two articles, both dealing with the development and etiology of alcohol dependence ("alcoholism"). Although important studies have been conducted on the etiology of other drug use, the course of development of alcohol dependence has received the most research attention. The first article, by Tarter and Vanyukov (1994), presents a developmental behavior–genetic perspective. As the authors state, the liability to alcoholism is determined by both genetic and nongenetic components. This article describes a "developmental trajectory" in which phenotypic differences in temperament and developing personality traits interact with the social environment in ways that may culminate in the development of alcohol dependence.

The article by Kranzler and Anton (1994) provides insight into the neuropsychopharmacologic basis of the rewarding effects of alcohol consumption that appear to increase the risk of dependence. Specific subtypes of alcohol dependence are linked to specific neurotransmitter systems; the authors review studies where the serotonergic and opioidergic neurotransmitter systems have shown the most consistent results. This research has important implications for understanding the action of various pharmacotherapies that have been developed in the treatment of alcohol dependence.

Initiation and Progression in Adolescence

Once an individual has experimented with substances or initiated regular drug use, what factors determine an escalated course of problem development among adolescents and young adults? The third section contains two articles that are representative of research on this topic. The purpose of the first article, by Wills, McNamara, Vaccaro, and Hirky (1996), was to determine variables that characterize adolescents who show escalation in substance use (tobacco, alcohol, and marijuana) from early to middle adolescence. In the cohort of adolescents in the 7th to 9th grades, various subgroups of students were identified, including nonusers, minimal experimenters, late starters, and escalators. Those who escalated drug use were found to score higher on such measures as high life stress, nonadaptive coping, deviance-prone attitudes, and parental/peer drug use, as compared with those at less risk.

On the basis of data from the national longitudinal study of high-school graduates (the Monitoring the Future project), the authors of the second article (Schulenberg et al., 1996) investigated determinants of "binge drinking" (usually defined as drinking five or more drinks in a row) in young adults between the ages of 18 and 24. Being male, possessing low self-efficacy, and drinking primarily "to get drunk" were found to be risk factors for increasing binge drinking over time. These results have important implications for formulating effective prevention programs for excessive drinking in adolescents and young adults.

Maintenance and Course of Abuse

Although adolescent use of alcohol and drugs is a risk factor with harmful consequences among teens and young adults, does evidence exist showing that adolescent drug use predicts mental health problems in later adulthood? In the fourth section of this reader, Newcomb, Scheier, and Bentler (1993) address this question in a prospective, longitudinal design involving a sample of almost 500 participants who were assessed at four different times over a 12-year period, beginning when they were young adolescents. A measure of polydrug use was developed that included frequency of using some combination of alcohol, cigarettes, cannabis, cocaine, and other hard drugs. The findings showed that teenage polydrug use itself had few effects on adult mental health problems but that increased poly-drug use over time exacerbated several indicators of adult mental problems (e.g., measures of psychoticism and suicide ideation). More research on the combined course of development of both mental health and addictive disorders is needed in order to improve programs designed to prevent dual-disorder or comorbidity problems in later life.

Prevention and Harm Reduction

Part V focuses on the topic of prevention and harm reduction. Most psychologists, along with public health specialists, define prevention in terms of three goals. The goal of primary prevention programs is to prevent the initiation of drug or alcohol use; programs such as DARE (Drug

Abuse Resistance Education) and those designed to prevent smoking among early adolescents share this goal. Once an individual has already initiated drug use, the goal of secondary prevention is to reduce the harmful consequences of alcohol or other drug use (harm reduction) and to prevent further escalation of problem use, abuse, or dependency. Although harm reduction approaches (such as training young adults responsible or controlled drinking skills) accept abstinence as the "least harmful" option, supporters of harm reduction encourage any decrement in harmful consequences (e.g., reduced blackouts or fewer fights or accidents due to excessive drinking) as an acceptable goal. Finally, the goal of tertiary prevention applies to individuals who have already developed an addictive behavior pattern (substance abuse or dependence): Here the goal is to prevent further harm or to reduce risk of relapse for those in treatment (relapse prevention).

The first of the four articles in this section, by Donaldson and his colleagues (1995), is a study of the effectiveness of primary prevention programs in public and private schools designed to prevent the onset of alcohol or other drug use. Findings from four waves of longitudinal data collected annually from the 5th to the 8th grade with a large sample (12,000 students) demonstrated that resistance-skills training (teaching students refusal skills to combat active social pressure to use drugs) was found to be an effective strategy for preventing the onset of drug use, but only if it is administered in the context of an interactive teaching program that also provides information about peer norms and attitudes about drug use. A potentially harmful counterproductive effect was found, however, for adolescents attending public schools who received only resistance training. These findings parallel those of other studies showing school-based primary prevention programs such as DARE that focus exclusively on alcohol or drug refusal skills (without the added discussion of peer norms in an interactive teacher–student classroom setting) to be largely ineffective in preventing initiation of drug use.

The second article, by Jessor, Van Den Bos, Vanderryn, Costa, and Turbin (1995), focuses on protective factors in adolescent problem behavior. Jessor and his colleagues have pioneered in the development of an influential comprehensive model of adolescent problem behavior that includes alcohol and drug abuse, delinquency, and sexual precocity. Their aim in this longitudinal study of 7th- to 9th-grade adolescents was to identify protective factors (based on measures of personality, perceived environment, and behavior systems) that may mitigate the impact of risk factors (variables that increase the likelihood of drug use and other problem behaviors). Results showed that protective factors do indeed moderate the relation of risk factors to problem behavior. These findings provide valuable information about designing effective prevention programs for adolescents.

The final two articles in this section deal with the controversial topic of controlled drinking. Those who advocate a strict disease model of alcoholism claim that abstinence is the only acceptable goal of treatment, whereas those who support a more behavioral, harm reduction model are open to the possibility that some people with serious drinking problems can learn to moderate or control their alcohol consumption. Rosenberg's article (1993) provides a review of research studies that have attempted to predict controlled drinking outcomes by alcoholics and other problem drinkers. Although no single personal factor (e.g., demographic characteristics, family history of alcoholism, and so forth) consistently predicted a controlled drinking outcome, convincing evidence exists that a lower level of severity of alcohol dependence, along with a belief that controlled drinking is possible, are positively associated with reduced drinking levels.

In the next article, Collins (1993) describes her research on "drinking restraint"—defined as a cognitive preoccupation with control over drinking. Similar to the notion of "restrained eating" (a cognitive preoccupation with diet and control over food intake), drinking restraint may be associated with failures to regulate consumption and increased probability of "losing control" or triggering a bout of binge drinking. The parallels between restraint over eating (dieting) and alcohol consumption (drinking restraint) are interesting and provocative.

Screening and Assessment

Four articles are included in the following section on screening and assessment. Screening individuals for potential alcohol or drug problems is an important assessment goal. The first article, by Errico and his colleagues (1990), describes one such screening instrument, the Neurological Impairment Scale (NIS). As with other screening instruments, the NIS is a brief, self-report instrument in the form of a 50-item symptom checklist. Results from this study show that this screening instrument reliably differentiated between alcoholic and control subjects, who were also assessed using a comprehensive battery of neuropsychological tests.

A more detailed assessment instrument, the Addictive Severity Index (ASI), is described in the second article, by McDermott and his coauthors (1996). The ASI is a widely used structured interview designed to assess seven areas of problem functioning: medical, employment, alcohol use, drug use, legal, family–social, and psychiatric problems. As such, the ASI provides a more comprehensive assessment of an individual's life problems associated with their alcohol or drug use and provides a valuable instrument for treatment matching and individualized intervention programs. This article reports a series of analyses that confirm the validity and reliability of the various scales of the ASI.

The third article in this section, by Insenhart and Silversmith (1996), provides data showing that response styles (test-taking attitudes) on the

MMPI-2 are related to alcohol problems among inpatients in treatment for alcohol dependence. Results confirmed that three distinct response style subgroups could be identified (defensive, straightforward, and exaggerated styles) and related to subgroups of alcohol dependency as identified by two independent alcohol assessment instruments.

The fourth and final article in this section describes a questionnaire designed to assess motivation for change among problem drinkers: the Stages of Change Readiness and Treatment Eagerness Scale (SOCRATES), developed by Miller and Tonigan (1996). This scale is designed to assess personal motivation to change drinking behavior (readiness for treatment) and is derived from the "Stages of Change" model, described in further detail by Prochaska, Diclemente, and Norcross (1992; see the first article in Part X of this book). Miller and Tonigan provide data on the reliability of the scale and a factor analysis of items; one such factor, defined as problem recognition, was found to be related to intensity of alcohol consumption and related problems. Treatment programs that attempt to match interventions to the patient's readiness to change may help to increase treatment effectiveness and reduce drop-out rates.

Diagnosis and Comorbidity

The four articles in Part VII extend the topic of screening and assessment to diagnosis and comorbidity. The topic of comorbidity or "dual diagnosis" refers to the coexistence of primary health or psychiatric conditions among many individuals who have been diagnosed as having an alcohol or drug problem. The first paper in this series (Johnson et al., 1995) presents the findings of a large sample of primary health care patients with alcohol abuse and dependence who were also diagnosed for potential comorbid psychiatric or health problems. Results showed that patients with alcohol or other drug problems were diagnosed with substantial psychiatric comorbidity and reported poorer health functioning than did patients without any psychiatric disorders. The second article, by Mueser, Bellack, and Blanchard (1992), narrows the focus of comorbidity to schizophrenia and substance abuse conditions. The article provides a review of the prevalence of this comorbid disorder, including the clinical effects of substance abuse on the course of the psychiatric illness. The article concludes with a discussion of principles of treatment for these dual-diagnosed patients.

Nathan's article (1991) on substance use disorders in the *DSM-IV* provides a history and overview of how substance abuse and dependence are defined (diagnostic criteria) in the latest edition of the *Diagnostic and Statistical Manual of Mental Disorders*. The *DSM-IV* distinguishes between alcohol or substance abuse (drinking or drug use in situations that cause problems or increase the risk of harm) and dependence (drinking or drug use that is thought to be primarily determined by physical tolerance and avoidance of withdrawal symptoms). Nathan draws attention to three important issues: (a) guidelines to distinguish behaviors associated with substance abuse from psychiatric disorders with similar behavioral consequences, (b) the predictive validity of possible alcoholic subtypes based on family history, and (c) the relationship of organic brain syndromes to intoxication and withdrawal.

The final article, by Ito, Miller, and Pollock (1996), provides results from a meta-analysis of studies that have investigated the relationship between alcohol consumption and aggressive behavior. Many of these studies explored the theoretical explanations of how alcohol may increase aggression by decreasing sensitivity to cues that would normally inhibit aggressive responding. Results show that three social–psychological variables may exert a moderating effect: provocation to aggression, frustration, and self-focused attention. The studies found that the aggressiveness of intoxicated participants relative to sober ones increased as a function of frustration but decreased as a function of provocation and self-focused attention. These findings may benefit programs designed to prevent alcohol-induced aggression (e.g., domestic violence).

Family Dynamics and Family Impact

A family history of alcohol problems is often predictive of increased risk of drinking problems among offspring. The three articles in Part VIII all address different aspects of family dynamics, and the impact of a family history of alcohol dependence. Studies of this kind are important in terms of differentiating the shared influence of genetics, family dynamics, and environment on the development of drinking problems in children of alcoholics. In the first article, by Harden and Pihl (1995), boys with an average age of 12 who came from families with an extensive history of paternal alcoholism differed from controls of similar age and IQ on several measures: cognitive function, cardiovascular reactivity, and parent-rated conduct problems. Boys with a positive family history of alcoholism performed most poorly on neuropsychological tests of frontal-lobe function (e.g., impaired memory function). The authors discuss how these factors may increase the risk of alcohol abuse in these high-risk youth, with important implications for prevention and treatment.

In the second article, Chassin and her colleagues (1996) report the results of a longitudinal study testing the effects of parental alcoholism on adolescent substance abuse. Findings indicate that male adolescents with alcoholic fathers and adolescents with drug-using peers developed more substance use over time than did adolescents without alcoholic fathers (especially girls) or without drug-using peers. Family environmental factors (e.g., stress levels and father's monitoring of child behavior) were found to be possible mediators of paternal alcoholism effects.

The third article in this section, by Newlin and Thomson (1990), provides a literature review of one possible psychobiological marker for alcoholism: response to an acute administration of alcohol, and how this may differ between individuals with and without a family history of alcoholism. Although some investigators have claimed that sons of alcoholic fathers are less sensitive to the effects of alcohol, Newlin and Thomson theorize that sons of alcoholics exhibit greater sensitivity to the effects as blood-alcohol levels increase, compared with sons of nonalcoholics, but show greater tolerance to the negative effects as blood-alcohol levels begin to fall. Newlin and Thomson's theoretical formulations, if confirmed, strongly suggest that the male offspring of alcoholic fathers may find alcohol more reinforcing because they are likely to experience heightened feelings of pleasure and euphoria on initial intoxication, and have a greater tolerance against anxiety and depression as blood-alcohol levels drop.

Treatment Approaches and Models

Four articles describe different treatment approaches and models in Part IX. Because no single approach appears to be more effective than others in the treatment of addictive behavior problems, a wide variety of treatment alternatives are currently available. As a result, interest in matching patients to the best available treatment (treatment matching) is currently a "hot topic" in addiction treatment research. As the first paper by Tucker and her coauthors (1995) shows, there may be common environmental factors associated with recovery from alcohol problems, whether or not formal treatment has been implemented. In their study of three groups of abstinent problem drinkers with different help-seeking histories (no treatment, Alcoholics Anonymous [AA] only, or treatment combined with AA), common environmental events were associated with successful recovery for former problem drinkers in all three groups over a 4-year period (2 years before and 2 years after becoming abstinent). Events common to recovery (molar environmental contexts) included decreased problems related to health, legal issues, and intimate and family relations for all participants, regardless of exposure to prior treatment. This article is an excellent example of research that has studied the "natural history" of recovery for individuals who resolve alcohol or drug problems on their own.

Treatment matching is the focus of the second article, by Longabaugh and colleagues (1995). Treatment matching research is designed to determine if patients with particular individual differences respond differentially to various addiction treatment approaches. In this study, patients were randomly assigned to one of three treatments: brief broad-spectrum treatment, relationship enhancement therapy, or a cognitive–behavioral treatment program. One important matching result from the 18-month follow-up showed that relationship enhancement therapy was significantly more effective in increasing abstinence for those patients who had a social network unsupportive of abstinence. The authors conclude that patient relationships should be assessed prior to relationship enhancement therapy.

Yet another treatment approach, that of contingency contracting, is explored in the next article, by Higgins and his colleagues (1995). In this treatment outcome study, cocaine-dependent outpatients were randomly assigned to one of three treatment conditions: (a) a behavioral intervention based on the community reinforcement approach with a contingency incentive program in which cocaine abstinence was reinforced by giving participants vouchers that could be exchanged for retail items, (b) a control condition of standard counseling, or (c) a third control condition of community reinforcement therapy without the added contingency incentive. Although follow-up results showed significant improvements in all three treatment conditions, only those receiving the contingency contracting also showed significant improvements in efficacy ratings (confidence in resisting relapse).

Behavioral intervention programs such as that reported by Higgins are often applied in combination with pharmacotherapies for drug dependence. In a comprehensive review article by O'Brien (1996), various pharmacotherapies are reviewed in terms of treatment efficacy. The results of his review suggest that although controlled studies reveal that some medications can be effective in the treatment of patients dependent on nicotine, alcohol, or opiates, no medications have been developed thus far that have demonstrated effectiveness in the treatment of patients dependent on cocaine, cannabinoids, sedatives, or hallucinogens. Considerable research effort is now underway to evaluate the effectiveness of other intervention approaches that combine pharmacotherapy with other behavioral or psychosocial treatments.

Planning and Managing Treatment and Recovery

The topic of treatment is continued in Part X on planning and managing treatment and recovery. Four articles are reprinted in this section. One of the most influential models in the addictive behavior change literature is the "Stages of Change" model described in the article by Prochaska, Diclemente, and Norcross (1992). Originally developed as a model of how people progress through various stages in their attempt to give up smoking, the model has been subsequently applied to a wide variety of addictive behaviors, as illustrated in this article. The key assumption of this model is that people progress through several stages (defined as precontemplation, contemplation, preparation, action, and maintenance) in attempting to modify an addictive behavior. Treatments that attempt to match interventions to the patient's unique "stage" are recommended; for patients in the precontemplation or contemplation stages, motivational enhancement strategies may be more effective than "action" strategies such as skills training, for example.

In the maintenance stage of behavior change, treatment approaches are often designed to maintain treatment gains and prevent relapse. Carroll (1996) provides a concise review of relapse prevention (RP) as a treatment for addictive behavior problems. RP treatment methods are designed to teach patients coping skills to prevent lapses to alcohol or drug use and to help those who have relapsed to get "back on track" in their recovery process. In a review of almost 25 randomized controlled trials of this approach, Carroll reports that across substances of abuse but most strongly for smoking cessation, there is evidence for the effectiveness of RP compared with no-treatment control conditions. Outcomes in which RP appears to hold particular promise include reducing the severity of relapses when they occur and enhanced durability of effects (RP often has a "delayed emergent" effect in which many patients show gradual improvement over time as they practice and implement new coping responses). Studies have also indicated that RP may have better results for patients at higher levels of impairment along such dimensions as psychopathology or severity of dependence.

In the third article, McLellan and his colleagues (1994) report on the similarity of outcome predictors across opiate, cocaine, and alcohol treatments. (McLellan and colleagues also developed the Addiction Severity Index described in section 6.) Patients receiving treatment for these addictive behaviors in a variety of treatment centers were followed for a period of 6 months. As reported in Tucker's paper in Part IX, the McLellan team found that outcomes were predicted by similar factors, regardless of the drug used or the type of treatment setting. Greater relapse rates at follow-up were predicted only by greater severity of alcohol and drug use at treatment admission, not by the number of services received during treatment. Other findings revealed that more severe psychiatric, employment, and family problems at admission predicted poorer social adjustment at follow-up; for patients receiving treatment services for these problems, however, outcome was more positive. These findings indicate that successful treatment approaches need to respond to a wide variety of patient problems and not be restricted solely to a focus on substance abuse.

The final article in this section addresses the vocational rehabilitation of drug abusers. In his review of the literature on this topic, Platt (1995) covers a number of variables thought to affect the vocational rehabilitation of drug users, along with programs that have been established to promote employment in this population. The author notes that a number of successful programs have been demonstrated in this regard (e.g., Employment

Assistance Programs). Employment is also often used as a source of reinforcement to maintain abstinence in the community reinforcement approach.

Issues in Specific Populations

Part XI presents four articles on the final topic of issues in specific populations with substance abuse problems. The relationship between life stressors and drinking problems among late-life problem drinkers is explored in the first article by Brennan and Moos (1990). Compared with nonproblem drinkers in late life, problem drinkers reported significantly more negative life events, chronic stressors, and deficits in social resources. Important gender differences were also noted (e.g., problem-drinking older men report more stressors related to finances and friends, whereas their female counterparts report more negative life events and ongoing marital difficulties).

In the second article, Bowser and Word (1993) report the results of a study comparing African–American adolescent crack cocaine users and nonusers in a San Franciso housing project. Interviews with all participants revealed that the long-term quality of family, peer, and community interactions appeared to differentiate crack users from nonusers. For example, before starting crack use, users were more likely to spend time alone or with friends at holidays than with their immediate family; users were also less likely to recall pleasant childhood memories. These results can be used to better inform community and peer-based prevention programs for African American youth who are at risk for drug problems.

Another culture at risk for alcohol and substance use problems is the Native American population, particularly among adolescents and young adults. In the third article in this section, Moncher, Holden, and Trimble (1990) provide a comprehensive review of alcohol and drug problems among American Indian youth, their families, and their communities. The need for culturally appropriate prevention technology is addressed, along with suggestions on how to cope with problems of stereotyping and stigmatization.

In the final article in this section, Catalano and his colleagues (1993) address culturally appropriate prevention programs for drug abuse, using data from a study of alcohol and drug use in 5th grade African American and European American students. Comparisons between the two ethnic groups showed that although European American children have higher rates of initiation to tobacco and alcohol use, risk factors for other drug use are the same for both groups. Implications of these findings for developing culturally appropriate drug abuse prevention programs are discussed.

This selection of readings from journals published by the APA is meant to provide a sample of the diverse psychological research on addictive behaviors. However, no single volume can do justice to this exciting and rapidly expanding field. Other work, some of equal importance, has had to be left out because of page limitations. To delve deeper into the field, readers might consult the references at the end of each chapter, which provide a further wealth of studies. We hope that, eventually, this volume will energize at least a few to contribute their insights and analyses to this growing field.

I

AN EPIDEMIOLOGICAL OVERVIEW

1

COMPARATIVE EPIDEMIOLOGY OF DEPENDENCE ON TOBACCO, ALCOHOL, CONTROLLED SUBSTANCES, AND INHALANTS: BASIC FINDINGS FROM THE NATIONAL COMORBIDITY SURVEY

JAMES C. ANTHONY, LYNN A. WARNER, AND RONALD C. KESSLER

The aim of this article is to report basic descriptive findings from new research on the epidemiology of drug dependence syndromes, conducted as part of the National Comorbidity Survey (NCS). In this study, our research team secured a nationally representative sample and applied standardized diagnostic assessments in a way that allows direct comparisons across prev-

Reprinted from *Experimental and Clinical Psychopharmocology*, 2, 244–268. (1994).

The National Comorbidity Survey (NCS) is a collaborative epidemiologic investigation of the prevalence, causes, and consequences of psychiatric morbidity and comorbidity in the United States. The NCS is supported by U.S. Public Health Service Grants MH 46376 and MH 49098 with supplemental support from the National Institute on Drug Abuse and W. T. Grant Foundation Grant 90135190.

Preparation of this article was supported by the National Institute on Drug Abuse Addiction Research Center. We acknowledge H. Chilcoat for valuable research assistance.

alence estimates and correlates of tobacco dependence, alcohol dependence, and dependence on other psychoactive drugs (Kessler et al., 1994).

For this overview of the survey's findings, a primary goal has been to answer two basic epidemiologic questions about drug dependence involving tobacco, alcohol, controlled drugs such as cocaine, and inhalants: First, in the population under study, what proportion of persons now qualifies as a currently active or former case of drug dependence? Second, where are the affected cases more likely to be found within the sociodemographic structure of the study population?

In addition, population estimates presented in this article shed light on the epidemiology of dependence on tobacco, alcohol, and the following individual drugs and drug groups: cannabis; heroin; cocaine; psychostimulants other than cocaine; analgesic drugs; a drug group consisting of anxiolytic, sedative, and hypnotic drugs; psychedelic drugs; and inhalant drugs. The following population estimates are presented for each of these listed drugs, including tobacco and alcohol: (a) lifetime prevalence of drug dependence, evaluated in relation to criteria published in the *Diagnostic and Statistical Manual of Mental Disorders*, Third Edition, Revised (DSM–III–R; American Psychiatric Association, 1987); (b) lifetime prevalence of extramedical drug use, defined to encompass illicit drug use as well as patients taking prescribed medicines to get high, taking more than was prescribed, or taking medicines for other reasons not intended by the doctor; and (c) the proportion of extramedical users who had become drug dependent.

Using estimates such as these, we seek to describe the broad population experience with forms of psychoactive drug use that generally occur without scrutiny or control by prescribers, pharmacists, or other health practitioners. Although conceding many reasons people might deny or underreport their illicit drug use or drug problems, we draw attention to how often illicit drug use and symptoms of drug use disorders are acknowledged in survey research of this type. For example, on the basis of confidential interviews conducted for the Epidemiologic Catchment Area (ECA) survey more than 10 years ago, we found that one in three adult Americans (30.5%) reported a history of recent or past illicit drug use. On the basis of self-report alone, 20% of these illicit drug users had a history of dependence on controlled substances or a related drug disorder. Not counting tobacco dependence, about one in six adult Americans (17%) met diagnostic criteria for either an alcohol or drug disorder, or both (Anthony & Helzer, 1991). These are substantial estimates that convey the public health significance of drug use and drug dependence in the United States, and they are far too large to be due to the type of exaggeration and overreporting sometimes found in surveys of drug use in early adolescence (Johnston, O'Malley, & Bachman, 1992). If a correction could be made for underreporting, these substantial estimates would be even larger.

In the 14 years since the start of the ECA surveys, the population's drug experience has changed in important ways, with passage through a now-subsiding epidemic of crack smoking and other cocaine use (Harrison, 1992; Kandel, 1991). The NCS chronicles results of these changes and draws strength from some methodological refinements that were not part of the ECA research plan: (a) a nationally representative sample of 15–54-year-olds; (b) a more complete assessment of extramedical drug use, applying measurement strategies developed for the National Household Survey on Drug Abuse (NHSDA; U.S. Department of Health and Human Services [USDHHS], 1993); (c) deliberate alignment of diagnostic criteria and the measurement strategies used to assess dependence on alcohol, tobacco, and other drugs, so as to allow comparisons across drug groups; and (d) more thorough adjustment for nonresponse biases introduced by designated respondents who declined to be assessed, perhaps for reasons connected to alcohol or drug dependence.

The descriptive estimates presented in this overview set the stage for ongoing research in which we are testing hypotheses about suspected determinants and consequences of drug dependence, including links between drug dependence and other psychiatric conditions such as anxiety and mood disorders (Kessler, 1995). These findings may interest pharmacologists and other scientists who are concerned about the population's drug experience outside the boundaries of laboratory and clinical research and practice. Those who study the reinforcing functions of drug use and dependence liability of individual drugs may gain useful insights by considering comparative aspects of the epidemiology of tobacco, alcohol, and other drug dependence, including epidemiologic evidence on the transition from a single occasion of drug use toward the development of drug dependence, a topic of considerable interest within the clinical and research community (e.g., see Anthony, 1991; Glantz & Pickens, 1992; Henningfield, 1992). Investigators also will find these population estimates useful as they seek to substantiate the potential public health significance of their pharmacologic studies or to analyze public policies. Finally, these estimates may have value for primary care practitioners and family doctors, as well as psychologists, psychiatrists, or other specialists who prescribe psychoactive drugs or who need to anticipate how frequently the health status of their patients might be complicated by a history of dependence on tobacco, alcohol, or other drugs.

METHOD AND MATERIALS

The NCS was based on a stratified, multistage area probability sample of persons 15 to 54 years old in the noninstitutionalized civilian population in the 48 coterminous United States, including a representative sample of students living in campus group housing. Fieldwork was carried out by the professional field staff of the Survey Research Center at the University of Michigan between September 14, 1990 and February 6, 1992. To allow midcourse adjustments and adaptation to unanticipated problems, the fieldwork was organized in relation to timed release of six replicate subsamples, each designed to be representative of the study population. Overall response rate was 82.4%, with a total of 8,098 participants. A more detailed discussion of the NCS sampling design and its implementation has been given by Kessler et al. (1994).

After sampling, 1 of the 158 specially trained survey interviewers met with each designated respondent to administer the Composite International Diagnostic Interview (CIDI), as adapted for the NCS to yield detailed information about a broad range of psychiatric disorders, including drug dependence (Cottler et al., 1991; Robins et al., 1988; Wittchen, 1995). These interviewers participated in a 7-day study-specific training program in the use of the CIDI before beginning fieldwork. They were trained to follow a protocol intended to engage the designated respondents' interest in the survey and to reinforce survey participation; to secure a private location for the interview, which most often was within the place of residence; to develop trust and rapport with the respondent and to obtain informed consent before starting the interview; to administer the survey questions, as worded, in a fixed sequence; and to record each subject's responses in a precoded response booklet. The interviewers were not given special training in psychopathology or psychopharmacology, and they were not made aware of any key hypotheses under study or of our research team's interest in the reinforcing functions served by drug use. The highly structured and standardized interview schedule also was used to gather information on suspected correlates and consequences of psychiatric disorders, including educational attainment, occupation, and other characteristics of designated respondents or their households.

Because previous surveys have provided some evidence that survey nonrespondents have more psychiatric disorders than respondents, a supplemental nonresponse survey was conducted in tandem with the main NCS survey. This was done by selecting a random subsample of designated respondents who initially were not interviewed either because of refusal or (in rare cases) inability to contact after many attempts. These persons were asked to complete a short-form version of the diagnostic interview.

Assessment of Alcohol and Other Drug Use

Respondents were asked separate questions on their use of alcoholic beverages, tobacco, and the other individual drugs and drug groups listed below. The survey questions on the frequency and recency of taking controlled substances and inhalants were nearly identical to standardized assessments developed for the NHSDA, now sponsored by the Office of Applied Studies within the Substance Abuse and Mental Health Services Administration. These questions clarified our focus on illicit use of Schedule I drugs such as marijuana, heroin, and LSD, as well as extramedical use of cocaine and other drugs that can be obtained through legitimate medical channels. They were phrased to encompass use of these drugs and medicines "on your own, either without your own prescription from a doctor, or in greater amounts or more often than prescribed, or for any reason other than a doctor said you should take them" (USDHHS, 1993). In addition, respondents were asked whether they had started to feel dependent on a drug while taking it in accord with a doctor's prescription. Ensuing survey questions covered topics such as age of onset, frequency, and recency of extramedical drug use for each of the following individual drugs and drug groups, which were adapted from NHSDA conventions: heroin; other opioids and analgesics that can be obtained through medical channels (e.g., morphine, propoxyphene, codeine); cannabis (marijuana, hashish, or both); psychedelic drugs (e.g., LSD, peyote, mescaline); inhalant drugs (e.g., gasoline or lighter fluids, spray paints, amyl nitrite, nitrous oxide); cocaine (including crack cocaine and freebase); psychostimulants other than cocaine (e.g., dextroamphetamine, methamphetamine); and anxiolytic, sedative, and hypnotic drugs (e.g., secobarbital and diazepam, as well as more recently introduced compounds such as flurazepam, alprazolam, and triazolam).

Consistent with the NHSDA and ECA surveys, the NCS assessment strategy included a detailed verbal description of each drug group and lists of qualifying drugs that were read to each participant, but it did not include the NHSDA colored pill card with pictures of different pharmaceutical products. Furthermore, the NCS interviewer read the questions and recorded each participant's answers on a precoded response form. This approach was consistent with prior ECA surveys on drug dependence but was in contrast with the NHSDA approach of allowing the respondent to self-administer survey questions on drug use. When interviewers administer the questions, it is possible to reduce the impact of low levels of literacy and reading achievement among participants and to use interview skip outs and branching patterns that can shorten the interview and distribute its coverage to other important topics such as suspected risk factors and use of mental health and other medical services. Although we acknowledge that some population groups may report more drug use when they self-administer NHSDA questionnaires (Schober, Caces, Pergamit, & Branden, 1992), we have made a direct comparison of NCS and 1991 NHSDA estimates, generally finding that the estimates were very close to one another, and that the NHSDA estimate always was located within the 95% confidence interval for the corresponding NCS estimate. We return to this topic in the Discussion section.

NCS questions on the use of alcoholic beverages followed a similar NHSDA format and elicited information about age of onset, frequency, recency, and quantity of drinking. Respondents also were asked whether they had consumed at least 12 drinks in any single year of their lives.

Diagnostic Assessment of Alcohol and Other Drug Dependence

The CIDI diagnostic assessment of alcohol and other drug dependence for the NCS was based on DSM–III–R criteria, translated into standardized survey questions for administration by a trained lay interviewer. As in the ECA program method used for Diagnostic Interview Schedule diagnoses (Robins, Helzer, Croughan, & Radcliff, 1985), each participant's answers to the survey questions have been recorded and converted to a machine-readable format, and a computer program has been used to determine whether the diagnostic criteria have been met. As summarized recently by Wittchen (1995), World Health Organization field trials and other methodological studies have provided evidence that the CIDI assessments for alcohol and other drug dependence have acceptable levels of interrater reliability and test-retest reliability, and generally are congruent with independently made standardized clinical diagnoses.

DSM–III–R criteria require evidence concerning nine manifestations of alcohol or other drug dependence grouped under the heading of Criterion A, modeled loosely after the original Edwards-Gross concept for an alcohol dependence syndrome (Edwards & Gross, 1976). The list of nine manifestations covers a range of signs or symptoms, such as those that occur in the context of a drug withdrawal syndrome, as well as behavioral manifestations of drug dependence such as unsuccessful attempts to stop or cut down on drug use, and sustained use despite recognition that it is related to social, psychological, or physical problems. To qualify for a DSM–III–R drug dependence diagnosis, at least three of these nine Criterion A manifestations must be met. In addition, Criterion B requires that the disturbance has persisted for at least one month or that presenting features of drug dependence have appeared repeatedly over a longer period of time. The CIDI includes two or more survey items designed to tap the domains represented by each of the nine Criterion A manifestations, as well as questions concerning Criterion B. The CIDI lifetime diagnosis for alcohol or other drug dependence is not made unless there is positive evidence that the respondent meets both Criterion A and Criterion B.

This assessment of alcohol or other drug dependence was administered whenever participants reported occasions of extramedical use of controlled substances or inhalants in their lifetimes, or when they reported consuming 12 or more drinks in any one year. For the assessment, identical standardized questions were asked for alcohol, controlled substances, and inhalants. By holding constant both the diagnostic criteria and the manner in which the criteria were assessed, we sought to reduce methodologic variation that otherwise might distort comparisons between alcohol and the other drugs. It was not possible to control for these differences in the ECA surveys (Anthony, 1991; Anthony & Helzer, 1991).

Two other methodologic contrasts between the ECA surveys and the NCS also should be mentioned in relation to controlled substances. First, in contrast with the NCS, the ECA surveys did not check for drug dependence (*Diagnostic and Statistical Manual of Mental Disorders*, 3rd ed., DSM–III; American Psychiatric Association, 1980) when a participant reported use of a medicine in accord with a doctor's prescription, even if that use had led to feelings of dependence. Second, the NCS included inhalants when assessing drug dependence (DSM–III–R), whereas the ECA surveys did not. As in the ECA surveys, dependence was assessed whenever participants reported at least several occasions of extramedical drug use, under the assumption that even as few as six occasions might be sufficient for development of drug dependence, but that drug dependence would be extremely rare or improbable among persons who had used the drug no more than several times.

Assessment of Tobacco Use and Dependence

When the NCS fieldwork started, there were insufficient funds to allow NCS assessment of tobacco use and tobacco dependence during an already lengthy interview. Midway through fieldwork, supplemental funding and interview time became available for inclusion of a CIDI section on DSM–III–R tobacco dependence designed to be parallel to the CIDI assessment for DSM–III–R dependence on alcohol and other drugs, but also including a few standardized questions on behaviors specific to tobacco smoking. Because of the NCS replicate sampling plan, it was possible to administer the tobacco assessment to a representative subsample of NCS participants, consisting of 4,414 persons, or 55% of the total NCS sample.

This assessment of tobacco dependence included questions about daily tobacco smoking but not about more infrequent or irregular smoking. Special analyses of the 1991 NHSDA data have been completed to fill this gap of information. The 1991 NHSDA was conducted midway through the NCS fieldwork, with a nationwide probability sample of persons 12 years of age and older and with survey assessments of drug use already described in this article. The NHSDA survey questions ascertain whether tobacco cigarettes were smoked, even on a single occasion, so that the resulting estimates for tobacco use correspond to the NCS estimates on alcohol use on at least one occasion and extramedical use of other drugs on at least one occasion. To conform with the NCS, the NHSDA analyses were re-stricted to 15–54-year-olds.[1]

Quality Control Measures During Fieldwork

The interviewers were monitored by 18 regional supervisors respon-sible for editing completed interviews before they were forwarded to the national field office. In addition, central field office staff reviewed inter-views as soon as they were received from supervisors. Whenever errors were found or important information was missing, the interview assignments were sent back to the field for resolution, and the respondents were recon-tacted to clarify their answers.

Analysis Procedures

We present survey-based population estimates for the lifetime prev-alence of extramedical drug use and the lifetime prevalence of drug depen-dence in relation to alcohol, tobacco, and the other individual drugs or drug groups previously listed. Each prevalence estimate for drug use is a proportion in which the numerator consists of the estimated number of persons who have had at least one occasion of extramedical drug use in their lifetimes, whereas the denominator is the total study population. Each population prevalence estimate for drug dependence has the same denom-inator, but the numerator is the estimated number of persons who qualify for the CIDI lifetime diagnosis for drug dependence according to DSM–III–R criteria. In addition, we report for each individual drug or drug group estimated proportions of drug users in the study population who had de-veloped drug dependence. In concept, these proportions may be regarded as estimates of the lifetime prevalence of drug dependence among users in the study population. Algebra can be used to show that each proportion is equal to the lifetime prevalence of drug dependence in the study pop-ulation, divided by the lifetime prevalence of drug use in the study popu-lation. Because we had to rely on NHSDA estimates for tobacco use, it was necessary to apply the algebraic method when we estimated the pro-portion of tobacco smokers who had developed tobacco dependence, and standard errors have not been estimated for these tobacco estimates.

We also present estimates for the strength of association between drug dependence and plausible determinants of drug dependence, including fixed characteristics such as birth year (age) and sex, as well as potentially mod-ifiable characteristics such as employment status; Table 1 gives a frequency

[1]These NHSDA analyses were conducted by Howard Chilcoat at the Etiology Branch of the National Institute on Drug Abuse, Addiction Research Center.

TABLE 1
Description of National Comorbidity Survey Sample in Relation to Selected Characteristics

Characteristic	Men	Women	Total
Sex			
Male			3,847
Female			4,251
Age			
15−24	868	900	1,768
25−34	1,211	1,415	2,626
35−44	1,128	1,114	2,242
45+	640	822	1,462
Race			
White	2,931	3,153	6,084
Black	427	584	1,011
Hispanic	362	371	733
Other	127	143	270
Employment			
Working	3,029	3,010	6,039
Student	525	552	1,077
Homemaker	6	483	489
Other	287	206	493
Education (in years)			
0−11	739	735	1,474
12	1,228	1,451	2,679
13−15	947	1,185	2,132
16+	933	880	1,813
Income (in thousands of dollars)			
00−19	963	1,381	2,344
20−34	993	1,038	2,031
35−69	1,364	1,358	2,722
70+	527	474	1,001
Household composition			
Live alone	688	510	1,198
Live with spouse	2,025	2,319	4,344
Live with other	814	586	1,400
Live with parent	320	836	1,156
Marital status			
Married or cohabiting	2,051	2,359	4,410
Separated, widowed, or divorced	503	750	1,253
Never married	1,293	1,142	2,435
Religion			
Protestant	2,006	2,469	4,475
Catholic	1,063	1,187	2,250
No preference	301	292	593
Other	477	303	780
Region			
Northeast	722	831	1,553
Midwest	993	1,084	2,077
South	1,352	1,529	2,881
West	780	807	1,587
Urbanicity			
Metropolitan	1,702	1,886	3,588
Other urban	1,277	1,452	2,729
Nonurban	868	913	1,781

Note. Unweighted sample data from the National Comorbidity Survey in the coterminous United States, 1990−1992.

distribution for each variable considered in this analysis on the basis of unweighted NCS sample data. To index the strength of association between drug dependence and each variable listed in Table 1, we have produced an estimate for the odds ratio. When a particular characteristic has no association with being a currently or formerly active case of drug dependence, the odds ratio estimate will be 1.0, or indistinguishable from 1.0 within the limits of survey precision. An odds ratio above 1.0 signals a positive association, whereas an odds ratio between 0.0 and 1.0 signals an inverse association (Fleiss, 1981). The odds ratios for this analysis have been estimated using logistic regression models and the Statistical Analysis System's PROC LOGISTIC (SAS Institute, 1988).

Aside from the unweighted sample data given in Table 1, all results reported in this article are based on conventional procedures for analysis of complex sample survey data. We have used weights to compensate for variation in sample selection probabilities as well as poststratification adjustment factors that compensate for survey nonresponse as well as other potential sources of survey error. Corresponding weights and poststratification adjustment factors also have been taken into account in the 1991 NHSDA estimates for tobacco use reported hereinafter.

Because of the complex sample design and weighting, standard errors of proportions were estimated using the Taylor series linearization method (Woodruff & Causey, 1976). The PSRA-TIO program in the OSIRIS IV statistical analysis and data management package was used to make these calculations (University of Michigan, 1981). Standard errors of odds ratios were estimated using the method of Balanced Repeated Replication in 44 design-based balanced subsamples (Kish & Frankel, 1970). These analytic procedures have been described in more detail by Kessler et al. (1994).

RESULTS

How Many 15–54-Year-Old Americans Have Developed Drug Dependence?

Table 2 shows lifetime prevalence estimates and a standard error for each estimate on the basis of CIDI interviews administered to the 15–54-year-old NCS study population between late 1990 and early 1992. According to Table 2 (see column 2), an estimated 24.1% of this study population had developed tobacco dependence (±1.0%), whereas 14.1% had developed alcohol dependence (±0.7%), and 7.5% (±0.4%) had developed dependence on at least one of the controlled substances or inhalant drugs listed in Table 2. Thus, in rank order, a history of tobacco dependence appeared most frequently in this study population, affecting about 1 in 4

TABLE 2
Estimated Prevalence of Extramedical Use and Dependence in Total Study Population and Lifetime Dependence Among Users

Drug categories	Proportion with a history of dependence		Proportion with a history of extramedical use		Dependence among extramedical users	
	P	SE	P	SE	P	SE
Tobacco[a]	24.1	1.0	75.6	0.6	31.9	—
Alcohol	14.1	0.7	91.5	0.5	15.4	0.7
Other drugs	7.5	0.4	51.0	1.0	14.7	0.7
Cannabis	4.2	0.3	46.3	1.1	9.1	0.7
Cocaine	2.7	0.2	16.2	0.6	16.7	1.5
Stimulant	1.7	0.3	15.3	0.7	11.2	1.6
Anxiolytics, etc.[b]	1.2	0.2	12.7	0.5	9.2	1.1
Analgesics	0.7	0.1	9.7	0.5	7.5	1.0
Psychedelics	0.5	0.1	10.6	0.6	4.9	0.7
Heroin	0.4	0.1	1.5	0.2	23.1	5.6
Inhalants	0.3	0.1	6.8	0.4	3.7	1.4

Note. Weighted estimates from the National Comorbidity Survey data gathered in 1990–1992 for persons 15–54 years old (*n* = 8,098). Dash indicates data not estimated. *P* = Estimated prevalence proportion.
[a]*n* = 4,414. [b]Anxiolytics, sedatives, and hypnotic drugs, grouped.

persons. Alcohol dependence was next most prevalent, having affected about 1 in 7 persons. A history of dependence on other drugs followed, in aggregate having affected about 1 in 13 persons.

Not counting tobacco and alcohol, cannabis accounted for more dependence than any other drug or drug group: In the NCS study population, 4.2% qualified for the lifetime diagnosis of cannabis dependence (Table 2, row 4, column 2). Dependence on cocaine, including crack cocaine, was next in rank: An estimated 2.7% of the 15–54-year-old study population had developed cocaine dependence. Prevalence estimates for only two other drug categories were above 1.0%: Dependence on psychostimulants other than cocaine (e.g., amphetamines) was 1.7%, and dependence upon anxiolytic, sedative, or hypnotic drugs was 1.2% (Table 2, row 7, column 2).

Within the Study Population, Where Was Drug Dependence Found?

Drug dependence was not distributed randomly within the study population; some groups were affected more than others. This can be seen in Table 3 in which logistic regression was used to produce odds ratio estimates that show the strength of association between drug dependence and various selected prevalence correlates such as age and sex.

TABLE 3
Demographic Correlates of Tobacco, Alcohol, and Other Drug Dependence

Characteristic	Tobacco OR	Tobacco 95% CI	Alcohol OR	Alcohol 95% CI	Other Drugs OR	Other Drugs 95% CI
Sex						
Male	1.18	0.99, 1.40	2.81*	2.29, 3.44	1.62*	1.24, 2.13
Female	1.00	—	1.00	—	1.00	—
Age						
15–24	0.48*	0.35, 0.64	1.41*	1.08, 1.84	2.64*	1.28, 5.45
25–34	0.96	0.70, 1.33	1.65*	1.27, 2.16	3.50*	1.92, 6.38
35–44	1.00	0.80, 1.25	1.65*	1.35, 2.02	3.08*	1.64, 5.79
45+	1.00	—	1.00	—	1.00	—
Race						
White	1.00	—	1.00	—	1.00	—
Black	0.45*	0.33, 0.60	0.35*	0.25, 0.50	0.54*	0.37, 0.79
Hispanic	0.59*	0.38, 0.92	1.00	0.72, 1.39	0.86	0.56, 1.34
Other	0.61	0.36, 1.05	0.59	0.24, 1.42	0.53	0.20, 1.42
Employment						
Working	1.00	—	1.00	—	1.00	—
Student	0.45*	0.30, 0.67	0.72*	0.51, 0.99	0.69	0.46, 1.02
Homemaker	1.53*	1.08, 2.18	0.72*	0.56, 0.92	1.59*	1.00, 2.51
Other	1.81*	1.31, 2.48	2.39*	1.72, 3.33	3.31*	2.10, 5.21
Education (in years)						
0–11	1.68*	1.14, 2.46	1.53*	1.23, 1.91	1.50*	1.04, 2.16
12	1.85*	1.34, 2.54	1.45*	1.14, 1.84	1.47*	1.08, 1.98
13–15	1.47*	1.04, 2.08	1.36*	1.05, 1.76	1.32	0.89, 1.94
16+	1.00	—	1.00	—	1.00	—
Income (in thousands of dollars)						
00–19	1.36	0.99, 1.86	1.59*	1.17, 2.18	2.11*	1.35, 3.31
20–34	1.44*	1.05, 1.98	1.27	0.91, 1.78	1.43	0.85, 2.41
35–69	1.24	0.91, 1.69	1.23	0.87, 1.72	1.21	0.72, 2.05
70+	1.00	—	1.00	—	1.00	—
Household composition						
Live alone	1.00	—	1.00	—	1.00	—
Live with spouse	1.05	0.80, 1.38	0.49*	0.38, 0.64	0.59*	0.41, 0.85
Live with other	0.87	0.59, 1.28	0.52*	0.36, 0.74	0.67	0.44, 1.02
Live with parent	0.39*	0.28, 0.56	0.43*	0.32, 0.59	0.44*	0.28, 0.69
Marital status						
Married or cohabiting	2.14*	1.79, 2.57	0.98	0.80, 1.20	1.08	0.75, 1.54
Separated, widowed, divorced	2.12*	1.59, 2.84	1.31	0.98, 1.75	1.37	0.86, 2.17
Never married	1.00	—	1.00	—	1.00	—
Religion						
Protestant	0.77	0.57, 1.04	0.60*	0.45, 0.80	0.51*	0.36, 0.71
Catholic	0.70*	0.50, 0.99	0.56*	0.42, 0.75	0.46*	0.33, 0.65
No preference	1.00	—	1.00	—	1.00	—
Other	0.75	0.46, 1.26	0.77	0.54, 1.10	0.82	0.48, 1.39
Region						
Northeast	1.05	0.79, 1.42	1.36*	1.01, 1.82	1.25	0.08, 1.78
Midwest	1.04	0.76, 1.42	1.34*	1.03, 1.75	0.86	0.63, 1.16
South	1.00	—	1.00	—	1.00	—
West	0.93	0.69, 1.25	1.51*	1.07, 2.14	1.79*	1.31, 2.46

TABLE 3   (*Continued*)

Characteristic	Tobacco		Alcohol		Other Drugs	
	OR	95% CI	OR	95% CI	OR	95% CI
Urbanicity						
Metropolitan	0.79	0.58, 1.07	1.00	0.74, 1.36	1.92*	1.33, 2.77
Other urban	0.85	0.59, 1.22	1.08	0.82, 1.41	1.72*	1.18, 2.51
Nonurban	1.00	—	1.00	—	1.00	—

Note. Dashes indicate data not estimated. OR = odds ratio; CI = confidence interval.
$p < .05$.

Sociodemographic Variation: Sex, Age, and Race–Ethnicity

Men were somewhat more likely than women to have been affected by dependence on alcohol and by dependence on controlled substances or inhalants, but not by tobacco dependence. When we compared the odds of dependence for men versus the odds of dependence for women, the odds ratio was 2.81 for alcohol dependence (95% confidence interval [CI] = 2.29, 3.44) and 1.62 for controlled substances or inhalants (95% CI = 1.24, 2.13). In contrast, the observed odds ratio was 1.18 for tobacco dependence, no more than slightly greater than the odds ratio value (1.0) that is expected under the null hypothesis of no association. Moreover, the 95% CI for the association between tobacco dependence and sex had a span from 0.99 to 1.40, trapping the null value of 1.0. Thus, the evidence is balanced toward a male excess in the prevalence of dependence on alcohol, controlled substances, or inhalants within this study population, but not toward a male excess in prevalence of tobacco dependence.

With respect to age, a history of tobacco dependence was least common among 15–24-year-olds, whereas a history of dependence on alcohol, controlled substances or inhalants was least common among 45–54-year-olds. As shown in Table 3, the odds of tobacco dependence among 15–24-year-olds were about one-half the odds of tobacco dependence among 45–54-year-olds (odds ratio [OR] = 0.48; 95% CI = 0.35, 0.64). However, compared with 45–54-year-olds, tobacco dependence was no more common among 25–34-year-olds (OR = 0.96) or 35–44-year-olds (OR = 1.0).

In contrast, a history of alcohol dependence was least common among 45–54-year-olds. By comparison with these older adults, the 15–24-year-olds were an estimated 1.41 times more likely to qualify for a lifetime alcohol dependence diagnosis (OR = 1.41; 95% CI = 1.08, 1.84); the corresponding odds ratio was 1.65 for the 25–34-year-olds (95% CI = 1.27, 2.16) and for the 35–44-year-olds (95% CI = 1.35, 2.02).

A history of dependence on controlled substances or inhalants was most likely to be found among young adults, and was least likely to be found among 45–54-year-olds. By comparison with 45–54-year-olds, the estimated odds of dependence on these drugs were 2.64 times greater among 15–24-year-olds, 3.50 times greater among 25–34-year-olds, and 3.08 times greater among 35–44-year-olds.

Compared with White Americans, the African-American segment of the study population was less likely to have a history of tobacco dependence (OR = 0.59), alcohol dependence (OR = 0.35), or dependence on other drugs (OR = 0.54); Hispanic Americans also were less likely than White Americans to have a history of tobacco dependence, but this was not the case for alcohol dependence ($p > .05$) or dependence on other drugs ($p > .05$). These inverse associations between drug dependence and being African American or Hispanic American also were found in multiple logistic regression analyses that held constant employment and two primary indicators of socioeconomic status: educational achievement and income (data not shown in a table).

Employment and Socioeconomic Status

To study variation in occurrence of drug dependence by employment status at the time of assessment, individuals who primarily were working for pay have been compared with students, homemakers, and others (e.g., those who had been recently laid off or terminated and not yet reemployed; other persons no longer in the active labor force). In comparison with employed workers, students generally were a lower lifetime prevalence group for dependence on tobacco (OR = 0.45) and alcohol (OR = 0.72), but not for other drugs such as marijuana, cocaine, or inhalants (OR = 0.69; $p > .05$). A history of alcohol dependence was observed less frequently among homemakers versus employed workers (OR = 0.72), but homemakers were somewhat more likely to have been affected by dependence on tobacco (OR = 1.53) and by dependence on other drugs (OR = 1.59). Prevalence of dependence on alcohol, tobacco, and other drugs was especially common among persons recently laid off but not yet reemployed and other individuals not working in the paid labor force at the time of the assessment. Compared with employed workers, these unemployed persons were an estimated 1.81 times more likely to have a history of tobacco dependence, 2.39 times more likely to have a history of alcohol dependence, and 3.31 times more likely to have a history of dependence on controlled substances or inhalants (Table 3). These moderately strong associations between unemployment and dependence on alcohol, tobacco, or other drugs also were found in multiple logistic regression analyses that held constant age, sex, education, income, and a selection of other potentially confounding variables (data not presented in a table).

Low educational achievement also had a moderately strong association with a history of dependence on tobacco, alcohol, or other drugs, with or without statistical adjustment using the multiple logistic regression model. For persons with 0–11 years of schooling compared with persons who went to school for more than 15 years, the history of tobacco dependence was associated with lower educational achievement (OR = 1.68), as was a history of alcohol dependence (OR = 1.53) and also a history of dependence on other drugs (OR = 1.50). A similar profile of modest but statistically significant associations was observed when comparing persons with 12 years of schooling to those with more than 15 years (Table 3).

It is interesting to note that lower educational achievement was associated with dependence on tobacco and alcohol even among persons who had completed more than 12 years of schooling. This can be seen in the odds ratios that contrast persons with 13–15 years of education with those who attended school for 16 years or more (for 13–15 years vs. 16+ years, OR = 1.47 for tobacco dependence; OR = 1.36 for alcohol dependence).

In general, a lower annual income was associated with having been affected by drug dependence (Table 3). For example, persons earning less than $20,000 per year were 2.11 times more likely to have a history of dependence on controlled substances or inhalants compared with persons whose annual income was $70,000 or more (95% CI = 1.35, 3.31). For tobacco dependence, the strongest association was observed in the contrast between persons with incomes of $20,000 to $34,000 per year versus those with annual income of $70,000 or more (OR = 1.43; 95% CI = 1.05, 1.98).

Household Composition

Most of the study population (n = 4,344) consisted of married persons living with a spouse (with or without other family members), but a considerable number of respondents (n = 1,198) were living alone in their households (see Table 1). Compared with those living alone, individuals living with their spouses were just as likely to have lifetime tobacco dependence (OR = 0.87), but were less likely to qualify as recent or past cases of alcohol dependence (OR = 0.49) or dependence on controlled drugs or inhalants (OR = 0.59), as presented in Table 3. Inverse associations also were observed for persons living with their parents in relation to tobacco, alcohol, and other drugs. In part, these inverse associations should be understood in relation to sex: Within the study population, a large majority of persons living with parents were women, as shown in Table 1.

Marital Status and Religious Preference

In this study population, there was a tendency for a history of tobacco dependence to be more common among persons who were currently married or living with partners as if married (see "married" in Table 3) and among formerly married individuals (separated, divorced, or widowed), and less common among persons who were never married; this was not the case for dependence on alcohol or other drugs (Table 3). On the other hand, there were fairly consistent associations involving religious preference, with a history of dependence found more frequently among persons who professed no religious preference, and by comparison, least frequently among Catholics (OR = 0.70 for tobacco; OR = 0.56 for alcohol; OR = 0.46 for other drugs). In addition, Protestants had lower prevalence of dependence on alcohol (OR = 0.60) and controlled substances or inhalants (OR = 0.51) in a contrast to persons with no religious preference, but the odds ratio estimate for tobacco dependence among Protestants was closer to the null value of 1.0 and the association was not statistically significant by conventional standards (OR = 0.77; p > .05).

Location of Residence

For dependence on controlled substances or inhalants, there were nonrandom distributions in relation to both region of the country and urban-nonurban location of residence. Compared with residents of states in the South, individuals living in the West were found to be an estimated 1.79 times more likely to have developed dependence on these drugs. Residents of metropolitan areas were most likely to have a history of dependence on controlled substances or inhalants (OR = 1.92), followed by residents of other urban areas (OR = 1.72), and residents of nonurban areas were least likely to have been drug dependent.

Alcohol dependence also was associated with region of the country, but not with metropolitan or other urban environments. In a comparison with residents of the South, the odds of alcohol dependence were about 50% greater among persons living in the West (OR = 1.51) and about 35% greater among persons living in the Northeast (OR = 1.36) or in the Midwest (OR = 1.34).

In contrast with dependence on alcohol or other drugs, tobacco dependence was distributed essentially at random in relation to region of the country and urbanicity. All of the tobacco odds ratios corresponding to region and urban and nonurban residence were close to the null value of 1.0 and the associated confidence intervals had spans from below 1.0 to above 1.0 (Table 3).

Drug Use and the Transition to Drug Dependence

Lifetime prevalence proportions for drug dependence in the study population are determined in part by how many persons have tried each type of drug at least once and survived to be interviewed, and in part by how many of these surviving drug users had proceeded to become drug dependent. For example, considerably fewer members of the study population had tried tobacco than alcohol (75.6% lifetime prevalence for tobacco use vs. 91.5% for alcohol use, as shown in Table 2, column 4). However, dependence was more likely to occur among tobacco smokers than among alcohol drinkers: Of the tobacco smokers, 31.9% had developed tobacco dependence, whereas only 15.4% of the alcohol drinkers had developed alcohol dependence (Table 2, column 6). In consequence, within the total study population, the lifetime prevalence of tobacco dependence (24.1%) was greater than the lifetime prevalence of alcohol dependence (14.1%), even though more persons had consumed alcohol (91.5%) than had smoked tobacco (75.6%).

When controlled substances and inhalants were considered as a single group, the data showed that slightly more than one half of the study population had taken one or more of these drugs for extramedical reasons (51.0%) and 14.7% of the users had developed dependence on at least one of the listed drugs (Table 2, row 3, columns 4 and 6). Nonetheless, one might expect considerable variation in the prevalence of extramedical drug use and in the transition from drug use to drug dependence, across individual drugs and drug groups.

After alcohol and tobacco, cannabis was the next most frequently used drug listed in Table 2, but it ranked low in relation to our index of dependence among users (Table 2, column 6). Within the study population, an estimated 46.3% had used cannabis at least once, but only 9.1% of the users had developed cannabis dependence: For every user with a history of cannabis dependence, there were 10 users who had not become dependent. By comparison, an estimated 16.2% of the study population had tried cocaine at least once, and 16.7% of them had qualified as cocaine dependent: For each cocaine user with a history of cocaine dependence, there were 5 users who had not become dependent (Table 2, columns 4 and 6).

An estimated 15.3% had used psychostimulants other than cocaine (e.g., amphetamines) for extramedical reasons, and 11.2% of these users had progressed to develop dependence on these drugs. Corresponding estimates for the anxiolytic, sedative, or hypnotic drugs were 12.7% and 9.2%, respectively. An estimated 9.7% of the study population had used analgesic drugs for extramedical reasons; 7.5% of these analgesic users had become dependent (Table 3, columns 4 and 6).

An estimated 10.6% of the 15–54-year-old study population reported using psychedelic drugs at least once, 6.8% reported use of inhalants, and 1.5% reported using heroin. An estimated 4.9% of the psychedelics users qualified for the dependence diagnosis. Among inhalant users, an estimated 3.7% qualified as dependent. By comparison, among heroin users in this sample, 23.1% had become dependent (Table 2).

Age and Drug Dependence by Drug Group

To some extent, age-associated variation in drug dependence that was observed in our logistic regression analyses should be understood in relation to differences in prevalence of drug use, in addition to other factors. For example, a history of tobacco use was less common among 15–24-year-olds as compared with older age groups (see Table 4 and Figure 1); this by itself might be sufficient to account for lower lifetime prevalence of tobacco dependence in the comparison of young versus older persons. However, the NCS data also highlighted the importance of age-related differences in the transition from tobacco use to tobacco dependence. In analyses that considered smokers only, we found that 15–24-year-old smokers were less likely than older smokers to have developed tobacco dependence (Table 4 and Figure 1).

For two groups of medically prescribed drugs, namely, the analgesics and the anxiolytic, sedative, and hypnotic drugs, the survey-based estimates for lifetime prevalence of dependence were higher for older age groups versus the youngest age group, despite generally lower prevalence of extramedical use among older adults. This was true for lifetime prevalence of dependence among extramedical users of these drugs as well as for lifetime prevalence of dependence among all persons (Table 4 and Figure 1).

A substantially different pattern was observed for marijuana, cocaine, psychostimulants other than cocaine, and the psychedelic drug group, which showed comparatively lower lifetime prevalence of dependence in the oldest age group, along with generally lower lifetime prevalence of extramedical drug use (Table 4 and Figure 1).

Alcohol offered a unique profile, with 45–54-year-olds having a relatively high lifetime prevalence of alcohol use (93.1%) but a relatively low prevalence of alcohol dependence (10.1%) as compared with the other age groups. Alcohol also is noteworthy because the lifetime prevalence of dependence among drinkers was about 10% for persons 45–54 years of age, considerably less than estimates of about 16% that were observed for all three younger age groups (Table 4 and Figure 1).

Drug Dependence by Drug Group and by Sex

In relation to lifetime prevalence of drug dependence and lifetime prevalence of extramedical use, the rank ordering of individual drugs and drug groups was generally identical for men and women (Table 5 and Figures 2 and 3). The exception can be seen in relation to a sex difference in the ranking of psychedelic drugs, which had been taken by 14.1% of men as compared with 7.2% of women.

In respect to 6 out of 10 individual drugs or drug groups, the lifetime prevalence estimates for dependence among users were roughly similar for

TABLE 4
Estimated Prevalence Proportion (*P*) of Extramedical Use and
Dependence in Total Study Population and Lifetime Dependence
Among Users by Age

Drug and age (years)	Proportion with a history of extramedical use		Proportion with a history of dependence		Dependence among users	
	P	*SE*	*P*	*SE*	*P*	*SE*
Tobacco[a]						
15–24	64.4	1.1	15.2	1.7	23.6	—
25–34	76.4	0.8	26.5	2.1	34.7	—
35–44	80.1	1.3	27.2	1.5	34.0	—
45+	82.7	1.4	27.2	2.3	32.9	—
Total	75.6	0.6	24.1	1.0	31.9	—
Alcohol						
15–24	82.5	1.1	13.6	1.1	16.5	1.3
25–34	95.0	0.7	15.6	1.1	16.4	1.1
35–44	94.9	0.8	15.6	1.0	16.4	1.0
45+	93.1	0.8	10.1	1.0	10.7	1.1
Total	91.5	0.5	14.1	0.7	15.4	0.7
Cannabis						
15–24	36.5	2.1	5.6	0.9	15.3	2.3
25–34	61.6	1.8	5.0	0.5	8.1	0.7
35–44	52.1	1.6	4.4	0.7	8.5	1.3
45+	25.5	1.9	0.8	0.4	3.1	1.5
Total	46.3	1.1	4.2	0.3	9.1	0.7
Cocaine						
15–24	10.6	1.0	2.6	0.6	24.5	4.8
25–34	26.9	1.6	4.2	0.4	15.5	1.9
35–44	17.2	1.4	2.6	0.4	15.3	2.4
45+	4.4	0.7	0.5	0.3	11.8	6.0
Total	16.2	0.6	2.7	0.2	16.7	1.5
Stimulants						
15–24	11.5	1.1	1.6	0.4	13.5	2.9
25–34	20.3	1.1	2.8	0.7	13.9	3.2
35–44	18.7	1.1	1.4	0.3	7.7	1.7
45+	7.2	0.8	0.5	0.2	6.5	2.0
Total	15.3	0.7	1.7	0.3	11.2	1.6
Anxiolytics, etc.[b]						
15–24	8.6	0.9	0.2	0.1	2.1	1.1
25–34	16.0	1.2	1.1	0.3	6.8	2.0
35–44	16.0	0.9	1.9	0.4	11.7	2.4
45+	8.0	1.0	1.6	0.6	20.3	6.9
Total	12.7	0.5	1.2	0.2	9.2	1.1
Analgesics						
15–24	10.9	1.0	0.2	0.1	1.6	0.7
25–34	12.0	0.8	0.8	0.1	6.8	1.0
35–44	9.1	0.8	1.0	0.2	11.5	2.9
45+	5.3	0.9	0.9	0.5	16.3	7.6
Total	9.7	0.5	0.7	0.1	7.5	1.0
Psychedelics						
15–24	8.3	0.7	0.7	0.2	8.8	2.5
25–34	14.9	1.1	0.7	0.2	4.5	1.3
35–44	12.8	1.0	0.5	0.1	3.8	1.1
45+	3.5	0.6	0.02	0.02	0.6	0.6
Total	10.6	0.6	0.5	0.1	4.9	0.7

Table continues

TABLE 4 (*Continued*)

Drug and age (years)	Proportion with a history of extramedical use		Proportion with a history of dependence		Dependence among users	
	P	SE	P	SE	P	SE
Heroin						
15–24	0.7	0.3	0.1	0.1	20.1	10.1
25–34	1.7	0.3	0.3	0.1	15.0	6.0
35–44	2.7	0.5	0.8	0.4	31.8	10.7
45+	0.7	0.3	0.1	0.05	10.7	7.7
Total	1.5	0.2	0.4	0.1	23.1	5.6
Inhalants						
15–24	8.1	1.0	0.6	0.3	7.9	3.8
25–34	9.9	0.8	0.1	0.1	1.5	0.7
35–44	5.7	0.7	0.1	0.1	2.6	1.4
45+	1.8	0.5	0.04	0.04	2.2	2.3
Total	6.8	0.4	0.3	0.1	3.7	1.4
Any drug group[c]						
15–24	42.8	1.8	7.4	1.1	17.3	2.3
25–34	64.7	1.7	9.5	0.9	14.7	1.2
35–44	56.4	1.6	8.5	0.9	14.9	1.5
45+	31.5	1.8	2.9	0.8	9.2	2.5
Total	51.0	1.0	7.5	0.4	14.7	0.7

Note. Weighted estimates from the National Comorbidity Survey data gathered in 1990–1992 for persons 15–54 years old ($n = 8{,}098$). Dashes indicate data not estimated.
[a] Tobacco use estimates from the 1991 National Household Survey on Drug Use, as described in the *Assessment of Alcohol and Other Drug Use* section, $n = 4{,}414$. Dependence among users estimated by the algebraic method described in the *Analysis Procedures* section; standard errors not estimated.
[b] Anxiolytics, sedatives, and hypnotic drugs, grouped.
[c] "Any drug group" refers to the aggregate category comprising the controlled substances and inhalant drugs, but not alcohol or tobacco.

men and women. For example, slightly more than 30% of the tobacco smokers had developed tobacco dependence, and slightly more than 22% of the heroin users had developed heroin dependence—regardless of sex. Minimal male-female differences in the prevalence of dependence among users were observed for cocaine, analgesics, hallucinogens, and inhalants (Table 5 and Figure 4).

In contrast, for alcohol and cannabis, male users were somewhat more likely than female users to have developed dependence (Table 5 and Figure 4). Furthermore, with respect to the drug group that included anxiolytics, sedatives, and hypnotics, female users were somewhat more likely than male users to have developed dependence. For example, an estimated 14% of men (±0.8%) and 11.5% of women (±0.8%) reported extramedical use of at least one anxiolytic, sedative, or hypnotic drug. Among these extramedical users, an estimated 6.6% of the men (±1.0%) and 12.3% of the women (±2.2%) had developed dependence on this class of drugs (Table 5).

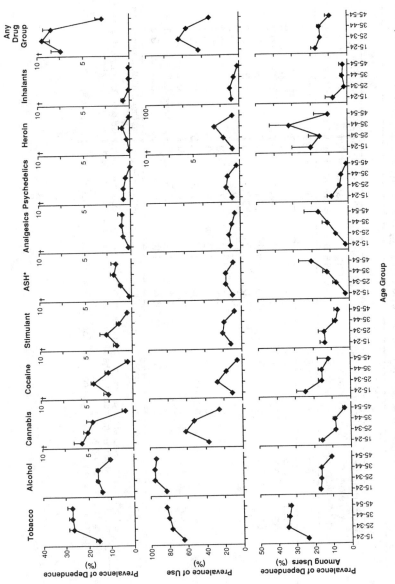

Figure 1. Drug-specific estimates for the lifetime prevalence of drug dependence (first row of graphs), lifetime prevalence of drug use (second row of graphs), and lifetime prevalence of drug dependence among extramedical drug users (third row of graphs), based on estimates presented in Table 4. Weighted estimates based on standardized assessment of 8,098 Americans 15–54-years-old, who were selected by probability sampling and interviewed for the National Comorbidity Survey, 1990–1992. The scale for individual graphs has been tailored for each set of estimates, with variation across rows and within rows. Error bars have been used to show the precision (standard error) of each estimate whenever possible. No error bar has been drawn when the standard error was quite small (i.e., half the height of the diamond symbol used to depict the point estimate) or in the case of tobacco dependence among users (see *Analysis Procedures* section). ASH = anxiolytic, sedative, and hypnotic drugs, grouped (e.g., secobarbital and diazepam, as well as more recently introduced compounds such as flurazepam, alprazolam, and triazolam); "Any drug group" = aggregate category comprising the controlled substances and inhalant drugs, but not alcohol or tobacco; † = change in scale.

COMPARATIVE EPIDEMIOLOGY OF DRUGS   23

TABLE 5
Estimated Prevalence Proportion (P) of Extramedical Use and Dependence in Total Study Population and Lifetime Dependence Among Users by Sex

Drug	Men Proportion with a history of extramedical use P	SE	Men Proportion with a history of dependence P	SE	Men Dependence among male users P	SE	Women Proportion with a history of extramedical use P	SE	Women Proportion with a history of dependence P	SE	Women Dependence among female users P	SE
Tobacco[a]	78.3	0.8	25.6	1.4	32.7	—	73.1	0.7	22.6	1.3	30.9	—
Alcohol	93.5	0.5	20.1	1.0	21.4	1.0	89.6	0.7	8.2	0.7	9.2	0.8
Cannabis	51.7	1.3	6.2	0.6	12.0	1.1	41.0	1.5	2.3	0.3	5.5	0.7
Cocaine	19.5	0.9	3.5	0.4	18.0	1.9	12.9	0.7	1.9	0.3	14.9	2.0
Stimulants	18.4	0.8	1.8	0.4	9.7	1.9	12.2	0.8	1.6	0.3	13.3	2.0
Anxiolytics, etc.[b]	14.0	0.8	1.0	0.1	6.6	1.0	11.5	0.8	1.4	0.3	12.3	2.2
Analgesics	11.6	0.7	0.8	0.2	6.7	1.6	7.9	0.5	0.7	0.1	8.6	1.4
Psychedelics	14.1	0.8	0.7	0.2	5.0	1.1	7.2	0.6	0.3	0.1	4.7	1.2
Heroin	2.2	0.2	0.5	0.2	22.3	6.5	0.9	0.2	0.2	0.1	25.2	12.9
Inhalants	9.4	0.7	0.4	0.2	4.1	1.7	4.3	0.4	0.1	0.1	2.7	2.0
Drug group[c]	55.8	1.3	9.2	0.7	16.4	1.2	46.4	1.5	5.9	0.5	12.6	1.0

Note. Weighted estimates from the National Comorbidity Survey data gathered in 1990–1992 for persons 15–54-years-old (*n* = 8,098). Dashes indicate data not estimated.

[a] Tobacco use estimates from the 1991 National Household Survey on Drug Use, as described in the *Assessment of Alcohol and Other Drug Use* section, *n* = 4,414. Dependence among users estimated by the algebraic method described in the *Analysis Procedures* section; standard errors not estimated.

[b] Anxiolytics, sedatives, and hypnotic drugs, grouped.

[c] "Drug group" refers to the aggregate category comprising the controlled substances and inhalant drugs, but not alcohol or tobacco.

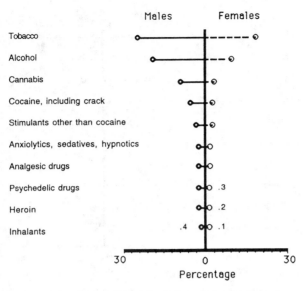

Figure 2. Estimated lifetime prevalence of drug dependence, by sex, based on estimates presented in Table 5.

DISCUSSION

Comparison of Prevalence Estimates

On the basis of general consensus, a DSM–III–R task panel on drug dependence decided to modify the Edwards–Gross alcohol dependence concept and to adopt this modification as a unified construct that would

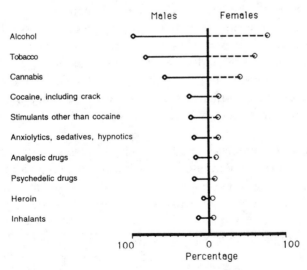

Figure 3. Estimated lifetime prevalence of extramedical drug use, by sex, based on estimates presented in Table 5.

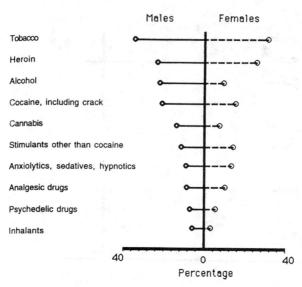

Figure 4. Estimated lifetime prevalence of drug dependence among extramedical drug users, by sex, based on estimates presented in Table 5.

apply to all psychoactive drugs (Kosten & Kosten, 1991; Kosten, Rounsaville, Babour, Spitzer, & Williams, 1987). As a result of this development, for the first time in an epidemiologic field survey we have been able to hold constant the diagnostic criteria for drug dependence as they are applied to users of tobacco, alcohol, controlled substances, and inhalants and to reduce marked between-drug differences in diagnostic assessments for drug dependence. In doing so, we found that a substantial proportion of the 15–54-year-old population in the United States—about 1 in 13 persons or 7.5%—has been affected by dependence on controlled substances or inhalants. By comparison, almost twice as many had developed alcohol dependence, about 14%, and about three times as many, 24.1%, had developed tobacco dependence at some time in life up to the time of the survey. The extent to which the nation's health is compromised by this history of drug dependence is likely to be a topic of investigation for many years.

To place the potential health and social burdens of drug dependence in context with the burden of other psychiatric morbidity, it may be useful to compare lifetime prevalence estimates for dependence on individual drugs with the lifetime prevalence of selected DSM–III–R anxiety and mood disorders ascertained by the CIDI method, which our research group has reported in a separate publication (Kessler et al., 1994). To illustrate, for this article we have estimated that cannabis dependence has affected 4.2% of the study population. This places the prevalence of cannabis dependence in rank between panic disorder (3.5% prevalence) and generalized anxiety disorder (5.1% prevalence) or agoraphobia without panic disorder (5.3% prevalence).

Comparatively, a history of cocaine dependence was found in 2.7% of the study population. Cocaine dependence was almost as prevalent as antisocial personality disorder (3.5% prevalence), and was about 70% more common than bipolar disorder (1.6% prevalence). Alcohol dependence (14.1%) was somewhat more common than simple phobia (11.3%) and social phobia (13.3%), whereas tobacco dependence at 24.1% was more prevalent than major depressive disorder at 17.1% (Kessler et al., 1994).

Checked against ECA estimates for lifetime prevalence of drug dependence, the NCS values generally were similar. To illustrate, ECA versus NCS estimates for cannabis disorders both were close to 4% (4.4% vs. 4.2%, respectively); for psychostimulants other than cocaine, both estimates were 1.7%; for the sedative drug group, both estimates were 1.2% (Anthony & Helzer, 1991).

One noteworthy exception involved cocaine, in that less than 1% of the ECA study population qualified for a cocaine disorder, whereas 2.7% of the NCS study population did so. In part, this difference can be attributed to a change in diagnostic criteria: DSM–III criteria used for the ECA covered cocaine abuse, but did not provide for the diagnosis of cocaine dependence (Anthony & Trinkoff, 1989). In addition, the most recent epidemic of cocaine dependence in the United States also can account for some of the observed increase.

To test whether the NCS estimates for lifetime prevalence of alcohol use and illicit drug use were consistent with those from the NHSDA conducted in 1991, we reanalyzed the NHSDA data to conform with the age and sex groups created for the NCS analyses within the age range from 15 to 54 years. This seemed to be especially necessary in light of observations about the importance of privacy and self-administration strategies in survey research about illicit drug use (e.g., see Schober et al., 1992). Nonetheless, in many instances, the NCS observed estimates were slightly higher than corresponding NHSDA estimates, particularly among older adults; in others, they were no more than slightly lower, particularly among 15–24-year-olds. However, for each comparison, the NHSDA estimate was well within the range defined by 95% CI for the corresponding NCS estimate (data not shown in a table).

There are no prior national survey estimates for tobacco dependence, but a recent population survey of young adults in the Detroit, Michigan area found that 74% of 21–30-year-olds had smoked tobacco at least once; among these smokers, 27% had developed DSM–III–R tobacco dependence (Breslau, Fenn, & Peterson, 1993). By comparison, estimates from the nationally representative NCS for roughly the same age group were not too different: Of the 25–34-year-olds, 76.4% had smoked and 34.7% had developed DSM–III–R tobacco dependence.

Comparison With Prevalence Estimates for Other Nations

To be sure, there are some countries in which the lifetime prevalence of alcohol dependence or tobacco dependence appear to equal or exceed the values observed in the NCS, most notably South Korea (e.g., see Lee et al., 1990a, 1990b). However, we are aware of no epidemiologic evidence on countries in which prevalence of dependence on controlled substances exceeds the values we found for 15–54-year-old noninstitutionalized residents of the coterminous United States (e.g., see Bland, Orn, & Newman, 1988; Canino et al., 1987; Compton et al., 1991; Hwu, Yeh, & Chang, 1989; Lee et al., 1990a; Wells, Bushnell, Hornblow, Joyce, & Oakley-Browne, 1989; Wittchen, Essau, von Zerssen, Krieg, & Zaudig, 1992).

Comparative Epidemiology of Tobacco, Alcohol, and Other Drug Dependence

Epidemiologic analyses of population data often begin with a consideration of birth year or age, sex, and race. This approach draws on a long tradition of including these variables on birth records and death certificates, which in many places have been the main sources of epidemiologic data. In addition, it generally is necessary to take these three inborn variables into account before assessing evidence about potentially modifiable risk factors or conditions that can be leveraged for prevention and control of disease. Moreover, birth year, sex, and race are fixed characteristics that cannot be modified by changes in conditions such as disease experience or toxic exposures.

In contrast, when we turn to the epidemiologic study of potentially modifiable conditions such as educational attainment, employment status, and access to material wealth, we face the possibility that these characteristics might influence the occurrence of disease and also might be influenced by disease. It is in this context that the limitations of cross-sectional survey data and the advantages of prospective or longitudinal data become most apparent. Reasoning along these lines, we caution against the causal interpretation of cross-sectional survey results, and we note that lifetime prevalence ratios or odds ratios from lifetime prevalence analyses typically cannot be interpreted as risk ratios or relative risk estimates (Kramer, Von Korff, & Kessler, 1980).

Even though they should not be given causal interpretation, the cross-sectional associations and odds ratios of the type estimated for this study can point out segments of the population where currently active or former cases of drug dependence are more or less likely to be found. In addition to highlighting the location of these cases within the population, cross-sectional odds ratios serve to index the strength of each observed association, whether causal or noncausal. Together with our basic prevalence estimates, the observed patterns of association (or lack thereof) represent the beginning steps for a comparative epidemiology of tobacco dependence, alcohol dependence, and dependence on controlled substances.

Scanning across odds ratio estimates from our analyses, one can find many commonalities and some noteworthy differences in the associations with dependence on tobacco, alcohol, and other drugs. Many of the observed associations are consistent with prior research, recently summarized by us and by others (e.g., Anthony, 1991; Anthony & Helzer, 1991; Anthony & Helzer, in press; Hawkins, Catalano, & Miller, 1992; Kandel, 1991). For example, sex (being a man) had a moderate degree of association with alcohol dependence and other drug dependence but not with tobacco dependence. This finding converges with other evidence showing an increasing health burden of tobacco smoking among women, and perhaps a declining burden among men (e.g., Adams, Gfroerer, & Rouse, 1989; Johnston et al., 1992).

Another comparative difference was observed in the associations with age, especially in the contrast of 45–54-year-olds with 15–24-year-olds. The 45–54-year-olds were more likely to have a history of current or past tobacco dependence; they were less likely to have a history of dependence on alcohol or on other drugs. However, age-specific prevalence estimates for individual controlled substances prompt a slightly different conclusion about two classes of drugs that are available by prescription. Namely, compared with 15–24-year-olds, the oldest adult extramedical drug users under study were more likely to have become dependent on analgesic drugs and on anxiolytic, sedative, or hypnotic drugs, which are used widely for legitimate medical reasons. This aspect of the 45–54-year-old population's drug experience differs from its experience with alcohol, Schedule I drugs such as heroin, and inhalant drugs.

These relationships between age and drug dependence, generally consistent with prior survey findings in the United States, may be understandable as a reflection of variation in drug availability or level of drug involvement across different birth cohorts, periods, or segments of the life span (Kandel, 1991). Alternately, there are two general epidemiologic observations that may clarify underlying issues of interpretation.

The first general observation involves the force of drug-related mortality, which can have an important but nearly hidden impact on age-specific estimates from cross-sectional assessments. At the time of assessment, each age group under study consists of survivors from one or more original birth cohorts (e.g., live births in a given year, or in a given span of years). At some point, mortality associated with drug dependence starts to contribute to the loss of drug-dependent persons from each birth cohort. Although the force of drug-related mortality can be in operation for all ages of drug users, accumulated attrition due to dependence-related deaths becomes an increasingly important factor in successive years of adulthood.

In this respect, alcohol provides a good illustration. As shown in Figure 1, the lower lifetime prevalence of dependence observed among the oldest drinkers might be due partly to a premature mortality that is secondary to alcohol dependence.

There also was a sharp drop in prevalence of heroin dependence across the two oldest age groups surveyed: 2.7% for 35–44-year-olds versus 0.7% for 45–54-year-olds. Among 2,242 participants age 35–44 years in the NCS sample, there were 64 heroin users, but among 1,462 participants age 45–54 years, there were only 13 heroin users. Based on the experience of these heroin users, we were able to estimate that almost one third of the 35–44-year-old heroin users in the study population had a history of heroin dependence, but we had too few users to produce a corresponding estimate for the 45–54-year-old heroin users. In the context of this discussion, it is informative that within this group of 13 people who were 45–54-years-old and who had used heroin at some point in their lives, there was only one user with a history of heroin dependence. We speculate that premature mortality associated with heroin dependence might account for these sharp differences in the observed heroin experience of these two older adult age groups within our study population.

The second general epidemiologic observation that merits consideration when studying age and drug dependence relates current age to the transitions from adolescence through age 34, which recent evidence pegs as the main period of risk for initiating drug use and drug dependence (e.g., see Anthony, 1991; Kandel, Murphy, & Karus, 1985). At the time of assessment in 1990–1992, the 15–24-year-olds had just started to pass through this main risk period. The importance of this fact might be seen most clearly in relation to the analgesics and the anxiolytic-sedative-hypnotic drug group. For these drugs, the proportion of extramedical users age 15–24 years who had developed a history of dependence was low, relative to the other age groups (Figure 1). This may reflect that these birth cohorts have just entered the high-risk period, and with passing time, their experience may prove to be more like the experience of their elders.

In relation to these NCS findings, two other associations deserve special comment:

African Americans and Drug Use

There is a widespread popular belief that African Americans are especially vulnerable to drug dependence, perhaps because of their overrepresentation in certain clinical samples. However, consistent with evidence from other recent epidemiologic surveys, the NCS estimates indicate that tobacco dependence, alcohol dependence, and dependence on other drugs are more common among White non-Hispanic Americans than among African Americans (e.g., see Anthony & Helzer, 1991; Kandel, 1991; Lillie-Blanton, Anthony, & Schuster, 1993).

Residence in a Nonurban Area

Alcohol and tobacco are widely available throughout the United States, but the illicit availability of controlled substances seems to vary considerably. Perhaps reflecting these different patterns of availability, residents of nonurban areas were a lower prevalence group for dependence on controlled substances but not for dependence on tobacco or alcohol (see Table 3). Analogously, the ECA survey in the Durham-Piedmont population of North Carolina found somewhat lower prevalence of drug disorders among inhabitants of rural areas compared with those living in urban areas (Anthony & Helzer, 1991).

Transition From Drug Use to Drug Dependence

When ECA results were published, some readers were surprised to find that many of the individuals who had used heroin or other controlled substances on more than five occasions had not developed drug dependence or other drug disorder, even though prior research on Vietnam veterans had indicated as much. For example, among heroin users in the ECA sample, only 44% had become a case of heroin dependence or heroin abuse as defined by DSM–III criteria. The corresponding estimates were close to 20% for extramedical users of cannabis, psychostimulants other than cocaine, and anxiolytics or sedative-hypnotic drugs (Anthony & Trinkoff, 1989). Similarly, Helzer (1985) and Robins (1993) have reported that most Vietnam veterans who used heroin and other opioid drugs in Vietnam did not become dependent taking these drugs while overseas.

Although not directly comparable to these ECA estimates based on the experience of individuals who had used drugs on more than five occasions, the NCS estimates also suggest that a large majority of persons who have initiated extramedical drug use have not proceeded to develop drug dependence. Even for drugs known for their dependence liability (e.g., tobacco, cocaine, heroin), the proportion of drug users who were found to have become dependent was in a range from 20–40%. Considering these prevalence estimates on the transition from drug use to drug dependence, it is noteworthy that NCS interviewers were able to develop trust and rapport sufficient to elicit reports of illegal drug-taking behavior from many participants. We speculate that many participants who acknowledge past illicit behavior also may be willing to report personal problems and other symptoms of drug dependence that they have experienced. At the same time, we acknowledge a strong possibility that some drug-dependent participants did not report on these problems with completeness or total accuracy, which would tend to attenuate the proportion of dependent persons among extramedical drug users.

On conceptual grounds, it can be argued that the transition from drug use to drug dependence in the population is determined partly by the reinforcing functions served by drug-taking and associated behaviors, with a linkage back to profiles of drug activity discovered through laboratory research (e.g., see Schuster, 1989; Thompson, 1981). In addition, this transition seems to be determined in part by other factors, some linked to the reinforcing functions of drug use, and some not so readily studied inside the laboratory (e.g., see Brady, 1989; Glantz & Pickens, 1992; Schuster, 1989). In theory, the array of these interrelated factors includes relative drug availability and opportunities for use of different drugs as well as their cost; patterns and frequencies of drug use that differ across drugs; different profiles of vulnerabilities of individuals whose extramedical use starts with one drug versus another, as well as both formal and informal social controls and sanctions against drug use or in its favor, which might be exercised either within intimate social fields such as the family or workplace or by larger units of social organization. Considered all together, the array of theoretically plausible determinants of the transition from drug use to drug dependence runs a span from the microscopic (e.g., the dopamine receptor) through the macroscopic (e.g., social norms for or against drug use; international drug-control policies).

A better understanding of these sources of variation, as well as attention to methodological features of cross-sectional survey research, would help us account for the rank ordering of individual drugs and drug groups in relation to the prevalence of extramedical drug use and in relation to the proportion of extramedical users who were found to have developed dependence. It is of considerable interest that the rank ordering by prevalence of extramedical drug use was quite similar for both men and women, differing only by the higher prevalence of psychedelic drug use among men.

The rank ordering in relation to transitions from drug use to drug dependence was not the same as that seen for prevalence of extramedical drug use. In addition, the ranking of drugs in relation to the use-to-dependence transition showed some variation across male and female drug users and across age groups. For both men and women, and for all but the oldest age group of drug users, tobacco and heroin were top ranked; psychedelic drugs and inhalants were at the bottom. There were male-female differences in lifetime prevalence of dependence among extramedical drug users only for alcohol and cannabis. An estimated 21.4% of the male alcohol drinkers had developed dependence, compared with an estimated 9.2% of female drinkers. Corresponding male and female estimates for cannabis were 12% and 5.5%, respectively. It is noteworthy that alcohol and cannabis had higher rank among men, whereas the anxiolytics-sedatives-hypnotic drug group was higher ranked for women (Table 5).

Notwithstanding these general observations, some attention should be given to the fact that 15–24-year-old drug users had a comparatively high lifetime prevalence of drug dependence in connection with cocaine and alcohol and with Schedule I drugs such as marijuana. To illustrate, for cocaine, almost 25% of the 15–24-year-old users had developed dependence. By comparison, only 15% of the 25–44-year-old cocaine users had developed dependence. To the extent that the 15–24-year-olds have many remaining years at risk, their already high value may become even higher, but for a possibly compensating influence. Namely, it has been observed that early onset illicit drug users (e.g., those who initiate illicit drug use before age 17) seem to be at increased risk for developing drug problems compared with drug users with a later start (e.g., after age 17), even when statistical adjustments are made for differences in duration of drug use (e.g., see Anthony & Petronis, 1993; Robins & Przybeck, 1985). It follows that the cumulative occurrence of drug dependence at first might be especially high among 15–24-year-old drug users, but then might decline as the lower risk experience of later onset drug users is added to this birth cohort's total drug experience. This is an empirical question that deserves continued study, including future analyses of the NCS data on the experience of individual birth cohorts born since 1935.

Future Directions for Research and Other Implications

Future directions for research on these topics can be guided by careful consideration of the present study's deficiencies. Foremost among these limitations is a cross-sectional study design that has placed heavy reliance on retrospective self-report methods, constraining scientific inference about risk and risk factors in relation to drug dependence. Given unbounded resources, we would have liked to make a prospective investigation of each drug's users, starting well before drug use had begun, with periodic observations sustained through periods of risk for drug dependence and other drug-related hazards, including the risk of drug-induced death. Instead, for cost containment, as in the ECA program, the annual NHSDA, and other large-scale epidemiologic surveys, we have sampled the population's experience cross-sectionally and have measured retrospectively. This approach leaves out the experiences of people who have died, as well as those who failed to recall and report their drug involvement with accuracy. Thus, it is useful to remember that on one side lifetime prevalence estimates based on self-reports are hemmed in by the seriousness of death, on the other side by long-forgotten or casual drug involvement that doesn't seem worth mentioning at the time of assessment. To the extent that some conditions may be associated with considerable risk of death (e.g., heroin dependence in the United States), this commonly used study design actually can yield an undercount of morbidity: Many seriously affected persons have died. To the extent that other conditions may be regarded as inconsequential and pointless to mention (e.g., taking a puff on someone else's marijuana cigarette without inhaling), the same approach can yield an overcount of morbidity: Many mildly affected persons are neglected.

As noted previously in this section, cross-sectional survey designs also can lead to misinterpreted time relationships. For example, in this study, it appears that low educational achievement might signal an increased risk of alcohol dependence. In fact, the cross-sectional evidence of this study does not clarify whether alcohol dependence is a risk factor for low educational achievement, whether low education is a risk factor for alcohol dependence, whether the relationship is reciprocal, or whether unmeasured antecedents might explain the observed associations between education and alcohol dependence. In this instance, we are fortunate to have recently published evidence from a prospective study, which found excess risk of alcohol disorders among adults who had not received high school or college diplomas compared with college graduates (Crum, Bucholz, Helzer, & Anthony, 1992; Crum, Helzer, & Anthony, 1993). Of course, whether cross-sectional or prospective, the evidence from a single observational study does not always lead to clear inferences about cause and effect; our study is no exception. As in experimental research, systematic replication is essential, and ultimately causal inferences must be based on judgments about the available evidence.

Limitations of more secondary importance include a restriction of the sampling frame to noninstitutionalized residents who could be sampled from identified dwelling units. Anthony and Trinkoff (1989) and Anthony and Helzer (1991) have discussed and demonstrated how overall prevalence rates for drug dependence and related conditions change very little when institutional residents (and by extension, the homeless) are included within the survey sampling frame. However, it should be acknowledged that this overall generalization might not hold for population subgroups with especially high rates of drug-related incarceration (e.g., young men of African-American heritage).

Current interest in hair analysis and other bioassays for illicit drug use raises a legitimate question about interview assessments of drug dependence (e.g., see Kidwell, 1992). Defined in terms of DSM–III–R diagnostic criteria and case definitions, drug dependence is a psychiatric disturbance for which recent drug use is but one indicator. Except in unusual circumstances, these diagnostic criteria for drug dependence can be assessed only by means of interviews or examinations, either with designated respondents themselves or with informants for these respondents. Given the size of the NCS sample and restricted resources, it was not possible to interview informants.

Against this background of study limitations, it is important to focus on the two epidemiologic questions for which this type of cross-sectional field study is indispensable: (a) In the population, what proportion of persons has been affected by drug dependence? and (b) Comparing subgroups, where in the population are cases of drug dependence more likely to be found? Although the answers to these questions do not constitute definitive evidence with regard to cause and effect relationships or mechanisms of action, these answers have an important public health value. As mentioned in our introduction, these answers can be of use to members of the scientific community and can serve to guide program and policy decisions.

In this respect, the most important implications of this study's results may concern its quantitative findings about the prevalence and location of drug dependence within the population, and the transition from drug use to drug dependence, now assessed with epidemiologic estimates on the basis of an NCS sample designed to generalize to a large segment of the American population. The NCS draws attention to the relative frequency of dependence on tobacco, alcohol, controlled substances, and inhalants, disclosing that many more Americans age 15–54 have been affected by drug dependence than by other psychiatric disturbances now accorded a higher priority in mental health service delivery systems, prevention, and government-sponsored research programs. NCS findings on prevalence correlates add to a growing body of evidence that African Americans do not seem to be more vulnerable to drug dependence by virtue of their race, and these findings also point toward some population segments such as homemakers, in which excess drug dependence has been suspected but never demonstrated clearly. Finally, the NCS results highlight an increasingly well-documented observation that many drug users, perhaps a vast majority, do not seem to make a transition to drug dependence. For them, instead, drug use lacks the major complications associated with clinically defined syndromes of drug dependence. In a time of increasing concern about government expenditures for health and health care reform, the distinction between drug use and drug dependence deserves greater consideration, with commensurate allocation of resources in the direction of drug dependence syndromes that affect public health and society all too commonly.

REFERENCES

Adams, E. H., Gfroerer, J. C., & Rouse, B. A. (1989). Epidemiology of substance abuse including alcohol and cigarette smoking. *Annals of the New York Academy of Sciences, 562*, 14–20.

American Psychiatric Association. (1980). *Diagnostic and statistical manual of mental disorders (3rd. ed.)*. Washington, DC: Author.

American Psychiatric Association. (1987). *Diagnostic and statistical manual of mental disorders (3rd ed., rev.)*. Washington, DC: Author.

Anthony, J. C. (1991). The epidemiology of drug addiction. In N. S. Miller (Ed.), *Comprehensive handbook of drug and alcohol addiction* (pp. 55–86). New York: Marcel Dekker.

Anthony, J. C., & Helzer, J. E. (1991). Syndromes of drug abuse and dependence.

In L. N. Robins & D. A. Regier (Eds.), *Psychiatric disorders in America* (pp. 116–154). New York: Free Press.

Anthony, J. C., & Helzer, J. E. (1995). Epidemiology of drug dependence. In M. Tsaung, M. Tohen, & G. Zahner (Eds.), *Textbook of psychiatric epidemiology*. New York: Wiley.

Anthony, J. C., & Petronis, K. R. (1993). *Early-onset drug use and risk of later drug problems*. Manuscript submitted for publication.

Anthony, J. C., & Trinkoff, A. M. (1989). United States epidemiologic data on drug use and abuse: How are they relevant to testing abuse liability of drugs? In M. W. Fischman & N. K. Mello (Eds.), *Testing for abuse liability of drugs in humans* (NIDA Research Monograph No. 92, pp. 241–266). Rockville, MD: National Institute of Drug Abuse.

Bland, R. C., Orn, H., & Newman, S. C. (1988). Lifetime prevalence of psychiatric disorders in Edmonton. *Acta Psychiatrica Scandinavica, 77* (Suppl. 338), 24–32.

Brady, J. V. (1989). Issues in human drug abuse liability testing: Overview and prospects for the future. In M. W. Fischman & N. K. Mello (Eds.), *Testing for abuse liability of drugs in humans* (NIDA Research Monograph No. 92, pp. 357–370). Rockville, MD: National Institute of Drug Abuse.

Breslau, N., Fenn, N., & Peterson, E. L. (1993). Early smoking initiation and nicotine dependence in a cohort of young adults. *Drug and Alcohol Dependence, 33,* 129–137.

Canino, G. J., Bird, H. R., Shrout, P. E., Rubio-Stipec, M., Bravo, M., Martinez, R., Sesman, M., & Guevara, L. M. (1987). The prevalence of specific psychiatric disorders in Puerto Rico. *Archives of General Psychiatry, 44,* 727–735.

Compton, W. M., Helzer, J. E., Hwu, H.-G., Yeh, E.-K., McEvoy, L., Tipp, J. E., & Spitznagel, E. L. (1991). New methods in cross-cultural psychiatry: Psychiatric illness in Taiwan and the United States. *American Journal of Psychiatry, 148,* 1697–1704.

Cottler, L., Robins, L. N., Grant, B., Blaine, J., Towle, I., Wittchen, H.-U., Sartorius, N., Burke, J., Regier, D., Helzer, J., & Janca, A. (1991). The CIDI-core substance abuse and dependence questions: Cross cultural and nosological issues. *British Journal of Psychiatry, 159,* 653–658.

Crum, R. M., Bucholz, K. K., Helzer, J. E., & Anthony, J. C. (1992). The risk of alcohol abuse and dependence in adulthood: The association with educational level. *American Journal of Epidemiology, 135,* 989–999.

Crum, R. M., Helzer, J. E., & Anthony, J. C. (1993). Level of education and alcohol abuse and dependence in adulthood: A further inquiry. *American Journal of Public Health, 83,* 830–837.

Edwards, G., & Gross, M. M. (1976). Alcohol dependence: Provisional description of a clinical syndrome. *British Medical Journal, 1,* 1058–1061.

Fleiss, J. E. (1981). *Statistical methods for rates and proportions*. New York: Wiley.

Glantz, M., & Pickens, R. (Eds.). (1992). *Vulnerability to drug abuse*. Washington, DC: American Psychological Association.

Harrison, L. D. (1992). Trends in illicit drug use in the United States: Conflicting results from national surveys. *The International Journal of the Addictions, 27,* 817–847.

Hawkins, J. D., Catalano, R. F., & Miller, J. Y. (1992). Risk and protective factors for alcohol and other drug problems in adolescence and early adulthood: Implications for substance abuse prevention. *Psychological Bulletin, 112,* 64–105.

Helzer, J. E. (1985). Specification of predictors of narcotic use versus addiction. In L. N. Robins (Ed.), *Studying drug abuse* (pp. 173–205). New Brunswick, NJ: Rutgers University Press.

Henningfield, J. E. (1992). Occasional drug use: Comparing nicotine with other addictive drugs. *Tobacco Control, 1,* 161–162.

Hwu, H.-G., Yeh, E.-K., & Chang, L.-Y. (1989). Prevalence of psychiatric disorders in Taiwan defined by the Chinese Diagnostic Interview Schedule. *Acta Psychiatric Scandinavica, 79,* 136–147.

Johnston, L. D., O'Malley, P. M., & Bachman, J. G. (1992). *Smoking, drinking, and illicit drug use among American secondary school students, college students and young adults, 1975–1991. Vol. 2. College students and young adults* (National Institutes of Health Publication No. 93-3481). Washington, DC: U.S. Government Printing Office.

Kandel, D. B. (1991). The social demography of drug use. *The Milbank Quarterly, 69,* 365–402.

Kandel, D. B. (1992). Epidemiological trends and implications for understanding the nature of addiction. In C. P. O'Brien & J. H. Jaffe (Eds.), *Addictive states* (pp. 23–40). New York: Raven.

Kandel, D. B., Murphy, D., & Karus, D. (1985). Cocaine use in young adulthood: Patterns of use and psychosocial correlates. In N. J. Kozel & E. H. Adams (Eds.), *Cocaine use in America: Epidemiologic and clinical perspectives* (NIDA Research Monograph No. 61, pp. 76–110). Rockville, MD: National Institute of Drug Abuse.

Kessler, R. C. (in press). The epidemiology of psychiatric comorbidity. In M. Tsaung, M. Tohen, & G. Zahner (Eds.), *Textbook of psychiatric epidemiology.* New York: Wiley.

Kessler, R. C., McGonagle, K. A., Zhao, S., Nelson, C., Hughes, M., Eshleman, S., Wittchen, H.-U., & Kendler, K. (1994). Lifetime and 12-month prevalence of DSM–III–R psychiatric disorders in the United States: Results from the National Comorbidity Survey. *Archives of General Psychiatry, 51,* 8–19.

Kidwell, D. A. (1992). *Discussion: Caveats in testing for drugs of abuse.* In M. M. Kilbey & K. Asghar (Eds.), *Methodological issues in epidemiological, prevention, and treatment research on drug-exposed women and their children* (NIDA Research Monograph No. 117, pp. 98–120). Rockville, MD: National Institute of Drug Abuse.

Kish, L., & Frankel, M. R. (1970). Balanced repeated replications for standard errors. *Journal of the American Statistical Association, 65,* 1071–1094.

Kosten, T. A., & Kosten, T. R. (1991). Criteria for diagnosis. In N. S. Miller (Ed.),

Comprehensive handbook of drug and alcohol addiction (pp. 263–283). New York: Marcel Dekker.

Kosten, T. R., Rounsaville, B. J., Babor, T. F., Spitzer, R. L., & Williams, J. B. (1987). Substance-use disorders in DSM–III–R. Evidence for the dependence syndrome across different psychoactive substances. *British Journal of Psychiatry, 151,* 834–843.

Kramer, M., Von Korff, M., & Kessler, L. (1980). The lifetime prevalence of mental disorders: Estimation, uses and limitations. *Psychological Medicine, 10,* 429–435.

Lee, C. K., Kwak, Y. S., Yamamoto, J., Rhee, H., Kim, Y. S., Han, J. H., Choi, J. O., & Lee, Y. H. (1990a). Psychiatric epidemiology in Korea: Part I. Gender and age differences in Seoul. *The Journal of Nervous and Mental Disease, 178,* 242–246.

Lee, C. K., Kwak, Y. S., Yamamoto, J., Rhee, H., Kim, Y. S., Han, J. H., Choi, J. O., & Lee, Y. H. (1990b). Psychiatric epidemiology in Korea: Part II. Urban and rural differences. *The Journal of Nervous and Mental Disease, 178,* 247–252.

Lillie-Blanton, M., Anthony, J. C., & Schuster, C. R. (1993). Probing the meaning of racial ethnic group comparisons in crack cocaine smoking. *Journal of American Medical Association, 269,* 993–997.

Robins, L. N. (1993). Vietnam veterans' rapid recovery from heroin addiction: A fluke or normal expectation? *Addiction, 88,* 1041–1054.

Robins, L. N., & Przybeck, T. R. (1985). Age of onset of drug use as a factor in drug and other disorders. In C. L. Jones & R. J. Battjes (Eds.), *Etiology of drug abuse* (NIDA Research Monograph No. 56, pp. 178–192). Rockville, MD: National Institute of Drug Abuse.

Robins, L. N., Helzer, J. E., Croughan, J., & Radcliff, K. S. (1985). National Institute of Mental Health Diagnostic Interview Schedule: Its history, characteristics, and validity. *Archives of General Psychiatry, 38,* 381–389.

Robins, L. N., Wing, J., Wittchen, H.-U., Helzer, J. E., Babor, T. F., Burke, J., Farmer, A., Jablenski, A., Pickens, R., Regien, D. A., Sartorius, N., & Towle, L. H. (1988). The Composite International Diagnostic Interview: An epidemiological instrument suitable for use in conjunction with different diagnostic systems and in different cultures. *Archives of General Psychiatry, 45,* 1069–1077.

SAS Institute. (1988). *SAS 6.03* [Computer program]. Cary, NC: Author.

Schober, S., Caces, M., Pergamit, M., & Branden, L. (1992). Effect of mode of administration on reporting of drug use in the National Longitudinal Survey. In C. F. Turner, J. T. Lessler, & J. C. Gfroerer (Eds.), *Survey measurement of drug use: Methodological studies* (pp. 267–276; DHHS Publication No. ADM 92-1929). Washington, DC: U.S. Government Printing Office.

Schuster, C. R. (1989). Testing and abuse liability of drugs in humans. In M. W. Fischman & N. K. Mello (Eds.), *Testing for abuse liability of drugs in humans* (NIDA Research Monograph No. 92, pp. 1–6). Rockville, MD: National Institute of Drug Abuse.

Thompson, T. (1981). Behavioral mechanisms and loci of drug dependence: An overivew. In T. Thompson & C. E. Johanson (Eds.), *Behavioral pharmacology of human drug dependence* (NIDA Research Monograph No. 37, pp. 1–10). Rockville, MD: National Institute of Drug Abuse.

U.S. Department of Health and Human Services. (1993). *National household survey on drug abuse: Main findings 1991* (DHHS Publication No. SMA 93-1980). Washington, DC: U.S. Government Printing Office.

University of Michigan. (1981). *OSIRIS VII* [Computer program]. Ann Arbor, MI: Institute for Social Research, The University of Michigan.

Wells, J. E., Bushnell, J. A., Hornblow, A. R., Joyce, P. R., & Oakley-Browne, M. A. (1989). Christchurch psychiatric epidemiology study, Part 1: Methodology and lifetime prevalence for specific psychiatric disorders. *Australian and New Zealand Journal of Psychiatry, 23,* 315–326.

Wittchen, H.-U. (1995). Reliability and validity studies of the WHO Composite International Diagnostic Interview (CIDI): A critical review. *Journal of Psychiatric Research.*

Wittchen, H.-U., Essau, C. A., von Zerssen, D., Krieg, J.-C., & Zaudig, M. (1992). Lifetime and six-month prevalence of mental disorders in the Munich Follow-Up Study. *European Archives of Psychiatry and Clinical Neuroscience, 241,* 247–258.

Woodruff, R. S., & Causey, B. D. (1976). Computerized method for approximating the variance of a complicated estimate. *Journal of the American Statistical Association, 71,* 315–321.

II

PERSPECTIVES ON ETIOLOGY

2

ALCOHOLISM: A DEVELOPMENTAL DISORDER

RALPH E. TARTER AND MICHAEL VANYUKOV

Alcoholism, or its more precise taxonomic designation, psychoactive substance use disorder, alcohol abuse or dependence (American Psychiatric Association, 1987), can be displayed at any age between early adolescence and late life. Its manifestation is commonly preceded by certain deviant psychological features that are extant since childhood (Tarter, Alterman, & Edwards, 1985). However, because the presence of psychological disturbances do not invariably portend an alcoholism outcome, a facilitating environment is also required.

Figure 1 schematically illustrates the etiology of alcoholism considered from a developmental behavior–genetic perspective. The Gaussian curve at the top of the figure depicts the distribution of phenotypes for temperament traits in the population. Certain temperament phenotypes, as discussed later, appear to be associated with the increased liability to alcoholism. Because temperament traits are measurable in neonates and infants

Reprinted from the *Journal of Consulting and Clinical Psychology, 62*, 1096–1107. (1994).
Copyright © 1994 by the American Psychological Association. Used with permission of the author.

Work on this article was supported by Grants AA08746 and DA05605 from the National Institute on Alcohol Abuse and Alcoholism.

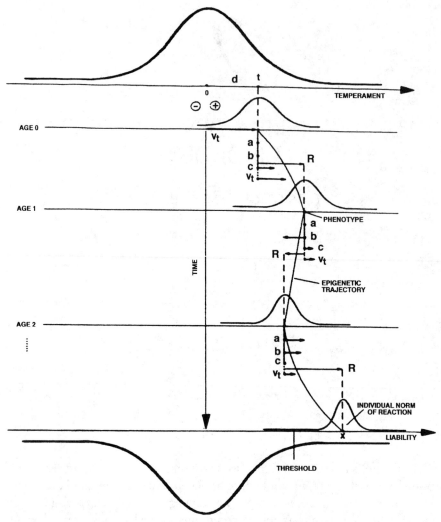

Figure 1. Development of alcoholism. Deviation (d) in temperament (t) comprises a vector (v_t) which, in combination with other vectors (a, b, c, . . .), biases the person toward or away from a threshold diagnosis of alcoholism. Here, the liability is shown to shift with age because the constituent vectors fluctuate throughout life. (R = overall vector.)

and have significant heritability, they can be viewed as the primary characteristics from which more complex psychological traits develop concomitant to continuous and reciprocal interactions with the environment.

The liability to alcoholism is determined by genetic and nongenetic components. This liability can be conceptualized as a trait that, as depicted at the bottom of Figure 1, is normally distributed in the population. Importantly, the liability trait is in a state of flux throughout the lifespan because of unfolding ontogenetic processes.

Consistent with the multifactorial model of inheritance (Falconer, 1965; Kendler & Eaves, 1986) alcoholism is the label for conditions that are manifest when the individual's liability phenotype surpasses a threshold of severity. The shaded region in the Gaussian distribution at the bottom of Figure 1 encompasses the segment of the population that manifests the "beyond-the-threshold" condition; that is, the population who qualify for the diagnosis of alcoholism. Although developmental behavior–genetic methods are appropriate for understanding the etiology of the full range of alcohol consumption behaviors under the distribution, the following discussion is confined to only the segment of the population that surpasses the liability threshold, that is, cases that qualify for a diagnosis of alcoholism.

From the developmental behavior–genetic perspective, the cardinal task for understanding the etiology of alcoholism is to clarify how phenotypic differences in temperament and developing personality traits, which constitute the basis of psychological individuality in the population, culminate eventually in alcoholism for some individuals and not for others. This process can be understood as a developmental trajectory. The quality of interaction with the environment, regulated in large part by the child's behavior, determines the force and direction of the trajectory. Consequent to interactions with the environment during development, behaviors are successively established that increase the risk for an alcoholism outcome.

In this fashion, behavior, considered in relation to the outcome phenotype of alcoholism, can be conceptualized as a vector so that it influences the acquisition of subsequent behaviors during ontogeny; this process is referred to as *epigenesis*. As shown in Figure 1, the first vector is presumed to be temperament phenotype because this is the earliest form of reliably measured behavior after birth. The magnitude of the vector is determined at the outset by the deviation (d) from the population mean in either the positive or negative direction. A central thesis is that temperament deviations in infants and young children negatively affect the quality of the parent–child relationship so that the ensuring behavior disposition of the child increases the risk for alcoholism. These behavior dispositions, constituting vectors, are represented in Figure 1 as a, b, c, ... Vt so that their combined influence defines the overall vector (R). It can be seen that the position of R varies, depending on the interactions among the constituent vectors across age. Hence, successive vectors during the lifespan, consisting of all genetic and nongenetic influences, determine the person's position on the liability trait for alcoholism at any given time. In the example provided, the hypothetical individual develops the affected condition of alcoholism. However, the same conceptual framework applies to cases where the person does not develop alcoholism. Furthermore, depending on the changing constituents of R, it can be seen how both "spontaneous" remission and rapid development of dependence can occur.

A final point with regard to the developmental process pertains to the concept of "norm of reaction." As shown in Figure 1, this is the range of potential change for the particular phenotype. In other words, limits are attached to the capacity to influence the magnitude of change that can be expected for a given individual. For example, for a child with Down's syndrome, environmental stimulation has limitations with respect to augmenting intellectual ability. In the same manner, with respect to the alcoholism phenotype, there are limits regarding the magnitude of change that can be accomplished. Hence, for some individuals, it may not be possible to shift the liability phenotype into the normative range as, for example, those individuals at the extreme end of the distribution of affected cases.

The developmental trajectory to an alcoholism outcome can have a short or long duration and can occur at any time between early adolescence and late adulthood (Helzer, Burman, & McEvoy, 1991). Importantly, outcome among young people who abuse alcohol has been shown to be determined by the number of risk factors (Bry, McKeon, & Pandina, 1982) and that their dynamic interplay over time influences the direction of the developmental trajectory (Labouvie, Pandina, & Johnson, 1991). Existing evidence suggests that higher genetic predisposition leads to earlier age onset alcoholism (Cloninger, Bohman, & Sigvardssen, 1981; McGue, Pickens, & Svikis, 1992). Hence, large deviation in temperament trait expression would be expected to be associated with the risk for an earlier age onset of alcoholism, whereas later age of onset of alcoholism would be expected to be associated with more normative temperament phenotypes and greater adverse environmental circumstances. Consistent with this proposition, behavioral deviancy in childhood is more common in early age onset alcoholism, whereas less genetic influence is present in later-age-onset alcoholism (Cloninger et al., 1981).

DEVELOPMENTAL CONTEXT OF ALCOHOLISM

The discussion up to this point argued for a process-oriented approach to understanding the etiology of early age onset alcoholism. Central to this perspective is the position that alcoholism is a multidimensional endpoint phenotype that is preceded by a succession of intermediary phenotypes of which the first are detectable relatively early in life in the form of temperament deviations. Within the lifespan perspective, a person's phenotype, through reciprocal interactions with multiple environments, can propel or project the person to problematic involvement with alcohol. Importantly, in this context, problematic involvement develops over time, however short or long the interval.

This approach to understanding alcoholism etiology has several parallels with other more accepted developmental disorders. Specifically, alcoholism, like more traditionally accepted developmental disorders, has the common feature of suboptimal acquisition of age-appropriate cognitive, emotional, or behavioral skills. Individuals at high risk for alcoholism have been found, for example, to be impaired on measures of cognitive capacity, particularly involving attentional and visuospatial ability, compared with children at low risk (Pihl, Peterson, & Finn, 1990). Also, attention-deficit disorder and conduct disorder commonly precede the onset of alcoholism (Robins & Rutter, 1990). It can be concluded from these findings that alcoholism—for many individuals, especially when the alcoholism outcome is first manifest early in life—is the culmination of a developmental disorder.

From the developmental perspective, adverse interactions in the home such as physical abuse, parental absenteeism, and poor discipline practices augment the child's liability to alcoholism. Emerging evidence points to the importance of family interaction patterns in shaping the trajectory by inculcating behaviors in the child that promote the likelihood of alcohol (and other drug) initiation. For example, greater mutual dissatisfaction between parent and child (Tarter, Blackson, Martin, Seilhamer, Pelham, & Loeber, 1993) and less effective discipline practices (Tarter, Blackson, Martin, Loeber, & Moss, 1993) have been observed in families where there is substance abuse, there is a stronger association between parent–child dissatisfaction and ineffective discipline with externalizing and internalizing tendencies in the children, compared with normal families. Significantly, association with peers promoting drug use has been found to be related to the combined influence of negative affect and deficient parental monitoring (Chassin, Pillow, Currna, Molina, & Barrera, 1993). These findings indicate how, among high-risk individuals, adverse interactions with the familial environment can orient the child toward enhanced risk for a negative outcome (which is depicted by the shaded area in Figure 1).

Concomitant as well as subsequent to parental interaction, the peer reference group influences the child's position on the liability trait. This latter influence can be either positive or negative and has the effect of deflecting the child toward the normative range or toward the affected range. For example, an adverse home environment has been shown to propel the child to affiliations with nonnormative peers (Wills, 1990). This fosters acceptance or at least tolerance of deviance (Jessor, Donovan, & Costa, 1991) that, in turn, is well recognized to predispose individuals to alcohol use. Viewed within an ontogenetic perspective, it can be seen why alcohol use and abuse among adolescents is also commonly intertwined with other behavioral deviations, such as school truancy, risk taking, gang affiliation, and so forth. However, the main point to be made is that the person's phenotype on the liability trait for alcoholism is not static. Rather, concomitant to developmental processes and changing circumstances at home and in the social environment, the phenotype (and by definition, the risk for alcoholism) fluctuates over time.

From the standpoint of alcoholism, prevention, the practical task is straightforward, albeit difficult. The manifold components of the liability trait for alcoholism, need to be disaggregated so that interventions can be implemented that effectively shift the phenotype toward normality. The same general principle applies to the treatment of alcoholics. Indeed, the observation that a substantial proportion of alcoholics change to nonalcoholic status without receiving an intervention points to instability of the multidimensional phenotype labeled "alcoholism" (Hasin, Grant, & Endicott, 1990). This instability of the liability phenotype is also starkly illustrated by the common observation that heavy drinking by young adults does not invariably portend surpassing the threshold for clinical alcoholism. The factors responsible for these phenomena have not been intensively studied, perhaps because they are not congruent with the generally held conception about the etiology and natural history of alcoholism as a progressive disorder. Nonetheless, from the practical standpoint, recognizing the instability of the liability phenotype should lend confidence to designing effective interventions that could affect alcoholism risk.

In summary, the liability to alcoholism is conceptualized as a latent trait consisting of genetic and nongenetic factors. The components of the trait vary between individuals in the population because of unique genetic constitution and idiosyncratic environmental experiences. Furthermore, the components of the liability trait change over time within the individual concomitant to changing biological maturation and quality of interactions with the environment. Considered from a developmental perspective, it appears to be essential that prevention and treatment interventions have an individual focus in which the main objective is to first decompose the factors constituting the liability phenotype and then apply procedures that effectively shift the phenotype toward the normal or subthreshold segment of the liability trait. The ensuing discussion examines the outset liability as it appears to be manifest early in life from a behavior–genetic framework and concludes with brief discussion of the ramifications of this approach for prevention, treatment, and diagnosis.

TEMPERAMENT PHENOTYPES ASSOCIATED WITH THE ELEVATED RISK FOR ALCOHOLISM

Allport (1961) provides a definition that captures the meaning of temperament:

Temperament reflects "the characteristic phenomena of an individual's nature, including his susceptibility to emotional stimulation, his customary strength and speed of response, the quality of his prevailing mood, and all the peculiarities of fluctuation and intensity of mood, these being phenomena regarded as dependent on constitutional makeup, and therefore largely hereditary in origin." (p. 34)

Although there is uncertainty regarding the exact complement of temperament traits or dimensions, strong empirical evidence nonetheless implicates significant heritability (contribution of genotypic variation on phenotypic variation in the population) for several traits. The following discussion examines the evidence for temperament deviations as risk factors for alcoholism according to the dimensions reported by Rowe and Plomin (1977). These authors identified six dimensions based on integration and analysis of the traits investigated in the New York Longitudinal Study (Thomas & Chess, 1984) and the Colorado Adoption project (Plomin & DeFries, 1983). These latter two investigations constitute the most comprehensive effort aimed at determining the impact of temperament on psychological development and psychosocial adjustment. Significantly, a genetic influence has been documented for the traits investigated in these two investigative programs (Cyphers, Phillips, Fulker, & Mrazek, 1990). Hence, the complement of temperament traits proposed by Rowe and Plomin (1977) is the most parsimonious and empirically based description of temperament. The traits identified are (a) behavior activity level, (b) attention span–persistence, (c) emotionality, (d) "soothability," (e) sociability, and (f) reaction to food. The following discussion succinctly reviews the evidence implicating an association between risk for alcoholism and deviation on these traits, with the exception of reaction to food, which has not received empirical study. (For more detailed reviews of the association between temperament phenotypes and alcoholism risk, see Tarter & Edwards [1988] and Tarter [1988].)

BEHAVIOR ACTIVITY LEVEL

This is an extensively researched temperament dimension. It has also been hypothesized to consist of two components, vigor and tempo (Buss & Plomin, 1975). Rapid behavioral tempo has been implicated to be associated with an increased risk for alcoholism (Vaillant, 1983); however, no research has been conducted regarding the influence of vigor on alcoholism risk.

Evidence from diverse sources indicates that high activity level is associated with a heightened risk for alcoholism. Although not emanating from temperament theory, longitudinal (Jones, 1968; McCord & McCord, 1960; Robins, 1966), adoption (Cantwell, 1972; Goodwin, Schulsinger, Hermansen, Guze, & Winokur, 1975), and retrospective studies (Tarter, McBride, Buonpane, & Schneider, 1977) point to an association between alcoholism and high behavioral activity level in childhood. It has been estimated that up to 40% of male alcoholics have childhood histories of hyperactivity (Wood, Wender, & Reimherr, 1983).

In addition, sons of alcoholic men score higher on ratings of behavioral activity level than sons of nonalcoholic men (Tarter, Kabene, Escallier, Laird, & Jacob, 1990). The possibility is thus raised that the phenotype of high behavioral activity level is a risk factor for alcoholism, inasmuch as male offspring of alcoholics are at high risk to also develop this disorder.

With the exception of one study (Moss, Blackson, Martin, & Tarter, 1992), behavioral activity level has been measured with rating scales. In the recently completed study by Moss et al. (1992), activity level was directly measured in sons of drug and alcohol abusers and compared with offspring of non-drug-abusing, nonalcoholic men using an actigraph attached to the participant's wrist. Measurements were taken while the youngster was in a resting condition and also during performance on two tasks requiring behavioral suppression and sustained attention. The boys in the experimental group demonstrated higher behavioral activity level than that of the children of nonalcoholic fathers while performing the tasks but not during the resting condition. These findings provide objective evidence for an association between heightened risk status for alcohol and drug abuse and the behavioral phenotype of high activity level. It is also noteworthy that the higher behavioral activity level found in the children of substance abusers was not concomitant to a conduct disorder. Hence, it can be tentatively concluded that this behavioral phenotype, although commonly aggregated with conduct disorder, is related to the risk for alcoholism and probably also to other types of drug abuse.

EMOTIONALITY

This temperament trait refers to the propensity to be easily and intensely aroused. Children of alcoholics reported greater emotional reactivity measured by scores on the neuroticism trait than offspring of nonalcoholics (Sher, Walitzer, Wood, & Brent, 1991). It is noteworthy that negative affect and anxiety are common features of youths who consume alcohol (Mezzich, Tarter, Kirisci, Clark, Bukstein, & Martin, 1993) and in offspring of alcoholics (Chassin, Rogush, & Barrera, 1991); however, these findings are not consistent across all studies (Windle, 1990). Somatic and behavioral symptoms of anxiety are commonly present among boys who develop alcoholism early in life (Gomberg, 1982). In a Swedish cohort of older teenagers and young adults reporting for mandatory military registration, it was observed that susceptibility to emotional distress was associated with quantity of alcohol consumed (Rydelius, 1983a, 1983b). Significantly, in children of alcoholics, it has been found that scores on the temperament trait of emotionality covaried with negative affect, which, in combination with stress and parental rearing skills, promoted affiliation with negative peer influences (Chasin et al., 1993). Furthermore, a susceptibility to autonomic nervous system arousal among individuals at high risk for alcoholism has been reported (Finn, Zeitouni, & Pihl, 1990). Taken together, the psychological and psychophysiological findings point to the likelihood that high emotionality is a phenotype for alcoholism risk.

"SOOTHABILITY"

This trait characterizes the individual's rapidity in returning to baseline level after emotional arousal. To date, no direct examination of this temperament trait has been undertaken. However, indirect evidence, marshaled from several studies, suggests that young men who are at a high risk for alcoholism experience a greater stress-dampening effect from ethanol than those who are at a low risk (Sher & Levenson, 1982). One interpretation of these results is that alcohol consumption by high-risk young men facilitates an otherwise deficient homeostasis. Consequently, they experience a stronger reinforcing effect from alcohol consumption. Thus, although the evidence is still tenuous, there is indication that the phenotype of low "soothability" may be associated with an increased risk for alcoholism.

ATTENTION SPAN–PERSISTENCE

Up to 40% of male alcoholics have been reported to qualify for an attention-deficit disorder–residual type (Wood et al., 1983). Research findings using neurocognitive tests, rating scales, and structured interviews confirm the high prevalence of attentional disturbances among children and young adults who, as a group, are at high risk for alcoholism (Alterman & Tarter, 1983; Tarter, Hegedus, Goldstein, Shelly, & Alterman, 1984). Also, young alcoholics scored lower than older alcoholics on tasks requiring motor persistence (Alterman, Tarter, Petrarulo, & Baughman, 1984); this finding is contrary to what would be expected if the deficit were only the consequence of an alcoholism history and suggests that poor task persistence antedates the alcoholism. It is also noteworthy that neurophysiological investigations reveal deviations on the P300 wave component of event-related potentials (Begleiter, Porjesz, & Kissin, 1984). The P300 wave is consensually recognized to reflect attentional mechanisms. Thus, on the basis of limited available evidence, it appears that attentional limitations and goal impersistence are associated with the risk for alcoholism.

Significantly, the findings pointing to low attentional capacity in high-risk individuals are based on various types of measurements evaluating different components of attention. Research has yet to be undertaken that is directed to delineating the particular facets of attention that are specifically associated with heightened risk.

SOCIABILITY

Systematic research on this temperament dimension has not been conducted with respect to the risk for alcoholism. Some evidence has been presented that indicates that high scores on the personality trait of extraversion are more common among alcoholics (Barnes, 1983); however, these findings are limited by the fact that the scores could have been confounded by the established chronic course of the alcoholism. The trait "inhibition to the unfamiliar" closely approximates sociability and has been shown to have important developmental ramifications (Kagan & Saidman, 1991); however, its relevance to alcoholism etiology has not been studied.

It appears that many alcoholics present as sociable when, in fact, the behavior constitutes a disinhibited interpersonal style. Hence, although overly facile and having an extraverted quality, the behavior is actually reflective of a poor self-control or dysregulation. This conclusion is buttressed by the observation that an antisocial personality disorder is a common comorbid condition of alcoholism.

It is also noteworthy that studies of alcoholics, studies of individuals at high risk, and prospective studies of individuals who subsequently became alcoholic, have documented frequently features such as aggressivity (Kellam, Ersminger, & Simon, 1980), sensation seeking (Zuckerman, 1972), impulsivity (McCord, 1972), and social nonconformity (Robins, 1966). These characteristics do not represent the attributes of normative sociability but rather behavioral disinhibition.

Complementing this conclusion are the results of several studies indicating that individuals who obtain a low sociability score on the California Psychological Inventory (in conjunction with a high behavioral disinhibition score measured by the MacAndrew Scale of the Minnesota Multiphasic Personality Inventory) obtain a greater stress-dampening effect from alcohol, compared with individuals whose scores are more normative (Sher & Levenson, 1982). Because alcohol is more reinforcing among individuals who score low on the trait of sociability, the possibility is raised that habitual alcohol consumption is more likely to occur. In effect, pharmacological disposition may covary with temperament phenotype. Germane to the present discussion, however, is the conclusion that the phenotype predisposing to alcoholism appears to be behavioral disinhibition, although, at first glance, the individual may present as extraverted. This conclusion concurs with the recent finding that parental alcoholism was unrelated to sociability in offspring (Chasin et al., 1993).

SUMMARY

On the basis of published results, the behavior–genetic approach appears to be a heuristic strategy for determining the psychological characteristics associated with the risk for alcoholism. As noted earlier, certain temperament phenotypes appear to be associated with a high risk for alcoholism. The temperament phenotypes that, to date, have been most implicative are high activity level, high emotionality, low sociability, low attention span–persistence, and low "soothability." It is emphasized, however, that an alcoholism outcome is not determined directly by temperament phenotype; rather, as depicted in Figure 1, this outcome is the culmination of the epigenetic process. The outset point, temperament phenotype, interacts with the social environment throughout the lifespan to determine risk status. Furthermore, it should be emphasized that factors in addition to temperament deviation (e.g., biochemical, physiological) may also affect the risk for alcoholism. Finally, it is important to note that a temperament deviation is not a necessary condition to predispose to an alcoholism outcome; it can be seen in Figure 1 that a normative temperament phenotype in the context of either adverse biological or environmental circumstances also can culminate in this outcome. After a brief examination of issues surrounding the need to concisely define the outcome—namely, alcoholism—the focus of the discussion then turns to how temperament–environment interactions underlie the developmental trajectory to alcoholism.

ALCOHOLISM PHENOTYPE

Research into etiology has been hampered by a lack of consensus regarding the taxonomic criteria for defining alcoholism; that is, an objective quantifiable description of the threshold on the continuum. The necessary or defining attribute for alcoholism has yet to be specified. Not surprisingly, therefore, consensus regarding the denotative meaning of this clinical condition remains elusive (Tarter, Moss, Arria, & Mezzich, 1992). In the American Psychiatric Association classification system, alcoholism is a multidimensional phenotype applied to individuals who exceed an arbitrary number of adverse consequences concomitant to alcohol consumption behavior. Hence, not surprisingly, the population who is labeled *alcoholic* is very heterogeneous with respect to clinical presentation and natural history. Without a clear specification of the outcome phenotype, alcoholism, it is not possible to elucidate specific etiologic mechanisms and associated developmental pathways. For example, there are manifold permutations of symptoms that could qualify an individual for a diagnosis of alcoholism (Tarter, Arria, Moss, Edwards, & Van Thiel, 1987). Thus, to clarify the etiology of alcoholism, the endpoint multidimensional phenotype needs to be specified better than currently practiced. Research focusing on particular phenotypic features of alcoholism constitute important progress in this direction for improving understanding of the interaction between genetic and environmental influences on producing specific outcomes (Heath, Meyer, Jardine, & Martin, 1991).

Recently, a first step in documenting phenotypic heterogeneity was undertaken in the form of a proposal of a method for quantifying 10 endpoints according to their severity (Tarter, 1990). This approach contradicts current efforts to identify pure alcoholic subtypes based on the dimensions of personality, comorbid psychiatric disorder, familial transmission patterns, or natural history. Referring to Figure 1, it is apparent that the pathway to alcoholism is unique for each individual. Hence, efforts to cluster alcoholics into distinct groups are unlikely to be successful, particularly if numerous dimensions relevant to treatment intervention are considered. Tarter (1990) proposed 10 salient dimensions that are integral to both etiology and maintenance of problems with alcohol consumption. Thus, rather than assigning this heterogeneous population with the one label of alcoholism, outcome is instead quantified across 10 domains. These 10 dimensions, evaluated by the Drug Use Screening Inventory are substance abuse; psychiatric disorder; behavior problems; work problems; social maladjustment; peer relations; health disturbances; social skill deficits; family problems; and leisure and recreation. By ranking severity of alcohol and drug involvement using the Drug Use Screening Inventory across 10 dimensions, it should be possible to more effectively target interventions to specific areas of disturbance and possibly calibrate the intensity of a particular intervention (e.g., inpatient, day hospital, outpatient) to the measured level of severity of disorder. However, germane to the context of this discussion, it can be readily appreciated that when alcoholism is considered as a multidimensional phenotype, the development trajectory is influenced by numerous factors that are unique to each person. From the standpoint of treatment, this conclusion underscores the need for individualized intervention and not a program in which each person receives the same type and intensity of intervention. From the standpoint of etiology, this conclusion buttresses recent findings pointing to the importance of the unshared environment (Reiss, Plomin, & Hetherington, 1991). From the standpoint of taxonomy, this conclusion calls into question the validity of the DSM system in general and the value of using labels such as alcoholism and alcohol dependence specifically (Tarter et al., 1992). Hence, by improving precision in the measurement of specific dimensions, the developmental trajectory, linking predisposing temperament phenotypes to particular consequences of alcohol consumption, can be better understood.

In summary, for research into alcoholism etiology to progress, concerted effort must be directed to elucidating the characteristics predisposing to specific phenotypic features encompassed within the multidimensional category of alcoholism. For example, the factors underlying pharmacological tolerance, craving, drinking pattern, and the biomedical consequences of drinking (e.g., cirrhosis) are, in all probability, very diverse. Whereas the research conducted to date has typically specified the outcome variable to be dichotomous (alcoholic vs. nonalcoholic), this clinically diagnosed endpoint of alcoholism itself encompasses a very heterogeneous population with respect to etiologic determinants, natural history, and behavioral presentation. Increased precision of measurement and greater specificity of endpoint phenotypes are thus necessary to further an understanding of alcoholism etiology.

PHENOTYPE–ENVIRONMENT INTERACTIONS

The developmental approach is based on the premise that primordial behavioral characteristics (e.g., temperament phenotypes), modified during the course of ontogeny, establish the psychological propensities that are associated with a high risk for alcoholism. This developmental trajectory occurs through interaction between the individual and the environment. In effect, the individual seeks out, as well as uniquely reacts to, the social environment. The person's psychological disposition and others in the social environment thus are mutually influenced by the quality of these interactions. For example, peers commonly cluster on the same behaviors, particularly for substance use and social deviancy (Kandel, Davies, & Baydar, 1990). Also it is well established that individuals respond to environmental stimuli according to their particular psychological characteristics. Thus, the person's psychological makeup mediates the quality of interaction with the environment to shape the developmental process; this iterative process has been referred to as the *organismic specificity hypothesis* (Wachs & Gandour, 1983). This framework for elucidating etiology is heuristic for investigating behavior epigenesis; that is, the successive acquisition of phenotypes according to the characteristics of previous phenotypes. Conceptualized as a Markov chain analysis, antecedent behavior probabilistically affects the expression of subsequent behavior to orient the person toward or away from an alcoholism outcome.

To illustrate this developmental model, Figure 2 and the discussion given later provides an example of one hypothetical trajectory to an alcoholism outcome. The temperament phenotype, high behavioral activity level, predisposes an individual to a series of outcomes that ultimately

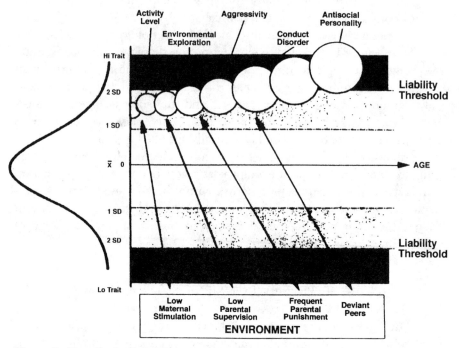

PHENOTYPE

Figure 2. Hypothetical developmental trajectory to alcoholism.

manifests as alcoholism. It is noteworthy that each of the processes depicted in Figure 2 that are implicated to influence behavioral development has been documented in the empirical literature; however, to date, investigations of alcoholism have not been conducted to encompass the chaining of the behavioral trajectory in a prospective study of alcoholism etiology.

On the basis of studies of animals and humans, substantial evidence has been accrued that demonstrates that variability in behavioral activity level in the population is influenced strongly by genotypic differences. The variation of this trait can be theoretically described within a Gaussian distribution consisting of infinite phenotypes. Infants manifesting a high behavioral activity level are prone to exchanges with the social environment that promote the development of conduct problems and deviancy. Available evidence indicates that high behavioral activity level in early childhood is associated with a propensity for extensive environmental exploration (Gandour, 1989); notably, this propensity, characterized as a sensation-seeking motivational style, is common among adolescent alcohol and drug abusers (Zuckerman, 1972). Unrestricted exploration of the environment can be associated with ineffective parental supervision; this factor has also been shown to be characteristic of youths at risk for substance abuse (Tarter et al., 1993) and conduct problems (Patterson, DeBaryshe,

& Ramsey, 1989). In addition, free-ranging access to the environment potentially sets the stage for conflict with caretakers. It is salient to note that children having a high behavioral activity level experience more severe punishment than other children (Webster-Stratton & Eyberg, 1982) and, in this regard, it is noteworthy that children at high risk for substance abuse are subjected to more severe and inconsistent disciplinary practices than other children (Tarter et al., 1993) and that there is also greater mutual dissatisfaction between parent and child (Tarter, Blackson, Martin, Seilhamer, et al., 1993). Thus, the temperament phenotype of high activity level, expressed in early childhood, predisposes to interactions with the environment which promote social maladjustment.

However, as pointed out by Thomas and Chess (1984), an effective environment in responding to the child's behavior can mitigate deviancy and maladjustment. Particularly, a mismatch between the child and caretakers with respect to behavioral and affective disposition has been hypothesized to be a critical factor. In a longitudinal research study conducted at the Center for Education and Drug Abuse Research, preliminary evidence has been accrued, indicating that the similarity between substance-abusing fathers and 10- to 12-year-old sons, with respect to a composite trait of "difficult affective temperament," is related to magnitude of behavior problems in the child (Blackson, Tarter, Martin, & Moss, 1994). Other research has shown that high behavioral activity in childhood of individuals who have a family history of alcoholism can promote drinking behavior in adulthood, although they are not alcoholic themselves (Pelham, Lang, Atkeson, Murphy, Gnagy, & Greiner, unpublished manuscript). The point to be made is that the interactions between the child and caretaker are mutually influential so as to affect the course of the child's psychological development.

A distressed home environment and disruptive behavior by the child in that environmental context do not necessarily result in problems that come to the attention of professionals. Thus, problems may remain unnoticed until the child enters school, where normative behavior patterns are essential for adjustment. Thus, although aggressive and oppositional behavior in the home can be tolerated, even if not effectively managed, such behavior in the school environment is problematic. These types of conduct problems are common among children at high risk for substance abuse (Mezzich, Tarter, Moss, & Hsieh, unpublished manuscript) and predispose them to conflicts with teachers as well as to social marginalization by normative-behaving peers. In reaction to this situation, the child is likely to select and affiliate with similar-behaving deviant peers. Hence, behavior disturbances, extant before entering school, become more firmly established so that a suprathreshold phenotype of conduct disorder is eventually manifest. By adolescence, this conduct disorder almost invariably includes alcohol and drug use.

In this developmental scenario, alcohol and drug use are intertwined with conduct problems and ultimately a conduct disorder that carries a risk of about 0.5 for developing into an antisocial personality disorder in adulthood (Farrington, 1991). Hence, the age at which the person first qualifies for a suprathreshold diagnosis of alcoholism (or other substance abuse) is variable; this disorder can occur at any time after the onset of conduct problems in childhood when the person initiates consumption as part of a generalized pattern of deviancy.

In summary, alcoholism etiology cannot be understood in the context of a specific cause–effect relationship. The aforementioned scenario, by illustrating one hypothetical developmental pathway to alcoholism, demonstrates how temperament phenotype early in life develops into successive behavioral phenotypes that eventually place the person onto a trajectory for this adverse outcome. Because the interactions between each child's phenotype and the environment are unique, every person in the population who develops alcoholism has an idiosyncratic etiology and natural history.

EPIGENETIC MODEL

The preceding discussion examined a developmental pathway to alcoholism based on a deviation in only one temperament trait, activity level. It is ultimately necessary to delineate the unique configuration of each person's temperament, involving conjointly all trait dimensions, to understand the etiology of alcoholism. Even within a framework of five temperament traits, as discussed herein, and the theoretically infinite number of phenotypes for each trait, it becomes apparent why every person in the population has a distinctive temperament makeup.

One configuration of phenotype that has received substantial interest is the difficult temperament. Individuals described as having a difficult temperament are characterized as having negative mood, high social withdrawal, high rigidity, high behavioral activity level, dysrhythmicity in eating, sleep and daily activity, and low task orientation (Thomas & Chess, 1977). Significantly, a difficult temperament in early childhood is associated with an increased risk for both internalizing and externalizing behavior disorder by late childhood and adolescence (Maziade et al., 1990).

An association between difficult temperament in childhood and subsequent alcohol and drug use has been reported (Lerner & Vicary, 1984). In addition, children of alcohol and drug abusers have been shown to score higher than offspring of nonabusing parents on the difficult temperament index, derived from the revised Dimensions of Temperament Scale (Tarter et al., 1990; Tarter, Blackson, Martin, Loeber, et al., 1993; Tarter, Blackson, Martin, Seilhamer, et al., 1993). Furthermore, it has been observed that a difficult temperament displayed in late childhood mediates the effects of parental history of substance abuse on the child's expression of behavior disturbance (Blackson et al., 1994).

Little is known regarding the mechanisms by which difficult temperament in childhood influences psychological development and initiation subsequently of alcohol and drug use. In one study, it was observed that there is greater mutual dissatisfaction between mother and son in families where the father is a substance abuser (Tarter et al., 1993) and that the magnitude of dissatisfaction correlated negatively with family cohesion and organization. This finding suggests that the environmental context combined with a suboptimal temperament predisposes a person to maladjustment, including hyperactivity, aggressiveness, and delinquency in the offspring. It is also noteworthy that male offspring of substance abusers experience more severe and less consistent disciplinary practices than children of nonabusing parents (Tarter et al., 1993). Taken together, these results indicate that a child who displays a difficult temperament, especially if living in a family where there is parental substance abuse, manifest behavioral features that have been frequently observed to predispose him or her to substance abuse. Furthermore, the magnitude of expression of these latter behavioral features in the child is related to assortative mating for these characteristics by the child's parents (Vanyukov, Moss, Plail, Blackson, Mezzich, & Tarter, 1993).

The epigenetic approach to alcoholism etiology is directed to delineating how behavioral phenotypes successively emerge concomitant to person–environment interaction patterns. The quality of these interactions, as previously discussed, is determined by the conjoint characteristics of the individual and the social environment. In one preliminary examination of the heuristic value of the epigenetic approach, a Markov chain analysis was conducted on a sample of 48 adolescents who qualified for a diagnosis of psychoactive substance use disorder (Tarter, Kirisci, Hegedus, Mezzich, & Vanyukov, 1949). It was found that a difficult temperament in childhood was present in 35% of the sample. Within this subsample, several different psychiatric disorders subsequently emerged, of which conduct disorder, attention-deficit disorder, and anxiety disorder were most prevalent. Alcohol or another drug abuse disorder next emanated from one of these disorders. The implications of these findings are twofold: (a) the pathways linking temperament to substance abuse are variable; and (b) the breadth of intermediary outcomes ultimately produce a population of alcoholics having limitless heterogeneity.

In summary, an epigenetic paradigm is heuristic for uncovering the developmental pathways to alcoholism and other variations of drug abuse. These pathways are determined by the unique quality of person–environment interactions that, in turn, determines the acquisition of successive behavioral phenotypes. This temporal organization and patterning of behavior constitutes the developmental trajectory that orients the person toward or away from an alcoholism outcome.

IMPLICATIONS OF THE DEVELOPMENTAL BEHAVIOR GENETIC PERSPECTIVE

The variability of temperament traits has a polygenic basis (Buss & Plomin, 1984; Plomin, 1990). Interindividual differences in the liability to alcoholism, as the developmental product of these traits, therefore, also have a polygenic basis. Emerging methods in molecular genetics potentially afford the opportunity to delineate how multiple genes located on different chromosomes underlie variation in behavior phenotypes, such as temperament. Particularly, quantitative trait loci (QTL) methods of analysis are being developed to elucidate the genetic substrate of behavior that could potentially have important applications for understanding alcoholism etiology. For example, research with rodents has shown that QTL technology can inform about the genetic basis underlying variation in alcohol tolerance (McClearn, Plomin, Gora-Maslak, & Crabbe, 1991). As noted previously, different aspects of alcoholism topology may have different substrates; however, research, to date, has not attempted to clarify the various behavioral phenotypes that may contribute to the liability to alcoholism using QTL methods.

PREVENTION OF ALCOHOLISM

Although the greatest period of risk for the onset of alcoholism is in the first half of life, the developmental behavior–genetic perspective encompasses the whole lifespan. The lifespan applicability of the behavior–genetic perspective stems mainly from the premise that it is the quality of interaction between the person having a particular psychological disposition and the social environment that determines the behavior response patterns and emotional reactions. In turn, these define, to a large degree, the initiation of habitual consumption of alcoholic beverages. At an age when alcohol is accessible and known by the consumer to have desired psychoactive effects, this usually occurring by late childhood, it is possible at any time thereafter for alcoholism to develop.

The model presented in Figure 1 conceptualizes how prevention research can be undertaken within the developmental behavior–genetic perspective. The psychological (temperament) disposition as discussed earlier, is a vector that orients the person toward or away from alcoholism or a drug abuse outcome. However, myriad environmental factors affect both the force and directional components of the vector. For example, the child's family could exercise a negative impact on the child and, thus, enhance the risk for an adverse outcome. Offsetting this influence, other influences in the environment can potentially reduce the risk. Thus, risk at any time is determined by the aggregate of environmental factors, positive and negative, interacting with psychological disposition. By disaggregating these factors with the aim of bolstering the positive ones and attenuating the negative ones, the risk for an alcoholism outcome can be diminished.

The implications of this approach to prevention are substantial. Specifically, it underscores the need to implement preventions that are tailored to one or more of the following objectives: changing the psychological characteristics of the individual; changing the environment; or changing the quality of interactions between the person and the environment. With respect to changing the person, the armamentarium of strategies ranging from pharmacologic to behavior modification methods may be effective in reducing risk status by shifting behavior toward the more normative range. However, because psychological interventions are less intrusive, they are arguably preferred to biological interventions for modifying the liability. Normative behavior, once established, is then a vector for further normative development. Changing the environment could also reduce risk by shifting the person toward normative behavior. For example, reducing accessibility to alcohol and drugs and preventing tobacco use in public places has the effect of forcing compliance with normative behavior. Placing the person in a social context or subculture that redefines normative behavior so that habitual alcohol use is negatively sanctioned constitutes another potentially effective environmental manipulation. Common observation of the radical behavioral and attitudinal changes that occur among individuals who join certain religious subcultures underscores the potency of environmental intervention.

Finally, preventive measures should be implemented that modify the quality of person–environment interaction patterns that are identifiable developmental vectors for future maladjustment. In this regard, interventions may be effective that are targeted to interaction patterns in particular environmental contexts (e.g., family, school, job), so that the individual's behavior is modified toward normality. As discussed previously, there appears to be a complex relationship between the child's difficult temperament, quality of parental rearing, and disruptive behavior in children of substance-abusing parents. Improving the parenting quality for parents of children who display a difficult temperament may thus promote normative development and ultimately reduce the risk for alcoholism and substance abuse.

In summary, prevention research can make a substantive contribution to reducing alcohol and drug abuse in society by the adoption of a developmental behavior–genetic perspective. On delineating the behaviors constituting vectors for the adverse outcome, it is then possible to identify those individuals who are at high risk to whom tailored interventions should be targeted.

TREATMENT OF ALCOHOLISM

Paralleling the strategy for individualized prevention, the approach to treatment requires modification of factors that have contributed to the suprathreshold diagnosis of drug abuse or alcoholism. The objective of treatment intervention is to disaggregate the factors contributing to severe problem involvement with drugs or alcohol (defined by surpassing the diagnostic threshold) and then implementing interventions that could shift the person toward the normative ranges. As shown in Figure 1, this involves shifting the person's phenotype as an affected condition of alcoholism (Figure 1, shaded area) to the normative area under the curve. Because the person's position on the liability trait is uniquely determined by genetic predisposition, in conjunction with shared and unshared environmental experiences, it is clear that interventions need to be targeted to those specific components that are liability enhancing. Consequently, standardized treatment programs that do not account for individuality in etiology and natural history are likely to be less successful than interventions that are tailored to specific components of the liability. This approach to treatment emphasizes the development of intervention resources and implementation of intervention modality on a case-by-case basis that addresses the person's unique etiologic determinants.

As pointed out previously, there are many factors that could trigger problem involvement with drugs and alcohol. The DUSI (Gordian Group, 1991; Tarter & Hegedus, 1992) is one efficient method for quantifying the severity of alcohol- and drug-related problems across 10 domains of health, psychiatric functioning, and psychosocial functioning so that areas in need of intervention can be efficiently detected. The goal of treatment is to deflect the person away from the severe end of the continuum in those domains that are responsible for maintaining problem involvement with drugs or alcohol. As with prevention intervention, there are three basic strategies in which the person can be deflected from the suprathreshold, or clinically affected range, to the normative range. These include changing the person's dispositional behavior pattern, changing the person's environment, and changing the quality of interaction between the person and the environment. Thus, whether the intervention is directed toward prevention or treatment, the task is to disaggregate the unique configuration of each individual's psychological and environmental factors that underlie the risk or manifestation of problem drinking.

REFERENCES

Allport, G. (1961). *Pattern and growth in personality*. New York: Holt, Rinehart, Winston.

Alterman, A., & Tarter, R. (1983). The transmission of psychological vulnerability. Implications for alcoholism etiology. *Journal of Nervous and Mental Disease, 171*, 147–154.

Alterman, A., Tarter, R., Petrarulo, E., & Baughman, T. (1984). Evidence for impersistence in young male alcoholics. *Alcoholism: Clinical and Experimental Research, 8*, 448–450.

American Psychiatric Association. (1987). *Diagnostic and statistical manual of mental disorders (3rd ed., rev.)*. Washington, DC: Author.

Barnes, G. (1983). Clinical and prealcoholic personality characteristics. In B. Kissin & H. Begleiter (Eds.), *The pathogenesis of alcoholism* (Vol. 6, pp. 113–195). New York: Plenum Press.

Begleiter, H., Porjesz, B., & Kissin, B. (1984). Event-related brain potentials in children at risk for alcoholism. *Science, 225*, 1493–1495.

Blackson, R., Tarter, R., Martin, C., & Moss, H. (1994). Temperament mediates the effects of family history of substance abuse on externalizing and internalizing child behavior. *American Journal of Addiction, 3*, 58–66.

Bry, B. H., McKeon, P., & Pandina, R. J. (1982). Extent of drug use as a function of number of risk factors. *Journal of Abnormal Psychology, 91*, 273–279.

Buss, A., & Plomin, R. (1975). *A temperament theory of personality development*. New York: Wiley.

Buss, A., & Plomin, R. (1984). *Temperament: Early developing personality traits*. Hillsdale, NJ: Erlbaum.

Cantwell, D. (1972). Psychiatric illness in families of hyperactive children. *Archives of General Psychiatry, 27*, 414–417.

Chassin, L., Pillow, D., Curran, P., Molina, B., & Barrera, M. (1993). Relation of parental alcoholism to early adolescent substance use: A test of three mediating mechanisms. *Journal of Abnormal Psychology, 102*, 3–19.

Chassin, L., Rogush, F., & Barrera, M. (1991). Substance use and symptomatology among adolescent children of alcoholics. *Journal of Abnormal Psychology, 100*, 449–463.

Cloninger, C., Bohman, M., & Sigvardssen, S. (1981). Inheritance of alcohol use: Cross-fostering analyses of adopted men. *Archives of General Psychiatry, 38*, 861–868.

Cyphers, L., Phillips, K., Fulker, D., & Mrazek, D. (1990). Twin temperament during the transition from infancy to early childhood. *Journal of the American Academy of Child Psychiatry, 29*, 392–397.

Falconer, D. (1965). The inheritance of liability to certain diseases estimated from the incidence among relatives. *Annals of Human Genetics, 29*, 51–86.

Farrington, D. (1991). Antisocial personality from childhood to adulthood. *The Psychologist, 4*, 389–394.

Finn, P., Zeitouni, N., & Pihl, R. (1990). Effects of alcohol on psychophysiological hyperactivity to nonaversive and aversive stimuli in men at high risk for alcoholism. *Journal of Abnormal Psychology, 99*, 79–85.

Gandour, M. (1989). Activity level as a dimension of temperament in toddlers: Its relevance for the organismic specificity hypothesis. *Child Development, 60*, 1092–1098.

Gomberg, E. (1982). The young male alcoholic: A pilot study. *Journal of Studies on Alcohol, 43*, 683–701.

Goodwin, D., Schulsinger, F., Hermansen, L., Guze, S., & Winokur, G. (1975). Alcoholism and the hyperactive child syndrome. *Journal of Nervous and Mental Disease, 160*, 349–353.

Gordian Group. (1991). *Drug Use Screening Inventory* [Available from the author at P.O. Box 1587, Hartsville, SC 29550].

Hasin, D., Grant, B., & Endicott, J. (1990). The natural history of alcohol abuse: Implications for definitions of alcohol use disorders. *American Journal of Psychiatry, 147*, 1537–1541.

Heath, A., Meyer, J., Jardine, R., & Martin, N. (1991). The inheritance of alcohol consumption in a general population twin study: II. Determinants of consumption frequency and quantity consumed. *Journal of Studies on Alcohol, 52*, 425–433.

Helzer, J., Burman, A., & McEvoy, L. (1991). Alcohol abuse dependence. In L. Robins & D. Regier (Eds.), *Psychiatric disorders in America* (pp. 81–115). New York: Free Press.

Jessor, R., Donovan, J., & Costa, F. (1991). *Beyond adolescence. Problem behavior and young adult development.* Cambridge, England: Cambridge University Press.

Jones, M. (1968). Personality correlates and antecedents of drinking patterns in adult males. *Journal of Consulting and Clinical Psychiatry, 32*, 2–12.

Kagan, J., & Saidman, N. (1991). Infarct predictors of inhibited and uninhibited profiles. *Psychological Science, 2*, 40–44.

Kandel, D., Davies, M., & Baydar, N. (1990). The creation of interpersonal contexts: Homophily in dyadic relationships in adolescence and young adulthood. In L. Robins & M. Rutter (Eds.), *Straight and devious pathways from childhood to adulthood* (pp. 221–241). Cambridge, England: Cambridge University Press.

Kellam, S., Ersminger, M., & Simon, M. (1980). Mental health in first grade and teenage drug, alcohol, and cigarette use. *Drug and Alcohol Dependence, 5*, 273–304.

Kendler, K., & Eaves, L. (1986). Models for the joint effect of genotype and environment on liability to psychiatric illness. *American Journal of Psychiatry, 14*, 279–289.

Labouvie, E., Pandina, R., & Johnson, V. (1991). Developmental trajectories of substance use in adolescence. Difference and predictors. *International Journal of Behavioral Development, 14*, 305–328.

Lerner, J., & Vicary, J. (1984). Difficult temperament and drug use: Analysis from the New York Longitudinal Study. *Journal of Drug Education, 14*, 1–8.

Maziade, M., Caron, C., Cote, R., Merrette, C., Bernier, H., Laplante, B., Boutin, P., & Thivierge, J. (1990). Psychiatric status of adolescents who had extreme temperaments at age 7. *American Journal of Psychiatry, 147*, 1531–1537.

McClearn, G., Plomin, R., Gora-Maslak, G., & Crabbe, J. (1991). The gene chase in behavioral science. *Psychiatry and Science, 2*, 222–229.

McCord, J. (1972). Etiological factors in alcoholism: Family and personal characteristics. *Quarterly Journal of Studies on Alcohol, 33*, 1020–1027.

McCord, W., & McCord, J. (1960). *Origins of alcoholism.* Stanford, CA: Stanford University.

McGue, M., Pickens, R., & Svikis, D. (1992). Sex and age effects on the inheritance of alcohol problems: A twin study. *Journal of Abnormal Psychology, 101*, 3–17.

Mezzich, A., Tarter, R., Moss, H., & Hsieh, Y. *Substance abuse vulnerability in three groups of prepubertal children of substance abusing fathers.* Unpublished manuscript.

Mezzich, A., Tarter, R., Kirisci, L., Clark, D., Bukstein, O., & Martin, C. (1993). Subtypes of early age onset alcoholism. *Alcoholism in Clinical and Experimental Research, 17*, 767–770.

Moss, H., Blackson, T., Martin, C., & Tarter, R. (1992). Heightened motor activity level in male offspring of substance abusing fathers: Association with temperament, behavior and psychiatric diagnosis. *Biological Psychiatry, 32*, 1135–1147.

Patterson, G., DeBaryshe, B., & Ramsey, E. (1989). A developmental perspective on antisocial behavior. *American Psychologist, 44*, 329–335.

Pelham, W., Lang, A., Atkeson, B., Murphy, D., Gnagy, E., & Greiner, A. *Stress-induced alcohol consumption in parents interacting with confederate children: Effects of child behavior, offspring psychopathology, and family history of alcohol problems.* Unpublished manuscript.

Pihl, R., Peterson, J., & Finn, P. (1990). Inherited predisposition to alcoholism: Characteristics of sons of male alcoholics. *Journal of Abnormal Psychology, 99*, 291–301.

Plomin, R. (1990). The role of inheritance in behavior. *Science, 248*, 183–188.

Plomin, R., & DeFries, J. C. (1983). The Colorado adoption project. *Child Development, 54*, 276–289.

Reiss, D., Plomin, R., & Hetherington, M. (1991). Genetics and psychiatry: An unheralded window on the environment. *American Journal of Psychiatry, 148*, 283–291.

Robins, L. (1966). *Deviant children grown up: A sociological and psychiatric study of sociopathic personality.* Baltimore: Williams and Wilkins.

Robins, L., & Rutter, M. (1990). *Straight and devious pathways from childhood to adulthood* (pp. 1–389). Cambridge, England: Cambridge University Press.

Rowe, D., & Plomin, R. (1977). Temperament in early childhood. *Journal of Personality Assessment, 41*, 150–156.

Rydelius, P. (1983a). Alcohol-abusing teenage boys: Testing a hypothesis on the relationship between alcohol abuse and social background factors, criminality and personality in teenage boys. *Acta Psychiatrica Scandinavica, 68*, 368–380.

Rydelius, P. A. (1983b). Alcohol-abusing teenage boys: Testing a hypothesis on alcohol abuse and personality factors using a personality inventory. *Acta Psychiatrica Scandinavica, 68*, 381–385.

Sher, K., & Levenson, R. (1982). Risk for alcoholism and individual differences in the stress–response-dampening effect of alcohol. *Journal of Abnormal Psychology, 19*, 350–367.

Sher, K., Walitzer, K., Wood, P., & Brent, E. (1991). Characteristics of children of alcoholics: Putative risk factors, substance use and abuse, and psychopathology. *Journal of Abnormal Psychology, 100*, 427–488.

Tarter, R. (1988). Are there inherited behavioral traits which predispose to substance abuse? *Journal of Consulting and Clinical Psychology, 36*, 189–196.

Tarter, R. (1990). Evaluation and treatment of adolescent substance abuse: A domain tree method. *American Journal of Drug and Alcohol Abuse, 61*, 1–46.

Tarter, R., Alterman, A., & Edwards, K. (1985). Vulnerability to alcoholism in men. A behavior–genetic perspective. *Journal of Studies on Alcohol, 46*, 329–356.

Tarter, R., Arria, A., Moss, H., Edwards, K., & Van Thiel, D. (1987). DSM-III criteria for alcohol abuse. Association with alcohol consumption behavior. *Alcoholism: Clinical and Experimental Research, 11*, 541–543.

Tarter, R., Blackson, T., Martin, C., Loeber, R., & Moss, H. (1993). Characteristics and correlates of child discipline practices in substance abuse and normal families. *American Journal on Addiction, 2*(1), 18–25.

Tarter, R., Blackson, T., Martin, C., Seilhamer, R., Pelham, W., & Loeber, R. (1993). Mutual dissatisfaction between mother and son in substance abuse and normal families. Association with child behavior problems. *American Journal on Addiction, 2*(2), 1–10.

Tarter, R., & Edwards, K. (1988). Psychological factors associated with the risk for alcoholism. *Alcoholism: Clinical and Experimental Research, 12*, 471–480.

Tarter, R., & Hegedus, A. (1992). The Drug Use Screening Inventory. Its application in the evaluation and treatment of alcohol and drug abuse. *Alcohol, Health and Research World, 15*, 65–75.

Tarter, R., Hegedus, A., Goldstein, G., Shelly, C., & Alterman, A. (1984). Adolescent sons of alcoholics: Neuropsychological and personality characteristics. *Alcoholism: Clinical and Experimental Research, 8*, 216–222.

Tarter, R., Kabene, M., Escallier, E., Laird, S., & Jacob, T. (1990). Temperament deviation and risk for alcoholism. *Alcoholism: Clinical and Experimental Research, 14*, 380–382.

Tarter, R., Kirisci, L., Hegedus, A., Mezzich, A., & Vanyukov, M. (1994). Heterogeneity of adolescent alcoholism. *Annals of the New York Academy of Science*, *708*, 172–180.

Tarter, R., McBride, H., Buonpane, N., & Schneider, D. (1977). Differentiation of alcoholics: Childhood history of minimal brain dysfunction, family history, and drinking pattern. *Archives of General Psychiatry, 34*, 761–768.

Tarter, R., Moss, H., Arria, A., & Mezzich, A. (1992). Psychiatric diagnosis of alcoholism: Critique and reformulation. *Alcoholism: Clinical and Experimental Research, 16*, 106–116.

Thomas, A., & Chess, S. (1977). *Temperament and development.* New York: Brunner/ Mazel.

Thomas, A., & Chess, S. (1984). Genesis and evolution of behavioral disorders. From infancy to early adult life. *American Journal of Psychiatry, 140*, 1–8.

Vaillant, G. (1983). *The natural history of alcoholism.* Cambridge, MA: Harvard University Press.

Vanyukov, M., Moss, H., Plail, J., Blackson, T., Mezzich, A., & Tarter, R. (1993). Antisocial symptoms in preadolescent boys and their parents: Association with cortisol. *Psychiatric Research, 46*, 9–17.

Wachs, T., & Gandour, M. (1983). Temperament, environment, and six-month cognitive–intellectual development: A test of the organismic specificity hypothesis. *International Journal of Behavioral Development, 6*, 135–152.

Webster-Stratton, C., & Eyberg, S. (1982). Child temperament: Relationship with child behavior problems and parent–child interactions. *Journal of Clinical Child Psychology, 11*, 123.

Wills, T. (1990). Multiple networks and substance use. *Journal of Social and Clinical Psychology, 9*, 78–90.

Windle, M. (1990). Temperament and personality attributes of children of alcoholics. In M. Windle & J. Searles (Eds.), *Children of alcoholics: A critical review of the literature* (pp. 129–167). New York: Guilford Press.

Wood, D., Wender, P., & Reimherr, F. (1983). The prevalence of attention deficit disorder, residual type, or minimal brain dysfunction in a population of male alcoholic patients. *American Journal of Psychiatry, 140*, 95–98.

Zuckerman, M. (1972). Drug usage as one manifestation of a "sensation seeking" trait. In E. Keup (Ed.), *Drug abuse: Current concepts and research* (p. 154). Springfield, IL: Charles C Thomas.

3

IMPLICATIONS OF RECENT NEUROPSYCHOPHARMACOLOGIC RESEARCH FOR UNDERSTANDING THE ETIOLOGY AND DEVELOPMENT OF ALCOHOLISM

HENRY R. KRANZLER AND RAYMOND F. ANTON

Recently renewed interest in pharmacotherapies for alcoholism stems largely from new insights into the putative neuropharmacologic basis for alcohol consumption, dependence, and related disabilities. Several recent review articles (Bohn, 1993; Jaffe, Kranzler, & Ciraulo, 1992; Litten & Allen, 1991) provide a comprehensive discussion of this area. Rather than attempt to deal exhaustively with this rapidly developing area, we focus principally on medications that affect two neurochemical systems: the serotonergic and opioidergic systems. Pharmacologic manipulation of these systems appears to hold the greatest promise for providing efficacious treatments for relapse prevention in alcoholics.

Reprinted from the *Journal of Consulting and Clinical Psychology*, 62, 1116–1126. (1994). Copyright © 1994 by the American Psychological Association. Used with permission of the author.

This work was supported by grants AA03510, AA00143, and AA09568 from the National Institute on Alcohol Abuse and Alcoholism.

The article begins with a review of preclinical and clinical developments as they relate to the role of the serotonergic and opioidergic neurotransmitter systems in alcohol self-administration and alcoholism. Throughout the article, generic names are used to refer to all medications. For all medications approved for clinical use in the United States, the generic name, on its first appearance in the text, is followed by the medication's trade name, which appears in parentheses. Subsequent sections review recent developments in diagnosis and subtyping, as they relate to a neuropsychopharmacologic perspective on alcoholism. Finally, the impact that recent findings in the molecular genetics of alcoholism may have on developments in the neuropsychopharmacologic and typologic approaches to alcoholism are discussed.

The ultimate aim of this article is to frame these developments in terms of the insight that they provide into the etiology and development of alcoholism. However, it will be evident to the reader that the empirical literature is greatest for the neuropsychopharmacologic perspective; it is substantially less well developed for the typologic approach and is least well developed in the area of molecular genetics.

SEROTONERGIC NEUROTRANSMISSION IN ALCOHOLISM

It has generally been thought that the identification of a biological abnormality in alcoholics would permit specific pharmacologic interventions to be used to remedy the condition. On the basis of knowledge gained and techniques available from both preclinical and clinical research in other psychiatric disorders, the serotonin systems has been a prime candidate in the search for a biological basis for alcoholism. Of particular note is the convergence of findings that support the role of serotonin (5-HT) as a neurochemical modulator of mood and impulse control, both of which are of central significance in alcoholism and other addictive disorders (Coccaro & Murphy, 1990).

A growing literature has shown abnormalities to exist in 5-HT neurotransmission in alcoholics. These abnormalities include low cerebrospinal fluid (CSF) levels of 5-hydroxyindoleacetic acid (5-HIAA), the major metabolite of 5-HT (Gorelick, 1989; Roy, Virkkunen, & Linnoila, 1990). This has been interpreted to mean that alcoholics have diminished 5-HT neurotransmission (Ballenger, Goodwin, Major, & Brown, 1979). Furthermore, an inverse relationship between CSF 5-HIAA levels and the time elapsed since alcohol was last consumed has been found in alcoholics (Banki, 1981). This suggests that 5-HT release resulting from acute ethanol consumption may serve to "normalize" low brain levels of 5-HT in alcoholics (Ballenger et al., 1979). Other investigators have shown low CSF 5-HIAA levels to be associated with a variety of impulsive behaviors, including aggressivity (Brown, Goodwin, Ballenger, Goyer, & Major, 1979; Linnoila, Virkkunen, Scheinin, Rimon, & Goodwin, 1983), attempted and completed suicide (Asberg, Schalling, & Traskman-Bendz, 1987), and impulsive fire setting (Virkkunen, Nuutila, Goodwin, & Linnoila, 1987). Consistent with these findings in humans, studies in animals have linked 5-HT to aggression and readiness to ingest alcohol (Roy, Linnoila, & Virkkunen, 1987).

However, serotonergic neurotransmission is complex, and the level of 5-HT in the brain is only one mechanism by which behavior may be affected. Very different behavioral effects have also been observed in relation to subtypes of 5-HT receptors (Hoyer, 1990; Murphy, 1990). Although there is no universal agreement concerning many of the specific elements of 5-HT receptor classification, four major classes appear to exist: $5\text{-}HT_1$, $5\text{-}HT_2$, $5\text{-}HT_3$, and $5\text{-}HT_4$ (Hoyer, 1990). Several $5\text{-}HT_1$ receptor subtypes have also been identified, including $5\text{-}HT_{1A}$, $5\text{-}HT_{1B}$, $5\text{-}HT_{1C}$, and $5\text{-}HT_{1D}$ (Lucki & Wieland, 1990). In addition to the diversity of receptor types, there exists variability in the mechanisms whereby receptor stimulation is translated into changes in neuronal function. These complexities in both receptor type and mechanism of signal transduction may help to explain how a single neurotransmitter can exert a wide variety of effects and potentially can play a pathophysiologic role in a variety of disorders, including alcoholism (Hamon et al., 1990; Murphy, 1990).

SEROTONERGIC AGONIST EFFECTS ON ALCOHOL CONSUMPTION

Myers and Melchior (1977a), Naranjo, Sellers, and Lawrin (1986), and Gorelick (1989) have reviewed the extensive experimental literature that links 5-HT neurotransmission to alcohol consummatory behavior. A wide variety of 5-HT agonists (i.e., agents that produce effects like those produced by 5-HT itself) markedly reduce alcohol consumption on animals (Naranjo et al., 1986). Serotonin uptake inhibitors (SUIs) increase the concentration of 5-HT in the neuronal synapse. These drugs also produce a decrease in intracranial self-stimulation, an animal model that appears to provide a proxy measure for self-administration of psychoactive substances, including ethanol (Naranjo et al., 1984).

Data on the effects of SUIs on alcohol consumption in humans are more limited, and the effects are less potent than those in animals. These studies have been conducted in a variety of subject groups, including nonalcoholic volunteers, heavy drinkers (who were neither diagnosed as alcohol dependent nor seeking alcoholism treatment), and clinical samples of alcoholics. Both acute (Amit et al., 1985) and chronic (Naranjo et al., 1984) administration of zimelidine, an SUI that was removed from clinical trials because of toxicity, have shown that it attenuates ethanol consumption in subjects who were neither seeking treatment to help reduce their drinking nor counseled to do so. Other SUIs that have been tested for their effects on alcohol consumption in humans include citalopram (Naranjo et al., 1987), viqualine (Naranjo et al., 1989), and fluoxetine (Prazac; Naranjo, Kadlec, Sanhueza, Woodley-Remus, & Sellers, 1990). These studies have shown that the SUIs are well tolerated and that they can reduce drinking in nondepressed, heavy drinkers who are not seeking alcoholism treatment. The magnitude of the decrease, however, is not dramatic. For example, in heavy drinkers, 60 mg of fluoxetine per day (a dose that is three times that generally used to treat depression) decreased daily mean alcohol intake from 8.7 drinks during a baseline period to 6.9 drinks during the 4-week trial.

Studies of diagnosed alcoholics have yielded more mixed results. When alcoholics on an inpatient unit were given the opportunity to drink alcohol, pretreatment with up to 80 mg of fluoxetine per day initially reduced alcohol consumption. This effect, however, did not persist into the second week of the inpatient trial (Gorelick & Paredes, 1992). Kranzler et al. (1995) found that fluoxetine, at a maximal dosage of 60 mg per day in alcohol-dependent outpatients, was not significantly better than placebo treatment in reducing alcohol consumption. Finally, Kranzler, Del Boca, Korner, and Brown (1993) described a trial of fluvoxamine, another SUI, which was so poorly tolerated that the trial was discontinued. Despite these variable and modest effects on alcohol consumption in alcoholics, a role may emerge for SUIs in the multimodal treatment of alcoholism, possibly in conjunction with skills training in relapse prevention (Gallant, 1993; Marlatt, 1985).

SUBTYPES OF 5-HT RECEPTORS AND EFFECTS ON ALCOHOL CONSUMPTION

Several studies of animals and humans have used serotonergically active drugs that are selective for subtypes of 5-HT receptors. Agonists that are selective for the 5-HT_{1A} receptor have been shown both to reduce alcohol consumption in animals and to reduce anxiety and alcohol consumption in alcohol-dependent humans. Recent studies (Engel et al., 1992; Svensson, Fahlke, Hard, & Engel, 1993) have shown that the selective 5-HT_{1A} agonists 8-OH-DPAT and ipsapirone reduce both ethanol intake and the preference for ethanol in a free-choice situation. Similarly, the 5-HT_{1A} agonists gepirone and buspirone (BuSpar) have been shown to reduce ethanol consumption in rodents (Knapp, Benjamin, & Pohorecky, 1992; Privette, Hornsby, & Myers, 1988). Buspirone has produced a similar effect in monkeys (Collins & Myers, 1987). Taken together, these animal studies suggest that drugs that stimulate 5-HT_{1A} receptors produce substantial reductions in alcohol consumption.

Preclinical studies have also implicated $5\text{-HT}_2/5\text{-HT}_{1C}$ and 5-HT_3 receptors in alcohol consumption. Many of these studies (Fadda, Garan, Marchel, Colombo, & Gessa, 1991; Knapp & Pohorecky, 1992; Meert, Awouters, Niemegeers, Schellekens, & Janssen, 1991; Myers, Lankford, & Bjork, 1993) have shown that antagonists (i.e., drugs that block stimulation) of these receptors reduce alcohol consumption. However, other studies (Myers & Lankford, 1993; Svensson et al., 1993) have failed to show effects on alcohol consumption after treatment with such agents.

One approach to reducing alcohol consumption is the treatment of comorbid anxiety in anxious alcoholics (Kranzler & Liebowitz, 1988). This approach is based on evidence that anxious alcoholics drink to alleviate anxiety (Meyer, 1986). Consequently, use of a medication to reduce anxiety would theoretically reduce the drive to consume alcohol. Several recent trials with the anxiolytic buspirone address this hypothesis.

A double-blind trial of buspirone in outpatient alcoholics (Bruno, 1989) showed significantly greater retention in treatment and greater decreases in anxiety and depression scores in buspirone-treated patients, compared with the placebo group. Both groups showed significant declines in alcohol consumption during study participation, with no differential reduction as a consequence of buspirone treatment. The investigators did not examine whether the severity of the patients' anxiety interacted with the effects of the medication to reduce alcohol consumption. Tollefson, Montague-Clouse, and Tollefson (1992), in a study of abstinent alcoholics with comorbid generalized anxiety disorder, found that buspirone-treated subjects were less likely to discontinue medication treatment prematurely and had greater reductions in anxiety than did placebo-treated subjects. Although a subjective, global measure of improvement in drinking was observed for the active drug group, measures of alcohol consumption were not included in Tollefson et al.'s study. Kranzler et al. (1993) showed that in anxious alcoholics, those receiving buspirone in a 12-week outpatient trial were significantly more likely to remain in treatment and slower to return to heavy drinking during the study than were placebo-treated patients. Furthermore, patients who received the active drug reported fewer drinking days during the 6-month posttreatment follow-up period. In contrast to these three reports, Malcolm et al. (1992) found no advantage for buspirone over placebo on measures of either anxiety or alcohol consumption in alcoholics with symptoms of generalized anxiety that persisted beyond inpatient alcoholism treatment.

In general, these studies have shown buspirone to be safe and effective in reducing anxiety when used in a well-selected subgroup of alcoholics with substantial comorbid anxiety. Perhaps the most consistent and potent effect of the medication has been enhanced retention in treatment, compared with placebo. However, the impact of treatment with buspirone on risk of relapse to heavy drinking remains unclear. More research is needed to address this question.

Other studies of alcoholics or heavy drinkers have sought to produce reductions in alcohol consumption directly through effects on other 5-HT receptor subtypes. Ritanserin, which acts as an antagonist (i.e., blocker) at $5\text{-}HT_2/5\text{-}HT_{1C}$ receptor sites, has been reported to decrease drinking in alcoholics (Monti & Alterwain, 1991). A large multicenter trial is currently underway to evaluate the drug's effects in mild-to-moderate alcohol dependence. Similarly, Toneatto and colleagues (1991) found that the specific $5\text{-}HT_3$ antagonist ondansetron (Zofran) produced a greater reduction in alcohol consumption than did placebo in heavy drinkers who were not seeking alcoholism treatment. More clinical investigation with these selective serotonergic drugs is needed before definitive statements can be made regarding their usefulness for the treatment of alcoholism.

INTERACTION OF SEROTONERGIC AND DOPAMINERGIC SYSTEMS WITH ALCOHOL EFFECTS

The neurotransmitter dopamine has been implicated in the behavioral reinforcement produced by several drugs that are abused by humans, most notably the stimulant drugs (e.g., amphetamine, cocaine), but alcohol as well (Di Chiara & Imperato, 1988; Weiss, Bloom, & Koob, 1991). Interactions between serotonergic and dopaminergic systems have been shown to exist and may be of importance in the reinforcing effects of alcohol.

Several serotonergic drugs that reduce alcohol consumption in animals and humans interact with the dopamine system. For example, the $5\text{-}HT_2/5\text{-}HT_{1C}$ antagonist ritanserin decreases dopamine release in the substantia nigra (Ugedo, Grenhoff, & Svensson, 1987). Administration of $5\text{-}HT_3$ antagonists reduces dopamine activity in mesolimbic areas (Wozniak, Pert, & Linnoila, 1990) and has been shown to inhibit alcohol-induced stimulation of dopamine release in the nucleus accumbens (Carboni, Acquas, Frau, & Di Chiara, 1989). In contrast, $5\text{-}HT_3$ agonists enhance dopamine release (Costall, Domeney, Naylor, & Tyers, 1987). These effects may explain why some $5\text{-}HT_3$ antagonists have been shown to block the discriminative stimulus effects of alcohol (Grant & Barrett, 1991). The interaction of buspirone and other $5\text{-}HT_{1A}$ agonists with the dopamine system (Eison & Temple, 1986) may also help to explain the effects of these drugs on alcohol consumption.

Considerably more work is needed to elucidate the interaction between serotonergic and dopaminergic neurotransmission. Given that both systems have been implicated in alcohol-consummatory behavior, a clearer understanding of their interaction may provide unique opportunities for insights into the pathophysiology of alcoholism and for designing novel pharmacological treatments for the disorder.

OPIOIDERGIC NEUROTRANSMISSION IN ALCOHOLISM

The fundamental role that endogenous opioids play in reinforcement suggests that these substances play an important role in the pathophysiology of addictive disorders, including alcoholism. As with 5-HT, abnormalities in opioidergic neurotransmission have been shown to be present in alcoholics (Topel, 1988; Trachtenberg & Blum, 1987). Decreased basal levels of beta-endorphin have been found in the plasma (Aguirre, Del Arbol, Raya, Ruiz-Requena, & Irles, 1990), and CSF (Genazzani et al., 1981) of alcoholics, compared with that of nonalcoholic subjects. Enhanced pituitary release of cortisol and beta-endorphin (an endogenous opioid) by alcoholics after the administration of naloxone (Narcan), an opiate blocker, also provides a connection between alcoholism and opioidergic neurotransmission (Kemper et al., 1990).

The literature on animals helps to illuminate this issue as well. Beta-endorphin is self-administered by rats, leading to the postulate that altered sensitivity to beta-endorphin may be of pathophysiologic significance in both alcoholism and drug dependence (Van Ree, 1979, 1986). Furthermore, mice that were selectively bred for high voluntary ethanol consumption were found to have low levels of endogenous opioids before ethanol consumption (Blum & Topel, 1986). In contrast, beta-endorphin is increased in both the plasma and brain of rats who are fed alcohol (Eskelson, Hameroff, & Kanel, 1980). Acute ethanol treatment of alcohol-drinking mice produced an increase in hypothalamic release of beta-endorphin that was not observed in mice who consumed no ethanol (Gianoulakis & Gupta, 1986).

Similar findings have been obtained in humans who are at increased risk of alcoholism. Gianoulakis et al. (1989) found that unaffected adult children of alcoholics had basal levels of beta-endorphin that were comparable with those of abstinent alcoholics and significantly lower than those of unaffected adults who lacked a family history of alcoholism. Furthermore, when given alcohol, the adult children of alcoholics showed a significantly greater increase (i.e., a "normalization") in beta-endorphin levels, resulting in levels comparable with those observed following alcohol administration to adult children of nonalcoholics. Despite these intriguing findings, beta-endorphin, which is released from the pituitary gland, provides at best a limited reflection of events occurring within specific areas of the brain that control alcohol consumption.

OPIOIDERGIC EFFECTS OF ALCOHOL CONSUMPTION

There also exists an extensive literature reflecting the role of opioid-ergic neurotransmission in alcohol consumption and related phenomena. Small doses of the opioidergic agonist morphine have been shown to enhance ethanol intake in laboratory animals (Hubbell et al., 1986; Myers & Critcher, 1982). Tetrahydropapaveroline (THP), which is a biological precursor of morphine, is a condensation product of acetaldehyde and dopamine. THP binds to opioid receptors, producing effects similar to those of other opioid agonists (Myers & Melchior, 1977b).

In contrast, opioid antagonists (i.e., blockers) decrease ethanol consumption and self-administration (Altshuler, Phillips, & Feinhandler, 1980; De Witte, 1984; Hubbell et al., 1986). This is true both for naloxone, which is short-acting and administered intravenously (De Witte, 1984; Hubbell et al., 1986; Siviy, Calcagnetti, & Reid, 1982), and for naltrexone (Trexan), which is longer acting and administered orally (Altshuler et al., 1980; Crabtree, 1984; Myers, Borg, & Mossberg, 1986). Both of these agents antagonize opioid receptors without significant agonist effects at these or other receptors. Interestingly, in rats, naloxone was found to reduce ethanol intake by decreasing the duration of a drinking bout, rather than by affecting either the latency to drink or the initial phase of drinking (Siviy et al., 1982). This effect parallels what has been reported in a trial of the orally active drug naltrexone in alcoholics (Volpicelli, O'Brien, Alterman, & Hayashida, 1992). Naloxone has also been shown to block a variety of alcohol-related effects, including ethanol consumption induced by THP (Myers & Critcher, 1982), ethanol-induced increases in locomotor activity (Middaugh, Read, & Boggan, 1978), and ethanol dependence (Blum, Futterman, Wallace, & Schwertner, 1977).

As is true for the 5-HT system, opioidergic neurotransmission involves a variety of neuronal receptor types. The major classes of opioid receptors are mu, kappa, and delta, with some evidence for the existence of subtypes within these classes (Adler, Goodman, & Pasternak, 1990; Brownstein, 1993). Alcohol may differentially affect these receptor types, making it theoretically possible to identify medications with selective effects for use in the treatment of alcoholism. In animal models, ethanol in high concentrations inhibits opioid receptor binding, specifically that involving the delta receptor (Hiller, Angel, & Simon, 1981). Work by Froehlich et al. (Froehlich, Zweifel, Harts, Lumeng, & Li, 1991) has shown a primary role for the enkephalinergic system in the reinforcing effects of ethanol consumption. They have also shown that specific antagonism of delta receptors (for which the enkephalins, a second species of endogenous opioids, have greatest affinity) appears to be responsible for the decreased alcohol consumption observed with opioid antagonists.

OPIOID ANTAGONIST EFFECTS IN ALCOHOLICS

Two recent placebo-controlled trials of naltrexone (50 mg/day) in alcohol-dependent patients have shown the drug to be efficacious in relapse prevention. Volpicelli et al. (1992) studied male veterans enrolled in an intensive outpatient treatment program after an inpatient's stay. They found that, during the 12-week study, naltrexone reduced the number of drinking days, the craving for alcohol, and the risk of relapse to heavy drinking. Naltrexone was particularly effective in the prevention of relapse to heavy drinking among patients who sampled alcohol. In an effort to replicate and extend these findings, O'Malley et al. (1992) evaluated naltrexone and two manual-guided psychotherapies in a sample of alcohol-dependent outpatients. They found that naltrexone treatment produced decreases in drinking days, in the intensity of drinking, and in alcohol-related problems. Among patients who drank during the study, the active drug was especially effective in preventing relapse to heavy drinking when paired with relapse prevention psychotherapy, compared with routine clinical management. In both studies, the active drug was well tolerated and produced no serious adverse effects.

In summary, a substantial body of data suggests that opioidergic neurotransmission plays an important role in the reinforcement of alcohol-consummatory behavior and in the development of alcohol dependence. Opioidergic medications may reduce either the risk of developing alcoholism or the risk of relapse to heavy drinking among alcohol-dependent individuals. Ongoing research in the clinical application of these medications can be expected to define more clearly their role in the treatment of alcoholism.

INTERACTION OF OPIOIDERGIC AND DOPAMINERGIC SYSTEMS WITH ALCOHOL EFFECTS

As with the serotonergic system, there is also evidence for interaction between the opioidergic system and dopaminergic neurotransmission. Although direct reinforcing effects have been shown to exist for endogenous opioids such as enkephalins (Froehlich et al., 1991) and beta-endorphin (Van Ree, 1979, 1986), opioidergic effects on dopaminergic neurotransmission may also be important in the reinforcing effects of ethanol. The anatomic colocalization of endogenous opioids and dopamine in the brain reflects the interplay between these two systems, which may have particular relevance for the usefulness of an opioidergic drug to influence dopamine-mediated behaviors. Alcohol-induced release of dopamine in the nucleus accumbens (NAc) is associated with the motor stimulant and reinforcing effects of ethanol (Di Chiara & Imperato, 1988). Alcohol increases the release of dopamine in the NAc when administered involuntarily (McBride, Murphy, Lumeng, & Li, 1990), and in a free-choice situation (Weiss et al., 1991). In rat lines bred for alcohol preference, animals that readily consume ethanol have lower basal levels of dopamine in the NAc than do animals who consume lower levels of ethanol (Murphy, McBride, Lumeng, & Li, 1987). Opioid receptor agonists (e.g., morphine, beta-endorphin), whether injected peripherally (Rada, Mark, Pothos, & Hoebel, 1991), centrally (Iyengar, Kim, Marien, McHugh, & Wood, 1989) or directly into the ventral tegmentum (Kalivas & Duffy, 1990), also increase dopamine levels in the NAc. Furthermore, naloxone, when administered intraperitoneally, blocked the effects of ethanol on striatal dopamine turnover (Reggiani, Barbaccia, Spano, & Trabucchi, 1980).

SUMMARY OF THE EFFECTS OF SEROTONERGIC AND OPIOIDERGIC NEUROTRANSMISSION ON ALCOHOL CONSUMPTION

The administration of serotonergic agonists and opioid antagonists appears consistently to reduce alcohol consumption in animals. Whether these effects are attributable to shared effects on dopaminergic neurons remains to be determined. However, a direct comparison of the effect of these medications on alcohol consumption in animals has been reported. Hubbell et al. (1991), on the basis of a series of experiments with the opioid antagonist nalmefene and the SUI fluoxetine, concluded that opioidergic effects are more salient, with respect to alcohol consumption, than are serotonergic effects. In humans, the SUIs, which increase 5-HT in the synaptic cleft and thereby indiscriminately stimulate a variety of presynaptic and postsynaptic 5-HT receptor subtypes, have produced modest and somewhat inconsistent reductions in alcohol consumption. The availability of agents that bind selectively to 5-HT receptor subtypes may make it possible to refine the understanding of the role of serotonergic neurotransmission in alcohol-consummatory behavior and thereby to enhance clinical efficacy. Opioid antagonists appear to produce more consistent reductions in alcohol consumption in clinical samples. The majority of work in this area has been done using naltrexone, a nonselective antagonist of mu, kappa, and delta opioid receptors. Although evidence has begun to appear that implicates the delta receptor in the reinforcing effects of alcohol (Froehlich et al., 1991), this work is preliminary and clinical evaluation must await the availability of delta-specific agents that are approved for human use.

SUBTYPES OF ALCOHOLICS AND THEIR RELATIONSHIP TO NEUROPSYCHOPHARMACOLOGY

Alcoholism is both complex and multidimensional. It has been characterized as a set of disorders, the "alcoholisms" (Jacobson, 1976), a term that reflects its phenomenologic and etiologic heterogeneity (Gilligan, Reich, & Cloninger, 1987). Various typologic approaches have been used over the past 150 years in an effort to order the diversity of phenomena associated with alcoholism (Babor & Lauerman, 1986). "One-dimensional" typologies that are based on etiological variables, presenting symptoms, or drinking patterns have been shown to be poor independent predictors of outcome status (Babor, Dolinsky, Rounsaville, & Jaffe, 1988). Consequently, Babor et al. (1992) derived a typology that is based on initial evaluation and prospective follow-up of a cohort of alcoholics in inpatient rehabilitation. The dichotomous typology that they derived resembled in some respects one that was proposed earlier by Cloninger (1987), although these two typologies also differ in some important ways (see Table 1). Together, they provide an approach with potential usefulness for matching alcoholics to specific pharmacotherapies. However, this literature is not nearly as well developed as the neuropsychopharmacologic literature. The relative usefulness of these typologic approaches for understanding the etiology, natural history, and response to treatment in alcoholism requires substantially greater empirical evaluation.

Cloninger's Type 1–Type 2 distinction is based on a cross-fostering analysis in Sweden of men who were adopted as children (Cloninger, Bohman, & Sigvardsson, 1981). This approach enabled the investigators to examine the relative contributions of genetic and environmental factors in the development of alcoholism. It also led them to conclude that there are two different forms of the disorder. According to Cloninger's typology, Type 1 alcoholics are characterized by the late onset of problem drinking, rapid development of behavioral tolerance to alcohol, prominent guilt and anxiety related to drinking, and infrequent fighting and arrests when drinking. In contrast, Type 2 alcoholics are characterized by spontaneous alcohol-seeking behavior, early onset of an inability to abstain from alcohol, frequent fighting and arrests when drinking, and the absence of guilt and fear concerning drinking. Cloninger (1987) theorized that this distinction includes basic dimensions of personality structure, which he linked to neuropharmacologic substrates for various behaviors, including aggressivity and alcohol consumption. Differences in three basic personality traits are hypothesized to underlie the differences in the two subgroups. According to Cloninger, Type 1 alcoholics may be characterized by high reward dependence, high harm avoidance, and low novelty seeking. In contrast, Type 2 alcoholics may be characterized by high novelty seeking, low harm avoidance, and low reward dependence. Although work by Schuckit, Irwin, and

TABLE 1

Comparative Features of Two Typologies of Alcoholism

Variable	Late onset		Early onset	
	Type 1[a]	Type A[b]	Type 2[a]	Type B[b]
Age of onset (years)	After 25	$M > 30$	Before 25	$M < 22$
Gender specificity	Male or female	Male:female = 0.8	Male limited	Male:female = 1.7
Sociopathy	Low	Low	High	High
Binge drinking	Frequent	Infrequent	Infrequent	Frequent
Inability to abstain	Uncommon	Uncommon	Common	Common
Comorbid depression	High	Low	Low	High
Heritability	Low	Probably low	High	Probably high

[a]Type 1 and Type 2 are groups in a typology proposed in Cloninger's work (1987; Cloninger, Bohman, & Sigvardsson, 1981). [b]Type A and Type B are groups in a typology proposed by Babor, Hofmann, DelBoca, Hesselbrock, Meyer, Dolinsky, and Rounsaville (1992).

Mahler (1990) has failed to provide empirical support for this tridimensional personality scheme, Cloninger's typology has generated substantial research interest.

The typology proposed by Babor et al. (1992) was derived from an empirical clustering technique, applied to data obtained from 321 male and female alcoholics. The analysis identified two homogeneous subtypes that may have important implications both for prognosis and for treatment matching. One group, designated Type A, is characterized by later onset of problem drinking, fewer childhood risk factors, less severe alcohol dependence, less drug use, fewer alcohol-related problems, less psychopathology, and a better response to traditional alcoholism treatment. The other group, termed Type B, is characterized by childhood and familial risk factors, early onset of alcohol problems, greater severity of dependence, polydrug use, a more chronic treatment history (despite their younger age), greater psychopathology, and a poorer prognosis after alcoholism treatment. Cloninger's Type 1 alcoholic shares with the Type A alcoholic a later onset of alcohol-related problems and the absence of antisocial characteristics. Cloninger's Type 2 alcoholic shares with the Type B alcoholic an early onset of alcohol-related problems and the presence of antisocial characteristics, particularly when intoxicated.

Given that Cloninger's Type 2 ("male-limited") alcoholism is less common and more heritable than Type 1 ("milieu-limited") alcoholism, the etiologic implications of that typology are more evident than they are for the typology of Babor et al. However, the greater familial loading for alcoholism among Type B alcoholics identified by Babor et al. is consistent with greater heritability of that subtype. An important advantage for the typology of Babor et al. is that it has demonstrated predictive validity (Kadden, Cooney, Getter, & Litt, 1989; Litt, Babor, DelBoca, Kadden, & Cooney, 1992). Although these investigations (Kadden et al., 1989; Litt et al., 1992) were concerned with matching subtypes of alcoholic patients to psychotherapeutic treatments, the results suggest that empirically derived, multivariate typological classifications, as well as specific indicators (such as psychiatric severity and sociopathy), may provide a useful basis for predicting course and selecting treatment. Whereas some investigators have sought prospectively to match alcoholic subtypes to pharmacologic treatment (Gerra et al., 1992), this effort to refine pharmacotherapy for alcoholism has not been widely used.

Given the absence of a clear empirical basis on which to match alcoholic subtypes to specific pharmacotherapies, a major aim in this article is to highlight the substantial theoretical basis for such an approach, in an effort to stimulate research in this area. Practical difficulties in the application of such an approach also have to be addressed; these are, however, beyond the scope of this article. Some discussion of this issue may be found in work reported by Lamparski, Roy, Nutt, and Linnoila (1991) and by Brown, Babor, Litt, and Kranzler (1994).

The hypothesis by Cloninger (1987), that specific neurotransmitter systems underlie a tridimensional personality structure, is of heuristic value. Specifically, dopamine is hypothesized to modulate novelty seeking, which refers to frequent exploratory behavior and intensely pleasurable responses to novel stimuli. This notion is based on evidence that dopaminergic neurons predominate in those brain regions (such as the caudate and NAc) that subserve both behavioral activation and the reinforcing effects of several appetitive behaviors, including the self-administration of various drugs of abuse (Di Chiara & Imperato, 1988). Serotonin is hypothesized to modulate harm avoidance, which refers to a tendency to respond intensely to aversive stimuli and their conditioned signals. Related to this is a substantial literature on the role of 5-HT in the control of mood, impulsivity, aggression, and alcohol preference and consumption (Coccaro & Murphy, 1990; Naranjo et al., 1986; Roy et al., 1990). Finally, norepinephrine (NE) is hypothesized to modulate reward dependence or the resistance to extinction of previously rewarded behavior.

Biological and clinical data from recent work by Buydens-Branchey and her colleagues (Buydens-Branchey, Branchey, & Noumair, 1989; Buydens-Branchey, Branchey, Noumair, & Lieber, 1989) may help to clarify some differences that exist between the typologies discussed earlier. These investigators distinguished between early-onset and late-onset alcoholism in a sample of patients consecutively admitted to a rehabilitation program. The typologic distinction drawn by these investigators from clinical description closely resembles the typology of Babor et al. (1992) in the areas of familial alcoholism, antisocial behavior, and comorbid mood disorder. Among the patients studied by Buydens-Branchey, Branchey, and Noumair (1989), those with early-onset alcoholism were found to have been incarcerated more frequently for violent crimes, to have made more suicide attempts, and to have been depressed more often than patients with later onset of their alcoholism. Furthermore, among the early-onset group, there existed an inverse relationship between a measure of central serotonergic activity (the ratio of plasma tryptophan, which is the major precursor in the synthesis of 5-HT, to other amino acids competing for brain entry) and measures of depression and aggressivity (Buydens-Branchey, Branchey, Noumair, & Lieber, 1989). This, together with increased depressive symptoms in early-onset alcoholics, suggests that drugs that enhance 5-HT function, such as the SUIs, may be particularly useful in the treatment of this alcoholic subtype.

In an effort to assess the role of serotonergic neurotransmission in alcoholism, Benkelfat et al. (1991) conducted a pharmacologic challenge study in alcoholics using m-cholorophenylpiperazine, a serotonergic partial agonist. They found that the drug elicited euphoria and craving for alcohol in early-onset alcoholics but not in late-onset alcoholics. These data are consistent with the argument by Cloninger (1987) that low harm avoidance, which is hypothesized to result from decreased serotonergic tone in the central nervous system, is a central element in Type 2 alcoholism. A recent study, in which plasma levels of 5-HT and tryptophan were measured in subjects with and subjects without depression (some of whom received alcohol), provides support for the idea that 5-HT neurotransmission may also underlie the depressive effects of alcohol (Pietraszek et al., 1991). Finally, Lee and Meltzer (1991) examined neuroendocrine responses to the serotonergic agents L-5-hydroxytryptophan (L-5-HTP, a precursor of 5-HT) and MK-212 (a direct $5\text{-}HT_2/5\text{-}HT_{1C}$ receptor agonist) in alcoholic and nonalcoholic subjects. They found a blunted cortisol response to L-5-HTP and a blunted prolactin response to MK-212 in the alcoholic subjects, who mainly had early-onset disorder. In addition, the alcoholic group reported more "alcohol-like" effects of MK-212 and more restlessness, irritability, and anxiety than did the control group. One interpretation of these findings is that alcoholics (especially those with early onset) have an abnormally low capacity to synthesize 5-HT. The presence of this chronic deficiency results in an adaptive up-regulation of 5-HT receptors, making the system more sensitive to 5-HT agonist drugs. These findings are consistent with the earlier work of Ballenger et al. (1979), who demonstrated decreased 5-HT turnover in alcoholics, and Banki (1981), who found that the decrease in 5-HT turnover in alcoholics is correlated with the duration of their abstinence from alcohol.

In summary, there is growing empirical evidence for a dichotomous typology of alcoholism, of which one subtype is characterized by greater depression, binge drinking, and antisocial behavior. Furthermore, the neuropharmacologic substrate for these pathologic mood and behavioral dimensions may be linked through abnormalities in serotonergic neurotransmission. However, if serotonergic medications prove to be more efficacious in the treatment of early-onset alcoholism, as may be predicted, then the extent to which this effect is mediated by primary effects on mood, rather than on alcoholism per se, needs to be considered. Opioidergic neurotransmission has been shown to influence the intensity of drinking, with minimal effects on mood. On this basis, one may hypothesize that opioidergic medications will have more potent direct effects on alcohol dependence. Additionally, a final common (i.e., dopaminergic) pathway may exist for some of the effects on alcohol consumption produced by both serotonergic and opioidergic drugs.

NEUROPSYCHOPHARMACOLOGY AND MOLECULAR GENETICS

Recent developments in genetic research have made it possible to begin a systematic examination of the molecular basis of alcoholism. However, this literature is much newer and not as fully developed as either the neuropsychopharmacologic or the nosologic literature.

In addition to providing a basis for the identification of potentially efficacious pharmacotherapies, an outgrowth of the improved understanding of the neuropharmacologic basis of alcoholism has been the identification of candidate genes for molecular-level investigations. The search for neurochemical differences among alcoholic subtypes and between alcoholics and nonalcoholic samples has begun to generate hypotheses that can be tested using the rapidly developing technology of molecular genetics. Although this work is still in a very early stage, we discuss some recent developments that may bear directly on the issues that have been the focus of this article.

Whereas investigations into the molecular genetics of alcoholism have largely focused on candidate genes that are not directly relevant to alcohol's neuropharmacologic effects (Goldman, 1988), attention has recently been focused on the DNA sequence that codes for the synthesis of the D_2 dopamine receptor protein. Based on the evidence that dopaminergic neurotransmission may represent a common pathway for both serotonergic and opioidergic effects on alcohol consumption, this approach has theoretical appeal. A number of studies have provided support for an increased risk of alcoholism, particularly severe alcoholism, as a function of the frequency of the minor allele of the D_2 dopamine receptor gene (Blum et al., 1990; 1991; Comings et al., 1991; Parsian et al., 1991). However, a substantial number of studies have failed to demonstrate such an association (Bolos et al., 1990; Gelernter et al., 1991; Goldman et al., 1992; Goldman et al., 1993; Turner et al., 1992). In a meta-analysis of that literature, Gelernter, Goldman and Risch (1993) hypothesized that the association observed by some investigators between alcoholism and the minor allele at the D_2 dopamine receptor gene is due to sampling error and ethnic variation in allele frequencies, rather than to a physiologically important association.

Other investigators have begun to examine the association between alcoholism and genes coding for proteins involved in serotonergic neurotransmission. On the basis of the evidence linking early-onset alcoholism (Type 2 or Type B) with serotonergic abnormalities, this effort appears to be most promising in early-onset alcoholics. In Finnish alcoholics with impulsive behaviors, Nielsen et al. (1994) found an association between CSF levels of 5-HIAA, the major metabolite of 5-HT, and genotype for tryptophan hydroxylase, the enzyme that catalyzes the first step in 5-HT synthesis from tryptophan. There was no association between these measures in Finnish alcoholics without impulsive behaviors or in the control group. Although these findings require replication, they suggest that impulsive behaviors, which are more common in the Type 2 alcoholic sample of Cloninger's research and the Type B alcoholic sample of Babor et al.'s research and which have been linked to low levels of CSF 5-HIAA (Asberg et al., 1987; Brown et al., 1979; Linnoila et al., 1983; Virkkunen et al., 1987), are genetically influenced. With continued research into neuropharmacologic differences between early-onset and late-onset alcoholics, other serotonergic candidate genes (e.g., those coding for the 5-HT transporter or the various 5-HT receptor subtypes) and possibly other neurotransmitter systems (e.g., opioidergic, glutaminergic, GABAergic) may be implicated.

SUMMARY

In conclusion, there is a growing preclinical and clinical literature that has begun to elucidate the neuropharmacologic basis for alcohol consumption. This literature suggests that medications may come to play an important role in the treatment of alcoholism, specifically as adjuncts to psychosocial treatment in the prevention of relapse to heavy drinking. Although serotonergic and opioidergic neurotransmissions have been implicated in the control of alcohol-consummatory behavior, limited or contradictory evidence exists, particularly concerning the specific receptor subtypes involved in the reinforcing effects of alcohol. Whether these systems are primary in alcohol reinforcement or whether they are through modulation of a third system (e.g., dopamine) remains to be ascertained. Similarly, the application of differing research methodologies has yielded typologies of alcoholism that have considerable overlap, as well as several important differences. Application of these typologies appears to provide a strategy for the exploration of patient-treatment matching, which may serve to identify subgroups of alcoholics who would benefit differentially from specific medications. Finally, there has been considerable interest generated by recent molecular genetic studies of alcoholism. More work in this area is undoubtedly forthcoming. Developments in these three areas of investigation (i.e., neuropharmacology, nosology, and molecular genetics) are, to a growing degree, interdependent; new insights in each area are likely soon to yield findings in other domains. An aim of this article has been to clarify the areas of connection among these domains and, in so doing, to enhance the prospect for growth in each area through cross-fertilization.

REFERENCES

Adler, B., Goodman, R. R., & Pasternak, G. W. (1990). Opioid peptide receptors. In A. Bjorklund, T. Hokfelt, & M. J. Kuhar (Eds.), *Handbook of chemical neuroanatomy, Vol. 9: Neuropeptides in the CNS, part II* (pp. 359–393). Amsterdam: Elsevier.

Aguirre, J. C., Del Arbol, J. L., Raya, J., Ruiz-Requena, M. E., & Irles, J. R. (1980). Plasma β-endorphin levels in chronic alcoholics. *Alcohol, 7*, 409–412.

Altshuler, H., Phillips, P., & Feinhandler, D. (1980). Alteration of ethanol self-administration by naltrexone. *Life Sciences, 26*, 679–688.

Amit, Z., Brown, Z., Sutherland, A., Rockman, G., Gill, K., & Selvaggi, N. (1985). Reduction in alcohol intake in humans as a function of treatment with zimelidine: Implications for treatment. In C. A. Naranjo & E. M. Sellers (Eds.), *Research advances in new psychopharmacological treatments for alcoholism*. Amsterdam: Elsevier.

Asberg, M., Schalling, D., & Traskman-Bendz, L. (1987). Psychobiology of suicide, impulsivity, and related phenomena. In H. Y. Meltzer (Ed.), *Psychopharmacology: The third generation of progress* (pp. 665–668). New York: Raven Press.

Babor, T. F., Dolinsky, Z., Rounsaville, B., & Jaffe, J. (1988). Unitary vs. multidimensional models of alcoholism treatment outcome: An empirical study. *Journal of Studies on Alcohol, 49*, 167–177.

Babor, T. F., Hofmann, M., DelBoca, F. K., Hesselbrock, V., Meyer, R. E., Dolinsky, Z. S., & Rounsaville, B. (1992). Types of alcoholics: I. Evidence for an empirically-derived typology based on indicators of vulnerability and severity. *Archives of General Psychiatry, 8*, 599–608.

Babor, T. F., & Lauerman, R. J. (1986). Classification and forms of inebriety: Historical antecedents of alcoholic typologies. *Recent Developments in Alcoholism, 4*, 113–144.

Ballenger, J. C., Goodwin, F. K., Major, L. F., & Brown, G. L. (1979). Alcohol and central serotonin metabolism in man. *Archives of General Psychiatry, 36*, 224–227.

Banki, C. J. (1981). Factors influencing monamine metabolites and tryptophan in patients with alcohol dependence. *Journal of Neural Transmission, 50*, 98–101.

Benkelfat, C., Murphy, D. L., Hill, J. L., George, D. T., Nutt, D., & Linnoila, M. (1991). Ethanol like properties of the serotonergic partial agonist, m-chlorophenylpiperazine in chronic alcoholic patients. *Archives of General Psychiatry, 48*, 383.

Blum, K., Futterman, S., Wallace, J., & Schwertner, H. (1977). Naloxone-induced inhibition of ethanol dependence in mice. *Nature, 265*, 49–51.

Blum, K., Noble, E. P., Sheridan, P. J., Finley, O., Montgomery, A., Ritchie, T., Ozkaragoz, T., Fitch, R. J., Sadlack, F., Sheffield, D., Dahlmann, T., Halbardier, S., & Nogami, H. (1991). Association of the A1 allele of the D_2 dopamine receptor gene with severe alcoholism. *Alcohol, 8*, 409–416.

Blum, K., Noble, E. P., Sheridan, P. J., Montgomery, A., Ritchie, T., Jagadeeswaran, P., Nogami, H., Briggs, A. H., & Cohn, J. B. (1990). Allelic association of human dopamine D_2 receptor gene in alcoholism. *Journal of American Medical Association, 263*, 2055–2060.

Blum, K., & Topel, H. (1986). Opioid peptides and alcoholism: Genetic deficiency and chemical management. *Function Neurology, 1,* 71–83.

Bohn, M. J. (1993). Pharmacotherapy of alcoholism. *Psychiatric Clinics of North America* (Vol. 16, No. 4, pp. 679–692). Baltimore: Williams & Wilkins.

Bolos, A. M., Dean, M., Lucas-Derse, S., Ramsburg, M., Brown, G. L., & Goldman, D. (1990). Population and pedigree studies reveal a lack of association between the dopamine D_2 receptor gene and alcoholism. *Journal of the American Medical Association, 24,* 3156–3160.

Brown, G., Goodwin, F., Ballenger, J., Goyer, P. F., & Major, L. F. (1979). Aggression in humans correlates with cerebrospinal fluid metabolites. *Psychiatry Research, 1,* 131–139.

Brown, J., Babor, T. F., Litt, M. D., & Kranzler, H. R. (1994). The type A/type B distinction: Subtyping alcoholics according to indicators of vulnerability and severity. In T. F. Babor, V. Hesselbrock, R. E. Meyer, & W. Shoemaker (Eds.), *Types of alcoholics: Evidence from clinical, experimental and genetic research.* New York: New York Academy of Sciences, 708, 23–33.

Brownstein, M. J. (1993). A brief history of opiates, opioid peptides, and opioid receptors. *Proceedings of the National Academy of Sciences of the United States of America, 90,* 5391–5393.

Bruno, F. (1989). Buspirone in the treatment of alcoholic patients. *Psychopathology, 22*(Suppl.), 49–59.

Buydens-Branchey, L., Branchey, M. H., & Noumair, D. (1989). Age of alcoholism onset. I. Relationship to psychopathology. *Archives of General Psychiatry, 46,* 225–240.

Buydens-Branchey, L., Branchey, M. H., Noumair, D., & Lieber, C. S. (1989). Age of alcoholism onset. II. Relationship of susceptibility to serotonin precursor availability. *Archives of General Psychiatry, 46,* 231–236.

Carboni, E., Acquas, E., Frau, R., & Di Chiara, G. (1989). Differential inhibitory effects of a 5-HT$_3$ antagonist on drug-induced stimulation of dopamine release. *European Journal of Pharmacology, 164,* 515–519.

Cloninger, C. R. (1987). Neurogenetic adaptive mechanisms in alcoholism. *Science, 236,* 410–416.

Cloninger, C. R., Bohman, M., & Sigvardsson, S. (1981). Inheritance of alcohol abuse: Cross-fostering analysis of adopted men. *Archives of General Psychiatry, 38,* 861–868.

Coccaro, E. F., & Murphy, D. L. (Eds.). (1990). *Serotonin in major psychiatric disorders.* Washington, DC: American Psychiatric Press.

Collins, D. M., & Myers, R. D. (1987). Buspirone attenuates volitional alcohol intake in the chronically drinking monkey. *Alcohol, 4,* 49–56.

Comings, D. E., Comings, B. G., Muhleman, D., Dietz, G., Shahbahrami, B., Tast, D., Knell, E., Kocsis, P., Baumgarten, R., Kovacs, B. W., Levy, D. L., Smith, M., Borison, R., Evans, D., Klein, D. N., MacMurray, J., Tosk, J. M., Sverd, J., Gysin, R., & Flanagan, S. (1991). The dopamine D_2 receptor locus as a modifying gene in neuropsychiatric disorders. *Journal of the American Medical Association, 266,* 1793–1800.

Costall, B., Domeney, A. M., Naylor, R. J., & Tyers, M. B. (1987). Effect of the 5-HT$_3$ antagonist GR 38032F on raised dopaminergic activity in the meso-limbic system of the rat and marmoset brain. *British Journal of Pharmacology, 92,* 881–884.

Crabtree, B. L. (1984). Review of naltrexone, a long-acting opiate antagonist. *Clinical Pharmacy, 3,* 273–280.

De Witte, P. (1984). Naloxone reduces alcohol intake in a free-choice procedure event when both drinking bottles contain saccharine sodium or quinine sub-stances. *Neuropsychobiology, 12,* 73–77.

Di Chiara, G., & Imperato, A. (1988). Drugs abused by humans preferentially increase synaptic dopamine concentrations in the mesolimbic system of freely moving rats. *Proceedings of the National Academy of Sciences of the United States of America, 85,* 5274–5278.

Eison, A. S., & Temple, D. L., Jr. (1986). Buspirone: Review of its pharmacology and current perspectives on its mechanism of action. *American Journal of Medicine, 80*(Suppl.), 1–9.

Engel, J. A., Fahlke, C., Hard, E., Johannessen, K., Svensson, L., & Soderpalm, P. (1992). *Serotonergic and dopaminergic involvement in ethanol intake. Clinical Neuropharmacology, 15*(Suppl. 1), 64A–65A.

Eskelson, C. D., Hameroff, S. R., & Kanel, J. S. (1980). Ethanol increases serum beta-endorphin levels in rats. *Anesthesia and Analgesia, 59,* 537–538.

Fadda, F., Garau, B., Marchel, F., Colombo, G., & Gessa, G. (1991). MDL 72222, a selective 5-HT$_3$ receptor antagonist, suppresses voluntary ethanol consump-tion in alcohol-preferring rats. *Alcohol and Alcoholism, 26,* 107–110.

Froehlich, J. C., Zweifel, M., Harts, J., Lumeng, L., & Li, T.-K. (1991). Importance of delta opioid receptors in maintaining high alcohol drinking. *Psychophar-macology, 103,* 467–472.

Gallant, D. (1993). Amethystic agents and adjunct behavioral therapy and psy-chotherapy. *Alcoholism: Clinical and Experimental Research, 17,* 197–198.

Gelernter, J., Goldman, D., & Risch, N. (1993). The A1 allele at the D$_2$ dopamine receptor gene and alcoholism. *Journal of the American Medical Association, 269,* 1673–1677.

Gelernter, J., O'Malley, S., Risch, N., Kranzler, H. R., Krystal, J., Merikangas, K., Kennedy, J. L., & Kidd, K. K. (1991). No association between an allele at the D$_2$ dopamine receptor gene (DRD2) and alcoholism. *Journal of the American Medical Association, 266,* 1801–1807.

Genazzani, A., Nappi, G., Facchinetti, F., Mazzella, G. L., Parrini, D., Sinforiani, E., Petaraglia, F., & Savoldi, F. (1981). Central deficiency of β-endorphin in alcohol addicts. *Journal of Clinical Endocrinology and Metabolism, 55,* 583–586.

Gerra, G., Caccavari, R., Delsignore, R., Bocchi, R., Fertonani, G., & Passeri, M. (1992). Effects of fluoxetine and Ca-acetyl-homotaurinate on alcohol intake in familial and nonfamilial alcohol patients. *Current Therapeutic Research, 52,* 291–295.

Gianoulakis, C., & Gupta, A. (1986). Inbred strains of mice with variable sensitivity to ethanol exhibit differences in the content and processing of β-endorphin. *Life Sciences, 39,* 2315–2325.

Gianoulakis, C., Beliveau, D., Angelogianni, P., Meaney, M., Thavundayil, J., Tawar, V., & Duams, M. (1989). Different pituitary beta-endorphin and adrenal cortisol response to ethanol in individuals with high and low risk for future development of alcoholism. *Life Sciences, 45,* 1097–1109.

Gilligan, S., Reich, T., & Cloninger, C. R. (1987). Etiologic heterogeneity in alcoholism. *Genetic Epidemiology, 4,* 395–414.

Goldman, D. (1988). Molecular markers for linkage of genetic loci contributing to alcoholism. In M. Galanter (Ed.), *Recent developments in alcoholism* (Vol. 6, pp. 333–349). New York: Plenum.

Goldman, D., Brown, G. L., Albaugh, B., Robin, R., Goodson, S., Trunzo, M., Akhta, L., Lucas-Derse, S., Long, J., Linnoila, M., & Dean, M. (1993). DRD2 dopamine receptor genotype, linkage disequilibrium, and alcoholism in American Indians and other populations. *Alcoholism: Clinical and Experimental Research, 17,* 199–204.

Goldman, D., Dean, M., Brown, G. L., Bolos, A. M., Tokola, R., Virkkunen, M., Linnoila, M. (1992). D_2 dopamine receptor genotype and cerebrospinal fluid homovanillic acid, 5 hydroxyindoleacetic acid and 3-methoxy-r-hydroxphenylglycol in Finnish and American alcoholics. *Acta Psychiatrica Scandinavica.*

Gorelick, D. A. (1989). Serotonin reuptake blockers and the treatment of alcoholism. In M. Galanter (Ed.), *Recent developments in alcoholism* (Vol. 7, pp. 267–281). New York: Plenum.

Gorelick, D. A., & Paredes, A. (1992). Effect of fluoxetine on alcohol consumption in male alcoholics. *Alcoholism: Clinical and Experimental Research, 16,* 261–265.

Grant, K. A., & Barrett, J. D. (1991). Blockade of the discriminative stimulus effects of ethanol with 5-HT_3 receptor antagonists. *Psychopharmacology, 104,* 451–456.

Hamon, M., Lanfumey, L., El Mestikawy, S., Boni, C., Miguel, M. C., Bolanos, F., Schechter, L., & Gozlou, H. (1990). The main features of central 5-HT1 receptors. *Neuropsychopharmacology, 3,* 349–360.

Hiller, J. M., Angel, L. M., & Simon, E. J. (1981). Multiple opiate receptors: Alcohol selectively inhibits binding to delta receptors. *Science, 214,* 468–469.

Hoyer, D. (1990). Serotonin 5-HT3, 5-HT4 and 5-HT-M receptors. *Neuropsychopharmacology, 3,* 371–383.

Hubbell, C., Czirr, S., Hunter, G., Beaman, C. M., LeCann, N. C., & Reid, L. D. (1986). Consumption of ethanol solution is potentiated by morphine and attenuated by naloxone persistently across repeated daily administrations. *Alcohol, 3,* 39–54.

Hubbell, C. L., Marglin, S. H., Spitalnic, S. J., Abelson, M. L., Wild, K. D., & Reid, L. D. (1991). Opioidergic, serotonergic and dopaminergic manipulations and rats' intake of a sweetened alcoholic beverage. *Alcohol, 8,* 355–367.

Iyengar, S., Kim, H., Marien, M., McHugh, D., & Wood, P. L. (1989). Modulation of mesolimbic dopaminergic projections by beta-endorphin in the rat. *Neuropharmacology, 28,* 123–128.

Jacobson, G. R. (1976). *The alcoholisms: Detection, diagnosis, and assessment.* New York: Human Sciences Press.

Jaffe, J. H., Kranzler, H. R., & Ciraulo, D. A. (1992). Drugs used in the treatment of alcoholism. In J. Mendelson & N. Mello (Eds.), *Medical diagnosis and treatment of alcoholism* (pp. 421–461). New York: McGraw-Hill.

Kadden, R. M., Cooney, N. L., Getter, H., & Litt, M. (1989). Matching alcoholics to coping skills or interactional therapies: Posttreatment results. *Journal of Consulting and Clinical Psychology, 57,* 698–704.

Kalivas, P. W., & Duffy, P. (1990). Effect of acute and daily neurotensin and enkephalin treatments on extracellular dopamine in the nucleus accumbens. *Journal of Neuroscience, 10,* 2940–2949.

Kemper, A., Koalick, F., Thiele, H., Retzow, A., Rathsack, R., & Nickel, B. (1990). Cortisol and beta-endorphin response in alcoholics and alcohol abusers following a high naloxone dosage. *Drug and Alcohol Dependence, 25,* 319–326.

Knapp, D. J., Benjamin, D., & Pohorecky, L. A. (1992). Effects of gepirone on ethanol consumption, exploratory behavior, and motor performance in rats. *Drug Development Research, 26,* 319–341.

Knapp, D. J., & Pohorecky, L. A. (1992). Zacopride, a 5-HT$_3$ receptor antagonist, reduces voluntary ethanol consumption in rats. *Pharmacology, Biochemistry and Behavior, 41,* 847–850.

Kranzler, H. R., Burleson, J. A., Korner, P., DelBoca, F. K., Bohn, M. J., & Liebowitz, N. (1995) Fluoxetine treatment of alcoholism: A placebo-controlled trial. *American Journal of Psychiatry.*

Kranzler, H. R., Del Boca, F., Korner, P., & Brown, J. (1993). Adverse effects limit the usefulness of fluvoxamine for the treatment of alcoholism. *Journal of Substance Abuse Treatment, 10,* 283–287.

Kranzler, H. R., & Liebowitz, N. (1988). Anxiety and depression in substance abuse: Clinical implications. In S. Frazier (Ed.), *Anxiety and depression, medical clinics of North America* (Vol. 72, pp. 867–885). Baltimore: Williams & Wilkins.

Lamparski, D. M., Roy, A., Nutt, D. J., Linnoila, M. (1991). The criteria of Cloninger et al. and von Knorring et al. for subgrouping alcoholics: A comparison in a clinical population. *Acta Psychiatrica Scandinavica, 83,* 497–502.

Lee, M. A., & Meltzer, H. Y. (1991). Neuroendocrine responses to serotonergic agents in alcoholics. *Biological Psychiatry, 30,* 1017–1030.

Linnoila, M., Virkkunen, M., Scheinin, M., Rimon, R., & Goodwin, F. K. (1983). Low cerebrospinal fluid 5-H1AA concentration differentiates impulsive from nonimpulsive violent behavior. *Life Sciences, 33,* 2609–2614.

Litt, M. D., Babor, T. F., DelBoca, F. K., Kadden, R. M., & Cooney, N. (1992). Types of alcoholics: II. Application of an empirically-derived typology to treatment matching. *Archives of General Psychiatry, 8*, 609–614.

Litten, R. Z., & Allen, J. P. (1991). Pharmacotherapies for alcoholism: Promising agents and clinical issues. *Alcoholism: Clinical and Experimental Research, 15*, 620–633.

Lucki, I., & Wieland, S. (1990). 5-Hydroxytryptamine 1A receptors and behavioral responses. *Neuropsychopharmacology, 3*, 481–493.

Malcolm, R., Anton, R. F., Randall, C. L., Johnston, A., Brady, K., & Thevos, A. (1992). A placebo-controlled trial of buspirone in anxious inpatient alcoholics. *Alcoholism: Clinical and Experimental Research, 16*, 1007–1013.

Marlatt, G. A. (1985). Relapse prevention: Theoretical rationale and overview of the model. In G. A. Marlatt & J. R. Gordon (Eds.), *Relapse prevention* (pp. 3–70). New York: Guilford Press.

McBride, W. J., Murphy, J. M., Lumeng, L., & Li, T.-K. (1990). Serotonin, dopamine, and GABA involvement in alcohol drinking of selectively bred rats. *Alcohol, 7*, 199–205.

Meert, T. F., Awouters, F., Niemegeers, C. J., Schelleckens, K. H., & Janssen, P. A. J. (1991). Ritanserin reduces abuse of alcohol, cocaine, and fentanyl in rats. *Pharmacopsychiatry, 24*, 159–163.

Meyer, R. E. (1986). Anxiolytics and the alcoholic patient. *Journal of Studies on Alcohol, 47*, 269–273.

Middaugh, L. D., Read, E., & Boggan, W. O. (1978). Effects of naloxone on ethanol induced alterations of locomotion activity in C57BL/6 mice. *Pharmacology, Biochemistry and Behavior, 9*, 157–160.

Monti, J. M., & Alterwain, P. (1991). Ritanserin decreases alcohol intake in chronic alcoholics. *Lancet, 337*, 60.

Murphy, D. L. (1990). Neuropsychiatric disorders and the multiple human brain serotonin receptor subtypes and subsystems. *Neuropsychopharmacology, 3*, 457–471.

Murphy, J. M., McBride, W. J., Lumeng, L., & Li, T.-K. (1987). Contents of monoamines in forebrain regions of alcohol-preferring (P) and nonpreferring (NP) lines of rats. *Pharmacology, Biochemistry and Behavior, 26*, 389–392.

Myers, R. D., Borg, S., & Mossberg, R. (1986). Antagonism by naltrexone of voluntary alcohol selection in the chronically drinking macaque monkey. *Alcohol, 3*, 383–388.

Myers, R., & Critcher, E. (1982). Naloxone alters alcohol drinking induced in the rat by tetrahydropapaveroline (THP) infused ICV. *Pharmacology, Biochemistry and Behavior, 16*, 827–836.

Myers, R. D., & Lankford, M. F. (1993). Failure of the 5-HT$_2$ receptor antagonist, ritanserin, to alter preference for alcohol in drinking rats. *Pharmacology, Biochemistry and Behavior, 45*, 233–237.

Myers, R. D., Lankford, M. F., & Bjork, A. (1993). Irreversible suppression of alcohol drinking in cyanamide treated rats after sustained delivery of the 5-HT$_2$ antagonist amperozide. *Alcohol, 10,* 117–125.

Myers, R. D., & Melchior, C. L. (1977a). Alcohol and alcoholism: Role of serotonin. In W. B. Essman (Ed.), *Serotonin in health and disease* (Vol. 2, pp. 373–430). New York: Spectrum Publication.

Myers, R., & Melchior, C. L. (1977b). Alcohol drinking: Abnormal intake caused by tetrahydropapaveroline in brain. *Science, 196,* 554–556.

Naranjo, C. A., Kadlec, K. E., Sanhueza, P., Woodley-Remus, D., & Sellers, E. M. (1990). Fluoxetine differentially alters alcohol intake and other consummatory behaviors in problem drinkers. *Clinical Pharmacology and Therapeutics, 47,* 490–498.

Naranjo, C. A., Sellers, E. M., & Lawrin, M. O. (1986). Modulation of ethanol intake by serotonin uptake inhibitors. *Journal of Clinical Psychiatry, 47*(Suppl.), 16–22.

Naranjo, C. A., Sellers, E. M., Roach, C. A., Woodley, D. V., Sanchez-Craig, M., & Sykora, K. (1984). Zimelidine-induced variations in alcohol intake by nondepressed heavy drinkers. *Clinical Pharmacology and Therapeutics, 35,* 374–381.

Naranjo, C. A., Sellers, E. M., Sullivan, J. T., Woodley, D. V., Kadlec, K., & Sykora, K. (1987). The serotonin uptake inhibitor citalopram attenuates ethanol intake. *Clinical Pharmacology and Therapeutics, 41,* 266–274.

Naranjo, C. A., Sullivan, J. T., Kadlec, K. E., Woodley-Remus, D. V., Kennedy, G., & Sellers, E. M. (1989). Differential effects of viqualine on alcohol intake and other consummatory behaviors. *Clinical Pharmacology and Therapeutics, 46,* 301–309.

Nielsen, D. A., Goldman, D., Virkkunen, M., Tokola, R., Rawlings, R., & Linnoila, M. (1994). Suicidality and 5-hydroxyindoleacetic acid concentration associated with a tryptophan hydroxylase polymorphism. *Archives of General Psychiatry, 51,* 34–38.

O'Malley, S. S., Jaffe, A. J., Chang, G., Schottenfeld, R. S., Meyer, R. E., & Rounsaville, B. (1992). Naltrexone and coping skills therapy for alcohol dependence: A controlled study. *Archives of General Psychiatry, 49,* 894–898.

Parsian, A., Todd, R., Devor, E. J., O'Malley, K. L., Suarez, B. K., Reich, T., & Cloninger, C. R. (1991). Alcoholism and alleles of the human D$_2$ dopamine receptor locus. *Archives of General Psychiatry, 48,* 655–663.

Pietraszek, M. H., Urano, T., Sumioshi, K., Serizawa, K., Takahashi, S., Takada, Y., & Takada, A. (1991). Alcohol-induced depression. Involvement of serotonin. *Alcohol & Alcoholism, 26,* 155–159.

Privette, T. H., Hornsby, R. I., & Myers, R. D. (1988). Buspirone alters alcohol drinking induced in rats by tetrahydropapaveroline injected into brain monoaminergic pathways. *Alcohol, 5,* 147–152.

Rada, P., Mark, G. P., Pothos, E., & Hoebel, B. G. (1991). Systemic morphine simultaneously decreases extracellular acetylcholine and increases dopamine in the nucleus accumbens of freely moving rats. *Neuropharmacology, 30,* 1133–1136.

Reggiani, A., Barbaccia, M., Spano, P., & Trabucchi, M. (1980). Role of dopaminergic-enkephalinergic interactions in the neurochemical effects of ethanol. *Substance and Alcohol Actions/Misuse, 1,* 151–158.

Roy, A., Linnoila, M., & Virkkunen, M. (1987). Serotonin and alcoholism. *Substance Abuse, 8,* 21–27.

Roy, A., Virkkunen, M., & Linnoila, M. (1990). Serotonin in suicide, violence, and alcoholism. In E. F. Coccaro & D. L. Murphy (Eds.), *Serotonin in major psychiatric disorders* (pp. 187–208). Washington, DC: American Psychiatric Press.

Schuckit, M. A., Irwin, M., & Mahler, H. M. (1990). Tridimensional personality questionnaire scores of sons of alcoholic and nonalcoholic fathers. *American Journal of Psychiatry, 147,* 481–487.

Siviy, S., Calcagnetti, D., & Reid, L. (1982). A temporal analysis of naloxone's suppressant effect on drinking. *Pharmacology, Biochemistry and Behavior, 16,* 173–175.

Svensson, L., Fahlke, C., Hard, E., & Engel, J. A. (1993). Involvement of the serotonergic system in ethanol intake in the rat. *Alcohol, 10,* 219–224.

Tollefson, G. D., Montague-Clouse, J., & Tollefson, S. L. (1992). Treatment of comorbid generalized anxiety in a recently detoxified alcohol population with a selective serotonergic drug (Buspirone). *Journal of Clinical Psychopharmacology, 12,* 19–26.

Toneatto, T., Romach, M. K., Sobell, L. C., Sobell, M. B., Somer, G. R., & Sellers, E. M. (1991). Ondansetron, a 5-HT$_3$ antagonist, reduces alcohol consumption in alcohol abusers. *Alcoholism: Clinical and Experimental Research, 15,* 382.

Topel, H. (1988). Beta-endorphin genetics in the etiology of alcoholism. *Alcohol, 5,* 159–165.

Trachtenberg, M., & Blum, K. (1987). Alcohol and opioid peptides: Neuropharmacological rationale for physical craving of alcohol. *American Journal of Drug and Alcohol Abuse, 13,* 365–372.

Turner, E., Ewing, J., Shilling, P., Smith, T. L., Irwin, M., Schuckit, M., & Kelsoe, J. R. (1992). Lack of association between an RFLP near the D$_2$ dopamine receptor gene and severe alcoholism. *Biological Psychiatry, 31,* 285–290.

Ugedo, L., Grenhoff, J., & Svensson, T. H. (1987). Modulation and excitation of nigral dopamine cell activity by the 5-HT$_2$-antagonist ritanserin. *Neuroscience, 22*(Suppl.), S42.

Van Ree, J. M. (1979). Reinforcing stimulus properties of drugs. *Neuropharmacology, 18,* 963–969.

Van Ree, J. M. (1986). Role of pituitary and related neuropeptides in alcoholism and pharmacodependence. *Progress in Neuropsychopharmacology and Biological Psychiatry, 10,* 219–228.

Virkkunen, M., Nuutila, A., Goodwin, F. K., & Linnoila, M. (1987). CSF monoamine metabolites in male arsonists. *Archives of General Psychiatry, 44,* 241–247.

Volpicelli, J., O'Brien, C., Alterman, A., & Hayashida, M. (1992). Naltrexone in the treatment of alcohol dependence. *Archives of General Psychiatry, 49,* 867–880.

Weiss, F., Bloom, F. E., & Koob, G. F. (1991, December). *Effects of ethanol self-administration on accumbens dopamine release: Strain differences between alcohol-preferring (P) and genetically heterogenous Wistar rats.* Paper presented at the 30th annual meeting of the American College of Neuropsychopharmacology, San Juan, Puerto Rico.

Wozniak, K. M., Pert, A., & Linnoila, M. (1990). Antagonism of 5-HT$_3$ receptors attenuates the effects of ethanol on extracellular dopamine. *European Journal of Pharmacology, 187,* 287–289.

III

INITIATION AND PROGRESSION IN ADOLESCENCE

4

ESCALATED SUBSTANCE USE: A LONGITUDINAL GROUPING ANALYSIS FROM EARLY TO MIDDLE ADOLESCENCE

THOMAS ASHBY WILLS, GRACE McNAMARA, DONATO VACCARO, AND A. ELIZABETH HIRKY

This research was conducted to determine variables that characterize adolescents who show escalation in substance use over the period from early to middle adolescence. In recent years it has been recognized that although many teenagers engage in experimentation with tobacco or alcohol, only some go on to develop substance use problems in late adolescence or early adulthood (Glantz & Pickens, 1992; Kandel & Yamaguchi, 1985). Accordingly, a focus in research has been to determine factors that discriminate adolescents who develop high-intensity use from those who never use cigarettes or alcohol or those who remain at a low level of

Reprinted from the *Journal of Abnormal Psychology, 105,* 166–180. (1996). Copyright © 1996 by the American Psychological Association. Used with permission of the author.

This research was supported by National Institute on Drug Abuse Grant R01-DA-05950. We thank the superintendents of the school districts for their support; the parents and participating students for their cooperation; and Kate DuHamel, Angela Riccobono, Mark Spellman, Jody Wallach, and Caroline Zeoli for assistance with the research.

experimentation (Brook, Cohen, Whiteman, & Gordon, 1992; Kaplan & Johnson, 1992). In this article we consider methodological issues for research on escalation, discuss the theoretical basis for predictions about escalated use, and report data from a study that provides a direct examination of escalation during adolescence and tests theoretical predictions about the process.

EPIDEMIOLOGY AND METHODOLOGY FOR ESCALATED USE

Epidemiologic data from general population samples of adolescents show a steady increase in prevalence of tobacco, alcohol, and other substance use over the period from 12 years to 18 years of age (Johnston, O'Malley, & Bachman, 1989). Retrospective reports indicate that initial experience with substances typically occurs during the 7th or 8th grade (Johnston et al., 1989) and that the frequency and number of substances used increases over the period of adolescence (Kandel & Yamaguchi, 1985). In later adolescence, lifetime prevalence rates for several substances are substantial, whereas rates for heavy use are considerably lower (Johnston et al., 1989). These data imply that a subgroup of adolescents engages in rapid escalation to high-intensity substance use, whereas others engage only in minimal experimentation. However, at present there is little descriptive information on patterns of escalation from data that are based on repeated measures of substance use during adolescence.

The pattern of findings from longitudinal studies suggests that a particular subgroup of adolescents is vulnerable to escalated substance use. Two methodological approaches have been used to investigate this issue. One approach, multiple regression analysis of data obtained on two occasions during adolescence, tests whether a given variable is related to substance use at the second measurement point, with control for level of substance use at the initial measurement. This method has been used in several studies of variables related to substance use (e.g., Chassin, Presson, Sherman, Corty, & Olshavsky, 1984; Christiansen, Smith, Roehling, & Goldman, 1989; Wills, 1986). However, the regression approach has some ambiguity because it cannot necessarily distinguish a variable related to change in experimental (but limited) use from a variable related to steady increase in use. This is a concern because epidemiologic data suggest the group of experimenters could be large relative to the group of escalators; hence, regression analyses could be likely to detect predictors of experimental use as well as of escalation and would have no way to distinguish these two types of effects.

A second approach to studying escalation is represented in long-term studies that examine a particular type of escalation. Retrospective analyses have found that adults with substance abuse problems typically began illicit drug use before 15 years of age (Robins & Przybeck, 1985). With respect to longitudinal studies, Kaplan and colleagues (Kaplan & Johnson, 1992; Kaplan, Martin, Johnson, & Robbins, 1986) followed a sample with data from the 7th-grade survey administration into young adulthood and used reports from the follow-up about whether a participant had engaged in daily marijuana use at some time in his or her life. These investigators found that emotional distress at the time of initial drug use and perceived negative affect reduction were related to the index of escalated use. Kandel and Davies (1992) followed a sample of high-school student into young adulthood and used regression analyses to test variables related to reports of daily marijuana use at some time prior to the follow-up. This study found that reports of early onset, deviant peer affiliations, low religious partici-pation, low educational expectations, and parental substance use were all related to the criterion index. Though these studies have provided valuable contributions, the indices of escalation were based on retrospective reports, and investigators have suggested that research is required with closer spaced longitudinal data to measure predictor variables at the time when escala-tion takes place (see, e.g., Kandel & Davies, 1992).

Determining the factors that distinguish escalated substance users from other types of users helps to resolve methodological questions about escalation. We used a grouping analysis approach in the present research. Data on substance use and theoretically derived variables were obtained at yearly intervals during the period (from 7th grade to 9th grade) when escalation is predicted to occur, and clustering analysis was used to deter-mine empirical patterns of substance use over time. Discriminant function analysis was then used to test whether study variables differentiated ado-lescents who escalated from adolescents who showed other patterns of use or nonuse. The grouping approach can test for variables that characterize a subgroup of persons who show rapid escalation in substance use and which distinguish this group from persons who show patterns of nonuse or experimentation.

THEORETICAL ISSUES

We used constructs from several theoretical models of adolescent sub-stance use. Constructs were included from stress-coping theory (e.g., Wills & Filer, 1996), problem behavior theory (e.g., Jessor & Jessor, 1977), and peer-association theory (e.g., Elliott, Huizinga, & Ageton, 1985; Patterson, DeBaryshe, & Ramsey, 1989). We also included measures of parental sub-stance use in order to address issues from recent research on the role of parental use and risk status (e.g., Chassin, Rogosch, & Barrera, 1991; Sher, Walitzer, Wood, & Brent, 1991). Though these constructs have usually been discussed as risk factors for substance use in general, they are also relevant for predictions about escalation (Kaplan & Johnson, 1992). In the following sections, we discuss how these models are relevant for escalated substance use.

Stress-Coping Model

The stress-coping model construes high-intensity substance use as a function of life stress and coping resources (Wills & Shiffman, 1985). Life stress is a demonstrated risk factor for adolescent substance use and has been construed as promoting substance use through increasing emotional distress or undermining perceptions of control (Newcomb & Harlow, 1986; Wills, 1986, 1990). A high level of stress around the time of initial trial would theoretically be conducive to escalation in use (cf. Kaplan et al., 1986). Coping responses in theory can be either protective or risk-promoting with respect to substance use (Wills & Hirky, 1996). Adaptive mechanisms include a behavioral approach (i.e., engaging in problem solving and direct action to resolve a problem) and a cognitive approach (i.e., using internal strategies to minimize emotional distress through reinterpreting problematic situations). Adaptive coping is predicted to decrease the likelihood of escalation because it would result in resolution of problems and would help build normative competencies (Blechman & Wills, 1992; Cole, 1991). Nonadaptive mechanisms, such as dealing with problem situations through anger, avoidance, or helplessness, are predicted to increase the likelihood of escalation because they do not contribute to resolution of problems and may alienate potential supporters (cf. Cooper, Russell, & George, 1988; Hirschman, Leventhal, & Glynn, 1984; Rhode, Lewinsohn, Tilson, & Seeley, 1990). Finally, the stress-coping model as well as other models (e.g., Brook, Brook, Gordon, Whiteman, & Cohen, 1990; Kandel & Davies, 1992) construe emotional support from parents as an important protective factor, and parental support is a demonstrated protective factor for adolescent substance use (Brook et al., 1992; Wills, Vaccaro, & McNamara, 1992). Thus, we predicted that parental support is inversely related to escalation of substance use.

Problem Behavior Model

The problem behavior theory (Jessor & Jessor, 1977) includes constructs ranging from distal to proximal factors in substance use. *Distal* factors are value and attitude variables reflecting involvement in conventional goals. For example, a large difference between value on independence and value on achievement is predicted to predispose the adolescent to deviant rather than conventional activity. In the social control structure, a positive relationship with parents is posited as a distal factor, presumably because it is associated with more conventional attitudes. Affiliation with deviant peers is posited to be a *proximal* risk factor because it provides modeling of, and social reinforcement for, deviant behavior. These predictions have been shown to be related to substance use in studies of high-school and college students (e.g., Jessor, Chase, & Donovan, 1980). Although problem behavior theory has focused on predicting heavy use rather than escalation, the theory does propose that substance use arises from a dynamic balance of instigations and controls (Jessor & Jessor, 1977, p. 23). Thus, this theory could generate the prediction that adolescents with relatively more instigation toward deviant behavior and relatively fewer controls would be prone to escalated substance use.

Peer-Affiliation Models

Differential-affiliation models focus on the peer group as the pathway to substance use. It is assumed that acceptance in a substance-using peer group provides access to necessary resources (e.g., cigarettes), an opportunity to learn how to engage in the behavior, and observational evidence that the behavior can be performed without catastrophic consequences (Elliott et al., 1985; Mosbach & Leventhal, 1988). Both problem behavior theory and peer-association theory predict that affiliation with deviant peers is associated with onset of substance use. With regard to escalation, it is posited in some models that involvement in a deviant peer group leads to escalation of use. This is predicted to occur not only because the peer group provides reinforcement for deviant behavior, but also because the group members are themselves alienated from conventional goals such as academic achievement (Patterson et al., 1989). Thus, a closed system may develop in which members of the group reinforce each others' detachment from conventional goals and increased substance use. This leads to the prediction that affiliation with substance-using peers is related to escalation in drug use over time.

To provide a direct examination of escalation, we obtained data from an adolescent sample at yearly intervals during the time period when escalated substance use is predicted to occur. Constructs from three theoretical models were measured. We predicted that a subgroup of adolescents would show steady escalation in substance use over the study period, whereas other subgroups would show minimal use or nonuse. The research tested predictions from three theoretical models about how stress-coping factors, deviance-prone attitudes, and peer affiliations are relevant for distinguishing the subgroup of escalators from the nonusers and experimenters.

METHOD

Quesionnaires were administered to participants at yearly intervals over a 3-year period, beginning in 7th grade and continuing through 9th grade. The questionnaire included items on substance use and a number of psychosocial scales.

Participants and Procedure

The participants were 1,702 adolescents in public school districts in lower Westchester County, New York. The school districts are in mixed urban–suburban communities that are representative of the state population (U.S. Department of Commerce, 1992). At the initial survey administration, mean age of participants was 12.4 years. Self-reported ethnic identification indicated that the sample was 29% African American, 23% Hispanic, and 37% White, and that it included comparable proportions of female (47%) and male (53%) participants. Data on family structure indicated that 53% of participants were living with both biological parents, 34% were in a single-parent structure (primarily single mothers, sometimes with relatives), and 13% were in a blended family (one biological parent and one stepparent). Data on parental education using a 6-point scale indicated that $M = 3.70$ ($SD = 1.37$) for fathers and $M = 3.72$ ($SD = 1.35$) for mothers. In each case the median and modal levels of parental education was high school graduate, so the families can be characterized as working class on the average.

Data were obtained through a self-report questionnaire administered to students in classrooms by project staff. The questionnaire took approximately 40 min to administer. The staff members followed a standardized protocol in giving instructions to students and answering questions about individual items. The survey was administered under confidential conditions, and a Certificate of Confidentiality protecting the data was obtained from the U.S. Public Health Service. Questionnaires were identified only with a code number; participants were told that they should not write their name on the survey and that their answers were strictly confidential.

The questionnaire was administered together with a biochemical measure. During the questionnaire administration, participants provided a sample of expired air, which was analyzed for carbon monoxide (CO) with automated equipment (the Breath CO Analyzer, Vitalograph Corporation, Lenexa, KS). Measurement of CO in expired air provides a biochemical indicator of recent cigarette smoking. Participants were informed that the breath samples provided an indication of cigarette smoking, a procedure shown in some studies to increase the validity of self-reported substance use (e.g., Murray, O'Connell, Schmid, & Perry, 1987). The CO result was labeled only with a code number, and participants were informed that these data also were strictly confidential.

Students participated under a consent procedure in which parents were sent a notice informing them of the nature of the study and the breath measurement. A parent could elect to have his or her child excluded from the data collection if he or she wished. Participants were informed that they could refuse or discontinue participation at the time of the survey. *Completion rate* was defined as the number of usable questionnaires obtained in a given wave divided by the total class enrollment from school lists. For the three waves of data collection the completion rate was 92%, 88%, and 84%, respectively, with case loss from parental and student refusals being less than 1% in each wave, and the majority of case loss occurring because of student absenteeism.

The initial data collection with 7th graders occurred between November 1990 and March 1991. The questionnaire was readministered in Fall 1991, when participants were in the 8th grade, and in Fall 1992, when they were in the 9th grade. *Retention rate* was defined as the number of cases providing usable data from 7th through 9th grades divided by 1,702. A total of 1,184 cases provided usable data for 7th through 9th grades (retention rate = 70%).

Measures

The questionnaire included demographic items and scales for the psychosocial variables. For psychosocial scales, unless noted otherwise the items were administered using a 5-point Likert response scale with anchor points *not at all true* and *very true*.[1] All scores were constructed such that a higher score indicated more of the named construct. Similar measures have been used in prior adolescent research on life stress (e.g., Chassin, Pillow, Curran, Molina, & Barrera, 1993; Newcomb & Harlow, 1986); coping and competence (e.g., Cole, 1991; Harter, 1986; Wills, 1986; Wills et al., 1992); and deviant behavior (Elliott et al., 1985; Jessor et al., 1980). Scale structure was verified with factor analysis (principal-factor method, varimax rotation) and internal consistency (Cronbach alpha) analysis.

Demographic Information

The participant was asked about his or her age, sex, and ethnic group membership. An item on family composition asked what adult or adults the participant currently lived with (8 options). Two questions asked about the level of education for mother and father, respectively; responses were on a 6-point scale, with anchor points *grade school* and *post college* (masters, doctoral, or other professional education).

---

[1]Measures of behavioral and intimacy competence, self-esteem, and perceived control were added beginning with the 8th-grade survey. There was initial concern about 7th-grade students completing a lengthy questionnaire. In the 7th-grade survey, a 4-point response scale was used for measures of support, coping, competence, and affect. This was changed to a 5-point scale in the 8th and 9th grades to try to reduce negative skew (i.e., means toward the high end of the scale) for these variables, which it did not. When tabled comparisons of means across measurement points are made, the relevant 7th-grade variables are transformed to a 5-point scale; statistical tests are performed on data in their original metric.

Parental Support

Perceived availability of parental support was indexed with a 12-item measure that was based on a functional model of social support (Wills et al., 1992). The measure contains a 5-item scale for emotional support (e.g., "I can share my feelings with my parent," Cronbach alpha over measurements = .82–.88) and a 7-item scale for instrumental support (e.g., "If I need help with school work I can ask my parent about it," α = .76–.83). Participants were instructed to describe their feelings about the parent whom they talked to the most; this was done to insure that the support data were not biased by the prevalence of single-parent structures in the sample.

Affective States

On the basis of mood adjectives from Zevon and Tellegen (1982), we used a 24-item inventory to index affective states during the past month. The measure contained 12-item scales for negative affect (e.g., tense, sad, worried; α = .88–.91) and positive affect (e.g., happy, interested, relaxed; α = .83–.88).

Negative Life Events

A 20-item checklist of negative life events was based on previous inventories of adolescent life events (Newcomb & Harlow, 1986; Wills, 1986). Participants were presented with an item and asked to indicate whether the event had occurred during the previous year, using a dichotomous (yes–no) response scale. The inventory included 11 events that occurred to family members (e.g., "Somebody in my family had a serious illness") and 9 events that occurred directly to the child (e.g., "I had a serious accident"). The score for negative life events was based on the total set of 20 items (α = .67–.71).

Perceived Competence

A 32-item inventory derived from the Perceived Competence Scale for Adolescents (Harter, 1985) taps five domains of competence as perceived by the respondent. The measures were a 7-item scale for academic competence (e.g., "I like school because I do well in class," α = .67–.71), a 7-item scale for peer social competence (e.g., "I find it easy to make friends with other kids," α = .64–.68), and a 7-item scale for adult social competence (e.g., "I feel that I'm well liked by adults," α = .65–.69). Also included were a 6-item scale for behavioral competence ("I usually behave and do the right thing," α = .65–.68) and a 5-item scale for intimacy competence (e.g., "I have close friends I can share secrets with," α = .65–.67).

Deviance Proneness

Four measures tapped core constructs from problem behavior theory (Jessor & Jessor, 1977). Three measures were 4-item value scales administered with the stem "How important is it to you." Scales were for value on independence (e.g., "To decide for yourself about how to spend your free time," α = .66–.74), value on achievement (e.g., "To get at least a B average this year," α = .74–.76), and value on religion (e.g., "To be able to turn to prayer when you're facing a personal problem," α = .80–.81). The value scales were administered with 4-point response scales, with anchor points *not at all important* to *very important*. Following the protocol of Jessor and Jessor (1977), a score was computed for the difference of the first two scales (value on independence − value on achievement); this is termed the *value discrepancy score*. A 10-item scale on tolerance for deviance was administered with the stem "How wrong do you think it is:" followed by examples of deviant acts (e.g., "Take things that don't belong to you," "Damage school property on purpose;" α = .91–.92). Responses were on a 4-point scale, with anchor points *not at all wrong* to *very wrong*.

Coping Processes

A 32-item intention-based measure, indexing coping processes used to deal with typical adolescent problems, was derived from previous research (Carver, Scheier, & Weintraub, 1989; Stone & Neale, 1984; Wills, 1986). Coping measures were introduced to participants with the statement "Here are some things that people may do when they have a problem." Participants were presented with general descriptions of eight coping goals together with 3–4 descriptors for each goal. After reading the definitions, participants were asked to indicate the extent to which they used each type of coping for a given problem; responses were on 5-point scales, with anchor points *never do this* and *very often do this*. Four problem types were assessed: problems with parents, school, sadness, and health. The coping items were administered with a stem for each problem type; for example, "When I have a problem with school work, I _____ ." The coping dimensions were as follows (general definition to participant in parentheses): behavioral coping ("Do something to try to solve the problem;" alpha coefficient over problems = .75–.78), cognitive coping ("Do something to see the problem in a different way;" α = .77–.78), anger coping ("Get mad at people;" α = .79–.80), physical exercise ("Do physical exercise;" α = .85–.87), avoidant coping ("Avoid the problem;" α = .73–.78), social entertainment or hanging out ("Hang out with other kids;" α = .87–.88), substance use coping ("Use substances to feel better;" α = .89–.91), and helpless coping ("Give up on the problem;" α = .80–.81). Scores for a given coping dimension were computed by summing responses over the four problem types.

Esteem and Control

Measures were included to index positive and negative dimensions of self-esteem (see Fleming & Watts, 1980) and perceived control (see Paulhus, 1983); items were selected through previous research with adolescents (Wills, 1985). The four measures were based on 5-item scales for positive self-regard (e.g., "I feel that I have a number of good qualities;" α = .85– .88), negative self-image (e.g., "I often feel discouraged about myself;" α = .83–.84), positive perceived control (e.g., "When I make plans, I'm pretty sure I can make them work;" α = .76–.78), and lack of control (e.g., "I feel I have little control over things that happen to me;" α = .67–.69).

Family Substance Use

Questions about substance use (weekly or more often) by parents and siblings, respectively, included items for cigarette smoking, alcohol use (beer or wine), and liquor (whiskey, scotch, rum). Each item was coded for analysis on a 3-point scale (*None use, one use, two use*).

Peer Substance Use

Three items asked the particpant whether any of his or her friends smoked cigarettes, drank beer or wine, or smoked marijuana. Responses were on 5-point scales, with response points *none, one, two, three,* and *four or more.*

Substance Use

Substance use by the participant was measured with three items that asked about the typical frequency of his or her cigarette, alcohol, and marijuana use. Items were introduced to participants with the stem: "How often do you smoke cigarettes/drink alcohol/smoke marijuana?" Responses were on 6-point scales, with scale points *never used, tried once-twice, used four-five times, usually use a few times a month, usually use a few times a week,* and *usually use every day.* A fourth item, with a 3-point response scale (*no, happened once,* and *happened twice or more*) asked whether there was a time in the last month when the participant had three or more drinks on one occasion. The indices of cigarette, alcohol, and marijuana use were substantially intercorrelated, and the correlations increased with age; internal consistency (Cronbach alpha) for the four-item scale was .69, .69, and .81 for the 7th through 9th grades, respectively. Thus, the four items were combined in a composite score, consistent with methodological research (Hays, Widaman, DiMatteo, & Stacy, 1987; Needle, Su, & Lavee, 1989). The composite score was on an 18-point scale, where 0 indicated nonuse of any substance and 17 indicated daily use of tobacco, alcohol, and marijuana plus heavy drinking twice or more in the past month.

RESULTS

Clustering Analysis

To determine empirical patterns of substance use over time, we used clustering analysis of longitudinal data on substance use. Clustering procedures group cases on the basis of similarity in absolute level on the input data. For the present analyses, the composite substance use scores for a participant at 7th, 8th, and 9th grades (i.e., three data points for each participant) were used as input to a disjoint clustering procedure (Proc Fastclus; SAS Institute, 1988). This analysis uses a fast clustering algorithm, which operates on large data sets by assigning all participants to clusters on the basis of the Euclidean distance from quantitative seed variables. After initial estimates of cluster centroids, an iterative procedure follows in which cluster seeds are replaced by cluster means, repeating until changes in the cluster means become small. On the basis of clustering parameters including the pseudo-F statistic (Milligan & Cooper, 1985), we selected a 5-cluster solution. Table 1 presents the mean substance use score over three waves for each of the five substance use groups.

The empirical clusters included a group termed *stable nonusers* ($n = 586$; 50% of the sample) who showed almost complete nonuse of substances at all three measurement points; the 9th-grade mean score of 0.79 indicates that the typical adolescent in this cluster had tried one substance on one occasion at some time in his or her life. A second group, labeled *minimal experimenters* ($n = 309$; 26% of the sample) had scores representing a minimal level of use at all three measurement points. A group labeled *late starters* ($n = 161$; 14% of the sample) showed experimental levels in 7th and 8th grades but increased in 9th grade. There were two types of escalation represented in the data. A group labeled *escalator 1* ($n = 76$; 6% of the sample) showed elevated substance use at 7th grade and increased in use throughout the study period. A group labeled *escalator 2* ($n = 51$; 4% of the sample) also showed early onset and showed a large increase in substance use over the study period.[2]

To provide a fine-grained picture of the groups indicated by the cluster analysis, we included the percentage rates for each substance use index over the three measurements in Table 1. Noteworthy for the escalator 2 group are the steady increase in involvement with all types of substances

---

[2]To test the replicability of the cluster solution, we drew a series of random 60% subsamples from the data set and specified a five-factor solution. The same essential clusters were found across the samples. We visually inspected the pattern of actual substance use scores across waves for all the cases and found that they were in accord with the means from the clustering results. There were some cases who showed a decrease in substance use over time, usually beginning from a minimal level, or a peak in 8th grade with minimal levels before and after; these cases (approximately 22 cases, or 2% of the sample) were classified by the algorithm as minimal experimenters.

TABLE 1

Percentage Rates and Means for Substance Use Indices Over 7th-, 8th-, and 9th-Grade Measurements, by Cluster Group

Index	Stable nonuser			Minimal experimenter			Late starter			Escalator 1			Escalator 2		
	7th	8th	9th	7th	8th	9th	7th	8th	9th	7th	8th	9th	7th	8th	9th
Smoking															
Never	92	89	76	55	30	23	49	27	6	14	2	7	22	11	2
1–2 times	7	11	20	37	48	45	40	40	17	33	11	8	31	13	2
4–5 times	1	1	4	6	19	26	11	23	26	20	21	21	25	19	0
Monthly	0	0	1	1	2	5	0	8	20	16	29	14	14	17	10
Weekly	0	0	0	1	1	1	0	2	12	8	11	13	2	13	14
Daily	0	0	0	1	1	0	0	0	19	9	26	37	6	28	73
Alcohol															
Never	76	69	60	31	12	14	44	20	4	22	10	4	31	13	0
1–2 times	22	28	35	50	50	48	46	51	17	34	15	24	37	13	2
4–5 times	2	2	5	17	31	33	10	26	42	30	37	29	20	34	8
Monthly	1	0	0	1	6	5	0	3	32	13	31	37	8	30	45
Weekly	0	0	0	0	1	0	0	1	4	0	5	7	4	6	24
Daily	0	0	0	0	1	0	0	0	0	0	3	0	0	4	22
Marijuana															
Never	100	100	99	98	99	93	99	99	60	91	63	45	92	60	2
1–2 times	0	0	1	2	1	6	1	1	27	5	21	24	4	17	6
4–5 times	0	0	0	0	0	1	0	0	9	3	8	18	2	9	16
Monthly	0	0	0	0	0	0	0	0	1	1	3	9	0	6	22
Weekly	0	0	0	0	0	0	0	0	1	0	2	4	1	4	33
Daily	0	0	0	0	0	0	0	0	1	0	3	0	1	4	22
Heavy drink															
None	97	97	96	88	79	90	86	83	40	58	42	41	75	45	8
Once	3	3	4	9	17	9	14	13	36	24	24	32	14	21	12
≥ Twice	0	0	0	4	4	1	0	3	24	18	34	27	12	34	81
Mean substance use score	0.38	0.47	0.79	1.63	2.59	2.65	1.42	2.52	6.44	4.07	6.92	7.54	3.31	6.89	13.82
Group n		586			309			161			76			51	

Note. Values for smoking, alcohol, marijuana, and heavy drinking are percentages, summing to 100 down each column. Means for composite substance use score are on a 0–17 scale; for scoring, see text.

over the study period and the high level of use at the 9th-grade measurement, which for this group showed weekly or daily use of substances and an 81% rate of frequent heavy drinking in the past month. The escalator 1 group had early onset and increased over the study period but had considerably lower levels of use, for example, a 37% rate of daily smoking in 9th grade compared with 73% for the escalator 2 group and a 27% rate of frequent heavy drinking compared with 81% for the other group. The late starter group showed only experimental levels of use in the 8th grade, but at the 9th grade measurement was generally comparable to the escalator 1 group except for a lower rate of daily cigarette smoking (19% daily smokers compared with 37% for the escalator 1 group).

Demographic and Attrition Analyses

The distribution of demographic characteristics across the five substance use groups for 7th-grade data was tested with chi-square analysis. The overall chi-square was nonsignificant for gender, $\chi^2(4, N = 1178) = 2.6$, ns, and for ethnicity, $\chi^2(8, N = 1056) = 13.3$, ns. For family structure, $\chi^2(8, N = 1181) = 15.0$, $p = .06$, adolescents from single-parent families were overrepresented in the escalator 2 group. For parental education (coded as high school vs. college), $\chi^2(4, N = 1029) = 10.8$, $p < .05$, adolescents from families with high-school education were overrepresented in the two escalator groups. These findings are consistent with prior research (e.g., Jessor et al., 1980; Murray, Perry, O'Connell, & Schmid, 1987; Needle, Su, & Doherty, 1990; Newcomb & Bentler, 1988b). Though demographic effects for the substance use groups were not striking, subsequent multivariate analyses were replicated with demographic controls.

In analyses for attrition, participants who stayed in the panel were compared with persons who left the panel (attriters). These analyses showed that attriters differed from panel members ($p < .01$ by t test) on family structure (more single and blended), more life events, lower academic and behavioral competence, more anger and avoidant coping, more friends, substance use, and more own substance use. They did not differ on gender, ethnicity, parental education, parental support, religiosity, tolerance for deviance, parental substance use, or sibling substance use. In absolute terms, in 7th grade the mean substance use score on an 18-point scale was 1.26 for panel members compared with 1.96 for those who left by 8th grade; in 8th grade the mean score for panel members was 1.95 compared with 2.53 for those who left by 9th grade. The effects are consistent with other school-based research (e.g., Kandel, Kessler, & Margulies, 1978; Newcomb & Bentler, 1988a) in that persons with lower academic performance and greater substance use are more likely to leave the cohort, but the magnitude of attrition does not present serious basis for the analytic sample.

TABLE 2
Means and Univariate ANOVA for Selected Variables, by Substance Use Group

Variable-grade	Range	Substance use group					F
		Stable nonuser	Minimal exper.	Late starter	Escalator 1	Escalator 2	
Emot. support	5–25						
7		21.24	19.73_a	19.60_a	18.77_a	18.70_a	12.31****
8		19.42	17.78_a	17.29_{ab}	15.98_{bc}	15.13_c	16.96****
9		19.20	17.69_a	16.36_b	17.58_{ab}	14.62	16.44****
Academic comp.	7–35						
7		26.10_a	25.69_a	24.45_b	22.71_c	24.19_{bc}	9.42****
8		26.27_a	25.70_a	24.33_b	23.40_b	23.74_b	9.15****
9		26.64_a	26.09_a	24.72_b	24.00_{bc}	22.80_c	12.16****
Anger coping	4–20						
7		8.74	9.49_a	10.02_a	10.43_a	12.38	10.57****
8		8.85	10.05	10.97_a	11.67_{ab}	12.83_b	19.70****
9		8.88_a	9.36_a	10.96_b	10.61_b	13.04	18.13****
Value discr.	±12						
7		-0.95	-0.11_a	-0.07_a	0.49_a	1.70	12.87****
8		-0.75	0.28_a	0.53_a	0.86_a	2.53	21.16****
9		-0.21	0.45_a	1.37_b	0.93_{ab}	2.46	19.30****
Hangout coping	4–20						
7		10.51_a	11.15_{ab}	11.61_b	13.24	15.16	12.00****
8		9.87	11.12_a	11.42_{ab}	12.60_{bc}	14.15_c	11.73****
9		10.09_a	10.53_{ab}	12.70_c	11.61_b	13.98_c	13.69****
Behav comp.	6–30						
8		21.96	20.01	19.06	17.63_a	16.38_a	37.74****
9		22.01	20.19	18.14_a	18.20_a	15.78	47.97****
Neg events	20–40						
7		23.28	23.94	24.57	25.51_a	26.08_b	25.34****
8		23.05	24.15	24.89_a	25.52_{ab}	26.43_b	36.50****
9		23.09	23.87	25.19	25.30_a	27.31_a	45.07****

	Grade	Scale						F
Parent smoking	7	1–3	1.56a	1.63a	1.80b	1.80b	2.00b	8.85****
	8		1.56	1.66a	1.87b	1.76ab	2.00b	9.34****
	9		1.57a	1.57a	1.81b	1.76b	1.90b	7.05****
Parent liquor	7	1–3	1.13a	1.14a	1.14a	1.37b	1.24b	6.75****
	8		1.17a	1.20a	1.18a	1.18a	1.38	2.35*
	9		1.16a	1.22a	1.32b	1.39b	1.35b	7.27****
Friend smoking	7	1–5	1.62	2.14a	2.39a	3.88	3.29	60.57****
	8		2.12	3.22	3.61	4.57a	4.38a	78.04****
	9		3.13	3.82	4.47a	4.64ab	4.90b	45.41****
Friend beer	7	1–5	1.25	1.62a	1.56a	2.68b	2.43b	37.97****
	8		1.48	2.27	2.71	3.16a	3.64a	60.70****
	9		2.22	2.95	4.06a	4.15a	4.68	75.45****
Friend marij.	7	1–5	1.06a	1.11a	1.08a	1.28	1.49	9.22****
	8		1.10	1.40a	1.35a	2.43b	2.64b	58.62****
	9		1.63	2.06	3.27a	3.61a	4.57	96.40****
Carbon monoxide	7	ppm	3.79a	3.70a	3.70b	4.04b	3.88ab	1.58
	8		2.84a	2.77a	2.88a	2.76a	3.55	4.54***
	9		2.59a	2.67a	3.17	5.21b	5.51b	41.48****
No. of cases			586	309	161	76	51	

Note. Pairwise comparisons are for comparisons of cell means across a row; means with common subscript are not significantly different ($p < .05$). Exper. = experimenter; emot. = emotional; comp. = competence; discr. = independence – achievement value discrepancy score; neg = negative; marij. = marijuana; ppm. = parts per million. For 7th-grade measures of support, competence, and coping, mean values are for data transformed to a 1–5 response scale (see Footnote 1); analysis of variance (ANOVA) test is for data in their original metric. Behavioral competence was not measured in the 7th-grade questionnaire. Degrees of freedom for F test are as follows: for numerator, $df = 4$; for denominator, $df = 1,085$–$1,177$.

$*p < .05.$ $***p < .001.$ $****p < .0001.$

Variables Discriminating Substance Use Groups

We performed univariate analyses to test whether study variables were comparable across the five substance use groups. The one-way analysis of variance provides an F test indicating whether there is significant variation in a given predictor across groups. Pairwise comparisons were used to test whether two particular cell means differed significantly. Analyses were performed with the general linear-models procedure (Proc GLM; SAS Institute, 1988), which provides pairwise tests that account for the different sizes of the groups.

Results indicated that almost all the study variables showed significant differences across the empirical substance use groups. (Recall that the clustering analysis did not involve any of the predictor variables.) At the 7th-grade measurement, the two groups of participants who escalated had significantly ($p < .0001$ unless otherwise noted) more of the following: life stress, low parental support, low academic competence, deviant attitudes (e.g., greater independence-achievement value discrepancy), and nonadaptive modes of coping (i.e., anger, hanging out, helplessness, and substance use coping). In addition, these groups showed significantly more parental substance use (cigarettes and liquor) and more peer substance use (cigarettes, alcohol, and marijuana).[3] Comparable analyses indicated that these across-group differences were replicated in 8th- and 9th-grade data. Significant differences at these measurements indicated that escalators also scored lower on behavioral competence, positive control, and positive esteem ($p < .01$) and higher on negative esteem and negative control.[4]

Results for selected variables, those included in subsequent discriminant analyses, are presented in Table 2, with pairwise comparisons of cell means.[5] Pairwise tests for the 7th-grade data indicated a pattern in which stable nonusers generally were significantly lower on risk factors and sig-

---

[3]Because of the possibility that group differences could be driven by differences in the participants' initial substance use levels, analyses of variance for 7th-grade data were repeated including the 7th-grade substance use score as a covariate. All the reported variables remained significant with this control; thus, these effects are not attributable to initial substance use level. The pairwise comparisons in Table 2 are based on unadjusted means because these indicate the actual differences between the groups.

[4]Teacher ratings were also obtained on students' competence and other attributes. These used the same items completed by the students, worded for a third-part format. The ratings were done at approximately the same time as the student questionnaire was administered, but teachers did not know what students said about themselves on the questionnaire. Hence, the teacher ratings represent an independent source. Measures included scales for academic, peer, adult, behavioral, and intimacy competence (from Harter, 1985) and scales for novelty seeking and generalized self-control (from Wills, Vaccaro, & McNamara, 1994). Effects in the teacher ratings corroborated those in the self-report data, with significant differences found for academic competence, adult competence, behavioral competence, self-control, and novelty seeking; escalator groups were lower on competence and self-control and higher on novelty seeking. Teacher data generally did not add unique predictive power in stepwise analyses; hence, they are not reported in detail here.

[5]A complete table of results for all variables, including analyses of variance and correlation matrices, is available from Thomas Ashby Wills.

nificantly higher on protective factors, compared with all other groups. The escalator 1 and escalator 2 groups generally were significantly higher on risk factors and lower on protective factors, compared with nonusers and minimal experimenters. In most cases the two escalator groups did not differ significantly in the pairwise comparisons, although the escalator 2 group had more extreme values. (The pairwise test has lower power for this comparison because of the smaller group sizes.) The late starter group usually occupied an intermediate position, for example being elevated above the experimenter group on risk factors but lower than the escalator groups; pairwise comparisons typically indicated nonsignificant differences from either experimenter or escalator groups, but variables can be noted where late starters were significantly different from both groups (e.g., negative life events). These comparisons were replicated in 8th- and 9th-grade data. Results for the CO measurement showed the groups did not differ at the 7th-grade measurement (when rates of smoking were low), but in 8th grade the escalator 1 group was significantly elevated and in 9th grade both escalator groups were significantly elevated above other groups, paralleling the self-report data on cigarette smoking.[6]

Multivariate Analyses

The univariate tests presented previously are not necessarily independent, because the predictor variables may be intercorrelated. Correlation analyses, presented for selected variables in the Appendix, indicated that correlations among the predictor variables were significant and substantial in some cases. Because of the intercorrelations among the predictor variables, multivariate analyses were performed to determine variables with independent discriminating power. For the multivariate test, discriminant function analysis was used. With five known criterion groups and a set of predictor variables, this procedure derives a linear additive function that maximizes the ratio of between–within group variation, then derives a second function orthogonal to the first that provides the next maximal amount of separation, and so on up to four functions (Stevens, 1986). The overall ability of the predictor set to discriminate the groups is indexed by Wilks's lambda, a 0–1 statistic representing the ratio of residual variation to total (explained + residual) variation; a lower value of lambda thus indicates greater discriminating ability. For analyses of escalation, the aim is to use variables that are measured before escalation occurs; accordingly,

---

[6]There was an overall decrease in mean levels of CO from 7th grade to 8th grade. There is no obvious explanation for this effect, because the instruments and measurement protocol were identical throughout the study. We believe that the decrease may reflect seasonal ambient levels. In 7th grade students were surveyed during the fall and some were surveyed in February and March, whereas in the 8th and 9th grades, all students were surveyed between October and December. The decrease (e.g., from 3.8 parts per million to 2.8 parts per million among nonusers) may reflect a small change in ambient level of CO during the heating season.

variables from the 7th grade were used because these measurements were obtained prior to escalation. Variables from the 8th grade were also analyzed because these measurements were obtained prior to the subsequent increase for the late starter group.[7]

We used a combined rational and empirical procedure to select a set of variables for analysis. Initially we selected eight variables, covering the theoretical domains of the study, that were the most significant univariate discriminators of substance use groups in the 7th- and 8th-grade data. A stepwise discriminant analysis was then performed with the complete set of measures (using Proc Stepdisc; SAS Institute, 1988) to determine whether additional variables with independent discriminating power were present in either 7th- or 8th-grade data. These analyses indicated that friends' beer drinking, friends' marijuana use, and parental liquor use had independent discriminating power net of the eight selected variables. Thus, a set of 11 variables was designated for analysis; behavioral competence was included in the 8th-grade analysis because it was also a highly significant univariate discriminator. The set of designated variables was then entered in discriminant function analysis with forced entry of the complete set of variables (using Proc Candisc; SAS Institute, 1988).[8]

Results for the two measurement points are presented in Tables 3 and 4. The tables include the structure matrix (zero-order correlations of the predictor variables with the discriminant functions), the standardized coefficients for predictor variables on the discriminant functions in the multivariate solution, and the value of each discriminant function at the group centroids. The structure correlations, comparable to item loadings on factors in a factor analysis, are useful for substantive interpretation of the nature of each discriminant function. The canonical coefficients, comparable to partial regression coefficients in a multiple regression analysis, indicate the discriminating ability of a given variable net of all others in the model. Though the discriminant analysis with forced entry of predictors does not provide an exact test for the significance of each predictor, the

---

[7]Missing data, an important consideration in longitudinal studies, were dealt with in the following manner. Data points that were missing within scales (e.g., 1 item missing in a 6-item scale) were screened up to a limit of 25% missing within scales, using BMDP-AM (Dixon, 1992). The data screening procedure in BMDP-AM using this criterion indicated that data within scales were missing at random, across all scales and waves. Missing items were replaced using the method of stepwise regression on nonmissing items within the scale.

[8]The measure of substance use as a coping mechanism was not included in the analyses because of some concern that it was too closely related to level of substance use. In the 7th-grade data, the measure of substance use coping when added to the set of designated variables decreased the Wilks's lambda to .67; in the 8th-grade data, this measure when added to the set of designated variables decreased the Wilks's lambda to .50. Other research has shown that coping motives are strongly related to high-intensity substance use both among adolescents (Wills & Cleary, 1995) and among adults (Cooper, Russell, & George, 1988); attention to detailed assessment of perceived coping functions of substances should be considered for further research with escalated substance use.

TABLE 3
Seventh Grade Data: Canonical Discriminant Analysis
With 1,088 Observations

Variable	Discriminant function			
	1	2	3	4
Structure matrix				
Friends smoking	.81	−.30	−.06	.06
Friends beer	.62	−.17	.34	−.34
Neg. life events	.52	.24	−.16	.31
Anger coping	.30	.43	−.01	.10
Value discrepancy	.34	.38	−.03	−.20
Hangout coping	.34	.34	.26	.11
Friends marijuana	.29	.28	.58	.09
Parent liquor	.24	−.26	.36	.14
Parent smoking	.27	.30	−.31	.36
Academic competence	−.31	.23	.16	−.43
Emotional support	−.33	−.13	.40	.45
Standardized canonical coefficients				
Friends smoking	.61	−.47	−.30	.20
Friends beer	.30	−.21	.32	−.63
Neg. life events	.24	.32	−.16	.31
Hangout coping	.20	.21	.32	.06
Value discrepancy	.15	.40	−.04	−.21
Parent smoking	.11	.29	−.36	.32
Parent liquor	.14	−.35	.44	.10
Anger coping	.08	.36	.04	.04
Friends marijuana	−.03	.39	.57	.21
Academic competence	−.03	.43	.10	−.50
Emotional support	−.16	−.06	.41	.66
Eigenvalue	.327	.036	.019	.012
% of assoc.	83	9	5	3
Group means on canonical variables				
Stable nonuser	−.430	−.022	.079	.043
Min. experimenter	.045	.020	−.078	−.172
Late starter	.302	.057	−.269	.153
Escalator 1	1.482	−.494	.137	.027
Escalator 2	1.369	.675	.266	.033

Note. Neg. = negative; assoc. = association; min. = minimal. For the discriminant functions, the significance levels are as follows: for Function 1 and Function 2, $p < .0001$; for Function 3, $p < .05$.

significance of the discriminant functions can be tested with a residual procedure based on the eigenvalues (Stevens, 1986).

In the 7th-grade data, the discriminant analysis indicated a significant solution, with Wilks's $\lambda = .70$, approximate $F(44, 4107) = 8.94$, $p < .0001$. There were three significant discriminant functions. The first function was the major one, accounting for 83% of the total association. The nonuser group had a low score on this function, the experimenter and late starter

TABLE 4
Eighth Grade Data: Canonical Discriminant Analysis
With 1,057 Observations

Variable	Discriminant function			
	1	2	3	4
Structure matrix				
Friends smoking	.71	−.20	−.45	−.28
Friends beer	.62	−.14	.05	.09
Friends marijuana	.54	.75	−0.1	.21
Neg. life events	.48	−.12	.26	.18
Anger coping	.38	−.08	.13	.11
Hangout coping	.28	.08	.19	.02
Value discrepancy	.37	.02	.51	−.18
Parent smoking	.21	−.22	.30	.45
Parent liquor	.08	.16	.42	−.08
Academic competence	−.24	.08	.16	−.68
Emotional support	−.33	.02	−.08	−.04
Behavioral competence	−.51	.04	−.09	−.03
Standardized canonical coefficients				
Friends smoking	.52	−.16	−.79	−.50
Friends beer	.25	−.56	.39	.22
Friends marijuana	.29	1.12	−.16	.21
Neg. life events	.26	−.21	.28	.06
Value discrepancy	.21	−.01	.55	−.29
Anger coping	.20	−.06	−.01	.06
Parent smoking	.06	−.27	.28	.50
Academic competence	.03	.05	.37	−.78
Hangout coping	.02	.12	.15	−.01
Emotional support	−.07	.02	−.02	−.04
Parent liquor	−.10	.21	.37	−.20
Behavioral competence	−.20	−.04	.03	.31
Eigenvalue	.547	.064	.020	.010
% of assoc.	85	10	3	2
Group means on canonical variables				
Stable nonuser	−.642	.089	.010	.039
Min. experimenter	.236	−.067	−.017	−.159
Late starter	.633	−.508	.020	.113
Escalator 1	1.487	.429	−.420	.098
Escalator 2	1.860	.532	.473	.052

Note. Neg. = negative; assoc. = association; min. = minimal. For the discriminant functions, significance levels are as follows: for Function 1 and Function 2, $p < .0001$; for Function 3, $p < .05$.

groups had progressively greater values, and the two escalator groups scored high on this function. The structure correlations indicated that the function was defined by a higher level of life stress and friends' substance use; a moderate level of parental substance use, deviance-prone attitudes, and hangout coping; and a moderately low level of parental support. The standardized discriminant function coefficients indicated that friends' smoking had strong discriminating ability whereas life stress, friends' beer drinking, and hangout coping had moderate discriminating ability, and parental support and parental substance use had lower but not trivial coefficients. Thus, at 7th grade, variables from several theoretical domains had independent effects for discriminating the group of participants who escalated from those who did not. Moreover, data for the major discriminant function indicated a scaled effect such that participants who remained nonusers had a low score, experimenters and late starters were slightly elevated, and participants who eventually escalated had a high score on the function.[9]

The first discriminant function was large relative to the second and third functions. Thus, interpretation for the latter two is qualified, because these represent specific contrasts net of a large primary effect. The second discriminant function contrasted the escalator 2 group, high on this function, from the escalator 1 group, low on this function. This function was defined by greater anger, deviance-prone attitudes, hanging out, and life stress, and among peers more deviant (marijuana) use and less normative (cigarette and alcohol) use, together with greater academic competence and less parental liquor use. Thus, the group of extreme escalators had generally greater deviance and stress at 7th grade relative to the less extreme escalators but also had greater academic competence at this measurement point. The third discriminant function contrasted the late starters (low on the function) with the two groups of escalators (high on the function). This function was largely defined by friends' marijuana use, parental liquor use, and parental support. Thus, the late starters had relatively lower levels of support, deviant peer use, and parental liquor use at this time, relative to the escalators.

In 8th-grade data, the discriminant analysis indicated a significant solution, with Wilks's $\lambda = .59$, approximate $F(48, 4012) = 12.29$, $p < .0001$. There were three significant discriminant functions. The first discriminant function again was the major one, accounting for 85% of the total association. Nonusers had a low value on this function, the escalator 1 and escalator 2 groups had high values on this function (with the escalator 1 group now highest), and the late starter group showed an intermediate level. The first function was defined by variables similar to the previous measurement. Canonical coefficients indicated moderate to high discriminating ability for most of the entered variables. However, parental smoking, academic competence, hanging out, and parental support had smaller coefficients at this measurement point.

---

[9]These analyses were replicated with demographic controls, including one index for gender, two indices for ethnicity (African American vs. other and Hispanic vs. other), two indices for family structure (single parent vs. other and blended family vs. other), and one index for parental education (coded as high-school graduate or less vs. college or more). These analyses did not substantially change the results; the nature of the discriminant functions, their relative contributions to explained between-group variation, and the canonical coefficients for the predictor variables were all quite similar across the analyses.

The second discriminant function was largely defined by friends' marijuana use and contrasted the two escalator groups (high on this function) with the late starter group (low on this function). Canonical coefficients indicated that the discriminating ability of this function was largely contributed by friends' marijuana use. (Note that standardized coefficients greater than 1.0 can and typically do occur in discriminant analysis.) Thus, both escalator groups had more deviant peer use at this measurement point, compared with the late starters. The third function was defined largely by more deviance-prone attitudes, more parental liquor use, and lower friends' smoking, and contrasted the escalator 2 group (high on this function) with the escalator 1 group (low on this function). This indicates the extreme escalators had more deviant attitudes and more parental liquor use, relative to the less extreme escalators.

DISCUSSION

In this research, repeated measures of substance use were obtained from a representative sample of adolescents, and analyses were conducted on patterns of use over time. The empirical classification showed that a group with rapid escalation of substance use can be identified within the general population of adolescents, together with a larger group who show minimal levels of use over the period from early to middle adolescence. The escalation indicated in self-reported substance use was corroborated by a biochemical indicator and thus is not interpretable as inflated reporting by a subgroup of teenagers. Discriminant function analysis was used to test whether variables from three theoretical domains could differentiate escalators from other groups of users or nonusers. Multivariate results showed that the group of escalators was discriminated from other groups on a number of variables and that these findings obtained with control for demographic characteristics. Though analyses showed some evidence of differential attrition of persons with more substance use, this type of attrition would work against the detection of variables affecting escalation, so any attrition bias in the results would operate in a conservative direction for analyses testing predictors of escalation.

The results support these general conclusions, which are discussed subsequently in more detail. First, psychosocial variables measured in 7th grade, a time when levels of substance use were low for all groups, showed significant ability to discriminate the subgroup of adolescents who eventually escalated. Thus, the variables are predictors of escalation. Second, variables from several theoretical models showed independent effects for distinguishing the various groups of users and nonusers. This finding is consistent with previous research showing that adolescent substance use is related to a number of different risk and protective factors (e.g., Hawkins,

Catalano, & Miller, 1992; Newcomb, Maddahian, & Bentler, 1986; Wills, Vaccaro, & McNamara, 1994). Third, the great majority of between-group association was accounted for by a single discriminant function, with substance use groups arrayed monotonically on this function: nonusers were lowest, minimal experimenters were slightly elevated, and the escalator groups were highest on the function. Thus, escalated substance use in adolescence can be predicted by risk loading in Zucker's (1994) terms, with escalators having a high level of risk factors and a low level of protective factors, whereas persons who remained nonusers or minimal experimenters have very different levels on these factors. The combination of factors representing a high risk loading can be characterized as greater life stress, lower parental support, more parental substance use, more deviant attitudes and maladaptive coping, lower self-control ability, and greater affiliation with peers who use substances (particularly marijuana). In the context of current knowledge about the prognostic significance of early onset and progression (Glantz & Pickens, 1992; Kandel & Davies, 1992; Robins & Przybeck, 1985), the present results suggest that the group of escalators is of serious concern with respect to vulnerability for substance abuse.

A specific conclusion from this study concerns the contrast between experimenters and abstainers. Results showed the group of experimenters to be systematically distinguished from the group of abstainers. Although some comparisons were nonsignificant, as would be expected from the low risk loading of the experimenters, significant pairwise differences showed the experimenters to have slightly higher levels of stress, maladaptive coping, and deviance-prone attitudes, and slightly lower levels of parental support and self-control; these differences were replicated over the period from 7th to 9th grade. This contrasts somewhat with the suggestion of Shedler and Block (1990), who analyzed data from follow-up of a sample of 85 participants who were recruited through a university nursery school in Berkeley, California, and had been previously studied at 7 and 11 years of age. These investigators concluded that persons classified at 18 years of age as abstainers (never tried marijuana or any other drug) were psychologically maladjusted compared with persons classified as experimenters (used marijuana ≤ monthly and used ≤ 1 other drug). The studies are not directly comparable, among other reasons because the mean age for the present participants was 14.4 years at the last measurement, whereas the participants in the Shedler and Block analysis were somewhat older. It is possible that experimentation in later adolescence could be more developmentally normative than experimentation in 7th–9th grade. The present data from a community sample of adolescents, using empirical classification of substance use patterns, are consistent with the finding of Shedler and Block (1990) that a proportion of adolescents showed experimental levels of use and that heavy users showed evidence of adjustment problems. However, the data are inconsistent with their suggestion that abstention from drug use during early adolescence indicates risk for maladjustment. Further research with different measures and different age groups is indicated to investigate the generality of this conclusion.

Theoretical Issues

In this section, we discuss issues concerning the theoretical import of the findings. A first issue arises because the present data show that the group of escalators had prior experience with smoking and alcohol use at the initial measurement. Although this is consistent with research on early onset (Robins & Przybeck, 1985), there is a question as to whether the observed group differences in variables such as life stress or maladaptive coping simply represent consequences of prior use or other factors. We think this is unlikely for several reasons. First, prospective analyses have shown that variables such as negative life events and low family support precede changes in substance use (e.g., Newcomb & Bentler, 1988a; Newcomb & Harlow, 1986; Wills, 1986; Wills, Vaccaro, McNamara, & Hirky, 1993), so it is unlikely that the temporal ordering of relationships is reversed. Second, we found that the between-group differences in study variables were obtained with control for initial level of substance use, so it is not likely that the observed differences are simply consequences of level of use. Third, a common rival explanation for findings in predictive analyses is that the putative predictors are all caused by a third factor. The grouping methodology is not immune to this issue, but in the present case it is not clear what the third factor might be, as we included constructs from several theoretical models of substance use and demonstrated that the findings obtained with control for gender, ethnicity, family structure, and socioeconomic status. Given that differences in study variables were observed prior in time to subsequent escalation and that rival explanations are excluded, it is plausible to conclude that the variables are predictors of escalation. The results of the present grouping analysis indicate that if an adolescent enters 7th grade experiencing such factors as high stress, low parental support, and low academic competence, he or she is more vulnerable to rapid escalation in substance use. It should be noted that reciprocal relationships are possible, and structural modeling approaches have the ability to test formal models of distal and proximal relationships and to test for reciprocal effects (e.g., Chassin et al., 1993; Newcomb & Bentler, 1988a; Wills, DuHamel, & Vaccaro, 1995). Each approach provides a complementary set of advantages.

As a second theoretical issue, we emphasize that variables from several domains had independent effects for discriminating escalators from other participants. The present study could have detected differential effects if they existed (e.g., experimentation predicted by life stress while escalation was predicted by peer use), but this was not found. Instead, constructs from stress-coping theory, problem behavior theory, and peer affiliation models all had loadings on the major discriminant function. Though previous research has sometimes focused on what are presented as competing theories, we have found in this and other research with empirical classification methods (Wills, Vaccaro, & McNamara, 1994) that a group representing problem youth differs on several theoretical dimensions. In principle this could be construed as indicating a process of independent multifactorial causation, that factors such as coping patterns, peer affiliations, negative life events, and commitment to academic achievement are all relevant for adolescents' substance use but derive from different domains of predictors. An alternative formulation is that variables put forth by different theories represent diverse manifestations of a common underlying factor. Though no single study can resolve this issue, recent theory and research have suggested deficits in self-regulation ability as a substrate for development of risk (e.g., Khantzian, 1990; Miller & Brown, 1991; Sher & Trull, 1994; Tarter & Mezzich, 1992; Wills, DuHamel, & Vaccaro, 1995; Zuckerman, 1994). Thus, the theoretical issue may be less a focus on testing competing theories and more a focus on working toward a general model to understand why various attributes cluster for adolescents who develop problem behavior.

A specific theoretical comment concerns the difference between the escalator 1 and escalator 2 groups. Lacking prior descriptive data and theory, we did not predict this difference, but we think the manifest difference between the groups should be discussed. Present data indicate that the escalator 1 group actually had a higher level of substance use than the other group at the initial measurement point but that the escalator 2 group had more extreme escalation, thus showing that escalation is not merely predictable from base level. The theoretical question is to account for the difference between these two groups. Our suggestion, following from the previous discussion, is that the extreme escalator group had greater risk loading from particularly important variables from early on. We also suggest that the moderate escalator group experienced an improvement in circumstances over the study period, for example, showing relative improvements in family support and academic competence, and less change in deviant attitudes and deviant peer affiliations, whereas some of these characteristics deteriorated for the extreme escalator group. It is possible that an environmental change (e.g., improved parental economic circumstances or marital relationship, tutoring or counseling for the student) augmented the protective factors for the first group (cf. Conger et al., 1990; Grych & Fincham, 1990; Takeuchi, Williams, & Adair, 1991; Wills, McNamara, & Vaccaro, 1995). We postulate that a change in the adolescent's life situation would restrain a process that otherwise could result in more adverse outcome. We note that the difference is a relative one, because both groups showed substantial rates of substance use in the 9th grade, but the suggestion is that the moderate escalator group is at reduced risk compared with the extreme escalator group. Though these interpretations are post hoc, we suggest that considering dynamic aspects of the longitudinal data provides an approach to accounting for group differences in patterns of substance use.

Further Questions

This study indicates that some persons enter adolescence experiencing less parental support and more life stress, having less adaptive patterns of coping and competence, and beginning to gravitate into groups of peer substance users. To the extent that these factors continue into middle adolescence and countervailing factors are not operative, the person becomes embedded in a matrix of active users, a greater frequency of use makes the experience-regulating functions of substances more salient, and the adolescent is primed to continue substance use at increasing rates (Wills & Cleary, 1995). Several further questions about the escalation process may help to understand more about escalated substance use. Research beginning with younger samples may help to clarify whether early onset is part of a process involving differences in self-regulation of cognition and emotion, with concomitant effects on parent–child relationships (Rothbart & Ahadi, 1994; Tarter, Moss, & Vanyukov, 1995). Detailed study of peer groups would help to understand how adolescents with high-risk characteristics enter peer groups and how the interactions among group members affect behavior over time in either a competence-promoting or a risk-promoting direction (cf. Mosbach & Leventhal, 1988; Steinberg, Dornbusch, & Brown, 1992; Wills, DuHamel, & Vaccaro, 1995). Analyses of panel data would help to clarify the importance of lagged or reciprocal relationships among substance use, maladaptive coping, and other variables. Research is also suggested on the prognostic significance of experimentation and late starting; though the level of use among experimenters was a minimal one over the present study period, this does not necessarily imply that experimentation is risk free, and research is required to investigate how experimentation or late starting may be related to substance use at later ages (cf. Chassin, Presson, Sherman, & Edwards, 1990). Finally, implications for prevention should be considered. The present results suggest escalators represent a particularly high-risk target group, and research on the design of preventive interventions for these persons may provide approaches that are appropriate and effective.

REFERENCES

Blechman, E. A., & Wills, T. A. (1992). Process measures in interventions for drug-abusing women: From coping to competence. In M. M. Kilbey & K.

Asghar (Eds.), *Methodological issues in epidemiological, prevention, and treatment research on drug-exposed women* (pp. 314–343). Rockville, MD: National Institute on Drug Abuse.

Brook, J. S., Brook, D. W., Gordon, A. S., Whiteman, M., & Cohen, P. (1990). The psychosocial etiology of adolescent drug use: A family interactional approach. *Genetic, Social, and General Psychology Monographs, 116,* 111–267.

Brook, J., Cohen, P., Whiteman, M., & Gordon, A. S. (1992). Psychosocial risk factors in the transition from moderate to heavy use or abuse of drugs. In M. Glantz & R. Pickens (Eds.), *Vulnerability to drug abuse* (pp. 359–388). Washington, DC: American Psychological Association.

Carver, C. S., Scheier, M. F., & Weintraub, J. K. (1989). Assessing coping strategies. *Journal of Personality and Social Psychology, 56,* 267–283.

Chassin, L. A., Pillow, D. R., Curran, P. J., Molina, B., & Barrera, M. (1993). Relation of parental alcoholism to early adolescent substance use: A test of three mediating mechanisms. *Journal of Abnormal Psychology, 102,* 3–19.

Chassin, L. A., Presson, C. C., Sherman, S. J., Corty, E., & Olshavsky, R. W. (1984). Predicting the onset of cigarette smoking in adolescents: A longitudinal study. *Journal of Applied Social Psychology, 14,* 224–243.

Chassin, L. A., Presson, C. C., Sherman, S. J., & Edwards, D. A. (1990). The natural history of cigarette smoking: Predicting young-adult smoking outcomes from adolescent smoking patterns. *Health Psychology, 9,* 701–718.

Chassin, L., Rogosch, F., & Barrera, M. (1991). Substance use and symptomatology among adolescent children of alcoholics. *Journal of Abnormal Psychology, 100,* 449–463.

Christiansen, B. A., Smith, G. T., Roehling, P. V., & Goldman, M. S. (1989). Alcohol expectancies predict adolescent drinking behavior one year later. *Journal of Consulting and Clinical Psychology, 57,* 93–99.

Cole, D. A. (1991). Preliminary support for a competency-based model of depression in children. *Journal of Abnormal Psychology, 100,* 181–190.

Conger, R. D., Elder, G. H., Jr., Lorenz, F. O., Conger, K. J., Simons, R. L., Whitbeck, L. B., Huck, S., & Melby, J. N. (1990). Linking economic hardship to marital quality and instability. *Journal of Marriage and the Family, 52,* 643–656.

Cooper, M. L., Russell, M., & George, W. H. (1988). Coping, expectancies, and alcohol abuse: A test of social learning formulations. *Journal of Abnormal Psychology, 97,* 218–230.

Dixon, W. J. (Ed.). (1992). *BMDP statistical software manual.* Berkeley: University of California Press.

Elliott, D. S., Huizinga, D., & Ageton, S. S. (1985). *Explaining delinquency and drug use.* Beverly Hills, CA: Sage Publications.

Fleming, J. S., & Watts, W. A. (1980). The dimensionality of self-esteem. *Journal of Personality and Social Psychology, 39,* 921–929.

Glantz, M. D., & Pickens, R. W. (1992). Vulnerability to drug abuse: Introduction and overview. In M. Glantz & R. Pickens (Eds.), *Vulnerability to drug abuse* (pp. 1–14). Washington, DC: American Psychological Association.

Grych, J. H., & Fincham, F. D. (1990). Marital conflict and children's adjustment. *Psychological Bulletin, 108,* 267–290.

Harter, S. (1985). *Manual for the self-perception profile for children and adolescents.* Department of Psychology, University of Denver.

Harter, S. (1986). Processes underlying the construction, maintenance, and enhancement of the self-concept in children. In J. Suls & A. G. Greenwald (Eds.), *Psychological perspectives on the self* (Vol. 3, pp. 137–181). Hillsdale, NJ: Erlbaum.

Hawkins, J. D., Catalano, R. F., & Miller, J. Y. (1992). Risk and protective factors for alcohol and other drug problems in adolescence and early adulthood. *Psychological Bulletin, 112,* 64–105.

Hays, R. D., Widaman, K. F., DiMatteo, M. R., & Stacy, A. W. (1987). Structural equation models of current drug use. *Journal of Personality and Social Psychology, 52,* 134–144.

Hirschman, R. S., Leventhal, H., & Glynn, K. (1984). The development of smoking behavior. *Journal of Applied Social Psychology, 14,* 184–206.

Jessor, R., Chase, J. A., & Donovan, J. E. (1980). Psychosocial correlates of marijuana use and problem drinking in a national sample of adolescents. *American Journal of Public Health, 70,* 604–613.

Jessor, R., & Jessor, S. L. (1977). *Problem behavior and psychosocial development.* New York: Academic Press.

Johnston, L. D., O'Malley, P. M., & Bachman, J. G. (1989). *Drug use, drinking, and smoking; National survey results from high school, college, and young adult populations 1975–1988.* Rockville, MD: National Institute on Drug Abuse.

Kandel, D. B., & Davies, M. (1992). Progression to regular marijuana involvement: Phenomenology and risk factors for near-daily use. In M. Glantz & R. Pickens (Eds.), *Vulnerability to drug abuse* (pp. 211–253). Washington, DC: American Psychological Association.

Kandel, D. B., Kessler, R. C., & Margulies, R. Z. (1978). Antecedents of adolescent initiation into stages of drug use. In D. B. Kandel (Ed.), *Longitudinal research on drug use* (pp. 73–100). New York: Wiley.

Kandel, D. B., & Yamaguchi, K. (1985). Developmental patterns of the use of legal, illegal, and prescribed drugs. In C. L. Jones & R. J. Battjes (Eds.), *Etiology of drug abuse* (pp. 193–235). Rockville, MD: National Institute on Drug Abuse.

Kaplan, H. B., & Johnson, R. J. (1992). Relationships between circumstances surrounding initial illicit drug use and escalation of use: Moderating effects of gender and early adolescent experiences. In M. Glantz & R. Pickens (Eds.), *Vulnerability to drug abuse* (pp. 299–358). Washington, DC: American Psychological Association.

Kaplan, H. B., Martin, S. S., Johnson, R. J., & Robbins, C. A. (1986). Escalation of marijuana use. *Journal of Health and Social Behavior, 27,* 44–61.

Khantzian, E. J. (1990). Self-regulation and self-medication factors in alcoholism and the addictions. In M. Galanter (Ed.), *Recent developments in alcoholism* (Vol. 8, pp. 255–271). New York: Plenum Press.

Labouvie, E. W., Pandina, R. J., & Johnson, V. (1991). Developmental trajectories of adolescent substance use. *International Journal of Behavioral Development, 14,* 305–328.

Miller, W. R., & Brown, J. M. (1991). Self-regulation as a conceptual basis for the prevention of addictive behaviors. In N. Heather, W. Miller, & J. Greeley (Eds.), *Self-control and the addictive behaviors* (pp. 3–79). Sydney, Australia: Maxwell Macmillan.

Milligan, G. W., & Cooper, M. C. (1985). Examination of procedures for determining the number of clusters in a data set. *Psychometrika, 50,* 159–179.

Mosbach, P., & Leventhal, H. (1988). Peer group identification and smoking. *Journal of Abnormal Psychology, 97,* 238–245.

Murray, D. M., O'Connell, C. M., Schmid, L. A., & Perry, C. L. (1987). The validity of smoking self-reports by adolescents. *Addictive Behaviors, 12,* 7–15.

Murray, D. M., Perry, C. L., O'Connell, C., & Schmid, L. (1987). Seventh-grade cigarette, alcohol, and marijuana use: Distribution in a North Central U.S. metropolitan population. *International Journal of the Addictions, 22,* 357–376.

Needle, R. H., Su, S., & Doherty, W. J. (1990). Divorce, remarriage, and adolescent substance use. *Journal of Marriage and the Family, 52,* 157–169.

Needle, R., Su, S., & Lavee, Y. (1989). A comparison of the empirical utility of three composite measures of adolescent drug involvement. *Addictive Behaviors, 14,* 429–441.

Newcomb, M. D., & Bentler, P. M. (1988a). Impact of adolescent drug use and social support on problems of young adults: A longitudinal study. *Journal of Abnormal Psychology, 97,* 64–75.

Newcomb, M. D., & Bentler, P. M. (1988b). The impact of family context, deviant attitudes, and emotional distress on adolescent drug use. *Journal of Research in Personality, 22,* 154–176.

Newcomb, M. D., & Harlow, L. L. (1986). Life events and substance use among adolescents. *Journal of Personality and Social Psychology, 51,* 564–577.

Newcomb, M. D., Maddahian, E., & Bentler, P. M. (1986). Risk factors for drug use among adolescents: Concurrent and longitudinal analyses. *American Journal of Public Health, 76,* 525–531.

Patterson, G. R., DeBaryshe, B. D., & Ramsey, E. (1989). A developmental perspective on antisocial behavior. *American Psychologist, 44,* 329–335.

Paulhus, D. (1983). Sphere-specific measures of perceived control. *Journal of Personality and Social Psychology, 44,* 1253–1265.

Robins, L. N., & Przybeck, T. R. (1985). Age of onset of drug use as a factor in drug and other disorders. In C. L. Jones & R. J. Battjes (Eds.), *Etiology of drug abuse* (pp. 178–192). Rockville, MD: National Institute on Drug Abuse.

Rohde, P., Lewinsohn, P. M., Tilson, M., & Seeley, J. R. (1990). Dimensionality of coping and its relation to depression. *Journal of Personality and Social Psychology, 58,* 499–511.

Rothbart, M. K., & Ahadi, S. A. (1994). Temperament and the development of personality. *Journal of Abnormal Psychology, 103,* 55–66.

SAS Institute. (1988). *SAS/STAT user's guide* (Release 6.03 Edition). Cary, NC: Author.

Shedler, J., & Block, J. (1990). Adolescent drug use and psychological health. *American Psychologist, 45,* 612–630.

Sher, K. J., & Trull, T. (1994). Personality and disinhibitory psychopathology: Alcoholism and antisocial personality disorder. *Journal of Abnormal Psychology, 103,* 92–102.

Sher, K. J., Walitzer, K. S., Wood, P. K., & Brent, E. E. (1991). Characteristics of children of alcoholics: Putative risk factors, substance use and abuse, and psychopathology. *Journal of Abnormal Psychology, 100,* 427–448.

Steinberg, L., Dornbusch, S. M., & Brown, B. B. (1992). Ethnic differences in adolescent achievement: An ecological perspective. *American Psychologist, 47,* 723–729.

Stevens, J. (1986). *Applied multivariate statistics for the social sciences.* Hillsdale, NJ: Erlbaum.

Stone, A. A., & Neale, J. M. (1984). A new measure of daily coping. *Journal of Personality and Social Psychology, 46,* 892–906.

Takeuchi, D. T., Williams, D. R., & Adair, R. K. (1991). Economic stress in the family and children's emotional and behavioral problems. *Journal of Marriage and the Family, 53,* 1031–1041.

Tarter, R. E., & Mezzich, A. C. (1992). Ontogeny of substance abuse: Perspectives and findings. In M. Glantz & R. Pickens (Eds.), *Vulnerability to drug use* (pp. 149–177). Washington, DC: American Psychological Association.

Tarter, R. E., Moss, H. B., & Vanyukov, M. M. (1995). Behavior genetic perspective of alcoholism etiology. In H. Begleiter and B. Kissin (Eds.), *Alcohol and alcoholism* (Vol. 1, pp. 294–326). New York: Oxford University Press.

U.S. Department of Commerce. (1992). *1990 census of the population: Social and economic characteristics (New York).* Washington, DC: Government Printing Office.

Wills, T. A. (1985). Stress, coping, and tobacco and alcohol use in early adolescence. In S. Shiffman & T. A. Wills (Eds.), *Coping and substance use* (pp. 67–94). Orlando, FL: Academic Press.

Wills, T. A. (1986). Stress and coping in early adolescence: Relationships to smoking and alcohol use in urban school samples. *Health Psychology, 5,* 503–529.

Wills, T. A. (1990). Stress and coping factors in the epidemiology of substance use. In L. T. Kozlowski, H. M. Annis, H. D. Cappell, F. B. Glaser, M. S. Goodstadt, Y. Israel, H. Kalant, E. M. Sellers, & E. R. Vingilis (Eds.), *Research advances in alcohol and drug problems* (Vol. 10, pp. 215–250). New York: Plenum Press.

Wills, T. A., & Cleary, S. D. (1995). Stress-coping model for alcohol-tobacco interactions in adolescence. In J. B. Fertig & J. P. Allen (Eds)., *Alcohol and tobacco: From basic science to clinical practice* (pp. 107–128). Bethesda, MD: National Institute on Alcohol Abuse and Alcoholism.

Wills, T. A., DuHamel, K., & Vaccaro, D. (1995). Activity and mood temperament as predictors of adolescent substance use: Test of a self-regulation mediational model. *Journal of Personality and Social Psychology, 68*, 901–916.

Wills, T. A., & Filer, M. (1996). Stress-coping model of adolescent behavior problems. In T. H. Ollendick & R. J. Prinz (Eds.), *Advances in clinical child psychology* (Vol. 18, pp. 91–132). New York: Plenum Press.

Wills, T. A., & Hirky, A. E. (1996). Coping and substance abuse: A theoretical model and review of the evidence. In M. Zeidner & N. S. Endler (Eds.), *Handbook of coping: Theory, research, and applications* (pp. 279–302). New York: Wiley.

Wills, T. A., McNamara, G., & Vaccaro, D. (1995). Parental education related to adolescent stress-coping: and substance use. *Health Psychology, 14*, 464–478.

Wills, T. A., & Shiffman, S. (1985). Coping and substance use: A conceptual framework. In S. Shiffman & T. A. Wills (Eds.), *Coping and substance use* (pp. 3–24). Orlando, FL: Academic Press.

Wills, T. A., Vaccaro, D., & McNamara, G. (1992). Life events, family support, and competence in adolescent substance use: A test of vulnerability and protective factors. *American Journal of Community Psychology, 20*, 349–374.

Wills, T. A., Vaccaro, D., & McNamara, G. (1994). Novelty seeking, risk taking, and related constructs as predictors of adolescent substance use: An application of Cloninger's theory. *Journal of Substance Abuse, 6*, 1–20.

Wills, T. A., Vaccaro, D., McNamara, G., & Hirky, A. E. (1993, August). *Family support prospectively related to adolescents' competence and substance use.* Paper presented at the 101st Annual Convention of the American Psychological Association, Toronto, Ontario, Canada.

Zevon, M. A., & Tellegen, A. (1982). The structure of mood change: An idiographic and nomothetic analysis. *Journal of Personality and Social Psychology, 43*, 111–122.

Zucker, R. A. (1994). Pathways to alcohol problems: A developmental account of the evidence for multiple alcoholisms and contextual contributions to risk. In R. A. Zucker, J. Howard, & G. M. Boyd (Eds.), *The development of alcohol problems* (pp. 255–289). Bethesda, MD: National Institute on Alcohol Abuse and Alcoholism.

Zuckerman, M. (1994). Impulsive unsocialized sensation seeking. In J. E. Bates & T. D. Wachs (Eds.), *Temperament: Individual differences at the interface of biology and behavior* (pp. 219–255). Washington, DC: American Psychological Association.

APPENDIX
Correlations Among Predictors for Discriminant Analyses, 7th and 8th Grade Data

Predictor	1	2	3	4	5	6	7	8	9	10	11	12
1. Friends smoking	—	.58	.24	.17	.18	.20	.36	.05	.15	-.15	-.19	-.27
2. Friends beer	.56	—	.24	.19	.16	.16	.51	.10	.10	-.16	-.18	-.28
3. Negative events	.30	.29	—	.29	.17	.21	.24	.14	.14	-.31	-.30	-.39
4. Anger coping	.17	.16	.28	—	.22	.36	.16	.10	.08	-.27	-.21	-.39
5. Value discrepancy	.15	.16	.13	.15	—	.23	.15	.07	.13	-.18	-.22	-.26
6. Hangout coping	.16	.13	.16	.29	.19	—	.14	.06	.07	-.19	-.12	-.27
7. Friends marijuana	.32	.47	.25	.12	.11	.08	—	.09	.08	-.17	-.17	-.23
8. Parent liquor	.09	.10	.17	.06	.05	.03	.09	—	.17	-.09	-.10	-.11
9. Parent smoking	.14	.10	.17	.13	.09	.05	.09	.15	—	-.11	-.05	-.17
10. Academic competence	-.22	-.18	-.38	-.23	-.12	-.12	-.11	-.08	-.09	—	.23	.40
11. Emotional support	-.19	-.15	-.32	-.24	-.18	-.08	-.13	-.11	-.07	.22	—	.34
12. Behavioral competence	—	—	—	—	—	—	—	—	—	—	—	—

Note. Correlations for 7th grade data are below the diagonal, and correlations for 8th grade data are above the diagonal. Approximate significance levels are as follows: $r = |.07|$, $p < .01$; $r = |.08|$, $p < .001$; $r = |.09|$, $p < .0001$.

5

ADOLESCENT RISK FACTORS FOR BINGE DRINKING DURING THE TRANSITION TO YOUNG ADULTHOOD: VARIABLE- AND PATTERN-CENTERED APPROACHES TO CHANGE

JOHN SCHULENBERG, KATHERINE N. WADSWORTH,
PATRICK M. O'MALLEY, JERALD G. BACHMAN,
AND LLOYD D. JOHNSTON

The period between adolescence and adulthood is a critical developmental transition characterized by new social contexts, additional responsibilities and privileges, and opportunities and incentives for important developmental change in self-definition. During this transition, diversity in life paths becomes more clearly manifest (Sherrod, Haggerty, & Feath-

Reprinted from *Developmental Psychology, 32,* 659–674. (1996). Copyright © 1996 by the American Psychological Association. Used with permission of the author.

This article is based in part on a paper presented at the fifth biennial meeting of the Society for Research on Adolescence, San Diego, California, February 11, 1994. This study was supported by grants from the National Institute on Alcohol Abuse and Alcoholism (AA09143) and the National Institute on Drug Abuse (DA01411) and by the Survey Research Center's Angus Campbell Fellowship. We acknowledge the helpful comments of Lois Hoffman, Jeylan Mortimer, and Robert Zucker on a previous version of this article. We thank Sharon Leech, Jinyun Liu, and Brian O'Keefe for their assistance with data management and analysis and the entire Monitoring the Future staff for assistance on this project.

erman, 1993). Variability in the timing and content of developmental milestones increases, and there is a widening of opportunities for successes and failures. Although there is continuity in functioning and adjustment between adolescence and young adulthood for most young people, many troubled adolescents become exemplary young adults, and likewise, some dysfunctional young adults come from the ranks of well-functioning adolescents (Aseltine & Gore, 1993).

Because of their characteristic blend of continuity and discontinuity, developmental transitions represent opportunities for addressing key developmental issues (Petersen, 1993; Schulenberg, Maggs, & Hurrelmann, 1997). They provide a unique vantage point for examining questions about selection and socialization, and in particular about the robustness of initial individual differences in the face of pervasive change associated with the transition. Some important questions are, To what extent can success or failure during the transition be predicted in advance? What are the pretransitional risk factors for increased or new difficulties during the transition? For those experiencing earlier difficulties, what are the pretransitional protective factors against continued difficulties during the transition? With respect to adolescent predictors of problem behaviors during the transition to young adulthood, these questions reflect an important gap in the literature. Filling this gap, according to Jessor, Donovan, and Costa (1991), would have important practical implications regarding the rationale for and targets of early intervention, as well as larger theoretical implications regarding the specification of structures and pathways of development across the life span.

In this investigation, we focus on one specific problem behavior, binge drinking, and several personality and social context characteristics that have been found to be risk factors for binge drinking during adolescence. Our central question is whether it is possible to predict change in binge drinking during the transition to young adulthood as a function of adolescent personality and social context characteristics. We address this question with national panel data, using both variable- and pattern-centered approaches (cf. Magnusson & Bergman, 1988) to predicting change. The use of both approaches, focusing on change in binge drinking in the total sample and on change in the form of different trajectories of binge drinking, respectively, permits a more comprehensive consideration of our central question.

FREQUENT BINGE DRINKING DURING THE TRANSITION TO YOUNG ADULTHOOD

Binge drinking, typically defined as having five or more drinks in a row, is the most ubiquitous problem behavior during adolescence and young adulthood. A recent survey revealed that 28% of the nation's high school seniors and 40% of those 21 to 22 years old had engaged in binge drinking at least once within the previous 2 weeks (Johnston, O'Malley, & Bachman, 1994). Although some drinking short of intoxication may not be a cause for concern for some, there is little doubt that binge drinking—particularly if frequent—is an important health-compromising behavior. Specifically, frequent binge drinking makes one vulnerable to ongoing problems with alcohol (e.g., over half the young adults who binge drink at least once a week exhibit signs of alcohol abuse or dependence; Hilton, 1991); it increases one's vulnerability to other health-compromising behaviors, including violence, unprotected or unwanted sexual intercourse, use of illicit drugs, and driving while intoxicated (e.g., Baer, 1993); and it may contribute to cognitive decrements when sober (Parker, Parker & Harford, 1991).

Our concern with frequent binge drinking stems not only from its prevalence and health-compromising consequences and concomitants but also from literature suggesting that ongoing problem behaviors, including binge drinking, may reflect difficulties with the transition to young adulthood. Hurrelmann (1990) asserted that excessive substance use should be viewed as a signal of inadequate coping with developmental tasks. In discussing the reciprocity between substance abuse and difficulties with developmental tasks, Baumrind and Moselle (1985) argued that substance abuse consolidates existing difficulties and inhibits further development (see also Pandina, Labouvie, Johnson, & White, 1990). Thus, frequent binge drinking may serve as a way of coping with the transition that is ultimately ineffective and therefore may increase difficulties. By focusing on frequent binge drinking, our results should have broader implications for the understanding of functioning and adjustment during the transition to young adulthood.

PERSONALITY AND SOCIAL CONTEXT RISK FACTORS FOR ALCOHOL USE

The predominant theoretical perspectives on substance use converge in their emphasis on multiple risk factors, with each, in varying degrees, highlighting personality and social context influences (see Petraitis, Flay, & Miller, 1995, for a review). Accordingly, we took a multiple risk factor approach, using adolescent personality and social context characteristics to predict concurrent and subsequent binge drinking.[1] We viewed personality

---

[1] Although it is likely that substance use has some reciprocal impact (e.g., Baumrind & Moselle, 1985), our implied causal model is consistent with the evidence indicating that the predominant causal direction during adolescence and young adulthood is from personality and social context to substance use (e.g., Labouvie & McGee, 1986; Stein et al., 1987).

influences as preceding social context influences. That is, in line with the evidence that individuals seek and construct social contexts that are consistent with and reinforce their personality (Block, Block, & Keyes, 1988; Caspi, Elder, & Bem, 1988; Lerner, 1982; Nurmi, 1993), we expected personality influences to be more enduring than social context influences on binge drinking over time (Kandel, Kessler, & Margulies, 1978; Stein, Newcomb, & Bentler, 1987).

The focus on both concurrent and long-term prediction permitted a test of the robustness of the adolescent risk factors (i.e., whether adolescent risk factors for concurrent binge drinking are also risk factors for increased binge drinking over time), as well as of the emergence of risk factors (i.e., whether adolescent characteristics that are not risk factors for concurrent binge drinking are risk factors for increased binge drinking over time; see Chassin, Presson, Sherman, & Edwards, 1991, for a similar analysis with respect to cigarette smoking). We attempted to select characteristics for which there was theoretical or empirical evidence suggestive of their robustness. We relied on relevant cross-sectional and longitudinal studies, especially those few longitudinal studies that have attempted to predict change in substance use during the transition to young adulthood (e.g., Chassin et al., 1991; Donovan, Jessor, & Jessor, 1983; Kandel, Simcha-Fagan, & Davies, 1986; Stein et al., 1987).

Personality Characteristics

Decades of research have documented the importance of personality influences on alcohol use during adolescence and young adulthood (see Zucker, Boyd, & Howard, 1994). Consistent with the relevant literature, we considered personality characteristics in broad terms and included personality and behavioral attributes (e.g., Block et al., 1988; Brook, Whiteman, Gordon, & Cohen, 1986). Three of the four personality domains that we selected have been consistently found to relate to alcohol and other drug use: (a) antisociality–alienation (e.g., Block et al., 1988; Brook, Cohen, Whiteman, & Gordon, 1992; Jessor & Jessor, 1977); (b) low conventionality (e.g., Chassin et al., 1991; Jessor et al., 1991; Newcomb & Bentler, 1988); and (c) low personal control orientation (e.g., Jessor et al., 1991; Newcomb & Harlow, 1986; Sadava & Thompson, 1986). The fourth domain was self-esteem and identity. Evidence regarding the link between self-esteem and substance use is equivocal (e.g., Kaplan, 1985; Labouvie & McGee, 1986; Newcomb, Bentler, & Collins, 1986), and limited evidence suggests an inverse relationship between identity (e.g., relating to purpose in life) and substance use (e.g., Newcomb & Harlow, 1986).

In regard to the possible long-term robustness of risk factors in these four personality domains, the evidence is strongest for low conventionality (e.g., Donovan et al., 1983; Jessor et al., 1991; Newcomb & Bentler, 1988;

Stacy, Newcomb, & Bentler, 1991). Consistent with the notion that it is a central characteristic of deviance proneness (Jessor & Jessor, 1977), low conventionality in adolescence appears to make one vulnerable to increased binge drinking during the transition to young adulthood. Although there is little direct evidence regarding the domain of antisociality–alienation, the extensive literature on childhood aggressive and antisocial antecedents of adolescent substance use and deviancy (e.g., Block et al., 1988; Caspi, Lynam, Moffitt, & Silva, 1993; Kellam, Simon, & Ensminger, 1983; Loeber, 1982) suggests that those high in this domain during adolescence are vulnerable to increased binge drinking during the transition; however, other evidence suggests that this personality domain may not have long-term predictive power across the transition (Zucker, 1994). Although the direct evidence for personal control orientation is limited and mixed (e.g., Chassin et al., 1991; Jessor et al., 1991), the successful negotiation of the transition is partly dependent on adolescent planfulness and self-efficacy (e.g., Clausen, 1991; Nurmi, 1993; Werner & Smith, 1992), suggesting that to the extent that increased binge drinking reflects difficulties with the transition, low personal control orientation may be a robust predictor. Finally, although the limited evidence regarding the robustness of self-esteem and identity is equivocal (e.g., Jessor et al., 1991; Kaplan, 1985; Newcomb et al., 1986), those low in this domain toward the end of adolescence may well be more prone to difficulties with the transition (Erikson, 1968), including increased binge drinking.

Drinking Motivations and Expectations

Drinking motivations and expectations also reflect personality characteristics (e.g., Brennan, Walfish, & Aubuchon, 1986; Ellickson & Hays, 1991) but are typically viewed separately because they are more proximal to alcohol use (e.g., Stacy et al., 1991). Although the most common reasons cited for drinking among young people are social motivations (Johnston & O'Malley, 1986), personal motivations may be more highly related to eventual problems with drinking (e.g., Goldman, Brown, Christiansen, & Smith, 1991). For example, drinking to get drunk is associated with binge drinking and intoxication (e.g., Wechsler & Isaac, 1992; Windle & Barnes, 1988), and drinking to cope with problems is associated with frequency and quantity of drinking (e.g., Hesselbrock, O'Brien, Weinstein, & Carter-Menendez, 1987). Both drinking to get drunk and drinking to cope were included in the present study, along with expected future alcohol use (e.g., Ellickson & Hays, 1991). To the extent that these three constructs represent the function and importance of alcohol in one's life, they should predict increased binge drinking during the transition as potential stressors expand and opportunities for binge drinking increase.

Social Context Characteristics

Alcohol use is such an integral part of many peer activities during adolescence that it is not surprising that the peer social context includes some of the most powerful concurrent predictors of alcohol and other drug use (e.g., Chassin, 1984; Hawkins, Catalano, & Miller, 1992; Kandel, 1980; Oetting & Beauvais, 1987). Nevertheless, this predictive power appears to dissipate quickly as individuals make new social contacts during the transition (e.g., Kandel et al., 1986; Stein et al., 1987). We focused on perceived peer deviance and the quantity of free time spent with peers, both of which have been found to be positively and strongly related to alcohol use (e.g., Bachman, O'Malley, & Johnston, 1984; Brook et al., 1992; Dishion & Loeber, 1985; Kandel, 1980; Silbereisen & Noack, 1988). To tap the quality of peer attachments, we focused on loneliness, which has been found to be inversely related to alcohol use (e.g., Olmstead, Guy, O'Malley, & Bentler, 1991; Windle, 1992).

Gender Differences

Consistent with the wealth of relevant evidence, we expected that binge drinking would be more common among men than women (e.g., Johnston et al., 1994; Wechsler & Isaac, 1992) and that men would be more likely than women to increase their binge drinking during the transition (e.g., Blane, 1979; Donovan et al., 1983; Schulenberg, Bachman, O'Malley, & Johnston, 1994). Although there is evidence on gender differences in the etiology of alcohol abuse and dependence (e.g., Brennan et al., 1986; Jessor et al., 1991) that is suggestive of gender differences in the robustness of adolescent risk factors, other evidence suggests that personality risk factors operate in similar ways for men and women (e.g., Jessor & Jessor, 1977; Radliff & Burkhart, 1984; Windle & Barnes, 1988). We included a focus on gender interactions to examine whether the robustness of the risk factors varied by gender.

Variable- and Pattern-Centered Approaches to Change

The increased diversity in life paths during the transition raises questions about the best way to study stability and change. Consistent with the developmental literature in general, the most common strategies for studying stability and change in substance use have been variable-centered ones. By definition, these approaches provide information about change over time in variables aggregated across individuals, whether the focus is on predictors of deviations from average change over time (e.g., longitudinal structural equation models) or on group-level differences in average change over time (e.g., repeated measures analysis of variance). As powerful and widely used as they are, these approaches are not necessarily the best way to study stability and change (Nesselroade, 1992). By focusing on average change and not attending to individual patterns of stability and change, variable-centered approaches may inadequately portray intraindividual change for even the majority of individuals in a given sample (e.g., Block & Robins, 1993; Labouvie, Padina, & Johnson, 1991; Magnusson & Bergman, 1988). This is especially likely during a developmental transition, when increased heterogeneity is expected.

An exclusive reliance on a variable-centered approach would be inadequate for our purposes. In addition to the evidence for wide interindividual variation in patterns of increased and decreased alcohol use during the transition to young adulthood (Elliott, Huizinga, & Menard, 1989; Grant, Harford, & Grigson, 1988), different types of alcoholism have been recognized that are defined in part by whether the onset of abusive drinking occurs prior to, during, or after this transition (e.g., Cloninger, 1987; Zucker, 1989, 1994). Because these different developmental pathways of alcohol use and abuse are likely to have different antecedents, failure to consider the different pathways could hinder efforts to predict change in binge drinking. Thus, as a complement to a traditional variable-centered approach, we used a pattern-centered approach (e.g., Block, 1971; Cairns, 1986) to focus on distinct patterns of intraindividual change in binge drinking. Increasingly, studies have used this type of pattern-centered approach to examine trajectories of substance use (e.g., Chassin et al., 1991; Donovan et al., 1983; Labouvie et al., 1991) and other developmental phenomena ranging from self-concept (e.g., Block & Robins, 1993) to delinquency (e.g., Elliott et al., 1989). In previous research, we identified and validated six trajectories of binge drinking (defined later; Schulenberg, O'Malley, Bachman, Wadsworth, & Johnston, 1996). In the present study, pattern-centered analyses were undertaken to predict the different trajectories as a function of adolescent personality and social context characteristics.

This combined focus on both variable- and pattern-centered analyses has been recommended in the alcohol and developmental literatures (Labouvie et al., 1991; Magnusson & Bergman, 1988; Ozer & Gjerde, 1989). Variable-centered analyses provide a straightforward way to identify risk factors that, in theory, apply to "everyone in general." The relatively complex pattern-centered analyses provide a way to identify risk factors specific to certain types of individuals defined by their initial and subsequent levels of binge drinking. Inconsistencies between findings from the two analyses serve to identify risk factors that operate conditionally, dependent on one's level of binge drinking, and consistencies serve to identify "unconditional" risk factors. We combined the two approaches in an effort to gain additional perspective on the prediction of continued and increased problem drinking during the transition to young adulthood.

METHOD

Four waves of national panel data were obtained from the Monitoring in Future project, an ongoing study of adolescents and young adults conducted at the University of Michigan's Institute for Social Research. The project has surveyed nationally representative samples of approximately 17,000 high school seniors each year since 1975, using questionnaires administered in classrooms. Approximately 2,400 individuals are randomly selected from each senior year cohort for follow-up. Follow-up surveys are conducted on a biennial basis, using mailed questionnaires. The biennial follow-up surveys begin 1 year after high school for one random half of each cohort and 2 years after high school for the other half (the two random halves were combined for these analyses). Study procedures are described in detail elsewhere (Bachman, Johnston, & O'Malley, 1991; Johnston et al., 1994).

Sample

The sample included respondents from the 1976–1987 cohorts who participated in the first three follow-up surveys (spanning ages 18 to 24). Five separate questionnaire forms were distributed randomly within schools at senior year. Three of the forms (A, B, and C) contained relevant personality and social context items, with little overlap in items across the forms. A total of 6,862 weighted cases (56.9% women) were included in the analyses of these three forms. All analyses were conducted on the weighted sample.[2]

Although retention rates for any one follow-up averaged 75% to 80%, the pattern-centered analyses made it necessary to restrict the sample to respondents present at all four waves, resulting in a retention rate of 62.6%. To determine the effects of attrition, multiple regression analyses were conducted to predict retention as a function of the senior year variables used in this study. The equations were significant, with the amount of variance accounted for in retention being less than 7%. Background characteristics were most predictive of retention: those retained were significantly more likely to be female, White, and have higher grade point averages (GPAs) than those excluded. With few exceptions (e.g., hostility, "hanging out" with friends), none of the other variables, including senior year binge drinking, predicted retention. Thus, although attrition was not random with respect to some important background characteristics, it was largely unrelated to the variables that were of primary concern in this study.

---

[2]Because respondents with more frequent senior year illicit drug use were oversampled for follow-up by a factor of 3, they required a corrective weighting of .333.

Measures

The outcome measure in all analyses was binge drinking. Senior year predictors included background variables, personality characteristics, drinking motivations and expectations, and social context characteristics.[3] Correlations among the variables are presented in the Appendix.

Binge Drinking

Binge drinking was measured with a single item concerning the frequency of having five or more drinks in a row during the past 2 weeks. Possible responses ranged from *none* (1) to *10 or more times* (6). This is a standard self-report measure of binge drinking (e.g., Kusserow, 1991; Wechsler & Isaac, 1992), and previous analyses with data from the Monitoring the Future project (e.g., Johnston & O'Malley, 1986) support its validity.

For the pattern-centered analyses, respondents were placed in seven trajectory groups on the basis of their patterns of binge drinking across the four waves: Chronic, Decreased, Increased, Fling, Rare, Never, and Remaining. These trajectories are defined in Table 1. In keeping with our focus on potentially problematic use of alcohol, and consistent with a standard indicator of problem drinking (i.e., weekly binge drinking; e.g., Blane, 1979; Hilton, 1991), the first four trajectories involved frequent binge drinking, defined as two or more episodes of binge drinking in a 2-week period. The other two primary trajectories, Rare and Never, involved no frequent binge drinking. In a previous analysis, the trajectories were derived conceptually and confirmed with cluster analyses, and the construct validity of the trajectories was demonstrated by showing that they corresponded to changes in negative consequences of drinking, loss of control of drinking, attitudes about heavy drinking, and peer heavy drinking (Schulenberg et al., 1996). It was also found that the trajectories coincided with change in illicit drug use, suggesting some correspondence of the binge drinking trajectories to other problem behaviors.

Sample sizes and percentages for each trajectory group for the total sample and by gender are included in Table 1. Over 90% of the sample fit into one of the six primary trajectory groups, with over a third never engaging in any binge drinking. Consistent with the epidemiological evidence (e.g., Hilton, 1991), compared with men, women were underrepresented

---

[3]Because the sample was restricted to those who provided valid binge drinking data at all four waves, missing data on the predictors was minimal (i.e., less than 17% of the respondents were missing any predictors, and among them, nearly half were missing only one predictor and none was missing more than half of the predictors). Because it would have been unnecessarily restrictive to limit the sample to those with nonmissing data on all predictors, we imputed within-gender by binge drinking trajectory group means for missing data. Preliminary analyses conducted without imputation provided results that were very similar to those obtained after imputation.

TABLE 1
Binge Drinking Trajectories: Subsample Sizes and Percentages for the Total Sample by Gender

Binge trajectory	Description	Men		Women		Total	
		n	%	n	%	n	%
Chronic	Frequent binge drinking at every wave.	352	11.9	112	2.9	464	6.8
Decreased	Frequent binge drinking at Wave 1, decreased to no frequent binge drinking by Wave 4.	392	13.3	409	10.5	801	11.7
Increased	No frequent binge drinking at Wave 1, increased to frequent binge drinking by Wave 4.	405	13.7	265	6.8	670	9.8
Fling	No frequent binge drinking at Wave 1 and Wave 4, frequent binge drinking at Wave 2 or Wave 3, or both.	273	9.2	386	9.9	659	9.6
Rare	Some binge drinking during at least one wave, but no frequent binge drinking.	426	14.4	670	17.1	1,096	16.0
Never	No binge drinking at any wave.	720	24.3	1,784	45.7	2,504	36.5
Remaining	Some frequent binge drinking, but pattern over time does not correspond to any of the categories above.	390	13.2	278	7.2	668	9.7
Total		2,958	100.0	3,904	100.0	6,862	100.0

Note. *Binge drinking* is defined as having 5 or more drinks in a row at least once in the past 2 weeks. *Frequent binge drinking* is defined as having 2 or more binge drinking episodes in the past 2 weeks. Modal ages: Wave 1 (senior year) = 18, Wave 2 = 19–20, Wave 3 = 21–22, Wave 4 = 23–24. Weighted *ns* are presented.

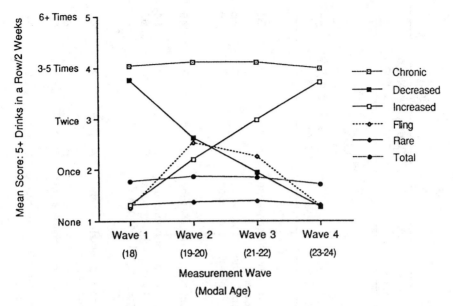

Figure 1. Mean scores for five or more drinks in a row in the past 2 weeks by binge drinking trajectory.

in the Chronic and Increased groups and overrepresented in the Never group.

The mean binge drinking scores for each trajectory group (excluding the Never and Remaining groups) are illustrated in Figure 1. Total sample mean scores are also included, showing slightly but significantly higher means at Waves 2 and 3. As is clear, this normative trajectory cannot adequately portray the various embedded differential change trajectories. As would be expected given the trajectory definitions, there were no within-trajectory gender differences in the means (in the total sample, means were higher for men than for women).

Background Variables

Background variables measured at senior year included gender, ethnicity, parental education level, and high school GPA.[4] These variables are listed in Table 2, and as indicated, each was a "core" variable (present in all questionnaire forms).

Personality Characteristics

In selecting measures from the available data, we focused on characteristics consistent with those used in relevant literature. Across the

---

[4]O'Malley, Bachman, and Johnston (1988) investigated period, age, and cohort effects in the Monitoring the Future data and demonstrated that by far the dominant factor in alcohol use was age. As a partial control for other effects, senior year cohort was included in preliminary analyses but was not significant, and therefore it was excluded from the final models.

TABLE 2
Predictors and Sample Items

Scale	Sample item	Survey form	No. of items	α
Background				
Gender (0 = male, 1 = female)		Core	1	—
Ethnicity (0 = non-White, 1 = White)		Core	1	—
Parental education level		Core	1	—
High School GPA		Core	1	—
Personality				
Antisociality–Alienation				
Hostility	"During the last 12 months, how often have you hurt someone badly enough to need bandages or a doctor?"	B	3	.51
Social intolerance	"It's not really my problem if others are in trouble and need help."	C	4	.66
Social–political apathy	"How much do you think about the social problems of the nation and the world, and about how they might be solved?"	C	2	.69
Conventionality				
Social conservatism	"Too many young people are sloppy and just don't care how they look."	B	2	.45
Risk taking	"I get a real kick out of doing things that are a little dangerous."	B	2	.84
Promarriage value	"Most people will have fuller and happier lives if they choose legal marriage rather than staying single, or just living with someone."	C	3	.67
Personal Control Orientation				
Obedience	"I feel that a good citizen should go along with whatever the government does even if he disagrees with it."	A	2	.47
Family role efficacy	"How good do you think you would be as a parent?"	B	3	.67
Self-efficacy	"When I make plans, I am almost certain that I can make them work."	C	3	.58
Work role readiness	"How well do you think your experiences and training have prepared you to be a good worker on a job?"	C	1	—

Affect and identity				
Identity focus	"How important is it to find purpose and meaning in your life?"	A	1	—
Positive self-esteem	"I take a positive attitude toward myself."	C	4	.77
Drinking motivations/expectations				
Drink to get drunk	"The most important reasons for your drinking include to feel good or get high."	A	3	.82
Drink to cope	"The most important reasons for your drinking include to get away from your problems or troubles."	A	3	.60
Expected future use	"Do you think you will be drinking 5 years from now?"	A	1	—
Social context				
Evenings out	"During a typical week, on how many evenings do you go out for fun and recreation?"	Core	1	—
Perceived peer norms for school misconduct	"How do you think most of the students in your class would feel if you cheated?"	A	3	.52
Hanging out with friends	"How often do you get together with friends, informally?"	B	2	.52
Loneliness	"I often wish I had more good friends."	C	4	.57

Note. Higher scores correspond with higher levels of the attribute indicated by the variable label. Some sample items have been paraphrased. Dashes indicate that no value is computed for alpha. GPA = grade point average.

three forms, four personality domains were included: (a) antisociality–alienation, (b) conventionality, (c) personal control orientation, and (d) affect and identity. These domains are listed in Table 2 along with the corresponding scales, reliability information, and sample items. Factor analyses were used to form the scales as well as to provide minimum evidence concerning discriminant validity.

Antisociality–alienation included three scales: Hostility, including threats and acts of aggression (e.g., similar to Stacy et al., 1991); Social Intolerance, including a distinct lack of concern for others; and Social–Political Apathy (e.g., similar to the alienation construct in Jessor & Jessor, 1977). Conventionality included three scales: Social Conservatism (e.g., similar to the liberalism construct in Stein et al., 1987) and Promarriage Value, both reflecting traditional orientations, and Low Risk-Taking (e.g., similar to Brook et al., 1986). Personal Control Orientation included four scales: Self-Efficacy, based on Nowicki and Strickland's (1973) Internal Locus of Control subscale; Obedience to Authority; and because of the salience of family and work decisions during the transition, Family Role Efficacy and Work Role Readiness (comprises 1 item). Affect and Identity included a Positive Self-Esteem scale based on Rosenberg (1965), and an item concerning identity focus (similar to the purpose-in-life construct in Newcomb & Harlow, 1986).

Drinking Motivations and Expectations

To measure the reason for using alcohol, we included scales of Drinking to Get Drunk (e.g., similar to Wechsler & Isaac, 1992) and Drinking to Cope (e.g., similar to Jessor & Jessor, 1977). In addition, we included an item concerning expected future use of alcohol (similar to Ellickson & Hays, 1991).

Social Context Characteristics

Social context measures included two indicators of quantity of time spent with friends—frequency of evenings out and of hanging out with friends (e.g., similar to Brook et al., 1992); Perceived Peer Norms for School Misconduct (e.g., similar to Jessor & Jessor, 1977); and Loneliness (e.g., similar to Newcomb & Bentler, 1988).

RESULTS

Findings based on the variable- and pattern-centered approaches are presented separately. The evidence of gender differences in the etiology of alcohol abuse and dependence (see introductory section) suggested the possibility that some risk factors would operate differently for men and women. Based on preliminary analyses, several gender by risk factor interactions were tested, and the final models include the interactions that were found to be significant. The three separate questionnaire forms made it necessary to conduct three parallel sets of analyses.

Variable-Centered Approach

In the variable-centered analyses, binge drinking in the total sample was considered as a function of the senior year predictors. To provide a baseline, we first examined concurrent binge drinking and then change in binge drinking between senior year and Wave 4. Hierarchical multiple regression analyses were conducted. The findings are summarized in Table 3.[5] To facilitate presentation, results from the three questionnaire forms were combined, and coefficients for core items were averaged across the three forms. Because of the large sample size for the variable-centered analyses, only coefficients that reached .01 level of significance are discussed.

Senior Year Binge Drinking

Predictors were added sequentially in four blocks: background variables, personality characteristics, social context characteristics, and Gender × Risk Factor interactions (in Form A, drinking motivations and expectations were added as a separate block after the personality block). Each block added significantly to the amount of variance accounted for, except for gender interaction in Form C. The final model accounted for 33.7%, 27.4%, and 18.2% of the variance in binge drinking in Forms A, B, and C, respectively.

As shown in Table 3, background risk factors ($p < .01$) for senior year binge drinking included being male and being White. In addition, lower GPA was a background risk factor. Personality risk factors included those reflecting higher antisociality–alienation (higher hostility, social intolerance, and social–political apathy) and lower conventionality (lower social conservatism and promarriage value, and higher risk taking). None of the personal control orientation predictors was significant, with one exception: The significant gender interaction revealed that lower family role efficacy was a risk factor for men ($\beta = -.08$) but not women ($\beta = .01$). Neither of the affect and identity predictors was significant. Drinking motivation and expectation risk factors included higher levels of drinking to get drunk, drinking to cope, and expected future use; the significant gender interactions revealed that both drinking to get drunk and expected future use were significantly stronger for men ($\beta = .41$ and .19, respectively) than

---

[5]Standardized coefficients are presented to facilitate interpretation. Tables of unstandardized regression coefficients and standard errors are available from the authors.

TABLE 3
Summary of Multiple Regression (Variable-Centered) Results Predicting Senior Year (SY) Binge Drinking and Change in Binge Drinking: Standardized Regression Coefficients

Predictors	Form	Senior year binge drinking	Wave 4 binge drinking
		Background	
Gender (C = male, 1 = female)	Core	−.14***	−.19***
Ethnicity (0 = non-White, 1 = White)	Core	.06***	.05*
Parent education	Core	−.01	.03
High School GPA	Core	−.11***	−.05*
Senior year binge drinking	Core	—	.24***
		Personality	
Antisociality–Alienation			
Hostility	B	.14***	.00
Social intolerance	C	.07***	.01
Social-political apathy	C	.08***	.00
Conventionality			
Social conservatism	B	−.08***	−.09***
Risk taking	B	.13***	.04
Promarriage value	C	−.11***	−.05**
Personal Control Orientation			
Obedience	A	−.04*	.01
Family role efficacy	B	−.03	−.03
Self-efficacy	C	−.04*	−.10***
Work role readiness	C	.01	−.03
Affect and Identity			
Identity focus	A	.01	−.03
Positive self-esteem	C	.00	.01

Drinking motivations/expectations

	Form		
Drink to get drunk	A	.33***	.14***
Drink to cope	A	.05**	−.02
Expected future use	A	.17***	.11***
Social context			
Evenings out	Core	.19***	.04
Peer norms for misconduct	A	.03	.02
Hanging out with friends	B	.13***	.03
Loneliness	C	−.04*	−.04*
Gender interactions			
Gender × Family Role Efficacy	B	.05**	—
Gender × Drink to Get Drunk	A	−.10***	−.06**
Gender × Expected Future Use	A	−.05**	—
Gender × Evenings Out	Core	−.05*	—
Gender × SY Binge Drinking	Core	—	−.04*
Gender × Risk Taking	B	—	.05*

	R^2	F	df	R^2	F	df
A	.34	82.58***	14	.22	46.49***	14
B	.27	72.80***	12	.18	39.33***	13
C	.18	38.17***	13	.21	43.07***	14

Note. For core items, coefficients were averaged across the three questionnaire forms, and modal significance levels are presented. Dashes indicate a nonsignificant interaction, excluded from the equation. Form A, $n = 2,287$; Form B, $n = 2,328$; Form C, $n = 2,247$. GPA = grade point average.
*$p < .05$. **$p < .01$. ***$p < .001$.

women (β = .28 and .16, respectively). Social context risk factors included those reflecting greater quantity of time spent with friends (higher frequency of evenings out and of hanging out with friends).

Change in Binge Drinking Over Time

To examine change in binge drinking over time, we predicted Wave 4 binge drinking and included Wave 1 binge drinking as a predictor in the first block. The four blocks (five in Form A) were again added to the equation sequentially, and except for the personality block in Form A and the social context block in Forms A and B, each block added significantly to the amount of variance accounted for. The final model accounted for 22.3%, 18.1%, and 21.3% of the variance in Wave 4 binge drinking in the three forms, respectively. As indicated in Table 3, there was moderate instability in binge drinking between adolescence and young adulthood (i.e., Wave 1 binge drinking β = .24).[6]

In examining the senior year predictors as possible risk factors for a relative increase in binge drinking over time, we sought to determine which were robust (i.e., risk factors for both senior year binge drinking and for a relative increase in binge drinking over time) and which were "emergent" (i.e., risk factors for a relative increase in binge drinking over time but not for senior year binge drinking). As shown in Table 3, robust senior year risk factors included being male; lower social conservatism and pro-marriage value, both reflecting lower conventionality; and higher levels of drinking to get drunk and expected future use. Based on a significant gender interaction, drinking to get drunk was a significantly stronger robust risk factor for men (β = .17) than for women (β = .13). Noticeably absent from this list of robust risk factors were those concerning antisociality–alienation and social context. Finally, the only emergent risk factor was lower self-efficacy; those lower in self-efficacy at senior year were not at risk (or perhaps only very slightly so, with $p < .05$) for senior year binge drinking, but they were quite distinctly at risk for increased binge drinking over time.

Thus, the variable-centered analyses were successful in identifying significant adolescent risk factors for increased binge drinking during the transition to young adulthood, with the success of the overall prediction being relatively modest. We now turn to the pattern-centered analyses to consider an alternative strategy for predicting change.

---

[6]These coefficients ranged from .19 to .30 across the three forms. Because of measurement error and the inclusion of the several other variables in the models, these coefficients reflect lower bound estimates of stability. For example, O'Malley, Bachman, and Johnston (1983) estimated the 3-year stability of binge drinking to be .65, adjusting for measurement error (see also Schulenberg et al., 1994).

Pattern-Centered Approach

The purpose of the pattern-centered analyses was to examine whether the senior year predictors could differentiate between diverging trajectories (i.e., initially similar but subsequently different in level of binge drinking). Four pairwise comparisons were considered: (a) *Chronic versus Decreased*, (b) *Fling versus Rare*, (c) *Increased versus Rare*, and (d) *Increased versus Fling*.[7] Because we were predicting a dichotomous outcome, logistic regression analyses were conducted.[8] Findings are summarized in Table 4, with coefficients combined across the three forms to facilitate interpretation (see Footnote 5). Because of the modest subsample sizes of some of the trajectory groups, we focus on coefficients with a $p < .05$ significance level.

Chronic Versus Decreased

The Chronic and Decreased groups had similarly high (but significantly different) binge drinking means at senior year, with both groups averaging about three to five binge drinking episodes within the previous 2 weeks (4.03 and 3.78, respectively)[9]; by Wave 4, however, the two groups were quite different (see Figure 1). Because respondents in these two groups were already involved in frequent binge drinking at senior year and were thus clearly vulnerable to future frequent binge drinking (e.g., Bachman et al., 1984; Newcomb & Bentler, 1988), it is appropriate to consider significant predictors of decreased frequent binge drinking over time as "protective factors" against continued frequent binge drinking during the transition (e.g., we do not view protective factors as simply the opposite of risk

---

[7]The Never trajectory was excluded from consideration of diverging trajectories for three reasons: (a) our focus on diverging trajectories required comparison of trajectories that were as similar as possible in initial binge drinking level, which made the Rare group rather than the Never group the appropriate match for the Increased and Fling groups; (b) preliminary analyses showed that the Rare and Never groups were significantly different on several of the senior year personality and social context characteristics, arguing against combining the two groups; and (c) because respondents in the Never group never engaged in any binge drinking across the four waves of measurement, it is highly unlikely that they were at risk for problematic drinking and thus were not of primary concern in this study.

[8]Maximum likelihood estimates (MLE) and standard errors from the logistic regression analyses are analogous to those obtained in ordinary least squares estimation in standard linear regression models. The $-2 \log L$ chi-square statistic is analogous to the omnibus F statistic in linear regression. There is no widely accepted statistic for estimating the percent of variance accounted for in logistic regression models (DeMaris, 1992).

[9]This lack of statistical equality in initial level of binge drinking between the chronic and decreased trajectories suggested an alternative explanation for any significant predictor in this comparison (i.e., that it was predicting difference in initial level, not subsequent divergence). To consider this alternative explanation, we reran the analyses for this comparison and included initial binge drinking in the equations. The standardized coefficients for initial binge drinking were .13, .15, and .08 for Forms A, B, and C, respectively (significant in the first two only). The inclusion of initial binge drinking had no impact on coefficients for the other predictors, with two minor exceptions: In Form A, the coefficient for drink to get drunk dropped from .11 ($p < .05$) to .10 ($p < .07$); in Form B, the coefficient for hostility increased from $-.07$ ($p < .12$) to $-.09$ ($p < .05$). With these two minor exceptions, the findings provide strong evidence against the alternative explanation.

TABLE 4
Summary of Logistic Regression (Pattern-Centered) Results Predicting Trajectory Membership: Standardized Regression Coefficients

Predictors	Form	Chronic vs. decreased	Fling vs. rare	Increased vs. rare	Increased vs. fling
		Background			
Gender (0 = male, 1 = female)	Core	-.26***	-.02	-.21***	-.20***
Ethnicity (0 = non-White, 1 = White)	Core	.06	.01	.01	.01
Parent education	Core	.06	.06	.04	-.04
High School GPA	Core	-.06	-.01	-.06	-.04
		Personality			
Antisociality–Alienation					
Hostility	B	-.07	.02	.07	.04
Social intolerance	C	.03	.04	.01	-.02
Social-political apathy	C	-.03	.00	.04	.03
Conventionality					
Social conservatism	B	-.05	-.09*	-.12**	-.02
Risk taking	B	.03	-.05	.00	.06
Promarriage value	C	-.03	-.02	-.07	-.06
Personal Control Orientation					
Obedience	A	.00	-.03	.09	.12*
Family role efficacy	B	-.05	-.02	-.11**	-.07
Self-efficacy	C	-.11*	.00	-.10*	-.09
Work role readiness	C	-.10*	-.01	-.06	-.04
Affect and Identity					
Identity focus	A	.11*	-.03	-.11*	-.07
Positive self-esteem	C	.01	-.03	.00	.02

Drinking motivations/expectations

Predictor	Form				
Drink to get drunk	A	.11*	.04	.13**	.08
Drink to cope	A	.05	.01	.02	.04
Expected future use	A	.10	.02	.03	.04
Social context					
Evenings out	Core	.00	.04	.08*	.05
Peer norms for misconduct	A	-.01	.00	.02	.03
Hang out with friends	B	.01	.08	-.02	-.11*
Loneliness	C	-.14**	-.01	-.04	-.01
Gender interactions					
Gender × Social Intolerance	C	—	-.09*	—	.13*
Gender × Loneliness	C	—	—	.09*	—
Gender × Risk Taking	B	—	—	—	.11*
Gender × Drink to Get Drunk	A	—	—	—	-.12*
Gender × Hanging Out	B	—	—	—	-.12*

	-2 log L χ^2	df	-2 log L χ^2	df	-2 log L χ^2	df	-2 log L χ^2	df
A	44.66***	11	7.08 (ns)	11	51.87***	11	45.29***	12
B	49.11***	10	17.62 (ns)	10	67.88***	10	36.81***	12
C	57.74***	12	15.64 (ns)	13	44.30***	13	30.33**	13

Note. In each pair, the first trajectory listed = 1 and the second = 0. Weighted *ns* for Forms A, B, and C, respectively: chronic (138, 165, 161), decreased (218, 301, 282), increased (222, 245, 203), fling (224, 225, 210), rare (350, 376, 370). For core items, coefficients were averaged across the three questionnaire forms, and modal significance levels are presented. Dashes indicate nonsignificant interactions, excluded from equation.

*p < .05. **p < .01. ***p < .001.

factors but rather as predictors that come into play once future vulnerability is established; cf. Hawkins et al., 1992; Rutter, 1994). As shown in Table 4, the model was significant in all three forms.

Before considering what distinguished these two groups, it is instructive to note their comparability on several risk factors for senior year binge drinking (from the variable-centered analyses). Both groups had equally high levels of antisociality–alienation, drinking to cope, expected future use, and time spent with friends; and equally low levels of GPA and conventionality. Turning to their differences, Table 4 shows that the senior year protective factors against continued frequent binge drinking over time were being female; higher self-efficacy and work role readiness, both reflecting a more internal control orientation; lower identity focus, reflecting less concern with identity exploration; less drinking to get drunk; and greater loneliness, perhaps reflecting less satisfaction with senior year social relationships.

Increased Versus Fling Versus Rare

By definition, none of the respondents in the Increased, Fling, or Rare groups reported any frequent binge drinking at senior year. As illustrated in Figure 1, their low levels of binge drinking at senior year were statistically equivalent (1.31, 1.25, and 1.30, respectively). The three groups were also similar on many of the risk factors for senior year binge drinking, with all three having equally high GPAs and equally low levels of antisociality–alienation and expected future alcohol use. Pairwise comparisons of the three groups were conducted to (a) identify senior year risk factors for initiating any frequent binge drinking after high school (common to the Fling and Increased groups) and (b) distinguish the senior year risk factors for a time-limited "fling" with frequent binge drinking (characteristic only of the Fling groups) from the senior year risk factors for a sustained increase in frequent binge drinking over time (characteristic only of the Increased group). As shown in Table 4, the models for the *Fling versus Rare* comparisons were not significant,[10] and those for the other two comparisons were significant.

Across the comparisons of *Fling versus Rare* and *Increased versus Rare*, the only common senior year risk factor was lower social conservatism, indicating that this risk factor was important in predicting the post-high-school initiation of any frequent binge drinking but not in predicting its eventual course once initiated. Common to both of the comparisons of *Fling versus Rare* and *Increased versus Fling* was the significant Gender × Social Intolerance interaction, indicating that higher social intolerance was

---

[10]Although the omnibus tests in this comparison were not significant, the specific risk factors reaching significance were of particular conceptual interest and worthy of consideration. Our pattern-centered focus argued against combining these two groups in subsequent analyses.

a risk factor for a time-limited fling with frequent binge drinking among men (β = .16 and −.16, respectively) but not women (β = −.04 and .07, respectively).

The comparisons of *Increased versus Rare* and *Increased versus Fling* yielded similar results. In addition to gender, predictors of similar magnitude across the two comparisons included obedience ($p < .06$ in the former comparison, significant in the latter); self-efficacy (significant in the former comparison, $p < .12$ in the latter); and among men, drinking to get drunk (in the former comparison, this risk factor was significant for men, β = .22, but not women, β = −.05). These findings suggest that being male, lower personal control orientation, and higher levels of drinking to get drunk (among men) are senior year risk factors for post-high-school initiation of frequent binge drinking that becomes a sustained increase in frequent binge drinking over time.

Risk factors unique to the comparison of *Increased versus Rare* included lower family role efficacy and identity focus and higher frequency of evenings out. Also, lower loneliness was a risk factor for men (β = −.16) but not women (β = .07). These risk factors were thus important in predicting a sustained increase in frequent binge drinking in contrast to no frequent binge drinking. Risk factors unique to the comparison of *Increased versus Fling* were found only for women. Lower frequency of hanging out with friends (β = −.21 for women, .02 for men) and higher levels of risk-taking (β = .16 for women, −.06 for men) were risk factors for a sustained increase in frequent binge drinking as opposed to a time-limited fling, indicating that these factors became important for women only after they initiated frequent binge drinking.

Summary

From the variable-centered analyses, significant senior year risk factors for concurrent binge drinking included being male and being White; lower GPA, and conventionality; and higher levels of antisociality–alienation, drinking to get drunk, drinking to cope, expecting future use of alcohol, and quantity of time spent with friends. Significant gender interactions revealed that lower family-role efficacy was a risk factor for men only, and both drinking to get drunk and expected future use were stronger risk factors for men than women. Among these risk factors for senior year binge drinking, however, only male gender, lower conventionality, and higher drinking to get drunk and expected future use were robust risk factors for increased binge drinking over time. In addition, lower self-efficacy emerged as a senior year risk factor for increased binge drinking over time.

These conclusions were elaborated on and qualified by the pattern-centered findings. Consistent with the variable-centered results, being male, lower self-efficacy, and higher drinking to get drunk (especially among men) were senior year risk factors for a sustained increase in binge drinking over time among initial nonfrequent binge drinkers; likewise, being female, higher self-efficacy, and lower drinking to get drunk were senior year protective factors against continued frequent binge drinking among initial frequent binge drinkers. In contrast, lower social conservatism was a conditional risk factor that was important only when predicting initiation into any post-high-school frequent binge drinking. Furthermore, some predictors that were not significant in the variable-centered analyses were found to be significant in the pattern-centered analyses (e.g., social intolerance, loneliness).

DISCUSSION

The transition to young adulthood is a critical sorting point in life, a time of important and lasting changes in functioning and adjustment. Whether the a priori prediction of these changes is possible reflects a salient theoretical issue regarding the strength of pretransitional individual differences in the face of a powerful developmental transition. In this investigation, we examined whether risk factors for concurrent binge drinking in adolescence predicted change in binge drinking during the transition to young adulthood. We addressed this question with national panel data, using both variable- and pattern-centered approaches to change.

Variable-Centered Findings: Robust and Emergent Risk Factors for Binge Drinking

Robust Risk Factors

In the variable-centered analyses, five of the senior year risk factors for concurrent binge drinking were found to also be risk factors for increased binge drinking over time, including being male, lower social conservatism and promarriage value, and greater drinking to get drunk and expected future use. The gender difference coincides with the wealth of evidence showing that during adolescence and young adulthood, men are more likely than women to drink (e.g., Johnston et al., 1994; Wechsler & Isaac, 1992); to increase their drinking over time (e.g., Donovan et al., 1983; Schulenberg et al., 1994); and to have problems with alcohol (e.g., Hilton, 1991). Explanations for this expected finding range from cultural to physiological ones. For example, a decline in alcohol use during the transition is associated with pregnancy and with marriage, and women tend to marry earlier than men (e.g., Bachman, O'Malley, Johnston, Rodgers, & Schulenberg, 1992). In addition, women weigh less than men on average and metabolize alcohol faster, indicating that five or more drinks in a row may be a more deviant behavior for women. It is noteworthy that only one of the gender interactions was significant, suggesting little difference between men and women in the adolescent characteristics that make one vulnerable to increased binge drinking during the transition to young adulthood.

Social conservatism and promarriage value both represent conventionality, and it is noteworthy that among all of the significant senior year personality and social context risk factors for concurrent binge drinking, only lower conventionality remained a robust risk factor. This expected finding is consistent with Jessor and Jessor's (1977) problem behavior theory, a theory that underscores the importance of low conventionality for deviance proneness (Donovan et al., 1983; Jessor et al.; 1991), and with the research of Newcomb and Bentler (1988) and their colleagues (Stacy et al., 1991; Stein et al., 1987), who have found that social conformity (based on law abidance, liberalism, and religious commitment) is one of the only adolescent personality characteristics that predicts change in substance use during the transition to young adulthood. As we note later, however, there were some conditions to this risk factor.

The finding that none of the risk factors in the antisociality–alienation domain was robust is consistent with other research indicating that adolescent delinquency and hostility have no direct impact on adult use of alcohol and other drugs (e.g., Kandel et al., 1986; Stacy et al., 1991). Of course, the adolescent antisociality–alienation risk factors were not unrelated to young adulthood binge drinking (see Appendix), but the regression analyses revealed that the relationships were fully mediated by senior binge drinking and other predictors. The lack of direct linkage suggests some discontinuity in these relationships during the transition to young adulthood that could be due in part to increased drinking not related to antisociality–alienation factors during the transition (cf. Loeber, 1982; Zucker, 1989, 1994). Alternatively, the lack of robustness in the antisociality–alienation domain may have been partly due to limitations associated with our measures and sample (e.g., the lack of high school dropouts) (see the section *Limitations and Future Directions*, which appears later).

The connection between the motive of drinking to get drunk and heavy drinking has been recognized for over four decades (Straus & Bacon, 1953; see also Johnston & O'Malley, 1986; Wechsler & Isaac, 1992). Our findings extend this literature by showing that drinking to get drunk is also an adolescent risk factor for increased binge drinking over time. Whether this risk factor reflects the importance of getting drunk to the adolescent or simply a dose-response relationship, its robustness suggests its salience in the development of alcohol abuse and dependence during the transition to young adulthood. The finding that expected future use is a robust risk factor offers evidence of its long-term predictive validity (Ellickson & Hays, 1991).

In line with the evidence that personality influences on substance use are more enduring than social context influences (e.g., Kandel et al., 1978; Stein et al., 1987), we found personality risk factors to be more robust than social context risk factors. Although this finding suggests that personality influences on binge drinking precede social context influences, an interpretation consistent with the evidence that individuals seek and construct social context supportive of their personality (e.g., Block et al., 1988; Caspi et al., 1988; Lerner, 1982; Nurmi, 1993), it also may reflect that personality is less changeable than the social context during the transition.

Emergent Risk Factors

Only self-efficacy was found to be an emergent risk factor (i.e., predictive of change in binge drinking over time but not of concurrent binge drinking). Previous research has shown that low internal control is related to alcohol and other drug use during adolescence and young adulthood (e.g., Newcomb & Harlow, 1986; Sadava & Thompson, 1986). The finding that this risk factor remained hidden in high school and then emerged during the transition suggests that as the opportunities for both binge drinking and expressing self-direction increase during the transition, the inverse relationship between the two becomes stronger.

Pattern-Centered Findings: Trajectories of Differential Change in Binge Drinking

Unconditional and Conditional Risk Factors

Consistencies and inconsistencies between the pattern- and variable-centered findings represent opportunities to consider possible conditional risk factors. For three predictors (gender, self-efficacy, drinking to get drunk), the variable- and pattern-centered approaches generally yielded the same conclusion, suggesting that these three were "unconditional" in the sense that they predicted future binge drinking regardless of level of senior year binge drinking. In contrast, lower social conservatism was found to be a conditional risk factor. Although the variable-centered analyses indicated, in theory, that this risk factor was unconditional, the pattern-centered findings revealed that it operated only when the individual had not already engaged in frequent binge drinking. Once frequent binge drinking was initiated (either at senior year or after high school), social conservatism had no predictive power on the course of binge drinking, a finding that serves to qualify the literature on low conventionality and deviance proneness (e.g., Jessor et al., 1991; Newcomb & Bentler, 1988).

Trajectories of Change

In addition to qualifying the variable-centered analyses, the pattern-centered analyses provided evidence on the predictability of diverging trajectories of binge drinking. The Chronic and Decreased groups were similar in senior year binge drinking and statistically identical on such characteristics as antisociality–alienation, conventionality, and time spent with friends. These two groups were thus clearly at risk for continued frequent binge drinking. But those who appeared to have a relatively more concrete plan for the future (e.g., higher self-efficacy and work role readiness), a relatively greater dissatisfaction with the present (i.e., higher loneliness), and a relatively lower desire to drink to get drunk were more likely to discontinue their frequent binge drinking. Although frequent binge drinking may only be a necessary condition of alcoholism, and certainly not a sufficient one, these findings begin to address an important gap in the literature regarding the characteristics that distinguish developmentally limited alcoholism from ongoing antisocial alcoholism (Zucker, 1994).

The Increased, Fling, and Rare trajectories were statistically identical in their low levels of binge drinking, antisociality–alienation, and time spent with friends. The latter two trajectories were hardly distinguishable in the analyses, suggesting that a time-limited fling with frequent binge drinking is due more to present situational factors than to any long-standing individual characteristics. In contrast, the risk factors that distinguished the Increased trajectory from the other two indicated that adolescents low on internal orientation and conventionality and who drink primarily to get drunk are vulnerable for a post-high-school initiation and subsequent long-term increase in frequent binge drinking during the transition to young adulthood. This group may also be vulnerable to experiencing difficulties during the transition (Schulenberg et al., 1996), perhaps related to their increased frequent binge drinking. Again, although frequent binge drinking may only be a necessary condition of alcoholism, this group may well be on the path to what Zucker (1994) has labeled "late-onset, negative-affect alcoholism."

Limitations and Future Directions

An important strength of this study was the use of national, multiple-cohort panel data spanning a 6-year period between late adolescence and young adulthood. However, because the sample was limited to those who were high school seniors, generalizability to high school dropouts may be limited. This could be remedied by beginning longitudinal studies earlier in the life-span, which would also provide a better perspective on the antecedents of the trajectories. Binge drinking is certainly worthy of the intensive examination given here, but it is only one element of the personality–behavioral matrix that constitutes problem behaviors. Although our previous findings regarding the correspondence between the binge drinking trajectories and illicit drug use (Schulenberg et al., 1996) suggest the generality of the findings from the present study to other problem behaviors, conclusive evidence awaits additional research.

We were limited to measures available in the data set, a common and perhaps forgivable limitation of secondary analyses of national panel data (Brooks-Gunn, Phelps, & Elder, 1991). Corroboration of our findings from other studies would be useful in this regard. Because items were distributed across three separate questionnaire forms, it was not possible to include all predictors in one equation, raising some concern about the interrelationships among some of the risk factors. Nevertheless, because each personality domain included predictors from two or more forms, and because the core variables behaved similarly in the three forms, it is likely that the simultaneous consideration of all predictors would yield conclusions quite similar to ours. Finally, because both predictors and outcomes were self-report, some effects may have been inflated, and future research would benefit by gathering additional data from external sources.

There were sufficiently clear patterns in our statistically significant findings to argue for their substantive significance. Nevertheless, although our coefficients represent lower bound effect sizes due to measurement error, many of the significant coefficients were relatively small in magnitude. Our modest success suggests the limits of predicting change in alcohol and other drug use during the transition to young adulthood on the basis of pretransitional characteristics alone (cf. Chassin et al., 1991; Donovan et al., 1983; Kandel et al., 1986; Stein et al., 1987). As a first and necessary step in our ongoing research on the causes of change in binge drinking during the transition, this study focused on the long-term prediction of change in binge drinking as a function of adolescent characteristics. As such, we did not address the possibility of change in the personality and social context characteristics over time. It is possible that the lack of robustness of some senior risk factors was because the change in binge drinking corresponded to change in the risk factor. Alternatively, because many personality attributes tend to be quite stable during the transition to young adulthood (e.g., McGue, Bacon, & Lykken, 1993), the lack of robustness may be due to a change in the relationship between binge drinking and the given personality attribute over time. Of course, any of these changes occur within the larger context of social role changes during the transition, and as previous analyses of data from the Monitoring the Future project have shown, changes in binge drinking correspond to changes in living arrangements and marital status (Bachman et al., 1984, 1992). Building on the findings from the present study, we are pursuing this issue in our ongoing research (Schulenberg, Wadsworth, O'Malley, Bachman, & Johnston, 1995; Wadsworth, Schulenberg, O'Malley, Bachman, & Johnston, 1994).

Conclusions and Implications

Ideally, considerations of risk and protective factors ought to span time frames characterized by the heightened potential for vulnerability. The period between adolescence and young adulthood is a critical developmental transition as well as a time of heightened vulnerability to escalating problem drinking. We identified a group of individuals who appeared relatively free of problem behaviors during adolescence but had become problem drinkers by the end of the transition. Although experiences during the transition undoubtedly contributed to the initiation and escalation of frequent binge drinking, a noteworthy senior risk factor for this group was low internal control orientation. This suggests that they may have lacked the necessary planfulness (Clausen, 1991; Nurmi, 1993) or ego resiliency (Block et al., 1988) during adolescence to begin to negotiate successfully the transition, and increased frequent binge drinking was likely both a contributor to and outcome of this lack of internality. We also identified a group that was at high risk for continued frequent binge drinking who instead had decreased their frequent binge drinking over time. For this group, the senior year protective factors against a long-term pattern of problem drinking included a higher internal control orientation, along with a sense of dissatisfaction with their current social context and a sense of connection to future roles.

There has been perennial recognition of the need to combine nomothetic and idiographic approaches. Almost 60 years ago, Allport (1937) argued for an intermediate position: "There is no reason why we should not learn from every generalization about human nature that we can. At the same time we need to be alert for concepts and methods that enable us to understand patterned individuality" (p. 12). Over the years, others have echoed this sentiment (e.g., Block, 1971; Nesselroade, 1992). This study underscores the advantages of combining variable- and pattern-centered approaches in an attempt to identify common and more individualistic predictors of change. It also demonstrates the utility of an interdisciplinary approach that combines developmental psychology and large-scale survey research (Brooks-Gunn et al., 1991; Jackson & Antonucci, 1994). The confluence of developmental conceptualizations and large representative samples of individuals followed over time offers needed opportunities for advancing our understanding of interindividual differences and similarities in intraindividual change.

REFERENCES

Allport, G. W. (1937). *Pattern and growth in personality.* New York: Holt, Rinehart & Winston.

Aseltine, R. H., Jr., & Gore, S. (1993). Mental health and social adaptation following the transition from high school. *Journal of Research on Adolescence, 3,* 247–270.

Bachman, J. G., Johnston, L. D., & O'Malley, P. M. (1991). *Monitoring the Future project after seventeen years: Design and procedures* (Monitoring the Future Occasional Paper No. 33). Ann Arbor, MI: Institute for Social Research.

Bachman, J. G., O'Malley, P. M., & Johnston, L. D. (1984). Drug use among young adults: The impacts of role status and social environments. *Journal of Personality and Social Psychology, 47,* 629–645.

Bachman, J. G., O'Malley, P. M., Johnston, L. D., Rodgers, W., & Schulenberg, J. (1992). *Changes in drug use during the post-high school years* (Monitoring the Future Occasional Paper No. 35). Ann Arbor, MI: Institute for Social Research.

Baer, J. S. (1993). Etiology and secondary prevention of alcohol problems with young adults. In J. S. Baer, G. M. Marlatt, & R. J. McMahon (Eds.), *Addictive behaviors across the life span: Prevention, treatment, and policy issues* (pp. 111–137). Newbury Park, CA: Sage.

Baumrind, D., & Moselle, K. A. (1985). A developmental perspective on adolescent drug use. *Advances in Alcohol and Substance Use, 5,* 41–67.

Blane, H. T. (1979). Middle-aged alcoholics and young drinkers. In H. T. Blane & M. E. Chafetz (Eds.), *Youth, alcohol, and social policy* (pp. 5–38). New York: Plenum Press.

Block, J. (1971). *Lives through time.* Berkeley, CA: Bancroft Books.

Block, J., Block, J. H., & Keyes, S. (1988). Longitudinally foretelling drug usage in adolescence: Early childhood personality and environmental precursors. *Child Development, 59,* 336–355.

Block, J., & Robins, R. W. (1993). A longitudinal study of consistency and change in self-esteem from early adolescence to early adulthood. *Child Development, 64,* 909–923.

Brennan, A. F., Walfish, S., & Aubuchon, P. (1986). Alcohol use and abuse in college students. 1. A review of individual and personality correlates. *The International Journal of the Addictions, 21,* 449–474.

Brook, J. S., Cohen, P., Whiteman, M., & Gordon, A. S. (1992). Psychosocial risk factors in the transition from moderate to heavy use or abuse of drugs. In M. Glantz & R. Pickens (Eds.), *Vulnerability to drug abuse* (pp. 359–388). Washington, DC: American Psychological Association.

Brooks, J. S., Whiteman, M., Gordon, A. S., & Cohen, P. (1986). Dynamics of childhood and adolescent personality traits and adolescent drug use. *Developmental Psychology, 22,* 403–414.

Brooks-Gunn, J., Phelps, E., & Elder, G. H., Jr. (1991). Studying lives through time: Secondary data analyses in developmental psychology. *Developmental Psychology, 27,* 899–910.

Cairns, R. B. (1986). Phenomena lost: Issues in the study of development. In J.

Valsiner (Ed.), *The individual subject and scientific psychology* (pp. 97–112). New York: Plenum Press.

Caspi, A., Elder, G. H., Jr., & Bem, D. J. (1988). Moving away from the world: Life-course patterns of shy children. *Developmental Psychology, 24*, 824–831.

Caspi, A., Lynam, D., Moffitt, T. E., & Silva, P. A. (1993). Unraveling girls' delinquency: Biological, dispositional, and contextual contributions to adolescent misbehavior. *Developmental Psychology, 29*, 19–30.

Chassin, L. (1984). Adolescent substance use and abuse. *Advances in Child Behavioral Analysis and Therapy, 3*, 99–152.

Chassin, L., Presson, C. C., Sherman, S. J., & Edwards, D. A. (1991). Four pathways to young-adult smoking status: Adolescent social-psychological antecedents in a Midwestern community sample. *Health Psychology, 10*, 409–418.

Clausen, J. A. (1991). Adolescent competence and the shaping of the life course. *American Journal of Sociology, 96*, 805–842.

Cloninger, C. R. (1987). Neurogenetic adaptive mechanisms and alcoholism. *Science, 236*, 410–416.

DeMaris, A. (1992). *Logit modeling: Practical applications.* Newbury Park, CA: Sage.

Dishion, T. J., & Loeber, R. (1985). Adolescent marijuana and alcohol use: The role of parents and peers revisited. *American Journal of Drug and Alcohol Abuse, 11*, 11–25.

Donovan, J. E., Jessor, R., & Jessor, L. (1983). Problem drinking in adolescence and young adulthood: A follow-up study. *Journal of Studies on Alcohol, 44*, 109–137.

Ellickson, P. L., & Hays, R. D. (1991). Antecedents of drinking among young adolescents with different alcohol use histories. *Journal of Studies on Alcohol, 52*, 398–408.

Elliott, D. S., Huizinga, D., & Menard, S. (1989). *Multiple problem youth: Delinquency, substance use, and mental health problems.* New York: Springer-Verlag.

Erikson, E. H. (1968). *Identity, youth, and crisis.* New York: Norton.

Goldman, M. S., Brown, S. A., Christiansen, B. A., & Smith, G. T. (1991). Alcoholism and memory: Broadening the scope of alcohol-expectancy research. *Psychological Bulletin, 110*, 137–146.

Grant, B. F., Harford, T. C., & Grigson, M. B. (1988). Stability of alcohol consumption among youth: A national longitudinal survey. *Journal of Studies on Alcohol, 49*, 253–260.

Hawkins, J. D., Catalano, R. F., & Miller, J. Y. (1992). Risk and protective factors for alcohol and other drug problems in adolescence and early adulthood: Implications for substance use prevention. *Psychological Bulletin, 112*, 64–105.

Hesselbrock, V. M., O'Brien, J., Weinstein, M., & Carter-Menendez, N. (1987). Reasons for drinking and alcohol use in young adults at high risk and at low risk for alcoholism. *British Journal of Addiction, 82*, 1335–1339.

Hilton, M. E. (1991). The demographic distribution of drinking problems in 1984.

In W. B. Clark & M. E. Hilton (Eds.), *Alcohol in America: Drinking practices and problems* (pp. 87–101). Albany: State University of New York Press.

Hurrelmann, K. (1990). Health promotion for adolescents: Preventive and corrective strategies against problem behavior. *Journal of Adolescence, 13*, 231–250.

Jackson, J. S., & Antonucci, T. C. (1994). Survey methodology in life-span human development research. In S. H. Cohen & H. W. Reese (Eds.), *Life-span developmental psychology: Methodological contributions* (pp. 65–94). Hillsdale, NJ: Erlbaum.

Jessor, R., Donovan, J. E., & Costa, F. M. (1991). *Beyond adolescence: Problem behavior and young adult development.* New York: Cambridge University Press.

Jessor, R., & Jessor, S. L. (1977). *Problem behavior and psychological development: A longitudinal study of youth.* New York: Academic Press.

Johnston, L. D., & O'Malley, P. M. (1986). Why do the nation's students use drugs and alcohol? Self-reported reasons from nine national surveys. *Journal of Drug Issues, 16*, 29–66.

Johnston, L. D., O'Malley, P. M., & Bachman, J. G. (1994). *National survey results on drug use from the Monitoring the Future Study, 1975–1993.* Rockville, MD: National Institute on Drug Abuse.

Kandel, D. B. (1980). Drug and drinking behavior among youth. *Annual Review of Sociology, 6*, 235–285.

Kandel, D. B., Kessler, R. C., & Margulies, R. S. (1978). Antecedents of adolescent initiation into states of drug use: A developmental analysis. *Journal of Youth and Adolescence, 7*, 13–40.

Kandel, D., Simcha-Fagan, O., & Davies, M. (1986). Risk factors for delinquency and illicit drug use from adolescence to young adulthood. *The Journal of Drug Issues, 16*, 67–90.

Kaplan, H. B. (1985). Testing a general theory of drug abuse and other deviant adaptations. *Journal of Drug Issues, 22*, 477–492.

Kellam, S. G., Simon, M. B., & Ensminger, M. E. (1983). Antecedents in first grade of teenage substance use and psychological well-being: A ten-year community-wide perspective study. In D. F. Ricks & B. S. Dohrenwend (Eds.), *Origins of psychopathology* (pp. 17–42). Cambridge, England: Cambridge University Press.

Kusserow, R. P. (1991). *Youth and alcohol: A national survey—Drinking habits, access, attitudes and knowledge.* Rockville, MD: Department of Health and Human Services.

Labouvie, E. W., & McGee, C. R. (1986). Relation of personality to alcohol and drug use in adolescence. *Journal of Consulting and Clinical Psychology, 54*, 289–293.

Labouvie, E. W., Padina, R. J., & Johnson, V. (1991). Developmental trajectories of substance use in adolescence: Differences and predictors. *International Journal of Behavioral Development, 14*, 305–328.

Lerner, R. M. (1982). Children and adolescents as producers of their own development. *Developmental Review, 2*, 342–370.

Loeber, R. (1982). The stability of antisocial and delinquent child behavior: A review. *Child Development, 53*, 1431–1446.

Magnusson, D., & Bergman, L. R. (1988). Individual and variable-based approaches to longitudinal research on early risk factors. In M. Rutter (Ed.), *Studies of psychosocial risk: The power of longitudinal data* (pp. 45–61). New York: Cambridge University Press.

McGue, M., Bacon, S., & Lykken, D. T. (1993). Personality stability and change in early adulthood: A behavioral genetic analysis. *Developmental Psychology, 29*, 96–109.

Nesselroade, J. R. (1992). Adult personality development: Issues in assessing constancy and change. In R. A. Zucker, A. I. Rabin, J. Aronoff, & S. Frank (Eds.), *Personality structure in the life course* (pp. 221–275). New York: Springer.

Newcomb, M. D., & Bentler, P. M. (1988). *Consequences of adolescent drug use: Impact on the lives of young adults.* Newbury Park, CA: Sage.

Newcomb, M. D., Bentler, P. M., & Collins, C. (1986). Alcohol use and dissatisfaction with self and life: A longitudinal analysis of young adults. *Journal of Drug Issues, 16*, 479–494.

Newcomb, M. D., & Harlow, L. L. (1986). Life events and substance use among adolescents: Mediating effects of perceived loss of control and meaninglessness in life. *Journal of Personality and Social Psychology, 51*, 564–577.

Nowicki, S., & Strickland, B. R. (1973). A locus of control scale for children. *Journal of Consulting and Clinical Psychology, 40*, 148–154.

Nurmi, J. E. (1993). Adolescent development in an age-graded context: The role of personal beliefs, goals, and strategies in the tackling of developmental tasks and standards. *International Journal of Behavioral Development, 16*, 169–189.

Oetting, E. R., & Beauvais, F. (1987). Peer cluster theory: Drugs and the adolescent. *Journal of Counseling and Development, 65*, 17–22.

Olmstead, R. E., Guy, S. M., O'Malley, P. M., & Bentler, P. M. (1991). Longitudinal assessment of the relationship between self-esteem, fatalism, loneliness, and substance use. *Journal of Social Behavior and Personality, 6*, 749–770.

O'Malley, P. M., Bachman, J. G., & Johnston, L. D. (1983). Reliability and consistency of self-reports of drug use. *International Journal of the Addictions, 18*, 805–824.

O'Malley, P. M., Bachman, J. G., & Johnston, L. D. (1988). Period, age, and cohort effects on substance use among young Americans: A decade of change, 1976–1986. *American Journal of Public Health, 78*, 1315–1321.

Ozer, D. J., & Gjerde, P. F. (1989). Patterns of personality consistency and change from childhood through adolescence. *Journal of Personality, 57*, 483–507.

Pandina, R. J., Labouvie, E. W., Johnson, V., & White, H. R. (1990). The relationship between alcohol and marijuana use and competence in adolescence. *Journal of Health and Social Policy, 1*, 89–108.

Parker, E. S., Parker, D. A., & Harford, T. C. (1991). Specifying the relationship between alcohol use and cognitive loss: The effects of frequency of consumption and psychological distress. *Journal of Studies on Alcohol, 52,* 366–373.

Petersen, A. C. (1993). Creating adolescents: The role of context and process in developmental trajectories. *Journal of Research on Adolescence, 3,* 1–18.

Petraitis, J., Flay, B. R., & Miller, T. Q. (1995). Reviewing theories of adolescent substance use: Organizing pieces of the puzzle. *Psychological Bulletin, 117,* 67–86.

Radliff, K. G., & Burkhart, B. R. (1984). Sex differences in motivations for and effects of drinking among college students. *Journal of Studies on Alcohol, 45,* 26–32.

Rosenberg, M. (1965). *Society and the adolescent self image.* Princeton, NJ: Princeton University Press.

Rutter, M. (1994). Concepts of causation, tests of causal mechanisms, and implications for intervention. In A. C. Petersen & J. T. Mortimer (Eds.), *Youth unemployment and society* (pp. 147–171). New York: Cambridge University Press.

Sadava, S. W., & Thompson, M. M. (1986). Loneliness, social drinking, and vulnerability to alcohol problems. *Canadian Journal of Behavioral Science, 18,* 133–139.

Schulenberg, J., Bachman, J. G., O'Malley, P. M., & Johnston, L. D. (1994). High school educational success and subsequent substance use: A panel analysis following adolescents into young adulthood. *Journal of Health and Social Behavior, 35,* 45–62.

Schulenberg, J., Maggs, J., & Hurrelmann, K. (Eds.). (1997). *Health risks and developmental transitions during adolescence.* New York: Cambridge University Press.

Schulenberg, J., O'Malley, P. M., Bachman, J. G., Wadsworth, K. N., & Johnston, L. D. (1996). Getting drunk and growing up: Trajectories of binge drinking during the transition to young adulthood. *Journal of Studies on Alcohol, 57,* 289–309.

Schulenberg, J., Wadsworth, K. W., O'Malley, P. M., Bachman, J. G., & Johnston, L. D. (1995, March). *Diverging trajectories of binge drinking: Young adulthood as a critical juncture in the natural history of alcohol abuse.* Paper presented at the 1995 Biennial Meetings of the Society for Research in Child Development, Indianapolis, IN.

Sherrod, L. R., Haggerty, R. J., & Featherman, D. L. (1993). Introduction: Late adolescence and the transition to adulthood. *Journal of Research on Adolescence, 3,* 217–226.

Silbereisen, R. K., & Noack, P. (1988). On the constructive role of problem behavior in adolescence. In N. Bolger, A. Caspi, G. Downey, & M. Moorehouse (Eds.), *Persons in context: Developmental processes* (pp. 152–180). Cambridge, England: Cambridge University Press.

Stacy, A. W., Newcomb, M. D., & Bentler, P. M. (1991). Personality, problem drinking, and drunk driving: Mediating, moderating, and direct-effect models. *Journal of Personality and Social Psychology, 60,* 795–811.

Stein, J. A., Newcomb, M. D., & Bentler, P. M. (1987). An 8-year study of multiple influences on drug use and drug use consequences. *Journal of Personality and Social Psychology, 53,* 1094–1105.

Straus, R., & Bacon, S. (1953). *Drinking in college.* New Haven, CT: Yale University Press.

Wadsworth, K. W., Schulenberg, J., O'Malley, P. M., Bachman, J. G., & Johnston, L. D. (1994, February). *Personality, social context, and binge drinking: Patterns of change from adolescence to young adulthood.* Paper presented at the 5th Biennial Meetings of the Society for Research on Adolescence, San Diego, CA.

Wechsler, H., & Isaac, N. (1992). "Binge" drinkers at Massachusetts colleges: Prevalence, drinking style, time trends, and associated problems. *The Journal of the American Medical Association, 267,* 2929–2931.

Werner, E. E., & Smith, R. S. (1992). *Overcoming the odds: High risk children from birth to adulthood.* Ithaca, NY: Cornell University Press.

Windle, M. (1992). A longitudinal study of stress buffering for adolescent problem behaviors. *Developmental Psychology, 28,* 522–530.

Windle, M., & Barnes, G. M. (1988). Similarities and differences in correlates of alcohol consumption and problem behaviors among male and female adolescents. *International Journal of the Addictions, 23,* 707–728.

Zucker, R. A. (1989). Is risk of alcoholism predictable? A probabilistic approach to a developmental problem. *Drugs and Society, 3,* 69–93.

Zucker, R. A. (1994). Pathways to alcohol problems and alcoholism: A developmental account of the evidence for multiple alcoholisms and for contextual contributions to risk. In R. A. Zucker, J. Howard, & G. M. Boyd (Eds.), *The development of alcohol problems: Exploring the biopsychosocial matrix of risk* (pp. 255–289). Rockville, MD: National Institute on Alcohol Abuse and Alcoholism.

Zucker, R. A., Boyd G., & Howard, J. (Eds.). (1994). *The development of alcohol problems: Exploring the biopsychosocial matrix of risk.* Rockville, MD: National Institute of Alcohol Abuse and Alcoholism.

APPENDIX
Scale and Item Intercorrelations by Questionnaire Form

Form A

Variable	1	2	3	4	5	6	7	8	9	10	11	12
1. Senior year binge drinking	—											
2. Wave 4 binge drinking	.37	—										
3. Gender (0 = male, 1 = female)	−.21	−.27	—									
4. Ethnicity (0 = non-White, 1 = White)	.12	.11	−.01	—								
5. Parental education	−.02	.04	−.03	.12	—							
6. High school GPA	−.22	−.14	.13	.12	.20	—						
7. Obedience	−.15	−.08	.03	.01	−.04	.06	—					
8. Identity focus	−.07	−.10	.21	−.08	−.06	.03	.01	—				
9. Drink to get drunk	.48	.31	−.08	.13	.02	−.20	−.17	−.05	—			
10. Drink to cope	−.01	−.06	.05	−.07	−.07	.00	.06	.04	.05	—		
11. Expected future use	.33	.26	−.09	.17	.09	−.05	−.17	−.07	.37	−.33	—	
12. Evenings out	.28	.16	−.07	.10	−.04	−.13	−.11	−.02	.26	−.07	.20	—
13. Peer norms for misconduct	.20	.16	−.26	.01	−.07	−.13	−.09	−.07	.20	.03	.14	.14

Form B

Variable	1	2	3	4	5	6	7	8	9	10	11
1. Senior year binge drinking	—										
2. Wave 4 binge drinking	.34	—									
3. Gender (0 = male, 1 = female)	−.21	−.26	—								
4. Ethnicity (0 = non-White, 1 = White)	.11	.10	−.04	—							
5. Parental education	−.02	.04	−.04	.18	—						
6. High school GPA	−.21	−.15	.14	.13	.21	—					
7. Risk taking	.29	.20	−.28	.09	.05	−.16	—				
8. Hostility	.27	.13	−.17	.01	−.04	−.14	.19	—			
9. Social conservatism	−.18	−.17	.07	−.14	−.08	.01	−.15	−.08	—		
10. Family role efficacy	−.10	−.10	.13	.01	.02	.12	−.13	−.06	.08	—	
11. Evenings out	.36	.19	−.06	.12	−.00	−.12	.20	.17	−.19	−.02	—
12. Hang out with friends	.32	.17	−.09	.07	−.08	−.20	.23	.15	−.14	−.02	.45

Form C

	1	2	3	4	5	6	7	8	9	10	11	12	13
1. Senior year binge drinking	—												
2. Wave 4 binge drinking	.40	—											
3. Gender (0 = male, 1 = female)	-.17	-.24	—										
4. Ethnicity (0 = non-White, 1 = White)	.10	.08	-.05	—									
5. Parental education	-.01	.02	-.06	.16	—								
6. High school GPA	-.20	-.14	.12	.11	.20	—							
7. Social intolerance	.18	.14	-.28	.08	-.05	.13	—						
8. Social-political apathy	-.12	-.04	-.16	-.02	.17	-.16	-.15	—					
9. Promarriage value	-.19	-.15	.02	.02	.00	-.14	-.08	.07	—				
10. Self-efficacy	-.10	-.13	-.03	.00	.13	-.17	-.12	.15	.14	—			
11. Work role preparation	-.03	-.06	.03	-.02	.01	-.14	-.07	.08	.04	.13	—		
12. Self-esteem	-.03	-.02	-.09	-.04	.10	-.18	-.10	.18	.05	.35	.23	—	
13. Evenings out	.31	.19	-.06	.12	.00	.10	.06	-.09	-.17	-.04	-.01	.04	—
14. Loneliness	-.08	-.05	-.01	-.05	-.08	-.07	.00	-.01	-.05	-.24	-.11	-.31	-.19

Note. In general, coefficients ≥ .07 are significant at $p < .001$, and coefficients ≥ .05 are significant at $p < .05$. GPA = grade point average.

IV

MAINTENANCE AND COURSE OF ABUSE

6

EFFECTS OF ADOLESCENT DRUG USE ON ADULT MENTAL HEALTH: A PROSPECTIVE STUDY OF A COMMUNITY SAMPLE

MICHAEL D. NEWCOMB, LAWRENCE M. SCHEIER, AND P. M. BENTLER

Despite the common assumption that drug use causes emotional distress and psychopathology, there is little scientific evidence for this belief beyond anecdotal and correlational findings. For example, it has been noted that drugs are often used to improve mood and relieve emotional distress (Labouvie, 1986; Newcomb, Chou, Bentler, & Huba, 1988) and that psychiatric impairment is frequently observed in drug-abusing populations (e.g., Bukstein, Brent, & Kaminer, 1989; Ford, Hillard, Giesler, Lassen, & Thomas, 1989). Such associations lead many to conclude (perhaps prematurely) that drug use impairs mental health (e.g., Ross, Glaser, & Germanson, 1988; Rounsaville, Weissman, Chrits-Christoph, Wilber, &

Reprinted from *Experimental and Clinical Psychopharmacology*, *1*, 215–241. (1993). Copyright © 1993 by the American Psychological Association. Used with permission of the author.

This research was supported by Grant DA 01070 from the National Institute on Drug Abuse.

169

Kleber, 1982). However, a clear resolution of whether drug abuse truly contributed to or simply co-occurs with psychopathology and emotional distress has evaded researchers (e.g., Kandel, Davies, Karus, & Yamaguchi, 1986). Research on the associations between drug use and mental health has emerged primarily from three sources: (a) studies of treatment and clinical samples, (b) cross-sectional examinations of more general samples, and (c) analyses of prospective data.

TREATMENT AND CLINICAL STUDIES

Most evidence regarding the relationship between psychopathology and drug use comes from clinical samples (e.g., Hesselbrock, Meyer, & Keener, 1985; Ross et al., 1988). In general, these studies reveal that drug abuse is strongly associated with psychopathology before, during, and somewhat less after treatment (e.g., Dorus & Senay, 1980; Kosten, Rounsaville, & Kleber, 1988). However, several confounds typically preclude drawing causal inferences regarding drug abuse and psychopathology from these treatment data. These include the presence of many diverse psychiatric symptoms, inconsistent diagnostic practices, different patient population characteristics, and premorbid symptoms that may be misconstrued as sequelae. The most limiting problem, however, is that all patients have some type of severe problem or dysphoria. Thus, they are distressed individuals willing to seek help, whose pathology is manifest and a problem; the development of drug abuse and psychopathology has already occurred and the developmental process cannot be observed accurately. Results from such samples cannot be generalized to nonclinical, community samples.

CROSS-SECTIONAL STUDIES

Findings from cross-sectional studies reveal moderate to strong associations between drug use and psychopathology. For example, Gold, Washton, and Dackis (1985) screened a subset of cocaine abusers who called a national hotline and reported high levels of self-reported depression (83%), irritability (87%), paranoid feelings (65%), and suicide attempts (5%), with users reporting an average of 4 years of drug use. Based on their general population sample, Newcomb, Bentler, and Fahy (1987) reported several significant associations between cocaine use and psychopathology. For example, compared with male nonusers, male cocaine users reported higher levels of anxious mood, impaired cognitive functions, and impaired motivation. They also reported greater hostility, negative affect, a lack of purpose in life, and proneness toward psychotic thinking. Likewise, female cocaine users, when compared with their nonusing counterparts, reported greater levels of depressed and anxious mood, impaired cognitive functions, greater hostility, and greater proneness toward psychotic thinking, along with a host of other distressful symptoms. Kandel (1984) reported that heavier marijuana users were more likely to be hospitalized for mental health problems, were less happy about life, and were more likely to consult a mental health professional as compared with lower level users. However, all these analyses were cross-sectional, so that the causal directions remain obscure.

PROSPECTIVE STUDIES

A few longitudinal studies have examined the mental health consequences of drug use in general community populations, and varied findings have emerged (e.g., Kandel et al., 1986; Newcomb & Bentler, 1988a, 1988b). Some have reported causal relationships between drug use and deteriorated emotional health (e.g., Dackis & Gold, 1983; Newcomb & Bentler, 1988a, 1988b). Others have suggested that, though much accepted as common knowledge, evidence for causal relationships between early drug use and later deficits in emotional development is "hard to verify scientifically" (Newcomb & Bentler, 1988b, p. 64). For example, adequate controls for preexisting conditions and important confounds may not have been made. In addition, several studies have reported apparently positive effects from moderate alcohol use, including greater positive affect, stress reduction, and limited improvements in cognitive performance (Baum-Baicker, 1985; Kandel et al., 1986; Newcomb & Bentler, 1988a, 1988b; Newcomb, Bentler, & Collins, 1986).

EXPLANATORY MODELS

Several theoretical models have been advanced to explain the association between drug use–abuse and psychopathology. These explanations range from biochemical to psychosocial processes. Several of these perspectives are summarized here.

Biochemical Mechanisms

Recent attention has been directed at the biological mechanisms of drugs on mood changes and the possible pharmacological treatments for drug and alcohol addiction (e.g., Gawin & Kleber, 1984, 1985; Gold et al., 1985; Kleber & Gawin, 1984). Several researchers have suggested that chronic drug use or abuse creates long-term changes in brain chemistry and synaptic transmission (e.g., Dackis & Gold, 1985; Wise, 1984).

Expectancies

A different literature documents the critical role of psychosocial expectations and learning on drug reactions and effects (e.g., Adesso, 1985; Newcomb et al., 1988; Sher & Levenson, 1982). Ethical and scientific restrictions limit these experiments to short-term outcomes and prevent controlled study of the long-term consequences of chronic drug use. With the exception of alcohol, much of this research has been limited to animal experiments, which cannot be generalized with accuracy to humans (for a review, see Adesso, 1980). Nevertheless, prospective studies have begun to address these causal mechanisms in community samples (e.g., Newcomb et al., 1988; Stacy, Newcomb, & Bentler, 1991a). This leaves unresolved whether psychopharmacological, psychobehavioral, or lifestyle changes from chronic drug use create long-term mental health consequences.

Self-Medication and Biphasic Mechanisms

Alcohol and drug use can have paradoxical or biphasic psychological effects. Initially, alcohol and other drugs are used for their positive acute benefits to improve mood, reduce stress, and relieve emotional discomfort (Dackie & Gold, 1983; Newcomb et al., 1988; Sadava, Thistle, & Forsythe, 1978). These acute positive effects are often followed by emotional and cognitive distress and are exacerbated with continued, recurring, and chronic alcohol and drug consumption (e.g., Beckman, 1980; Bibbs & Chambless, 1986; Keykin, Levy, & Wells, 1987; Malow, West, Williams, & Sutker, 1989). Both learning and opponent process theories have been used to explain drug addiction mechanisms (e.g., Shipley, 1987).

Some hypothesize that drug use may be a form of self-medication: to relieve dysphoria and cope with stress (Khantzian & Treece, 1985; Kleber & Gawin, 1984; Wills, 1985). Barrett (1985) suggested that drug abusers increase their drug use to achieve an affective homeostasis, relying on previously learned psychological reactions and expectancies from ingestion. With increasing physiological and psychological tolerance, drug abusers require greater amounts of the drug to prevent emotional distress, which potentiates an abusive and addictive cycle (Barrett, 1985; Marlatt, Baer, Donovan, & Kivlahan, 1988; Washton & Gold, 1984). Moreover, a drug-abusing lifestyle may create economic, medical, relationship, and work problems that can lead to secondary emotional problems (Newcomb, 1988; Newcomb & Bentler, 1988a). Refuge from these accumulating psychological strains may be sought in continued or increased drug use, which then reinforces the addictive cycle.

Developmental Disruption

Adolescence is an essential developmental period during which rapid emotional, social, biological, and cognitive growth occur (e.g., Newcomb, 1987). It is a time to consolidate psychological, emotional, cognitive, and problem-solving growth and maturity to assume adult roles and responsibilities (Havighurst, 1972). Disruption of this process through precocious development, persistent drug use, or other interference may impair the learning of adequate psychological adaptational skills necessary for adult roles and responsibilities and create or exacerbate psychopathology (Newcomb, 1987; Newcomb & Bentler, 1988a).

Some Problems in Longitudinal Research

Although prospective studies offer hope for disentangling causal sequences, there are several limitations with earlier research. Often, only a few measures of mental health were used. Kandel et al. (1986) only used scales of depression and psycosomaticism, whereas Newcomb and Bentler (1988a) examined a wider, but still restricted, array of mental health constructs. A more diverse set of mental health measures is necessary to capture precise and specific effects of drug use on psychological functioning.

The maturational course and development of psychological states unfold throughout life. To study these patterns requires long-term prospective data (e.g., Gollob & Reichardt, 1987; Newcomb et al., 1987). Most studies designed to assess influences of drug use on mental health have spanned relatively brief time periods, which prohibit investigation of major developmental transitions (e.g., Kandel et al., 1986; Newcomb & Bentler, 1988a). In their earlier longitudinal investigation, Newcomb and Bentler (1988a) found some limited support for negative effects from early drug use. It is quite possible that effects may be more pronounced over longer periods of time (e.g., Hartka et al., 1989). Certain developmental processes (i.e., including psychological disorders) may take many years to unfold, making it likely that more severe disturbances might only be identified over lengthy periods of time (e.g., Weissman et al., 1984).

In some cases (e.g., Kandel et al., 1986), composite drug use measures were used. This practice obscures potential differential mental health effects related to specific drugs and prevents examination of across-time drug-specific effects (Newcomb, in press; Newcomb & Bentler, 1988a, 1988b).

Finally, most research depicts drug use at discrete points in time that reflect static "snapshots" of drug involvement and do not capture dynamic, evolving patterns of use. Such static measures of drug use are certainly incomplete, because they do not reflect changes (increases or decreases) or stability of drug use behaviors as they evolve over time. A more comprehensive approach involves comparing early and later drug use measures to capture dynamic drug use transition. One important reason for making this distinction in drug use patterns is to understand whether drug use during adolescence alone affects later mental health or whether any subsequent changes (i.e., escalation, discontinuation) in drug use behaviors influence subsequent mental health. In other words, are teenagers doomed to suffer throughout life because of their adolescent drug use, or do subsequent changes in their drug use patterns alter the effects of earlier drug use?

IMPORTANCE OF THIS RESEARCH

Although research has documented the comorbidity of psychopathology and drug abuse in treatment samples, no causal priority between these disorders has been established, and little clarification has emerged from general community samples (Newcomb et al., 1987). It is unclear whether high rates of comorbidity in treatment populations also exist in community samples. Most important is the need to determine in a rigorous, empirical manner if and how teenage drug use and dynamic changes into adulthood are associated with or exacerbate mental health problems in later life.

This study was designed to answer the following research questions: (a) Does teenage drug use or do changes in subsequent drug use affect psychological functioning in adulthood? (b) Do static measures of adolescent polydrug and use of specific drugs better predict changes in psychological functioning than dynamic measures of the same drugs that capture changes in drug use patterns over an 8-year period reflected in residual variances? and (c) What specific types of mental health are most vulnerable to which type and pattern of adolescent drug use?

To answer these questions, we use latent-variable structural equation models (SEMs) to analyze four waves of data spanning a 12-year period. Numerous measures of drug use were gathered in early and late adolescence and young adulthood, and constructs of psychological functioning, emotional distress, traditional attitudes (social conformity), and interpersonal contact (social support) from late adolescence were used to predict a wide range of mental health constructs in adulthood. The study spanned a 12-year period in its entirety, with early adolescent drug use measures obtained at baseline (1976) and follow-up measures obtained at Year 13 (1988), although causal inferences can only be made over the last 8 years (because Year 1 and Year 5 drug use data were combined).

This research cannot determine definitively whether types and extents of teenage drug use (and subsequent dynamic changes in these patterns of drug involvement) caused or created increments or decrements for various types of mental health functioning over time. Such precise and unequivocal conclusions can only be made with true experimental designs, including random assignment (e.g., Newcomb, 1990). Such strict control cannot ethically be imposed on long-term issues of drug use and psychopathology. Therefore, we chose the most powerful, nonexperimental method available to study these evolving relationships so that we can make the strongest conclusions regarding potential causal inferences and effects. This approach involves testing appropriate prospective data in complex SEMs and meeting as many causal criteria as possible (Newcomb, 1990, 1994). We were able to conform with most criteria under which a causal inference may be made (Newcomb, 1987, 1990). The one critical criterion that this research and all other nonexperimental designs cannot meet is the need to control for all possible confounds and spurious influences. We controlled for the most likely "omitted third variable" problem by including numerous measures of social support and social conformity (e.g., Newcomb & Bentler, 1988a), but these clearly do not capture the universe of all potential confounding influences. Nevertheless, we believe that these conclusions will provide strong support for likely causal effects from teenage drug use and dynamic changes in their drug use patterns over time on various types of mental health functioning in adulthood.

METHOD

Sample

The sample was initially contacted as 7th- through 9th-grade students in 11 Los Angeles County schools and was followed for 12 years so that we could study adolescent and adult growth, development, and drug use. The sample for this study includes 487 participants who provided data in Year 1 (1976), Year 5 (1980), Year 9 (1984), and Year 13 (1988). A description of this sample as adults at Year 13 is given in Table 1. The sample is ethnically mixed (about one third non-White), has a mean age of about 25.5 years, and contains more women than men (which has been an unfortunate feature from Year 1). Most are high school graduates with an average of 2 years of college, more than two thirds have full-time jobs, and about half are living with a mate. More complete descriptions of the sample and the scope of the research project are reported elsewhere (Newcomb, 1992; Newcomb & Bentler, 1988a, 1988b; Stacy, Newcomb, & Bentler, 1991a, 1991b).

Newcomb (1992) provided extensive attrition analyses across the entire 12 years of this study. Overall, these analyses show that gender and ethnic composition have been only slightly altered by attrition. Likewise, there were only minor differences in Year 1 drug use prevalence rates between dropouts and retained subjects over the 12-year period. Moreover,

TABLE 1
Description of Sample

Variable	Men (n = 136)	Women (n = 351)	Total (N = 487)
Age (years)			
M	25.46	25.49	25.48
Range	24–28	24–27	24–28
Ethnicity (%)			
Black	8	15	13
Hispanic	10	11	11
White	71	62	64
Asian	10	11	11
Other	1	1	1
Education (years)			
M	14.65	14.03	14.21
Range	10–18	10–18	10–18
No. of children (%)			
None	78	64	68
One	15	21	19
Two	6	11	9
Three or more	1	4	4
Income for past year (%)			
Under $5,000	7	19	16
$5,000–$15,000	28	26	26
$15,000–$30,000	44	46	46
Over $30,000	21	9	12
Living situation (%)			
Alone	9	8	8
Parents	19	19	19
Spouse	41	41	41
Cohabitation	8	8	8
Dormitory	2	0	1
Roommates	14	13	13
Other	7	11	10
Current life activity (%)			
Military	3	0	2
Junior college	3	2	2
Four-year college	9	5	6
Part-time job	5	7	6
Full-time job	73	67	69
Child rearing/homemaker	1	15	11
Other	4	4	4

participants who remained in the study were quite similar to dropouts on numerous drug and personality measures obtained at Year 1.

Measures

Adolescent Drug Use Scales

In Year 1, frequency-of-use scales for 5 classes of drugs were generated: alcohol (beer, wine, and liquor), cigarettes (one item), marijuana (cannabis and hashish), cocaine (one item), and hard drugs (including downers, heroin, inhalants, psychedelics, and uppers). Year 1 drug use items were rated on 5-point anchored scales that ranged from *never* (1) to *regularly* (5). In Year 5, the same 5 drug use scales were created from identical substances as in Year 1 except for hard drugs, which in Year 5 were expanded to include 14 different substances. Year 5 drug items were rated on 7-point anchored scales, ranging from *never* (1) to *more than once a day* (7), for the past 6 months. All 10 drug use scales were standardized, and then the same scales from Year 1 and Year 5 were averaged to produce 5 composite drug use scales reflecting drug use during adolescence.

These five scales of adolescent drug use were used to reflect a Polydrug Use latent construct that captured the extent of using multiple substances during early and late adolescence. In addition, the residual variables from each of the five scales were used to capture the specific use of each separate drug and were tested as predictors. This procedure allowed us to separate the general effects of polydrug use, quite prevalent among adolescents (e.g., Clayton & Ritter, 1985), as a latent construct, from the effects of using specific types of drugs, as captured in the residual variables of the specific drug use scales (after prediction from the common factor: see Newcomb, 1994). This method has been described by Newcomb (1990), with numerous examples elsewhere (e.g., Newcomb, 1988; Newcomb & Bentler, 1988a, 1988b). The one difficulty with this procedure, when used with first-order latent factor models, is that systematic and random errors are confounded in the residual variables (Newcomb, 1994). Because of this limitation, we primarily focus on large effects of these specific, residual variables (i.e., Stacy et al., 1991a, 1991b).

Increased Drug Use

Five young adult drug use scales (Year 9) consisted of the same items and rating scales as in Year 5 and were used to reflect a latent construct of Polydrug Use. For theoretical purposes, we wanted to use these drug use measures to construct variables that reflect change in drug use from adolescence to young adulthood. In other words, we wanted to compare drug use measures from adolescence to those in young adulthood to capture dynamic changes (increased, decreased, or remained the same) of evolving drug involvement after adolescence to young adulthood and determine whether these generated changes in psychological functioning and emotional distress into adulthood.

Dynamic changes in drug use can be captured in several ways from repeated assessments. Without a time-series design, differences can be represented as change scores. For example, $V2 - V1$ would represent the change in a variable V from Occasion 1 to Occasion 2. In earlier, preliminary work, we tested this typical method to capture these changes in drug use over time as difference scores (Newcomb & Bentler, 1989). This quite common method created several difficulties, such as floor and ceiling effects, and numerous paradoxical or uninterpretable results. Because of these difficulties, which are commonly encountered with change or difference scores (e.g., Cronbach & Furby, 1970; Woody & Costanzo, 1990), we used an alternative procedure in the present analyses. Furthermore, differences among observed scores do not adequately reflect changes in a latent variable, and even latent variables created from simple difference scores may not adequately reflect the stability of that latent construct (e.g., Nesselroade & Bartsch, 1977).

J. Cohen and Cohen (1983) suggested an hierarchical multiple regression approach as an alternative to difference scores with repeated measure data. However, this approach exaggerates the cross-sectional associations at the follow-up wave of data, which confounds change effects with contemporaneous correlations. This approach is also restricted to measured variables and is not extended to latent variables or unmeasured constructs.

We took J. Cohen and Cohen's (1983) basic approach and extended it to resolve both of these difficulties and unresolved issues. To deal with the follow-up confound problems, we needed at least three waves of data. Dwyer (1983) pointed out that to establish causal order between events, more than two measurement waves are necessary. We restricted our drug use follow-up measures (Year 9) to a data wave earlier than the dependent or consequence constructs (Year 13) but later than the independent variables or baseline measure (Years 1 and 5). Therefore, our change (residual) scores preceded our dependent measures by 4 years and did not capitalize on contemporaneous associations. Furthermore, we took J. Cohen and Cohen's approach and applied it to latent constructs by using the disturbance term of later Polydrug Use after prediction from earlier Polydrug Use as a change (residual) score to predict consequences at a later time. Similarly, we used measured-variable residual variables to simultaneously capture change in use of specific drugs.

These innovative procedures certainly deviate necessarily from the inadequate recommendations of J. Cohen and Cohen (1983). They reflect significant improvements in method (SEMs), confounds (three waves of data instead of two), and interpretation (change precedes effects). Our solution uses residualized latent and measured-variable scores from young adulthood to predict changes in mental health measures into adulthood. That is, if $F2 = B*F1 + D2$, where $F1$ and $F2$ are the latent variables F measured at Occasions 1 and 2, and B is the usual optimal regression weight, $D2$ represents the part of $F2$ that is not predictable from $F1$ (Bentler, 1989). In our models, we evaluate the usual effects of $F1$ on various subsequent outcome latent variables (in adulthood), but, in addition, we permit D2 to be correlated with other factors at Time 1 (Year 9) and evaluate the "causal" effects of D2 on a variety of other factors measured at Time 3 (Year 13).

In other words, we use residual or disturbance terms as change variables. These residual variables reflect that portion of drug use that is not stable over time, capturing whether drug use increased, decreased, or remained the same from one assessment to the next. In our structural equation models, the residual variables reflect changes in each of the five types of drugs, as well as changes in polydrug use as captured by latent constructs. These residual variables are constructed so that higher values reflect increased drug use and they are labeled accordingly.

Adolescent Psychosocial Scales

We included three other constructs from late adolescence (Year 5) to control for across-time stability and spurious confound effects on later psychopathology. A construct of Emotional Distress was reflected in three scales: self-derogation (seven items; Kaplan & Pokorny, 1969); (low) self-acceptance (four items; Stein, Newcomb, & Bentler, 1986); and depression (four items; Newcomb, Huba, & Bentler, 1986). This Emotional Distress construct served as a general distress measure to control for stability in the later mental health measures. Support for the use of a general distress construct is provided by both Scheier and Newcomb (1993) and Tanaka and Huba (1984).

Deviant or unconventional attitudes and behavior are strongly associated with drug use (McGee & Newcomb, 1992). To control for such possible confounds, we included a construct of Social Conformity from adolescence to reflect rejection or adherence to conventional values. This latent factor was reflected in three multiitem scales: law abidance, (low) liberalism, and religious commitment (Newcomb & Bentler, 1988a, 1988b; Stein et al., 1986).

Finally, a latent factor of Social Support during adolescence was included. This construct was captured by four four-item scales measuring the supportiveness of relationships with parents, family, adults, and peers (Newcomb & Bentler, 1988b). Social Support is an important protective factor against psychopathology and positive influence on emotional health (e.g., S. Cohen & Wills, 1985; Newcomb & Bentler, 1988b) that must be represented in the present analyses.

Adult Outcome Measures

Adult mental health status was captured by 27 measured variables used to reflect nine latent constructs: Emotional Distress, Self-Derogation,

Psychoticism, Depression, Purpose in Life, Suicide Ideation, Anxiety, Hostility, and Disorganized Thinking. The confirmatory factor structure and more complete description of all items and scales are presented elsewhere (Scheier & Newcomb, 1993).

The adult Emotional Distress construct had two indicators. These were repeated assessments of the same depression and (low) self-acceptance scales used in adolescence. The Self-Derogation scale was also repeated in adulthood but was not used as an indicator of the Emotional Distress construct as during adolescence. To gain greater sensitivity and specificity in adult affective functioning, we created a separate Self-Derogation construct with two indicators: one scale each of positive and negative self-image (Harlow, Newcomb, & Bentler, 1986).

The Magic Ideation (Magid) Scale (Eckblad & Chapman, 1983) was used to create indicators of a latent construct of Psychoticism. The 30 dichotomous items assess schizotypy and a predisposition to psychosis. These items were randomly parceled into three 10-item subscales (Magid 1, 2, and 3; Newcomb & Bentler, 1988a).

A Depression construct was reflected by four subscales of the 20-item Center for Epidemiologic Studies–Depression Scale (CES-D; Radloff, 1977). The CES-D emphasizes the affective component of depression. The subscales were derived from previous factor analyses and included positive affect (the elevated mood items), negative affect, impaired motivation, and impaired relationships (Harlow et al., 1986).

A construct of Purpose in Life (PIL) was hypothesized to reflect three scales created from a slight modification of the 20-item Crumbaugh and Maholick (1964) measure. Previous exploratory and confirmatory factor analytic work verified the unidimensionality of the measure and the reliability of three scales of these 20 seven-point Likert-type items as indicators of a latent construct (PIL 1, 2, and 3; Harlow, Newcomb, & Bentler, 1986, 1987).

A Suicide Ideation construct was reflected by four items; two from the Petrie and Chamberlain (1983) Suicide Behavior Subscale ("I have been thinking about ways to kill myself" and "I have told someone I want to kill myself") and two additional items we created ("I have made attempts to kill myself" and "I imagine my life will end with suicide"; Harlow et al., 1986).

Separate constructs of Anxiety and Hostility were derived from a modified version of the Hopkins Symptom Checklist (Uhlenhuth, Balter, Mellinger, Cisin, & Clinthorne, 1983). Three items with the largest factor loadings from each scale were chosen as indicators for each construct.

Finally, three four-item scales reflected a construct of Disorganized Thinking: thought disorganization, (less) deliberateness, and (less) diligence (Stein et al., 1986).

RESULTS

Descriptive statistics for all adolescent, young adult, and adult variables are given in Table 2. The right-hand column presents point-biserial correlations of each variable with gender of the respondent and reveals several mean differences. The largest accounted for less than 4% of the variance between men and women. Only a few researchers have found sex differences in psychological consequences of alcohol and drug use (e.g., Robbins, 1989). The many variables needed in our model require a large sample for stable and reliable results. Separate analyses by sex would reduce our sample size to unacceptable numbers (e.g., Bentler & Chou, 1987; Marsh, Balla, & McDonald, 1988; Tanaka, 1987). Therefore, we had to combine our samples of men and women in our SEMs, even though this sacrifices our ability to examine gender-specific mental health consequences of drug use.

We now turn to our SEM analyses. Although a few of our variables may be considered quasi-continuous or border on categorical (i.e., drug use items, not the scales), categorical methods cannot currently be practically implemented with such a large model (Newcomb, 1990). More important, Hays and Huba (1988) demonstrated clearly that conclusions reached when drug use frequency items were analyzed by several different procedures all arrived at similar conclusions. Finally, the present analyses are based on presumed linear relationships among the variables and are not designed to test for potential curvilinear or other nonlinear patterns, as at least one other study has noted may exist between drug use and psychological variables (Shedler & Block, 1990).

Confirmatory Factor Analyses

Before developing our structural or path model, we conducted a confirmatory factor analysis (CFA) to assess how well the observed measures reflected the hypothesized latent constructs. This analysis also allowed us to examine the correlations among the unobserved latent factors. Change in Polydrug Use from adolescence to young adulthood was captured as a disturbance term (with higher values reflecting Increased Polydrug Use). We accomplished this by allowing the adolescent Polydrug Use construct to predict the young adult Polydrug Use construct, and the residual (or disturbance) variable of this adult latent factor represents Increased Polydrug Use. Cross-time correlated residuals were included a priori for repeatedly measured variables. In addition, we correlated residuals of cocaine and hard drugs at each time to capture their unique similarities as measures of extremely illicit or hard drugs.

The fit of the model was adequate according to several criteria, $\chi^2(932, N = 487) = 1,761.01$, $p < .001$, Comparative Fit Index (CFI; Ben-

TABLE 2
Summary of Descriptive Statistics

Latent construct/ measured variable	M	No. of items	Range	SD	Skew	Kurtosis	Mean sex difference[a] r_{pb}
Adolescent Drug Use			Adolescence (Years 1 and 5)				
Alcohol frequency	—	6	−1.33–2.49	—	0.13	−0.91	−.03
Cigarette frequency	—	2	−0.85–2.22	—	0.95	0.07	.12**
Cannabis frequency	—	4	−0.60–3.25	—	1.73	2.67	.01
Cocaine frequency	—	2	−0.30–5.15	—	3.46	15.42	.06
Hard drug frequency	—	19	−0.33–8.74	—	4.16	33.31	.07
Emotional Distress							
Depression	7.66	4	4–18	3.25	0.85	−0.49	.03
Self-acceptance	15.89	4	4–20	3.12	−0.67	0.04	−.03
Self-derogation	2.41	7	0–10	2.79	0.87	−0.08	.09*
Social Conformity							
Liberalness	9.99	4	4–19	2.57	0.22	0.10	.03
Law abidance	13.15	4	4–20	3.96	−0.21	−0.70	.13**
Religious commitment	15.44	4	4–20	3.98	−0.71	−0.28	.14**
Social Support							
Relationships with:							
Parents	15.99	4	6–20	3.39	−0.78	−0.09	.03
Family	14.55	4	4–20	4.14	−0.57	−0.46	−.02
Adults	17.11	4	7–20	2.27	−0.70	0.40	.09*
Peers	16.74	4	6–20	2.74	−1.08	1.12	.04

Young Adult Drug Use							
Alcohol use	—	3	-1.62–2.17	—	-0.01	-1.04	-.09*
Cigarette use	—	2	-0.66–1.79	—	1.06	-0.69	-.07
Cannabis use	—	2	-0.65–3.63	—	1.46	1.02	.00
Cocaine use	—	2	-0.60–3.65	—	1.55	1.31	-.01
Hard drug use	—	14	-0.40–9.12	—	3.91	21.26	-.05
Adulthood (Year 13)							
Emotional Distress							
Depression	7.24	4	4–20	2.99	1.36	2.25	.02
Self-acceptance	16.06	4	4–20	2.91	-0.94	0.91	-.06
Self-Derogation							
Positive self-image	5.77	2	4–6	0.55	-2.26	3.95	-.11*
Negative self-image	10.97	5	10–15	1.28	1.24	0.70	.05
Purpose in Life (PIL)							
PIL 1	11.42	6	4.3–14	1.68	-0.97	0.87	-.06
PIL 2	10.84	7	3.6–14	1.71	-0.70	0.36	-.06
PIL 3	11.13	7	3.5–14	1.59	-0.65	0.78	.03
Psychoticism							
Magid 1	21.60	10	20–28	1.69	1.20	1.18	.07
Magid 2	16.22	10	14–21	1.32	0.90	0.54	.05
Magid 3	28.78	10	18–35	1.91	-0.50	5.68	.03
Suicide Ideation							
Told someone kill self	1.18	1	1–4	0.47	2.76	7.61	-.04
Think about killing self	1.25	1	1–4	0.54	2.31	5.56	-.05
Life end with suicide	1.10	1	1–4	0.39	4.35	21.01	-.06
Tried to kill self	1.09	1	1–4	0.38	5.05	29.45	.06

Table continues

TABLE 2 (Continued)

Latent construct/measured variable	M	No. of items	Range	SD	Skew	Kurtosis	Mean sex difference[a] r_{pb}
			Adulthood (Year 13)				
CES-D							
Positive affect	2.42	4	0.50–3	0.60	−1.00	0.32	−.12**
Negative affect	0.50	5	0–2.8	0.54	1.30	1.52	.16***
Impaired social relations	0.26	3	0–3	0.41	2.29	7.52	.00
Impaired cognitions	0.57	8	0–2.75	0.44	0.90	1.00	.10*
Hostility							
Hostility 1	2.47	1	1–5	0.86	0.25	−0.09	.19***
Hostility 2	2.36	1	1–5	0.80	0.34	0.20	.16***
Hostility 3	2.00	1	1–4	0.80	0.50	−0.21	.16***
Anxiety							
Anxiety 1	2.43	1	1–5	0.87	0.27	−0.27	.01
Anxiety 2	2.56	1	1–5	0.83	0.07	−0.29	.00
Anxiety 3	2.18	1	1–5	0.83	0.60	0.40	−.09*
Disorganized Thinking							
Deliberateness	13.46	1	4–20	3.04	−0.24	−0.10	−.06
Diligence	15.80	1	6–20	2.75	−0.60	0.32	.03
Thought disorganization	8.89	1	4–18	2.89	0.52	0.00	.06

Note. Dashes for adolescent drug use indicate standardized scale scores were used averaging over early and late adolescence, and dashes for young adult drug use indicate standardized scale scores were also used. Magid = magic ideation; CES-D = Center for Epidemiologic Studies–Depression Scale.

[a] A positive correlation indicates that women had the larger value.

* $p \leq .05$. ** $p \leq .01$. *** $p \leq .001$.

tler, 1990) = .92. The CFI is a sample-size adjusted analogue to the Normed Fit Index (Bentler & Bonett, 1980) and indicates the amount of covariation in the data accounted for by the hypothesized model. A rule of thumb is not to reject a model when the ratio of the model's chi-square to the degrees of freedom is less than 2.00 (Bentler, 1980; Bentler & Bonett, 1980). This ratio for the CFA model was 1.89, indicating an adequate model fit. Standardized factor loadings and residual variables (variances) of the observed variables for the CFA model are depicted in Figure 1.

As hypothesized, all factor loadings for the measured variables on the latent factors were sizable and significant ($p < .001$). The adolescent Polydrug Use construct largely reflected marijuana, which had the largest loading, followed in magnitude by alcohol and cigarette use and to a lesser extent by cocaine and hard drug use. Similarly, marijuana use had nearly the largest factor loading on the young adult Polydrug Use construct; however, in this case, cocaine use had a larger loading than alcohol and cigarette use.

Table 3 presents the intercorrelations among the 13 latent factors and Increased Polydrug Use residual variable. For the adolescent latent constructs, adolescent Polydrug Use was strongly and significantly associated with less Social Conformity and moderately correlated with less Social Support, more adolescent Emotional Distress, and more adult Psychoticism. The stability correlation of adolescent Emotional Distress with adult Emotional Distress was of moderate magnitude and larger than with the other adult constructs. Adolescent Emotional Distress was also significantly correlated with all but one of the other adult mental health constructs (excluding Psychoticism). This generally supports our use of the adolescent Emotional Distress construct as a broad measure of adolescent psychological distress and control for stability effects of most adult mental health constructs.

Adolescent Polydrug Use significantly predicted young adult Polydrug Use ($\beta = .74$), leaving 45% of residual variance that we interpret as changes (increases or decreases) in Polydrug Use from adolescence to young adulthood. Increased Polydrug Use was correlated significantly with adolescent Social Conformity and only Psychoticism of the adult mental health constructs.

Structural Model Analyses

The same factor structure or measurement portion of the CFA model was used as the basis for our initial structural or path model. Correlations among all of the adolescent latent factors and Increased Polydrug Use variable (residual) were allowed to be estimated freely. We estimated unidirectional paths from each adolescent construct (and Increased Polydrug Use) to every adult construct, capturing possible causal relationships in a

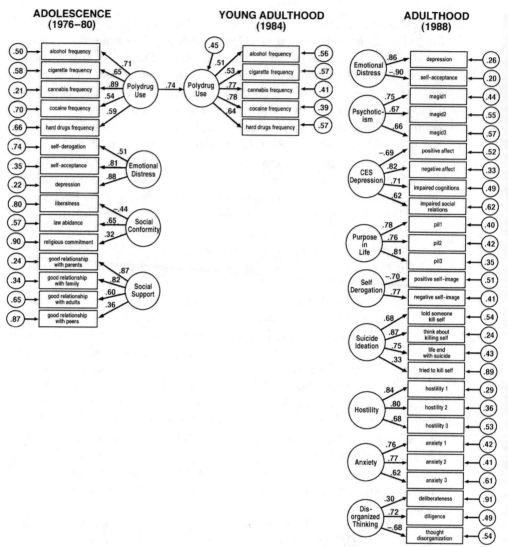

Figure 1. Final confirmatory factor analysis model. (Large circles represent latent constructs, rectangles are measured variables, and small circles with numbers are residual variables. Factor loadings are standardized and all are significant [$p < .001$]. Not depicted in the figure are two-headed arrows [i.e., correlations] joining each possible pair of factors. Estimates for these correlations are given in Table 3. CES = Center for Epidemiologic Studies; magid = magic ideation; pil = purpose in life.)

saturated fashion (Newcomb, 1994). The disturbance terms of all dependent (adult) latent factors were allowed to intercorrelate freely. Each of the residual variables from the five specific types of adolescent drug use was allowed to predict its analogous measure in adulthood. The residuals of each of these five young adult drug use measures represent increased use

TABLE 3
Factor Intercorrelations for the Confirmatory Factor Analysis Model

Variable	1	2	3	4	5	6	7	8	9	10	11	12	13	14
Adolescence														
1. Adolescent Polydrug Use	—													
2. Increased Polydrug Use[a]	.00	—												
3. Emotional Distress	.14**	.01	—											
4. Social Conformity	-.70***	-.24**	-.38***	—										
5. Social Support	-.22***	-.12*	-.64***	.52***	—									
Adulthood														
6. Emotional Distress	.08	.04	.41***	-.20**	-.34***	—								
7. Psychoticism	.21***	.32***	.08	-.25***	-.10*	.19***	—							
8. CES-D	-.02	.06	.27***	-.09	-.24***	.74***	.31***	—						
9. Purpose in Life	-.10*	-.01	-.39***	.25***	.33***	-.86***	-.21***	-.68***	—					
10. Self-Derogation	.08	.01	.39***	-.22**	-.32***	.88***	.34***	.71***	-.75***	—				
11. Suicide Ideation	.03	.12*	.26***	-.12*	-.16**	.62***	.26***	.57***	-.63***	.62***	—			
12. Hostility	.05	-.01	.32***	-.12*	-.19***	.56***	.20***	.64***	-.57***	.63***	.42***	—		
13. Anxiety	.04	.08	.25***	-.05	-.09	.28***	.21***	.44***	-.35***	.37***	.23***	.55***	—	
14. Disorganized Thinking	.08	.01	.17**	-.24**	-.14*	.65***	.26***	.53***	-.61***	.57***	.32***	.46***	.28***	—

Note. Significance level is determined by a critical ratio of the unstandardized parameter estimate divided by its standard error. CES-D = Center for Epidemiologic Studies–Depression Scale.

[a]This measure reflects increased drug use from adolescence (Years 1–5) to young adulthood (Year 9).

*p < .05. **p < .01. ***p < .001.

of each drug. Finally, within-time correlated residuals for cocaine and hard drugs were retained, and residuals for repeatedly measured psychosocial variables were correlated across time.

As expected, this initial structural model had an identical fit to the CFA model. This initial structural model only tests standard across-time paths, those between latent constructs (Newcomb, 1994). To capture more detailed, subtle, and comprehensive patterns in these data, we continued our development of this structural model by testing for specific or nonstandard paths across time (Newcomb, 1990, 1994; Newcomb & Bentler, 1988a, 1988b). Specific nonstandard paths were added on the basis of empirical importance and substantive interpretations. Empirical guidance was obtained from stepwise Lagrangian multiplier tests (Chou & Bentler, 1990). In some cases, the sign of a parameter estimate was opposite to the corresponding covariance; these parameters were regarded as suppressor effects and were not included. Specification searches were restricted to only three types of specific or nonstandard across-time structural paths and were considered in the following sequence: (a) adolescent latent factors and Increased Polydrug Use variable to measured variables in adulthood; (b) measured-variable residual terms in adolescence and those five residuals reflecting increases in specific types of drug use to adult latent factors; and (c) adolescent measured-variable residuals and five increased specific drug use residuals to adult measured variables. After paths were added with the Lagrangian test, we made final model adjustments by deleting nonsignificant parameters with the Wald test (Chou & Bentler, 1990). This procedure of additions and then deletions of model parameters has been found to be the best modification strategy to capture the "true" model (Chou & Bentler, 1990; MacCallum, 1986).

A final structural model was obtained with an adequate fit, $\chi^2(856, N = 487) = 1,215.31, p < .001$; CFI = .96. Figure 2 depicts the significant paths between latent factors in this final structural model. Correlations among adult latent construct residuals were omitted from the figure for ease of depiction but are presented in Table 4.

Adolescent Polydrug Use did not significantly predict any of the mental health latent constructs in adulthood. On the other hand, Increased Polydrug Use was significantly associated with increased adult Psychoticism and Suicide Ideation. The effect on Psychoticism should be interpreted with caution, because no comparable baseline measure was available to control for its stability and adolescent Emotional Distress did not serve this function.

Several nondrug effects between adolescent Emotional Distress and adult latent constructs were also apparent. Adolescent Emotional Distress increased adult Emotional Distress, Self-Derogation, Suicide Ideation, Hostility, Disorganized Thinking, and decreased Purpose in Life. Adolescent

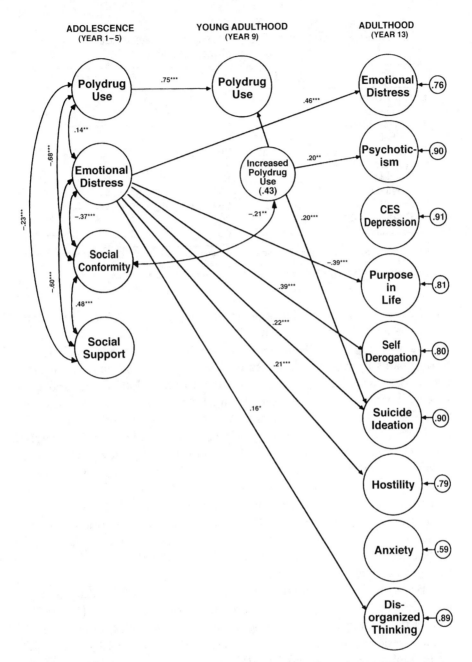

Figure 2. Final structural model of the across-time effects between latent constructs. (Large circles represent latent factors, and small circles with numbers reflect residual variances. Path coefficients are standardized, and significance levels were determined by critical ratios on unstandardized coefficients [*p < .05; **p < .01; ***p < .001]. Other nonstandard regression effects from this same final model that do not relate latent constructs to one another are given in Table 5. Correlations among the residuals of adult latent factors are given in Table 4. CES = Center for Epidemiologic Studies.)

TABLE 4
Correlations Among the Factor Residuals in Adulthood From the Final Structural Model

Factor	1	2	3	4	5	6	7	8	9
1. Emotional Distress	—								
2. Psychoticism	.00[a]	—							
3. CES-D	.89	.11*	—						
4. Purpose in Life	−.84	.00[a]	−.78	—					
5. Self-Derogation	.86	.11*	.78	−.70	—				
6. Suicide Ideation	.62	.00[a]	.61	−.63	.58	—			
7. Hostility	.60	.00[a]	.55	−.60	.61	.39	—		
8. Anxiety	.48	.00[a]	.24	−.51	.48	.22*	.45	—	
9. Disorganized Thinking	.78	.00[a]	.43	−.69	.59	.31	.34	.00[a]	—

Note. Unless otherwise noted, all residual correlations are significant at $p < .001$ level (*$p < .01$). CES-D = Center for Epidemiologic Studies–Depression Scale.
[a]Parameter was nonsignificant and constrained at zero in the final structural model.

Social Conformity and Social Support had no significant, direct effects on any of the adult latent constructs.

Table 5 contains a summary of all specific or nonstandard effects reflecting paths from adolescent measured-variable residuals and latent factors to the various adult mental health measures (both latent and observed). These paths are all from the final structural model and must be considered in concert with results from the same model given in Figure 2 and Table 4. These specific or nonstandard paths provide a detailed picture of more specific influences of both drug and nondrug adolescent variables on adult mental health (see Newcomb, 1994). Although many of these effects are relatively small, they represent partial regression coefficients, indicating unique contributions beyond stability and baseline controls. Table 5 is organized into three sections on the basis of the content of the predictor variables: adolescent drug effects, increased drug use effects, and nondrug effects. These effects are numerous, and only selected ones are discussed here (all are presented in Table 5).

By far the largest nonstandard regression effect involving drug use was from adolescent Polydrug Use to one indicator of Psychoticism (Magid 1). Among the various adolescent drug use predictor variables, specific use of alcohol (residual) had five significant across-time effects: higher alcohol use in adolescence decreased later CES-D, impaired cognitions (apparent beneficial effects), and PIL 3 and increased one indicator of Suicide Ideation ("think about killing self") and one indicator of Anxiety. Adolescent cigarette use increased adult impaired cognitions, Magid 3, and thought disorganization and decreased PIL 2, positive self-image, and deliberateness. Adolescent cannabis frequency had four significant nonstandard effects: increased CES-D and Magid 3 and decreased positive self-image and "tried

TABLE 5
Nonstandard Effects Not Depicted in Figure 2

Predictors		Consequences		Standardized parameter estimate
Observed	Latent	Observed	Latent	
	Polydrug Use	Adolescent drug effects		
Alcohol freq.		Magid 1	CES-D	.25**
Alcohol freq.		Impaired cognitions		-.12**
Alcohol freq.		PIL 3		-.07*
Alcohol freq.		Think about killing self		-.08**
Alcohol freq.		Anxiety 3		.07*
Cigarette freq.		Magid 3		.12**
Cigarette freq.		Impaired cognitions		.10*
Cigarette freq.		PIL 2		.07*
Cigarette freq.		Positive self-image		-.09**
Cigarette freq.		Deliberateness		-.08*
Cigarette freq.		Thought disorganization	CES-D	-.11*
Cannabis freq.		Positive self-image		.07*
Cannabis freq.		Tried to kill self		.17**
Cannabis freq.		Magid 3		-.12*
Cannabis freq.		Magid 3		-.10*
Cocaine freq.		Magid 2		.11*
Hard drug freq.		Magid 3		.10*
Hard drug freq.		PIL 2		.09*
Hard drug freq.		Negative self-image		-.06*
Hard drug freq.		Told someone kill self		.13***
Hard drug freq.				.07*

Table continues

TABLE 5 (Continued)

Predictors		Consequences		Standardized parameter estimate
Observed	Latent	Observed	Latent	
		Increased drug use effects		
Increased alcohol use	Increased Polydrug Use	Positive affect		−.13**
Increased alcohol use	Increased Polydrug Use	Impaired relations		.18***
Increased alcohol use	Increased Polydrug Use	Anxiety 3		.15**
Increased cigarette use		Impaired relations		−.14**
Increased cigarette use		PIL 1		−.06**
Increased cigarette use		Positive self-image		.09**
Increased cigarette use		Think about killing self		.05*
Increased cannabis use		Deliberateness		−.15**
Increased cannabis use			Purpose in Life	−.06*
Increased cannabis use			Psychoticism	.11**
Increased cannabis use		Magid 1		.11*
Increased cannabis use		Positive affect		−.17***
Increased cannabis use		Negative affect		.09**
Increased cannabis use		Tried to kill self		−.15**
Increased cannabis use		Hostility 1		.09**
Increased cannabis use		Thought disorganization		.10**
Increased cannabis use			Emotional Distress	.14***
Increased cannabis use			Purpose in Life	−.14***
Increased cannabis use			Self-Derogation	.16**
Increased cocaine use		Impaired relations		.14**
Increased cocaine use		Negative self-image		.06**
Increased cocaine use		Tried to kill self		.14**
Increased hard drug use		Negative affect		−.10**
Increased hard drug use		Impaired relations		.08*
Increased hard drug use		Hostility 1		−.07*
Increased hard drug use		Anxiety 2		.07*

Predictor		Outcome	
Increased hard drug use		Psychoticism	.14**
Increased hard drug use		Disorganized Thinking	.12*

Nondrug effects

Predictor	Mediator	Outcome	
Self-derogation	Emotional Distress	Impaired relations	.13**
Self-derogation	Emotional Distress	Positive affect	-.25***
Self-derogation	Emotional Distress	PIL 2	-.08*
Self-derogation	Emotional Distress	Told someone kill self	.08*
Self-derogation	Emotional Distress	Anxiety 1	.07*
Self-derogation	Emotional Distress	Diligence	.15*
Self-derogation		Negative affect	.09**
Self-derogation		Impaired cognitions	.14***
Self-derogation		Impaired relations	.12**
Self-derogation		Hostility 2	.07*
Self-derogation		Hostility 3	.11**
Self-derogation		Psychoticism	.12*
Self-derogation		Self-Derogation	.07*
Self-derogation		Anxiety	.13*
Self-derogation		Disorganized Thinking	.09*
Self-acceptance		Magid 3	.08*
Self-acceptance		CES-D	-.13*
Self-acceptance		Negative affect	-.14**
Self-acceptance		Impaired cognitions	-.18***
Self-acceptance		Negative self-image	-.10**
Self-acceptance		Think about killing self	-.07*
Self-acceptance		Hostility	-.20***
Self-acceptance		Hostility 3	.06*
Self-acceptance		Anxiety	-.31***
Self-acceptance		Disorganized Thinking	.13*
Self-acceptance		Thought disorganization	-.15***

Table continues

NEWCOMB, SCHEIER, AND BENTLER

TABLE 5 (Continued)

Predictors		Consequences		Standardized parameter estimate
Observed	Latent	Observed	Latent	
Nondrug effects				
Depression		Magid 2		.17***
Depression		Magid 3		.11**
Depression			CES-D	.15*
Depression		Negative affect		.21**
Depression		Impaired cognitions		.31***
Depression		Impaired relations		.14**
Depression		Negative self-image		.12**
Depression			Purpose in Life	−.13**
Depression		PIL 1		.13**
Depression			Hostility	.35***
Depression			Anxiety	.53***
Depression		Anxiety 2		.21***
Depression		Anxiety 3		.14**
Depression			Disorganized Thinking	.21**
Depression		Deliberateness		−.15**
Depression		Thought disorganization		.24***
Depression			Suicide Ideation	.10*
	Social Conformity	Hostility 2		−.07*
	Social Conformity	Diligence		−.10*
Liberalness			Purpose in Life	−.07*
Liberalness		Deliberateness		−.08*
Law abidance			Self-Derogation	.11**
Law abidance		Tried to kill self		.09*
Law abidance		Diligence		.10*
Religious commitment		Positive self-image		.07*
Religious commitment		Negative self-image		−.06*

Teen predictor	Adult outcome variable	Coefficient
Religious commitment	Purpose in Life — PIL 2	.07*
Religious commitment	Psychoticism — Tried to kill self	.11**
Social Support	Depression	−.05*
Social Support	Negative affect	−.15***
Social Support	Impaired cognitions	−.08*
Social Support	Impaired relations	−.11*
Good relations with parents	Impaired relations	.12*
Good relations with parents	Life end with suicide	.07*
Good relations with parents	Tried to kill self	−.12*
Good relations with parents	Deliberateness	−.14**
Good relations with parents	Tried to kill self	−.16*
Good relations with parents	Deliberateness	.19***
Good relations with parents	Thought disorganization	−.18***
Good relations with family	Positive self-image	.08*
Good relations with family	Think about killing self	−.10**
Good relations with family	Life end with suicide	−.14**
Good relations with family	Tried to kill self	−.15***
Good relations with adults	Diligence	−.10*
Good relations with adults	Positive self-image	.09*
Good relations with adults	Anxiety — Hostility 3	−.12**
Good relations with adults	Anxiety — Magid 2	−.09*
Good relations with peers	Positive self-image	−.08*
Good relations with peers	Hostility 3	−.08*
Good relations with peers	Think about killing self	−.07*
Good relations with peers	Life end with suicide	−.08*

Note. All observed predictors are from the residual of that variable. Magid = magic ideation; CES-D = Center for Epidemiologic Studies–Depression Scale; PIL = Purpose in Life.

*p < .05. **p < .01. ***p < .001.

to kill self." Only one effect was noted for adolescent cocaine use: It increased one indicator of Psychoticism. Adolescent hard drug use increased negative self-image, "told someone kill self," and Magid 2 and decreased PIL 2.

Increases in Polydrug Use and specific types of drug use had a variety of effects on mental health in adulthood and are presented in the second section of Table 5. Increased Polydrug Use exacerbated impaired relationships and Anxiety 3 and reduced positive affect. Increased consumption of alcohol into young adulthood had 3 specific effects: improved self-image, reduced impaired relations (apparent beneficial effects), and decreased PIL 1. Increased cigarette use decreased Purpose in Life and deliberateness and heightened thoughts about killing self. Increased cannabis use had 10 specific effects on adult mental health functioning: greater Psychoticism (and Magid 1), negative affect, Hostility 1, thought disorganization, Emotional Distress, and Self-Derogation. Increased cannabis involvement also reduced Purpose in Life, positive affect, and attempts to kill self. Increased cocaine use exacerbated impaired relations, negative self-image, and attempts to kill self. Finally, increased hard drug use had 6 significant nonstandard effects related to heightened Psychoticism, Disorganized Thinking, impaired relations, and Anxiety 2, and it also reduced negative affect and Hostility 1.

Other specific or nonstandard effects from adolescent predictors to adult mental health functioning were quite numerous and are presented in the third section of Table 5. For instance, Emotional Distress increased impaired relations, Anxiety 1, diligence, and "told someone kill self" and decreased positive affect and PIL 2. These results confirm our use of a general Emotional Distress construct to control for adolescent levels of subsequent mental health measures (Scheier & Newcomb, 1993). The fewest nondrug, specific effects of adolescent variables were for Social Conformity and its indicators. Both adolescent Emotional Distress and Social Support, in conjunction with their specific indicators, had numerous significant effects on adult mental health functioning. Among some of the larger effects was adolescent depression increasing both Hostility and Anxiety in adulthood. Social Support and various good relations with family and friends as a teenager ameliorated or reduced numerous types of mental health problems as an adult.

DISCUSSION

Mental health and psychological functioning evolve over time in response to various internal and external forces. To test whether drug use affects mental health and psychological development, one must account for the effects of known or likely influences of these outcomes. In our final path model, changes in mental health due to drug use could not be attributed to spurious influences related to conventionality or traditionalism (Social Conformity); parental, peer, or family support (Social Support); or prior levels of Emotional Distress. All of these likely factors were included as baseline controls. If drug use and emotional distress are generated by the same underlying cause or vulnerability to psychopathology, this research design would reveal no unique, direct effects from earlier drug use to later mental health problems (e.g., Garber & Hollon, 1991; Newcomb & Bentler, 1988a). Although comorbidity between mental disorders and alcohol and drug abuse is quite high in both community and institutional samples (e.g., Regier et al., 1990), we found that drug use may precede or exacerbate mental health problems.

Drug Use Consequences

The Adolescent and Increased Polydrug Use constructs had unequal influences on adult mental health. Adolescent Polydrug Use had no significant effects on any adult constructs and only one specific effect on a measured variable in adulthood (Magid 1). In contrast, Increased Polydrug Use had five significant long-term negative effects on adult mental health. Those who increased their polydrug use from adolescence to young adulthood expressed greater Psychoticism and Suicide Ideation, as general latent constructs, and specifically more impaired relations, Anxiety 3, and less positive affect than when they were teenagers. At least in terms of Polydrug Use (reflecting a high level of drug involvement akin to drug abuse— Newcomb, 1992; Newcomb & Bentler, 1988b), substance use as a teenager had few long-term detrimental effects on mental health functioning. This is in contrast to the more numerous mental health adversities associated with increased drug involvement from adolescence into adulthood.

Use of specific substances also adversely influenced several aspects of mental health, although many of these effects were small in magnitude. These effects were more prevalent for increases in specific substances but also included several specific adolescent drug use measures. In our discussion, we focus on effects of .10 or higher and give less attention to smaller, though significant, influences.

Cannabis use had the greatest number of unique effects on the outcome measures. Chronic marijuana consumption has been associated with an "amotivational syndrome," based on the belief that excessive drug consumption leads to emotional disenfranchisement (Baumrind & Moselle, 1985), perceived parental detachment (Brook, Gordon, Brook, & Brook, 1989), impairments in cognitive functioning (Ferraro, 1980), and deficits in academic performance (Mellinger, Somers, Davidson, & Manheimer, 1976). Others have failed to confirm that marijuana precipitates declines in mental health or intellectual functioning (e.g., Ginsberg & Greeley,

1978; Kandel, 1978). Kandel reviewed relevant research and found little evidence that teenage marijuana use preceded the problems associated with amotivation and concluded that many of these problems actually preceded marijuana use. Our data indicate that adolescent and, particularly, increased cannabis use had several long-term negative mental health consequences. Thus, the mental health consequences of cannabis use may be more pronounced subsequent to adolescence rather than during the teenage years.

Adolescent cigarette use was related to increased Magid 3 and decreased deliberateness and had four other smaller effects. Increased cigarette use was also related to decreased deliberateness and had two smaller adverse effects. Previously (Newcomb & Bentler, 1988b), we reported that cigarette use increased emotional distress and also had damaging effects on other areas of life functioning. This earlier study spanned 4 years (in contrast to the present 12-year study) and suggests that the negative psychosocial consequences of cigarette use occur over a relatively short period of time and may not persist over a greater length of time. The long-term major adversity of cigarette smoking may be largely physical.

Cocaine use has been associated with emotional deterioration and psychosocial problems in clinical (e.g., Chitwood, 1985; Kosten et al., 1988) and survey populations (Newcomb & Bentler, 1986, 1987, 1988a, 1988b). Kosten et al. reported more disturbance on a range of psychosocial outcomes among addicts who increased their cocaine use over a 2.5-year period while in treatment for opioid dependence. On the other hand, Newcomb and Bentler (1986) found no serious short-term consequences from cocaine use in their general population study, although teenagers were followed for only 1 year and the extent of their cocaine consumption was limited. Discussing their findings, Newcomb and Bentler (1986) reported, "cocaine use in this more or less normal adolescent sample, generated no significant increases or decreases in eight measures of emotional distress" (p. 272). Negative effects may take longer to emerge (e.g., Newcomb & Bentler, 1988a), as is typical with psychiatric disturbances (e.g., Lewinsohn, Duncan, Stanton, & Hautzinger, 1986). Contrary to these earlier findings from adolescence, we found four specific negative effects in adulthood associated with adolescence and increased cocaine use into young adulthood. Higher cocaine use during adolescence increased one indicator of Psychoticism in adulthood, whereas increased cocaine use exacerbated impaired relations, negative self-image, and attempts to kill self. Petronis, Samuels, Moscicki, and Anthony (1990) also found that cocaine use was associated with risk of making a suicide attempt.

Specific use of hard drugs during adolescence was associated with increased later negative self-image, one indicator of Psychoticism (Magid 2), thoughts about suicide, and reduced PIL 2; these generally reflect exacerbated personal alienation, self-dislike, and bizarre beliefs. The extreme legal sanctions, psychoactive potency, and social awkwardness associated with using hard drugs (their use is generally not condoned even by peer groups) may contribute to these adverse effects. Equally alarming, increased hard drug use was moderately associated with increased Psychoticism and Disorganized Thinking and had small, but significant, influences on increasing Anxiety 2 and impaired relationships and reducing hostility (only one indicator) and negative affect. We found similar effects of teenage hard drug use on suicidal ideation over a 4-year period (Newcomb & Bentler, 1988a), and Ward and Schuckit (1980) reported that polydrug users (including hard drugs) had self-destructive ideation. The various potent sympathomimetic, sedating, anesthetic, or euphoriant properties of these drugs (i.e., hypnotics, stimulants, inhalants, and narcotics) may provide immediate, but temporary relief from psychic distress; however, when use is excessive or escalates over prolonged periods of time, hard drugs create several types of adverse mental health consequences.

There were both adverse and beneficial effects on adult mental health from specific early alcohol use and increased alcohol use, when other drug effects were controlled. The adverse consequences were related to indicators of Purpose in Life (lower), Anxiety (higher), and Suicide Ideation (higher).

Positive effects from alcohol use may be attributed to the fact that alcohol, for most of society, is legal and does not carry the social, moral, and legal ramifications associated with illicit drugs. Current laws prohibit alcohol use during adolescence; however, in general, use of alcohol receives fewer negative social sanctions and may be considered by many as a necessary social link in making the transition between adolescence and adulthood (e.g., Jessor, 1986). Also, alcohol is generally consumed in social situations that may reinforce positive expectancies in ways unlike other drugs, whose effects are more personal. Therefore, it is not too surprising that alcohol has some limited beneficial effects generally related to affect (reduced CES-D), social relations (reduced impaired relations), and self-perception (increased positive self-image). Similar beneficial effects of alcohol have been noted in our earlier research (Newcomb & Bentler, 1988a, 1988b) and other studies (e.g., Kandel et al., 1986).

Nondrug Relationships

Numerous developmental patterns unrelated to drugs were evident in the final SEM. Most of those effects related to adolescent Emotional Distress and its specific measured-variable indicators and reflect synergistic influences over time among various types of psychopathology or mental health. They also demonstrate how dysphoric affect and poor self-regard (Emotional Distress in adolescence) can have a generalized disruptive influence on many aspects of adult mental health (emotions, attitudes, and perceptions) and social (impaired relations) functioning. Emotional Distress also increased diligence, a finding that was unexpected. One possible interpretation is that heightened diligence may be an attempt to cope with or control the chaos and helplessness of inner turmoil. In other words, more diligence may be one way to impose structure, order, and predictability on a life plagued with dissatisfaction and distress.

Various indicators of adolescent Social Conformity influenced several aspects of adult psychological functioning. Adherence to conventionality had both positive and negative effects on adult mental health status and may reflect the mixed blessing of following social norms (e.g., Shedler & Block, 1990). For instance, law abidance increased Self-Derogation and attempts to kill self (as did religious commitment). On the other hand, more adolescent Social Conformity and law abidance increased later diligence, and religious commitment enhanced self-image.

Finally, Social Support and many of the indicators of the Social Support construct enhanced emotional health and may be protective forces. These variables decreased Anxiety and various indicators of Suicide Ideation, reduced negative affect, and improved social relations. Like Brook et al. (1989), we speculate that early disenfranchisement from traditional socialization influences and supportive interpersonal connections may exacerbate feelings of alienation and poor self-regard during this critical development period and may result in both increases in drug use and increased dysphoria. The latter finding is reinforced by the higher levels of depression in adulthood for those youth reporting low Social Support during adolescence. The one inconsistent finding to this pattern was that good relations with parents in adolescence increased adult Psychoticism. It is possible that overinvolvement with parents during adolescence may be antithetical to the development tasks of this age, which are to separate and individuate from parents and establish one's own intimate support network (e.g., Havighurst, 1972). As many family theorists indicate (e.g., Bowen), overinvolvement with parents may lead to psychotic conditions, as noted in our findings.

Theoretical Implications

Our findings are especially important when we consider that adolescence is a period of life during which critical emotional, social, and psychological skills and competencies are acquired, tested, and refined (e.g., Erikson, 1968). These involve acquisition of adult social roles, leaving home, attending college, beginning independent living, employment, marriage, and parenthood, to name just a few. Failure to acquire and master these competencies can result in serious emotional deficits and psychopathology (Havighurst, 1972). Conceivably, drug-abusing or frequent drug-using teenagers may have insufficient or inadequate socialization experiences, fail to cope successfully with various age-related stressors and transitions, and may be alienated from institutions from which many coping skills can be acquired and learned (i.e., family and schools). These drug-using, disaffected youth may become depressed and blame themselves for their inadequacies, and some may believe that increased tension arising from self-doubt and persistent thoughts of failure and negative self-image can be assuaged through continued or increased drug involvement, in the hope of alleviating this emotional distress. Our findings suggest that disruption to developmental mechanisms through precocious, continued, or escalated drug use may cause long-term emotional harm.

Several theoretical explanations have been suggested to explain why drug-abusing or heavily drug-involved youth lack adequate coping skills. Baumrind and Moselle (1985) suggested that adolescent drug use creates an hiatus from normal developmental processes, leaving youth without the necessary skills and cognitive abilities to adequately meet life's challenges. Alternatively, Newcomb (1987; Newcomb & Bentler, 1988a, 1988b) suggested that drug-involved youth accelerate their development and pass over important developmental experiences needed to acquire critical life skills. One example from our research includes abandonment of socially valued educational pursuits (Weng, Newcomb, & Bentler, 1988). Our present data do not directly test these hypotheses, although they emphasize the importance of the later transitional years between adolescence and adulthood, such that drug abuse during this critical developmental period may disrupt normal development and create serious mental health consequences.

Several researchers have suggested that drug abuse does not cause mental illness, but rather, that drug abuse causes unconventional behaviors (e.g., Kaplan, Johnson, & Bailey, 1988) that lead to detachment and alienation from important social institutions (i.e., school and family). Over time, such experiences may reduce feelings of purpose in life, create social and interpersonal deficits, heighten anxiety and hostility, or even lead to thoughts about suicide. These resulting cognitions, behavior, and affect reflect deficits in emotional functioning (e.g., B. P. Dohrenwend, Shrout, Egri, & Mendelsohn, 1980). This hypothesis is consistent with D. P. Dohrenwend's (1961) drift theory, which suggests that mental illness is a cause of disorganized social living, ultimately promulgating a downward socioeconomic and functional spiral of the mentally ill. It is known from studies of clinical populations that drug-abusing lifestyles can incur severe economic hardships, medical complications, and often serious emotional difficulties that may further reinforce a downward drift (Khantzian & Schneider, 1986; Weiss, Mirin, Griffin, Michael, & Sollogub, 1986). As more treatment alternatives become available to these individuals, including pharmacologic modalities, it becomes increasingly important to refine and sharpen clinical distinctions between mental health problems that are primary and secondary substance abuse disorders (e.g., Meyer, 1986).

One must also pay attention to problems associated with dual diagnosis of substance abuse and other disorders (Ford et al., 1989; Khantzian & Treece, 1985; Regier et al., 1990; Rounsaville & Kleber, 1985). Intervention with drug abusers requires difficult decisions to be made regarding choice of treatment and problems associated with complicated and interrelated presenting symptoms. It is possible that the developmental trajectory of psychopathology—when not accompanied with drug abuse—departs from a similar emotional dysfunction with substance abuse (e.g., Khantzian & Schneider, 1986). In addition, poor social and cognitive skills of long-term drug abusers may hinder treatment and recovery and require direct remediation over a lengthy period. If early initiation and continued use of drugs impair mental and emotional functioning, as we have shown, this heightens the importance of prevention efforts to delay drug use onset and to provide alternative affective coping and social skills (e.g., Hawkins, Lishner, & Catalano, 1985).

Limitations

There are several limitations to this study. First, the data were based on self-report measures and their possible biases (e.g., Stacy, Widaman, Hays, & DiMatteo, 1985). Others have noted that self-report measures of drug use are valid and have provided empirical tests to underscore these claims (e.g., Needle, Jou, & Su, 1989). Notwithstanding, error in measurement could be minimized through use of collateral and independent reports of drug use, although this information was not available for these data.

Second, although youth may confront a number of important developmental tasks during the transition from adolescence to young adulthood, negotiation of other life periods may also produce stress and disequilibrium that could motivate individuals to use or abuse drugs. Even though this study focused on one developmental period that represents a considerably long span of the life course, manifestation of the negative effects of drug abuse may not surface until even later in life, into older adulthood. Certainly, it would be valuable to reassess these adults further along their developmental course to determine whether the patterns we observed continue unabated into their later adult lives.

Third, and corollary to the previous limitation, the time lag in this study may underestimate the causal relationships between adolescent measures and subsequent adult psychological functioning, if such processes occur over a shorter period of time (e.g., Gollog & Reichardt, 1987). On the other hand, viewed from a life span perspective, our time span may have limited our ability to make generalizations regarding the effects of drug use on developmental processes to later and more extended periods of development.

Fourth, we did not assess psychiatric impairment with standard clinical diagnostic criteria (i.e., the *Diagnostic and Statistical Manual of Mental Disorders*, 3rd. ed., rev.; American Psychiatric Association, 1987). Rather, we used standard and proven epidemiological assessment tools that have demonstrated validity and reliability in general community studies. Although standard diagnostic assessment is most appropriate with clinical populations (e.g., Ford et al., 1989), these categorical decision criteria are less appropriate and useful with community samples. They are impractical, have little utility with low base-rate pathology, and are cost-prohibitive. Most important, however, is that they are dichotomous and therefore are restricted to only one or a few diagnostic "hits" (dual or triple diagnoses at most) and do not capture the true range of psychopathology that is subclinical in extent. Accordingly, the measures used in this study provided a broad, but still limited, assessment of psychopathology, as well as capturing the full range of disturbance in each type of psychopathology. A wider selection of assessments along with a broader definition of psychopathology may strengthen the effects observed between drug use and psychopathology.

Fifth, our assessments of drug use represented frequency of consumption and did not determine drug abuse, alcoholism, or other criteria of drug dependencies. The associations between use and abuse of drugs appeared to vary on the basis of the particular substance (Newcomb, 1992), and our present findings were restricted to frequency of drug use.

Sixth, because of the necessarily complex nature of our analyses, requiring inclusion and consideration of numerous influences to make the strongest causal inferences possible, we chose not to provide simple descriptive statistics regarding how much greater risk for a particular type of psychopathology is associated with a specific increment in drug use. Although these figures could be provided, they would be erroneous and misleading, because they could not reflect important confounds, other controls, and shared variance of critical constructs. Therefore, the public health significance of our various findings must be inferred from the size and significance of the standardized path estimates. In general, the effects were modest to moderate in magnitude.

Seventh, data for both men and women were analyzed together. As with other studies of survey data (e.g., Johnston, O'Malley, & Bachman, 1988), patterns of drug use may differ between sexes, although we did not find substantial differences in drug use patterns. Previous analyses on this sample conducted separately by sex have revealed few substantial gender differences in substantive, prospective results (Newcomb et al., 1988; Stein, Newcomb, & Bentler, 1987). Conducting analyses separately by sex would have produced too small of samples and compromised the robustness of our statistical techniques (e.g., Tanaka, 1987). Notwithstanding, collapsing data across sexes (and other demographic characteristics) may have masked potential gender differences in linkages between adolescent drug use and adult psychological functioning.

Finally, several other explanations for declines in psychological functioning due to drug use could not be directly explored. For example, drug use may alter neurophysiology and thereby impair neuropsychological functioning (e.g., Becker & Kaplan, 1986). Structural brain changes induced through chronic drug use and concomitant neuropsychological impairment may by synergistic and difficult to separate. Quite possibly, acute cognitive impairment resulting from early drug use may motivate heightened drug use to relieve distress or avoid the deficits. This may mask further cognitive impairment or facilitate misattribution of decrements in functioning to drug-induced behavioral changes. Various biochemical models of addiction need to be considered (e.g., cocaine and dopamine depletion), which suggest that drug abuse may precipitate neurochemical changes that alone may contribute to both acute and chronic neuropsychological impairment.

REFERENCES

Adesso, V. J. (1980). Experimental studies of human drinking behavior. In H. Rigter & J. C. Crabbe (Eds.), *Alcohol tolerance and dependence* (pp. 123–155). Amsterdam: Elsevier.

Adesso, V. J. (1985). Cognitive factors in alcohol and drug use. In M. Galizio & S. A. Maisto (Eds.), *Determinants of substance abuse: Biological, psychological, and environmental factors* (pp. 179–208). New York: Plenum Press.

American Psychiatric Association. (1987). *Diagnostic and statistical manual of mental disorders* (3rd ed., rev.). Washington, DC: Author.

Barrett, R. J. (1985). Behavioral approaches to individual differences in substance abuse: Drug-taking behavior. In M. Galizio & S. A. Maisto (Eds.), *Determinants of substance abuse: Biological, psychological, and environmental factors* (pp. 150–175). New York: Plenum Press.

Baum-Baicker, C. (1985). The psychological benefits of moderate alcohol consumption: A review of the literature. *Drug and Alcohol Dependence, 15*, 305–322.

Baumrind, D., & Moselle, K. A. (1985). A developmental perspective on adolescent drug use. *Advances in Alcohol and Substance Use, 5*, 41–67.

Becker, J. T., & Kaplan, R. F. (1986). Neurophysiological and neuropsychological concomitants of brain dysfunction in alcoholics. In R. E. Meyer (Ed.), *Psychopathology and addictive disorders* (pp. 263–292). New York: Guilford Press.

Beckman, L. (1980). Perceived antecedents and effects of alcohol consumption in women. *Journal of Studies on Alcohol, 41*, 518–530.

Bentler, P. M. (1980). Multivariate analysis with latent variables: Causal modeling. *Annual Review of Psychology, 31*, 419–456.

Bentler, P. M. (1989). *EQS structural equations program manual*. Los Angeles: BMDP Statistical Software.

Bentler, P. M. (1990). Comparative fit indexes in structural models. *Psychological Bulletin, 107*, 238–246.

Bentler, P. M., & Bonett, D. G. (1980). Significance tests and goodness of fit in the analysis of covariance structures. *Psychological Bulletin, 88*, 588–606.

Bentler, P. M., & Chou, C.-P. (1987). Practical issues in structural modeling. *Sociological Methods & Research, 16*, 78–117.

Bibbs, J. L., & Chambless, D. L. (1986). Alcohol use and abuse among diagnosed agoraphobics. *Behavior Research and Therapy, 24*, 49–58.

Brook, J. S., Gordon, A. S., Brook, A., & Brook, D. W. (1989). The consequences of marijuana use on intrapersonal and interpersonal functioning in black and white adolescents. *Genetic, Social, and General Psychology Monographs, 115*, 351–369.

Bukstein, O. G., Brent, D. A., & Kaminer, Y. (1989). Comorbidity of substance abuse and other psychiatric disorders in adolescents. *American Journal of Psychiatry, 146*, 1131–1141.

Chitwood, D. D. (1985). Patterns and consequences of cocaine use. In N. J. Kozel & E. H. Adams (Eds.), *Cocaine use in America: Epidemiologic and clinical perspectives* (pp. 111–129). Rockville, MD: National Institute on Drug Abuse.

Chou, C.-P., & Bentler, P. M. (1990). Model modification in covariance structure modeling: A comparison among likelihood ratio, Lagrange multiplier, and Wald tests. *Multivariate Behavioral Research, 25*, 115–136.

Clayton, R. R., & Ritter, C. (1985). The epidemiology of alcohol and drug abuse among adolescents. *Advances in Alcohol and Substance Abuse, 4*, 69–97.

Cohen, J., & Cohen, P. (1983). *Applied multiple regression/correlation for the behavioral sciences* (2nd ed.). Hillsdale, NJ: Erlbaum.

Cohen, S., & Wills, T. A. (1985). Stress, social support, and the buffering hypothesis. *Psychological Bulletin, 98*, 310–357.

Cronbach, L. J., & Furby, L. (1970). How we should measure change—or should we? *Psychological Bulletin, 74*, 68–80.

Crumbaugh, J. C., & Maholick, L. J. (1964). An experimental study in existentialism: The psychometric approach to Frankl's concept of noogenic neurosis. *Journal of Clinical Psychology, 20*, 200–207.

Dackis, C. A., & Gold, M. S. (1983). Opiate addiction and depression—cause or effect? *Drug and Alcohol Dependence, 11*, 105–109.

Dackis, C. A., & Gold, M. S. (1985). New concepts in cocaine addiction: The dopamine depletion hypothesis. *Neuroscience Behavioral Review, 9*, 469–477.

Dohrenwend, B. P., Shrout, P. E., Egri, G., & Mendelsohn, F. S. (1980). Nonspecific psychological distress and other dimensions of psychopathology. *Archives of General Psychiatry, 37*, 1229–1236.

Dohrenwend, D. P. (1961). The social psychological nature of stress: A framework for causal inquiry. *Journal of Abnormal and Social Psychology, 62*, 294–302.

Dorus, W., & Senay, E. C. (1980). Depression, demographic dimensions, and drug abuse. *American Journal of Psychiatry, 137*, 699–704.

Dwyer, J. H. (1983). *Statistical models for the social and behavioral sciences.* New York: Oxford University Press.

Eckblad, M., & Chapman, L. J. (1983). Magical ideation as an indicator of schizotypy. *Journal of Consulting and Clinical Psychology, 51*, 215–225.

Erikson, E. H. (1968). *Identity, youth and crisis.* New York: Norton.

Ferraro, D. P. (1980). Acute effects of marijuana on human memory and cognition. In R. C. Peterson (Ed.), *Marijuana research findings: 1980* (pp. 98–119). Rockville, MD: National Institute on Drug Abuse.

Ford, J., Hillard, J. R., Giesler, L. J., Lassen, K. L., & Thomas, H. (1989). Substance abuse/mental illness: Diagnostic issues. *American Journal of Drug and Alcohol Abuse, 15*, 297–307.

Garber, J., & Hollon, S. D. (1991). What can specificity designs say about causality in psychopathology research? *Psychological Bulletin, 110*, 129–136.

Gawin, F. H., & Kleber, H. D. (1984). Cocaine abuse treatment: Open pilot study with desipramine and lithium carbonate. *Archives of General Psychiatry, 41*, 903–909.

Gawin, F. H., & Kleber, H. D. (1985). Neuroendocrine findings in chronic cocaine abusers: A preliminary report. *British Journal of Psychiatry, 147*, 569–573.

Ginsberg, I. J., & Greeley, J. R. (1978). Competing theories of marijuana use: A longitudinal study. *Journal of Health and Social Behavior, 19*, 22–34.

Gold, M. S., Washton, A. M., & Dackis, C. A. (1985). Cocaine abuse: Neurochemistry, phenomenology, and treatment. In N. J. Kozel & E. H. Adams (Eds.), *Cocaine use in America: Epidemiologic and clinical perspectives* (pp. 130–150). Rockville, MD: National Institute on Drug Abuse.

Gollob, H. F., & Reichardt, C. S. (1987). Taking account of time lags in causal models. *Child Development, 58*, 80–92.

Harlow, L. L., Newcomb, M. D., & Bentler, P. M. (1986). Depression, self-derogation, substance use, and suicide ideation: Lack of purpose in life as a mediational factor. *Journal of Clinical Psychology, 42*, 5–21.

Harlow, L. L., Newcomb, M. D., & Bentler, P. M. (1987). Purpose in Life test assessment using latent variable. *British Journal of Clinical Psychology, 26*, 235–236.

Hartka, E., Johnstone, B. M., Leino, V., Motoyoshi, M., Temple, M. J., & Fillmore, K. M. (1989, June). *Trends in drinking and depression in several longitudinal samples: An exploratory analysis from the collaborative alcohol-related longitudinal project.* Paper presented at the meeting of the Life History Research Society, Montreal, Quebec, Canada.

Havighurst, R. J. (1972). *Developmental tasks and education* (3rd ed.). New York: McKay.

Hawkins, J. D., Lishner, D., & Catalano, R. F. (1985). Childhood predictors and the prevention of adolescent substance abuse. In C. L. Jones & R. J. Battjes

(Eds.), *Etiology of drug abuse: Implications for prevention* (pp. 75–126). Rockville, MD: National Institute on Drug Abuse.

Hays, R. D., & Huba, G. (1988). Reliability and validity of drug use items differing in the nature of their response options. *Journal of Primary Prevention, 6,* 73–97.

Hesselbrock, M. N., Meyer, R. E., & Keener, J. J. (1985). Psychopathology in hospitalized alcoholics. *Archives of General Psychiatry, 42,* 1050–1055.

Jessor, R. (1986). Adolescent problem drinking: Psychosocial aspects and developmental outcomes. In R. K. Silbereisen, K. Eyferth, & G. Rudinger (Eds.), *Development as action in context* (pp. 241–264). Berlin: Springer-Verlag.

Johnston, L. D., O'Malley, P. M., & Bachman, J. G. (1988). *Illicit drug use, smoking, and drinking by America's high school students, college students, and young adults: 1975–1987.* Rockville, MD: National Institute on Drug Abuse.

Kandel, D. B. (1978). Convergences in prospective longitudinal surveys of drug use in normal populations. In D. Kandel (Ed.), *Longitudinal research on drug use: Empirical findings and methodological issues* (pp. 3–38). Washington, DC: Hemisphere.

Kandel, D. B. (1984). Marijuana users in young adulthood. *Archives of General Psychiatry, 41,* 200–209.

Kandel, D. B., Davies, M., Karus, D., & Yamaguchi, K. (1986). The consequences in young adulthood of adolescent drug involvement. *Archives of General Psychiatry, 43,* 746–754.

Kaplan, H. B., Johnson, R. J., & Bailey, C. A. (1988). Explaining adolescent drug use: An elaboration strategy for structural equations modeling. *Psychiatry, 51,* 142–163.

Kaplan, H. B., & Pokorny, A. D. (1969). Self-derogation and psychosocial adjustment. *Journal of Nervous and Mental Disease, 149,* 421–434.

Keykin, E. Y., Levy, J. C., & Wells, V. (1987). Adolescent depression, alcohol and drug abuse. *American Journal of Public Health, 77,* 178–182.

Khantzian, E. J., & Schneider, R. J. (1986). Treatment implications of a psychodynamic understanding of opioid addicts. In R. E. Meyer (Ed.), *Psychopathology and addictive disorders* (pp. 323–333). New York: Guilford Press.

Khantzian, E. J., & Treece, C. (1985). *DSM-III* psychiatric diagnosis of narcotic addicts: Recent findings. *Archives of General Psychiatry, 42,* 1067–1071.

Kleber, H. D., & Gawin, F. H. (1984). Cocaine abuse: A review of current and experimental treatments. In J. Grabowski (Ed.), *Cocaine: Pharmacology, effects, and treatment of abuse* (pp. 111–129). Rockville, MD: National Institute on Drug Abuse.

Kosten, T. R., Rounsaville, B. J., & Kleber, H. D. (1988). Antecedents and consequences of cocaine abuse among opioid addicts: A 2.5-year follow-up. *Journal of Nervous and Mental Disease, 176,* 176–181.

Labouvie, E. W. (1986). Alcohol and marijuana use in relation to adolescent stress. *International Journal of the Addictions, 21,* 333–345.

Lewinsohn, P. M., Duncan, E. M., Stanton, A. K., & Hautzinger, M. (1986). Age at first onset for nonbipolar depression. *Journal of Abnormal Psychology, 95,* 378–383.

MacCallum, R. (1986). Specification searches in covariance structure analyses. *Psychological Bulletin, 100,* 107–120.

Malow, R. M., West, J. A., Williams, J. L., & Sutker, P. B. (1989). Personality disorders classification and symptoms in cocaine and opioid addicts. *Journal of Consulting and Clinical Psychology, 57,* 765–767.

Marlatt, G. A., Baer, J. S., Donovan, D. M., & Kivlahan, D. R. (1988). Addictive behaviors: Etiology and treatment. *Annual Review of Psychology, 39,* 223–252.

Marsh, H. W., Balla, J. R., & McDonald, R. P. (1988). Goodness-of-fit indexes in confirmatory factor analysis: The effect of sample size. *Psychological Bulletin, 103,* 391–410.

McGee, L., & Newcomb, M. D. (1992). General deviance syndrome: Expanded hierarchical evaluations at four ages from early adolescence to adulthood. *Journal of Consulting and Clinical Psychology, 60,* 766–776.

Mellinger, G. D., Somers, R. H., Davidson, S. T., & Manheimer, D. I. (1976). The amotivational syndrome and the college student. *Annals of the New York Academy of Science, 282,* 37–55.

Meyer, R. E. (1986). How to understand the relationship between psychopathology and addictive disorders: Another example of the chicken and the egg. In R. E. Meyer (Ed.), *Psychopathology and addictive disorders* (pp. 3–16). New York: Guilford Press.

Needle, R. H., Jou, S. C., & Su, S. S. (1989). The impact of changing methods of data collection on the reliability of self-reported drug use of adolescents. *American Journal of Drug and Alcohol Abuse, 15,* 275–289.

Nesselroade, J. R., & Bartsch, T. W. (1977). Multivariate experimental perspectives on the construct validity of the trait-state distinction. In R. B. Cattell & R. M. Dreger (Eds.), *Handbook of modern personality theory* (pp. 221–238). New York: Hemisphere.

Newcomb, M. D. (1987). Consequences of teenage drug use: The transition from adolescence to young adulthood. *Drugs and Society, 1,* 25–60.

Newcomb, M. D. (1988). *Drug use in the workplace: Risk factors for disruptive substance use among young adults.* Dover, MA: Auburn House.

Newcomb, M. D. (1990). What structural modeling techniques can tell us about social support. In I. G. Sarason, B. R. Sarason, & G. R. Pierce (Eds.), *Social support: An interactional view* (pp. 26–63). New York: Wiley.

Newcomb, M. D. (1992). Understanding the multidimensional nature of drug use and abuse: The role of consumption, risk factors, and protective factors. In M. D. Glantz & R. Pickens (Eds.), *Vulnerability to drug abuse* (pp. 255–298). Washington, DC: American Psychological Association.

Newcomb, M. D. (1994). Drug use and intimate relationships among women and men: Separating specific from general effects in prospective data using structural equations models. *Journal of Consulting and Clinical Psychology.*

Newcomb, M. D., & Bentler, P. M. (1986). Cocaine use among adolescents: Longitudinal associations with social context, psychopathology, and use of other substances. *Addictive Behaviors, 11,* 263–273.

Newcomb, M. D., & Bentler, P. M. (1987). Cocaine use among young adults. *Advances in Alcohol and Substance Abuse, 6,* 73–96.

Newcomb, M. D., & Bentler, P. M. (1988a). *Consequences of adolescent drug use: Impact on the lives of young adults.* Newbury Park, CA: Sage.

Newcomb, M. D., & Bentler, P. M. (1988b). Impact of adolescent drug use and social support on problems of young adults: A longitudinal study. *Journal of Abnormal Psychology, 97,* 64–75.

Newcomb, M. D., & Bentler, P. M. (1989, September). *Effects of specific drug use and cross-time dynamics: A structural equations approach.* Paper presented at the National Institute on Drug Abuse Technical Review, Longitudinal Studies of Drug Abuse, Rockville, MD.

Newcomb, M. D., Bentler, P. M., & Collins, C. (1986). Alcohol use and dissatisfaction with self and life: A longitudinal analysis of young adults. *Journal of Drug Issues, 16,* 479–494.

Newcomb, M. D., Bentler, P. M., & Fahy, B. (1987). Cocaine use and psychopathology: Associations among young adults. *International Journal of the Addictions, 22,* 1167–1188.

Newcomb, M. D., Chou, C.-P., Bentler, P. M., & Huba, G. J. (1988). Cognitive motivations for drug use among adolescents: Longitudinal tests of gender differences and predictors of change in drug use. *Journal of Counseling Psychology, 35,* 426–438.

Newcomb, M. D., Huba, G. J., & Bentler, P. M. (1986). Life change events among adolescents: An empirical consideration of some methodological issues. *Journal of Nervous and Mental Disease, 174,* 280–289.

Petrie, K., & Chamberlain, K. (1983). Hopelessness and social desirability as moderating variables in predicting suicide behavior. *Journal of Consulting and Clinical Psychology, 51,* 485–487.

Petronis, K. R., Samuels, J. F., Moscicki, E. K., & Anthony, J. C. (1990). An epidemiologic investigation of potential risk factors for suicide attempts. *Social Psychiatry and Psychiatric Epidemiology, 25,* 193–199.

Radloff, L. S. (1977). The CES-D scales: A self-report depression scale for research in the general population. *Applied Psychological Measurement, 1,* 385–401.

Regier, D. A., Farmer, M. E., Rae, D. S., Locke, B. Z., Keith, S. J., Judd, L. L., & Goodwin, F. K. (1990). Comorbidity of mental disorders with alcohol and other drug abuse: Results from the epidemiologic catchment area (ECA) study. *Journal of the American Medical Association, 264,* 2511–2518.

Robbins, C. (1989). Sex differences in psychosocial consequences of alcohol and drug abuse. *Journal of Health and Social Behavior, 30,* 117–130.

Ross, H. E., Glaser, R. B., & Germanson, T. (1988). The prevalence of psychiatric disorders in patients with alcohol and other drug problems. *Archives of General Psychiatry, 45,* 1023–1031.

Rounsaville, B. J., & Kleber, H. D. (1985). Psychotherapy/counseling for opiate addicts: Strategies for use in different treatment settings. *International Journal of the Addictions, 20,* 869–896.

Rounsaville, B. J., Weissman, M. M., Chrits-Christoph, K., Wilber, C., & Kleber, H. (1982). Diagnosis and symptoms of depression in opiate addicts: Course and relationship to treatment outcomes. *Archives of General Psychiatry, 39,* 151–156.

Sadava, S. W., Thistle, R., & Forsythe, R. (1978). Stress, escapism, and patterns of alcohol and drug use. *Journal of Studies on Alcohol, 39,* 725–736.

Scheier, L. M., & Newcomb, M. D. (1993). Multiple dimensions of affective and cognitive disturbance: Latent-variable models in a community sample. *Psychological Assessment, 5,* 230–234.

Shedler, J., & Block, J. (1990). Adolescent drug use and psychological health: A longitudinal inquiry. *American Psychologist, 45,* 612–630.

Sher, K. J., & Levenson, R. W. (1982). Risk for alcoholism and individual differences in the stress-response-dampening effect of alcohol. *Journal of Abnormal Psychology, 91,* 350–367.

Shipley, T. C. (1987). Opponent process theory. In H. T. Blane & K. E. Leonard (Eds.), *Psychological theories of drinking and alcoholism* (pp. 346–387). New York: Guilford Press.

Stacy, A. W., Newcomb, M. D., & Bentler, P. M. (1991a). Cognitive motivation and problem drug use: A nine-year longitudinal study. *Journal of Abnormal Psychology, 100,* 502–515.

Stacy, A. W., Newcomb, M. D., & Bentler, P. M. (1991b). Personality, problem drinking, and drunk driving: Mediating, moderating, and direct-effect models. *Journal of Personality and Social Psychology, 60,* 795–811.

Stacy, A. W., Widaman, K. F., Hays, R., & DiMatteo, M. R. (1985). Validity of self-reports of alcohol and other drug use: A multitrait-multimethod assessment. *Journal of Personality and Social Psychology, 49,* 219–232.

Stein, J. A., Newcomb, M. D., & Bentler, P. M. (1986). Stability and change in personality: A longitudinal study from early adolescence to young adulthood. *Journal of Research in Personality, 20,* 276–291.

Stein, J. A., Newcomb, M. D., & Bentler, P. M. (1987). Personality and drug use: Reciprocal effects across four years. *Personality and Individual Differences, 8,* 419–430.

Tanaka, J. S. (1987) "How big is big enough?": Sample size and goodness of fit in structural equation models with latent variables. *Child Development, 58,* 134–146.

Tanaka, J. S., & Huba, G. J. (1984). Confirmatory hierarchical factor analysis of psychological distress measures. *Journal of Personality and Social Psychology, 46,* 621–635.

Uhlenhuth, E. H., Balter, M. B., Mellinger, G. D., Cisin, I. H., & Clinthorne, J. (1983). Symptom checklist syndromes in the general population: Correlations with psychotherapeutic drug use. *Archives of General Psychiatry, 40,* 1167–1173.

Ward, N. G., & Schuckit, M. A. (1980). Factors associated with suicidal behavior in polydrug abusers. *Journal of Clinical Psychiatry, 41*, 379–385.

Washton, A. M., & Gold, M. S. (1984). Chronic cocaine abuse: Evidence for adverse effects on health and functioning. *Psychiatric Annals, 14*, 733–743.

Weiss, R. D., Mirin, S. M., Griffin, M. L., Michael, J. L., & Sollogub, A. C. (1986). Psychopathology in chronic cocaine abusers. *American Journal of Drug and Alcohol Abuse, 12*, 17–29.

Weissman, M. M., Wickramaratne, P., Merikangas, K. R., Leckman, J. F., Prusoff, B. A., Caruso, K. A., Kidd, K. K., & Gammon, D. (1984). Onset of major depression in early adulthood. *Archives of General Psychiatry, 41*, 1136–1143.

Weng, L.-J., Newcomb, M. D., & Bentler, P. M. (1988). Factors influencing non-completion of high school: A comparison of methodologies. *Educational Research Quarterly, 12*, 8–22.

Wills, T. A. (1985). Stress, coping, and tobacco and alcohol use in early adolescence. In S. Shiffman & T. A. Wills (Eds.), *Coping and substance use* (pp. 67–94). San Diego, CA: Academic Press.

Wise, R. A. (1984). Neural mechanisms of the reinforcing action of cocaine. In J. Grabowski (Ed.), *Cocaine: Pharmacology, effects, and treatment of abuse* (pp. 15–33). Rockville, MD: National Institute on Drug Abuse.

Woody, E. Z., & Costanzo, P. R. (1990). Does marital agony precede marital ecstasy? A comment on Gottman and Krokoff's "Marital Interaction and Satisfaction: A Longitudinal View." *Journal of Consulting and Clinical Psychology, 58*, 499–501.

V

PREVENTION AND HARM REDUCTION

7

RESISTANCE-SKILLS TRAINING AND ONSET OF ALCOHOL USE: EVIDENCE FOR BENEFICIAL AND POTENTIALLY HARMFUL EFFECTS IN PUBLIC SCHOOLS AND IN PRIVATE CATHOLIC SCHOOLS

STEWART I. DONALDSON, JOHN W. GRAHAM,
ANDREA M. PICCININ, AND WILLIAM B. HANSEN

The United States has the highest rate of substance abuse of any industrialized country (see Falco, 1992). Approximately 18 million Americans experience health-related problems as a result of alcohol use (National Institute on Alcohol Abuse and Alcoholism, 1987). Alcohol use is a major risk factor for liver disease, and it is a factor in approximately one

Reprinted from *Health Psychology*, 14, 291–300. (1995). Copyright © 1995 by the American Psychological Association.

This research was supported by National Institute on Alcohol Abuse and Alcoholism Grant R01AA06201. We wish to acknowledge the outstanding work of Gaylene Gunning, Kathie Heller, Mike Hennesy, Bill Howells, Beth Lundy, Dana Mann, Sallye O'Guynn, Jill Pearson, Kelly Rippentrop, Laura Ross, and Bobbie Searl in the completion of various aspects of this project. We also thank the teachers and administrators of the Los Angeles and San Diego County school districts for their invaluable assistance in carrying out this research. Special thanks to Barbara Melamed, Allan Wicker, and Robert Gable for many insightful comments that undoubtedly improved this article.

half of all homicides, suicides, and motor vehicle fatalities (U.S. Department of Health and Human Services [DHHS], 1991).

The social development of millions of children and adolescents is substantially hindered by alcohol and other substance use (Dryfoos, 1991). For example, unwanted pregnancy, delinquency, and school failure are often associated with adolescent substance use (see Hawkins, Catalano, & Miller, 1992). Primary prevention programs are important because the earlier that adolescents start using alcohol and other substances, the more likely it is that they will abuse alcohol and drugs (Robins & Pryzbeck, 1985).

Early efforts (during the 1960s and 1970s) to prevent the onset of alcohol and drug use allegedly failed because they were based on faulty assumptions or flawed program theory (Botvin, 1990; Ellickson, 1993; Falco, 1992); for example, programs relying on scare tactics, moral exhortations, or provision of factual information about drugs, or those based on strategies to enhance an adolescent's character or personality, have generally been shown to be ineffective.

Recent prevention efforts reflect a better understanding of what leads children and adolescents to begin using alcohol and drugs, particularly social pressures. Although the conclusions from reviews of the effectiveness of social influence prevention programs are not entirely consistent, much (but not all) of the evidence is favorable. For example, although Moskowitz (1989) concluded that little evidence exists to support the efficacy of primary prevention programs, meta-analyses have shown consistent positive effects for behavior, attitudes, and knowledge outcomes (e.g., Bangert-Drowns, 1988, mean $ES = .41$, $N = 33$; Rundall & Bruvold, 1988, mean $ES = .27$, $N = 76$; Tobler, 1986, mean $ES = .30$, $N = 98$; see also Lipsey & Wilson, 1993). The most comprehensive review to date revealed that prevention programs based on social influence models that were evaluated in the 1980s had predominantly positive effects (63%), with a few effects being neutral (26%) or negative (11%; Hansen, 1992). However, most prevention programs based on social influence consist of a bundle of strategies whose effects on various populations and under various conditions need to be sorted out (cf. Coie et al., 1993; Flay, 1985; Hansen, 1992, 1993).

SOCIAL INOCULATION THEORY

Social inoculation theory is often used to guide the development of prevention programs (e.g., see Evans, 1983; Evans, Raines, & Hanselka, 1984). This perspective recognizes that as children reach early adolescence, they experience greatly increased vulnerability and mobility, experiment with potential lifestyles, and seek independence (often in the form of rebellion) from adult authority figures (Evans, 1984). An adolescent's decision to drink alcohol or use drugs is believed to depend on his or her ability to resist the often overwhelming situational social pressures common in early adolescence.

Inoculation against the inevitable social influences of early adolescence is the primary focus of resistance-skills training. Adolescents are first taught how to recognize social pressure from peers, older siblings and their friends and associates, and the media. Next they are trained to cope with high-pressure situations by developing social skills to refuse explicit alcohol and drug offers without experiencing negative social consequences (e.g., losing friends, being stereotyped by peers). The development of adequate refusal skills is the main goal of resistance-skills training.

EVALUATIONS OF RESISTANCE-SKILLS TRAINING

Although substance-specific assertiveness (Wills, Baker, & Botvin, 1989) and resistance self-efficacy (Hays & Ellickson, 1990) appear inversely related to substance use, numerous evaluations of the impact to resistance-skills training have failed to show overall program effects (e.g., Dielman, Kloska, Leech, Schulenberg, & Shope, 1992; Hansen & Graham, 1991; Shope, Dielman, Butchart, Campanelli, & Kloska, 1992). Evaluations of the most widely used school-based prevention program in the United States, Project DARE (Drug Abuse Resistance Education), also reveal very small prevention effects (e.g., the ES ranged from .00 to .11 across eight studies, mean $ES = .06$; Ennett, Tobler, Ringwalt, & Flewelling, 1994). Recent theory-driven mediation or process analyses (Donaldson, Graham, & Hansen, 1994) have isolated theory failure not program failure (see Chen, 1990; Donaldson, 1995; Lipsey, 1993), as the reason for null effects. That is, resistance-skills training programs significantly improved adolescents' refusal skills, but refusal skills failed to predict subsequent alcohol, tobacco, and marijuana use.

Some studies suggest that prevention interventions are differentially effective on the basis of participant characteristics (e.g., Ellickson & Bell, 1990; Graham, Johnson, Hansen, Flay, & Gee, 1990; Shope et al., 1992) and that traditional analyses based on all adolescents in a prevention program often fail to detect important effects. Most resistance-skills training programs are based on the assumption that adolescents do not believe alcohol use is acceptable behavior and therefore do not necessarily want to try to begin using alcohol. The problem, according to this perspective, is that they lack the appropriate social skills to refuse offers of alcohol made by their peers, older siblings, and others; in other words, adolescents are not necessarily motivated to begin using alcohol, but they simply do not know how to refuse without experiencing negative social consequences. Therefore, the extent to which adolescents' beliefs about the acceptability of alcohol use moderate the relationship between refusal skills and subsequent alcohol use is one of the main issues examined in this research.

Some data suggest that the failure of resistance-skills training may be due to counterproductive effects or unintended consequences offsetting the benefits of the training (e.g., Donaldson et al., 1994; Graham, Donaldson, Hansen, Rohrbach, & Unger, 1995). For example, adolescents frequently overestimate their peers' use of alcohol and other drugs (see Hansen, 1992). An adolescent's perception of the prevalence of offers of alcohol, cigarettes, and marijuana in his or her school predicts subsequent use of alcohol and drugs and mediates the effects of successful normative education interventions (Donaldson et al., 1994). One potential counterproductive effect of resistance-skills training may be that it increases prevalence estimates: Adolescents receiving resistance-skills training may believe that they are being trained to resist alcohol offers because many such offers are still being made in their school environment.

PRIOR EVALUATIONS OF THE ADOLESCENT ALCOHOL PREVENTION TRIAL

Data from the Adolescent Alcohol Prevention Trial (AAPT), a longitudinal drug prevention trial that examines two social psychology-based strategies for preventing the onset of adolescent alcohol and drug use (described in more detail below), were used to test hypotheses in the present study. Two prior outcome evaluations of the AAPT have been published elsewhere (Donaldson et al., 1994; Hansen & Graham, 1991). These AAPT evaluations, as well as mediation analyses based on the Midwestern Prevention Project (MacKinnon et al., 1991), suggest that social influence prevention programs succeed by enhancing an adolescent's ability to resist passive social pressure (e.g., social modeling and overestimation of peer use), not by teaching resistance skills to combat active social pressure (see Graham, Marks, & Hansen, 1991).

This article probes further the question of why prior evaluations of resistance-skills training have failed to show program effects. Unlike prior AAPT evaluations that have focused on specific subsamples, participant data from all AAPT interventions (fifth grade plus seventh-grade booster and seventh grade only; described in detail below) across all school settings (public schools and private Catholic schools) were available for us to test hypotheses in this research.

HYPOTHESES

An assumption of social inoculation theory is that adolescents are not motivated to begin using alcohol but that they lack the appropriate social skills to refuse it. Refusal skills may, therefore, predict subsequent alcohol use only when adolescents believe that drinking is inappropriate. Hypothesis 1, therefore, was that seventh-grade refusal skills would significantly predict eighth-grade alcohol use for those adolescents who believe it is inappropriate for adolescents to drink alcohol but not for those adolescents who believe it is acceptable for adolescents to drink alcohol.

Teaching adolescents the necessary skills to refuse alcohol and drug offers, in the absence of normative education curricula, may send them a counterproductive message. That is, they may come to believe that the reason they are being taught how to refuse offers of alcohol and drugs is that offers are or soon will be prevalent in their school environment. Because beliefs about prevalence predict the onset of alcohol and drug use, this unintended consequence of resistance-skills training could represent a counterproductive effect that offsets any beneficial effects of resistance training. Hypothesis 2 was that resistance-skills training would increase adolescents' beliefs about the prevalence of alcohol, cigarette, and marijuana offers.

METHOD

Participants

Participants were 11,995 students (53% female and 47% male; 45.3% European American, 37.4% Hispanic, 12.6% Asian, 3% African American, and 1.7% other ethnic groups) from 130 school units (52% attending public schools and 48% attending private Catholic schools) in Los Angeles and San Diego County who received one of four Adolescent Alcohol Prevention Trial (AAPT) curricula. Each analysis presented in this article is based on a subsample of the AAPT participants. The criteria used to select subsamples are described below.

Adolescent Alcohol Prevention Trial

Although other researchers have looked at the effectiveness of drug prevention programs that target both active and passive forms of social influence, a unique feature of the AAPT design was that it allowed for the separate examination of the effects of each program component. That is, the AAPT was designed to examine the active ingredients in social influence-based adolescent drug prevention programs. We accomplished

TABLE 1
The Adolescent Alcohol Prevention Trial 2 × 2 Factorial Design

Resistance training	Normative education	
	No	Yes
No	Informative only	Information + normative education
Yes	Information + resistance training	Information + resistance training + normative education

this by randomly assigning school units to one of four experimental conditions: (a) information about consequences of use (information only), (b) resistance training (resistance-skills training + information about consequences of use), (c) normative education (normative education + information about consequences of use), and (d) the combined condition (resistance-skills training + normative education + information about consequences of use). Table 1 summarizes this 2 × 2 factorial design.

Experimental Design

We divided elementary and junior high schools into 130 independent school units, which were based on junior high school feeder patterns and geographical considerations. Using a procedure designed to maximize pretest comparability on relevant measures (Graham, Flay, Johnson, Hansen, & Collins, 1984), we randomly assigned the 130 school units to one of the four experimental conditions. Approximately 62% of the participants received the main version of one of the programs (i.e., conditions) in fifth grade and a follow-up booster program in seventh grade (all seventh-grade booster programs were condensed versions that emphasized the main issues presented during the original program). The remaining 38% of the participants received the main version of one of the programs in seventh grade only. The main programs are described below.

Information Only

Condition 1, information only, consisted of four 45-min lessons about health and the social consequences of using alcohol and other drugs. All of the interventions implemented in this study were developed at a time when providing information about the consequences of use was considered a standard school-based approach for preventing alcohol and drug use onset. Therefore, the information-only condition served as a standard-treatment comparison group (i.e., a treatment-as-usual control group).

Resistance Training

Condition 2, resistance training, was designed to teach adolescents how to refuse explicit drug offers in a socially acceptable manner. Resistance training consisted of four lessons about consequences of using substances and five lessons that help students identify and resist (i.e., refusal skills) pressure by peers and advertisements to use alcohol and other substances. For example, resistance-training curricula included lessons covering the types of social pressure (e.g., friendly, teasing, threats, tricks, dares, lies, and silent pressure), techniques to say "no," assertiveness and refusal practice, reports of personal resistance experiences, and parent–child interviews about peer and media pressure. Student commitments to resist pressure to drink alcohol were videotaped (a detailed description of AAPT curricula is provided in Hansen, Graham, Wolkenstein, & Rohrbach, 1991).

Normative Education

The theoretical basis for developing normative education can be traced back to the attitude–belief theory of Ajzen and Fishbein (1973), the problem behavior theory of Jessor and Jessor (1977) as applied to the social cultural model, and social cognitive–learning theory (Bandura, 1977, 1986). In short, beliefs about the prevalence and acceptability of alcohol and drug use by adolescents' peers have been shown to be substantial risk factors for the onset of adolescent alcohol and drug use. Normative education curricula are designed specifically to combat the influence of passive social pressures (e.g., social modeling and overestimation of adolescent alcohol and drug use; see Graham et al., 1991).

Condition 3, normative education, included four lessons about consequences and five lessons that corrected erroneous perceptions of prevalence and acceptability of alcohol and drug use among peers and established a conservative normative school climate regarding substance use. Sample lessons include a survey and discussion about the prevalence of alcohol use among students, an exercise on class opinions about alcohol use, homework to interview a parent about appropriate and inappropriate uses of alcohol, a class discussion of appropriate and inappropriate uses of alcohol, homework to interview a nondrinker, a lesson on developing positive friendships that include nondrinking as a positive quality, and videotaped alcohol rap songs and personal opinion statements (see Hansen et al., 1991).

The Combined Condition

Condition 4, the combined condition, included three lessons about the consequences of use, three-and-one-half lessons teaching resistance skills, and three-and-one-half lessons establishing conservative norms (see Hansen et al., 1991).

Measures

Alcohol Use

The main dependent variable used to test the first hypothesis was recent alcohol use. An alcohol-use index was created that consisted of three items. The first two items were "How many drinks of alcohol have you had in the past month?" and "... in the past week?" Response categories for these alcohol use items were as follows: 1 = *none or only sips for religious service*, 2 = *only sips (not for religious service)*, 3 = *part or all of one drink*, 4 = *2 to 4*, 5 = *5 to 10*, 6 = *11 to 20*, 7 = *21 to 100*, and 8 = *more than 100*. The third item was "How many days in the last month (30 days) have you had alcohol to drink?" The response categories were as follows: 1 = *none*, 2 = *1*, 3 = *2 or 3*, 4 = *4 to 7*, 5 = *8 to 14*, and 6 = *15 to 30*. Alcohol-use measures taken prior to the interventions (main or boosters) at seventh grade (pretest) and 1 year later in the eighth grade (posttest) were used in the present study. The three alcohol-use items were standardized ($M = 0$, $SD = 1$) and averaged separately for the participants in the fifth- versus seventh-grade interventions. Alpha coefficients for each scale were good: for seventh-grade alcohol use $\alpha = .88$ and for eighth-grade alcohol use $\alpha = .90$. The reliability of a similar set of items used in a comparable sample has also been reported elsewhere to be very good (Graham, Flay, Johnson, Hansen, Grossman, & Sobel, 1984).

Refusal Skills

Refusal skills were measured by a behavioral assessment procedure described in some detail by Graham, Rohrbach, Hansen, Flay, and Johnson (1989) and Rohrbach, Graham, Hansen, Flay, and Johnson (1987). Approximately one third of the AAPT participants were randomly selected to complete the behavioral assessment procedure. Participants were removed from their classrooms one at a time. A same-sex classmate (previously trained) then role-played a persistent offer of alcohol to the participant. Each participant's response was observed by (a) two classmates (the offerer and another student observer of the opposite sex), (b) two adult data collectors, and (c) the actual participant. After the role-playing, each of the observers completed a questionnaire about the participant's performance. Several items assessed the skill with which the offer was rejected. These items included ratings of amount of eye contact, loudness of voice, and posture. There were also two general items asking how well the student stood up for him- or herself and how well the student resisted the offer of alcohol. In the present study, we measured the refusal skills of seventh-graders by the standardized average of (a) the standardized average of the classmates' ratings, (b) the standardized average of the adult data collectors' ratings, and (c) the standardized average of the self-reports, collected after the programs in seventh grade. Coefficient alpha was .60 for the three independent assessments (peer, adult data collectors, and self-reports) of refusal skills in the present study.

Alcohol-Use Acceptability

Prior to the seventh-grade interventions (including boosters) the participants completed a pretest questionnaire. This instrument contained two scenarios of adolescent alcohol use (in the first scenario the user was 14 years old, and in the second, 17 years old). Participants indicated whether or not they believed it was acceptable for the character in each scenario to drink alcohol. In addition, they were asked "Do you think it is OK for people your age to drink alcohol every now and then (do not count alcohol at a religious service)?" Response categories for this item were as follows: 1 = *definitely yes*, 2 = *mostly yes*, 3 = *mostly no*, 4 = *definitely no*. Participants answering "definitely yes," "mostly yes," or "mostly no" to any of these questions were classified as believing it was acceptable for adolescents to drink alcohol (*OK to drink alcohol* = 1). Participants answering "definitely no" to all of the questions were classified as believing it was not acceptable for adolescents to drink alcohol (*OK to drink alcohol* = −1).

Perceived Prevalence of Offers

A process questionnaire was administered immediately after the implementation of the main and booster versions of the seventh-grade programs. The process questionnaire contained questions that assessed the participants' beliefs about the prevalence of alcohol, cigarette, and marijuana offers at their school. Three items answered in seventh grade were used to measure the participants' beliefs about the prevalence of offers at their school: "A lot of people in my school offer alcoholic drinks to their friends," "A lot of people who go to my school offer cigarettes to their friends," and "A lot of people who go to my school offer marijuana to their friends." Response categories for the items were as follows: 1 = *strongly disagree*, 2 = *disagree*, 3 = *agree*, and 4 = *strongly agree*. These three items were standardized and averaged. The alcohol-offers item was also analyzed separately.

Data Analysis

Two program group membership variables were dummy-coded as follows. Participants receiving resistance training were assigned a 1 for the variable resistance training. Those who did not receive resistance training were assigned a −1. Participants receiving normative education received a 1 for the variable normative education. Those who did not receive normative education received a −1. The Resistance Training × Normative

Education interaction term was constructed by multiplying the variables resistance training and normative education.

Both hypotheses were tested separately for those adolescents who received interventions in fifth grade followed by a booster program in seventh grade versus those who received interventions in seventh grade only. Furthermore, prior research established that adolescents attending public school report substantially higher prevalence of alcohol and drug offers in their schools than those attending private Catholic schools (Donaldson et al., 1994). Therefore, we also examined the effects of resistance training on prevalence estimates of drug and alcohol offers (i.e., Hypothesis 2) separately for adolescents attending public schools versus private Catholic schools.

Test of Hypothesis 1

We conducted prospective analyses assessing the extent to which alcohol use among eighth-grade students was predicted by their refusal skills measured in seventh-grade (a) for adolescents who believed it was acceptable to drink alcohol, and (b) for adolescents who believed it was not acceptable to drink alcohol. The Refusal Skills × Alcohol-Use Acceptability interaction was also examined. Six latent variable structural equation models (three for the fifth-grade interventions, and three for the seventh-grade interventions) were analyzed using LISREL VII (see Jöreskog & Sörbom, 1989). Gender, ethnicity (European American vs. other), type of school (public vs. private), seventh-grade alcohol use (pretest), resistance training, normative education, and the Resistance Training × Normative Education interaction were controlled for in each analysis. Seventh-grade alcohol use (the covariate), refusal skills, and eighth-grade alcohol use were modeled as latent constructs, whereas the program variables and demographic controls were single-item manifest indicators. One of the primary advantages of conducting latent variable analyses (vs. standard hierarchical regression) is that findings are not attenuated by measurement error.

As described above, only a randomly selected one third of the participants completed the behavioral assessment procedure. Therefore, analyses involving seventh-grade refusal skills are based on approximately one third of the AAPT participants. All of the analyses reported in this article are based on the participants who had data available for the variables of interest in each analysis.

Test of Hypothesis 2

The hypothesis that training in resistance skills increases prevalence estimates was examined using an analysis of covariance (ANCOVA) in combination with three specific, a priori, orthogonal contrasts. First, in order to determine if the four program conditions had a differential impact on seventh-grade students' estimates of the prevalence of offers, the Resistance Training × Normative Education interaction was examined. Gender, ethnicity, and seventh-grade alcohol use (pretest) were controlled for, and separate analyses were conducted for, those in the fifth-grade versus seventh-grade interventions. Furthermore, because prior analyses have discovered large differences in absolute prevalence estimates across school settings (e.g., Donaldson et al., 1994), each analysis was also done separately for those attending the public schools versus private Catholic schools.

Second, after adjusting for the control variables, we performed three orthogonal contrasts to understand specific differences in prevalence estimates among the four experimental program conditions. The contrasts included (a) resistance training versus all of the other programs (i.e., information only, normative education, and the combined condition), which directly tests Hypothesis 2; (b) combined condition versus normative education and information only, which assesses the effect of providing both resistance training and normative education; and (c) normative education versus information only, which examines how the program designed to affect prevalence estimates (i.e., normative education) compares with the standard treatment-as-usual control group (i.e., information only).

From a conceptual standpoint, we were interested in how adolescents in the various conditions perceived the prevalence of drug offers in their school environments. Because the unit of assignment was the school unit (described earlier in this section), analyses at the individual level are essentially based on quasi-experimental data. One strategy for retaining the experimental aspect of the design, often used when statistical power is inadequate, is to statistically correct for the intraclass correlation using multilevel or hierarchial linear modeling techniques (e.g., see Aitkin & Longford, 1986; Bryk & Raudenbush, 1987; Kreft, 1994). However, the most conservative and intuitively interpretable experimental analysis, school-level analysis, also allows the researcher to rule out the possibility that individual-level findings are simply due to a high intraclass correlation. Therefore, school units receiving the fifth- and seventh-grade interventions were combined, and the analysis was repeated using an aggregate measure (school level) of prevalence of drug offers. The school-level analysis was conducted separately for the public schools and private Catholic schools.

RESULTS

Alcohol Use

Fifth-Grade Interventions

There was a significant inverse relationship between seventh-grade refusal skills and eighth-grade alcohol use ($b = -.21$, $SE = .10$, $p < .05$)

for the adolescents participating in the fifth-grade interventions who believed that it was not acceptable to drink (n = 495). The same analysis for adolescents who believed that it was acceptable to drink (n = 346) revealed a positive but nonsignificant relationship between seventh-grade refusal skills and eighth-grade alcohol use (b = .09, SE = .08, ns). Furthermore, there was a significant Refusal Skills × Alcohol Use Acceptability interaction (b = .06, SE = .03, p < .05) for the adolescents participating in the fifth-grade interventions. A summary of the results, including model fit indices for each analysis, is displayed in Table 2.

Seventh-Grade Interventions

There was a significant inverse relationship between seventh-grade refusal skills and eighth-grade alcohol use (b = −.14, SE = .05, p < .01) for those adolescents participating in the seventh-grade-only interventions who believed that it was not acceptable to drink (n = 573). For adolescents who believed that it was acceptable to drink (n = 377), there was not a significant relationship between seventh-grade refusal skills and eighth-grade alcohol use (b = .001, SE = .07, ns). However, the Refusal Skills × Alcohol Use Acceptability interaction was not statistically significant (b = .02, SE = .03, ns) for those adolescents participating in the seventh-grade interventions (see Table 2).

TABLE 2
Summary of LISREL Analyses Using Seventh-Grade Refusal Skills to
Predict Eighth-Grade Alcohol Use

Analysis	N	b	SE	t	GFI	RMSR	ρ
Fifth-grade interventions							
Adolescents believing it is okay to drink	346	.087	.079	1.10	.963	.055	.962
Adolescents believing it is not okay to drink	495	−.206	.100	−2.04*	.966	.050	.939
Refusal Skills × Okay to Drink interaction	841	.062	.028	2.23*	.980	.041	.959
Seventh-grade interventions							
Adolescents believing it is okay to drink	377	.001	.070	0.01	.976	.048	.995
Adolescents believing it is not okay to drink	573	−.140	.050	−2.52**	.972	.053	.960
Refusal Skills × Okay to Drink interaction	950	.015	.027	0.55	.989	.039	.989

Note. GFI = goodness-of-fit index, RMSR = root mean square residual.
*p < .05. **p < .01.

Perceived Prevalence of Offers

Public Schools

There was a significant Resistance Training × Normative Education interaction on seventh graders' estimates of the prevalence of drug and alcohol offers for adolescents participating in the fifth-grade interventions (drug offers, $F[1, 914] = 14.36, p < .01$; alcohol offers, $F[1, 2185] = 20.08, p < .01$) and for those participating in the seventh-grade interventions (drug offers, $F[1,914] = 16.90, p < .01$; alcohol offers, $F[1, 925] = 10.77, p < .01$). The follow-up contrast of resistance training with the other programs showed that adolescents who received resistance training had significantly higher prevalence estimates of drug offers (fifth-grade interventions, $F[1, 2135] = 18.49, p < .01$; seventh-grade interventions, $F[1, 914] = 21.20, p < .01$) and alcohol offers (fifth-grade interventions, $F[1, 2185] = 20.83, p < .01$; seventh-grade interventions, $F[1, 925] = 20.71, p < .01$) than adolescents receiving the other curricula. Furthermore, those adolescents receiving both resistance training and normative education (the combined condition) had significantly lower prevalence estimates of drug offers (fifth-grade interventions, $F[1, 2135] = 8.69, p < .01$; seventh-grade interventions, $F[1, 914] = 9.55, p < .01$) and alcohol offers (fifth-grade interventions, $F[1, 2185] = 8.56, p < .01$; seventh-grade interventions, $F[1, 925] = 7.25, p < .01$) than adolescents in the normative education and information-only conditions. The difference in prevalence estimates between the normative education and information-only conditions was not significant. A summary of these findings is displayed in Tables 3 and 4.

Private Catholic Schools

There was also a significant Resistance Training × Normative Education interaction on perceived prevalence of drug and alcohol offers for adolescents participating in the fifth-grade interventions (drug offers, $F[1, 1242] = 7.67, p < .01$; alcohol offers, $F[1, 1253] = 11.71, p < .01$) and seventh-grade interventions (drug offers, $F[1, 1632] = 9.54, p < .01$; alcohol offers, $F[1, 1647] = 11.94, p < .01$) delivered in the private Catholic schools. However, the pattern of results found in the private Catholic schools differed from the pattern described for the public schools.

The contrast of resistance training with other programs was not significant for those adolescents in the fifth-grade interventions who were attending private Catholic schools. This finding was mainly due to high prevalence estimates in the information-only condition, not a substantially different pattern of results (i.e., the combined and normative education conditions still had the lowest prevalence estimates). However, for Catholic school adolescents participating in the seventh-grade interventions, resistance-training participants had significantly lower prevalence-of-offers

TABLE 3
Effects of Resistance-Skills Training on Estimates of Drug Offers

Experimental conditions	Fifth-grade interventions								Seventh-grade interventions							
	Public school students (n = 2,142)				Private school students (n = 1,249)				Public school students (n = 921)				Private school students (n = 1,639)			
	M	SD	F	df	M	SD	F	df	M	SD	F	df	M	SD	F	df
Interaction tests																
Resistance Training × Normative Education interaction			14.36**	(1, 2135)			7.67**	(1, 1242)			16.90**	(1, 914)			9.54**	(1, 1632)
Resistance training	.17	.04			.08	.06			.23	.06			−.16	.05		
Normative education	.01	.04			−.22	.06			.01	.07			.00	.05		
Combined condition	−.15	.04			−.15	.06			−.27	.07			−.01	.04		
Information only	.00	.05			.31	.06			−.03	.06			.15	.05		
Orthogonal contrasts																
Resistance training versus all other programs			18.49**	(1, 2135)			2.48	(1, 1242)			21.20**	(1, 914)			12.85**	(1, 1632)
Other programs	−.05	.04			−.03	.05			−.10	.07			.05	.05		
Combined condition versus normative education + information only			8.69**	(1, 2135)			8.84**	(1, 1242)			9.55**	(1, 914)			2.21	(1, 1632)
Normative education + information only	.00	.04			−.05	.06			−.02	.06			.08	.05		
Normative education versus information only			0.02	(1, 2135)			43.67**	(1, 1242)			.18	(1, 914)			4.42*	(1, 1632)

*$p < .05.$ **$p < .01.$

TABLE 4
Effects of Resistance-Skills Training on Estimates of Alcohol Offers

Experimental conditions	Fifth-grade interventions								Seventh-grade interventions							
	Public school students (n = 2,192)				Private school students (n = 1,260)				Public school students (n = 932)				Private school students (n = 1,654)			
	M	SD	F	df	M	SD	F	df	M	SD	F	df	M	SD	F	df
Interaction tests																
Resistance Training × Normative Education interaction			20.08**	(1, 2185)			11.71**	(1, 1253)			10.77**	(1, 925)			11.94**	(1, 1647)
Resistance training	.14	.04			.04	.04			.17	.05			−.10	.04		
Normative education	.02	.03			−.17	.04			−.04	.06			−.04	.03		
Combined condition	−.12	.03			−.12	.04			−.19	.05			.01	.03		
Information only	−.13	.04			.28	.04			.00	.05			.11	.04		
Orthogonal contrasts																
Resistance training versus all other programs			20.83**	(1, 2185)			.82	(1, 1253)			20.71**	(1, 925)			8.31**	(1, 1647)
Other programs	−.04	.03			−.01	.04			−.07	.05			.03	.04		
Combined condition versus normative education + information only			8.56**	(1, 2185)			11.55**	(1, 1253)			7.25**	(1, 925)			.29	(1, 1647)
Normative education + information only	.00	.03			.06	.04			−.02	.05			.04	.04		
Normative education versus information only			0.80	(1, 2185)			51.63**	(1, 1253)			0.21	(1, 925)			7.14**	(1, 1647)

** p < .01.

RESISTANCE SKILLS AND ALCOHOL USE   229

estimates than those participating in the other programs (drug offers, $F[1, 1632] = 12.85$, $p < .01$; alcohol offers, $F[1, 1647] = 8.31$, $p < .01$). The combined condition versus normative education plus information only contrast was significant for the fifth-grade interventions (drug offers, $F[1, 1242] = 8.84$, $p < .01$; alcohol offers, $F[1, 1253] = 11.55$, $p < .01$), but not for the seventh-grade interventions. Furthermore, those adolescents receiving normative education had significantly lower prevalence estimates than those receiving information only (fifth-grade interventions, drug offers, $F[1, 1242] = 43.67$, $p < .01$, alcohol offers, $F[1, 1253] = 51.63$, $p < .01$; seventh-grade interventions, drug offers, $F[1, 1632] = 4.42$, $p < .05$, alcohol offers, $F[1, 1647] = 7.14$, $p < .01$; see Tables 3 and 4).

School-Level Analysis

The pattern of results was very similar at the school level of analysis. For the public schools ($n = 73$ school units), there was a significant Resistance Training $\times$ Normative Education interaction for the aggregate measure of prevalence of drug offers, $F(1, 68) = 5.89$, $p < .05$. The public schools that received resistance training had significantly higher prevalence estimates than all of the other public schools combined, $F(1, 68) = 8.73$, $p < .01$. Furthermore, the public schools receiving the combined condition interventions had significantly lower prevalence estimates than those receiving normative education and information only, $F(1, 68) = 4.81$, $p < .05$.

For the private Catholic schools ($n = 57$ school units), the Resistance Training $\times$ Normative Education interaction was not statistically significant. However, as was demonstrated across the fifth- and seventh-grade interventions at the individual level of analysis, normative education schools had significantly lower prevalence estimates than information-only schools, $F(1, 52) = 16.54$, $p < .01$.

DISCUSSION

In contrast with other recent work, the present findings indicate that resistance-skills training may effectively delay the onset of alcohol use when adolescents believe it is not acceptable to drink. For adolescents who did not meet this basic assumption of social inoculation theory, refusal skills did not predict subsequent alcohol use. This finding was consistent across fifth- and seventh-grade interventions and provides at least one reason why previous research on resistance training reveals either very small (Ennent et al., 1994) or no overall program effects (see Dielman et al., 1992; Donaldson et al., 1994; Hansen & Graham, 1991; Shope et al., 1992).

The potentially harmful effect examined in this research was that resistance-skills training increases estimates of alcohol, cigarette, and marijuana offers. Rather convincing evidence supported this hypothesis for adolescents attending public school but not for those attending private Catholic school. Public school students who received the resistance-training condition reported significantly higher levels of alcohol and drug offers than did all of the other conditions combined, regardless of whether they received the intervention of the fifth or seventh grade. However, when resistance-skills training was delivered in combination with normative education (i.e., the combined condition), the harmful effect did not occur. In fact, adolescents receiving the combined program report significantly lower prevalence estimates than those receiving normative education or information only. These findings further underscore the importance of the need for participants' beliefs to concur with basic program assumptions. That is, it appears that resistance training may be an effective strategy in public schools as long as adolescent beliefs about the acceptability and prevalence of use and offers are conservative.

The resistance-training condition did not significantly increase prevalence estimates for those attending private Catholic school. For those in the fifth-grade interventions, the pattern of prevalence estimates was in line with what was expected. Adolescents receiving normative education and the combined program reported the lowest prevalence estimates. Although the pattern for the adolescents receiving the seventh-grade interventions was somewhat similar to the pattern found for those in the fifth-grade interventions, the differences between conditions were noticeably smaller for those participating in the seventh-grade interventions. Generally speaking, the results suggest, first, that normative education interventions delivered in private Catholic schools may be more effective when delivered in fifth grade as opposed to seventh grade, at least with respect to correcting misperceptions of the prevalence of alcohol and drug offers, and, second, that resistance training does not have the same harmful effect in the private Catholic schools as it does in public schools.

The absolute level of prevalence estimates was much higher for those attending public school than it was for those attending private Catholic school (Donaldson et al., 1994). Generally, the public schools studied were much larger and had a much more diverse student body (probably including many more adolescents who exhibited problem behaviors, such as smoking). For example, the average number of seventh-grade students in the public schools was 252 ($SD = 45$) versus 39 ($SD = 13$) for the private Catholic schools. Thus, the public school students probably had much less information about total peer prevalence of offers and use than those attending the much smaller and more homogeneous private Catholic schools. Adolescents in the public schools also reported significantly higher levels of eighth-grade cigarette and marijuana use, but there was not a significant difference in eighth-grade alcohol use.

The results of this study suggest that in environments with potentially high levels of drug and alcohol use and offers (e.g., many of the public schools studied), providing resistance-skills training programs alone may send the wrong message. This finding is especially important because many programs implemented in public schools today rely primarily, and in some cases exclusively, on resistance-skills training or "just say no" strategies.

Strengths and Limitations

One major strength of this investigation is that the hypotheses about beneficial and counterproductive effects of resistance-skills training were tested in the context of a large experimental prevention trial. This enabled us to examine the hypotheses (with reasonable levels of statistical power) under a variety of conditions, for important subgroups of adolescents, and, where appropriate, at both the individual and school levels of analysis. Below, several limitations associated with the hypothesis tests are discussed.

It is important to note that our prospective analyses predicting eighth-grade alcohol use with seventh-grade refusal skills are not based on experimental data. That is, we demonstrated only that a subgroup of adolescents who had good resistance skills in seventh grade tended to have lower alcohol use in eighth grade. Furthermore, because the unit of random assignment was the school unit, analyses of the effects of resistance training on prevalence estimates at the individual level are essentially based on quasi-experimental data. However, analyses conducted at the experimental level (i.e., the school unit) revealed virtually the same pattern of results and, thus, rule out the possibility that the intraclass correlation alone accounts for the findings.

Although the number of sessions across the four experimental conditions in the AAPT was not equal, prior evaluations have demonstrated convincingly that unequal sessions alone do not explain program effects (see, e.g., Hansen & Graham, 1991). The results of the prevalence-estimate analyses presented in this study further illustrate the implausibility of this rival hypothesis.

The dependent measures (i.e., eighth-grade alcohol use and seventh-grade prevalence estimates) were based on only one method of measurement (self-reports). Although we (e.g., Donaldson et al., 1994; Graham, Flay, Johnson, Hansen, Grossman, & Sobel, 1984; Graham et al., 1990, 1991) and others (Biglan, Gallison, Ary, & Thompson, 1985; Pechacek, Murray, Luepker, Mittlemark, & Johnson, 1984) have found evidence for the validity and reliability of the type of items used in this investigation, caution should always be used when interpreting analyses based on only one method of the measurement (Donaldson, 1995; Graham, Collins, Donaldson, & Hansen, 1993).

Finally, the hypotheses were tested using data from the AAPT participants who had complete information available on the variables of interest. This raises the following questions: (a) Do the findings generalize to U.S. adolescents and (b) do the findings generalize to those adolescents participating in the AAPT who had incomplete data? First, neither hypothesis test was based on a random sample of U.S. adolescents. This is a common limitation of large-scale experimental studies conducted in field settings. Second, generalizations about findings of the AAPT must obviously take into account the characteristics of the schools and adolescents who were selected for the study.

For those participating in the AAPT, data were missing primarily for one of three reasons: (a) planned missing data, (b) internal omissions, and (c) attrition. Refusal skills were assessed on a randomly selected one third of the participants (i.e., planned missing data). Therefore, the missing data mechanism is random and should not compromise the generalizability of the findings (Graham & Donaldson, 1993). Graham, Hofer, and Piccinin (1994) have shown that data missing because of internal omissions are likely to be caused by either a random or an accessible missing data mechanism (i.e., measured and accounted for in the analysis) and are not likely to bias the type of ANCOVA analyses conducted in this study. However, data missing because of attrition are more problematic and require more complex analyses.

Approximately 80% of the original sample of AAPT participants completed the eighth-grade posttest questionnaires. Hansen, Tobler, and Graham (1990) found that differential attrition in drug prevention interventions most often causes researchers to underestimate program effects. Although we conducted traditional attrition analyses (see Hansen, Collins, Malotte, Johnson, & Fielding, 1985) and failed to discover problems caused by differential attrition in this study, recent work suggests that these tests may not always be adequate to rule out attrition bias (Graham & Donaldson, 1993). A more rigorous approach for understanding the effects of attrition involves modeling the missing data mechanism or the reasons why participants drop out. Simply stated, attrition does not bias results if the missing data mechanism is either random or measured and is included in the analyses. Recent work tracking and analyzing the AAPT participants who were originally missing at posttest has revealed that only 5%–10% appear to be missing because of alcohol- and drug-related reasons, and suggests that the problem of attrition bias in prevention intervention research may be overstated (Graham, Donaldson, Hansen, & Hofer, 1994). However, the external validity of the findings presented in this article must be viewed in light of data missing because of participant attrition.

Implications and Conclusion

The results of this investigation have direct implications for future prevention programming. Prevention programs that use resistance-skills training should attempt to create or reinforce conservative beliefs about the prevalence and acceptability of adolescents' use of alcohol, cigarettes, and marijuana. As shown in this investigation, teaching active resistance skills in combination with normative education appears to be an effective prevention strategy.

This study also has implications for the evaluation of future prevention programs. Most prevention programs include multiple strategies for preventing adolescent substance abuse. The phenomena under investigation are typically complex, multidimensional, context dependent, and contingent on multiple factors. Although the simple "black-box" experimental approach (i.e., summative evaluations of a treatment group vs. control group) used to evaluate most programs is reasonable for interventions that are less complex and unidimensional and produce direct and immediate effects (e.g., chemotherapy, such as lithium for depression or aspirin for headache), they do not accurately represent the complexity of most interventions for substance-use prevention (see Donaldson et al., 1994; Hansen, 1993; Lipsey, 1988). That is, they leave us in the dark about the mechanisms through which prevention efforts succeed or fail and typically do not inform us about for whom and under what conditions specific components of a program work best.

Preventing alcohol and drug abuse is obviously very challenging, but an extremely worthwhile investment of professional time. An understanding of the basic social psychological processes underlying the onset of use, and its prevention, is critical for developing a generalizable knowledge base that can be used to consistently design successful programs. Although this research is, admittedly, only a small step toward understanding the complexity of social influence-based prevention programming, the findings illustrate the value of systematically investigating why (or the processes through which effects occur), for whom, and under what conditions specific strategies delay, or fail to delay, the onset of adolescent alcohol and drug use.

REFERENCES

Aitkin, M. A., & Longford, N. (1986). Statistical modeling in school effectiveness studies. *Journal of the Royal Statistical Society, 149A*, 1–43.

Ajzen, I., & Fishbein, M. (1973). Attitudinal and normative variables as predictors of specific behaviors. *Journal of Personality and Social Psychology, 27*, 41–57.

Bandura, A. (1977). *Social learning theory*. Englewood Cliffs, NJ: Prentice Hall.

Bandura, A. (1986). *Social foundations of thought and action: A social cognitive theory*. Englewood Cliffs, NJ: Prentice Hall.

Bangert-Drowns, R. L. (1988). The effects of school-based substance use education—A meta-analysis. *Journal of Drug Education, 18*, 243–264.

Biglan, A., Gallison, C., Ary, D., & Thompson, R. (1985). Expired air carbon monoxide and saliva thiocyanate: Relationships to self-reports of marijuana and cigarette smoking. *Addictive Behaviors, 10,* 137–144.

Botvin, G. J. (1990). Substance abuse prevention: Theory, practice, and effectiveness. In M. Tonry & J. Q. Wilson (Eds.), *Drugs and crime* (pp. 461–519). Chicago: University of Chicago Press.

Bryk, A. S., & Raudenbush, S. W. (1987). Applying Hierarchical Linear Model to measurements of change problems. *Psychological Bulletin, 101,* 147–158.

Chen, H. T. (1990). *Theory-driven evaluations.* Newbury Park, CA: Sage.

Coie, J. D., Watt, L. F., West, S. G., Hawkins, J. D., Asarnow, J. R., Markman, H. J., Ramey, S. L., Shure, M. B., & Long, B. (1993). The science of prevention: A conceptual framework and some directions for a national research program. *American Psychologist, 48,* 1013–1022.

Dielman, T. E., Kloska, D. D., Leech, S. L., Schulenberg, J. E., & Shope, J. T. (1992). Susceptibility to peer pressure as an explanatory variable for the differential effectiveness of an alcohol misuse prevention program in elementary schools. *Journal of School Health, 62,* 233–237.

Donaldson, S. I. (1995). Worksite health promotion: A theory-driven empirically based perspective. In G. P. Keita & S. L. Sauter (Eds.), *Job stress intervention: Current practices and new directions.* Washington, DC: American Psychological Association.

Donaldson, S. I., Graham, J. W., & Hansen, W. B. (1994). Testing the generalizability of intervening mechanism theories: Understanding the effects of adolescent drug use prevention interventions. *Journal of Behavioral Medicine, 17,* 195–216.

Dryfoos, J. G. (1991). *Adolescents at risk: Prevalence and prevention.* New York: Oxford University Press.

Ellickson, P. L. (1993). School-based drug prevention: What should it do? What has to be done? In R. Coombs & D. Ziedonis (Eds.), *Handbook of drug abuse prevention* (pp. 93–120). Englewood Cliffs, NJ: Prentice Hall.

Ellickson, P. L., & Bell, R. M. (1990). Drug prevention in junior high school: A multisite longitudinal test. *Science, 247,* 1299–1305.

Ennett, S. T., Tobler, N. S., Ringwalt, C. L., & Flewelling, R. L. (1994). How effective is drug abuse resistance education? A meta-analysis of project DARE outcome evaluations. *American Journal of Public Health, 84,* 1394–1401.

Evans, R. I. (1983). Deterring smoking in adolescents: Evolution of a research program in applied social psychology. *International Review of Applied Psychology, 32,* 71–83.

Evans, R. I. (1984). A social inoculation strategy to deter smoking in adolescents. In J. D. Matarazzo, S. M. Weiss, J. A. Herd, N. E. Miller, & S. M. Weiss (Eds.), *Behavioral health: A handbook of health enhancement and disease prevention* (pp. 765–774). New York: Wiley.

Evans, R. I., Raines, B. E., & Hanselka, L. (1984). Developing data-based communications in social psychological research: Adolescent smoking prevention. *Journal of Applied Social Psychology, 14,* 289–295.

Falco, M. (1992). *The making of a drug-free America: Programs that work.* New York: Random House.

Flay, B. R. (1985). Psychosocial approaches to smoking prevention: A review of findings. *Health Psychology, 4,* 449–488.

Graham, J. W., Collins, N. L., Donaldson, S. I., & Hansen, W. B. (1993). Understanding and controlling for response bias: Confirmatory factor analysis of multitrait–multimethod data. In R. Steyer, K. F. Wender, & K. F. Widamen (Eds.), *Psychometric methodology: Proceedings of the 7th European Meeting of the Psychometric Society in Trier* (pp. 585–590). New York: Verlag.

Graham, J. W., & Donaldson, S. I. (1993). Evaluating interventions with differential attrition: The importance of nonresponse mechanisms and use of follow-up data. *Journal of Applied Psychology, 78,* 119–128.

Graham, J. W., Donaldson, S. I., Hansen, W. B., & Hofer, S. M. (1994). *Attrition in prevention research. How big a problem?* Unpublished manuscript.

Graham, J. W., Donaldson, S. I., Hansen, W. B., Rohrbach, L. A., & Unger, J. (1995). *Tracing the process of longitudinal prevention program effects with hierarchical data and complex missing data patterns.* Manuscript submitted for publication.

Graham, J. W., Flay, B. R., Johnson, C. A., Hansen, W. B., & Collins, L. M. (1984). Group comparability: A multiattribute utility measurement approach to the use of random assignment with small numbers of aggregated units. *Evaluation Review, 8,* 247–260.

Graham, J. W., Flay, B. R., Johnson, C. A., Hansen, W. B., Grossman, L. M., & Sobel, J. L. (1984). Reliability of self-report measures of drug use in prevention research: Evaluation of the Project SMART questionnaire via the test–retest reliability matrix. *Journal of Drug Education, 14,* 175–193.

Graham, J. W., Hofer, S. M., & Piccinin, A. M. (1994). Analysis with missing data in drug prevention research. In L. M. Collins & L. A. Seitz (Eds.), *Advances in data analysis for prevention intervention research* (NIDA Research Monograph No. 142, pp. 13–63). Washington, DC: U.S. Department of Health and Human Services.

Graham, J. W., Johnson, C. A., Hansen, W. B., Flay, B. R., & Gee, M. (1990). Drug use prevention programs, gender, and ethnicity: Evaluation of three seventh-grade Project SMART cohorts. *Preventive Medicine, 19,* 305–313.

Graham, J. W., Marks, G. S., & Hansen, W. B. (1991). Social influence processes affecting adolescent substance use. *Journal of Applied Psychology, 76,* 291–298.

Graham, J. W., Rohrbach, L. A., Hansen, W. B., Flay, B. R., & Johnson, C. A. (1989). Convergent and discriminant validity for assessment of skill in resisting a role play alcohol offer. *Behavior Assessment, 11,* 353–379.

Hansen, W. B. (1992). School-based substance abuse prevention: A review of the state of the art in curriculum, 1980–1990. *Health Education Research: Theory and Practice, 7,* 403–430.

Hansen, W. B. (1993). School-based alcohol prevention programs. *Alcohol, Health, & Research World, 17,* 54–60.

Hansen, W. B., Collins, L. M., Malotte, C. K., Johnson, C. A., & Fielding, J. E. (1985). Attrition in prevention research. *Journal of Behavioral Medicine, 8,* 261–275.

Hansen, W. B., & Graham, J. W. (1991). Preventing alcohol, marijuana, and cigarette use among adolescents: One-year results of the Adolescent Alcohol Prevention Trial. *Preventive Medicine, 20,* 414–430.

Hansen, W. B., Graham, J. W., Wolkenstein, B. H., & Rohrbach, L. A. (1991). Program integrity as a moderator of prevention program effectiveness: Results for fifth-grade students in the Adolescent Alcohol Prevention Trial. *Journal of Studies on Alcohol, 52,* 568–579.

Hansen, W. B., Tobler, N. S., & Graham, J. W. (1990). Attrition in substance abuse prevention research: A meta-analysis of 85 longitudinally-followed cohorts. *Evaluation Review, 14,* 677–685.

Hawkins, J. D., Catalano, R. F., & Miller, J. M. (1992). Risk and protective factors for alcohol and other drug problems in adolescence and early adulthood: Implications for substance abuse prevention. *Psychological Bulletin, 112,* 64–105.

Hays, R. D., & Ellickson, P. L. (1990). How generalizable are adolescents' beliefs about pro-drug pressures and resistance self-efficacy? *Journal of Applied Social Psychology, 220,* 321–340.

Jessor, R., & Jessor, S. L. (1977). *Problem behavior and psychosocial development.* New York: Academic Press.

Jöreskog, K. G., & Sörbom, D. (1989). *LISREL VII: User's reference guide.* Mooreville, IN: Scientific Software.

Kreft, I. G. G. (1994). Multilevel models for hierarchically nested data: Potential applications in substance abuse prevention research. In L. M. Collins & L. A. Seitz (Eds.), *Advances in data analysis for prevention intervention research* (NIDA Research Monograph No. 142, pp. 148–183). Washington, DC: U.S. Department of Health and Human Services.

Lipsey, M. W. (1988). Practice and malpractice in evaluation research. *Evaluation Practice, 9,* 5–24.

Lipsey, M. W. (1993). Theory as method: Small theories of treatments. *New Directions for Program Evaluation, 57,* 5–38.

Lipsey, M. W., & Wilson, D. B. (1993). The efficacy of psychological, educational, and behavioral treatment: Confirmation from meta-analysis. *American Psychologist, 48,* 1181–1209.

MacKinnon, D. P., Johnson, C. A., Pentz, M. A., Dwyer, J. H., Hansen, W. B., Flay, B. R., & Wang, E. Y. (1991). Mediating mechanisms in a school-based drug prevention program: First-year effects of the Midwestern Prevention Project. *Health Psychology, 10,* 164–172.

Moskowitz, J. M. (1989). The primary prevention of alcohol problems: A critical review of the research literature. *Journal of Studies on Alcohol, 50,* 54–88.

National Institute on Alcohol Abuse and Alcoholism. (1987). *Sixth special report* to the U.S. congress on alcohol and health. Washington, DC: U.S. Department of Health and Human Services.

Pechacek, T. F., Murray, D. M., Luepker, R. V., Mittlemark, M. B., & Johnson, C. A. (1984). Measurement of adolescent smoking behavior: Rationale and methods. *Journal of Behavioral Medicine, 7*, 123–140.

Robins, L. N., & Pryzbeck, T. R. (1985). Age of onset of drug use as a factor in drug and other disorders. In C. L. Jones & R. J. Battjes (Eds.), *Etiology of drug abuse: Implications for prevention* (NIDA Research Monograph No. 56, DHHS Publication No. ADM 85-1335, pp. 178–192). Washington, DC: U.S. Government Printing Office.

Rohrbach, L. A., Graham, J. W., Hansen, W. B., Flay, B. R., & Johnson, C. A. (1987). Evaluation of resistance skills training using multitrait-multimethod role play skills assessment. *Health Education Research, 2*, 401–407.

Rundall, T. G., & Bruvold, W. H. (1988). A meta-analysis of school-based and alcohol use prevention programs. *Health Education Quarterly, 15*, 317–334.

Shope, J. T., Dielman, T. E., Butchart, A. T., Campanelli, P. C., & Kloska, D. D. (1992). An elementary school-based alcohol misuse prevention program: A follow-up evaluation. *Journal of Studies on Alcohol, 53*, 106–121.

Tobler, N. S. (1986). Meta-analysis of 143 adolescent drug prevention programs: Quantitative outcome results of program participants compared to a control or comparison group. *Journal of Drug Issues, 16*, 537–567.

U.S. Department of Health and Human Services. (1991). *Healthy people 2000: National health promotion and disease prevention objectives* (DHHS Publication No. PHS 91-50212). Washington, DC: U.S. Government Printing Office.

Wills, T. A., Baker, E., & Botvin, G. J. (1989). Dimensions of assertiveness: Differential relationships to substance use in early adolescence. *Journal of Consulting and Clinical Psychology, 4*, 473–478.

8

PROTECTIVE FACTORS IN ADOLESCENT PROBLEM BEHAVIOR: MODERATOR EFFECTS AND DEVELOPMENTAL CHANGE

RICHARD JESSOR, JILL VAN DEN BOS, JUDITH VANDERRYN, FRANCES M. COSTA, AND MARK S. TURBIN

Research on adolescent involvement in problem behavior, indeed, on adolescent behavior and development more generally, has become more complex in recent years. Multivariate inquiries now map both social and personal influences over time and are displacing single-variable, single-domain, cross-sectional approaches (Jessor, 1993). Increased complexity is also evident in studies that go beyond traditional concerns with demon-

Reprinted from *Developmental Psychology*, 31, 923–933. (1995). Copyright © 1995 by the American Psychological Association. Used with permission of the author.

This study is a report from the research project, "Contraceptive and Health Behavior Over Time in Adolescence," supported by Grant 91-1194-88 from the William T. Grant Foundation, R. Jessor, principal investigator. Support from the MacArthur Foundation Research Network on Successful Adolescent Development Among Young in High-Risk Settings is gratefully acknowledged. We are grateful to the officials of the school district involved for their gracious and extended cooperation. The contributions of John Donovan to this report are appreciated. The article has benefited particularly from the comments and suggestions of Gary H. McClelland and Arnold J. Sameroff.

strating "main effects" to explore interactive relations among predictor variables as well, and to examine whether those interactions moderate predicted linkages with behavior. The latter kind of complexity is the focus of this article. We report an investigation of the relationships between psychosocial protective factors and involvement in problem behavior in adolescence: alcohol and drug abuse, delinquency, and sexual precocity. The effects of protective factors and their role as moderators of the relationship between risk factors and problem behavior are examined cross-sectionally as well as over time.

Interest in protective factors emerged initially from work in developmental psychopathology. The observation, among children similarly exposed to risk for psychopathology, that many nevertheless escaped its impact or consequences led Garmezy and others (Garmezy, 1985; Garmezy & Masten, 1986; Rutter, 1987; Werner, 1989a, 1989b) to articulate variables that might be protective, that is, that might serve to moderate, buffer, or insulate against risk. Variation in risk alone had preoccupied various researchers, but the new attention to protective factors provided a basis for investigators to account for individual differences in outcome in which exposure to risk was essentially held constant. More recently, the possibility of protective factors mitigating the impact of risk has been extended beyond psychopathology to involvement in adolescent drug and alcohol abuse (Brook, Whiteman, Cohen, & Tanaka, 1992; Felix-Ortiz & Newcomb, 1992; Hawkins, Catalano, & Miller, 1992; Stacy, Newcomb, & Bentler, 1992; Stacy, Sussman, Dent, Burton, & Flay, 1992; Wills, Vaccaro, & McNamara, 1992).

Although the concept of risk, borrowed largely from epidemiology, is widely understood, the same is not true for protection. Risk factors are those conditions or variables that are associated with a higher likelihood of negative or undesirable outcomes—morbidity or mortality, in classical usage, or, more recently, behaviors that can compromise health, well-being, or social performance. There has been far less consensus about the concept and operationalization of protective factors. Protection has sometimes been defined simply as the absence of risk or as the low end of a risk variable. Rutter (1987) argued most forcefully, however, that protective factors and risk factors should be treated as conceptually distinct rather than as opposite ends of a single dimension, and that view is now coming to be shared by most others (Felix-Ortiz & Newcomb, 1992; Hawkins et al., 1992; Jessor, 1991; Luthar & Zigler, 1991; Pellegrini, 1990). In this latter perspective, protective factors are considered independent variables that can have their own direct effects on behavior but that, in addition, can moderate the relation between risk factors and behavior.

Protective factors are conceptualized as decreasing the likelihood of engaging in problem behavior: through direct personal or social controls against its occurrence (e.g., strong religious commitment or predictable parental sanctions); through involvement in activities that tend to be incompatible with or alternatives to problem behavior (e.g., activities with the family or with church groups); and through orientations toward and commitments to conventional institutions (e.g., schools) or to adult society more generally. In contrast, risk factors are conceptualized as increasing the likelihood of engaging in problem behavior: through direct instigation or encouragement (e.g., failure or frustration instigating a coping response, or models and influence from peers); through increased vulnerability for normative transgression (e.g., low self-esteem); and through greater opportunity to engage in problem behavior (e.g., membership in an antisocial peer group).

Research on risk and protective factors has often shown them to be negatively related, but that relationship ought not to be seen as a logical necessity. Rather, it may simply reflect a particular history of personal experience or a particular organization of the social ecology; for example, in those contexts in which protection is high, risk is usually low, and vice versa. These empirical relations notwithstanding, it remains logically possible, for example, to find high risk accompanied by high protection, rather than high risk necessarily implying low protection. An adolescent may well have antisocial friends and yet be committed to and involved in school. Although risk and protection may be inversely related empirically, the conceptual perspective is that they are best treated as orthogonal.

As already noted, the influence of protective factors, whether in relation to substance abuse or to any other adolescent problem behavior, is to lessen the likelihood of its occurrence. When protective factors serve, in addition, as moderators, they modify the relation between risk and problem behavior: That relationship, linear and positive when protection is low or absent, is markedly attenuated when protection is high. This description of a differential relation of risk to problem behavior at different levels of protection is another way of specifying an interaction between risk and protection in their relation to adolescent involvement in problem behavior.

A large number of protective factors, ecological as well as personal, have been explored as moderators of the relationship of risk to behavioral outcomes. Garmezy (1985) organized protection variables into three categories: (a) dispositional attributes, that is, individual differences, such as high self-efficacy; (b) family attributes, such as parental support and affection; and (c) extrafamilial circumstances, such as support from other adults, or strong community integration. In research on alcohol and drug abuse, the protective factors studied have ranged from bonding to conventional society (Hawkins et al., 1992) to supportive relations with parents (Felix-Ortiz & Newcomb, 1992; Wills et al., 1992) to high religiosity and law abidance (Felix-Ortiz & Newcomb, 1992; Stacy, Newcomb, & Bentler, 1992) to self-efficacy in social relations (Stacy, Sussman, et al., 1992).

Our own approach to the delineation of protective factors in adolescence has relied on the systematic implications of problem-behavior theory

(Jessor, Donovan, & Costa, 1991; Jessor, Graves, Hanson, & Jessor, 1968; Jessor & Jessor, 1977). In each of the three psychosocial explanatory systems in the theory—the personality system, the perceived environment system, and the behavior system—the variables are specified either as instigators to or controls against involvement in problem behavior. Investigations are analogous to risk factors, and controls are analogous to protective factors. Although the risk and protective factors used in this study originate from a particular theory, their commonality with the variables used by others, as noted earlier, will be obvious.

Seven protective variables were used in the present research: (a) positive orientation to school, (b) positive orientation to health, and (c) intolerant attitudes toward deviance (and, in later waves, religiosity) from the personality system; (d) positive relations with adults, (e) the perception of strong social controls or sanctions for transgression, and (f) awareness of friends who model conventional behavior, from the perceived environment system; and (g) actual involvement in prosocial behaviors, such as volunteer work and family activities, from the behavior system. Six risk variables were used: (a) low expectations for success, (b) low self-esteem, and (c) a general sense of hopelessness about life, from the personality system; (d) awareness of friends who model involvement in problem behavior and (e) a greater orientation toward friends than toward parents, from the perceived environment system; and (f) poor school achievement (and, in later waves, school dropout), from the behavior system. The measurement of each of these variables and its rationale as a risk or protective factor are elaborated in the Method section.

In research in which multiple risk factors and multiple protective factors have been assessed, there has been growing interest in the amount of risk or the amount of protection as a key parameter, as well as in the various types of risk or protection represented by the specific measures. Findings have shown substantial linear relations between the number of different risk factors and a variety of outcomes (Bry, 1983; Garmezy, 1985; Jessor et al., 1968, Chapter 11; Newcomb, Maddahian, & Bentler, 1986; Sameroff, Seifer, Baldwin, & Baldwin, 1993; Sameroff, Seifer, Barocas, Zax, & Greenspan, 1987; Small & Luster, 1994; Werner, 1989a, 1989b). Rutter (1979) also advocated counting the number of risk (and protective) factors because he found that different risk factors potentiated each other. A counting or cumulative approach to risk and protective factors focuses on variation in the number of different risk or protective factors involved. Exploring this approach is a salient concern of the present investigation, although we also examine the role of particular risk and protective factors.

Unlike earlier research on the moderating role of protective factors, in which the concern was with psychopathology or, more recently, with substance abuse, the focus of the present study is on the larger domain of adolescent problem behavior, including problem drinking, illicit drug use, delinquent behavior, and early sexual intercourse. The aim of the present research is to explore the role of psychosocial protective factors in adolescent problem behavior. Our first concern is to determine whether protective factors are, indeed, associated with lower levels of involvement in problem behavior. Our second concern is to determine whether protective factors moderate the relationship between risk and problem-behavior involvement. And our third concern is to determine whether protective factors are related to change in adolescent problem behavior over subsequent time.

METHOD

Study Design and Procedure

The data used in this article were collected as part of a longitudinal study of problem behavior and health-related behavior in adolescence. Begun in the spring of 1989, the study has involved four annual waves of data collection on middle school and high school youths. Participants were in Grades 7 to 9 at Wave 1 when data were collected in six middle schools and four high schools in a large metropolitan school district in the Rocky Mountain region. Participating schools were chosen for the study by the school district administration to maximize representation of Hispanic and Black students from inner-city areas.

Active parental and personal consent was sought for all students enrolled in the selected schools. Letters describing the study were written to the parents and the students, and signed consent forms were returned to the school. All of the letters and consent forms were written in both English and Spanish. Study participants were released from class to take part in large-group administration sessions. Bilingual versions of the questionnaire were available for those students who preferred to work in Spanish. Each student received a token payment of $5 for each wave.

Participants

A total of 2,410 students in Grades 7, 8, and 9 participated in the first wave of the study in 1989. Although participation rates varied from school to school, questionnaires were filled out by 67% of the middle school students (Grades 7 and 8) and by 49% of the high school students (Grade 9). The less-than-desirable initial participation rate was due largely to the necessity of obtaining active parental consent and to the difficulty of eliciting a response from many of the parents. Comparisons of the Wave-1 participants with nonparticipants, using school record data, show that the participant sample did represent the full range of scores on grade point average, standardized achievement test scores, disciplinary actions, and school absences, although participants were, on the average, more conventional than nonparticipants on these indicators.

At the Wave-2 (1990) data collection, questionnaires were completed by 2,016 students, or 84% of the Wave-1 sample. At Wave 3 (1991), 1,974 students (82% of the Wave-1 sample) filled out questionnaires, and, in Wave 4, 1,782 students (74% of the Wave-1 sample) took part. Overall, 1,591 students filled out all four annual questionnaires; they represent 66% of the Wave-1 sample. The effect of the attrition of 819 participants, after Wave 1, was examined. (The non-four-wave participants included participants having only one [n = 212], two [n = 215], or three [n = 392] waves of data.) Their Wave-1 scores on 12 selected measures from the questionnaire were compared with the Wave-1 mean scores of the 1,591 four-wave participants on those same measures. The attrition subsample was less conventional or more problem-prone on 9 of the measures, and there was no difference on 3 of the measures. Despite those mean differences, the intercorrelations among the measures were similar in both groups. A test of the equality of the covariance structure matrices in the two groups, based on nine representative variables, yielded a goodness-of-fit index of .997. Although the chi-square of 79.8 was significant ($p < .001$), it was only slightly more than twice the 36 degrees of freedom. Thus, despite the bias toward greater conventionality in the participating four-wave sample, relations among their measures would not be very different had the attrition not occurred.

Forty-three percent of the four-wave longitudinal sample are male, and equal proportions of the sample are in the 7th-, 8th-, and 9th-grade starting cohorts. With respect to race/ethnicity, 36% of the sample are White, 36% Hispanic, 22% Black, 4% Asian, and 2% Native American. Forty-five percent of the participants are from intact families; 22% have a stepparent living with them (usually stepfather); 29% live with one parent (usually mother); and 3% live with other relatives or guardians. The analyses presented in this article were carried out using data from all the White, Hispanic, and Black participants with four complete waves of data ($N = 1,486$).

Measurement of Risk and Protection

Six measures of risk and 7 measures of protection were obtained from the Wave-1 (1989) data, and they are used as continuous variables in later multivariate analyses of problem behavior involvement. To establish an index of the number of risk factors and protective factors, however, we dichotomized scores on each measure to represent the presence or absence of that risk factor or protective factor using the procedure described later. An overall Risk Factor Index (RFI) and an overall Protective Factor Index

(PFI) were then developed on the basis of summative scores that characterized each participant. Dichotomization of scores on each of the individual measures of risk or protection was done so as to yield roughly the extreme 30% of participants on that measure, thus maximizing the likelihood that the risk factor or the protective factor was indeed present. An extreme score on a measure was assigned the value of 1, indicating the presence of risk or of protection on the different measures. A score of 0 indicates no risk or no protection on the respective measures.

Measures of Protection

Three protective factors represent the personality system. Positive Orientation To School is a nine-item scale measuring attitudes toward school (e.g., "How do you feel about going to school?") and personal value on academic achievement (α = .79). Having a positive orientation toward school constitutes protection against involvement in problem behavior because it reflects positive engagement with a conventional social institution and commitment to its goals. Such an orientation toward conventionality is not compatible with engaging in behaviors that are considered inappropriate by adults and that may also jeopardize school achievement. Positive Orientation Toward Health is a two-component index based on the standardized score on a 7-item scale of personal value on health (α = .67) added to the standardized score on a 10-item scale of personal beliefs about the health consequences of various behaviors such as smoking and eating junk food (α = .76). A positive orientation toward health constitutes protection because it represents a personal control against involvement in behaviors, such as substance use, that can be damaging to or incompatible with health. Attitudinal Intolerance of Deviance is a 10-item attitude scale assessing the judged "wrongness" of certain delinquent-type behaviors, including physical aggression, theft, and property damage (α = .90). Intolerance of deviance constitutes protection because it reflects a commitment to conventional values and disapproval of norm-violative activities, and it serves as a direct personal control against involvement in such activities. Protection in the personality system is thus indicated by a positive orientation toward school, a positive orientation toward health, and high intolerance of deviance.

Three protective factors represent the perceived involvement system. Positive Relations With Adults was measured by four questions assessing a respondent's relationships with parents and other adults, including the extent to which parents show interest in the respondent and whether the respondent is able to discuss personal problems with an adult (α = .61). More positive relations with adults constitute protection because adults provide support for conventional behavior and sanctions against problem behavior. Perceived Regulatory Controls was measured by a two-component index based on the standardized score on a seven-item scale assessing the presence of family rules about getting homework done, dating, curfew, doing chores, and so on ($\alpha = .57$), added to the score on one question about expected sanctions from friends for involvement in deviant behavior. Perception of greater regulatory controls in the social environment constitutes protection because it increases the likelihood that the adolescent will be deterred from problem behaviors, and it helps make clear the types of behavior that are unacceptable to others. Friends Models for Conventional Behavior, a four-item scale assessing the proportion of friends who are in school clubs, attend religious services, are in community or church youth groups, and get good grades in school ($\alpha = .75$), constitutes protection because it reflects greater involvement with conventional peers and more time spent in conventional activities. Protection in the perceived social environment is thus indicated by positive relations with adults, high regulatory controls, and high friends models for conventional behavior.

One measure of protection represents the behavior system. Prosocial Activities is a three-item index that combines involvement and time spent in family activities, in volunteer activities, and in school clubs other than sports. High involvement in prosocial activities constitutes protection because prosocial activities preempt time to become involved in problem behavior and also promote orientations and social networks incompatible with the latter.

The operationalization of protection is thus based on answers to the questionnaire that yield characterizations of the respondent, of the social environment as perceived by the respondent, and of the respondent's behavior.

Measures of Risk

Three risk factors represent the personality system. Expectations for Success is a two-component index consisting of the standardized score on a four-item scale of expectations for academic achievement ($\alpha = .85$) added to the standardized score on a nine-item scale of perceived life chances in the opportunity structure ($\alpha = .90$). Together, these components assess anticipated positive life outcomes in various areas such as school, family life, employment, friendships, finances, and so on. Low expectation of achieving these valued life goals constitutes risk for involvement in problem behavior because it can serve to pressure an adolescent toward alternative means, such as substance use or delinquency, to achieve some of those same goals. Self-Esteem is a six-item scale measuring participants' beliefs about their abilities and attributes in various domains, including social skills, academic competence, and personal attractiveness ($\alpha = .66$). A low sense of self-worth and low confidence in one's ability to handle challenges and responsibilities constitute risk because engaging in problem behavior can be a way to cope with such negative feelings. Hopelessness is a two-component index consisting of the standardized score on a four-item scale of depression (α = .85) added to the standardized score on a four-item scale of alienation (α = .67). Together, these components assess feelings of depression, anxiety, hopelessness, and social alienation. Disengagement from societal norms and feeling isolated from others constitute risk because the social influences that usually serve as controls against engaging in problem behavior are attenuated, and the sense of vulnerability may lead to coping through problem behavior. Risk in the personality system is thus indicated by low expectations for success, low self-esteem, and high hopelessness.

Two risk factors represent the perceived environment system. Friends Models for Problem Behavior is a four-item scale assessing perceived models among friends for cigarette smoking, alcohol use, marijuana use, and sexual intercourse (α = .75). Exposure to friends who model involvement in problem behavior constitutes risk because models (a) provide an opportunity to learn how to engage in the behavior, (b) offer access to supplies that may be necessary for carrying out the behavior, such as cigarettes, alcohol, or other drugs, and (c) indicate that problem behavior is characteristic of the peer group. The Friend Orientation Index is a two-component measure based on standardized scores on two three-item scales, one measuring perceived agreement or compatibility between parents and friends (α = .71) and the other measuring the relative influence of parents and friends on the respondent's outlook, life choices, and behavior (α = .56). Lower parents–friends agreement and higher friends'-relative-to-parents' influence both indicate greater orientation to friends and constitute risk because parents represent and exercise controls against deviant or norm-violative behavior and generally serve as models for conventional values, attitudes, and activities. Risk in the perceived involvement system is thus indicated by high friends models for problem behavior and high orientation to friends relative to parents.

One measure of risk, School Record Grade Point Average, represents the behavior system. Grade point averages in the bottom 28% of the distribution were considered a risk factor. Low school achievement constitutes risk because it may reflect detachment from school, may lower expectations for success in other life areas such as work, may have a negative impact on self-esteem, and may contribute to a sense of personal hopelessness.

Establishing the RFI and the PFI

The RFI and the PFI were computed by adding the dichotomized scores (0 to 1) on the six risk and the seven protective measures, respectively. Scores on the RFI could range from 0 to 6, and scores on the PFI could range from 0 to 7. For respondents missing scores on measures in an index, the missing values were replaced with the mean of the scores for the relevant gender, cohort, and race/ethnicity subgroup.

The RFI and the PFI are summative indexes rather than scales and, as such, would not be expected to show high alpha reliabilities. The RFI had an alpha reliability of .54; the mean inter-item correlation was .16. The PFI had an alpha reliability of .59; the mean inter-item correlation was .17. Corrected item—total correlations for both indexes ranged from .15 to .41. Given the widely varied content of the indexes, these psychometric properties indicated a reasonable degree of internal coherence for both of them.

The Pearson correlation of −.42 (−.39 for the male and −.46 for the female participants) between the RFI and the PFI was in the expected negative direction. The magnitude of this correlation indicated that the two measures, although empirically related as might be expected, shared only a modest proportion of variance and reflected relatively distinct constructs. The magnitude of this correlation between the measures of risk and protection was, incidentally, quite similar to that found in two other recent studies, namely, −.35 in both Wills et al. (1992) and Felix-Ortiz and Newcomb (1992).

Female students had a slightly higher mean score on the RFI than did male students (1.8 vs. 1.6), $F(1, 1484) = 8.0$, $p < .01$, and also on the PFI (2.2 vs. 1.8), $F(1, 1484) = 21.7$, $p < .001$. Mean scores on the RFI were highest for Hispanics (2.1), followed by Blacks (1.7) and Whites (1.3), $F(2, 1483) = 33.7$, $p < .001$. Mean scores on the PFI were highest for Blacks (2.4), followed by Whites (2.1) and Hispanics (1.8), $F(2, 1483) = 15.4$, $p < .001$. Cohort scores on the RFI showed an increase in mean as age increased: 1.5, 1.7, and 2.0 for the 7th, 8th, and 9th graders, respectively, $F(2, 1483) = 15.1$, $p < .001$. Mean scores on the PFI decreased, but not significantly, after 7th grade: 2.2, 2.0, and 2.0 for 7th, 8th, and 9th graders, respectively.

Measurement of Problem Behavior

The Multiple Problem Behavior Index (MPBI) assesses four different areas of adolescent problem behavior: (a) problem drinking (score range = 3–24), based on reports of frequency of drunkenness, frequency of high volume drinking (5 or more drinks per occasion), and negative consequences of drinking ($\alpha = .81$); (b) delinquent-type behavior (score range = 10–50), including self-reports of physical aggression, vandalism, theft, and lying ($\alpha = .85$); (c) marijuana involvement (score range = 0–8), as reflected in reports of whether the adolescents ever use, frequency of use, availability of marijuana, and the number of times the adolescents have been high ($\alpha = .71$); and (d) sexual intercourse experience (score range = 1–2), based on respondents' reports of whether they had ever had sexual intercourse.[1] Measures of the four components of the index were transformed into T scores (mean of 50 and standard deviation of 10) and summed.[2]

Male students had a significantly higher MPBI mean score than did female students (202.4 vs. 198.1), $F(1, 1484) = 7.4$, $p < .01$; mean MPBI score for Hispanics was highest (206.6), followed by Blacks (196.9) and Whites (194.9), $F(1, 1483) = 24.6$, $p < .001$; and mean scores across cohorts increased from 191.2 to 200.7 to 208.4 for the 7th-, 8th-, and 9th-grade cohorts, respectively, $F(1, 1483) = 42.9$, $p < .001$. The MPBI has an alpha of .75; it has been well established as an important criterion measure in considerable previous work (Jessor & Jessor, 1977).

Analytic Procedures

Hierarchical multiple regression was used in both cross-sectional and longitudinal analyses to assess, first, whether protection is related to adolescent involvement in problem behavior; second, whether protection moderates the relationship between risk and problem-behavior involvement; and third, whether protection is related to change in adolescent problem-behavior involvement over time.[3]

The demonstration of a moderator effect for protection requires the demonstration of a significant Risk × Protection interaction. Multiple regression provides for the statistical testing of a moderator effect for continuous variables (here the RFI and the PFI) by including their product or interaction term at a later step in the regression equation (Baron & Kenny, 1986; Cohen, 1978; Saunders, 1956). A hierarchical incremental F test then shows whether the product term, the interaction, adds predictability over and above the account provided by the additive model using just the two predictors.

---

[1]Mean scores are 4.40 for the problem drinking measure, 16.27 for delinquent-type behavior, 1.68 for marijuana involvement, and 1.22 for sexual intercourse experience. Intercorrelations among these measures are as follows: problem drinking correlates .50, .59, and .34 with delinquent-type behavior, marijuana involvement, and sexual intercourse experience, respectively; delinquent-type behavior correlates .51 and .28 with marijuana involvement and sexual intercourse experience, respectively; and the latter two measures correlate .34. All correlations are significant at $p < .001$.

[2]In the Wave-1 data, eight outlying high scores on the MPBI were recoded to approximately three standard deviations above the mean, thereby ensuring a less skewed distribution for the analyses presented in this article.

[3]Five demographic variables are included in all these analyses as control measures: gender, two indicators of race/ethnicity, an index of socioeconomic status, and cohort. The first ethnicity variable contrasts Whites with Hispanics and Blacks, and the second ethnicity variable contrasts Hispanics with Blacks. The SES index is a three-item measure combining participant's reports of mother's and father's educational attainment and father's occupation ($\alpha = 82$). If any of the components of this measure were missing, the remaining information was used alone. Cohorts refers to Wave-1 grade in school: Grade 7, 8, or 9.

RESULTS

The Results section is organized into two parts. The first part is based on cross-sectional data from Wave 1 (1989) and examines whether protective factors are related to adolescent involvement in problem behavior and, in addition, whether they moderate the relationship between risk factors and problem-behavior involvement. The second part examines whether antecedent protection is related to change in adolescent involvement in problem behavior over time, using the longitudinal data on later problem-behavior involvement in Waves 2 (1990), 3 (1991), and 4 (1992).

Cross-Sectional Analyses of Protection and Problem Behavior

We ran hierarchical multiple regression analyses to predict the Wave-1 criterion measure of adolescent involvement in problem behavior, the MPBI. A set of five demographic control measures—gender, two ethnic status dummy variables (White vs. Minority; Hispanic vs. Black), family socioeconomic status (SES), and grade in school (cohort)—was entered in Step 1. In Steps 2 and 3, respectively, the RFI and the PFI were entered. Finally, in Step 4, the cross-product, RFI × PFI, was entered as the interaction term. A significant increase in the multiple R^2 following the entry of the interaction term into a regression analysis already containing the RFI and PFI predictors provides evidence for a moderator effect (see Cohen & Cohen, 1983, pp. 320–324). Results of the hierarchical regression analyses are shown in Table 1.

The demographic control measures entered in Step 1 account for a significant portion of the variance in adolescent problem behavior; the R^2 with the MPBI is .10. With the entry of the RFI in Step 2, there is a substantial and significant increment in the amount of variance explained; the R^2 now reaches .23, and the R^2 change of .132 is also highly significant. When the PFI is entered in Step 3, the R^2 increases to .24. The .013 increment is significant and indicates that the PFI accounts for unique variance in the MPBI score in addition to the variance it shares with the RFI, the latter already having been entered. As the unstandardized regression coefficients show, both the RFI (7.96) and the PFI (−1.25) are significantly related to variation in adolescent problem behavior in the direction expected. The data, thus far, provide support for the effect of protection: The higher the number of protective factors, the lower the involvement in problem behavior. The data also support the wealth of previous findings about the effect of risk: The higher the number of risk factors, the greater the involvement in problem behavior.

When the interaction term, RFI × PFI, is added in Step 4, the R^2 change of .004 is also statistically significant. Thus, controlling for sociodemographic factors, and taking into account the effects of the RFI and

TABLE 1

Cross-Sectional Hierarchical Regression Analysis of the Risk Factor and Protective Factor Indexes With the Multiple Problem Behavior Index: Wave 1 (1989)

Step/Predictor measures	β at final step[a]	R^2	R^2 change
1. Demographic controls		.10***	
Gender	−4.86***		
White or Minority	−1.21*		
Hispanic or Black	2.53**		
Socioeconomic status	−.08		
Cohort	6.56***		
2. Add Risk Factor Index	7.96***	.23***	.132***
3. Add Protective Factor Index	−1.25*	.24***	.013***
4. Add Risk × Protection interaction	−.85***	.25***	.004**

[a]Unstandardized regression coefficients are reported because standardized coefficients are inappropriate with interaction terms (see Aiken & West, 1991, pp. 40−47).
*$p \leq .05$. **$p \leq .01$. ***$p \leq .001$.

the PFI, there is still a significant increment in the prediction of problem behavior contributed by the Risk × Protection interaction. This finding provides empirical support for the moderating effect of protection on the relationship between risk and problem behavior in adolescence. The significant regression coefficient of −.85 for the interaction term indicates that the effect of protection is to lessen the impact of risk more when protection is high than when protection is low or absent.

The moderator effect of protection on the relationship between risk and involvement in problem behavior is illustrated in Figure 1. Using the regression analysis findings reported in Table 1, we plotted the predicted values of the MPBI score, for different levels of protection, against the level of risk. The ordinate in Figure 1 represents the predicted degree of involvement in problem behavior (the predicted MPBI score); the abscissa represents degree of risk (the RFI score); and the three regression lines represent three different levels of protection from highest protection (PFI score = 7) to lowest protection (PFI score = 1) to an absence of protection (PFI score = 0). The interaction effect is evident. When protection is absent (PFI score = 0), increasing the level of risk shows the largest effect, as illustrated by the steep slope of the regression line. At the minimal level of protection (PFI score = 1), the slope of the regression line is slightly less steep. It is when protection is high (PFI score = 7) that it has a pronounced effect: Increasing the level of risk now makes only a modest difference, that is, the slope of the regression line is relatively shallow. High risk is associated with high involvement in problem behavior when protection is absent or low but not when protection is high. In fact, under

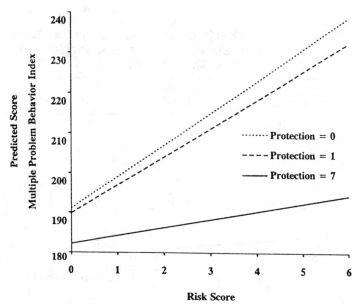

Figure 1. The moderator effect of protection on the relationship of risk to problem behavior: predicted curves.

the condition of highest protection, the predicted MPBI score for high risk is not much higher than the predicted scores for low risk.

The curves in Figure 1 are predicted from the regression equation represented in Table 1; it is also possible to illustrate the moderator role of protection by plotting curves from the actual data. Both the RFI and the PFI were dichotomized as close to the median as possible—at 0 or 1 versus 2 or more—and the significant interaction yielded by a two-way analysis of variance, $F(1, 1482) = 7.3$, $p < .01$, was plotted in Figure 2. The curves, now based on the four cell means, again illustrate the greater impact of high protection on the risk–problem behavior relation than of low protection.

Replicating the Cross-Sectional Analyses

Parallel cross-sectional hierarchical multiple regressions were carried out for the Wave-2, Wave-3, and Wave-4 data. (In Waves 3 and 4, a new, five-item measure of risk, Dropout Proneness, $\alpha = .86$, was added to the RFI, and a new, four-item measure of protection, Religiosity, $\alpha = .88$, was added to the PFI.) In each of the three subsequent data waves, the total set of predictor measures accounted for a portion of the variance in the MPBI criterion measure similar to that shown in Table 1 for the Wave-1 data: 25%, 26%, and 24%, respectively. In each of the subsequent waves, the demographic controls were significant, but now they accounted for less than 5% of the variance; the RFI and PFI each added a significant incre-

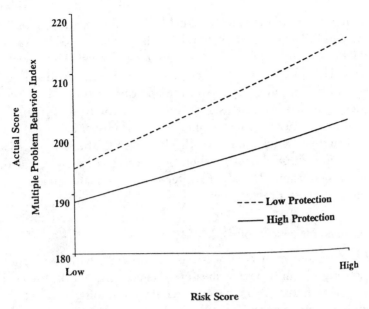

Figure 2. The moderator effect of protection on the relationship of risk to problem behavior: actual curves.

ment in variance accounted for; and the RFI × PFI interaction term added a further significant increment in Wave 2 and in Wave 3 (.008, $p < .001$, in each), but not in Wave 4. Thus, the four separate, cross-sectional replications yielded a similar pattern of findings in respect to both the direct and the moderator role of protective factors, except for the nonsignificant interaction in Wave 4. This robustness of outcome obtained although the sample was increasing in age from Wave 1 to Wave 4 and moving from a middle school to a high school context.

Although gender and race/ethnicity were among the demographic controls in all of these analyses, sample size was large enough to permit analyses within gender and race/ethnicity subgroups. Hierarchical multiple regressions were run for male and female students separately, and for White, Hispanic, and Black youths separately, again using the Wave-1 (1989) data. The findings for these subgroups were, with some exceptions, similar to the findings already reported for the total sample.

For female students, the total set of predictors accounted for 29% of the variance in problem behavior involvement; for male students, it was 20%. For both genders, the cohort measure had a significant unstandardized regression coefficient among the demographic controls. For both genders, the RFI and the PFI each added a significant increment to the R^2. And the addition of the RFI × PFI interaction term added a further significant increment (.005, $p < .05$) for the young women, but it did not reach significance for the young men.

When the analyses were carried out for the three race/ethnicity subgroups, the total set of predictors yielded R^2s of .23, .26, and .18 for Whites, Hispanics, and Blacks, respectively (all significant at $p < .001$). Among the demographic controls, cohort had a significant B coefficient for all three subgroups. The addition of the RFI and the PFI each yielded significant increments in R^2 in all groups. And the addition of the RFI $\times$ PFI interaction term yielded a further significant increment in R^2 for the Whites (.005, $p < .05$), a near significant increment for Hispanics (.005, $p < .06$), and a nonsignificant increment for Blacks. Overall, the five subgroup replications mimic those shown in Table 1 for the total sample, but the absence of a significant RFI $\times$ PFI interaction for male students and for Blacks is an important exception.

Analyzing the Components of the MPBI

Although our primary concern in this article is with the higher order construct of problem behavior, measured here by the MPBI, the generality of the present findings can be explored by examining each of the four problem-behavior components of the MPBI as a separate criterion measure. Hierarchical regressions were again carried out, but now separately for problem drinking, marijuana involvement, delinquent-type behavior, and sexual intercourse experience, again using the Wave-1 data. The pattern of findings for each behavior is consonant with that for the MPBI composite index overall: the demographic controls account for between 4% and 12% of the variance in the four problem behavior measures; the RFI and PFI each add a significant increment in variance accounted for (except for the PFI for sexual intercourse experience); and the RFI $\times$ PFI interaction term adds a further significant increment in variance accounted for when problem drinking (.003, $p < .05$), marijuana involvement (.004, $p < .01$), and delinquent-type behavior (.005, $p < .01$) are the criterion measures, but not when the criterion measure is sexual intercourse experience. (The sexual intercourse experience measure has the limitation of being a simple dichotomy in these analyses. It should also be mentioned that when the PFI is "unpacked," as in analyses reported later, protection does add a significant increment in variance for this measure.) The total set of predictors yielded R^2s of .16, .21, .21, and .12, respectively, for those four component behaviors, somewhat less than for the composite MPBI, but each a significant R^2 in magnitude.

Thus far, the analyses have shown that counting the number of protective factors yields a measure—the PFI—that is inversely related to adolescent involvement in problem behavior, a finding that is relatively robust over four waves of data, across gender and racial/ethnic subgroups, and across different specific problem behaviors, except for sexual intercourse experience. In addition, the role of protection as moderator of the relation of risk to problem behavior has also received support from the significant

JESSOR, VAN DEN BOS, VANDERRYN, COSTA, AND TURBIN

RFI × PFI interaction in the total sample analysis and in three out of the five subgroup analyses. Although small, the significant interaction effect is of substantial theoretical importance. We return to the difficulty of detecting interaction effects in field studies, and the usually small magnitudes that are found, in the Discussion.

Analyzing Risk and Protective Factors as Continuous Measures

The use of cumulative indexes for risk and protection, that is, counting the number of different risk factors or protective factors, results in treating those factors as equally weighted and, in a sense, as mutually substitutable. Although useful for conceptual purposes, such analyses do obscure the differential importance that particular risk or protective factors may have in regard to adolescent problem-behavior outcomes. To permit an exploration of the differential contribution of the separate measures of risk factors and protective factors, we "unpacked" the Wave-1 RFI and PFI in a series of hierarchical multiple regressions with the MPBI as the criterion. The data are shown in Table 2.

Table 2 presents the bivariate relations between each predictor measure and the criterion, the standardized beta coefficients at the final step, and the R^2 and R^2 change at each step. It is worth pointing out immediately that using the total set of 5 controls plus, now, 13 separate risk and protection measures yields a final R^2 of .48, twice the amount of variance accounted for by the 5 controls plus only the 2 RFI and PFI measures in Table 1. The final R^2 in Table 2 is similar to the level of variance in problem behavior accounted for in much of our earlier work (Jessor, Donovan, & Costa, 1991; Jessor & Jessor, 1977) using a set of about 16 predictor measures from problem-behavior theory. Also apparent in Table 2, both unpacked sets of risk factors and protective factors add a significant increment in the R^2 beyond that of the demographic controls.

At the bivariate level, there is a small negative correlation between SES and involvement in problem behavior, and a small positive correlation between cohort (grade in school or, for the most part, chronological age) and involvement in problem behavior among the demographic measures. Among the risk factors, the strongest bivariate relationship is between the criterion and Friends Models for Problem Behavior, followed by Grade Point Average and Expectations for Success. Among the protective factor measures, the most substantial predictor is Attitudinal Intolerance of Deviance, followed by Positive Orientation to School, Perceived Regulatory Controls, and Friends Models for Conventional Behavior.

The standardized betas in Table 2 mirror the strength of the bivariate relations. Among the demographic controls, the beta for cohort is significant; among the risk factors, Friends Models for Problem Behavior has the largest beta coefficient, with Expectations for Success, Self-Esteem, and

TABLE 2
Cross-Sectional Hierarchical Multiple Regression Analysis of the Separate Risk Factor and Protective Factor Measures With the Multiple Problem Behavior Index: Wave 1 (1989)

Step/predictor measures	Pearson r[a]	β at final step[b]	R^2	R^2 change
1. Demographic controls			.10***	
Gender	−.07	−.01		
White or minority	−.13	.01		
Hispanic or Black	.14	.03		
Socioeconomic status	−.17	−.02		
Cohort	.23	.05**		
2. Add risk factors			.43***	.328***
Expectations for Success	−.28	−.07**		
Self-Esteem	−.16	.17**		
Hopelessness	.11	.01		
Friends Models, Problem Behavior	.62	.46***		
Friend Orientation	.19	.01		
Grade Point Average	−.32	−.06**		
3. Add protective factors			.48***	.054***
Positive Orientation, School	−.32	−.06*		
Positive Orientation, Health	−.19	.03		
Intolerance of Deviance	−.48	−.26***		
Positive Relations, Adults	−.18	.00		
Perceived Regulatory Controls	−.24	.01		
Friends Models, Conventional Behavior	−.21	−.02		
Prosocial Activities	−.14	.00		

[a]All Pearson correlations are significant at $p \leq .01$ or better. [b]Beta values are standardized partial regression coefficients.
*$p \leq .05$. **$p \leq .01$. ***$p \leq .001$.

Grade Point Average significant but considerably smaller; and, among the protective factor measures, Attitudinal Intolerance of Deviance has the largest beta, with Positive Orientation to School also being significant.

When unpacked multiple regression analyses were run for each of the four adolescent problem behaviors separately, the pattern of findings is quite similar with regard to the relative importance of the different risk and protective factor measures. For all four problem behaviors, the risk factor measure with the consistently largest significant beta weight is Friends Models for Problem Behavior, and the protective factor measure playing that same role is Attitudinal Intolerance of Deviance. Expectations for Success has a significant beta for three of the problem behaviors, Self-Esteem for two, Hopelessness for two, and Grade Point Average for one, among the other risk factors. Among the other protective factor measures, both Positive Orientation to School and Friends Models for Conventional Behavior have significant betas for two of the problem behaviors, and Prosocial Activities has a significant beta for one of the behaviors.

At the level of the individual risk and protective factors measures, then, there is a robustness of findings, both across the composite index of problem-behavior involvement and across its components, with respect to the key influence of Friends Models for Problem Behavior and Attitudinal Intolerance of Deviance, and some consistency for several of the other measures in each domain.

Longitudinal Analyses of Protection and Change in Problem Behavior

The four-wave, longitudinal design of the study provides an opportunity to examine whether antecedent protection has implications for change in adolescent involvement in problem behavior with subsequent development. Hierarchical multiple regression analysis was again used, only now with the Wave-1 MPBI score entered at Step 1 as a control, so that the criterion measure was change in the level of involvement in problem behavior in subsequent years, that is, by Wave 2, Wave 3, and Wave 4.[4] The data predicting change in MPBI by Wave 2 (1990), Wave 3 (1991), and Wave 4 (1992) are shown in Table 3. Because the RFI × PFI interaction term was not significant as a predictor in any subsequent year, that step is omitted from the table.

The total amount of variance explained in change in multiple problem behavior involvement declines as the time interval lengthens, from 46% by Wave 2, to 34% by Wave 3, to 28% by Wave 4. As can be seen in Table 3, the Wave-1 MPBI score entered at Step 1 accounts for a substantial amount of variance in the subsequent MPBI scores at Waves 2, 3, and 4. With respect to change in multiple problem behavior involvement, cohort has a significant beta coefficient in Waves 2 and 4, gender in Waves 3 and 4, and SES in Wave 4 only, when demographic controls are entered at Step 2. When the Wave-1 RFI is entered at Step 3, there is a significant increment in R^2 for all three waves, and the same is true when the Wave-1 PFI is added at Step 4. What is of special interest to note in Table 3 is that the PFI shows a significant beta coefficient in each of the three time intervals, whereas that is not true for the RFI in any of the time intervals.[5]

Despite stability in the MPBI score over time and development, change in multiple problem-behavior involvement does, indeed, show predictability during adolescence. Of the two key theoretical measures, the RFI and the PFI, it is the antecedent number of protective factors that

[4]The Wave-2, -3, and -4 MPBI measures were constructed similarly to the Wave-1 (1989) MPBI. In each wave, there were eight outlier scores recoded to approximately three standard deviations above the mean. Alpha reliability is .74, .74, and .73 for the Wave-2, -3, and -4 MPBI, respectively. The Pearson correlation of the Wave-1 MPBI with the Wave-2, -3, and -4 MPBI is .67, .57, and .50, respectively.

[5]These analyses were replicated with a three-item MPBI, dropping the sexual experience item because it permits change in only one direction. The outcome for all three follow-up waves is essentially identical to the findings for the four-item MPBI used here.

TABLE 3

Longitudinal Hierarchical Multiple Regression Analysis of the Wave-1 (1989) Risk Factor and Protective Factor Indexes With Change in Multiple Problem Behavior by Wave 2 (1990), Wave 3 (1991), and Wave 4 (1992)

Step/predictor measures	Wave 2 (1990)			Wave 3 (1991)			Wave 4 (1992)		
	β at final step[a]	R^2	R^2 change	β at final step[a]	R^2	R^2 change	β at final step[a]	R^2	R^2 change
1. Wave-1 MPBI score		.45***			.32***			.25***	
2. Add demographic controls		.46***	.005*		.33**	.006*		.27***	.016***
Gender	−.01			−.04*			−.08***		
White or minority	.03			.03			.01		
Hispanic or Black	.02			.04			.02		
Socioeconomic status	−.02			.00			.06*		
Cohort	−.04*			−.02			−.08***		
3. Add Wave-1 Risk Factor Index	.04	.46***	.003**	.03	.33***	.003*	.04	.27***	.004**
4. Add Wave-1 Protective Factor Index	−.07**	.46***	.003**	−.08***	.34***	.005***	−.10***	.28***	.007***

Note. MPBI = Multiple Problem Behavior Index.
[a]Standardized regression coefficients, betas, are reported.
[b]$p \leq .05$. **$p \leq .01$. ***$p \leq .001$.

emerges consistently as the significant predictor of change in problem-behavior involvement—the greater the earlier protection, the greater the reduction in MPBI in subsequent years.

DISCUSSION

Psychosocial protective factors appear to play an important role in the etiology and the developmental course of adolescent problem behavior. The present findings argue, therefore, that scientific attention should be broadened beyond its traditional preoccupation with risk factors to encompass variation in protection as well. Protective factors have been shown to relate both directly and indirectly to adolescent involvement in problem behavior—the greater the protection, the less the problem behavior—and, in interaction with risk factors, protective factors can moderate their relation to problem behavior. The overall findings show robustness across four separate waves of data, across gender and race/ethnicity subgroups, and in relation to multiple outcome criteria. The findings also obtain whether an index of the number of risk and protective factors was used or whether the actual continuous measures themselves were used.

The relation of protection to development change in adolescence has special significance, given the importance of problem behavior as a characteristic of that life stage. When change in involvement in problem behavior was the criterion—whether over a 1-, 2-, or 3-year interval—it was the PFI that had a significant beta weight at the final step in the regression analysis, not the RFI. What this suggests is that, although risk does have a stronger relation to variation in problem-behavior involvement than protection, antecedent protection has a stronger relation to change (here diminution) in problem behavior than antecedent risk. To the extent this is true, it would have significant implications for intervention efforts seeking to reduce problem-behavior involvement during adolescence.

Although not statistically significant in every analysis, the empirical support for a moderator role for protection—a significant RFI × PFI interaction—was nevertheless substantial; this may well be the most important finding of the study for theory. It corroborates a differential or variable impact of protection on the relation between risk and problem behavior—its major impact being evident when protection is high, and its influence being more limited when protection is low or absent—a pattern in accord with Rutter's (1987) earlier conceptualization.

The importance we placed on having established a significant Risk × Protection interaction may seem questionable given the small amount of additional or unique variance (about 1%) that is accounted for in most of the analyses. As McClelland and Judd (1993) pointed out, however, "moderator effects are notoriously difficult to detect in nonexperimental field studies" (p. 377) in contrast to the apparent ease with which such effects are found in experiments. A study by Grossman et al. (1992) provides an illustration; they were able to describe "the power of . . . protective factors as independent predictors . . . after risk was taken into account" (p. 546) but then found it necessary to report their "second general finding . . . the absence of any interactions" (p. 547). When interactions are detected in nonexperimental studies, it is the usual case, as in the present study, that they involve only 1% to 3% of the total variance (Chaplin, 1991).

In a telling statistical analysis, and using the present data set as a case study, McClelland and Judd (1993) demonstrated that "jointly extreme observations are crucial for detecting interactions" (p. 382); this is precisely what is achieved by the deliberate assignment of cases in an experiment, but in field studies, the investigator has to work with whatever joint distribution of predictors happens to obtain. Given their argument, the detection of significant interactions in the present study is, indeed, noteworthy. Despite the small magnitude of those interactions, they provide strong support for the theoretical inference sought about the relation between protection and risk, namely, that protection can moderate the influence of risk on problem behavior in adolescence.

In establishing the measures of risk and protection, we followed a strategy that relied on counting the number of different risk factors or protective factors present, emphasizing thereby the amount of risk or protection rather than particular factors or particular patterns of factors. That strategy was clearly useful in revealing both the direct and moderator effects of protection and, to that extent, showing that magnitude of risk and protection is an important parameter, as others have also shown (Bry, 1983; Sameroff et al., 1987; Small & Luster, 1994). When the RFI and the PFI were unpacked (see Table 2), however, the differential importance of the different risk and protective factors became apparent. Although shared variance affected which measure might achieve a significant beta at the expense of another, it was clear that the most powerful protective factor was a personal control, Attitudinal Intolerance of Deviance, and next was a personal orientation and commitment to a conventional institution, Positive Orientation to School. Among the risk factors, the most powerful one was a measure of instigation in the perceived social environment, Friends Models for Problem Behavior, followed by Low Expectations for Success in regard to conventional goals, and personal vulnerability in terms of Low Self-Esteem and Hopelessness. With respect to both prevention and intervention, these findings suggest targets for program design and practices in family management.

An inquiry that engages both risk and protective factors cannot escape questioning about their separateness as domains of independent variables. The most frequent challenge is that risk and protection are really opposite ends of the same variables, hence highly correlated inversely, rather than being orthogonal. We have dealt with this problem in the introduction by specifying conceptual properties of protective factors that are deliberately different from the conceptual properties of risk factors in relation to problem behavior. Protective factors were conceptualized as variables that reflect involvement with and commitment to conventional society, that control against nonnormative activities, and that refer to activities incompatible with normative transgression. With respect to the actual measures we used to operationalize risk and protection, they seem to us to be rather clear indicators, although one or two may well be arguable. In the end, it is the empirical findings that buttress the case we have tried to make. First, the RFI and PFI share only a modest proportion (18%) of common variance. Second, measures that might most clearly seem opposite ends of a single variable, for example, Friends Models for Problem Behavior and Friends Models for Conventional Behavior, are only correlated $-.20$, and indeed, in the hierarchical multiple regressions for Delinquent-Type Behavior and also for Marijuana Involvement, both of these two predictor measures retained a significant beta weight at the final step. Thus, it is neither obvious nor useful to assume that being high on one of the measures implies being low on the other.

Third, to pursue this example further, these two measures have quite different correlations with other measures, for example, with Prosocial Activities (.32 for Friends Models for Conventional Behavior and $-.11$ for Friends Models for Problem Behavior) or with the MPBI itself ($-.21$ for Friends Models for Conventional Behavior and .62 for Friends Models for Problem Behavior).

Another seemingly obvious example might be the risk factor, Grade Point Average, and the protective factor, Positive Orientation to School. Although related as expected, their correlation is, again, small (.28), and their relations to other measures are quite different. Grade Point Average correlated .36 with SES; by contrast, Positive Orientation to School correlated only .13 with SES. The respective correlations of Grade Point Average and Positive Orientation to School with Positive Orientation to Health are .14 and .42, with Attitudinal Intolerance of Deviance are .21 and .45, with Positive Relations With Adults are .10 and .30, and with Perceived Regulatory Controls are .14 and .37. The results of the present study seem to us to provide support for the heuristic value of making a conceptual distinction between protection and risk, and for efforts to operationalize that distinction with distinctive measures.

The generality of the findings for the direct effects of protection across both genders and all three racial/ethnic subgroups was pervasive. With respect to the moderator effects of protection, generality was more limited; although evident for the total sample and for the female, White, and Hispanic subgroups, a significant interaction was not found for male students or for Blacks. With respect to gender differences, a somewhat greater proportion of total variance in problem behavior is accounted for among the women than among the men (29% vs. 20%), but no other consistent difference was apparent. With respect to the racial/ethnic differences, the Black sample data accounted for the smallest proportion of variance of any subgroup (18%), and the Black sample was by far the smallest subgroup (n = 346). But it is not obvious why no significant interaction was achieved because there was a direct effect of protection for Blacks, and Blacks also had the highest mean score on the PFI of all three ethnic groups.

The findings we have reported are limited in important ways. The less-than-desirable initial sample participation rate and the subsequent attrition certainly impose limits on the generality of the inferences that can be drawn. The conceptual effort to distinguish risk and protective factors, while salutary, could benefit from further theoretical elaboration, and the empirical support for the distinction, presented earlier, is not immune from alternative interpretation. It is also the case that the measures used, even those about the social environment, are all limited to self-reports from questionnaires, that is, all are provided by the same individual. The possibility, therefore, that common method variance has influenced the findings cannot be ruled out. It would be desirable in future research to have external validity established for the measures used. Measures independent of self-report, especially those for the ecological variables, would clearly be a step forward. Furthermore, the measurement of protection could certainly be made more exhaustive in regard to family, neighborhood, and institutional factors. Finally, deliberate sampling to maximize jointly extreme scores on the risk and protective predictors would permit stronger tests of their interaction.

Despite these limitations, the study has illuminated the role of protective factors in adolescent problem behavior and development. Greater recognition of the direct and moderator effects of protection should provide a strong stimulus for more sophisticated theorizing and, equally important, for the development of prevention and intervention efforts targeted at enhancing protection as well as at reducing risk.

REFERENCES

Aiken, L. S., & West, S. G. (1991). *Multiple regression: Testing and interpreting interactions.* Newbury Park, CA: Sage.

Baron, R. M., & Kenny, D. A. (1986). The moderator–mediator variable distinction in social psychological research: Conceptual, strategic, and statistical considerations. *Journal of Personality and Social Psychology, 51,* 1173–1182.

Brook, J. S., Whiteman, M., Cohen, P., & Tanaka, J. S. (1992). Childhood precursors of adolescent drug use: A longitudinal analysis. *Genetic, Social, and General Psychology Monographs, 118,* 195–213.

Bry, B. H. (1983). Predicting drug abuse: Review and reformulation. *International Journal of the Addictions, 18,* 223–233.

Chaplin, W. F. (1991). The next generation of moderator reach in personality psychology. *Journal of Personality, 59,* 143–178.

Cohen, J. (1978). Partialed products are interactions; partialed powers are curve components. *Psychological Bulletin, 85,* 858–866.

Cohen, J., & Cohen, P. (1983). *Applied multiple regression/correlation analysis for the behavioral sciences* (2nd ed.). Hillsdale, NJ: Erlbaum.

Felix-Ortiz, M., & Newcomb, M. D. (1992). Risk and protective factors for drug use among Latino and White adolescents. *Hispanic Journal of Behavior Science, 14,* 291–309.

Garmezy, N. (1985). Stress-resistant children: The search for protective factors. In J. E. Stevenson (Ed.), *Recent research in developmental psychopathology. Journal of Child Psychology and Psychiatry Book Supplement No. 4* (pp. 213–233). Oxford, England: Pergamon Press.

Garmezy, N., & Masten, A. S. (1986). Stress, competence, and resilience: Common frontiers for therapist and psychopathologist. *Behavior Therapy, 17,* 500–521.

Grossman, F. K., Beinashowitz, J., Anderson, L., Sakurai, M., Finnin, L., & Flaherty, M. (1992). Risk and resilience in young adolescents. *Journal of Youth and Adolescence, 21,* 529–550.

Hawkins, J. D., Catalano, R. F., & Miller, J. Y. (1992). Risk and protective factors for alcohol and other drug problems in adolescence and early adulthood: Implications for substance abuse prevention. *Psychological Bulletin, 112,* 64–105.

Jessor, R. (1991). Risk behavior in adolescence: A psychosocial framework for understanding and action. *Journal of Adolescent Health, 12,* 597–605.

Jessor, R. (1993). Successful adolescent development among youth in high-risk settings. *American Psychologist, 48,* 117–126.

Jessor, R., Donovan, J. E., & Costa, F. M. (1991). *Beyond adolescence: Problem behavior and young adult development.* Cambridge, England: Cambridge University Press.

Jessor, R., Graves, T. D., Hanson, R. C., & Jessor, S. L. (1968). *Society, personality and deviant behavior: A study of a tri-ethnic community.* New York: Holt, Rinehart, & Winston.

Jessor, R., & Jessor, S. L. (1997). *Problem behavior and psychosocial development: A longitudinal study of youth.* New York: Academic Press.

Luthar, S. S., & Zigler, E. (1991). Vulnerability and competence: A review of research on resilience in childhood. *American Journal of Orthopsychiatry, 61,* 6–22.

McClelland, G. H., & Judd, C. M. (1993). Statistical difficulties of detecting interactions and moderator effects. *Psychological Bulletin, 114,* 376–390.

Newcomb, M. E., Maddahian, E., & Bentler, P. A. (1986). Risk for drug use among adolescents: Concurrent and longitudinal analyses. *American Journal of Public Health, 76,* 525–531.

Pellegrini, D. S. (1990). Psychosocial risk and protective factors in childhood. *Journal of Developmental and Behavioral Pediatrics, 11,* 201–209.

Rutter, M. (1979). Protective factors in children's response to stress and disadvantage. In W. M. Kent & J. E. Rolf (Eds.), *Primary prevention of psychopathology* (Vol. 3, pp. 49–74). Hanover, NH: University Press of New England.

Rutter, M. (1987). Psychosocial resilience and protective mechanisms. *American Journal of Orthopsychiatry, 57,* 316–331.

Sameroff, A. J., Seifer, R., Baldwin, A., & Baldwin, C. (1993). Stability of intelligence from preschool to adolescence: The influence of social and family risk factors. *Child Development, 64,* 80–97.

Sameroff, A. J., Seifer, R., Barocas, R., Zax, M., & Greenspan, S. (1987). Intelligence quotient scores of 4-year-old children: Social-environmental risk factors. *Pediatrics, 79,* 343–350.

Saunders, D. R. (1956). Moderator variables in prediction. *Educational and Psychological Measurement, 16,* 209–222.

Small, S. A., & Luster, T. (1994). Adolescent sexual activity: An ecological risk-factor approach. *Journal of Marriage and the Family, 56,* 181–192.

Stacy, A. W., Newcomb, M. D., & Bentler, P. M. (1992). Interactive and higher-order effects of social influences on drug use. *Journal of Health and Social Behavior, 33,* 226–241.

Stacy, A. W., Sussman, S., Dent, C. W., Burton, D., & Flay, B. (1992). Moderators of peer social influence in adolescent smoking. *Personality and Social Psychology Bulletin, 18,* 163–172.

Werner, E. E. (1989a). Children of the garden island. *Scientific American, 260,* 106–111.

Werner, E. E. (1989b). High-risk children in young adulthood: A longitudinal study from birth to 32 years. *American Journal of Orthopsychiatry, 59,* 72–81.

Wills, T. A., Vaccaro, D., & McNamara, G. (1992). The role of life events, family support, and competence in adolescent substance use: A test of vulnerability and protective factors. *American Journal of Community Psychology, 20,* 349–374.

9

PREDICTION OF CONTROLLED DRINKING BY ALCOHOLICS AND PROBLEM DRINKERS

HAROLD ROSENBERG

Few issues have sparked as much controversy in alcohol studies as the question of controlled drinking (CD). Specifically, must all alcoholics or problem drinkers be counseled to abstain from alcohol for the rest of their lives, or can some of them—by their own efforts, with therapy, or seemingly spontaneously—drink in a moderate, controlled, and harm-free manner? Several definitions are necessary before we take up this question.

The first question is, what is CD? Definitions of CD have varied, but usually have included some limit on the amount and frequency of consumption (e.g., maximum of 3 oz of alcohol per day) and the condition that the drinking results in neither signs of dependence (e.g., withdrawal syndrome) nor social, legal, or health problems (Heather & Tebbutt, 1989).

Reprinted from *Psychological Bulletin, 113*, 129–139. (1993). Copyright © 1993 by the American Psychological Association. Used with permission of the author.

This project was supported in part by a Summer Stipend Award from Bradley University. I thank Seymour Rosenberg for his helpful comments on many earlier drafts of this article; Carole Fisher and Brian Spencer, librarians at Mapperley Hospital, Nottingham, England, for their assistance in acquiring reprints; and the anonymous reviewers for their helpful critique of a previous version.

Some investigators have included one or both of the following in the definition of CD: (a) The drinking does not result in intoxication, and (b) the drinker experiences a sense of mastery or control over the drinking (Reinert & Bowen, 1968). These latter two conditions are less frequently included by researchers, probably because such internal states cannot be directly corroborated by collateral sources, as drinking and its consequences can be. Other terms that have been proposed to describe drinking that is controlled include *moderate drinking* (Marlatt, 1989) and *nonproblem drinking* (Heather & Tebbutt, 1989).

Another definitional issue concerns criteria for alcoholism and problem drinking. In general, the terms *alcoholism* and *alcohol dependence* are used interchangeably and are indicated by loss-of-control drinking, markedly increased tolerance, withdrawal symptoms on cessation of consumption, and a compulsion to drink. Some authors have identified alcoholism/ dependence with a list of symptoms or negative consequences of alcohol dependence (e.g., Polich, Armor, & Braiker, 1981), others have used the criteria in the third edition of the *Diagnostic and Statistical Manual of Mental Disorders* (*DSM-III*; American Psychiatric Association, 1980), and still others have used specially developed scales such as the Alcohol Dependence Scale (Skinner & Allen, 1982) or Severity of Alcohol Dependence Questionnaire (SADQ; Stockwell, Murphy, & Hodgson, 1983).

The term *problem drinker* is usually reserved for persons who display few if any signs of dependence although problem drinkers often drink excessively (e.g., more than 21 standard drinks of 0.5 oz of alcohol per week) and suffer one or more alcohol-related problems such as drunken driving arrests, occupational or social dysfunction, and health problems. When describing each study reviewed in the present article, I note whether the subjects were reported to be alcoholics or problem drinkers.

The modern history of research on CD began 3 decades ago, when Davies (1962) produced a storm of comment and research with his report that a long-term follow-up of 93 alcoholics treated at Maudsley Hospital revealed 7 who were "normal" drinkers. Davies was not the first to report cases of CD, but his article provoked much protest (replies published in *Quarterly Journal of Studies on Alcohol*, 1963, 24, 109–121, 321–332, and 727–735) and has remained so prominent that some two decades later Edwards (1985) questioned Davies's interpretation of the results.

Some who oppose CD argue that stable CD in alcoholics is so rare that there is no point recommending it for clients (e.g., McCrady, 1985; Stockwell, 1986). However, estimates of the frequency of CD vary considerably, in part because definitions of CD and other outcome categories vary (Heather & Tebbutt, 1989; Miller, 1985). In addition, the frequency of CD may vary depending on the ideology of the treatment service, type of patient sampled, and country and time period during which CD was studied (Gerard & Saenger, 1966; Peele, 1987).

Reviews of treatment outcome, the natural history of alcohol consumption, and laboratory- and hospital-based drinking by alcoholics have revealed that CD is not rare and, depending on the population studied, is no less frequent than abstinence (Heather & Robertson, 1981; Lloyd & Salzberg, 1975; Marlatt, 1983; Pattison, Sobell, & Sobell, 1978; Polich et al., 1981). In a review of studies across many different treatment sites, Miller (1983) found that moderate drinking occurred in 25–90% (M = approximately 65%) of CD-treated samples. Moreover, in long-term follow-up studies (>15 years) of alcoholic patients treated in abstinence-oriented programs, controlled drinkers constituted 10–30% of the treated sample, abstainers constituted an additional 10–30%, and relapsers were often the largest outcome group (Hyman, 1976; McCabe, 1986; Nordstrom & Berglund, 1987; Vaillant & Milofsky, 1982).

Others have challenged the value of CD with the argument that it cannot be sustained and inevitably results in relapse. The empirical evidence is mixed. In some studies, periods of uncontrolled drinking frequently followed CD in alcoholics who attended abstinence-oriented treatment (e.g., Finney & Moos, 1981; Watson, 1987). In other studies, however, CD was sustained during follow-up periods of at least 1 year (e.g., Miller & Baca, 1983; Pettinati, Sugarman, DiDonato, & Maurer, 1982; Polich et al., 1981; Vaillant & Milofsky, 1982). Instability of drinking is not confined to CD in any case, and many alcoholics' drinking patterns—whether controlled, abstinent, or uncontrolled—change several times within a matter of months or years (e.g., Watson & Pucel, 1985; Yates & Norris, 1981). Uncontrolled drinking is a frequent occurrence following periods of both abstinence *and* CD, and periods of relapse are likely whether an alcoholic attempts CD or abstinence.

Although it was not possible to address all the important issues in CD in the present review, some of them are mentioned briefly here. For one, whereas CD is widely accepted in the United Kingdom (Robertson & Heather, 1982; Rosenberg, Melville, Levell, & Hodge, 1992), there is considerable opposition to CD in American and Canadian alcohol treatment programs (Brochu, 1990; Miller, 1986; Rush & Ogborne, 1986) and relatively few American treatment programs openly offer CD training. Despite the widespread opposition to CD in North America, however, a variety of interventions to help alcoholics and problem drinkers moderate their drinking have been evaluated. These interventions include self-recording of drinking and blood alcohol content; setting daily and weekly consumption limits; and pacing drinking by sipping, diluting, and alternating alcoholic and nonalcoholic beverages (Alden, 1988; Sanchez-Craig, Annis, Bornet, & MacDonald, 1984). Another important issue is the value of CD training and CD goals to prevent more harmful drinking and the development of alcohol dependence by high-risk problem drinkers (Marlatt, 1987; Sanchez-Craig, Wilkinson, & Walker, 1987). The value of CD is enhanced by the evidence that some problem drinkers may be more likely to sustain CD than abstinence (Polich et al., 1981; Sanchez-Craig et al., 1984). As summarized in the Institute of Medicine (IOM; 1990) review on matching alcohol treatments to individual needs, "Uniform goals for all individuals may be a simpler approach, but the notion of different goals for different individuals seems more consistent with the heterogeneity of alcohol problems and the individuals who manifest them" (p. 296).

If we accept the propositions that a meaningful proportion of alcoholics and problem drinkers do moderate their drinking and that CD does not inevitably result in relapse, the question is, which alcoholics and problem drinkers are able to control their drinking? As Marlatt (1983) asked in his review of the CD controversy, "What type of individual responds best to an abstinence treatment goal compared to a goal of controlled drinking? Is it possible to match clients to a treatment goal that best fits their abilities and beliefs?" (p. 1106). An answer to this question has implications for both theoretical issues relating to the nature of alcoholism and practical issues related to client-treatment matching (Edwards et al., 1988).

The most recent comprehensive review of patient characteristics associated with CD was performed by Heather and Robertson (1981). Other more recent reviews (Edwards et al., 1988; Hill, 1985; Miller, 1983; Peele, 1987) have briefly addressed this question, but no comprehensive review has been published since that of Heather and Robertson. In their review, Heather and Robertson summarized nine investigations of possible predictors of CD. They noted four conditions reliably associated with CD: lower severity of drinking symptoms, younger age, regular employment, and less contact with Alcoholics Anonymous (AA). Successful abstinence was predicted by three indexes: prior abstinence, greater previous contact with AA, and a self-label of "alcoholic." In short, the data to 1980 indicated that (a) lower severity of a drinking problem (measured in various ways) was predictive of a CD outcome and (b) an alcoholic self-concept and an abstinence orientation were associated with an abstinent outcome.

In the present review, I examined recent research on the factors that appear to predict CD by alcoholics and problem drinkers and the methodological issues to be considered in the evaluation and design of research on this question. I found that no single factor has been uniformly predictive, although severity of dependence and client attitudes about CD and abstinence have received considerable support. Moreover, the search for pretreatment predictors of an ultimate drinking status has been hindered by an unrealistic assumption that presumably enduring personal characteristics create a stable outcome. Instead, predicting CD may be more successful if the drinker is seen as an active agent in his or her drinking who is subject to multiple influences, some of which are relatively enduring personal characteristics and some of which are relatively transient environmental events.

SEVERITY OF DEPENDENCE

No patient characteristic has received more attention as a predictor of CD than severity of dependence. The severity hypothesis (Orford & Keddie, 1986a) maintains that the greater an alcoholic's physical dependence on alcohol, the less likely it is that the person will be able to control his or her alcohol consumption. Therefore, CD is considered achievable by alcoholics with fewer signs of dependence and by incipient problem drinkers; individuals whose alcoholism is of greater severity and who do not abstain are considered the most likely to relapse.

Finney and Moos (1981) investigated variables associated with outcome in alcoholic patients who had attended any one of five residential, abstinence-oriented treatment programs. Their study included measures of pretreatment demographic and drinking patterns; life events; treatment experiences (e.g., number of sessions, attendance of AA meetings, and ingestion of disulfiram); and posttreatment after care, family environment, and work environment. Results did not reveal any significant demographic differences between abstainers and moderate drinkers at 6-month follow-up, but they did support the severity hypothesis in that moderate drinkers reported fewer physical symptoms and fewer hangovers before treatment than did the 6-month abstainers. In addition, the moderate drinkers had consumed less alcohol per typical drinking day before entering treatment.

Foy, Nunn, and Rychtarik (1984), in their initial study and a 5–6-year follow-up study (Rychtarik, Foy, Scott, Lokey, & Prue, 1987) of an inpatient CD treatment program for chronic alcoholics, also noted the relationship of CD to severity of dependence. The number of moderate-drinking days during early follow-up (7–12 months posttreatment) was associated with fewer pretreatment symptoms of dependence, but neither the number of abstinent days nor the number of abusive-drinking days was associated with the number of dependence symptoms. This result provides some support for the severity hypothesis, but the long-term follow-up revealed that the number of "major withdrawal symptoms" was no longer correlated with consumption 5–6 years after treatment. Maisto, Sobell, and Sobell (1980), in a 2-year follow-up study of alcoholic patients who participated in their individualized behavior therapy studies (M. B. Sobell & Sobell, 1973, 1976), also found no significant association between severity and posttreatment drinking.

Vaillant and Milofsky (1982) reported a long-term (33 years) follow-up of a sample of 456 adolescents, 110 of whom met their criteria for "alcohol abuse" at some time during follow-up. Their classification of alcohol abuse included subjects who were problem drinkers and others who were alcohol dependent. Vaillant and Milofsky compared 18 "asymptomatic drinkers" (i.e., controlled drinkers) with 49 men who had abstained for at least 12 months at some time subsequent to their drinking problem. Consistent with the severity hypothesis, the asymptomatic drinkers had fewer symptoms on Vaillant and Milofsky's Problem Drinking Scale (PDS) of physical dependence and social deviance, and only one third met *DSM-III* criteria for alcohol dependence. In contrast, 80% of the 49 "alcohol abusers" who then abstained were alcohol dependent according to *DSM-III* criteria, and most had had at least nine symptoms on the PDS.

Helzer et al. (1985) interviewed a sample of 393 former alcoholic patients from a variety of institutions to assess the frequency of drinking outcomes, including CD and occasional drinking. Severity of dependence was associated with outcome in the sense that moderate drinkers had later onsets of drinking per se, of regular drinking, of first intoxication, and of problem drinking (all of which may have been correlated in their subject sample). The moderate and occasional drinkers had the lowest lifetime number of assessed medical, social, and legal problems related to alcohol. Both the Vaillant and Milofsky (1982) and Helzer et al. investigations are laudable for the length of follow-up and for the sampling of populations not typically studied. However, Helzer et al.'s restrictive definition of CD and Vaillant and Milofksy's inclusion of limited binge drinking in the definition of abstinence limit the generalizability of their results (Heather & Tebbutt, 1989; Miller, 1985; Peele, 1987).

In a 10–12-year follow-up of a Maudsley Hospital sample of patients diagnosed as alcoholics, Edwards, Duckitt, Oppenheimer, Sheehan, and Taylor (1983) reported that the controlled drinkers had relatively low scores on their measure of dependence. In a subsequent and more extensive and sophisticated treatment of the follow-up data, Edwards et al. (1988) evaluated the association of intake variables with two multivariate dimensions of outcome (C. Taylor et al., 1986). A worse outcome on the first outcome dimension (i.e., heavier drinking with poor adjustment) was predicted by more alcohol-related troubles (and a higher Eysenck Neuroticism score) at intake. Outcome on the second dimension was not correlated with drinking problems or severity at intake.

The aforementioned studies were conducted with patients who were typically chronic, hospitalized alcoholics. The severity hypothesis also has received support from studies of the effectiveness of CD training for problem drinkers. This research has shown that problem drinkers frequently reduce their consumption to moderate, nonproblem levels and maintain such levels during follow-up of 1 or more years (e.g., Alden, 1988; Miller, Leckman, Delaney, & Tinkcom, 1992; Sanchez-Craig et al., 1984).

Additional support comes from research by Miller and his associates, who examined predictors of outcome in four studies of outpatient problem drinkers who participated in CD training programs. Lower severity of dependence at intake was predictive of CD outcome in two studies (Miller & Baca, 1983; Miller & Joyce, 1979), but the evidence was equivocal in two others (Miller et al., 1992; Miller, Pechacek, & Hamburg, 1981). Specifically, Miller and Joyce (1979) found that abstainers at 3-month follow-up had significantly higher scores on the Michigan Alcoholism Screening Test (MAST; Selzer, 1971) than did controlled and uncontrolled drinkers. In a separate investigation with a 2-year follow-up, abstainers again had significantly higher MAST scores than did controlled drinkers (Miller & Baca, 1983).

In a long-term follow-up of problem drinkers who participated in behavioral self-control training, Miller et al. (1992) found an equal proportion of their abstainers and asymptomatic (i.e., controlled) drinkers diagnosable at intake as alcohol dependent using *DSM-III* criteria. On another measure of severity, however, a significantly greater proportion of both abstainers and unremitted drinkers were classified as more impaired at intake than were drinkers who were later classified as asymptomatic or improved-but-impaired. Finally, Miller et al. (1981) found that controlled drinkers had significantly higher MAST scores and significantly greater consumption at intake than did less improved drinkers, but there were no subjects abstaining at follow-up to allow for a comparison of the two types of successful outcome.

As Miller et al. (1992) demonstrated, different measures of severity may be differentially predictive of outcome. Measures of severity examined in the present review included withdrawal symptoms, *DSM-III* criteria, drinking history, specially developed scales, and the MAST, many of which are correlated with each other (Orford & Keddie, 1986a; Skinner & Allen, 1982). The convergence of results supporting the severity hypothesis is impressive given that the researchers used different indexes of severity, sampled different populations of drinkers, and compared different types of outcomes, but it is still not clear which measures of severity are most predictive of CD.

The present review and the earlier one by Heather and Robertson (1981) generally support the severity hypothesis. Several researchers, however, have reported that measures of severity of dependence were not associated with outcome (Elal-Lawrence, Slade, & Dewey, 1986; Heather, Rollnick, & Winton, 1983; Maisto et al., 1980; Orford & Keddie, 1986b). In addition, the nature of the relationship between severity and CD has not yet been established. One possibility is that the likelihood of CD decreases monotonically as severity of dependence increases, and at some point severity is so great that the probability of CD is zero. Alternatively, although CD generally declines as severity increases, there may be plateaus in severity in which changes in level of severity do not matter. Also, even at the highest levels of severity, perhaps some alcoholics are able to control their drinking as a result of other factors. Finally, a significant association between the two variables does not necessarily mean that lower severity is the cause of CD.

PERSUASION AND BELIEFS

The other major predictor of CD that has been investigated is what Orford and Keddie (1986a, 1986b) termed the persuasion or indoctrination hypothesis. According to this hypothesis, outcome is influenced by the degree to which an alcoholic or problem drinker believes in the necessity of abstinence versus the degree to which the person is persuaded that CD is attainable. The indexes used to measure patient beliefs varied considerably among the studies in which this hypothesis was examined. I reviewed both the results of these studies and the methodological issues raised by the diversity of indexes of persuasion.

Evidence in support of the persuasion hypothesis includes results showing an inverse relationship between CD and patients' beliefs about the necessity of maintaining abstinence and the inevitability of loss of control. Heather et al. (1983) pitted the persuasion hypothesis against the severity hypothesis in a study of the 6-month posttreatment drinking patterns of alcoholic patients in an abstinence-oriented British alcohol treatment unit. They measured subjective sense of control with a multi-item self-report survey of expectations of loss of control and of moderate drinking. Patients who resumed drinking at a "harm-free" level (fewer than five drinks per day and no negative consequences) scored significantly lower on the scale of subjective dependence than did the abstainers and relapsers. Scores on a measure of physical severity of dependence (the SADQ; Stockwell et al., 1983), however, were not predictive of drinking during follow-up. Similarly, Orford and Keddie (1986b), in a 1-year assessment of patients in an English alcohol treatment unit, found that both the patients' expectations of being able to control their drinking and the type of treatment (abstinence vs. CD) were associated with outcome, but physical dependence was not predictive of outcome.

Contrary to the results of these British studies, patients' beliefs were not related to drinking outcome in a sample of American male alcoholic patients studied by Watson, Jacobs, Pucel, Tilleskjor, and Hoodecheck (1984). There are several explanations why Watson et al. may not have found persuasion predictive. First, they defined rejection of abstinence on the basis of two interview questions regarding subjects' perception of loss of control and moderate drinking in "all, some, or no alcoholics," rather than the subject's perception of the likelihood of being able to moderate his own drinking. Second, Watson et al. measured CD using collateral reports of the degree to which the patient's drinking was controlled or uncontrolled, and it is unclear whether collaterals had the same operational definition of CD. Finally, Watson et al. studied patients in an abstinence-oriented program in a Veterans Administration hospital, a setting in which the patients might expect little or no support for expressing a belief in moderate drinking.

Another measure of persuasion is a patient's decision to pursue CD or abstinence after treatment (often referred to as goal choice). Studies in which goal choice has been evaluated as a predictor of CD have yielded inconsistent results. Booth, Dale, and Ansari (1984) found that client drinking status at 1-year follow-up was associated with goal choice at discharge from an English alcohol treatment unit. However, they also found that most patients drank problematically or in excess of the CD limit at some time during follow-up, whether their goal was abstinence or CD. In another study of English alcoholic patients, Elal-Lawrence et al. (1986, 1987) found that goal choice *at intake* was not related to outcome, but goal choice *at discharge* was predictive of outcome.

In a study of alcohol-dependent Swedish outpatients, Ojehagen and Berglund (1989) found no difference in the number of abusive-drinking days per month among patient groups who had a consistent abstinence goal, a consistent CD goal, or a drinking goal that changed during a 2-year follow-up period. All groups averaged about 2 abusive-drinking days per month, but patients who consistently chose abstinence drank significantly more on those abusive-drinking days than did the other goal choice groups. In addition, goal choice was stable across the 2 years for only a little over half the patients, and it was not uncommon for goal choice to change more than once during follow-up.

Another measure of persuasion is self-label as an alcoholic. Miller et al. (1992) found that self-acceptance of the label "alcoholic" or "problem drinker" at intake was associated with abstinence at outcome, whereas no asymptomatic drinkers perceived themselves as alcoholic and most rated themselves at intake as nonproblem drinkers. Similarly, Miller and Joyce (1979) found that abstainers' mean self-rating as "alcoholic" (M = 5.0) was significantly higher than the mean self-ratings of controlled drinkers and relapsers, although the latter two groups still perceived themselves as "alcoholic" (mean ratings = 4.3 and 4.6, respectively, on a scale of 1–5).

Other indexes of persuasion include the client's exposure to AA and exposure to CD training. Several investigations since Heather and Robertson's (1981) have provided support for their finding that controlled drinkers attended AA less frequently than abstainers both before and after treatment (Elal-Lawrence et al., 1986, 1987; Finney & Moos, 1981). Exposure to CD training also has been predictive of CD outcome, perhaps as a result of both a change in persuasion and the content of CD training. Elal-Lawrence et al. (1987) reported that the controlled drinkers in their study had received CD training more frequently than the other outcome groups, but this was confounded with the fact that more of the controlled drinkers also had had inpatient treatment during which CD training was offered. Maisto et al. (1980) reported that randomly assigning a subject to a CD goal, regardless of whether CD training was received, was associated with more CD days during follow-up.

The results of these studies lend support to the persuasion hypothesis, but they also raise a number of important questions. First, what is the source of a problem drinker's persuasion? Patients' beliefs about the efficacy of CD may be present before treatment, may result from indoctrination during treatment, and may change after discharge as a result of posttreatment experiences. In addition, a client's persuasion that abstinence is necessary may be a result, as well as an antecedent, of unsuccessful attempts at CD.

Second, what specific beliefs constitute the persuasion that CD is a likely personal outcome for an individual problem drinker? For example, how important is the expectation that one is able to control one's drinking? Heather, Winton, and Rollnick (1982) found that the item on their Subjective Dependence Scale that measured patients' belief in their own ability to drink moderately did not predict harm-free drinking, but knowledge of and belief in the saying "First drink, then drunk" did. In addition, how can researchers distinguish a genuine and realistic belief in CD from an unrealistic fantasy of CD?

Third, how stable are a drinker's beliefs over time? In the studies of belief I reviewed, subjective dependence or goal choice was typically measured only once and its predictive value was tested some months later. However, individuals' expectancy of drinking moderately, their perception of themselves as an alcoholic, and their goal choice may change during and after treatment (Ojehagen & Berglund, 1989).

The studies in the present review support the persuasion hypothesis, and patients' attitudes and beliefs probably have value in goal planning. However, an assessment of the full value of this hypothesis requires a better understanding of the nature and source of the different beliefs that constitute persuasion, psychometric analyses of the measures of persuasion, and prospective studies that include repeated measurement of both beliefs and drinking during follow-up.

OTHER PREDICTORS

In addition to severity and persuasion, which have received the most attention, a variety of other patient characteristics also have been found to be significant predictors of CD. In this section I summarize the results of studies in which the relationship between CD and frequency of treatment, pretreatment drinking style, psychological and social stability, demographic characteristics, family history of drinking, referral source, and posttreatment adjustment and drinking was evaluated.

Frequency of Treatment

Evidence from three investigations indicates that the fewer the number of treatment episodes for alcohol problems, the greater the likelihood of CD (Finney & Moos, 1981; Maisto et al., 1980; Saunders & Kershaw, 1979). Explanations of this statistical relationship may be cast in terms of both the persuasion hypothesis and the severity hypothesis. Multiple treatment experiences may, as the persuasion hypothesis implies, influence a patient's identity as an alcoholic and strengthen his or her belief in the need for abstinence. Multiple treatment episodes also may reflect deterioration or severity as well as access to and willingness to seek professional care.

Pretreatment Drinking Style

Two studies suggest that drinking style, perhaps independent of severity of dependence, is associated with CD. For example, Elal-Lawrence et al. (1986) found that both relapsers and controlled drinkers had shorter periods of abstinence before treatment than did abstainers. They also found that controlled drinkers were significantly more likely than abstainers to have been continuous drinkers (98% vs. 80%). These proportions, although statistically significantly different, reveal that the majority of both abstainers and controlled drinkers drank continuously before admission.

McCabe (1986) conducted a 16-year follow-up study of alcohol-dependent patients treated in a British alcohol treatment unit and found that the only significant predictor of outcome was assignment to Jellinek's (1960) typology. Specifically, epsilon type (i.e., bout) drinkers were most likely to be problem or dependent drinkers or to have died by the time of follow-up. Patients originally classified as gamma type (loss-of-control) drinkers and delta type (inability-to-abstain) drinkers were about evenly split between good outcome (abstinence or CD) and bad outcome (relapse, problem drinking, or death).

Psychological and Social Stability

Employment and good social and psychological functioning are considered prognostic of better outcome in several types of psychological disorders. Outcome studies have shown that such functioning is predictive of CD. In studies reviewed by Heather and Robertson (1981), pretreatment employment was predictive of CD (Hyman, 1976; Polich et al., 1981; Vogler, Weissbach, & Compton, 1977), and in two more recent studies, moderate drinking and abstinence were associated with better pretreatment employment (Elal-Lawrence et al., 1986) and having a skilled occupation at intake (Edwards et al., 1988).

In a long-term (M = 20 years) follow-up of Swedish inpatients treated for alcoholism, Nordstrom and Berglund (1987) found that social stability (e.g., not having a criminal record, having a stable work record, and being married) on first admission was more frequent among those who ultimately became social drinkers than among those who abstained. Rychtarik et al. (1987) found that the fewer the pretreatment social supports (spouse, contact with living children, and permanent housing), the greater a patient's average daily consumption at the 5–6-year follow-up.

With regard to psychological functioning, Finney and Moos (1981) found that a measure of psychological well-being at intake differentiated controlled drinkers from abstainers 6 months later, with controlled drinkers having a greater sense of well-being. Nordstrom and Berglund (1987) found that patients who eventually abstained had been assessed at admission 20 years earlier as displaying signs of "personality disturbance" (i.e., interpersonal dependence, immaturity, psychopathy, lack of commitment, or coldness) more frequently than patients who became social drinkers. Edwards et al. (1988) found that poorer outcome at follow-up was associated with psychological test scores that had indicated neuroticism some 10 years previously.

Demographic Characteristics

Age, education, gender, and other background characteristics have been included as demographic variables in studies of predictors of CD, albeit without a theoretical rationale. In two studies reviewed by Heather and Robertson (1981)—those by Polich et al. (1981) and Vogler et al. (1977)—younger age was associated with CD during follow-up. Similarly, Maisto et al. (1980) found younger age correlated with "days functioning well" (i.e., abstinence plus CD days). In a number of studies, however, age failed to predict CD (Finney & Moos, 1981; Helzer et al., 1985; Miller & Joyce, 1979; Nordstrom & Berglund, 1987). Perhaps both younger and older problem drinkers may be more likely to practice CD than middle-aged abusers (cf. Drew, 1968), and studies in which mean ages among outcome groups are simply compared are not suitable for examining such a nonlinear relationship.

The amount of formal education has not been found to be a consistent predictor of outcome. In one investigation, education was not a significant variable in controlled consumption (Miller & Joyce, 1979), but in two other studies less education was associated with CD (Maisto et al., 1980; Miller et al., 1981).

Many investigators have either studied only men or selected only men for follow-up (Edwards et al., 1988; Foy et al., 1984; Nordstrom & Berglund, 1987; Vaillant & Milofksy, 1982; Watson et al., 1984). In several studies that included both men and women, gender was associated with outcome and women appeared more likely to moderate their drinking than men. Elal-Lawrence et al. (1986) found that whereas 25% of their abstainers were women, approximately 40% of their CD and relapsed groups were female; Miller and Joyce (1979) also found more women (40%) in their CD group than in their abstinent and uncontrolled groups (11% and 16%, respectively); and Helzer et al. (1985) noted that 15% of the women they studied became controlled drinkers, compared with 4% of the men. Sanchez-Craig, Leigh, Spivak, and Lei (1989) studied male and female problem drinkers recruited by advertisements to participate in brief CD training programs. During the 1-year follow-up, women reported a significantly greater reduction in the number of heavy-drinking days than did men, although both sexes showed a significant treatment effect.

In contrast to these studies, Bromet and Moos (1979) found more male than female controlled drinkers and Orford and Keddie (1986b) found similar proportions of men and women in their outcome groups. In addition, the relationship between gender and CD is unclear because there may be sampling bias in the women who seek treatment, are accepted for treatment, and are available for follow-up. It is also unclear what female psychological characteristics, either alone or in interaction with treatment experiences, increase the probability of moderate drinking. Moreover, it may be easier for women to meet the consumption limits for CD because of size differences. If the quantity/frequency limit for CD in a study is the same for men and women, more women may meet the criteria for CD because women, on average, are smaller, drink less, and may require less alcohol to achieve an intoxicating blood alcohol level than larger men, who consume more drinks and fail to meet CD limits.

Family History of Drinking

The degree to which heredity predisposes a person to alcohol abuse and dependence has yet to be established. In a recent review and critique of the major twin studies and adoption studies that have been interpreted as conclusive demonstrations of the genetic contribution to alcoholism, Searles (1988) noted that the interacting roles of heredity and the environment in problem drinking have not been adequately studied to warrant definitive conclusions about the genetic etiology of alcoholism.

Whatever contributions heredity and the environment make to the etiology of alcoholism, it is reasonable to examine the empirical relationship between a family history of alcoholism and CD. The results of CD prediction studies in which parental or family history of alcoholism was assessed are mixed.

Miller and Joyce (1979) found subjects' ratings of their father's status as a drinker on a scale from 1 (*abstainer*) to 5 (*alcoholic*) was significantly different for their three outcome groups, with the fathers of abstainers having a higher average rating (4.2) than the fathers of controlled drinkers (2.9) and relapsers (3.1). Miller et al. (1992) found that the relatives of controlled drinkers had significantly fewer symptoms of alcoholism, whereas abstainers and drinkers who were improved-but-still-impaired had family histories of alcoholism. Interestingly, fewer than half of Miller et al.'s uncontrolled drinkers reported family histories of alcoholism.

In contrast to the preceding findings, Elal-Lawrence et al. (1986) did not find a significant difference among groups on the frequency of drinking problems in subjects' parents and, paradoxically, found that controlled drinkers more frequently had a positive family history of problem drinking (50%) than did abstainers (33%) and relapsers (27%). Finally, two other studies did not yield a significant association between outcome and parental or familial alcoholism (Edwards et al., 1988; Nordstrom & Berglund, 1987).

Referral Source and Status

The relationship between CD and referral source and status has been examined in two studies. In one, abstainers (44%) were more likely to have been referred by their physicians than were relapsers (23%) and controlled drinkers (18%) (Elal-Lawrence et al., 1986). Related to source of referral is the willingness with which an individual seeks alcohol treatment. Clinical lore holds that coerced patients are less motivated and less likely to succeed than those who volunteer to enter therapy. However, Watson, Brown, Tilleskjor, Jacobs, and Pucel (1988) found that referral status as voluntary versus coerced (court commitment or reported social pressure to enter treatment) was not related to reinstitutionalization, to drinking in the week before outcome appraisal, or to collaterals' reports of the patients' level of control over consumption.

Posttreatment Characteristics

As noted previously, participation in AA following treatment is associated more frequently with abstinence than with moderate drinking (Elal-Lawrence et al., 1987; Heather & Robertson, 1981). Perhaps those who are abstinent decide to attend AA and undecided patients who attend AA are influenced to maintain abstinence. Patients who pursue moderate drinking would not find support for that goal choice in AA, and it is not surprising that they do not have the same after-care experience.

Finney and Moos (1981) measured several aspects of posttreatment family environment at 6-month follow-up. Moderate drinkers had returned to families that were more recreation oriented than those of the abstainers, although there were no significant differences in other aspects of family environment. Of course, the recreation orientation of the moderate drinkers' families may have been significantly greater before treatment as well. The moderate drinkers also differed from the relapsers and abstainers regarding spouses' drinking. Moderate drinkers (83%) were more likely to have a spouse who drank moderately at the 6-month assessment than were the abstainers (45%) or relapsers (53%). This appeared to be a change from pretreatment, when a higher proportion of the spouses of patients who became moderate drinkers were heavy drinkers. Another relevant factor in CD seems to be changing the conditions under which an individual drinks. Controlled drinkers often report altering the persons with whom, the places where, and the types of beverages they drink (Elal-Lawrence et al., 1987).

Curiously, the moderate drinkers studied by Finney and Moos (1981) reported a more aversive posttreatment work environment than the abstainers. Work-related stress seems likely to provoke heavier rather than moderate drinking, but perhaps the presence of a spouse who drinks moderately and other supports buffer such stress, perhaps some specific stressful event is required to provoke heavier consumption, or perhaps increased work stress takes some time to result in heavier drinking (Finney and Moos noted a higher relapse rate at the 2-year follow-up for 6-month controlled drinkers vs. abstainers).

Although the quantity and frequency of drinking often change during follow-up (J. R. Taylor, 1987; Watson & Pucel, 1985; Yates & Norris, 1981), success per se (i.e., either controlling one's drinking or abstaining) has been predictive of continued success. Maisto et al. (1980) found that "days functioning well" (controlled plus abstinent days) during the final 6 months of a 2-year follow-up was predicted by the same index in the previous 6 months. Rychtarik et al. (1987) found that the number of abstinent days in the 6 months prior to the 5–6-year follow-up correlated with the number of abstinent days during the latter 6 months of the 1st year's follow-up.

Remaining abstinent for a time has been recommended as an important break from problem drinking before pursuing moderate consumption. This period of abstinence provides an opportunity for improvement of physical health and cognitive abilities and may enhance self-efficacy about coping with urges to drink (Heather & Robertson, 1981; Sanchez-Craig et al., 1987). The necessity of an initial period of abstinence for controlled drinking was not empirically supported in three of the post-1980 studies (Elal-Lawrence et al., 1987; Finney & Moos, 1981; Nordstrom & Berglund, 1987), but Sanchez-Craig and Lei (1986) found that abstinence or light drinking during the first 3 weeks of treatment predicted later CD in a group of outpatient problem drinkers. The value of an initial period of abstinence may vary depending on physical health and other factors, and continued evaluation of its predictive value is warranted.

Most extant research on CD has been concerned with pretreatment variables and presumably enduring personal characteristics. Increased attention to patient characteristics, social environments, interpersonal experiences, and significant life events that occur after or independently of treatment may yield new findings about the factors that predict CD. Also, it should be emphasized that conclusions about the relative efficacy of CD and abstinence are based primarily on group data of patients in treatment. Predicting the likelihood that an individual will drink moderately or abstain is probably best conducted in the context of a therapeutic relationship in which multiple patient characteristics are considered, support and training for the client's goal choice are provided, and posttreatment circumstances and consumption are monitored to permit intervention if drinking becomes uncontrolled.

METHODOLOGICAL ISSUES

A variety of methodological issues confront researchers designing studies on the factors associated with CD. Some of these issues are specific to CD research, but others arise in the research of treatment outcome of many disorders.

First, variations in the operational definitions of drinking patterns provide for sometimes widely different definitions of CD and abstinence (Heather & Tebbutt, 1989). For example, investigators of CD differ on the limitations of the quantity and frequency of drinking and only some studies include assessment of the psychosocial consequences of drinking. Also, it is rare to include assessment of self-efficacy or a sense of mastery over drinking. Definitions of abstinence also vary. For example, Vaillant and Milofsky (1982) defined abstinence as including limited binge drinking lasting no more than 1 week, whereas others preclude all drinking during the follow-up period.

Second, there is ample empirical evidence that problem drinkers change from one drinking status to another during posttreatment follow-up (e.g., Watson & Pucel, 1985; Yates & Norris, 1981). Performing several assessments of drinking during a longitudinal study would provide the researcher with an estimate of the stability of a subject's drinking status. Repeated measurement of drinking and predictors during the follow-up would also allow researchers to evaluate the influence of events or changes in subject characteristics that occur contemporaneously with changes in drinking. Researchers also might consider the advantages of measuring the number of CD or abstinent days within a meaningful time frame rather than assigning a subject to an outcome category at some relatively fixed point in time (L. C. Sobell & Sobell, 1989).

Repeated measurement of predictors, along with repeated assessment of drinking, also would allow researchers to evaluate the changing psychological, physiological, and environmental factors that contribute to maintenance of a stable drinking outcome over time. For example, a client's abstinence may be caused initially after treatment by poor physical health and a belief in the need for abstinence to recover that health. Several months later, the client's abstinence may be based no longer on health concerns but on social support and the reinforcing changes in interpersonal relationships that have accompanied abstinence. Some months or years later, the person's continued abstinence may be due to his or her adoption of an identity as a "recovering alcoholic" and the development of a repertoire of coping skills to deal with occasional high-risk temptations to drink.

Third, researchers rely heavily on subject self-report for data about predictor characteristics and alcohol consumption and its consequences during follow-up. The conditions under which the self-reports of alcoholics and problem drinkers are obtained are likely to affect their accuracy. Self-reports typically agree with collateral sources of information (e.g., reports by significant others and archival records) when subjects are alcohol free, given assurances of confidentiality, and interviewed in a clinical or research setting (O'Farrell & Maisto, 1987; L. C. Sobell & Sobell, 1990). Researchers can reduce the possibility that self-reports may underestimate (or overestimate) drinking by attending to the factors that increase accuracy and obtaining collateral information when feasible.

A fourth issue is the selection of a time frame for the assessment of outcome status. The time frame is the number of weeks or months at the conclusion of follow-up during which drinking behavior and outcome are assessed. In addition to selecting the time frame for assessing drinking, researchers select the duration of the follow-up period: the number of months or years after treatment until drinking is assessed. Given the potential for significant change in drinking, Nathan and Lansky's (1978) proposal of a follow-up period of at least 2 years' duration in alcohol treatment outcome research is especially relevant to CD studies. As noted previously, researchers also need to decide whether to assess drinking throughout the follow-up period or for a selected time frame at the end of follow-up.

It has yet to be examined empirically, but the time period over which the researcher assesses the predictor variables may influence the predictive value of the characteristics being measured. The most reliable lengths of time over which to measure a subject's drinking style, withdrawal symptoms, commitment to abstinence or CD, social support, and psychological adjustment to improve their predictive value have not been established.

The sample selected for study also may influence the apparent predictors of CD. In the studies included in the present review, inpatients or outpatients in a treatment or training program were typically examined. The characteristics that predict CD in untreated alcoholics and problem drinkers have been largely unstudied (but see Smart, 1975–1976; Tuchfeld, 1981). Likewise, the outcome orientation of the treatment program from which subjects are selected may be important. Some patients attend abstinence-oriented programs, others particpate in CD training programs, and others select their own drinking goal. In addition, some samples are not suitable for evaluating some variables. For example, it would be difficult to evaluate the predictive value of severity of dependence in subjects who were primarily nondependent.

Finally, which outcome groups are compared may affect conclusions about the prediction of CD. In some studies, all three general types of outcome—CD, abstinence, and relapse—were compared (e.g., Booth et al., 1984; Elal-Lawrence et al., 1986, 1987; Miller & Joyce, 1979); in others, only controlled drinkers and abstainers were compared (e.g., Finney & Moos, 1981; Miller & Baca, 1983; Nordstrom & Berglund, 1987; Orford & Keddie, 1986b); and in others, controlled drinkers were combined with abstainers in a success category for comparison with unsuccessful subjects (e.g., McCabe, 1986; Sanchez-Craig & Lei, 1986). Still other researchers used idiosyncratic comparisons (e.g., Heather et al., 1983, compared abstainers with all other outcome categories together and then compared harm-free drinkers with all other outcome categories together), and some did not compare distinct outcome groups, but rather correlated drinking during follow-up with selected predictor variables (e.g., Foy et al., 1984; Maisto et al., 1980) or correlated intake characteristics with dimensions of outcome (Edwards et al., 1988). Some of the diversity in findings may be the result of differences in the particular contrasts.

TOWARD A CONCEPTUAL INTEGRATION

What conclusions can be drawn about the prediction of CD? The research I reviewed indicates that lower severity of dependence, a belief in CD, employment, younger age, psychological and social stability, and female gender have been associated with CD, although no single characteristic has been consistently predictive and the influence of posttreatment factors on CD has been relatively unexamined.

On the basis of their 1981 review, in which they also concluded that severity of drinking symptoms, persuasion, employment, and age were predictive of CD, Heather and Robertson outlined a tentative decision tree for clients who wish to control their drinking. They recommended an initial period of abstinence followed by either an abstinence-oriented intervention, a minimal CD intervention, or an intensive CD intervention, the choice of which is based on three factors: (a) the client's severity of drinking symptoms (low to moderate vs. severe), (b) the client's age (under vs. over 40 years), and (c) the client's employment status (regular employment vs. unemployed or casual employment). Noting the relative lack of data on female clients at that time, Heather and Robertson recommended applying the decision guide only to male clients.

This guide reflects current thinking on matching clients to treatments and outcome goals, but the value of indicators at initial assessment may be limited by contraindications among predictors. For example, Orford and Keddie (1986a) found that it was difficult in practice to recommend an outcome goal based on pretreatment characteristics because severity of dependence, drinking patterns, problem duration, family history of alcoholism, and goal choice did not covary in a predictable manner. Clients display some characteristics that indicate an abstinent course might be best and other characteristics that indicate that CD is the more likely outcome.

Elal-Lawrence et al. (1986), on the basis of their pattern of findings, proposed that it is not any one pretreatment factor that is predictive, but the congruence or incongruence among an individual's drinking history, expectation of abstinence, and physical health that is predictive. Controlled drinking results when there is a congruent relationship among a client's acceptance of a nonabstinence ideology, lack of expectation or experience with abstinence, and good physiological status. An abstinence outcome shares the good physiological status but combines it with an abstinence ideology and the expectation of or experience of abstinence in the past. Relapse is the result of an incongruent relationship among factors: a poor physiological history (e.g., liver damage) and a lack of expectation or experience of abstinence, but an abstinence ideology.

Although the congruence/incongruence formulation implies that a change in one or more of the cardinal factors (physical health, abstinence ideology, or abstinence expectations) could result in a change in an individual's drinking status, it does not explicitly reflect the role of precipitating events in drinking outcome or address the role of the individual as an active agent in the unfolding *process* of drinking decisions and actions.

One of the chief limitations of current research on and formulations of the prediction of drinking outcome is that most investigations seem to have been based on a constant-risk assumption (Shiffman, 1989). That is, researchers have attempted to identify presumably enduring patient characteristics that place an individual at constant risk for relapse or increase the likelihood of abstinence or CD. In his review of conceptual issues in relapse in substance abuse, Shiffman (1989) argued for the influence of three types of variables in relapse in substance abuse: (a) enduring personal characteristics (e.g., severity of dependence, personality, and demographic characteristics), (b) background variables (e.g., posttreatment and social support, general stress level, and occupational functioning), and (c) precipitants (fast-changing, transient phenomena such as major life events). The same argument can be made for the prediction of CD.

Current methodologies in CD prediction studies do not fully reflect the influence of all three types of factors or represent drinking as a developmental process. However, it seems likely that persons who experience drinking problems, like persons who experience other types of psychological dysfunction, have "individual courses . . . shaped by an interactive combination of personality characteristics, psychopathology, environmental supports, treatment, and luck; by growth, development, hard work, and persistence" (Harding & Strauss, 1985, p. 348). Such a contextual and idiographic approach presents methodological challenges for research on the precipitants of outcome in alcohol problems, but it may contain a fuller answer to the question of which alcoholics and problem drinkers will control their drinking.

REFERENCES

Alden, L. E. (1988). Behavioral self-management controlled-drinking strategies in a context of secondary prevention. *Journal of Consulting and Clinical Psychology, 56,* 280–286.

Booth, P. G., Dale, B., & Ansari, J. (1984). Problem drinkers' goal choice and treatment outcome: A preliminary study. *Addictive Behaviors, 9,* 357–364.

Brochu, S. (1990). Abstinence versus nonabstinence: The objectives of alcoholism rehabilitation programs in Quebec. *Journal of Psychoactive Drugs, 22,* 15–21.

Bromet, E. J., & Moos, R. (1979). Prognosis of alcoholic patients: Comparisons of abstainers and moderate drinkers. *British Journal of Addiction, 74,* 183–188.

Davies, D. L. (1962). Normal drinking in recovered alcohol addicts. *Quarterly Journal of Studies on Alcohol, 23,* 94–104.

Drew, L. R. H. (1968). Alcoholism as a self-limiting disease. *Quarterly Journal of Studies on Alcohol, 29,* 956–967.

Edwards, G. (1985). A later follow-up of a classic case series: D. L. Davies' 1962 report and its significance for the present. *Journal of Studies on Alcohol, 36,* 181–190.

Edwards, G., Brown, D., Oppenheimer, E., Sheehan, M., Taylor, C., & Duckitt, A. (1988). Long term outcome for patients with drinking problems: The search for predictors. *British Journal of Addiction, 83,* 917–927.

Edwards, G., Duckitt, A., Oppenheimer, E., Sheehan, M., & Taylor, C. (1983). What happens to alcoholics? *Lancet, 2,* 269–270.

Elal-Lawrence, G., Slade, P. D., & Dewey, M. E. (1986). Predictors of outcome type in treated problem drinkers. *Journal of Studies on Alcohol, 47,* 41–47.

Elal-Lawrence, G., Slade, P. D., & Dewey, M. E. (1987). Treatment and follow-up variables discriminating abstainers, controlled drinkers and relapsers. *Journal of Studies on Alcohol, 48,* 39–46.

Finney, J. W., & Moos, R. H. (1981). Characteristics and prognoses of alcoholics who became moderate drinkers and abstainers after treatment. *Journal of Studies on Alcohol, 42,* 94–105.

Foy, D. W., Nunn, L. B., & Rychtarik, R. G. (1984). Broad-spectrum behavioral treatment for chronic alcoholics: Effects of training controlled drinking skills. *Journal of Consulting and Clinical Psychology, 52,* 218–230.

Gerard, D. L., & Saenger, G. (1966). *Out-patient treatment of alcoholism.* Toronto, Ontario, Canada: University of Toronto Press.

Harding, C. M., & Strauss, J. S. (1985). The course of schizophrenia: An evolving concept. In M. Alpert (Ed.), *Controversies in schizophrenia* (pp. 339–353). New York: Guilford Press.

Heather, N., & Robertson, I. (1981). *Controlled drinking.* New York: Methuen.

Heather, N., Rollnick, S., & Winton, M. (1983). A comparison of objective and subjective measures of alcohol dependence as predictors of relapse following treatment. *British Journal of Clinical Psychology, 22,* 11–17.

Heather, N., & Tebbutt, J. (1989). Definitions of nonabstinent and abstinent categories in alcoholism treatment outcome classifications: A review and proposal. *Drug and Alcohol Dependence, 24,* 83–93.

Heather, N., Winton, M., & Rollnick, S. (1982). An empirical test of "a cultural delusion of alcoholics." *Psychological Reports, 50,* 379–382.

Helzer, J. E., Robins, L. N., Taylor, J. R., Carey, K., Miller, R. H., Combs-Orme, T., & Farmer, A. (1985). The extent of long-term moderate drinking among alcoholics discharged from medical and psychiatric treatment facilities. *New England Journal of Medicine, 312,* 1678–1682.

Hill, S. Y. (1985). The disease concept of alcoholism: A review. *Drug and Alcohol Dependence, 16,* 193–214.

Hyman, M. M. (1976). Alcoholics 15 years later. *Annals of the New York Academy of Sciences, 273,* 613–623.

Institute of Medicine. (1990). *Broadening the base of treatment for alcohol problems.* Washington, DC: National Academy Press.

Jellinek, E. M. (1960). *The disease concept of alcoholism.* New Brunswick, NJ: Hillhouse.

Lloyd, R. W. J., & Salzberg, H. C. (1975). Controlled social drinking: An alternative to abstinence as a treatment goal for some alcohol abusers. *Psychological Bulletin, 82,* 815–842.

Maisto, S. A., Sobell, M. B., & Sobell, L. C. (1980). Predictors of treatment outcome for alcoholics treated by individualized behavior therapy. *Addictive Behaviors, 5,* 259–264.

Marlatt, G. A. (1983). The controlled-drinking controversy: A commentary. *American Psychologist, 38,* 1097–1110.

Marlatt, G. A. (1987). Research and political realities: What the next twenty years hold for behaviorists in the alcohol field. *Advances in Behavior Research and Therapy, 9,* 165–171.

McCabe, R. J. R. (1986). Alcohol-dependent individuals sixteen years on. *Alcohol and Alcoholism, 21,* 85–91.

McCrady, B. S. (1985). Comments on the controlled drinking controversy. *American Psychologist, 40,* 370–371.

Miller, W. R. (1983). Controlled drinking: A history and critical review. *Journal of Studies on Alcohol, 44,* 68–83.

Miller, W. R. (1985). How prevalent are controlled drinking outcomes? A commentary on Helzer et al., 1985. *Bulletin of the Society of Psychologists in Addictive Behaviors, 4,* 207–212.

Miller, W. R. (1986). Haunted by the Zeitgeist: Reflections on contrasting treatment goals and concepts of alcoholism in Europe and the United States. *Annals of the New York Academy of Sciences, 472,* 110–129.

Miller, W. R., & Baca, L. M. (1983). Two-year follow-up of bibliotherapy and therapist-directed controlled drinking training for problem drinkers. *Behavior Therapy, 14,* 441–448.

Miller, W. R., & Joyce, M. A. (1979). Prediction of abstinence, controlled drinking, and heavy drinking outcomes following self-control training. *Journal of Consulting and Clinical Psychology, 47,* 773–775.

Miller, W. R., Leckman, A. L., Delaney, H. D., & Tinkcom, M. (1992). Long-term follow-up of behavioral self-control training. *Journal of Studies on Alcohol, 53,* 249–261.

Miller, W. R., Pechacek, T. F., & Hamburg, S. (1981). Group behavior therapy for problem drinkers. *International Journal of the Addictions, 16,* 829–839.

Nathan, P. E., & Lansky, D. (1978). Common methodological problems in research on the addictions. *Journal of Consulting and Clinical Psychology, 46,* 713–726.

Nordstrom, G., & Berglund, M. (1987). A prospective study of successful long-term adjustment in alcoholic dependence: Social drinking versus abstinence. *Journal of Studies on Alcohol, 48,* 95–103.

O'Farrell, T. J., & Maisto, S. A. (1987). The utility of self-report and biological measures of alcohol consumption in alcoholism treatment outcome studies. *Advances in Behavior Research and Therapy, 9,* 91–125.

Ojehagen, A., & Berglund, M. (1989). Changes of drinking goals in a two-year out-patient alcoholic treatment program. *Addictive Behaviors, 14,* 1–9.

Orford, J., & Keddie, A. (1986a). Abstinence or controlled drinking in clinical practice: Indications at initial assessment. *Addictive Behaviors, 11,* 71–86.

Orford, J., & Keddie, A. (1986b). Abstinence or controlled drinking in clinical practice: A test of the dependence and persuasion hypotheses. *British Journal of Addiction, 81,* 495–504.

Pattison, E. M., Sobell, M. B., & Sobell, L. C. (Eds.). (1978). *Emerging concepts of alcohol dependence.* New York: Springer.

Peele, S. (1987). Why do controlled-drinking outcomes vary by investigator, by country and by era? Cultural conceptions of relapse and remission in alcoholism. *Drug and Alcohol Dependence, 20,* 173–201.

Pettinati, H. M., Sugarman, A. A., DiDonato, N., & Maurer, H. S. (1982). The natural history of alcoholism over four years after treatment. *Journal of Studies on Alcohol, 43*, 201–215.

Polich, J. M., Armor, D. J., & Braiker, H. B. (1981). *The course of alcoholism: Four years after treatment.* New York: Wiley.

Reinert, R. E., & Bowen, W. T. (1968). Social drinking following treatment for alcoholism. *Bulletin of the Menninger Clinic, 32*, 280–290.

Robertson, I., & Heather, N. (1982). A survey of controlled drinking treatment in Britain. *British Journal on Alcohol and Alcoholism, 17*, 102–105.

Rosenberg, H., Melville, J., Levell, D., & Hodge, J. E. (1992). A 10-year follow-up survey of acceptability of controlled drinking in Britain. *Journal of Studies on Alcohol, 53*, 441–446.

Rush, B., & Ogborne, A. C. (1986). Acceptability of nonabstinence treatment goals among alcoholism treatment programs. *Journal of Studies on Alcohol, 47*, 146–150.

Rychtarik, R. G., Foy, D. W., Scott, T., Lokey, L., & Prue, D. M. (1987). Five–six-year follow-up of broad-spectrum behavioral treatment for alcoholism: Effects of training controlled drinking skills. *Journal of Consulting and Clinical Psychology, 55*, 106–108.

Sanchez-Craig, M., Annis, H. A., Bornet, A. R., & MacDonald, K. R. (1984). Random assignment to abstinence and controlled drinking: Evaluation of a cognitive-behavioral program for problem drinkers. *Journal of Consulting and Clinical Psychology, 52*, 390–403.

Sanchez-Craig, M., & Lei, H. (1986). Disadvantages of imposing the goal of abstinence on problem drinkers: An empirical study. *British Journal of Addiction, 81*, 505–512.

Sanchez-Craig, M., Leigh, G., Spivak, K., & Lei, H. (1989). Superior outcome of females over males after brief treatment for the reduction of heavy drinking. *British Journal of Addiction, 84*, 395–404.

Sanchez-Craig, M., Wilkinson, D. A., & Walker, K. (1987). Theory and methods for secondary prevention of alcohol problems: A cognitively based approach. In W. M. Cox (Ed.), *Treatment and prevention of alcohol problems: A resource manual* (pp. 287–331). New York: Academic Press.

Saunders, W. M., & Kershaw, P. W. (1979). Spontaneous remission from alcoholism—A community study. *British Journal of Addiction, 74*, 251–265.

Searles, J. R. (1988). The role of genetics in the pathogenesis of alcoholism. *Journal of Abnormal Psychology, 97*, 153–167.

Selzer, M. L. (1971). The Michigan Alcoholism Screening Test: The quest for a new diagnostic instrument. *American Journal of Psychiatry, 127*, 89–94.

Shiffman, S. (1989). Conceptual issues in the study of relapse. In M. Gossop (Ed.), *Relapse and addictive behaviour* (pp. 149–179). London: Routledge & Kegan Paul.

Skinner, H. A., & Allen, B. A. (1982). Alcohol dependence syndrome: Measurement and validation. *Journal of Abnormal Psychology, 91*, 199–209.

Smart, R. G. (1975–1976). Spontaneous recovery in alcoholics: A review and analysis of the available research. *Drug and Alcohol Dependence, 1,* 277–285.

Sobell, L. C., & Sobell, M. B. (1989). Treatment outcome evaluation methodology with alcohol abusers: Strengths and key issues. *Advances in Behavior Research and Therapy, 11,* 151–160.

Sobell, L. C., & Sobell, M. B. (1990). Self-report issues in alcohol abuse: State of the art and future directions. *Behavioral Assessment, 12,* 77–90.

Sobell, M. B., & Sobell, L. C. (1973). Alcoholics treated by individualized behavior therapy: One year treatment outcome. *Behaviour Research and Therapy, 11,* 599–618.

Sobell, M. B., & Sobell, L. C. (1976). Second year treatment outcome of alcoholics treated by individualized behavior therapy: Results. *Behaviour Research and Therapy, 14,* 195–215.

Stockwell, T. (1986). Cracking an old chestnut: Is controlled drinking possible for the person who has been severely alcohol dependent? *British Journal of Addiction, 81,* 455–456.

Stockwell, T., Murphy, D., & Hodgson, R. (1983). The Severity of Alcohol Dependence Questionnaire: Its use, reliability and validity. *British Journal of Addiction, 78,* 145–155.

Taylor, C., Brown, D., Duckitt, A., Edwards, G., Oppenheimer, E., & Sheehan, M. (1986). Alcoholism and the patterning of outcome: A multivariate analysis. *British Journal of Addiction, 81,* 815–823.

Taylor, J. R. (1987). Controlled drinking studies: Methodological issues. *Drugs and Society, 1,* 83–107.

Tuchfeld, B. (1981). Spontaneous remission in alcoholics: Empirical observations and theoretical implications. *Journal of Studies on Alcohol, 42,* 626–641.

Vaillant, G. E., & Milofsky, E. S. (1982). Natural history of male alcoholism: IV. Paths to recovery. *Archives of General Psychiatry, 39,* 127–133.

Vogler, R. E., Weissbach, T. A., & Compton, J. V. (1977). Learning techniques for alcohol abuse. *Behaviour Research and Therapy, 15,* 31–38.

Watson, C. G. (1987). Recidivism in "controlled drinker" alcoholics: A longitudinal study. *Journal of Clinical Psychology, 43,* 404–412.

Watson, C. G., Brown, K., Tilleskjor, C., Jacobs, L., & Pucel, J. (1988). The comparative recidivism rates of voluntary- and coerced-admission male alcoholics. *Journal of Clinical Psychology, 44,* 573–581.

Watson, C. G., Jacobs, L., Pucel, J., Tilleskjor, C., & Hoodecheck, E. (1984). The relationship of beliefs about controlled drinking to recidivism in alcoholic men. *Journal of Studies on Alcohol, 45,* 172–175.

Watson, C., & Pucel, J. (1985). Consistency of posttreatment alcoholics' drinking patterns. *Journal of Consulting and Clinical Psychology, 53,* 679–683.

Yates, F. E., & Norris, H. (1981). The use made of treatment: An alternative approach to the evaluation of alcoholism services. *Behavioural Psychotherapy, 9,* 291–309.

10

DRINKING RESTRAINT AND RISK FOR ALCOHOL ABUSE

R. LORRAINE COLLINS

Restraint is one of a number of constructs that are shared among addictive behaviors. Herman and Mack (1975) introduced the restraint construct as a way of accounting for differences in the eating behavior of dieters and the obese as compared with normal-weight individuals. Working from Nisbett's (1972) *set-point* theory and Schachter's (1968) notions concerning the role of externality in obesity, Herman and Mack described restrained individuals as being concerned about weight and restrained in their eating habits (i.e., below their set point) but likely to respond to external cues for eating. Over the years Herman and colleagues (e.g., Herman & Kozlowski, 1979; Herman & Polivy, 1984; Polivy & Herman, 1985) have elaborated on these original notions. As they see it, restraint is involved in the regulation of intake of addictive substances such as food, cigarettes, and alcohol (Herman & Kozlowski, 1979). According to the

Reprinted from *Experimental and Clinical Psychopharmacology*, 1, 44–54. (1993). Copyright ©1993 by the American Psychological Association. Used with permission of the author.

Portions of this article were presented at the Sixth Annual International Conference on the Treatment of Addictive Behaviors, Santa Fe, New Mexico, in January 1993. Preparation of this article was supported by National Institute on Alcohol Abuse and Alcoholism Grant R01-AA07595, awarded to R. Lorraine Collins.

boundary model of eating (Herman & Polivy, 1984), this regulation occurs within physiologically mediated upper and lower boundaries. Within these boundaries there exists a zone of "biological indifference" within which consumption is mediated by nonphysiological factors such as social influences and cognitions. Persons who seek to keep their intake below the biological upper boundary (e.g., dieters) set up a new upper boundary, within the zone of biological indifference. In order not to breach this more restrictive upper boundary, the individual relies on cognitive regulation. Cognitive regulation is less sensitive to physiological and bodily needs that typically help with regulating consumption. Therefore, it is more difficult to maintan regulation within this new upper boundary, and failures to regulate (i.e., consumption beyond the new upper boundary) are more likely to occur.

CONCEPTUALIZATIONS OF THE DRINKING RESTRAINT CONSTRUCT

Drinking Restraint as Cognitive Preoccupation With Control Over Drinking

Citing commonalities between the consumption patterns of dieters and certain types of drinkers, Ruderman and McKirnan (1984) introduced the *drinking restraint construct*. They defined restrained drinkers as persons preoccupied with controlling their alcohol intake. Restrained drinkers are somewhat analogous to dieters, because both are cognitively and behaviorally preoccupied with controlling their intake. When regulation fails, both groups may subsequently engage in excessive consumption.

Ruderman and McKirnan (1984) presented the drinking restraint construct as a context for testing Marlatt and Gordon's (1980) notion that a "slip" in perceived control over drinking would lead to overindulgence in alcohol (i.e., the abstinence violation effect; AVE). By linking restraint to the AVE, Ruderman and McKirnan provided a context for examining the cognitive processes involved in the regulation (or failure to regulate) alcohol intake as well as a means of testing an important component of Marlatt and Gordon's *relapse prevention* model. They began their research by using a "preload" paradigm borrowed from the literature on restrained eating (cf. Herman & Mack, 1975; Ruderman & Christensen, 1983; Tomarken & Kirschenbaum, 1984) to test the role of a drinking violation in restrained drinkers' propensity to binge drink. Fifty male students who scored high and low on their measure of drinking restraint participated in a taste test of wines. This taste-rating task served as an unobtrusive measure of alcohol consumption (cf. Higgins & Marlatt, 1975). The taste test was preceded by the required consumption of a preload of two glasses of wine (the violation). The results indicated that restrained drinkers consumed more than unrestrained drinkers, regardless of preload.

A follow-up study included the wine preload, but this time subjects were given the choice of making taste ratings of either wine or a nonalcoholic soda. It was predicted that following the preload, restrained drinkers would be more likely to choose to rate an alcoholic beverage. The results indicated that restrained drinkers generally were more likely to choose to rate an alcoholic beverage. In addition, restrained drinkers who had consumed a preload were less likely to choose an alcoholic beverage than restrained drinkers who had not consumed a preload. There was no such difference for unrestrained drinkers. Generally, the results from these two experiments indicated that the violation (represented by a preload) did not increase alcohol consumption among restrained drinkers. Ruderman and McKirnan (1984) concluded that their findings did not substantiate predictions derived from the AVE.

Although Ruderman and McKirnan's (1984) work provided an excellent start to understanding the processes involved in drinking restraint, they have conducted no further research on the topic. Collins and colleagues (Collins, George, & Lapp, 1989; Collins & Lapp, 1991, 1992) have pursued research on drinking restraint as involving a cognitive preoccupation with limiting drinking, particularly as it pertains to the AVE and the processes involved in the move from social drinking to problem drinking. This program of research is described in a later section of this review. For now, I describe an alternative conceptualization of drinking restraint.

Drinking Restraint as Response Conflict

Bensley (1989) has characterized drinking restraint as involving cycles of intentional overcontrol of alcohol consumption (abstinence or light drinking) alternating with drinking binges that represent lapses in control. These extremes in drinking styles were said to represent a *response conflict* in which individuals try to maintain a balance between the competing impulse to drink and the resistance of these impulses. The drinking behavior evident in a particular situation is a function of whether the approach (drinking) or avoidance (not drinking) gradient of this conflict is momentarily stronger. The "loss of control" evident in binge drinking may be due to alcohol's (physiologically mediated) role as a disinhibitor of the inhibitory response conflict. Bensley (1991) provided cross-sectional evidence of drinking as response conflict in a survey of female and male university students. When compared with unrestrained drinkers, restrained drinkers reported more impulses to drink as well as more inhibitions against drinking. They also exhibited more cyclic drinking (alternating patterns of light and heavy drinking), more extreme patterns of drinking, more loss of control drinking, and more externality on a measure of drinking-related locus of control. These findings were interpreted as being consistent with the response conflict conceptualization of drinking restraint.

Bensley (née Southwick) also has characterized drinking restraint as a risk factor for alcohol abuse. She and her colleagues have conducted questionnaire (Bensley, 1991; Curry, Southwick, & Steele, 1987; Southwick & Steele, 1987) and laboratory (Bensley, 1989; Bensley, Kuna, & Steele, 1988, 1990) studies to test predictions derived from their conceptualization of restraint as involving response conflict and external responsiveness. Curry, Southwick, and Steele began by developing a measure of drinking restraint (the Drinking Restraint Scale) from which they found that restraint was related to heavy drinking, the experience of intoxication, and other negative consequences of alcohol use, as well as an external style of controlling alcohol consumption.

In a subsequent laboratory analog study, the role of external responsiveness as a risk factor for restrained drinkers was tested in a delay-of-gratification paradigm (Bensley et al., 1988). Restrained and unrestrained university students were asked to participate in taste ratings of beers. When the subjects' preferred beer became unavailable, they were given the choice of either waiting for their preferred beer or proceeding with taste ratings of nonpreferred beers. Restrained drinkers tended to choose delay and their decision to delay was more influenced by an external characteristic of the beer (i.e., the difference in taste between their preferred beer and the available nonpreferred beer). Moreover, restrained drinkers who chose immediate gratification with the nonpreferred beer tended to increase their beer consumption. This latter finding was interpreted as being indicative of the propensity to binge as a function of a self-perceived failure to control drinking by deciding to delay. Bensley (1989) provided further evidence of the role of external responsiveness in the drinking behavior of restrained drinkers. She found that restrained drinkers were more responsive to the taste of beer. That is, when compared with unrestrained drinkers, restrained drinkers drank significantly more of their preferred beer and drank similar amounts of their nonpreferred beer.

In another laboratory study, subjects were required to consume a preload of two glasses of wine. Persons who had successfully maintained restraint consumed more wine in a taste-rating task than did unsuccessfully restrained drinkers (Bensley et al., 1990). For the successful restrained drinkers, the preload was said to represent a violation of restraint. As such, the results were interpreted as indicating that violations placed successfully restrained individuals at risk for excessive drinking.

In other studies, Southwick and Steele (1987) tested the notion that restraint was related to control style and found that restrained individuals were low in generalized self-control. Interestingly, there was no relationship between drinking restraint (as measured by the Drinking Restraint Scale; Curry, Southwick & Steele, 1987) and eating restraint (as measured by the

Eating Restraint Scale; Herman & Polivy, 1980). This finding suggests that restraint is not a generalized response across different consummatory behaviors.

To date, the research conducted by Bensley and colleagues (Bensley, 1989, 1991; Bensley et al., 1988, 1990; Curry, Southwick, & Steele, 1987; Southwick & Steele, 1987) has indicated a myriad of relationships among restraint and a variety of personality and drinking-related variables. However, the conceptual meaningfulness of these relationships has not been fully described. A key conceptual question concerns the nature and psychometric properties of the Drinking Restraint Scale (DRS) as a measure of drinking restraint. As will become evident, whether the DRS assesses restraint as a unitary construct (approach or avoidance) or is multifaceted (assesses both the approach and avoidance gradients of the response conflict) can be crucial to understanding the relationships between its scores and other variables. Examination of the items of the DRS suggests that it could be a multifaceted measure; however, only total DRS scores have been used in the research to date. If the internal structure of the DRS is not unitary, then many of the relationships reported so far may be spurious. No psychometric analysis of the internal structure of the DRS has been undertaken. There are also key conceptual relationships that have not been well elucidated. For example, how does external responsiveness relate to response conflict? One would assume that external responsiveness would have an effect on the approach gradient. However, the findings to date do not clearly show this possibility. Generally then, although the research of Bensley and her colleagues has provided certain key threads of relationships and ideas, they have yet to be woven into a meaningful understanding of processes related to drinking restraint as response conflict.

MEASUREMENT OF DRINKING RESTRAINT

The method used to measure drinking restraint is important, because restraint is a complex phenomenon that seems to involve competing tendencies. Ruderman and McKirnan's (1984) and Bensley's (1989, 1991) conceptualizations of drinking restraint share the notion that it represents a risk factor for alcohol abuse, and both base their scales on existing measures of eating restraint. Although their measures differed somewhat in format and content, both developed unitary drinking restraint questionnaires. Ruderman and McKirnan developed the Restrained Drinking Scale (RDS), and Bensley and colleagues (Curry, Southwick, & Steele, 1987) developed the Drinking Restraint Scale (DRS). Subsequent research by Collins and colleagues (Collins et al., 1989; Collins & Lapp, 1992) has led to the development of a multifactored measure of drinking restraint, the Temptation and Restraint Inventory. Each of these measures is now discussed in turn.

Restrained Drinking Scale

The RDS (Ruderman & McKirnan, 1984), the first measure of restrained drinking, contains 23 items adapted from two existent measures of eating restraint: the Restraint Scale (Herman & Polivy, 1980) and the Three-Factor Eating Questionnaire (Stunkard, 1981). Each RDS item (e.g., "Do feelings of guilt about drinking too much help you to control your intake?") was rated on a 9-point Likert scale in which "1" indicated lack of preoccupation and "9" indicated a high degree of such preoccupation. The RDS was developed as a unitary measure, in which level of restraint was based on a total score across all items. Analyses based on scores from a sample of male university students indicated item-total correlations ranging from .19 to .61 and good internal consistency (Cronbach α = .81). In Ruderman and McKirnan's research, scores on the RDS were moderately correlated with self-reported drinking. Median splits were used to differentiate restrained and unrestrained drinkers. In comparison with unrestrained drinkers, restrained drinkers consumed more in taste ratings of wines and, in a subsequent study, were more likely to choose to drink an alcoholic beverage rather than a nonalcoholic soda.

Drinking Restraint Scale

The DRS (Curry, Southwick, & Steele, 1987) was directly modeled on Herman and Polivy's (1980) Restraint Scale. It consisted of alcohol-related modifications of 7 of the 10 Restraint Scale items, with item-total correlations ranging from .20 to .50. The first 3 DRS items (e.g., "How would your present level of drinking compare to your ideal level?") are rated on 7-point Likert scales, and the remaining 4 items (e.g., "Do you feel that you give too much time and thought to drinking?") are rated in terms of frequency of occurrence. The possible range of scores was 6 to 27, and internal consistency for a sample of female and male university students was moderately good (Cronbach α = .68). Men tended to score significantly higher than women. Higher DRS scores were related to heavy drinking, a more external style of controlling alcohol consumption, and alcohol-related problems.

Development of the Temptation and Restraint Inventory: A Multifactored Measure of Drinking Restraint

Because both the RDS and the DRS were adapted from existing measures of restrained eating, it was reasoned that they should reflect the complexities and controversies found in such measures (cf. Heatherton, Herman, Polivy, King, & McGree, 1988). One such controversy is whether measures of restraint assess only successful regulation of intake (restraint only) or both aspects of the theoretical cycle involved in the restraint construct, namely, restriction (i.e., regulation of intake) and disinhibition (i.e., yielding to temptation by temporarily suspending regulation).

The most commonly used measure of eating restraint, the Restraint Scale (Herman & Polivy, 1980), which served as a model for both the RDS (Ruderman & McKirnan, 1984) and the DRS (Curry, Southwick, & Steele, 1987), was developed as a unitary measure. Even so, psychometric analyses of the Restraint Scale have identified a bifactorial structure that roughly corresponds to the notion that restraint involves both restriction and disinhibition of intake (e.g., Blanchard & Frost, 1983; Heatherton et al., 1988; Lowe, 1984; Ruderman, 1983). Psychometric analyses of the other commonly used measure of eating restraint, the Three-Factor Eating Questionnaire (Stunkard, 1981; Stunkard & Messick, 1985), also have identified these competing tendencies (Collins, Lapp, Helder, & Saltzberg, 1992; Westenhoefer, 1991). The Three-Factor Eating Questionnaire served as a model for some of the items of the RDS. Even with evidence of the multifactored nature of both of the measures of eating restraint on which the RDS and DRS were based, the internal structure of both of these scales had never been examined when Collins et al. (1989) began research on drinking restraint.

Collins and colleagues (Collins et al., 1989) began with the premise that the meaningfulness of research on the drinking restraint construct was linked to the internal structure and psychometric properties of the instrument used to measure it. This led us to examine the internal structure of the RDS, which seemed the most promising of the two existent measures. Collins et al. (1989) posited that the RDS was not a unitary measure, as conceived by Ruderman and McKirnan (1984). Cluster analyses of the RDS items, as rated by male and female university students, showed that it was consistently partitioned into four clusters, formed by 13 of the 23 items. Based on content, these clusters were named (a) *Govern*, 3 items pertaining to difficulty controlling alcohol intake (e.g., "Do you find that once you start drinking it is difficult for you to stop?"); (b) *Restrict*, 3 items pertaining to attempts to limit drinking (e.g., "Do you ever cut back your drinking in an attempt to change your drinking habits?"); (c) *Emotion*, 3 items describing negative affect as a reason for drinking (e.g., "When you feel lonely are you more likely to drink?"); and (d) *Consume*, 4 items describing frequency and occasions for heavy drinking (e.g., "How often do you go on drinking binges?"). In separate multiple regression equations predicting maximum consumption per occasion (excessive drinking) and weekend (typical) drinking, the RDS clusters exhibited the following relationships to alcohol consumption. The Restrict cluster predicted lower levels of self-reported drinking, the Govern and Emotion clusters predicted higher levels of drinking, and the Consume cluster was confounded with self-reported drinking. For example, Collins et al. (1989) found that a total RDS score minus the items of the Consume cluster accounted for only 2% of the variance in drinking. Given these results, the Consume cluster has not been included in our subsequent modifications of the RDS. In summary, Collins et al. (1989) had shown that the RDS was multifaceted, with components that had both a positive and a negative relationship to self-reported drinking. Also of methodological note, we treated restraint as a continuous variable, rather than in the dichotomous fashion favored in previous research (cf. Bensley, 1991; Bensley et al., 1990; Ruderman & McKirnan, 1984).

Collins and Lapp (1992) subsequently replicated this multiple component structure of the RDS in a sample of male and female community residents. In addition, we enhanced the earlier modification of the RDS by developing new items that complemented the three RDS clusters and expanded on the cognitive preoccupation said to characterize restrained drinkers. The new items were presented in the same format as those of the RDS to circumvent any differential response style biases arising from the use of different scales. Responses from a random half of the community sample were entered into an exploratory factor analysis from which two factors were extracted. Based on the content of these items, the factors were named Cognitive Preoccupation (CP) and Concern About Drinking (CAD). The CP factor contains three items that refer to thoughts about drinking (e.g., "Is it hard to distract yourself from thinking about drinking?"). The three items of the CAD factor pertained to plans to reduce drinking and worry about controlling drinking (e.g., "Does the sight and smell of alcohol make you think about limiting your drinking?"). These two factors were confirmed with the remaining half of the community sample, and each factor exhibited an adequate level of internal consistency (Cronbach αs; CP = .82, CAD = .78).

Correlational analyses indicated significant relationships among the three RDS clusters (Govern, Restrict, and Emotion), CP, and CAD. All five factors were then combined to form a new, integrated measure of drinking restraint, the Temptation and Restraint Inventory (TRI). Higher order factor analysis indicated that the TRI contains two second-order factors. Based on content, one factor was named Cognitive and Emotional Preoccupation (CEP), and the other factor was named Cognitive and Behavioral Control (CBC). The CEP second-order factor was composed of Govern, Emotion, and Cognitive Preoccupation and referred to thoughts about drinking and negative emotions. The CBC second-order factor was composed of Restrict and Concern about Drinking and referred to thoughts about limiting drinking and attempts to cut down on drinking. Consistent with the bifactorial structure inherent in the restraint construct, the CEP factor predicted higher levels of weekly alcohol consumption, and the CBC factor predicted slightly lower levels of weekly alcohol consumption. An interaction indicated that weekly alcohol consumption was lower among individuals who were highly preoccupied with alcohol (CEP) but were attempting to control their alcohol intake (CBC). Consumption was higher in those who were highly preoccupied but not engaged in control behaviors. Weekly alcohol consumption remained essentially unchanged by the subjects' level of control (CBC) among individuals who were low on the CEP factor.

A similar regression on drinking-related problems, as measured by scores on the Short Michigan Alcoholism Screening Test (SMAST; Selzer, Vinokur, & van Rooijen, 1975), indicated that CEP significantly predicted an increase in SMAST score, whereas neither CBC nor the interaction of the two factors of the TRI was significantly related to SMAST scores. Collins and Lapp (1992) interpreted this pattern of results as suggesting that being preoccupied with drinking is the key to placing some individuals at risk for excessive drinking, whereas attempts and plans to control drinking exerts a moderating influence on alcohol consumption. Generally, the results of this study provided support for the characterization of drinking restraint as involving a reciprocal relationship between regulated (CBC) and unregulated or excessive (CPC) alcohol intake. The properties of the TRI are consistent with the conceptualization of drinking restraint as involving a cognitive preoccupation with controlling alcohol intake as well as the notion that measures of restraint should capture both aspects of the cycle of successful and unsuccessful regulation.

ABSTINENCE VIOLATION EFFECT AND RESTRAINED DRINKING

Ruderman and McKirnan (1984) introduced the drinking restraint construct in the context of providing a test of the abstinence violation effect described by Marlatt and Gordon (1980) in their original presentation of the relapse prevention model. Marlatt (1985) presented a reformulation of the abstinence violation effect (AVE), in which the role of attributions was elaborated. The AVE reportedly occurs when an individual chooses to abstain from substance use but experiences a lapse (i.e., initial use or overuse of the substance). Reactions to the lapse are theoretically contingent on causal attributions concerning the reason for the lapse and affective reactions to the attribution (Marlatt, 1985). Individuals who attribute the cause of the lapse to internal, stable, and global aspects of the self are more likely to see the lapse as a generalized failure (e.g., lack of willpower) and to experience negative affect related to this pessimistic self-attribution. These reactions occur along a continuum of intensity. In an attempt to repair the negative affective state, the individual continues or increases substance use to the point of excess.

An analogous phenomenon may occur for restrained social drinkers who, because of their preoccupation with controlling their alcohol intake, voluntarily set limits on their consumption. When successful, the setting of limits will maintain regulated consumption. However, limit setting on the part of the restrained drinker may serve as a sufficient condition for experiencing what Collins, Lapp, and Izzo (1991) have labeled the limit violation effect (LVE), when drinking limits are violated. That is, the restrained drinker's setting of limits may initially produce successful regulation of alcohol intake. However, the experience of a limit violation (i.e., the failure to regulate alcohol consumption) may result in an episode of excessive–binge drinking. The LVE suggests that excessive drinking occurs when restrained drinkers blame themselves for the violation, experience negative affective reactions to this attribution, and then drink to repair their mood (cf. Marlatt, 1985). Because continuing to drink represents a further violation, a negative cycle of restraint, violation, and excessive drinking may develop over time.

The paradox suggested by both the restraint construct and the AVE–LVE is that, for some individuals, the typical clinical prescription to limit one's intake of a substance may actually "set one up" to overindulge in that substance. If researchers and clinicians can identify those individuals who are at risk for this reaction or delineate the processes involved in this paradoxical reaction, then they may be able to intervene or provide alternative prescriptions.

Abstinence Violation Effect in Clinical Samples

The AVE provides a description of the processes that may place restrained drinkers at risk for alcohol abuse. However, the evidence for the occurrence of the AVE is inconsistent. Most of this evidence comes from clinical samples recovering from excessive use of a variety of addictive substances. Several studies have supported the notion that the AVE is an important predictor of lapses in the control of smoking (Curry, Marlatt, & Gordon, 1987), relapse following alcohol treatment (Ross, Miller, Emmerson, & Todt, 1989), dieting lapses among overweight women (Ogden & Wardle, 1990), and outcome among very low-calorie dieters (Mooney, Burling, Hartman, & Brenner-Liss, 1992). Limited support for the AVE was found in a study of relapse among opiate addicts (Bradley, Gossop, Brewin, Phillips, & Green, 1992). In contrast, the AVE was not supported in an examination of attributional style and relapse situations in a sample of illicit drug users (Birke, Edelmann, & Davis, 1990). Hall, Havassy, and Wasserman (1990) failed to find support for the AVE when they examined the return to substance use among persons (smokers, opiate users, and alcoholics) who had just completed abstinence-oriented treatment programs.

The inconsistent support for the occurrence of the AVE among clinical samples may have resulted from conceptual and methodological limitations and inconsistencies in the research to date. A common and important conceptual limitation is the characterization of the AVE–LVE as an all-or-none reaction. In theory, the AVE–LVE is predicted to occur along a continuum of intensities, and the threshold for the occurrence of excessive consumption has not been identified. It is possible that low levels of substance use (a lapse) will not engage the AVE, particularly if the violation is not accompanied by negative affective reactions, self-attribution for its occurrence, or both. Even so, some studies have characterized any level of use following abstinence as indicative of the likely occurrence of the AVE.

Many studies have failed to assess the impact of negative affect and the personal commitment to abstinence, two key components of the AVE. The failure to assess the role of negative affect is fairly common (e.g., Birke et al., 1990; Bradley et al., 1992; Mooney et al., 1992; Ogden & Wardle, 1990) and has not precluded finding support for the AVE (e.g., Mooney et al., 1992; Ogden & Wardle, 1990). A personal commitment to abstinence and limit setting also is essential for the occurrence of the AVE–LVE; yet, many studies fail to assess this commitment and may invoke participation in an abstinence-oriented treatment program as being indicative of this commitment (Birke et al., 1990; Mooney et al., 1992; Ogden & Wardle, 1990).

The role of the attributional component of the AVE–LVE, and its measurement, varies among clinical studies. In some studies, attributions have neither been assessed nor described (Hall et al., 1990; Ross et al., 1989). When attributions are considered, the measures often are inconsistent. Some studies have used generalized measures of attributional style (e.g., Birke et al., 1990; Bradley et al., 1992; Ogden & Wardle, 1990), whereas others have used content-specific attribution measures (Curry, Marlatt, & Gordon, 1987; Mooney et al., 1992; Ogden & Wardle, 1990). Given the variety of inconsistencies in the conceptualization and measurement of the components of the AVE, it is no wonder that a variety of claims have been made about the occurrence of the AVE among clinical samples. More controlled research is necessary before any conclusions can be made about the relevance of the AVE for explaining the processes involved in relapse.

Abstinence Violation Effect in Restrained Drinkers

In research involving restrained drinkers, Ruderman and McKirnan (1984) failed to find support for the AVE in two studies in which male social drinkers were required to consume an alcohol preload (two glasses of wine) representing a drinking violation. In contrast to the hypothesized increase in consumption, they found that restrained drinkers simply consumed more than unrestrained drinkers, irrespective of the preload. Bensley et al. (1990) also reported failure to find a restraint-violation effect when using a preload methodology. They reported increased consumption in a taste-rating task following a wine preload but no significant effects of consumption on mood.

A key limitation of these laboratory tests of the AVE–LVE was the requirement that subjects consume a preload of wine. Although subjects cooperated with the request to consume the preload, this requirement is likely to have removed their sense of responsibility for violating their drinking limits. In effect, the attributional component of the AVE–LVE, which is pivotal in theory, was probably not engaged in these experiments. Consequently, the LVE may not have been observed because a key provision for its occurrence was inadvertently overlooked. In addition, these studies used unitary measures of drinking restraint, based on total scores, which are likely to have represented preoccupation with alcohol or the propensity to drink heavily. As such, the findings for restrained drinkers may be spurious.

Collins and Lapp (1991) conducted a cross-sectional test of the AVE–LVE based on questionnaires administered to a community sample of 323 social drinkers. Subjects completed the RDS as well as a Drinking Attributional Style Questionnaire (DASQ), a content-specific measure of the causal attributions for drinking-related situations. The DASQ contains a factor of causal attributions for positive drinking-related situations (which we characterized as *self-enhancement*) and a second factor of causal attributions for negative situations (which we characterized as *self-blame*). Thus, this test of the AVE–LVE included consideration of the role of the various aspects of restraint, as well as attributions specific to drinking.

Separate hierarchical multiple regression equations were conducted for each of three self-reported drinking variables, which served as analogues of regulated and unregulated alcohol consumption. The three variables were (a) minimum number of drinks on a single occasion (representing successful restraint), (b) maximum number of drinks on a single occasion (lapses), and (c) SMAST scores (alcohol problems resulting from a pattern of unregulated consumption). Results of a multivariate multiple regression indicated that two aspects of restraint (Restrict and Govern) predicted minimum drinking, which was not predicted by either attributional style. Maximum drinking was predicted by attributions for positive situations as well as Restrict and Govern. For both minimum and maximum drinking, individuals were seemingly balanced between the inclination to drink and exerting behavioral control over drinking behavior. The self-enhancement inherent in the role of positive attributions for predicting maximum drinking (i.e., drinking to have a good time) may indicate an inclination or ability to reassert control over alcohol intake following specific episodes of heavy drinking. Drinking-related problems (SMAST scores) were predicted by attributions for negative situations (self-blame) and Govern. This seemed to mean that the individual was preoccupied with drinking but was not engaging in the behaviors that help regulate drinking. In addition, they blamed themselves for negative drinking outcomes. This self-blaming attribution could lessen the individual's sense of efficacy for controlling alcohol intake, thereby interfering with the recovery from episodes of heavy drinking. The cumulative result of repeated failures to recover and the related excessive drinking is the experience of drinking-related problems. Because the pattern of results were consistent with predictions derived from the AVE–LVE, Collins and Lapp (1991) interpreted them as providing support for Marlatt's (1985) reformulation of the AVE.

The cross-sectional test of the AVE was followed by a laboratory analog test of the LVE (Collins, Lapp, & Izzo, 1993) among a community sample of young, male social drinkers. We used modeling of alcohol consumption (Collins & Marlatt, 1981) to precipitate limit violations. We reasoned that modeling of heavy drinking would lead to the violation of prestated drinking limits without evoking the conceptual and methodological problem inherent in explicitly requiring subjects to violate limits, as is done with the preload methodology. The subtle influences contained in the modeling procedure maintained the possibility that subjects would make personal attributions for violating their drinking limits. We assessed negative affect (tension, depression, and anger) by using subscales of the Shortened Profile of Mood States (Shacham, 1983) and behavioral aspects of the LVE, with a procedure that gave subjects the choice of continuing to drink.

To assess drinking limits, Collins et al. (1993) asked subjects to provide an estimate of the number of beers they were likely to consume during the 30-min drinking session. This enquiry was embedded in a more general screening interview that took place a few days before the drinking session. The drinking session occurred in a laboratory bar and subjects were served alcoholic beer. Each subject was randomly paired with a confederate, and the pairs were instructed to "get to know each other" while drinking as they normally would in a bar. Confederates were trained to model *light* (one to two 12-oz glasses of nonalcoholic beer) or *heavy* (four to five glasses) drinking during the session, but they did not explicitly encourage the subjects to drink. All participants in a particular session were exposed to the same type of modeled drinking behavior. After the drinking session, subjects were invited to voluntarily participate in a rating of the taste characteristics of two whiskeys. The number of shots of whiskey subjects requested served as the measure of the subject's inclination to continue drinking (our behavioral measure of sequelae to the LVE).

The results indicated that the modeling manipulation was effective. Total beer consumption varied as a function of modeling, such that subjects in the heavy condition drank significantly more than subjects in the light condition. Subjects in the heavy condition also were more likely to violate their prestated drinking limit, whereas those in the light condition tended to drink less than their prestated limit. Postdrinking negative affect (the affective component of the LVE) occurred as a function of the violation of limits. This effect was evident in increases in depression and anger, which varied as a function of excess drinking (actual consumption minus prestated drinking limit) coupled with particular aspects of drinking restraint.

Although the affective component of the LVE was present, the expected behavioral sequelae to the LVE was not evident. Rather than the predicted increased inclination to drink (i.e., ordering more shots of whiskey), the number of shots ordered decreased as a function of increased negative affect. This finding was unexpected, because in contrast to the LVE, it indicated a lessened tendency to continue drinking as a function of experiencing negative affect. A post hoc consideration of the attributional component of the LVE indicated that in the heavy condition, subjects had attributed their increased consumption to external influences. Being able to attribute their behavior to external influences is likely to have precluded the occurrence of a more intense LVE, which would include the behavioral sequelae of ordering more shots.

There are two other methodological limitations that may explain Collins et al.'s (1993) failure to observe behavioral aspects of limit violation. The LVE experienced in this laboratory analog was not of such intensity as to produce a behavioral reaction, and the time frame of the study was too limited. As noted previously, the AVE–LVE is experienced across a range of intensities. The extent of the violation in this study (M = 93 ml, just over 3 oz) may not have been sufficient to produce an LVE of enough intensity to precipitate the behavioral reaction of deciding to continue drinking. That is, subjects felt badly after drinking beyond their limits but may not have felt badly enough to decide to "blow" the evening by continuing to drink. Even if they felt badly, to the extent that they could make external attributions for their drinking (particularly to partner influences), they did not experience an LVE of enough intensity to produce a behavioral reaction.

With regard to the time frame of the Collins et al. (1993) study, subjects experienced a single drinking episode that occurred over a relatively short span of time (30 min). The negative affect experienced in a single, short episode of limit violation may not have been enough to precipitate a full-blown LVE reaction, which includes the decision to continue drinking. Interestingly, in a study of obese binge eaters, Eldredge and Agras (1992) failed to find a behavioral reaction to negative mood induction in a laboratory. However, the mood induction did produce more binge eating on the following day. It is possible that a similar phenomenon, a delayed binge, occurred among our sample of social drinkers.

Rather than precipitating drinking, single episodes of limit violation or violations of restricted duration may initially serve to reinstate vigilance and effort related to controlling alcohol intake. This might explain Collins et al.'s (1993) finding of a decrease in the number of shots ordered as a function of experiencing negative affect. The move to excessive drinking is most likely to occur with repeated failures to regulate alcohol intake, self-attribution, and related experiences of the LVE over longer durations of time.

SUMMARY AND CONCLUSION

Research on drinking restraint is in its relative infancy. The pioneering work of Ruderman and McKirnan (1984) and the contributions of Bensley and colleagues (cf. Bensley, 1991; Curry, Southwick, & Steele, 1987) have provided a solid conceptual and methodological base from which to examine processes related to risk for alcohol abuse. Collins and colleagues have conducted survey and laboratory research that have provided support for restraint as a multifaceted construct, which includes the temptation to drink and attempts to regulate consumption (Collins et al., 1989; Collins & Lapp, 1991, 1992; Collins et al., 1993). A psychometrically sound measure that includes both of these tendencies has been developed, and their relationship to self-reported drinking conforms to our predictions (Collins et al., 1989; Collins & Lapp, 1982). Drinking restraint also has provided a context for testing the affective and attributional aspects of the AVE–LVE (Collins & Lapp, 1991; Collins et al., 1993). However, for a myriad of reasons, behavioral aspects of the LVE have not been produced in the laboratory. The next step in our program of research is to conduct field studies of phenomena related to restraint and the LVE. The aim of this new research is to understand the precipitants and correlates of the cycle of restraint and excessive drinking. In field studies, my colleagues and I hope to examine the naturalistic occurrence of the LVE and to learn more about the ways in which restraint operates as a risk factor for alcohol abuse. The results of this research will have implications for our theoretical and practical understanding of the move from social drinking to problem drinking, as well as the relapse process.

REFERENCES

Bensley, L. S. (1989). The heightened role of external responsiveness in the alcohol consumption of restrained drinkers. *Cognitive Therapy and Research, 13,* 623–636.

Bensley, L. S. (1991). Construct validity evidence for the interpretation of drinking restraint as a response conflict. *Addictive Behaviors, 16,* 139–150.

Bensley, L. S., Kuna, P. H., & Steele, C. M. (1988). The role of external responsiveness in drinking restraint. *Cognitive Therapy and Research, 12,* 261–278.

Bensley, L. S., Kuna, P. H., & Steele, C. M. (1990). The role of drinking restraint success in subsequent alcohol consumption. *Addictive Behaviors, 15,* 491–496.

Birke, S. A., Edelmann, R. J., & Davis, P. E. (1990). An analysis of the abstinence violation effect in a sample of illicit drug users. *British Journal of Addiction, 85,* 1299–1307.

Blanchard, F. A., & Frost, R. O. (1983). Two factors of restraint: Concern for dieting and weight fluctuation. *Behaviour Research and Therapy, 21,* 259–267.

Bradley, B. P., Gossop, M., Brewin, C. R., Phillips, G., & Green, L. (1992). Attributions and relapse in opiate addicts. *Journal of Consulting and Clinical Psychology, 60,* 470–472.

Collins, R. L., George, W. H., & Lapp, W. M. (1989). Drinking restraint: Refinement of a construct and prediction of alcohol consumption. *Cognitive Therapy and Research, 13,* 423–440.

Collins, R. L., & Lapp, W. M. (1991). Restraint and attribution: Evidence of the abstinence violation effect in alcohol consumption. *Cognitive Therapy and Research, 15,* 69–84.

Collins, R. L., & Lapp, W. M. (1992). The Temptation and Restraint Inventory for measuring drinking restraint. *British Journal of Addiction, 87,* 625–633.

Collins, R. L., Lapp, W. M., Helder, L., & Saltzberg, J. A. (1992). Cognitive restraint and impulsive eating: Insights from the Three-Factor Eating Questionnaire. *Psychology of Addictive Behaviors, 6,* 47–53.

Collins, R. L., Lapp, W. M., & Izzo, C. V. (1991, August). *Affective and behavioral aspects of the limit violation effect.* Poster presented at the 99th Annual Convention of the American Psychological Association, San Francisco.

Collins, R. L., Lapp, W. M., & Izzo, C. V. (1993). *Affective and behavioral reactions to the violation of limits on alcohol consumption.* Manuscript submitted for publication.

Collins, R. L., & Marlatt, G. A. (1981). Social modeling as a determinant of drinking behavior: Implications for prevention and treatment. *Addictive Behaviors, 6,* 233–239.

Curry, S., Marlatt, G. A., & Gordon, J. R. (1987). Abstinence violation effect: Validation of an attributional construct with smoking cessation. *Journal of Consulting and Clinical Psychology, 55,* 145–149.

Curry, S., Southwick, L., & Steele, C. (1987). Restrained drinking: Risk factor for problems with alcohol? *Addictive Behaviors, 12,* 73–77.

Eldredge, K. L., & Agras, W. S. (1992, November). *A laboratory test of the role of negative mood and cognition in dietary disinhibition*. Poster presented at the meeting of Association for Advancement of Behavior Therapy, Boston.

Hall, S. M., Havassy, B. E., & Wasserman, D. A. (1990). Commitment to abstinence and acute stress in relapse to alcohol, opiates, and nicotine. *Journal of Consulting and Clinical Psychology, 58,* 175–181.

Heatherton, T. F., Herman, C. P., Polivy, J., King, G. A., & McGree, S. T. (1988). The (mis)measurement of restraint: An analysis of conceptual and psychometric issues. *Journal of Abnormal Psychology, 97,* 19–28.

Herman, C. P., & Kozlowski, L. T. (1979). Indulgence, excess, and restraint: Perspectives on consummatory behavior in everyday life. *Journal of Drug Issues, 9,* 185–196.

Herman, C. P., & Mack, D. (1975). Restrained and unrestrained eating. *Journal of Personality, 43,* 647–660.

Herman, C. P., & Polivy, J. (1980). Restrained eating. In A. J. Stunkard (Ed.), *Obesity* (pp. 208–225). Philadelphia: W. B. Saunders.

Herman, C. P., & Polivy, J. (1984). A boundary model for the regulation of eating. In A. J. Stunkard & E. Stellar (Eds.), *Eating and its disorders* (pp. 141–156). New York: Raven Press.

Higgins, R. L., & Marlatt, G. A. (1975). Fear of interpersonal evaluation as a determinant of alcohol consumption in male social drinkers. *Journal of Abnormal Psychology, 84,* 644–651.

Lowe, M. R. (1984). Dietary concern, weight fluctuation and weight status: Further explorations of the Restraint Scale. *Behaviour Research and Therapy, 22,* 243–248.

Marlatt, G. A. (1985). Cognitive factors in the relapse process. In G. A. Marlatt & J. R. Gordon (Eds.), *Relapse prevention* (pp. 128–200). New York: Guilford Press.

Marlatt, G. A., & Gordon, J. R. (1980). Determinants of relapse: Implications for the maintenance of behavior change. In P. O. Davidson & S. M. Davidson (Eds.), *Behavioral medicine: Changing health lifestyles* (pp. 410–452). New York: Guilford Press.

Mooney, J. P., Burling, T. A., Hartman, W. M., & Brenner-Liss, D. (1992). The abstinence violation effect and very low calorie diet success. *Addictive Behaviors, 17,* 319–324.

Nisbett, R. E. (1972). Hunger, obesity, and the ventromedial hypothalamus. *Psychological Review, 79,* 433–453.

Ogden, J., & Wardle, J. (1990). Control of eating and attributional style. *British Journal of Clinical Psychology, 29,* 445–446.

Polivy, J., & Herman, C. P. (1985). Dieting and binging: A causal analysis. *American Psychologist, 40,* 193–201.

Ross, S. M., Miller, P. J. Emmerson, R. Y., & Todt, E. H. (1989). Self-efficacy, standards, and abstinence violation: A comparison between newly sober and long-term sober alcoholics. *Journal of Substance Abuse, 1,* 221–229.

Ruderman, A. J. (1983). The Restraint Scale: A psychometric investigation. *Behaviour Research and Therapy, 21,* 253–258.

Ruderman, A. J., & Christensen, H. (1983). Restraint theory and its applicability to overweight individuals. *Journal of Abnormal Psychology, 92,* 210–215.

Ruderman, A. J., & McKirnan, D. J. (1984). The development of a Restrained Drinking Scale: A test of the abstinence violation effect among alcohol users. *Addictive Behaviors, 9,* 365–371.

Schachter, S. (1968). Obesity and eating. *Science, 161,* 751–756.

Selzer, M. L., Vinokur, A., & van Rooijen, L. (1975). A self-administered short Michigan Alcoholism Screening Test (SMAST). *Journal of Studies on Alcohol, 36,* 117–126.

Shacham, S. (1983). A shortened version of the Profile of Mood States. *Journal of Personality Assessment, 47,* 305–306.

Southwick, L., & Steele, C. M. (1987). Restrained drinking: Personality correlates of a control style. *Journal of Drug Issues, 17,* 349–358.

Stunkard, A. J. (1981). "Restrained eating": What it is and a new scale to measure it. In L. A. Cioffi, W. P. T. James, & T. B. Itallie (Eds.), *The body weight regulatory system: Normal and disturbed mechanisms* (pp. 243–251). New York: Raven Press.

Stunkard, A. J., & Messick, S. (1985). The Three-Factor Eating Questionnaire to measure dietary restraint, disinhibition and hunger. *Journal of Psychosomatic Research, 29,* 71–83.

Tomarken, A. J., & Kirschenbaum, D. S. (1984). Effects of plans for future meals on counterregulatory eating by restrained and unrestrained eaters. *Journal of Abnormal Psychology, 93,* 458–472.

Westenhoefer, J. (1991). Dietary restraint and disinhibition. Is restraint a homogeneous construct? *Appetite, 16,* 45–55.

VI

SCREENING AND ASSESSMENT

11

SCREENING FOR NEUROPSYCHOLOGICAL IMPAIRMENT IN ALCOHOLICS

AUSTIN L. ERRICO, SARA J. NIXON, OSCAR A. PARSONS, AND JOHN TASSEY

Neuropsychological screening techniques first became popular in the 1940s and 1950s when it was still believed that brain damage could be identified by some general manifestation (Lezak, 1983). As the complexities of brain pathology became better appreciated, the need for a multidimensional approach to neuropsychological assessment became apparent. Subsequently, screening techniques have assumed a new role. They can provide useful information to help identify areas for further inquiry in populations in which neurological disorders are more frequent than in the general population but occur at base rates that are unknown or are so low that thorough neuropsychological or neurological examination of each person in that population is impractical or prohibitively costly (Lezak, 1983).

Reprinted from *Psychological Assessment: A Journal of Consulting and Clinical Psychology, 2,* 45–50. (1990). Copyright ©1990 by the American Psychological Association. Used with permission of the author.

This research was supported by Grants AA01464 and AA06135 from the National Institute for Alcohol Abuse and Alcoholism to Oscar A. Parsons.

For example, neuropsychological screening is useful in the examination of patients seeking psychiatric treatment as well as for at-risk groups such as elderly or alcoholic persons, who may show no obvious neurological impairment (Goldstein, 1986; Yozawitz, 1986).

Traditionally, neuropsychological screening instruments (see Berg, Franzen, & Wedding, 1987, for review) have been developed as performance measures of cognitive functioning (e.g., the Mini-Mental Status exam [Folstein, Folstein, & McHugh, 1975], the Mental Status Examination [Taylor, Abrams, Faher, & Almy, 1980], and the Short Portable Mental Status Questionnaire [Pfeiffer, 1975]). A less common method has been to rely on a patient's self-report of perceived deficiency.

In one study, Chelune, Heaton, and Lehman (1986) administered the Patient's Assessment of Own Functioning Inventory (PAF), the Minnesota Multiphasic Personality Inventory (MMPI), and a comprehensive battery of cognitive tests to a group of patients with suspected or diagnosed brain dysfunction and to a group of normal control subjects. The PAF is a self-report questionnaire used to obtain patient ratings of cognitive and neurological difficulties. Patients were found to have greater neuropsychological impairment and reported more PAF complaints than did control subjects. Self-ratings, however, were more strongly associated with patients' MMPI results than with their test performance. Similar results were found in another study (Shelton & Parsons, 1987) using sober alcoholic and nonalcoholic control subjects. Alcoholic subjects performed poorer on neuropsychological tests and reported significantly more impairment on all PAF scales than did control subjects. Performance differences were not found to be related to PAF complaints, and measures of anxiety and depression were correlated significantly with self-reported impairment.

Thus, in studies using general neuropsychological referrals and alcoholic patients, the subjects' complaints, as measured by the PAF, were more reflective of their affective states than of their actual abilities (Chelune et al., 1986; Shelton & Parsons, 1987). Is this an inherent problem of all self-report data, or can a patient's perceived dysfunction be used to screen for neuropsychological impairment? Additional studies using other instruments need to be conducted before conclusions can be reached about the clinical utility of self-report questionnaires.

Recent studies (O'Donnell, DeSoto, & Reynolds, 1984; O'Donnell, Reynolds, & DeSoto, 1984) have suggested that a new self-report inventory, the Neuropsychological Impairment Scale (NIS) could reliably and validly predict neuropsychological impairment in normal as well as in neuropsychiatric populations.

The NIS is a 50-item self-report scale designed to assess complaints indicative of brain damage (e.g., forgetfulness, bumping into things, and trouble learning). The test consists of eight subscales: Global Measure of Impairment (GMI), Total Items Checked (TIC), Symptom Intensity Measure (SIM), Lie scale (LIE), General scale (GEN), Pathognomic scale (PAT), Learning–Verbal scale (LV), and Frustration scale (FRU). Normative data have been obtained from 62 separate groups (e.g., churches, civic organizations, schools, and work settings) in urban, suburban, and rural areas (N = 2,150). Separate norms have been computed on 300 neuropsychiatric patients, including substance abusers, schizophrenics, and patients with neurologic, affective, anxiety, impulse, adjustment, and personality disorders (O'Donnell & Reynolds, 1983).

Validity studies (O'Donnell, DeSoto, & Reynolds, 1984; O'Donnell & Reynolds, 1983; O'Donnell, Reynolds, & DeSoto, 1984) have been conducted comparing the NIS with tests known to be sensitive to cognitive dysfunction. In one study (O'Donnell, Reynolds, & DeSoto, 1984), the GMI and SIM subscales were shown to significantly correlate with performance measures from the Halstead-Reitan Battery known to be sensitive to brain dysfunction (i.e., the Halstead Impairment Index, Category Test, Part B of the Trail-Making Test, and the Tactual Performance Test Localization). Validity was also assessed in a second study (O'Donnell, DeSoto, & Reynolds, 1984). An optimal (not cross-validated) NIS scale score was defined as impaired if the T-score value exceeded 60. T-scores were derived from the normative data (N = 2,150) previously mentioned. Using the Halstead Impairment Index as their criterion for brain damage (impairment was defined by a score equal to or exceeding .5), O'Donnell, DeSoto, & Reynolds (1984) reported the NIS scales demonstrated between 68% and 91% sensitivity and between 43% and 86% "specificity" in 41 patients referred for neuropsychological evaluation. Test–retest correlation coefficients for five NIS scales (GMI, LIE, PAT, TIC, & SIM) were shown to be between .52 and .87 for 25 neuropsychiatric patients (Mdn = .78) and between .65 and .92 for 82 undergraduate psychology students. These correlation coefficients were significant in both samples, $p < .01$ and $p < .001$, respectively. In sum, although the data are limited, it appears that the NIS may be both a valid and a reasonably reliable predictor of neuropsychological impairment.

The NIS may provide a useful measure for screening alcoholic persons who are considered at risk for neuropsychological deficits. Early detection of cognitive impairment in alcoholics undergoing treatment could provide valuable information in the structuring of effective rehabilitation programs, ultimately saving both clinicians and patients time and unnecessary frustration. However, a critical issue in valid neuropsychological assessment is control of nonneurological variables that are known to affect cognitive performance. The influence of age and education are probably the most well-cited examples (Heaton, Grant, & Matthews, 1986; Parsons & Prigatano, 1978). In addition, affective states such as anxiety and depression have been implicated as possible variables that may affect cognitive performance in alcoholics and thus should be monitored (Grant, 1987; Parsons, 1989). For a neuropsychological screening instrument to be considered valid, it should not only be related to measures of impairment, but the relationship should be relatively independent of the influence of non-neurological variables.

In determining whether the NIS could serve as a valid indicator of neuropsychological impairment in alcoholics, we asked the following questions:

1. Do detoxified alcoholics undergoing treatment score differently on the NIS than nonalcoholic subjects?
2. Is the NIS a reliable instrument when used with alcoholics?
3. Is the NIS related to cognitive impairment as evaluated by standard neuropsychological tests known to be sensitive to brain dysfunction; and if so, is this relationship independent of other variables that have been shown or hypothesized to affect neuropsychological performance, such as age, education, anxiety, and depression?
4. Is performance on the NIS related to drinking behaviors in alcoholics?

METHOD

Subjects

A total of 73 male alcoholics from the Oklahoma City Veterans Administration Medical Center inpatient alcohol treatment program and 36 community control subjects, recruited through newspaper ads and civic organizations, volunteered for this study. All of the subjects were between 24 and 60 years of age, with at least a sixth-grade education and a minimum Shipley Institute of Living vocabulary age of 13.0 (low-average level of intelligence as measured by vocabulary; Shipley, 1940). The two groups, alcoholic and control, were equated on age (M = 42.5 ± 9.7 and M = 43.0 ± 8.5, respectively) and on number of years of education (M = 12.7 ± 2.2 and M = 12.7 ± 1.8, respectively). All of the subjects gave informed consent and were paid for their participation. The alcoholic subjects reported an average of 11.5 years of problem drinking and a typical consumption of 361.2 g of absolute ethanol per drinking day. They also met the National Council of Alcoholism criteria for alcoholism (Criteria Committee, National Council on Alcoholism, 1972). None of the control subjects had a history of alcohol abuse; their typical consumption averaged 39.2 g of absolute ethanol per drinking day. Subjects were carefully screened but were not ruled out for medications, drug abuse, psychiatric history, and medical problems that could possibly affect brain functioning.

Those subjects with positive screening variables were included because they typified inpatient alcoholics. Comparison on baseline neuropsychological measures revealed no differences between these and "cleaner" alcoholic subjects (Yohman, Schaeffer, & Parsons, 1988). Finally, subjects with histories of neurological disorders were excluded from this study.

Tests and Procedures

All of the subjects were given the NIS, which requires subjects to rate the intensity with which they experience various symptoms. Subjects use a 4-point scale, with higher ratings associated with increasing intensities. The GMI is the total raw-score sum of the 45 neuropsychological items (LIE scale not included); the TIC also provides a global indicator of impairment; and the SIM is derived by dividing GMI by TIC. The LIE scale consists of five items that assess test-taking attitude. The GEN asks questions about difficulties in mental efficiency, alertness, and endurance; the PAT is made up of items that frequently suggest the presence or history of neuropsychological impairment; the LV reflects complaints of verbal communication and learning problems; and the FRU contains items reflecting undue affective and motivational reactions.

The NIS was given to alcoholic subjects approximately 7 days after their admission to the treatment program and was readministered during the 4th week of hospitalization. Control subjects were given the NIS only once. All of the subjects were administered a 4-hr test battery consisting of several self-report questionnaires, including the Beck Depression Inventory (BDI; Beck, Ward, Mendelson, Mock, & Erbaugh, 1961) and the Spielberger State–Trait Anxiety Inventory (AI; Spielberger, Gorsuch, & Lushene, 1970), along with a variety of neuropsychological tests. The tests selected have been found to be sensitive to brain dysfunction and to discriminate alcoholic from nonalcoholic subjects. Descriptions of these measures are given elsewhere (Yohman et al., 1988). Alcoholics were tested on this battery approximately 3 weeks after admission to the hospital. Alcoholics were readministered the AI and BDI during their 4th week of hospitalization. The neuropsychological tests measured three clusters of cognitive functioning: learning and memory, problem-solving and perceptual–motor skills, and an overall performance index, which is the mean level of performance on all tests. (See Table 1.) Raw test scores for the alcoholics were placed in a common metric by transferring them to standard T scores (50 ± 10) based on the distributions in the nonalcoholic control sample. Specific results on the neuropsychological data are given elsewhere (Yohman et al., 1988); suffice it to say that alcoholics performed significantly poorer than did control subjects on all of the neuropsychological test clusters. Finally, subjects were given a structured interview in which they were asked about their drinking histories for the last 6 months,

TABLE 1
Neuropsychological Tests

Test	Reference
Learning and memory	
Wechsler Memory Scale–Logical Memory[a]	Russell, 1975
Wechsler Memory Scale–Visual Reproduction	Russell, 1975
Symbol–Digit Paired Associates	Ryan & Butters
Luria Memory Words	Luria, 1966
Face–Name Paired Associates	Schaeffer & Parsons, 1987
Verbal Paired Associates	Yohman & Parsons, 1985
Performance index	
Consists of all of the tests listed	
Problem-solving	
Block Design (WAIS–R)	Wechsler Adult Intelligence Scale–Revised (Wechsler, 1981)
Twenty Questions	Laine & Butters, 1982
Abstraction Test	Shipley, 1940
Hypothesis Testing Procedure	Levine, 1966
Adaptive Skills Battery	Jones & Lanyon, 1981
Conceptual Level Analogy Test	Willner, 1970
Perceptual–motor	
Digit Symbol (WAIS–R)	Wechsler Adult Intelligence Scale–Revised (Wechsler, 1981)
Rennick Repeatable Battery	Rennick, Russell, Kempler, & Schwartz, 1972
Lafayette Pegboard	
Sentence Writing	
Trail-Making, Test B	

[a]Only the delayed recall data were used in the analysis.

in order to obtain values for various recent drinking practices. These include typical quantity consumed per occasion (TQ), frequency of typical drinking (TF), typical Quantity × Frequency (TQF), maximum quantity drunk (MQ), frequency of maximum drinking (MF), the maximum Quantity × Frequency (MQF), and the quantity frequency index (QFI; Cahalan, Cisin, & Crossley, 1969); the latter is the sum of the amount of absolute alcohol for wine, beer, and liquor consumed, multiplied by the frequency for each. Finally, a chronicity (CHRON) measure was obtained. (See Table 3.) Alcoholics were asked how long alcohol had been a problem in their lives, and control subjects were asked how long they had been drinking socially.

RESULTS

To address our first question, alcoholic and control group differences on all NIS scales were assessed by a multivariate analysis of variance. Scores on all eight scales served as the dependent measures; means and standard deviations are presented in Table 2. Using the Wilks's criterion, a significant group main effect was found, $F(8, 100) = 5.03$, $p < .0001$. To investigate the independent influence of each test, eight univariate analyses of variance were conducted. The groups differed significantly on all scales except the LIE scale. The groups were also found to differ on the AI and BDI, with alcoholic subjects scoring significantly higher than control subjects.

In order to investigate the test–retest reliability of the NIS (Question 2), the scale was readministered to all alcoholic subjects ($n = 73$) 3 weeks after initial testing (4 weeks abstinent from alcohol). Correlations ranged from .52 to .80 (Table 3); all were significant ($p < .001$). Depression and anxiety scores were also found to significantly decrease over this time: BDI, $M = .90 \pm .74$ versus $M = 5.4 \pm 5.6$, $t(67) = 6.6$, $p < .001$; AI, $M = 54.6 \pm 13.5$ versus $M = 51.3 \pm 11.6$, $t(67) = 2.8$, $p < .01$.

Question 3 was answered by performing bivariate correlations between each of the NIS scales and the three clusters of neuropsychological tests. Control subjects showed only one significant relationship: The SIM scale was negatively correlated with problem-solving performance, $r(34) = -.40$, $p < .05$. In alcoholic subjects, on the other hand, five of the NIS scales (PAT, GMI, LV, SIM, and TIC) were significantly and inversely related to most of the neuropsychological clusters, as well as the performance index (Table 4). The GEN scale significantly correlated with the learning/memory and performance indexes and showed trends with the

TABLE 2
Means and Standard Deviations of NIS Scales and Affective Measures

	Group			
	Alcoholics ($n = 73$)		Controls ($n = 36$)	
Scale	M	SD	M	SD
NIS				
PAT	5.1	5.4	1.3	2.1
GMI	35.4	23.2	16.7	10.0
GEN	8.3	6.6	4.8	3.2
LV	6.9	6.0	3.8	3.0
SIM	1.6	0.4	1.2	0.2
TIC	21.7	10.3	13.9	7.4
LIE	7.1	2.7	7.5	3.2
FRU	8.6	5.1	4.0	2.3
Affective measure				
BDI	9.0[a]	7.4[a]	3.6	3.4
AI	54.6[a]	13.5[a]	44.5	7.2

Note. NIS = Neuropsychological Impairment Scale; PAT = Pathognomic Scale; GMI = Global Measure of Impairment; GEN = General Scale; LV = Learning–Verbal Scale; TIC = Total Items Checked; SIM = Symptom Intensity Measure; LIE = Lie Scale; FRU = Frustration Scale; BDI = Beck Depression Inventory; AI = Spielberger State Anxiety Inventory.
[a]$n = 69$.

TABLE 3
Test–Retest Coefficients and Paired *t*-Tests of NIS and Affective Measures for Alcoholics

Scale	Test–retest coefficients[a] (n = 73)	Paired t-tests (n = 73)	p level
NIS			
PAT	.80	3.66	.0005
GMI	.76	4.35	.0001
GEN	.70	2.04	.045
LV	.76	1.47	.1463
SIM	.67	5.32	.0001
TIC	.78	3.12	.0026
LIE	.52	−0.41	.680
FRU	.69	5.10	.0001
Affective measure			
BDI	.76[b]	6.64[b]	.0001
AI	.70[b]	2.78[b]	.007

Note. NIS = Neuropsychological Impairment Scale; PAT = Pathognomic Scale; GMI = Global Measure of Impairment; GEN = General Scale; LV = Learning–Verbal Scale; TIC = Total Items Checked; SIM = Symptom Intensity Measure; LIE = Lie Scale; FRU = Frustration Scale; BDI = Beck Depression Inventory; AI = Spielberger State–Trait Anxiety Inventory.
[a] All test–retest coefficients were significant at the .0001 level.
[b] n = 69.

other clusters. Only the LIE and FRU scales were not significantly correlated with task performance, although trends between FRU and the neuropsychological measures were in the expected negative direction.

To further investigate Question 3, stepwise multiple regression analyses were used to predict alcoholics' neuropsychological performance, based

TABLE 4
Pearson Correlations for Alcoholics

Test	L/M	PROB	PERC	PERF	CHRON	TQF	MQF	BDI	AI
PAT	−.28*	−.28*	.21	−.33**	.26*	.20	.15	.44**	.29*
GMI	−.30*	−.30*	−.31*	−.38**	.27*	.25*	.07	.65**	.54**
GEN	−.24*	−.22	−.22	−.28**	.26*	.06	−.12	.56**	.41**
LV	−.30*	−.35**	.41**	−.43**	.23	.28**	.04	.60**	.51**
SIM	−.33**	−.38**	−.31**	−.43**	.14	.39**	.31**	.62**	.56**
TIC	.23	−.24*	−.25*	−.30*	.31**	.20	.03	.55**	.44**
LIE	.19	.12	.06	.15	−.02	−.01	−.05	−.16	−.25*
FRU	.11	−.07	.06	.10	.11	.28*	.12	.61**	.64**
BDI	−.28*	−.26*	−.19	−.32**	.09	.28*	.14	—	—
AI	−.28*	−.30**	−.22	−.33**	.07	.25*	.13	—	—

Note. L/M = Learning and Memory; PROB = Problem-Solving; PERC = Perceptual–Motor; PERF = Performance Index; TQF = Typical Quantity × Frequency; CHRON = Chronicity; MQF = Maximum Quantity × Frequency; BDI = Beck Depression Inventory; AI = Spielberger State–Trait Anxiety Inventory; GMI = Global Measure of Impairment; PAT = Pathognomic Scale; GEN = General Scale; LV = Learning–Verbal Scale; TIC = Total Items Checked; SIM = Symptom Intensity Measure; LIE = Lie Scale; FRU = Frustration Scale.
*p < .05. **p < .01.

on NIS scores, age, education, and anxiety and depression ratings. The performance index was used as our dependent variable inasmuch as previous research has shown similar indexes to be among the more sensitive indicators of brain dysfunction (Parsons & Prigatano, 1978; Reitan & Davison, 1974). As expected from previous research (Heaton et al., 1986; Parsons & Prigatano, 1978), age and education were each found to significantly predict performance. Anxiety was also found to significantly contribute to the model. The amount of variance accounted for by each of these variables was as follows: education = 26%, age = 26%, and anxiety rating = 4%. When anxiety was excluded from the model, depression also reached significance, accounting for 3.4% of the variance. This finding suggests that contrary to the theoretically different states they are designed to assess, the AI and BDI appeared to be measuring similar (i.e., overlapping) dimensions. By adding the NIS subscales to the regression model, neither the anxiety nor depression rating significantly predicted performance, but instead the SIM scale accounted for 6% of the variance. Moreover, the variability accounted for by age and education remained the same (52% total), suggesting that the SIM scale predicted performance relatively independent of age and education but shared much of the variance with that accounted for by AI and BDI. When the SIM scale was replaced by the LV scale, a similar pattern emerged, with LV accounting for 4% of the variance. Thus, although affective measures initially predicted performance, these effects disappeared when demographics and cognitive complaints as measured by the SIM and LV scale were accounted for. These results are summarized in Table 5.

Factor analysis (varimax rotation) of the eight drinking-related questions indicated that three variables—CHRON, TQF, and MQF—best described drinking behavior for the alcoholic subjects used in this study. A

TABLE 5
Stepwise Regression Models Predicting Neuropsychological Performance in Alcoholics

Measure	Model			
	1	2	3	4
Age	26%	26%	26%	26%
Education	26%	26%	26%	26%
AI	4%	omitted	ns	ns
BDI	ns	3.4%	ns	ns
SIM	omitted	omitted	6%	omitted
LV	omitted	omitted	omitted	4%

Note. Percentages refer to the variance accounted for by given variable. AI = Spielberger State–Trait Anxiety Inventory; BDI = Beck Depression Inventory; SIM = Symptom Intensity Measure; LV = Learning–Verbal Scale; ns = nonsignificant; Model 1 = age, education, AI, BDI; Model 2 = age, education, BDI; Model 3 = age, education, AI, BDI, SIM; Model 4 = age, education, AI, BDI, LV.

correlational analysis revealed that CHRON and TQF were significantly positively related to four of the NIS scales (Table 4). The three drinking variables were also significantly negatively related to the performance index: CHRON, $r(74) = -.24$, $p < .05$; TQF, $r(74) = -.34$, $p < .01$; and MQF, $r(73) = -.27$, $p < .05$.

DISCUSSION

Previous research has suggested that self-report questionnaires concerning disability are not valid indicators (i.e., screening tests) of neuropsychological impairment but are more reflective of a patient's affective status. Recent studies by O'Donnell and Reynolds (1983; O'Donnell, Reynolds, & DeSoto, 1984) have suggested that the NIS could serve as a reliable and valid screening instrument in neuropsychiatric populations. The purpose of this study was to investigate whether the NIS could serve as a screening instrument in an alcoholic sample. Although several aspects of our data appeared to be encouraging, further analysis led us to be wary of the NIS's usefulness as a clinical screening instrument, a conclusion consistent with Franzen (1989). On the positive side, the data revealed five findings.

First, most NIS scales demonstrated reasonable test–retest reliability in the 73 alcoholics who were given the test again. Paired t tests of the difference between test and retest scores showed that cognitive and neurological complaints as assessed by six (SIM, PAT, GEN, FRU, TIC, and GMI) of the eight scales significantly decreased after 3 weeks (Table 3). Similarly, depression and anxiety scores were also found to significantly decrease over this time. Whether the decline in self-reported symptoms is exclusively indicative of a recovery in neuropsychological function or reflective of improved affect remains an empirical question. Second, the mean GMI score for our 73 alcoholic subjects ($M = 35.45 \pm 23.23$) was comparable with that reported by O'Donnell and Reynolds (1983) for 28 substance abuse subjects ($M = 37.37 \pm 23.64$). Unfortunately, means on the other NIS measures for O'Donnell and Reynolds's sample were not reported, prohibiting us from making other comparisons. Third, in agreement with work indicating a positive relation between neuropsychological performance and alcoholic drinking behavior (Schaeffer & Parsons, 1986), some NIS scales were also found to correlate with measures of alcohol consumption. Fourth, our alcoholic subjects scored significantly higher than the control subjects on all six clinical scales, indicating greater symptomatology in the former group. Finally, all six of these scales were inversely related to neuropsychological performance in alcoholics but not in control subjects. Thus, the higher the alcoholics' NIS scale scores, the poorer the performance on neuropsychological tests. This relationship, however, was modest, reflecting only about 16% shared variance between the NIS scores and the performance index.

Nevertheless, the last result was somewhat encouraging, given our previous unsuccessful attempt to relate neuropsychological performance with self-reported symptoms (Shelton & Parsons, 1987). However, in the present investigation, unlike in our previous study, anxiety and depression were significantly correlated with neuropsychological impairment. The issue of whether the NIS is reflective only of disturbed affect or is also indicative of organic impairment calls into question its clinical usefulness in an alcoholic population. Recall that stepwise multiple regression analyses found that only SIM and LV subscales of the NIS significantly predicted overall performance. Both of these scales also shared considerable variance with the AI or BDI, or both. Intercorrelational analyses of the BDI, AI, LV, and SIM scales revealed that these variables were significantly correlated with each other, M $r(74)$ = .62, p < .001. Because cognitive and neurological symptomatology are likely to be exacerbated by a subject's affective status as well as organic pathology (Beck, 1967; Miller, 1975; Parsons, 1977; Parsons, Maslow, Morris, & Denny, 1964), it is conceivable that the NIS scales may be reflective of this "affective" component, rather than brain damage or dysfunction. This view is supported by the higher correlations between the NIS and affective measures than between the NIS and the performance index (Table 4). This is interesting in light of the fact that affective states are sometimes implicated as important variables mediating cognitive performance in alcoholics (Grant, 1987; Parsons, 1989). Our data suggest that affective symptoms appear to be more powerful determinants of complaints than of neuropsychological impairment. These results are consistent with previous attempts to predict cognitive dysfunction from self-report questionnaires (Chelune et al., 1986; Shelton & Parsons, 1987).

In sum, previous research (Shelton & Parsons, 1987) has suggested that alcoholics' subjective perceptions of their dysfunction are more reflective of their affective status than of their actual impairment. Results from this study using the NIS support this trend. Like the PAF, the NIS was found to be more strongly related to emotional distress than cognitive impairment. Given this, our recommendation is that the NIS (and other self-report impairment inventories) be used only as a supplemental tool for identifying specific neurological and cognitive complaints and that it not be relied on as the only means of screening alcoholics who may be in need of neuropsychological assessment.

REFERENCES

Beck, A. T. (1967). *Depression: Clinical, experimental, and theoretical aspects*. New York: Hoebner.

Beck, A. T., Ward, C. H., Mendelson, M., Mock, J. E., & Erbaugh, J. K. (1961). An inventory for measuring depression. *Archives of General Psychiatry, 4,* 561–571.

Berg, R., Franzen, M., & Wedding, D. (1987). *Screening for brain impairment: A manual for mental health practice.* New York: Springer Publishing.

Cahalan, V., Cisin, I., & Crossley, H. M. (1969). *American drinking practices.* New Brunswick, NJ: Rutgers Center for Alcohol Studies.

Chelune, G., Heaton, R., & Lehman, R. (1986). Neuropsychological and personality correlations of patients' complaints of disability. In G. Goldstein (Ed.), *Advances in clinical neuropsychology* (Vol. 3, pp. 95–126). New York: Plenum Press.

Criteria Committee, National Council on Alcoholism. (1972). Criteria for the diagnosis of alcoholism. *American Journal of Psychiatry, 129,* 127–135.

Folstein, M., Folstein, S., & McHugh, P. (1975). Mini-mental state: A practical method of grading the cognitive state of patients for the clinician. *Journal Psychiatric Residents, 12,* 189–198.

Franzen, M. D. (1989). Screening instruments. *Reliability and validity in neuropsychological assessment* (pp. 247–248). New York: Plenum Press.

Goldstein, G. (1986). The neuropsychology of schizophrenia. In I. Grant & K. M. Adams (Eds.), *Neuropsychological assessment of neuropsychiatric disorders* (pp. 147–171). New York: Oxford University Press.

Grant, I. (1987). Alcohol and the brain: Neuropsychological correlates. *Journal of Consulting and Clinical Psychology, 55,* 310–324.

Heaton, R. K., Grant, I., & Matthews, C. G. (1986). Differences in neuropsychological test performance associated with age, education, and sex. In I. Grant & K. M. Adams (Eds.), *Neuropsychological assessment of neuropsychiatric disorders* (pp. 147–171). New York: Oxford University Press.

Jones, S. L., & Lanyon, R. I. (1981). Relationship between adaptive skills and outcome of alcoholism treatment. *Journal of Studies on Alcohol, 42,* 521–525.

Laine, M., & Butters, N. (1982). A preliminary study of the problem-solving strategies of detoxified long-term alcoholics. *Drug and Alcohol Dependence, 10,* 235–242.

Levine, M. (1966). Hypothesis behavior by humans during discrimination learning. *Journal of Experimental Psychology, 71,* 331–338.

Lezak, M. D. (1983). *Neuropsychological assessment* (2nd ed.). New York: Oxford University Press.

Luria, A. R. (1966). *Higher cortical functions in man.* New York: Basic Books.

Miller, W. R. (1975). Psychological deficit in depression. *Psychological Bulletin, 82,* 238–260.

O'Donnell, W. E., De Soto, C. B., & Reynolds, D. McQ. (1984). Sensitivity and specificity of the Neuropsychological Impairment Scale (NIS). *Journal of Clinical Psychology, 40,* 553–555.

O'Donnell, W. E., & Reynolds, D. McQ. (1983). *Neuropsychological Impairment Scale (NIS) manual*. Annapolis, MD: Annapolis Neuropsychological Services.

O'Donnell, W. E., Reynolds, D. McQ., & De Soto, C. B. (1984). Validity and reliability of the Neuropsychological Impairment Scale (NIS). *Journal of Clinical Psychology, 40,* 549–552.

Parsons, O. A. (1977). Neuropsychological deficits in chronic alcoholics: Facts and fancies. *Alcoholism: Clinical and Experimental Research, 1,* 51–56.

Parsons, O. A. (1989). Impairment in sober alcoholics' cognitive functioning: The search for determinants. In T. Løberg, C. A. Marlott, W. R. Miller, & P. E. Nathan (Eds.), *Addictive behaviors: Prevention and early identification* (pp. 101–116). Lisse, The Netherlands: Swets & Zerlinger.

Parsons, O. A., Maslow, H., Morris, F., & Denny, J. P. (1964). Trail-Making Test performance in relation to certain experimenter, test, and subject variables. *Perceptual and Motor Skills, 19,* 199–206.

Parsons, O. A., & Prigatano, G. P. (1978). Methodological considerations in clinical neuropsychological research. *Journal of Consulting and Clinical Psychology, 46,* 608–619.

Pfeiffer, E. (1975). A Short Portable Mental Status Questionnaire for the assessment of organic brain deficit in elderly patients. *Journal of the American Geriatrics Society, 23,* 433–441.

Reitan, R. M., & Davison, L. A. (1974). *Clinical neuropsychology: Current status and applications.* Washington, DC: Winston.

Rennick, P. M., Russell, M., Kempler, H., & Schwartz, M. (1972, May). *The effect of d-amphetamine on cognitive and perceptual–motor functions of hyperkinetic children.* Paper presented at the meeting of the Midwestern Psychological Association, Chicago.

Russell, E. W. (1975). A multiple scoring method of assessment of complex memory factors. *Journal of Consulting and Clinical Psychology, 43,* 800–809.

Ryan, C., & Butters, N. (1980). Learning and memory impairments in young and old alcoholics: Evidence for the premature-aging hypothesis. *Alcoholism: Clinical and Experimental Research, 4,* 288–293.

Schaeffer, K. W., & Parsons, O. A. (1986). Drinking practices and neuropsychological performance in alcoholics and social drinkers. *Alcohol, 3,* 175–180.

Schaeffer, K. W., & Parsons, O. A. (1987). Learning impairment in alcoholics using an ecologically relevant test. *The Journal of Nervous and Mental Disease, 175,* 213–218.

Shelton, M. D., & Parsons, O. A. (1987). Alcoholics' self-assessment of their neuropsychology functioning in every day life. *Journal of Clinical Psychology, 43,* 395–403.

Shipley, W. C. (1940). A self-administering scale for measuring intellectual impairment and deterioration. *Journal of Psychology, 9,* 371–377.

Spielberger, C. D., Gorsuch, R. L., & Lushene, R. E. (1970). *Test manual for the State–Trait Anxiety Inventory.* Palo Alto, CA: Consulting Psychologists Press.

Taylor, M. A., Abrams, R., Faher, R., & Almy, G. (1980). Cognitive tasks in the

Mental Status Examination. *The Journal of Nervous and Mental Disease, 168*, 167–170.

Wechsler, D. (1981). *WAIS-R manual: Wechsler Adult Intelligence Scale–Revised.* New York: Harcourt, Brace & Jovanovich.

Willner, A. E. (1970). Toward the development of a more sensitive clinical test of abstraction: The Analogy Test. *Proceedings of the 78th Annual Convention of the American Psychological Association, 5*, 553–554.

Yohman, J. R., & Parsons, O. A. (1985). Intact verbal paired associate learning in alcoholics. *Journal of Clinical Psychology, 41*, 844–851.

Yohman, J. R., Schaeffer, K. W., & Parsons, O. A. (1988). Cognitive training in alcoholic men. *Journal of Consulting and Clinical Psychology, 56*, 67–72.

Yozawitz, A. (1986). Applied neuropsychology in a psychiatric center. In I. Grant & K. M. Adams (Eds.), *Neuropsychological assessment of neuropsychiatric disorders* (pp. 121–146). New York: Oxford University Press.

12

CONSTRUCT REFINEMENT AND CONFIRMATION FOR THE ADDICTION SEVERITY INDEX

PAUL A. McDERMOTT, ARTHUR I. ALTERMAN, LAWRENCE BROWN, ARTURO ZABALLERO, EDWARD C. SNIDER, AND JAMES R. McKAY

The Addiction Severity Index (ASI; McLellan, Luborsky, Woody, & O'Brien, 1980) is one of the most widely used assessment devices in the field of substance abuse. It has been used by numerous researchers in studies of treatment outcome and as a clinical assessment tool in thousands of treatment facilities (McLellan et al., 1992). The instrument has been translated into at least nine languages. It is, therefore, somewhat surprising given the ASI's extensive use that there are still relatively little data on its reliability and validity.

As commonly applied, the ASI is used in patient interviews to gather information across seven areas of problem functioning: medical, employment, alcohol, drugs, legal, family–social, and psychiatric. A composite

Reprinted from *Psychological Assessment*, 8, 182–189. (1996). Copyright © 1996 by the American Psychological Association. Used with permission of the author.

This research was supported in part by National Institute of Drug Abuse Center Grants DA-05186 and DA-060142, National Institute of Drug Abuse Grant DA-05858, and the U.S. Department of Veterans Affairs.

score (CS) is computed frequently for each area by weighing and summing scores for items that reflect more current functioning (i.e., functioning thought to be potentially alterable). CSs have been recommended for use in treatment outcome studies whose focus is on change (McLellan, Luborsky, Cacciola, Griffith, McGahan, & O'Brien, 1985). As such, CSs are based solely on information reported by patients. In addition, McLellan et al. (1980) provided an interviewer severity rating (ISR) for each area. ISRs are intended to reflect an interviewer's perception of need for treatment as based on all ASI information. They are a partial function of patient self-report and of the interviewer's interpretation of that information.

In the article introducing the ASI, McLellan et al. (1980) reported interrater reliability for ISRs in six problem areas (the alcohol and drug areas were initially merged to form a substance abuse area). Independent ISRs were produced from videotapes of 25 interviews, yielding a coefficient of approximately .90 for each area. A second study (McLellan et al., 1985) examined ISR interrater reliability across 30 videotaped cases. Reliability remained appreciable with a low of .70 for the drug problem area and .94 for the psychiatric problem area. Moreover, 3-day stability of ISRs reached .92 or higher across problem areas.

A more stringent evaluation was conducted by Hodgins and el-Guebaly (1992). Rather than rely on conventional correlation indexes (expressions of direction and strength of association), they applied intraclass coefficients (reflecting concordance of direction and level, or agreement). Working with 15 substance abusers in treatment for primary mental disorders, they had six judges independently observe interviews through one-way mirrors and thereafter produce ISRs. Coefficients ranged from a high of .96 for the alcohol and legal areas to a low of .30 for the employment area. Alterman, Brown, Zaballero, and McKay (1994) and Stoffelmayr, Mavis, and Kasim (1994) have further reported marginal reliability for ISRs.

ASI CSs also show a mixed psychometric history. As noted, these scores derive from a succinct compilation of item-level information provided by patients. Specifically, patient responses to questions pertaining to the past 30 days or to follow-up periods are arithmetically weighted for each problem area. Inasmuch as several items contribute to each area CS, estimates of internal consistency are feasible. In this context, Hodgins and el-Guebaly (1992), working with 152 substance abusers in treatment for primary psychiatric disorders, found alpha coefficients ranging from .88 for the medical area to .48 for the legal area, with an average alpha of only .68 across all seven areas. More promising results were reported by Hendricks, Kaplan, Van Limbeck, and Geerlings (1989) in a study of 142 Dutch detoxification patients. Except for an alpha coefficient of .58 for the employment area, all CSs exceeded .70. On the other hand, Alterman et al.

(1994) found internal consistency for three of the seven areas (employment, drugs, and legal) to be less than .70.

It has been suggested (Hendricks et al., 1989; Hodgins & el-Guebaly, 1992) that, notwithstanding intended treatment utility of CSs, the quantity of preselected items is too limited and the content focus too broad to constitute reasonably homogeneous measures. In turn, the relevance of the ISR indexes is diminished because they are hypothetically grounded in the same item content as CSs.

Within this frame, our article reports on a series of analyses to reconstruct and confirm the validity and reliability of the ASI's hypothesized problem scales. The investigation enlisted a large and diverse sample of substance abuse patients and sought to identify internally homogeneous and meaningful addiction problem scales (thereby replacing CS-type indexes) and to substantiate the unique relationship of each scale to presumably dependent severity ratings by clinical interviewers.

METHOD

Participants

The primary sample (N = 990) was drawn from two independent treatment centers, all participants being methadone maintenance opiate patients. The Addiction Research and Treatment Center provided 633 patients from six treatment sites located in Brooklyn and Manhattan, New York. An additional 357 were male veterans undergoing treatment at the Veterans Affairs (VA) Medical Center, Philadelphia, Pennsylvania. The combined cohort contained 784 men and 206 women (ages 19–69 years; M = 38.9, SD = 7.6), with 53.0% being African American, 27.5% Hispanic (26.4% Puerto Rican), and 19.5% Caucasian. In addition, 41.2% identified themselves as Catholic, 27.9% Protestant, 7.8% Islamic, and 0.4% Jewish. Approximately 9% were in controlled environments (drug or alcohol clinics, prisons, psychiatric or medical facilities) where average time in the environment was 13.5 days (median = 9.5; range = 1–90).

A secondary sample (N = 244) was formed to assess the ASI's concurrent and predictive validity. It consisted of male patients at the VA Medical Center who volunteered to participate in a treatment outcome study that focused on effects of methadone maintenance with antisocial and nonantisocial individuals. Patients included 181 from the primary sample and an additional 63 recruited over a $2\frac{1}{2}$-year period. Ages ranged from 24 to 56 years (M = 40.7, SD = 5.0), with African Americans comprising 58.6%, Caucasians 37.3%, and others 4.1%. On the average, these patients had undergone 2.4 (SD = 1.6; range = 0–13) previous treatment attempts.[1]

Instrumentation

ASI is a 40- to 60-min semistructured interview of 155 items pertaining to patient sociodemographic status and to problems in the seven areas noted previously. On completion of an interview, the interviewer records an interviewer severity rating (ISR) for each problem area (9 = *extreme problem* and 0 = *no problem*). The ISRs are to represent the interviewer's overall assessment of need for additional treatment as based on patient report of lifetime and recent difficulties. ISRs, according to instruction (McLellan et al., 1992), are to emerge from consideration of quantified historical problem information and the patient's personal assessment of the gravity of the current problem as well as need for treatment (applying a 0- to 4-point scale: 4 = *extremely* and 0 = *not at all severe*). As determined by McLellan et al. (1980), Hendricks et al. (1989), and Hodgins and el-Guebaly (1992), the latter patient personal assessments appear to be at least as important as the quantitative lifetime problem items in determining the ISRs.

Of the 155 items, 16 evaluate present employment potential and are not designed to reflect morbidity or employment problems. Four other items are common to the alcohol and drug areas and, as such, cannot be regarded as unique to either area. Three additional items, although relevant to problem functioning, are multicategorical (nondichotomous nominal scales) and three are contingency items associated with rare circumstances (i.e., items not administered to most patients, as contingent on response to a previous item). Consequently, the 16 nonproblem, 4 compound, 3 categorical, and 3 contingency items were eliminated from subsequent analyses, leaving 129 problem items. Thus, the medical problem area contained 8 unique items, the employment problem area 5 items, alcohol area 11 items, drug 28, legal 26, family–social 29, and psychiatric 22. Items comprised a wide range of point-scales including dichotomous (*yes* vs. *no*), ordinal scales (Hollingshead occupational ranks), Likert scales with symmetric anchors (*no, indifferent, yes*) and asymmetric anchors (*not at all, slightly, to considerably, extremely*), and interval scales (e.g., "How much money did you receive?").

Other instruments served as validity criteria used with the secondary sample. The Structured Clinical Interview for *DSM–III–R* (SCID; Spitzer, Williams, Gibbon, & First, 1990) is a semistructured interview designed to produce diagnoses of major psychiatric disorders. Substantial test–retest

---

[1]Detailed patient demographics and medical information for both the primary and secondary samples may be obtained by writing to Paul A. McDermott.

reliability has been established (Williams et al., 1992) for most Axis I disorders, including the disorders used in this investigation. The Revised Psychopathy Checklist (PCL–R; Hare, 1991) is a device for rating interview responses. Responses are scored on a 3-point scale corresponding to presence, possible presence, or absence of each of 20 symptoms connoting psychopathic personality structure or antisocial lifestyle. Although the PCL–R may be applied to assess independently a dimension of personality structure and one of lifestyle, the welter of evidence on psychometric integrity pertains to the PCL–R total score. The reported average alpha coefficient is .88 and interrater reliability is .86–.93 across clinical and forensic samples (Hare et al., 1990). The Beck Depression Inventory (BDI; Beck & Steer, 1993) is a self-report scale containing 21 symptoms and expressions of attitude. Responses are recorded on a 4-point Likert scale and summed to represent overall intensity of depressive thought and attitude. Evidence supporting BDI reliability and validity is abundant (Cohen, Swerdlik, & Phillips, 1995). Finally, the State–Trait Anxiety Inventory (STAI; Spielberger, Gorsuch, & Lushene, 1970) is a self-report device presenting two 20-item scales: the state scale focusing on present manifestations of anxiety, and the trait scale focusing on long-term manifestations. The scales have appreciable internal consistency (.83–.94), appropriate retest reliability, and construct validation (Gaudry, Vagg, & Spielberger, 1975).

In addition, two types of treatment outcome measures were obtained. The total of felony arrests was determined directly from state police reports over the 2-year period following ASI administration. For the 7 months following ASI administration, weekly urine toxicology screens tested for presence of opiates, cocaine, barbiturates, and related addictive substances.

Procedure and Analysis

Participants from the Addiction Research and Treatment Center were administered the ASI between 2 and 4 weeks after initiation of methadone treatment. Those at the VA Medical Center were evaluated on program entry. Participants comprising the secondary sample at the VA Medical Center also were administered the SCID, PCL–R, BDI, and STAI in three 1- to 2-hr sessions within 2–6 weeks after program entry. These participants were compensated for their time in evaluation sessions. All participants were volunteers recruited in accordance with federal, university, and American Psychological Association ethical guidelines.

All evaluations were conducted by trained clinical staff, following a 2-month period of instruction including workshops, simulations, videotaped trials, and demonstration of independent concurrence with other staff. Clinical staff attended a 2-day workshop conducted by the author of the PCL–R. The ASI, PCL–R, BDI, and STAI were administered by B.A.

and M.A. level psychology staff, whereas M.A. and Ph.D. level clinicians administered the SCID. Ph.D. psychologist supervisors monitored all evaluations. Cumulative felony arrests were obtained directly from state-level police records. Urine specimens were collected approximately weekly by medical staff through a procedure that visually verified specimen retrieval. Laboratory toxicology yielded either positive or negative results for each substance each week. To provide comparable metrics across substances and to adjust for patient failures to submit specimens, toxicology was converted to percentage of positive specimens over 7 months.

The analytic strategy proceeded in five stages, the first four involving the primary sample and the fifth the secondary sample. First, items were assigned to the seven hypothetical problem scales according to the rational–inductive structure proposed by McLellan et al. (1992). Differential item point-scales were converted linearly to a common scaled-score form ($M = 10$, $SD = 3$) as preparation for item analyses and later summation by unit weighting (Wainer, 1976; Wang & Stanley, 1970). Thereafter, the items comprising each theoretical problem scale were submitted to series of item analyses, including item-total correlations, conditional alpha for the deletion of each item (Cronbach, 1990), item difficulty (popularity) and variability indexes, and coefficient alpha for overall sum of unit-weighted item scores. The immediate goal was to produce seven potential scales with respective internal consistency $\geq.70$, no item operating to suppress internal consistency, and acceptable variability (no item-total $r < .20$ or $\geq .80$; see Allen & Yen, 1970, and Hennyssen, 1971, on item analysis).

In the second stage, the proposed scales were subjected to confirmatory analysis. Conventional components or factor analysis are not appropriate for this purpose because the underlying point-scales mix binary- and continuous-scale items and the structure assumes mutually exclusive scale membership for all items. Common factoring or principal components analysis in such instances will yield difficulty factors and other spurious dimensions that are defined more by the peculiar distributional character of items than by emergent latent traits (Gorsuch, 1983; Parry & McArdle, 1991). Alternatively, oblique item cluster analysis makes no assumption regarding item point-scales while permitting mutually exclusive scale membership. Thus, to confirm composition of the seven proposed problem scales, items were subjected to oblique, multiple-group, principal components cluster analysis (Anderberg, 1973; Harman, 1976), where hypothesized scale membership was based on the first-stage item analyses, and items were permitted to migrate iteratively to problem scales that better explained item variance. Essentially, the proportion of item variance predicted by other items in the hypothesized correct scales was compared with the variance predicted by items in the empirically best alternative scales. A principal component was extracted for each final scale and cluster loadings calculated for each item. The loadings are interpreted in a manner similar to factor loadings. Inasmuch as the components are oblique, interscale correlations are computed and must not exceed conventional criteria (.50 for clinical measures; McDermott, 1993).

In the third stage, resultant item scales were introduced to higher-order factor analysis (as advised by Gorsuch, 1983) and to variance partitioning so as to reveal scale variation that was both unique and reliable. A score was calculated for each scale by unit-weighting (Wainer, 1976) of standardized item scores, and the seven scores were submitted to exploratory principal factoring by using squared multiple correlations as initial communality estimates. Retained factors were rotated to simple structure using orthogonal varimax and oblique promax criteria and hyperplane count. Whereas scale communality indicated the proportion of common variance within each scale, specificity (i.e., coefficient alpha − communality) reflected the proportion of variance that is unique to each scale. Specificity indexes that were greater than error variance (1 − alpha) were deemed significant and estimates of the proportion of each scale's variance that is both unique and reliable.

In the fourth stage, convergent and divergent construct validity was assessed by relating the refined scales to corresponding interviewer severity ratings (ISRs). Canonical variance analysis (van den Wollenberg, 1977) applied the summary scores for the seven problem scales as the first variate set and the seven ISRs as the second set. The method is especially useful for identifying the unique magnitude and pattern of contributions of each problem scale to specific ISRs. In addition, the complete overlap of problem scale and ISR variability was established through canonical redundancy analysis (Miller & Farr, 1971) based on the full bimultivariate model (as recommended by Thorndike & Weiss, 1973).

In the final stage, concurrent validity was assessed by correlating the refined scales with SCID, PCL–R, BDI, and STAI measures obtained for the VA Medical Center secondary sample at the initiation of methadone maintenance treatment. Canonical variance analyses explored the ability of ASI scales to predict treatment outcome in terms of future positive toxicology for substance abuse and future felony arrests.

RESULTS

One ASI item was invariant for the sample and so was dropped from subsequent analysis. Of the 128 items remaining, 83 survived first-stage item analyses, with the medical problem scale containing 7 items, employment problem scale 3 items, alcohol scale 11, drug 15, legal 12, family–social 15, and psychiatric 20. Three items produced higher item-total rs and internal consistency when valence was reversed (i.e., original response keying reflected increasing health rather than morbidity) and thereafter appeared in that form. Nine of the drug items recounted recent usage of different substances and, whereas item analytic parameters for the individual items signaled elimination, the nine were combined to form an acceptably reliable composite of "Days of drug problems during past 30 days." Thus, 75 items emerged from item analyses.

Confirmatory analysis assessed the proposition that items comprising the seven scales were more highly related to hypothesized scale co-members than to items comprising other scales. Iterative migration confirmed placement of 74 of the 75 items (one legal-scale item, "Number of days of illegal activity during past 30 days," was more related to drug items and that item was discarded). Overall, 36.7% of item variance was accounted for by the solution, the least amount of item variance explained for the family–social scale (24.7%) and most variance for the employment scale (76.8%).

Table 1 presents the component items for each problem scale, the multiple R^2 statistics confirming strongest relationship with the hypothesized scales, oblique cluster structure loadings, and variance explained. Posted also are alpha coefficients and item-total rs. Note that, as per stated criteria, all scales yielded alpha coefficients $\geq .70$ (range = .71 – .90) and no item produced an item-total $r < .20$ or $\geq .80$.

Third-stage common factoring began with the bivariate interscale correlation matrix. No scales correlated higher than the stated .50 upper limit (highest r, .49, found for overlap of the family–social and psychiatric scales; unsigned bivariate r, $M = .19$, $SD = .11$).

Before factoring, the correlation matrix for the seven problem scales was examined by using Bartlett's chi-square criteria (Geweke & Singleton, 1980), rejecting the likelihood of an identity matrix ($p < .0001$) and indicating ($p < .0001$) that no more than two viable dimensions could be extracted. Common factoring proceeded with extraction of two-factor models, rotated to varimax and promax criteria at power (k) 2 through 7. With maximum hyperplane count found for $k = 2$, an identical factor pattern was discovered for both the orthogonal varimax and oblique promax solutions. The first dimension accounted for 16.2% of total variance and (on the basis of salient loadings) was defined primarily by the medical and psychiatric problem scales. The second dimension accounted for 14.5% of variance and was defined by the employment and family–social scales. Considering the interfactor correlation (.36), the model explained 22.6% of total variance, thus indicating that most variance among the first-order scales was not common variance.[7]

The partitioning of variance (common, specific, and error) showed that, for almost every scale, unique variance exceeded common variance and that, for all scales, the amount of unique and reliable variance was

---

[2]Detailed tables displaying results of these and subsequent analyses may be obtained by writing to Paul A. McDermott.

TABLE 1

Confirmatory Oblique Principal Components Structures and Reliability for Addiction Severity Index

Scale and item[b]	Structure loading[c]	R^2 with[a]		Item–total r[d]
		Own scale	Competing scale	
Medical problems				
Patient rating of severity of medical problems	.84	.71	.11	.69
Patient rating of need for medical treatment	.83	.68	.10	.67
Suffers from chronic medical problems	.76	.57	.05	.63
Days suffered medical problems during past 30 days	.75	.56	.09	.58
Takes pills for medical problems	.65	.43	.02	.51
Receives a medical pension	.41	.17	.03	.32
No. of lifetime hospitalizations	.40	.16	.03	.30
Item variance explained = 46.8%				
Coefficient alpha = .79				
Employment problems				
Patient rating of severity of employment problems	.91	.83	.11	.78
Patient rating of need for employment counseling	.88	.77	.09	.71
No. of days of employment problems during past 30 days	.84	.70	.07	.65
Item variance explained = 76.8%				
Coefficient alpha = .85				
Alcohol problems				
Patient rating of severity of alcohol problems	.80	.64	.02	.68
Patient rating of need for alcohol treatment	.78	.61	.02	.67
Days intoxicated during past 30 days	.76	.58	.01	.62
Days used alcohol during past 30 days	.75	.56	.02	.62
Days of alcohol problems during past 30 days	.75	.56	.01	.62
Money spent on alcohol over past 30 days	.69	.48	.01	.57

Table continues

TABLE 1 (Continued)

| Scale and item[b] | Structure loading[c] | R^2 with[a] | | Item–total r[d] |
		Own scale	Competing scale	
Alcohol problems				
Years used alcohol to intoxication	.61	.37	.02	.53
Years used alcohol overall	.56	.32	.02	.48
No. of previous alcohol treatments	.43	.18	.02	.42
No. of previous alcohol detoxes	.40	.16	.01	.38
No. of times had DTs	.25	.07	.00	.21
Item variance explained = 41.2%				
Coefficient alpha = .84				
Drug problems				
Patient rating of severity of drug problems	.85	.72	.08	.68
Days of drug problems during past 30 days	.82	.67	.04	.63
Amount of drug usage during past 30 days	.80	.65	.07	.62
Money spent on drugs during past 30 days	.69	.47	.02	.49
Patient rating of need for drug treatment	.67	.45	.05	.47
No. of previous drug treatments	.37	.20	.05	.38
No. of previous drug detoxes	.25	.06	.03	.27
Item variance explained = 45.22%				
Coefficient alpha = .78				
Legal Problems				
Months of lifetime incarceration	.76	.57	.01	.58
No. of arrests for robbery	.65	.42	.00	.42
No. of arrests for weapons offenses	.64	.41	.01	.42
No. of arrests for parole/probation violations	.60	.36	.02	.43

No. of arrests for assault	.58	.33	.01	.37
No. of arrests for drug charges	.47	.22	.01	.33
No. of arrests for burglary, larceny	.43	.18	.01	.28
No. of arrests for homicide, manslaughter	.36	.13	.01	.22
On probation or parole	.35	.12	.00	.25
Patient rating of severity of legal problems	.30	.09	.06	.29
Patient rating of need for legal counseling	.29	.09	.07	.28
Item variance explained = 26.62%				
Coefficient alpha = .71				

Family–social problems

Patient rating of severity of social problems	.69	.47	.09	.55
Patient rating of need for family treatment	.68	.46	.08	.54
Patient rating of family problems	.67	.45	.10	.54
Patient rating of need for social treatment	.67	.46	.07	.52
Conflicts with close friends at any time	.47	.22	.05	.37
Conflicts with sexual partner or spouse at any time	.46	.21	.05	.35
Conflicts with neighbors at any time	.45	.21	.05	.36
Dissatisfaction with free time	.44	.19	.05	.33
Conflicts with siblings at any time	.41	.17	.04	.32
Days of conflicts with others during past 30 days	.41	.17	.04	.30
Dissatisfaction with living arrangements	.40	.16	.03	.31
Conflicts with mother at any time	.40	.16	.04	.30
Days of conflicts with family during past 30 days	.39	.15	.05	.28
Dissatisfaction with marital status	.36	.12	.03	.27
Conflicts with neighbors during past 30 days	.33	.11	.01	.25
Item variance explained = 24.7%				
Coefficient alpha = .77				

Table continues

TABLE 1 (Continued)

Scale and item[b]	Structure loading[c]	R^2 with[a]		Item–total r[d]
		Own scale	Competing scale	
Psychiatric problems				
Patient rating of psychiatric problems	.80	.63	.21	.72
Patient rating of need for psychiatric treatment	.79	.62	.21	.72
Days of anxiety during 30 days	.70	.50	.12	.62
Days of psychiatric problems during past 30 days	.69	.48	.10	.61
Anxiety over lifetime	.67	.45	.13	.59
Suicidal thoughts over lifetime	.65	.42	.10	.60
Days of depression during past 30 days	.65	.43	.09	.58
Depression over lifetime	.65	.42	.10	.58
Psychiatric medications over lifetime	.63	.40	.07	.58
Days of trouble understanding during past 30 days	.60	.37	.08	.55
Trouble understanding over lifetime	.59	.34	.07	.53
Suicide attempts over lifetime	.57	.32	.05	.52
No. of inpatient psychiatric treatments	.54	.29	.02	.50
Days of psychiatric medication during past 30 days	.40	.29	.06	.48
Violence over lifetime	.52	.27	.11	.47
Hallucinations over lifetime	.51	.26	.03	.47
Receives a psychological or psychiatric pension	.50	.25	.03	.46
Days of suicidal thoughts during past 30 days	.41	.17	.02	.37
Days of hallucinations during past 30 days	.40	.16	.02	.38
Days of violent behavior during past 30 days	.40	.16	.08	.35
Item variance explained = 36.1%				
Coefficient alpha = .90				

Note. $N = 990$. DT = Delirium tremens.

[a]Based on confirmatory cluster analysis, where hypothesized item-scale membership is determined through previous rational–clinical theory and item analyses. R^2 for an item's own scale indicates the proportion of item variance predicted by other items in the hypothesized correct scale, whereas R^2 for an item's competing scale indicates variance predicted by items in the empirically best alternative scale. [b]Item wording is abbreviated or altered for convenient presentation in the table. [c]Correlations between respective items and the oblique principal component permeating each scale, as derived in confirmatory, multiple-group, principal components cluster analysis (Anderberg, 1973; Harman, 1976). Interpretation is similar to that of factor loadings. [d]Each value is a Pearson product–moment coefficient with respective item excluded from total scale score.

substantial (M = 58%, SD = 13%, range = 37%–79%). This result supports interpretation of each scale as a distinct and reliable measure.

Canonical variance analysis related the set of seven problem scales (fully based on patient self-report) to the seven ISRs (based on patient self-report and interviewer interpretation thereof). Wilks's lambda was less than .01, where multivariate $F(49, 4959)$ = 151.9, significant at $p < .0001$. All seven possible canonical relationships were statistically significant ($p < .0001$), indicating seven distinct patterns of relationship between the problem scales and ISRs. As recommended by Thorndike and Weiss (1973), canonical structure loadings were used to inform the different relationships.

The highest salient loadings for each variate pair revealed that each problem scale was most closely related to its corresponding ISR. This indicated that the respective ISRs are primarily related to the unique variation in corresponding problem scales rather than reflecting a general halo or Barnum effect (Furnham & Schofield, 1987). Canonical redundancy estimates also showed that, overall, 49.1% of the variation in ISRs is predictable from known variation in problem scales.

Concurrent validity for various ASI scales was supported through correlations ($p < .001$, unless otherwise indicated) with external measures. The legal problems scale correlated .42 with the total psychopathy index of the PCL–R (Hare, 1991), the strongest relationship ($r = .47$) having been found with the PCL–R measure of criminal versatility. Legal problems also predicted ($r = .38$) the number of future arrests over 2 years. Psychiatric problems correlated .42 with STAI (Spielberger, Gorsuch, & Lushene, 1970) state anxiety, .41 with STAI trait anxiety, .44 with BDI (Beck & Steer, 1993) depression, and .52 with the sum of SCID (Spitzer et al., 1990) psychiatric disorders, the highest correlation (.57) being with SCID's measure of lifetime major depression.

Concurrent relationship between the alcohol problems scale and the SCID diagnosis of lifetime alcohol disorders was .45. Drug problems correlated .20 ($p < .02$) with the sum of SCID diagnoses for lifetime disorders involving sedatives, opiates, cocaine, and related substances, and .25 ($p < .002$) with percentage of positive urine tests for barbiturates, opiates, and cocaine.

Most important, the seven ASI scales were able to predict significantly (canonical R = .40, $p < .004$) the percentage of positive urine toxicology screens for opiates, cocaine, and barbiturates. When applied for prediction of all treatment outcomes (positive urine screens plus total arrests), they produced a canonical R of .59, $p < .01$.

DISCUSSION

Former evaluations of the construct and criterion validity of the ASI have generally produced encouraging results (Kosten, Rounsaville, &

Kleber, 1983; McLellan et al., 1985). Such work has typically established a close relationship between ASI information and independent patient charts and test data. Sometimes the ASI information was represented by ISRs and sometimes by CSs (mathematical composites of selected ASI items; McGahan, Griffith, Parente, & McLellan, 1990). Of course, the ISRs are actually interviewer impressions of the import of patient self-reports. CSs, although entirely self-report, have limited value unless they are grounded in psychometrically homogeneous and meaningful scales that convey unique and reliable constructs.

One investigator (Rogalski, 1987) did attempt to resolve construct structure by using a principal component solution based on a selected 51 of the 129 scalable items. It is unfortunate that the sample of 190 self-identified substance abusers undermet accepted minimal subject-to-item ratio (Comrey, 1988; Guadagnoli & Velicer, 1988) and no rationale was advanced for inclusion or exclusion of ASI items.

The current strategy has operated from the premise that valid scales must conform to constructs that have known clinical relevance (Dawis, 1987) and consequential validity (Messick, 1989). To this end, the concept of addiction problem areas was preserved by refining the rational–inductive item sets commonly applied in treatment centers. The refinements essentially identified the more homogeneous and robust aspects of each addiction problem area and thereafter subjected the new scales to confirmatory analysis and variance partitioning. It was found that the transformed ASI scales are relatively independent and that they each retain a substantial amount of variability that is both unique and reliable.

This enhances the potential utility of the scales for clinical work, in which it is necessary to gather large amounts of information through diverse question formats and it is important to know that theoretically distinct types of information are neither spurious nor redundant. The refined problem scales also open the feasibility of useful typological research. That is, various investigators (Kosten et al., 1983; McLellan et al., 1980) have recognized the value of understanding prototypic patient profiles across the addiction problem areas. However, such inquiry to date has relied on profiles formed from ISRs or CSs of unscaled ASI item sets. The new scales provide a more reliable and direct foundation for ASI patient profiles that can be explored through hierarchical cluster and classification analysis.

As added enhancement for those who would apply refined ASI scales in research or practice, we have developed convenient SAS (Statistical Analysis Systems Institute) computer code that can transform and standardize item-level ASI data and compute raw problem scale scores. Moreover, the code transforms raw scores into area-conversion T scores (Thorndike, 1982). Unlike linear T scores, the normalized standard scores preserve the percentile comparability of given *T* scores across scales, as well as the familiar *M* = 50 and *SD* = 10.[3]

The analyses further illustrate that the ISRs, so often used by clinicians to summarize impressions, are highly related to the information conveyed by the refined scales. Indeed, the pattern of relationship is not so simple as to constitute a general bias for or against patient problems across problem scales. Instead, the ISR associated with each respective problem scale appears to be rooted mainly, and appropriately, in the patient reports for the specific scale. This discovery also lends support to the notion that interviewer impressions are potentially useful, although results will undoubtedly vary as a function of interviewer training.

CONCLUSION

It should be recognized that this series of studies was based on a specific population—methadone maintenance patients from urban centers of eastern states. It will be necessary to test the generality of the proposed ASI structure for other reference groups and locales. Nonetheless, this sample was large and relatively diverse and the interviewers were competent. The sample and attendant analyses of ASI data should provide a good starting point for future construct validity and treatment outcome research.

REFERENCES

Allen, M. J., & Yen, W. M. (1970). *Introduction to measurement theory*. Belmont, CA: Wadsworth.

Alterman, A. L., Brown, L. S., Zaballero, A., & McKay, J. (1994). The interviewer severity ratings and composite scores of the ASI: A further look. *Drug and Alcohol Dependence, 34*, 201–209.

Anderberg, M. R. (1973). *Cluster analysis for applications*. New York: Academic Press.

Beck, A. T., & Steer, R. A. (1993). *Beck Depression Inventory manual*. San Antonio, TX: Psychological Corporation.

Cohen, R. J., Swerdlik, M. E., & Phillips, S. M. (1995). *Psychological testing and assessment* (3rd ed.). Mountain View, CA: Mayfield.

Comrey, A. L. (1988). Factor-analytic methods of scale development in personality and clinical psychology. *Journal of Consulting and Clinical Psychology, 56*, 754–761.

---

[3]Whereas by design the ASI problem scales all show positive skewness (beta value *M* = 1.39, *SD* = 0.94), the extent of skewness varies widely (range = 0.32–2.79). Area conversion maintains interpretive equivalence across scales by assigning standard scores according to corresponding raw-score percentiles as expected under the normal curve.

Cronbach, L. J. (1990). *Essentials of psychological testing* (5th ed.). New York: Harper-Collins.

Dawis, R. V. (1987). Scale construction. *Journal of Counseling Psychology, 34,* 481–489.

Furnham, A., & Schofield, B. (1987). Accepting personality test feedback: A review of the Barnum effect. *Current Psychological Research & Reviews, 6,* 162–178.

Gaudry, E., Vagg, P., & Spielberger, C. D. (1975). Validation of the state–trait distinction in anxiety research. *Multivariate Behavioral Research, 10,* 331–341.

Geweke, J. F., & Singleton, K. I. (1980). Interpreting the likelihood of ratio statistic in factor models when sample size is small. *Journal of the American Statistical Association, 75,* 133–137.

Gorsuch, R. L. (1983). *Factor analysis* (2nd ed.). Hillsdale, NJ: Erlbaum.

Guadagnoli, E., & Velicer, W. (1988). Relations of sample size to the stability of component patterns. *Psychological Bulletin, 103,* 265–275.

Hare, R. D. (1991). *The Revised Psychopathy Checklist.* Toronto: Multi-Health Systems.

Hare, R. D., Harpur, R. J., Hakstain, A. R., Forth, A. E., Hart, S. D., & Newman, J. P. (1990). The Revised Psychopathology Checklist: Reliability and factor structure. *Psychological Assessment, 2,* 338–341.

Harman, H. H. (1976). *Modern factor analysis* (3rd ed.). Chicago: University of Chicago Press.

Hendricks, V. M., Kaplan, C. D., Van Limbeck, H., & Geerlings, P. (1989). The Addiction Severity Index: Reliability and validity in a Dutch addict sample. *Journal of Substance Abuse Treatment, 6,* 133–141.

Hennyssen, S. (1971). Gathering, analyzing, and using data on test items. In R. L. Thorndike (Ed.), *Educational measurement* (2nd ed., pp. 130–159). Washington, DC: American Council on Education.

Hodgins, D. C., & el-Guebaly, N. (1992). More data on the Addiction Severity Index: Reliability and validity with the mentally ill substance abuser. *Journal of Nervous and Mental Disease, 180,* 197–201.

Kosten, T. R., Rounsaville, B. J., & Kleber, H. D. (1983). Concurrent validity of the Addiction Severity Index. *Journal of Nervous and Mental Disease, 171,* 606–610.

McDermott, P. A. (1993). National standardization of uniform multisituational measures of child and adolescent behavior pathology. *Psychological Assessment, 5,* 413–424.

McGahan, P. L., Griffith, J. A., Parente, R., & McLellan, A. T. (1990). *Composite scores from the Addiction Severity Index.* Philadelphia: Veterans Administration and National Institute on Drugs and Alcohol.

McLellan, A. T., Kushner, H., Metzger, D., Peters, R., Smith, L., Grissom, G., Pettinati, H., & Argeriou, M. (1992). The fifth edition of the Addiction Severity Index: Historical critique and normative data. *Journal of Substance Abuse Treatment, 9,* 199–213.

McLellan, A. T., Luborsky, L., Cacciola, J., Griffith, J., McGahan, P., & O'Brien, C. P. (1985). *Guide to the Addiction Severity Index: Background, administration, and field testing results*. Rockville, MD: U.S. Department of Human Services.

McLellan, A. T., Luborsky, L., Woody, G. E., & O'Brien, C. P. (1980). An improved diagnostic evaluation instrument for substance abuse patients. *Journal of Nervous and Mental Disease, 168*, 26–33.

Messick, S. (1989). Validity. In R. L. Linn (Ed.), *Educational measurement* (3rd ed., pp. 13–103). New York: American Council on Education and Macmillan.

Miller, J. K., & Farr, S. D. (1971). Bimultivariate redundancy: A comprehensive measure of interbattery relationship. *Multivariate Behavioral Research, 6*, 313–324.

Parry, C. D. H., & McArdle, J. J. (1991). An applied comparison of methods for least-squares factor analysis of dichotomous variables. *Applied Psychological Measurement, 15*, 35–46.

Rogalski, C. J. (1987). Factor structure of the Addiction Severity Index in an inpatient detoxification sample. *International Journal of Addictions, 22*, 981–992.

Spielberger, C. D., Gorsuch, R. L., & Lushene, R. E. (1970). *Test manual for the State–Trait Anxiety Inventory*. Palo Alto, CA: Consulting Psychologists Press.

Spitzer, R. L., Williams, J. B. W., Gibbon, M., & First, M. B. (1990). *Structured Clinical Interview for DSM–III–R*. Washington, DC: American Psychiatric Association.

Stoffelmayr, B. E., Mavis, B. E., & Kasim, R. F. (1994). The longitudinal stability of the Addiction Severity Index. *Journal of Substance Abuse Treatment, 11*, 372–378.

Thorndike, R. L. (1982). *Applied psychometrics*. Boston: Houghton Mifflin.

Thorndike, R. M., & Weiss, D. J. (1973). A study of the stability of canonical correlations and canonical components. *Educational and Psychological Measurement, 33*, 123–134.

van den Wollenberg, A. L. (1977). Redundancy analysis: An alternative to canonical correlation analysis. *Psychometrika, 42*, 207–219.

Wainer, H. (1976). Estimating coefficients in linear models: It don't make no nevermind. *Psychological Bulletin, 83*, 213–217.

Wang, M. W., & Stanley, J. C. (1970). Differential weighting: A review of methods and empirical studies. *Review of Educational Research, 40*, 663–705.

Williams, J. B. W., Gibbon, M., First, M. B., Spitzer, R. L., Davies, M., Borus, J., Howes, M. J., Kane, J., Pope, H. C., Jr., Rounsaville, B., & Wittchen, H-U. (1992). The Structured Clinical Interview for DSM–III–R (SCID): II. Multisite test–retest reliability. *Archives of General Psychiatry, 49*, 630–636.

13

MMPI-2 RESPONSE STYLES: GENERALIZATION TO ALCOHOLISM ASSESSMENT

CARL E. ISENHART AND DANIEL J. SILVERSMITH

Meehl and Hathaway (1946) were among the first researchers to suggest that personality inventories were susceptible to both conscious "faking" and unconscious self-deception. In their landmark Minnesota Multiphasic Personality Inventory (MMPI; Meehl & Hathaway, 1946) work, they devised the Lie (L) and Correction (K) scales (Merydith & Wallbrown, 1991) to assess response bias. The L scale assesses overall frankness in the individual's approach to the instrument. High L scores are indicative of an unsophisticated attempt to present oneself in a favorable light. The K scale assesses a more subtle attempt to respond defensively and is indicative of an attempt to deny problems and demonstrate no need for psychological treatment (Butcher, 1990). Baer, Wetter, and Berry (1992), in

Reprinted from *Psychology of Addictive Behaviors*, 10, 115–123. (1996). Used with permission of the author.

Some of the data presented in this article were collected as part of a multisite evaluation conducted by the Program Evaluation and Resource Center at the Palo Alto Veterans Affairs Medical Center under the auspices of the Mental Health and Behaviorial Sciences Service, Veterans Affairs Central Office.

their meta-analysis of 25 MMPI studies that compared honest responders with participants who underreported psychopathology, found mean effect sizes of just under one standard deviation for the *L* and *K* scales.

The third original Validity scale, the Infrequency scale (*F*), was devised by Hathaway and McKinley (1943). Elevations on the *F* scale are found with individuals who are admitting to problems that are endorsed by fewer than 10% of the general population and could be indicative of psychosis, random responding, exaggeration of symptoms, or a "cry for help" (Butcher, 1990). Berry, Baer, and Harris (1991) found a mean effect size of over two standard deviations for the *t*-scaled *F* in their meta-analysis of 18 studies that examined malingering on the MMPI.

There has been copious research analyzing the power of the MMPI-2 Validity scales to identify fake-bad and fake-good response styles. Graham, Watts, and Timbrook (1991) and Cassisi and Workman (1992) found that the MMPI-2 Validity scales accurately assess the individual's response style. Within psychiatric populations, Butcher (1990) identified four distinct validity profile configurations and associated test-taking attitudes: Profile 1, open and frank (moderate elevations on the *F* scale and low *L* and *K* scores); Profile 2, virtuous and perfectionistic (high *L* and *K* scores and a moderate-to-low *F*); Profile 3, reluctant and resistant to acknowledge most problems (high *K* scores and moderate-to-low *L* and *F* scores); and Profile 4, a "plea for help" (high *F* scores and low *L* and *K* scores).

Butcher (1990) hypothesized that the client's assessed test-taking attitude may be generalized to his or her approach to treatment: Profile 1 patients are problem oriented, are willing to discuss their problems, and are relatively easy to engage in psychological treatment; Profile 2 patients perceive their psychological adjustment to be good, refuse to engage in self-criticism, remain aloof early in treatment, and maintain rigid beliefs and moralistic attitudes; Profile 3 patients are reluctant to disclose personal weaknesses, appear resistant in therapy, and tend to reluctantly enter treatment at the insistence of another; Profile 4 patients present nonspecific problems that involve several life areas, are unable to focus on specific issues in therapy, feel vulnerable to the demands of the environment, and are unable to cope with their problems. Thus, understanding the patient's response style (by the validity profile) is critical to interpreting MMPI and MMPI-2 results and possibly to predicting the individual's attitude toward treatment.

Most psychological tests do not have the built-in validity checks that have been devised for the MMPI and MMPI-2. Without response style information, it is possible that scores that should be attributed to response style are interpreted solely in terms of the construct(s) supposedly being measured, which may lead to misdiagnoses and inappropriate treatment. This is of particular concern with a substance-abusing population in which there are concerns about the accuracy of self-report substance use information. In addition, previous work has demonstrated that a socially desirable response set influences Alcohol Use Inventory (AUI; Skinner & Allen, 1983) and Inventory of Drinking Situations (IDS; Isenhart, 1993) scores. Therefore, we hypothesized that a defensive profile (high L and K and low F) would result not only in spuriously low MMPI-2 clinical scales but also in spuriously low scale scores on the AUI and IDS. Similarly, an exaggerated profile (low L and K and high F) would result in spuriously high scale scores on the AUI and IDS.

The goals of this study included determining the number and types of validity profiles in a sample of inpatient alcohol abusers, assessing whether response styles identified by the MMPI-2 can be generalized to other assessment instruments, and establishing and testing calibration equations for future classification.

METHOD

Participants

Five hundred thirty-eight men (300 in the first sample and 238 in the second sample) who met the *Diagnostic and Statistical Manual of Mental Disorders* (3rd. ed., rev.; DSM–III–R, American Psychiatric Association, 1987) criteria for alcohol abuse or dependence and who were admitted to a large midwestern Veterans Affairs Medical Center for inpatient substance abuse rehabilitation were included in the study. The first sample consisted of consecutive-admissions patients who completed the assessment battery as part of the initial clinical assessment before entering the program. The second sample consisted of patients consecutively admitted to the program and who requested to participate in a Veterans Affairs-wide program evaluation study. Only patients with alcohol as their primary drug of choice were included (although they could be abusing other drugs).

Program

The participants took part in a 21-day, inpatient program that was based on the principles of Alcoholics Anonymous and included group and individual counseling, educational lectures, and self-help activities. Participation in the treatment program made the patients eligible to participate in the study. The patients were expected to complete the program and follow-up with all recommended aftercare activities (e.g., self-help groups and relapse groups). In addition to substance use disorders, patients also experienced a range of additional Axis I disorders (especially anxiety and mood disorders) and were typically "influenced" to seek treatment by a variety of external sources (e.g., courts, spouses, and employers). Although some patients were detoxified on the unit in which the program operated, most patients were medically and psychiatrically stable on admission because any acute detoxification is conducted in county detoxification centers, on a medical unit, or both. The assessments used in this process were completed after a wide range of time following the patient's last drink. Although the assessment was completed within 3 working days of the patient's admission, some patients may have consumed alcohol the day before their admission whereas others may have not been using for weeks before admission (e.g., they may have been in jail or may have been court ordered to remain alcohol-free and complete inpatient programming).

Instruments

Alcohol Use Inventory (AUI)

The AUI (Horn, Wanberg, & Foster, 1985, 1987) measures various dimensions of an individual's alcohol abuse. The primary scales assess the short-term benefits related to alcohol use, styles of use, consequences from use, and concerns and acknowledgments regarding alcohol abuse and treatment. The six second-order scales assess enhanced functioning from alcohol use, extent of obsessive drinking, alcohol-related life disruption (two scales), anxiety resulting from alcohol abuse, and awareness of problems related to alcohol use. The third-order scale is a broad measure of alcohol dependence. Horn et al. (1987) reported 1-week test–retest reliability coefficients ranging from .54 to .89 on the primary scales, from .80 to .94 on the secondary scales, and .89 on the tertiary scale. Construct validity was demonstrated by comparing each of the AUI scales with the Michigan Alcoholism Screening Test (MAST; Selzer, 1971) and Daily Amount of Alcohol Consumed (DAAC; Skinner & Allen, 1983).

Inventory of Drinking Situations (IDS)

The IDS (Annis, 1982) was developed to assess the frequency of heavy drinking over the past year in the specific high-risk situations identified by Marlatt and Gordon (1980, 1985). Isenhart (1991, 1993) examined the psychometrics of the instrument and made modifications resulting in a shorter version that assesses four high-risk situations: Negative Emotions (NE; feeling pessimistic about life), Social Pressure (SP; feeling pressure from the environment to use), Testing Personal Control (TC; thinking a few drinks could be managed without losing control), and Pleasant Emotions (PE; feeling happy when things are going well). The instrument's psychometrics have been evaluated and demonstrate good factorial validity, internal consistency (alpha), and unique variance (Isenhart, 1993).

Background Information

All participants from the second sample provided background information by using an intake information form designed for the program evaluation project (Maude-Griffin, Finney, & Moos, 1992). The form requested demographic information including: age, education, employment status, occupation, income, and marital status. Also, severity of alcohol dependence was assessed by using a self-report rating scale on which each participant indicated the extent he experienced each of the nine *DSM–III–R* symptoms of alcohol dependence during the prior 3 months. Each rating ranged from 1 (*never*) to 5 (*almost every day*) so that the total scores ranged from 9 to 45.

Procedure

On admission into the program, patients completed a psychological test battery that included the instruments used in this study. Only consistent MMPI-2 response styles were considered; therefore, participants with inconsistent patterns as demonstrated by Variable Response Inventory raw scores greater than 13, True Response Inventory raw scores greater than 13 or less than 5, or both inventories were not included in analyses (Graham, 1990). Seventeen participants (6%) were eliminated from the first sample, leaving a total of 283 participants, and 7 participants (3%) were eliminated from the second sample, leaving a total of 231 participants.

The same cluster-analytic procedures were conducted on both samples to cross-validate the results from the first sample on the second sample. Specifically, both samples were used to ascertain the appropriate number of significant clusters to retain for further analysis. Cluster analyses were performed on both samples (Ward's minimum variance method was used) by utilizing the *L*, *F*, and *K* scores. The procedures described by Calinski and Harabasz (1974) and Duda and Hart (1973) were used to determine the number of clusters. Milligan and Cooper (1985) reported that these procedures were some of the most accurate techniques for determining the significant number of clusters in a data set.

The stability of the classification procedures was evaluated by using the procedures described by Wells-Parker, Anderson, Pang, and Timken (1993). Calibration equations, using discriminant analysis, were generated from the first sample and applied to the second sample to predict group membership. These predicted group memberships were cross-tabulated with the actual group memberships generated from the cluster analysis of the second sample. These researchers recommended the following criterion to evaluate group correspondence: If the number of cases in a cell represents at least 50% of all cases in the respective row and column, then a cluster group generated by cluster analysis (or some other solution) corresponds to a cluster group generated by a different solution (in this case, discriminant analysis).

One concern is that the differences in the identified profiles could be attributed to severity of alcohol dependence and not to response bias. Therefore, the DSM–III–R alcohol severity ratings were used to compare the severity of alcohol dependence between the identified clusters in the second sample. It is assumed that if the severity ratings are similar, then the identified differences are likely due to response bias. However, if the severity ratings differ, then the identified differences in profile elevations could be due to severity of alcohol dependence, and, consequently, the profiles may reflect genuine differences in psychological distress. An analysis of variance (ANOVA) (along with the Scheffé post hoc analysis, if appropriate) was used to assess for severity differences between the identified cluster groups.

Multivariate analyses of variance and ANOVAs (along with the Scheffé post hoc analysis, if appropriate) were used to assess the differences between the three subgroups in the second sample on the primary, secondary, and tertiary AUI scales and on the IDS scales. We hypothesized that there would be a significant main affect for subgroup. That is, the MMPI-2 response pattern found in each cluster group would generalize to the other alcohol assessment instruments and influence the mean subscale scores.

RESULTS

Examination of the demographic characteristics of Samples 1 and 2, respectively, showed that most participants were middle-aged (42.85 [11.65] and 43.75 [12.35]); most were divorced (35% and 36%), married (25% and 20%), or single (24% and 27%); and most had at least completed high school (45% and 34%) and many had some post–high school training (42% and 52%). The average DSM–III–R alcohol dependence severity rating for the second sample was 25.36 (SD = 10.26), which suggests a moderate level of dependency.

Three clusters were identified in the first sample. Cluster 1, the *exaggerated* group (n = 19, 7%), had a highly elevated F score (M = 104.21), a moderate L score (M = 49.53), and a low K score (M = 35.79). Cluster 2, the *straightforward* group (n = 168, 59%), had a moderately elevated F score (M = 63.99) and moderate L (M = 47.93) and K (M = 42.79) scores. Cluster 3, the *defensive* group (n = 96, 34%), had a slightly elevated L score (M = 56.71) relative to F (M = 49.42) and K (M = 53.90).

The second sample was subjected to the same cluster-analytic procedures as the first. This analysis supported keeping three clusters on which to perform additional analyses. The exaggerated group (n = 30, 13%) displayed a very high F scale score ($M = 106.87$), a moderate L score ($M = 47.40$), and a low K score ($M = 35.90$). The straightforward group ($n = 139$, 60%) displayed a moderately elevated F score ($M = 62.74$) and moderate L ($M = 48.42$) and K ($M = 42.66$) scores. The defensive group ($n = 62$, 27%) displayed slight elevations on L ($M = 54.06$) and K ($M = 57.10$) relative to F ($M = 46.68$).

The unstandardized canonical discriminant function coefficients generated from the first sample showed that the first discriminant function accounted for 91% of the variance and that the second discriminant function accounted for 9% of the variance. The multiple correlations squared for the two functions were, respectively, .8511 and .4510. This suggests that the use of both functions significantly increases the accuracy of classifying participants into cluster groups.

The calibration equations generated from the first sample were then applied to the second sample and produced similar subgroups (in terms of scale elevations and percentage of cases in each subgroup). Figure 1 reflects the similarities of the subgroups of both samples.

The results of the cross-tabulation of the cluster groups from the second sample with the calibration-derived groups (developed from the first sample) are shown in Table 1. The results were significant, $\chi^2(4, N = 231) = 359.72$, $p < .000005$, and showed in each case that the number of cases in each cell represents more than 50% of the cases in the respective row and column. This finding supports the stability of the cluster groups across the two samples.

The results of the analysis of the alcohol dependence severity ratings were significant, $F(2, 225) = 9.42$, $p = .0001$. Post hoc analysis showed that the defensive group ($M = 21.74$, $SD = 9.55$) significantly differed from the straightforward group ($M = 27.15$, $SD = 9.81$) and the exaggerated group ($M = 28.87$, $SD = 11.13$). No other significant differences were found. Thus, the defensive group reported significantly lower levels of alcohol dependency than did the other two groups, both of whom reported average levels of dependency.

The subgroups from the second sample (based on the discriminant functions developed from the first sample) were then compared on the AUI and IDS subscales (the primary, secondary, and tertiary AUI scales were analyzed separately). We expected that if the participant's MMPI-2 response style "generalized" to the AUI and IDS, then the defensive, straightforward, and exaggerated groups should have generally low, middle, and high scale elevations, respectively, on the two alcohol assessment scales.

AUI and IDS data were available on a total of 207 participants: 29 exaggerated, 103 straightforward, and 75 defensive. AUI validity can be evaluated by examining for decile differences equal to or greater than three between the Disruption 1 and Disruption 2 scales (Horn et al., 1987). A review of the differences between these scales showed that 30 (15%) had

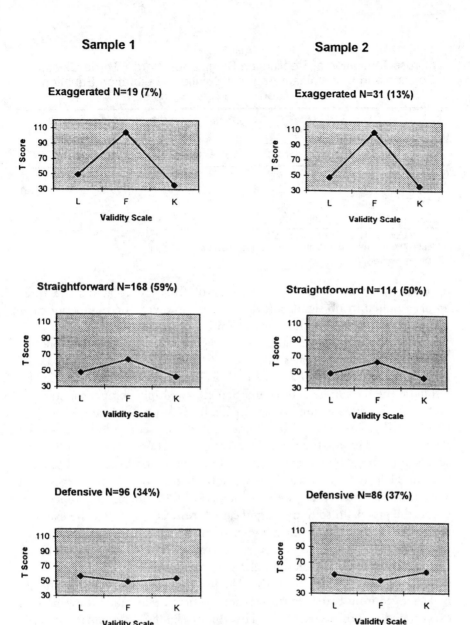

Sample 1

Sample 2

Exaggerated N=19 (7%)

Exaggerated N=31 (13%)

Straightforward N=168 (59%)

Straightforward N=114 (50%)

Defensive N=96 (34%)

Defensive N=86 (37%)

Figure 1. The Minnesota Multiphasic Personality Inventory-2 Validity scale mean score configurations of both samples on the basis of cluster analysis by using Ward's minimum variance method. *L* = Lie scale; *F* = Infrequency scale; *K* = Correction scale.

an absolute difference equal to or greater than three. Of these, 19 (63%) suggested a defensive response pattern (i.e., the Disruption 1 score, consisting of more "obvious" indicators of alcohol dependency, was higher than the Disruption 2 scale, which consists of more "subtle" indicators of alcohol

TABLE 1
Cross-Tabulation of Replication Sample for Ward's Three-Cluster Solution and Discriminant Analysis Solution (Calibration Equations) Generated From First Sample

Groups based on Ward's clustering for replication sample	Groups based on discriminant functions for first sample			
	Group 1	Group 2	Group 3	Total
Group 1	62[a]	0	0	62
Group 2	24	114[a]	1	139
Group 3	0	0	30[a]	30
Total	86	114	31	231

Note. $\chi^2(4, N = 231) = 359.72$, $p < .000005$.
[a]At least 50% of the cases fell into corresponding clusters.

dependency). Analysis of the frequency of these AUIs across the three groups resulted in no significant differences; however, the number of cases was likely too low to warrant any definitive conclusions.

Multivariate analyses identified a significant effect for subgroup on both the AUI primary scales ($V = 0.5275$), $F(34, 378) = 3.98$, $p < .0005$, and the secondary scales ($V = 0.2537$), $F(12, 400) = 4.84$, $p < .0005$. The results of the univariate F tests and Scheffé's multiple comparison analysis of the AUI subscales are shown in Table 2. With few exceptions, the exaggerated group received the highest AUI scale scores, followed by the straightforward group, then the defensive group. There were no statistically significant subgroup differences on the Gregarious and Sustained Drinking and the Help Before subscales. Also, note that for the Receptiveness and Awareness subscales there were no statistically significant differences between the groups in spite of a significant F test. Of 24 scales, the exaggerated group scored significantly higher than the straightforward and defensive groups on 9 and 18 scales, respectively. The straightforward group scored significantly higher than the defensive group on 14 scales. These subscale trends are reflected in the Alcohol Involvement scale. The decile ranks ranged from two to four to six for the defensive, straightforward, and exaggerated groups, respectively. This highly significant summary scale, $F(2, 204) = 28.13$, $p < .0005$, difference, and the individual subscale differences, suggest that scores on the AUI must be interpreted in light of response style.

Multivariate analysis ($V = 0.2440$), $F(8, 396) = 6.88$, $p < .0001$, identified subgroup as a main effect among three of four IDS subscales as shown in Table 3. The exaggerated group scored significantly higher than the defensive group on two (NE and TC) scales, the exaggerated group scored higher than the straightforward groups on one scale (NE), and the straightforward group scored higher than the defensive group on one (NE) scale.

TABLE 2
Alcohol Use Inventory Scale Scores of the Subgroups

Subgroup	Exaggerated		Straightforward		Defensive		F
	M	SD	M	SD	M	SD	
Primary scale							
Social Improvement	5.24$_a$	2.61	5.19$_a$	2.95	3.52$_b$	2.30	9.81***
Mental Improvement	2.48$_a$	1.77	1.84$_a$	1.72	0.87$_b$	1.22	14.02***
Mood Management	6.72$_a$	0.9963	5.25$_b$	2.08	3.76$_c$	2.31	24.49***
Marital Coping	1.62$_a$	2.39	1.17$_a$	1.91	0.40$_b$	0.9005	6.99**
Gregarious Drinking	5.00	2.25	4.65	2.56	5.17	2.57	0.9266
Compulsive Drinking	4.76$_a$	2.77	3.35$_b$	2.53	1.85$_c$	2.08	17.25***
Sustained Drinking	6.66	3.61	6.85	3.38	5.93	3.31	1.64
Loss of Control	9.86$_a$	3.85	7.10$_b$	3.88	5.37$_c$	3.56	15.31***
Role Maladaptation	6.45$_a$	3.71	5.53	3.50	4.35$_b$	2.86	5.05**
Delirium	6.03$_a$	3.89	2.52$_b$	2.66	1.68$_b$	1.93	28.93***
Marital Problems	1.55	2.21	1.49$_a$	2.11	0.67$_a$	1.37	4.66*
Quantity	6.17$_a$	2.52	5.15	2.78	4.35$_b$	2.26	6.97**
Guilt and Worry	6.62$_a$	2.11	5.67$_a$	2.45	4.43$_b$	2.65	9.84***
Help Before	3.66	2.14	2.82	2.15	2.65	2.01	2.46
Receptiveness	17.14	2.61	16.56	2.83	15.61	3.70	3.17*
Awareness	12.52	3.79	12.26	9.38	9.72	3.94	3.14*
Secondary scale							
Enhanced	10.90	13.31	7.87	3.91	6.60$_b$	3.08	5.41**
Obsessed Drinking	11.17$_a$	5.50	9.86$_a$	4.85	7.44$_b$	4.01	8.97***
Disruption 1	22.45$_a$	8.50	16.58$_b$	8.24	13.27$_c$	6.96	14.59***
Disruption 2	9.24$_a$	2.80	7.53$_b$	2.80	6.23$_c$	2.65	13.64***
Anxious Concern	16.45$_a$	3.42	13.39$_b$	4.76	9.88$_c$	5.20	23.03***
Receptive Awareness	29.66$_a$	5.31	27.98$_a$	5.67	25.33$_c$	6.85	6.73**
Tertiary scale							
Alcohol Involvement	41.17$_a$	13.45	30.03$_b$	13.11	20.97$_c$	11.94	28.13***

Note. Means with different subscripts differ significantly at $p < .05$.
*$p < .05$. **$p < .01$. ***$p < .001$.

TABLE 3
Inventory of Drinking Situations Scale Scores of the Subgroups

Scale	Exaggerated		Straightforward		Defensive		F
	M	SD	M	SD	M	SD	
Negative Emotions	57.82$_a$	8.37	51.52$_b$	10.12	43.22$_c$	11.25	24.39***
Social Pressure	52.82	10.77	50.66	10.73	47.24	12.15	3.17*
Testing Control	54.68$_a$	12.67	49.97	10.40	46.71$_b$	9.11	6.28**
Pleasant Emotions	51.04	12.12	52.19	9.79	49.72	9.46	1.29

Note. Means with different subscripts differ significantly at $p < .05$.
*$p < .05$. **$p < .01$. ***$p < .001$.

DISCUSSION

This study identified and cross-validated the number and types of validity profiles in a sample of participants seeking treatment for alcoholism, determined that response style (as measured by the L, F, and K scales) tended to generalize to alcohol assessment instruments, and generated classification strategies for future patients and participants. Three validity scale clusters were labeled *straightforward*, *defensive*, and *exaggerated*. Evidence of cluster validity was found in the similar validity scale means and percentages of the second sample. Clearly, these are three distinct groups with three distinct response styles. The analysis identified three clusters instead of the four suggested by Butcher (1990). The missing group was the K-score, subtly dominated defensive group. It is likely that this subgroup was not identified because the difference between it and the defensive group described here was not robust enough in this clinical population to have been recognized. That is, for this sample, there was little discrimination between obvious defensiveness (as measured by L) and more subtle defensiveness (as measured by K). Another possibility is that the high-K validity profiles are frequently seen in patients in the "later stages" of successful therapy (Butcher, 1990). Because the MMPI-2 data were collected pretreatment, there were no later stage patients and, therefore, the K-score dominated group was not identified.

One issue has to do with the confounding of response bias with genuine distress levels: Do the validity profile differences between these groups represent response bias or do they represent genuine clinical differences in symptomatology? One way this issue was addressed in this project was to assess differences in DSM–III–R severity ratings for alcohol dependency across the three groups. The defensive group scored significantly lower than the other two groups. One possible interpretation is that this group had lower levels of dependency and, consequently, had lower levels of psychological distress that were reflected in lower MMPI-2 clinical profiles. However, another interpretation is that this group may have been minimizing both their level of alcohol dependency and their level of psychological distress. That is, because the alcohol dependency severity ratings were also self-report, the results may be attributed to a guarded response style. This issue will need to be examined in future projects by comparing validity profiles to non–self-report measures of severity levels (e.g., physical or emotional health). If the results presented here were due to bias, then these non–self-report measures of severity would not differ between the groups. However, if the non–self-report measures do suggest severity differences between the groups, then the results reported here may not represent bias per se but rather differences in severity.

Consistent with expectations, the AUI and IDS results are associated with participants' MMPI-2 response pattern (e.g., exaggerated MMPI-2 profiles occurred with highly elevated AUI and IDS scale scores). However, there were no significant differences among the subgroups on the AUI Gregarious and Sustained Drinking, Help Before, Receptiveness, and Awareness subscales. All three groups scored within the average range on the Gregarious Drinking subscale. Drinking gregariously (i.e., convivial or festive drinking at bars, parties, or with friends) may be more socially acceptable than isolated drinking. Therefore, the defensive group would be less likely to deny this style, and the exaggerated group would be less likely to overendorse this style. The same rationale may apply to the sustained subscale. That is, sustained drinking is seen as no more pathological than binge drinking so that the groups would not tend to over- or underendorse items on this scale.

One possible explanation for the absence of differences on the Help Before scale is that participants viewed past treatment as separate from present levels of distress. The Receptiveness and Awareness subscales assess the extent the patient acknowledges that his or her life is in crisis, help is needed, and that he or she will follow the suggestions of the counselor. It is likely that given these scales' apparent high face validity, most patients (regardless of cluster type) wanted to appear cooperative, whether genuine or not.

Comparisons among groups on the IDS subgroups were consistent with expectations. It is interesting to note that the scale that consistently differed between the three groups was the willingness to endorse using alcohol in response to negative affect. The concept of drinking in response to negative affect is a familiar indication of a substance use disorder. Therefore, participants trying to deny (exaggerate) their problems would under- or overendorse these items. However, drinking around others (SP) and in association with feeling happy (PE; as in celebrating) is not necessarily associated with problematic drinking. Therefore, a participant trying to deny (exaggerate) his or her problems would not under- or overendorse these items. It appears, therefore, that the content of the scale items, specifically if the items are indicative of a substance use disorder, influences whether a particular response pattern will bias the results.

This study demonstrated the effects of response styles on a psychological test battery. Results clearly suggest that response style as measured by MMPI-2 L, F, and K scores remains consistent across other tests. Although the AUI and the IDS are invaluable tools in the assessment of alcohol-dependent patients, response style must be considered when interpreting these and possibly other instruments.

Of most clinical relevance is the extent assessed response bias (as measured by the MMPI-2) can be generalized to nontest and non–self-report assessments. For example, it would be of particular interest and a good future topic to examine the relationship between MMPI-2 validity profiles and other assessment outcomes (e.g., collateral reports of patients' alcohol use) and level of participation in treatment activities (e.g., group attendance or level of attendance in aftercare activities).

The results of this study can only be generalized to the population in the sample: working class, mostly White, alcohol-abusing men. Issues unique to women, non-Whites, and nonalcohol drug abusers need to be examined in future studies along with examining the relationships between response style and treatment involvement and outcome.

REFERENCES

American Psychiatric Association. (1987). *Diagnostic and statistical manual of mental disorders* (3rd ed., rev.). Washington, DC: Author.

Annis, H. M. (1982). *Inventory of Drinking Situations*. Toronto, Ontario, Canada: Addiction Research Foundation of Ontario.

Baer, R. A., Wetter, M. W., & Berry, D. T. (1992). Detection of underreporting of psychopathology on the MMPI: A meta-analysis. *Clinical Psychology Review, 12*, 509–525.

Berry, D. T., Baer, R. A., & Harris, M. J. (1991). Detection of malingering on the MMPI: A meta-analysis. *Clinical Psychology Review, 11*, 585–598.

Butcher, J. N. (1990). *MMPI-2 in psychological treatment*. New York: Oxford University Press.

Calinski, R. B., & Harabasz, J. (1974). A dendrite method for cluster analysis. *Communications in Statistics, 3*, 1–27.

Cassisi, J. E., & Workman, D. E. (1992). The detection of malingering and deception with a short form of the MMPI-2 based on the L, F, and K scales. *The Journal of Clinical Psychology, 48*, 54–58.

Duda, R. O., & Hart, P. E. (1973). *Pattern classification and scene analysis*. New York: Wiley.

Graham, J. R. (1990). *MMPI-2 Assessing personality and psychopathology*. New York: Oxford University Press.

Graham, J. R., Watts, D., & Timbrook, R. E. (1991). Detecting fake-good and fake-bad MMPI-2 profiles. *Journal of Personality Assessment, 57*, 264–277.

Hathaway, S. R., & McKinley, J. C. (1943). *The Minnesota Multiphasic Personality Schedule*. Minneapolis: University of Minnesota Press.

Horn, J. L., Wanberg, K. W., & Foster, F. M. (1985). *Guidelines for understanding alcohol use and abuse: The Alcohol Use Inventory (AUI)*. Baltimore, MD: PsychSystems.

Horn, J. L., Wanberg, K. W., & Foster, F. M. (1987). *Guide to the Alcohol Use Inventory*. Minneapolis, MN: National Computer Systems.

Isenhart, C. E. (1991). Factor structure of the Inventory of Drinking Situations. *Journal of Substance Abuse, 3*, 59–71.

Isenhart, C. E. (1993). Psychometric evaluation of a short form of the Inventory of Drinking Situations. *Journal of Studies on Alcohol, 54*, 345–349.

Marlatt, G. A., & Gordon, J. R. (1980). Determinants of relapse: Implications for the maintenance of behavior change. In P. Davidson & S. Davidson (Eds.), *Behavioral medicine: Changing health lifestyles* (pp. 410–452). New York: Brunner/Mazel.

Marlatt, G. A., & Gordon, J. R. (Eds.). (1985). *Relapse prevention: Maintenance strategies in the treatment of addictive behaviors.* New York: Guilford Press.

Maude-Griffin, P. M., Finney, J. W., & Moos, R. H. (1992). *Multi-site evaluation of VA inpatient substance abuse treatment: Measures and conceptual domains.* Palo Alto, CA: Program Evaluation and Resource Center and HSR&D Center for Health Care Evaluation.

Meehl, P. E., & Hathaway, S. R. (1946). The K factor as a suppressor variable in the MMPI. *Journal of Applied Psychology, 30*, 526–564.

Merydith, S. P., & Wallbrown, F. H. (1991). Reconsidering response sets, test-taking attitudes, dissimulation, self-deception, and social desirability. *Psychological Reports, 69*, 891–905.

Milligan, G. W., & Cooper, M. C. (1985). An examination of procedures for determining the number of clusters in a data set. *Psychometrika, 50*, 159–179.

Selzer, M. L. (1971). The Michigan Alcoholism Screening Test: The quest for a new diagnostic instrument. *American Journal of Psychiatry, 127*, 1653–1658.

Skinner, H. A., & Allen, B. A. (1983). Differential assessment of alcoholism: Evaluation of the Alcohol Use Inventory. *Journal of Studies on Alcohol, 44*, 852–862.

Wells-Parker, E., Anderson, B., Pang, M., & Timken, D. (1993). An examination of cluster-based classification schemes for DUI offenders. *Journal of Studies on Alcohol, 54*, 209–218.

14

ASSESSING DRINKERS' MOTIVATION FOR CHANGE: THE STAGES OF CHANGE READINESS AND TREATMENT EAGERNESS SCALE (SOCRATES)

WILLIAM R. MILLER AND J. SCOTT TONIGAN

Motivation for change is a multifaceted construct, historically regarded as a prerequisite for responsiveness to treatment (Beckman, 1980; Dean, 1958). In treating alcohol problems, lack of motivation has sometimes been understood as resulting from client trait defense mechanisms such as denial, which pose formidable obstacles to recovery (Clancy, 1961; Moore & Murphy, 1961). Within this perspective, motivation may be judged in a binary manner: one either is motivated or is unmotivated and in denial (Clancy, 1964; DiCicco, Unterberger, & Mack, 1978). The pop-

Reprinted from *Psychology of Addictive Behaviors*, 10, 81–89. (1996). Copyright © 1996 by the Educational Publishing Foundation. Used with permission of the author.

This research was funded in part by Grant U10-AA08435 from the National Institute on Alcohol Abuse and Alcoholism. We gratefully acknowledge the collaboration of the Project MATCH Research Group in collecting and compiling the study data and in reviewing drafts of this article.

355

ular concept of "bottoming out" suggests a developmental point at which the person shifts from unmotivated to motivated status by virtue of having endured a sufficient volume of suffering to instigate change.

Alternatively, motivation for change has been construed as a fluctuating state of balance between the pros and cons of a behavior (Janis & Mann, 1977). In this view, motivational states vary along one or more continuous dimensions, influenced by a variety of factors in the social environment. Client motivation for change in problem drinking has been shown to be substantially influenced by therapist style and environmental characteristics (Miller, 1985; Miller, Benefield, & Tonigan, 1993).

Building on the latter approach, Prochaska and DiClemente (1982, 1986) developed a transtheoretical model depicting a sequence of stages through which people progress as they initiate and maintain behavior change. The first of these is termed *precontemplation*, a state of unawareness of a problem or need for change. As problem awareness increases, the person enters a state of ambivalence or *contemplation*, in which pros and cons are weighed (Miller & Rollnick, 1991). Over time, the decisional balance may tip in favor of change, as adverse consequences (cons) outweigh the perceived advantages of status quo (pros), a process paralleling the idea of bottoming out. In their original model, Prochaska and DiClemente (1986) termed this point of shifting balance the *determination* stage but subsequently deleted this stage and then more recently reinstated it, reconceptualizing this transitional period as a *preparation* phase (Prochaska & DiClemente, 1992; Prochaska, DiClemente, & Norcross, 1992). Next the person moves into an *action* stage in which efforts are made to change behavior. If these initial efforts are successful, the *maintenance* stage involves relapse prevention (Marlatt & Gordon, 1985), taking steps to protect against reversion to the prior behavior pattern. Given that behavior change is not perfectly maintained on the first try in most cases, a *relapse* stage was also described, from which the person may revert back to action or cycle again through contemplation, determination–preparation, action, and maintenance in order to achieve lasting behavior change.

Motivation for change in problem drinking has been measured in a variety of ways. Therapist judgments of motivation during treatment have been found to be predictive of client outcomes (Brown & Miller, 1993; cf. Leake & King, 1977). Open-ended questions about motivation for drinking and for change have been included in structured interviews (e.g., Miller & Marlatt, 1984). A decisional balance approach requires assessment of perceived reasons for and against change (Janis & Mann, 1977). Rollnick and his colleagues (Heather, Rollnick, & Bell, 1993; Rollnick, Heather, Gold, & Hall, 1992) have provided a scale of readiness for change in drinking, and Cox, Klinger, and Blount (1991) have described a goal-focused Motivational Structure Questionnaire.

Prochaska and DiClemente (1992) developed the University of

Rhode Island Change Assessment (URICA) with items marking stages of change from their transtheoretical model (McConnaughy, Prochaska, & Velicer, 1993). The URICA was designed to be useable for a broad range of concerns and asks the respondent general questions about "your problem." Although the URICA yields scales corresponding to four stages of change from the transtheoretical model (precontemplation, contemplation, action, and maintenance), analyses have focused primarily on cluster profiling of respondents (DiClemente & Hughes, 1990; Prochaska & DiClemente, 1992). The Stages of Change Readiness and Treatment Eagerness Scale (SOCRATES) was originally developed as a parallel measure of the stages of change described by Prochaska and DiClemente, with item content specifically focused on problem drinking.

In this article we introduce the SOCRATES, describing how it was developed, and presenting the results of two psychometric evaluations of its item pool. The first of these provides factor structure and internal consistency information from a large clinical sample. The second demonstrates the test–retest reliability of SOCRATES in a smaller sample. On the basis of these analyses, a 19-item version is commended for future use, and its potential applications are discussed.

DEVELOPMENT OF THE SOCRATES

An initial set of items for the SOCRATES was drafted by William R. Miller in 1987 and circulated for comment by about a dozen colleagues in substance abuse treatment research. A 32-item version (2.0) was then developed by using 5-point Likert scales, ranging from 5 (*strongly agree*) to 1 (*strongly disagree*), with four 8-item scales intended to correspond logically to the precontemplation (P), contemplation (C), determination (D), and action (A) stages. Maintenance stage items were not included in the original version because it was intended for use with clients initially presenting for treatment, but as discussed below this omission was later corrected in the interest of including all stages. The factor structure of Version 2.0 was tested with a sample of 224 clients (81% male, 54% Hispanic and 42% non-Hispanic White, and a mean age of 31 years) in treatment for alcohol dependence (Miller et al., 1990a, 1990b). Cronbach alpha coefficients of internal consistency were computed for the entire scale (.72) and for the four subscales ($P = .84$, $C = .67$, $D = .90$, $A = .89$). The P subscale was negatively correlated with the remaining three scales ($r = -.42$, $-.77$, and $-.43$, respectively), which were themselves positively intercorrelated ($r = .41-.64$). A factor analysis using alpha extraction with varimax rotation yielded four factors in the underlying structure of the dataset, which shared modest amounts of variance (range: 1%–20%). Several items loaded significantly on two different factors. One clear pattern was that precontemplation (negation of a problem) and determination items (recognition of a problem) formed a single robust first factor, representing opposite sides of the same dimension of problem recognition.

A third version of SOCRATES was then prepared, substituting for or rewording items that loaded on two factors. A fifth scale marking the maintenance (M) stage was also added to Version 3.0. An initial factor analysis of this 40-item version was completed with a population of heavy drinkers recruited through general medicine clinics of a Veterans Affairs Medical Center, indicating a clearer factor structure corresponding more closely to the a priori scales, and six items were again modified. After these changes, a further factor analysis was conducted with a new Veterans Affairs population ($N = 125$; Luckie, 1994), which identified 2 problematic items that were reworded for greater consistency with their factors. The resulting 1991 Version 5.0 was used in the present studies, for which a shorter (20-item) version was also developed, consisting of the 4 items from each scale with strongest scale loadings.

METHOD

The short form of SOCRATES 5.0 was included in the pretreatment assessment battery for Project MATCH, a multisite clinical trial of psychosocial treatments for alcohol problems (Project MATCH Research Group, 1993). The instrument was administered 1,726 clients as a paper-and-pencil questionnaire, embedded within a larger self-assessment packet. Five sites were outpatient treatment programs, and at five sites clients were seen for aftercare following residential or day treatment. At the Albuquerque site only, the full 40-item SOCRATES 5.0 was administered. For analyses of the overall sample, the short-form items were extracted from the full form for the 226 Albuquerque clients and were included in the total sample.

The SOCRATES short form was also included in a separate cross-site reliability study conducted with Project MATCH interviewers from all sites. The instrument was administered as part of a self-assessment battery completed twice (with a 2-day interval between administrations) by 82 heavy drinkers recruited specifically for this psychometric study. The sample included clients from several sources who had received treatment but were continuing to drink, as well as heavy drinkers who had never sought treatment. Details of the methodology of the full reliability study are provided in the overview article by Del Boca and Brown (1996) at the beginning of this issue.

TABLE 1
Description and Comparison of Full Project MATCH
Population (*N* = 1,726) and Sample Providing Complete SOCRATES
Instruments (*N* = 1,672)

Characteristic	Full Project MATCH sample		SOCRATES subsample	
	Outpatient (*n* = 952)	Aftercare (*n* = 774)	Outpatient (*n* = 924)	Aftercare (*n* = 748)
Age				
M	38.88	41.92	38.88	41.80
SD	10.72	11.11	10.74	11.07
Total SDU[a]				
M	796.31	1,405.66	794.94	1,401.55
SD	630.22	1,130.58	629.07	1,128.78
Gender				
Male	688	619	666	599
Female	264	155	258	149
Ethnicity				
White	762	622	745	599
Black	53	116	51	113
Hispanic	116	27	108	27
Other	21	9	20	9

Note. SOCRATES = Stages of Change Readiness and Treatment Eagerness Scale.
[a]One standard drink unit (SDU) = 0.5 oz (15 ml) of ethanol (see Miller, Heather, & Hall, 1991).

RESULTS

Study 1

Of the 1,726 cases included in the Project MATCH baseline sample, 1,672 (97%) completed SOCRATES with no missing items. The demographics for this sample are shown in Table 1, in comparison with characteristics of the full MATCH sample. No significant differences were observed, indicating that the responding sample was representative of the total MATCH population.

Patterns of intercorrelations among the original stage subscales were examined. Consistent with our prior findings, the P and D scales were inversely related in both outpatient ($r = -.70$) and aftercare samples ($r = -.62$). The A and M scales were also found to be strongly related ($r = .69$ and .56). Other intercorrelations were modest [range for outpatients was .01 (A and C) to $-.27$ (P and A) and for aftercare was .03 (P and C) to $-.42$ (P and A)]. This suggested a further analysis to determine the proportion of variance unique to each of the five scales, which was computed by subtracting from 1.0 and squared multiple correlation (R^2) of each scale with all other scale scores. All original scales, with the exception of C, shared about half of their variance with all other scales combined (range: .48–.51 for outpatients, .56–.66 for aftercare samples, and .43–.53 for the full sample). The C scale, specifically designed to tap ambivalence (Miller & Rollnick, 1991), shared almost no variance with the other scales (98%, 95%, and 99% unique variance, respectively).

The large sample of Study 1 provided an ideal opportunity to examine the factor structure underlying items designed to assess the stages of change. The 20 items of the SOCRATES short form were subjected to factor analysis by using both orthogonal and nonorthogonal rotations. Alpha extraction was used to minimize communality estimates (Tabachnick & Fidell, 1989). One item (6) from the original P scale, "The only reason I'm here is that somebody made me come," proved to be problematic. Its factor loading was low, and we failed to anticipate that this item would be confusing at follow-up and in contexts other than presentation for treatment. Further, within the scales described below, this would be the only item requiring reverse scaling. We therefore eliminated this item, resulting in a 19-item SOCRATES.

With a criterion of eigenvalues greater than 1.0, both orthogonal and nonorthogonal approaches yielded a three-factor solution, with factor content remaining relatively constant between orthogonal and nonorthogonal rotations. The primary difference between approaches was a switching of the order of the first two factors. This was true whether the entire sample (N = 1,672) was examined or whether the study arms (outpatient and aftercare) were analyzed separately. The orthogonal solution yielded a more straightforward interpretation for the entire sample, with three factors accounting for 45% of the item response variance. Item loadings for the three factors are shown in Table 2. Assignment of items to factors was based on their absolute magnitude, giving interpretive weight to only those loadings exceeding ±.30. For two items in which more complex loading occurred (i.e., loadings > ±.30 on two factors), the larger of the loadings was used to assign the item to a factor.

The first factor, Taking Steps, accounted for 27% of the item response variance and included eight items, all of the original A and M items. This factor is thus equivalent to the sum of our original A and M scales.

The second factor, Recognition, accounted for an additional 11% of the variance and combined seven items of the original P and D scales. Here, D items loaded in a positive direction, and original P items loaded in a negative direction. The three items from the original P scale had been reverse scaled before scoring, so to simplify scoring and interpretation, given their negative loadings, the responses to these items were simply added to the original D items to calculate the Recognition scale rather than being reverse scaled and then subtracted.

The third factor, Ambivalence, accounted for a further 7% of variance and included all four contemplation items. Thus the items written to tap ambivalence appear to represent a construct different from recognition and taking steps. Three similar factors have been reported from analyses of the

TABLE 2
Factor Analysis of the 19-Item SOCRATES: MATCH Baseline Sample

SOCRATES item	Original scale	Factor loadings		
		Taking steps	Recognition	Ambivalence
Taking Steps				
10. I have already changed my drinking, and I am looking for ways to keep from slipping back into my old pattern.	M	.81	.09	-.02
14. I am actively doing things now to cut down or stop drinking.	A	.76	.22	-.04
19. I am working hard to change my drinking.	A	.76	.28	-.05
4. I have already started making some changes in my drinking.	A	.73	.15	.00
9. I'm not just thinking about changing my drinking, I'm already doing something about it.	A	.69	.25	-.06
20. I have made some changes in my drinking, and I want some help to keep from going back to the way I used to drink.	M	.68	.16	.06
15. I want help to keep from going back to the drinking problems that I had before.	M	.46	.45	.00
5. I was drinking too much at one time, but I've managed to change my drinking.	M	.40	-.24	.16
Recognition				
11. I have serious problems with drinking.	P	.09	.80	-.02
16. I know that I have a drinking problem.	P	.15	.76	-.03
18. I am an alcoholic.	D	.22	.68	-.18
13. My drinking is causing a lot of harm.	D	.15	.62	-.01
8. I am a problem drinker.	D	.03	.61	.04
3. If I don't change my drinking soon, my problems are going to get worse.	D	.12	.60	.05
1. I really want to make changes in my drinking.	P	.16	.38	.04
Ambivalence				
17. There are times when I wonder if I drink too much.	C	.04	.06	.66
2. Sometimes I wonder if I am an alcoholic.	C	-.07	-.07	.58
12. Sometimes I wonder if I am in control of my drinking.	C	.00	-.06	.55
7. Sometimes I wonder if my drinking is hurting other people.	C	.07	.30	.31

Note. $N = 1,672$. SOCRATES = Stages of Change Readiness and Treatment Eagerness Scale. The original subscales of SOCRATES include M = maintenance, A = action, P = precontemplation, C = contemplation, and D = determination.

TABLE 3
Distributional Characteristics of the Factor Analytically Derived SOCRATES Scales

SOCRATES scale	Outpatient (*n* = 924)	Aftercare (*n* = 748)	Combined (*n* = 1,672)
Ambivalence			
M	14.68	13.95	14.35
SD	3.50	4.17	3.82
Skewness	−.65	−.50	−.61
Kurtosis	.13	−.44	−.11
Recognition			
M	30.54	32.60	31.46
SD	4.01	3.20	3.81
Skewness	−.88	−1.62	−1.15
Kurtosis	.38	2.59	.95
Taking Steps			
M	30.50	35.28	32.64
SD	5.82	3.80	5.55
Skewness	−.44	−1.02	−.81
Kurtosis	−.06	2.47	.51

Note. *N* = 1,672. SOCRATES = Stages of Change Readiness and Treatment Eagerness Scale.

SOCRATES at other sites (e.g., Isenhart, 1994; Morgan, Morgenstern, Blanchard, McCrady, & Langenbucher, 1995; Prescott & Børtveit, 1995). As reflected in Table 2, all items had loadings > .30 on the scales to which they were assigned, and only one item (15) had a loading > .30 on another scale. Also shown in Table 2 are the original scale assignments of items. All items were scored in the same direction to yield the three factor scales.

Because the factor structure of SOCRATES produces three rather than five separate dimensions, we do not recommend use of the original scale names because this instrument does not appear to measure the stage constructs as conceived by Prochaska and DiClemente (1982, 1986). Rather the scales of SOCRATES seem better understood as continuously distributed motivational processes that may underlie stages of change. Distributional characteristics of the three factors are reported in Table 3. To aid with interpretation of factor scale scores, we provide normative decile rankings in Table 4, on the basis of the Project MATCH clinical sample described in Table 1. It must be noted that these norms should not be applied to nonclinical (e.g., general) populations.

The internal consistency of each scale was calculated by using the full sample (*N* = 1,672). Cronbach alphas were .83 for Taking Steps, .85 for Recognition, and .60 for Ambivalence. Horn, Wanberg, and Foster (1987) specified the range of .70 to .80 to be optimal for alpha, in balancing scale fidelity and breadth of measurement. For the full SOCRATES (39 items, again omitting Item 6), the corresponding alphas were slightly higher: .89 for Taking Steps, .90 for Recognition, and .66 for Ambivalence. Factor analyses were conducted on the 39-item version to determine the

TABLE 4
Decile Rankings for the Three SOCRATES Scales for the Outpatient (*n* = 924), Aftercare (*n* = 748), and Combined Samples

Decile ranking (%)	Ambivalence (Range: 4–20)			Recognition (Range: 7–35)			Taking Steps (Range: 8–40)		
	O	A	C	O	A	C	O	A	C
10	10	8	8	25	28	26	22	30	25
20	12	10	11	27	30	28	26	32	29
30	13	12	13	29	32	30	28	33	30
40	14	13	14	30	33	31	30	35	32
50	15	15	15	31	34	33	31	36	33
60	16	16	16	32	35	34	32	36	35
70	16	16	16	34	35	35	33	38	36
80	18	18	18	35	35	35	36	39	38
90	19	19	19	35	35	35	38	40	40

Note. SOCRATES = Stages of Change Readiness and Treatment Eagerness Scale.
O = outpatient; A = aftercare; C = combined.

replicability of the obtained factors from the 19-item version. Parallel to the shorter version, and using alpha extraction and varimax rotation, three factors emerged. Combined, these factors accounted for 44% of total item variation and mirrored the item content of the three factors obtained from the shorter SOCRATES version. Factor 1, Recognition, consisted of all of the 8 determination items and 6 of the 7 precontemplation items. Three items from other scales (but not from the 19-item version) loaded on Factor 1 (maintenance: 25, 5 and contemplation: 12). Factor 2 (Taking Steps) consisted of the 8 action items and 4 of the 8 maintenance items. No items from other scales loaded on this second factor. Finally, the third factor, Ambivalence, consisted of 4 of the 8 contemplation items.

The SOCRATES scales also appear to measure three constructs with relatively little overlap. Ambivalence was unrelated to Recognition (r = .03) and Taking Steps (r = .03). Recognition and Taking Steps were positively and modestly related (r = .33).

Do the motivational dimensions measured by the SOCRATES covary with baseline measures of problem severity? Table 5 shows correlations of the SOCRATES scales with three alcohol consumption variables (total standard drinks consumed, number of drinks per drinking day, and total abstinent days in the 90 days before the most recent drink) and five problem scales derived from the Alcohol Use Inventory (Horn et al., 1987). The strongest correlations, reflecting up to 15% common variance, suggest a positive relationship between problem severity and Recognition.

At the Albuquerque MATCH site only, the complete 40-item SOCRATES was administered. A total of 216 (96%) participants answered all 40 items. These 159 (74%) male and 57 (26%) female participants reported a mean age of 33.2 years. Self-reported ethnicity was White non-

TABLE 5
Pearson Correlations Among Three SOCRATES Scales and Selected Intake Measures of Alcohol Consumption and Five Alcohol Problem Scales in the AUI

Intake measure	SOCRATES Scale		
	Ambivalence	Recognition	Taking Steps
Total SDU	−.03	.23	.11
Drinks per drinking day	−.10	.26	.15
Proportion abstinent days	−.06	−.06	−.04
AUI			
Loss of control	−.12	.39	.14
Role maladaptation	−.14	.29	.12
Delirium	−.12	.24	.08
Hangover	−.13	.31	.09
Marital	.02	.13	.04

Note. Correlations > .07 were statistically significant at $p < .001$. $N = 1,672$. SOCRATES = Stages of Change Readiness and Treatment Eagerness Scale; SDU = standard drink unit; AUI = Alcohol Use Inventory.

Hispanic for 48%, with 44% Hispanic, 1% Black, and 7% other (primarily Native American). Computing correlations between scale scores for the 39-item and 19-item versions, we found $r = .88$ for Ambivalence, .96 for Recognition, and .94 for Taking Steps. The strong comparability reflected here, the small differences in alphas for the two versions, and the cleaner factor structure with 19 items all indicated that the shorter SOCRATES may be preferable and adequately samples the underlying constructs.

Study 2

Participants in the cross-site reliability study were 65 male and 17 female, with a mean age of 30.7 years and 13.9 years of education. Many had been treated for alcohol problems ($M = 1.7$ times). By self-identified ethnicity, 53 were White non-Hispanic, 16 Hispanic, 3 African American, 7 Native American, and 4 of other identification.

The internal consistency of SOCRATES scales in the Study 2 sample ($N = 82$) is shown in Table 6. The excluded Item 6 was unrelated to any of the three factors in this sample, which consists of participants who were not presenting for treatment but had agreed to participate in a test–retest reliability study of assessment instruments. It is sensible, therefore, that they would deny that "the only reason I'm here is that somebody made me come." This finding further supported our decision to exclude Item 6 from the R scale. Test–retest reliabilities for the 19-item SOCRATES are also shown in Table 6. The intraclass correlations ranged from .82 to .94,

TABLE 6
Test−Retest Estimates of Reliability and Internal Item Consistency

SOCRATES scale	ICC	r	Cronbach α	
			Test	Retest
Ambivalence	.82	.83	.88	.87
Recognition	.94	.99	.95	.95
Taking Steps	.91	.93	.95	.96

Note. N = 82. ICC = intraclass correlation; SOCRATES = Stages of Change Readiness and Treatment Eagerness Scale.

not substantially smaller than the corresponding Pearson *r* values, reflecting excellent test−retest explicability.

Table 7 reports distributional characteristics for the scales of the 19-item version of the SOCRATES at initial testing and at retesting 2 days later. Although test−retest replicability was high as reported above, we observed a significant increase in mean Recognition scores at the second administration. A plausible explanation is a reactive effect of the first testing, in that assessment alone may raise problem awareness and alter drinking behavior (Bien, Miller, & Tonigan, 1993).

DISCUSSION

The findings of these two studies indicate that the SOCRATES yields three reliable, continuously distributed, and relatively orthogonal scales

TABLE 7
Distributional Characteristics of Test−Retest SOCRATES Scales

SOCRATES scale	Test	Retest	p^a
Ambivalence			
M	10.49	9.83	.04
SD	5.11	4.72	
Skewness	.22	.49	
Kurtosis	−1.16	−.90	
Recognition			
M	16.93	19.86	.00
SD	9.71	10.84	
Skewness	.27	.31	
Kurtosis	−1.64	−1.61	
Taking Steps			
M	25.28	25.38	.82
SD	10.57	10.24	
Skewness	−.05	−.13	
Kurtosis	−1.32	−1.28	

Note. N = 82. SOCRATES = Stages of Change Readiness and Treatment Eagerness Scale.
[a]*p* values derived from two tailed test−retest paired *t* tests.

that are replicable in a 2-day test–retest situation. The shorter 19-item form provides scores that converge well with the results of the longer version, and given its greater simplicity and clearer factor structure we recommend use of the 19-item version in further applications. Internal consistency was lowest for the Ambivalence scale, although its test–retest replicability was sound. This scale lagged behind the others in internal consistency across five versions of the instrument and may reflect an inherent difficulty of measuring ambivalence directly (rather than as a balance of pros and cons). In our clinical sample, scale alphas ranged from .60 to .85, not dissimilar from the findings of DiClemente and Hughes (1990) with URICA scales in a population seeking treatment for alcohol problems (.69 to .82). In our test–retest sample, alphas ranged from .87 to .96, perhaps inflated by the smaller sample size. Mean Recognition and Taking Steps scores were higher in the treatment-seeking (Study 1) sample, and the variance on all scales was markedly higher in Study 2 (cf. Tables 3 and 7). Psychometric characteristics of instruments are affected by a truncated range, and from this perspective SOCRATES also appears to be reliable with nonclinical samples containing a wide range of states of readiness and change efforts.

There are some inherent limitations in using a clinical sample to develop and norm measures of motivation. Clearly individuals presenting for treatment are not representative of self-perceptions within a general population. The decile rankings provided here cannot be used to judge an individual's status relative to drinkers in general. Samples used throughout the development of SOCRATES were heavy drinkers seen in clinical settings, primarily because this is the population for whom the SOCRATES was originally intended. It is quite possible, however, that this instrument would show a different structure and alter relationships with other variables in a more heterogeneous sample.

It is also important to note that the SOCRATES does not provide a comprehensive assessment of all possible motivational vectors. It most directly samples the person's recognition of drinking problems, ambivalence or uncertainty about drinking, and taking steps to change. Other potentially important motivational factors are not directly queried in SOCRATES, such as self-efficacy, outcome expectancies, specific pros and cons of change, and social support for drinking or abstinence.

SOCRATES scores may be useful for a variety of clinical and research purposes. We have provided clients with feedback of their scores, as a starting point for discussion of their motivation for change (Miller, Zweben, DiClemente, & Rychtarik, 1992). Changes in SOCRATES scores could reflect the impact of an intervention on problem recognition, ambivalence, and taking steps toward change. Baseline values may also be predictive of compliance with change efforts. Luckie (1994) found that SOCRATES scores (summing C + D scales of Version 4.0 to produce an *awareness* measure) predicted whether Veterans Affairs patients who were notified of their at-risk drinking returned for a check-up evaluation. SOCRATES variables may also be helpful in combination with other measures to better understand the structure of motivation and readiness for change. Curtin, Stephens, and Greaves (1992) found in a college sample that after severity of use and problems had been taken into account, a measure of benefits (pros) of change in drinking was negatively related to P, modestly and positively related to C and D, and more strongly and positively related to A and M scales of SOCRATES 4.0. With these factors and self-efficacy taken into account, a measure of the perceived costs (cons) of change was positively related only to the C scale, consistent with its intent to measure ambivalence (both pros and cons).

We are continuing research and development with the SOCRATES instrument. Sums of scales may be useful, as may profile analyses of clients' score patterns. Parallel forms have been developed for assessing motivation to change other drug use and for evaluating the motivation of significant others to participate in efforts to change the alcohol or other drug use of a loved one. (Current SOCRATES forms are available on request from William R. Miller and J. Scott Tonigan.) Further research will focus on the ability of SOCRATES scales to predict change efforts and outcomes.

REFERENCES

Beckman, L. J. (1980). An attributional analysis of Alcoholics Anonymous. *Journal of Studies on Alcohol, 41*, 714–726.

Bien, T. H., Miller, W. R., & Tonigan, J. S. (1993). Brief interventions for alcohol problems: A review. *Addiction, 88*, 315–336.

Brown, J. M., & Miller, W. R. (1993). Impact of motivational interviewing on participation and outcome in residential alcoholism treatment. *Psychology of Addictive Behaviors, 7*, 211–218.

Clancy, J. (1961). Procrastination: A defense against sobriety. *Quarterly Journal of Studies on Alcohol, 22*, 269–276.

Clancy, J. (1964). Motivation conflicts of the alcohol addict. *Quarterly Journal of Studies on Alcohol, 25*, 511–520.

Cox, W. M., Klinger, E., & Blount, J. P. (1991). Alcohol use and goal hierarchies: Systematic motivational counseling for alcoholics. In W. R. Miller & S. Rollnick (Eds.), *Motivational interviewing: Preparing people to change addictive behavior* (pp. 260–271). New York: Guilford Press.

Curtin, L., Stephens, R. S., & Greaves, C. K. (1992, November). *Relative utility of self-efficacy and outcome expectancies in predicting readiness of change in drinking behavior.* Paper presented at the annual meeting of the Association for Advancement of Behavior Therapy, Boston, MA.

Dean, S. I. (1958). Treatment of the reluctant client. *American Psychologist, 13*, 627–630.

Del Boca, F. K., & Brown, J. M. (1996). Issues in the development of reliable measures in addictions research: Introduction to Project MATCH assessment strategies. *Psychology of Addictive Behaviors, 10*, 67–74.

DiCicco, L., Unterberger, H., & Mack, J. E. (1978). Confronting denial: An alcoholism intervention strategy. *Psychiatric Annals, 8*, 596–606.

DiClemente, C. C., & Hughes, S. O. (1990). Stages of change profiles in outpatient alcoholism treatment. *Journal of Substance Abuse, 2*, 217–235.

Heather, N., Rollnick, S., & Bell, A. (1993). Predictive validity of the Readiness to Change Questionnaire. *Addiction, 88*, 1667–1677.

Horn, J. L., Wanberg, K. W., & Foster, F. M. (1987). *Guide to the Alcohol Use Inventory (AUI)*. Minneapolis, MN: National Computer Systems.

Isenhart, C. E. (1994). Motivational subtypes in an inpatient sample of substance abusers. *Addictive Behaviors, 19*, 463–475.

Janis, I. L., & Mann, L. (1977). *Decision-making: A psychological analysis of conflict, choice, and commitment*. New York: Free Press.

Leake, G. J., & King, A. S. (1977). Effect of counselor expectations on alcoholic recovery. *Alcohol Health and Research World, 11*(3), 16–22.

Luckie, L. F. (1994). *Brief alcohol screening and intervention in a primary health care setting*. Unpublished doctoral dissertation, University of New Mexico.

Marlatt, G. A., & Gordon, J. R. (Eds.). (1985). *Relapse prevention*. New York: Guilford Press.

McConnaughy, E. A., Prochaska, J. O., & Velicer, W. F. (1983). Stages of change in psychotherapy: Measurement and sample profiles. *Psychotherapy: Theory, Research and Practice, 20*, 368–375.

Miller, W. R. (1985). Motivation for treatment: A review with special emphasis on alcoholism. *Psychological Bulletin, 98*, 84–107.

Miller, W. R., Benefield, R. G., & Tonigan, J. S. (1993). Enhancing motivation for change in problem drinking: A controlled comparison of two therapist styles. *Journal of Consulting and Clinical Psychology, 61*, 455–461.

Miller, W. R., Heather, N., & Hall, W. (1991). Calculating standard drink units: International comparisons. *British Journal of Addiction, 86*, 43–47.

Miller, W. R., & Marlatt, G. A. (1984). *Manual for the Comprehensive Drinker Profile*. Odessa, FL: Psychological Assessment Resources.

Miller, W. R., Meyers, R. J., Hester, R. K., Delaney, H., Montgomery, H. A., & Abbott, P. J. (1990a, February). *The effectiveness of the community reinforcement approach: Preliminary findings of a clinical replication trial*. Paper presented at the 5th International Conference on Treatment of Addictive Behaviours, Sydney, Australia.

Miller, W. R., & Rollnick, S. (1991). *Motivational interviewing: Preparing people to change addictive behavior*. New York Guilford Press.

Miller, W. R., Tonigan, J. S., Montgomery, H. A., Abbott, P. J., Meyers, R. J., Hester, R. K., & Delaney, H. D. (1990b, November). *Assessment of client motivation for change: Preliminary validation of the SOCRATES instrument.* Paper presented at the annual meeting of the Association for Advancement of Behavior Therapy, San Francisco.

Miller, W. R., Zweben, A., DiClemente, C. C., & Rychtarik, R. G. (1992). *Motivational Enhancement Therapy manual: A clinical research guide for therapists treating individuals with alcohol abuse and dependence* (Vol. 2, Project MATCH Monograph Series). Rockville, MD: National Institute on Alcohol Abuse and Alcoholism.

Moore, R. C., & Murphy, T. C. (1961). Denial of alcoholism as an obstacle to recovery. *Quarterly Journal of Studies on Alcohol, 22,* 597–609.

Morgan, T. J., Morgenstern, J., Blanchard, K., McCrady, B. S., & Langenbucher, J. (1995, May). *Assessing the factor structure of the SOCRATES with treatment and non-treatment seekers.* Paper presented at the 7th International Conference on Treatment of Addictive Behaviors, Leeuwenhorst, the Netherlands.

Prescott, P., & Børtveit, T. (1995, May). *Psychometric characteristics of SOCRATES, DrInC, and DrInC-R in a Norwegian outpatient clinic sample: How do they compare with other studies?* Paper presented at the 7th International Conference on Treatment of Addictive Behaviors, Leeuwenhorst, the Netherlands.

Prochaska, J. O., & DiClemente, C. C. (1982). Transtheoretical therapy: Toward a more integrative model of change. *Psychotherapy: Theory, Research, and Practice, 19,* 276–288.

Prochaska, J. O., & DiClemente, C. C. (1986). Toward a comprehensive model of change. In W. R. Miller & N. Heather (Eds.), *Treating addictive behaviors: Processes of change* (pp. 3–27). New York: Plenum Press.

Prochaska, J. O., & DiClemente, C. C. (1992). Stages of change in the modification of problem behaviors. *Progress in Behavior Modification, 28,* 183–218.

Prochaska, J. O., DiClemente, C. C., & Norcross, J. C. (1992). In search of how people change: Applications to addictive behaviors. *American Psychologist, 47,* 1102–1114.

Project MATCH Research Group. (1993). Project MATCH: Rationale and methods for a multisite clinical trial matching patients to alcoholism treatment. *Alcoholism: Clinical and Experimental Research, 17,* 1130–1145.

Rollnick, S., Heather, N., Gold, R., & Hall, W. (1992). Development of a short Readiness to Change Questionnaire for use in brief, opportunistic interventions among excessive drinkers. *British Journal of Addiction, 87,* 743–754.

Tabachnick, B. G., & Fidell, L. S. (1989). *Using multivariate statistics* (2nd ed.). New York: Harper & Row.

VII

DIAGNOSIS AND COMORBIDITY

15

PSYCHIATRIC COMORBIDITY, HEALTH STATUS, AND FUNCTIONAL IMPAIRMENT ASSOCIATED WITH ALCOHOL ABUSE AND DEPENDENCE IN PRIMARY CARE PATIENTS: FINDINGS OF THE PRIME MD-1000 STUDY

JEFFREY G. JOHNSON, ROBERT L. SPITZER, JANET B. W. WILLIAMS, KURT KROENKE, MARK LINZER, DAVID BRODY, FRANK deGRUY, AND STEVEN HAHN

A number of studies conducted in the past decade have established that alcohol abuse and dependence (AAD) are relatively common in primary care settings, affecting 3% to 20% of primary care patients (e.g., Buchsbaum, Buchanan, Lawton, & Schnoll, 1991; Cherpitel, 1991; Cleary

Reprinted from the *Journal of Consulting and Clinical Psychology*, 63, 133–140. (1995). Copyright © 1995 by the American Psychological Association. Used with permission of the author.

This research was supported in part by an unrestricted educational grant from Roerig and Pratt Pharmaceuticals, divisions of Pfizer, Inc. We acknowledge gratefully the valuable comments and suggestions provided by Deborah Hasin and the statistical assistance provided by Mark Davies during the preparation of this article.

373

et al., 1988; Coulehan, Zettler-Segal, Block, McClelland, & Schulberg, 1987; Cyr & Wartman, 1988; Hurt, Morse, & Swenson, 1980; Leckman, Umland, & Blay, 1984; Powers & Spickard, 1984; Rydon, Redman, Sanson-Fisher, & Reid, 1992; Von Korff et al., 1987). A substantial body of research has also demonstrated that primary care physicians fail to recognize the presence of AAD in between 33% and 90% of their patients who have these disorders (Borus, Howes, Devins, Rosenberg, & Livingston, 1988; Cleary et al., 1988; Coulehan et al., 1987; Leckman et al., 1984; Moore & Malitz, 1986; Reid, Webb, Hennrikus, Fahey, & Sanson-Fisher, 1986; Rydon et al., 1992; see Kamerow, Pincus, & Macdonald, 1986; Schulberg & Burns, 1988).

Insofar as chronic heavy alcohol consumption has been associated with increased risk for a number of life-threatening illnesses (Adams, Yuan, Barboriak, & Timm, 1993; Eckardt et al., 1981; Gorelick, 1990; Mendelson, Babor, Mello, & Pratt, 1986; Schultz, Rice, & Parker, 1990), it has been proposed that researchers should develop methods that may bring about increased recognition of AAD and other psychiatric disorders by primary care physicians (e.g., Cyr & Wartman, 1988; Schulberg, 1991). Improved recognition of AAD appears to be of particular importance because research has demonstrated that feedback and advice provided by physicians and nurses can contribute to significant reductions in problem drinking (e.g., Anderson, 1993; Anderson & Scott, 1992; Kristenson, Ohlin, Hulten-Nosslin, Trell, & Hood, 1983; see also Babor, Ritson, & Hodgson, 1986).

This article presents findings of the PRIME–MD 1000 study (Spitzer et al., 1992) regarding the psychiatric comorbidity, health status, and functional impairment of primary care patients diagnosed with AAD. The PRIME–MD 1000 study was conducted to validate and assess the clinical usefulness of a new diagnostic system, entitled Primary Care Evaluation of Mental Disorders" (PRIME–MD), that was developed for the purpose of facilitating the recognition of a range of psychiatric disorders, including AAD, by primary care physicians.

Although numerous studies have examined the prevalence and recognition of AAD in primary care settings, very little research has investigated the extent to which primary care patients with AAD suffer from comorbid psychiatric disorders, poor health, and impaired functioning (see Wells, Burnam, Benjamin, & Golding, 1990). The handful of studies that have addressed these issues in primary care settings have yielded conflicting findings; perhaps this is due in large measure to the use of different definitions and methodologies. Thus, whereas Buchan, Buckley, Deacon, Irvine, and Ryan (1981) reported that primary care patients who were problem drinkers had higher rates of mental and physical illness, as well as more social and marital problems than control-group patients,

Tracy, Gorman, and Leventhal (1992) reported conversely that drinkers reported fewer illness symptoms than patients who abstained from alcohol use.

Although previous research indicates that patients in alcohol treatment programs tend to suffer from substantial psychiatric comorbidity and functional impairment (e.g., Mendelson et al., 1986; Powell et al., 1992; Powell, Penick, Othmer, Bingham, & Rice, 1982; Ross, Glaser, & Germanson, 1988; Schuckit, 1985), it has not been established whether the same is true of the larger population of primary care patients with mild to moderate AAD. A major goal of the present research, therefore, was to assess the psychiatric comorbidity, health status, and functional impairment of primary care patients with AAD.

METHOD

Participants

The mean age of the 1,000 patients who participated in the PRIME–MD 1000 Study was 55 years ($SD = 16.5$), with a range of 18 to 91 years; 60% were female, 58% were White, and 28% were college graduates. The most common types of physical disorders were hypertension (48%), arthritis (23%), diabetes (17%), heart disease (15%), and pulmonary disease (8%). Study participants were selected from four academic medical center primary care clinics, each directed by one of the authors: New England Medical Center General Medical Associates (hospital-based group practice); Bronx Municipal Hospital Center, Albert Einstein College of Medicine (city hospital clinic); Walter Reed Army Medical Center General Medicine Clinic (for both active-duty and retired military personnel and their families); and the University of South Alabama College of Medicine (family practice clinic). Participants were excluded from the study if they failed to provide informed consent, were less than 16 years of age, or were too demented or physically ill to participate. The first 369 patients who were entered into the study were selected by convenience but independently of the participating physicians' knowledge or suspicion that a patient had any psychopathology. The remaining 631 participants were either consecutively selected (one site) or selected with a site-specific procedure to ensure random sampling. Within all four sites, the convenience sample and the randomly selected sample did not differ with respect to age, sex, ethnicity, education, level of functioning, health status, or frequency of PRIME–MD diagnoses. A more detailed description of the sample is provided by Spitzer et al. (1993).

Instruments

The PRIME–MD Diagnostic System

The PRIME–MD Diagnostic System (Spitzer et al., 1993, 1994) has two components: a one-page screening instrument referred to as the Patient Questionnaire (PQ), which is completed by the patient before seeing the physician, and a Clinician Evaluation Guide (CEG), which is a structured clinical interview administered by the physician to patients who give positive responses on the PQ. The CEG assesses patients for the five groups of mental disorders most commonly encountered in primary care settings: mood, anxiety, alcohol, eating, and somatoform disorders. The PQ includes 26 yes-or-no questions about symptoms and signs experienced during the past month, the following three of which are adapted from the CAGE alcohol screening questionnaire (Ewing, 1984): (a) Have you thought you should cut down on your use of alcohol? (b) Has anyone complained about your drinking? (c) Have you felt guilty or upset about your drinking? A fourth PQ alcohol screening question assesses heavy drinking by asking whether the patient has consumed five or more drinks on a single day during the past month. If any of the four alcohol screening items are checked yes (i.e., "the patient screens positive" for AAD), the physician administers the alcohol module of the CEG, beginning with open-ended follow-up questions about each of the endorsed PQ items to determine their clinical significance.

Next, five additional CEG questions are asked, addressing the maladaptive use of alcohol during the past 6 months in the following areas: (a) Continued alcohol use despite being told by a physician to stop drinking because of a health problem; (b) Repeated alcohol use, intoxication, or hangovers while working, going to school, or taking care of other important responsibilities; (c) Repeated missing of work, school, or other important responsibilities because of alcohol use or being hung over; (d) Repeated problems getting along with other people while using alcohol; (e) Repeated automobile driving after having consumed several drinks or drinking too much. "Probable alcohol abuse or dependence" is diagnosed if any of these five items is endorsed by the patient, or if the patient's responses to the follow-up questions indicate that the patient's alcohol use has caused clinically significant impairment or distress during the past 6 months. Whereas some CEG items assess symptoms of alcohol abuse in accordance with the *Diagnostic and Statistical Manual of Mental Disorders* (3rd ed., rev. [DSM–III–R]; American Psychiatric Association, 1987; 4th ed. [DSM–IV], American Psychiatric Association, 1993), and others assess symptoms of alcohol dependence, the PRIME–MD system does not yield a differential diagnosis of alcohol abuse and alcohol dependence. Furthermore, the diagnosis is considered "probable" because further information may in some cases be needed to confirm the diagnosis.

In an assessment of the validity of PRIME–MD diagnoses, a subset of 431 patients, selected regardless of their screening and diagnostic status on the PQ and CEG, were reinterviewed by mental health professionals who were not informed of the PRIME–MD diagnostic findings, using a telephone-administered semistructured psychiatric interview. Reinterview by telephone was used because of its convenience and demonstrated similarity to the findings of face-to-face research interviews (Potts, Daniels, Burnam, & Wells, 1990; Wells, Burnam, Leake, & Robins, 1988). To permit assessment of the diagnostic criteria for the disorders assessed by physicians with the CEG, the telephone interview included the same diagnostic criteria used in the alcohol, anxiety, eating, and mood CEG modules. In addition, several open-ended questions from the Structured Clinical Interview for DSM–III–R (SCID; Spitzer, Williams, Gibbon, & First, 1992) were also included so as to permit assessment of psychopathology not elicited by the briefer and more structured CEG. Furthermore, as in the standard administration of the SCID, the mental health interviewer was encouraged to ask follow-up questions to clarify ambiguous responses to structured interview items.

Findings generally supported the validity of physician diagnoses obtained using the PRIME–MD system. The specificity and overall predictive power of physician diagnoses were consistently high for specific diagnoses, ranging from .84 to .99. Agreement between physician and mental health professional diagnoses, although modest, approximated the levels of agreement among mental health professionals using structured diagnostic interviews. With regard to AAD, a pairwise kappa of .71 was obtained between physician and mental health professional diagnoses, indicating good chance-corrected agreement. The sensitivity, specificity, and overall accuracy of physician AAD diagnoses using the PRIME–MD system were .81, .98, and .98 respectively, with physicians failing to detect the presence of AAD in 3 patients who were diagnosed with AAD by the mental health professionals and diagnosing AAD in 7 patients who were not diagnosed with AAD by the mental health professionals. The construct validity of the PRIME–MD diagnostic system was also supported by findings that patients who were diagnosed using the PRIME–MD system reported impaired functioning, as well as elevated health care utilization, in comparison with patients who did not receive PRIME–MD diagnoses. Furthermore, the concurrent validity of PRIME–MD was supported by strong relationships that were obtained between PRIME–MD diagnoses of mood, anxiety, and somatoform disorders and corresponding patient self-rated severity scales.

The Medical Outcomes Study Short Form General Health Survey (SF–20)

The SF–20 (Stewart, Hays, & Ware, 1988) is a 20-item self-report questionnaire that assesses six dimensions of health-related quality of life (physical, social, and role functioning, mental health, bodily pain, and general health perceptions). Scores on all six SF–20 scales range from 0 to 100, with higher scores indicating better health and less functional impairment; a 5-point reduction in SF–20 scale scores is generally considered clinically significant. Considerable support for the reliability and validity of the SF–20 has been reported (e.g., Nelson et al., 1983; Read, Quinn, & Hoefer, 1987; Stewart et al., 1988; Stewart et al., 1989).

Procedure

After providing informed consent, all 1,000 patients completed the PQ; 877 patients completed the SF–20. Then, before they examined each patient's responses to the PQ, participating physicians recorded how well they knew the patient on a 3-point scale ranging from *not at all well* (1) to *fairly well* (3), and whether they already knew that the patient was currently suffering from AAD or any other PRIME–MD mental disorder. Next, physicians examined the PQ and administered the CEG to all of their patients who screened positive on the PQ. One hundred twenty-four of the 1,000 patients (71% male; mean age = 49.9) gave affirmative responses to one or more PQ alcohol screening items and were thus administered the CEG alcohol module. After completing the CEG, participating physicians recorded all of the current health problems experienced by the patient, as well as their ratings of the patient's physical health on a 5-point scale ranging from (1) *excellent* to (5) *poor*.

RESULTS

Prevalence and Physician Recognition of Alcohol Abuse and Dependence (AAD)

Of the one hundred twenty-four patients who responded affirmatively to one or more PQ screening items, 51 (72% male; mean age = 53.4) were diagnosed by their physicians with AAD on the basis of the information obtained using the CEG. Thus, the overall prevalence of AAD in this sample was 5%, with specific prevalences of 10% in male patients and 2% in female patients. The mean age of the patients diagnosed with AAD was 53.4 years, which did not differ significantly from the mean age of 55.3 years for the remainder of the sample, $t(962) = 0.78$, $p > .05$.

A positive association was obtained between the number of PQ alcohol items endorsed by patients and the likelihood of an AAD diagnosis being assigned. Thus, whereas 16 of the 75 patients (21%) who endorsed a single PQ alcohol item were diagnosed with AAD, 20 of the 33 patients (61%) who endorsed two PQ alcohol items and 15 of the 16 patients

(94%) who endorsed three or four PQ alcohol items were diagnosed with AAD. The four PQ alcohol screening items varied substantially with regard to their sensitivity (se), specificity (sp), and positive predictive power (ppp): (PQ item 1) "Have you thought you should cut down on your use of alcohol?" (se = .76, sp = .96; ppp = .53); (PQ item 2) "Has anyone complained about your drinking?" (se = .39, sp = .99; ppp = .91); (PQ item 3) "Have you felt guilty or upset about your drinking?" (se = .33, sp = .99; ppp = .77); (PQ item 4) "Was there ever a single day in which you had five or more drinks of beer, wine, or liquor?" (se = .62, sp = .95; ppp = .41).

Of the 36 patients who were diagnosed with AAD and who were known "somewhat" or "fairly well" by their physicians, only 21 (58%) had been identified by their physicians as having a current alcohol problem before the administration of the PRIME–MD system. Insofar as 15 new cases of AAD were thus identified using PRIME–MD as a standard, the PRIME–MD system brought about a 71% increase in the recognition of AAD among patients who had some previous relationship with their physicians.

Psychiatric Comorbidity

Table 1 presents the prevalence rates, odds ratios, and results of chi-square tests with regard to the distribution of each disorder diagnosed using the PRIME–MD system in the 51 patients diagnosed with probable alcohol abuse or dependence, in comparison with the remaining 949 patients. Patients with AAD had substantial psychiatric comorbidity, with 47% receiving one or more additional PRIME–MD diagnoses; 33%, 22%, 6%, and 14% of patients with AAD were diagnosed with mood, anxiety, eating, and somatoform disorders, respectively. However, the psychiatric comorbidity rate associated with AAD was somewhat less than the comorbidity rates associated with mood (65%), anxiety (82%), eating (84%), and somatoform (73%) disorders. Of the 949 patients who were not diagnosed with AAD, 35% received one or more PRIME–MD diagnoses, with 26%, 18%, 3%, and 14% diagnosed with mood, anxiety, eating, and somatoform disorders, respectively. Odds ratios and chi-square tests were computed to determine whether patients with AAD would have an elevated likelihood of receiving each of the specific PRIME–MD diagnoses. Odds ratios (OR) are defined as the odds that a case (of AAD) will be diagnosed with a given disorder, divided by the odds that a control (non-AAD patient) will be so diagnosed. A Bonferroni correction procedure was implemented to control for the probability that multiple comparisons would inflate the likelihood of a Type II error, with a resulting alpha level of .002. Results were that, although the 51 patients with AAD tended to have somewhat higher prevalences of mood, anxiety, and eating disorders than the 949

TABLE 1
Prevalence and Odds Ratios for PRIME-MD Psychiatric Disorders in Patients Diagnosed With AAD, in Comparison With Patients Not Diagnosed With AAD

PRIME-MD disorder	Prevalence (%) in AAD patients ($n = 51$)	Prevalence (%) in all other patients ($n = 949$)	Odds ratio	χ^2	p
Any PRIME-MD disorder	47.1	35.2	1.64	2.91	.0881
Any mood disorder	33.3	25.5	1.46	1.50	.2204
MDD	21.6	11.0	2.23	5.35	.0207
With dysthymia	3.9	5.8	0.66	0.32	.5739
Without dysthymia	17.6	5.2	3.94	13.81	.0002
Recurrence or partial remission of MDD	5.9	6.2	0.94	0.02	.8997
Dysthymia	3.9	8.0	0.47	1.12	.2890
Minor depression	3.9	6.5	0.58	0.55	.4579
Any anxiety disorder	21.6	17.5	1.30	1.21	.2722
Generalized anxiety disorder	5.9	7.1	0.82	0.10	.7481
Panic disorder	3.9	3.6	1.10	0.02	.8993
Anxiety disorder NOS	11.8	8.7	1.39	1.47	.2261
Any somatoform disorder	13.7	13.9	0.98	0.00	.9705
Hypochondriasis	2.0	2.2	0.88	0.01	.9048
Multisomatoform disorder	9.8	8.1	1.23	0.18	.6682
Somatoform pain disorder	0.0	0.8	—	0.43	.5103
Somatoform disorder NOS	3.9	4.2	0.93	0.01	.9190
Any eating disorder	5.9	3.1	1.98	1.25	.2639
Binge eating disorder	5.9	2.8	2.13	1.53	.2155
Bulimia	0.0	0.1	—	0.05	.8166
Eating disorder NOS	0.0	0.1	—	0.05	.8166

Note. Dashes indicate that the odds ratio could not be computed, because of empty cells. PRIME-MD = Primary Care Evaluation of Mental Disorders; AAD = alcohol abuse or dependence; MDD = major depressive disorder; NOS = not otherwise specified.

patients without AAD, only in the case of major depressive disorder without dysthymia was this difference statistically significant (OR = 3.94), $x^2(1, N = 1000) = 13.81, p < .0005$.

Health and Functional Status of Patients With AAD

A series of seven analyses of variance (ANOVAs) were conducted, to compare the health and functional status of primary care patients with AAD with that of two other patient groups: (a) patients with no psychiatric disorders and (b) patients with other psychiatric disorders. As Table 2 indicates, significant overall differences on all six SF–20 scales were obtained among the three groups, with the mean scores of the AAD group in all instances intermediate between the scores of the no-diagnosis group and the other psychiatric diagnosis group. Post hoc Scheffé pairwise comparisons revealed that patients with AAD had significantly lower SF–20 scores, indicating poorer functioning, than patients who had no psychiatric diagnoses on five of the six SF–20 scales, but also revealed that AAD patients had significantly higher scores than patients with other psychiatric diagnoses on four SF–20 scales. Identical findings were obtained when analyses of covariance (ANCOVAs) were conducted, controlling for the effects of age, educational status, minority status, number of types of physical disorders, and site. A seventh ANOVA, conducted to compare physicians' health ratings of patients in these three groups was also statistically significant, $F(2, 988) = 51.73$, $p < .0001$. Scheffé post hoc pairwise comparisons revealed that physicians rated the health of patients with no psychiatric disorders ($M = 2.30$, $SD = 0.96$) as significantly better than that of both patients with AAD ($M = 2.86$, $SD = 1.14$) and patients with other psychiatric disorders ($M = 2.94$; $SD = 0.90$).

To determine whether the intermediate health and functional status of AAD patients was associated with the presence or absence of psychiatric comorbidity in these patients, a series of seven ANOVAs was conducted. The following specific research questions were addressed by means of these analyses: (a) Do the health and functional status of AAD patients with

TABLE 2
SF-20 Scores of Patients With AAD, Other PRIME-MD Diagnoses, and No PRIME-MD Diagnoses

	Diagnostic status					
	Patients with no psychiatric diagnoses ($n = 544$)		AAD patients ($n = 44$)		Patients with other psychiatric diagnoses ($n = 289$)	
Variable[a]	M	SD	M	SD	M	SD
Physical functioning	77.8	24.4	67.6	29.5[b]	58.7	27.5[b]
Social functioning	89.3	22.1	76.6	28.4[b]	68.4	33.2[b]
Role functioning	85.0	32.8	68.1	44.8[b,c]	51.7	45.4[b]
Mental health	80.8	13.4	70.3	20.6[b,c]	56.2	20.0[b]
Bodily pain	67.1	26.2	59.1	29.5[c]	44.0	24.9[b]
General health perceptions	65.4	24.0	51.2	27.7[b,c]	38.9	23.5[b]

Note. SF-20 = Medical Outcomes Study Short Form General Health Survey; AAD = alcohol abuse or dependence; PRIME-MD = Primary Care Evaluation of Mental Disorders.
[a]Statistically significant analysis of variance ($p < .001$). [b]Significantly different from no-psychiatric-diagnoses group (Scheffé post hoc test). [c]Significantly different from other-psychiatric-diagnoses group (Scheffé post hoc test).

co-occurring psychiatric disorders tend to differ from those of patients without any psychiatric disorders? (b) Do the health and functional status of AAD patients without co-occurring psychiatric disorders tend to differ from those of patients without any psychiatric disorders? and (c) Do the health and functional status of AAD patients with co-occurring psychiatric disorders tend to differ from those of AAD patients without co-occurring psychiatric disorders?

As Table 3 indicates, the results of these ANOVAs were that significant overall differences were obtained between the three groups on all six SF–20 scales. Post hoc Scheffé pairwise comparisons revealed that AAD patients without psychiatric comorbidity did not differ with respect to health and functional status from patients who had no psychiatric disorders. By contrast, AAD patients with one or more co-occurring psychiatric disorders had significantly lower scores than patients who had no psychiatric diagnoses on all six SF–20 scales and had lower scores than AAD patients without psychiatric comorbidity on five SF–20 scales. Identical findings were obtained when ANCOVAs were conducted, controlling for the effects of age, educational status, minority status, number of types of physical disorders, and site. A seventh ANOVA, conducted to compare physicians' health ratings of patients in these three groups, was also statistically significant, $F(2, 655) = 14.49$, $p < .0001$. Scheffé post hoc pairwise comparisons revealed that physicians rated the health of AAD patients with psychiatric comorbidity ($M = 3.38$, $SD = 0.97$) as significantly poorer than

TABLE 3
SF-20 Scores of AAD Patients With and Without Psychiatric Comorbidity and of Patients With No Psychiatric Diagnoses

	Diagnostic status					
	Patients with no psychiatric diagnoses ($n = 544$)		AAD patients without psychiatric comorbidity ($n = 24$)		AAD patients with psychiatric comorbidity ($n = 20$)	
Variable[a]	M	SD	M	SD	M	SD
Physical functioning	77.8	24.4	76.9	24.5	56.0	31.5[b,c]
Social functioning	89.3	22.1	86.9	21.1	63.8	31.4[b,c]
Role functioning	85.0	32.8	80.8	37.6	52.4	48.7[b,c]
Mental health	80.8	13.4	85.8	9.1	51.8	14.2[b,c]
Bodily pain	67.1	26.2	65.8	30.9	51.4	26.5[b]
General health perceptions	65.4	24.0	66.5	22.3	32.8	22.1[b,c]

Note. SF-20 = Medical Outcomes Study Short Form General Health Survey; AAD = alcohol abuse or dependence.
[a]Statistically significant analysis of variance (ANOVA), $p < .001$. For bodily pain, ANOVA was statistically significant, $p < .05$. [b]Significantly different from patients with no psychiatric diagnoses (Scheffé post hoc test). [c]Significantly different from AAD patients without psychiatric comorbidity (Scheffé post hoc test).

that of both AAD patients without psychiatric comorbidity (M = 2.38, SD = 1.09) and patients with no psychiatric disorders (M = 2.30, SD = 0.96).

It was also of interest to determine whether AAD patients with co-occurring psychiatric disorders differed with respect to health and functional status from patients without AAD who were diagnosed with other psychiatric disorders. A series of six t tests were thus conducted to compare the SF–20 scores of these groups. The results were that the two groups did not differ on the SF–20 scales for physical functioning, $t(277) = 0.44$, $p > .05$; social functioning, $t(277) = 1.13$, $p > .05$; role functioning, $t(277) = 0.06$, $p > .05$; mental health, $t(277) = 1.00$, $p > .05$; bodily pain, $t(277) = 1.31$, $p > .05$; or general health perceptions, $t(277) = 1.13$, $p > .05$. The means and standard deviations for the two groups are presented in the third columns of Tables 1 and 2. Results of a seventh t test indicated that physicians rated the health of AAD patients with psychiatric comorbidity (M = 3.38, SD = 0.97) as somewhat poorer, $t(355) = 2.28$, $p = .023$, than that of patients without AAD who were diagnosed with other psychiatric disorders (M = 2.94, SD = 0.90), although this difference failed to attain statistical significance when a Bonferroni procedure was used to adjust for the effects of multiple comparisons on the probability of producing a Type I error, which resulted in an alpha level of .007.

Finally, a t test was conducted to determine whether AAD patients with psychiatric comorbidity would report more alcohol-related problems than AAD patients without psychiatric comorbidity. The results were that AAD patients with psychiatric comorbidity reported a mean of 3.79 alcohol-related problems on the PQ and CEG (SD = 1.82), whereas AAD patients without psychiatric comorbidity reported a mean of 2.89 alcohol-related problems on the PQ and CEG (SD = 1.09). This difference was statistically significant, $t(49) = 2.18$, $p < .025$.

DISCUSSION

The principal findings of the present research were as follows: (a) Use of the PRIME–MD diagnostic system brought about a 71% increase in physician recognition of AAD. (b) Although nearly half of the 51 patients diagnosed with AAD had co-occurring psychiatric disorders, patients with AAD had fewer co-occurring psychiatric disorders than did patients with mood, anxiety, eating, and somatoform disorders. (c) Furthermore, although patients with AAD reported poorer health and greater functional impairment than did patients without any psychiatric disorders, they reported less impairment than did patients who were diagnosed with other psychiatric disorders. (d) Only those AAD patients who had one or more co-occurring psychiatric disorders reported poorer health and greater functional impairment than that of patients without any psychiatric disorders.

The present findings are consistent with previous findings indicating that primary care patients with AAD are likely to suffer from substantial psychiatric comorbidity and to have poorer health and greater functional impairment than primary care patients with no psychiatric diagnoses (e.g., Buchan et al., 1981). The present findings are also consistent with previous reports that individuals with AAD in the general population are at elevated risk for the presence of co-occurring psychiatric disorders (e.g., Regier et al., 1990). However, the present findings also indicate that primary care patients with AAD may tend to have fewer co-occurring psychiatric disorders, better health, and less functional impairment than patients with a range of other psychiatric disorders. Furthermore, the present findings suggest that those primary care patients with AAD who have one or more co-occurring psychiatric disorders may be substantially more likely to suffer from poor health and functional impairment than primary care patients with AAD who do not have any co-occurring psychiatric disorders.

It is noteworthy that Powell et al. (1992) have reported, similarly, that inpatients in an alcoholism treatment program who had one or more co-occurring psychiatric disorders reported greater distress and more alcohol-related problems than inpatients in the same treatment program who had no co-occurring psychiatric disorders, although other research has demonstrated that individuals under treatment for alcoholism tend to have poor health and impaired functioning regardless of psychiatric comorbidity (e.g., Mendelson et al., 1986; Ross et al., 1988; Schuckit, 1985). Insofar as the health and functional status of individuals in the general population with AAD has not yet been well investigated (Wells et al., 1990), it will be important for further research to determine whether the present findings, as well as those of Powell et al. (1992), will be confirmed in samples of individuals with AAD who are not currently under treatment for alcoholism.

It is possible that the widespread belief that people identified as problem drinkers typically suffer from poor health, impaired functioning, or both has resulted in part from a clinician's illusion effect (Cohen & Cohen, 1984), whereby conclusions derived from the study of severely disturbed patients—who are most frequently seen in treatment settings—are generalized to patients with less severe conditions (see Rogers et al., 1993; Stewart et al., 1993). Consistent with this hypothesis, Corrigan et al. (1986) have reported that patients in general hospital medical wards who were identified as suffering from alcoholism were less severely dependent on alcohol than a comparison group of patients, diagnosed with alcoholism, who were admitted for treatment to a psychiatric hospital. Further research should therefore evaluate the short- and long-term consequences of mild, moderate, and severe forms of AAD on health and daily functioning.

A substantial proportion of patients with current drinking problems have only mild to moderate symptoms of alcoholism (e.g., Powers & Spickard, 1984; Robins & Regier, 1991). As noted earlier, the present findings indicate that primary care AAD patients without co-occurring psychiatric disorders—who have relatively mild cases of AAD—may tend to have relatively few health problems and little functional impairment, compared with primary care patients who have no psychiatric disorders. It is noteworthy that problem drinking tends to be a transient condition that often leads to spontaneous remission (e.g., Hasin, Grant, & Endicott, 1990) and that individuals often cease or moderate their drinking when they become aware that they are suffering from the negative consequences of alcohol abuse (see Tracy et al., 1992; Wells et al., 1990). Nonetheless, because AAD is often a progressive condition that ultimately produces deleterious health consequences (e.g., Hasin et al., 1990; Schuckit, Smith, Anthenelli, & Irwin, 1993), it is clear that physicians should advise all such patients to cease or moderate their consumption of alcohol.

Fortunately, research has demonstrated that, by providing problem drinkers with information and brief counseling regarding the risks associated with continued heavy drinking, health professionals can contribute to significant reductions in their patients' alcohol consumption (e.g., Anderson, 1993; Anderson & Scott, 1992; Babor et al., 1986; Kristenson et al., 1983). The efficacy of such interventions may be due in part to resultant increases in patients' awareness that they are suffering from the effects of alcohol abuse (see Tracy et al., 1992; Wells et al., 1990). However, increased AAD intervention in primary care settings will be predicated on improved physician recognition of AAD (see Schulberg, 1991). Like the findings of previous researchers (e.g., Cleary et al., 1988; Cyr & Wartman, 1988; Leckman et al., 1984; Rydon et al., 1992), our findings demonstrate that routine screening can contribute to substantial increases in physician recognition of AAD in primary care settings. By enabling physicians to evaluate and diagnose AAD as well as other treatable psychiatric disorders, the PRIME–MD diagnostic system provides physicians with detailed information that can be used to facilitate intervention efforts.

Interpretation of the present findings should take into account some important considerations. Our finding that AAD patients who had no co-occurring psychiatric disorders did not suffer from significantly impaired health and functioning does not appear to be an artifact brought about by a large number of false-positive diagnoses, for two reasons: (a) the AAD prevalence rate of 5% for this study was relatively low in comparison with other studies that have reported AAD prevalence rates in primary care settings as high as 20% (e.g., Cyr & Wartman, 1988) and (b) AAD diagnoses obtained using the PRIME–MD diagnostic system had a very high specificity (.98) when compared with diagnoses of the same patients made by mental health professionals, indicating that participating physicians were unlikely to have made many false-positive diagnoses of AAD. It is also important to note that the PRIME–MD diagnostic system, developed for the purpose of facilitating rapid diagnostic evaluation in primary care settings, does not provide exhaustive evaluations of alcohol abuse or dependence. Clearly, somewhat different findings might have been obtained if the CEG, as well as lengthy structured clinical interviews focusing in greater detail on alcohol-related problems, had been administered to all 1,000 patients by experienced mental health professionals. Furthermore, the possibility cannot be ruled out that a number of patients reporting clinically significant alcohol abuse were not identified by means of the PRIME–MD system. Therefore, further investigations will need to be conducted so that the questions addressed by the present research might be more conclusively studied.

REFERENCES

Adams, W. L., Yuan, Z., Barboriak, J. J., & Rimm, A. A. (1993). Alcohol-related hospitalizations of elderly people: Prevalence and geographic variation in the United States. *Journal of the American Medical Association, 270,* 1222–1225.

American Psychiatric Association. (1987). *Diagnostic and statistical manual of mental disorders* (3rd ed., rev.). Washington, DC: Author.

American Psychiatric Association. (1993). *Diagnostic and Statistical Manual of Mental Disorders* (4th ed.). Washington, DC: Author.

Anderson, P. (1993). Management of alcohol problems: The role of the general practitioner. *Alcohol & Alcoholism, 28,* 263–272.

Anderson, P., & Scott, E. (1992). The effect of general practitioners' advice to heavy drinking men. *British Journal of Addiction, 87,* 891–900.

Babor, T. F., Ritson, E. B., & Hodgson, R. J. (1986). Alcohol-related problems in the primary health care setting: A review of early intervention strategies. *British Journal of Addiction, 81,* 23–46.

Borus, J. F., Howes, M. J., Devins, N. P., Rosenberg, R., & Livingston, W. W. (1988). Primary health care providers' recognition and diagnosis of mental disorders in their patients. *General Hospital Psychiatry, 10,* 317–321.

Buchan, I. C., Buckley, E. G., Deacon, G. L. S., Irvine, R., & Ryan, M. P. (1981). Problem drinkers and their problems. *Journal of the Royal College of General Practitioners, 31,* 151–153.

Buchsbaum, D. G., Buchanan, R. G., Lawton, M. J., & Schnoll, S. H. (1991). Alcohol consumption patterns in a primary care population. *Alcohol & Alcoholism, 26,* 215–220.

Cherpitel, C. J. S. (1991). Drinking patterns and problems among primary care patients: A comparison with the general population. *Alcohol & Alcoholism, 26,* 627–633.

Cleary, P. D., Miller, M., Bush, B. T., Warburg, M. M., Delbanco, T. L., & Aronson, M. D. (1988). Prevalence and recognition of alcohol abuse in a primary care population. *The American Journal of Medicine, 85,* 466–471.

Cohen, P., & Cohen, J. (1984). The clinician's illusion. *Archives of General Psychiatry, 41*, 1178–1182.

Corrigan, G. V., Webb, M. G. T., & Unwin, A. R. (1986). Alcohol dependence among general medical inpatients. *British Journal of Addiction, 81*, 237–246.

Coulehan, J. L., Zettler-Segal, M., Block, M., McClelland, M., & Schulberg, H. C. (1987). Recognition of alcoholism and substance abuse in primary care patients. *Archives of Internal Medicine, 147*, 349–352.

Cyr, M. G., & Wartman, S. A. (1988). The effectiveness of routine screening questions in the detection of alcoholism. *Journal of the American Medical Association, 259*, 51–54.

Eckardt, M. J., Harford, T. C., Kaelber, C. T., Parker, E. S., Rosenthal, L. S., Ryback, R. S., Salmoiraghi, G. C., Vanderveen, E., & Warren, K. R. (1981). Health hazards associated with alcohol consumption. *Journal of the American Medical Association, 246*, 648–666.

Ewing, J. A. (1984). Detecting alcoholism: The CAGE questionnaire. *Journal of the American Medical Association, 252*, 1905–1907.

Gorelick, P. B. (1990). Stroke from alcohol and drug abuse: A current social peril. *Postgraduate Medicine, 88*, 171–178.

Hasin, D. S., Grant, B., & Endicott, J. (1990). The natural history of alcohol abuse: Implications for definitions of alcohol use disorders. *American Journal of Psychiatry, 147*, 1537–1541.

Hurt, R. D., Morse, R. M., & Swenson, W. M. (1980). Diagnosis of alcoholism with a self-administered alcoholism screening test: Results of 1,002 patients receiving general examinations. *Mayo Clinic Proceedings, 55*, 365–370.

Kamerow, D. B., Pincus, H. A., & Macdonald, D. I. (1986). Alcohol abuse, other drug abuse, and mental disorders in medical practice: Prevalence, costs, recognition, and treatment. *Journal of the American Medical Association, 255*, 2054–2057.

Kristenson, H., Ohlin, H., Hulten-Nosslin, B., Trell, E., & Hood, B. (1983). Identification and intervention of heavy drinking in middle-aged men: Results and follow-up of 24–60 months of long-term study with randomized controls. *Journal of Alcoholism, Clinical and Experimental Research, 7*, 203–209.

Leckman, A. L., Umland, B. E., & Blay, M. (1984). Prevalence of alcoholism in a family practice center. *The Journal of Family Practice, 18*, 867–870.

Mendelson, J. H., Babor, T. F., Mello, N. K., & Pratt, H. (1986). Alcoholism and prevalence of medical and psychiatric disorders. *Journal of Studies on Alcohol, 47*, 361–366.

Moore, R. D., & Malitz, F. E. (1986). Underdiagnosis of alcoholism by residents in an ambulatory medical practice. *Journal of Medical Education, 61*, 46–52.

Nelson, E., Conger, B., Douglass, R., Gephart, D., Kirk, J., Page, R., Clark, A., Johnson, K., Stone, K., Wasson, J., & Zubkoff, M. (1983). Functional health status levels of primary care patients. *Journal of the American Medical Association, 249*, 3331–3338.

Potts, M. K., Daniels, M., Burnam, M. A., & Wells, K. B, (1990). A structured interview version of the Hamilton Depression Rating Scale: Evidence of reliability and versatility of administration. *Journal of Psychiatric Research, 24,* 335–350.

Powell, B. J., Penick, E. C., Nickel, E. J., Liskow, B. I., Riesenmy, K. D., Campion, S. L., & Brown, E. F. (1992). Outcomes of co-morbid alcoholic men: A 1–year follow-up. *Alcoholism: Clinical and Experimental Research, 16,* 131–138.

Powell, B. J., Penick, E. C., Othmer, E., Bingham, S. F., & Rice, A. S. (1982). Prevalence of additional psychiatric syndromes among male alcoholics. *Journal of Clinical Psychiatry, 43,* 404–407.

Powers, J. S., & Spickard, A. (1984). Michigan alcoholism screening test to diagnose early alcoholism in a general practice. *Southern Medical Journal, 77,* 852–856.

Reid, A. L. A., Webb, G. R., Hennrikus, D., Fahey, P. P., & Sanson-Fisher, R. W. (1986). Detection of patients with high alcohol intake by general practitioners. *British Medical Journal, 293,* 735–738.

Read, L. J., Quinn, R. J., & Hoefer, M. A. (1987). Measuring overall health: An evaluation of three important approaches. *Journal of Chronic Diseases, 40*(Suppl.), 7S–22S.

Regier, D. A., Farmer, M. E., Rae, D. S., Locke, B. Z., Keith, S. J., Judd, L. L., & Goodwin, F. K. (1990). Comorbidity of mental disorders with alcohol and other drug abuse: Results from the Epidemiological Catchment Area (ECA) Study. *Journal of the American Medical Association, 264,* 2511–2518.

Robins, L. N., & Regier, D. A. (1991). *Psychiatric disorders in America: The Epidemiologic Catchment Area Study.* New York: Free Press.

Rogers, W. H., Wells, K. B., Meredith, L. S., Sturm, R., & Burnam, M. A. (1993). Outcomes for adult depressed outpatients under pre-paid or fee-for-service financing. *Archives of General Psychiatry, 50,* 517–525.

Ross, H. E., Glaser, F. B., & Germanson, T. (1988). The prevalence of psychiatric disorders in patients with alcohol and other drug problems. *Archives of General Psychiatry, 45,* 1023–1031.

Rydon, P., Redman, S., Sanson-Fisher, R. W., & Reid, A. L. A. (1992). Detection of alcohol-related problems in general practice. *Journal of Studies on Alcohol, 53,* 197–202.

Schuckit, M. A. (1985). The clinical implications of primary diagnostic groups among alcoholics. *Archives of General Psychiatry, 42,* 1043–1049.

Schuckit, M. A., Smith, T. L., Anthenelli, R., & Irwin, M. (1993). Clinical course of alcoholism in 636 male inpatients. *American Journal of Psychiatry, 150,* 786–792.

Schulberg, H. C. (1991). Mental disorders in the primary care setting: Research priorities for the 1990s. *General Hospital Psychiatry, 13,* 156–164.

Schulberg, H. C., & Burns, B. J. (1988). Mental disorders in primary care: Epidemiologic, diagnostic, and treatment research directions. *General Hospital Psychiatry, 10,* 79–87.

Schultz, J. M., Rice, D. P., & Parker, D. L. (1990). Alcohol related mortality and years of potential life lost: United States, 1987. *Morbidity and Mortality Weekly Report, 39,* 173–178.

Spitzer, R. L., Williams, J. B. W., Gibbon, M., & First, M. B. (1992). The Structured Clinical Interview for DSM–III–R (SCID): I. History, rationale, and description. *Archives of General Psychiatry, 49,* 624–629.

Spitzer, R. L., Williams, J. B. W., Kroenke, K., Linzer, M., deGruy, F., Hahn, S. R., Brody, D., & Johnson, J. G. (1994). The PRIME–MD 1000 Study: Validation and clinical utility of a new procedure for diagnosing mental disorders in primary care. *Journal of the American Medical Association.*

Stewart, A. L., Greenfield, S., Hays, R. D., Wells, K., Rogers, W. H., Berry, S. D., McGlynn, E. A., & Ware, J. E. (1989). Functional status and well-being of patients with chronic conditions: Results from the Medical Outcomes Study. *Journal of the American Medical Association, 262,* 907–913.

Stewart, A. L., Sherbourne, C. D., Wells, K. B., Burnam, A., Rogers, W. H., Hays, R. D., & Ware, J. E. (1993). Do depressed patients in different treatment settings have different levels of well-being and functioning? *Journal of Consulting and Clinical Psychology, 61,* 849–857.

Tracy, J. I., Gorman, D. M., & Leventhal, E. A. (1992). Reports of physical symptoms and alcohol use: Findings from a primary health care sample. *Alcohol & Alcoholism, 27,* 481–491.

Von Korff, M., Shapiro, S., Burke, J. D., Teitlebaum, M., Skinner, E. A., German, P., Turner, R. W., Klein, L., & Burns, B. (1987). Anxiety and depression in a primary care clinic: Comparison of Diagnostic Interview Schedule, General Health Questionnaire, and practitioner assessments. *Archives of General Psychiatry, 44,* 152–156.

Wells, K. B., Burnam, M. A., Benjamin, B., & Golding, J. M. (1990). Alcohol use and limitations in physical functioning in a sample of the Los Angeles general population. *Alcohol & Alcoholism, 25,* 673–684.

Wells, K. B., Burnam, M. A., Leake, B., & Robins, L. N. (1988). Agreement between face-to-face and telephone administered versions of the depression section of the NIMH Diagnostic Interview Schedule. *Journal of Psychiatric Research, 22,* 207–220.

16

COMORBIDITY OF SCHIZOPHRENIA AND SUBSTANCE ABUSE: IMPLICATIONS FOR TREATMENT

KIM T. MUESER, ALAN S. BELLACK, AND JACK J. BLANCHARD

Alcohol and drug abuse–dependence have long been recognized to interfere with the diagnosis and treatment of major psychiatric disorders (e.g., Parker, Meiller, & Andrews, 1960). As the prevalence of substance abuse has grown in the general population following the cultural revolution of the 1960s, so has the problem of treating patients with comorbid psychiatric illness and substance abuse (Kushner & Mueser, 1993). This problem is particularly acute for patients with severe, chronic psychiatric illnesses, such as schizophrenia, who appear to be at increased vulnerability to abuse drugs or alcohol (Ananth et al., 1989). Substance abuse in schizophrenia has been associated with a more severe course of the disorder, including an earlier age of illness onset (Mueser et al., 1990), more severe symptomatology, and an increased rate of psychiatric hospitalization

Reprinted from the *Journal of Consulting and Clinical Psychology*, 60, 845–856. (1992). Copyright © 1992 by the American Psychological Association. Used with permission of the author.

Preparation of this article was supported by National Institute of Mental Health Grants MH38636, MH39998, and MH41577.

(Cleghorn et al., 1991; Drake et al., 1990). In light of the wide range of cognitive, affective, and social impairments characteristic of schizophrenia (Morrison, Bellack, & Mueser, 1988; Nuechterlein & Dawson, 1984b), the treatment of patients with comorbid substance abuse disorders presents a formidable challenge to both clinicians and the mental health system as a whole. There is a pressing need for more effective psychotherapeutic interventions to improve the outcome of schizophrenia patients who abuse drugs or alcohol. In the absence of such treatments, these patients are doomed to a poor quality of life, housing instability, and repeated relapses and rehospitalizations, with society paying the high economic costs of managing this erratic illness in the community.

This article focuses on the problems of substance abuse in schizophrenia and its treatments to help therapists optimize the outcome of this dual-diagnosis population. We organized our review to first describe research on the prevalence, assessment, and impact of substance abuse on the course of schizophrenia. Second, we review studies on the effects of substance abuse on cognitive factors in schizophrenia and consider the implications of these effects for treatment. Third, we summarize the principles of treating substance abusing schizophrenia patients, we review the limited treatment outcome research in this area, and we identify avenues for future research that may improve the efficacy of existing treatment technologies.

EPIDEMIOLOGY OF SUBSTANCE ABUSE IN SCHIZOPHRENIA

Estimates of the prevalence of substance abuse disorders in schizophrenia have ranged from as low as 10% to over 65% during the life of the patient (Ananth et al., 1989; Bowers & Swigar, 1983; Mueser et al., 1990). This wide range of prevalence estimates can be accounted for by methodological differences across studies, including the procedures used to sample the study populations, assessment techniques, and the demographic characteristics of the subjects.

The setting from which the sample of schizophrenia patients is drawn has an important influence on the observed rates of substance abuse prevalence, with acute care settings (e.g., emergency room) yielding higher rates than chronic inpatient environments (Galanter, Castaneda, & Ferman, 1988). Different approaches to defining and assessing substance abuse also result in varying estimates of prevalence; the use of structured interviews to establish substance abuse–dependence diagnoses is more reliable than self-report scales or chart review (Drake et al., 1990). Patient demographic characteristics are also important correlates of substance abuse, and differences in these characteristics across study samples have a corresponding effect on estimated prevalence rates. For example, gender (i.e., male) and

TABLE 1
Demographic and Clinical Predictors of Substance Abuse in Schizophrenia

Variable	Correlate with substance abuse
Gender	Male
Age	Young
Education	Low
Premorbid social-sexual adjustment	Good
Age of first hospitalization	Early
Treatment compliance	Poor
Relapse rate	High
Symptom severity	Higher suicidality

age (i.e., youth) are both predictive of substance abuse disorders, so that samples with a preponderance of young males, as is the case with many studies of young chronic patients (e.g., Pepper, Kirshner, & Ryglewicz, 1981; Safer, 1987), tend to yield high estimates of the prevalence of substance abuse. Demographic and clinical predictors of substance abuse in schizophrenia are summarized in Table 1.

The vast majority of studies have examined the prevalence of substance abuse in schizophrenia patients receiving treatment for their psychiatric disorder. A methodological limitation of the approach is that epidemiological surveys based on clinical populations tend to overestimate rates of comorbidity in comparison to community-based surveys, because there is a tendency for each type of disorder to independently lead to seeking medical care (i.e., "Berkson's fallacy"; Berkson, 1946). Thus, surveying patients in the general population is the optimal method for estimating the prevalence of substance abuse comorbidity in schizophrenia. Only one large-scale community-based comorbidity study has been conducted, the National Institute of Mental Health (NIMH) Epidemiologic Catchment Area (ECA) program (Regier et al., 1990), which evaluated substance abuse and other psychiatric disorders using structured clinical interviews with over 20,000 individuals. Although the major focus of this study was on the assessment of substance abuse and psychiatric disorders among people living in the community, institutionalized samples of psychiatric patients were also included to obtain an adequate sample size of severe psychiatric disorders.

The results of the ECA study provide strong evidence that psychiatric patients in general, and especially schizophrenia patients, are much more prone to substance abuse disorders than people in the general population. Table 2 summarizes the estimated prevalence rates from the ECA study for alcohol abuse and drug abuse in the general population and in three diagnostic groups (schizophrenia, affective disorder, and anxiety disorder).

TABLE 2
Lifetime Prevalence (%) and Odds Ratios (ORs) of Substance Abuse Disorder for Schizophrenia, Affective Disorder, and Anxiety Disorder

Psychiatric disorder	Any substance abuse or dependence		Any alcohol diagnosis		Any other drug diagnosis	
	%	OR	%	OR	%	OR
General population	16.7	—	13.5	—	6.1	—
Schizophrenia	47.0	4.6	33.7	3.3	27.5	6.2
Affective	32.0	2.6	21.8	1.9	19.4	4.7
Anxiety	23.7	1.7	17.9	1.5	11.9	2.5

Note. Dashes indicate data not available. Odds ratios = ratio of the odds of having the substance abuse disorder in the psychiatric diagnostic group to the odds of the disorder in the remaining population. Based on data from the National Institute of Mental Health Epidemiological Catchment Area study (Regier et al., 1990).

For example, it can be seen from Table 2 that 16.7% of the general population had a history of substance abuse disorder, compared with 47.0% of the schizophrenia patients, 32.0% of the affective disorder patients, and 23.7% of people with an anxiety disorder. The odds ratios (ORs) included in Table 2 reflect the odds of having a substance abuse disorder in a psychiatric diagnostic group (e.g., schizophrenia) to the odds of substance abuse in people not in the diagnostic group (e.g., nonschizophrenics). Thus, in the ECA study the chances of a person with schizophrenia having a substance abuse or dependence disorder were more than four times greater than a person who does not have schizophrenia (i.e., OR = 4.6).

It is apparent from the ECA study, as well as many other less rigorous epidemiological studies (e.g., Ananth et al., 1989; Barbee, Clark, Crapanzano, Heintz, & Kehoe, 1989; Bernadt & Murray, 1986; Magliozzi, Kanter, Csernansky, & Hollister, 1983; Mueser et al., 1990; Siris et al., 1988), that substance abuse in schizophrenia patients is a common clinical problem. Although the lifetime prevalence rate of substance abuse in schizophrenia is close to 50%, estimates of recent or current substance abuse are generally in the range of 20% to 40% (e.g., Drake, Osher, & Wallach, 1989; Mueser et al., 1990). Alcohol is consistently the substance most commonly abused by schizophrenia patients, although there is a high correlation between alcohol abuse and drug abuse, particularly marijuana and stimulants (Barbee et al., 1989; Mueser et al., 1990).

It should be noted that the vast preponderance of data on comorbid substance abuse in schizophrenia has been on North Americans (mainly from the United States), and that these estimates may not apply to schizophrenia patients in other parts of the world. It is widely understood that rates and types of substance abuse differ markedly throughout the world (Austin, Macari, & Lettieri, 1978) and that culture is an important determinant of the propensity to develop an addictive disorder to a particular type of substance (Westermeyer, 1986). However, relatively little data are available from non-North American samples of schizophrenia patients. Selected studies from England (Bernadt & Murray, 1986), Spain (Peralta & Cuesta, 1992), and Croatia (Koretic & Hotujac, 1987) suggest a lower rate of substance abuse in schizophrenia than in North American samples. It is unknown whether the apparently lower rates of comorbid substance abuse in non-American samples reflect a truly lower rate of comorbidity or whether it is due to some type of measurement artifact, such as method of assessment or selection of patients. These findings raise intriguing questions in need of research as to whether cross-cultural and cross-national differences in the course and outcome of schizophrenia may be due, in part, to differences in comorbid substance abuse.

Assessment

The accurate assessment of comorbid disorders is essential to planning effective treatments, but it is rendered difficult by the broad impact of schizophrenia on interpersonal functioning, and the psychotomimetic effects of substance abuse. To make the diagnosis of schizophrenia, it must first be established that the patient has experienced a clear deterioration in social, work, or self-care functioning in the absence of substance abuse, as well as having at least some of the following symptoms: delusions, prominent hallucinations, incoherence or looseness of associations, catatonic behavior, or flat or inappropriate affect (American Psychiatric Association, 1987). Clinicians who attempt to diagnose schizophrenia without assessing either history of substance abuse or the possibility of covert drug or alcohol abuse run a grave risk of misdiagnosis and, consequently, mistreatment (Alterman, Erdlen, LaPorte, & Erdlen, 1982; R. C. W. Hall, Popkin, & DeVaul, 1977).

Alcohol and commonly abused "street" drugs can produce a range of transient psychotic symptoms similar to those found in schizophrenia. Chronic alcohol abuse or withdrawal from alcohol can cause hallucinations and delusions (Schuckit, 1989; Victor & Hope, 1958). Amphetamine abuse has been found to produce a temporary psychotic state that is clinically indistinguishable from schizophrenia (R. C. W. Hall, Popkin, Beresford, & Hall, 1988), and chronic cocaine abuse or overdoses of cocaine can cause paranoia and delirium (Welti & Fishbain, 1985). Similarly, cannabis abuse can induce panic and paranoid symptoms (Hollister, 1986). Finally, hallucinogens, such as LSD, phencyclidine (PCP), and psilocybin, cause a variety of psychotic symptoms (e.g., Hensala, Epstein, & Blacker, 1967) and have served as useful animal models for schizophrenia (Javitt, 1987). In short, acute or chronic substance abuse or withdrawal from psychoactive drugs can cause many of the same symptoms found in schizophrenia. It is imperative, therefore, when making a diagnosis of schizophrenia to rule out the acute effects of substance abuse or withdrawal symptoms by questioning the patient and significant others about psychoactive substance use. If substance abuse has occurred in the past, but there is evidence of schizophrenic symptomatology in the absence of recent abuse (e.g., within the past month), a diagnosis of schizophrenia can be reliably made.

According to the *Diagnostic and Statistical Manual of Mental Disorders* (3rd ed., rev.; *DSM–III–R*; American Psychiatric Association, 1987), the diagnosis of *substance dependence* requires at least three of the following symptoms to have been present for 1 month or to have occurred repeatedly for a longer period: substance taken in larger amounts or for longer periods than intended; increased tolerance, withdrawal symptoms; use of substance to relieve withdrawal symptoms; excessive amounts of time spent obtaining, using, or recovering from the effects of the substance; persistent desire or unsuccessful attempts to stop or cut down substance use, continued use of substance despite knowledge of the deleterious social, psychological, or physical effects; giving up or decreasing important activities (e.g., work or hobbies) because of substance use; and frequent intoxication or withdrawal effects experienced during fulfillment of significant obligations (e.g., intoxicated at work, at school, or when caring for children). The diagnosis of *substance abuse* is invoked to characterize maladaptive patterns of substance use that do not meet criteria for dependence and requires recurrent substance use in situations where use is physically hazardous (e.g., driving a car or operating machinery while intoxicated) or continued substance use despite knowledge that such use has negative effects on social, occupational, or physical functioning.

Once the diagnosis of schizophrenia is established, several factors can interfere with the assessment of a comorbid substance abuse disorder. Perhaps the most significant problem is the reliability of patients' self-reports about their own substance abuse. The validity of self-reports of primary substance abusers is often questionable, both for concurrent abuse (Donovan & Marlatt, 1988) and retrospective ratings (Aiken, 1986). These problems are compounded when the patient has another major psychiatric disorder (Lehman, Myers, & Corty, 1989). Schizophrenia patients often deny substance abuse for fear of losing basic psychiatric treatment services and entitlements (Ridgely, Goldman, & Willenbring, 1990). Furthermore, once patients are identified as substance abusers they tend to receive less outpatient treatment, suggesting that these patients are viewed as difficult by mental health-care workers (Solomon, 1986; Solomon & Davis, 1986).

Another difficulty encountered when assessing substance abuse in schizophrenia patients is the problem of determining the negative effects of abuse on patient functioning. Schizophrenia patients usually have a range of impairments in their social, occupational, and psychological functioning, and evaluating the deleterious effects of substance abuse on a baseline of poor functioning raises questions about the validity of these indices of functioning. Drake et al. (1989) have reported that the effects of alcohol on schizophrenia patients frequently involve a change in the patient's clinical condition, compliance with treatment, or housing stability, but that many patients do not develop the full alcohol dependence syndrome (see also Bunt, Galanter, Lifshutz, & Castaneda, 1990; Chen et al., 1992).

The most commonly used methods for assessing substance abuse disorders in schizophrenia are hospital records, structured clinical interviews, self-report scales, reports from significant others or treatment staff, and biological assays. There are both advantages and disadvantages to each of these methods, as outlined in Table 3. Structured clinical interviews probably provide the most reliable information because of the standardized, rigorous approach to collecting information, although these interviews are time-consuming and require extensive training to administer properly. Pristach and Smith (1990) suggested that some schizophrenia patients are willing to acknowledge substance abuse on self-report questionnaires but deny substance abuse in interviews. Although most self-report scales developed for primary addiction populations have not been validated for psychiatric patients (Toland & Moss, 1989), there is mixed evidence suggesting that the Michigan Alcoholism Screening Inventory can be useful for detecting alcoholism in schizophrenia patients (Drake et al., 1990; Gorelick, Irwin, Schmidt-Lackner, & Marder, 1990).

Whereas each approach to assessment has its limitations, in practice many patients freely admit to recent or past substance abuse when questioned. There is a greater tendency for patients to acknowledge alcohol abuse than drug abuse. We advise interviewers to assure patients in advance that information about their substance abuse is needed strictly for diagnostic and treatment purposes, and there will be no legal or financial repercussions for full disclosure. The optimal method for assessing substance abuse is to tap multiple sources of information, including clinical records, patients, treatment team members, and relatives (when available). Clinicians are often privy to changes in mental status or other aspects of functioning induced by even low levels of substance abuse. Drake et al. (1990) showed that case managers are excellent resources who can provide reliable, valid ratings of substance abuse.

Reasons for Substance Abuse in Schizophrenia

The most prominent hypothesis to account for the high rate of substance abuse in psychiatric disorders is self-medication (Khantzian, 1985). According to this hypothesis, patients abuse alcohol and drugs to decrease distress caused by major symptoms, particularly anxiety and depression. It has been suggested that schizophrenia patients prefer to abuse stimulants

TABLE 3

Advantages and Disadvantages of Different Methods for the Assessment of Substance Abuse in Schizophrenia

Method	Examples	Advantages	Disadvantages
Chart review		Utilizes collateral sources of information.	Low sensitivity results in underestimates of substance abuse.
Structural clinical interviews	SCID	Highly reliable due to standardized method of obtaining information.	Time consuming. Patient may deny abuse in personal interview.
Self-report questionnaires	MAST	Time efficient. Patients may acknowledge abuse on questionnaires when they don't in interviews.	Unknown validity for psychiatric patients.
Significant others reports	Family History Research Diagnostic Criteria	Provides independent information about patients' behavior in natural environment.	Subject to relatives' attributions about patients' illness and substance abuse.
Treatment provider ratings	Case manager ratings	Incorporates clinical information using multiple sources.	Lack of standardized assessment questions may limit reliability of ratings.
Biological assays	Urine toxicology analysis	Highly reliable results about current substance use.	Impractical in most clinical settings. Provides no information on extent or consequences of abuse. Detects only very recent substance abuse.

Note. SCID = Structured Clinical Interview for the *Diagnostic and Statistical Manual of Mental Disorders* (3rd ed.; rev.) (Spitzer, Williams, Gibbon, & First, 1990). MAST = Michigan Alcoholism Screening Test (Selzer, 1971). Family history research diagnostic criteria are from Andreasen, Endicott, Spitzer, and Winokur (1977) and Andreasen, Rice, Endicott, Reich, and Coryell (1986). Case manager ratings are from Drake et al. (1990).

(e.g., amphetamines or cocaine) to overcome the negative symptoms of schizophrenia (Schneier & Siris, 1987), but this finding has not been replicated in recent studies (Mueser, Yarnold, & Bellack, 1992), including the large ECA study (Regier et al., 1990). At this time, the preponderance of evidence indicates that the drug choice of schizophrenia patients is determined by availability, rather than the specific central nervous system effects of the drugs. Alcohol is consistently the most commonly abused substance of schizophrenia patients, as well as of the general population. After alcohol, drug choice for schizophrenia patients varies over time and as a function of the demographic characteristics of the sample. For example, Mueser et al. (1992) reported that in 1983–1986 cannabis was the most commonly abused illicit drug among schizophrenia patients, whereas in 1986–1990 cocaine became the most popular drug among schizophrenia patients, a change in pattern similar to that in the general population (Pope, Ionescu-Pioggia, Aizley, & Varma, 1990).

Schizophrenia patients give a number of reasons for abusing drugs, some of which are consistent with the self-medication hypothesis. Many patients report that alcohol temporarily relieves chronic psychotic symptoms, such as delusions of reference and hallucinations (Freed, 1975; Hansen & Willis, 1977). Most patients describe the use of drugs or alcohol to "get high," relax, or alleviate boredom, and patients frequently report that drug use stimulates and energizes them (Dixon, Haas, Weiden, Sweeney, & Frances, 1991; Test, Wallisch, Allness, & Ripp, 1989). From the patient's perspective, self-medication is an attractive explanation for substance abuse behavior, and one that is frequently used by a wide variety of people who abuse drugs or alcohol (e.g., Kushner, Sher, & Beitman, 1990). Despite patients' reports, there is little evidence supporting self-medication as an explanation for why schizophrenia patients are more vulnerable to substance abuse. If more symptomatic patients were more likely to abuse drugs or alcohol, this would support the self-medication hypothesis. However, studies of symptomatology in substance abusing schizophrenia patients have produced contradictory findings (e.g., Barbee et al., 1989; Cleghorn et al., 1991; Dixon et al., 1991; Mueser et al., 1990; Negrete, Knapp, Douglas, & Smith, 1986; Sevy, Kay, Opler, & van Praag, 1990). Thus, the self-medication hypothesis appears to be of limited value in explaining the high rate of substance abuse in schizophrenia patients.

The situational context in which schizophrenia patients abuse drugs and alcohol provides important clues about the environmental determinants of substance abuse. The abuse of illicit drugs (e.g., marijuana and cocaine) in schizophrenia patients usually occurs in a social setting, and similarly, about half of alcohol abuse also occurs in a social context (Dixon, Haas, Weiden, Sweeney, & Frances, 1990). The social nature of substance abuse in schizophrenia suggests that such behavior may meet patients' social-affiliative needs for acceptance and interpersonal contact. Examining the social context in which each patient abuses drugs is vital to designing effective treatment. Interventions may be required to bolster the ability of patients to resist peer pressure to abuse drugs or alcohol or to alter the composition of patients' social networks, thus reducing their exposure to substance abusing peers.

Etiologically, substance abuse in schizophrenia patients appears to be determined by both the availability of drugs and alcohol in the patient's peer group and, to a lesser extent, genetic factors as well. Family studies have found that schizophrenia patients with a history of substance abuse–dependence do not differ from nonabusing patients in the number of relatives with a schizophrenia-spectrum disorder, but that the abusing patients have more relatives with histories of substance abuse and affective disorders (Dixon et al., 1991; Gershon et al., 1988). Thus, environmental and biological factors appear to contribute to the high rate of substance abuse in schizophrenia, whereas patients describe euphoric or other relaxing effects of drugs as reasons for abusing drugs.

Clinical Effects of Substance Abuse

Relatively little longitudinal research has been conducted to examine the effects of substance abuse on the course of schizophrenia. Most studies have been retrospective and raise questions about whether observed correlations reflect the consequences of substance abuse or patient selection factors. Nevertheless, there are some notable trends in the data. There is compelling evidence that stimulant abuse (e.g., cocaine and amphetamines) can precipitate onset of schizophrenia at an earlier age in biologically vulnerable people (Breakey, Goodell, Lorenz, & McHugh, 1974: Richard, Liskow, & Perry, 1985; Tsuang, Simpson, & Kronfol, 1982). The mechanism underlying this effect is unclear, but it has been suggested that repeated stimulant abuse may alter the dopamine system (which is believed to be involved in the pathogenesis of schizophrenia), resulting in behavioral sensitization and the development of schizophrenic symptoms (Lieberman, Kinon, & Loebel, 1990). Stimulant abuse, even in relatively small quantities, can also precipitate symptom relapses and hospitalizations (e.g., Lieberman et al., 1989).

Alcohol abuse has not been linked to an earlier onset of schizophrenia (e.g., Barbee et al., 1989), although it has been associated with a higher vulnerability to relapses in prospective research (Drake et al., 1990). Soni and Brownlee (1991) reported that schizophrenia patients who were alcohol abusers had lower serum fluphenazine (a neuroleptic medication) levels and more hospitalizations, which suggests that these patients were in poor therapeutic control compared with nonabusers. Furthermore, schizophrenia patients who abuse alcohol or drugs are often less compliant with their neuroleptic treatment (Drake et al., 1989) and report discontinuing neuroleptics during phases of substance abuse because of concerns about medication-drug interactions (Pristach & Smith, 1990). The poor outcome of schizophrenia patients who are substance abusers appears to be due to a combination of the psychomimetic effects of the drugs themselves (e.g., Knudsen & Vilmar, 1984), as well as noncompliance with treatments that are generally effective with this population (e.g., medication).

In addition to the impact of substance abuse on schizophrenia symptoms and rehospitalization, substance abuse is associated with an increased risk of suicide. Young male schizophrenia patients with a history of substance abuse are particularly vulnerable to suicidal ideation and attempts (Cohen, Test, & Brown, 1990; Landmark, Cernovsky, & Merskey, 1987). The link between substance abuse and suicidal behavior is not limited to schizophrenia. Substance abuse is also implicated in a high proportion of suicides among the general population (Fowler, Rich, & Young, 1986), and it has been repeatedly found that people with primary substance disorders have a high mortality for suicide (Hesselbrock, Meyer, & Keener, 1985; Whitters, Cadoret, & Widmer, 1985). The relation between suicide and substance abuse in schizophrenia is of special clinical concern because all patients with schizophrenia have an elevated risk of suicide (Roy, 1986), which is apparently increased further by concomitant substance use. It is not known whether schizophrenia and substance abuse are simply independent risk factors for suicide, or whether substance abuse potentiates the willingness to act on suicidal ideation in a subset of vulnerable schizophrenia patients. Suicidal ideation is a strong correlate of depression in schizophrenia. The association between substance abuse and suicide in schizophrenia suggests that treatments targeted at dual-diagnosis patients may need to address depression to improve long-term outcome.

Cognitive Effects of Substance Abuse

Cognitive deficits have been hypothesized to be central to the etiology and course of schizophrenia (e.g., Nuechterlein & Dawson, 1984a). Cognitive theories of schizophrenia have emphasized the pre-eminent role of impairments in information processing, attention, and memory (for reviews, see Braff, 1991; Nuechterlein & Dawson, 1984b). Schizophrenia patients, however, often demonstrate a generalized cognitive deficit across measures of cognitive functioning (Braff et al., 1991; Chapman & Chapman, 1973). Although the cognitive correlates of schizophrenia have received extensive investigation, a neglected issue concerns the role that comorbid alcohol and drug use may play in the etiology or exacerbation of these cognitive deficits. In this section, we review briefly the cognitive sequelae of alcohol and drug use to highlight the potential importance of these effects in schizophrenia patients with comorbid substance abuse.

In reviewing the neurocognitive correlates of alcoholism, we focus on the impairments observed in non-Korsakoff alcoholics and do not discuss the deficits that characterize the relatively uncommon Wernicke-Korsakoff syndrome (which results from chronic alcoholism and thiamin deficiency; see Greenberg & Diamond, 1985). Long-term alcohol abuse has been found to be associated with increased neurocognitive impairment: Neuropsychological paradigms have found deficits in abstract reasoning, learning, attention and information processing, complex perceptual-motor abilities, and memory in people with histories of alcoholism (e.g., Grant, 1987; Grant, Adams, & Reed, 1986; Parsons & Leber, 1981; Tarter & Edwards, 1985).

An important limitation in much of this literature is that most studies have been conducted with recently detoxified alcoholics. Few studies have been conducted after longer periods of abstinence (e.g., months or years) to determine the durability of these cognitive deficits. Accumulating evidence, however, suggests that there is long-term recovery of some cognitive functioning after continued abstinence (Adams, Grant, & Reed, 1980; Grant, Adams, & Reed, 1984), although cognitive impairment may persist despite months or years of sobriety (Brandt, Butters, Ryan, & Bayog, 1983; Fabian & Parsons, 1983; Parsons, Schaeffer, & Glenn, 1990; Ryan, DiDario, Butters, & Adinolfi, 1980). The enduring effects of alcohol on cognitive functioning, despite abstinence, may be due to irreversible neurological insult. For example, it has been proposed that alcohol abuse can lead to long-term impairment in memory through permanent damage to diencephalic structures (Brandt et al., 1983).

Although less research has been conducted on the neurocognitive effects of nonalcohol psychoactive drug use, evidence indicates a cause for concern (Reed & Grant, 1990). Polydrug abuse has been found to be related to neuropsychological impairment, particularly in verbal and perceptual-motor abilities (Grant et al., 1978; Grant & Judd, 1976), and electroencephalograph abnormalities (Grant & Judd, 1976). More specifically, recent studies also suggest that cognitive impairments may be associated with cocaine abuse (Herning, Glover, Koeppl, Weddington, & Jaffe, 1990; O'Malley & Gawin, 1990). The attribution of neurocognitive and neuropathological findings to a single drug or class of drugs is, however, a difficult task given the prevalent use of multiple substances in abusers (e.g., Grant et al., 1978; Mueser et al., 1990). Results from the ECA study (Regier et al., 1990) document the high rate of comorbidity between alcohol and drug use disorders: 21.5% of individuals with an alcohol use disorder also had another drug abuse–dependence disorder in their lifetime, whereas of those individuals with a drug use disorder, 47.3% also had a lifetime history of alcohol abuse–dependence.

In addition to the cognitive deficits outlined previously, neuroanatomical abnormalities have also been found to be associated with substance abuse, especially alcoholism. Neuroimaging studies indicate that suical widening and ventricular dilation in alcoholics appear to be the most frequent findings (Jernigan et al., 1991; Jernigan, Pfefferbaum, & Zatz, 1986; Ron, 1987; Wilkinson, 1987). As with neurocognitive deficits, some structural abnormalities may slowly resolve with prolonged abstinence (Ron, 1987; Wilkinson, 1985, 1987). These findings are interesting because cortical atrophy and ventricular enlargement have been observed to occur in at least a subpopulation of schizophrenics (for a review, see Raz & Raz, 1990). Thus, individuals with schizophrenia, who may have neuroanatomical abnormalities associated with this disorder, may be at heightened risk for even greater neuropathology if they also abuse alcohol.

The precise etiology of the observed cognitive and neuropathological findings associated with alcohol and drug use is not yet clear. These deficits are probably best viewed as determined by multiple factors. Thus, pathological findings may be the result of the direct neurotoxic effects of abused substances or may be related to neuromedical risk factors that abusers are exposed to, including head trauma, cerebral vascular disease, nutritional deficit, and liver dysfunction (Adams & Grant, 1986; Grant et al., 1984).

The foregoing review suggests that long-term substance abuse, particularly alcohol abuse–dependence, may further impair the already compromised cognitive functioning of schizophrenia patients. Additionally, the prevalence of neurocognitive impairments and neuroanatomical anomalies associated with schizophrenia itself may conceivably make these patients even more vulnerable than other individuals to the pernicious cognitive and neuropathological effects of alcohol and drug abuse. Despite the accumulation of data regarding the prevalence of substance use disorders in schizophrenia, there are no systematic studies of the cognitive correlates of substance abuse in this population. Thus, many questions regarding the cognitive effects of concomitant substance abuse in schizophrenia await further study: If comorbid substance abuse in schizophrenia results in further cognitive impairment, is this impairment simply additive or does a different pattern of cognitive disturbance emerge in abusing versus nonabusing patients? Furthermore, does the potential cognitive impairment associated with substance abuse in schizophrenia ameliorate with abstinence? How do neuroleptics and adjunctive medications interact with abused substances with regard to cognitive functioning? Given that male schizophrenia patients, in comparison to female schizophrenia patients, typically have an earlier age of onset and poorer course of illness (Goldstein, 1988; Lewine, 1981; Loranger, 1984), as well as a greater prevalence of neuroanatomical anomalies (Andreasen, Ehrhardt, et al., 1990; Andreasen, Swayze, et al., 1990; Raz & Raz, 1990), are there gender differences in the cognitive effects of substance abuse in schizophrenia?

A final area of concern regards the treatment implications of the possible cognitive deficits associated with alcohol and drug abuse. Studies conducted with schizophrenia patients and individuals with alcohol use disorders suggest that cognitive deficits have important implications for the efficacy of treatment interventions. For example, memory impairments in schizophrenia patients have been shown to be related to greater severity of social skills deficits prior to treatment and to predict poorer acquisition of these behaviors after participation in a social skills training program (Mueser, Bellack, Douglas, & Wade, 1991). With regard to the treatment of alcoholism, there is some suggestion that pretreatment neuropsychological impairment is related to a greater likelihood of relapse (Parsons, 1987). Although these findings are preliminary in nature, they do indicate a need to integrate research on cognitive functioning when considering treatment for schizophrenia patients with comorbid substance abuse.

TREATMENT

Drug and alcohol use by schizophrenia patients is one of the most pressing problems facing the mental health system. We discussed previously the widespread abuse of substances by schizophrenia patients, particularly by younger male patients. To some extent the epidemiological data understate the problem. In many urban hospitals and community mental health centers abuse is so common that it is assumed that any new patient has a problem with substances until it is proven otherwise. Excessive substance use by schizophrenics has most of the same social, health, economic, and psychiatric consequences that it has for other individuals. Moreover, as indicated previously, it has additional serious consequences for comorbid patients. It increases the risk of symptom exacerbation and relapse, it may compromise the efficacy of neuroleptics, and it decreases compliance with treatment. It often serves as a significant source of conflict in families that are already under great stress, a pernicious circumstance for schizophrenia patients who are highly vulnerable to heightened stress (Hooley, 1985). Substance use also has deleterious cognitive effects that are superimposed on an information-processing system that is already compromised (Bellack, 1992).

Clearly substance abuse by schizophrenia patients cannot be ignored. However, until recently it has been given scant attention by mental health professionals. The public health system, where most schizophrenia patients are treated, has traditionally been compartmentalized such that treatment for psychiatric and substance use problems has been provided by different agencies. This arrangement has many advantages; however, it has proven to be a disaster for dually diagnosed patients, particularly those with schizophrenia (Drake, Osher, & Wallach, 1991). It is now well known that schizophrenia patients have difficulty navigating diverse treatment and social service programs and tend to "fall between the cracks" (Bachrach, 1981). This problem has been compounded for dually diagnosed patients as they present special problems that traditional substance abuse and psychiatric programs have neither been willing nor been able to deal with, even when patients have been able to access treatment facilities (McLellan, Luborsky, Woody, O'Brien, & Druley, 1983).

Substance abuse and psychiatric treatment programs have evolved a different ethos or philosophy over time (Minkoff, 1991). The majority of addiction programs are based on the 12-step approach characteristic of Alcoholics Anonymous (AA). They use confrontation as a therapeutic tool (i.e., to get the patient to realize the consequences of abuse and accept himself or herself as an addict), and they emphasize the need for self-control and personal responsibility. They also often require abstinence as a precondition for participation in treatment rather than as a goal and tend to eschew the use of substances of all kinds (including prescribed medications). These strategies are all counterproductive with schizophrenia patients. This may not be an ideal approach with patients who have cognitive deficits and may be at increased vulnerability to the effects of interpersonal stress. They often are unable to admit to errors or problems or to see the connection between their behavior and their symptoms or life situations (Bellack, Mueser, Wade, Sayers, & Morrison, 1992). Thus, they may be unable to realistically agree to abstinence early on in treatment, and confrontational strategies may be stress-provoking and increase the risk of relapse. Finally, they generally require the long-term use of neuroleptics and other medications, which conflicts with AA's philosophy.

Psychiatric treatment programs traditionally emphasize tolerance, support, and caring. These attributes are desirable for treating schizophrenia but may not be helpful for dealing with substance abuse. Substance use is often ignored or discounted by psychiatric staff until and unless it interferes with treatment or creates a crisis in the family, at which time the patient may be referred to a primary substance abuse program for ancillary care. Thus, neither traditional substance abuse programs nor psychiatric programs are sufficient for dually diagnosed patients and in some cases they may be countertherapeutic.

Treatment Needs

The problem of substance abuse in schizophrenia has generated a large literature, but to date there have been no double-blind controlled trials of an intervention specifically designed to deal with this pernicious combination. Hence, the following discussion is derived from conceptual papers, a handful of published uncontrolled trials and demonstration projects, and our own experience. Surprisingly, there is a broad agreement on a number of requirements for effective treatment. First and foremost is the contention that dually diagnosed patients need a special program that integrates elements of both psychiatric and substance abuse treatment (Drake, Osher,

& Wallach, 1991; Lehman et al., 1989). These elements can derive from geographically distinct programs, but only if both interventions are concurrent and actively coordinated (Drake, McLaughlin, Pepper, & Minkoff, 1991). Sequencing separate treatments for each condition is thought to be ineffective. Single programs that combine the diverse elements needed are apt to do a better job of integration, be more cost efficient, and be easier for patients to navigate. However, such programs run counter to established practice, and few exist.

A second requirement for effective treatment is careful assessment (Lehman et al., 1989; Test et al., 1989). Schizophrenia is by itself a heterogeneous entity, and the addition of substance abuse simply creates more permutations. To be effective, a program must consider individual differences in both substance use patterns and psychiatric status. Patients differ in the type of substance(s) used, and the degree of use varies from recreational to abuse to dependence. As discussed previously, the reasons for use also differ, and include social pressure, boredom, and the desire to feel and act normal. Patients also differ in the degree to which they can actively participate in programs, assume responsibility for their behavior, and use self-control to withstand temptation.

This variability is particularly germane to substance abuse strategies. For example, one of the most promising techniques for primary substance abusers is relapse prevention (S. M. Hall, Wasserman, & Havassy, 1991; Marlatt & Gordon, 1985; Schiffman, 1992). This is a cognitive-behavioral approach in which patients are taught to avoid relapses by anticipating and avoiding risk situations, learning social skills to deal with social pressures and using cognitive coping skills to help control urges and prevent minor lapses from leading to full-blown relapses. This approach is likely to be helpful for patients whose substance use often occurs in predictable social situations. This approach may have limited applicability for patients with notable cognitive impairment, who might be unable to learn to anticipate problem situations and use the requisite cognitive strategies (Bellack, Morrison, & Mueser, 1989).

It is doubtful that relapse prevention training, if provided in a vacuum, will have a substantive effect on substance abuse in schizophrenia. However, embedding training in relapse prevention into a comprehensive treatment program for schizophrenia, including psychosocial interventions such as social skills training (Carey, Carey, & Meisler, 1990; Morrison & Bellack, 1984), behavioral or psychoeducational family therapy (Mueser & Glynn, 1990), and assertive community-based case management (Bond, McDonel, Miller, & Pensec, 1991; Stein & Test, 1980), is more likely to decrease substance abuse and improve the course of the illness. Treatment for substance abuse in schizophrenia needs to be integrated with broad-based psychosocial rehabilitation strategies because no clear line demarks substance abuse problems from social and symptom problems characteristic of the illness. Thus, a schizophrenia patient who abuses drugs or alcohol in social settings may not only need to be taught to recognize and cope more effectively with these situations but may also benefit from social skills training aimed at helping the patient establish relationships with non-abusing peers. Similarly, a patient who is the object of excessive parental criticism who abuses substances as an attempt to cope with or avoid this negative affect may require relapse prevention training combined with family intervention designed to ameliorate the affective climate of the family. This approach to integrating treatments is consistent with the fact that education about the deleterious effects of substance abuse is already provided in family therapy programs (e.g., Falloon, Boyd, & McGill, 1984) and some approaches to social skills training (e.g., symptom management training; Liberman & Corrigan, 1993).

Reducing the use of addictive substances is a difficult process under the best of circumstances, and treatment programs for nonpsychiatrically impaired abusers have had only limited success, with little evidence suggesting differential outcomes for different treatment models (Nathan & Skinstad, 1987; Sobell, Toneatto, & Sobell, 1990). Yet, many more people are able to quit on their own than through treatment (Tucker & Sobell, 1992). Factors that facilitate abstinence and controlled use of substances include high levels of motivation to quit, the ability to exert self-control in the face of temptation (urges), and social support or social pressure. Unfortunately, the schizophrenic abuser often has limitations in each of these areas. As indicated previously, schizophrenic abusers typically have difficulty perceiving (or accepting) the dangers of continued use, and thus are not highly motivated to reduce consumption. Many patients continue to experience disruptive (psychotic) symptoms and unpleasant emotions and have residual cognitive impairment even when the acute phase of the illness is in remission. Hence, they have limited ability to exert self-control and cope with the stresses of craving for substances or social pressure to imbibe. A great many schizophrenia patients are socially isolated and lack the social support and the stimulus to abstain provided by spouse, children, job, and friends (Osher & Kofoed, 1989).

Schizophrenia and substance abuse are not simply additive, but tend to exacerbate one another, dramatically complicating the treatment process. Consequently, treatment programs must be multidimensional, long term, and flexible (Drake, McLaughlin, Pepper, & Miakoff, 1991; Test et al., 1989). Osher and Kofoed (1989) have conceptualized treatment as a four-stage process. The patient must first be *engaged* in treatment, a process that might entail many false starts over months or years. Next, the individual must be *persuaded* to "accept long-term abstinence-oriented treatment" (p. 1027); this also is typically a gradual process (Kofoed & Keys, 1988). Once these two stages have been achieved, the individual is ready for *active treatment*, which involves teaching the skills needed to remain sober. Finally, the patient must be taught *relapse prevention* skills. The latter two stages require a variety of nonconfrontational elements commonly used in treatment of primary substance abusers, including social skills training (Morrison & Bellack, 1984), problem-solving training (Monti, Abrams, Kadden, & Cooney, 1989), and Marlatt's relapse prevention program (Marlatt & Gordon, 1985).

Special consideration must also be given to the psychiatric side of the equation. Effort must be directed to modify the maladaptive living situation that many chronic schizophrenia patients endure, including hopelessness, joblessness, poverty, boredom, and social isolation. Families must be involved when possible, and social support should be increased. An adequate medication regime must be determined, and the patient must be taught the value of compliance. Finally, the diverse elements of the program and other social service and medical needs must be coordinated by an intensive case management system (Drake, Osher, & Wallach, 1991; Test et al., 1989).

We would be remiss if we did not emphasize that substance abuse by schizophrenia patients is a societal problem, not simply a problem for the mental health establishment. It is, in part, a consequence of reinstitutionalization and the associated failure to provide enough resources to fund mental health and social services in the community on the one hand, coupled with mental health's failure to adequately deal with the causes of drug use and availability of drugs in the country. The mental health establishment is quite capable of developing effective treatment programs for the dually diagnosed patient. However, mental health professionals are unlikely to make a significant dent in the problem until and unless the United States resolves the broader societal issues and provides adequate funding to care for these disadvantaged and severely handicapped individuals. Schizophrenia patients are more like their peers than they are different from their peers. If drug use is common in their environment, they are at least as vulnerable as their peers unless they are so handicapped that they cannot access suppliers (Mueser et al., 1992). If mental health professionals expect substance abusers to abstain or minimize use, they must provide an alternative to poverty, boredom, and hopelessness.

Conclusion

The literature on substance abuse and schizophrenia is concentrated in the past 10 years, and particularly in the past 5 years. These dual dysfunctions have undoubtedly coexisted for some time, but they have only recently drawn the attention of the scientific and mental health establishments. This surge of interest is probably associated with the increase in illicit substance abuse over the past 25 years in our society, especially the recent "crack" cocaine epidemic.

This has been a frustrating topic to review, as so little is known about the causes, effects, or treatment of schizophrenia patients with comorbid substance abuse disorders. It has been easy to raise questions and identify issues in need of further study, but we can draw few firm conclusions other than that substance abuse is a pernicious problem for schizophrenia patients that has reached crisis proportions. In addition to the specific questions raised in each section of this article, we can conclude with one general recommendation: Understanding and solving this problem will require collaboration by experts on schizophrenia and substance abuse. Traditionally, these two groups have worked independently in separate programs, published in different journals, and received research funds from separate agencies (e.g., National Institute on Drug Abuse, National Institute on Alcohol Abuse and Alcoholism, and NIMH). Integration is essential at all levels to develop effective treatment strategies for this population.

REFERENCES

Adams, K. M., & Grant, I. (1986). Influence of premorbid risk factors on neuropsychological performance in alcoholics. *Journal of Clinical and Experimental Neuropsychology, 8,* 362–370.

Adams, K. M., Grant, I., & Reed, R. (1980). Neuropsychology in alcoholic men in their late thirties: One-year follow-up. *American Journal of Psychiatry, 137,* 928–931.

Aiken, L. S. (1986). Retrospective self-reports by clients differ from original reports: Implications for the evaluation of drug treatment programs. *The International Journal of the Addictions, 21,* 767–788.

Alterman, A. I., Erdlen, D. L., LaPorte, D. J., & Erdlen, F. R. (1982). Effects of illicit drug use in an inpatient psychiatric population. *Addictive Behaviors, 7,* 231–242.

American Psychiatric Association. (1987). *Diagnostic and statistical manual of mental disorders* (3rd ed., rev.). Washington, DC: Author.

Ananth, J., Vandewater, S., Kamal, M., Brodsky, A., Gamal, R., & Miller, M. (1989). Mixed diagnosis of substance abuse in psychiatric patients. *Hospital and Community Psychiatry, 40,* 297–299.

Andreasen, N. C., Ehrhardt, J. C., Swayze, V. W., Alliger, R. J., Yuh, W. T. C., Cohen, G., & Ziebell, S. (1990). Magnetic resonance imaging of the brain in schizophrenia. *Archives of General Psychiatry, 47,* 35–44.

Andreasen, N. C., Endicott, J., Spitzer, R. L., & Winokur, G. (1977). The family history method using diagnostic criteria. *Archives of General Psychiatry, 34,* 1229–1235.

Andreasen, N. C., Rice, J., Endicott, J., Reich, T., & Coryell, W. (1986). The family history approach to diagnosis. *Archives of General Psychiatry, 43,* 421–429.

Andreasen, N. C., Swayze, V. W., Flaum, M., Yates, W. R., Arndt, S., & Mc-Chesney, C. (1990). Ventricular enlargement in schizophrenia evaluated with computed tomographic scanning: Effects of gender, age, and stage of illness. *Archives of General Psychiatry, 47*, 1008–1015.

Austin, G. A., Macari, M. A., & Lettieri, D. J. (Eds.). (1978). Research issues 23: International drug use. Rockville, MD: National Institute on Drug Abuse, U.S. Department of Health, Education, and Welfare.

Bachrach, L. L. (1981). Continuity of care for chronic mental patients: A conceptual analysis. *Archives of General Psychiatry, 138*, 1449–1456.

Barbee, J. G., Clark, P. D., Crapanzano, M. S., Heintz, G. C., & Kehoe, C. E. (1989). Alcohol and substance abuse among schizophrenic patients presenting to an emergency psychiatric service. *Journal of Nervous and Mental Disease, 177*, 400–407.

Bellack, A. S. (1992). Cognitive rehabilitation for schizophrenia: Is it possible? Is it necessary? *Schizophrenia Bulletin, 18*, 43–50.

Bellack, A. S., Morrison, R. L., & Mueser, K. T. (1989). Social problem solving in schizophrenia. *Schizophrenia Bulletin, 15*, 101–116.

Bellack, A. S., Mueser, K. T., Wade, J., Sayers, S. L., & Morrison, R. L. (1992). The ability of schizophrenics to perceive and cope with negative affect. *British Journal of Psychiatry, 160*, 473–480.

Berkson, J. (1946). Limitations of the application of four-fold tables to hospital data. *Biometric Bulletin, 2*, 47–53.

Bernadt, M. W., & Murray, R. M. (1986). Psychiatric disorder, drinking and alcoholism: What are the links? *British Journal of Psychiatry, 148*, 393–400.

Bond, G. R., McDonel, E. C., Miller, L. D., & Pensec, M. (1991). Assertive community treatment and reference groups: An evaluation of their effectiveness for young adults with serious mental illness and substance abuse problems. *Psychosocial Rehabilitation, 15*, 31–43.

Bowers, M. B., & Swigar, M. E. (1983). Vulnerability to psychosis associated with hallucinogen use. *Psychiatry Research, 9*, 91–97.

Braff, D. L. (1991). Information processing and attentional abnormalities in the schizophrenic disorders. In P. E. Magaro (Ed.), *Cognitive bases of mental disorders* (pp. 262–307). Newbury Park, CA: Sage.

Braff, D. L., Heaton, R., Kuck, J., Cullum, M., Moranville, J., Grant, I., & Zisook, S. (1991). The generalized pattern of neuropsychological deficits in outpatients with chronic schizophrenia with heterogeneous Wisconsin Card Sorting Test results. *Archives of General Psychiatry, 48*, 891–898.

Brandt, J., Butters, N., Ryan, C., & Bayog, R. (1983). Cognitive loss and recovery in long-term alcohol abusers. *Archives of General Psychiatry, 40*, 435–442.

Breakey, W. R., Goodell, H., Lorenz, P. C., & McHugh, P. R. (1974). Hallucinogenic drugs as precipitant of schizophrenia. *Psychological Medicine, 4*, 255–261.

Bunt, G., Galanter, M., Lifshutz, H., & Castaneda, R. (1990). Cocaine/"crack" dependence among psychiatric inpatients. *American Journal of Psychiatry, 147,* 1542–1546.

Carey, M. P., Carey, K. B., & Meisler, A. W. (1990). Training mentally ill chemical abusers in social problem solving. *Behavior Therapy, 21,* 511–518.

Chapman, L. J., & Chapman, J. P. (1973). *Disordered thought in schizophrenia.* New York: Appleton-Century-Crofts.

Chen, C., Balogh, M., Bathija, J., Howanitz, E., Plutchik, R., & Conte, H. R. (1992). Substance abuse among psychiatric inpatients. *Comprehensive Psychiatry, 33,* 60–64.

Cleghorn, J. M., Kaplan, R. D., Szechtman, B., Szechtman, H., Brown, G. M., & Franco, S. (1991). Substance abuse and schizophrenia: Effect on symptoms but not neurocognitive function. *Journal of Clinical Psychiatry, 52,* 26–30.

Cohen, L. J., Test, M. A., & Brown, R. L. (1990). Suicide and schizophrenia: Data from a prospective community treatment study. *American Journal of Psychiatry, 147,* 602–607.

Dixon, L., Haas, G., Weiden, P. J., Sweeney, J., & Frances, A. J. (1990). Acute effects of drug abuse in schizophrenic patients: Clinical observations and patients' self-reports. *Schizophrenia Bulletin, 16,* 69–79.

Dixon, L., Haas, G., Weiden, P. J., Sweeney, J., & Frances, A. J. (1991). Drug abuse in schizophrenic patients: Clinical correlates and reasons for use. *American Journal of Psychiatry, 148,* 224–230.

Donovan, D. M., & Marlatt, D. A. (Eds.). (1988). *Assessment of addictive behaviors.* New York: Guilford Press.

Drake, R. E., McLaughlin, P., Pepper, B., & Minkoff, K. (1991). Dual diagnosis of major mental illness and substance disorder: An overview. In K. Minkoff & R. E. Drake (Eds.), *Dual diagnosis of major mental illness and substance disorder* (pp. 3–12). San Francisco: Jossey-Bass.

Drake, R. E., Osher, F. C., Noordsy, D. L., Hurlbut, S. C., Teague, G. B., & Beaudett, M. S. (1990). Diagnosis of alcohol use disorders in schizophrenia. *Schizophrenia Bulletin, 16,* 57–67.

Drake, R. E., Osher, F. C., & Wallach, M. A. (1989). Alcohol use and abuse in schizophrenia: A prospective community study. *Journal of Nervous and Mental Disease, 177,* 408–414.

Drake, R. E., Osher, F. C., & Wallach, M. A. (1991). Hopelessness and dual diagnosis. *American Psychologist, 46,* 1149–1158.

Fabian, M. S., & Parsons, O. A. (1983). Differential improvement of cognitive functions in recovering alcoholic women. *Journal of Abnormal Psychology, 92,* 87–95.

Falloon, I. R. H., Boyd, J. L., & McGill, C. W. (1984). *Family care of schizophrenia.* New York: Guilford Press.

Fowler, R. C., Rich, C. L., & Young, D. (1986). San Diego suicide study II: Substance abuse in young cases. *Archives of General Psychiatry, 43,* 962–965.

Freed, E. X. (1975). Alcoholism and schizophrenia: The search for perspectives. *Journal of Studies on Alcohol, 36,* 853–881.

Galanter, M., Castaneda, R., & Ferman, J. (1988). Substance abuse among general psychiatric patients: Place of presentation, diagnosis and treatment. *American Journal of Drug and Alcohol Abuse, 142,* 211–235.

Gershon, E. S., DeLisi, L. E., Hamovit, J., Nurhberger, J. I., Jr., Maxwell, M. E., Schreiber, J., Dauphinais, D., Dingman, C. W., II, & Guroff, J. J. (1988). A controlled family study of chronic psychosis. *Archives of General Psychiatry, 45,* 328–336.

Goldstein, J. M. (1988). Gender differences in the course of schizophrenia. *American Journal of Psychiatry, 145,* 684–689.

Gorelick, D. A., Irwin, M. R., Schmidt-Lackner, S., & Marder, S. (1990). Alcoholism among male schizophrenic inpatients. *Annals of Clinical Psychiatry, 2,* 19–22.

Grant, I. (1987). Alcohol and the brain: Neuropsychological correlates. *Journal of Consulting and Clinical Psychology, 55,* 310–324.

Grant, I., Adams, K. M., Carlin, A. S., Rennick, P. M., Judd, L. L., & Schoof, K. (1978). The collaborative neuropsychological study of polydrug users. *Archives of General Psychiatry, 35,* 1063–1074.

Grant, I., Adams, K. M., & Reed, R. (1984). Aging, abstinence, and medical risk factors in the prediction of neuropsychologic deficit in long-term alcoholics. *Archives of General Psychiatry, 41,* 710–718.

Grant, I., Adams, K. M., & Reed, R. (1986). Intermediate-duration (subacute) organic mental disorder of alcoholism. In I. Grant (Ed.), *Neuropsychiatric correlates of alcoholism* (pp. 37–60). Washington, DC: American Psychiatric Press.

Grant, I., & Judd, L. L. (1976). Neuropsychological and EEG disturbances in polydrug users. *American Journal of Psychiatry, 133,* 1039–1042.

Greenberg, D. A., & Diamond, I. (1985). Wernicke-Korsakoff syndrome. In R. E. Tarter & D. A. Van Thiel (Eds.), *Alcohol and the brain: Chronic effects* (pp. 295–314). New York: Plenum Press.

Hall, R. C. W., Popkin, M. K., Beresford, T. P., & Hall, A. K. (1988). Amphetamine psychosis: Clinical presentations and differential diagnosis. *Psychiatric Medicine, 6,* 73–79.

Hall, R. C. W., Popkin, M. K., & DeVaul, R. (1977). The effect of unrecognized drug abuse on diagnosis and therapeutic outcome. *American Journal of Drug and Alcohol Abuse, 4,* 455–465.

Hall, S. M., Wasserman, D. A., & Havassy, B. E. (1991). Relapse prevention. In R. W. Pickins, C. G. Leukefeld, & C. R. Schuster (Eds.), *Improving drug abuse treatment* (Research monograph No. 106, pp. 279–292). Rockville, MD: U.S. Department of Health and Human Services.

Hansell, N., & Willis, G. L. (1977). Outpatient treatment of schizophrenia. *American Journal of Psychiatry, 134,* 1082–1086.

Hensala, J. D., Epstein, L. J., & Blacker, K. H. (1967). LSD and psychiatric inpatients. *Archives of General Psychiatry, 16,* 554–559.

Herning, R. I., Glover, B. J., Koeppl, B., Weddington, W., & Jaffe, J. H. (1990).

Cognitive deficits in abstaining cocaine abusers. In J. W. Spence & J. J. Boren (Eds.), *Residual effects of abused drugs on behavior* (National Institute on Drug Abuse Research Monograph No. 101, pp. 167–178). Washington, DC: National Institute on Drug Abuse.

Hesselbrock, M. N., Meyer, R. E., & Keener, J. J. (1985). Psychopathology in hospitalized alcoholics. *Archives of General Psychiatry, 42,* 1050–1055.

Hollister, L. F. (1986). Health aspects of cannabis. *Pharmacology Review, 38,* 1–20.

Hooley, J. (1985). Expressed emotion: A review of the critical literature. *Clinical Psychology Review, 5,* 119–140.

Javitt, D. C. (1987). Negative schizophrenic symptomatology and the PCP (phencyclidine) model of schizophrenia. *Hillside Journal of Psychiatry, 9,* 12–35.

Jernigan, T. L., Butters, N., DiTraglia, G., Schaeffer, K., Smith, T., Irwin, M., Grant, I., Schuckit, M., & Cermack, L. S. (1991). Reduced cerebral grey matter observed in alcoholics using magnetic resonance imaging. *Alcoholism: Clinical and Experimental Research, 15,* 418–427.

Jernigan, T. L., Pfefferbaum, A., & Zatz, L. M. (1986). Computed tomography correlates in alcoholism. In I. Grant (Ed.), *Neuropsychiatric correlates of alcoholism* (pp. 21–36). Washington, DC: American Psychiatric Press.

Khantzian, E. J. (1985). The self-medication hypothesis of addictive disorders: Focus on heroin and cocaine dependence. *American Journal of Psychiatry, 142,* 1259–1264.

Knudsen, P., & Vilmar, T. (1984). Cannabis and neuroleptic agents in schizophrenia. *Acta Psychiatrica Scandinavica, 69,* 162–174.

Kofoed, L. L., & Keys, A. (1988). Using group therapy to persuade dual-diagnosis patients to seek treatment. *Hospital and Community Psychiatry, 39,* 1209–1211.

Koretic, D., & Hotujac, L. (1987). Alcohol intake by schizophrenics. *Alcoholism, 23,* 37–42.

Kushner, M. G., & Mueser, K. T. (1993). *Psychiatric comorbidity with alcohol disorders.* National Institute on Alcohol Abuse and Alcoholism Eighth Special Report to the U.S. Congress on Alcohol and Health. (Available from: U.S. Department of Health and Human Services, Public Health Service, Alcohol, Drug Abuse, and Mental Health Administration, National Institute on Alcohol Abuse and Alcoholism, 5600 Fishers Lane, Rockville, MD 20857)

Kushner, M. G., Sher, K. J., & Beitman, B. D. (1990). The relation between alcohol problems and the anxiety disorders. *American Journal of Psychiatry, 147,* 685–695.

Landmark, J., Cernovsky, Z. Z., & Merskey, H. (1987). Correlates of suicide attempts and ideation in schizophrenia. *British Journal of Psychiatry, 151,* 18–20.

Lehman, A. F., Myers, C. P., & Corty, E. (1989). Assessment and classification of patients with psychiatric and substance abuse syndromes. *Hospital and Community Psychiatry, 40,* 1019–1025.

Lewine, R. R. (1981). Sex differences in schizophrenia: Timing or subtypes? *Psychological Bulletin, 90,* 432–444.

Liberman, R. P., & Corrigan, P. W. (1993). Designing new psychosocial treatments for schizophrenia. *Psychiatry: Interpersonal and Biological Processes.*

Lieberman, J. A., Jody, D., Geisler, S., Vital-Herne, J., Alvir, J. M. J., Walsleben, J., & Woerner, M. G. (1989). Treatment outcome of first episode schizophrenia. *Psychopharmacology Bulletin, 25,* 92–96.

Lieberman, J. A., Kinon, B. J., & Loebel, A. D. (1990). Dopaminergic mechanisms in idiopathic and drug-induced psychoses. *Schizophrenia Bulletin, 16,* 97–110.

Loranger, A. W. (1984). Sex differences in age at onset of schizophrenia. *Archives of General Psychiatry, 41,* 157–161.

Magliozzi, J. R., Kanter, S. L., Csernansky, J. G., & Hollister, L. E. (1983). Detection of marijuana use in psychiatric patients by determination of urinary delta-9-tetrahydrocannabino-11-oic acid. *Journal of Nervous and Mental Disease, 171,* 246–249.

Marlatt, G. A., & Gordon, J. R. (Eds.). (1985). *Relapse prevention: Maintenance strategies in the treatment of addictive behaviors.* New York: Guilford Press.

McLellan, A. T., Luborsky, L., Woody, G. E., O'Brien, C. P., & Druley, K. A. (1983). Predicting response to alcohol and drug abuse treatments. *Archives of General Psychiatry, 40,* 620–625.

Minkoff, K. (1991). Program components of a comprehensive integrated care system for seriously mentally ill patients with substance disorders. In K. Minkoff & R. E. Drake (Eds.), *Dual diagnosis of major mental illness and substance disorder* (pp. 13–28). San Francisco: Jossey-Bass.

Monti, P. M., Abrams, D. B., Kadden, R. M., & Cooney, N. L. (1989). *Treating alcohol dependence.* New York: Guilford Press.

Morrison, R. L., & Bellack, A. S. (1984). Social skills training. In A. S. Bellack (Ed.), *Schizophrenia: Treatment, management, and rehabilitation* (pp. 247–279). New York: Grune & Stratton.

Morrison, R. L., Bellack, A. S., & Mueser, K. T. (1988). Deficits in facial-affect recognition and schizophrenia. *Schizophrenia Bulletin, 14,* 67–83.

Mueser, K. T., Bellack, A. S., Douglas, M. S., & Wade, J. H. (1991). Prediction of social skill acquisition in schizophrenic and major affective disorder patients from memory and symptomatology. *Psychiatry Research, 37,* 281–296.

Mueser, K. T., & Glynn, S. M. (1990). Behavioral family therapy for schizophrenia. In M. Hersen, R. M. Eisler, & P. M. Miller (Eds.), *Progress in behavior modification* (Vol. 26, pp. 122-147). Newbury Park, CA: Sage.

Mueser, K. T., Yarnold, P. R., & Bellack, A. S. (1992). Diagnostic and demographic correlates of substance abuse in schizophrenia and major affective disorder. *Acta Psychiatrica Scandinavica, 85,* 48–55.

Mueser, K. T., Yarnold, P. R., Levinson, D. F., Singh, H., Bellack, A. S., Kee, K., Morrison, R. L., & Yadalam, K. G. (1990). Prevalence of substance abuse in schizophrenia: Demographic and clinical correlates. *Schizophrenia Bulletin, 16,* 31–56.

Nathan, P. E., & Skinstad, A. H. (1987). Outcomes of treatment for alcohol problems: Current methods, problems, and results. *Journal of Consulting and Clinical Psychology, 55,* 332–340.

Negrete, J. C., Knapp, W. P., Douglas, D. E., & Smith, W. B. (1986). Cannabis affects the severity of schizophrenic symptoms: Results of a clinical survey. *Psychological Medicine, 16,* 515–520.

Nuechterlein, K. H., & Dawson, M. E. (1984a). A heuristic vulnerability/stress model of schizophrenic episodes. *Schizophrenia Bulletin, 10,* 300–312.

Nuechterlein, K. H., & Dawson, M. E. (1984b). Information processing and attentional functioning in the developmental course of schizophrenic disorders. *Schizophrenia Bulletin, 10,* 160–203.

O'Malley, S. S., & Gawin, F. H. (1990). Abstinence symptomatology and neuropsychological impairment in chronic cocaine abusers. In J. W. Spence & J. J. Boren (Eds.), *Residual effects of abused drugs on behavior* (National Institute on Drug Abuse Research Monograph No. 101, pp. 179–190). Washington, DC: National Institute on Drug Abuse.

Osher, F. C., & Kofoed, L. L. (1989). Treatment of patients with psychiatric and psychoactive substance abuse disorder. *Hospital and Community Psychiatry, 40,* 1025–1030.

Parker, J. B., Meiller, R. M., & Andrews, G. W. (1960). Major psychiatric disorders masquerading as alcoholism. *Southern Medical Journal, 53,* 560–564.

Parsons, O. A. (1987). Do neuropsychological deficits predict alcoholics' treatment course and recovery? In O. A. Parsons, N. Butters, & P. E. Nathan (Eds.), *Neuropsychology of alcoholism: Implications for diagnosis and treatment* (pp. 273–290). New York: Guilford Press.

Parsons, O. A., & Leber, W. R. (1981). The relationship between cognitive dysfunction and brain damage in alcoholics: Causal, interactive, or epiphenomenal? *Alcoholism: Clinical and Experimental Research, 5,* 326–343.

Parsons, O. A., Schaeffer, K. W., & Glenn, S. W. (1990). Does neuropsychological test performance predict resumption of drinking in post-treatment alcoholics? *Addictive Behaviors, 15,* 297–307.

Pepper, B., Kirshner, M. C., & Ryglewicz, H. (1981). The young adult chronic patient: Overview of a population. *Hospital and Community Psychiatry, 32,* 463–469.

Peralta, V., & Cuesta, M. J. (1992). Influence of cannabis abuse on schizophrenic psychopathology. *Acta Psychiatrica Scandinavica, 85,* 127–130.

Pope, H. G., Ionescu-Pioggia, M., Aizley, H. G., & Varma, D. K. (1990). Drug use and life style among college undergraduates in 1989: A comparison with 1969 and 1978. *American Journal of Psychiatry, 147,* 998–1001.

Pristach, C. A., & Smith, C. M. (1990). Medication compliance and substance abuse among schizophrenic patients. *Hospital and Community Psychiatry, 41,* 1345–1348.

Raz, S., & Raz, N. (1990). Structural brain abnormalities in the major psychoses: A quantitative review of the evidence from computerized imaging. *Psychological Bulletin, 108,* 93–108.

Reed, R. J., & Grant, L. (1990). The long-term neurobehavioral consequences of substance abuse: Conceptual and methodological challenges for future research. In J. W. Spence & J. J. Boren (Eds.), *Residual effects of abused drugs on behavior* (National Institute on Drug Abuse Research Monograph No. 101, pp. 10–56). Washington, DC: National Institute on Drug Abuse.

Regier, D. A., Farmer, M. E., Rae, D. S., Locke, B. Z., Keith, S. J., Judd, L. L., & Goodwin, F. K. (1990). Comorbidity of mental disorders with alcohol and other drug abuse. *Journal of the American Medical Association, 264,* 2511–2518.

Richard, M. L., Liskow, B. I., & Perry, P. J. (1985). Recent psychostimulant use in hospitalized schizophrenics. *Journal of Clinical Psychiatry, 46,* 79–83.

Ridgely, M. S., Goldman, H. H., & Willenbring, M. (1990). Barriers to the care of persons with dual diagnoses: Organizational and financing issues. *Schizophrenia Bulletin, 16,* 123–132.

Ron, M. A. (1987). The brain of alcoholics: An overview. In O. A. Parsons, N. Butters, & P. E. Nathan (Eds.), Neuropsychology of alcoholism: Implications for diagnosis and treatment (pp. 11–20). New York: Guilford Press.

Roy, A. (1986). Suicide in schizophrenia. In A. Roy (Ed.), *Suicide* (pp. 97–112). Baltimore: Williams & Wilkins.

Ryan, C., DiDario, B., Butters, N., & Adinolfi, A. (1980). The relationship between abstinence and recovery of function in male alcoholics. *Journal of Clinical Neuropsychology, 2,* 125–134.

Safer, D. J. (1987). Substance abuse by young adult chronic patients. *Hospital and Community Psychiatry, 38,* 511–514.

Schiffman, S. (1992). Relapse process and relapse prevention in addictive behaviors. *The Behavior Therapist, 15,* 9–11.

Schneier, F. R., & Siris, S. G. (1987). A review of psychoactive substance use and abuse in schizophrenia: Patterns of drug choice. *Journal of Nervous and Mental Disease, 175,* 641–650.

Schuckit, M. A. (1989). *Drug and alcohol abuse* (3rd ed.). New York: Plenum Press.

Selzer, M. L. (1971). The Michigan Alcoholism Screening Test: The quest for a new diagnostic instrument. *American Journal of Psychiatry, 127,* 1653–1658.

Sevy, S., Kay, S. R., Opler, L. A., & van Praag, H. M. (1990). Significance of cocaine history in schizophrenia. *Journal of Nervous and Mental Disease, 178,* 642–648.

Siris, S. G., Kane, J. M., Frechen, K., Sellew, A. P., Mandeli, J., & Frasano-Dube, B. (1988). Histories of substance abuse in patients with postpsychotic depressions. *Comprehensive Psychiatry, 29,* 550–557.

Sobell, L. C., Toneatto, A., & Sobell, M. B. (1990). Behavior therapy. In A. S. Bellack & M. Hersen (Eds.). *Handbook of comparative treatments for adult disorders* (pp. 479–505). New York: Wiley.

Solomon, P. (1986). Receipt of aftercare services by problem types: Psychiatric, psychiatric/substance abuse and substance abuse. *Psychiatric Quarterly, 87,* 180–188.

Solomon, P., & Davis, J. M. (1986). The effects of alcohol abuse among the new chronically mentally ill. *Social Work in Health Care, 11*, 65–74.

Soni, S. D., & Brownlee, M. (1991). Alcohol abuse in chronic schizophrenics: Implications for management in the community. *Acta Psychiatrica Scandinavica, 84*, 272–276.

Spitzer, R. L., Williams, J. B. W., Gibbon, M., & First, M. B. (1990). *Structured Clinical Interview for DSM–III–R—Patient edition* (SCID–P, Version 1.0). Washington, DC: American Psychiatric Press.

Stein, L. I., & Test, M. A. (1980). An alternative to mental hospital treatment: Conceptual model, treatment program, and clinical evaluation. *Archives of General Psychiatry, 37*, 392–397.

Tarter, R. E., & Edwards, K. L. (1985). Neuropsychology of alcoholism. In R. E. Tarter & D. H. Van Thiel (Eds.), *Alcohol and the brain: Chronic effects* (pp. 217–242). New York: Plenum Press.

Test, M. A., Wallisch, L. S., Allness, D. J., & Ripp, K. (1989). Substance use in young adults with schizophrenic disorders. *Schizophrenia Bulletin, 15*, 465–476.

Toland, A. M., & Moss, H. B. (1989). Identification of the alcoholic schizophrenic: Use of clinical laboratory tests and the MAST. *Journal of Studies on Alcohol, 50*, 49–53.

Tsuang, M. T., Simpson, J. C., & Kronfol, Z. (1982). Subtypes of drug abuse with psychosis. *Archives of General Psychiatry, 39*, 141–147.

Tucker, J. A., & Sobell, L. C. (1992). Influences on help-seeking for drinking problems and on natural recovery without treatment. *The Behavior Therapist, 15*, 12–14.

Victor, M., & Hope, J. M. (1958). The phenomenon of auditory hallucinations in chronic alcoholism. *Journal of Nervous and Mental Disease, 126*, 451–481.

Welti, C. V., & Fishbain, D. A. (1985). Cocaine-induced psychosis and sudden death in recreational cocaine users. *Journal of Forensic Sciences, 30*, 873–880.

Westermeyer, J. (1986). *A clinical guide to alcohol and drug problems.* New York: Praeger.

Whitters, A. C., Cadoret, R. J., & Widmer, R. B. (1985). Factors associated with suicide attempts in alcohol abusers. *Journal of Affective Disorders, 9*, 19–23.

Wilkinson, D. A. (1985). Neuroradiologic investigations of alcoholism. In R. E. Tarter & D. H. Van Thiel (Eds.), *Alcohol and the brain: Chronic effects* (pp. 183–215). New York: Plenum Press.

Wilkinson, D. A. (1987). CT scan and neuropsychological assessments of alcoholism. In O. A. Parsons, N. Butters, & P. E. Nathan (Eds.), *Neuropsychology of alcoholism: Implications for diagnosis and treatment* (pp. 76–102). New York: Guilford Press.

17

SUBSTANCE USE DISORDERS
IN THE *DSM–IV*

PETER E. NATHAN

The Substance Use Disorders Work Groups, formed in early 1988 at the beginning of the process of developing the fourth edition of the *Diagnostic and Statistical Manual of the Mental Disorders* (*DSM–IV*), includes Marc A. Schuckit as the chair and Thomas J. Crowley, John E. Helzer, Peter E. Nathan, and George Woody as members.

A guiding principle in this group's deliberations continues to be the awareness, shared with other *DSM–IV* work groups, of the disruptive impact of frequent changes in the nomenclature on clinical practice and research. As a consequence, we resolved early on to recommend changes in operational criteria only if data suggested strongly that modification in the existing revised *DSM–III* (*DSM–III–R*: American Psychiatric Association, 1987) criteria would yield substantial benefits.

The work group has spent more of its time considering alternative concepts and definitions of substance abuse and dependence and their im-

Reprinted from the *Journal of Abnormal Psychology*, 100, 356–361. (1991). Copyright © 1991 by the American Psychological Association. Used with permission of the author.

The views expressed in this article are those of the authors and do not represent the official positions of the American Psychiatric Association or its Task Force on *DSM–IV*.

pact on possible modifications in the criteria for abuse and dependence than on any other single issue. This allocation of time and attention is not surprising: the abuse–dependence distinction is of central importance to the diagnosis of the substance use disorders. Because of the attention the work group has paid to this issue, and because I was one of two work group members charged with coordinating this effort on behalf of the group, the group's deliberations on the abuse–dependence distinction are extensively considered in this report.

The work group has also accomplished a number of other tasks during the 28 months of its existence; three of the most important are described in some detail in this article. They include the development of guidelines for distinguishing behaviors that accompany the abuse of specific substances from other psychiatric disorders with similar behavioral consequences, evaluation of the predictive validity of proposed alcoholic subtypes based on family history of abuse–dependence, and reexamination of the diagnostic relation between the organic brain syndromes and intoxication and withdrawal.

Work group members have also undertaken a range of other tasks of relevance to a new edition of the DSM. These tasks include: rewording the section on solvents; reanalyzing and adding to the data in support of nicotine and caffeine abuse categories; considering the data in support of the inclusion of the anabolic steroids as a diagnostic subgroup; evaluating the clinical significance of long-term or protracted abstinence syndromes associated with the stimulants, opiates, and depressants; reworking the text and descriptions of marijuana-related problems; and reconsidering the diverse criteria for remission from substance dependence.

PSYCHOACTIVE SUBSTANCE ABUSE AND DEPENDENCE

Evolution of Diagnostic Conceptions of Abuse and Dependence

Alcoholism and drug dependence appeared in DSM–I (American Psychiatric Association, 1952), the first broadly conceived American nomenclature, as subsets of *sociopathic personality disturbance*, a catch-all diagnostic category that also included antisocial behavior and the sexual deviations, including homosexuality. DSM–II (American Psychiatric Association, 1968) categorized all four patterns of behavior essentially the same way. In both these editions of the instrument, the implication of this placement of these conditions was the same: Persons who exhibited any of the four constituted a threat to societal order different from—perhaps more serious than—that posed by the victims of other mental or emotional disorders.

DSM–III (American Psychiatric Association, 1980) moved away

from the implicit moralizing that burdened those portions of *DSM–I* and *DSM–II* devoted to substance abuse and dependence, the sexual deviations, and antisocial behavior. It did so, in part, by allocating a separate category to the substance use disorders, thereby eliminating the guilt by association implicit in their *DSM–I* and *DSM–II* placement. In addition, the text of the *DSM–III* highlighted research findings that implicated sociocultural and genetic factors in the etiology of these disorders, thereby emphasizing the role scientists and clinicians had begun to play in their study and treatment.

DSM–III Conception of Abuse and Dependence

DSM–III divided the substance use disorders into two major categories, abuse and dependence. This decision reflected findings from several longitudinal studies begun in the 1970s, notably those of Cahalan and his colleagues and of Fillmore, that showed that substantial numbers of problem drinkers do not progress to alcohol dependence (e.g., Cahalan, 1970; Fillmore, 1988; Roizen, Cahalan, & Shanks, 1978). Recently, Hasin, Grant, and Endicott (1990), who investigated the natural history of abuse and dependence, also found a significant number of persons with a history of abuse who had never progressed to dependence; this finding further justified a category of abuse separate from dependence.

Spitzer, Williams, and Skodol (1980) defined the *DSM–III* conception of substance abuse as

> a pattern of pathological use for at least one month that causes impairment in social or occupational functioning. Examples . . . include inability to reduce or discontinue use or remaining intoxicated throughout the day. (p. 153)

They also characterized the *DSM–III* concept of substance dependence by

> the presence of either tolerance or withdrawal. For alcohol and cannabis dependence, impairment in social or occupational functioning is also required. In the case of tobacco, the presence of a serious physical disorder that the individual knows is exacerbated by tobacco use is also considered evidence of dependence. (Spitzer et al., 1980, p. 155)

The empirical data accumulated over the years in support of the validity of the *DSM* criteria for (largely) alcohol abuse and dependence have, with some exceptions (e.g., Schuckit, Schwei, & Gold, 1986), found the distinction between abuse and dependence predictive of disorder severity and treatment outcome to a moderate degree (e.g., Hermos, Locastro, Glynn, Bouchard, & De Labry, 1988; Kosten & Kosten, 1990; Rounsaville, Dolinsky, Babor, & Meyer, 1987). Other predictors, however, including age of onset and intensity of alcohol or drug use (e.g., Schuckit, 1985), family history of substance abuse–dependence (e.g., Buydens-Branchey, Branchey,

& Noumaier, 1989), and number and severity of comorbid conditions, especially antisocial personality (e.g., Hesselbrock, Meyer, & Keener, 1985; Hesselbrock, Weidenman, & Reed, 1985; Rounsaville, Spitzer, & Williams, 1986; Stabenau, 1984), have predicted both severity and outcomes at least as robustly.

Critiques of the DSM–III Criteria for Abuse–Dependence

Extensive critiques of the *DSM–III* criteria for abuse and dependence have been published (e.g., Rounsaville, 1987; Rounsaville et al., 1986; Schuckit, Zisook, & Mortola, 1985). Most authors have based their critiques on the voluminous literature on the sensitivity, specificity, and utility of the *DSM–III* criteria. Though widely hailed as less stigmatizing and more reliable than its predecessors, *DSM–I* and *DSM–II*, and despite the empirical data in support of its concurrent and predictive validity cited above, the *DSM–III* concepts of abuse and dependence were widely criticized.

Rounsaville (1987) identified the following seven key problems with which most critics of the *DSM–III* have appeared to agree.

1. The substance use disorder section of the *DSM–III* does not adequately conceptualize or denote the coexistent features of these disorders. Most clinicians and researchers agree that there is much more to substance use and abuse than simply the use of psychoactive drugs. The criteria for abuse and dependence in the *DSM–III* do not reflect this clinical diversity.

2. The *DSM–III* conceptualization of the substance use disorders is unhelpfully atheoretical. By contrast, the consensus statement of the World Health Organization (WHO) Working Group 4 (World Health Organization, 1981) represents a cogent and convincing statement of the need for a theory-driven conceptualization of the substance use disorders. The WHO model proposed in that statement, influenced by Edwards and Gross's (1976) alcohol dependence syndrome (described later), is a complex, dynamic scheme based on behavioral principles that puts forward a "system of reinforcement which initiates and perpetuates substance taking and dependence" (Rounsaville, 1987, p. 183).

3. Tolerance is a poor criterion for determining dependence. Tolerance in *DSM–III* is not specified in a complex manner, even though clinical tolerance phenomena are complex and varied. As well, wide individual differences in initial levels of tolerance to drugs are the rule rather than the exception.

Accordingly, it is easy for nontolerant persons to meet the tolerance criterion the way it is written in *DSM–III*.

4. The relation between substance abuse and substance dependence is inconsistent and illogical in several substance categories in *DSM–III*. As the dependence criteria are written, they include—and sometimes mix—two different concepts: *psychological* dependence characterized by a pathological pattern of use and *physiological* dependence demonstrated by a substance-specific withdrawal syndrome.

5. Efforts to achieve consistency of diagnostic criteria across different groups of drugs have produced meaningless criteria in particular instances. The limiting, time-linked phrases, *one-month duration* and *intoxicated throughout the day* are examples. They were not derived empirically, and in many instances, they do not accord with clinical experience.

6. Blackouts are incorrectly defined in the alcohol abuse and dependence criteria.

7. Quantity and frequency of drug use are inconsistent features of the criteria for the substance use disorders, though this information is frequently of diagnostic significance. The absolute quantity and frequency of drug use are listed as considerations in diagnosing substance use disorders in only two specific instances.

DSM–III–R Conception of Abuse and Dependence

The DSM–III–R conception of abuse and dependence owes a heavy debt to the alcohol dependence syndrome, described by Edwards and Gross in 1976 and elaborated by Edwards, Arif, and Hodgson in 1981 and by Edwards in 1986. As described by Rounsaville and Kranzler (1989) in a review of the theoretical basis and empirical grounding for *DSM–III–R*, the alcohol dependence syndrome develops

> in accordance with behavioral principles via a system of reinforcement that initiates and perpetuates substance taking and dependence. The positive and negative reinforcement contingencies involved in heavy alcohol use lead to the development of a core set of symptoms designated as the *dependence syndrome*; it is seen as multidimensional with *biologic, social, and behavioral components*. The cardinal feature of this syndrome is impaired control over alcohol use. The syndrome elements, most of which are incorporated into *DSM–III–R* criteria, are as follows: 1) narrowing of the substance use repertoire such that substance use becomes stereotyped around a regular schedule of almost continuous or daily consumption; 2) salience of substance-taking behavior such that, despite negative consequences, substance use is given

higher priority than are other activities that previously had been important; 3) increased tolerance; 4) withdrawal symptoms; 5) substance use to avoid withdrawal; 6) subjectively experienced compulsion to use the substance; and 7) readdiction liability. (pp. 324–326)

The substance dependence syndrome concept was probably attractive to the drafters of *DSM–III–R*, at least in part, because it appears to address most of the seven key problems with the *DSM–III* approach to the substance use disorders identified by Rounsaville (1987). Thus, the substance dependence syndrome constitutes a theoretical, integrating statement about substance dependence that clarifies the relationship between abuse and dependence, diminishes the importance of both tolerance and withdrawal in the diagnosis of dependence, reduces the clinician's need for knowledge of either blackout or drug quantity or frequency, and permits, at least to some extent, the incorporation of coexisting features of the substance use disorders in the diagnostic formulation.

The construct of a substance dependence syndrome seems to be valid for drugs other than alcohol, the drug for which the construct was originally developed (e.g., Phillips et al., 1987; Stripp, Burgess, Pattison, Pead, & Holman, 1990; Sutherland et al., 1986). The syndrome has also been independently validated for alcohol by research workers other than Edwards and his colleagues (e.g., Babor, Cooney, & Lauerman, 1987; Drummond, 1990).

Concerns About the DSM–III–R Conception of Abuse–Dependence

Despite the apparent advantages of conceptual reliance on the substance dependence syndrome in the *DSM–III–R*, the criteria for abuse and dependence that result from this reliance have presented some problems for diagnosticians and clinicians. Thus, moving away from the greater emphasis in the *DSM–III* on the physical aspects of dependence (exemplified by tolerance and withdrawal symptoms) has appeared to some to contradict both widespread clinical conviction and empirical data about the predictive validity of these symptoms (e.g., Hasin, Endicott, & Keller, 1989; Kosten & Kosten, 1990; Rounsaville et al., 1987). As well, shifting the criteria away from social consequences of alcohol abuse and dependence has seemed to some to be a movement away from a central feature of the syndrome. The *DSM–III–R* criteria for abuse and dependence, some have claimed, have also increased the heterogeneity of dependence (by lowering the threshold for its diagnosis), obscured traditional concepts of the substance use disorders (by embracing a dimensional mode of abuse–dependence and thereby eschewing the traditional categorical model on which the disease model of alcoholism has rested), and reduced the saliency of the concept of abuse (by reducing it to a residual category), despite some empirical evidence to the contrary (e.g., Hasin et al., 1990).

Perhaps most telling, though, is the decision on the part of the drafters of the *DSM–III–R* to restructure the *DSM–III* system for diagnosing abuse and dependence by making a rather marked change away from the *DSM–III* criteria in favor of the *DSM–III–R* criteria, without subjecting each of the two sets of criteria to empirical testing for concurrent and predictive validity. Despite encouraging empirical and conceptual reports on the advantages of the substance dependence syndrome (e.g., Babor, Cooney, & Lauerman, 1987; Babor, Lauerman, & Cooney, 1987; Skinner & Goldberg, 1986), a direct comparison of the *DSM–III* and *DSM–III–R* criteria with a range of patients in a range of clinical settings is requisite to a fully informed decision on the differential predictive validity of the two sets of criteria.

Decisions on Conceptions of Abuse–Dependence in DSM–IV

Decisions on a range of questions about the abuse–dependence criteria in *DSM–IV* will have to be made by the work group. They will be made empirically, after data have been analyzed on the concurrent and predictive validity of the *DSM–III* and *DSM–III–R* criteria from several sets of studies.

A principal source of these data will be six field trials, which will survey 800 patients diverse in age, ethnicity, gender, and treatment status who suffer from a range of substance use disorders. The patients' abuse–dependence will be diagnosed according to criteria from the *DSM–III*, the *International Classification of Diseases and Related Health Problems* (10th ed.; World Health Organization, 1990), or the *DSM–III–R*, as well as a set of criteria proposed for the *DSM–IV* pending the evaluation of their reliability and validity. In the proposed *DSM–IV* criteria, shown in Table 1, abuse does not represent a residual category, as it does in *DSM–III–R*; instead, abuse is diagnosed according to a distinct and specific set of behaviors. Dependence incorporates the *DSM–III–R* emphasis on compulsive use as well as the *DSM–III* reliance on impairment in social and occupational functioning and pathological use. Tolerance or withdrawal symptoms or both are required for the diagnosis of dependence in the proposed *DSM–IV* criteria.

In addition, several existing sets of previously unanalyzed clinical data will be examined. These data were gathered from general population samples (e.g., the Epidemiologic Catchment Area projects) as well as from several groups of persons who used cocaine, heroin, and alcohol. The abuse or dependence by these persons will be diagnosed according to the proposed *DSM–IV* criteria as well as by those from at least one of the three other diagnostic systems.

Patients in both the field trials and the unanalyzed data sets have been or will be followed for a minimum of a month—in some instances,

TABLE 1
Diagnostic Criteria for Psychoactive Substance Abuse and Dependence (Draft, October 1990)

A. Psychoactive substance abuse involves a pattern of repeated problems with the substance as indicated by at least two of the following:

 (1) substance taken in larger amounts or over a longer period than intended;
 (2) persistent desire or unsuccessful efforts to cut down or control substance use;
 (3) a great deal of time spent on activities necessary to obtain the substance (e.g., visiting multiple doctors or driving long distances) or take the substance (e.g., chain-smoking);
 (4) continued substance use despite knowledge of persistent or recurrent social, psychological, or physical problems caused or exacerbated by the use of the substance (e.g., daily cigarette smoking despite knowledge of a heightened risk of lung cancer, cocaine use despite cocaine-induced depression, or continued drinking despite an ulcer made worse by alcohol consumption);
 (5) recurrent substance use resulting in inability to fulfill major role obligations at work, school, or home [examples include (a) repeated absences or poor work performance related to substance use, (b) substance-related absences, suspensions, or expulsions from school, and (c) neglect of children or household responsibilities because of substance use];
 (6) recurrent substance use in situations in which it is physically hazardous (e.g., driving an automobile or operating a machine when impaired by substance use);
 (7) important social, occupational, or recreational activities given up or reduced because of substance use; or
 (8) recurrent substance-related legal or interpersonal problems (examples include substance-related arrests and traffic accidents, and physical fights related to substance use).

B. Psychoactive substance dependence involves, additionally, one or both of the following:

 (1) *tolerance*, defined by (a) the need for markedly increased amounts of the substance in order to achieve intoxication or desired effect, (b) markedly diminished effect with continued use of the same amount of the substance, or (c) evidence of the ability to function adequately at doses or blood levels of the substance that produce significant impairment in a casual user (e.g., consuming a fifth of whiskey or its equivalent per day); or
 (2) *evidence of withdrawal*, characterized by a withdrawal syndrome observed after reduction or cessation of substance use or in response to a challenge with an antagonist.

substantially more—to determine the course of the substance use disorder, including such indexes of outcome as whether or not drinking or drug use resumes, pattern of the resultant alcohol- or drug-related problems, presence and severity of alcohol or drug withdrawal symptoms, occurrence and nature of comorbidity, and when relevant, the nature of subsequent alcohol- or drug-related diagnoses. (Although significantly longer follow-up intervals would be desirable, given that relapses also occur after many months of sobriety, the pragmatics of research and its funding have, to this time, limited such follow-up intervals in outcome research.)

After analysis of unanalyzed data sets as well as those from the field trials, the differential predictive and concurrent validity of the four sets of diagnostic criteria will be analyzed. Although the ultimate validation of criteria for abuse or dependence will be how well abuse and dependence independently predict course of illness, other relevant predictors will include number and malignancy of substance-related signs and symptoms, associated physical, psychological, psychiatric, social, familial, and vocational status, and response to treatment and other measures of involvement in treatment.

SUBSTANCE USE AND OTHER PSYCHIATRIC DISORDERS

The work group completed a critical review of the behavioral consequences of use and abuse of the substances, depressants and stimulants, for which data that relate to psychiatric syndromes is most plentiful. These substances yield a high frequency of depressive, anxious, and psychotic behaviors, which usually disappear when use of the substance is discontinued. The review concluded that the significance of anxiety, depression, and psychosis for the diagnosis, prognosis, or treatment of persons who use drugs that depress or stimulate brain function during intoxication and withdrawal must be viewed very differently than the same behaviors in persons who are not abusing alcohol, benzodiazepines, or barbiturates, on the one hand, and cocaine, crack, the amphetamines, or the over-the-counter and prescription weight-reducing drugs, on the other.

To sharpen the difficult diagnostic distinctions that must be made at such times, members of the Substance Use Disorder Work Group have been in close contact with members of the other relevant work groups to develop guidelines for *DSM–IV*. It seems clear even now, for example, early in the process of reviewing this material, that persons must be drug-free between 4–6 weeks before they can be reliably diagnosed with a psychiatric disorder exclusive of the effects of their drug use.

PREDICTIVE VALIDITY OF ALCOHOLIC SUBTYPES

The work group reviewed data on the potential clinical importance of identifying alcoholics with alcoholic family members. This review was largely motivated by two research programs, both started in the 1970s, which reported that a family history of alcoholism affected behavioral outcomes. Goodwin's early findings (summarized in Goodwin, 1983) suggested that such persons might be different behaviorally from alcoholics without such a family history. Research by Cloninger and his colleagues (e.g., Cloninger, Bohman, Sigvardsson, & Van Knorring, 1985; Sigvardsson, Cloninger, & Bohman, 1985) has suggested that men with a family history of alcoholism might experience an earlier onset of problems and a more severe clinical course. Although still influential, these studies have been widely criticized for methodological weaknesses (e.g., Lester, 1988; Murray et al., 1983). (More recently, research by Finn and Pihl, 1987, 1988, has demonstrated that men with and without a paternal history of alcoholism differ in cardiovascular reactivity to unavoidable shock, which further supports the likelihood that family history of alcoholism may predict differential behavioral outcomes.)

A search of the psychiatric and psychological literature was conducted for every empirical study of familial alcoholism from 1970 to the present. The exact prevalence of alcoholics with a family history of alcoholism was found to differ depending on the research methods used. With the most restrictive criteria (definitive diagnosis of alcoholism in biological parents), between 20% and 35% of alcoholics entering treatment had an alcoholic father, mother, or both. When alcoholism is defined less restrictively and is extended to include any first- or second-degree relative, almost two thirds of alcoholics entering treatment have a family form of the disorder.

Alcoholics with a family history of alcoholism are reported to develop their alcohol-related problems earlier, to demonstrate more intense symptoms of physical dependence on alcohol, and to be likely to show more severe social consequences of their drinking. However, such alcoholics tend to come from families with more psychopathology of many kinds. This increased prevalence of psychopathology, in turn, rather than simply the familial alcoholism, may be responsible for the earlier onset and more severe course of alcohol-related problems. Also, more alcoholics with a family history of the disorder fulfill criteria for a preexisting antisocial personality disorder, a finding that can also help to explain the behavioral differences between alcoholics with and without a family history.

This review concluded that whereas familial alcoholism does convey some useful information about the future clinical course of a person's alcoholism, once additional variables are controlled, inclusion of a diagnosis of familial alcoholism into *DSM–IV* does not appear justifiable.

ORGANIC DISORDERS ASSOCIATED WITH SUBSTANCE USE

DSM–III–R lists and details 19 diagnoses that describe behaviors associated with alcohol or drug intoxication or withdrawal. It also includes 6 organic mental syndromes of chronic behavioral disorders that involve memory loss, hallucinations, delusions, affective disorder, anxiety, and personal disorder. *DSM–III–R* proscribes diagnosis of the former in the presence of the latter, yet the variability of both the intoxication or withdrawal states and the organic mental syndromes is such that a great deal of diagnostic ambiguity can result, especially when a patient is in the midst of the chronic abuse of several substances.

The work group's review of these complex issues suggests that reliable decision rules may be generated to enable simultaneous diagnosis of both intoxication or withdrawal states and organic mental syndromes, as well as psychiatric comorbidity, an additional complicating factor in cases of polydrug abuse–dependence. After consulting 150–200 articles on the phenomenology of these disorders, the review concluded that the distinction between intoxication or withdrawal disorders and organic mental syndromes may have outlived its usefulness. An appropriate substitute may be a new system that names and describes the substances abused, the manner in which they have been used, and the consequences of that use (e.g., alcohol intoxication mood disorder, pentobarbital withdrawal delirium, cocaine delusional disorder, as well as simpler conditions like cocaine intoxication, alcohol withdrawal, and cannabis intoxication).

REFERENCES

American Psychiatric Association. (1952). *Diagnostic and statistical manual of mental disorders* (1st ed.). Washington, DC: Author.

American Psychiatric Association. (1968). *Diagnostic and statistical manual of mental disorders* (2nd ed.). Washington, DC: Author.

American Psychiatric Association. (1980). *Diagnostic and statistical manual of mental disorders* (3rd ed.). Washington, DC: Author.

American Psychiatric Association. (1987). *Diagnostic and statistical manual of mental disorders* (Rev. 3rd ed.). Washington, DC: Author.

Babor, T. F., Cooney, N. L., & Lauerman, R. J. (1987). The drug dependence syndrome concept as a psychological theory of relapse behavior: An empirical evaluation. *British Journal of Addiction, 82,* 393–405.

Babor, T. F., Lauerman, R. J., & Cooney, N. L. (1987). In search of the alcohol dependence syndrome: A cross-national study of its structure and validity. In P. Paakkanen & P. Sulkunen (Eds.), *Cultural studies on drinking and drinking practices* (pp. 75–82). Helsinki, Finland: Social Research Institute on Alcohol Studies.

Buydens-Branchey, L., Branchey, M. H., & Noumair, D. (1989). Age of alcoholism onset: Relationship to susceptibility. *Archives of General Psychiatry, 46,* 225–230.

Cahalan, D. (1970). *Problem drinkers: A national survey.* San Francisco: Jossey-Bass.

Cloninger, C. R., Bohman, M., Sigvardsson, S., & VonKnorring, A. (1985). Psychopathology in adopted-out children of alcoholics: The Stockholm Adoption Study. In M. Galanter (Ed.), *Recent developments in alcoholism* (pp. 37–51). New York: Plenum Press.

Drummond, D. C. (1990). The relationship between alcohol dependence and alcohol-related problems in a clinical population. *British Journal of Addiction*, 85, 357–366.

Edwards, G. (1986). The alcohol dependence syndrome: A concept as stimulus to enquiry. *British Journal of Addiction*, 81, 171–183.

Edwards, G., Arif, A., & Hodgson, R. (1981). Nomenclature and classification of drug and alcohol related problems. *Bulletin of WHO*, 59, 225–242.

Edwards, G., & Gross, M. M. (1976). Alcohol dependence: Provisional description of a clinical syndrome. *British Medical Journal*, 1, 1058–1061.

Fillmore, K. M. (1988). *Alcohol use across the life course: A critical review of 70 years of international longitudinal research*. Toronto: Addiction Research Foundation.

Finn, P. R., & Pihl, R. O. (1987). Men at risk for alcoholism: The effect of alcohol on cardiovascular response to unavoidable shock. *Journal of Abnormal Psychology*, 96, 230–236.

Finn, P. R., & Pihl, R. O. (1988). Risk for alcoholism: A comparison between two different groups of sons of alcoholics on cardiovascular reactivity and sensitivity to alcohol. *Alcoholism: Clinical and Experimental Research*, 12, 742–747.

Goodwin, D. W. (1983). Familial alcoholism: A separate entity? *Substance and Alcohol Actions and Misuse*, 4, 129–136.

Hasin, D. S., Endicott, J., & Keller, M. B. (1989). RDC alcoholism in patients with major affective syndromes: Two-year course. *American Journal of Psychiatry*, 146, 318–323.

Hasin, D. S., Grant, B., & Endicott, J. (1990). The natural history of alcohol abuse: Implications for definitions of alcohol use disorders. *American Journal of Psychiatry*.

Hermos, J. A., Locastro, J. S., Glynn, R. J., Bouchard, G. R., & De Labry, L. O. (1988). Predictors of reduction and cessation of drinking in community-dwelling men: Results from the normative aging study. *Journal of Studies on Alcohol*, 49, 363–368.

Hesselbrock, M. N., Meyer, R. E., & Keener, J. J. (1985). Psychopathology in hospitalized alcoholics. *Archives of General Psychiatry*, 42, 1050–1055.

Hesselbrock, M. N., Weidenman, M. A., & Reed, H. B. C. (1985). Effect of age, sex, drinking history and antisocial personality on neuropsychology of alcoholism. *Journal of Studies on Alcohol*, 46, 313–319.

Kosten, T. A., & Kosten, T. R. (1990). *The dependence syndrome concept as applied to alcohol and other substances of abuse*. Unpublished manuscript, Yale University.

Lester, D. (1988). Genetic theory: An assessment of the heritability of alcoholism. In C. D. Chaudron & D. A. Wilkinson (Eds.), *Theories on alcoholism* (p. 1–28). Toronto: Addiction Research Foundation.

Murray, R. M., Clifford, C., Gurling, H. M. D., Topham, A., Clow, A., & Bernadt, M. (1983). Current genetic and biological approaches to alcoholism. *Psychiatric Developments*, 2, 179–192.

Phillips, G. T., Gossop, M. R., Edwards, G., Sutherland, G., Taylor, C., & Strang,

J. (1987). The application of the SODQ to the measurement of the severity of opiate dependence in a British sample. *British Journal of Addiction, 82,* 691–699.

Roizen, R., Cahalan, D., & Shanks, P. (1978). Spontaneous remission among untreated problem drinkers. In D. B. Kandel (Ed.), *Longitudinal research on drug use: Empirical findings and methodological issues* (pp. 197–221). Washington, DC: Hemisphere.

Rounsaville, B. J. (1987). An evaluation of the DSM–III substance-use disorders. In G. Tischler (Ed.), *Treatment and classification in psychiatry* (pp. 175–194). New York: Cambridge University Press.

Rounsaville, B. J., Dolinsky, Z. S., Babor, T. F., & Meyer, R. E. (1987). Psychopathology as a predictor of treatment outcome in alcoholics. *Archives of General Psychiatry, 44,* 505–513.

Rounsaville, B. J., & Kranzler, H. R. (1989). The *DSM–III–R* diagnosis of alcoholism. *Annual Review of Psychiatry, 8,* 323–340.

Rounsaville, B. J., Spitzer, R. L., & Williams, J. B. W. (1986). Proposed changes in *DSM–III* substance use disorders: Description and rationale. *American Journal of Psychiatry, 143,* 463–468.

Schuckit, M. A. (1985). The clinical implications of primary diagnostic groups among alcoholics. *Archives of General Psychiatry, 42,* 1043–1049.

Schuckit, M. A., Schwei, M. G., & Gold, E. (1986). Prediction of outcomes in inpatient alcoholics. *Journal of Studies on Alcohol, 47,* 151–155.

Schuckit, M. A., Zisook, S., & Mortola, J. (1985). Clinical implications of *DSM–III* diagnoses about alcohol abuse and alcohol dependence. *American Journal of Psychiatry, 142,* 1403–1408.

Sigvardsson, S., Cloninger, C. R., & Bohman, M. (1985). Prevention and treatment of alcohol abuse: Uses and limitations of the high risk paradigm. *Social Biology, 32,* 185–193.

Skinner, H. A., & Goldberg, A. E. (1986). Evidence for a drug dependence syndrome among narcotic users. *British Journal of Addiction, 81,* 479–484.

Spitzer, R. L., Williams, J. B., & Skodol, A. E. (1980). *DSM–III:* The major achievements and an overview. *American Journal of Psychiatry, 137,* 151–160.

Stabenau, J. R. (1984). Implications of family history of alcoholism, antisocial personality, and sex differences in alcohol dependence. *American Journal of Psychiatry, 141,* 1178–1182.

Stripp, A. W., Burgess, P. M., Pattison, P. E., Pead, J., & Holman, C. P. (1990). An evaluation of the psychoactive substance dependence syndrome in its application to opiate users. *British Journal of Addictions, 85,* 621–627.

Sutherland, G., Edwards, G., Taylor, C., Phillips, G., Gossop, M., & Brady, R. (1986). The measurement of opiate dependence. *British Journal of Addiction, 81,* 485–494.

World Health Organization. (1981). Memorandum: Nomenclature and classification of drug- and alcohol-related problems. *Bulletin of WHO, 59,* 225–242.

World Health Organization. (1990). *International classification of diseases and related health problems* (10th ed.). Geneva: Author.

18

ALCOHOL AND AGGRESSION: A META-ANALYSIS ON THE MODERATING EFFECTS OF INHIBITORY CUES, TRIGGERING EVENTS, AND SELF-FOCUSED ATTENTION

TIFFANY A. ITO, NORMAN MILLER, AND VICKI E. POLLOCK

Statistics on the co-occurrence of alcohol and violent crimes suggest a troubling link between alcohol and aggression. Perpetrators of violent crimes are more likely intoxicated during the commission of their crime than are perpetrators of nonviolent crimes (Murdoch, Pihl, & Ross, 1990).

Reprinted from *Psychological Bulletin, 120,* 60–82. (1996). Copyright © 1996 by the American Psychological Association. Used with permission of the author.

This work was supported by an American Psychological Association Minority Fellowship, National Science Foundation Grant SBR-9319752, National Institute for Alcohol and Alcoholism Grants RO1-AA08031 and KO2-AA0146, and Alcohol Beverage Foundation Grant ABMRF.

We thank Shelley Duval and Virginia Duval for theoretical discussions on self-focused attention; John Musciente and Darren Urada for assistance in locating the studies, computing effect sizes, and serving as judges; and Brad J. Bushman, Kate B. Carey, Michael J. Cody, Michael E. Dawson, Mitchell Earleywine, Blair T. Johnson, Sheila T. Murphy, and Stephen J. Read for helpful comments on drafts. We presented portions of this article at the 1994 annual meeting of the Research Society on Alcoholism, Maui, Hawaii.

Such findings have fueled a large body of research addressing the relationship between intoxication and aggression. Both qualitative (e.g., Gustafson, 1993; Moss & Tartar, 1993; Pihl, 1983; Pihl, Peterson, & Lau, 1993; Taylor, 1983; Taylor & Chermack, 1993; Taylor & Leonard, 1983) and quantitative (Bushman & Cooper, 1990; Steele & Southwick, 1985) reviews have quite clearly shown that intoxication can increase aggression. A theoretical understanding of this relationship, however, remains unresolved.

In this article, we use meta-analytic procedures to explore the role of situational factors in moderating the relation between alcohol and aggression. Theories emphasizing the way in which attention is allocated to various situational cues are important in this context (e.g., Taylor & Chermack, 1993; Taylor & Leonard, 1983; Zeichner & Phil, 1979). Two specific variants are a model based on alcohol's anxioloytic effect and Steele and Southwick's (1985) inhibition conflict model. Other situationally determined variables that may vary within the context of an aggression-eliciting situation are provocation, frustration, and self-focused attention. For decades, researchers have examined the relation between alcohol and aggression using paradigms that contain either a provoking or frustrating event. Although the roles of provocation and frustration have figured prominently in experimental research on aggression per se, interestingly, there has been little explicit theoretical concern about their effects on aggression by intoxicated individuals. Similarly, focus of attention historically has been an important variable in the social psychological literature on aggression, but very little attention has been paid to understanding how it may affect the aggressive behavior of intoxicated participants. Consequently, in this meta-analysis, we also assess the moderating role of provocation, frustration, and self-focused attention in alcohol-induced aggression.

WHY DOES ALCOHOL SOMETIMES INCREASE AGGRESSION?

The literature on the effects of alcohol on aggression is extremely large, and an examination of all the facets of it is beyond the scope of a single article. For instance, behavioral changes following alcohol consumption may be directly attributable to its pharmacological effects, but at this time there is no clear understanding of the specific mechanism that causes alcohol to increase aggression. Among the effects of acute and chronic alcohol administration are altered permeability of cell membranes, as well as disruptions of voltage-gated ion channels (Hunt, 1985) and secondary messengers (Hoffman & Tabakoff, 1990). Whereas some research has emphasized the roles of tetrahydroisoquinolines (e.g., Myers, Melchior, & Swartzwelder, 1980) and endorphins (e.g., Gianoulakis & Gupta, 1986) as biological mediators of alcohol effects, other research has focused on alcohol-induced changes in the neurotransmitters dopamine and serotonin as mechanisms that underlie behavioral reinforcement resulting from alcohol intake (Koob & Bloom, 1988). Despite this extensive animal and human research, however, there is no known direct causal link between specific biological and behavioral changes induced by alcohol.

In human behavioral research, a large body of survey data indicates that social drinkers expect alcohol to increase aggression (Lindman & Lang, 1994; Rohsenow, 1983; Roizen, 1983; Southwick, Steele, Marlatt, & Lindell, 1981). It is, therefore, likely that people possess the expectation not only that alcohol will facilitate aggression but also that such antinormative behavior will be met with greater tolerance if it is displayed by an intoxicated rather than a sober person (Critchlow, 1986; Lang & Sibrel, 1989; Sobell & Sobell, 1973; but see Gustafson, 1991b, for an alternative outcome). It has, therefore, been suggested that the increased aggression in intoxicated participants reflects, at least to some degree, their attempt to fulfill this expectation or role-play the part of the "aggressive drunk" (Brown, Goldman, Inn, & Anderson, 1980; Lang, 1983; MacAndrew & Edgerton, 1969; Marlatt & Rohsenow, 1980). Moreover, the appropriateness of this social role may be especially salient to participants in the experiments reviewed in this meta-analysis because their procedures are likely to prime the alcohol–aggression expectation through the display of aggression-related cues (e.g., shock apparatus and competitive games). Finally, the very fact that a scientist studies both alcohol and aggression may reinforce these expectancies in participants. Thus, under an expectancy-driven conceptualization of alcohol-facilitated aggression, it is assumed that people possess the expectation that alcohol can increase aggression and that such beliefs facilitate aggression following alcohol consumption.

Despite the expectation people possess for alcohol to increase aggression, substantial unexplained variability characterizes the relation between alcohol and aggression. For example, although survey data show that people expect alcohol to increase aggression, this same data show that aggression is not always expected to follow intoxication. When respondents were asked to indicate whether alcohol always, usually, or sometimes makes them aggressive, only 1% reported that they always expected aggression (Roizen, 1983). In addition, a meta-analytic assessment of the independent contributions of pharmacological and expectancy effects on intoxicated aggression revealed significant heterogeneity among both sets of effect sizes (Hull & Bond, 1986). These findings suggest that situational factors play an important role in determining whether and to what degree aggression increases following alcohol consumption. Consequently, we discuss five situational factors that we examined in our meta-analysis. For this purpose, we group them under the next two main headings.

COGNITIVE THEORIES OF INTOXICATED AGGRESSION

Alcohol has been observed to cause many forms of cognitive impairments. Intoxication appears to narrow attention (Huntley, 1973; Moskowitz & DePry, 1968), interfere with memory processes (Birnbaum, Johnson, Hartley, & Taylor, 1980; Birnbaum & Parker, 1977; Craik, 1977; Jones & Jones, 1977; Rosen & Lee, 1976), and diminish the ability to engage in abstract thinking (Tartar, Jones, Sompson, & Vega, 1971). Applying this array of consequences to the explanation of aggressive behavior, several researchers have proposed what we refer to as cognitive theories of alcohol-induced aggression. These cognitive theories have also been referred to as attentional hypotheses (Gustafson, 1993) and cognitive theoretical perspectives (Taylor & Chermack, 1993). For example, Pernanen (1976) argued that intoxication decreases the number of cues to which a person can attend. An intoxicated person may not correctly perceive the reasons for other people's behavior, making the actions of others appear more arbitrary and provocative than they would to a sober perceiver. As a consequence, Pernanen believed intoxicated individuals are more likely to respond with aggression. Taylor and colleagues (Taylor & Chermack, 1993; Taylor & Leonard, 1983) argued that alcohol-induced impairments render intoxicated individuals able to attend to only the most salient and dominant cues, which are typically those that instigate an aggressive response. According to this view, the propensity for aggression is increased when alcohol is consumed because inhibitory cues are less salient to intoxicated persons. In addition, Zeichner and Pihl (1979) showed that when an experimental procedure directly manipulated the correlation between the amount of aversive stimulation participants received with the amount of aggression they had displayed, sober participants decreased their aggressive behavior relative to a condition in which aggression and aversive stimulation were experimentally controlled to be uncorrelated. By contrast, intoxicated participants appeared unaffected by the contingency between own aggression and amount of aversive stimulation received, displaying equally high levels of aggression in both conditions. This led Zeichner and Pihl to suggest that alcohol increases aggression by affecting the ability to correctly perceive the negative consequences of one's aggression.

The assumption that alcohol impairs a person's ability to perceive and respond to aggression inhibiting cues but has less effect on one's ability to perceive and respond to instigating stimuli is common to these cognitive theories. However, alcohol does not uniformly increase aggression. All people do not become aggressive every time they have a drink. Thus, a crucial question that these theories leave unanswered is *when* intoxication increases aggression.

Anxiolysis: Disinhibition Theories Revisited

Arousal of anxiety is an inherent feature of situations in which aggression is elicited; therefore, to understand how and when alcohol increases aggression, it is necessary to understand the role of anxiety. Specifically, anxiety can be conceptualized as a warning signal indicating the potential for aversive consequences (Spielberger, 1972). Aggression-eliciting situations are typically fraught with such potential. For example, social disapproval may ensue if others perceive aggression as unreasonable. In addition, an aggressive action may elicit fear of retaliation. Functionally, the experience of anxiety serves to suppress behaviors that are associated with its arousal, and this could account for why aggression is not overtly displayed every time it is instigated.

There has been debate as to whether alcohol reliably decreases anxiety–stress. Sayette's (1993) appraisal-disruption model proposes that the temporal ordering between alcohol consumption and exposure to anxiety-eliciting cues determines whether intoxication is anxiolytic. Specifically, Sayette argued that alcohol produces anxiolysis by disrupting appraisal of the situation as anxiolytic. Therefore, anxiolysis most likely occurs when alcohol consumption precedes exposure to the anxiety-eliciting cues. For studies in this dataset, the source of anxiety-provoking cues is the experimental task itself (e.g., cues indicating social disapproval of aggression or possible retaliation), to which participants are not exposed until after they have consumed alcohol. Studies in this review, therefore, meet the condition set by Sayette for anxiolysis with respect to the temporal ordering of alcohol consumption and exposure to anxiety-provoking cues, suggesting that intoxicated participants in these studies should experience relatively less anxiety than sober ones. In summary, we believe that intoxication dampens the arousal of anxiety in the studies in the present dataset and that this, in turn, weakens the suppression of aggression (Gray, 1987; Pihl et al., 1993; Taylor & Chermack, 1993; Washburne, 1956). It is, therefore, predicted that alcohol may increase aggression in situations in which anxiety would normally both be aroused and act to inhibit it. We refer to this model as the anxiolysis–disinhibition model.

The anxiolysis–disinhibition model leads to the hypothesis that the greatest difference in aggression between sober and intoxicated individuals occurs when anxiogenic cues are greatest. If anxiogenic cues are weak, then little suppression of aggression would be expected in either sober or intoxicated persons. However, as the intensity of anxiogenic cues increases, sober persons should be more likely to experience anxiety than those who are intoxicated and, hence, be more inclined to suppress aggression. By contrast, intoxicated persons would be expected to behave in a fashion relatively free from the effects of such suppression. Therefore, a crucial test of this model is whether the difference between the aggressive behavior of intoxicated and sober persons increases as a function of the degree to which situational factors induce anxiety.

Inhibition Conflict

Alternatively, Steele and colleagues (Steele & Josephs, 1990; Steele & Southwick, 1985) have suggested inhibition conflict as the mechanism by which alcohol increases the likelihood of aggressive behavior. Inhibition conflict refers to a type of response conflict that occurs when a behavior is instigated by one set of strong cues and, simultaneously, is inhibited by another set of strong cues. The two primary tenets of the theory are that (a) alcohol impairs cognitive processing and, in particular, narrows the range of cues to which a person can attend; and (b) as a consequence of this narrowed attentional range, an intoxicated person who is confronted with a situation that elicits high-inhibition conflict is able to process and respond only to the most salient behavioral cues. Consider, for example, an individual who experiences a strong provocation to assault another person at work. If sober, this person should be able to process not only the instigating cue of provocation but also other cues that signal the normative constraints that make physical aggression inappropriate in the workplace. By contrast, an intoxicated person whose attentional focus has been narrowed by alcohol may lack the cognitive resources to attend adequately to both sets of cues. Steele and colleagues argued that because instigating cues are usually more salient and immediate, whereas inhibiting cues often require the retrieval of personal standards of behavior and cognitively demanding estimations of future consequences, the intoxicated person typically will be influenced more by the instigating cue. Thus, an intoxicated person is more likely to aggress than a sober one.

The experience of inhibition conflict is one manifestation of what Steele has referred to as *alcohol myopia*—the general narrowing of attention following alcohol consumption (Steele & Josephs, 1990). Alcohol myopia may be responsible for a wide range of behaviors, such as drunken self-inflation and decreases in psychological stress when intoxicated. We focus only on the more specific concept of *inhibition conflict* because it is thought to moderate alcohol's aggression facilitating effects (Steele & Josephs, 1990).

More important, Steele and colleagues (Steele & Josephs, 1990; Steele & Southwick, 1985) argued that only an interaction between alcohol's pharmacological effects and features of the situation that affect inhibition conflict alter the balance of cues bearing on a response. Hence, not all situations necessarily increase aggression among intoxicated individuals. If a situation is low in inhibition conflict—because the instigating cues are weak, the inhibiting cues are weak, or both sets of cues are weak—then intoxicated and sober persons process cues similarly and, therefore, behave similarly. According to Steele and Josephs, in a situation low in inhibition conflict, intoxication "would only block inhibiting cues that are already weak or weaken inhibiting cues against a response tendency that was weak to begin with" (p. 923). That is, the combination of high-inhibition conflict and intoxication is expected to increase aggression (p. 925).

Steele and Southwick (1985) meta-analytically assessed the predictive utility of the inhibition conflict model. They confirmed that situations likely to elicit high, as compared with low, levels of inhibition conflict were associated with a larger difference in the degree to which the extremity of the behavior of intoxicated participants exceeded that of controls. Because Steele and Southwick were interested in the effect of alcohol on social behaviors in general, the researchers of the 34 studies in their dataset investigated a wide range of behaviors (e.g., gambling and eating) not solely aggression. In the present analysis, we specifically assessed the effects of inhibition conflict on aggression. Whereas our sample of studies was culled from 49 reports that assessed aggressive behaviors under intoxication, fewer than half of the 34 studies reviewed by Steele and Southwick were concerned with aggression.

Both the anxiolysis–disinhibition and inhibition conflict models assume that responsiveness to inhibiting cues is affected by intoxication, but the explanations they offer for this differ somewhat. The anxiolysis–disinhibition model is concerned with the specific inhibiting cue of anxiety, whereas the inhibition conflict model does not specify any one source of inhibiting cues. Moreover, the inhibition conflict model focuses on the *relative* strength between inhibiting and instigating cues. Therefore, each model may provide specific insight into how aggression is increased when alcohol is consumed.

SOCIAL PSYCHOLOGICAL MODERATORS
OF AGGRESSIVE BEHAVIOR

We next address whether other social psychological variables— namely, provocation, frustration, and self-focused attention—which have been previously shown to moderate aggressive behavior in sober individuals, similarly affect intoxicated participants.

Provocation

A provoking stimulus can be very effective in increasing aggression for several reasons. By thwarting or angering a person, it may directly elicit negative affect and angry or emotional aggression (Averill, 1982; Berkowitz, 1989; Feshbach, 1964). Alternatively, or in parallel with this emotional responding, cognitive factors such as the belief in "an eye for an eye" may lead people to respond in a tit-for-tat fashion to provocation (Axelrod, 1984; Gouldner, 1960). In fact, actually experiencing physical discomfort as a result of an attack may not even be required. Merely knowing that someone intended to attack can be sufficient to induce aggression (Greenwell & Dengerink, 1973).

Another way in which provocation can increase aggression is by serving as a suitable external justification for a behavior that normally is considered inappropriate. Concern about violating such normative proscriptions may be associated with anxiety, the awareness of which serves to inhibit aggressive behavior. Consequently, people usually behave in a non-aggressive manner, unless a suitable external justification for aggression can be found. Thus, attack or provocation by another person can serve as a triggering event that provides justification for aggressive retaliation. Because the norm of reciprocity sanctions aggression in retaliation to another's attack, provocation frees the individual to aggress. Provocation can, therefore, serve the dual roles of instigation and excuse for aggression.

The effect of provocation on aggression has long been investigated in sober participants; although it also frequently appears as a central feature of experimental paradigms in research on aggression and alcohol (e.g., Kelly, Cherek, Steinberg, & Robinson, 1988; Richardson, 1981; Shuntich & Taylor, 1972), relatively little attention has been paid to its theoretical importance in this latter literature. Pernanen (1976) and Gustafson (1993) have both emphasized that level of provocation should be considered in interpreting findings in the alcohol and aggression literature. In fact, in his analysis of the role of provocation, Gustafson suggested that alcohol facilitates aggression only when provocation is present and that, in the absence of provocation, sober and intoxicated persons will behave similarly. According to Gustafson, then, absence of provoking stimuli may serve as a boundary condition on alcohol's aggression facilitating effects.

Inherent in Gustafson's (1993) view on the importance of provocation in alcohol-related aggression is the assumption that intoxicated individuals inhibit their aggression in the absence of provocation in the same manner as sober participants. Specifically, it is assumed that intoxicated individuals will aggress only if a triggering provocation is experienced. Gustafson based this conclusion on a somewhat informal review of results and, unfortunately, provides no theoretical explanation for his conclusion. Moreover, this prediction is not consistent with evidence showing that alcohol increases aggression among intoxicated participants, even in low-provocation conditions (e.g., Gustafson, 1985a, 1986a; Taylor & Gammon, 1976; Taylor & Sears, 1988).

Extant research, therefore, supports a prediction quite different from that of Gustafson (1993). Moreover, theoretical analyses suggest instead that the difference between the aggressive behavior of intoxicated and sober persons should be *greatest* when provocations are absent. Under conditions of low provocation, sober participants are likely to observe normative constraints and behave relatively nonaggressively. By contrast, intoxicated participants seem less responsive to these normative constraints (perhaps because violating these norms is not associated with anxiety) and instead tend to display more aggression than sober participants, even in circumstances under which controls do not experience provocation.

A similar theoretical argument was used by Bettencourt and Miller (1996) to account for the decrease in gender differences in aggression under provocation. Their meta-analysis shows that men are consistently more aggressive than woman when provocation is absent, but this gender difference diminishes when provocation is introduced. At only moderate levels of provocation, the strong gender difference found in its absence is no longer seen. Although social roles dictate that aggression by women is more unacceptable than that by men, provocation apparently frees women from this social role proscription by providing an external justification, thereby enabling them to display levels of aggression more comparable with that of men. Consequently, we hypothesize that the aggressive behavior of intoxicated individuals will exceed that of sober ones under conditions of low provocation. When provoked, sober participants will behave more aggressively than when unprovoked. Intoxicated participants may also respond to provocation with increased aggression; but, because they are already inclined to behave in a relatively aggressive manner, the additional instigation and justification provided by provocation should not increase their aggression as much as it does for sober participants (i.e., a type of ceiling effect). Thus, the difference between the aggressive behavior of intoxicated and sober individuals seems likely to diminish as provocation increases.

Frustration

Just as provoking events are a frequent feature of paradigms investigating the effects of intoxication on aggression, these paradigms also frequently include frustrating events. The role of frustration in aggression also has a long history in the social psychological literature, stimulated by the publication of the frustration–aggression hypothesis (Dollard, Doob, Miller, Mowrer, & Sears, 1939). Although much of this research has been dedicated to refuting the assertion that aggression is an invariant consequence of frustration, this body of evidence, nevertheless, persuasively indicates that frustration can instigate aggression (for a review, see Berkowitz, 1989). *Frustration*, defined as blocking an ongoing goal-directed behavior, may operate in a manner similar to provocation and serve both as an instigator and an external justification for violating normative constraints against aggression. Consequently, we predict that frustration will be related to alcohol-potentiated aggression in the same manner as provocation. Specifically, we expect that the aggressive behavior of intoxicated participants will exceed that of sober ones when frustrations are minimal, but as frustration increases and the aggressive behavior of sober participants increases correspondingly, intoxicated and sober participants will behave more similarly.

In his statement on the role of provocation in alcohol-facilitated aggression, Gustafson (1993) did not distinguish between provocation and frustration. Rather, he considered frustration to be a form of provocation (p. 23). Even though we predict that provocation and frustration will have similar directions of influence on the difference in aggression between sober and intoxicated participants, we nevertheless believe that it is theoretically important to distinguish between them and to assess their influences separately. Hence, we constrain the use of the term *provocation* to a negative affect that arises as a direct result of being attacked, or perceiving attack, by another person. In keeping with most prior discussion, we use the term *frustration* to refer to the blocking of ongoing goal-directed behaviors.[1] In the research on aggression, frustration is often situationally or task induced (Carlson & Miller, 1988).

Self-Focused Attention

Whatever their differences, the anxiolysis–disinhibition and inhibition conflict models both predict that intoxication typically is associated with decreased responsiveness to inhibiting cues and subsequent increases in aggression. Inducing self-focused attention, however, may increase attention to inhibiting cues. *Self-focus* refers to a state in which a self-regulatory process is initiated, personal standards of appropriate behavior become salient, and attempts are made to comply with these standards (Carver, 1979; Carver & Scheier, 1981, 1990; Duval & Wicklund, 1972). When salient, these standards inhibit impulsive, self-indulgent behavior. Self-focused attention in sober participants is associated with increased prosocial behavior (Duval, Duval, & Neely, 1979; Gibbons & Wicklund, 1982; M. Rogers, Miller, Mayer, & Duval, 1982; also shown meta-analytically by Carlson, Charlin, & Miller, 1988; Carlson & Miller, 1987) and less antisocial behavior such as aggression (Carver, 1975; Scheier, Fen-

---

[1]We note that the dimension of human agency may also be an important factor in aggression-inducing events. Meta-analytic evidence suggests that interpersonal sources of instigating events induced twice the magnitude of aggression (relative to control conditions) as that produced by nonpersonal sources, even when intensity of the negative event was controlled (Carlson & Miller, 1998). We note also that the definition of *aggression-eliciting* events excludes a class of negative events, namely, nonhuman provocations that do not necessarily interfere with a goal-directed activity (e.g., extremes in temperature). Although this category logically exists, and is represented in the larger literature on aggression, it was not present among the studies in this dataset. We, therefore, do not consider them in our analysis.

igstein, & Buss, 1974) and cheating (Diener & Wallbom, 1976). Similarly, deindividuation, which is characterized by a loss of individual identity and a subsequent lack of concern with personal standards of behavior (Diener, 1980), has been associated with increased aggression (Lightdale & Prentice, 1994; Prentice-Dunn & Rogers, 1980; R. W. Rogers & Prentice-Dunn, 1981).

It is unclear, however, whether the self-regulatory processes associated with self-focused attention operate in the same manner in intoxicated as in sober individuals. In particular, Hull (1981; Hull, Levenson, Young, & Sher, 1983; see also Washburne, 1956) argued that alcohol interferes with the likelihood of focusing attention on self by inhibiting the encoding of self-relevant information. In support of this view, when asked to make a speech about what they like and dislike about their bodies, intoxicated participants used fewer self-relevant pronouns than those sober (Hull et al., 1983). Hull argued that a desire to decrease self-focused attention, and thereby avoid both assessments of how well one is meeting behavioral standards and the ensuing guilt associated with failure to meet them, may motivate people to drink (Hull & Young, 1983a, 1983b; Hull, Young, & Jouriles, 1986). Heatherton and Baumeister (1991) advocated a similar position.

Despite these findings, Hull and Reilly (1983) suggested that self-focusing manipulations can counteract the intoxication-induced tendency to avoid the focus on self. This position is consistent with data obtained by Bailey, Leonard, Cranston, and Taylor (1983), who increased self-focus in half of their participants by placing a mirror and video camera in the experimental room (common manipulations used to induce self-focus), telling them their session would be videotaped and making a point of calling them by their names. Self-focused participants, both in the placebo (nonalcoholic beverage) and alcohol conditions, chose to administer a lower intensity of shocks to their competitive opponent than non-self-focused participants. The effects of self-focusing manipulations were also investigated by Ross and Pihl (1988), who assessed the performance of intoxicated and sober participants on a complex reaction time task in which behavioral regulation presumably would lead participants to strive for better performance. Both sober and intoxicated participants who performed the task in front of mirrors and a video camera responded faster and made fewer errors than those who did not receive the self-focusing manipulation. Self-focus also appeared to interact with alcohol ingestion such that performance was most improved for intoxicated self-focused participants.

Ross and Pihl (1988) speculated that their self-focused intoxicated participants, who knew they had received alcohol, were attempting to compensate for its deleterious effects. Self-focus presumably made salient to them the behavioral standard of not appearing drunk and impaired and, thereby, motivated them to exhibit superior performance. If this explanation is correct, then it suggests that the intoxicated participants overcompensated for the effects of intoxication in that their absolute performance levels exceeded that of sober participants. An alternative interpretation is that the narrowed attentional focus accompanying intoxication served to intensify their self-focused state by decreasing sensitivity to other stimuli that had the potential to distract attention from self. Sober participants may be relatively less affected by self-focusing cues because their wider range of attentional focus allows them to attend to other stimuli that ordinarily compete with self for attention.[2]

These prior outcomes suggest alternative hypotheses about the relationship of self-focus and aggressive behavior after alcohol consumption. According to Hull (1981), intoxicated participants are less likely to be affected by situational factors that ordinarily encourage self-focused attention in sober participants because alcohol interferes with the encoding of self-relevant information. This view leads to the prediction that when compared with the aggressive behavior of sober participants, intoxicated ones will be relatively unaffected by level of self-focus. The difference between the aggressive behavior of intoxicated and sober participants should, therefore, increase as situational factors encouraging self-focused attention increase. This may be especially likely when subtle self-focusing cues are present. Alternatively, the data collected by Bailey et al. (1983) and Ross and Pihl (1988) suggest that self-focused attention decreases aggression in intoxicated participants as well as sober ones. Moreover, in Ross and Pihl, the performance of intoxicated participants was more strongly affected by self-focusing manipulations than that of sober participants, suggesting that although aggressive behavior may be less likely when attention is focused on self, it may be even more unlikely among intoxicated self-focused persons.

METHOD

Literature Searches

We used three methods to locate studies for the meta-analysis. First, *PsycInfo* (1967–1994), *Medline* (1966–1994), and *Current Contents* (1989–1994) databases were searched through May 1994 using the keywords *alcohol*, *intoxication*, and *ethanol*, cross-referenced with *aggression*, *antisocial behavior*, *anger*, and *attack*. Second, we reviewed the reference lists of three previous meta-analyses on the effects of alcohol on human

---

[2]We thank Blair Johnson for suggesting this line of thought.

behavior (Bushman & Cooper, 1990; Hull & Bond, 1986; Steele & South-wick, 1985). Third, we examined relevant journals (e.g., *Quarterly Journal of Studies on Alcohol*) published in June, July, and August 1994.

Criteria for Inclusion

We included studies in the meta-analysis if they fulfilled four criteria. First, studies had to be published in a journal. Second, they had to include at least one measure of aggression. Third, data necessary for computing an effect size had to be included in the published report. Finally, studies had to compare at least one experimental condition in which alcohol was consumed with a condition in which it was not. This comparison condition could be a placebo condition (participants expect to consume alcohol but actually receive a nonalcoholic beverage), a control condition (participants both expect and receive a nonalcoholic beverage), or a condition in which no drink was consumed. Although it could be informative to analyze effect sizes separately as a function of the type of control group used, two considerations argue against doing so. First, such an analysis would have low power because few studies compared an alcohol condition with one in which no drink was consumed. Second, we found type of control group was confounded with other potentially important variables such as dose of alcohol. For these reasons, we collapsed across type of control group (cf. Bushman & Cooper, 1990; and Steele & Southwick, 1985), which is conservative because variation among control groups decreases the likelihood of detecting significant effects, relative to analyses in which control groups are homogeneous.

A total of 49 studies satisfied the inclusion criteria (and are indicated in the reference section by an asterisk). Dates of publication ranged from April 1972 to August 1994. One article (Rohsenow & Bachorowski, 1984) contained three independent experiments, each satisfied the inclusion criteria. Of the 47 articles from which the 49 studies were extracted, 22 were included in Bushman and Cooper's (1990) meta-analysis, 13 were included in Steele and Southwick's (1985) meta-analysis, and 3 were included in Hull and Bond's (1986) meta-analysis (see Appendix A for the list). These figures represent an overlap of 8 studies between Bushman and Cooper and Steele and Southwick and 1 study between Steele and Southwick and Hull and Bond. Eighteen studies (38%) are uniquely represented in our meta-analysis.

Rating of Potential Moderator Variables

We used judges' ratings, based on the information contained in blinded copies of each study's method section and made without knowledge of the study's results or corresponding effect sizes, to assess the contextual level of each moderator variable within each study. We made ratings of the five theoretical variables—anxiety, inhibition conflict, provocation, frustration, and self-focused attention—for all studies by two judges (Tiffany Ito and a graduate student in psychology) on 9-point scales possessing no descriptive adjectives other than that a value of 9 indicated a high level of the variable in question. We present the operational definitions used by the judges in Appendix B. In addition, Appendix B includes examples (not given to the judges before the ratings) of a study that received the most extreme rating for each end-point of the rated variables. Judges first independently rated a subset of eight studies and discussed discrepancies with the other authors of this article. To avoid systematic bias, we made ratings for each of the five variables across studies before proceeding to the next variable. We randomly determined the order in which each judge made his or her ratings for the five variables, and the order was different for each judge. Additionally, the studies were in a different random order for each judge. These procedures correspond to those discussed and recommended in Miller and Carlson (1990) and Miller, Lee, and Carlson (1991).

The judges also rated a sixth variable, *task complexity*—defined as the degree to which response measures and features of the experimental task require habitual, routine, low level, familiar, easy mental activity as opposed to effortful, complex, novel, mentally difficult activity. Analyses revealed no significant effects of degree of task complexity on effect size. We did not, therefore, give it further consideration.

We instructed the judges to take within- and between-subject experimental manipulations into account when making their ratings. Therefore, it was possible for a single study to contribute more than one rating per variable if the judges determined that the level of that variable was manipulated within the study. For example, the judges made 50 ratings of self-focused attention. For 48 of the studies, the judges agreed that the level of self-focus did not vary across conditions within the same study; therefore, they assigned a single rating of self-focused attention to each study. However, self-focused attention was manipulated in one study, so they assigned two ratings on the self-focus variable. They used similar procedures to rate within-study differences for the other theoretical variables. In total, the judges made 77 ratings of anxiety, 54 ratings of inhibition conflict, 91 ratings of provocation, and 74 ratings of frustration.

Descriptive statistics and reliabilities of the judges' ratings are shown in Table 1. Although the validity of these ratings could not be assessed (e.g., by correlating judges' ratings with manipulation check effect sizes) because the data necessary for such an assessment were not included in the primary sources, these rating procedures have been shown to have convergent and construct validity in other research (e.g., Carlson et al., 1988; Carlson & Miller, 1987; Eagly & Steffen, 1986; Miller & Carlson, 1990;

TABLE 1
Descriptive Statistics and Reliabilities of Judges' Ratings for Moderator Variables

Variable	All studies			k	Excluding the two most extreme outliers		
	M	SD	Reliability		M	SD	Reliability
Anxiety	6.43	2.38	.88***	77	6.39	2.39	.88***
Inhibition conflict	5.71	3.16	.94***	54	5.71	3.19	.93***
Provocation	3.95	2.73	.90***	91	3.93	2.73	.90***
Frustration	3.88	2.67	.78***	74	3.94	2.68	.79***
Self-focused attention	3.41	1.81	.81***	50	3.42	1.85	.78***

Note. Ratings were made of 49 separate studies. Multiple ratings per study were possible, with the total number shown as *k*. Reliability is shown as the Pearson product–moment correlation coefficient of the two judges' ratings. All variables were rated on 9-point scales, with a value of 9 indicating the highest levels of anxiety, inhibition conflict, provocation, frustration, and self-focused attention.
***$p < .001$.

Miller et al., 1991). Moreover, the reliabilities of the judges' ratings, as defined by the Pearson product–moment correlation coefficient, were generally high in magnitude, and all exceeded .75 (see Table 1). In view of this, we performed moderator analyses on the average of the ratings made by the two judges.

Coding of Study Characteristics

We coded information on 10 characteristics of each study. We coded three of these originally as continuous variables but later made them categorical because of the characteristics of their respective distributions. These variables are (a) dose of alcohol (two categories), (b) time allowed for ingestion (three categories), and (c) time allowed for absorption (four categories). We coded the remaining seven study characteristics into either dichotomous or trichotomous categories. The dichotomous variables are (a) presence of nonaggressive response alternatives, (b) possibility of retaliation, and (c) gender. The trichotomous variables are (a) experimenter knowledge of drink content, (b) distraction of participants during beverage consumption, (c) participants' drinking history, and (d) type of response measure. Two coders independently extracted the information from a subset of 26 studies. Agreement between them was 97%, by assessing the number of agreements divided by the total number of characteristics extracted. Disagreement between the coders typically occurred over whether a certain piece of information could be reliably determined. For example, many studies did not clearly state how long the alcohol absorption period was, but it might have been possible to estimate this value. Disagreement occurred when one coder estimated the value but the other coded the study as missing this information. Ultimately, we adopted the conservative strategy of coding a study as missing the information, unless the relevant information was clearly and unambiguously stated in the method section. Given the high agreement between coders and our decision to adopt a conservative strategy in cases of ambiguous information, only one coder extracted study characteristics from the remaining studies.

Computation of Effect Sizes

Following Hedges (1981) and Hedges and Olkin (1985), we used d as the effect size index, representing the difference between the experimental and control group mean and divided by the pooled standard deviation (SD). We corrected these d values for bias resulting from small sample size (Hedges & Olkin, 1985). In this meta-analysis, a positive effect size indicates that more aggressive behavior was displayed by participants who were administered alcohol relative to those in the control condition. The pooled SD was based on individual cell SDs whenever possible, but when not reported, we obtained estimates of pooled SDs from analysis of variance results. We performed computations with the meta-analytic program $DSTAT$ (Johnson, 1993).

Frequently, studies reported enough data to compute multiple effect sizes. There were three different sources of multiple effect sizes: (a) comparison of more than one dose of alcohol with a control group (e.g., a low-dose and a high-dose group), (b) data on more than one dependent measure (e.g., no. of shocks administered and intensity of shocks), and (c) manipulation of other independent variables in addition to the alcohol–no alcohol variable. Indiscriminantly including multiple within-study effect sizes in the meta-analysis would violate assumptions about their independence and could, thereby, bias outcomes. We adopted the following strategies, therefore, for all datasets used in the analyses reported herein. If a study's researchers administered more than one alcohol dose (as was the case for seven studies), we randomly selected one of the doses and included in the analysis only those effect sizes that reflected the comparison of the selected dose with the control condition. If a study reported data on multiple dependent measures, we calculated effect sizes for all possible measures, then averaged them together into a single index.

For the last source of multiple effect sizes, manipulation of other independent variables besides dose of alcohol, we considered the random selection and averaging strategies inadequate because the different conditions within a study often had bearing on the theoretical questions addressed in this analysis. For example, a study might cross a manipulation of alcohol dose with a manipulation of provocation. Because we hypothesize that provocation will moderate effect size, it would be inappropriate to average effect sizes that represent different levels of provocation. Similarly, important information on the effects of different levels of provocation would be lost if we only randomly selected one effect size from such studies.

As a result, we used a shifting unit of analysis approach (Bushman & Cooper, 1990; Cooper, 1989), which represents a compromise between the independence assumption and the desire to retain as much information as possible. More specifically, use of the shifting unit of analysis means that, for each of the five variables of theoretical interest, we included all of the effect sizes relevant to that analysis. As previously indicated, judges were instructed to take within-study conditions into account when making their ratings, resulting in 77, 54, 91, 74, and 50 separate ratings of anxiety, inhibition conflict, provocation, frustration, and self-focused attention, respectively. We created five separate datasets, one for each variable with effect sizes that corresponded to the conditions rated for that particular variable. For example, in the self-focused attention dataset, where 48 of the 49 studies were judged to lack within-study variation in level of self-focused attention, the 48 studies contributed one effect size each. For the remaining study, which contained within-study variation in self-focused attention, we entered two effect sizes into the dataset. One represented the difference between sober and intoxicated participants in a condition low in self-focus, and the other represented the difference between participants sober and intoxicated in a condition high in self-focus. We used similar procedures for the other four datasets.

We created a sixth dataset in which each study was allowed to contribute only one effect size by averaging together all effect sizes from the same study. We used this dataset to obtain the mean effect size across all studies, irrespective of potential variation in any of the five variables of theoretical interest. We also used this dataset for the categorical analyses of study characteristics (e.g., whether participants were distracted during the beverage consumption period) because these characteristics displayed no within-study variation. The only exception was the analysis on participant gender. It was possible in three studies to compute separate effect sizes for male and female participants, and a fourth study included only female participants. The analysis on gender was, therefore, based on 50 effect sizes.

Distributions of Variables

The distribution of ratings of anxiety was negatively skewed and that of self-focused attention was positively skewed. We used logarithmic transformations to normalize these variables. Provocation, frustration, and inhibition conflict were each bimodally distributed, and consequently were dichotomized. Low values ranged from 1 to 4, 1.5 to 4.5, and 1 to 4; high values ranged from 5 to 9, 6 to 9, and 6 to 9 for provocation, frustration, and inhibition conflict, respectively. The dichotomization of inhibition conflict is consistent with results from Steele and Southwick (1985), who reported that a 2-point scale for inhibition conflict yielded the most reliable judgments. Also, as suggested earlier, the distribution of alcohol dose was biomodal. Dose was, therefore, dichotomized, with low doses ranging from 0.23 to 1.00 ml of alcohol/kg of body weight and high doses ranging from 1.20 to 1.30 ml/kg. We used these transformed variables in all subsequent analyses.

Data Analysis Strategy

We used regression analyses to assess the effect of the continuously distributed moderator variables (anxiety and self-focused attention) on effect size. The specific regression analyses used were designed for meta-analytic data (Hedges & Olkin, 1985) and provide a test of model specification, Q_E, in which a significant value indicates that the model is not sufficient to account for heterogeneity among the effect sizes. For inhibition conflict, provocation, and frustration, we performed categorical analyses. We first categorized effect sizes as a function of the moderator variable, then we assessed the degree of within- and between-category homogeneity. A well-specified model in which variability in the effect sizes is explained by the category distinctions would result in *homo*geneity within each category but *heter*ogeneity between the categories. Between-category homogeneity is assessed by Q_B, which has an approximate χ^2 distribution with degrees of freedom (df) equal to $p - 1$, where p is the number of categories in the model. When there are only two categories in the model, Q_B is analogous to a pairwise comparison. Within-category homogeneity is assessed by Q_W, which has an approximate χ^2 distribution with $m - 1$ df, where m is the number of effect sizes in each category (Hedges & Olkin, 1985). Both statistics test the assumption of homogeneity; significant values are indicative of heterogeneity in the effect sizes.

Regardless of whether we used regression or categorical models, we performed all analyses on effect sizes that were weighted by the inverse of their variance (Hedges & Olkin, 1985). In addition, we included dose of alcohol administered to participants in the experimental condition as a factor in each analysis. All significance tests are two-tailed, unless stated otherwise.

RESULTS

Overall Effect of Alcohol on Aggressive Behavior

The mean effect size of 0.54 across the 49 studies had a 95% confidence interval (CI) that excluded 0, CI = 0.45–0.63, indicating that intoxication increased aggression. By Cohen's (1988) standards, this is considered a medium effect size. (Effect sizes of d = 0.20, 0.50, and 0.80 are considered small, medium, and large in magnitude, respectively.) In addition, there was significant heterogeneity among these effect sizes, $Q(48)$ = 285.19, p < .0001. Most effect sizes ranged from −1.0 to 1.0, but two substantially exceeded this range, d = 7.81 and 5.99, respectively. When we removed these two extreme values, the difference in aggressive behavior between intoxicated and sober participants remained significant: The mean effect size was 0.47, and the 95% CI again excluded 0, CI = 0.38–0.56. Removing these extreme values did not result in homogeneity among effect sizes, $Q(46)$ = 78.92, p < .005. Although the general pattern of results did not change when we removed the two most extreme outliers, the possibility that their large magnitude was due to unique features of the original experiments led us to exclude them from subsequent analyses. Despite the substantial independence of our dataset from that of Bushman and Cooper (1990), our mean effect size is similar to the mean of 0.43 obtained in their analysis.

As indicated in the criteria for study inclusion, we extracted all effect sizes in this analysis from published reports. Rosenthal (1979) and Wachter (1988) have argued that because studies obtaining null results are less likely to be published, analyzing data from only published reports biases results in favor of obtaining a mean effect size that differs significantly from 0. This has been labeled the *file drawer problem*. A fail-safe n, which represents the number of studies obtaining null results that would be needed to render the obtained mean effect size nonsignificant, was calculated to assess threat of the file drawer problem in this analysis. Rosenthal (1991) suggested that a conservative tolerance level for the fail-safe n is $5k + 10$, where k is the number of effect sizes. Thus, for 49 effect sizes, it should exceed 255. The obtained fail-safe n of 2,826 based on the mean effect size of the 49 studies (or 1,863 when the two most extreme effect sizes are removed) suggests that a file drawer problem is unlikely. In other words, there would need to be 2,826 unpublished studies with null results to render the overall mean effect size obtained in this meta-analysis equal to 0.

Given the significant mean effect size indicating that alcohol increases aggression, it is reasonable to expect that dose of alcohol consumed is related to effect size, with larger effect sizes associated with higher doses. To test this, we compared the effect sizes of studies that administered low as opposed to high doses. We omitted from this analysis the two most extreme outliers and one additional study (Boyatzis, 1974) that did not specify dose. As expected, higher alcohol doses were associated with larger effect sizes, M = 0.53, CI = 0.41–0.65, than lower doses, M = 0.35, CI = 0.21–0.50, Q_B = 3.43, p < .03, one-tailed.[3] As evidenced by the exclusion of 0 from both CIs, even low doses of alcohol (0.23 to 1.00 ml/kg) increased aggression.

Mechanisms of Increased Aggression in Intoxicated Individuals

Role of Anxiety

We have suggested that the increased aggression of intoxicated participants might be due to their decreased sensitivity to anxiety-provoking situational cues, which in a sober participant would serve to inhibit aggression. Specifically, the aggressive behavior of intoxicated participants is expected to most greatly exceed that of sober ones as the intensity of anxiety-provoking cues increases. We tested this with a regression analysis. To account for the effects of alcohol dose, we entered dose into the analysis with the anxiety ratings. The regression coefficients and test of model specification are shown in Table 2. As expected, level of anxiety was a significant predictor of effect size, such that the difference between intoxicated and sober participants increased as level of anxiety increased, $B = 0.58$, $p < .001$. Nonetheless, the test of specification for this model was significant, indicating that heterogeneity among the effect sizes was present, $Q_E = 141.07$, $p < .001$.

To explicitly assess whether the influence of anxiety-provoking cues differs as a function of dose, we regressed anxiety onto effect size separately for studies in the high- and low-dose subsets. Regression coefficients and tests of model specification for these analyses are also shown in Table 2. In both subsets, the regression coefficient for anxiety was positive. In the high-dose subset, the coefficient was significant, $B = 0.70$, $p < .001$, but the coefficient in the low-dose subset reached only marginal significance, $B = 0.43$, $p < .08$, two-tailed. Despite the absolute difference between these coefficients, they did not differ significantly from each other, $t = 0.49$. Also, in the high-dose subset, no significant heterogeneity was present in the model, $Q_E = 23.17$, but heterogeneity remained in the low-dose subset, $Q_E = 117.22$, $p < .001$.

Inhibition Conflict

Table 3 shows the mean effect size and CIs as a function of both level of inhibition conflict and alcohol dose. The difference in mean effect size

[3]We performed comparable analyses on the five other datasets as well. With the exception of anxiety, all analyses were consistent with the conclusion that alcohol-induced aggression increases when larger alcohol doses are consumed. That is, in the inhibition conflict, provocation, frustration, and self-focused attention datasets, higher doses were associated with significantly larger mean effect sizes than lower alcohol doses. The only exception was the anxiety dataset, in which we entered anxiety and dose into a regression equation. Dose was not a significant predictor of effect size in this analysis, $B = -0.11$, $p < .20$. It should also be noted that the effect of dose in the self-focus dataset reached only marginal significance with a two-tailed test, $p < .10$. (The regression coefficients for dose when entered into the anxiety and self-focus regression equations are shown in Tables 2 and 6, respectively.)

TABLE 2
Regression Analyses of Anxiety and Alcohol Dose

Dataset and predictor	B	β	Q_E	k
All studies			141.07***	74
Anxiety	0.58***	0.32		
Dose	−0.11	−0.11		
Low-dose subset			117.22***	39
Anxiety	0.43	0.16		
High-dose subset			23.17	35
Anxiety	0.70***	0.56		

Note. Dose was dichotomized, with low values ranging from 0.23 to 1.00 ml/kg and high values ranging from 1.20 to 1.30 ml/kg. B denotes unstandardized regression coefficient. β denotes standardized regression coefficient. Q_E denotes test of model specification. Significant Q_E values indicate that the model is inadequate to account for heterogeneity among effect sizes. In addition, the two studies contributing the most extreme outliers were excluded. In the low-dose subset, the regression coefficient for anxiety was marginally significant, $p < .08$, two-tailed.
***$p < .001$.

between studies with high and low levels of inhibition conflict was significant, $Q_B = 17.46$, $p < .001$, such that larger effect sizes were associated with higher levels of inhibition conflict. It should be noted, however, that the CIs for both means excluded 0. Thus, even when inhibition conflict was low, intoxicated participants exhibited more aggression than sober ones. Significant heterogeneity was present among only the low-inhibition conflict effect sizes, $Q_W = 52.98$, $p < .001$.

To assess potential moderating effects of dose, we separated the dataset into low- and high-dose subsets and examined the means as a function of inhibition conflict (see Table 3, lower panel). Dose did not moderate

TABLE 3
Categorical Analysis of Inhibition Conflict and Alcohol Dose

Dataset and variable class	k	$M\,d_+$	95% CI for d_+		Q_W	Q_B
			Lower	Upper		
All studies						17.46***
Low-inhibition conflict	22	0.27	0.14	0.40	52.98***	
High-inhibition conflict	29	0.65	0.53	0.78	17.61	
Low-dose studies						5.67*
Low-inhibition conflict	16	0.24	0.08	0.39	46.71***	
High-inhibition conflict	8	0.64	0.35	0.93	6.34	
High-dose studies						7.52**
Low-inhibition conflict	5	0.22	−0.05	0.50	2.84	
High-inhibition conflict	21	0.65	0.52	0.79	11.26	

Note. d_+ denotes effect sizes weighted by the reciprocal of their variances. CI denotes confidence interval. Q_W tests within-category homogeneity; Q_B tests between-category homogeneity. Significant values indicate rejection of the hypothesis of homogeneity. One study (Boyatzis, 1974) lacked dose information, so it was excluded from all analyses involving dose. In addition, the two studies contributing the most extreme outliers were excluded. Significance tests are two-tailed.
*$p < .05$. **$p < .01$. ***$p < .001$.

the tendency for effect size to increase with higher levels of inhibition conflict. High-inhibition conflict was associated with larger effect sizes than low-inhibition conflict within both the high-dose, $Q_B = 7.52$, $p < .006$, and low-dose subsets, $Q_B = 5.67$, $p < .02$.

Other Social Psychological Moderators

The analyses of anxiety and inhibition conflict suggest that both factors may have predictive utility in explaining how alcohol increases aggression. However, neither accounted for all of the variation in effect sizes. We obtained significant heterogeneity in the overall regression analysis of anxiety. According to Steele and Josephs (1990), intoxication should increase aggression only when higher doses of alcohol have been administered and when inhibition conflict is high. In our analyses, however, intoxication increased aggression even at low doses and low levels of inhibition conflict. Moreover, as mentioned, dose did not moderate the effect of inhibition conflict, and there was significant heterogeneity among the low-inhibition conflict studies. These outcomes suggest that the relationship between alcohol and aggression may depend on other factors. We examine next the role of three such factors: provocation, frustration, and self-focused attention.

Provocation

We predicted that the difference in aggression between sober and intoxicated participants would decrease as intensity of provocation increased. As shown by the means and CIs in Table 4, this was the pattern

TABLE 4
Categorical Analysis of Provocation and Alcohol Dose

Dataset and variable class	k	M d_+	95% CI for d_+		Q_W	Q_B
			Lower	Upper		
All studies						4.10*
Low provocation	55	0.65	0.56	0.74	77.75*	
High provocation	33	0.50	0.40	0.61	59.44**	
Low-dose studies						6.23**
Low provocation	24	0.54	0.39	0.70	52.32***	
High provocation	12	0.23	0.04	0.42	33.28***	
High-dose studies						0.63
Low provocation	30	0.70	0.59	0.82	22.64	
High provocation	21	0.63	0.50	0.76	14.32	

Note. d_+ denotes effect sizes weighted by the reciprocal of their variances. CI denotes confidence interval. Q_W tests within-category homogeneity; Q_B tests between-category homogeneity. Significant values indicate rejection of the hypothesis of homogeneity. One study (Boyatzis, 1974) lacked dose information, so it was excluded from all analyses involving dose. In addition, the two studies contributing the most extreme outliers were excluded.
*$p < .05$. **$p < .01$. ***$p < .001$.

we obtained. Lower levels of provocation were associated with larger effect sizes than higher levels of provocation, $Q_B = 4.10$, $p < .05$. Note, however, that both CIs exclude 0. Hence, under low as well as high provocation, intoxicated participants behaved more aggressively than did those who were sober.

To assess whether the effect of provocation was moderated by alcohol dose, we divided the dataset as a function of dose, and analyses on provocation were repeated. The lower panel of Table 4 shows that, in the low-dose subset, lower levels of provocation were associated with larger effect sizes, $Q_B = 6.23$, $p < .01$. For the high-dose subset, the means were in the same direction, but the difference was not significant, $Q_B = 0.63$. Even though the aggressive behavior of intoxicated and sober participants became more similar as the intensity of provocation increased (viz., smaller mean effect sizes), intoxicated participants consistently remained more aggressive than sober ones. This latter effect is revealed by the exclusion of 0 from all CIs, even those in which intensity of provocation was high.

Frustration

Table 5 shows that both low and high levels of frustration were associated with mean effect sizes that differed from 0 (i.e., the 95% CIs excluded 0). However, contrary to our expectation that sober and intoxicated participants would behave more similarly when frustration was high, the results show that higher levels of frustration were associated with larger, not smaller, mean effect sizes, $Q_B = 6.69$, $p < .01$. We observed this same pattern in the low-dose subset, $Q_B = 16.48$, $p < .001$. Such a comparison

TABLE 5
Categorical Analysis of Frustration and Alcohol Dose

Dataset and variable class	k	$M\,d_+$	95% CI for d_+ Lower	Upper	Q_W	Q_B
All studies						6.69**
Low frustration	52	0.42	0.33	0.51	86.38**	
High frustration	20	0.66	0.50	0.82	54.17***	
Low-dose studies						16.48***
Low frustration	28	0.23	0.11	0.36	55.33**	
High frustration	19	0.67	0.50	0.83	54.10***	
High-dose studies						NA
Low frustration	23	0.58	0.45	0.70	15.38	
High frustration	1	0.54	−0.35	1.43	NA	

Note. d_+ denotes effect sizes weighted by the reciprocal of their variances. CI denotes confidence interval. Q_W tests within-category homogeneity; Q_B tests between-category homogeneity. Significant values indicate rejection of the hypothesis of homogeneity. One study (Boyatzis, 1974) lacked dose information, so it was excluded from all analyses involving dose. The two studies contributing the most extreme outliers were excluded.
**$p < .01$. ***$p < .001$.

TABLE 6
Regression Analyses on Self-Focused Attention and Alcohol Dose

Dataset and predictor	B	β	Q_E	k
All studies			70.77**	47
Self-focused attention	−0.42*	−0.22		
Dose	0.16	0.19		
Low-dose subset			43.52***	20
Self-focused attention	−0.77***	−0.44		
High-dose subset			16.71	27
Self-focused attention	0.95*	0.44		

Note. Dose was dichotomized, with low values ranging from 0.23 to 1.00 ml/kg and high values ranging from 1.20 to 1.30 ml/kg. B denotes unstandardized regression coefficients. β denotes standardized regression coefficient. Q_E denotes test of model specification. Significant values indicate that the model is inadequate to account for heterogeneity among effect sizes. The two studies contributing the most extreme outliers were excluded. The regression coefficient for dose was marginally significant, $p < .10$, two-tailed.
*$p < .05$. **$p < .01$. ***$p < .001$.

could not be made within the high-dose subset, however, because there was only one effect size in the high-frustration–high-dose cell.

Self-Focused Attention

The results of the regression analysis on self-focused attention are shown in Table 6. Following the same strategy as with the analysis of anxiety, we included dose as a predictor in the equation with self-focused attention. The results indicate that self-focused attention was a significant predictor of effect size, $B = -0.42$, $p < .05$. The negative sign of the regression coefficient indicates that as self-focused attention increased, sober and intoxicated participants behaved more similarly.

To assess whether the effect of self-focused attention was moderated by dose, we conducted separate regression analyses on the low- and high-dose subsets of the studies. The results from the low-dose subset replicate those in the overall sample (see Table 6); higher levels of self-focused attention were associated with smaller effect sizes, $B = -0.77$, $p < .001$. By contrast, we observed the opposite relationship within the high-dose subset of the studies. In this latter set, higher levels of self-focused attention were associated with larger effect sizes, $B = 0.95$, $p < .05$. That is, when higher alcohol doses were administered, *greater* levels of self-focus were associated with *larger* differences in the aggressiveness of intoxicated and sober participants. The coefficients for the low- and high-dose subsets differed reliably, $t(43) = 4.10$, $p < .01$.

Study Characteristics

Categorical moderator analyses of study characteristics are shown in Table 7. Although ancillary to the major theoretical questions, we summarize these results for descriptive purposes.

TABLE 7
Tests of Categorical Models of Study Characteristics

Variable and class	k	$M\ d_+$	95% CI for d_+ Lower	95% CI for d_+ Upper	Q_W	Q_B
Presence of nonaggressive response alternatives						10.70***
Available	17	0.27_a	0.12	0.42	41.28***	
Not available	30	0.58_b	0.47	0.70	26.94	
Possibility of retaliation						18.80***
Possible	29	0.64_a	0.52	0.76	17.02	
Not possible	17	0.23_b	0.09	0.37	42.17***	
Experimenter knowledge of drink content						19.78***
Blind	13	0.21_a	0.06	0.36	30.09**	
Not blind	8	0.65_b	0.43	0.87	2.86	
Not clearly stated	26	0.63_b	0.49	0.76	26.19	
Distracted during consumption of alcohol						16.91***
Distracted	15	$0.24_{a,c}$	0.10	0.39	40.25***	
Not distracted	6	$0.56_{c,d}$	0.29	0.84	6.05	
Not clearly stated	26	$0.63_{b,d}$	0.51	0.76	16.42	
Time allowed for ingestion (in min)						9.10**
5–17	21	$0.37_{a,c}$	0.22	0.49	55.18**	
20–30	17	$0.47_{c,d}$	0.32	0.61	12.95	
Not clearly stated	9	$0.74_{b,d}$	0.53	0.94	1.70	
Time allowed for absorption (in min)						10.29**
10–15	14	0.47_c	0.28	0.66	33.65**	
20–25	13	$0.31_{a,c}$	0.16	0.45	18.54	
30–45	16	$0.63_{b,c}$	0.47	0.79	15.90	
Not clearly stated	4	$0.69_{c,b}$	0.33	1.04	0.54	
Drinking history						28.39***
Light–moderate social	21	0.62_a	0.48	0.75	26.05	
Heavy social	4	-0.05_b	-0.26	0.17	1.61	
Missing	22	0.62_a	0.47	0.77	11.33	
Type of response measure						17.27***
Direct behavior	42	0.56_a	0.45	0.66	56.64	
Verbal–questionnaire	4	0.02_b	-0.21	0.25	5.01	
Both	1	0.51	0.10	0.92	—	
Gender[a]						1.60
Men	46	0.49_a	0.39	0.58	76.23	
Men and women	4	0.27_a	-0.06	0.60	7.69	

Note. d_+ denotes effect sizes weighted by reciprocal of their variances. CI denotes confidence interval. Q_W tests within-category homogeneity; Q_B tests between-category homogeneity. Significant values indicate rejection of the hypothesis of homogeneity. Q_W is not reported for those categories consisting of only one case. The two most extreme outliers were excluded from all analyses. Therefore, $k = 47$. Within each category dimension, means with different subscripts differ at $p < .05$. [a] Separate effect sizes for men and women were calculated from three separate studies. In addition, one study included only female participants. As a result, $k = 50$ for the analysis of gender.
*$p < .05$. **$p < .01$. ***$p < .001$.

Presence of Nonaggressive-Response Alternatives

Many studies used paradigms that forced participants to engage in some type of aggression. For example, participants could choose how intense a shock to deliver but lacked the option of not delivering a shock. Gustafson (1993) suggested that increased aggression following intoxication may be restricted to situations in which aggression is the only response alternative available. As shown in Table 7, studies lacking a nonaggressive-response alternative yielded a significantly larger mean effect size than those in which a nonaggressive-response alternative was available, Q_B = 10.70, p < .001. However, intoxicated participants behaved more aggressively than sober ones, even when a nonaggressive-response alternative was available (i.e., the CI excluded 0). Caution should be used when interpreting these results because subsequent follow-up analyses revealed that studies in which aggression was the only response alternative also tended to administer higher alcohol doses than studies in which nonaggressive alternatives were available, $t(31)$ = 5.65, p < .0001.

Possibility of Retaliation

Studies in which it was possible for the target of the participant's aggression to retaliate were associated with a larger mean effect size than those in which retaliation was not possible. This finding is somewhat difficult to interpret, however, because possibility of retaliation tended to covary with other theoretically important variables. For example, a concern about retaliation was the source of inhibiting cues in many studies that received high ratings of inhibition conflict. Similarly, fear of retaliation often contributed to ratings of high anxiety.

Experimenter Knowledge of Drink Content

To examine the consequence of the experimenter's knowledge of drink content, we classified studies into one of three categories: experimenter blind to drink content, experimenter not blind, and not enough information reported to determine the experimenter's knowledge. Although all three categories were associated with positive mean effect sizes and CIs that excluded 0, the mean effect size was smaller in the experimenter blind category, compared with categories in which the experimenter was not blind or not enough information was provided, $\chi^2(2)$ = 10.41, p < .005, and $\chi^2(2)$ = 16.88, p < .0001, respectively. This outcome, also obtained by Bushman and Cooper (1990), is consistent with the literature on experimenter expectancy effects (e.g., Rosenthal, 1976).

Distraction During Consumption of Alcohol

There were three categories of studies in this analysis: participants definitely distracted, participants definitely not distracted, and not enough information provided for an accurate classification. Although all yielded CIs that excluded 0, studies in which participants were distracted during the alcohol consumption period had a significantly smaller mean effect size than those studies for which no clear information was provided, $\chi^2(2) = 15.71$, $p < .0005$.

Time Allowed for Ingestion and for Absorption

Q_B values for both analyses of time allowed for ingestion and for absorption were significant, indicating that these variables moderate the degree to which alcohol augments aggression. In the case of ingestion time, this effect seems to be primarily due to the difference between studies allowing 5 to 17 min for ingestion and those in which no accurate information on time allowed for ingestion could be obtained, $\chi^2(2) = 9.08$, $p < .01$. Larger effect sizes were associated with studies that did not clearly report the time for ingestion. The effect of time allowed for absorption seems most attributable to the difference between studies allowing 20 to 25 min for absorption and those allowing 30 to 45 min, $\chi^2(2) = 9.08$, $p < .01$, with larger effect sizes in the latter group. However, it should be noted that time for absorption tended to be confounded with dose, such that studies administering higher doses tended to allow more time for absorption.

Drinking History, Type of Response Measure, and Gender

Although the significant Q_B values for drinking history and type of response measure suggest that these variables also moderate effect size, we refrain from conclusions concerning them because of their substantial covariation, as well as the small number of studies within some of the variable classes. In addition, both variables tended to covary with participant gender, such that a history of heavy social drinking among the participants and use of verbal measures were associated with the inclusion of female participants. Thus, we were unable to make an assessment of the individual moderating effects of each variable.

DISCUSSION

Anxiety and Inhibition Conflict

Many formulations take the view that increased aggression following alcohol consumption is a consequence of decreased sensitivity to cues that inhibit aggression (e.g., Taylor & Chermack, 1993; Taylor & Leonard, 1983; Zeichner & Pihl, 1979). One model focuses on the role of anxiety in inhibiting aggression. It argues that to the extent that intoxication is associated with anxiolysis, intoxication blocks responsivity to this behavioral inhibition system. Similarly, the inhibition conflict model proposed by Steele and colleagues (Steele & Josephs, 1990; Steele & Southwick, 1985) describes how decreased sensitivity to inhibiting cues, in conjunction with intoxication, facilitates aggression.

Our results provide some support for both models. Considering the anxioloysis–disinhibition model first, this model argues that when anxiety arousing cues are very low in intensity, they have little inhibiting effect on either sober or intoxicated participants, thus yielding small effect sizes. When instead such cues are stronger in intensity, their effects in sober participants is to strongly inhibit their aggression. Therefore, if intoxicated participants ignore these latter cues, there is a large difference in the aggressiveness of the two groups, reflected by large effect sizes. As predicted, effect size (reflecting the greater aggression of intoxicated participants relative to that of sober controls) increased as intensity of anxiety-provoking cues increased. There was also a tendency for the effect of anxiety to be strongest in those studies administering relatively high-alcohol doses. This is consistent with the interpretation that at lower alcohol doses, and presumably lower levels of alcohol-related cognitive impairments, both intoxicated and sober participants are relatively responsive to anxiety-provoking cues that serve to inhibit aggression. As alcohol dose increases and various aspects of cognitive functioning are correspondingly impaired, intoxicated participants may experience anxiolysis. Their behavior would, therefore, be relatively free from anxiety-related inhibition, leading to increased aggression in intoxicated relative to sober persons.

The analysis of inhibition conflict revealed that increased levels of inhibition conflict were associated with larger effect sizes. However, our results do not completely support the inhibition conflict model because Steele (Steele & Josephs, 1990; Steele & Southwick, 1985) argued that the aggressive behavior of intoxicated persons should exceed that of sober ones only when both inhibition conflict and alcohol dose are high. Our results show that the combination of high-inhibition conflict and high dose is associated with increased aggression. In conflict to other predictions of this model, however, intoxicated participants were also significantly more aggressive than sober ones when inhibition conflict was high but alcohol dose was low and when both inhibition conflict and dose were low. Indeed, as seen by inspection of Table 3 and contrary to the inhibition conflict model, there is no hint that dose moderates the effect of inhibition conflict.

The conceptual independence of these two models also warrants consideration. Some of the study characteristics judged to be anxioloytic were also judged as contributing to high levels of inhibition conflict. One such example, as mentioned earlier, is the degree to which the experimental paradigm suggests the possibility of retaliation. It could be argued that the specification of anxiolysis is simply one way in which the potency of aggression inhibiting cues is decreased in situations of high-inhibition conflict. However, the anxiolysis–disinhibition model is distinct from, and perhaps preferable to, the inhibition conflict model because it allows for the possibility that inhibiting cues are attended to as fully as instigating cues but that aggression nevertheless increases in intoxicated people. In other words, in contrast to inhibition conflict, the anxiolysis–disinhibition model is more parsimonious because it only requires the assumption that the psychological effect of the inhibiting cues differs depending on whether one is sober or intoxicated.

Zeichner, Pihl, Niaura, and Zacchia (1982) illustrated this difference between the anxiolysis–disinhibition and inhibition conflict models. In their study, intoxicated and sober participants were given the opportunity to shock a "bogus" partner, and the partner was said to have the ability to deliver aversive stimulation to the participants in the form of irritating noise. No partner in fact existed. One third of both groups of participants were given attentional instructions that required them to write down after each trial the level of shock they selected for their partner and the level of noise they received back from their partner. Because the level of noise that participants received was programmed to correlate perfectly with the intensity of shock they chose to deliver to their partners, the attentional instructions should have forced these participants to attend to the consequences of their aggressive behavior. This, in turn, should have inhibited aggression. Instead, intoxicated participants in this condition were more aggressive than their sober counterparts. As Pihl et al. (1993) summarized,

> the acutely intoxicated participants were not more aggressive because they were unaware, verbally or cognitively, of what they were doing and of the consequences of their behavior but because that knowledge no longer served an inhibitory function, perhaps because it no longer produced fear. (p. 132)

The inhibition conflict model seemingly predicts the opposite pattern of results. Forcing participants to attend to the negative consequences of their aggressive behavior should make the inhibiting cues relatively more salient than instigating cues. Consequently, with a narrowed range of attentional focus, intoxicated participants would be expected to attend more exclusively to these salient inhibiting cues (Steele & Josephs, 1990, Footnote 1). The inhibition conflict model would, therefore, predict that intoxicated participants in the forced attention condition would behave less aggressively than those in the other two conditions, which clearly was not the case. Alternatively, even if forcing them to attend to the negative consequences of their aggressive behavior only made the salience of the inhibiting cues more similar to that of the provoking cues, these participants should have behaved less aggressively or should not have differed from sober controls, leaving the outcome still contrary to the inhibition conflict model.

Although intensity of anxiety-provoking cues and level of inhibition conflict did moderate effect size, neither completely accounted for the relation between aggression and intoxication. Significant heterogeneity among effect sizes remained in the analyses of anxiety and inhibition conflict. Consequently, we conclude that although knowledge of the intensity of anxiety-provoking cues and level of inhibition conflict provides some predictive utility the effect of alcohol on aggression is a complex process with multiple determinants. A full understanding of the relation between alcohol and aggression, therefore, requires attention to other moderating variables.

Provocation and Frustration

The presence and intensity of provocation is one additional factor that can moderate the tendency for intoxicated people to behave more aggressively than sober ones. Gustafson (1993) has argued that provocation moderates the effect of alcohol on aggression, such that alcohol increases aggression only in situations in which provocation is present. Two aspects of our analysis challenge that conclusion. First, the obtained direction of effect is opposite to that predicted by Gustafson and is in accord with our theoretically derived prediction. That is, the difference in aggression between intoxicated and sober participants actually decreased rather than increased as intensity of provocation increased.

Second, it appears that Gustafson's (1993) conclusion was based on the assumption that provocation affects the difference in behavior between intoxicated and sober participants through its effects on the behavior of those intoxicated. By contrast, we suspect that provocations have their strongest effect on sober people because intoxicated people display relatively greater levels of aggression, even in the absence of provocation. As evidence of this, we calculated the mean effect size of those studies that received a provocation rating of 1 (the lowest possible rating). The mean of these 26 effect sizes was 0.56, CI = 0.43–0.69, indicating that even among studies with the lowest level of provocation, the aggressive behavior of intoxicated participants reliably exceeded that of sober ones. Hence, it is likely that the smaller effect size associated with higher levels of provocation is largely the result of an increased display of aggression by sober participants in response to provocation.

When we examined this difference in effect size as a function of provocation separately within the low- and high-dose studies, the same direction of effect was obtained in both subsets. In the low-dose studies, the greater aggressiveness of intoxicated participants relative to that of sober ones was reliably reduced under high levels of provocation. In the high-dose studies, however, although provocation produced a similar direction of effect, it did not evidence reliability. In summary then, provocation reduces the difference in aggression between intoxicated and sober participants, although the source of these effects remains unspecified. They may be due to the provocation's instigating or angering effects or because it provides suitable rationale for aggression, which might otherwise be considered an inappropriate behavior.

Originally, we expected provocation and frustration to have similar directions of influence on effect size, but this was not the case. Whereas higher levels of provocation were associated with smaller effect sizes, higher levels of frustration were associated with larger effect sizes. In retrospect, we believe that these opposing effects become theoretically understandable when they are linked to paradigm characteristics associated with the high-frustration as compared with high-provocation studies in this dataset. Aggressive behaviors can be categorized into two types: (a) instrumental and affective or (b) hostile (e.g., Baron, 1977; Feshbach, 1964; Geen, 1990). The main goal of affective aggression is to inflict harm, whereas instrumental aggression is enacted in the service of attaining some other goal, such as money or status. Of course, any aggressive act may contain elements of both intent to harm and instrumentality. Nevertheless, one motive can dominate.

In this dataset, many studies in which high levels of provocation were induced used the reaction time–competition paradigm. The male participant in this paradigm believed that he was competing with another participant who was said to be located in a separate room (e.g., Jeavons & Taylor, 1985). The loser of each competitive trial received a shock, the intensity of which was determined by his opponent. For trials on which the participant won, he received no shock but was given feedback about the intensity he would have received had he lost. No opponent in fact existed, and the shock intensity feedback was preprogrammed by the experimenter. This feedback was manipulated to indicate that the opponent sometimes selected relatively high-intensity shocks for the participant. We believe that experiencing such provocative behavior from a stranger with whom no prior interaction has occurred, and in particular no prior *negative* interaction has occurred, would serve to anger and irritate the participant. Aggression displayed by the participant against the opponent is, therefore, likely motivated by a desire to harm the opponent and retaliate against him for the pain he has actually or intended to inflict.

By contrast, the studies judged as high in frustration tended to be teacher–learner studies, or modifications of the paradigm, which we believe are more likely to elicit instrumental aggression. The participant, in the role of teacher (or supervisor, in the modified paradigm), was thought to experience frustration to the extent that a partner performed poorly and jeopardized the participant's likelihood of obtaining a monetary incentive.[4] In many cases, this monetary incentive was quite sizable (e.g., approximately $80 in Gustafson, 1986a), so the motivation to obtain it should be substantial. In addition, participants were sometimes explicitly informed that their aggression could be instrumental in obtaining their monetary reward (e.g., Gustafson, 1985b).

The increased aggression among intoxicated participants under conditions of high frustration may, therefore, be attributable to differences in perceived instrumental value between sober and intoxicated participants. After all, there is the potential that even low-intensity shocks could be effective in improving the learner's performance. Sober and less impaired participants may be more likely to consider this. Moreover, sober participants who do use higher intensity shocks may be more likely than intoxicated ones to notice that their relatively aggressive behavior is not having the intended effect (i.e., is not improving the learner's performance). As a consequence, their aggressive behavior may become less responsive to increases in frustration (i.e., continued poor performance by the learner). By contrast, intoxicated participants may be less likely to realize that their continued and escalating use of aggression is relatively ineffective. If so, the difference in aggression between intoxicated and sober participants should increase as a function of frustration. The likelihood that aggression would begin to lose its instrumental value for sober participants is particularly high in this dataset, given the fact that participants' goal-directed behavior was always completely thwarted. That is, no matter how much aggression participants displayed, they were never able to reach their desired goal.

Additionally, in a teacher–learner study, the participant is charged with the task of teaching or supervising another person. To some extent then, poor performance by the partner reflects poorly on the participant's ability as a teacher–supervisor (Rule & Percival, 1971). Sober participants, as relatively less impaired, are likely to be more sensitive to this contingency than their intoxicated counterparts. They may appear to be less responsive to increases in frustration because they do not want to be seen as severely punishing another person for something for which they themselves are partly responsible.

Finally, the different effects we obtained for frustration and provocation may be attributable to differences in the perceived appropriateness of aggression in response to these two events. As we have already argued,

---

[4]The only difference between a teacher–learner study and what we refer to as the "modified version" is that in the latter, participants are explicitly told that the task performed by their bogus partner requires concentration but no learning (e.g., Gustafson, 1986a). We retain the term *teacher–learner* to refer to both versions of this paradigm, regardless of whether learning is involved, for two reasons: (a) to link the modified paradigm with the larger body of work that is descended from Buss's (1961) original development of the paradigm and (b) the two versions of the paradigm do not differ in the feature that is of theoretical interest, namely, the extent to which a participant's valued goal is blocked.

the belief in an eye-for-an-eye may make aggression in retaliation to a provocation acceptable. However, there may be greater ambiguity as to whether it is appropriate to take one's frustrations out on another person. Frustrated individuals may, therefore, be more likely to wrestle with their conscience than those provoked. The greater aggression displayed by intoxicated, frustrated participants may reflect their decreased sensitivity to these concerns.[5]

Paradigm differences between high-frustration and high-provocation studies may, therefore, explain the different effects obtained as a function of provocation and frustration. In particular, paradigm characteristics that elicit angry as compared with instrumental aggression appear important. It should be noted that, whereas high frustration appeared to be associated with instrumental aggression in the current dataset, this covariation does not necessarily appear in the larger literature on aggression. Inductions of task frustration may typically lack the interpersonal aspects that elicit instrumental aggression and instead evoke affective aggression. For example, frustration elicited by one's inability to complete an ostensibly easy task increases aggression relative to individuals who experience task success (Geen, 1968). This aggression could in no way facilitate completion of the task, rendering an instrumental motivation for it unlikely. Thus, it may be that had the research paradigms of the studies in our meta-analysis invoked noninterpersonal, task frustration, our parallel predictions for frustration and provocation would have been upheld.

We conducted an internal analysis to test the hypothesis that provocation and frustration would have similar directions of effect when frustration was likely to elicit affective aggression. We divided studies on the basis of the predominant type of aggression likely instigated (affective or instrumental), then compared effect sizes as a function of level of provocation and frustration. The determining characteristics of aggression type were whether (a) features of the experimental paradigm provided participants with a desirable goal and (b) aggression could be perceived as useful in achieving the goal. We coded the aggression as instrumental in nature if both conditions were met. Otherwise, we considered the aggression primarily affective in nature. The mean effect sizes as a function of level of frustration in Table 8 show that the unexpected reverse outcome obtained in the main analysis—namely, smaller, rather than larger, effect sizes under low levels of frustration—was substantially attenuated when the frustrating event elicited affective aggression. Moreover, the absolute magnitude of the reverse frustration effect obtained in the main analysis (as compared with Table 5) is even larger among the subset of studies limited to include only those in which frustration elicited instrumental aggression.

To provide a conceptual comparison, we conducted this same analysis

---

[5]We thank a reviewer for this suggestion.

TABLE 8
Categorical Analysis of Frustration and Provocation as a Function of Type of Aggression

Variable and class	Instrumental aggression							Affective aggression						
			95% CI for d_+							95% CI for d_+				
	k	$M d_+$	Lower	Upper	Q_W	Q_B		k	$M d_+$	Lower	Upper	Q_W	Q_B
Frustration						14.67***							40.59***
Low	20	0.23	0.08	0.38	35.75*			31	0.51	0.40	0.62	40.51	
High	17	0.66	0.50	0.83	54.04***			3	0.57	−0.10	1.23	0.04	
Provocation						0.18							8.77*
Low	15	0.37	0.19	0.54	35.12***			39	0.75	0.64	0.86	29.35	
High	2	0.26	−0.18	0.70	2.18			31	0.52	0.41	0.63	56.08*	

Note. d_+ denotes effect sizes weighted by reciprocal of their variances. CI denotes confidence interval. Q_W tests within-category homogeneity; Q_B tests between-category homogeneity. Significant values indicate rejection of the hypothesis of homogeneity.
*$p < .05$. ***$p < .001$.

as a function of level of provocation (see Table 8). When we only considered those studies that elicited affective aggression, as expected, the effect of provocation replicates that obtained in the main analysis: Low provocation was associated with larger effect sizes than high provocation. By contrast, when we examined the subset of studies that elicited instrumental aggression, the absolute magnitude of the difference between low and high provocation was smaller and nonsignificant. Although these outcomes do not completely confirm our hypotheses about the role of type of aggression, they are consistent with it. We are cautious in our interpretation, however, due to the fact that there were only two effect sizes in the high-provocation, instrumental aggression cell (Lang, Goeckner, Adesso, & Marlatt, 1975; Zeichner, Allen, Giancola, & Lating, 1994) and only three in the high-frustration, affective aggression cell (Cherek, Steinberg, & Manno, 1985; Kelly, Cherek, Steinberg, & Robinson, 1988; Taylor, Schmutte, & Leonard, 1977).

These opposing directions of effect for provocation and frustration were interesting although unexpected. In the larger experimental literature on aggression per se (wherein only the behavior of sober participants is considered), the magnitude of the effects may differ, but provocation and frustration typically operate in a similar direction (meta-analysis; Carlson & Miller, 1988; Geen, 1990). Their opposite effects on the difference between sober and intoxicated aggression in the current dataset suggest that greater attention needs to be paid to the unique aspects of the paradigms in which they are induced. We, therefore, echo a concern—first voiced by Pernanen (1976) and later by Gustafson (1993)—that features of the paradigms that affect frustration and provocation need to be considered when interpreting results of studies on the alcohol–aggression relation. We also think that it may be useful to attend to the motives for aggression that are aroused in different situations (i.e., instrumental as compared with affective aggression).

Self-Focused Attention

The negative relationship between effect size and self-focus in the overall dataset and in the subset of low-dose studies indicates that the tendency for intoxicated participants to behave more aggressively than sober ones is reduced when attention is focused on self. In other words, intoxicated participants behave more similarly to those sober as self-focus increases. Because intoxication generally increases aggression, this finding suggests that self-focus differentially exerts greater inhibitory effects on intoxicated participants. That is, self-focused participants are seemingly able to overcome the aggression-inducing consequences of alcohol ingestion. There are at least two possible explanations for such a pattern. First, intoxicated participants have been shown to overcome alcohol-induced impairments when motivated to concentrate on their performance. For example, intoxicated participants who were told to "try to stay sober" showed better motor and cognitive performance than those not given this instruction (Young & Pihl, 1980; see also Gustafson & Kallmen, 1990a, 1990b, 1990c; Myrsten, Lamble, Frankenhaeuser, & Lundberg, 1979; Ross & Pihl, 1988; Williams, Goldman, & Williams, 1981). Ross and Pihl argued that focusing attention on self can induce such a compensatory process. To the extent that intoxicated participants are more influenced by self-focusing cues than sober participants, as our results indicate, it appears that they actually overcompensate and regulate their behavior even more stringently than sober participants. Alternatively, the narrowed attentional focus accompanying intoxication may intensify a self-focused state by decreasing sensitivity to other, potentially distracting stimuli. Sober participants may be relatively less affected by self-focusing cues because their wider range of attentional focus exposes them to cues that compete with self for attention. These explanations are not incompatible; both processes may occur.

The fact that effect size and self-focus were positively related in the high-dose subset of studies may be a function of the relatively weak strength of the self-focusing cues in this dataset. Explicit manipulations of self-focus were rare in the dataset, and we made ratings of self-focus on the basis of subtle variations in situational cues. Not surprisingly, on average, self-focus was low (viz., below the scale midpoint in 70% of the studies). In this dataset, it is therefore reasonable to expect that as alcohol dose and the cognitive impairment associated with it increased, intoxicated participants would be less affected by the relatively weak self-focusing cues. The unimpaired sober participants may still be influenced by the self-focusing cues, leading them to behave less aggressively than those intoxicated who had been given higher doses.

The different effect of self-focus as a function of dose may also be explained by the finding that intoxication typically decreases the likelihood of focusing attention on self (Hull et al., 1983). The self-focusing cues in this dataset may have been sufficient to overcome this general tendency in those intoxicated participants who had consumed lower doses. Because they may have started out at a lower level of self-focus than sober ones, the aggressive behavior of intoxicated participants may have been more greatly affected than that of sober ones. This would account for the negative relation between effect size and self-focus when lower doses had been consumed. As dose increased, the likelihood of focusing on self may correspondingly decrease, such that stronger self-focusing cues are required if attention is to be redirected to self. The relatively weak self-focusing cues in this dataset may, therefore, have had little effect on the intoxicated participants who had received higher doses. These same cues should still have effected sober ones, resulting in a positive relation between effect size and self-focus when higher doses are involved.[6] It should be noted that the mean judges' ratings of self-focus did not differ as a function of dose ($p >$ .05), indicating that the different relation observed between self-focus and effect size as a function of dose is not attributable to differences in the intensity of self-focusing cues between high- and low-dose studies.

Study Characteristics

This review has focused on a number of potentially important moderators of the relation between alcohol and aggression. One issue that needs to be stressed is that it is often not possible in the existing literature to assess separately the effect of other theoretically relevant factors because the variables of interest tend to covary within studies. Our analysis has revealed many instances of this. For example, the display of aggression differs as a function of gender (Eagly & Steffen, 1986); but, in the alcohol and aggression literature, inclusion of female participants has tended to covary with a history of heavier social drinking among the participants and use of verbal measures of aggression—both of which could influence effect size. We, therefore, found it impossible to assess the independent influences of these three variables. Because each of these variables is of potential theoretical and practical importance, systematic investigation of their independent effects would be welcomed.

Similarly, we were unable to reach a strong conclusion about certain paradigmatic features, such as the influence of the availability of nonaggressive-response alternatives. Gustafson (1993) argued that alcohol increases aggression only in situations in which participants are forced to make an aggressive response. We attempted to test this hypothesis by dividing studies as a function of whether nonaggressive-response alternatives were present in an experiment. Unfortunately, these two categories differed significantly in mean dose of alcohol given to the participants, thereby precluding assessment of whether observed differences in effect size were due to dose effects or to the type of response alternatives.

Implications for Future Research

The analyses on the moderator variables in this meta-analysis produced a number of interesting results. However, like any meta-analytic research whose researchers examine the effects of moderator variables by comparing subsets of studies or ordering studies in terms of their judged or coded level on the moderator of interest, the obtained relation between the moderator (e.g., anxiety) and effect size (e.g., the difference in aggression between sober and intoxicated participants) is correlational in nature.

---

[6]We thank a reviewer for this suggestion.

Hence, it needs to be followed up by experimental research. In this section, we briefly suggest future experimental research linked to the specific effects we have obtained.

Anxiety and Inhibition Conflict

Although not strongly emphasized in our report, our judges' ratings of anxiety and inhibition conflict showed strong covariation. Indeed, in an analysis in which each study was allowed to contribute one rating per variable, the correlation between ratings of anxiety and inhibition conflict was so high as to suggest singularity of the two concepts ($r = 91$, $p < .001$, when corrected for reliability of the judgments). Despite this, we have tried to outline differential predictions made by the anxioloysis–disinhibition and inhibition conflict models. Before such predictions can be adequately tested, however, independent manipulations of the two models are required, assuming that they do indeed possess discriminative construct validity. Frankly, we are at a loss to generate independent manipulations. Operationalizations of anxiety (e.g., presence of a high-status observer who has control over the participant with respect to an important outcome) that come to mind would also serve as inhibiting cues that increase inhibition conflict, and vice versa. The conceptual independence of anxiety and inhibition conflict and their relation in moderating alcohol-induced aggression, therefore, requires greater attention. As previously discussed, the possibility of retaliation often contributed to ratings of both high-anxiety and high-inhibition conflict in this dataset. A wider range of operationalizations of anxiety and inhibition conflict should be explored to eliminate the possibility that the obtained effects are unique to threat of retaliation. In summary, at the very least, a wider variety of manipulations of anxiety and inhibition conflict and an elaborated conceptual analysis of their potential discriminative construct validity is warranted.

Provocation and Frustration

In our analysis of provocation and frustration, it was apparent that the distinction between these concepts was confounded with other variables. In particular, our discussion suggests the need to separately manipulate the type of aggressive responses elicited by provocation and frustration manipulations. Specifically, it calls for experimental researchers to examine separately the effects of alcohol for *provocations* experimentally designed to elicit instrumental versus affective aggression and, in parallel, for inductions of *frustration* designed to elicit instrumental versus affective aggression. Perhaps also important is the need for experiments whose researchers orthogonally examine these effects when the instigatory source is human versus environmental. With respect to this latter call, it is worth noting that in our dataset, many of the frustration inductions depended on human agency (a "stupid" partner in the teacher–learner paradigm), as opposed to environmental circumstances (e.g., extreme temperatures or task failure). Provocation may also be induced either by human agency or environmental circumstances. It may be important that the definition of provocation given to our judges constrained it to instances of human agency.

We also note that many of the paradigms used to study alcohol and aggression are fairly provoking (e.g., a shock machine is present, a participant is involved in competition). As a result, studies that received the lowest rating on the provocation dimension most likely reflected a condition of low, as opposed to no, provocation. It would be of interest to compare the aggression of intoxicated and sober participants under conditions in which provocation was judged below threshold, so as to determine whether the relation between provocation and effect size holds in the absence of provocation. Similarly, some amount of anxiety and inhibition conflict likely existed even in those studies that received the lowest ratings on these variables. Hence, our results do not specifically address the relationship between alcohol and aggression under situations of no anxiety or no inhibition conflict.

Self-Focus

The concept of *self-focus* contains two components: One refers to personal standards for ideal behavior, whereas the other represents impulsive inclination. It would be useful to develop separate measures of each component, so as to determine whether they are effected equally as a consequence of alcohol ingestion and its dose. It is possible that the attentional deficits induced by intoxication primarily interfere with the encoding of one, the other, or both of these components. Alternatively, or in addition, intoxication may interfere with the high order cognitive process of comparing an adequate cognitive representation of each.

Other Issues

It would also be useful to determine whether changes in motivation or ability are responsible for the results obtained herein. On the one hand, proscriptions against drinking and driving imply that alcohol has inevitable capacity reduction consequences. On the other hand, Ross and Pihl (1988) have concluded that the

> pharmacological action of alcohol may be counteracted when subjects are motivated to "act sober," either by experimenters setting a behavioral standard of sober performance, or by manipulations aimed at forcing the subjects to take personal responsibility for their performance. (p. 116)

The influence of self-focused attention at lower doses is consistent with this conclusion. Clearly, however, at high enough doses, alcohol exerts behavioral effects that cannot be overcome by increased motivation. The data that we reviewed are not sufficient to address this issue, but determination of the relative contributions of changes in ability and motivation could help clarify the effects of alcohol on behavior in general, and on aggressive behavior in particular.

CONCLUSION

In closing, we emphasize that although this meta-analysis confirms the causal role of alcohol in increasing aggression (see also Bushman & Cooper, 1990; and Steele & Southwick, 1985), we do not view aggression as an inevitable consequence of intoxication. Laboratory studies such as those in this analysis are specifically designed to facilitate aggression by creating situations in which participants feel comfortable displaying it should they desire to do so. By contrast, most real-world settings contain many fewer aggression-instigating cues and many more inhibiting ones.

REFERENCES

References marked with an asterisk indicate studies included in the meta-analysis.

Averill, J. R. (1982). *Anger and aggression: An essay on emotion.* New York: Springer-Verlag.

Axelrod, R. (1984). *The evolution of cooperation.* New York: Basic Books.

*Bailey, D. S., Leonard, K. E., Cranston, J. W., & Taylor, S. P. (1983). Effects of alcohol and self-awareness on human physical aggression. *Personality and Social Psychology Bulletin, 9,* 289–295.

*Bailey, D. S., & Taylor, S. P. (1991). Effects of alcohol and aggressive disposition on human physical aggression. *Journal of Research on Personality, 25,* 334–342.

Baron, R. A. (1977). *Human aggression.* New York: Plenum Press.

*Bennett, R. M., Buss, A. H., & Carpenter, J. A. (1969). *Quarterly Journal of Studies on Alcohol, 30,* 870–877.

Berkowitz, L. (1989). Frustration–aggression hypothesis: Examination and reformulation. *Psychological Bulletin, 106,* 59–73.

Bettencourt, B. A., & Miller, N. (1996). Gender differences in aggression as a function of provocation: A meta-analysis. *Psychological Bulletin, 119,* 422–447.

Birnbaum, I. M., Johnson, M. K., Hartley, J. T., & Taylor, T. H. (1980). Alcohol and elaborative schemas for sentences. *Journal of Experimental Psychology: Human Leaning and Memory, 6,* 293–300.

Birnbaum, I. M., & Parker, E. S. (1977). Acute effects of alcohol on storage and retrieval. In I. M. Birnbaum & E. S. Parker (Eds.), *Alcohol and human memory* (pp. 99–108), Hillsdale, NJ: Erlbaum.

*Bond, A., & Lader, M. (1987). The effects of alcohol on behavioural aggression and cardiac and electrodermal activity monitored during an aversive task. *Journal of Psychophysiology, 1,* 229–240.

*Boyatzis, R. E. (1974). The effects of alcohol consumption on the aggressive behavior of men. *Quarterly Journal of Studies on Alcohol, 35,* 959–972.

Brown, S. A., Goldman, M. S., Inn, A., & Anderson, L. R. (1980). Expectations of reinforcement from alcohol: Their domain and relation to drinking patterns. *Journal of Consulting and Clinical Psychology, 48,* 419–426.

Bushman, B. J., & Cooper, H. M. (1990). Effects of alcohol on human aggression: An integrative research review. *Psychological Bulletin, 107,* 341–354.

Buss, A. H. (1961). *The psychology of aggression.* New York: Wiley.

Carlson, M., Charlin, V., & Miller, N. (1988). Positive mood and helping behavior: A test of six hypotheses. *Journal of Personality and Social Psychology, 55,* 1–17.

Carlson, M., & Miller, N. (1987). Explanation of the relation between negative mood and helping. *Psychological Bulletin, 102,* 91–108.

Carlson, M., & Miller, N. (1988). The differential effects of social and nonsocial negative events on aggressiveness. *Sociology and Social Research, 72,* 155–158.

Carver, C. S. (1975). Physical aggression as a function of objective self-awareness and attitudes toward punishment. *Journal of Experimental Social Psychology, 11,* 510–519.

Carver, C. S. (1979). A cybernetic model of self-attention processes. *Journal of Personality and Social Psychology, 8,* 1251–1281.

Carver, C. S., & Scheier, M. F. (1981). *Attention and self-regulation: A control theory approach to human behavior.* New York: Springer-Verlag.

Carver, C. S., & Scheier, M. F. (1990). Origins and functions of positive and negative affect: A control-process view. *Psychological Review, 97,* 19–35.

*Cherek, D. R., Steinberg, J. L., & Manno, B. R. (1985). Effects of alcohol on human physical aggressive behavior. *Journal of Studies on Alcohol, 46,* 321–328.

Cohen, J. (1988). *Statistical power analyses for the behavioral sciences* (2nd ed.). Hillsdale, NJ: Erlbaum.

Cooper, H. M. (1989). *Integrating research: A guide for literature reviews.* Newbury Park, CA: Sage.

Craik, F. I. M. (1977). Similarities between the effects of aging and alcoholic intoxication on memory performance, construed within a "levels of processing" framework. In I. M. Birnbaum & E. S. Parker (Eds.), *Alcohol and human memory* (pp. 9–21). Hillsdale, NJ: Erlbaum.

Critchlow, B. (1986). The powers of John Barleycorn. *American Psychologist, 41,* 751–764.

Current Contents [Database]. (1989–1994, July). Philadelphia: Institute for Scientific Information [Producer]. Available from: Ovid Technologies.

Diener, E. (1980). Deindividuation: The absence of self-awareness and self-regulation in group members. In B. P. Paulus (Ed.), The psychology of group influence (pp. 209–242). Hillsdale, NJ: Erlbaum.

Diener, E., & Wallbom, M. (1976). Effects of self-awareness on antinormative behavior. Journal of Research in Personality, 10, 107–111.

Dollard, J., Doob, L., Miller, N., Mowrer, O., & Sears, R. (1939). Frustration and aggression. New Haven, CT: Yale University Press.

Duval, S., Duval, V. H., & Neely, R. (1979). Self-focus, felt responsibility, and helping behavior. Journal of Personality and Social Psychology, 37, 1769–1778.

Duval, S., & Wicklund, R. A. (1972). A theory of objective self-awareness. New York: Academic Press.

Eagly, A. H., & Steffen, V. J. (1986). Gender and aggressive behavior: A meta-analytic review of the social psychological literature. Psychological Bulletin, 100, 309–330.

Feshbach, S. (1964). The function of aggression and the regulation of aggressive drive. Psychological Review, 71, 257–272.

*Ganter, A. B., & Taylor, S. P. (1992). Human physical aggression as a function of alcohol and threat of harm. Aggressive Behavior, 18, 29–36.

Geen, R. G. (1968). Effects of frustration, attack, and prior training in aggressiveness upon aggressive behavior. Journal of Personality and Social Psychology, 9, 316–321.

Geen, R. G. (1990). Human aggression. Pacific Grove, CA: Brooks/Cole.

Gianoulakis, C., & Gupta, A. (1986). Inbred strains of mice with variable sensitivity to ethanol exhibit difference in the content and processing of beta-endorphins. Life Sciences, 39, 2315–2325.

Gibbons, F. X., & Wicklund, R. A. (1982). Self-focused attention and helping behavior. Journal of Personality and Social Psychology, 43, 462–474.

Gouldner, A. W. (1960). The norm of reciprocity. American Sociological Review, 25, 161–178.

Gray, J. A. (1987). The psychology of fear and stress. New York: Cambridge University Press.

Greenwell, J., & Dengerink, H. A. (1973). The role of perceived versus actual attack in human physical aggression. Journal of Personality and Social Psychology, 26, 66–71.

*Gustafson, R. (1984). Alcohol, frustration, and direct physical aggression: A methodological point of view. Psychological Reports, 55, 959–966.

*Gustafson, R. (1985a). Alcohol and aggression: Pharmacological versus expectancy effects. Psychological Reports, 57, 955–966.

*Gustafson, R. (1985b). Alcohol-related aggression: A further study of the importance of frustration. Psychological Reports, 57, 683–697.

*Gustafson, R. (1985c). Frustration as an important determinant of alcohol-related aggression. *Psychological Reports, 57,* 3–14.

*Gustafson, R. (1986a). Alcohol, frustration, and aggression: An experiment using the balanced placebo design. *Psychological Reports, 59,* 207–218.

*Gustafson, R. (1986b). Threat as a determinant of alcohol-related aggression. *Psychological Reports, 58,* 287–297.

*Gustafson, R. (1987). Alcohol and human physical aggression: An experiment using a "backward" balanced placebo design. *Journal of Social Behavior and Personality, 2,* 135–144.

*Gustafson, R. (1988). Beer intoxication and physical aggression in males. *Drug and Alcohol Dependence, 21,* 237–242.

*Gustafson, R. (1989). Alcohol and the validation of experimental aggression paradigms: The Taylor reaction time procedure. *Drug and Alcohol Dependence, 23,* 49–54.

*Gustafson, R. (1990). Wine and male physical aggression. *Journal of Drug Issues, 20,* 75–86.

*Gustafson, R. (1991a). Aggressive and nonaggressive behavior as a function of alcohol intoxication and frustration in women. *Alcoholism: Clinical and Experimental Research, 15,* 886–892.

Gustafson, R. (1991b). Alcohol and outcome expectancies: Tolerance for socially nonacceptable behaviors. *Psychology Reports, 69,* 67–74.

*Gustafson, R. (1991c). Male physical aggression as a function of alcohol, frustration, and subjective mood. *International Journal of the Addictions, 26,* 255–266.

*Gustafson, R. (1991d). Male physical aggression as a function of alcohol intoxication and frustration: Experimental results and methodological considerations. *Alcoholism: Clinical and Experimental Research, 15,* 158–164.

*Gustafson, R. (1992). Alcohol and aggression: A replication study controlling for potential confounding variables. *Aggressive Behavior, 18,* 21–28.

Gustafson, R. (1993, September). What do experimental paradigms tell us about alcohol-related aggressive responding. *Journal of Studies on Alcohol* (Suppl. 11), 20–29.

Gustafson, R., & Kallmen, H. (1990a). Alcohol and the compensation hypothesis: A test with cognitive and psychomotor tasks. *Perceptual and Motor Skills, 71,* 1367–1374.

Gustafson, R., & Kallmen, H. (1990b). Effects of alcohol on cognitive performance measured with Stroop's Color–Word Test. *Perceptual and Motor Skills, 71,* 99–105.

Gustafson, R., & Kallmen, H. (1990c). Effects of alcohol on prolonged cognitive performance measures with Stroop's Color–Word Test. *Psychological Reports, 67,* 645–650.

Heatherton, T. F., & Baumeister, R. F. (1991). Binge eating as escape from self-awareness. *Psychological Bulletin, 110,* 86–108.

Hedges, L. V. (1981). Distribution theory for Glass's estimator of effect size and related estimators. *Journal of Educational Statistics, 6,* 107–128.

Hedges, L. V., & Olkin, I. (1985). *Statistical methods for meta-analysis.* New York: Academic Press.

Hoffman, P. L., & Tabakoff, B. (1990). Ethanol and guanine nucleotide binding proteins: A selective interaction. *FASEB Journal, 4,* 2612–2622.

Hull, J. G. (1981). A self-awareness model of the causes and effects of alcohol consumption. *Journal of Abnormal Psychology, 90,* 586–600.

Hull, J. G., & Bond, C. F. (1986). Social and behavioral consequences of alcohol consumption and expectancy: A meta-analysis. *Psychological Bulletin, 99,* 347–360.

Hull, J. G., Levenson, R. W., Young, R. D., & Sher, K. J. (1983). Self-awareness-reducing effects of alcohol consumption. *Journal of Personality and Social Psychology, 44,* 461–473.

Hull, J. G., & Reilly, N. P. (1983). Self-awareness, self-regulation, and alcohol consumption: A reply to Wilson. *Journal of Abnormal Psychology, 92,* 514–519.

Hall, J. G., & Young, R. D. (1983a). The self-awareness-reducing effects of alcohol: Evidence and implications. In J. Suls & A. G. Greenwood (Eds.), *Psychological perspectives on the self* (Vol. 2, pp. 159–190). Hillsdale, NJ: Earlbaum.

Hull, J. G., & Young, R. D. (1983b). Self-consciousness, self-esteem, and success–failure as determinants of alcohol consumption in male social drinkers. *Journal of Personality and Social Psychology, 44,* 1097–1109.

Hull, J. G., Young, R. D., & Jouriles, E. (1986). Applications of the self-awareness model of alcohol consumption: Predicting patterns of use and abuse. *Journal of Personality and Social Psychology, 51,* 790–796.

Hunt, W. A. (1985). *Alcohol and biological membranes.* New York: Guilford Press.

Huntley, M. J. (1973). Effects of alcohol and fixation-task difficulty on choice reaction time to extrafoveal stimulation. *Quarterly Journal of Studies on Alcohol, 34,* 89–103.

*Jeavons, C., & Taylor, S. P. (1985). The control of alcohol-related aggression: Redirecting the inebriate's attention to socially appropriate conduct. *Aggressive Behavior, 11,* 93–101.

Johnson, B. T. (1993). *DSTAT 1.10: Software for the meta-analytic review of research literatures* [Manual]. Hillsdale, NJ: Erlbaum.

Jones, B. M., & Jones, M. K. (1977). Alcohol and memory impairment in male and female social drinkers. In I. M. Birnbaum & E. S. Parker (Eds.), *Alcohol and human memory* (pp. 127–138). Hillsdale, NJ: Erlbaum.

*Kelly, T. H., Cherek, D. R., & Steinberg, J. L. (1989). Concurrent reinforcement and alcohol: Effects on human aggressive behavior. *Journal of Studies on Alcohol, 50,* 399–405.

*Kelly, T. H., Cherek, D. R., Steinberg, J. L., & Robinson, D. (1988). Effects of provocation and alcohol on human physical aggressive behavior. *Drug and Alcohol Dependence, 21,* 105–121.

Koob, G. F., & Bloom, F. E. (1988, November 4). Cellular and molecular mechanisms of drug dependency. *Science, 242,* 715–723.

Lang, A. R. (1983). Drinking and disinhibition: Contributions from psychological research. In R. Room & G. Collins (Eds.), *Alcohol and disinhibition: Nature and meaning of the link* (National Institute for Alcohol and Alcoholism Research Monograph No. 12, pp. 48–87). Washington, DC: U.S. Government Printing Office.

*Lang, A. R., Goeckner, D. T., Adesso, V. J., & Marlatt, G. R. (1975). Effects of alcohol on aggression in male social drinkers. *Journal of Abnormal Psychology, 84,* 508–518.

Lang, A. R., & Sibrel, P. A. (1989). Psychological perspectives on alcohol consumption and interpersonal aggression: The potential role of individual differences in alcohol-related criminal violence. *Criminal Justice and Behavior, 16,* 299–324.

*Laplace, A. C., Chermack, S. T., & Taylor, S. P. (1994). Effects of alcohol and drinking experience on human physical aggression. *Personality and Social Psychology Bulletin, 20,* 439–444.

*Leonard, K. E. (1984). Alcohol consumption and escalatory aggression in intoxicated and sober dyads. *Journal of Studies on Alcohol, 45,* 75–80.

*Leonard, K. E. (1989). The impact of explicit aggressive and implicit nonaggressive cues on aggression in intoxicated and sober males. *Personality and Social Psychology Bulletin, 15,* 390–400.

Lightdale, J. R., & Prentice, D. A. (1994). Rethinking sex differences in aggression: Aggressive behavior in the absence of social roles. *Personality and Social Psychology Bulletin, 20,* 34–44.

Lindman, R. E., & Lang, A. R. (1994). The alcohol–aggression stereotype: A cross-cultural comparison of beliefs. *International Journal of the Addictions, 29,* 1–13.

MacAndrew, C., & Edgerton, R. B. (1969). *Drunken comportment.* Chicago: Aldine.

Marlatt, G. A., & Rohsenow, D. J. (1980). Cognitive processes in alcohol use: Expectancy and the balanced placebo design. In N. Mello (Ed.), *Advances in substance abuse* (Vol. 1, pp. 159–199). Greenwich, CT: JAI Press.

Medline [Database]. (1966–1994, July). Bethesda, MD: National Library of Medicine [Producer]. Available from: Ovid Technologies.

Miller, N., & Carlson, M. (1990). Valid theory-testing meta-analyses further question the negative state relief model of helping. *Psychological Bulletin, 107,* 215–225.

Miller, N., Lee, J.-Y., & Carlson, M. (1991). The validity of inferential judgments when used in theory-testing meta-analysis. *Personality and Social Psychology Bulletin, 17,* 335–343.

Moskowitz, H., & DePry, D. (1968). Differential effect of alcohol on auditory vigilance and divided-attention tasks. *Quarterly Journal of Studies on Alcohol, 29,* 54–63.

Moss, H. B., & Tartar, R. E. (1993). Substance abuse, aggression, and violence. *American Journal on Addictions, 2*, 149–160.

*Murdoch, D., & Pihl, R. O. (1985). Alcohol and aggression in a group interaction. *Addictive Behaviors, 10*, 97–101.

Murdoch, D., Pihl, R. O., & Ross, D. (1990). Alcohol and crimes of violence: Present issues. *International Journal of the Addictions, 25*, 1065–1081.

Myers, R. D., Melchior, C., & Swartzwelder, H. S. (1980). Amine-aldehyde metabolites and alcoholism: Fact, myth, or uncertainty. *Substance and Alcohol Actions/Misuse, 1*, 223–238.

Myrsten, A.-L., Lamble, R., Frankenhaeuser, M., & Lundberg, A. (1979). Interaction of alcohol and reward in an achievement situation. *Psychopharmacology, 62*, 211–215.

Pernanen, K. (1976). Alcohol and crimes of violence. In B. Kissin & H. Begleiter (Eds.), *The biology of alcoholism: Vol. 4. Social aspect of alcoholism* (pp. 351–441). New York: Plenum Press.

Pihl, R. O. (1983). Alcohol and aggression: A psychological perspective. In E. Gottheil, K. A. Druley, T. E. Skoloda, & H. M. Waxman (Eds.), *Alcohol, drug abuse, and aggression* (pp. 292–313). Springfield, IL: Charles C Thomas.

Pihl, R. O., Peterson, J. B., & Lau, M. A. (1993, September). A biosocial model of the alcohol–aggression relationship. *Journal of Studies on Alcohol* (Suppl. 11), 128–139.

*Pihl, R. O., Smith, M., & Farrell, B. (1984). Alcohol and aggression in men: A comparison of brewed and distilled beverages. *Journal of Studies on Alcohol, 45*, 278–282.

*Pihl, R. O., & Zacchia, C. (1986). Alcohol and aggression: A test of the affect–arousal hypothesis. *Aggressive Behavior, 12*, 367–375.

*Pihl, R. O., Zeichner, A., Niaura, R., Nagy, K., & Zacchia, C. (1981). Attribution and alcohol-mediated aggression. *Journal of Abnormal Psychology, 90*, 468–475.

Prentice-Dunn, S., & Rogers, R. W. (1980). Effects of deindividuating situational cues and aggressive models on subjective deindividuation and aggression. *Journal of Personality and Social Psychology, 39*, 104–113.

PsycINFO [Database]. (1967–1994, July). Washington, DC: American Psychological Association [Producer]. Available from: Silver-Platter.

*Richardson, R. (1981). The effect of alcohol on male aggression toward female targets. *Motivation and Emotion, 5*, 333–344.

Rogers, M., Miller, N., Mayer, F. A., & Duval, S. (1982). Personal responsibility and salience of the request for help: Determinants of the relation between negative affect and helping behavior. *Journal of Personality and Social Psychology, 43*, 956–970.

Rogers, R. W., & Prentice-Dunn, S. (1981). Deindividuation and anger-mediated interracial aggression: Unmasking regressive racism. *Journal of Personality and Social Psychology, 41*, 63–73.

Rohsenow, D. J. (1983). Drinking habits and expectancies about alcohol's effects for self versus other. *Journal of Counseling and Clinical Psychology, 51,* 752–756.

*Rohsenow, D. J., & Bachorowski, J. (1984). Effects of alcohol expectancies on verbal aggression in men and women. *Journal of Abnormal Psychology, 93,* 418–432.

Roizen, R. (1983). Loosening up: General population views of the effects of alcohol. In R. Room & G. Collins (Eds.), *Alcohol and disinhibition: Nature and meaning of the link* (National Institute of Alcohol and Alcoholism Research Monograph No. 12, pp. 236–257). Washington, DC: U.S. Government Printing Office.

Rosen, L. J., & Lee, C. L. (1976). Acute and chronic effects of alcohol use on organizational processes in memory. *Journal of Abnormal Psychology, 85,* 309–317.

Rosenthal, R. (1976). *Experimenter effects in behavioral research* (rev. ed.). New York: Appleton-Century-Crofts.

Rosenthal, R. (1979). The "file drawer problem" and tolerance for null results. *Psychological Bulletin, 86,* 638–641.

Rosenthal, R. (1991). Meta-analysis: A review. *Psychonomic Medicine, 53,* 247–271.

Ross, D. F., & Pihl, R. O. (1988). Alcohol, self-focus, and complex reaction-time performance. *Journal of Studies on Alcohol, 49,* 115–125.

Rule, B. G., & Percival, E. (1971). The effects of frustration and attack on physical aggression. *Journal of Experimental Research in Personality, 5,* 111–118.

Sayette, M. A. (1993). An appraisal-disruption model of alcohol's effect on stress responses in social drinkers. *Psychological Bulletin, 114,* 459–476.

Scheier, M. F., Fenigstein, A., & Buss, A. H. (1974). Self-awareness and physical aggression. *Journal of Experimental Social Psychology, 10,* 264–273.

*Schmutte, G. T., Leonard, K. E., & Taylor, S. P. (1979). Alcohol and expectations of attack. *Psychological Reports, 45,* 163–167.

*Schmutte, G. T., & Taylor, S. P. (1980). Physical aggression as a function of alcohol and pain feedback. *Journal of Social Psychology, 110,* 235–244.

*Shuntich, R. J., & Taylor, S. P. (1972). The effects of alcohol on human physical aggression. *Journal of Experimental Research in Personality, 6,* 34–38.

Sobell, M. B., & Sobell, L. A. (1973). Individualized behavior therapy for alcoholics. *Behavior Therapy, 4,* 49–72.

Southwick, L., Steele, C. M., Marlatt, A., & Lindell, M. (1981). Alcohol-related expectancies: Defined by phase of intoxication and drinking experience. *Journal of Consulting and Clinical Psychology, 49,* 713–721.

Spielberger, C. D. (1972). Anxiety as an emotional state. In C. D. Spielberger (Ed.), *Anxiety: Current trends in theory and research* (Vol. 1, pp. 23–49). New York: Academic Press.

Steele, C. M., & Josephs, R. A. (1990). Alcohol myopia: Its prized and dangerous effects. *American Psychologist, 45,* 921–933.

Steele, C. M., & Southwick, L. (1985). Alcohol and social behavior I: The psychology of drunken excess. *Journal of Personality and Social Psychology, 48*, 18–34.

Tartar, R. E., Jones, B. M., Simpson, C. D., & Vega, A. (1971). Effects of task complexity and practice on performance during acute alcohol intoxication. *Perceptual and Motor Skills, 33*, 307–318.

Taylor, S. P. (1983). Alcohol and human physical aggression. In E. Gottheil, K. A. Druley, T. E. Skoloda, & H. M. Waxman (Eds.), *Alcohol, drug abuse, and aggression* (pp. 280–291). Springfield, IL: Charles C Thomas.

Taylor, S. P., & Chermack, S. T. (1993, September). Alcohol, drugs, and human physical aggression. *Journal of Studies on Alcohol* (Suppl. 11), 78–88.

*Taylor, S. P., & Gammon, C. B. (1976). Aggressive behavior of intoxicated subjects: The effect of third party intervention. *Journal of Studies on Alcohol, 37*, 917–930.

*Taylor, S. P., Gammon, C. B., & Capasso, D. R. (1976). Aggression as a function of the interaction of alcohol and threat. *Journal of Personality and Social Psychology, 34*, 938–941.

Taylor, S. P., & Leonard, K. E. (1983). Alcohol and human physical aggression. In R. G. Geen & E. I. Donnerstein (Eds.), *Aggression: Theoretical review. Vol. 2: Issues in research* (pp. 77–101). New York: Academic Press.

*Taylor, S. P., Schmutte, G. T., & Leonard, K. T. (1977). Physical aggression as a function of alcohol and frustration. *Bulletin of the Psychonomic Society, 9*, 217–218.

*Taylor, S. P., Schmutte, G. T., Leonard, K. E., & Cranston, J. W. (1979). The effects of alcohol and extreme provocation on the use of a highly noxious electric shock. *Motivation and Emotion, 3*, 73–81.

*Taylor, S. P., & Sears, J. D. (1988). The effects of alcohol and persuasive social pressure on human physical aggression. *Aggressive Behavior, 14*, 237–243.

Young, J. A., & Pihl, R. O. (1980). Self-control of the effects of alcohol intoxication. *Journal of Studies on Alcohol, 41*, 567–571.

Wachter, K. W. (1988, September 16). Disturbed by meta-analysis? *Science, 24*, 1407–1408.

Washburne, C. (1956). Alcohol, self and the group. *Quarterly Journal of Studies on Alcohol, 17*, 108–123.

*Weisman, A. M., & Taylor, S. P. (1994). Effect of alcohol and risk of physical harm on human physical aggression. *Journal of General Psychology, 121*, 67–76.

Williams, R. M., Goldman, M. S., & Williams, D. L. (1981). Expectancy and pharmacological effects of alcohol on human cognitive and motor performance: The compensation for alcohol effect. *Journal of Abnormal Psychology, 90*, 267–270.

*Zeichner, A., Allen, J. D., Giancola, P. R., & Lating, J. M. (1994). Alcohol and aggression: Effects of personal threat on human physical aggression and affective arousal. *Alcoholism: Clinical and Experimental Research, 18*, 657–663.

*Zeichner, A., & Pihl, R. O. (1979). Effects of alcohol and behavior contingencies on human aggression. *Journal of Abnormal Psychology, 88*, 153–160.

*Zeichner, A., & Pihl, R. O. (1980). Effects of alcohol and instigator intent on human aggression. *Journal of Studies on Alcohol, 41*, 265–276.

*Zeichner, A., Pihl, R. O., Niaura, R., & Zacchia, C. (1982). Attention processes in alcohol-mediated aggression. *Journal of Studies on Alcohol, 43*, 714–724.

APPENDIX A:
OVERLAP OF STUDIES WITH OTHER META-ANALYSES

The following studies from the present dataset were also included in the following prior meta-analyses on the relation of alcohol and social behavior:

Bushman & Cooper (1990) Meta-Analysis

Bailey et al. (1983)
Gustafson (1985b)
Gustafson (1985c)
Gustafson (1986a)
Gustafson (1986b)
Gustafson (1987)
Gustafson (1988)
Gustafson (1990)
Gustafson (1991c)
Jeavons & Taylor (1985)
Pihl et al. (1984)
Pihl & Zacchia (1986)
Pihl et al. (1981)
Schmutte et al. (1979)
Schmutte & Taylor (1980)
Shuntich & Taylor (1972)
Taylor & Gammon (1976)
Taylor et al. (1976)
Taylor et al. (1977)
Taylor et al. (1979)
Taylor & Sears (1988)
Zeichner et al. (1982)

Hull & Bond (1986) Meta-Analysis

Lang et al. (1975)
Pihl et al. (1981)
Rohsenow & Bachorowski (1984)

Steele & Southwick (1985) Meta-Analysis

Bennett et al. (1969)
Boyatzis (1974)
Lang et al. (1975)
Pihl et al. (1981)
Schmutte & Taylor (1980)
Shuntich & Taylor (1972)
Taylor & Gammon (1976)
Taylor et al. (1976)
Taylor et al. (1977)
Taylor et al. (1979)
Zeichner & Pihl (1979)
Zeichner & Pihl (1980)
Zeichner et al. (1982)

Bushman & Cooper's (1990) Descriptive Summary

(but not in their main meta-analysis)
Boyatzis (1974)
Gustafson (1984)
Lang et al. (1975)
Leonard (1984)
Rohsenow & Bachorowski (1984)

APPENDIX B:
ATTENTION AND CUE SALIENCE VARIABLES EXTRACTED FROM EACH STUDY

These are the definitions judges used to rate the levels of anxiety, inhibition conflict, provocation, frustration, and self-focused attention of each study. All variables were rated on 9-point scales; examples are provided of studies which, according to the ratings obtained from the judges, represented the endpoints of each scale.

Anxiety

This criteria is the extent to which the overall experimental circumstances effected the participants by increasing their anxiety, making them excited, worried, highly alert, or attentive. Such a state is usually aroused by the perception of threat to self (either physical or psychological) or worry over potential or actual negative consequences for the self. Endpoints are

> 2 = participating in a reaction time–competition study in which the fear of receiving shocks has been removed (e.g., Ganter & Taylor, 1992)

9 = participating in a reaction time–competition study (e.g., Taylor et al., 1977) where there is concern about beating an opponent on a reaction time task and receiving shocks for losing.

Inhibition Conflict

This criteria is the degree to which the participant's response is simultaneously pressured by instigating and inhibiting cues (Steele & Southwick, 1985). High-inhibition conflict is assigned when conflicting pressures are strong and relatively equal. If inhibiting cues involve the possibility for negative consequences, these consequences should be directly linked to the participant's behavior. Endpoints are

1 = ability to negatively evaluate another person without fear of retaliation (e.g., Rohsenow & Bachorowski, 1984)

9 = participating in a reaction time–competition paradigm (e.g., Taylor et al., 1977) where there are cues instigating the delivery of high-intensity shocks to an opponent, while fear of receiving high-shock levels from that opponent simultaneously inhibits aggression.

Provocation

This criteria is the extent to which negative affect would arise as a direct result of being attacked or provoked by another person. It depends on the extent to which the participant perceives malicious or aggressive intent (i.e., how the participant perceives the situation, irrespective of the actual intentions of the actor). Endpoints are

1 = Trial 1 in a reaction time–competition study before any high-intensity provoking shocks have been received from an opponent (e.g., Jeavons & Taylor, 1985)

9 = learning that an opponent planned to deliver a shock that was twice as high as one's pain threshold in a reaction time–competition study (e.g., Taylor et al., 1979).

Frustration

This criteria is the extent to which an ongoing, goal-directed behavior is blocked or thwarted. The source of frustration could be another person or an event. Endpoints are

1 = participating in a reaction time–pain perception study in which the participant's task is to respond as quickly as possible to a tone and in so doing, deliver a shock to one's partner (e.g., Pihl et al., 1984)

9 = the crucial trials where the teacher–supervisor in a teacher–learner study sees that he or she will not win an amount ($80) because

the learner–partner has made too many mistakes on a simple task (e.g., Gustafson, 1986a).

Self-Focused Attention

This is the degree to which the participant's attention is focused on self because of circumstances in the experimental setting that cause the participant to be the object of his or her attention and the degree to which experimental situation induces self-evaluation for internal concerns or standards (but not self-presentational concerns). Endpoints are

1–2 = participating in a teacher–learner study (e.g., Gustafson, 1986a) where attention is directed toward supervising another person
9 = performing a task in front of a mirror and video camera (Bailey et al., 1983).

VIII

FAMILY DYNAMICS
AND FAMILY IMPACT

19

COGNITIVE FUNCTION, CARDIOVASCULAR REACTIVITY, AND BEHAVIOR IN BOYS AT HIGH RISK FOR ALCOHOLISM

PHILIP W. HARDEN AND ROBERT O. PIHL

Behavioral genetic methods have been used to identify individuals with a predisposition to develop alcoholism (Goodwin, 1984) and have spurred attempts to identify characteristics, either biological or environmental, that distinguish them from the general population. Empirically derived markers observed prior to the onset of alcoholism may reflect underlying etiologic mechanisms. However, it is widely accepted that the causes of alcoholism are multidetermined and that alcoholics and their vulnerable family members form a heterogeneous population (Pihl, Peterson, & Finn, 1990; Sher, 1991). The specific effect of any single marker will probably not be as important to etiology as the total number of operative risk factors (Tarter, 1988). Research into vulnerability for alcohol-

Reprinted from the *Journal of Abnormal Psychology, 104*, 94–103. (1995). Copyright © 1995 by the American Psychological Association. Used with permission of the author.

This research was supported in part by the Medical Research Council of Canada. We thank Allison Coogan, Helen Fiona Drake, Peter Giancola, and Rachel Young for their research assistance and Rhonda Amsel for her statistical advice.

ism should benefit, then, from diverse approaches to identifying the most probable set of risks.

We examined two sets of characteristics associated with paternal alcoholism that may contribute to both the onset and advancement of alcoholism (Peterson, Finn, & Pihl, 1992; Pihl & Peterson, 1992). The first of these concerns the stress-dampening response to alcohol. Autonomic nervous system reactivity, particularly cardiovascular response to aversive and nonaversive stimuli, has distinguished the at-risk group from normal controls and offspring from families where alcoholism is limited to a single member (Finn & Pihl, 1987, 1988). This autonomic hyperreactivity is moderated by alcohol. Daughters of male multigenerational alcoholics have also exhibited electrodermal reactivity to novelty that was normalized by a moderate dose of alcohol (Stewart, Finn, Peterson, & Pihl, 1994). Drinking may serve the function of normalizing states of hyperarousal in these individuals, and their informal attempts to self-medicate could develop into alcohol dependence over time.

If hyperreactivity is associated with etiology, then it should predate experimentation with alcohol and correlate with behaviors or traits related to alcohol use, such as conduct disorder, extroversion, or anxiety. In previous studies with adults, cardiovascular response was induced by the threat of electric shock. Research with children presented an opportunity to evaluate autonomic nervous system response to less aversive stimuli. If alternative induction procedures are successful, the generality of the hyperreactivity phenomenon would be enhanced. During mental stress, heart rate reactivity occurs independently of somatic activity and metabolic demand. Cardiac response to laboratory stressors is also fairly representative of heart rate response to a number of naturalistic, "real-world" challenges, especially in cardiovascularly hyperreactive individuals (Turner, 1989). Enhanced cardiovascular arousal during a competitive mental arithmetic task was therefore expected to characterize the high-risk group.

The second characteristic is a profile of cognitive dysfunction drawn from neuropsychological tests designed to test the functional integrity of the frontal lobes (Peterson et al., 1992). Several research groups attempted to delineate patterns of cognitive functioning that represent the at-risk population and obtained mixed results. This had led some to discount cognitive impairment as an etiological factor in alcoholism (Alterman & Hall, 1989). However, variable methodologies may have contributed to this confusion. Studies have not always screened for potential confounds of cognitive ability such as craniocerebral injury, birth trauma, febrile seizures, and fetal alcohol syndrome (West & Prinz, 1987). The definition of high risk has sometimes permitted the inclusion of participants with limited genetic predisposition. Results have also differed according to the battery of tests administered. Comprehensive neuropsychological test batteries were typically designed to localize lesions and cranial trauma, not selective cognitive impairments in neurologically intact but behaviorally disordered individuals. This approach to test selection has been criticized for its failure to account for numerous biological and environmental variables (e.g., race, gender, development, personality traits, immunocompetence, medical disorders, toxin exposure) that affect brain function and test performance (Hartman, 1992). Neuro-psychological testing in high-risk individuals is relevant if the assessment of functional competence defines the objective.

The neuropsychological hypothesis we pursued asserted that high-risk status would be associated with deficits of the executive functions associated with the frontal lobe. Dysfunctions of the anterior cortex are not usually detected by regular intelligence testing. The influence of the frontal lobes is exerted at the highest levels of hierarchical cognitive integration, response sequencing, strategic planning, and internal representation (Perecman, 1987). Extensive input from posterior and basal systems are received through lateralized and hierarchical neural networks. Subsystems of the frontal granular cortex mediate emotion, language, memory, motor, and attentional systems. Its putative operations include the temporal organization (i.e., the sequencing of behavior to attain a goal), problem-solving, selective attention, conditional learning, anticipation, the inhibition of competing alternatives, and verbal fluency (Fuster, 1989). This panoply of skills is often referred to as an executive function in order to convey a sense of mediation and interconnection with other cerebral structures (Shallice, 1988).

It is still unclear how cognitive deficits would influence the development of psychopathology. Peterson and Pihl (1990) have written about the importance of a neural comparator subsystem. Under conditions of novelty this circuit is thought to provide motivational tone and memory input during the evaluation of response alternatives. To alleviate uncertainty in potentially threatening circumstances, alternative outcomes are estimated and optimal problem solving strategies are evolved. Poor strategic thinking may lead to inaccurate judgments of circumstances, restricted evaluations of personal and social consequences, or a failure to inhibit inappropriate behavioral responses. Dysfunctional decision making in complex interpersonal transactions could elevate general stress and have a negative impact on social success. An assessment of executive functions in young high-risk people may provide insight into their ability to adapt to behavioral challenges.

We also investigated the relationship between autonomic and cognitive function, and the domain of behavioral or personality traits. The etiology of alcoholism has been frequently linked with personality structure. Most of the present evidence implicates either a constellation of disinhibited, impulsive, and antisocial behavior, or neuroticism, anxiety, and emotional lability (Sher & Trull, 1994). Because these characteristics are fairly stable, indications should be discernible in a prealcoholic sample. We collected parental ratings of antisocial behavior, anxiety, hyperactivity, and learning problems. Higher levels of behavioral disturbance, particularly conduct problems, were expected among sons of male multigenerational alcoholics (SOMMAs). Participants were also asked to self-report with the Junior Eysenck Personality Inventory. Either neuroticism or a combination of extroversion or psychoticism may differentiate the groups (H. J. Eysenck & Gudjonsson, 1989). Because most behavioral psychopathologies are comorbid with each other (Carey & DiLalla, 1994), no particular hypothesis concerning the specific type of personality structure common to this preadolescent to early adolescent SOMMA group was considered.

METHOD

Participants

Twenty-eight boys with a mean age of 12.1 years (range = 8–15 years) took part in the study; half were SOMMAs. Multigenerational alcoholism was defined as alcoholism in the father, paternal grandfather, and one other paternal male relative. According to a recent population study, positive family histories of this degree increase the odds of alcohol dependence by 167% (D. A. Dawson, Harford, & Grant, 1992). Children from families that reported no alcoholism in the parents, grandfather, or paternally related male relatives acted as controls. They were also similar on age (within 9 months of each other) and Full Scale IQ (within 10 points). Socioeconomic status variables (family income, occupations, and highest attained level of education) were also recorded.

High-risk boys were recruited through the Douglas Hospital McGill University Alcohol Research Centre. Alcoholism was defined by alcohol dependence criteria from the third edition of the *Diagnostic and Statistical Manual of Mental Disorders* (DSM–III; American Psychiatric Association, 1980) and was based on interviews with family members. For unavailable family members, the Family History Research Diagnostic Criteria (Endicott, Andreasen, & Spitzer, 1975) were used. The fathers of the boys in the index group were abstinent at the time of the study. Control group members were recruited with the permission of the Montreal Catholic School Commission, and through an advertisement in a community newspaper and posters at local YMCAs. Parents and participants were fully informed about the nature of the research and experimental procedures. Consent forms were signed prior to participation. Experimental procedures were approved by a McGill University ethics committee on human research.

To eliminate any possible relationship between cognitive performance and prior exposure to ethanol, boys with social drinking practices were excluded. An age cutoff of 15 years was set to ensure that social experimentation with alcohol would be minimal. Epidemiological surveys have indicated that 50% of boys age 15 and older engage in one or more monthly drinking episodes during which they consume 2–4 alcoholic beverages (Barnes & Welte, 1986). Self-report information about alcohol and drug use was gathered with a confidential questionnaire designed for the study. Maximum consumption reported by participants was two alcoholic beverages (usually wine), not more than twice a year. No marijuana or other drug use was reported.

Maternal alcohol consumption during pregnancy was retrospectively estimated by mothers on the health screening questionnaire. Recruitment criteria had excluded mothers with a history of alcohol abuse; thus, reported consumption levels were low. Mothers of high-risk boys reported an average consumption of 1.2 drinks per week. Mothers of low-risk boys estimated an average weekly consumption of 0.8 alcoholic beverages. Although there is no agreed upon "safe dose" of ethanol during fetal gestation (Niccols, 1994), prenatal exposure at these dose levels has not been related to fetal alcohol syndrome. Nevertheless, the relationship between maternal weekly alcohol consumption and cognitive performance was examined. No positive correlation existed in this data set between average weekly consumption and cognitive deficits.

A health history questionnaire screened for craniocerebral trauma, epilepsy, seizures, and psychiatric illness in the child. No prenatal or perinatal birth complications were reported. One mother and her family in the high-risk group were receiving family counseling subsequent to a divorce. No other referrals to mental health professionals had occurred.

Parents were asked if their son had ever been in trouble with the police or youth authorities. No study participant had ever been under the supervision of family services or been charged in court because of delinquent behavior. Single mothers headed three families in the SOMMA group and two among the controls. The three parental separations in the high-risk group had occurred within the past 5 years, one within the last 6 months. All high-risk boys had spent the majority of their development with both parents. There were no obvious deviations between the groups in parental socioeconomic status. All heads of families were employed, and their spouses were also usually employed outside the home. The average level of education among parents ranged from 12th grade to 2 years of college. Parental socioeconomic status data were applied to a Canadian socioeconomic index (Blishen, Carroll, & Moore, 1987). The mean score for heads of family was 52.8 for controls and 51.6 for the high-risk group. These levels represent medium socioeconomic backgrounds (Blakely & Harvey, 1988).

Cognitive Test Battery

Tests were assessed for their suitability with children aged 8 to 15 years. Of the many neuropsychological tests which purportedly ascertain the executive functions of the frontal lobes, four were selected whose validity has been established on patients with known neurological lesions of the frontal lobes. A memory test and a test of attention–impulsivity were also included.

Wechsler Intelligence Scale for Children—Revised (WISC–R; Wechsler, 1974)

The WISC–R measures the general level of intellectual function. All 12 subscales were administered.

Wisconsin Card Sorting Test (WCST; Heaton, 1981)

This is perhaps the most widely known test of frontal lobe function. Card sorting performance in children approaches adult standards by age 10 to 12 (Chelune & Baer, 1986). Although performance on the WCST is correlated with age, its sensitivity is not restricted by age (Chelune & Thompson, 1987). Of the several dependent measures that have been extrapolated from the Wisconsin, only perseverative responses and perseverative errors are specifically sensitive to frontal dysfunction.

Spatial Conditional Associate–Learning (SCAL; Milner, 1982)

This test has proved sensitive to dysfunctions of the frontal-hippocampal axis in neurological patients with bilateral frontal damage and extensive right hippocampal involvement. The right hippocampus is involved with spatial learning. Dysfunctional conditional learning is not related to discriminating between stimuli or in responding, but in the selection of the appropriate response to a stimulus (Petrides, 1987). The person taking the test must learn an arbitrary association between six white cards and six white lights randomly arranged on a table. Completion criteria for this administration were set at 15 consecutive correct matches or 60 trials. Incorrect matches were recorded as errors and served as the dependent variable.

Self-ordered Pointing (SOP), Concrete and Abstract versions (Petrides & Milner, 1982)

The SOP measures aspects of frontal control on working memory. One component of executive function is the monitoring of ongoing goal-oriented activity through the maintenance of active effort, temporal discrimination, and the comparison of results with original intentions. Executive dysfunctions result in a disorganization of mnemonic processes, rather than an amnesia of the kind associated with temporal lobe damage (Petrides, 1991). The task requires a flexible conceptual organization, response planning, and response inhibition. Two versions of the SOP were administered: (a) *Concrete*: representational drawings of familiar concrete objects (e.g., table, broom, stove); and (b) *Abstract*: drawings of abstract line figures that are more difficult to encode verbally. The spatial properties of the Abstract version have been found to impose a greater demand on right frontal processing. The inhibition of verbal encoding in the Abstract version results in a higher level of difficulty. The total number of errors committed was the dependent variable for each version.

Word Fluency (I. L. Thurstone & Thurstone, 1949)

A written version of Thurstone's verbal fluency task was administered. Each boy was asked to record in 5 min as many words as possible (excluding proper nouns) that began with the letter S. The test measures the ability to generate words, independently of vocabulary skills, within a phonemically controlled category. It has been argued that successful performance is an aspect of conscious attention and the ability to sustain behavior (Ramier & Hécaen, 1970). The coordination of the memory search is a function of frontal control. Positron-emission tomography scans during verbal fluency tests have indicated a bilateral activation of dorsolateral frontal, anterior cingulate, and parahippocampal cortex, with greater left hemispheric involvement. Word generation leads to a spreading activation in the temporal cortex. This activation must be inhibited for successful selection of words from within the assigned letter category (Frith, Friston, Liddle, & Frackowiak, 1991). The left dorsolateral frontal cortex exerts an inhibitory influence over word retrieval processing.

Wechsler Paired Associates, Recall (Wechsler, 1945)

This is a test of verbal memory from the Wechsler Memory Scale. Ten sets of paired words are read to the individual in three trials. One of the words subsequently serves as a cue for the recall of the matching component. Six of the paired words are easily associated; 4 are not. Number of errors on the three trials was the dependent variable.

Matching Familiar Figures Test (MFFT), 20-item revision (Cairns & Cammock, 1978)

This matching-to-sample task was originally regarded as a measure of conceptual tempo within the dimension of reflection–impulsivity. Latency to the first response and number of errors prior to a correct match were recorded as separate dependent measures. The MFFT has been widely used as a measure of both impulsivity and attention. However, the construct validity of conceptual tempo has not been supported by longitudinal research (Block, Gjerde, & Block, 1986). The dependent variable of response latency has consistently failed as a predictor of personality correlates. Response accuracy does relate, however, to important behavioral dimensions, although not impulsivity per se. The error-prone child has been described as rigid, unaccommodating, vulnerable, and susceptible to anxiety. Conversely, the accurate child is adaptable, sociable, emotionally secure, and skilled in applying information processing strategies.

Behavior and Personality Questionnaires

Conners Parent Rating Scale, 48-item version
(Goyette, Conners, & Ulrich, 1978)

Parents are posed 48 questions regarding their child's current behavior. Factor analysis supports 5 primary dimensions in this behavior rating scale: Conduct Problems, Anxiety, Learning Problems, Impulsive–Hyperactive, and Psychosomatic Problems. A Hyperactivity Index is also derived. Individual case ratings were converted to T-scores in order to portray their clinical significance.

Junior Eysenck Personality Questionnaire
(JEPQ; H. J. Eysenck & Eysenck, 1975)

The JEPQ is a self-report instrument adapted from the adult version for use with children age 7 to 16. It measures three primary personality traits: neuroticism (N), extroversion (E), and psychoticism (P) and also includes a measure of dissimulation (L; a "lie" scale). The relationship between scale elevations and adult or juvenile antisocial behavior has been extensively studied in many cross-cultural samples.

Psychophysiological Apparatus

Autonomic recordings were obtained with an 8 channel Grass model 7D polygraph. Signal frequency filters for the various channels were set in accordance with the Grass polygraph manuals to ensure adequate wave forms. Heart rate was recorded with a 7P4 electrocardiograph (EKG) tachograph preamplifier that is triggered by the EKG R wave. Changes in rates are based on the elapsed time of the beat-to-beat interval. Medi-Trace pellet electrodes were placed bilaterally on the chest. Peripheral cardiovascular vasoconstriction was measured in terms of digital blood volume amplitude (DBVA) and was read from a second 7P4 EKG tachograph. The output was set to display the pulse wave form from the 7P4 amplifier circuit.

The input signal was drawn from a Grass PTTI-6 photoelectric transducer attached to the nail of the third finger of the nondominant hand. A black cloth was draped over the hand to block artifacts from ambient light sources. A 7P3 preamplifier was used to record tension in the frontalis muscle from two Medi-Trace pellet electrodes arranged vertically over the brow of the left eye. The muscle tension signals were integrated using full-wave rectification and a time constant of .2 s. The bandwidth was .3 to 75 Hz. Skin conductance was measured with a 7P1 preamplifier set to psychogalvanic response. Skin resistance levels were transformed to skin conductance units (micromhos) by deriving the reciprocal of the original skin resistance values. Bilateral electrodermal activity was recorded with Beckman Biopotential Ag/AgCl electrodes (1 cm diameter), attached to the medial phalanges of the second and third fingers. Following the guidelines of Fowles, Fisher, and Tranel (1982), an electrolyte medium was prepared from an inert cream base mixed with a 0.19 saline solution to produce a 0.05 molar sodium chloride concentration. Chart speed was set at a rate of 5 mm/s. The mental arithmetic stimuli were presented binaurally through a Panasonic SR–52 audiocassette recorder and Realistic Nova 10 stereo headphones.

Experimental Procedures

Trained research assistants who were blind to the participant's risk status carried out the experimental procedures. All testing took place at McGill University. The length and number of sessions were dictated by school schedules and parental availability. Index participants were always accompanied to the University by a parent who would complete the questionnaires and the screening interview. Whenever possible testing was split over two sessions with the cognitive assessment occurring on the first visit and the stress test on the second visit when the surroundings were more familiar. The order in which the cognitive tests were administered was varied. Psychophysiological testing took place in a naturalistic, dimly lit room at McGill University. The boys were seated in a comfortable Lazyboy chair with the polygraph equipment located in an adjacent room. To demystify the experimental situation, the boys were permitted to view the equipment and to handle sample electrodes prior to their placement. The psychophysiological procedures were explained in age-appropriate language. The boys were encouraged to ask questions or express concerns. The mental arithmetic protocol was explained and practiced to ensure adherence to task protocols. An expectation of success was established by allowing the boys to win $2 during the practice session. This sum was carried over into the formal session. There was a 10-min adaptation period prior to testing to allow arousal associated with electrode placement to dissipate.

The mental arithmetic paradigm was an adaptation of a task described by Carroll, Turner, and Hellawell (1986). Eight audiotaped arithmetic problems were presented to the boys over headphones. Problems were selected from lists used in the Carroll et al. experiments, which had been rated as moderately difficult. Each arithmetic question was coupled with a suggested solution. The boys were required to respond immediately to the suggested solution by answering "right" or "wrong." They were told that a correct answer would win them $1 but that $1 would be lost for an incorrect response. Once each boy responded to the arithmetic question the experimental assistant provided him with feedback. The arithmetic problems that were presented would be hard for the older boys to solve quickly without pen and paper.

The performance feedback provided to the boys was fixed according to two prepared and counterbalanced orders. The number of wins and losses were thus held equal for all. Novelty, task difficulty, and pacing permitted the manipulation of feedback. In postexperimental debriefings no one questioned its accuracy.

In an effort to mitigate any sense of failure or loss of self-esteem resulting from the mental arithmetic paradigm, testing continued for a short period after the official 8 trials, and the boys were permitted to win $5. They earned a total of $25 for their participation.

RESULTS

An analysis of covariance (ANCOVA) procedure was adopted to analyze the cognitive battery. Tests were conducted to examine the principal statistical assumptions of normality, homogeneity of variance, and regression. Transformation of values for the SCAL and MFFT to their square root equivalents aided in the approximation of normal distributions. The psychophysiological data were examined with a multivariate ANCOVA for repeated measures, with baseline values as the covariates.

We selected participants whose age and IQ matched, because of the effect of developmental level on neuropsychological test performance. This issue is particularly important in the assessment of frontal lobe function. The frontal lobes reach adult-level maturation in terms of neuroanatomical structure (synaptic connectivity) and metabolic patterns of glucose uptake during early adolescence (Phelps, Barrio, Hoffmann, Huang, & Chugani, 1991). The timing of physiological maturation corresponds with the evidence of child neuropsychologists working from frontal lobe tests (Becker, Isaac, & Hynd, 1987; Chelune & Thompson, 1987; Welsh & Pennington, 1988; Welsh, Pennington, & Groisser, 1991). Although selection criteria ensured group similarities of age, WISC–R verbal IQ, and maternal alcohol consumption during pregnancy, these variables served as covariates in the analysis of cognitive tests.

Age and Grade Levels

Neither age or grade level differed between groups. The mean age of boys from families with male-limited alcoholism was 12.1 years (SD = 2.21), with a range between 8.8 and 15.1 years. Controls were age 12.2 (SD = 2.00), with a range between 9.6 to 15.4 years. SOMMAs had achieved a mean overall grade level of 6.1 (SD = 2.17), compared with a grade placement of 6.5 (SD = 1.91) for low-risk boys. Five of 14 high-risk boys (i.e., 36%) had failed to attain their proper grade placement. Only 1 of 14 controls (i.e., 7%) had experienced academic failure. According to Fisher's exact test there was a trend (p = .082) associated with SOMMA status and academic failure. Although the difference did not reach a .05 level of confidence, the trend has appeared early in their schooling.

Cognitive Test Battery

WISC–R

No group differences on the WISC–R were found. IQ scales were in the high average range, and there was no clinically significant scatter among the subtests. SOMMAs attained a mean Full Scale IQ score of 118 (SD = 14.5), a mean Verbal IQ of 114 (SD = 12.9), and a mean Performance IQ of 119 (SD = 14.4). Controls achieved a group mean Full Scale IQ of 115 (SD = 12.7), a Verbal IQ of 112 (SD = 13.4), and a Performance IQ of 115 (SD = 10.9).

Cognitive Tests

Seven dependent variables can be derived from the four putative tests of frontal lobe function. These seven have reliably distinguished between frontal lobe patients, patients with damage to nonfrontal cortical structures, and normal controls. They are perseverative responses and perseverative errors from the Wisconsin Card Sort; the number of words generated during written Word Fluency; the number of errors and the number of trials with an error prior to criterion in SCAL; and the number of errors committed on the Concrete and Abstract versions of the SOP. Given the ratio between sample size and outcome measures, a partial correlation analysis controlling for group status was conducted to reduce the number of dependent variables. The two Wisconsin Card Sort variables, perseverative errors and perseverative responses, were strongly correlated (.982), because the former is a subset of the latter. The perseverative response score was retained. SCAL errors and error-trials were highly correlated (.709). The error score

TABLE 1
Partial Correlations Among Frontal Tests Controlling for Group

Test	1	2	3	4	5
1. WCST: PR	1.00				
2. Word Fluency	−0.44*	1.00			
3. SCAL	0.46**	−0.33*	1.00		
4. SOP: C	0.32*	0.24	0.26	1.00	
5. SOP: A	0.53**	−0.21	0.33*	−0.27	1.00

Note. WCST: PR = Wisconsin Card Sorting Test: Perseverative Responses; SCAL = Spatial Conditional Associative–Learning; SOP: C = Self-ordered Pointing: Concrete; SOP: A = Self-ordered Pointing: Abstract.
*$p < .05$. **$p < .01$.

from the SCAL, rather than the number of error-trials, was retained because of its more normal distribution. The different versions of the SOP were designed with the intention of differentiating between spatial and verbal mediated processing. Although the test protocols for the versions are identical, they were considered as separate tests. Their relative independence was noted in the partial correlation matrix. The partial correlation coefficients of the five selected frontal variables are listed in Table 1. Because the scoring for Word Fluency reflected success at word production, the correlations between it and the other error-based measures were negative.

Two outcome measures can be extracted from the MFFT: latency and an error score. Because the conceptual validity of the latency variable is uncertain, only the error score was processed. The number of errors over the three trials of the Paired Associates test comprised the dependent variable for the seventh ANCOVA. To control for Type I error the alpha level was adjusted using a Bonferroni correction and set at $p < .008$.

In examining the relationship between the covariates, age and verbal IQ, and the dependent measures, a significant negative correlation between age and SCAL errors was noted. Older boys in both groups were more accurate learners than their younger counterparts. There was also a joint effect of age and IQ on Word Fluency. More words were produced as age and verbal IQ increased. There was a significant negative relationship between age and errors on the paired associates. Finally, there was a trend for SOP–Abstract performance to improve as verbal IQ rose. These effects underscore the need to mitigate confounds through comparative group composition and statistical adjustment.

Results from the analysis of the cognitive test battery supported the hypothesis that high-risk boys would perform more poorly on tests of frontal lobe function. Groups differed at $p < .008$ on four of the five frontal variables, SCAL, SOP–Concrete, WCST perseverative re-

TABLE 2
Covariate Adjusted Means and Standard Deviations
of Cognitive Measures

Variable	SOMMAs		Controls	
	M	SD	M	SD
SCAL[a]	6.3*	1.3	4.0	1.1
SOP: Concrete	5.6*	1.4	3.5	1.4
WCST	34.6*	14.3	17.9	9.7
Word Fluency	20.8*	6.8	31.4	10.9
Paired Associates	7.8	6.2	2.5	1.5
MFFT[a]	3.3	0.9	2.5	0.7
SOP: Abstract	6.6	2.5	5.2	3.1

Note. SOMMAs = sons of male multigenerational alcoholics; SCAL = Spatial Conditional Associative–Learning; SOP = Self-ordered Pointing; WCST = Wisconsin Card Sorting Test; MFFT = Matching Familiar Figures Test.
[a]Values are square-root transformed.
*SOMMA and control means differ significantly at the Bonferroni-corrected alpha level of $p <$ .008.

sponses,[1] and Word Fluency. SOMMAs also performed more poorly than control group boys on the Paired Associates memory test and the MFFT, although these differences did not exceed the Bonferroni-corrected alpha level. However, the proportion of the total variance accounted for by group membership in the Paired Associates ANCOVA was η^2 = .208, and for the MFFT it was η^2 = .159. Both these values would be regarded as large effects sizes in Cohen's (1977) terminology. There were no differences on the SOP–Abstract test. Error rates for the SOP–Abstract were higher than those on the SOP–Concrete for both groups. The difficulty of the SOP–Abstract is greater (M. Petrides, personal communication, February 8, 1994), and a floor effect may have resulted. Covariate adjusted means are reported in Table 2.

---

[1]The clinical relevance of WCST performance deficits in children is difficult to evaluate because testing norms and cutoffs do not exist. However, we may compare SOMMAs test scores to previously published data. Chelune and Thompson (1987) report means and standard deviations for perseverative responses and errors from two studies of age-matched samples of controls and children who had been referred for neurological evaluation. The first patient group (n = 15) had a mean age of 9.2 years and the second (n = 62) had a mean age of 13.4 years. There was a negative correlation between performance and age. Control boys in our study committed an average of 18.1 (SD = 10.1) perseverative responses, compared with a previously reported mean of 17.6 (SD = 14.4) for similarly aged participants. The younger of the patient samples had a mean age of 9.2 years and made 42.1 (SD = 29.8) perseverative responses, whereas the older group at 13.4 years made 25.2 (SD = 21.1) responses. SOMMAs, with a mean age of 12.1 years, made 34.4 (SD = 15.5) perseverative responses. Compared to the patient groups, the sons of alcoholics fit between the two patient groups, both in terms of age and performance. The patients in Chelune and Thompson's study were a heterogeneous group composed of suspected and confirmed cases of neurologic disorder. Of the 62 members in the older group, 53% were diagnosed as learning disabled, 31% with neurologic disease or trauma, and 16% with seizure disorder.

Psychophysiological Measures

Polygraph charts were scored manually, and a second rater randomly assessed portions to obtain reliability estimates. Correlation coefficients were significant ($p < .01$) for heart rate (.991), DBVA (.937), skin conductance (.988), and muscle tension (.912).

It took approximately 3.5 min to run the mental arithmetic paradigm. The eight arithmetic questions were presented through a prerecorded audio tape that regulated timing of the trials. The continuously recorded data were divided for scoring purposes into 3 subphases per trial to correspond with events that occurred during each trial. The first event was a brief 70 dB orienting tone that marked the onset of an 8-s subphase prior to the presentation of the question. The next subphase of approximately 8 s began with the arithmetic question and ended with the feedback supplied by the research assistant. The third trial subphase spanned 10 s to the onset of the next orienting tone. For heart rate, skin conductance, and muscle tension, output levels were sampled at 1-s intervals of the subphase, then averaged. Thus, for each of the three subphases per trial, over the 8 trials, 24 data points per channel were calculated. With DBVA, all pulse waves in a subphase were measured from peak to trough. These distances were then averaged to represent a DBVA data point. The units of analysis for the four psychophysiology channels were beats per minute (BPM) for heart rate, arbitrary units for DBVA, microvolt for muscle tension, and micromhos for skin conductance. Skin conductance units were transformed to their square root equivalents to improve homogeneity of variance (M. E. Dawson, Schell, & Filion, 1990). The DBVA values were transformed to log units. Baselines were derived by calculating the mean value of a 60-s span following the adaptation period.

The stress paradigm was represented by a $2 \times 2 \times 8 \times 3$ design (Group $\times$ Order of Feedback $\times$ Trial $\times$ Subphase) in a multivariate ANCOVA for repeated measures. Baseline values were entered as the covariate. Group and order were between-subjects factors, and trials and subphases were within-subjects factors. Baseline values are listed in Table 3.

Heart Rate

The hypothesis of greater cardiovascular reactivity was supported. A main effect for group status was found, $F(1, 23) - 5.26$, $p < .04$, which indicated that heart rate was more elevated for SOMMAs throughout the psychophysiological assessment. No other main effects or interactions reached statistical significance. The average baseline adjusted heart rate for SOMMAs during the stress test was 80.79 BPM ($SD = 2.25$); it was 76.62 BPM ($SD = 1.39$) for controls.

TABLE 3
Baselines for Psychophysiological Measures

Channel	SOMMAs		Controls	
	M	*SD*	*M*	*SD*
Heart rate BPM	73.88	8.97	74.01	10.16
DBVA (log units)	1.30	0.14	1.14	0.23
Skin conductance[a]	5.61	1.45	5.08	1.37
Muscle tension[b]	66.76	40.12	81.14	58.07

Note. SOMMAs = sons of male multigenerational alcoholics; BPM = beats per minute; DBVA = digital blood volume amplitude.
[a]in square-root micromhos. [b]in microvolts.

DBVA

Cardiovascular reactivity was also assessed by measuring peripheral vasoconstriction. Significantly reduced blood flow in the finger tip was noted in high-risk boys during the arithmetic task, $F(1, 23) = 7.30$, $p < .02$. There was no interaction with any other factor. The covariate adjusted mean was 1.083 ($SD = 0.059$) for SOMMAs and 1.220 ($SD = 0.039$) for controls. In terms of change from baseline, this represented a vasoconstriction in log units of -0.141 for sons of alcoholics versus a vasodilation of .011 for controls.

Skin Conductance

No effects were noted for mean skin conductance level.

Muscle Tension

There were no significant differences in tension measured from the frontalis muscles. Although it is possible that differences in other muscle groups might have influenced cardiovascular response, it was not evident in frontalis measurement.

Behavior and Personality Questionnaires

Conners Parent Rating Scale

Analyses of variance indicated that statistical significance was reached only on the Conduct Problems subscale, $F(1, 26) = 10.72$, $p < .004$, with SOMMAs identified as more problematic. There was also a nonsignificant trend for SOMMAs to exhibit more signs of anxiety, $F(1, 26) = 4.02$, $p < .06$. To appreciate the clinical significance of these findings age-normed T−scores were calculated. The SOMMA T−score mean for Conduct Problems was 77.7, more than 2 *SD*s above the general population mean.

Although scores for the high-risk group were higher on every Eysenck scale, there were no statistically valid differences. Scores from both groups were high in terms of P, E, and L and low on the N scale, although within published boundary limits. The mean for the P scale was 4.5 (SD = 2.4) for SOMMAs and 3.6 (SD = 1.8) for controls. The E scale mean was 18.4 (SD = 4.2) for SOMMAs and 17.8 (SD = 5.3) for controls. In terms of N, high-risk boys averaged 10.1 (SD = 3.4) and controls 8.9 (SD = 4.6). The L scale average for SOMMAs was 8.1 (SD = 3.7), whereas controls averaged 6.6 (SD = 2.9).

Relationship Between Reactivity, Cognition, and Behavior

Group dissimilarities were uncovered in the domains of autonomic reactivity, cognition, and behavior. The relationship between these three areas was addressed by calculating a partial correlation matrix that controlled for group status. The four variables that were entered were: (a) baseline-adjusted heart rate reactivity averaged over trials and subphases, (b) a composite of Z scores from all frontal tests to represent executive function, (c) the Conduct Problems score, and (d) the Anxiety score from the Conners scale. Had our sample been composed of social drinkers, we could have used alcohol consumption as a variable. Instead, we chose behaviors thought to contribute to the etiology of alcohol abuse.

After adjusting for the effect of group, two statistically significant relationships remained. The first was between heart rate reactivity and anxiety, which resulted in a Pearson product-moment correlation of .544, $p < .003$. A significant correlation of .358 existed between executive function and conduct problems, $p < .04$. The partial correlations along with the zero-ordered equivalents are listed in Table 4.

TABLE 4
Partial and Product-Moment Correlations Among Heart Rate,
Executive Function, and Behavior Scores

Variable	Heart rate		Executive function		Conduct problems	
	PC	PMC	PC	PMC	PC	PMC
Executive function	−.16	.30				
Conduct problems	−.18	.22	.36*	.71		
Anxiety	.54**	.62	.04	.31	.12	.33

Note. PC = partial correlation controlling for group; PMC = product-moment correlation.
*$p < .05$. **$p < .01$.

DISCUSSION

The results suggest a relationship between high-risk status in SOMMAs and their performance on frontal lobe tests, autonomic reactivity to stress, and patterns of disruptive behavior. After controlling for group differences, significant correlations remained between frontal ability and conduct problems, and between heart-rate reactivity and parent-rated anxiety levels. The attempted integration of neuropsychological, psychophysiological, and behavioral perspectives constitute strengths of the study, as does the assessment of a young at-risk population before their initiation to alcohol or drug use. The findings, particularly those from the cognitive battery, were reinforced by the controls imposed over potential confounds such as age disparities, fetal and infant illness, and involvement in delinquent lifestyles.

However, the generalizability of the study is restricted by the small sample size and limited data on the alcoholic fathers. None of the fathers of SOMMAs were actively alcoholic. The majority resided with their families and provided their children with a middle-class living standard. We were not able to characterize them further in terms of personality subtypes, whether primarily antisocial, anxious–depressive, or comorbid. Although vulnerability is strongly associated with the density of genetic loading in the family, information concerning the genetics of personality would help to clarify the associations between the factors and their probable contribution to outcome. This may be especially important in samples that are based solely on genetic loadings. The lifetime prevalence of diagnoses in one study of multigenerational alcoholics supported a model of depression spectrum disease (Finn, Kleinman, & Pihl, 1990), rather than antisocial personality disorder. Alcoholism is frequently comorbid with antisocial personality disorder, anxiety disorders, depressive disorders, and personality disorders. More information on the family would permit comparisons with known alcoholic groups. The lack of information on possible comorbidities reduces the ability to associate findings in the son with specific diagnoses in the father (Sher & Trull, 1994).

Cognitive Function

The results from cognitive testing were not commensurate with WISC–R evaluations of the intellectual potential (high-average Full Scale IQ) in our high-risk boys. Despite their high-average IQs, and although on average they had not yet completed primary school, there was a trend for greater SOMMA academic failure. Controls were matched for age and IQ and the remaining discrepancies were statistically removed; nevertheless, sons of alcoholics performed more poorly on most tests in the cognitive battery, but especially the frontal lobe measures. These results indicate measurable individual differences in information processing, within the context of a structurally intact neural system, for some members of the high-risk group. Significant differences in performance were found on two tests, the SOP and the SCAL, that are related to the function of two distinct regions of the dorsolateral frontal cortex. Positron emission research has distinguished between the abilities engaged by the SOP and those associated with the SCAL, tracing the former to the mid-dorsolateral area and the latter to the posterior aspect (Petrides, Alivisatos, Evans, & Meyer, 1993; Petrides, Alivisatos, Meyer, & Evans, 1993). These are principal connections between the dorsolateral cortex and other cortical sites such as the cingulate, posterior parietal, posterior premotor, visual, and linguistic areas. These distal areas provide sensory input, or, as may be the case with the cingulate gyrus, assist in the selection of competing response alternatives (J. V. Pardo, Pardo, Janer, & Raichle, 1990). The SOP is a task of temporal organization. It requires people to monitor their short-term working memory in order to select new target stimuli and to prevent the selection of previously chosen material. The monitoring of ongoing behavior, in the context of past and future performance and in accordance with external guidelines, comprises the executive aspect of frontal influence on memory function. The development and execution of planned, goal-oriented behavior is shaped in this way by frontal ability. Successful conditional-associate learning also requires the frontal mediation of memory. The SCAL tests the ability to retrieve the appropriate behavioral response when previously encountered environmental cues are presented. Performance in conditional learning bears on the ability of an individual to adapt behavior to meet external demands. SOMMAs took longer to learn the associations and made more errors doing so.

Perseverative responding was evident on the Wisconsin Card Sort Test. SOMMA performance was equivalent to previously reported preservation scores in a similarly aged, mixed sample of children with learning disabilities and neurologic conditions (Chelune & Thompson, 1987). Sons of alcoholics also experienced more difficulty on the written Word Fluency test. Research using positron-emission tomography indicates that both the frontal and temporal lobes are intimately involved in successful performance on this task. Deficits may relate either to cognitive strategies in organizing memory search and word retrieval, or an inability to maintain effort over the 5-min testing period (Randolph, Braun, Goldberg, & Chase, 1993). Discrepancies in the expected direction were noted on other cognitive measures, but these results did not exceed the probability that differences could be attributed to chance given the number of comparisons.

A significant association was found between executive cognitive function, defined as a composite of the frontal tests, and disruptive behavior. This is consistent with the literature implicating cognitive deficits in the course and development of conduct disorder and criminality. Moffitt (1993) reported that neuropsychological dysfunctions of verbal and executive functions were related to early onset conduct disorder and aggressiveness. They predicted antisocial behavior even after general intelligence, motivation, and environmental factors were accounted for. In our study SOMMAs were not involved in overt, identifiable delinquent behavior. The possibility remains that the boys engaged in antisocial acts without the awareness of parents or authorities. Anxiety traits tend to moderate aggression in preadolescent boys, and more covert means of expressing conduct disorder are typically followed (Hinshaw, Lahey, & Hart, 1993). Future studies of young SOMMAs would benefit by including self-reports of delinquent behavior. Moffitt also noted that cognitive deficits in conduct disordered children were typically mild. Although severely disturbed behaviorally, they would not be diagnosed as brain damaged on a neurological examination. Neuropsychological deficits that are apparent prior to adolescence have a disproportionate influence on developmental pathways to antisocial behavior (Hinshaw et al., 1993). How cognitive deficits affect the life course remains the subject of debate. Frontal dysfunction could exert a main effect, or transact with a disrupted family environment, leading to oppositional attitudes, school failure, negative emotional states, increased contact with antisocial peers, and hence a gateway to alcohol and drug use (Pihl & Peterson, 1992).

Psychophysiology

The mental arithmetic paradigm induced increased heart rate and peripheral vasoconstriction in SOMMAs relative to controls. This cardiovascular reactivity resulted from psychological challenge, rather than the threat of electric shock previously used with adults. The phenomenon of hyperreactivity in high-risk adult men is thereby extended to an earlier development period. The demonstration that some high-risk individuals must deal with physiological reactivity from a young age supports a model for the stress-dampening effects of alcohol.

The second correlation to emerge was that between heart-rate reactivity and anxiety. Cardiovascular hyperreactivity could be construed as a somatic component of anxiety. An association in young adolescents and adults between cardiovascular reactivity during mental stress and emotional coping has been reported in studies of familial hypertension (Vogele & Steptoe, 1993). In that research the interaction between a family history of hypertension and high trait anxiety, anger inhibition (hostility), and self-concealment identified individuals with exaggerated cardiovascular responses. This suggests a strong psychological component in the physiological response to environmental demands. Because cardiovascular reactivity may relate to suspected etiological mechanisms for alcoholism (the anxiety–depression and stress-dampening models), greater elaboration of the psychophysiological response is needed. Future work on SOMMAs would benefit by assessing their emotional state during stress and their customary coping skills. Given the correlation between heart-rate reactivity and anxiety, an unresolved question is whether study participants attached a positive or negative valence to their arousal. Associations between reactivity and variables such as body mass and parental blood pressure should also be evaluated.

Although this study has uncovered several potential risks, outcomes remain indeterminate because psychobiological factors operate in a dynamic psychosocial environment. The form and severity of psychopathologies can vary with the timing of developmental periods and the interplay of protective factors. Nevertheless, the risks are tangible and have the potential to inform our understanding of the etiology of alcoholism in this population. They may provide markers for diagnostic instruments and could serve as elements to be considered in structured treatment programs and preventive interventions designed to increase the competence of the vulnerable.

REFERENCES

Alterman, A. I., & Hall, J. G. (1989). Effects of social drinking and familial alcoholism risk on cognitive functioning: Null findings. *Alcoholism: Clinical and Experimental Research, 13*, 799–803.

American Psychiatric Association. (1980). *Diagnostic and statistical manual of mental disorders* (3rd ed.). Washington, DC: Author.

Barnes, G. M., & Welte, J. W. (1986). Patterns and predictors of alcohol use among 7–12th grade students in New York State. *Journal of Studies on Alcohol, 47*, 53–61.

Becker, M. G., Isaac, W., & Hynd, G. W. (1987). Neuropsychological development of nonverbal behaviors attributed to "frontal lobe" functioning. *Developmental Neuropsychology, 3*, 275–298.

Blakely, J. H., & Harvey, E. B. (1988). Market and non-market effects on male and female occupational status attainment. *Canadian Review of Sociology and Anthropology, 25*, 23–39.

Blishen, B. R., Carroll, W. K., & Moore, C. (1987). The 1981 socioeconomic index for occupations in Canada. *Canadian Review of Sociology and Anthropology, 24*, 465–488.

Block, J., Gjerde, P. F., & Block, J. H. (1986). More misgivings about the Matching Familiar Figures Test as a measure of reflection–impulsivity: Absence of construct validity in preadolescence. *Developmental Psychology, 22*, 820–831.

Cairns, E., & Cammock, T. (1978). Development of a more reliable version of the Matching Familiar Figures Test. *Developmental Psychology, 14*, 555–560.

Carey, G., & DiLalla, D. L. (1994). Personality and psychopathology: Genetic perspectives. *Journal of Abnormal Psychology, 103,* 32–43.

Carroll, D., Turner, J. R., & Hellawell, J. C. (1986). Heart rate and oxygen consumption during active psychological challenge: The effects of task difficulty. *Psychophysiology, 23,* 174–181.

Chelune, G. J., & Baer, R. A. (1986). Developmental norms for the Wisconsin Card Sorting Test. *Journal of Experimental and Clinical Neuropsychology, 8,* 219–228.

Chelune, G. J., & Thompson, L. L. (1987). Evaluation of the general sensitivity of the Wisconsin Card Sorting Test among younger and older children. *Developmental Neuropsychology, 3,* 81–89.

Cohen, J. (1977). *Statistical power analysis for the behavioral sciences* (rev. ed.). New York: Academic Press.

Dawson, D. A., Harford, T. C., & Grant, B. F. (1992). Family history as a predictor of alcohol dependence. *Alcoholism: Clinical and Experimental Research, 16,* 572–575.

Dawson, M. E., Schell, A. M., & Filion, D. L. (1990). The electrodermal system. In J. T. Cacioppo & L. G. Tassinary (Eds.), *Principles of psychophysiology: Physical, social, and inferential elements* (pp. 295–325). New York: Cambridge University Press.

Endicott, J., Andreasen, N., & Spitzer, R. L. (1975). *Family history research diagnostic criteria.* New York: New York Psychiatric Institute.

Eysenck, H. J., & Eysenck, S. B. G. (1975). *The Eysenck Personality Questionnaire (adult and junior) manual.* San Diego, CA: Educational and Industrial Testing Service.

Eysenck, H. J., & Gudjonsson, G. H. (1989). *The causes and cures of criminality.* New York: Plenum.

Finn, P. R., Kleinman, I., & Pihl, R. O. (1990). The lifetime prevalence of psychopathology in men with multigenerational family histories of alcoholism. *The Journal of Nervous and Mental Disease, 178,* 500–504.

Finn, P. R., & Pihl, R. O. (1987). Men at high risk for alcoholism: The effect of alcohol on cardiovascular response to unavoidable shock. *Journal of Abnormal Psychology, 96,* 230–236.

Finn, P. R., & Pihl, R. O. (1988). Risk for alcoholism: A comparison between two different groups of sons of alcoholics on cardiovascular reactivity and sensitivity to alcohol. *Alcoholism: Clinical and Experimental Research, 12,* 742–747.

Fowles, D. C., Fisher, A. E., & Tranel, D. T. (1982). The heart beats to reward: The effect of monetary incentive on heart rate. *Psychophysiology, 19,* 506–513.

Frith, C. D., Friston, K. J., Liddle, P. F., & Frackowiak, R. S. J. (1991). A PET study of word finding. *Neuropsychologia, 29,* 1137–1148.

Fuster, J. M. (1989). *The prefrontal cortex: Anatomy, physiology, and neuropsychology of the frontal lobe.* New York: Raven Press.

Goodwin, D. W. (1984). Studies of familial alcoholism: A review. *Journal of Clinical Psychiatry, 45,* 14–17.

Goyette, C. H., Conners, C. K., & Ulrich, R. F. (1978). Normative data for the revised Conners Parent and Teacher Rating Scale. *Journal of Abnormal Child Psychology, 6,* 221–236.

Hartman, D. E. (1992). Neuropsychological toxicology. In A. E. Puente & R. J. McCaffrey (Eds.), *Handbook of neuropsychological assessment: A biopsychosocial perspective* (pp. 485–507). New York: Plenum.

Heaton, R. K. (1981). *Wisconsin Card Sorting Test manual.* Odessa: Psychological Assessment Resources.

Hinshaw, S. P., Lahey, B. B., & Hart, E. L. (1993). Issues of taxonomy and co-morbidity in the development of conduct disorder. *Development and Psychopathology, 5,* 31–49.

Milner, B. (1982). Some cognitive effects of frontal-lobe lesions in man. *Philosophical Transactions of the Royal Society of London, Series B, 298,* 211–226.

Moffitt, T. E. (1993). The neuropsychology of conduct disorder. *Development and Psychopathology, 5,* 135–151.

Niccols, G. A. (1994). Fetal alcohol syndrome: Implications for psychologists. *Clinical Psychology Review, 14,* 91–111.

Pardo, J. V., Pardo, P. J., Janer, K. W., & Raichle, M. E. (1990). The anterior cingulate cortex mediates processing selection in the Stroop attentional conflict paradigm. *Proceedings of the National Academy of Sciences of the United States of America, 87,* 256–259.

Perecman, E. (1987). Consciousness and the meta-functions of the frontal lobes: Setting the stage. In E. Perecman (Ed.), *The frontal lobes revisited* (pp. 1–10). New York: IRBN Press.

Peterson, J. B., Finn, P. R., & Pihl, R. O. (1992). Cognitive dysfunction and the inherited predisposition to alcoholism. *Journal of Studies on Alcohol, 53,* 154–160.

Peterson, J. B., & Pihl, R. O. (1990). Information processing, neuropsychological function, and the inherited predisposition to alcoholism. *Neuropsychology Review, 1,* 343–369.

Petrides, M. (1987). Conditional learning and the primate frontal cortex. In E. Perecman (Ed.), *The frontal lobes revisited* (pp. 91–108). New York: IRBN Press.

Petrides, M. (1991). Frontal lobes and memory. In F. Boiler, J. Grafman, L. Squire, & G. Gainotti (Eds.), *Handbook of neuropsychology* (Vol. 3, pp. 75–90). Amsterdam: Elsevier Science Publishers.

Petrides, M., Alivisatos, B., Evans, A. C., & Meyer, E. (1993). Dissociation of human mid-dorsolateral from posterior dorsolateral frontal cortex in memory processing. *Proceedings of the National Academy of Sciences of the United States of America, 90,* 873–877.

Petrides, M., Alivisatos, B., Meyer, E., & Evans, A. C. (1993). Functional activation of the human frontal cortex during the performance of verbal working memory tasks. *Proceedings of the National Academy of Sciences of the United States of America, 90*, 878–882.

Petrides, M., & Milner, B. (1982). Deficits on subject-ordered tasks after frontal and temporal lobe lesions in man. *Neuropsychologia, 20*, 249–262.

Phelps, M. E., Barrio, J. R., Hoffmann, E. J., Huang, S. C., & Chugani, H. T. (1991). PET: A biochemical image of the brain at work. In N. A. Lassen, D. H. Ingvar, M. E. Raichle, & L. Friberg (Eds.), *Brain work and mental activity: Quantitative studies with radioactive tracers* (pp. 32–49). Copenhagen: Munksgaard.

Pihl, R. O. & Peterson, J. B. (1992). Etiology. In P. Nathan, N. Langenbucer, B. McCrady, & W. Frankenstein (Eds.), *Annual review of addictions research and treatment* (Vol. 2, pp. 153–175). Elmsford, NY: Pergammon Press.

Pihl, R. O., Peterson, J., & Finn, P. (1990). Inherited predisposition to alcoholism: Characteristics of sons of male alcoholics. *Journal of Abnormal Psychology, 99*, 291–301.

Ramier, A. M., & Hécaen, H. (1970). Role respectif des atteintes frontales et de la latéralisation lésionalle dans les déficits de la "fluence verbale" [The respective roles of frontal damage and the lateralization of lesions in verbal fluency deficits]. *Revue Neurologique, 123*, 17–22.

Randolph, C., Braun, A. R., Goldberg, T. E., & Chase, T. N. (1993). Semantic fluency in Alzheimer's, Parkinson's, and Huntington's disease: Dissociation of storage and retrieval failures. *Neuropsychology, 7*, 82–88.

Shallice, T. (1988). *From neuropsychology to mental structure.* New York: Cambridge University Press.

Sher, K. J. (1991). *Children of alcoholics: A critical appraisal of theory and research.* Chicago: University of Chicago Press.

Sher, K. J., & Trull, T. J. (1994). Personality and disinhibitory psychopathology: Alcoholism and antisocial personality disorder. *Journal of Abnormal Psychology, 103*, 92–102.

Stewart, S. H., Finn, P. R., Peterson, J. B., & Pihl, R. O. (1994). *The effects of alcohol on electrodermal orienting in daughters of familial alcoholic males.* Manuscript submitted for publication.

Tarter, R. E. (1988). The high-risk paradigm in alcohol and drug abuse research. In R. W. Pickens & D. S. Svikis (Eds.), *Biological vulnerability to drug abuse* (NIDA research monograph 89, pp. 73–86). Rockville, MD: U.S. Dept. of Health and Human Services.

Thurstone, I. L., & Thurstone, T. (1949). *Examiner manual for the SRA primary mental abilities.* Chicago: Scientific Resource Associates.

Turner, J. R. (1989). Individual differences in heart rate response during behavioral challenge. *Psychophysiology, 26*, 497–505.

Vogele, C., & Steptoe, A. (1993). Anger inhibition and family history as modulators of cardiovascular responses to mental stress in adolescent boys. *Journal of Psychosomatic Research, 37*, 503–514.

Wechsler, D. (1945). A standardized memory scale for clinical use. *Journal of Psychology, 19,* 87–95.

Wechsler, D. (1974). *Wechsler Intelligence Scale for Children-Revised.* New York: Psychological Corporation.

Welsh, M. C., & Bennington, B. F. (1988). Assessing frontal lobe functioning in children: Views from developmental psychology. *Developmental Neuropsychology, 4,* 199–230.

Welsh, M. C., Pennington, B. F., & Groisser, D. B. (1991). A normative-developmental study of executive function: A window on prefrontal function in children. *Developmental Neuropsychology, 7,* 131–149.

West, M. O., & Prinz, R. J. (1987). Parental alcoholism and childhood psychopathology. *Psychological Bulletin, 102,* 204–218.

20

THE RELATION OF PARENT ALCOHOLISM TO ADOLESCENT SUBSTANCE USE: A LONGITUDINAL FOLLOW-UP STUDY

LAURIE CHASSIN, PATRICK J. CURRAN, ANDREA M. HUSSONG, AND CRAIG R. COLDER

Parent alcoholism is a well-established risk factor for adult alcoholism, and recent data suggest that parent alcoholism also raises risk for alcohol and drug use during adolescence (Chassin, Rogosch, & Barrera, 1991; Hawkins, Catalano, & Miller, 1992). However, less is known about the mechanisms underlying this risk, particularly for adolescents. Theoretical speculations have included social environmental mechanisms, such as impaired parental monitoring and control and weak parent–adolescent bonds. More

Reprinted from the *Journal of Abnormal Psychology, 105*, 70–80. (1996). Copyright © 1996 by the American Psychological Association. Used with permission of the author.

This study was supported by National Institute on Drug Abuse Grant DA05227. We thank Kirsten Bech, Julie Kossak-Fuller, Polly Lewit, and Brooke Molina for coordinating the interviewing and data collection activities, and Jennifer Rose and Heather Montgomery for assistance in figure preparation. Many colleagues provided important advice on research design and on the latent growth curve modeling. We thank Kenneth J. Sher, Bengt Muthen, Phil Wood, David Francis, Jack McArdle, Mike Stoolmiller, Leona Aiken, Dave MacKinnon, Steve West, and Peter Bentler for their consultation on these issues.

biologically based theories have focused on potentially heritable personality traits related to substance use and on potentially heritable individual differences in alcohol effects (e.g., tendencies to derive greater positive reinforcement from alcohol). Recently, these diverse theories have been integrated into heuristic models postulating links between biologically based individual differences and social environmental mechanisms that interact to determine risk (see Sher, 1991, for a review).

Despite theoretical speculation, however, there have been few empirical studies to test these models with adolescent children of alcoholics (COAs; although some studies have examined mediators of parent substance use effects in the general population, e.g., Wills, Schrebman, Benson, & Vaccaro, 1994). There is also a lack of longitudinal model tests. Moreover, research on parent alcoholism has been limited by methodological problems, including an overreliance on treated samples and failures to consider co-occurring risk factors, such as other forms of parent psychopathology (Sher, 1991; West & Prinz, 1987). To address these problems, we conducted a longitudinal study of a community sample, considering parent alcoholism in the context of other risk factors for adolescent substance use (Chassin et al., 1991). Previously, we tested a cross-sectional model of parent alcoholism effects on adolescent substance use that focused on three domains of mediators: (a) parental monitoring of the adolescent's behavior and adolescents' affiliations with drug-using peers, (b) adolescents' stress and experience of negative affect, and (c) adolescents' temperamental emotionality and sociability (Chassin, Pillow, Curran, Molina, & Barrera, 1993). These domains were chosen because they are linked (either theoretically or empirically) with both parent alcoholism and adolescent substance use. The current study provides a longitudinal test of this model.

SOCIALIZATION PATHWAYS: PARENTING AND PEER AFFILIATION

Deficits in parental support and ineffective parental control practices have been frequently identified as risk factors for adolescent substance use (Hawkins et al., 1992). For the present study, the most relevant work is Patterson's social interactional theory of adolescent conduct problems (including substance use). Dishion, Patterson, and Reid (1988) found a cross-sectional relation between parent drug use and early adolescent drug use that was both direct (interpreted as the result of parental modeling and availability) and indirect (mediated through impaired parental control). Parent drug use was associated with decreased monitoring of the adolescent's activities, and this decreased monitoring was associated with membership in a drug-using peer group that was the proximal pathway into adolescent drug sampling. Our cross-sectional data (Chassin et al., 1993) supported a similar mechanism. The current study tested whether such impaired monitoring predicted growth over time in adolescent substance use and whether impaired monitoring mediated parent alcoholism effects on such growth.

STRESS AND NEGATIVE AFFECT REGULATION PATHWAYS

An alternative (but not mutually exclusive) pathway suggests that parent alcoholism is associated with environmental stress that produces negative affect. Negative affect can then lead to adolescent substance use in several ways. First, substance use may be adopted as a means of regulating negative affect. This mechanism is controversial with regards to adolescent substance use. Some researchers suggest that affect regulation may motivate substance abuse or adult substance use but has little impact on adolescent substance use initiation (Swaim, Oetting, Edwards, & Beauvais, 1989). However, other data link negative affect to earlier stages of adolescent substance use as well (Newcomb & Harlow, 1986; Paton, Kessler, & Kandel, 1977).

Perhaps more relevant for adolescent substance use is a mechanism that hypothesizes additional mediation through a drug-use-promoting peer group. Kaplan (1980) suggested that adolescents who suffer negative self-evaluations use deviant peer groups to restore damaged self-esteem. This peer group affiliation helps to repair self-image, but it also increases risk for delinquent behaviors. A similar mechanism may apply to adolescents who are experiencing negative affect.

Stress and negative affect pathways may help to explain the impact of parent alcoholism on adolescent substance use. Our cross-sectional data (Chassin et al., 1993) showed that parent alcoholism was associated with elevations in environmental stress that in turn were associated with negative affect. Negative affect had both a direct effect on use (consistent with negative affect regulation mechanisms) as well as an indirect effect, mediated through affiliations with drug-using peers (consistent with Kaplan's, 1980, self-derogation theory). In the current study, we tested whether a direct effect of negative affect (consistent with affect regulation) or an indirect effect of negative affect (consistent with self-derogation theory) or both, could explain the effects of parent alcoholism on growth over time in adolescent substance use.

TEMPERAMENT PATHWAYS: EMOTIONALITY AND SOCIABILITY

Temperament factors may also mediate the effects of parent alcoholism on offspring substance use. Tarter, Alterman, and Edwards (1985) suggested that COAs were more likely to be high in activity, low in persistence, slow to soothe after stress, and emotionally labile and disinhibited. Other research suggests that these characteristics are associated with substance use as well (Hawkins et al., 1992; Watson & Clark, 1993; Wills, DuHamel, & Vaccaro, 1995). Moreover, cross-sectional studies of college student COAs (Sher, Walitzer, Wood, & Brent, 1991) support a mediational role for "behavioral undercontrol." Thus, adolescent COAs may be at risk for substance use because they are temperamentally emotionally reactive and underregulated.

We focus on temperamental emotionality and sociability as potential mediators of parental alcoholism effects. We chose these temperament dimensions because they are recognized by most theoretical models of temperament (Goldsmith et al., 1987), they map readily onto adult personality dimensions (e.g., neuroticism and extraversion; Eysenck & Eysenck, 1969), and they represent key elements of major models of adolescent substance use (e.g., sociability should be important for peer influence models, and emotionality should be important for affect regulation models).[1] Our cross-sectional data found that maternal alcoholism was associated with heightened emotionality that, in turn, increased the likelihood of adolescents' experiencing negative affect that raised risk for substance use (Chassin et al., 1993). Sociability, however, was unrelated to parental alcoholism. The current study tested whether these temperamental mediators predicted growth over time in adolescent substance use.

In sum, although research suggests that COAs' elevated risk for substance use may be mediated through multiple pathways, few empirical studies have tested mediational models with this population, and longitudinal studies are particularly lacking. Although our cross-sectional model showed that multiple mediators made independent contributions to adolescents' substance use outcomes, these data cannot establish the temporal precedence of the risk factors to the outcomes. The current study provides a longitudinal test of our mediational model over a 3-year period. Through the use of latent growth curve modeling, we examined predictors of indi-

---

[1]An important temperamental mediator missing from our model is behavioral undercontrol. Many characteristics have been considered under this rubric (e.g., impulsivity, aggression, sensation seeking, and overactivity). However, we did not focus on this construct because different theoretical models of temperament lack clear consensus concerning its structure and operationalization. Even for more clearly defined subcomponents such as activity level, data are conflicting about whether the operative risk factor is activity level per se or associated conduct problems and disregulation (Windle, 1990), and there are complex relations between activity level and other dimensions of behavioral undercontrol (Wills et al., 1995). Finally, many operationalizations of behavioral undercontrol rely on indicators of antisocial behavior and, under these circumstances, behavioral undercontrol may be an indicator of co-occurring deviant behavior rather than being a temperamental characteristic that predisposes an individual to substance use (Nathan, 1988; Windle, 1990). For these reasons, we did not consider behavioral undercontrol in the current model. However, future examinations of this construct are very important if clear operational definitions can be provided, and recent research has suggested some measurement directions (e.g., Martin et al., 1994; White et al., 1994).

vidual differences in adolescents' rates of substance use growth. Specifically, we tested whether parent alcoholism predicted steeper growth in adolescent substance use and whether our hypothesized mediators could account for these parent alcoholism effects. We addressed methodological limitations of previous research by studying a community sample for whom parent alcoholism and co-occurring psychopathology were directly ascertained, and by using multiple reporters to minimize the impact of response biases.

METHOD

Participants

The total sample at Time 1 consisted of 454 adolescents, aged 10.5 to 15.5 years (M = 12.7, SD = 1.45) and their parents. COAs (n = 246) had at least one biological alcoholic parent who was also a custodial parent, and controls (n = 208) had no biological or custodial alcoholic parents. Because the current study used adolescent, mother, and father reports, we excluded 38 single-parent families and 87 two-parent families without complete data from both parents at Time 1. Sample retention was high. Of the 329 two-parent families with complete data at Time 1, only 8 families did not provide complete data at all three time points. Finally, 5 participants were identified as influential outliers and were excluded,[2] leaving a final sample of 316 families in the analyses.

We compared the 138 participants who were dropped from the analyses to the 316 who were retained using all available Time 1 data (adolescent report, parent report, and spouse reports on non-interviewed parents). T tests and chi-square comparisons showed that, at Time 1, the groups did not significantly differ in age, gender, father's alcoholism, parent antisocial personality, parent affective disorder, stress, emotionality, sociability, or negative affect. However, those dropped from analysis had higher Time 1 substance use, less parent monitoring, more peer substance use, more Hispanic parents, less educated parents, and more alcoholic mothers (p values ranged from <.10 to <.001). Although the groups were largely comparable on the variables of interest, some caution is warranted in generalization.

Of the 316 adolescents in the current sample, 47% were female, 21% Hispanic, and 89% lived with both biological parents. COAs and controls did not significantly differ in these characteristics. However, COAs had

---

[2]These outliers were 5 participants who reported extremely high use at Time 1 (more than 3.5 standard deviations above the mean) and steep decreases in use at Times 2 and 3. Their inclusion in the model produced estimation problems, with a large negative correlation between the intercept and slope factors and several models failing to converge. Although they may be a potentially important (albeit small) subsample when considering cessation of substance use, they cannot be appropriately modeled within our overall sample and thus were dropped from analyses.

less educated parents, more parents with lifetime diagnoses of affective disorders, and more parents with lifetime diagnoses of antisocial personality disorder (all $ps < .05$).

Recruitment

Recruitment procedures are presented in detail elsewhere (Chassin, Barrera, Bech, & Kossak-Fuller, 1992). COA families were recruited using court records ($n = 103$), wellness questionnaires from a health maintenance organization ($n = 22$), and community telephone surveys ($n = 120$). COAs had to be non-Hispanic Caucasian or Hispanic, Arizona residents, aged 10.5–15.5 years, and English speaking. Moreover, a biological and custodial parent had to meet the criteria of the *Diagnostic and Statistical Manual of Mental Disorders* (3rd ed., *DSM–III*; American Psychiatric Association, 1980) for alcohol abuse or dependence or Family History—Research Diagnostic Criteria (FH–RDC; Andreasen, Endicott, Spitzer, & Winokur, 1977), based on spouse reports (if the alcoholic parent was not interviewed). Demographically matched controls were recruited using telephone interviews. Controls were screened to match the COA participant in ethnicity, family composition, age, and socioeconomic status. Neither biological nor custodial parents could meet *DSM–III* criteria (or FH–RDC criteria) for alcohol abuse or dependence.

Recruitment biases are discussed in detail elsewhere (Chassin et al., 1992; Chassin et al., 1993). We required that the alcoholic parent be custodial as well as biological (so that the adolescent had the potential to be exposed to this parent's influence). This requirement produced an overrepresentation of two-parent families. Also, those who refused participation were more likely to be Hispanic. However, the sample was unbiased with respect to alcoholism indicators that were available in archival records. In support of the representativeness of the alcoholic sample, their comorbidities were similar to those reported in the Epidemiological Catchment Area Study (Helzer & Pryzbeck, 1988). However, the underrepresentation of single-parent families and the higher refusal rate for Hispanics suggests caution in generalization.

Procedure

The procedures are described in detail elsewhere (Chassin et al., 1991). Data were collected using three annual computer-assisted interviews with the adolescents and their parents. Confidentiality was reinforced with a Department of Health and Human Services Certificate of Confidentiality.

Measures

Parent Alcoholism and Associated Psychopathology

Lifetime *DSM–III* (American Psychiatric Association, 1980) diagnoses of alcohol abuse or dependence, affective disorder (major depression or dysthymia), and antisocial personality were obtained using a computerized version of the Diagnostic Interview Schedule (DIS, Version III; Robins, Helzer, Croughan, & Ratcliff, 1981). If only one parent was interviewed, alcoholism diagnoses for the other parent were made using spouse reports according to FH–RDC. For the current analyses, alcoholism diagnoses of the biological father and mother were each considered (separately) as dichotomous variables. Among the 316 families in the current analyses, 28 mothers and 151 fathers met these criteria.

Parents' affective disorders and antisocial personality disorders (using the DIS) were treated (separately) as control variables in the model. For each family, lifetime diagnoses of affective disorders and antisocial personality were considered as dichotomous variables, either present (in one or both parents) or absent.

Parent Monitoring of the Adolescent's Behavior

Parents' monitoring of their adolescent's behavior in the past 3 months was assessed by mother and father self-report (three items, e.g., "I had a pretty good idea of [the adolescent's] plans for the day"). Coefficient alphas over the three waves ranged from .74–.80 for father's monitoring and .77–.85 for mother's monitoring. A single score was computed for each parent using the mean of the three items.

Associations With Drug-Use Promoting Peers

Adolescents estimated how many of their friends used alcohol, marijuana, and other drugs occasionally and regularly, using items adapted from Johnston, O'Malley, and Bachman (1988). They also reported how their close friends would feel about their using marijuana, alcohol, and other drugs occasionally and regularly. Coefficient alpha was .89–.90 across waves for the six-item peer substance use measure and .89–.93 across waves for the seven-item peer tolerance of substance use measure. Because adolescent's reports of peer substance use and peer tolerance of substance use were highly correlated ($r = .59–.63$ across waves), the two scales were averaged to represent a drug-use promoting peer environment.

Adolescent Life Stress

Parents and adolescents reported on negative, uncontrollable life events that had occurred to the adolescent within the past 3 months (e.g., friend moved away, parent lost job, parent arrested). Events were taken from the Children of Alcoholics Life Events Schedule (Roosa, Sandler, Gehring, Beals, & Cappo, 1988) and the General Life Events Schedule for Children (Sandler, Ramirez, & Reynolds, 1986), supplemented with items from other child life events schedules. Each informant's score was a count of reported stressful events. Correlations among reporters across waves varied as follows: mothers with fathers, .48–.54; mothers with adolescents, .36–.45; and fathers with adolescents, .32–.44. For the structural modeling, the stress variable was a multiple-reporter composite manifest variable created using factor score regression weights.[3] Standardized factor loadings showed that each reporter's score loaded significantly, with parent data somewhat more heavily weighted (.75 for mother, .68 for father) than adolescent data (.57, averaged over waves).

Adolescent Negative Affect

Negative affect was measured using adolescent self-report of internalizing symptomatology, self-derogation, and perceived loss of control in the past 3 months. Internalizing symptomatology was assessed with seven items from the Achenbach Child Behavior Checklist (CBCL; Achenbach & Edelbrock, 1981; coefficient α = .78–.79 across waves). Sample items included the following: cried a lot; felt nervous, high-strung, or tense. Perceived loss of control was assessed by three items from Newcomb and Harlow (1986; coefficient α = .72–.76 across waves; e.g., "I felt I was not in control of my life"). Self-derogation was assessed using seven items from Rosenberg's (1979) scale (coefficient α = .81–.87 across waves). Intercorrelations among the three dimensions ranged from .50 to .66 across waves. For the structural modeling, adolescent negative affect was a composite manifest variable created using factor score regression weights.[4] Standardized factor loadings showed that each indicator significantly loaded on the construct with slightly greater weight on perceived control (−.86) than internalizing symptoms (.72) or self-derogation (−.66, averaged across waves).

---

[3]There were four endogenous variables that involved either multiple reporters or multiple indicators (stress, emotionality, sociability, and negative affect). These could not be used as multiple indicator latent factors because of the required number of parameters and the current sample size. To preserve maximal information, we created linear composite manifest variables using factor score regression weights. Longitudinal measurement models of each construct were estimated, with equality constraints placed on the loadings across time. Nested chi-square tests revealed no significant decrements in the model chi-square as a function of the imposed equality constraints, confirming that the constructs were structurally invariant over time. Accordingly, a single set of factor weights was used to create manifest linear composites for each construct at each time period. These manifest variables were corrected for unreliability (the measurement errors were set to [1-coefficient alpha] multiplied by the variance of the indicator; Bollen, 1989, p. 168).
[4]See Footnote 3.

Emotionality and Sociability

Emotionality and sociability were measured by parents' and adolescents' reports on a modification of the Emotionality, Activity, and Sociability Temperament Scale (Buss & Plomin, 1984). Coefficient alphas across reporters and waves ranged between .70 and .80 for emotionality and between .54 and .74 for sociability. Correlations between reporters for emotionality varied across waves as follows: mothers with fathers, .41–.45; mothers with adolescents, .21–.29; and fathers with adolescents, .19–.28. Correlations between reporters for sociability varied across waves as follows: mothers with fathers, .43–.46; mothers with adolescents, .38–.44; and fathers with adolescents, .22–.31. For the structural modeling, emotionality and sociability were multiple reporter composite manifest variables created using factor score regression weights.[5] Standardized factor loadings showed that each reporter's data significantly loaded for both constructs, with mothers' data weighing most heavily for sociability (.82) compared to father and adolescent (.56 and .53, respectively, averaged over waves), and parent data weighted more heavily (.69 for mother and .65 for father) than adolescent data (.39, averaged over waves) for emotionality.

Adolescent Substance Use

Adolescents self-reported their frequency of substance use in the past year (from none to daily use) on 12 items, including drinking beer–wine and hard liquor, drinking five or more drinks in a row, getting drunk on alcohol, and using eight illicit drugs. A substance use score was calculated by summing the responses to these 12 items.[6]

Because of the young age of the participants, the prevalence of substance use was generally low. Thus, the current study is best viewed as examining trajectories of substance use initiation (rather than substance abuse). However, by Wave 3 more than half of the COAs and one third of the controls used alcohol (with an average frequency among users of monthly use for COAs and occasional but less than monthly use for controls); 18% of the COAs and 6% of the controls used illegal drugs (with an average frequency among users of occasionally but less than monthly use for COAs and less than five times per year for controls); and 33% of

---

[5]See Footnote 3.

[6]Because different types of adolescent substance use might have different determinants, we re-estimated our models predicting growth in alcohol use and heavy alcohol use separately. (The lower prevalence of illicit drug use precluded a separate test.) There were no substantive changes in the findings. We also tested whether a two-factor model (separating alcohol and drug use) would be a better fit to the data than a one-factor overall substance use model. The chi-square difference test showed no significant improvement in fit for the two-factor model; the two factors were highly intercorrelated, and there was a large cross-loading such that heavy alcohol use loaded on both factors. For these reasons, we used an overall substance use score as the dependent measure.

the COAs and 13% of the controls had experienced a negative consequence of alcohol or drug use. Moreover, these prevalence rates should not be taken to minimize the significance of substance use in this sample, because substance use at these ages is prognostic of later substance abuse (Robins & Pryzbeck, 1985). For example, Robins and McEvoy (1990) found that, among individuals who retrospectively reported any use of illicit drugs before age 15, 87% reported a drug problem in adulthood. Among those who reported being drunk on alcohol before age 15, 84% reported an alcohol problem in adulthood.

RESULTS

Testing for Growth in the Endogenous Variables Over Time

We first tested for growth in the endogenous variables over time using latent growth curve modeling (LGC; McArdle, 1988; Meredith & Tisak, 1984, 1990; Muthen, 1991). All models were estimated using EQS (Version 3.0; Bentler, 1989) based on the sample covariance matrix and a column vector of means.[7]

Step 1: FOCUS Models

For each variable, we estimated a one-factor three-indicator Factor of Curves (FOCUS) model (McArdle, 1988), in which the indicators of the single latent factor were the Time 1, Time 2, and Time 3 measures of the variable. Eight models were estimated, one for each of the seven mediators and one for adolescent substance use. For each variable, an initial baseline model fixed all three factor loadings to 1.0 (representing no growth over time) while freely estimating the mean and variance of the latent factor. This no-growth model fit the data well for sociability, emotionality, and negative affect (i.e., all model chi-square test statistics were nonsignificant, all $ps > .15$). Because these three constructs showed no systematic change over time, they were represented in the structural model by their Time 1 scores.

However, this no-growth model did not hold for mother's and father's monitoring, stress, peer substance use, or adolescent substance use. Thus, a series of nested models were estimated to ascertain the shape of the growth. Adolescent substance use and peer use showed significant linear increases over time. Mother's monitoring showed a significant linear decrease over time. Finally, stress and father's monitoring showed no changes from Time 1 to 2, but a decrease from Time 2 to 3. Because there were only three measurement points, the pattern of growth observed for envi-

---

[7]The covariance matrix and vector of means are available from Patrick J. Curran.

ronmental stress and father's monitoring could not be modeled further using an LGC framework. Accordingly, we used the Time 1 measures of stress and father's monitoring in the final model because they best captured the pattern over two of the three time points while also allowing for prospective prediction of adolescent substance use growth.

Step 2: Two-Factor Intercept and Slope Models

Because adolescent substance use, peer use, and mother's monitoring showed significant linear growth, for these constructs we estimated models that separated the intercept of the growth curve (which represents the starting point of the growth curve at Time 1) from the slope component of the growth curve (which represents the shape of the growth over time). For each construct, we estimated a two-factor, three-indicator model. The first factor was defined by fixing all three of the loadings from the Time 1, 2, and 3 measures of the construct to 1.0; thus, it represented the initial level or intercept of the growth curve. The second factor fixed the first loading to 0 (thus not allowing the Time 1 measure to load on this factor), the second loading was fixed at 1.0, and the third loading was fixed at 2.0. This second factor represented the linear slope of the growth curve. The mean of each factor represents the group parameter, and the variance of each factor represents the individual variation of each adolescent around the group parameter.

For both mother's monitoring and peer use, these models showed nonsignificant variances in the slope factor. This suggests that, over time, the entire sample experienced increases in peer use and decreases in mother's monitoring, but that these changes were uniform across individuals. Because of the lack of individual variation in growth, we used the Time 1 measures of peer use and mother's monitoring in the structural model. However, for adolescent substance use, there was significant individual variation in growth over time. Thus, the goal of all further analyses was to predict this individual variation in substance use growth.

Summary

Analyses suggested that the Time 1 scores for the predictor variables were appropriate for use in the structural model to predict adolescent substance use growth over time. This was true either because the predictors showed no growth over time (for sociability, emotionality, and negative affect); because they showed uniform growth without individual variation (for mother's monitoring and peer use); or because the pattern of growth could not be modeled with three time points (for stress and father's monitoring). However, because adolescent substance use showed both significant linear growth and significant individual variation in growth over time, it was represented in our model by a latent intercept factor (representing

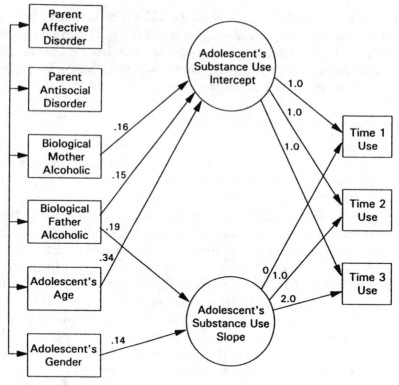

Figure 1. Direct effects model; $\chi^2(13, N = 316) = 24.5$, $p = .03$, Tucker–Lewis Fit Index = .95, Comparative Fit Index = .98. Only significant effects are shown. All coefficients are standardized and all ps < .05.

initial substance use levels) and a latent slope factor (representing rates of growth over time). Most important for the current study are predictors of the slope factor, because these are prospective predictors of individual rates of substance use growth over time.

Effect of Parent Alcoholism on Substance Use Growth

Our first question was whether parent alcoholism significantly predicted adolescents' substance use growth. To test this, we regressed the latent intercept and slope factors on mother's and father's alcoholism diagnosis, parent antisocial personality disorder, parent affective disorder, adolescent's age, and adolescent's gender (see Figure 1). A priori predicted paths were estimated from maternal and paternal alcoholism diagnosis to the substance use intercept and slope factors. This model was estimated and, on the basis of significant Lagrange Multiplier tests ($p < .01$), two paths from control variables were added: a path from adolescent age to substance use intercept, and from adolescent gender to substance use slope. This model fit the data well, $\chi^2(13, N = 316) = 24.5$, $p = .03$, Tucker–

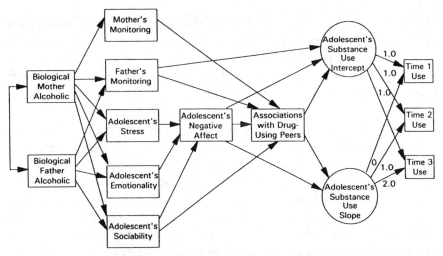

Figure 2. Hypothesized structural model.

Lewis Fit Index (TLI; Tucker & Lewis, 1973) = .95, Comparative Fit Index (CFI; Bentler, 1990) = .98.

Both maternal and paternal alcoholism and adolescent age significantly predicted the substance use intercept factor. Thus, for COAs and older adolescents, the substance use growth curve started at a significantly higher level than it did for non-COAs and younger adolescents. More important, paternal alcoholism and adolescent gender significantly predicted the slope factor. That is, adolescents with alcoholic fathers and boys showed steeper substance use growth over time than did adolescents with nonalcoholic fathers and girls.[8]

Mechanisms Associated With Parent Alcoholism Risk

We next tested hypothesized mediators of parent alcoholism effects on substance use growth. Figure 2 presents the hypothesized model that considers the effects of parent alcoholism operating through elevations in environmental stress (which then act to increase negative affect), temperamental emotionality and sociability, and parent monitoring of the adolescent's behavior. We also tested whether negative affect influenced

[8]The lack of maternal alcoholism effect on the slope factor was surprising. Because this effect might be due to the small number of alcoholic mothers in the subsample, we re-estimated this model using the full sample including single-parent families or those with noninterviewed parents. (This was possible because alcoholism diagnoses were available on all parents, even those who were not interviewed.) With the full sample, there was a marginally significant effect of maternal alcoholism on substance use slope ($p < .08$) such that adolescents with alcoholic mothers showed steeper substance use growth.

adolescent substance use both directly and indirectly (by increasing the likelihood of associating with drug-use-promoting peers). Paths from maternal alcoholism to father's monitoring and from father's monitoring directly to adolescent's initial levels of use (i.e., the intercept factor) were based on results from our earlier cross-sectional model (Chassin et al., 1993).

Before estimating the model, it was necessary to account for variance attributable to the control variables. Control variables were parent antisocial disorder, parent affective disorder, adolescent's age, and adolescent's gender. (Effects of ethnicity and parent education were not considered because they were unrelated to the dependent measure at any wave of measurement.) To accomplish this, the a priori hypothesized paths from the noncontrol variables were freely estimated; the structural disturbances between maternal and paternal monitoring, stress, emotionality, and sociability were freely estimated; and all paths from the control variables were fixed to zero. This model was estimated, the path from the control variable with the largest Lagrange Multiplier was freed, and the model was re-estimated until no Lagrange Multipliers from control variables exceeded 6.6 ($p < .01$). This resulted in the freeing of six paths from control variables: parent affective disorder to stress and to emotionality; parent antisocial disorder to father's monitoring; adolescent age to negative affect and to peer use; and adolescent gender to the substance use slope factor. Although this procedure capitalizes on chance in estimating the effects of the control variables, it provides a stringent test of the theoretical variables of interest. The final model fit the data well, $\chi^2(62, N = 316) = 88.6$, $p = .01$, TLI = .95, CFI = .98; see Figure 3 .

In terms of the parenting pathway, both maternal and paternal alcoholism were related to decreased paternal monitoring (although the relation was only marginally significant for father's alcoholism). In turn, adolescents whose fathers reported lower levels of monitoring were more likely to associate with drug-using peers, and these peer associations predicted increases in substance use over time. Adolescents whose fathers reported less monitoring of their behavior also had higher initial substance use levels.

In terms of the stress and negative affect pathway, maternal and paternal alcoholism significantly predicted higher levels of stress that in turn predicted higher levels of negative affect. Negative affect predicted greater associations with drug-using peers that in turn predicted both higher levels of initial substance use and steeper substance use growth.

In terms of temperament variables, maternal alcoholism was marginally related to heightened emotionality, which in turn was significantly associated with elevations in negative affect and, thus, contributed to the negative affect pathway. High levels of sociability were significantly related

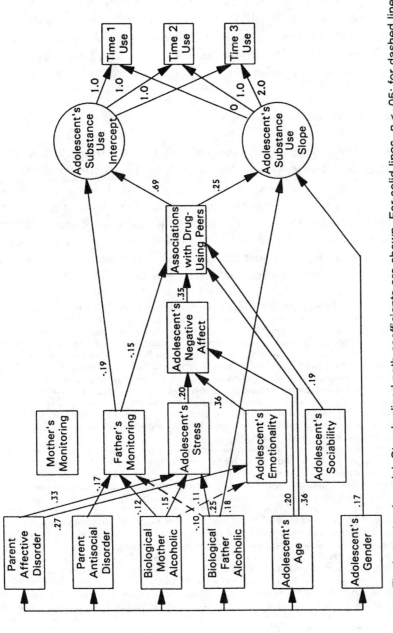

Figure 3. Final structural model. Standardized path coefficients are shown. For solid lines, *p* < .05; for dashed lines, *p* < .10; $\chi^2(62, N = 316) = 88.6$, *p* = .01, Tucker–Lewis Fit Index = .95, Comparative Fit Index = .98.

to associations with drug-using peers. However, sociability showed no significant relation to parent alcoholism.[9]

Finally, the direct effect of paternal alcoholism on the substance use slope factor remained significant even after the inclusion of the hypothesized mediators in the model. Thus, the mediators could not completely explain the paternal alcoholism effect.[10] The final model explained a moderate amount of the variance in the substance use slope factor ($R^2 = 13\%$) and a large amount of variance in the intercept factor ($R^2 = 61\%$).[11]

Hierarchical Model Testing

To test whether a single domain of mediators was sufficient to explain substance use outcomes or whether multiple pathways were necessary, we estimated three nested models in which the regression parameters for each mediating path were set to zero. That is, one model fixed all paths associated with parenting to zero, another fixed all paths associated with temperament to zero, etc. Compared to the full model in which all hypothesized paths were freely estimated, the added restrictions in each of these three models produced a significant decrement in model fit. Thus, each of

---

[9]Our exclusion of single-parent families might have underestimated the effect of parent alcoholism on temperament, because this selection might have eliminated the most temperamentally "at risk" families. To assess this, we calculated correlations between parent alcoholism and the temperament variables separately for single-parent and two-parent families (relying on maternal and adolescent report of temperament because fathers in single-parent families were typically not interviewed). There were no significant differences in the correlations between parent alcoholism and sociability for either reporter, and no differences in the correlations between parent alcoholism and emotionality using adolescent report. Using the mother's report, there were stronger relations between parent alcoholism and emotionality in the single-parent families than in the two-parent families. Thus, the magnitude of the links between parent alcoholism and emotionality might be stronger if single-parent families were included (at least for the mother's report).

[10]The use of lifetime diagnoses does not consider effects of the recency and severity of parent alcoholism (or of subclinical drinking problems in the control group). Accordingly, we re-estimated our model two other ways—operationalizing parent drinking problems as the number of alcohol-related consequences or dependency symptoms reported within the past year (among both alcoholic and control parents), and again considering the quantity–frequency of parents' alcohol consumption in the past year. All of the effects of paternal alcoholism were identical to those produced by the lifetime diagnoses. For maternal alcoholism, the links to father's monitoring, stress, and emotionality were weakened. Because we had only a small number of alcoholic mothers who were currently reporting drinking problems, this was a weaker test of maternal alcoholism effects. However, because only paternal alcoholism significantly predicted adolescents' substance use growth over time, these changes in the maternal alcoholism effects do not influence our conclusions. Parents' current use of other drugs might also be important. However, for current drug use (past 3 months) maternal use was at such low levels that analysis was not feasible, and paternal drug use did not significantly relate to the dependent variable over and above paternal alcoholism status. Accordingly, we did not consider parent current drug use in our multivariate model.

[11]Maximum likelihood estimation assumes that the observed data follow a multivariate normal distribution. Because our substance use scores were skewed, we re-estimated the model using manifest factor score regression composites of the intercept and slope of substance use, with robust maximum likelihood estimation from EQS (Bentler, 1989). No substantive differences were found.

the three mediating pathways was necessary to best reproduce the observed data.

Mediation of Parent Alcoholism Effects

The direct effects models reported earlier showed that both maternal and paternal alcoholism predicted the intercept factor and that paternal alcoholism predicted the slope factor. To test whether our psychosocial variables significantly mediated these effects, we computed z-ratios for the total indirect effects in EQS. In predicting the intercept factor, the total indirect effects for both maternal and paternal alcoholism were significant (z-ratios = 2.34 and 2.17 respectively, both ps < .05). In predicting the slope factor, the total indirect effect for paternal alcoholism was marginally significant (z-ratio = 1.85, p < .06).[12]

DISCUSSION

The current study provided a longitudinal test of parent alcoholism effects on adolescents' substance use growth and tested psychosocial mediators of these effects. As would be expected developmentally, our adolescent sample showed significant growth over time in their consumption of alcohol and illegal drugs. More important, however, latent growth curve modeling revealed significant individual differences in the rates of this growth, and paternal alcoholism significantly predicted steeper growth. Thus, adolescents with alcoholic fathers are not only more likely to use substances, but also increase their substance use at a more rapid rate than do their non-COA peers.

The finding that only paternal rather than maternal alcoholism predicted substance use growth over time was surprising. Because maternal alcoholism was associated with elevations in adolescents' initial levels of substance use, and because analyses of the full sample showed marginally significant prediction of substance use growth from maternal alcoholism, it would be premature to entirely rule out maternal alcoholism effects on adolescent substance use outcomes. Our ability to detect maternal alcoholism effects on substance use growth may have been weakened by the relatively small number of alcoholic mothers in the sample.

---

[12] Maternal alcoholism showed a marginally significant indirect effect on the slope factor when the hypothesized mediators were included in the model (z-ratio = 1.89, p < .06). However, in the absence of a direct effect of maternal alcoholism on substance use growth, this indirect effect is not clearly interpretable and is likely due to suppressor effects of the mediating variables. Even when we re-estimated the direct effects model with the full sample, the direct effect of maternal alcoholism on slope was only marginally significant. Given the lack of a direct effect of maternal alcoholism on substance use growth, we have not interpreted the marginally significant indirect effect.

We also asked whether COAs' substance use outcomes could be accounted for by impaired parental monitoring, elevated environmental stress and negative affect, and elevated emotionality and sociability, all of which were hypothesized to be related to affiliations with drug-using peers. Our hierarchical model testing confirmed that no one domain of mediators could sufficiently account for COAs' substance use outcomes. Rather, it was necessary to consider all three domains. These results are consistent with recent theory that postulates multiple interrelated pathways to substance use (Sher, 1991; Zucker, 1994), and it underlines the importance of a simultaneous consideration of these multiple risk factors.

The central question, however, was whether these multiple risk factors could account for individual variation in substance use growth (i.e., whether they significantly predicted the slope of the growth curve). Whereas predictors of the intercept factor represent cross-sectional relations (with ambiguous directions of effect), predictors of substance use slope represent prospective predictors of changes in substance use over time. Of course, significant prediction of the slope factor does not rule out bidirectional effects in which adolescent substance use and the mediators show reciprocal relations. Indeed, theoretically, such reciprocal relations are quite likely, particularly for constructs such as peer affiliations or parent monitoring (e.g., Fisher & Bauman, 1988). However, our significant predictors of the slope factor can confidently rule out a unidirectional "reverse" direction of effect in which adolescent substance use influences the mediators without any reciprocal effects. Finally, as with all observational longitudinal research, our prospective prediction of the slope factor cannot rule out "third variables" underlying these relations. Thus, we can specify the temporal precedence between our predictor variables and adolescents' substance use growth, but this does not imply a causal relation.

Our model accounted for 13% of the variance in this slope factor. This can be considered a moderate effect size (in Cohen's, 1988, terms) and is comparable to other prospective studies of adolescent substance use (Kandel, Kessler, & Margulies, 1978; Windle, 1990). Here, we discuss the implications of our findings for each of the hypothesized pathways, confining our interpretations to prediction of the slope factor (for a discussion of cross-sectional prediction, see Chassin et al., 1993). Moreover, because only paternal alcoholism showed a significant direct effect on substance use growth, we discuss our mediators in terms of their ability to account for this paternal alcoholism effect.

Parenting and Socialization Pathways

There was some support for father's monitoring as mediating the effects of paternal alcoholism on substance use growth. Father's alcoholism was associated with less paternal monitoring of adolescent behavior, which, in turn, predicted associations with drug-using peers. These peer associations prospectively predicted adolescents' growth in substance use involvement over time. These findings support family socialization models of adolescent substance use (Dishion et al., 1988; Hawkins et al., 1992) in suggesting that COAs are at risk for substance use growth in part because of impairments that occur in family socialization and behavioral management. The fact that the father's monitoring had unique effects (above and beyond a consideration of the mother's monitoring) is noteworthy because many studies of adolescent socialization consider only the mother's role in these parenting behaviors. Our data support the importance of the father's parenting behaviors as well.

However, this family socialization pathway could not fully explain the effects of the father's alcoholism on adolescents' substance use growth. Significant direct effects of the father's alcoholism remained, even when the hypothesized mediators were included in the model. This may be because monitoring is only one component of parenting thought to be important to adolescent substance use. More powerful effects might have been found if we had examined multiple aspects of parenting, including rule enforcement and parental supportiveness. Alternatively, our brief self-report measure of parent monitoring may have underestimated its importance.

Moreover, peers as well as parents are important socializing influences, and our findings showed that adolescents who (at the beginning of the study) had more friends who used drugs or tolerated the use of drugs also showed the steepest increase in substance use. This finding is in contrast to a recently reported longitudinal study (Farrell & Danish, 1993) that found no prospective effects of peer influences on subsequent gateway drug use in adolescents. The differences in findings may reflect the different ethnic composition of the samples. Farrell and Danish (1993) had a predominantly African American sample, and peer influences have been reported to be particularly small for this group (Farrell & Danish, 1993).

Stress and Negative Affect Models

The current findings also support stress and negative affect pathways as mediators of paternal alcoholism effects on adolescents' substance use growth. Paternal alcoholism was associated with elevations in environmental stress, which, in turn, were associated with heightened levels of negative affect. Negative affect was related to affiliation with drug-using peers, which significantly predicted increases in substance use over time. These findings support mechanisms such as Kaplan's (1980) self-derogation theory, which suggest that adolescents who experience low self-esteem (or lower levels of perceived control and higher levels of negative affect) are more likely to affiliate with deviant peer groups. This peer affiliation raises risk for delinquent behaviors, including substance use. As with socialization models, however, these mechanisms could not fully explain the effect of paternal alcoholism on substance use growth.

Unlike our cross-sectional results, there was no unique direct path from negative affect to substance use growth. Such an effect might have been predicted by a simple negative affect regulation model of adolescent substance use. As other researchers have suggested, negative affect regulation motives may be more important for later stages of substance "abuse" than for early adolescent substance use (Swaim et al., 1989). Alternatively, our annual measurement intervals may not be optimal for capturing simple negative affect regulation mechanisms that may operate over much briefer time windows. Nevertheless, that we found a unique direct path from negative affect to substance use cross-sectionally but not longitudinally raises the possibility that our cross-sectional finding represents a "reverse" direction of effect. That is, adolescent substance use may act to increase adolescents' levels of negative affect (Hansell & White, 1991). The most parsimonious interpretation of our longitudinal findings are that they support self-derogation mechanisms involving stress and negative affect rather than simple negative affect regulation models of use.[13]

Temperamental Emotionality and Sociability

Our findings did not support emotionality or sociability as mediators of paternal alcoholism effects because father's alcoholism was not significantly related to either construct. In terms of sociability, as Tarter et al. (1985) have speculated, previous notions of COAs as particularly sociable may have confused an outgoing, extroverted style with disinhibition (an indicator of behavioral undercontrol). Perhaps behavioral undercontrol is the "true" temperamental mediator of paternal alcoholism effects. Recent cross-sectional findings with college student COAs support this hypothesis (Sher et al., 1991). Temperamental bases for behavioral undercontrol could also be exacerbated by harsh or inconsistent parenting among alcoholic parents. However, recent adoptee data raise the possibility that behavioral undercontrol (as measured by aggression and antisociality) is not uniquely tied to parent alcoholism but rather mediates the effects of co-occurring parent antisocial personality (Cadoret, Yates, Troughton, Woodworth, & Stewart, 1995). This is consistent with our baseline data that found adolescents' externalizing symptoms to be predicted by parent antisocial per-

---

[13] It is also possible that direct negative affect regulation motives operate only within a subgroup of adolescents—those who do not have effective alternative strategies for coping with negative affect. However, other analyses of the current data show this moderating effect for measures of behavioral and cognitive coping strategies in cross-sectional but not longitudinal analyses (Hussong, 1995). Other measures of coping (e.g., drinking coping motives) might identify a subgroup of adolescents for whom direct negative affect regulation mechanisms are operative, but these effects were not found with our measures of behavioral and cognitive coping.

sonality rather than uniquely related to parent alcoholism (Chassin et al., 1991). Thus, although indicators of behavioral undercontrol and antisociality may be important predictors of adolescent substance use outcomes, more research is needed to determine whether these characteristics mediate the effects of parent alcoholism or of parents' co-occurring antisociality.

In terms of emotionality, the current study found links to maternal but not paternal alcoholism. However, our data may have underestimated the role of emotionality because of our exclusion of single-parent families, among whom links between parental alcoholism and emotionality were particularly strong. Thus, samples that include greater number of single-parent families might find a significant mediational role for emotionality.

Direct Effects of Paternal Alcoholism

Perhaps the most surprising finding was that (unlike our cross-sectional model) the direct effect of paternal alcoholism on substance use growth remained significant even after the inclusion of our psychosocial mediators. Thus, although these hypothesized mediators play a role in COAs' substance use, they could not fully explain the risk for escalating substance use that was associated with paternal alcoholism. How then can we interpret the direct effect of paternal alcoholism on growth curves of adolescent substance use? One possibility is that important mediators of paternal alcoholism effects were unmeasured by our study. For example, previous research has suggested that COAs may experience greater pharmacological benefits from substance use (Newlin & Thomson, 1990; Sher, 1991), and these benefits may mediate the effect of paternal alcoholism on substance use growth. Indeed, these pharmacological benefits would be more likely to determine substance use growth than adolescents' first use of substances because they require some experience with the substance to be operative. Both behavioral undercontrol and the pharmacological effects of substances are worthy of further investigation as potential mediators of parent alcoholism effects on adolescents' substance use growth.

Finally, although the current study corrected many of the methodological problems in earlier research (e.g., by using a longitudinal design, a community sample, multiple reporter data, and direct ascertainment of parent alcoholism), it is also important to recognize its limitations. First, the small number of alcoholic mothers in the sample limits our ability to detect maternal alcoholism effects. Second, the study included only three time points, limiting our ability to model patterns of growth for two of the psychosocial variables. Third, alcoholism was treated as a unitary disorder, and no attempt was made to subtype particular forms of alcoholism. Similarly, substance use was treated as a unitary variable, and models focused on specific substances or specific transitions between different stages of substance use involvement might produce different findings. Fourth, our use of two-parent families and our higher refusal rates of Hispanic subjects suggests caution in generalization and may have underestimated the importance of temperamental emotionality.

In sum, the current study provided a longitudinal test of parent alcoholism effects on adolescent substance use growth and tested hypothesized mediators of these effects. Findings showed that boys, adolescents with drug-using peers, and adolescents with alcoholic fathers had steeper substance use growth trajectories. Data were consistent with father's monitoring, stress, and negative affect as mediators of this paternal alcoholism effect. However, because the direct effect of father's alcoholism on substance use slope remained significant even after considering the hypothesized mediators, it is likely that other (unmeasured) mediators are necessary to fully explain paternal alcoholism risk. Mediators of interest for future research include behavioral undercontrol and COAs' psychopharmacological experiences of substance use effects.

REFERENCES

Achenbach, T. M., & Edelbrock, C. (1981). Behavioral problems and competencies reported by parents of normal and disturbed children aged four through sixteen. *Monographs of the Society for Research in Child Development, 46*(1, Serial No. 188).

American Psychiatric Association. (1980). *Diagnostic and statistical manual of mental disorders* (3rd ed.). Washington, DC: Author.

Andreasen, N. C., Endicott, J., Spitzer, R. L., & Winokur, G. (1977). The family history method using diagnostic criteria: Reliability and validity. *Archives of General Psychiatry, 34*, 1229–1235.

Bentler, P. M. (1989). *EQS Structural equations program manual*. Los Angeles: BMDP Statistical Software, Inc.

Bentler, P. M. (1990). Comparative fit indexes in structural models. *Psychological Bulletin, 107*, 238–246.

Bollen, K. A. (1989). *Structural equations with latent variables*. New York: Wiley.

Buss, A. H., & Plomin, R. (1984). *Temperament: Early developing personality traits*. Hillsdale, NJ: Erlbaum.

Cadoret, R. J., Yates, W. R., Troughton, E., Woodworth, G., & Stewart, M. (1995). Adoption study demonstrating two genetic pathways to drug abuse. *Archives of General Psychiatry, 52*, 42–52.

Chassin, L., Barrera, M., Bech, K., & Kossak-Fuller, J. (1992). Recruiting a community sample of adolescent children of alcoholics: A comparison of three subject sources. *Journal of Studies on Alcohol, 53*, 316–320.

Chassin, L., Pillow, D., Curran, P., Molina, B., & Barrera, M. (1993). Relation of parental alcoholism to early adolescent substance use: A test of three mediating mechanisms. *Journal of Abnormal Psychology, 102*, 3–19.

Chassin, L., Rogosch, R., & Barrera, M. (1991). Substance use and symptomatology among adolescent children of alcoholics. *Journal of Abnormal Psychology*, 100, 449–463.

Cohen, J. (1988). *Statistical power analysis for the social sciences*. Hillsdale, NJ: Erlbaum.

Dishion, T. J., Patterson, G. R., & Reid, J. R. (1988). Parent and peer factors associated with drug sampling in early adolescence: Implications for treatment. In E. R. Rahdert & J. Grabowski (Eds.), *Adolescent drug abuse: Analyses of treatment research* (pp. 69–93; NIDA Research Monograph No. 77, DHHS Publication No. ADM88-1523). Rockville, MD: National Institute on Drug Abuse.

Eysenck, H. J., & Eysenck, S. B. G. (1969). *Personality Structure and Measurement*. London: Routledge & Kegan.

Farrell, A. D., & Danish, S. J. (1993). Peer drug associations and emotional restraint: Causes or consequences of adolescents' drug use? *Journal of Consulting and Clinical Psychology, 61*, 327–334.

Fisher, L. A., & Bauman, K. E. (1988). Influence and selection in the friend–adolescent relationship: Findings from studies of adolescent smoking and drinking. *Journal of Applied Social Psychology, 18*, 289–314.

Goldsmith, H. H., Buss, A. H., Plomin, R., Rothbart, M. K., Thomas, A., Chess, S., Hinde, R., & McCall, R. (1987). Roundtable: What is temperament? Four approaches. *Child Development, 58*, 505–529.

Hansell, S., & Raskin White, H. (1991). Adolescent drug use, psychological distress, and physical symptoms. *Journal of Health and Social Behavior, 32*, 288–301.

Hawkins, J. D., Catalano, R. F., & Miller, J. Y. (1992). Risk and protective factors for alcohol and other drug problems in adolescence and early adulthood: Implications for substance use prevention. *Psychological Bulletin, 112*, 64–105.

Helzer, H. E., & Pryzbeck, T. R. (1988). The co-occurrence of alcoholism with other psychiatric disorders in the general population and its impact on treatment. *Journal of Studies on Alcohol, 49*, 219–224.

Hussong, A. (1995). [Coping as a moderator of the relation between negative affect and adolescent substance use]. Unpublished data, Arizona State University, Tempe.

Johnston, L., O'Malley, P., & Bachman, J. (1988). *Illicit drug use, smoking, and drinking by America's high school students, college students, and young adults, 1975–1987*. Washington, DC: U.S. Government Printing Office.

Kandel, D. B., Kessler, R. C., & Margulies, R. Z. (1978). Antecedents of adolescent initiation into stages of drug use. In D. B. Kandel (Ed.), *Longitudinal research on drug use* (pp. 73–100). New York: Wiley.

Kaplan, H. B. (1980). *Deviant behavior in defense of self*. New York: Academic Press.

Martin, C. S., Earleywine, M., Blackson, T. C., Vanyukov, M. M., Moss, H. B., & Tarter, R. E. (1994). Aggressivity, inattention, hyperactivity, and impulsivity in boys at high and low risk for substance abuse. *Journal of Abnormal Child Psychology, 22,* 177–203.

McArdle, J. (1988). Dynamic but structural modeling of repeated measures data. In J. R. Nesselroade & R. B. Catell (Eds.), *Handbook of multivariate experimental psychology.* New York: Plenum.

Meredith, W., & Tisak, J. (1984). *"Tuckerizing"* curves. Paper presented at the annual meeting of the Psychometric Society, Santa Barbara, CA.

Meredith, W., & Tisak, J. (1990). Latent curve analysis. *Psychometrika, 55,* 105–122.

Muthen, B. (1991). Analysis of longitudinal data using latent variable models with varying parameters. In L. M. Collins & J. Horn (Eds.), *Best methods for the analysis of change: Recent advances, unanswered questions, future directions* (pp. 1–17). Washington, DC: American Psychological Association.

Nathan, P. (1988). The addictive personality is the behavior of the addict. *Journal of Consulting and Clinical Psychology, 56,* 183–188.

Newcomb, M. D., & Harlow, L. L. (1986). Life events and substance use among adolescents: Mediating effects of perceived loss of control and meaninglessness in life. *Journal of Personality and Social Psychology, 51,* 564–577.

Newlin, D. B., & Thomson, J. B. (1990). Alcohol challenge with sons of alcoholics: A critical review and analysis. *Psychological Bulletin, 108,* 383–402.

Paton, S., Kessler, R., & Kandel, D. B. (1977). Depressive mood and adolescent illegal drug use: A longitudinal analysis. *Journal of Genetic Psychology, 131,* 267–289.

Robins, L. N., Helzer, J. E., Croughan, J., & Ratcliff, K. S. (1981). National Institute of Mental Health Diagnostic Interview Schedule: Its history, characteristics, and validity. *Archives of General Psychiatry, 38,* 381–389.

Robins, L. N., & McEvoy, L. (1990). Conduct problems as predictors of substance abuse. In L. N. Robins & M. Rutter (Eds.), *Straight and devious pathways from childhood to adulthood* (pp. 182–204). Cambridge, England: Cambridge University Press.

Robins, L. N., & Pryzbeck, T. R. (1985). Age of onset of drug use as a factor in drug and other disorders. In C. R. Jones & R. J. Battjes (Eds.), *Etiology of drug abuse: Implications for prevention* (pp. 178–192; NIDA Research Monograph No. 56, DHHS Publication No. ADM85-1335). Washington, DC: U.S. Government Printing Office.

Roosa, M. W., Sandler, I. N., Gehring, M., Beals, J., & Cappo, L. (1988). The Children of Alcoholics Life-Events Schedule: A stress scale for children of alcohol-abusing parents. *Journal of Studies on Alcohol, 49,* 422–429.

Rosenberg, M. (1979). *Conceiving the self.* New York: Basic Books.

Sandler, I. N., Ramirez, R., & Reynolds, K. (1986, August). *Life stress for children of divorce, bereaved, and asthmatic children.* Paper presented at the annual meeting of the American Psychological Association, Washington, DC.

Sher, K. J. (1991). *Children of alcoholics: A critical appraisal of theory and research.* Chicago: University of Chicago Press.

Sher, K. J., Walitzer, K. S., Wood, P. K., & Brent, E. E. (1991). Characteristics of children of alcoholics: Putative risk factors, substance use and abuse, and psychopathology. *Journal of Abnormal Psychology, 100*, 427–449.

Swaim, R. C., Oetting, E. R., Edwards, R., & Beauvais, F. (1989). Links from emotional distress to adolescent drug use: A path model. *Journal of Consulting and Clinical Psychology, 57*, 227–231.

Tarter, R. E., Alterman, A. I., & Edwards, K. L. (1985). Vulnerability to alcoholism in men: A behavior–genetic perspective. *Journal of Studies on Alcohol, 46*, 329–356.

Tucker, L. R., & Lewis, C. (1973). The reliability coefficient for maximum likelihood factor analysis. *Psychometrika, 38*, 1–10.

Watson, D., & Clark, L. A. (1993). Behavioral disinhibition versus constraint: A dispositional perspective. In D. M. Wegner & J. W. Pennebacker (Eds.), *Handbook of mental control* (pp. 506–527). New York: Prentice Hall.

West, M. O., & Prinz, R. J. (1987). Parental alcoholism and childhood psychopathology. *Psychological Bulletin, 102*, 204–218.

White, J. L., Moffitt, T. E., Caspi, A., Bartusch, D. J., Needles, D., & Stouthamer-Loeber, M. (1994). Measuring impulsivity and examining its relationship to delinquency. *Journal of Abnormal Psychology, 103*, 192–205.

Wills, T. A., DuHamel, K., & Vaccaro, D. (1995). Activity and mood temperament as predictors of adolescent substance use: Test of a self-regulation mediational model. *Journal of Personality and Social Psychology, 68*, 901–916.

Wills, T. A., Schrebman, D., Benson, G., & Vaccaro, D. (1994). Impact of parental substance use on adolescents: A test of a mediational model. *Journal of Pediatric Psychology, 19*, 537–556.

Windle, M. (1990). A longitudinal study of antisocial behaviors in early adolescence as predictors of late adolescent substance use: Gender and ethnic group differences. *Journal of Abnormal Psychology, 99*, 86–91.

Zucker, R. (1994). Pathways to alcohol problems and alcoholism: A developmental account of the evidence for multiple alcoholisms and for contextual contributions to risk. In R. Zucker, G. Boyd, & J. Howard (Eds.), *The development of alcohol problems: Exploring the biopsychosocial matrix of risk* (pp. 255–290; NIH Publication No. 94-3495). Rockville. MD: National Institute on Alcohol Abuse and Alcoholism.

21

ALCOHOL CHALLENGE WITH SONS OF ALCOHOLICS: A CRITICAL REVIEW AND ANALYSIS

DAVID B. NEWLIN AND JAMES B. THOMSON

Alcoholism and drug abuse are the most prevalent psychiatric disorders (Robins et al., 1984). Approximately 30% of American men and 8% of American women have experienced serious problems with these drugs. However, the etiologies of alcoholism and drug abuse are unclear. This ambiguity may be due, in part, to the fact that long-term use of toxic drugs (such as alcohol) may obscure factors that play a role in the etiology of alcoholism and drug addiction. Therefore, comparisons of, for example, alcoholics with nonalcoholics may elucidate effects of the disorder without shedding any light on its causes.

One approach to studying causation is to investigate individuals who are at risk for the disorder but who are asymptomatic at the time of testing.

Reprinted from *Psychological Bulletin*, 108, 383–402 (1990). Used with permission of the author.

This research was supported in part by New Investigator Research Award AA06433 from the National Institute on Alcoholism and Alcohol Abuse to David B. Newlin.

We would like to thank Diana Fishbein, Jeannette Johnson, and Mary Beth Pretorius for commenting on earlier versions of this article.

Characteristics of at-risk individuals may reveal factors that promote development of the disorder. At the same time, these characteristics are not obscured by the long-term consequences of the abuse of alcohol and other drugs.

Alcoholism tends to run in families (Cotton, 1979). Therefore, individuals with a family history of alcoholism are at elevated risk for developing the disorder in late adolescence and adulthood. Whether this elevated risk is environmentally or genetically mediated (or both), offspring of alcoholics may have psychological or biological characteristics that play important etiological roles in the development of alcoholism. Empirical research over the last decade has attempted to identify these potentially causative factors in high-risk individuals.

One important technique for studying at-risk individuals is to administer alcohol challenges to high- and low-risk groups. The purpose of this procedure is to determine whether high-risk individuals have deviant responses to alcohol that could begin to explain their increased risk for alcoholism. Perhaps high-risk individuals respond to alcohol differently than low-risk individuals, which could have implications for their motivation to drink. For example, high-risk individuals might experience greater euphoria from alcohol, fewer adverse reactions such as nausea or hangover, or greater tolerance for the drug. These potential characteristics have direct implications for understanding at-risk status. Although it is clear that some individuals with a family history of alcoholism are more likely to become alcoholics themselves, it is not known what increases their morbidity. This question is equally valid for genetic, environmental, and interactional models of risk.

The purpose of this article is to review those studies in which offspring of alcoholics have been administered alcohol challenges, to critically evaluate the methodologies used in this paradigm, and to offer an integrative model that attempts to resolve the many discrepancies in this literature. A methodological critique is badly needed to evaluate procedures that have been used many times in this area of investigation and have become de facto standards despite their limitations. Although model building may seem premature in this relatively new field, the literature has grown so rapidly that integrative analysis is needed to provide a focus for continuing research.

The central question in studies in which high- and low-risk individuals are challenged with alcohol has been whether individuals with a family history of alcoholism (FH+) are more or less sensitive to alcohol than subjects with no such history (FH−). In other words, the focus has been on the relative magnitude of the response to alcohol. We address this issue in our critical review of the literature, in part because this has been such an overriding theme in these studies. However, our integrative model attempts to go beyond the differential sensitivity issue to the motivational implications of these data. We argue that the motivation to drink (or to avoid negative consequences of drinking) is a key issue that may provide a theoretical link between high-risk status and final manifestation of alcoholism.

PSYCHOBIOLOGICAL MARKERS

A psychobiological marker is a characteristic, other than symptoms of the disease itself, that identifies those individuals in the population who are most likely to develop a specific disorder. This characteristic may be measured using psychological or biological means. In the case of alcoholism, it is a characteristic that can be measured in children or adolescents (before the development of the disorder) that has significant power for predicting who will and will not show alcoholic behavior in adulthood. In other words, individuals who manifest this characteristic are more likely to develop alcoholism.

How do we identify psychobiological markers of alcoholism? A direct implication of the definition of psychobiological markers is that alcoholics themselves will be much more likely than nonalcoholics to display these characteristics. However, it is possible that a result of this disorder (i.e., prolonged drinking) is to change the marker so that it is no longer measurable. For example, suppose that there is a specific neuroendocrine marker for alcoholism; individuals who possess this neuroendocrine marker are much more likely to develop alcoholism than those without this characteristic. Researchers might therefore hope to discover this marker by comparing the neuroendocrine profiles of alcoholics and nonalcoholics. However, it is possible that prolonged drinking produces toxic effects that change or obscure this marker. Assuming that the neuroendocrine characteristic plays a significant role in the etiology of alcoholism, it is plausible (if not likely) that alcohol could have both short- and long-term effects on this neuroendocrine system. Therefore, it is easy to see that other means would be needed to identify this marker.

This reasoning is equally applicable to responses to alcohol challenge. Alcoholics ought to have different responses to alcohol from nonalcoholics. If nothing else, they certainly ought to show greater tolerance for alcohol. However, this difference would not represent a psychobiological marker because it could easily be a result of prolonged drinking rather than a predisposing characteristic.

Therefore, research has been conducted with individuals at risk for alcoholism to identify characteristics that distinguish them from individuals at low risk for developing alcoholism. The rationale is the same whether the higher risk is due to genetic or environmental (or interactional) factors. Features that distinguish high- from low-risk groups may represent psychobiological markers for alcoholism. This is ultimately tested through long-term follow-up of those with and without the potential marker to determine who develops the disorder.

Alcoholism is not necessarily a single disorder with a dimensional etiology. A marker may be present for one type of alcoholism but not for other types, or multiple markers may reflect different etiological pathways. One does not have to assume that alcoholism has a single etiological pathway to justify the search for psychobiological markers. However, consideration of this issue may change the way in which results are interpreted. Similarly, a psychobiological marker for alcoholism is not necessarily specific to the disorder. The specificity question requires empirical examination of other high-risk groups (such as individuals with a family history of schizophrenia) to determine whether the marker is specific to offspring of alcoholics.

GENETIC FACTORS

There actually have been more reviews of genetic studies on alcoholism than the number of empirical studies on which the reviews comment. However, despite the large number of review articles, there have been very few critical reviews. Murray, Clifford, and Gurling (1983), Searles (1988), and Peele (1986) critically reviewed this literature and concluded that the evidence in favor of a genetic contribution to alcoholism is not strong. We briefly summarize the evidence in sufficient detail only to provide a background to alcohol-challenge studies. The high-risk paradigm does not depend on evidence for a genetic contribution to alcoholism; environmental risk is equally valid in the search for psychobiological markers for alcoholism. In addition, the study of offspring of alcoholics does not allow inferences concerning genetic versus environmental markers.

Much of the alcohol-challenge research has been motivated by evidence of genetic factors in alcoholism. Cotton (1979) reviewed evidence that alcoholism tends to run in families. She found that, of 4,329 alcoholic probands, 30.8% had an alcoholic parent, compared with 4.7% of 922 nonpsychiatric patients. This supports either genetic or environmental determination of alcoholism in many patients. Twin and adoption studies also have attempted to resolve the nature versus nurture question.

Overall drinking behavior, including normal social drinking, was reported to be significantly heritable in three studies of Scandinavian twins (Kaij, 1960; Kaprio et al., 1987; Partanen, Bruun, & Markkanen, 1966). However, in two other large twin studies, cited by Gurling, Murray, and Clifford (1981), no evidence was found for the heritability of normal drinking. Alcoholism concordance rates in twins were examined in four studies; Hrubec and Omenn (1981) and Kaij (1960) found evidence of significant heritability, whereas Gurling et al. (1981) and Partanen et al. (1966) found no such evidence. Differences in methodology and subject criteria may have contributed to the disparate results. However, in the two largest studies, Hrubec and Omenn (1981) and Partanen et al. (1966) found significant evidence for the heritability of alcoholism and overall drinking pattern, respectively.

The rationale behind adoption studies is that these designs allow separate relative measures of genetic and environmental components. Two large studies of northern European subjects with matched control groups (Bohman, 1978; Goodwin, Schulsinger, Hermansen, Guze, & Winokur, 1973) found alcoholism to be more common in adopted sons of alcoholics (SOAs) than in sons of nonalcoholics (SONAs). Both studies have been criticized on various grounds. Data for Bohman's entire adoptee population were presented in a later publication (Cloninger, Bohman, & Sigvardsson, 1981). When these data were presented in the format of Goodwin et al. (1973), the proband and control groups did not differ in alcoholism rates. Goodwin et al. (1973) found alcoholism in a significantly higher proportion of adopted SOAs, but heavy and problem drinking were more common among SONAs. When definitional criteria were redistributed to agree with common conceptions of alcoholism (including almost every study to be cited in this review), no significant differences remained between groups.

In two smaller studies of half-siblings raised with or without an alcoholic parent, Goodwin et al. (1974) and Schuckit, Goodwin, and Winokur (1972) both found that alcoholism rates were not increased significantly by living with the alcoholic parent. Together, these twin, adoption, and half-sibling studies suggest a strong hereditary component to alcoholism. On critical examination, however, the evidence appears less strong.

The widely cited conclusion that SOAs are 3 to 5 times more likely to become alcoholic may not reflect genetic factors. However, even if it were a valid estimate, this would indicate much lower genetic loading to alcoholism than, for example, schizophrenia. Offspring of schizophrenics are approximately 12.3 times more likely to develop schizophrenia than are offspring of nonschizophrenics (Faraone & Tsuang, 1985). Apparently, the genetic hypothesis for alcoholism does not account for a large proportion of the variance no matter what estimates are used, and the risk ratio can give a very misleading representation of the strength of the effect.

DEFINITIONAL ISSUES

One approach to the definitional problems (American Psychiatric Association, 1980; National Council on Alcoholism, 1972) noted earlier is to examine the alcoholic behavior found to be heritable in the genetic studies. Cloninger et al. (1981) described two forms of alcoholism on the basis of a multivariate analysis of their complete male adoptee data. Type 1, or milieu-limited, alcoholism usually was mild (only one registration for alcohol abuse) and, depending on the postnatal environment, could become severe (with hospitalization or treatment required). Type 2, or male-limited, alcoholism was moderate (two or three registrations for alcohol abuse, no treatment) and independent of environmental influence. There was an apparent logical problem with this formulation, however, because this moderate and highly heritable form of alcoholism usually occurred in sons of fathers with severe and extensively treated alcoholism (Cloninger, 1983). Moreover, Cloninger et al. reported that sons with severe alcoholism tended to have fathers with mild alcoholism, which they suggested is a less strictly heritable form of alcoholism. Public registration data is biased by the presence of antisocial behavior in both the fathers and sons. Antisocial behavior is much more likely to be called to the attention of authorities, so that it is more likely to be represented in the register.

Goodwin et al. (1973), on the other hand, found that heavy and problem drinking did not significantly differentiate adopted SOAs and adopted SONAs. Only alcoholism, determined by very strict and severe criteria, was found to be inherited. The limitations of Goodwin et al.'s study have already been discussed, and because of the small numbers and lack of replication, these results should not be overinterpreted. Nevertheless, Goodwin et al.'s results indicate a categorical difference in heritability between alcoholism with two (or fewer) related problems and alcoholism with three (or more) related problems. Cloninger et al. (1981) reported the highest heritability in a group roughly similar to the problem drinkers of Goodwin et al.'s study, although there was a higher percentage of problem drinkers among the control subjects than among the SOAs (14% vs. 19%) in the latter study.

One additional point should be mentioned before leaving this topic. Abel and Lee (1988) found that exposing rat sires to alcohol led to changes in offspring behavior. This raises the thorny issue of whether the heritable component of alcoholism is really due to genetic transmission in the traditional sense of the term or to changes in the sperm of the father resulting from exposure to alcohol. It is also possible that both effects are present. This issue requires further research before firm conclusions can be drawn. The implications of these results, if replicated, are that it may be necessary to study the grandsons of alcoholics when the father is not alcoholic. Another approach would be to restrict FH+ groups to individuals with alcoholic brothers and sisters rather than parents. These studies have not yet been performed.

Alcohol-challenge studies with the sons and daughters of alcoholics have had scientific influence beyond their number, in part because the results have been accepted without consideration of the theoretical and methodological assumptions made in this research paradigm. In this section, we summarize those studies in which SOAs (and one study of daughters of alcoholics) were given alcohol in challenge doses so that deviant responses in the high-risk group could be measured. The types of measures that have been used in these studies include blood alcohol concentration (BAC), acetaldehyde levels, other biochemical measures, electroencephalography (EEG), self-reported intoxication, static ataxia (body sway), other motor and cognitive measures, and a range of autonomic measures.

A central focus for this research paradigm has been the question of whether offspring of alcoholics are more or less sensitive to the effect of alcohol. The results on this question have been remarkably inconsistent, particularly because, at first glance, this seems to be a simple and straightforward question. Whether the offspring of alcoholics are more sensitive to alcohol is an important conceptual issue for which integrative analyses are needed. A summary of studies focusing on this issue is presented in Table 1.

Blood Alcohol Concentration

Schuckit (1981) hypothesized that alcohol metabolism is under genetic control and measured peak BAC in nonalcoholic college men who were FH+ ($n = 20$) or FH− ($n = 20$). In this and other studies, Schuckit used criteria similar to those of the *Diagnostic and Statistical Manual of Mental Disorders* (3rd ed.; American Psychiatric Association, 1980) without tolerance or withdrawal requirements. The groups were matched for demography, drinking history, and height:weight ratio. Subjects were administered 0.75 mg/kg of 95% ethanol, and BAC was measured regularly with blood drawn from a venous catheter for 5 hr. Blood alcohol curves for the two groups were almost identical. A review of other studies in which BAC was measured in SOAs revealed no group differences in average or peak BAC in any study (Lipscomb & Nathan, 1980; O'Malley & Maisto, 1985; Pollock et al., 1983a; Schuckit, 1984a, 1984b, 1985a; Schuckit, O'Connor, Duby, Vega, & Moss, 1981; Schuckit, Parker, & Rossman, 1983). Lex, Lukas, Greenwald, and Mendelson (1988) reported no significant differences in BAC between FH+ and FH− women given 0.56 g/kg alcohol.

Utne, Hansen, Winkler, and Schulsinger (1977) measured alcohol elimination rate in adoptees from the Danish adoption study (Goodwin et al., 1973). Ten SOAs were randomly selected, and 10 SONAs were matched for age and age at adoption. A dose between 0.27 and 0.36 g/kg

TABLE 1
Summaries of Alcohol-Challenge Studies

Study	Sample	N	Measure	SOA vs. SONA
Schuckit (1981)	College students	SOA = 20 SONA = 20	BAC	ns
Lex, Lukas, Greenwald, & Mendelson (1988)	Women	DOA = 6 DONA = 6	BAC	ns
Utne, Hansen, Winkler, & Schulsinger (1977)	General population	SOA = 10 SONA = 10	Alcohol elimination	ns
Schuckit & Rayses (1979)	College students	SOA = 20 SONA = 20	Acetaldehyde	SOA greater
Schuckit & Duby (1982)	College students	SOA = 30 SONA = 30	Flushing	SOA greater
Behar et al. (1983)	General population (8–15 yrs old)	SOA = 11 SONA = 11	Acetaldehyde, cortisol, norepinephrine, beta-endorphin	ns
Schuckit, Shaskan, Duby, Vega, & Moss (1982)	College students	SOA = 11 SONA = 11	Monoamine oxidase activity	ns
Schuckit, O'Connor, Duby, Vega, & Moss (1981)	College students	SOA = 22 SONA = 22	Dopamine-B-hydroxylase	ns
Schuckit (1984a)	College students	SOA = 20 SONA = 20	Cortisol	SOA less
Schuckit, Gold, & Risch (1987b)	College students	SOA = 30 SONA = 30	Cortisol	SOA less
Moss, Yao, & Maddock (1989)	College students	SOA = 10 SONA = 10	Cortisol	ns
Schuckit, Parker, & Rossman (1983)	College students	SOA = 44 SONA = 44	Prolactin	SOA less
Schuckit, Gold, & Risch (1987a)	College students	SOA = 30 SONA = 30	Prolactin	SOA less
Schuckit, Risch, & Gold (1988)	College students	SOA = 18 SONA = 18	Adrenocorticotropic hormone	SOA less

Table continues

TABLE 1 (*Continued*)

Study	Sample	N	Measure	SOA vs. SONA
Swartz, Drews, & Cadoret (1987)	Adoptees	SOA = 17 SONA = 12	Epinephrine	SOA greater (stress induced)
Newlin & Thomson (1990), Exp. 1	College students	SOA = 9 SONA = 9	Autonomic	SOA greater
Newlin & Thomson (1990), Exp. 2	College students	SOA = 11 SONA = 14 SONA = 10	Autonomic	SOA greater
Schuckit, Engstrom, Alpert, & Duby (1981)	College students	SOA = 20 SONA = 20	Electromyograph	SOA greater
Lipscomb, Carpenter, & Nathan (1979), Exp. 1	College students	SOA = 12 SONA = 12	Static ataxia	ns
Lipscomb & Nathan (1980)	College students	SOA = 12 SONA = 12	Static ataxia	ns
O'Malley & Maisto (1985)	College students	SOA = 24 SONA = 24	Static ataxia	ns
Schuckit (1985a)	College students	SOA = 34 SONA = 34	Static ataxia	SOA less
Newlin & Thomson (1990), Exp. 2	College students	SOA = 11 SONA = 14	Static ataxia	SOA greater
Lex, Lukas, Greenwald, & Men- delson (1988)	Women	DOA = 6 DONA = 6	Static ataxia	DOA less
Lipscomb & Nathan (1980)	College students	SOA = 12 SONA = 12	Intoxication	ns
Schuckit (1980c)	College students	SOA = 20 SONA = 20	Intoxication	SOA less
Schuckit (1984b)	College students	SOA = 20 SONA = 20	Intoxication	SOA less
Schuckit (1985a)	College students	SOA = 34 SONA = 34	Intoxication	ns
O'Malley & Maisto (1985)	College students	SOA = 24 SONA = 24	Intoxication	SOA less

Study	Population	Group (n)	Measure	Result
Vogel-Sprott & Chipperfield (1987)	College students	SOA = 21 SONA = 22	Intoxication	ns
Moss, Yao, & Maddock (1989)	College students	SOA = 10 SONA = 10	Intoxication	SOA less
Finn & Pihl (1987)	College students	SOA = 24 SONA = 12	Intoxication	ns
Lex, Lukas, Greenwald, & Mendelson (1988)	Women	DOA = 6 DONA = 6	Intoxication	ns
Kaplan, Hesselbrock, O'Connor, & Depalma (1988)	General population	SOA = 25 SONA = 24	Intoxication	SOA greater
Nagoshi & Wilson (1987)	College students	SOA = 35 SONA = 35	Intoxication	SOA greater
Moss, Yao, & Maddock (1989)	College students	SOA = 10 SONA = 10	Mood	SOA greater
Pollock et al. (1983)	General population	SOA = 31 SONA = 17	EEG alpha	SOA greater
Elmasian, Neville, Woods, Schuckit, & Bloom (1982)	General population	SOA = 15 SONA = 15	P300 amplitude and latency	SOA less
Schuckit, Gold, Croot, Finn, & Polich (1988)	College students	SOA = 21 SONA = 21	P300 latency	SOA less
Kaplan, Hesselbrock, O'Connor, & Depalma (1988)	General population	SOA = 25 SONA = 24	EEG alpha	ns
Vogel-Sprott & Chipperfield (1987)	College students	SOA = 21 SONA = 22	Motor tasks	SOA greater
Nagoshi & Wilson (1987)	College students	SOA = 35 SONA = 35	Motor tasks	ns
Levenson, Oyama, & Meek (1987)	College students	SOA = 112 SONA = 131	Stress-response dampening	SOA greater
Finn & Pihl (1987)	College students	SOA = 24 SONA = 12	Stress-response dampening	SOA greater
Swartz, Drews, & Cadoret (1987)	Adoptees	SOA = 17 SONA = 12	Stress-response dampening (epinephrine)	SOA greater

Note. SOA = son of alcoholic parents; SONA = son of nonalcoholic parents; BAC = blood alcohol concentration; DOA = daughter of alcoholic parents; DONA = daughter of nonalcoholic parents; EEG = electroencephalograph.

ethanol was administered intravenously, and alcohol elimination rate was calculated from the linear portion of the blood alcohol curve. No significant differences were found.

Lipscomb and Nathan (1980) examined 24 college men who were light or heavy drinkers and FH+ or FH−. The criteria for alcoholism were (a) the subject received medical treatment for alcoholism and (b) the subject was considered alcoholic by medical or religious authorities. Subjects were rewarded for accuracy in estimating BAC while receiving a programmed series of drinks. No group differences were found in the accuracy of BAC estimation for any session.

Acetaldehyde

Although it is relatively clear that SOAs and SONAs do not differ in BAC following consumption of alcohol, it is possible that they differ in terms of metabolites of alcohol. Schuckit and Rayses (1979) examined acetaldehyde levels in college students with ($n = 20$) and without ($n = 20$) first-degree relatives with alcoholism. Acetaldehyde, a metabolite of ethanol, causes facial flushing and nausea in many Asians (Harada, Agarwal, Goedde, Tagaki, & Ishikawa, 1982; Newlin, 1989; Wolff, 1972). It is not clear what characteristics of acetaldehyde buildup or facial flushing are protective against the development of alcoholism in Asians who flush in response to alcohol (Newlin, 1989). In contrast, Schuckit and Rayses (1979) suggested that acetaldehyde may mediate short-term effects of alcohol, such as heightened subjective intoxication. This apparent contradiction has not been resolved. Schuckit and Rayses (1979) gave their subjects 0.5 ml/kg 95% ethanol and mixer and measured acetaldehyde from blood samples taken at baseline and every 30 min for 180 min. Following alcohol administration, FH+ subjects had significantly higher acetaldehyde concentrations than did FH− subjects.

Shortly after publication of the Schuckit and Rayses (1979) study, Ericksson (1980) criticized their methodology and suggested that their results were based on mainly artifactually formed acetaldehyde. Subsequently, Schuckit and Duby (1982) assessed acetaldehyde concentrations with a method that had been modified to include Eriksson's (1980) suggestions for avoiding artifact. Schuckit and Duby (1982) compared 30 FH+ and a matched group of 30 FH− nonalcoholic college men. The procedure, described previously, involved administration of 0.59 g/kg 95% ethanol with mixer; blood samples were taken regularly for 5 hr. In addition, facial flushing was measured by ear plethysmograph and by observation (a technician, blind to experimental condition, using an ad hoc 7-point scale). Despite methodological problems, significantly more FH+ subjects (39%) than FH− subjects (13%) showed plethysmograph-measured flushing increases of 50% or more up to 60 min after consuming alcohol. Data were not presented more clearly for groups. A significant positive correlation ($r = .88$) was reported between observational flushing measured for 90 min and acetaldehyde levels for all 60 subjects. The two flushing measures, however, were not correlated. Schuckit and Duby admitted that "absolute acetaldehyde values are uncertain because of disagreements in the literature about methodology" (p. 417).

One other group of researchers (Behar et al., 1983) measured acetaldehyde in SOAs ($n = 11$) and SONAs ($n = 11$). Behar et al. recruited the children of hospitalized alcoholics who met the Feighner et al. (1972) criteria for primary alcoholism. SOAs and sons of parents with no family history of alcohol or psychiatric disorder were catheterized for blood samples and administered a drink containing 0.5 ml/kg ethanol. Breath and blood acetaldehyde were measured repeatedly for several hours, as were plasma cortisol, norepinephrine, epinephrine, and beta-endorphin levels. Behar et al. (1983) reported that blood acetaldehyde levels were not significantly different for the two groups at baseline or after consuming alcohol. Blood and breath acetaldehyde values were not correlated with each other. No significant differences between groups were found for plasma epinephrine, norepinephrine, cortisol, or beta-endorphin.

To summarize, the finding of equivalent BACs in SOAs and SONAs has been a very consistent one in this literature. Apparently, SOAs and SONAs do not differ in the pharmacokinetics of alcohol. Results concerning acetaldehyde must be considered highly tentative given the difficulty in measurement and failures to replicate.

Serum Biochemical Measures

Schuckit, Shaskan, Duby, Vega, and Moss (1982) measured platelet monoamine oxidase (MAO) activity after alcohol administration in nonalcoholic college men. Fifteen SOAs were matched with 15 SONAs on demographics, height:weight ratio, and drinking history. Subjects were screened for drug abuse and affective disorder. After fasting overnight, subjects were catheterized and given 0.59 g/kg ethanol with mixer. Platelet MAO activity was measured at baseline and 180 min after drinking. No significant group differences were found for baseline or 180-min blood MAO values.

Another enzyme, dopamine-B-hydroxylase (DBH), is also thought to be important in regulation of mood states and psychiatric disorders. Schuckit, O'Connor, et al. (1981) compared 22 FH+ nonalcoholic college men and a matched sample of FH− nonalcoholic men. After an overnight fast, subjects were catheterized and tested for DBH level by a technician blind to group. Subjects then drank 0.59 g/kg 95% ethanol and mixer, and blood samples were drawn every 30 min for 180 min. DBH levels at baseline and 180 min were analyzed, and no significant differences between groups were found. Post hoc correlational analyses fielded a significant positive relationship between drinks or drinking day and DBH level in FH+ men, which ran counter to experimental hypotheses.

Plasma cortisol was measured by Schuckit (1984a) for 20 pairs of nonalcoholic college men. Subjects with alcoholic first-degree relatives and matched subjects with no alcoholic first-degree relatives were catheterized after an overnight fast and given a drink containing 0.59 g/kg 95% ethanol. Venous blood was sampled at baseline and regularly for several hours. The groups differed significantly at 15, 30, 240, 270, and 300 min after alcohol consumption, with FH+ subjects lower in plasma cortisol. When data were analyzed as percent change from baseline, group differences were significant only at 240, 270, and 300 min after consumption. Schuckit did not rule out possible circadian changes in cortisol levels as an alternative explanation for the group differences.

Schuckit, Gold, and Risch (1987b) replicated these results in a later study that was placebo controlled. Following placebo, FH+ subjects had smaller increases in cortisol levels, which were significant only at 30 min after consumption. There were very small differences between groups at the low (0.75 ml/kg) ethanol dose, but larger differences at 90, 120, 150, and 180 min after consumption for the high ethanol dose. In this same study (Schuckit et al., 1987b), prolactin differences were greatest at the low ethanol dose.

Moss, Yao, and Maddock (1989) attempted to replicate Schuckit's cortisol results with 10 SOAs and 10 SONAs. They found no differences in cortisol levels as BAC rose or as it fell. Because the sample was so small, this may not represent a failure to replicate.

Serum prolactin (PRL) levels were measured in SOAs and controls in two studies. PRL, an anterior pituitary hormone, has been found to be elevated in chronic alcoholics (e.g., Van Theil & Lester, 1976). Schuckit et al. (1983) administered 0.59 g/kg 95% ethanol to 44 FH+ and 44 matched FH− nonalcoholic college men. The methodology was the same as for Schuckit (1984a), and samples were collected regularly for 4 hr after alcohol administration. Post hoc analyses found the two groups to differ significantly at 150 min after ethanol administration, with FH+ subjects showing lower PRL levels. This effect was replicated in a second experiment that included a placebo control (Schuckit, Gold, & Risch, 1987a) with 30 FH+ and 30 matched FH− subjects. In three separate sessions, each beginning at 9:00 a.m., subjects drank a placebo, 0.75 ml/kg ethanol, and 1.1 ml/kg ethanol, in random order, and blood was drawn every 30 min for 180 min. Thirty and 60 min after alcohol consumption, levels of PRL following the low dose were lower among FH+ subjects than among FH− subjects; following the higher dose, PRL levels were lower for FH+ subjects at 90, 120, and 150 min. There were no significant differences for placebo.

In an effort to determine whether the neuroendocrine differences in response to alcohol between SOAs and SONAs are due to central rather than peripheral events, Schuckit, Risch, and Gold (1988) assayed adrenocorticotropic hormone (ACTH) in 18 matched pairs of SOAs and SONAs. SOAs had lower levels of ACTH approximately 90 to 180 min after drinking the higher dose of alcohol (1.1 ml/kg).

In multivariate analysis (Schuckit, Risch, & Gold, 1988) of the same cortisol and PRL data from the earlier study (Schuckit et al., 1987a, 1987b), stepwise discriminant analysis revealed that maximum "terrible" feelings on the Subjective High Assessment Scale (SHAS; Judd et al., 1987) explained the most variance, followed by maximum low-dose PRL level, maximum high-dose cortisol level, and 210-min high-dose cortisol level. Not surprisingly, these same variables exhibited significant classification rates in a jackknife procedure. Seventy percent of the FH+ and 83% of the FH− subjects were correctly classified into their respective groups. In a principal-components analysis of the data, the subjective high measures segregated differently from the biochemical measures, although the first three factors significantly discriminated between groups.

The findings concerning stress hormones (particularly prolactin and cortisol) have been relatively consistent from Schuckit's laboratory. SOAs appear to have greater acute tolerance to alcohol (i.e., more rapid recovery from alcohol-induced changes) in relation to these neuroendocrine measures. Whether the greatest difference between SOAs and SONAs has been at the high or low dose has been less consistent. The differences in these hormones have typically been found well after alcohol was administered, usually from one to several hours after drinking. Moss et al.'s (1989) apparent failure to replicate is consistent with the high variability of these measures and does not seriously challenge the earlier results.

Electroencephalography

Pollock et al. (1983) reported EEG results from a subset of their longitudinal high-risk sample after the administration of 0.5 g/kg of 95% ethanol in currant juice. EEG data were collected from 31 SOAs and 17 control subjects in groups that did not differ in weekly alcohol consumption or in mean BAC. There were no overall main effects for risk, but SOAs showed significantly greater increases than controls in slow alpha energy at 30 min and 120 min after drinking. Decreases in fast alpha energy were found for both groups 30 and 60 min after drinking. Differences in mean alpha activity (combined fast and slow alpha) were significantly greater for SOAs at 30, 60, and 120 min after drinking for all scalp locations except the left occipital. Results including subjects previously dropped because of incomplete data suggested that the differences in mean alpha frequency were localized to the right and posterior scalp regions. Pollock et al. suggested that the changes in alpha frequency after alcohol consumption may reflect SOAs increased sensitivity to alcohol's effects.

Kaplan, Hesselbrock, O'Connor, and Depalma (1988) studied EEG responses to alcohol (two 12 oz. beers) in 25 SOAs and 24 SONAs. Both groups showed increases in alpha activity after drinking; there were no significant differences between groups. However, for SOAs, alpha activity was correlated with desire to drink alcohol, but for SONAs, it was correlated with perceived intoxication.

Using a weak criterion for primary alcoholism ("if drinking behavior interfered with his marriage or job"), Elmasian, Neville, Woods, Schuckit, and Bloom (1982) compared 15 SOAs and 15 SONAs matched for drinking habits, height:weight ratio, age, sex, and socioeconomic status. Each group was divided into three subgroups of 5 subjects each, who received either a placebo, a low-dose alcoholic drink (0.59 g/kg), or a high-dose alcoholic drink (0.94 g/kg), administered early in the morning after fasting. Subjects were asked to press a button in response to a target tone, and event-related potentials were recorded. For SOAs, both alcohol and placebo caused reduced amplitude and increased latency of response. The differences between groups were significant even though alcohol reduced the amplitude of the P300 component in both groups. SOAs were also less accurate at identifying target stimuli. It should be noted that the groups were extremely small in this study.

In a more recent study, Schuckit, Gold, Croot, Finn, and Polich (1988) found no differences in P300 latency between 21 FH+ and 21 FH− subjects after placebo or 0.75 ml/kg alcohol doses. However, FH+ subjects demonstrated a more rapid return to baseline in P300 latency after drinking the high (1.1 ml/kg) dose of alcohol (measured at 240 min).

The results with EEGs have been very tentative. Clearly, more research is needed before drawing conclusions concerning differences between SOAs and SONAs in terms of EEG responses to an alcohol challenge. This is potentially fertile ground for research.

Static Ataxia

Alcohol causes a robust increase in static ataxis, or body sway (Moskowitz, Daily, & Henderson, 1974). Static ataxia has been measured with a rope-and-pulley system to which subjects are connected with a harness. Measurements are made while the subject is standing, with eyes open or eyes closed.

Static ataxia has been used as a measure of motor performance in a number of studies of SOAs. Lipscomb, Carpenter, and Nathan (1979, Exp. 1) selected 12 male FH+ subjects whose first- or second-degree relatives had been treated for alcoholism or who were considered alcoholic by religious or medical authorities. Twelve male FH− subjects were matched for drinking pattern. Light and problem drinkers were excluded. Subjects were administered a series of drinks programmed to yield a peak BAC of 0.08%. Twice before and six times after alcohol consumption, body sway was measured by the movement of ropes attached to the subject's back and side while he stood with eyes open. FH+ subjects swayed significantly more than FH− subjects at baseline, although postdrinking sway showed no group differences when baseline scores were used as a covariate.

Lipscomb et al. (1979, Exp. 2) reported further data obtained from unselected and unmatched subjects. Twenty-one FH+ and 46 FH− subjects were exposed to the same drinking procedure, but sway was measured with subjects' eyes closed as well as open. FH+ subjects swayed significantly more than FH− subjects with eyes closed but not with eyes open, apparently at baseline.

Lipscomb and Nathan (1980) administered low, moderate, or high doses of alcohol to 12 FH+ and 12 FH− subjects who were heavy or light drinkers. Body sway was measured with subjects' eyes open (the same method that Lipscomb et al. (1979) used) but was collected only in the first session. No group differences were found.

Schuckit (1985a), in a study of 34 FH+ and 34 FH− nonalcoholic college men, measured body sway after placebo, low (0.75 ml/kg) or high (1.1 ml/kg) doses of alcohol. Schuckit measured body sway with the method of Lipscomb et al. (1979); subjects' eyes were open. Schuckit measured each subject three times for each measurement period and averaged the results. No significant group differences were found for baseline or placebo measurements, but FH+ subjects showed significantly less sway than FH− subjects 135 min after a low dose of alcohol. The difference was not significant for the high-alcohol dose. In an apparent attempt to replicate this effect, Schuckit and Gold (1988) found the low-dose body-sway measurement to be weakly related to familial history of alcoholism and entered the measurement after a number of other biochemical measures in a jackknife classification procedure. Body-sway results for both the low and high doses were found on the second factor to emerge in a principal-components analysis, and this factor accounted for 14% of the variance.

Newlin and Thomson (1990) recorded the static ataxia of 11 SOAs and 14 SONAs on a stabilometer board before alcohol consumption and as BAC increased during four separate sessions with 0.5 g/kg alcohol. SOAs showed greater alcohol-induced increases in static ataxia in the first and second (but not the third and fourth) sessions with alcohol.

One pilot study of women differing in family history of alcoholism has been reported. Lex et al. (1988) studied 6 FH+ and 6 FH− women who were given 0.56 g/kg ethanol; body sway was measured on a stabilometer platform. FH− women had significantly lower sway scores at a number of measurement points following alcohol consumption.

In summary, the results with static ataxia have been promising but inconsistent. Because static ataxia is a very reliable measure of the effect of alcohol, it would seem to be an appropriate measure for family-history studies. However, the methodology may be inadequate to yield consistent results across different laboratories. We would particularly expect different results from rope-and-pulley systems and stabilometer measures of static ataxia. A further complication is that the static ataxia measures may not differentiate between inner ear disturbances and the hyperactivity (or hypoactivity) caused by alcohol. Methodological research is needed to improve these measurement systems before definitive research can be carried out.

Subjective Responses to Alcohol

Schuckit (1980c) examined self-ratings of intoxication in 20 FH+ and a matched control group of 20 FH− nonalcoholic college men. After fasting and catheterization, subjects received 0.59 g/kg 95% ethanol. The SHAS, consisting of positive and negative adjectives relevant to mood, was administered every 30 min for 180 min after alcohol consumption. FH+ subjects reported significantly less subjective intoxication than did controls on both the SHAS and a 10-point ad hoc scale of "feeling high." However, FH− men had significantly higher BACs 60 min after drinking. Almost all of the SHAS items on which FH− subjects rated themselves significantly higher were positive in tone (e.g., "sexy," "joyful," "enjoy self," etc.).

Schuckit (1984b) later reexamined subjective intoxication after placebo, low, or high doses of alcohol. Matched groups of 20 FH+ and FH− nonalcoholic college men were examined using the methodology described for Schuckit (1980c), except that they received the three different levels of alcohol in three randomly ordered sessions. Subjects completed an ad hoc questionnaire before the first session, describing how they expected to feel after receiving alcohol. After drinking, they used a 36-point scale to indicate drug effect and intoxication at regular intervals for 4 hr. The two groups were similar in their expectations of intoxication level. No group differences were found for subjective intoxication after drinking a placebo beverage. For the low dose of alcohol (0.59 ml/kg 95% ethanol), mean self-ratings of drug effect and intoxication were lower for FH+ subjects. The group differences for the high dose (1.1 ml/kg) were not significant. Schuckit provided an interesting hypothesis for the findings, namely, that FH+ individuals do not accurately perceive intoxication until they are drunk and intoxication has become obvious.

Schuckit (1985a) again assessed subjective intoxication in a study of body sway in 34 FH+ and a matched group of 34 FH− nonalcoholic college men. The procedures were identical to those reported in Schuckit

(1984b), with the addition of the body sway assessment. Results showed that, for the high-alcohol dose, ratings of intoxication correlated positively ($r = .30$) with body sway and that, for FH+ subjects, body sway correlated negatively ($r = -.28$) with number of alcoholic relatives.

In a later multivariate analysis of various responses to an alcohol challenge, Schuckit and Gold (1988) found that maximum terrible feelings after the high dose of alcohol was the best single independent discriminator between FH+ and FH− men and that maximum terrible feelings loaded highly on the first factor in a principal-components analysis; this factor accounted for 46% of the total variance.

Another assessment of subjective intoxication in SOAs was conducted by O'Malley and Maisto (1985). Twenty-four nonalcoholic college-student SOAs and a matched group of 24 SONAs were examined. Diagnostic criteria for parental primary alcoholism were the same as in Schuckit (1980c), with the additional requirement of treatment for alcoholism. All subjects were moderate to heavy drinkers. Subjects in each group received placebo, a low dose (1.3 ml/kg), or a high dose (2.58 ml/kg) of 80 proof alcohol. Perceived intoxication (indicated on an 8-point scale), mood, and internal sensations were self-reported on two separate occasions after drinking. No group differences were found on measures of estimated quantity of alcohol consumed or expected effects of alcohol. Regardless of dose (including placebo), SOAs reported feeling significantly less intoxicated than did SONAs and reported less behavioral impairment at peak BAC. Two of six factors from the Sensation Scale, "central stimulant" and "anesthetic" were self-reported lower by SOAs. In a post hoc multiple regression analysis, O'Malley and Maisto found that scores on the preassessment of expectancy accounted for more of the variance in self-reports of intoxication in SOAs than in SONAs and that BAC contributed equally to both groups.

Vogel-Sprott and Chipperfield (1987) found no differences in self-reported intoxication between 21 FH+ men and 22 FH− men after they consumed 0.83 ml/kg of alcohol. Nagoshi and Wilson (1987) studied the responses of 35 FH+ and 35 matched FH− men on a host of measures when BAC was maintained at a plateau of approximately 0.10 g/dl for several hours. Contrary to prediction, FH+ subjects had significantly greater self-reported and tester-rated intoxication scores than FH− subjects. However, FH+ subjects also had significantly higher BACs than FH− subjects at some time points, and the significant intoxication comparisons represented 4 of 83 separate t tests.

Finn and Pihl (1987) found no significant differences in self-reported intoxication in 12 FH− men, 12 SOAs, and 12 SOAs with an alcoholic grandparent. However, there was a nonsignificant trend for higher risk subjects to report lower intoxication after drinking a 1.32 ml/kg dose of alcohol.

In Lex et al.'s (1988) pilot study of 6 FH+ and 6 FH− women, there were no significant differences on the SHAS. Moss et al. (1989) found that SOAs reported lower levels of intoxication in the descending limb of the BAC curve after drinking placebo, low, and high doses of alcohol. After both alcohol doses, SOAs reported nonsignificantly higher levels of intoxication while BAC rose. SOAs also reported greater confusion, less vigor, and more anger than SONAs after the high dose of alcohol. These effects were found in both the ascending and descending limbs of the BAC curves. Kaplan et al. (1988) found in their EEG study that SOAs reported greater intoxication than SONAs immediately after drinking alcohol, although there were no significant differences 30 min after drinking.

It is difficult to summarize the intoxication results because they have been very inconsistent in different laboratories. Resolution of this discrepancy requires consideration of the time in which the measurements were made, an issue discussed later in relation to our integrative model.

Motor or Muscle Responses

Motor or muscle performance has been assessed in several studies. Schuckit, Engstrom, Alpert, and Duby (1981) measured muscle-tension response to ethanol in 20 SOAs and a matched group of 20 SONAs. Electromyographic recordings (EMGs) with frontal placement were made at baseline and regularly for several hours after subjects drank 0.59 g/kg 95% ethanol. Recordings made at rest and during a task did not differ between groups at baseline, but SOAs had significantly lower resting EMGs 15 min after alcohol administration.

Vogel-Sprott and Chipperfield (1987) compared 21 SOAs and 22 SONAs on bead-stringing and hand-steadiness tasks before and after they drank 0.83 ml/kg alcohol. After drinking, SOAs were more impaired on the hand-steadiness measure and on a bead-stringing task during both the rising and falling blood alcohol curves. Nagoshi and Wilson (1987) found essentially no differences between 36 SOAs and 36 SONAs on a large battery of cognitive and motor tasks given following consumption of alcohol.

Chronic Tolerance

Newlin and Thomson (1990) studied the development of chronic tolerance during the rising blood alcohol curve in SOAs and SONAs. In a preliminary study, 9 college-age SOAs and 9 SONAs were selected on the basis of self-report data they provided about their biological fathers. Doses of 0.5 g/kg alcohol were administered on three separate days, and placebo was administered on a fourth day. A range of autonomic measures were recorded continuously before drinking and during the rising blood alcohol curve. Although there were no significant differences between groups in the first session, SOAs tended to develop sensitization (reverse tolerance) across sessions, whereas SONAs showed tolerance. These trends were significant for finger-pulse amplitude, finger temperature, and skin conductance. There were no significant differences in responses to the placebo challenge in the last session. In a replication study, 11 SOAs and 14 SONAs selected through the same procedures received 0.5 g/kg alcohol in four sessions and placebo in the fifth. SOAs became sensitized to alcohol across sessions (as reflected by pulse transit time), and showed greater development of chronic tolerance to alcohol-induced increases in static ataxia (measured with a stabilometer). In the first and second sessions, SOAs showed significantly greater alcohol-induced increases in static ataxia than SONAs, but SOAs showed no increases in static ataxia in the third and fourth sessions. SONAs tended to have a greater decrease in heart rate in response to the placebo. Newlin and Thompson (1990) interpreted the tolerance and sensitization results in terms of potential differences between SOAs' and SONAs' hedonic responses to alcohol during the rising blood alcohol curve.

Stress-Response Dampening

Stress-response dampening refers to the tendency of alcohol to reduce the magnitude of responses to a stressful challenge presented after alcohol has been administered (Levenson, Sher, Grossman, Newman, & Newlin, 1980). If stress-response dampening is greater in SOAs than SONAs, then alcohol has a greater effect on these high-risk individuals, and it can be concluded that SOAs are more sensitive to alcohol in this paradigm.

Levenson, Oyama, and Meek (1987) selected 112 FH+ men and women and 131 FH− men and women for a stress response dampening study with 1.0 g/kg alcohol and either a public speaking or threat of shock stressor. The FH+ group showed a significantly greater decrease in pulse transit time (to the ear) in response to both stressors under alcohol, and FH+ men showed significantly greater decreases in general motor activity in response to the shock stressor under alcohol. In the placebo condition, the response to the stressors did not differ according to familial history.

In a similar study, Finn and Pihl (1987) selected 12 FH− subjects, 12 SOAs with nonalcoholic grandparents, and 12 SOAs with one alcoholic grandparent. Alcohol (1.32 ml/kg) was administered before a signaled shock stressor. SOAs in the highest risk group showed a significantly larger increase in heart rate in response to alcohol and to the stressor without alcohol. Similarly, alcohol significantly decreased digital pulse volume to a greater extent in SOAs with an alcoholic grandparent and digital pulse volume showed a significantly greater decrease to alcohol in this group. More important, the responses of heart rate and digital pulse volume to the stressor were significantly dampened in the SOAs with an alcoholic grandparent in the alcohol condition.

Swartz, Drews, and Cadoret (1987) selected 17 FH+ male and female adoptees and 12 matched FH− adoptees. Epinephrine excretion in urine was measured at baseline, following a videogame stressor, and after subjects drank 0.5 ml/kg alcohol. Resting levels of epinephrine were significantly lower in FH+ individuals, and the stress-induced increase in epinephrine excretion was slightly (nonsignificantly) greater under the effect of alcohol. More important, the stress-induced increase was significantly greater in FH− subjects than in FH+ subjects, though Swartz et al. did not test the interaction reflecting a potentially greater stress-response dampening effect in the FH+ group.

The stress-response dampening studies have been relatively consistent. After consuming alcohol, SOAs show greater reductions in autonomic stress response than do SONAs. Sher and Levenson (1982) and Levenson et al. (1987) found that individuals selected on the basis of personality predictors of alcoholism also showed greater stress-response dampening than subjects without this personality risk.

METHODOLOGICAL ISSUES

Statistical Power

The statistical power of the high-risk design can be calculated. Statistical power has been calculated for a similar design, the familial–sporadic design in psychiatric epidemiology. Eaves, Kendler, and Schulz (1986) made a series of genetic and statistical assumptions about research designs in which psychiatric patients who do (familial) and do not (sporadic) have affected relatives are studied in relation to potential risk factors. Eaves et al. (1986) found that this design was inherently weak and required extremely large samples to increase the likelihood that risk factors would be detected. The design lacks power in part because sporadic cases are very likely to actually involve a genetic predisposition that simply has not been expressed in relatives. Therefore, the familial and sporadic cases do not differ in genetic makeup to any great degree.

The problem in high-risk designs is the opposite. The control group is not likely to have the genetic predisposition to alcoholism, but many of the experimental subjects (i.e., SOAs) do not have this predisposition either. Therefore, the groups are inherently heterogeneous (genetically, at least), and this greatly reduces the statistical power of the high-risk design (Sher, 1985). This heterogeneity is true only of genetic factors, however, and does not apply to social or familial influences (because, by definition, SOAs grew up in families with alcoholism). In addition, the risk of alcoholism in the general population is much higher than for the types of disorders studied by Eaves et al. (1986).

An initial power analysis run by Eaves (personal communication, November 1987) revealed greater statistical power in the high-risk design than the familial–sporadic design. The sample sizes needed to achieve adequate confidence of detecting a genetic marker are within those typically used in the SOA literature. The power for detecting environmental markers is even greater because the groups (SOAs vs. SONAs) are each homogeneous with regard to familial alcoholism.

To say that the high-risk design is more powerful than the familial–sporadic design does not really say that much, given the extremely low power of the latter. In addition, consideration of the inherently low power of high-risk designs suggests that many reported differences between SOAs and SONAs are actually false positives. This must be weighed against the consistency of results across studies, both within a laboratory and between laboratories, a point to which we return in our discussion of an integrative model.

Representativeness of Samples

We noted previously that SOAs are a heterogeneous group. Some of them will become alcoholics or drug abusers, and some will not. They are also heterogeneous in terms of the degree of family history of alcoholism or the percentage of relatives that are alcoholics. Some researchers (e.g., Finn & Pihl, 1987) have attempted to increase the degree of genetic vulnerability by selecting multigenerational SOAs (individuals who have an alcoholic parent and grandparent). This increases the likelihood that SOAs will themselves display signs of alcoholism before they enter the study.

Interestingly, in most of the studies we reviewed, problem drinkers were screened before subjects were selected. However, problem drinking could easily be prodromal to alcoholism, or a heritable condition, in the typical college-age subject. For example, Sher (1985) inadvertently included problem drinkers in a study of personality traits in SOAs and found significant group differences attributable only to those subjects.

The problem is that if the high-risk sample is to be representative of the high-risk population, then it must necessarily include some individuals who begin to display the psychopathology at an early age. This is particularly problematic for studies of alcohol challenge because the subjects are almost always over the age of 21. The mean age of onset of alcoholism is in the mid-20s (Robins et al., 1984) and is thought to be younger in men who are at the highest risk for a genetically transmitted form of alcoholism (Cloninger, 1983). However, it is possible that SOAs who carry the vulnerability to alcoholism but have not and will not express it are capable of revealing the deviant response to alcohol. This is the case when the phenotypic expression of the genetic vulnerability requires some environmental stressor or other condition for full manifestation of the disorder to occur.

Types of Alcoholism

We suggest that Cloninger's (1983) analysis of the archival data primarily reflects the modulation of the severity of alcoholic behavior by antisocial behavior and that typing may depend more critically on the presence or absence of psychopathy in men or somaticizing disorder in women. It is possible that offspring of alcoholics may differ to a significant degree depending on whether the affected parent, usually the father, has manifested antisocial behavior. In other words, it may be necessary to divide offspring of alcoholics in an alcohol-challenge study into those with an alcoholic parent who is psychopathic and those who do not have psychopathy in the family. We suggest that classification of the fathers as Type 1 (milieu limited) or Type 2 (male limited) may accomplish the same goal. More important, it is entirely possible that alcohol-challenge studies have recruited from different populations, in the sense that some samples are dominated by sons of Type 1 fathers and others by sons of Type 2 fathers. For example, it is likely that subjects sampled from large university samples are primarily sons of Type 1 fathers, whereas subjects recruited from lower socioeconomic communities that have a high rate of criminal behavior might be sons of Type 2 fathers. Research is needed in which SOA samples recruited from university and general populations are typed relative to the form of alcoholism represented in their families. At least in Scandinavia, the proportion of Type 1 alcoholics is much lower than that of Type 2 alcoholics (Cloninger et al., 1981). To the extent that this is the case in the United States, then most samples of SOAs are dominated by sons of Type 1 alcoholics (who are less likely to express antisocial behavior). This is particularly problematic in a search for a genetic marker if Cloninger's suggestion, that Type 1 alcoholism is less heritable than Type 2 alcoholism, is accurate. This problem may account for the inconsistencies between results from laboratories that recruit SOAs from different populations and may further dilute the genetic linkages often assumed in the high-risk challenge design.

Specificity for Positive Family History

An important question is whether any presumed psychobiological marker that predominates among SOAs is specific for alcoholism. In other words, is an individual who possesses the marker at elevated risk for disorders other than alcoholism? If this were the case, then it would not be valid to suggest that that marker played a direct causal role in the development of alcoholism but only that it was associated with a range of disorders sharing a common diathesis.

There is evidence that SOAs are at heightened risk for drug abuse and antisocial personality. Cadoret, Troughton, O'Gorman, and Heywood (1986) studied 242 male adoptees and 201 female adoptees in terms of their adult psychopathology. Men and women whose biological parent(s) had possible or definite alcohol problems were 4.3 times more likely to abuse drugs, but antisocial personality and other psychiatric disorders in a first-degree biological relative did not significantly increase the likelihood that the proband would abuse drugs. Similarly, probands with familial alcohol problems were 4.8 times as likely to manifest antisocial personality. There was some specificity, however. Familial antisocial personality increased the likelihood of alcohol abuse but not drug abuse.

It is possible that SOAs are at risk for an even broader spectrum of psychiatric disorders. However, it is also possible that the psychobiological marker itself is specific to alcoholism even when familial alcoholism is not. In other words, individuals who possess some distinct marker may be at greatly elevated risk only for alcoholism. In any case, the specificity of any potential psychobiological marker is an empirical question, and the specificity of that marker should be tested rather than assumed.

Specificity of Alcohol Response

A similar issue is whether the response to alcohol is specific to alcohol or is manifest with any drug or, indeed, any intense stimulus. No studies have been reported in which SOAs or FH+ individuals have been challenged with a drug other than alcohol. Therefore, there is no basis on which to suggest that any potentially deviant response to alcohol is specific to that particular drug.

The response may not even be specific to drugs as a particular class of stimuli. Finn and Pihl (1987) reported that multigenerational SOAs had enhanced responses to a shock stressor in the absence of alcohol. Newlin (1985) found that SOAs responded differently than SONAs to alcohol placebo. The heart rate decrease following placebo was greater in SOAs than in SONAs, which Newlin attributed to drug conditioning processes. Newlin and Thomson (1990) also found differences in placebo response between SOAs and SONAs, although in the opposite direction. In the latter study, subjects were given alcohol on four separate occasions prior to receiving the placebo, whereas Newlin (1985) administered placebo in the first session. Newlin and Thomson (1990) also found that SOAs became sensitized to the laboratory itself, as indicated by increasing baselines across sessions in this group.

It is entirely possible that SOAs have deviant responses to any intense stimulus, whether pharmacological, biological, or psychological. Again, specificity must be verified empirically rather than assumed. Potential non-specificity of response to stimuli may suggest a conceptual link between deviant responses to alcohol challenge and various cognitive and personality differences between SOAs and SONAs. In other words, deviant responses to a wide range of stimuli (in addition to alcohol) could reflect underlying differences in the organization of the nervous system that would also result in personality and cognitive differences between groups. The presumed psychobiological marker could be manifest in deviant responses to alcohol and a range of other responses that are not specific to alcohol.

Follow-Up

To date, no alcohol-challenge studies with FH+ and FH− subjects have included a long-term follow-up to determine whether those subjects (whether FH+ or FH−) that manifested the deviant response to alcohol later developed alcoholic behavior. This is a serious gap in the literature that is likely to be corrected in the future.

Laboratory Specificity

Schuckit and his colleagues (Schuckit, 1980a, 1980b, 1982b, 1982c, 1985b) have contributed the majority of data concerning alcohol challenges to FH+ and FH− men. Their methodology has been relatively constant across studies (in fact, many separate publications from this group represent results from the same experiment), and elements of their methodology have been adopted by other researchers in this field. Therefore, it may be useful to examine their methodology to determine in what ways it advances or undermines the alcohol-challenge paradigm. Also, it may be valuable to determine whether this methodology merits emulation.

Subject Selection Procedures

Schuckit's subjects have been routinely recruited from the undergraduate student population of the University of California at San Diego (UCSD). They are White and non-Jewish. Because of the relative affluence and high social functioning of these families, this population probably represents individuals whose relatives have less severe forms of alcoholism that are not associated with antisocial behavior (e.g., Type 1). Although there is some evidence that these individuals are at elevated risk for alcoholism, the risk is not great and it may be modulated strongly by environmental factors (Cloninger, 1987). It is also likely that UCSD students have primarily positive, nurturant home environments that would not encourage alcoholic behavior. Therefore, it is particularly important in this population to determine eventual risk for alcoholic behavior. Other researchers (e.g.,

Newlin, 1985; Newlin & Thomson, 1990) have also used university samples and are subject to the same criticism.

The only alcohol-challenge study to further divide SOAs was a stress-response dampening experiment by Finn and Pihl (1987). They used single- and multigeneration SOAs, which were interpreted roughly as environmental and genetic risk groups, respectively. Although we would not agree that single-generation SOAs are only at heightened environmental risk for alcoholism, Finn and Pihl found clear differences between the two groups. This suggests that further subdivision of SOAs, particularly into groups with and without familial psychopathy, is a potentially fruitful research strategy.

Finally, direct clinical and psychometric evaluation of family members could provide more definitive diagnoses for classifying family members in terms of antisociality and drug abuse. There is evidence that FH+ individuals' self-reports about their family members have some validity. Sher and Descutner (1986) found that siblings' reports of their biological father's drinking behavior were concordant when they answered questions from the Michigan Alcoholism Screening Test (Selzer, 1971; Selzer, Vinokur, & van Rooijen, 1975) phrased in terms of their father's drinking rather than their own. This was particularly true of items that were relatively observable, such as attendance at Alcoholics Anonymous and arrests for public intoxication and driving under the influence of alcohol. In addition, Levenson et al. (1987) found that responses to questionnaires mailed to the parents of their subjects were in good agreement with the offsprings' reports of their parents' drinking behavior. O'Malley, Carey, and Maisto (1986) also reported significant agreement between university students' reports of their parents' drinking practices and the reports of the actual parents. However, even though it may be possible to validly diagnose alcoholism by using offspring reports, it is unlikely that these reports would allow subtyping of the parent's alcoholic behavior (e.g., into Type 1 or Type 2 alcoholism).

Placebo

Early studies by Schuckit's laboratory were not placebo controlled. This is a potentially serious problem given evidence that SOAs and SONAs may differ in their responses to a placebo challenge (Newlin, 1985; Newlin & Thomson, 1990) and to a laboratory stressor in the absence of alcohol (Finn & Pihl, 1987). Later studies by Schuckit's laboratory included a placebo challenge and both low and high doses of alcohol challenge. In these reports, FH+ and FH− groups did not differ in terms of their placebo response, and their responses were generally minimal. However, Schuckit's placebo manipulation does not have the rigor of those employed in balanced-placebo studies (Rohsenow & Marlatt, 1981).

Therefore, it is likely that subjects could determine that they were drinking a placebo beverage on the basis of taste and other cues. Schuckit did not include a validity check on the placebo manipulation to determine whether it was successful.

The exact wording of the instructions in the placebo condition may be important for obtaining a robust placebo response (Kirsch & Weixel, 1988). The standard instructions in double-blind placebo studies involve telling the subjects that they will receive either placebo or alcohol and that they will not know and the experimenter will not know which is being administered. Alternatively, in deceptive-administration studies, subjects are told that they will receive alcohol in both conditions, but in fact, they receive alcohol in one condition and placebo in the other.

Kirsch and Weixel (1988) found that subjects were more likely to be deceived by deceptive administration than by a double-blind placebo and that the placebo responses were different in the two conditions. Kirsch and Weixel challenged the validity of the double-blind placebo design because it does not produce as robust a placebo effect. The rationale for telling subjects that they will receive either drug or placebo stems from ethical issues in treatment research (i.e., subjects might wish to seek alternative treatment if they knew that they might receive a placebo). The same concern does not apply in the present deceptive administration design, and the only ethical issue is deception relative to the placebo administration.

Schuckit and others have used double-blind placebo rather than deceptive administration and have generally not found a placebo effect of any significant magnitude. In contrast, Newlin (1985; Newlin & Thomson, 1990) used deceptive administration and found a robust placebo response, as well as differences in placebo response between SOAs and SONAs. Adoption of the balanced-placebo design (Hull & Bond, 1986; Marlatt & Rohsenow, 1980) in SOA challenge studies, as advocated in the preceding paragraphs, would also involve deceptive administration.

Alcohol Administration

Schuckit's subjects come into the laboratory at 7:00 a.m. and are administered alcohol at approximately 9:00 a.m. The alcohol is served in the form of 95% laboratory alcohol mixed in a 20% by volume solution with "sugarfree, noncaffeinated, carbonated beverage served at room temperature." It is not difficult to imagine that a significant number of subjects would become ill when drinking this beverage at 9:00 in the morning. Most social drinkers imbibe in the late afternoon and evening rather than in the morning. Jones (1974) found that the response to alcohol was greater in the morning than the evening hours, potentially reflecting conditioned tolerance at times when alcohol is normally consumed. Laboratory-grade alcohol is easily tasted in a 20% by volume beverage, and more palatable forms of alcohol are available.

Therefore, it is entirely possible that Schuckit's procedure of giving substantial quantities of alcohol in the early morning leads to illness and "terrible feelings" from alcohol. A major portion of the SHAS (Judd et al., 1977), adapted by Schuckit, includes such items as "nausea," "discomfort," and "feeling terrible," which Schuckit has grouped together on a terrible-feelings scale. This scale was the best single discriminator between SOAs and SONAs in a recent study (Schuckit & Gold, 1988) of multiple markers of alcohol challenge. This suggests that a very basic aspect of Schuckit's procedure may involve inducing illness that is greater in SONAs.

If it is true that a significant portion of Schuckit's subjects become ill or experience nausea because of the alcohol administration procedure, then this casts a different light on the biochemical measures he has used to measure the effect of alcohol. In other words, the differences in serum cortisol and PRL that Schuckit and his colleagues have found may be due to nausea and illness rather than to alcohol per se. Cortisol and PRL are stress hormones that are increased by a wide variety of stressors in both humans and animals (Martin & Reichin, 1987). Schuckit found that increases in these hormones were accompanied by increased terrible feelings and that the differences in hormones were greatest from 1 to 3 hours following alcohol, when headache, nausea, and other negative side effects are most prevalent.

This analysis suggests that differences between SOAs and SONAs in subjective intoxication (as measured by the terrible-feelings scale of the SHAS), serum cortisol, and PRL may actually have been due to nausea rather than the effect of alcohol. This would suggest that SONAs are more sensitive to these negative side effects of alcohol than are SOAs. This conclusion is of considerable theoretical importance if it is assumed that negative side effects tend to inhibit drinking behavior, but it is a very different conclusion from that of Schuckit and Gold (1988).

Novelty

Schuckit's procedure involves a highly novel laboratory environment to which subjects have not habituated. Newlin and Pretorius (1991) found that the response to alcohol challenge was suppressed in a novel environment, compared with response in the same environment when it was familiar to subjects. Newlin and Pretorius suggested that groups may differ in the rates and degree to which they habituate to a novel environment. In this case, SOAs may be more reactive to a novel laboratory environment (as they are to a laboratory stressor; Finn & Pihl, 1987) than are SONAs, so that SOAs show greater inhibition of the response to alcohol in the novel laboratory. This might account, in part, for Schuckit's finding that SOAs are less sensitive to alcohol than SONAs in a single session in the laboratory.

The simplest solution to this problem is to habituate subjects to the laboratory before giving them alcohol. Another solution is to give alcohol more than once, which also allows the measurement of chronic tolerance or sensitization to the drug. These procedures would tend to minimize the effect of laboratory novelty on the response to alcohol and the potential interaction of this factor with familial alcoholism.

Multiple Alcohol Challenges

Newlin and Thomson (1990) argued that there are many problems with using a single alcohol challenge in the high-risk paradigm and many advantages to administering alcohol on several different occasions (i.e., multiple alcohol challenges). A single alcohol challenge confounds sensitivity to the drug with acute tolerance (i.e., tolerance within a session), chronic tolerance (i.e., tolerance across multiple sessions), and inhibition caused by the novelty of the laboratory. Acute tolerance requires consideration of different responses in the rising and falling limbs of the blood alcohol curve. Schuckit's procedure often does not involve any measurement during the rising curve; his first measurement period is typically 30 or 60 min after alcohol has been consumed, which is beyond the peak BAC produced with his alcohol administration procedures. Therefore, it is not possible to compare responses in the rising and falling curves.

Clearly, the measurement of chronic tolerance requires multiple sessions. If there are adaptational trends (such as chronic tolerance or chronic sensitization) that occur over sessions with alcohol, these trends may be more important clinically than the response to the first challenge. Second, adaptational trends across sessions with multiple alcohol challenges may become apparent in responses that do not differ, or differ only to a limited degree, in the first session (Newlin & Thomson, 1990).

Finally, adaptation to the laboratory may be superimposed on the response to alcohol (Newlin & Pretorius, in press). It is difficult to predict the effect of this process on differences in the response to alcohol of SOAs and SONAs.

Dose Dependency

Schuckit's laboratory has been one of the few to use two alcohol doses. However, in most cases the difference between SOAs and SONAs has not been dose dependent. In some cases, the higher dose has shown differences between high- and low-risk groups, and in others, the low dose has shown effects. This raises the question of the extent to which the effect follows traditional pharmacological characteristics, such as dose dependency. Evidence that alcohol itself was the causative factor in these studies would be greatest if the highest dose produced the largest difference between groups.

It is possible, however, that a low dose allows the greatest manifestation of individual differences in drug response. If all subjects are heavily intoxicated, then few differences between groups may be apparent. In contrast, with a low dose, individual differences between groups could be expressed without ceiling effects. This question deserves further experimental research because it has direct implications for the choice of dose in individual-difference studies.

Social Interaction

The standard procedure of having an experimenter in the same room as the subject during studies of alcohol challenge may represent a methodological problem. Social interaction between the subject and the experimenter is an inevitable result of this procedure, particularly with measures that require verbal and nonverbal interaction for their completion. These researchers may be studying the effect of alcohol on social interaction rather than the effect of alcohol itself. Some measures, such as cortisol, PRL, and autonomic measures, may be particularly sensitive to the social atmosphere of the laboratory. This factor could interact with the novelty of the laboratory because the subject is required to deal with a new person in addition to a new laboratory. To minimize the confounding of social contact with the effect of alcohol, it may be necessary to place the subject alone in a subject chamber.

A DIFFERENTIATOR MODEL

As noted previously, the issue of whether SOAs are more or less sensitive to alcohol has been a central focus of alcohol-challenge studies. The psychobiological response to alcohol during the rising and falling limbs of the blood alcohol curve has been idealized in the set of curves at the top of Figure 1. Sensitivity to the drug is represented by the area under this curve. If two curves are of the same shape or are identical, as they may be for SOAs and SONAs, then the areas under the curve will be the same, and the curves can be compared by using the mean response over time. If alcohol is administered on several occasions (Newlin, 1989; Newlin & Thomson, 1990), then sensitivity may be conceptualized as the mean response across occasions, aside from any trends toward increasing responses (chronic sensitization) or declining responses (chronic tolerance).

Acute Tolerance

Schuckit's results showing reduced sensitivity to alcohol have been found during the declining blood alcohol curve, from 60 min to as much as 300 min after alcohol is consumed. For example, P300 latency in FH+

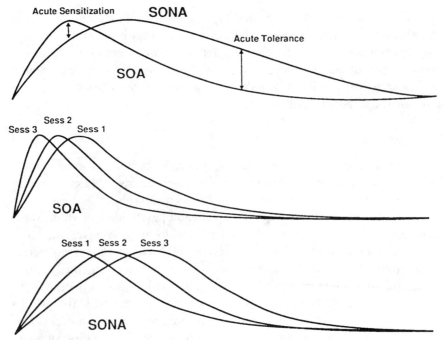

Figure 1. Schematic diagram of differentiator model. (In the first set of curves, note the greater acute sensitization during the ascending limb of the blood alcohol curve in sons of alcoholics [SOAs] and the greater acute tolerance in SOAs during the falling limb of the curve. This is indicated by a more rapid and robust onset of the effect of alcohol and more rapid return to baseline of the falling blood alcohol curve. In the second and third sets of curves, the accentuation of acute sensitization and acute tolerance across sessions in SOAs is illustrated. SONA = sons of nonalcoholic parents.)

men declined toward baseline more quickly than for FH− men 240 min after alcohol consumption, but not at baseline or 70 min following alcohol consumption (Schuckit, Gold, et al., 1988). As measured by serum PRL, SONAs had a larger response to alcohol at 60 min with the low dose and at 120 min with the high dose (Schuckit et al., 1987a); in another study, reduced PRL response was found in SOAs 150 min after alcohol consumption. Curves for serum cortisol diverged with the high dose at 90 min and thereafter (Schuckit et al., 1987b); in another study using analysis of covariance, the curves diverged at 240 min and beyond. Similarly, SONAs showed greater body sway than SOAs 135 min after the low dose (Schuckit, 1985a).

This tendency toward more rapid return to baseline in SOAs has been a very consistent finding under Schuckit's methodology. This trend is reflected in the top set of curves in Figure 1 as a reduced response to alcohol during the declining blood alcohol curve. We argue that this represents SOAs' greater acute tolerance for alcohol, compared with SONAs.

Acute tolerance is defined as the development of tolerance for a drug within a session in which the drug is administered. Acute tolerance may be measured several different ways. First, using steady-state pharmacokinetic procedures, the amount of the drug in the blood may be maintained at a constant level for long periods of time; because drug levels are constant, any decrease in response to the drug represents the development of acute tolerance. A second method is to assess the drug effect at equivalent blood drug levels on the rising and falling blood drug curves; acute tolerance is indicated when subjects show greater response to the drug during the rising curve than during the falling curve. A final method is to measure recovery rates from the drug. One group of subjects may be said to show greater development of acute tolerance if they recover more quickly from the effects of the drug. With all these measurement procedures, acute tolerance is indicated when response to the drug is less than that expected on the basis of the blood drug curve. For our example, we would suggest that SOAs show greater development of acute tolerance when they show less response during the declining blood alcohol curve than do SONAs. Acute sensitization is then defined as greater drug action than that expected on the basis of the blood drug curve.

However, Schuckit's procedure has also yielded results suggesting that SOAs are more sensitive to alcohol than SONAs. For example, Schuckit, Engstrom, et al. (1981) found that frontal muscle tension was lower in SOAs than SONAs only 15 min after alcohol was consumed. Elmasian et al. (1982) recorded event-related potentials immediately after alcohol consumption and 30 min later; the results indicated greater decreases in P300 latency among SOAs, although this effect was also found with placebo. In addition, Savoie, Emory, and Moody-Thomas (1988) found that FH+ men reported lower anxiety than FH− men during the ascending blood alcohol curve. These effects occurred during the rising blood alcohol curve, and they indicated that SOAs were more sensitive to alcohol than SONAs. These relationships are summarized in Figure 2.

Other researchers have also found that SOAs are more sensitive to alcohol during the rising blood alcohol curve. Newlin and Thomson (1990) reported that SOAs showed greater increases than SONAs in finger-pulse amplitude, skin temperature, and skin conductance during the rising blood alcohol curve in the third session with alcohol but not in the first session; similar nonsignificant trends were found for heart rate and general motor activity. Newlin and Thomson (1990) also found in a second experiment that SOAs had greater increases in pulse transit time in the fourth session with alcohol during the rising blood alcohol curve and greater increases in static ataxia in the first and second sessions. Unfortunately, Newlin and Thomson (1990) did not record these measures during the falling blood alcohol curve to determine whether SONAs would show smaller effects at the later time points. Nagoshi and Wilson (1987) found that SOAs reported greater intoxication following the first "topping" dose of alcohol

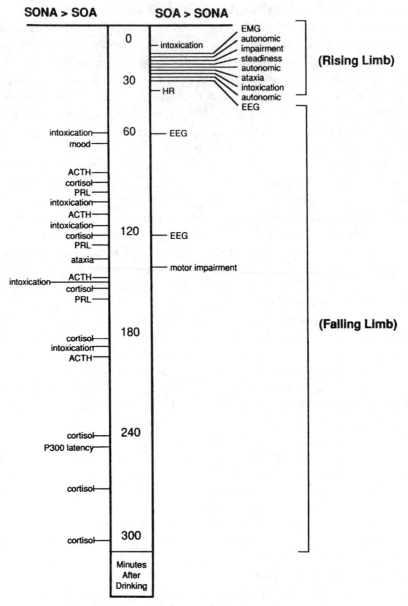

Figure 2. Summary of studies of sons of alcoholics (SOAs) and sons of nonalcoholics (SONAs) in terms of the timing of the effect. (The dependent measures that were greater in SOAs than in SONAs are illustrated to the right of the time line [time in minutes since consuming alcohol], and the measures that were greater in SONAs than in SOAs are illustrated to the left of the time line. The rising blood alcohol curve is represented by approximately the first 30 min after drinking [depending on dose and rate of drinking], and the falling blood alcohol curve is reflected by the remaining time. The effects for which SOAs showed greater responsivity than SONAs tended to occur during the rising blood alcohol curve, and effects for which SONAs showed greater responsivity than SOAs tended to occur during the falling curve. This pattern supports the differentiator model. EMG = electromyograph; EEG = electroencephalograph; PRL = prolactin; ACTH = adrenocorticotropic hormone; HR = heart rate.)

when BAC was increasing, and Kaplan et al. (1988) found that SOAs reported greater intoxication immediately after drinking two beers. O'Malley and Maisto (1985) reported that SOAs had greater impairment on some perceptual-motor tasks 10 and 35 min after drinking alcohol. This effect represents acute sensitization because the psychological response to the drug increases more rapidly than expected on the basis of the blood alcohol curve.

This effect is illustrated by the top set of curves in Figure 1, in which the psychological effects during the rising blood alcohol curve occur more rapidly for SOAs than SONAs, whereas the reverse is true during the falling blood alcohol curve. These relationships suggest an active Newtonian differentiator in SOAs that responds to the first differential or slope of the blood alcohol curve rather than to its level. In other words, the response to alcohol is accentuated when the slope is positive (during the rising blood alcohol curve) and attenuated when the slope is negative (during the falling blood alcohol curve). The former is acute sensitization and the latter is acute tolerance. This differentiator function is indicated in the top set of curves in Figure 1 by a curve for SOAs that represents the first differential of the curve for SONAs.

This differentiator model is hampered by the fact that there are no instances in which both acute sensitization and acute tolerance have been found in the same experiment. Moss et al. (1989) displayed self-reported intoxication curves that strongly support the differentiator model, but only acute tolerance on the falling curve was significant. The standard-error bars indicate that even though acute sensitization in SOAs was actually of greater magnitude than the statistically significant acute tolerance, the former was not significant because of greater variability. Moss et al. (1989) had 10 subjects per group; the two effects might both have been significant in a larger sample. Research that directly tests the model presented in Figure 1 is needed to establish that both effects can be found in the same subjects.

Many of the measures listed in Figure 2 were used by the same researchers (presumably using similar procedures). Moreover, many measures appear in both the left- and right-hand panels (e.g., self-reported intoxication and static ataxia). This indicates that the time-dependent pattern we noted does not appear to be due solely to different procedures or to specific measures. Therefore, this pattern does show some degree of generality despite the fact that greater acute sensitization and acute tolerance have not been reported in the same study.

The differentiator model goes a long way toward resolving the many discrepancies between results in the alcohol-challenge literature. As shown in Table 1, about as many studies have found that SOAs are more sensitive to alcohol as have reported the opposite. Consideration of the time factor reduces these inconsistencies markedly. It is clear that researchers need to consider the temporal factor in relation to the sensitivity issue.

Relation to Mood Effects

The differentiator model corresponds in interesting ways to reports of the differential mood and subjective responses to alcohol in normal social drinkers during the rising and falling blood alcohol curves. Babor, Berglas, Mendelson, Ellingboe, and Miller (1983) reported that "subjects tested while blood alcohol levels [BAL] were ascending ... described themselves as more elated, friendly, and vigorous. As BAL declined, subjects described themselves as more angry, depressed, and fatigued" (p. 53).

Euphoria and accompanying EEG alpha activity have been reported only during the rising blood alcohol curve. Lukas, Mendelson, Benedikt, and Jones (1986) measured EEG, "euphoria" on a joystick, and plasma ethanol levels in 18 young men as they drank 0.35 or 0.70 g/kg alcohol. Reports of euphoria on the joystick and transient episodes of alpha activity occurred at the same times on the rising blood alcohol curve. Reports of euphoria were reduced during the falling curve, and there was relatively little alpha activity at later time points. In contrast, following alcohol consumption, theta activity was increased during the entire recording session and closely matched the blood alcohol curve. Lukas, Mendelson, and Benedikt (1986) found similar results for euphoria during the rising blood alcohol curve.

There are also parallels to subjective responses to drugs other than alcohol. The "rush" or intense subjective high felt immediately after injection of cocaine or opiates can be differentiated from the less intense pleasurable feelings experienced during prolonged responses to these drugs (Kumor, Sherer, & Cascella, in press). Rush is most often experienced when drugs are injected intravenously or when a drug is inhaled, and both routes of drug administration are associated with very rapidly rising blood drug curves. In contrast, the high associated with the falling blood drug curve, or with slower routes of administration, such as by mouth or by "snorting," is both qualitatively and quantitatively different from that of rush. These observations also suggest that the slope of the rising blood drug curve may be an important determinant of the psychological response to drugs and that the subjective responses to these drugs are different in the rising and falling limbs of the blood drug curve.

These observations suggest that subjective responses to alcohol and to other drugs may be more sensitive to the slope of the blood drug curve than to its absolute level. It is as if the transition in state induced by the drug is more important than the state itself. This also suggests a differentiator model of the psychobiological response to drugs of abuse.

More important, it suggests that SOAs may be more sensitive to the drug during the rising blood alcohol curve, when euphoria is greatest, and less sensitive during the falling curve, when anxiety and depression are greatest. This would suggest that alcohol is more reinforcing for SOAs than for SONAs during both the rising and falling curves. SOAs may experience greater euphoria during the rising blood alcohol curve and experience less dysphoria during the falling curve. This double benefit may produce greater motivation to drink alcohol and thereby place SOAs at greater risk for alcoholism. We feel that this interpretation is more consistent with the available data than simple consideration of sensitivity to alcohol and more compelling as an interpretation of the relationship between these psychobiological markers and final manifestation of the disorder.

In other words, sensitivity to the drug must be related to the time and circumstances under which the response is measured. Sensitivity to the drug probably is a key component of the rewarding aspect of the response to alcohol, but that sensitivity must be understood in relation to the transition in blood alcohol rather than its absolute level. Most important, adaptational trends that occur over time are critically important and might be better measured with multiple alcohol challenges.

It is possible that this differentiator model has a pharmacokinetic substrate, even though SOAs and SONAs do not differ in peak blood alcohol levels or curves. First, it may be that SOAs and SONAs differ in the levels of psychoactive metabolites of alcohol, although the data on acetaldehyde are very weak. Second, Noe and Kumor (1983) suggested that small, low-flux compartments may have different absorption characteristics than larger central compartments. For this to account for the results of alcohol-challenge studies, a small, low-flux compartment critical to the response measures used in such studies would have to have faster absorption characteristics in SOAs and more rapid clearance during the falling blood alcohol curve. Noe and Kumor's (1983) analysis assumes that the area under the low-flux compartment's curve that is higher during the rising blood drug curve must be equal to the area between the small compartment's falling curve and that of the larger compartment. In other words, the total area under the curves of the two compartments must be equal. This analysis may be unlikely given alcohol's propensity to circulate throughout the body in relatively equal amounts but is worth considering because it leads to testable predictions.

Chronic Tolerance and Sensitization

This differentiator model has implications for chronic in addition to acute tolerance and sensitization. Chronic tolerance is defined as attenuation in the effect of a drug with repeated administrations across sessions rather than within a session. Conversely, chronic sensitization represents increasingly greater responses to a drug across sessions. There is no necessary assumption that acute and chronic tolerance reflect operation of the same mechanism.

If it is assumed that the differentiator is accentuated by repetition of the alcohol stimulus across sessions with alcohol, then the model predicts both greater chronic sensitization and chronic tolerance in SOAs compared with SONAs, depending on whether the response to alcohol is measured in the rising or falling blood alcohol curves. This is depicted by the two sets of curves at the bottom of Figure 2. As the differentiator in SOAs is accentuated, it leads to a more rapidly rising psychological response to the drug, and, at the same time, to a more rapidly decaying response after BAC has peaked. Newlin and Thomson (1990) found results consistent with greater chronic sensitization to alcohol in SOAs during the rising blood alcohol curve across three or four sessions with alcohol (Newlin, 1987). With stimulant measures (i.e., autonomic measures that were affected in an arousal-like manner), chronic sensitization was found in SOAs compared with SONAs; these measures were finger-pulse amplitude, finger temperature, and skin conductance in the first study and pulse transit time in the replication study. With a depressant measure, static ataxia, the reverse was found; SOAs showed greater increases in body sway only in the first and second sessions. There is a conceptual analogy between Schuckit's (1985a) body-sway results in a single session with alcohol, in which he found SOAs to have greater acute tolerance than SONAs, and Newlin and Thomson's (1990) results with body sway, in which they found greater chronic tolerance across four sessions with alcohol.

Greater acute tolerance has also been found with rats that were genetically selected for preference for oral alcohol (Gatto, Murphy, Waller, McBride, Lumeng, & Li, 1986). Gatto et al. found that alcohol-preferring rats (P rats) showed greater acute tolerance than alcohol-nonpreferring (NP) rats in their first exposure to the drug. This was found on a dynamic ataxia measure for which P rats showed more rapid recovery from alcohol compared with NP rats. In addition, P rats retained this acute tolerance for 10 days, whereas NP rats lost their acute tolerance.

These results suggest interesting parallels between rats that are genetically selected for alcohol preference and SOAs. Further research is needed to test the limits of this analogy. This would involve more research with P and NP rats to determine whether they show other effects similar to SOAs (e.g., chronic sensitization on stimulant measures), and with SOAs and SONAs to determine whether they show greater retention of acute tolerance (in addition to the findings already mentioned concerning initial display of acute tolerance). This could lead to a potentially very powerful boot-strapping line of research in which parallels between particular strains of animals and familial alcoholism in people are investigated.

Implications

If this analogy to a differentiator in SOAs is accurate, it has implications for a variety of responses other than alcohol. The model may explain presumed personality differences between those at high and low risk for alcoholism (Hennecke, 1984; Morrison & Schuckit, 1983; Saunders & Schuckit, 1981; Schuckit, 1982a, 1983; Tarter, Hegedus, Goldstein, Shelly, & Alterman, 1984). Sons of alcoholics may be particularly sensitive to the leading edge of psychological stimuli, such that their responses are accentuated early in the response to a stimulus and are blunted or habituated quickly when the response is repeated. This analysis might be profitably extended to habituation paradigms and personality measures that are related to the temporal dimensions of arousal to a wide range of different stimuli.

SUMMARY AND CONCLUSIONS

Many of the procedures in alcohol-challenge research have become de facto standards, even though they may tend to minimize the potential differences between SOAs and SONAs and may lead to alcohol-induced illness on the part of the subjects. Few researchers have acclimated their subjects to the novel laboratory environment or given alcohol more than once to study chronic tolerance or sensitization in these individuals. In addition, very few researchers have measured alcohol effects in SOAs and SONAs during both the rising and falling limbs of the blood alcohol curve. We argue that this is essential to resolve the issue of differences in sensitivity to alcohol as a function of familial alcoholism.

We have made a number of proposals for methodological improvements in alcohol-challenge research. We particularly stress that it is important to avoid making subjects ill during the procedure by giving them alcohol in impure form early in the morning in a very unpalatable mixture. There are sound empirical reasons for administering alcohol in a form and at a time that is similar to the usual drinking practices of normal social drinkers. This prevents both the confounding effects of illness and increases the generalizability of the results.

We have proposed a differentiator model of the response to alcohol, in which SOAs show both greater acute sensitization to and greater acute tolerance for alcohol than SONAs depending on whether the effect of alcohol is measured during the rising or falling limbs of the blood alcohol curve. This is a testable model that has many implications for research.

Despite problems with the alcohol-challenge literature, the early results are promising and easily justify continued research in this area. Alcoholism is a serious social problem that is difficult to prevent or treat in part, because practitioners do not yet understand the various etiologies of the disorder. It is clear that alcohol-challenge studies of SOAs and SONAs may further understanding of the etiology of alcoholism.

REFERENCES

Abel, E. L., & Lee, J. A. (1988). Paternal alcohol exposure affects offspring behavior but not body or organ weights in mice. *Alcoholism: Clinical and Experimental Research, 12,* 349–354.

American Psychiatric Association. (1980). *Diagnostic and statistical manual of mental disorders* (3rd ed.). Washington, DC: Author.

Babor, T. F., Berglas, S., Mendelson, J. H., Ellingboe, J., & Miller, K. (1983). Alcohol, affect, and disinhibition of verbal behavior. *Psychopharmacology, 80,* 53–60.

Behar, D., Berg, C. J., Rapoport, J. L., Nelson, W., Linnoila, M., Cohen, M., Bozevich, C., & Marshall, T. (1983). Behavioral and physiological effects of ethanol in high-risk and control children: A pilot study. *Alcoholism: Clinical and Experimental Research, 7,* 404–410.

Bohman, M. (1978). Some genetic aspects of alcoholism and criminality: A population of adoptees. *Archives of General Psychiatry, 35,* 269–276.

Cadoret, R. J., Troughton, E., O'Gorman, T. W., & Heywood, E. (1986). An adoption study of genetic and environmental factors in drug abuse. *Archives of General Psychiatry, 43,* 1131–1136.

Cloninger, C. R. (1983). Genetic and environmental factors in the development of alcoholism. *Journal of Psychiatric Treatment and Evaluation, 5,* 487–496.

Cloninger, C. R. (1987). Neurogenetic adaptive mechanisms in alcoholism. *Science, 236,* 410–416.

Cloninger, C. R., Bohman, M., & Sigvardsson, S. (1981). Inheritance of alcohol abuse: Cross-fostering analysis of adopted men. *Archives of General Psychiatry, 38,* 861–868.

Cotton, N. S. (1979). The familial incidence of alcoholism. *Journal of Studies on Alcohol, 40,* 89–116.

Eaves, L. J., Kendler, K. S., & Schultz, C. (1986). The familial sporadic classification: Its power for the resolution of genetic and environmental etiologic factors. *Journal of Psychiatric Research, 10,* 115–130.

Elmasian, R., Neville, H., Woods, D., Schuckit, M., & Bloom, F. (1982). Event-related brain potentials are different in individuals at high and low risk for developing alcoholism. *Proceedings of the National Academy of Science, 79,* 7900–7903.

Eriksson, P. C. (1980). Elevated blood acetaldehyde levels in alcoholics and their relatives: A reevaluation. *Science, 207,* 1383–1384.

Faraone, S. V., & Tsuang, M. T. (1985). Quantitative models of the genetic transmission of schizophrenia. *Psychological Bulletin, 98,* 41–66.

Feighner, J. P., Robins, E., Guze, S. B., Woodruff, R. A., Winokur, G., & Munoz, R. (1972). Diagnostic criteria for use in psychiatric research. *Archives of General Psychiatry, 26,* 57–63.

Finn, P. R., & Pihl, R. O. (1987). Men at high risk for alcoholism: The effect of alcohol on cardiovascular response to unavoidable shock. *Journal of Abnormal Psychology, 96,* 230–236.

Gatto, G. J., Murphy, J. M., Waller, M. B., McBride, W. J., Lumeng, L., & Li, T. K. (1987). Persistence of tolerance to a single dose of ethanol in the selectively bred alcohol-preferring P rat. *Pharmacology, Biochemistry, and Behavior, 28,* 105–110.

Goodwin, D. W., Schulsinger, F., Hermansen, L., Guze, S. B., & Winokur, G. (1973). Alcohol problems in adoptees raised apart from alcoholic biological parents. *Archives of General Psychiatry, 28,* 238–243.

Goodwin, D. W., Schulsinger, F., Moller, N., Hermansen, L., Winokur, G., & Guze, S. B. (1974). Drinking problems in adopted and nonadopted sons of alcoholics. *Archives of General Psychiatry, 31,* 164–169.

Gurling, H. M. D., Murray, R. M., & Clifford, C. A. (1981). Investigations into the genetics of alcohol dependence and into its effects on brain function. In L. Gedda, P. Parisi, & W. Nance (Eds.), *Twin research 3: Epidemiological and clinical studies.* New York: Alan R. Liss.

Harada, S., Agarwal, D. P., Goedde, H. W., Tagaki, S., & Ishikawa, R. (1982). Possible protective role against alcoholism for aldehyde dehydrogenase isozyme deficiency in Japan. *Lancet, ii,* 827.

Hennecke, L. (1984). Stimulus augmenting and field dependence in children of alcoholic fathers. *Journal of Studies on Alcohol, 45,* 486–492.

Hull, J. G., & Bond, C. F. (1986). Social and behavioral consequences of alcohol consumption and expectancy: A meta-analysis. *Psychological Bulletin, 99,* 347–360.

Hrubec, Z., & Omenn, G. S. (1981). Evidence of genetic predisposition to alcoholic cirrhosis and its biological end points by zygosity among male veterans. *Alcoholism: Clinical and Experimental Research, 5,* 207–215.

Jones, B. M. (1974). Circadian variation in the effects of alcohol on cognitive performance. *Quarterly Journal of Studies on Alcohol, 35,* 423–431.

Judd, L. L., Hubbard, R. B., Huey, L. Y., Attewell, P. A., Janowsky, D. S., & Takahashi, K. I. (1977). Lithium carbonate and ethanol induced 'highs' in normal subjects. *Archives of General Psychiatry, 34,* 463–467.

Kaij, L. (1960). *Alcoholism in twins.* Stockholm: Almkvist & Wiksell.

Kaplan, R. F., Hesselbrock, V. M., O'Connor, S., & Depalma, N. (1988). Behavioral and EEG responses to alcohol in nonalcoholic men with a family history of alcoholism. *Progress in Neuro-Psychopharmacology and Biological Psychiatry, 12,* 873–885.

Kaprio, J., Koskenvuo, M., Langinvainio, H., Romanov, K., Sarna, S., & Rose, R. J. (1987). Genetic influences on use and abuse of alcohol: A study of 5,638 adult Finnish twin brothers. *Alcoholism: Clinical and Experimental Research, 11,* 349–356.

Kirsch, I., & Weixel, L. J. (1988). Double-blind versus deceptive administration of a placebo. *Behavioral Neuroscience, 102,* 319–323.

Kumor, K. M., Sherer, M. A., & Cascella, N. G. (1989). Cocaine use in man: Subjective effects, physiologic responses and toxicity. In K. K. Redda, C. H. Walker, & G. Barnett (Eds.), *Cocaine, marijuana, and designer drugs: Chemistry, pharmacology, and behavior* (pp. 84–92). Cleveland, OH: CRC Press.

Levenson, R. W., Oyama, On. N., & Meek, P. S. (1987). Greater reinforcement from alcohol for those at risk: Parental risk, personality risk, and gender. *Journal of Abnormal Psychology, 96,* 242–253.

Levenson, R. W., Sher, K. J., Grossman, L., Newman, J., & Newlin, D. B. (1981). Alcohol and stress response dampening: Pharmacological effects, expectancy, and tension reduction. *Journal of Abnormal Psychology, 89,* 528–538.

Lex, B. W., Lukas, S. E., Greenwald, N. E., & Mendelson, J. H. (1988). Alcohol-induced changes in body sway in women at risk for alcoholism: A pilot study. *Journal of Studies on Alcohol, 49,* 346–356.

Lipscomb, T. R., Carpenter, J. A., & Nathan, P. E. (1979). Static ataxia: A predictor of alcoholism? *British Journal of Addiction, 74,* 289–294.

Lipscomb, T. R., & Nathan, P. E. (1980). Blood alcohol level discrimination: The effects of family history of alcoholism, drinking pattern, and tolerance. *Archives of General Psychiatry, 3,* 571–576.

Lukas, S. E., Mendelson, J. H., & Benedikt, R. A. (1986). Instrumental analysis of ethanol-induced intoxication in human males. *Psychopharmacology, 89,* 8–13.

Lukas, S. E., Mendelson, J. H., Benedikt, R. A., & Jones, B. (1986). EEG alpha activity increases during transient episodes of ethanol-induced euphoria. *Pharmacology, Biochemistry, and Behavior, 25,* 889–895.

Marlatt, G. A., & Rohsenow, D. J. (1980). Cognitive processes in alcohol use: Expectancy and the balanced placebo design. In N. K. Mell (Ed.), *Advances in substance abuse: Behavioral and biological research* (Vol. 1, pp. 159–199). Greenwich, CT: JAI Press.

Martin, J. B., & Reichin, S. (1987). *Clinical neuroendocrinology* (2nd ed.). Philadelphia: F. A. Davis.

Morrison, C., & Schuckit, M. A. (1983). Locus of control in young men with alcoholic relatives and controls. *Journal of Clinical Psychiatry, 44,* 306–307.

Moskowitz, H., Daily, J., & Henderson, R. (1974). *Acute tolerance to behavioral impairment in drinkers* (U.S. Department of Transportation Publication No. HS 009-2-322). Washington, DC: National Highway Traffic Safety Administration.

Moss, H. B., Yao, J. K, & Maddock, J. M. (1989). Responses by sons of alcoholic fathers to alcoholic and control drinks: Perceived mood, intoxication, and plasma prolactin. *Alcoholism: Clinical and Experimental Research, 13,* 252–257.

Murray, R. M., Clifford, C. A., & Gurling, H. M. (1983). Twin and adoption studies: How good is the evidence for a genetic role? *Recent Developments in Alcoholism, 1,* 25–48.

Nagoshi, C. T., & Wilson, J. R. (1987). Influence of family alcoholism history on alcohol metabolism, sensitivity and tolerance. *Alcoholism: Clinical and Experimental Research, 11,* 392–398.

National Council on Alcoholism. (1972). Criteria for the diagnosis of alcoholism. *Annals of Internal Medicine, 77,* 249–258.

Newlin, D. B. (1985). Offspring of alcoholics have enhanced antagonistic placebo response. *Journal of Studies on Alcohol, 46,* 490–494.

Newlin, D. B. (1987). Alcohol expectancy and conditioning in sons of alcoholics. *Advances in Alcohol and Substance Abuse, 6,* 33–58.

Newlin, D. B. (1989). The skin flushing response: Autonomic, self-report, and conditioned responses to repeated administrations of alcohol in Asian men. *Journal of Abnormal Psychology, 98,* 421–425.

Newlin, D. B., & Pretorius, M. B. (1991). Greater alcohol effect in a familiar than a novel environment in humans. *Journal for Studies on Alcohol.*

Newlin, D. B., & Thomson, J. B. (1990). *Tolerance and sensitization to alcohol in sons of alcoholics.* Manuscript submitted for publication.

Noe, D. A., & Kumor, K. M. (1983). Drug kinetics in low-flux (small) anatomic compartments. *Journal of Pharmaceutical Sciences, 72,* 718–719.

O'Malley, S. S., Carey, K. B., & Maisto, S. A. (1986). Validity of young adults' reports of parental drinking practices. *Journal of Studies on Alcohol, 47,* 433–435.

O'Malley, S. S., & Maisto, S. A. (1985). Effects of family drinking history and expectancies on responses to alcohol in men. *Journal of Studies on Alcohol, 46,* 289–297.

Partanen, J., Bruun, K., & Markkanen, T. (1966). *Inheritance of drinking behavior.* New Brunswick, NJ: Rutgers University Center of Alcohol Studies.

Peele, S. (1986). The implications and limitations of genetic models of alcoholism and other addictions. *Journal of Studies on Alcohol, 47,* 63–73.

Pollock, V. E., Volavka, J., Goodwin, D. W., Mednick, S. A., Gabrielli, W. F., Knop, J., & Schulsinger, F. (1983). The EEG after alcohol administration in men at risk for alcoholism. *Archives of General Psychiatry, 40,* 857–861.

Robins, L. N., Helzer, J. E., Weissman, M. M., Orvashel, H., Gruenberg, E., Burke, J. D., & Regier, D. A. (1984). Lifetime prevalence of specific psychiatric disorders in three sites. *Archives of General Psychiatry, 41,* 949–958.

Rohsenow, D. J., & Marlatt, A. G. (1981). The balanced placebo design: Methodological considerations. *Addictive Behaviors, 6,* 107–122.

Saunders, G. R., & Schuckit, M. A. (1981). MMPI scores in young men with alcoholic relatives and controls. *Journal of Nervous and Mental Disorders, 169,* 456–458.

Savoie, T. M., Emory, E. K., & Moody-Thomas, S. (1988). Acute alcohol intoxication in socially drinking female and male offspring of alcoholic fathers. *Journal of Studies on Alcohol, 49*, 430–435.

Schuckit, M. A. (1980a). Alcoholism and genetics: Possible biological mediators. *Biological Psychiatry, 15*, 437–477.

Schuckit, M. A. (1980b). Biological markers: Metabolism and acute reactions to alcohol in sons of alcoholics. *Pharmacology, Biochemistry, and Behavior, 13*(Suppl. 1), 9–16.

Schuckit, M. A. (1980c). Self-rating of alcohol intoxication by young men with and without family histories of alcoholism. *Journal of Studies on Alcohol, 41*, 242–249.

Schuckit, M. A. (1981). Peak blood alcohol levels in men at high risk for the future development of alcoholism. *Alcoholism: Clinical and Experimental Research, 5*, 64–66.

Schuckit, M. A. (1982a). Anxiety and assertiveness in the relatives of alcoholics and controls. *Journal of Clinical Psychiatry, 43*, 238–239.

Schuckit, M. A. (1982b). A prospective study of genetic markers in alcoholism. In E. Usdin & I. Hanin (Eds.), *Biological markers in psychiatry and neurology* (pp. 445–455). Oxford, England: Pergamon Press.

Schuckit, M. A. (1982c). A study of young men with alcoholic close relatives. *American Journal of Psychiatry, 139*, 791–794.

Schuckit, M. A. (1983). Extroversion and neuroticism in young men at higher and lower risk for alcoholism. *American Journal of Psychiatry, 140*, 1223–1224.

Schuckit, M. A. (1984a). Differences in plasma cortisol after ingestion of ethanol in relatives of alcoholics and controls: Preliminary results. *Journal of Clinical Psychiatry, 45*, 374–376.

Schuckit, M. A. (1984b). Subjective responses to alcohol in sons of alcoholics and controls. *Archives of General Psychiatry, 41*, 879–884.

Schuckit, M. A. (1985). Ethanol-induced changes in body sway in men at high alcoholism risk. *Archives of General Psychiatry, 42*, 375–379.

Schuckit, M. A., & Duby, J. (1982). Alcohol-related flushing and the risk for alcoholism in sons of alcoholics. *Journal of Clinical Psychiatry, 43*, 415–418.

Schuckit, M. A., Engstrom, D., Alpert, R., & Duby, J. (1981). Differences in muscle-tension response to ethanol in young men with and without family histories of alcoholism. *Journal of Studies on Alcohol, 42*, 918–924.

Schuckit, M. A., & Gold, E. O. (1988). A simultaneous evaluation of multiple markers of ethanol/placebo challenges in sons of alcoholics and controls. *Archives of General Psychiatry, 45*, 211–216.

Schuckit, M. A., Gold, E., & Risch, S. C. (1987a). Changes in blood prolactin levels in sons of alcoholics and controls. *American Journal of Psychiatry, 144*, 854–859.

Schuckit, M. A., Gold, E., & Risch, S. C. (1987b). Plasma cortisol levels following ethanol in sons of alcoholics and controls. *Archives of General Psychiatry, 44*, 942–945.

Schuckit, M. A., Gold, E., Croot, K., Finn, P., & Polich, J. (1988). P300 latency after ethanol in sons of alcoholics and controls. *Biological Psychiatry, 24,* 310– 315.

Schuckit, M. A., Goodwin, D. A., & Winokur, G. (1972). A study of alcoholism in half-siblings. *American Journal of Psychiatry, 128,* 1132–1136.

Schuckit, M. A., O'Connor, D. T., Duby, J., Vega, R., & Moss, M. (1981). Dopamine-B-hydroxylase activity levels in men at high risk for alcoholism and controls. *Biological Psychiatry, 16,* 1067–1075.

Schuckit, M. A., Parker, D. C., & Rossman, L. R. (1983). Ethanol-related prolactin responses and risk for alcoholism. *Biological Psychiatry, 18,* 1153–1159.

Schuckit, M., & Rayses, V. (1979). Ethanol ingestion: Differences in blood acetaldehyde concentrations in relatives of alcoholics and controls. *Science, 203,* 54–55.

Schuckit, M. A., Risch, S. C., & Gold, E. O. (1988). Alcohol consumption, ACTH level, and family history of alcoholism. *American Journal of Psychiatry, 145,* 1391–1395.

Schuckit, M. A., Shaskan, E., Duby, J., Vega, R., & Moss, M. (1982). Platelet monoamine oxidase activity in relatives of alcoholics: Preliminary study with matched control subjects. *Archives of General Psychiatry, 39,* 137–140.

Searles, J. S. (1988). The role of genetics in the pathogenesis of alcoholism. *Journal of Abnormal Psychology, 97,* 153–167.

Selzer, M. L. (1971). The Michigan Alcoholism Screening Test: The quest for a new diagnostic instrument. *American Journal of Pyschiatry, 127,* 1653–1658.

Selzer, M. L., Vinokur, A., & van Rooijen, L. (1975). A self-administered Short Michigan Alcoholism Screening Test (SMAST). *Journal of Studies on Alcohol, 36,* 117–126.

Sher, K. J. (1985). Excluding problem drinkers in high-risk studies of alcoholism: Effect of screening criteria on high-risk versus low-risk comparisons. *Journal of Abnormal Psychology, 94,* 106–109.

Sher, K. J., & Descutner, C. (1986). Reports of paternal alcoholism: Reliability across siblings. *Addictive Behaviors, 11,* 25–30.

Sher, K. J., & Levenson, R. W. (1982). Risk for alcoholism and individual differences in the stress-response-dampening effect of alcohol. *Journal of Abnormal Psychology, 91,* 350–367.

Swartz, C. M., Drews, V., & Cadoret, R. (1987). Decreased epinephrine in familial alcoholism: Initial findings. *Archives of General Psychiatry, 44,* 938–941.

Tarter, R. E., Hegedus, A. M., Goldstein, G., Shelly, C., & Alterman, A. I. (1984). Adolescent sons of alcoholics: Neuropsychological and personality characteristics. *Alcoholism: Clinical and Experimental Research, 8,* 216–222.

Utne, H. E., Hansen, F. V., Winkler, K., & Schulsinger, F. (1977). Ethanol elimination rate in adoptees with and without parental disposition towards alcoholism. *Journal of Studies on Alcohol, 38,* 1219–1223.

Van Thiel, D. H., & Lester, R. (1976). Alcoholism: Its effect on hypothalamic pituitary gonadal function. *Gastroenterology, 71,* 318–327.

Vogel-Sprott, M., & Chipperfield, B. (1987). Family history of problem drinking among young male social drinkers: Behavioral effects of alcohol. *Journal of Studies on Alcohol, 48,* 430–436.

Wolff, P. H. (1972). Ethnic differences in alcohol sensitivity. *Science, 175,* 449–450.

IX

TREATMENT APPROACHES
AND MODELS

22

MOLAR ENVIRONMENTAL CONTEXTS SURROUNDING RECOVERY FROM ALCOHOL PROBLEMS BY TREATED AND UNTREATED PROBLEM DRINKERS

JALIE A. TUCKER, RUDY E. VUCHINICH, AND MICHELE M. PUKISH

Recovery from alcohol problems is not reliably associated with time-limited treatments (e.g., Miller & Hester, 1986a) and depends more on the environmental contexts surrounding treatment than on client or treatment-specific characteristics (e.g., Moos, Finney, & Cronkite, 1990; Polich, Armor, & Braiker, 1981). Paths to recovery that do not involve

Reprinted from *Experimental and Clinical Psychopharmacology, 3*, 195–204. (1995). Copyright © 1995 by the American Psychological Association. Used with permission of the author.

This research was supported in part by a grant-in-aid award from the Office of the Vice President for Research at Auburn University and by Grant R-01-AA08972 from the National Institute on Alcohol Abuse and Alcoholism. Portions of this research were presented at the 101st Annual Convention of the American Psychological Association held in Toronto, Ontario, Canada, in August 1993.

We thank Angela Crawford for assistance in data collection; Kelaine Murnock for assistance in data coding; the Columbus, Georgia, Redeemer Lutheran Church, the Mobile, Alabama, Holy Cross Lutheran Church, Glen King, Wendy Reibert, Pamela and Howard Snide, and Stuart Tietzen for providing interview space off-campus; and Bonnie Beard for data entry.

treatment are common (e.g., Armor & Meshkoff, 1983; Hingson, Scotch, Day, & Culbert, 1980), but the process involved, including the role of environmental factors, has been investigated only recently (e.g., Snow, Prochaska, & Rossi, 1994; L. C. Sobell, Sobell, Toneatto, & Leo, 1993; Tucker & Gladsjo, 1993; Tucker, Vuchinich, & Gladsjo, 1994). Studying recovery and relapse patterns among untreated problem drinkers is important because (a) most problem drinkers never enter treatment, yet many recover without it; (b) knowledge about recovery and relapse processes derived from treatment samples may not generalize to untreated problem drinkers; and (c) influences on drinking outcomes cannot be separated from influences on help-seeking patterns unless both treated and untreated cases are studied (Tucker & Gladsjo, 1993).

Certain environmental circumstances appear to promote behavior change in both treated and untreated problem drinkers. Treatment outcome studies with lengthy follow-ups (e.g., Moos et al., 1990) have shown that successful outcomes are associated with fewer negative event occurrences and with greater client resource during the posttreatment interval. Studies of relapse after treatment (reviewed by Tucker, Vuchinich, & Gladsjo, 1990–1991) have shown similar associations between drinking and the posttreatment environment, whether assessed by negative event occurrences (e.g., Hore, 1971; Vuchinich & Tucker, 1994) or cognitive and emotional reactions to events (e.g., Marlatt & Gordon, 1980). Most studies of natural recovery (reviewed by L. C. Sobell, Sobell, & Toneatto, 1992) also have implicated environmental variables. For example, Klingemann (1991) and Tucker et al. (1994) studied untreated recovered problem drinkers and found that negative events in several areas (e.g., health, legal, or family problems) decreased from the pre- through the postrecovery period; Klingemann also found increased positive events after initial recovery. In addition, Tucker et al. included a group of untreated active problem drinkers and found increases in negative events over a comparable time period. In a similar study, L. C. Sobell et al. (1993) failed to find a relationship between events and recovery; however, events that occurred only during the year preceding abstinence were assessed, which may have been too brief to capture the broader life contexts that support recovery. Klingemann (1991) and Tucker et al. (1994) used longer intervals that spanned the pre- and postabstinence years.

The aforementioned research is consistent with Prochaska and DiClemente's (1986; Prochaska, DiClemente, & Norcross, 1992) long-term view of the behavior change process, although they did not focus on environmental variables. Whether treatment assisted or not, recovery appears to occur over several years that bracket the discrete act of quitting drinking or involvement in time-limited interventions and is heavily influenced by problem drinkers' life circumstances. The ubiquity of unsuccessful quit attempts among problem drinkers (Tucker et al., 1994) implies that many experience circumstances that motivate initial abstinence. Because only some maintain sobriety, long-term success may depend on circumstances during the postcessation period. This argues for assessing environmental circumstances over a lengthy interval surrounding initial abstinence.

Although environmental variables have been implicated in treated and untreated recoveries, their role in recoveries by participants in Alcoholics Anonymous (AA) has not been investigated. Including problem drinkers with different help-seeking histories is important to ascertain whether a core set of environmental circumstances surrounds recoveries achieved with and without interventions. In the current study, we investigated this issue using the methods of Tucker et al. (1994) and included abstinent problem drinkers who had received no assistance, AA only, or alcohol treatment plus AA.[1] Event occurrences were assessed during a 4-year period that spanned the 2 years before and 2 years after respondents initiated abstinence. If the pattern of events found in natural recovery studies (e.g., Klingemann, 1991; Tucker et al., 1949) are related to behavior change regardless of interventions, then all three help-seeking groups should evidence a similar pattern of increased negative events prior to recovery and increased positive events after recovery. If interventions were promoted by greater preresolution negative events, resulted in greater postresolution positive events beyond those associated with recovery alone, or both, this would be manifested as Group × Year interactions, in contrast to the year main effects hypothesized for events as part of a common recovery process.

METHOD

Participant Recruitment and Screening

Natural recoveries occur outside the treatment system and require the solicitation of subjects from the community. To avoid confounding the method of recruitment with subjects' help-seeking status, all subjects were solicited using newspaper advertisements in several Alabama and Georgia communities. The advertisements asked for research participants who had overcome a drinking problem with or without treatment. Similar studies (Klingemann, 1991; L. C. Sobell et al., 1992) that evaluated the representativeness of media-solicited samples have shown no evidence of selection bias, and use of this common method allows comparisons across studies.

---

[1]Previous research (e.g., Tucker & Gladsjo, 1993) has shown that relatively few problem drinkers in the United States received formal treatment without also participating in Alcoholics Anonymous. Thus, we did not include a treatment-only group.

Respondents to the advertisements completed questionnaires by mail, including the Michigan Alcoholism Screening Test (MAST; Seltzer, 1971), Alcohol Dependence Scale (ADS; Skinner & Horn, 1984), Drinking Problems Scale (DPS; Cahalan, 1970), and questions about demographic characteristics, drinking practices, and help-seeking history. Usable questionnaires were returned by 187 of 244 respondents (77%), who were not paid. Inclusion criteria for the interview portion of the study followed L. C. Sobell et al. (1992) and Tucker et al. (1994): (a) a minimum of 5-year drinking problem history prior to recovery; (b) currently abstinent from alcohol and other drugs for at least 2 years, but no longer than 10 years, to ensure stable recoveries without extending the recall period into the distant past; (c) an unweighted MAST score of ≥5, which is the cutpoint for alcohol problems; and (d) evidence of alcohol problems based on one or more of the following: alcohol dependence symptoms (e.g., severe shakes, tolerance), as assessed by the ADS; other alcohol-related negative consequences as defined by the Rand report (Polich et al., 1981; e.g., drunk driving arrests, job loss) and as assessed by the MAST and DPS; and quantity and frequency of alcohol consumption exceeding a monthly average of four standard drinks (55 g absolute ethanol) per drinking day, with ≥5 heavy drinking days per month involving consumption of six or more drinks (82 g ethanol).

Following L. C. Sobell et al. (1992), alcohol treatment was defined as any Antabuse (disulfiram) use or alcohol-related hospitalizations, counseling, or treatment program participation in which the primary focus was on drinking problems and the provider was qualified to offer alcohol treatment. Except for requiring AA participants to have attended two or more meetings, length of treatment or AA participation was not a selection criterion for two reasons: (a) Long-term drinking outcomes have not been reliably related to treatment duration or intensity (Miller & Hester, 1986b), and (b) we focused on separating variables common to recovery from variables associated with different help-seeking histories and thus did not evaluate the effectiveness of treatment or AA.

Sample Characteristics

Sixty-five respondents met the inclusion criteria. Primary reasons for exclusion were a nonabstinent drinking status (57%), abstinence of <2 years (13%) or >10 years (16%), and problem histories of <5 years (7%). Scheduling or communication problems prevented interviews with 5 eligible respondents. Interview data from 3 subjects were excluded, 2 because their collaterals reported that they had not abstained continuously and 1 because of extensive memory problems during the interview. The final sample therefore included 57 subjects: 21 treatment plus AA, 18 AA only, and 18 no assistance.

The help-seeking groups did not differ significantly on duration of problem drinking (M = 16.3 years, SD = 7.8) or abstinence (M = 6.8 years, SD = 4.0). As expected, treatment-plus-AA subjects reported more total help-seeking episodes (M = 2.9, SD = 1.4) than did AA-only subjects (M = 1.4, SD = 0.6), $t(37)$ = 3.52, p < .002, but lifetime AA attendance was similar across the groups (M = 953.1 meetings, SD = 727.3). Among treatment-plus-AA subjects, the percentages of help-seeking episodes comprised of alcohol treatment only, AA only, or both were 50.0%, 36.7%, and 13.3%, respectively. Treatments included inpatient (M = 1.10 episodes) and outpatient (M = 0.10 episodes) alcohol programs, alcohol-focused outpatient counseling by a nonphysician (M = 0.33), Antabuse (M = 0.23), and other (M = 0.14, e.g., residential).

The groups did not differ significantly with respect to age at resolution (M = 43.9, SD = 11.6 years), gender (80.7% male), race (96.5% Caucasian), and percentage married during the year prior to resolution (63.6%). No-assistance subjects had less education (M = 12.7, SD = 3.1) than did AA-only (M = 15.5, SD = 1.7, p < .01) and treatment-plus-AA (M = 14.5, SD = 2.8, p < .05) subjects, $F(2, 54)$ = 5.15, p < .01, who did not differ significantly. This difference had no consequence for subjects' income and employment status prior to resolution, which did not differ significantly across groups (mean income = $38,813, SD = 30,928; mean weeks employed = 43.02, SD = 17.03; 63% white-collar occupations). The similarities across groups indicated that any differences in events surrounding recovery could not be attributed to demographic differences.

Subject Interview Procedures

Subjects were interviewed individually in 1.5- to 2.5-hr sessions and were paid $10. After giving their written informed consent, they were administered a breath test (Alco-Sensor III, Intoximeters, St. Louis, MO) to verify no recent alcohol consumption. Subjects then were provided with recall aids suggested by research on memory for naturalistic events, which included calendars on which they recorded personally memorable events; lists of news events for each month of the interview period; popular TV shows, movies, and songs for each year covered; and photographs of different kinds and sizes of alcoholic beverages. Subjects had been asked to bring any materials that would aid recall (e.g., old appointment books). Following Tucker et al. (1994), the interview assessed, in order of administration, subjects' drinking patterns, event occurrences, and resolution and help-seeking patterns.

Drinking Practices

The Lifetime Drinking History (LDH; Skinner & Skeu, 1982) was used to assess drinking during the 3 years before subjects abstained. Subjects defined "phases" that involved a consistent drinking pattern or sustained abstinence and, within each phase involving drinking, reported (a) the frequency and quantity of alcohol consumption for their average and maximum drinking patterns; (b) the percentage of drinking that involved beer, wine, or liquor consumption; and (c) the percentage of drinking that occurred in the morning. High interview–reinterview reliabilities on the LDH have been found using treated (Skinner & Sheu, 1982; L. C. Sobell et al., 1988) and untreated (Gladsjo, Tucker, Hawkins, & Vuchinich, 1992) problem drinkers; good subject–collateral agreements have been observed using untreated problem drinkers (Gladsjo et al., 1992); and LDH indexes are significantly correlated with biochemical measures of liver dysfunction (Skinner, 1985).

Event Occurrences

As in Tucker et al. (1994), event occurrences were assessed using the Life Events Questionnaire (LEQ) developed specifically for use with alcoholics (Vuchinich, Tucker, & Harllee, 1986). The LEQ is a nonredundant compilation of five life events scales (Coddington, 1972; Dohrenwend, Krasnoff, Askenasy, & Dohrenwend, 1978; Holmes & Rahe, 1967; Raykel, Pruskoff, & Uhlenhuth, 1971; Sarason, Johnson, & Siegel, 1978) that assess 78 events in eight functional categories (i.e., work, residence, intimate relations, family relations, friendship and social activities, finances, physical health, and legal matters) and 15 miscellaneous "other" events. In the present study, we scored health habit changes separately from health problems because negative health problems may precede recovery, whereas positive health habit changes may accompany abstinence (L. C. Sobell et al., 1992, 1993). The LEQ has excellent reliability over a 2-week interval with inpatient alcoholics (Vuchinich et al., 1986) and sufficient accuracy as assessed by subject–collateral agreements using untreated problem drinkers (Gladsjo et al., 1972).

The LEQ was administered for the 4-year period that started 2 years before and continued for 2 years after subjects initiated abstinence. For each event reported, subjects indicated the date(s) of occurrence and whether the event had a positive or negative effect on their lives. If subjects could not recall an exact date, they indicated two dates within which they were certain an event occurred; the midpoint was used in the data analyses.

Resolution Patterns and Maintenance Factors

Subjects were asked how many times they had made serious but unsuccessful attempts to quit or moderate their drinking; their drinking goals in each attempt; and length of time required to achieve their current abstinence; and what motivated their recovery and what helped maintain it. Depending on their help-seeking status, they rated barriers to or incentives for alcohol treatment, AA, or both; these data are reported separately along with analyses of the questionnaire measures of alcohol problems (Tucker, 1995). Information also was gathered about each help-seeking episode.

Collaterals

Most subjects (82.3%) nominated a collateral, although this was not a requirement to avoid biasing the sample in favor of subjects with intact social networks. Collaterals (50% spouses, 11% other family members, and 39% friends) were not paid and were interviewed by telephone by an interviewer who was unaware of the subjects' responses; 76.1% had lived with the subjects during all or part of the assessment interval, and 69.6% had had daily contact. All but one collateral knew the subject well enough to report on the subjects' drinking and help-seeking status. Collaterals also completed the DPS and a Drinking Consequences Checklist (DCC; L. C. Sobell et al., 1992) regarding the subjects' drinking problems.

Collaterals verified that the 57 subjects retained in the sample had abstained for 2 or more years, and subject and collateral reports of the year when subjects began abstaining were highly correlated ($r = 95$, $p < .001$). All collaterals for no-assistance and AA-only subjects and all but six collaterals for treatment-plus-AA subjects verified subjects' help-seeking status. In the six discrepant cases, collaterals indicated the subjects had received an alcohol intervention, although the collaterals and subjects did not agree fully on the details.

Subject and collateral reports were significantly correlated on the DPS ($r = .62$, $p < .001$), DCC ($r = .63$, $p < .001$), and most measures of drinking practices (e.g., $r = .65$ for drinking days per month—average pattern, $p < .01$; 88.2%, 88.2%, and 94.1% agreement for whether subjects drank beer, wine, and liquor, respectively, during their average pattern). Lower, albeit significant, correlations were obtained for quantities of alcohol consumption (e.g., $r = .38$, $p < .05$, for milliliters of ethanol per day—average pattern), which are less amenable to collateral observation (cf. Gladsjo et al., 1992; L. C. Sobell et al., 1988). Also, on most measures, subjects reported greater alcohol use or alcohol problems than did collaterals. This is consistent with accurate reporting by both participants because subjects have greater access to their behavior. Overall, these data support the accuracy of subjects' reports and are consistent with previous findings using similar retrospective methods (Gladsjo et al., 1992; L. C. Sobell et al., 1988; Vuchinich, Tucker, & Harllee, 1988).

RESULTS

Event Occurrences Surrounding Recovery

Events reported on each LEQ subscale were summed separately for Years 1, 2, 3, and 4, and the subscales were analyzed in separate 3 × 4 (Group × Year) repeated measures analyses of variance (ANOVAs). Subjects initially abstained at the end of Year 2. As shown in Figure 1, significant year main effects were obtained for seven subscales: Health Problems, $F(3, 162) = 6.59$, $p < .0004$; Legal, $F(3, 162) = 7.49$, $p < .0001$; Family Relations, $F(3, 162) = 2.69$, $p < .05$; Intimate Relations, $F(3, 162) = 6.86$, $p < .0002$; Social, $F(3, 162) = 10.97$, $p < .0001$; Health Habits, $F(3, 162) = 22.61$, $p < .0001$; and Finances, $F(3, 162) = 14.67$, $p < .0001$. The analyses also revealed significant group main effects for the Legal subscale, $F(2, 54) = 5.27$, $p < .009$, and the Social subscale, $F(2, 54) = 3.21$, $p < .05$. There were significant Group × Year interactions, $Fs(6, 162) = 2.25$ and 2.21, $ps < .042$ and $.045$, for the Legal and Social subscales, respectively, which qualify the year and group main effects for both subscales. The interactions are shown in Figure 2. The ANOVAs for the Work, Residence, and Other subscales yielded no significant effects.

Scheffé's procedure was used to probe the year main effects (Kirk, 1968). Events in the legal, health problems, family relations, and intimate relations categories evidenced significant decreases over time. Significantly more legal events occurred during the 2 years preceding resolution compared with the 2 years following resolution ($p < .05$). For health problems ($p < .05$) and family relations ($p < .07$), more events were reported during the year preceding resolution compared with the other 3 years. The majority of events in these categories were negative (64%, 59%, and 64% for health problems, legal, and family relations, respectively), indicating that abstinence was associated with decreased problems. With one exception, the same pattern was found for intimate relations events: Significantly more events were reported in Years 1, 2, and 3 compared with Year 4 ($p < .01$); the majority of events were negative in Years 1 and 2 (52%) but were positive in Year 3 (73%). Thus, abstinence was associated with postresolution decreases in negative intimate relations events and with postresolution increases in positive events.

A different pattern was found in the social, health habit, and finances categories, which were composed of 19%, 29%, and 29% negative events, respectively. For all subscales, significantly more events were reported during the year immediately following resolution (Year 3) compared with the other 3 years ($ps < .01$). Recovery was thus associated with increased positive events in these categories.

To probe the significant interactions, we used simple main effects tests to compare the three groups at each year and to compare change over years

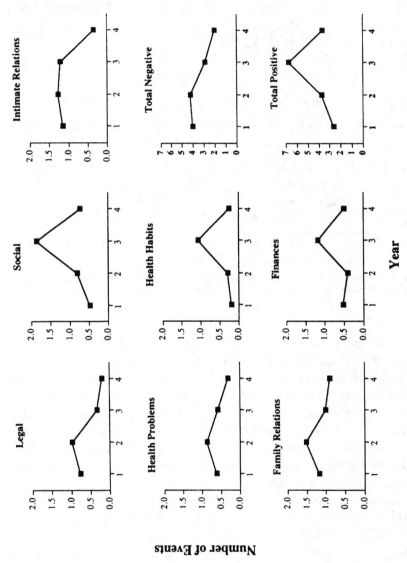

Figure 1. Mean event occurrences per year for significant year main effects collapsed across help-seeking groups on the Life Events Questionnaire. Participants in all groups initiated stable abstinence at the end of Year 2.

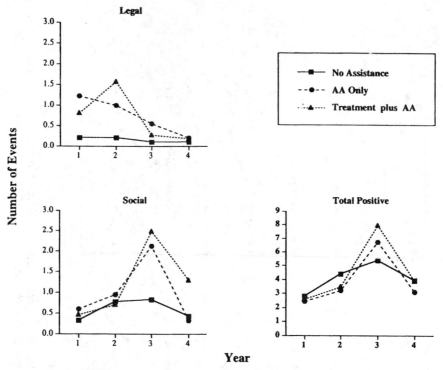

Figure 2. Mean event occurrences per year for significant interaction effects on the Life Events Questionnaire. AA = Alcoholics Anonymous.

within each group (α = .05, two-tailed, for each of the two sets of comparisons for each subscale). The year and group main effects for the legal and social subscales were primarily attributable to the two groups of subjects who had received assistance: AA-only and treatment-plus-AA subjects showed significant change over time in legal and social events ($ps < .02$), whereas no-assistance subjects did not. Compared with no-assistance subjects, assisted subjects reported more (negative) legal events during the 2 years before resolution and more (positive) social events during the year following resolution ($ps < .05$).

As shown in Figure 1, significant year main effects also were obtained for total negative, $F(3, 159) = 8.93$, $p < .0001$, and total positive, $F(3, 159) = 32.27$, $p < .0001$, events. Like the year main effects on the LEQ subscales, more negative events were reported during the 2 years before than during the 2 years after resolution, and more positive events were reported during the year following resolution compared with the other 3 years ($ps < .01$). As shown in Figure 2, a significant Group $\times$ Year interaction also was obtained for total positive events, $F(6, 159) = 2.22$, $p < .045$. Although all three groups experienced a significant change over time ($ps < .01$), there were group differences in the degree of increase during

Year 3 ($p < .01$). Receiving assistance, especially treatment, was associated with greater positive events during the first postresolution year.

A more fine-grained analysis of this group difference was performed on the sums of positive events during the 3-month quarters of Year 3. The analysis yielded a (near significant) group main effect, $F(2, 54) = 3.02$, $p < .058$, a time main effect, $F(3, 162) = 37.86$, $p < .0001$, and a Group × Time interaction, $F(6, 162) = 2.46$, $p < .027$. Comparisons showed that all groups reported significant decreases in positive events from the beginning to the end of Year 3. In addition, significant group differences were found during the first quarter (both assisted groups reported more events than did unassisted subjects) and during the second quarter (treatment-plus-AA subjects reported more events than the other two groups; $ps < .01$). Events also were categorized according to whether their effects were time limited (e.g., brief illness, vacation) or of extended duration (e.g., improved finances, social and intimate relations); 94.8% of the positive events reported in Year 3 had extended effects, some of which probably continued into Year 4.

In a similar analysis, we examined total negative events during the eight quarters of Years 2 and 3 (recall that the overall analysis revealed a significant decrease from the pre- through postresolution interval and no group differences). A significant time main effect was obtained, $F(7, 378) = 4.20$, $p < .0002$. Comparisons showed that negative events increased significantly during the last quarter of Year 2 and then decreased significantly throughout Year 3, with the lowest mean occurring during the second quarter ($ps < .01$). Most negative events in Years 2 (95.6%) and 3 (94.0%) had effects with extended duration. Together, these findings based on events within quarters surrounding the initiation of abstinence generally mirror at a more local level the patterns of positive and negative events observed over the longer 4-year assessment interval.

Drinking Practices and Resolution Patterns

With one exception, the three help-seeking groups reported similar drinking practices on the LDH. Treatment-plus-AA subjects reported more total phases ($M = 5.0$) than AA-only ($M = 3.0$) and no-assistance ($M = 2.89$) subjects, $F(2, 54) = 3.17$, $p < .05$, indicating greater variability in their preresolution drinking patterns. Otherwise, the groups reported similar percentages of phases to involve alcohol consumption (grand mean = 88.4%) and similar frequencies and quantities of drinking during their average and maximum drinking patterns (average pattern: $M = 20.12$ days per month, $SD = 6.71$, with a mean of 231.84 ml of ethanol consumed per drinking day, $SD = 154.67$; maximum pattern: $M = 9.13$ days per month, $SD = 6.66$, with a mean of 372.12 ml of ethanol consumed per drinking day, $SD = 199.21$). On the basis of average pattern drinking, the groups also reported similar percentages of liquor, beer, and wine consumption (56.8%, 38.9%, and 4.3%, respectively) and the percentage of morning drinking (12.2%).

Most subjects (84%) had prior serious but failed attempts to change their drinking ($M = 65.44$ attempts, $SD = 149.04$, range = 0–751). Moderation drinking ($M = 56.80$ attempts), rather than abstinence ($M = 8.63$), was the goal in most failed quit attempts, $F(1, 43) = 4.45$, $p < .041$. There were no significant group differences in the number of failed attempts, but 7 of 9 subjects who quit during their first attempt were in the no-assistance group, and 2 were in the AA-only group. When subjects successfully quit, 79% achieved abstinence within 6 days or less (75% within 1 day), and 21% gradually reduced their drinking over a mean of 6.3 months.

For the two assisted groups, initiation of stable abstinence occurred during a help-seeking episode for 30.8% of subjects, 5.1% quit many months or years after an episode, and 64.1% began abstaining several days or weeks before seeking help. The latter pattern was especially common among treatment-plus-AA subjects (85.7%) compared with AA-only subjects (38.9%), $\chi^2(1, N = 39) = 15.38$, $p < .001$.

Perceived Reasons for Resolution

Following Tucker et al. (1994), two independent raters categorized subjects' reported reasons for resolution ($M = 1.49$ reasons, range = 0–4) into 1 of the 10 LEQ categories or as being attributable to an alcohol-focused intervention. "Other" reasons were further categorized into religious influences or experiences and negative personal states (e.g., loss of dignity, no self-respect). The raters agreed on 93.1% of the assignments. The raters also categorized each reason as a negative or positive influence (94.3% agreement) and, similar to the scheme of Sobell et al. (1993), classified each subject into one of three categories defined by the temporal relationship between influences on recovery and the act of quitting drinking (90.6% agreement): (a) influences that occurred within hours or days before quitting drinking; (b) longer term influences that evolved over weeks, months, or years; and (c) a combination of immediate and long-term influences. Disagreements were resolved by discussion and consensus.

As shown in Table 1 and consistent with Tucker et al. (1994), health problems were cited the most frequently as motivating recovery. Smaller percentages of subjects cited reasons in all other LEQ categories except for residential and health habit changes. Like the preresolution event data, almost all reasons were negative. Among the two assisted groups, only 17.9% reported that an intervention motivated recovery.

Regarding temporal relationships between perceived influences on resolution and the act of quitting drinking, 22.8% of subjects reported only immediate influences, 56.1% reported only long-term influences, and

TABLE 1
Perceived Reasons for Resolution, Influences on Resolution Maintenance, and Other Health Habit Changes Reported by Participants Who Had Received No Assistance, AA Only, or Treatment Plus AA

Variable	% participants citing factor			
	No assistance	AA only	Treatment plus AA	All participants
Reasons for resolution				
Physical health problems	44.4	50.0	28.6	40.4
Illness or injury	(33.3)	(33.3)	(14.3)	(26.3)
Negative physical effects of drinking episodes	(11.1)	(16.7)	(14.3)	(14.1)
Family problems	22.2	22.2	28.6	24.6
Negative personal effects of drinking (e.g., no self-respect)	16.7	27.8	42.9	29.8
Marital problems	27.8	11.1	4.8	14.0
Religious experiences or reasons	16.7	11.1	4.8	10.5
Social problems	0.0	16.7	9.5	8.8
Legal problems	5.6	0.0	9.5	5.3
Financial problems	5.6	5.6	4.8	5.3
Work-related problems	0.0	11.1	0.0	3.5
Change in living arrangements	0.0	0.0	0.0	0.0
Other health habit changes	0.0	0.0	0.0	0.0
Intervention related	—	16.7	19.0	17.9
Resolution maintenance factors				
AA	—	72.2	52.4	61.5
Religious investment	33.3	22.2	23.8	26.3
Role of family members	50.0	5.5	9.5	21.1*
Spouse only	(11.1)	(0.0)	(9.5)	(7.0)
Changes in personal willpower	22.2	5.5	4.8	10.5
Other major lifestyle change (e.g., social activities, health habits)	5.5	16.7	4.8	8.8
Miscellaneous other factors[a]	16.7	16.7	14.3	15.8
Other health habit changes				
Increased physical activity	43.8	33.3	57.1	45.5
Dietary improvements	50.0	33.3	47.6	43.6
Attempts to quit smoking	50.0	50.0	24.0	40.0
Quit after stopping drinking	(18.8)	(44.4)	(24.0)	(29.1)
Quit before stopping drinking	(18.8)	(0.0)	(0.0)	(5.5)
Still trying to quit	(12.4)	(5.6)	(0.0)	(5.5)
Quit other drug use or abuse	18.8	44.4	42.9	36.4
Nonprescribed drugs (e.g., marijuana, cocaine)	(18.8)	(27.8)	(33.3)	(27.3)
Prescribed drugs (e.g., Valium, Xanax)	(0.0)	(16.7)	(9.5)	(9.1)

Note. Numbers in parentheses represent subsets of the total percentage for that variable. AA = Alcoholics Anonymous.
[a]Factors cited by less than 5% of subjects. No subject cited treatment as a maintenance factor.
*$p < .01$ (two-tailed).

17.5% reported both immediate and long-term influences (3.6% gave no reasons or the temporal dimension was unclear). Thus, as in Tucker et al. (1994), most subjects (73.5%) reported (a subset of) influences that evolved over a lengthy time period, a pattern also evident in the event data.

Resolution Maintenance Factors

Two raters categorized subjects' reports of factors that helped them remain abstinent (M = 1.33 factors, range = 1–5) into 1 of 17 maintenance categories used by Tucker et al. (1994) and Sobell et al. (1993) or as involving AA or alcohol treatment (97.4% agreement). The percentages of subjects citing each factor are shown in Table 1. Two findings were striking: Most assisted subjects attributed maintenance of abstinence to AA, but none of the treatment-plus-AA subjects attributed it to treatment. By contrast, no-assistance subjects were significantly more likely to cite the role of family members in maintenance.

Health Habit Changes

Table 1 shows the percentages of subjects who reported making health habit changes other than drinking; 52 subjects made at least one other change (M = 1.76, range = 0–5). Increased physical activity and dietary improvements were the most common, but quitting smoking and use of other drugs also occurred. Most changes occurred after subjects quit drinking.

DISCUSSION

The results of our study add to evidence that recovery from drinking problems is influenced by environmental variables that operate outside the context of interventions (e.g., Moos et al., 1990; Tucker et al., 1990–1991). As found previously (e.g., Klingemann, 1991; Tuchfeld, 1981; Tucker et al., 1994), negative events preceded abstinence in several areas of functioning and may motivate attempts to quit. Many quit attempts are unsuccessful, however, and the increased positive events that followed abstinence (especially during the first 3–6 months), coupled with the decreased negative events, may be critical contextual factors that support recovery. Although postabstinence increases in positive events were greater among problem drinkers who received interventions, event changes common to all groups were more pervasive than those related to help-seeking status. Moreover, most subjects reported positive health habit changes other than quitting drinking, which suggests that the environmental context surrounding recovery from drinking supported generalized positive changes in behavior patterns.

The finding that different contexts surrounded initial behavior change versus maintenance is consistent with the assumptions guiding relapse prevention (Marlatt & Gordon, 1985) and Miller's (1985; Miller & Rollnick, 1991) situational analysis of variables that motivate alcohol treatment entry and behavior change. It further suggests the potential value of assessing contextual factors when clients enter treatment. Motivation for change may be related to life–health areas in which clients have experienced negative events related to drinking (cf. Thom, 1987), and such contextual factors may provide a basis for treatment matching. For example, the success of behavioral marital therapy with problem drinkers (e.g., O'Farrell, Choquette, Cutter, Brown, & McCourt, 1993) suggests the utility of a focused, functional approach to treatment selection, although specific interventions have not been as well developed for other types of alcohol-related dysfunction. Matching conducted on the basis of such contextual variables may facilitate positive outcomes more so than matching done on the basis of stable drinker characteristics, drinking practices, and other standard diagnostic criteria that have characterized research to date (cf. Miller & Hester, 1986c).

More generally, the event complex surrounding recovery argues for a molar contextualist perspective (see Hayes, Hayes, & Reese, 1988; Vuchinich & Tucker, 1996) on the addictive behavior change process. Such a view emphasizes the broader temporal and environmental context that surrounds the often circumscribed act of quitting drinking. Emphasis is on understanding how changes in drinking emerge out of the dynamic historic and contemporary commerce of individuals with their life circumstances, rather than on identifying temporally contiguous events, feelings, or cognitions that immediately precede or "trigger" abstinence (e.g., Ludwig, 1985; L. C. Sobell et al., 1993). Our event data and subjects' perceived reasons for resolution[2] support this view by suggesting that (a) no single event or a category of events typically was the sole influence on recovery

---

[2]As discussed by Tucker, Vuchinich, and Gladsjo (1994), it is important to note that respondents' perceived reasons for quitting drinking and for maintaining abstinence are attributional measures that differ conceptually and methodologically from the objective measures of events surrounding initial abstinence. Both levels of analysis are probably important for understanding the recovery process; they may interact in complex ways, and relationships between the two variable classes merit further evaluation. However, most previous studies of natural recovery and studies of relapse processes after treatment have relied on participants to identify the relevant variables and have not objectively measured the surrounding environmental contexts. This risks obtaining reports that are more susceptible to attributional biases and may obscure environmental influences that operate over longer periods of time, such as those identified in the current study. As one example, when some participants cited changes in personal willpower as important for resolution maintenance, this may not indicate a causal role of increased willpower in recovery as much as it reflects a common attributional tendency of individuals to take credit for success by attributing it to internal, personal attributes, rather than to external events. Such attributional biases are less likely to operate when respondents report on observable events and behaviors that do not require subjective inferences and when reports are collected using structured inventories (Vuchinich et al., 1988).

(although occasionally an event within this broader complex might have provided the final impetus for change), and (b) in most cases, recovery involved a combination of short- and long-term influences that evolved over several years. Although others (e.g., Marlatt & Gordon, 1985; Prochaska et al., 1992) have emphasized the extended time frame of addictive behavior change, they focused largely on internal psychological processes that mediate change rather than on environmental variables. The role of environmental contexts thus has not been well explored in process-oriented studies of relationships among recovery attempts, relapse episodes, and help-seeking episodes over lengthy intervals.

In this regard, one of the study's more intriguing findings was that many subjects initiated abstinence days or weeks before receiving interventions, especially treatment, a finding also reported by Maisto, Sobell, Sobell, Lei, and Sykora (1988). Similarly, subjects' stated reasons for resolution and for maintenance suggested that interventions did not motivate behavior change but did assist with maintenance. These findings question the traditional role ascribed to interventions in motivating and producing behavior change and raise new questions about the functional value of interventions within the life contexts of problem drinkers (cf. Pringle, 1982). The variables critical for generating recovery attempts appear to reside outside the immediate context of interventions, but interventions may help consolidate initial changes in drinking and may provide a forum for addressing other alcohol-related problems (e.g., marriage, legal problems). This view is consistent with research on help-seeking (e.g., Thom, 1987), which has shown that alcohol treatment utilization often is motivated more by individuals' interest in resolving alcohol-related problems than in stopping drinking.

Differences in events attributable to help-seeking status were more limited than the common environmental changes associated with recovery. Nevertheless, problem drinkers who received interventions reported relatively more preresolution legal events, which is a well-worn path to receiving interventions (e.g., Weisner, 1990). Assisted subjects also experienced greater postabstinence improvements in social activities. Because all assisted problem drinkers participated in AA, it is not clear whether their reports of increased positive social events reflected involvement in AA or more global changes. Given that assisted subjects reported more postabstinence positive events in general, especially during the first several months after recovery, it appears that interventions facilitated naturally occurring improvements associated with recovery, particularly in the social area. The latter finding may prove important, given that social factors made up the only group difference in factors cited as important for maintenance. Many subjects in both assisted groups attributed maintenance to involvement in AA, which provides a supportive nondrinking social network, whereas no-assistance subjects were more likely to cite the role of family members. This suggests that social support is important for maintenance but that the groups obtained it from different sources.

Finally, Schachter (1982) suggested that individuals who can quit on their own never seek assistance, which should result in assisted subjects reporting relatively more failed quit attempts (cf. Cohen et al., 1989). We found no such differences, perhaps because of the wide variability in quit attempts in all groups. However, 7 of 9 subjects who quit on the first attempt were in the no-assistance group, and none were in the treatment-plus-AA group. Although the role of failed quit attempts in promoting help-seeking remains unclear, past failures appear to have been informative about drinking goals. As found by Tucker et al. (1994), moderation drinking, rather than abstinence, was the goal in most failed quit attempts, and these failures might have convinced subjects of the necessity of abstinence. Preference for moderation drinking in failed recovery attempts was similar across groups, even though two groups had participated in AA. The apparent lack of connection between drinking goals and receipt of an abstinence-oriented intervention is reminiscent of treatment outcome studies that showed inconsistent relationships between treatment program drinking goals and posttreatment drinking outcomes (see M. B. Sobell & Sobell, 1987).

Although our study yielded a coherent picture of the environmental contexts that surround recovery, the generality of the findings is potentially limited by the correlational design, retrospective data collection, modest sample size, and the predominately White, middle-class, male sample. However, until the variables that influence recovery and help-seeking processes are better investigated, prospective process-oriented studies will be difficult to conduct because bases for selecting problem drinkers for inclusion who are likely to achieve desired drinking outcomes or help-seeking pattern are not well established. Retrospective studies using preexisting groups with known outcomes should help identify the relevant variable classes, which then can be investigated prospectively. Confidence in the observed relationships in the current study is increased by the good subject–collateral agreements (cf. Gladsjo et al., 1992; L. C. Sobell et al., 1988) and because the study replicated and extended the findings of Klingemann (1991) and Tucker et al. (1994); note also that the Tucker et al. sample included more Blacks and more women, was conducted in another region of the United States, and showed similar results.

Thorough explication of variables common to recovery regardless of the path taken, and separation of those variables from influences on help-seeking, will require programmatic studies that variously include problem drinkers with different help-seeking experiences and different drinking outcomes, including abstinence, moderation, and problem drinking. Greater integration of the previously distinct literatures on recovery processes and help-seeking patterns is indicated, and the focus of clinical research should be expanded to include both treated and untreated problem drinkers.

REFERENCES

Armor, D. J., & Meshkoff, J. E. (1983). Remission among treated and untreated alcoholics. In N. K. Mello (Eds.), *Advances in substance abuse: Behavioral and biological research* (Vol. 3, pp. 239–269). Greenwich, CT: JAI Press.

Cahalan, D. (1970). *Problem drinkers: A national survey.* San Francisco: Jossey-Bass.

Coddington, R. D. (1972). The significance of life events as etiologic factors in the diseases of children. *Journal of Psychosomatic Research, 16,* 7–18.

Cohen, S., Lichtenstein, E., Prochaska, J. O., Rossi, J. S., Gritz, E. R., Carr, C. R., Orleans, C. T., Schoenbach, V. J., Biener, L., Abrams, D., DiClemente, C., Curry, S., Marlatt, G. A., Cummings, M. K., Emont, S. L., Giovino, G., & Ossip-Klein, D. (1989). Debunking myths about self-quitting: Evidence from 10 prospective studies of persons who attempt to quit smoking by themselves. *American Psychologist, 44,* 1355–1365.

Dohrenwend, B. S., Krasnoff, L., Askenasy, A. R., & Dohrenwend, B. P. (1978). Exemplification of a method for scaling life events: The PERI Life Events Scale. *Journal of Health and Social Behavior, 19,* 205–229.

Gladsjo, J. A., Tucker, J. A., Hawkins, J. L., & Vuchinich, R. E. (1992). Adequacy of recall of drinking patterns and event occurrences associated with natural recovery from alcohol problems. *Addictive Behaviors, 17,* 347–358.

Hayes, S. C., Hayes, L. J., & Reese, H. W. (1988). Finding the philosophical core: A review of Stephen C. Pepper's *World hypothesis: A study in evidence. Journal of the Experimental Analysis of Behavior, 50,* 97–111.

Hingson, R., Scotch, N., Day, N., & Culbert, A. (1980). Recognizing and seeking help for drinking problems. *Journal of Studies on Alcohol, 41,* 1102–1117.

Holmes, T. H., & Rahe, R. H. (1967). The Social Readjustment Rating Scale. *Journal of Psychosomatic Research, 11,* 213–218.

Hore, B. D. (1971). Live events and alcoholic relapse. *British Journal of Addiction, 6,* 25–37.

Kirk, R. E. (1968). *Experimental design: Procedures for the behavioral sciences.* Belmont, CA: Brooks/Cole.

Klingemann, H. K.-H. (1991). The motivation for change from problem alcohol and heroin use. *British Journal of Addiction, 86,* 727–744.

Ludwig, A. M. (1985). Cognitive processes associated with "spontaneous" recovery from alcoholism. *Journal of Studies on Alcohol, 46,* 53–58.

Maisto, S. A., Sobell, L. C., Sobell, M. B., Lei, H., & Sykora, K. (1988). Profiles of drinking patterns before and after outpatient treatment for alcohol abuse. In T. Baker & D. Cannon (Eds.), *Assessment and treatment of addictive behaviors* (pp. 3–27). New York: Praeger.

Marlatt, G. A., & Gordon, J. R. (1980). Determinants of relapse: Implications for the maintenance of behavioral change. In P. Davidson & S. Davidson (Eds.), *Behavioral medicine: Changing health lifestyles* (pp. 410–452). New York: Brunner/Mazel.

Marlatt, G. A., & Gordon, J. R. (1985). *Relapse prevention: Maintenance strategies in the treatment of addictive behaviors.* New York: Guilford Press.

Miller, W. R. (1985). Motivation for treatment: A review with special emphasis on alcoholism. *Psychological Bulletin, 98,* 84–107.

Miller, W. R., & Hester, R. K. (1986a). The effectiveness of alcoholism treatment: What research reveals. In W. R. Miller & N. Heather (Eds.), *Training addictive behaviors: Processes of change* (pp. 121–174). New York: Plenum.

Miller, W. R., & Hester, R. K. (1986b). Inpatient alcoholism treatment: Who benefits? *American Psychologist, 7,* 794–805.

Miller, W. R., & Hester, R. K. (1986c). Matching problem drinkers with optimal treatments. In W. R. Miller & N. Heather (Eds.), *Treating addictive behaviors: Processes of change* (pp. 175–203). New York: Plenum.

Miller, W. R., & Rollnick, S. (1991). *Motivational interviewing: Preparing people to change addictive behavior.* New York: Guilford Press.

Moos, R. H., Finney, J. W., & Cronkite, R. C. (1990). *Alcoholism treatment: Context, process, and outcome.* New York: Oxford University Press.

O'Farrell, T. J., Coquette, K. A., Cutter, H. S. G., Brown, E. D., & McCourt, W. F. (1993). Behavioral marital therapy with and without additional couples relapse prevention sessions for alcoholics and their wives. *Journal of Studies on Alcohol, 54,* 652–666.

Polich, J. M., Armor, D., & Braiker, H. B. (1981). *The course of alcoholism: Four years of treatment.* New York: Wiley.

Pringle, G. H. (1982). Impact of the criminal justice system on substance abusers seeking help. *Journal of Drug Issues, 12,* 275–283.

Prochaska, J. O., & DiClemente, C. C. (1986). Toward a comprehensive model of change. In W. R. Miller & N. Heather (Eds.), *Treating addictive behaviors: Processes of change* (pp. 3–27). New York: Plenum.

Prochaska, J. O., DiClemente, C. C., & Norcross, J. C. (1992). In search of how people change: Applications to addictive behaviors. *American Psychologist, 47,* 1102–1114.

Raykel, E. S., Pruskoff, B. A., & Uhlenhuth, E. H. (1971). Scaling of life events. *Archives of General Psychiatry, 25,* 340–347.

Sarason, I. G., Johnson, H. J., & Siegel, J. M. (1978). Assessing the impact of life changes: Development of the Life Experiences Inventory. *Journal of Consulting and Clinical Psychology, 46,* 932–946.

Schachter, S. (1982). Recidivision and self-cure of smoking and obesity. *American Psychologist, 37,* 436–444.

Seltzer, M. L. (1991). The Michigan Alcoholism Screening Test: The quest for a new diagnostic instrument. *American Journal of Psychiatry, 127,* 1653–1658.

Skinner, H. A. (1985). Lifetime drinking history. In D. J. Lettieri, J. E. Nelson, & M. A. Sayers (Eds.), *Alcoholism treatment assessment instruments* (NIAAA Treatment Handbook Series 2, pp. 512–527). Washington, DC: U.S. Government Printing Office.

Skinner, H. A., & Horn, J. L. (1984). *Alcohol Dependence Scale (ADS) user's guide.* Toronto: Addiction Research Foundation.

Skinner, H. A., & Sheu, W. (1982). Reliability of alcohol use indices: The Lifetime Drinking History and the MAST. *Journal of Studies on Alcohol, 43,* 1157–1170.

Snow, M. G., Prochaska, J. O., & Rossi, J. S. (1994). Processes of change in Alcoholics Anonymous: Maintenance factors in long-term sobriety. *Journal of Studies on Alcohol, 55,* 362–371.

Sobell, L. C., Sobell, M. B., Riley, D. M., Schuller, R., Pavan, D. S., Cancilla, A., Klajner, F., & Leo, G. (1988). The reliability of alcohol abusers' self-reports of drinking and life events that occurred in the distant past. *Journal of Studies on Alcohol, 49,* 225–232.

Sobell, L. C., Sobell, M. B., & Toneatto, T. (1992). Recovery from alcohol problems without treatment. In N. Heather, W. R. Miller, & J. Greeley (Eds.), *Self-control and addictive behaviors* (pp. 198–242). New York: Macmillan.

Sobell, L. C., Sobell, M. B., Toneatto, T., & Leo, G. I. (1993). What triggers the resolution of alcohol problems without treatment? *Alcoholism: Clinical and Experimental Research, 17,* 217–224.

Sobell, M. B., & Sobell, L. C. (1987). Conceptual issues regarding goals in the treatment of alcohol problems. *Drugs & Society, 1,* 1–37.

Thom, B. (1987). Sex differences in help-seeking for alcohol problems: 2. Entry into treatment. *British Journal of Addiction, 82,* 989–997.

Tuchfeld, B. S. (1981). Spontaneous remission in alcoholics: Empirical observations and theoretical implications. *Journal of Studies on Alcohol, 42,* 626–641.

Tucker, J. A. (1995). Predictors of help-seeking and the temporal relationship of help to recovery among treated and untreated recovered problem drinkers. *Addiction, 90,* 805–809.

Tucker, J. A., & Gladsjo, J. A. (1993). Help-seeking and recovery by problem drinkers: Characteristics of drinkers who attended Alcoholics Anonymous or formal treatment or who recovered without assistance. *Addictive Behaviors, 18,* 529–542.

Tucker, J. A., Vuchinich, R. E., & Gladsjo, J. A. (1990–1991). Environmental influences on relapse in substance use disorders. *International Journal of the Addictions, 25,* 1017–1050.

Tucker, J. A., Vuchinich, R. E., & Gladsjo, J. A. (1994). Environmental events surrounding natural recovery from alcohol-related problems. *Journal of Studies on Alcohol, 55,* 401–411.

Vuchinich, R. E., & Tucker, J. A. (1994). *Life events, alcoholic relapse, and behavioral theories of choice: A prospective analysis.* Manuscript submitted for publication.

Vuchinich, R. E., & Tucker, J. A. (1996). The molar context of alcohol abuse. In

L. Green & J. H. Kagel (Eds)., *Advances in behavioral economics* (Vol. 3). Norwood, NJ: Ablex.

Vuchinich, R. E., Tucker, J. A., & Harllee, L. M. (1986, August). *Individual differences in the reliability of alcoholics' reports of drinking*. Poster presented at the 94th Annual Convention of the American Psychological Association, Washington, DC.

Vuchinich, R. E., Tucker, J. A., & Harllee, L. M. (1988). Behavioral assessment. In D. M. Donovan & G. A. Marlatt (Eds.), *Assessment of addictive behaviors* (pp. 51–93). New York: Guilford Press.

Weisner, C. (1990). The alcohol treatment-seeking process from a problems perspective. Responses to events. *British Journal of Addiction, 85,* 561–569.

23

MATCHING TREATMENT FOCUS TO PATIENT SOCIAL INVESTMENT AND SUPPORT: 18-MONTH FOLLOW-UP RESULTS

RICHARD LONGABAUGH, PHILIP W. WIRTZ, MARTHA C. BEATTIE, NORA NOEL, AND ROBERT STOUT

In recent years, there has been an increasing focus in psychotherapy research toward identifying combinations of patient and treatment factors that increase treatment effectiveness (Beutler, 1991; Blatt & Felsen, 1993; Dance & Neufeld, 1988). As indicated by an examination of attribute-treatment interactions conducted previously in educational testing research (Cronbach & Snow, 1977), such study requires sophistication in research

Reprinted from the *Journal of Consulting and Clinical Psychology, 63*, 296–307. (1995). Copyright © 1995 by the American Psychological Association. Used with permission of the author.

Preparation of this article was supported in part by National Institute of Alcoholism and Alcohol Abuse Grant AA 05827, Environmental Treatment of Alcohol Abusers.

Richard Longabaugh was principal investigator. The therapy was carried out by Nora Noel, Lisa Wood, Peter Reid, Margaret Howard, Susan Norman, and Susan Swanson. Data were collected by Jennifer Udall, Ellen Weinstein, Andrew Frew, Richard Alves, Ray Brigidi, Charles Arouth, and Paul Canole. Thanks are expressed to Isabel McDevitt for her assistance in preparing this article.

design and variable measurement, as well as theory for guiding patient–treatment matching (Shoham-Salomon & Hannah, 1991; Smith & Sechrest, 1991).

In alcoholism treatment outcome research, a focus on patient–treatment matching effects has also become prominent and is currently a major thrust of investigation (Donovan & Mattson, 1994). Here, too, it has been concluded that theory must be an important ingredient in identifying patient–treatment matching effects (Finney & Moos, 1992).

Although treatment research has documented a (sometimes variable and weak) relationship between social factors and recovery from alcoholism (Gibbs & Flanagan, 1977; Moos, Finney, & Cronkite, 1990), little is known about the comparative efficacy of treatments designed to enhance the social conditions thought to be conducive for recovery. Relationship enhancement is a treatment that aims to increase a patient's investment in his or her social relationships and the support for abstinence of these relationships. The aim of the present study is to test whether different intensities of relationship enhancement treatment are more (or less) effective with patients characterized by different pretreatment levels of affiliative investment in their social network or support for abstinence by this social network. If there is a "threshold" level of relationship enhancement treatment intensity below which relationship enhancement treatment is not significantly more effective than an individually focused treatment modality, this would provide important information for the design of future relationship enhancement treatments.

THEORETICAL RATIONALE

Our theoretical approach, described elsewhere (Beattie et al., 1993; Longabaugh & Beattie, 1985; Longabaugh, Beattie, Noel, Stout, & Malloy, 1993), postulates that posttreatment alcohol involvement is a function of the person's previous alcohol involvement and psychological functioning. To the extent that the person is affiliatively or instrumentally invested in his or her social environment, both alcohol involvement and psychological functioning are each affected by support from this environment for alcohol involvement or abstinence and psychological well-being, respectively (Beattie et al., 1993). Characterizing the profiles of patients presenting for treatment on these variables suggests points for clinical intervention that should enhance treatment outcomes through a patient–treatment matching strategy (Longabaugh & Beattie, 1985). To test this theory for patient–treatment matching, we developed a randomized clinical trial to test the hypothesized set of conditions under which treatment interventions focusing on the patient's primary interpersonal relationships and world of work would be differentially effective from extended cognitive–behavioral treatment that focused exclusively on restructuring the individual patient's coping mechanisms.

The present report focuses on one aspect of the model: the patient's affiliative investment in his or her social network and the use of relationship enhancement therapy that aims to modify these relationships. This report clarifies the results of a previous analysis of this same patient population, in which outcomes achieved by patients at 12 months after treatment initiation were reported (Longabaugh et al., 1993). This earlier report compared extended cognitive–behavior (ECB) therapy with therapy that combined two intensities of a component of relationship enhancement. In this earlier report, it was hypothesized that a patient's pretreatment level of affiliative investment would interact with network posttreatment level of support for abstinence to predict level of abstinence following treatment. This prediction was supported. It was also hypothesized that treatment condition would interact with pretreatment investment and posttreatment support to produce matching effects. This prediction was not supported.

The present analysis differs from the previous report in four ways: (a) the length of follow-up is extended from 12 to 18 months from treatment initiation, (b) the two treatments that previously combined different intensities of relationship enhancement are separated and analyzed separately (called extended relationship enhancement [ERE] and brief broad spectrum [BBS] treatment), (c) the matching hypothesis focuses on the combination of pretreatment investment and pretreatment support for abstinence (rather than posttreatment support for abstinence, the subject of the earlier report), and (d) a latent growth model is used in data analysis rather than a repeated measures analysis of covariance (ANCOVA) model.

The question presently addressed is as follows: For which patient profiles will two intensities of relationship enhancement therapy increase treatment effectiveness? It is hypothesized that the effectiveness of relationship enhancement therapy depends on both the patient's pretreatment affiliative investment and support for abstinence. For this reason, a higher order interaction of treatment with support for abstinence and investment was expected.

METHOD

Patient Population

The study was conducted in an outpatient setting at a private, nonprofit psychiatric hospital in Providence, Rhode Island. Outpatient treatment was one option available to alcohol abusers seeking treatment after inpatient medical detoxification, partial hospital alcohol treatment, or as direct referrals from the community. The details of patient recruitment and the patient population are presented elsewhere (Longabaugh et al., 1993). Criteria for study inclusion were that the patient (a) be at least 18 years old, (b) have sufficient functioning to be treated in an outpatient setting, (c) have a positive score on the Alcohol Impairment Index (Armor, Polich, & Stambul, 1978), and (d) have alcohol abuse or dependence listed as a problem to be treated on the problem list of the patient's problem-oriented medical record used at this medical facility (Fowler & Longabaugh, 1975; Longabaugh, Fowler, Stout, & Kreibel, 1983). Of the 279 patients who met the criteria for study inclusion and who gave informed consent to participate in the research protocol, 229 patients (82%) completed the baseline assessment and were randomized to treatment condition.

The average age of patients was 38 years at study entry, and 69% were male. They averaged slightly more than high school education (13.1 years) and had stable residency; 28% of the patients lived alone. Their modal income was in the $15,000–$20,000 range. Half the sample (50%) had been arrested sometime in their lifetime; 10% had been imprisoned. Almost half (49%) had been previously hospitalized for alcohol-related reasons. Twenty-nine percent had a current non-substance-related Axis I diagnosis in accordance with the *Diagnostic and Statistical Manual of Mental Disorders* (3rd ed.; *DSM–III*; American Psychiatric Association, 1980), whereas 47% qualified for an Axis I diagnosis of substance abuse or dependence other than alcohol, as assessed by the Diagnostic Interview Schedule (DIS: Robins, Helzer, Croughan, & Ratcliff, 1981). Most patients (81%) had a *DSM–III* diagnosis of alcohol dependence. Estimated drinking over the past month on the Quantity-Frequency Index (Jessor, Graves, Hanson, & Jessor, 1968) averaged 5.2 oz. (approximately 147.42 g) of ethanol per day. When reporting daily drinking over the past 90 days through the time-line follow-back method (Sobell, Maisto, Sobell, & Cooper, 1979), they average 9.3 standard drinks per day and 13.2 standard drinks on drinking days. They reported being abstinent an average of 30% of the 90 days before treatment and likewise estimated that they were abstinent almost one third of the days over the past year. Almost one third had attended Alcoholics Anonymous in the past year.

Treatment

Patients were treated in one of three treatment conditions that used a social learning framework (Noel, Reid, Wood, Brinson, & Longabaugh,

1988) and that were structured to include a maximum of 20 outpatient sessions. Treatment began with one or two intake sessions. Of the 18 sessions scheduled to follow, the last two planned sessions were booster sessions, one scheduled to occur 3 months after completion of the initial course of treatment and a second session to occur 1 year following treatment initiation. In addition, two emergency sessions with the patient's primary therapist were available to the patient, at the discretion of patient and therapist.

BBS Treatment

In the introductory sessions, treatment assignment was explained to the patient and a general treatment plan was presented. The patient was asked to bring a significant other to at least one of these two sessions. An occupational therapist also attended as well as the professional who was to be the partner's therapist. Beyond these introductory sessions, BBS treatment consisted of four modules of differing intensities. Six sessions of cognitive–behavioral therapy were offered. These were provided in a group format, generally involving 6 to 8 patients. (When patients were unable to attend group sessions, individual sessions were offered as a substitute.) In this module, the focus was on the functional analysis of the antecedents and short and long range consequences of drinking. Treatment consisted of helping the patient modify these associations through cognitive–behavioral restructuring. Sessions were structured to focus on the following topics: stimulus control, rearranging consequences, restructuring cognitions, assertion training, problem solving for alternatives to drinking, and dealing with slips and relapses.

In a second module, four sessions were spent with an occupational therapist who focused on enhancing the patient's occupational behaviors (job seeking, job maintaining, or other goal-oriented activities). (This component of occupational enhancement was included to test hypotheses that were not under investigation in the present analysis.)

In a third module, four sessions were devoted to partners' therapy, where one or more significant others (e.g., spouse, child, parent, or friend) chosen by the patient were included in the treatment sessions. In these partners' sessions, the treatment focused on supporting the patient's abstinence and strengthening the relationship through improved communication, problem solving, and increasing social reinforcements.

The fourth module consisted of two didactic sessions that were offered to members of the larger social network identified by the patient. These didactic sessions were devoted to the subject of "alcohol abuse and how to help" (contingency management).

Ordinarily, delivery of these first four modules was completed within 4 months after treatment initiation. In addition to these four modules, the patient was offered two booster sessions for review and consolidation of gains. In BBS treatment, the patient was invited to bring a significant other to each of the two booster sessions.

ERE

To increase the intensity of the focus on primary relationships, ERE consisted of only three modules, two of which focused on relationship enhancement. The number of sessions allocated to partners' therapy was increased from four to eight. The focus of these sessions remained the same: (a) teaching techniques to help the relationship reinforce abstinence and deal with slips and (b) strengthening the relationship by enhancing reinforcements in the relationship and teaching communication and problem-solving skills. Because of the increase in the number of sessions devoted to the relationship, it was possible for the therapist to work on these relationship problems with greater intensity.

The two didactic sessions focusing on the patient's larger network were preserved, as were the six structured sessions devoted to cognitive–behavioral restructuring.

To maintain an equal number of treatment sessions across the three experimental treatment conditions while also increasing the intensity of the partners' therapy module, we eliminated the four-session occupational therapy module. In all other respects, ERE and BBS treatment were identical. As was the case for BBS treatment, the patient was asked to have a significant other accompany him or her to the booster sessions.

ECB Therapy

ECB therapy precluded participation of any significant others in the experimental treatment. Instead, the individually focused cognitive–behavioral therapy was intensified and extended over 16 treatment sessions. These sessions followed the two introductory sessions and preceded the two booster sessions (at which a significant other did not attend). ECB therapy was conducted in a group modality and was similar in its implementation to other cognitive therapies delivered in this format (Kadden, Cooney, Getter, & Litt, 1989; McCrady, Fink, Longabaugh, & Stout, 1983). The same topics were addressed in ECB therapy as was the case when this module was presented more briefly in the cognitive–behavioral module of the other two treatments: stimulus control, rearranging consequences, restructuring cognitions, assertion training, problem solving for alternatives to drinking, and dealing with slips and relapses. However, in ECB therapy, it was possible to spend more time on each topic, individualize its application to specific patients to a greater extent, and time the presentation of topics more flexibly to the events occurring in the patients' lives outside of treatment. Overall, ECB therapy was less structured in its implementation than its six-session counterpart delivered in BBS treatment and ERE.

Monitoring Treatment Delivery

A therapist's manual was developed and used by the treatment research supervisor (Nora Noel) and the research therapists in guiding treatment (Noel et al., 1988). The treatment research supervisor met weekly with therapists in each of the treatment conditions to supervise and assure implementation of the research protocol. Technique and cases were reviewed on a weekly basis. Therapists completed a checklist after each session to record those components of the treatment ingredients that were addressed within the session.

Assignment to Treatment Condition

Patients were randomized to treatment condition using Wei's (1978) urn randomization technique, balancing on four prognostic variables (Beattie et al., 1993; Longabaugh & Beattie, 1985; Longabaugh et al., 1993) and two additional factors. The six variables were alcohol involvement, psychological functioning, marital stability, employment stability, gender, and previous exposure to the social learning treatment model. The details and results of the assignment procedure have been previously described; the urn technique successfully balanced patients across treatment conditions (Longabaugh et al., 1993).

The Study Subsample

The sample used in the present analysis is the subsample of 188 patients (82% of the study sample) who had completed baseline testing and provided drinking data at one or more follow-up points. As our criterion for evaluability was "intention to treat," it was not necessary that the patient actually receive the treatment intended; rather, only that he or she complete baseline assessment and be informed of the randomly assigned treatment condition. Because of our use of the latent growth model for data analysis, it was not necessary that patients provide data at all five follow-up intervals.

Table 1 outlines the amount of treatment patients received in each of the three treatment conditions. Overall, patients received an average of 10.8 therapy visits across the three treatment conditions. There were no significant differences between treatments in the number of sessions patients received, except as prescribed by the research design. BBS treatment patients received an average of 2.75 cognitive–behavioral sessions, 1.81 partners' sessions, and 2.12 occupational enhancement sessions. ERE patients received an average of 2.85 cognitive–behavioral sessions, 4.00 partners' sessions, and no occupational enhancement sessions. ECB therapy patients received an average of 9.35 cognitive–behavioral sessions and no occupational or partners' sessions. In each condition, the average number of sessions received was slightly less than half those available for the condition. The large standard deviations indicate there was wide variability in the extent to which patients used the therapy available. This concern led to a more detailed description of within and between treatment variation in use of therapy modules. In Table 2 the number of patient visits to each of the therapists, cognitive–behavioral group therapist, partner's therapist, and occupational therapist, is reported for each treatment condition. As can be seen from Table 2, minimal exposure to the distinctive aspects of each treatment varied across treatment condition. For ECB, minimal exposure to treatment was defined as the patient attending at least one session of cognitive–behavioral treatment. Fifty-eight (84%) of those included in the intention to treat cohort met this criterion. For ERE, minimal exposure to treatment was defined as the patient attending at least one session with the Partner's therapist as well as one with the cognitive–behavioral therapist. Only 35 (56%) of the intention to treat cohort met this criterion. For BBS, minimal exposure to treatment was defined as attending at least one session with the occupational therapist, as well as one each with the cognitive–behavioral group therapist and partner's therapist. Thirty-seven (65%) of those included in the intention to treat cohort met this criterion. Thus, the acceptability or accessibility of ECB treatment, involving only one therapist and the patient, is greater than that of either ERE or BBS treatment, which involve inclusion of a significant other as well as one (the partner's therapist) or two (the occupational therapist) additional therapists. This confounding of differential exposure to treatment with treatment assignment raises the question as to whether any treatment matching effects observed may be the result of differential acceptability or accessibility of assigned treatment condition, rather than to the effects of the treatment actually received. To address this question, the analysis to be described was repeated including only patients receiving minimal treatment exposure.

TABLE 1
Means and Standard Deviations of Number of Visits, by Treatment

Variable	Extended cognitive–behavioral		Extended relational enhancement		Brief broad spectrum		Total sample	
	M	SD	M	SD	M	SD	M	SD
No. of introductory visits	1.81	0.99	1.81	1.10	1.89	1.03	1.84	1.03
Regular visits to individual or group therapist	9.35	7.24	2.85	2.61	2.75	2.44	5.21	5.75
Regular visits to partners' therapist			4.00	3.45	1.81	2.00	1.87	2.81
No. of family and friends evening visits			0.58	0.88	0.68	0.89	0.40	0.76
Regular visits to occupational therapist					2.12	1.91	0.64	1.43
No. of interim visits	0.07	0.26	0.35	0.96	0.12	0.43	0.18	0.63
No. of crisis visits	0.19	0.52	0.26	0.57	0.19	0.55	0.21	0.54
No. of booster visits	0.58	0.86	0.34	0.68	0.44	0.76	0.46	0.78
Total visits of all kinds	12.00	8.38	10.23	7.21	10.04	7.34	10.82	7.71

TABLE 2
Distribution of Visits, by Treatment Group

% (and n) visiting:

No. of visits	Individual group therapist			Partners' therapist		
	Extended cognitive–behavioral	Extended relational enhancement	Brief broad spectrum	Extended relational enhancement	Brief broad spectrum	Occupational therapist: brief broad spectrum
0	16 (11)	35 (22)	35 (20)	27 (17)	51 (29)	42 (24)
1	6 (4)	8 (5)	5 (3)	8 (5)	4 (2)	2 (1)
2	6 (4)	6 (4)	9 (5)	8 (5)	5 (3)	4 (2)
3	6 (4)	3 (2)	5 (3)	5 (3)	2 (1)	7 (4)
4	6 (4)	8 (5)	11 (6)	8 (5)	32 (18)	46 (26)
5	4 (3)	13 (8)	16 (9)	5 (3)	7 (4)	
6		23 (14)	19 (11)	3 (2)		
7	3 (2)	3 (2)		6 (4)		
8	3 (2)			24 (15)		
9	3 (2)			2 (1)		
10	1 (1)			3 (2)		
11	1 (1)					
14	3 (2)					
16	4 (3)					
17	36 (25)					
20	1 (1)					
M	9.35	2.85	2.75	4.00	1.81	2.12
SD	7.24	2.61	2.44	3.45	2.00	1.91

Data Collection Procedures: Pre- and Posttreatment

Patients agreeing to participate in the study were given a comprehensive assessment prior to treatment, and at this same time a significant other was interviewed. Subsequently, at 1-month intervals patients and significant others were interviewed by phone for monthly updates on the most important measures in the study. At 6-month intervals, both patient and significant other were interviewed more extensively in person whenever possible.

Variables and Their Measurements

Percentage Days Abstinent

The time-line follow-back procedure (Sobell et al., 1979) was used to measure estimated alcohol consumption. At baseline patients were interviewed concerning consumption during the 90 days prior to treatment. At subsequent monthly intervals patients provided the same information concerning consumption since last reporting. Significant others were also asked about patient drinking at these same intervals. Only patient data are used in the analyses reported here. However, reliability between patient and significant other indicates substantial agreement, particularly at follow-up. The correlation between patient and significant other reports of percent days abstinent prior to treatment is .60 and posttreatment correlations range from .76 to .84 (Stout, Beattie, Longabaugh, & Noel, 1989). Also of importance, Stout et al. (1989) conducted an analysis of mean differences in reported abstinent days between patient and significant other reports. On average the patient reported a few more days of abstinence than did the significant other, but this small discrepancy did not differ by treatment condition. From the information provided by the time-line follow-back procedure, a measure of percent days abstinent was operationally defined. The number of abstinent days reported by patients were aggregated across quarterly intervals to yield five 3-month blocks, extending from 3 months after treatment initiation to 18 months. (The period from 0 to 3 months from treatment initiation was excluded from the analysis, as a great preponderance of complete abstinence during this within-treatment period created a ceiling effect.) To better normalize the distribution of the dependent variable, we converted percent days abstinent to a log transformation using the formula $y = -\ln(101 - y)$.

Abstinent days were chosen over other possible indices of alcohol involvement because this measure has been used more often than any other measure in alcohol treatment outcome and matching studies (Babor et al., 1994; Longabaugh, 1993). It is at least as robust a measure of outcome as any other drinking measure.

Support of Alcohol Involvement Versus Abstinence

At baseline and 6-month intervals, patients were administered the Important People and Activities instrument (Clifford & Longabaugh, 1993; Longabaugh, Wirtz, & Clifford, 1995, unpublished manuscript). This instrument queries patients on their interpersonal network, who they have frequent contact with, how important these people are to them, how much they like them, and how these people respond to the patient's drinking, as well as the drinking patterns of these important others themselves. From this information, a single factor of support for alcohol involvement versus abstinence was developed (Longabaugh et al., 1993). In a summary of the factor, patients who perceive others as more accepting of their drinking and as being more likely to be drinkers themselves, are characterized as having interpersonal networks supportive of alcohol involvement. When the patient perceives others as less accepting of their drinking and more likely to be abstinent, his or her interpersonal network is characterized as supportive of abstinence.

Affiliative Social Investment

Various self-report measures were used to measure a person's affiliative social involvement. We expected that the value a person attaches to his or her relationships with others could be indexed both by measures of subjective value and by measures of amount of time spent in these relationships. Most of this information is captured in the Important People and Activities instrument, from which is abstracted the number of people in the patient's social network, the number of people in their network with whom they have daily contact, and the amount of contact they have with others important to them. In addition, subjective value is indexed in a composite score which is the average of the importance and liking ratings of the six most important others they named. As part of our intake form, we also determine the proportion of a person's life that has been spent married to the current partner and whether the patient currently lives alone or with others. From these data, a factor of affiliative social investment was derived (Longabaugh et al., 1993). To summarize, the index defining affiliative investment reflects the amount of time a person spends with other people important to him or her, as well as the subjective value of these people for the patient.

Data Analysis

A hierarchical latent growth modeling procedure (Bryk & Raudenbush, 1992) was chosen for testing the primary hypothesis. This model was favored over a more traditional repeated measures ANCOVA approach for three reasons: (a) greater analytic power, (b) a better capacity to accommodate missing data points, and (c) a perceived closer correspondence to the clinical phenomena we are attempting to understand. The two models share similarities: Both are linear models using the same (transformed) dependent measure. A disadvantage of the latent growth model is that it is new to the alcohol treatment research field and is thus unfamiliar to research consumers.

The effects of social support and affiliative investment on drinking outcome measures may vary across time; the hierarchical latent growth modeling procedure (which explicitly incorporates time into the model) permits each individual to be characterized in terms of his or her drinking level at the first follow-up and his or her rate of change in drinking behavior across the subsequent follow-ups. Conceptually this is roughly equivalent to creating a separate graphical plot for each patient, with up to 5 points plotted (one for each 3-month follow-up interval for which data are available for the patient), where the outcome variable is the vertical axis, and time (representing the dates of the follow-up interviews) is the horizontal axis. For each patient, a curve (formally called a latent growth curve) is then fit to these data so as to come as close as possible to all data points. This curve can be as simple as a straight line (i.e., a first-degree polynomial) or as complex as a fourth-degree polynomial (as there are five follow-up interviews included in the analysis: 4–6, 7–9, 10–12, 13–15, and 16–18 months after treatment initiation) and is of the same level of complexity for all patients.

Under this conceptualization, two questions were of primary interest to the study: (a) Is rate of change in percentage of days abstinent related to social support, affiliative investment, treatment condition, or a combination of social support, affiliative investment, and treatment condition? (b) Is percentage of days abstinent at any given follow-up related to social support, affiliative investment, treatment condition, or a combination of social support, affiliative investment and treatment condition?

Each patient can be characterized in terms of the "parameter estimates" of his or her growth curve; in the case of a linear specification these would be the slope and the intercept of the straight line characterizing the relationship between time and response to treatment. A second-degree polynomial specification would include a quadratic parameter estimate as well. Although the computational algorithm for deriving these parameter estimates is somewhat complex, conceptually the process can be described as a two-level regression. At the lower (follow-up) level, percentage of days abstinent is regressed on time of follow-up interview for each patient. At the higher (patient) level, the set of intercepts and slopes derived from the lower level are regressed on baseline abstinence level, treatment group, social support level, investment level, and all two-, three-, and four-way interactions between time, treatment group, social support level, and investment level. The four-way interaction is included to test for the possibility that treatment group differences in the Support × Investment interaction might change over time. Of primary interest to the study is the three-way Treatment Group × Support × Investment interaction.

In addressing the first question, a statistically significant effect associated with the Support × Investment × Treatment Group interaction would suggest that the effect of the Support × Investment × Treatment Group interaction on percentage of days abstinent changes across time. A nonsignificant interaction (suggesting that any possible effect of Support × Investment × Treatment Group interaction does not change significantly over time) lays the groundwork for pursuing the second question: Is the (relatively constant) interaction effect a statistically significant one?

This analysis was conducted twice, once for the primary analysis involving the entire intention to treatment sample ($n = 188$), and once again using only patients who met the minimal exposure to treatment criterion ($n = 130$).

RESULTS

To put the hypothesized matching effects into a familiar context, Table 3 presents the (untransformed) percentage of abstinent days for patients in each of the three treatment groups in the 3 months before treatment and for each of the five 3-month periods included in the analyses of follow-up. The table also includes the number of patients providing data at each of the observational periods. As can be seen from the table, the abstinence achieved by each treatment group was high and did not vary by treatment condition. During Months 15 to 18 after treatment initiation, ECB therapy patients averaged 86% days abstinent, ERE patients averaged 90% days abstinent and BBS treatment patients had 83% abstinent days. As reported in Table 4, these main effect differences between treatment conditions are not statistically significant.

It can also be seen that abstinence after treatment is much greater than prior to treatment. This is reflected in the significant effect for time in Table 4.

To facilitate presentation of the model tested, we presented the relationships depicted by the resulting parameter estimates in Table 4 at 15 and 18 months posttreatment in Figure 1, A and B, respectively. Figure 1 provides complementary views (i.e., each from a view which is 180 degrees opposite the perspective of the other) of the relationships between social support, investment, treatment group, and percentage of days abstinent between 15 and 18 months posttreatment initiation for patients whose baseline abstinence level was at the mean. It can be seen that, as expected, the extended relationship enhancement treatment was better than the

TABLE 3
Means and Standard Deviations of Untransformed Percentage of Days Abstinent, by Treatment Group and Time From Initiation of Treatment

| Treatment group | Baseline | | | Time since initiation of treatment | | | | | | | | | | | | | |
| | | | | 6 months | | | 9 months | | | 12 months | | | 15 months | | | 18 months | | |
	M	SD	n	M	SD	n	M	SD	n	M	SD	n	M	SD	n	M	SD	n
Extended cognitive–behavioral	35.17	32.39	69	92.59	16.28	65	89.37	22.42	65	87.03	24.28	63	85.43	28.90	62	86.51	26.92	58
Extended relationship enhancement	38.22	35.49	62	94.20	12.08	60	89.31	20.47	55	85.19	30.65	51	87.04	26.15	53	89.58	23.12	50
Brief broad-spectrum	26.11	29.50	57	89.23	22.03	55	90.05	21.02	51	88.76	23.55	50	84.67	27.39	50	82.99	27.47	57

TABLE 4
Statistical Significance of Model Parameter Estimates

Source	Numerator df[a]	F	p
Baseline	1	4.02	<.05
Treatment group	2	0.39	ns
Time	1	10.70	<.01
Social investment	1	0.43	ns
Social support	1	0.11	ns
Social investment × social support	1	3.60	ns
Time × social investment	1	0.81	ns
Time × social support	1	0.00	ns
Time × social investment × social support	1	0.20	ns
Time × treatment group	2	1.16	ns
Social investment × treatment group	2	1.50	ns
Social support × treatment group	2	0.81	ns
Social investment × social support × treatment group	2	4.28	<.02
Time × social investment × treatment group	2	0.73	ns
Time × social support × treatment group	2	4.37	<.02
Time × social support × social investment × treatment group	2	2.58	ns

[a]There are 163 degrees of freedom in the denominator for all tests presented in this table.

other two treatments for patients who initially reflected low levels of either social support for abstinence or investment in their social network. Contrary to expectations, however, patients who were comparatively low in both support and investment at treatment initiation, fared worse (on average) in this treatment than in either of the other two treatments (see Figure 1A). In contrast, the BBS treatment—which included a brief relationship enhancement component—was least effective for patients who were initially low in either support or investment (but not both) and was most effective for those who were initially either low in both support and investment (most apparent in Figure 1A) or high in both support and investment (most apparent in Figure 1B).

Statistical tests of the significance of each generic term in the model are presented in Table 4. Pretreatment percentage of days abstinent is positively predictive of posttreatment days abstinence, $p < .05$. The four-way interaction was found to be nonsignificant, $F(2, 163) = 2.58$, ns, providing no strong statistical support for the existence of a change across time in Support × Investment interaction differences between groups. With the four-way interaction reflecting nonsignificance, it was possible to test the primary hypothesis of the study, as reflected in the significant three-way Support × Investment × Group interaction, $F(2, 163) = 4.28$, $p < .02$. A priori contrasts revealed the difference in the Support × Investment in-

A

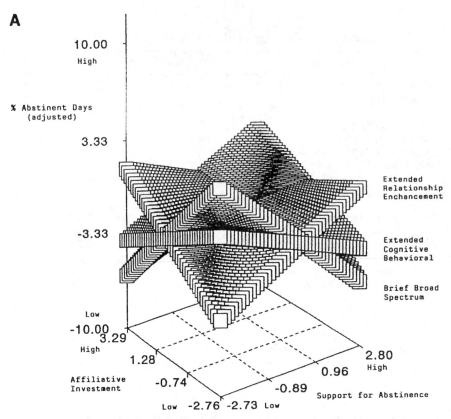

Figure 1A. Parameter estimate 15 months posttreatment.

teraction between the ERE treatment and the BBS treatment to be significant, $F(1, 163) = 7.96$, $p < .005$. Also significant was the contrast between ERE and ECB treatment, $F(1, 163) = 4.39$, $p < .04$. However, the difference in the Support × Investment interaction between the BBS treatment and the ECB treatment conditions was not found to be significant, $F(1, 163) = 0.13$, *ns*. The analysis which included only patients who met the criterion of minimal exposure to treatment criterion also revealed a statistically significant Investment × Support × Treatment interaction term, $F = 3.20$, $p < .05$, despite the greatly reduced number of denominator degrees of freedom (73). Other results of this analysis paralleled those of the primary analysis, indicating that differential exposure to minimal treatment was not responsible for the observed matching effects.

DISCUSSION

Two important findings emerge from this study. ERE treatment was found to be more effective than the other two treatment conditions in

B

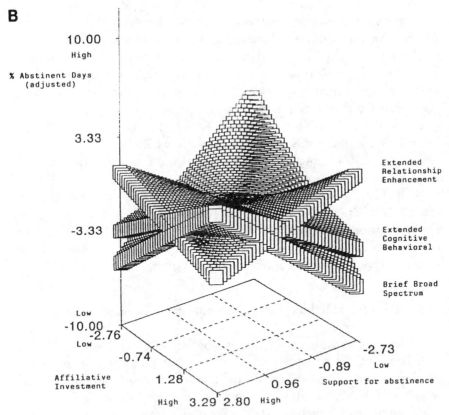

Figure 1B. Parameter estimate 18 months posttreatment.

increasing abstinence among those patients who began treatment highly invested in a network unsupportive of abstinence or with low investment in a network supportive of their abstinence. ERE was least effective with patients who were either uninvested in an unsupportive environment or were highly invested in a supportive environment. Conversely, BBS treatment was found to be more effective among patients who began treatment with either low investment in an unsupportive network or high investment in a supportive network. In ECB therapy, patients had outcomes that were relatively unaffected by pretreatment investment and support.

That ERE treatment was more efficacious than BBS treatment in attaining abstinence among patients entering treatment with relationship deficits suggests a possible "threshold" level of relationship enhancement treatment necessary to overcome these deficits. ERE and BBS treatment are the same in all respects except two. In ERE, the patient and significant other are offered up to eight sessions of relationship enhancement, whereas in BBS treatment they have only four sessions available to them. Instead, in BBS treatment, the patient receives up to four sessions of occupational enhancement, whereas in ERE there are none. Methodologically, exposure to vocational enhancement is totally confounded with the four session reduction in relationship enhancement sessions. Theoretically, however, the difference in exposure to relationship enhancement for patients differing in their affiliative investment is wholly pertinent, whereas the opportunity for such patients to receive occupational enhancement is irrelevant. Occupational enhancement is theoretically an inert active ingredient when applied to the affiliative investment dimension (Beattie et al., 1993). From the perspective of our theoretical model then, we interpret the differences between these two groups as attributable to the different exposures they have to relationship enhancement.

The fact that ERE was found to be less efficacious than the other two treatments in attaining abstinence among patients entering treatment with relationships characterized with both types of deficits suggests that there are limits to the extent to which relational deficits can be addressed with an ERE component of this intensity and duration.

Implications for Matching Patients to Specific Treatment

The primary question is, Under what set of conditions should a patient be assigned to a treatment condition that includes a focus on relationship enhancement? Second, how much therapeutic attention should be given to the relationship as a component of treatment?

Results of the present study suggest that the intensity of focus on relationship enhancement should be calibrated to the anticipated difficulty in dealing with problems in the patient's relationship to significant others. Where extended relationship treatment is most effective is when the patient is either less invested in highly supportive relationships, or highly invested in unsupportive relationships. The aim of ERE in this instance is to either increase the patient's affiliative investment in a supportive relationship or to increase the support for abstinence in relationships in which the patient is already highly invested.

ERE is comparatively least effective when the relationship is nonproblematic before treatment (i.e., high investment and high support for abstinence). It is also comparatively least effective when relationships are both highly problematic and of marginal importance to the patient (i.e., low support from relationships in which the patient is little invested).

In BBS treatment, a brief focus on the relationship, in combination with the other components of treatment, results in good outcome when the patient's relationships are nonproblematic (i.e., when the patient is highly invested in supportive relationships). In this instance, it would appear that a brief exposure to relationship enhancement is sufficient to assess and reinforce this resource for the patient. The BBS treatment patient also experiences markedly superior outcomes to those achieved in ERE when his or her social relationships are highly problematic for a direct intervention effort (i.e., when the patient has low investment in relationships which are also unsupportive of his or her abstinence). Here, the therapeutic task of both increasing the patient's investment in their existing social relationships and also modifying these relationships to be supportive of abstinence may be unachievable. From the patient's perspective, the therapeutic thrust might appear to be a distraction at best, and counterproductive at worst. In such cases, the brief therapeutic attention to primary relationships in BBS treatment may be sufficient to assess the inadvisability of attempting to change them and energizing the therapeutic focus toward increasing the patient's own coping skills, as accomplished in the ECB therapy modality, or in the cognitive–behavioral and vocational enhancement components of BBS treatment.

Figure 2 provides a visual schematic representation of our understanding of the observed results portrayed in Figure 1A and Figure 1B. In Figure 2, the effectiveness of individually focused extended cognitive therapy provides a useful context for interpretation. As portrayed by Figure 2 and consistent with the findings, the effectiveness of ECB therapy is unrelated to our characterization of the patient's interpersonal relationships. This is consistent with the rationale of ECB therapy, to develop the patient's cognitive and behavioral skills so that he or she can more effectively deal with whatever problematic areas exist. We expected, and it appears to be the

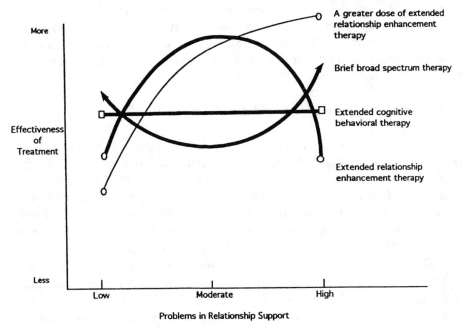

Figure 2. Schemas of effectiveness of treatment as a function of problem in relationship support and treatment type.

case, that cognitive–behavioral treatment does buffer the effects of problematic relationships.

Figure 2 highlights the conditions under which matching and mismatching occur. As can be seen from this schema, the relationship between difficulties in interpersonal relationships and effectiveness is expected to be curvilinear for both high- and low-intensity relationship enhancement treatments. In conditions of low relationship difficulty, ERE is mismatched to patient profile in that it is expending most of the therapeutic capital on a nonproblem. In contrast, both ECB therapy and BBS treatment allocate therapeutic resources to other problem areas and are more effective than ERE. In conditions of moderate difficulty in interpersonal relationships, ERE matches the patient profile well, allocating the bulk of treatment to focusing on these relationships. In contrast, BBS treatment with its brief attention to the relationship is mismatched to patient profile. The therapeutic effort is not sufficient to the task and the therapy is truncated. ECB therapy, working solely with the patient, is unable to achieve the effectiveness of extensive attention to relationships but avoids the pitfall of too brief a focus on problematic relationships. Last, in conditions of high relationship difficulty ERE is mismatched and least effective. ECB therapy and BBS treatment, which spend no and little time respectively on relationship enhancement, both achieve better outcomes.

A question for future research is whether more intensive relationship enhancement treatment than that provided in the present study would be effective in treating patients with the most problematic relationship profiles. (Such an effect would be portrayed by the hypothetic thin line in Figure 2.) Blatt and Felsen (1993) and McKay, Longabaugh, Beattie, Maisto, and Noel (1993) report findings suggestive of this hypothesis.

A Comparison of 18-Month and 12-Month Results

The present study has observed matching effects, whereas the analysis of 12-month outcomes of the same population did not find matching effects. It is informative to contrast the aims and methods of these two analyses. To review what was stated at the outset, there are four differences in design. First, the earlier study included data only through the 12-month follow-up period. In the present study, the follow-up period was extended through 18 months. Second, the earlier report used a repeated measures ANCOVA model, whereas the present study used a latent growth model. Third, the 12-month report combined two experimental groups which are differentiated in the present report, ERE and BBS treatment. Fourth, the 12-month outcome study used pretreatment investment and posttreatment support as the patient attribute matching variables, whereas the present study used pretreatment investment and pretreatment support as the matching patient attributes. This last fact by itself indicates that the results of the two studies cannot be directly compared. Nevertheless, we had included an Investment × Pretreatment Support × Treatment term in the 12-month analysis. The results were not reported because they were neither significant nor pertinent to the hypotheses tested in the earlier article.

In the present report, an interaction between Treatment × Investment by pretreatment support has been observed at the 18-month follow-up point. To examine which factors were involved in producing this discontinuity of results, we have conducted four analyses on the 12-month data set. Using the pretreatment investment and support variables as patient-matching factors and log-transformed percentage of days abstinent as the dependent variable, we ran two repeated measures ANCOVAs: the first one combined ERE and BBS treatment into a single treatment condition (described as "relationship enhancement" in the earlier article) to be compared with ECB therapy (described as "individually focused CB" in the earlier article); the second preserved ERE and BBS therapy as separate treatment conditions (as we have done in the present study). We also carried out a hierarchical latent growth model (HLM) analysis twice, once keeping ERE and BBS treatment separate and once combining them.

Inspection of the results of these four analyses indicates that, although the HLM increases the F values and decreases the p values in comparison with the repeated measures ANCOVA in both comparisons, it is the separation of the two relationship enhancement intensity conditions (ERE and BBS treatment) that brings about the significant differences between treatment groups. From these analyses it is clear that combining the two intensities of relationship enhancement treatment in the previous analysis resulted in loss of important information. Results of the present analyses allow us to considerably refine our earlier conclusions.

In the earlier report, we suggested that knowledge of the patient's pretreatment affiliative investment was an indicator of whether relationship enhancement treatment would be helpful to achieving patient sobriety. We concluded that relationship enhancement was likely to maximize outcome only for high investors who had support for abstinence following their treatment (an outcome that we could not predict before treatment assignment). By adding the patient's pretreatment support and the intensity of the relationship enhancement condition to the equation, we have found that we now have a sufficiently specified model that we can make matching predictions before treatment assignment.

Methodological Significance

The methodological implications of using the HLM procedure instead of the repeated measures ANCOVA approach used at the 12-month follow-up point may be of major significance for researchers doing longitudinal outcome studies. HLM, by permitting use of patients who have not completed all of the follow-up data points, appreciably increased the patient sample on which we were able to conduct our analysis of outcome, as well as the degrees of freedom available to conduct the analysis.

Our data set is quite comparable with others in the alcohol treatment literature, particularly where intention to treat (rather than exposure to treatment or completion of treatment) is the criterion for determining who is to be included in data analysis. "Intention-to-treat" studies are likely to lose a significant proportion of patients to follow-up, especially when the period for measuring outcome is extended over a long period of time. Particularly crucial to such multiple follow-up data points is the fact that a sizable portion of patients, although supplying some follow-up data, will miss other data points. In an analysis that requires all data points to be present, a sizable reduction in the robustness of the data analytic technique occurs. In contrast, HLM requires only one follow-up data point as a minimum for the patient to be included in the analysis.

Studies of patients who have completed treatment generally have much higher follow-up rates than the present study but constitute a partially self-selected population. To a lesser extent, this is also true of studies that have some minimum amount of exposure to treatment to be judged sufficient. In contrast, the primary analysis of the present study included all patients randomized to treatment, regardless of whether they ever showed up for even the first session.

The fact that our understanding of matching effects would have been incomplete without inclusion of a second-order matching variable suggests that other investigators be wary of oversimplification in the hypotheses and methodologies they develop for testing matching hypotheses. The strategy chosen for testing matching hypotheses should reflect the complexity of the theory (Longabaugh, Wirtz, DiClemente, & Litt, 1994). In this context, it should be noted that linear functions may also be too simple to model individual growth curves. In the present study, 75% of the sample provided complete data at all five follow-up points. This enabled the analytic procedure to converge on an admissible solution for the linear trend of the Investment × Support interaction over time. Attempts to model a higher order (e.g., quadratic) failed. Thus, these data provide no basis to assume a higher level of complexity.

Study Limitations

Several caveats must be stated. The advantages of the HLM procedure for data sets such as ours are attractive. However, HLM may carry its own limitations as well. It may be that patients with missing data points who would be excluded from the analysis may be unique in some kind of way that is correlated with the hypotheses. HLM assumes that the missing data points are randomly distributed. This may not be the case and, therefore, should be a focus for investigation in its own right. In the present study, we addressed this concern by redoing the analysis five times where we included patients who had data at at least only one follow-up data point, at least, two, three, four, and all five, respectively. The results of these analyses were similar and the conclusions remained the same. In this instance, these comparable results may not be surprising, as 75% of the patients in the original analysis completed all five follow-ups and 96.3% provided data at more than one follow-up point.

We have limited our drinking outcome to percentage of days abstinent. Other measures of drinking might well yield different results. We would anticipate such differences. It has elsewhere been argued that measures of drinking intensity, such as number of drinks per drinking day, and measures of drinking frequency, such as percentage of abstinent days, are orthogonal variables (Babor et al., 1994; Longabaugh & Clifford, 1992). And, in fact, after reviewing the literature Babor, Kranzler, and Lauerman (1987) concluded that measures of intensity and frequency have different negative consequences. Thus, ultimately it may be found that different treatment strategies need to be used to effect different dimensions of drinking outcome. In at least one instance, our own research has shown this to be true (Longabaugh, Rubin, et al., 1994).

All three treatment conditions involved a component of cognitive–behavioral therapy. Therefore, any generalizability possible from present results will be limited to other treatments having a core component of cognitive–behavioral therapy as well.

The greatest limitation to unambiguous interpretation of the findings reported is that each of the treatment modalities included in this study have involved several components postulated to be active ingredients. Because of the confounding of some of these components across treatments, it is impossible to conclude with certainty which variables produced the differences observed. Further research will be needed to do so. It will be necessary in parametric studies to separate and systematically vary different intensities of each purported active ingredient to determine the functional relationships between patient characteristic and treatment variable.

REFERENCES

American Psychiatric Association. (1980). *Diagnostic and statistical manual of mental disorders* (3rd ed.). Washington, DC: Author.

Armor, D. J., Polich, J. M., & Stambul, H. B. (1978). *Alcoholism and treatment.* New York: Wiley.

Babor, T. F., Kranzler, H. R., & Lauerman, R. J. (1987). Social drinking as a health and psychosocial risk factor: Anstie's limit revisited. In M. Galanter (Ed.), *Recent developments in alcoholism* (Vol. 5, pp. 373–402). New York: Plenum Press.

Babor, T. F., Longabaugh, R., Zweben, A., Fuller, R., Stout, R., Anton, R., & Randall, C. (1994, December). Issues in the definition and measurement of treatment outcome in alcoholism research. *Journal of Studies on Alcohol*, Suppl. 12, 101–111.

Beattie, M. C., Longabaugh, R., Elliott, G., Stout, R., Fava, J., & Noel, N. (1993). Effect of the social environment on alcohol involvement and subjective well-being prior to alcoholism treatment. *Journal of Studies on Alcohol*, 54, 283–296.

Beutler, L. E. (1991). Have all won and must all have prizes? Revisting Luborsky et al.'s verdict. *Journal of Consulting and Clinical Psychology*, 59, 226–232.

Blatt, S. J., & Felsen, I. (1993). Different kinds of folks may need different kinds of strokes: The effect of patients' characteristics on therapeutic process and outcome. *Psychotherapy Research*, 3, 245–259.

Bryk, A., & Raudenbush, S. W. (1992). *Hierarchical linear models*. Newbury Park, CA: Sage.

Clifford, P. R., & Longabaugh, R. (1993). *Manual for the administration of the Important People and Activities Instrument*. Unpublished manuscript, adapted for use by Project MATCH.

Cronbach, L. J., & Snow, R. E. (1977). *Aptitudes and instruction methods: A handbook for research on interactions*. New York: Irvington.

Dance, K. A., & Newfeld, R. W. J. (1988). Aptitude-treatment interaction research in the clinical setting: A review of attempts to dispel the "patient uniformity" myth. *Psychological Bulletin*, 104, 192–213.

Donovan, D. M., & Mattson, M. E. (1994, December). Alcoholism treatment matching research: Methodological and clinical approaches. *Journal of Studies on Alcohol*, Suppl. 12, 5–14.

Finney, J. W., & Moos, R. H. (1992). Four types of theory that can guide treatment evaluations. In H. Chen & P. H. Rossi (Eds.), *Using theory to improve program and policy evaluations* (pp. 15–27). New York: Greenwood Press.

Fowler, D. R., & Longabaugh, R. (1975). The problem-oriented record: Problem definition. *Archives of General Psychiatry*, 32, 831–834.

Gibbs, L. E., & Flanagan, J. (1977). Prognostic indicators of alcoholism treatment outcome. *International Journal of the Addictions*, 12, 1097–1141.

Jessor, R., Graves, T. D., Hanson, R. C., & Jessor, S. L. (1968). *Society, personality and deviant behavior: A study of a tri-ethnic community*. New York: Holt, Rinehart & Winston.

Kadden, R. M., Cooney, N. L., Getter, H., & Litt, M. D. (1989). Matching alcoholics to coping skills or interaction therapies: Posttreatment results. *Journal of Consulting and Clinical Psychology*, 57, 698–704.

Longabaugh, R. (1993, September). *The measurement of consumption and conse-*

quences in treatment outcome studies: Health services research on alcohol abuse and alcoholism. (Workshop supported by the Alcohol Research Utilization System.) Bethesda, MD: National Institute on Alcohol Abuse and Alcoholism.

Longabaugh, R., & Beattie, M. C. (1985). Optimizing the cost effectiveness of treatment for alcohol abusers (National Institute for Alcohol Abuse and Alcoholism Research Monograph-15. #85-132). Washington, DC: U.S. Government Printing Office.

Longabaugh, R., Beattie, M. C., Noel, N., Stout, R., & Malloy, P. (1993). The effect of social investment on treatment outcome. Journal of Studies on Alcohol, 54, 465–478.

Longabaugh, R., & Clifford, P. R. (1992). Program evaluation and treatment outcome. Annual Review of Addictions Research and Treatment, 2, 223–247.

Longabaugh, R., Fowler, D. R., Stout, R., & Kreibel, G. (1983). Validation for a problem focussed nomenclature. Archives of General Psychiatry, 40, 453–461.

Longabaugh, R., Rubin, A., Malloy, P., Beattie, M. C., Clifford, P. R., & Noel, N. (1994). Drinking outcomes of alcohol abusers diagnosed as antisocial personality disorder. Alcoholism: Clinical and Experimental Research, 18, 778–785.

Longabaugh, R., Wirtz, P. W., & Clifford, P. R. (1995). The Important People and Activities Instrument. Unpublished manuscript.

Longabaugh, R., Wirtz, P., DiClemente, C., & Litt, M. (1994, December). Issues in the development of client-treatment matching hypotheses. Journal of Studies on Alcohol, Suppl. 12, 46–59.

McCrady, B. S., Fink, E., Longabaugh, R., & Stout, R. (1983). Behavioral alcoholism treatment in the partial hospital. International Journal of Partial Hospitalization, 2, 83–95.

McKay, J. R., Longabaugh, R., Beattie, M. C., Maisto, S. A., & Noel, N. E. (1993). Does adding conjoint therapy to individually focused alcoholism treatment lead to better family functioning? Journal of Substance Abuse, 5, 45–59.

Moos, R. H., Finney, J. W., & Cronkite, R. C. (Eds.). (1990). Evaluating and improving alcoholism treatment programs. Alcoholism treatment: Context, process, and outcome (pp. 3–13). New York: Oxford University Press.

Noel, N. E., Reid, P., Wood, L. F., Brinson, M., & Longabaugh, R. (1988). BETA Project Therapist Manual, 1–136.

Robins, L. N., Helzer, J. E., Croughan, J., & Ratcliff, K. S. (1981). National Institute of Mental Health Diagnostic Interview Schedule: Its history, characteristics, and validity. Archives of General Psychiatry, 38, 381–389.

Shoham-Salomon, V., & Hannah, M. T. (1991). Client-treatment interaction in the study of differential change processes. Journal of Consulting and Clinical Psychology, 59, 217–225.

Smith, B., & Sechrest, L. (1991). Treatment of Aptitude × Treatment interactions. Journal of Consulting and Clinical Psychology, 59, 233–244.

Sobell, L. C., Maisto, S. A., Sobell, M. B., & Cooper, A. M. (1979). Reliability of alcoholics' self-reports of drinking and related behaviors one year prior to treatment in an outpatient treatment program. *Behavioral Research Therapy, 17*, 147–160.

Stout, R. L., Beattie, M. C., Longabaugh, R., & Noel, N. E. (1989). Factors affecting correspondence between patient and significant other reports of drinking [Abstract]. *Alcoholism: Clinical and Experimental Research, 12*, 336.

Wei, L. J. (1978). An application of an urn model to the design of sequential controlled clinical trials. *Journal of the American Statistical Association, 73*, 559–563.

24

OUTPATIENT BEHAVIORAL TREATMENT FOR COCAINE DEPENDENCE: ONE-YEAR OUTCOME

STEPHEN T. HIGGINS, ALAN J. BUDNEY, WARREN K. BICKEL, GARY J. BADGER, FLORIAN E. FOERG, AND DORIS OGDEN

This article describes 1-year outcomes from two controlled trials in which cocaine-dependent outpatients were randomly assigned either to a multicomponent behavioral treatment or to one of two control treatments. The behavioral treatment integrates the community reinforcement approach (CRA) with an incentive program in which patients earn vouchers exchangeable for retail items contingent on cocaine abstinence (Higgins, Budney, & Bickel, 1994). A total of four controlled trials supports the during-treatment efficacy of this intervention (Higgins et al., 1991, 1993; Higgins, Budney, Bickel, Foerg, et al., 1994; Silverman et al., 1994). However, outcomes beyond the 3- or 6-month trial periods have not been reported from any of these trials, leaving it unclear whether treatment gains were sustained after treatment termination. The present report describes

Reprinted from *Experimental and Clinical Psychopharmacology, 3*, 205–212. (1995). Copyright © 1995 by the American Psychological Association. Used with permission of the author.

This study was supported by Research Grants DA 06113 and DA 08076 and National Training Award DA 07242 from the National Institute on Drug Abuse.

results from assessments conducted at the end of treatment and 9 and 12 months after treatment entry in two of the four trials (Higgins et al., 1993; Higgins, Budney, Bickel, Foerg, et al., 1994). These two trials were selected because both (a) included random patient assignment, (b) followed identical 6-month schedules of treatment delivery and 6-month follow-up periods, and (c) were conducted in the same clinic. Treatment comparisons during the 6-month trials have been reported previously and are summarized only briefly here, with the focus of this report being on posttreatment comparisons.

METHOD

Participants

Seventy-eight individuals participated in the two trials. Their baseline characteristics are presented in Table 1. There were no significant differences in baseline characteristics between patients randomized to the complete behavioral treatment and the respective control groups in either trial (Higgins et al., 1993; Higgins, Budney, Bickel, Foerg, et al., 1994). Participants were residents of the local community who received free treatment as remuneration for their research participation. Inclusion criteria were that they be ≥18 years of age; meet *Diagnostic and Statistical Manual of Mental Disorders*, 3rd ed., rev. (DSM–III-R; American Psychiatric Association, 1987) criteria for cocaine dependence; and reside within the county in which the clinic was located. Exclusion criteria were opioid or sedative dependence, current psychosis, dementia, a medical condition precluding employment, plans to relocate outside the immediate area within 6 months, and pregnancy.

End of Treatment and Follow-Up Assessments

Baseline and during-treatment assessments have been described previously and are not repeated here (Higgins et al., 1993; Higgins, Budney, Bickel, Foerg, et al., 1994). End of treatment assessments were conducted at 6 months and follow-up assessments at 9 and 12 months after treatment entry by trained, bachelor's-level research assistants who were not blinded to participant treatment assignment. Assessments were conducted at the clinic in which treatment was provided if participants agreed or elsewhere when necessary. Urine specimens were always collected under staff observation. End of treatment assessments were scheduled at 6 months after treatment entry, independent of whether patients dropped out of treatment before that date. Participants were informed of the schedule of follow-up assessments during informed consent obtained at intake. End of treatment

TABLE 1
Participant Baseline Characteristics

Characteristics	Trial 1		Trial 2	
	CRA with vouchers	Counseling	CRA with vouchers	CRA
Demographics				
Mean age (years)	28.5 ± 4.8	30.1 ± 5.5	31.8 ± 3.9	30.9 ± 6.1
% Caucasian	100	100	90	80
% male	89	89	70	65
% never married	63	42	45	35
% ≤ 12 years education	89	89	70	85
% employed full time	68	58	35	55
Median weekly income ($) (interquartile range)[a]	200 (93–300)	337 (75–450)	200 (113–350)	200 (143–296)
Cocaine use				
Preferred route				
% intranasal	47	58	55	45
% intravenous	32	26	30	20
% freebase	21	11	15	35
% other	0	5		
Median grams per week (interquartile range)	2.0 (0.6–4.3)	2.5 (1.0–5.5)	2.7 (1.5–5.2)	2.4 (1.5–3.2)
Other drug dependence				
% alcohol dependent	47	63	45	65
% cannabis dependent	37	47	10	15

Note. $N = 19$ for both groups in Trial 1 and $N = 20$ for both groups in Trial 2. CRA = community reinforcement approach.
[a]Participants with no income were excluded from computations.

and follow-up measures of efficacy were cocaine abstinence documented via urinalysis testing, self-reported cocaine abstinence, Addiction Severity Index (ASI) composite scores (McLellan et al., 1985), and aftercare participation. The ASI is a structured interview administered by a trained staff member and assesses seven areas of functioning: alcohol, drug, employment, family–social, legal, medical, and psychiatric. Composite scores are weighted combinations of individual items that provide reliable, valid, and sensitive measures of problem severity during the 30 days prior to the interview. Composite scores vary from 0 to 1.0, with higher scores indicating greater impairment. Assessments took approximately 1 hour to complete, and participants were paid $35 per assessment.

Treatment Descriptions

Behavioral Treatment

The theoretical rationales and other details about this treatment have been described previously and are described only briefly here (Higgins, Budney, & Bickel, 1994). The treatment was 24 weeks in duration and consisted of CRA (see Sisson & Azrin, 1989) combined with an incentive program based on contingency-management procedures. Urine specimens were collected under staff observation according to a Monday, Wednesday, and Friday schedule during Treatment Weeks 1–12 and a Monday and Thursday schedule during Weeks 13–24. All specimens were screened for benzoylecgonine (a cocaine metabolite), and one randomly selected specimen per week was also screened for the presence of other abused drugs. Failure to submit a scheduled specimen was treated as a cocaine-positive result. Patients were informed of their urinalysis results immediately after submitting their specimens. Specimens collected during Weeks 1–12 that were negative for benzoylecgonine earned points that were recorded on vouchers and given to participants. Points were used to purchase retail items in the community. The value of points increased with each consecutive negative urinalysis test. Failure to submit a scheduled specimen or a cocaine-positive result reset the value of vouchers back to their initial value from which they could escalate again according to the same schedule. During Treatment Weeks 13–24, participants received a single Vermont State Lottery ticket per cocaine-negative urinalysis test.

CRA was implemented in 1- to 1.5-hr therapy sessions scheduled twice weekly for the initial 12 weeks and then once weekly during the final 12 weeks of treatment. Sessions focused on five general issues: (a) improving family relations, (b) providing skills training to minimize drug use, (c) providing vocational counseling, (d) assisting with developing new recreational activities and social networks, and (e) monitoring disulfiram therapy for those who abused alcohol. Patients were encouraged to enter aftercare following completion of the 24 weeks of treatment. This generally consisted of a once monthly brief (30 min) counseling session and a monthly random urinalysis test. Continuation of disulfiram therapy was also possible.

Drug Abuse Counseling

Drug abuse counseling was the control treatment in Trial 1. This treatment has been described previously and is only briefly described here (Higgins et al., 1993). Urinalysis monitoring was conducted under the same schedule as described above for the behavioral treatment, but results were not shared with patients or therapists. This treatment was designed to represent outpatient drug and alcohol counseling as it is commonly delivered, which typically does not involve regular urinalysis monitoring. During informed consent, patients in this group were informed that urinalysis testing was for research purposes only and that results would not be shared with therapists. Patients received $5 per urine specimen submitted independent of the results throughout the 24 weeks of treatment.

During weeks 1–12, counseling sessions consisted of one 2.5-hr group and one 1-hr individual therapy session per week based on a twelve-step model of drug abuse (see *Narcotics Anonymous*, 1988). That was reduced to one group or individual session per week during weeks 13–24. Therapists in this group were informed that disulfiram therapy was available for patients with alcohol dependence or abuse, but only one patient was recommended. As aftercare, patients assigned to this treatment were encouraged to participate regularly in Alcoholics Anonymous (AA) or Narcotics Anonymous (NA) and to participate in a once weekly personal growth group conducted in the same clinic in which treatment was provided. Follow-up assessments were conducted according to the same schedule and in the same manner as described above for the behavioral treatment.

CRA Without Vouchers

The control group for Trial 2 received CRA as described above but without the voucher program used during weeks 1–12 of treatment. Instead of vouchers, this control group simply received slips of paper noting their urinalysis results. During weeks 13–24 of treatment, this group was treated in the same manner as the CRA-with-vouchers group. The recommended aftercare plan and follow-up schedule for this group also was identical to the CRA-with-vouchers group.

Statistical Methods

Analyses corresponding to treatment comparisons during the 6-month trial were reported previously (Higgins et al., 1993; Higgins, Budney,

TABLE 2
Follow-Up Compliance: Trial 1

Compliance measures	6 months	9 months	12 months
Percent of participants assessed[a]			
CRA with vouchers[b]	100 (19/19)	100 (19/19)	89 (17/19)
Counseling	74 (14/19)	74 (14/19)	68 (13/19)
Median days early or late for scheduled assessment[c]			
CRA with vouchers	14 (3–17)[d]	6 (4–10)	9 (6–22)
Counseling	21 (11–39)	10 (1–20)	19 (3–36)

Note. CRA = community reinforcement approach.
[a]Values in parentheses indicate N. [b]Significant difference between treatments, $p \leq .05$, chi-square test. [c]Values in parentheses indicate interquartile range. [d]Significant difference between treatments, $p \leq .05$, Wilcoxon rank sum test.

Bickel, Foerg, et al., 1994). With regard to follow-up measures, urinalysis results and self-reported abstinence were analyzed using an intent-to-treat approach in which percents were calculated as the number of participants abstinent by the number of participants randomized. Treatment comparisons and changes over time on these dichotomous measures were performed using the computer program SAS PROC CATMOD (SAS, 1989) for categorical modeling including repeated measures designs. Treatment comparisons on categorical measures that were not repeated over time were performed using chi-square tests. Wilcoxon rank sum tests were used to compare treatments on deviation from scheduled assessment dates (Tables 2 and 5). ASI results were analyzed using BMDP program 5V designed to perform repeated measures analyses with incomplete observations (Dixon, 1988). This analysis uses a mixed model regression to obtain maximum likelihood estimates of fixed effects (i.e., time, treatment, and their interaction) while incorporating differences between participants as random effects. Means presented in Tables 4, 7, and 8 are linear combinations of the estimated regression parameters. Additionally, orthogonal contrasts were constructed to test two planned comparisons: comparing intake values to posttreatment values and testing for changes during the posttreatment follow-up period. Hypotheses related to the above comparisons and their interactions with treatment were tested via a Wald statistic. Statistical significance was determined at the 5% level in all analyses.

RESULTS

Trial 1: CRA With Vouchers Versus Drug Abuse Counseling

Follow-Up Compliance

Table 2 provides a breakdown of compliance across the two treatments at the 6-, 9-, and 12-month assessments. The number of patients who participated in the posttreatment assessments did not change significantly over time in either group, but more participants were assessed in the CRA-with-vouchers than drug abuse counseling groups, $\chi^2(1, N = 38)$ = 5.2, p = .02. Follow-up assessments were conducted significantly closer to the scheduled date in the CRA-with-vouchers group at the 6-month assessment. A total of four (21%) participants in the drug abuse counseling group failed to participate in any posttreatment assessments: one refused to participate and three could not be located. All individuals in the CRA-with-vouchers group participated in at least one posttreatment assessment.

Cocaine Abstinence

As previously reported, significantly longer durations of continuous cocaine abstinence were documented during the trial in the CRA-with-vouchers treatment than in the drug abuse counseling treatment (Higgins et al., 1993). For example, the percentages of participants in the CRA-with-vouchers group versus the drug abuse counseling group documented to have achieved at least 4, 8, and 16 weeks of continuous cocaine abstinence were 74% versus 16%, 68% versus 11%, and 42% versus 5%, respectively.

More participants were documented to be cocaine abstinent via urinalysis at the 6-, 9-, and 12-month assessments in the CRA-with-vouchers group than in the drug abuse counseling group, $\chi^2(1,N = 38) = 7.3$, p = .007 (Figure 1). This treatment difference was not simply an artifact of differential follow-ups in the two groups, as similar trends were observed

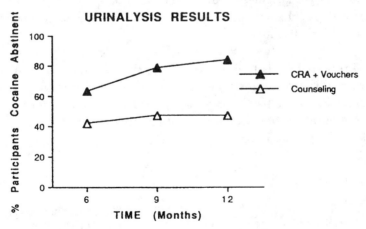

Figure 1. Percentages of participants randomized to the community reinforcement approach (CRA)-with-vouchers and drug abuse counseling groups whose urinalysis results were negative for cocaine at 6-, 9-, and 12-month posttreatment assessments.

TABLE 3
Percentage of Participants Reporting No Cocaine Use
in the Past 30 Days: Trial 1

Treatments[a]	6 months	9 months	12 months
CRA with vouchers	53 (10/19)	68 (13/19)	58 (11/19)
Counseling	42 (8/19)	42 (8/19)	32 (6/19)

Note. Percentages are calculated as number of participants documented divided by number of participants randomized (as shown in parentheses). CRA = community reinforcement approach. N = 19 per group.
[a]Intent-to-treat analysis.

in other analyses. For example, when percentages were calculated with missing participants excluded, 72%, 88%, and 96% of participants in the CRA-with-vouchers group were abstinent at the 6-, 9-, and 12-month assessments, respectively, versus 67%, 69%, and 69% in the drug abuse counseling group, respectively.

All participants reported recent cocaine use (i.e., during the past 30 days) on entering the study, and thus the posttreatment abstinence levels observed in both groups represent significant improvements from intake (Table 3). Although the posttreatment abstinence levels were higher on average in the CRA-with-vouchers group than in the drug abuse counseling group, those differences were not significant.

Significantly more participants in the CRA-with-vouchers group than in the drug abuse counseling group were documented to be cocaine abstinent across all three posttreatment assessments: 58% (11/19) versus 26% (5/19), respectively, $\chi^2(1, N = 38) = 3.9$, $p = .05$. Self-reported abstinence in the past 30 days across all three assessments also was higher in the CRA-with-vouchers group, but that difference was not significant: 42% (8/19) in CRA-with-vouchers group versus 26% (5/19) in drug abuse counseling, $\chi^2(1, N = 38) = 1.1$, ns.

Concordance between patients' self-reported cocaine abstinence and urinalysis results in this trial was excellent; that is, urinalysis results were negative in 98% of the instances (54/55) in which participants reported no cocaine use in the past 30 days and provided a specimen for urinalysis. In the one instance of discordance, self-reported abstinence was changed to indicate recent use in the results.

ASI Composite Scores

Participants in both treatment groups showed significant and comparable improvements from intake in ASI composite drug, alcohol, family–social, and psychiatric scores (Table 4). The only significant change over time during the posttreatment period was observed in composite psychiatric scores, which improved significantly in both groups during the 6-

TABLE 4
Addiction Severity Index Composite Scores: Trial 1

Scales	Intake	6 months	9 months	12 months
Medical				
CRA with vouchers	0.22 ± 0.07[a]	0.19 ± 0.07	0.15 ± 0.06	0.18 ± 0.08
Counseling	0.32 ± 0.07	0.25 ± 0.08	0.18 ± 0.07	0.13 ± 0.09
Employment				
CRA with vouchers	0.59 ± 0.06	0.58 ± 0.06	0.59 ± 0.07	0.61 ± 0.07
Counseling	0.51 ± 0.06	0.44 ± 0.06	0.52 ± 0.08	0.44 ± 0.08
Alcohol[b]				
CRA with vouchers	0.33 ± 0.05	0.21 ± 0.04	0.21 ± 0.04	0.16 ± 0.05
Counseling	0.35 ± 0.05	0.21 ± 0.05	0.13 ± 0.05	0.12 ± 0.06
Drug[b]				
CRA with vouchers	0.22 ± 0.02	0.14 ± 0.02	0.09 ± 0.02	0.09 ± 0.02
Counseling	0.26 ± 0.02	0.11 ± 0.02	0.12 ± 0.02	0.08 ± 0.02
Legal				
CRA with vouchers	0.19 ± 0.04	0.13 ± 0.05	0.12 ± 0.05	0.16 ± 0.04
Counseling	0.17 ± 0.03	0.17 ± 0.04	0.11 ± 0.05	0.10 ± 0.06
Family and Social[b]				
CRA with vouchers	0.29 ± 0.05	0.15 ± 0.05	0.08 ± 0.05	0.11 ± 0.05
Counseling	0.35 ± 0.05	0.15 ± 0.06	0.22 ± 0.04	0.20 ± 0.06
Psychiatric[b,c]				
CRA with vouchers	0.35 ± 0.04	0.28 ± 0.05	0.20 ± 0.04	0.18 ± 0.06
Counseling	0.37 ± 0.04	0.30 ± 0.06	0.23 ± 0.05	0.20 ± 0.06

Note. CRA = community reinforcement approach.
[a]Mean ± standard error of the mean based on maximum likelihood estimates associated with mixed-model regression analysis. [b]Significant difference between intake and posttreatment scores across both treatment groups, Wald test $p < .01$. [c]Significant decrease in scores during posttreatment follow-up period across both treatment groups, Wald test $p < .01$.

month follow-up period. No significant changes were observed in composite legal, medical, or employment scores.

Treatment Participation

As reported previously, more patients randomized to CRA with vouchers than drug abuse counseling completed 24 weeks of treatment (58% versus 11%; Higgins et al., 1993).

Consistent with that difference in completion rates, more participants in CRA with vouchers than drug abuse counseling entered aftercare: 21% (4/19) of participants in the CRA-with-vouchers group versus 0% in the drug abuse counseling group, $\chi^2(1, N = 38) = 4.5$, $p = .03$. The average duration of aftercare involvement among the four CRA-with-vouchers participants was 50 ± 11 days. Three of those participants received disulfiram during aftercare for an average duration of 23 ± 11 days. As expected, participation in aftercare was more likely during the first than the second half of the follow-up period.

There were no treatment differences in the number of participants who received treatment other than aftercare during the follow-up period: 16% (3/19) of participants in the CRA-with-vouchers group and 11%

(2/19) in the drug abuse counseling group were readmitted for outpatient treatment in our clinic, and the same percentages from each group entered residential treatment for drug abuse.

Because all participants in the drug abuse counseling group were instructed to enroll in AA or NA as part of their treatment, we assessed whether self-help participation was greater in the counseling group. Responses to an ASI item that asked whether patients received any outpatient services for drug or alcohol during the past 30 days, including AA or NA, were examined for each treatment. At the 6-, 9-, and 12-month assessments, 16% (3/19), 11% (2/19), and 11% (2/19), respectively, of participants in the drug abuse counseling group indicated receiving some form of outpatient care, while 37% (7/19), 21% (4/19), and 37% (7/19), respectively, of participants in the CRA-with-vouchers group did so. Thus, there was no evidence that the counseling group regularly attended NA or AA more than the CRA-with-vouchers group.

Trial 2: CRA With Versus Without Vouchers

Follow-Up Compliance

There were no significant treatment differences in the number of participants assessed posttreatment, but there was a significant decrease in both groups in the number of participants assessed over time, $\chi^2(2, N = 40) = 5.9$, $p = 0.05$ (Table 5). Interviews at the 12-month assessment were conducted significantly closer to the scheduled date in the group with vouchers. A total of 95% and 100% of participants assigned to CRA with and without vouchers participated in at least one assessment. One individual refused participation.

TABLE 5
Follow-Up Compliance: Trial 2

Compliance measures	6 months	9 months	12 months
Percent of participants assessed[a]			
CRA with vouchers	95 (19/20)	95 (18/20)	75 (15/20)
CRA	95 (19/20)	90 (18/20)	85 (17/20)
Median days early or late for scheduled assessment[b]			
CRA with vouchers	2 (0–20)	11 (2–15)	14 (7–17)[c]
CRA	12 (0–29)	11 (8–20)	20 (13–34)

Note. CRA = community reinforcement approach.
[a]Values in parentheses indicate the number of patients assessed per sample size. [b]Values in parentheses indicate interquartile range. [c]Significant differences between treatment groups, $p \le .05$, Wilcoxon test.

Cocaine Abstinence

As previously reported, the CRA-with-vouchers group achieved significantly greater durations of documented cocaine abstinence during the treatment period than the no-vouchers group (Higgins, Budney, Bickel, Foerg, et al., 1994). For example, the percentages of participants in the groups with versus without vouchers, documented to have achieved at least 4, 8, and 16 weeks of continuous abstinence, were 75% versus 55%, 55% versus 25%, and 30% versus 15%, respectively.

There were no significant treatment differences or changes over time in the number of participants documented to be cocaine abstinent via urinalysis at the 6-, 9-, and 12-month assessments. Percentages abstinent at those times in the vouchers versus no-vouchers groups were 80% (16/20) versus 75% (14/20), 70% (14/20) versus 65% (13/20), and 65% (13/20) versus 60% (12/20), respectively.

Self-reported cocaine abstinence levels are shown in Table 6. Because all participants entered treatment as recent cocaine users, abstinence levels observed through the three posttreatment assessments in both groups represented substantial improvements from intake. There was a trend toward greater posttreatment abstinence in the vouchers than no-vouchers groups, but it was not significant, $\chi^2(1, N = 40) = 2.4$, $p = 0.11$. There were no significant treatment differences in the number of participants who were abstinent across all three posttreatment assessments: 45% (9/20) versus 40% (8/20) of participants in the vouchers versus no-vouchers groups had negative urinalysis results across all assessments and 35% (7/20) versus 20% (4/20) reported zero days of cocaine use in the past 30 across all assessments in the vouchers versus no-vouchers groups.

Concordance between patients' self-reported cocaine abstinence and urinalysis results was also excellent in this trial and almost identical to results from Trial 1; that is, urinalysis results were negative in 98% (52/53) of the instances in which participants reported no cocaine use in the past 30 days and provided a specimen for urinalysis. In the one instance of discordance, self-reported abstinence was changed to indicate recent use in the results.

TABLE 6
Percentage of Participants Reporting No Cocaine Use
in the Past 30 Days: Trial 2

Treatments[a]	6 months	9 months	12 months
CRA with vouchers[a]	60 (12/20)	55 (11/20)	45 (9/20)
CRA	40 (8/20)	35 (7/20)	40 (8/20)

Note. Percentages are calculated as number of participants documented divided by number of participants randomized (as shown in parentheses). CRA = community reinforcement approach. $N = 20$ per group.
[a]Intent-to-treat analysis.

ASI Composite Scores

ASI composite alcohol and family-social scores improved significantly and comparably from intake through the posttreatment assessments in both treatment groups (Table 7). Significant improvements were also observed with composite drug and psychiatric scores, but the magnitude of improvement in those scores was significantly greater in the vouchers than in the no-vouchers groups. The treatment differences observed in the composite drug scores were primarily due to differences on the four items listed in Table 8. The treatment differences observed in the psychiatric scores were primarily due to differences on the following two items: (a) significant periods (3 or more consecutive days) of serious depression in the past 30 days that were not a direct result of drug/alcohol use and (b) significant periods of trouble understanding, concentrating, or remembering during the past 30 days that were not a direct result of drug/alcohol use.

Treatment Participation

As reported previously, significantly more patients assigned to the vouchers versus no-vouchers group completed 24 weeks of treatment, 75%

TABLE 7
Addiction Severity Index Composite Scores: Trial 2

Scales	Intake	6 months	9 months	12 months
Medical				
CRA with vouchers	0.11 ± 0.05[a]	0.11 ± 0.05	0.21 ± 0.07	0.17 ± 0.07
CRA	0.13 ± 0.06	0.12 ± 0.06	0.16 ± 0.07	0.19 ± 0.07
Employment				
CRA with vouchers	0.54 ± 0.05	0.55 ± 0.07	0.56 ± 0.05	0.59 ± 0.07
CRA	0.65 ± 0.05	0.62 ± 0.07	0.60 ± 0.06	0.60 ± 0.06
Alcohol[b]				
CRA with vouchers	0.29 ± 0.05	0.11 ± 0.04	0.14 ± 0.05	0.10 ± 0.04
CRA	0.40 ± 0.05	0.20 ± 0.04	0.20 ± 0.05	0.23 ± 0.05
Drug[b,c]				
CRA with vouchers	0.25 ± 0.02	0.05 ± 0.01	0.08 ± 0.02	0.07 ± 0.02
CRA	0.23 ± 0.02	0.10 ± 0.02	0.12 ± 0.02	0.12 ± 0.02
Legal				
CRA with vouchers	0.20 ± 0.05	0.09 ± 0.05	0.10 ± 0.05	0.09 ± 0.05
CRA	0.12 ± 0.04	0.13 ± 0.05	0.13 ± 0.05	0.14 ± 0.06
Family and Social[b]				
CRA with vouchers	0.36 ± 0.05	0.14 ± 0.04	0.14 + 0.04	0.16 ± 0.05
CRA	0.35 ± 0.05	0.13 ± 0.03	0.15 ± 0.05	0.19 ± 0.05
Psychiatric[b,d]				
CRA with vouchers	0.35 ± 0.05	0.13 ± 0.04	0.15 ± 0.05	0.09 ± 0.03
CRA	0.38 ± 0.05	0.31 ± 0.04	0.29 ± 0.05	0.29 ± 0.06

Note. CRA = community reinforcement approach.
[a]Mean ± standard error of the mean based on maximum likelihood estimates associated with mixed-model regression analysis. [b]Significant difference between intake and posttreatment scores across both treatment groups, Wald test $p < .01$. [c]Significant differences between treatment groups in change from baseline to posttreatment scores, Wald test $p < .01$. [d]Significant difference between treatment groups in change from baseline to posttreatment scores, Wald test $p < .05$.

TABLE 8
Selected Items From the Addiction Severity Index Composite Drug Scale

Items	Intake	6 months	9 months	12 months
Days of cocaine use in the past 30				
CRA with vouchers	11.0 ± 1.3[a]	0.9 ± 0.7	1.0 ± 0.8	0.9 ± 1.4
CRA	8.8 ± 1.3	2.4 ± 0.7	3.0 ± 0.8	2.3 ± 1.3
How many days in the past 30 have you experienced drug problems?				
CRA with vouchers	15.7 ± 1.9	0.9 ± 0.9	1.4 ± 1.3	1.8 ± 2.3
CRA	9.1 ± 1.9	2.6 ± 0.8	6.1 ± 1.2	6.1 ± 2.2
How troubled or bothered have you been in the past 30 days by drug problems?[b]				
CRA with vouchers	3.6 ± 0.3	0.9 ± 0.3	1.0 ± 0.3	0.9 ± 0.3
CRA	3.3 ± 0.2	1.7 ± 0.3	1.8 ± 0.3	1.6 ± 0.3
How important to you now is treatment for drug problems?[c]				
CRA with vouchers	3.9 ± 0.3	1.2 ± 0.4	1.6 ± 0.3	1.8 ± 0.3
CRA	3.6 ± 0.3	1.6 ± 0.4	1.6 ± 0.4	2.1 ± 0.3

Note. CRA = community reinforcement approach.
[a]Mean ± standard error of the mean based on maximum likelihood estimates associated with mixed-model regression analysis. [b]Ratings ranged from 0 (*not at all*) to 4 (*extremely*). [c]Ratings ranged from 0 (*not at all*) to 4 (*extremely*).

(15/20) versus 40% (8/20), respectively (Higgins, Budney, Bickel, Foerg, et al., 1994).

Consistent with that difference in completion rates, 70% (14/20) of participants in the vouchers group versus 30% (6/20) in the no-vouchers group enrolled in the aftercare program, $\chi^2(1, N = 40) = 6.4$, $p = .01$. Average duration of aftercare participation in the vouchers group was 136 ± 14 days; three of those patients received disulfiram during that period for an average duration of 104 ± 30 days. Average duration of aftercare participation in the group without vouchers was 95 ± 24 days; two of those patients received disulfiram during that period for an average duration of 28 ± 18 days. Duration of aftercare participation tended to be longer in the voucher group, but that difference was not significant. As expected, participation in aftercare in both treatment groups was more likely during the first than the second half of the follow-up period. Duration of disulfiram therapy during aftercare was not analyzed statistically because of the small sample sizes involved.

One participant from each treatment group was readmitted for outpatient treatment in our clinic during the follow-up period and none reported other outpatient or residential treatment.

DISCUSSION

There are three aspects of this study on which we wish to comment. First, this study should be considered preliminary, as both trials were designed for during-treatment rather than follow-up comparisons. Hence, initial hypotheses, power calculations, and so forth were all based on assessing short-term outcomes. That focus on during-treatment comparisons accounts, for example, for the relatively small sample sizes studied as well as the absence of controls regarding participation in other treatments during the follow-up period, although controlling that factor would be difficult. At least one other group has reported a similar exploratory follow-up study from a clinical trial on outpatient treatment for cocaine dependence (Carroll et al., 1994). Such studies (a) provide important information regarding the pattern of changes observed in clinical samples of cocaine-dependent individuals during treatment follow-up, (b) can reveal differences in the long-term efficacy of different treatments, and (c) can serve a heuristic function in the formulation of more effortful and costly long-term outcome studies.

Second, each of the treatments assessed in this trial was associated with substantial improvements from intake in cocaine abstinence and other important areas of functioning. These improvements were evident throughout the follow-up period. All participants entered treatment reporting recent (past 30 days) cocaine use, but that was improved by 40–60% through the posttreatment assessments. These improvements in cocaine use were associated with significant improvements in ASI composite drug, alcohol, family–social, and psychiatric scores, although not employment, legal, or medical scores. This profile of significant clinical improvements in cocaine use and other important areas of functioning during the 6–12 months after treatment entry is consistent with other recent reports on clinical samples of people who abuse cocaine (Alterman et al., 1994; Carroll, Power, Bryant, & Rounsaville, 1993; Carroll et al., 1994). Percentages of participants who sustained abstinence across all of the posttreatment assessments in the present study were 20–40%, with the remaining participants either drifting between periods of abstinence and use or maintaining use at a regular but reduced frequency compared to intake levels. These results demonstrate the simple but important point that cocaine-dependent patients can make significant progress during and after treatment entry in reducing their cocaine use and attendant problems. Unfortunately, in the absence of no-treatment or waiting list control groups in this or prior studies, it is impossible to determine the exact contribution of treatment to these improvements.

Third, the CRA-with-vouchers treatment appears to be more efficacious than the control treatments during follow-up consistent with during-treatment observations from these trials. Evidence was observed during the follow-up periods in both trials supporting greater improvements in cocaine use in the CRA-with-vouchers treatment than control treatments. The same was true for enrollment in aftercare, and there was evidence in one trial indicating greater reductions in psychiatric symptomatology with the CRA-with-vouchers treatment than with control treatment. The particular measures on which significant treatment differences were observed were not consistent across trials. For example, significant differences were observed in urinalysis results but not self-reports in the trial comparing CRA with vouchers and drug abuse counseling, while the converse was true in the trial comparing CRA with and without vouchers. We cannot account for these inconsistencies, and they weaken the case supporting the efficacy of this treatment. That said, the apparent inconsistencies across the two trials should be balanced against the consistent observation that whenever significant treatment differences or trends were observed, they favored the CRA-with-vouchers treatment over the control treatments.

What influence missing data had on outcome in this study is difficult to determine. The follow-up rates were relatively good for this population. The 79% follow-up rate in the drug abuse counseling group is comparable to what others have reported in follow-up studies of cocaine abusers, and the 95–100% follow-up rates observed with the other treatments appear somewhat higher than expected (Alterman et al., 1994; Carroll et al., 1993, 1994). Nevertheless, missing data are always a problem in such follow-up studies. The intent-to-treat analysis is a well-accepted way of dealing with missing data in substance abuse research (e.g., Nathan & Lansky, 1978). As used in this study, it describes the actual rate of abstinence observed in the entire sample of participants randomized to treatment. Using it in Trial 1 of this study, in which follow-up rates were significantly lower in the drug abuse counseling group, may have produced larger treatment differences than would have been observed in other analyses. However, we are confident it did not produce artifactual differences because, as noted above, the CRA-with-vouchers group still had up to 25% greater abstinence than the drug abuse counseling group using analyses that excluded missing participants. The mixed-model regression provides a reasonable approach to dealing with missing data for continuous measures like ASI composite scores where an intent-to-treat approach is not feasible. Others have also recently reported using regression models for dealing with missing data in follow-up studies of cocaine-dependent patients (Carroll et al., 1994).

Considering how few positive treatment differences have been reported in controlled trials for cocaine dependence, and how sorely needed are effective treatments for this disorder, the results supporting the efficacy of the CRA-with-vouchers treatment observed in this study appear promising and merit further study. To our knowledge, there is only one other report of a treatment difference during follow-up in a controlled trial on the treatment of cocaine dependence (Carroll et al., 1994). In that report, also an exploratory study, ASI composite cocaine scores indicated better outcomes during the year after treatment completion in participants treated with relapse prevention therapy compared to those who received a non-specific clinical management intervention. Interestingly, no significant treatment differences were observed in urinalysis results in that study, which is similar to the results observed in Trial 2 of the present study, in which significant treatment differences were observed on the ASI but not in urinalysis testing.

In summary, this follow-up study contributes new and important information on the progress of cocaine-dependent patients during the year after treatment entry. Consistent with prior reports from other clinics, significant clinical improvements in cocaine use and other areas of functioning were associated with all treatments. When treatment differences were observed during follow-up, they supported the efficacy of the CRA-with-vouchers over the control treatments consistent with during-treatment effects reported previously.

REFERENCES

Alterman, A. I., O'Brien, C. P., McLellan, A. T., August, D. S., Snider, E. C., Droba, M., Cornish, J. W., Hall, C. P., Raphaelson, A. H., & Schrade, F. X. (1994). Effectiveness and costs of inpatient versus day hospital cocaine rehabilitation. *The Journal of Nervous and Mental Disease, 182,* 157–163.

American Psychiatric Association. (1987). *Diagnostic and statistical manual of mental disorders* (3rd ed., rev.). Washington, DC: Author.

Carroll, K. M., Power, M-E. D., Bryant, K., & Rounsaville, B. J. (1993). One-year follow-up status of treatment seeking cocaine abusers: Psychopathology and dependence severity as predictors of outcome. *The Journal of Nervous and Mental Disease, 181,* 71–79.

Carroll, K. M., Rounsaville, B. J., Nich, C., Gordon, L. T., Wirtz, P. W., & Gawin, F. H. (1994). One-year follow-up of psychotherapy and pharmacotherapy for cocaine dependence. *Archives of General Psychiatry, 51,* 989–997.

Dixon, W. J. (Ed.). (1988). *BMDP statistical software manual* (Vol. 2). Berkeley, CA: University of California Press.

Higgins, S. T., Budney, A. J., & Bickel, W. K. (1994). Applying behavioral concepts and principles to the treatment of cocaine dependence. *Drug and Alcohol Dependence, 34,* 87–97.

Higgins, S. T., Budney, A. J., Bickel, W. K., Foerg, F. E., Donham, R., & Badger, G. J. (1994). Incentives improve outcome in outpatient behavioral treatment of cocaine dependence. *Archives of General Psychiatry, 54,* 568–576.

Higgins, S. T., Budney, A. J., Bickel, W. K., Hughes, J. R., Foerg, F., & Badger, G. (1993). Achieving cocaine abstinence with a behavioral approach. *American Journal of Psychiatry, 150,* 763–769.

Higgins, S. T., Delaney, D. D., Budney, A. J., Bickel, W. K., Hughes, J. R., Foerg, F., & Fenwick, J. W. (1991). A behavioral approach to achieving initial cocaine abstinence. *American Journal of Psychiatry, 148,* 1218–1224.

McLellan, A. T., Luborsky, L., Cacciola, J., Griffith, J., Evans, F., Barr, H. L., & O'Brien, C. P. (1985). New data from the Addiction Severity Index: Reliability and validity in three centers. *The Journal of Nervous and Mental Disease, 173,* 412–423.

Narcotics anonymous (5th ed.). (1988). Van Nuys, CA: World Service Office.

Nathan, P. E., & Lansky, D. (1978). Common methodological problems in research on addictions. *Journal of Consulting and Clinical Psychology, 46,* 713–726.

SAS Institute Inc. (1989). *SAS/STAT user's guide, version 6* (4th ed. Vol 1) Cary, NC: SAS Institute Inc.

Silverman, K., Higgins, S. T., Brooner, R. K., Montoya, I. D., Schuster, C. R., & Preston, K. L. (1994). *An effective treatment for cocaine abuse: Reinforcement of sustained abstinence.* Manuscript submitted for publication.

Sisson, R. W., & Azrin, N. H. (1989). The Community Reinforcement Approach. In R. K. Hester & W. R. Miller (Eds.), *Handbook of alcoholism treatment approaches: Effective alternatives* (pp. 242–258). New York: Pergamon Press.

25

RECENT DEVELOPMENTS IN THE PHARMACOTHERAPY OF SUBSTANCE ABUSE

CHARLES P. O'BRIEN

Over the past 20 years, there has been great progress in understanding the psychopharmacology of substance abuse. Receptors have been identified and cloned for opiates, cocaine, and marijuana. Endogenous transmitters have been identified for opioid and cannabinoid receptors, giving researchers the potential for understanding mechanisms by which these drugs interfere with normal function and produce behavioral effects. In addition, radical changes in thought about the nature of addictive disorders and the development of specific diagnostic criteria have occurred. Beginning with the third revised edition of the *Diagnostic and Statistical Manual of Mental Disorders* (*DSM–III–R*; American Psychiatric Association, 1987) and continuing with the fourth edition (*DSM–IV*; American Psychiatric Association, 1994), addiction (i.e., substance dependence) has been defined as a

Reprinted from the *Journal of Consulting and Clinical Psychology, 64*, 677–686. (1996). Copyright © 1996 by the American Psychological Association. Used with permission of the author.

This article was supported in part by the Veterans Affairs Medical Research Service and by Grant P50DA05186-09 from the National Institute on Drug Abuse.

behavioral disorder. Diagnostic emphasis is on the loss of control over substance use and the accompanying encroachment on normal activities rather than focusing on tolerance and physical dependence as in prior definitions. Early diagnosis is important because waiting until a person is "down and out" and the diagnosis is obvious simply reduces the probability of successful treatment. Tolerance and physical dependence are often present, but these are not required for the diagnosis of abuse or dependence. Tolerance simply refers to a reduction in drug effect with repeated use so that users can ingest large quantities of the drug without showing significant impairment. Physical dependence is a state of adaptation to the presence of the drug such that continued administration of the drug is necessary to maintain normal function. If the drug ingestion is stopped abruptly, symptoms and signs of a withdrawal syndrome occur that can be effectively treated with medication. Although much more is understood now about the nature of withdrawal than in the past, the treatment of withdrawal (detoxification) is no longer considered to be pivotal to long-term outcome of the addictive disorder. Of course, sedative withdrawal, including alcohol withdrawal, can be fatal if not appropriately medicated, but there are effective medications to reduce withdrawal symptoms. The long-term outcome does not depend on the type of detoxification, and the emphasis in good treatment programs is on prevention of relapse.

Another important change in thinking about addictive disorders is the acceptance of the notion that the brain may have lasting changes produced by repeated drug taking (Nestler, Hope, & Widnell, 1993). In the past, treatment of all substance abuse was similar and consisted of stopping the drug and using group therapy or other psychosocial support to encourage the patient to remain drug free. The treatment of substance abuse was not seen as a medical problem and often did not even include evaluation by a physician. If medications were involved at all, it was simply to ease the discomfort of withdrawal symptoms. While this strategy works well for some patients, the majority require complete medical evaluation including a psychiatric examination. Appendix A lists the medical options for patients after detoxification. This review emphasizes post-detoxification treatment. Unfortunately, the general public often confuses the treatment of withdrawal with the treatment of addiction. Effective treatment of addiction requires a long-term approach to reducing the risk of relapse and improving the ability of patients to function in society.

TREATMENT SUCCESS

A stable drug free state is not usually achieved with the initial course of treatment. Substance use disorders are similar to other chronic disorders such as arthritis or diabetes. Success of treatment is measured in terms of substantial reduction of symptoms, not cure. In these terms, the treatment success rates for addictive disorders are comparable to those of other chronic disorders, but if one expects a "cure," the success rate for any chronic disorder would be low (O'Brien & McLellan, 1996). As with better understood endocrine disorders, such as diabetes and hypothyroidism, some addictive disorders require maintenance medication.

The definition of success in the treatment of drug dependence varies with the type of drug. For heroin addiction, a success may include not only patients who achieve stable abstinence, but also those who show significant improvement in health and the ability to function after transfer to methadone treatment. In the treatment of cocaine abuse and addiction, complete abstinence is always the goal, but realistically many patients show tremendous improvement in functional measures while still admitting to occasional cocaine use. Continued treatment sessions should focus on preventing these lapses and they typically become further apart in time. For nicotine dependence, the course is usually different. When ex-smokers "slip" and use one or two cigarettes, they tend to relapse quickly to their prior level of dependence. This leads to the general observation that the success rate for the treatment of nicotine addiction among patients failing to stop on their own and seeking professional help is significantly worse than that for other common addictions such as heroin, cocaine, and alcohol.

Cost Effectiveness of Treatment

Over the past 10–15 years, insurance plans have covered brief inpatient treatment, usually up to 28 days. This is expensive, often not necessary, and may be ineffective over the long term unless it includes continuing outpatient follow-up care. Modern health care plans include coverage for substance abuse treatment but allow greater flexibility. Numerous studies have shown little or no difference in long-term outcome between inpatient and outpatient treatment except in costs (Annis, 1986; Alterman et al., 1992). Although there is still some controversy (Walsh et al., 1991), the preponderance of evidence supports the advantages of long-term outpatient care with brief hospitalizations only when needed.

When addictive disorders are considered along with other chronic disorders, the available treatments appear relatively successful. Unfortunately, there is a strong tendency to expect "cures" as though addiction were an acute illness, such as pneumonia or a fractured bone. Detoxification is not treatment; it is simply the beginning of a process that must be continued with variable intensity for several years or indefinitely. When treatment success is measured in terms of improvement 6 to 12 months after beginning treatment, the success rates in the literature vary from a low of 20% for nicotine dependence to a high of 75% for specific behavioral treatment of cocaine dependence (Fiore, Smith, Jorenby, & Baker,

1994; Higgins et al., 1995). Good methadone programs can expect success rates of 60% to 70% for heroin addicts while they remain in treatment (Ball & Ross, 1991). Treatment of addiction generally leads to savings in other areas, because untreated addiction produces monetary costs to society associated with employee absences, crime, incarceration, and medical costs for secondary disorders such as cancer and accidents. Comparisons of benefits to costs for patients in treatment have consistently yielded favorable ratios. For example, a large study of 11,000 methadone patients yielded a benefits-to-costs ratio of 4:1 (Hubbard et al., 1989), and another (Gerstein et al., 1994) yielded a 4.8:1 ratio for methadone patients in treatment and 12.6:1 for discharged methadone patients. For cocaine treatment programs, similar favorable ratios have been found. A recent RAND study (Everingham & Rydel, 1994) analyzed the cost of reducing cocaine use in the United States by 1%. This analysis showed that increasing treatment facilities would accomplish the reduction at a cost 23 times less than reducing supply in countries where cocaine is grown and 7.3 times less than increasing domestic law enforcement. These estimates are all the more impressive when it is noted that the RAND group conservatively estimated treatment of cocaine dependence as being only 13% effective when published data show 50% to 75% effectiveness for good treatment programs. These data from studies of the financial benefits of treatment suggest that inclusion of treatment for addiction in a national health plan would make good economic sense.

Should Medications Be Used?

The drug-free approach is listed first in Appendix A because it is preferable when feasible. Some treatment programs for substance abuse are founded on the philosophy that a drug-free approach is the only approach. "You can't treat a drug problem with a drug" is the oft-repeated phrase. This statement implies that all drugs are alike. In reality, there are abundant data showing the benefits of psychoactive medications in addictive disorders when they are specifically indicated to treat coexisting psychiatric disorders. An example would be lithium for a cocaine addict who also suffers from bipolar affective disorder. Psychoactive medication that has significant abuse potential should, of course, be avoided in patients with a history of substance abuse. Apart from treating accompanying psychiatric disorders, medication may be specifically indicated for the addiction itself. Short- and long-term maintenance strategies are listed in Appendix A.

Dual Diagnosis

The frequency of an additional psychiatric diagnosis depends on the population being studied. Some patients have psychiatric symptoms before initiating substance abuse. For them, the use of unauthorized drugs may constitute an attempt at treating their psychiatric disorder. The majority of psychiatric problems are found in long-time drug abusers, probably because of the accumulated effects of substance abuse on their nervous system and the pressures caused by social and occupational problems.

Depression is a frequent finding both in heroin addicts and in cocaine addicts. Depressive symptoms are usually self-limiting, and their appearance depends on the stage of the addiction. When beginning a course of methadone treatment, opiate addicts show a high frequency of depressive symptoms that clear after stabilization on methadone. Among patients whose symptoms persist and who meet criteria for a mood disorder, double-blind, placebo-controlled studies in methadone-maintained patients have demonstrated the efficacy of antidepressant medications (Woody, O'Brien, McLellan, & Evans, 1982). During withdrawal from cocaine, depressive symptoms are common, but in most cases, these symptoms resolve spontaneously in a few days. Studies in cocaine addicts that focus on depression are lacking. Psychoactive medications are routinely used when schizophrenia and anxiety disorders coexist with addictive disorders, but they have not been the subject of controlled studies in homogeneous populations. It should be emphasized that dual-diagnosis patients are best managed by a combination of psychoactive medication and psychotherapy.

OPIOID DEPENDENCE

Opiates are derivatives of the opium poppy, and opioids are nonopiates that act on the same receptors as opiates. Basic neuroscience discoveries have provided much information about how opiates and opioids act on the brain. Beginning with the specific receptors that are the initial site of drug action, there is considerable information about the physiological systems affected by this class of drugs. The endogenous opioid system is widely represented throughout the body. The well-known effects of drugs such as heroin include inhibition of pain perception and the production of relaxation and euphoria. In addition, there are important opioid effects on the endocrine, cardiovascular, gastrointestinal, and immune systems. Three types of receptors for this system (μ, δ, κ) have been identified and cloned. Three distinct families of peptide transmitters have been identified for these receptors: endorphins, enkephalins, and dynorphins, respectively. A common feature of most drugs that are abused by humans is that they activate the same reward system in the brains of experimental animals. Opioids produce an augmentation of dopamine (DA) levels in limbic brain regions such as the nucleus accumbens (NAc), similar to the augmentation produced by alcohol, cocaine, amphetamine, and nicotine. Although the mechanism for producing the DA increase is different for each drug, activation of this system seems to be important for the production of reward from drugs as well as reward from other activities such as sex or food. Other brain systems appear to be involved in the mechanisms of tolerance and physical dependence on opioids. When opioid drugs are taken regularly, their effects diminish (tolerance); if they are stopped abruptly, a withdrawal syndrome ensues. This pattern occurs when opiates are given to treat pain and, thus, fear of producing addiction causes many doctors to undertreat patients who are in pain. In reality, true addiction with drug-seeking behavior rarely occurs in the course of medical treatment. It is very important not to confuse the presence of tolerance and physical dependence with true addiction.

Opiate addiction has been a problem for the United States for well over 100 years and the availability of potent supplies of heroin has increased dramatically in the 1990s. Estimates of current heroin users are in the range of 750,000 to 1 million Americans (Kreek, 1992). Most of the efforts to deal with the problem over the past century have been legal rather than medical. Whereas some opioid addicts are able to detoxify and remain drug-free, the majority relapse, even after intensive psychotherapy. More importantly, many heroin addicts will not even consider a drug-free treatment approach. Maintenance treatment using methadone was developed in the 1960s. The essence of this treatment is the transfer of the patient from a short-acting opiate that must be taken by injection two to four times daily to a long-acting opioid that needs be taken only once daily by mouth. The effects of this transfer are remarkable. It requires relatively little effort on the part of the patient; thus, the treatment has wide appeal. The appeal of methadone is important from a public health perspective, as infections such as HIV and resistant tuberculosis threaten the general public as well as substance abusers.

Initially, most heroin addicts have poor motivation for changing their lives. When first introduced to methadone treatment, they still want to get "high" and mix other drugs with prescribed medication. With appropriate counseling in a structured program, the patient can make the transition from thinking as a street addict to behaving as a productive citizen. Methadone substitutes for heroin, reduces drug-seeking behavior and blocks opiate withdrawal symptoms. It stabilizes physiological systems because of its long duration of action, in contrast to the short action of heroin which produces ups and downs (Kreek, 1992). Typically, patients continue to use some heroin during the first few weeks or months on methadone. Methadone does not block the effects of heroin, but it produces cross-tolerance to heroin and all similar drugs. Thus, the effects of usual doses of heroin are diminished and over time the typical patient decreases heroin use further and then stops. The evidence shows that the improvement in all areas of function shown by methadone patients is produced by a combination of medication (methadone) and psychosocial intervention. When methadone dose is held constant at a level adequate for most patients (60 mg), there is an orderly relationship between the "dose" of psychotherapy and the outcome of treatment (McLellan, Arndt, Metzger, Woody, & O'Brien, 1993). Some improvement is seen with methadone alone, but with increments in psychosocial interventions, there is significantly greater improvement as measured by illicit drug use, psychiatric symptoms, family problems, and employment. Other studies have demonstrated that patients on methadone become healthier and have lower rates of exposure to infections, including HIV (Metzger et al., 1993).

The physiological stability produced by methadone is demonstrated in several ways. Patients report fewer sleep problems and less depression. Male patients report improved sexual performance. While on heroin, they were in and out of withdrawal, and when they found time for sex, they frequently experienced premature ejaculations. On methadone, sexual arousal and orgasm were reported to be delayed and sex was reported to be more satisfying (Mintz, O'Brien, & Goldschmidt, 1974). Women report irregular menses while on heroin, but on methadone there is at first a suppression of menstruation and then after about 6 to 12 months, a resumption of regular cycling. A similar stabilization is noted in the hypothalamic-pituitary-adrenal axis. Women can conceive while on methadone, and the babies are born physically dependent on the opioid. While on methadone, expectant mothers can receive good prenatal care, and the withdrawal syndrome in newborns is readily treated. Although it would be preferable to have women drug-free during pregnancy, babies born to methadone-treated mothers are significantly healthier than babies born of mothers using street heroin.

Length of Methadone Treatment

Appendix A lists both brief and long-term maintenance using methadone. Brief maintenance (extended detoxification) as defined by federal methadone regulations is up to 180 days of methadone treatment. This is enough time to give some patients a stable period during which they can organize their lives and become engaged in psychotherapy. Six months is too short for most patients, however, and the duration of methadone treatment should be determined by the patient's needs and not by an arbitrary time limit. Some patients require several years of stable methadone maintenance before they can be gradually detoxified by decreasing the dose of methadone. Many others require indefinite maintenance on this medication. For these patients, methadone should be considered as a hormone replacement therapy analogous to thyroxine for patients with hypothyroidism or prednisone for patients with Addison's disease. The endogenous opioid system is so complicated that a simple diagnostic test has not yet been devised that could demonstrate a primary or secondary deficiency state, if one existed. Some data measuring spinal fluid or plasma endogenous opioids from addicts do exist, however, but they are limited to individual peptides and do not give a clear picture of the overall system (O'Brien, 1992). There are also data from nonaddict populations showing that the system can be congenitally hyperactive resulting in babies born with stupor and respiratory depression that is reversed by opiate antagonists such as naloxone or naltrexone (Myer, Morris, Brase, Dewey, & Zimmerman, 1990). It is theoretically possible, therefore, that other individuals could be born with congenitally low endogenous opioids, possibly giving them a lower threshold for pain and making them more vulnerable to becoming opioid addicts. It is also possible, but not clearly demonstrated, that years of taking exogenous opiates such as heroin could suppress the production of endogenous opioids and create a need for lifetime methadone as "hormone replacement." This would explain why many former opioid addicts are unable to remain free of exogenous opioids despite apparently good motivation.

A hypothetical derangement of the endogenous opioid system would also be consistent with data demonstrating a protracted opioid withdrawal syndrome (Martin & Jasinski, 1969). Although the acute opioid withdrawal syndrome diminishes in a matter of 5 to 10 days whether treatment is received or not, a more subtle withdrawal syndrome lasting 6 months has been described under controlled inpatient conditions. Symptoms consist of sleep disturbance and dysphoria with accompanying disturbances in appetite, blood pressure, and cortisol rhythms. These symptoms would be expected to increase the probability of heroin use if the patient were in an environment where opiates were available.

Methadone Controversies

Despite overwhelming evidence demonstrating efficacy, methadone remains a controversial treatment (Institute of Medicine Report, 1990). Methadone produces clear functional improvement but not a cure. The patient remains physically dependent on a synthetic replacement medication and is capable of functioning normally. The general public expects methadone patients to be stuporous, but this is not the case for a properly regulated methadone patient. Tolerance develops to the sedating effects of opioids, and patients receiving methadone are quite alert (Zacny, 1995) and capable of operating motor vehicles and performing complex tasks such as teaching school or practicing law or medicine. Approximately 120,000 patients in the United States are receiving methadone as treatment for heroin addiction at present. Good programs, as defined by having adequate counseling staff and using adequate doses of methadone, have success rates of 60% to 70%. This is remarkable considering that the typical patient arrives with little motivation for change and numerous problems. Unfortunately, methadone programs are generally underfunded, and some programs do little more than dispense methadone. Although this is of some benefit, the full impact of methadone treatment requires a structured counseling–psychotherapy program. Eventually, frequent counseling sessions become unnecessary and patients can be trusted to take methadone at home. Legal requirements permit only limited doses to be prescribed for use at home, even for patients who have demonstrated their trustworthiness. An exception is "medical maintenance" that requires only monthly visits, but is available in only a few experimental programs (Novick, Pascarelli, & Joseph, 1988).

Other Medications for Opioid Dependence

LAAM is 1-α-acetylmethadol, a long-acting opioid that has been studied extensively in clinical trials before its approval by the Food and Drug Administration (FDA) in 1993. LAAM is similar to methadone, but its long half-life and even longer acting metabolites produce opiate effects for about 72 hr after a single daily ingestion. This makes LAAM very convenient because it requires dosing only three times per week and still provides physiological stability, in contrast to methadone which must be taken daily.

Buprenorphine belongs to another class of medications called partial agonists. It is currently approved for the treatment of pain, and it has shown good efficacy as a maintenance drug in several clinical trials among heroin addicts. As a partial μ opiate agonist, buprenorphine activates opiate receptors producing effects similar to heroin and methadone, but there is a "ceiling" such that higher doses produce no greater effect. In studies so far, overdose from buprenorphine has not been seen, and if heroin or other opioids are taken, their effects are attenuated or blocked by the presence of buprenorphine. This medication is expected to receive FDA approval, joining methadone and LAAM as a third option for "hormone replacement" in the treatment of heroin addicts. On the basis of experience from clinical trials so far, there are some heroin addicts who prefer methadone, others who prefer LAAM, and still others who feel that they get the best results from buprenorphine. As with other classes of medications, it is helpful for the clinician to have a selection of medications from which to choose.

Opioid Antagonist Treatment

The discovery of specific opiate receptor antagonists in the early 1970s gave rise to hopes for the "perfect" medication for the treatment of heroin addiction. Naltrexone seemed to be the answer because it specifically blocks μ opiate receptors and, to a lesser extent, κ receptors (Raynor et al., 1994), but it has little or no direct or agonist effects of its own. Naltrexone and its short-acting analog, naloxone, have high affinity for opiate receptors and displace drugs such as morphine or methadone, resulting in the sudden onset of withdrawal symptoms when given to people who are opioid dependent. If the heroin addict is first detoxified so that opiate receptors are gradually evacuated, naltrexone will bind to the receptors and prevent subsequent injections of heroin from having an effect. Numerous clinical trials showed that naltrexone was pharmacologically quite effective, and it was approved by the FDA in 1983. Unfortunately, naltrexone is a very underused medication in the treatment of heroin addiction. Unlike methadone, it has no positive psychoactive effects. Few street heroin addicts show any interest in this type of treatment, and few programs encourage patients to try it. It is a more complicated approach than methadone, and most physicians have not been trained in the use of this medication. Opioid-dependent health care workers such as physicians, pharmacists, and nurses often do well on naltrexone because it enables them to return to work with no risk of relapse although they work in areas with high drug availability. There is also evidence that naltrexone is helpful in preventing relapse in probationers who have a conditional release from prison after drug-related crimes (Brahen et al., 1984; Tilly et al., 1992).

Experience with naltrexone demonstrates that blocking opiate receptors does not impair normal function for most people. Studies in animals have implicated opiate receptors in a wide variety of functions such as control of appetite, sexual behavior, and of course, pain perception. Occasionally, normal volunteers given naltrexone report dysphoria or depression, but most former heroin addicts have few symptoms related to the antagonist. Some have remained on naltrexone for up to 10 years with no apparent change in appetite or pain perception and no impairment of ability to experience pleasure from sources such as sex or music.

Alcohol, covered in another review in this special section, has been found to act on several systems in the brain. Because of the animal studies showing that the endogenous opioid system is activated by alcohol, naltrexone was used to block opioid receptors in alcoholics. Naltrexone produced a reduction in alcohol craving and a lower rate of relapse when compared with controls in the same rehabilitation program receiving placebo. Alcoholic patients who did drink while on naltrexone reported that the expected "high" from alcohol was diminished or absent. This suggests that some of the effects of alcohol are mediated via opiate receptors. The initial clinical study by Volpicelli and colleagues (Volpicelli, Alterman, Hayashida, Muentz, & O'Brien, 1990; Volpicelli, Alterman, Hayashida, & O'Brien, 1992) was later confirmed by O'Malley et al. (1992). Subsequent human studies have demonstrated that alcohol produces a dose-related increase in plasma β-endorphin in young adults with a strong family history of alcoholism and, therefore, a high risk of developing alcoholism in the future. A control group with a negative family history for alcoholism showed a significantly smaller endorphin response to alcohol (Gianoulakis, 1994). β-endorphin is one of the endogenous opioids that is active at μ opiate receptors. Unfortunately, this peptide does not readily cross the blood brain barrier and there is currently no practical way to measure brain levels of these substances. In 1995, the FDA approved naltrexone as an adjunct in the treatment of alcoholism. Thus, a medication developed for the treatment of opiate addiction may turn out to have an important role in the treatment of alcoholism.

COCAINE DEPENDENCE

More than 23 million Americans are estimated to have used cocaine at some time in their lives although the number of current users decreased to 1.4 million in 1994 (Substance Abuse and Mental Health Administration, 1995). The number of frequent users has remained steady at around 800,000 individuals. Illicit cocaine is administered through the nasal mucosa ("snorting"), inhalation (free base, smoked cocaine, crack), or intravenous injection. People seek cocaine because it produces an intense euphoria, or "high." It also causes a dose-dependent increase in heart rate and blood pressure accompanied by increased arousal, improved performance on tests requiring alertness, and a sense of self-confidence and well-being. Intense euphoria occurs at higher doses, and it is followed, according to patient reports, by a desire for more drug. Involuntary motor activity, stereotyped behavior, and paranoia may occur after high or repeated doses.

An unknown proportion of cocaine users lose control and become addicts. The variables that influence this loss of control are not known specifically, but clinical data suggest that they include availability, route of administration, dose, frequency and preexisting vulnerability to addiction. Crack cocaine, in particular, is widely available and priced at $2 to $5 per unit dose in some major cities. This makes it very attractive to children. Generally, substance abuse is more common in male than in female users, and for cocaine, male users predominate at a ratio of 2:1. Male dominance is less for crack cocaine, however, as it is the form preferred by many young women; thus, cocaine use during pregnancy is commonly seen. Cocaine is often involved in a drugs-for-sex exchange, and an association between HIV infection and cocaine use has been documented (Edlin et al., 1994).

Recent studies on brain reward mechanisms have yielded important information on the ways that cocaine affects behavior. The reinforcing effects of cocaine and cocaine analogs correlate best with their effectiveness in blocking the DA transporter (Ritz, Lamb, Goldberg, & Kuhar, 1987). This reuptake blockade results in excess synaptic DA and thus increased dopaminergic stimulation at critical brain sites. However, cocaine also blocks both norepinephrine (NE) and serotonin (5HT) reuptake, and chronic use of cocaine produces changes in these systems as measured by reductions in the neurotransmitter metabolites MHPG (3-methoxy-4 hydroxyphenethyleneglycol) and 5-HIAA (5-hydroxyindoleacetic acid). Thus, neurotransmitters other than DA may be involved in the symptoms reported by patients after a period of heavy cocaine use.

Repeated administration of cocaine to laboratory rats results in a progressively increased behavioral response although the dose of cocaine remains constant. This phenomenon, called sensitization, has been a reliable finding in numerous studies where cocaine is administered once daily and motor activity is quantified. In human cocaine users, sensitization for the euphoria effect is not typically seen; to the contrary, many experienced users report requiring more cocaine over time to obtain euphoria (i.e., tolerance). Within a single laboratory session, reduced euphoric response (tachyphylaxis, rapid tolerance) has been reported by human users when the same dose is given repeatedly.

Sensitization in humans has been suggested as the mechanism for the paranoid, psychotic manifestations of cocaine use. This hypothesis is based on the observation that paranoia during a binge begins after several years of cocaine use (M = 35 months) in vulnerable users (Satel, Southwick, & Gawin, 1991b). Thus, repeated administration may be required to sensitize the patient to experience paranoia. The phenomenon of kindling has also been suggested as an explanation for cocaine-induced paranoia. Just as subthreshold electrical stimulation will produce seizures if given repeatedly, small doses of cocaine will eventually produce seizures in rats (Weiss, Post, Szele, Woodward, & Nierenberg, 1989). Thus, repeated exposure to cocaine may "kindle" limbic system activity resulting in the appearance of paranoid symptoms that were not produced by earlier cocaine use.

Sensitization (reverse tolerance) may involve conditioning, and thus it is interesting to note that human cocaine users often report a strong response similar to their response to cocaine on seeing the white powder before it is administered. This response has been measured in the laboratory in former cocaine users when they view scenes of cocaine preparation or use (O'Brien, 1992). Their reaction, which is presumed to be a conditioned response, consists of physiological arousal and increased craving for cocaine. Recently, limbic system activation as measured by increased regional cerebral blood flow has been reported in former cocaine addicts shown cocaine-related stimuli (Childress et al., 1995).

Cocaine is typically used intermittently, and thus, even heavy users experience periods of withdrawal or "crash." Cocaine withdrawal is manifested by subjective complaints including craving for cocaine, depression, fatigue, and sleepiness. Clinicians usually observe a slowed heart rate but no other objective signs of cocaine withdrawal. Studies of hospitalized cocaine users during withdrawal (Satel et al., 1991a) show gradual diminution of these symptoms over 1 to 3 weeks. A few patients have been studied using receptor imaging techniques and these indicate a down-regulation of dopamine receptors in the post-cocaine period that may persist for months (Volkow, Fowler, & Wolf, 1991). A residual mood disorder may be seen after cocaine withdrawal and, in some cases, antidepressant medication is indicated. Because cocaine withdrawal is usually mild, medical treatment of withdrawal symptoms is seldom required.

The challenge in the treatment of cocaine addiction is helping the patient to resist the urge to restart compulsive cocaine use. Intensive psychosocial rehabilitation programs involving individual and group psychotherapy based on the principles of Alcoholics Anonymous and behavioral treatments based on reinforcing cocaine-free urine tests can result in significant improvement in the majority of cocaine users (Alterman et al., 1992; Higgins et al., 1994). Follow-up studies have reported success rates of 60% to 75% at 7 to 12 months after being randomized to treatment. Numerous medications have been tried in an attempt to further improve the results of treatment programs, but nothing so far has had consistent success in controlled trials. One of the difficulties in studying medications for this indication is that cocaine addiction is improved by psychosocial interventions. In a medication study, therefore, it is necessary to provide counseling equally to both medication and control groups.

A variety of tricyclic antidepressants have been studied as aids to preventing relapse. Most notable has been the research on desipramine (DMI; Gawin et al., 1989) showing that craving for cocaine and reported use of cocaine were significantly reduced in outpatients randomized to this medication. It was hypothesized that DMI was helpful in nondepressed cocaine addicts because its effects on monoamine reuptake may restore neurotransmitter function during the postcocaine exhaustion period. Although DMI did seem to have an effect in white-collar, intranasal cocaine users, subsequent studies of DMI efficacy in other populations have been mixed. Other medications that influence the DA system have been tried. Amantadine, a drug that stimulates dopaminergic transmission may have short-term efficacy as an aid in detoxification (Alterman et al., 1992). The kindling phenomenon has been the target of studies using carbamazepine, an anticonvulsant, but several controlled studies in cocaine addicts have failed to demonstrate any benefit from this medication (Cornish et al., 1995). The selective serotonin reuptake inhibitors have also been studied. Fluoxetine has been reported to produce a significant reduction in cocaine use as measured by lower average urinary levels of the cocaine metabolite benzoylecgonine (Batki, Manfredi, Jacob, & Jones, 1993). This category of medication is still under investigation to determine whether these reductions are reliable and clinically significant. The partial opioid agonist, buprenorphine, has been reported to reduce cocaine self-administration in monkeys (Mello, Mendelson, Bree, & Lukas, 1989), but controlled clinical studies have not yielded positive results. As of 1995, no medication has produced consistently positive results in improving the relapse rate for cocaine dependence. The mainstay of treatment remains psychosocial and behavioral approaches, but recent basic research advances suggest that a medication will eventually be found that further improves the current success rates for psychosocial treatment.

NICOTINE

There is no doubt among scientists that nicotine provides the reinforcement for the smoking of tobacco and that nicotine is an addicting drug. Because smoking is the most common cause of preventable death and disease in the United States, nicotine can be considered to be the most important drug of abuse. The addiction produced by nicotine can be extremely resistant to treatment. In fact, the success rate for smokers who request professional help for their addiction is the poorest of any drug of abuse. Only about 20% are still abstinent 1 year after beginning a treatment program (Fiore et al., 1994). Some heavy smokers are able to give up cigarettes permanently without great difficulty, whereas others keep returning to smoking in spite of severe symptoms produced by emphysema or cancer.

Nicotine dependence meets the criteria for dependence as listed in DSM–IV (American Psychiatric Association, 1994). The subjective effects produced by nicotine have been compared with those of stimulants such as cocaine or amphetamine, although the magnitude is much less. The strength of the nicotine dependence is demonstrated not by the severity of the nicotine withdrawal syndrome (see Appendix B) but by the difficulty in resisting relapse. The majority of alcoholics, cocaine addicts, and heroin addicts who also smoke report more difficulty giving up cigarettes than in stopping their other addiction. Although there are many casual users of alcohol and cocaine, most nicotine users smoke regularly, with fewer than 10% taking a small enough dose (five cigarettes or less per day) to avoid dependence (American Psychiatric Association, 1994). Mood disorders (dysthymic disorder, affective disorder) are associated with nicotine dependence, but it is not known whether depressive symptoms develop during the course of nicotine dependence or whether they begin before nicotine use and perhaps predispose one to begin smoking. Depressive symptoms generally increase during smoking withdrawal, and this may be a factor in relapse to compulsive smoking.

Nicotine is readily absorbed through the lungs and also through the skin and mucous membranes. Absorption through the lungs produces discernible central nervous system effects in as little as 7 s. Thus, each puff produces some discrete reinforcement. If the smoker averages 10 puffs per cigarette, there are 200 reinforcements per pack. Usage tends to become ritualized so that the environmental cues, timing, paraphernalia, and situation become associated repetitively with the effects of nicotine. There is, therefore, ample opportunity for the development of conditioned cues or triggers. Smoking cues have now been demonstrated to both increase desire to smoke and to elicit smoking behavior under laboratory conditions (Droungas, Ehrman, Childress, & O'Brien, 1995).

Both stimulant and depressantlike effects follow the administration of nicotine. It produces a feeling of alertness, yet there is some muscle relaxation. In rat studies, there is evidence of activation of the limbic reward system and increased extracellular DA in the NAc region after nicotine injections. Nicotine affects other systems as well, including endogenous opioids and glucocorticoids.

Smokers report tolerance to the subjective effects of nicotine. Apparently, sensitivity to nicotine can be at least partially restored over a few hours because the first cigarette of the day after a night of abstinence typically gives the "best" feeling. After months of abstinence, resumption of smoking may again produce nausea. Naive smokers experience nausea at low nicotine blood levels, and tolerant smokers will experience nausea if nicotine levels are experimentally raised above usual levels. Intravenous nicotine produces a decrease in the number of cigarettes smoked and in the number of puffs (Russell, 1987). Falling nicotine blood levels may be one element of the urge to smoke the next cigarette. In some dependent smokers, correlations of nicotine level and smoking suggested that they were smoking to achieve a certain nicotine level and thus avoid withdrawal symptoms. In sum, there is support for the argument that smokers may be smoking to achieve the reward of nicotine effects and evidence that they are attempting to avoid the pain of nicotine withdrawal. The most likely hypothesis, of course, is that smoking is motivated by a combination of a pull toward the benefits of nicotine and an avoidance of the punishment of withdrawal.

Nicotine replacement therapy can reduce the symptoms of nicotine withdrawal. Smokers report that nicotine gum and the nicotine patch do not produce the same effects as smoking, and this may be due to their producing a steady moderate nicotine plasma level rather than the spikes produced by smoking. Nicotine replacement does, however, suppress the symptoms of nicotine withdrawal, and this helps in the first phase of treatment. More smokers are able to achieve abstinence, but within 6 months, most resume smoking. In controlled studies, there is a small but significant advantage for nicotine patch over placebo that persists for 6 to 12 months. Verified abstinence rates at 12 months follow-up are in the range of 20%, even for good treatment programs (Fiore et al., 1994). Efforts to improve the success rate using nicotine patch in combination with behavioral interventions and in combination with mecamylamine, a nicotine antagonist, show promise (Rose et al., 1994). Antidepressant medication may also be helpful because of the association between smoking and depression. Controlled clinical trials testing the effects of antidepressants on the outcome of treatment for nicotine dependence are not yet available.

MARIJUANA

Although marijuana is the most commonly used illegal drug, relatively few marijuana users seek treatment for marijuana dependence. There is clear evidence from laboratory studies in humans that marijuana can produce physical dependence (Jones, Benowitz, & Herning, 1981), but the typical user does not take the drug in sufficient quantity and with the regularity necessary to produce physical dependence so that withdrawal symptoms occur when use is interrupted. Cannabis smoke contains many chemicals, including 61 different cannabinoids. The cannabinoid that produces almost all of the characteristic pharmacological effects of smoked marijuana is Δ-9-tetrahydrocannabinol (THC). Basic research on the actions of marijuana has resulted in discoveries that may shed light on normal brain function. Specific cannabinoid receptors have now been identified in the brain (Devane, Dysarz, Johnson, Melvin, & Howlett, 1988), and these receptors have been cloned (Matsuda, Lolait, Brownstein, Young, & Bonner, 1990). Although the physiological role of these receptors has not yet been discovered, their wide distribution suggests that their role may be significant (Herkenham, 1993). The importance of these receptors is further suggested by their similar distribution across species with high densities in the cerebellum, cerebral cortex, hippocampus, and striatum. An endogenous ligand that is specific for these receptors has been reported (Devane et al., 1992). As this story unfolds, it will likely affect the understanding of marijuana abuse and dependence as well as increasing our understanding of the nervous system.

PSYCHEDELICS

Drugs that are ingested to experience hallucinations or a changed mental state constitute a small but important part of the total drug abuse problem. The best known drug in this category is lysergic acid diethylamide (LSD), whose hallucinogenic properties were discovered by accident 51 years ago. It is a remarkably potent compound producing significant psychedelic effects with a total dose of as little as 25 to 50 μg. LSD is an indoleamine, a group that includes DMT (N,N-dimethylamine) and psilocybin; the phenethylamines include mescaline, dimethoxymethylamphetamine (DOM), methylenedioxyamphetamine (MDA), and methylenedioxymethamphetamine, (MDMA, or "ecstasy"). Both groups have a strong affinity for $5\text{-}HT_2$ receptors (Titeler, Lyon, & Glennon, 1988), but they differ in their affinity for certain other subtypes of 5-HT receptors. There is good correlation between the relative affinity of these compounds for $5\text{-}HT_2$ receptors and their potency as hallucinogens in humans. Antagonists of $5\text{-}HT_2$ receptors such as ritanserin block the behavioral and electrophysiological effects of these drugs in animal models. Several of the 14 different subtypes of 5-HT receptors have been cloned, and it is now known that LSD interacts with other subtypes besides $5\text{-}HT_2$ at nanomolar concentrations (Peroutka, 1994).

Compulsive use of psychedelic drugs is unusual, and although tolerance does develop to the behavioral effects of LSD after three to four daily doses, no withdrawal syndrome has been observed. Over the years, there have been claims that LSD and, more recently, MDMA can enhance the effectiveness of psychotherapy and are therefore helpful in the treatment of addictions and other mental disorders. When the claims for LSD were tested by controlled treatment outcome studies, there was no evidence of benefit; at present, there is no evidence that any of these drugs are useful as medications. MDMA, the most recent claimed psychotherapy enhancer, also may have significant neurotoxicity. Degeneration of serotonergic nerve cells and axons has been found in rats after treatment with MDA and MDMA (Ricuarte, Byran, Strauss, Seiden, & Schuster, 1985). The cerebrospinal fluid of humans who are chronic MDMA users has been found to have low levels of 5-HT metabolites, a finding consistent with the animal studies.

SUMMARY

Addictive disorders are chronic and relapsing by definition. Compulsive drug-seeking behavior with attendant social dysfunction are essential features of the diagnosis, whereas tolerance and physical dependence are often present but are not required elements. Treatment of these disorders should always involve long-term psychosocial interventions, but there are now medications that can improve the results of treatment when medications are indicated. Coexisting psychiatric disorders should be treated specifically because these "dual diagnoses" strongly influence the outcome of treatment for addiction. Medications have been demonstrated to be helpful in the rehabilitation of patients dependent on nicotine, alcohol, or opiates. Much research has focused on the development of a medication to aid in the treatment of cocaine dependence, but thus far no medication has shown consistent benefits in controlled clinical trials. Except for coexisting psychiatric disorders, medications have not been demonstrated to be helpful in the management of patients dependent on cannabinoids, nonalcohol sedatives, or hallucinogens.

REFERENCES

Alterman, A. I., Droba, M., Antelo, R. E., Cornish, J. W., Sweeney, K. K., Parikh, G., & O'Brien, C. P. (1992). Amantadine may facilitate detoxification of cocaine addicts. *Drug and Alcohol Dependence, 31,* 19–29.

Alterman, A. I., O'Brien, C. P., McLellan, A. T., August, D. S., Snider, E. C., Droba, M., Cornish, J. W., Hall, C. P., Raphaelson, A. H., & Schrade, F. X. (1994). Effectiveness and costs of inpatient versus day hospital cocaine rehabilitation. *Journal of Nervous and Mental Disease, 182,* 157–163.

American Psychiatric Association. (1987). *Diagnostic and statistical manual of mental disorders* (3rd ed., rev.). Washington, DC: Author.

American Psychiatric Association. (1994). *Diagnostic and statistical manual of mental disorders* (4th ed.). Washington, DC: Author.

Annis, H. (1986). Is inpatient rehabilitation of the alcoholic cost effective? Con position. *Advances in Alcoholism and Substance Abuse, 5*(1–2), 175–190.

Ball, J. C., & Ross, A. (1991). *The effectiveness of methadone maintenance treatment.* New York: Springer-Verlag.

Batki, S. L., Manfredi, L., Jacob, P., III, & Jones, R. T. (1993). Fluoxetine for cocaine dependence in methadone maintenance: Quantitative plasma and urine cocaine/benzoylecgonine concentrations. *Journal of Clinical Psychopharmacology, 13,* 243–250.

Brahen, L. S., Henderson, R. K., Copone, T., et al. (1984). Naltrexone treatment in a jail work-release program. *Journal of Clinical Psychiatry, 45,* 49.

Childress, A. R., Mozley, D., Fitzgerald, J., Reivich, M., Jaggi, J., & O'Brien, C. P. (1995). Limbic activation during cue-induced cocaine craving. *Neuroscience Abstracts, 21,* 1956.

Cornish, J. W., Maany, I., Fudala, P. J., Neal, S., Poole, S. A., Volpicelli, P., & O'Brien, C. P. (1995). Carbamazepine treatment for cocaine dependence. *Drug and Alcohol Dependence, 38,* 221–227.

Devane, W. A., Dysarz, F. A., Johnson, M. R., Melvin, L. S., & Howlett, A. C. (1988). Determination and characterization of a cannabinoid receptor in rat brain. *Molecular Pharmacology, 34,* 605–613.

Devane, W. A., Hanus, L., Breuer, A., Pertwee, R. G., Stevenson, L. A., Griffin, G., Mandelbaum, A., Etinger, A., & Mechoulam, R. (1992). Isolation and structure of a brain constituent that binds to the cannabinoid receptor. *Science, 258,* 1946–1949.

Droungas, A., Ehrman, R. N., Childress, A. R., & O'Brien, C. P. (1995). Effect of smoking cues and cigarette availability on craving and smoking behavior. *Addictive Behaviors, 20,* 657–673.

Edlin, B. R., Irwin, K. L., Faruque, S., McCoy, C. B., Word, C., Serrano, Y.,

Inciardi, J. A., Bowser, B. P., Schilling, R. F., Holmberg, S. D., & Multicenter Crack Cocaine and HIV Infection Study Team. (1994). Intersecting epidemics-crack cocaine use and HIV infection among inner-city young adults. *New England Journal of Medicine, 331,* 1422–1427.

Everingham, S., & Rydell, C. (1994). *Controlling cocaine.* Santa Monica, CA: RAND.

Fiore, M. C., Smith, S. S., Jorenby, D. E., & Baker, T. B. (1994). The effectiveness of the nicotine patch for smoking cessation. *Journal of the American Medical Association, 271,* 1940–1946.

Gawin, F. H., Kleber, H. D., Byck, R., Rounsaville, B. J., Kosten, T. R., Jatlow, P. I., & Morgan, C. (1989). Desipramine facilitation of initial cocaine abuse. *Archives of General Psychiatry, 46,* 117–121.

Gerstein, D. R., Johnson, R. A., Harwood, H. J., Fountain, D., Suter, N., & Malloy, K. (1994). *Evaluating recovery services: The California Drug and Alcohol Assessment (CALDATA).* Sacramento: California Department of Alcohol and Drug Programs.

Gianoulakis, C. (1994). Genetics of alcoholism: Role of the endogenous opioid system. *Journal of Metabolism and Brain Disorders, 9,* 105–131.

Herkenham, M. A. (1993). Localization of cannabinoid receptors in brain: Relationship to motor and reward systems. In S. G. Korenman & J. D. Barchas (Eds.), *Biological basis of substance abuse* (Vol. 13, pp. 187–200). New York: Oxford University Press.

Higgins, S. T., Budney, A. J., Bickel, W. K., Badger, G. J., Foerg, F. E., & Ogden, D. (1995). Outpatient behavioral treatment for cocaine dependence: One-year outcome. *Experimental and Clinical Psychopharmacology, 3,* 205–212.

Higgins, S. T., Budney, A. J., Bickel, W. K., Foerg, F. E., Ogden, D., & Badger, G. J. (1994). *Outpatient behavioral treatment for cocaine dependence: One-year outcome.* Paper presented at College on Problems of Drug Dependence Symposium.

Hubbard, R. L., Marsden, M. E., Rachal, J. V., Harwood, H. J., Cavanaugh, E. R., & Ginzburg, H. M. (1989). *Drug abuse treatment: A national study of effectiveness.* Chapel Hill: University of North Carolina Press.

Institute of Medicine Report. (1990). The effectiveness of treatment. In D. R. Gerstein & H. J. Harwood (Eds.), *Treating drug problems* (pp. 132–199). Washington, DC: National Academy Press.

Jones, R. T., Benowitz, N. L., & Herning, R. I. (1981). Clinical review of cannabis tolerance and dependence. *Journal of Clinical Pharmacology, 21,* (Suppl.), 143S–152S.

Kreek, M. J. (1992). Rationale for maintenance pharmacotherapy of opiate dependence. In C. P. O'Brien & J. H. Jaffe (Eds.), *Addictive states* (pp. 205–230). New York: Raven Press.

Martin, W. R., & Jasinski, D. (1969). Psychological parameters of morphine in man tolerance, early abstinence, protracted abstinence. *Journal of Psychiatry Research, 7,* 9–16.

Matsuda, L. A., Lolait, S. J., Brownstein, M. J., Young, A. C., & Bonner, W. I. (1990). Structure of a cannabinoid receptor and functional expression of the cloned cDNA. *Nature, 346*, 561–564.

McLellan, A. T., Arndt, I. O., Metzger, D., Woody, G., & O'Brien, C. P. (1993). The effects of psychosocial services in substance abuse treatment. *Journal of the American Medical Association, 269*, 1959–1993.

Mello, N. K., Mendelson, J. H., Bree, M. P., & Lukas, S. E. (1989). Buprenorphine suppresses cocaine self-administration by rhesus monkeys. *Science, 245*, 859–862.

Metzger, D. S., Woody, G. E., McLellan, A. T., O'Brien, C. P., Druley, P., Navaline, H., DePhilippis, D., Stolley, P., & Abrutyn, E. (1993). Human immunodeficiency virus seroconversion along in- and out-of-treatment drug users: An 18-month prospective follow-up. *Journal of AIDS, 6*, 1049–1056.

Mintz, J., O'Brien, C. P., & Goldschmidt, J. (1974). Sexual problems of heroin addicts when drug free, on heroin, and on methadone. *Archives of General Psychiatry, 31*, 700–703.

Myer, E. C., Morris, D. L., Brase, D. A., Dewey, W. L., & Zimmerman, A. W. (1990). Naltrexone therapy of apnea in children with elevated cerebrospinal fluid β-endorphin. *Annals of Neurology, 27*, 75–80.

Nestler, E. J., Hope, B. T., & Widnell, K. L. (1993). Drug addiction: A model for the molecular basis of neural plasticity. *Neuron, 11*, 995–1006.

Novick, D. M., Pascarelli, E. F., & Joseph, H. (1988). Methadone maintenance patients in general medical practice: A preliminary report. *Journal of the American Medical Association, 259*, 3299–3302.

O'Brien, C. P. (1992). Opioid addiction. In A. Herz (Ed.), *Handbook of Experimental Pharmacology* (Vol. 104/II Opioids II, pp. 803–823). Berlin: Springer-Verlag.

O'Brien, C. P., Childress, A. R., McLellan, T., & Ehrman, R. (1990). Integrating systematic cue exposure with standard treatment in recovering drug dependent patients. *Addictive Behaviors, 15*, 355–365.

O'Brien, C. P., & McLellan, A. T. (1996). Myths about the treatment of addiction. *Lancet, 347*, 237–240.

O'Malley, S. S., Jaffe, J., Chang, G., Schottenfeld, R. S., Meyer, R. E., & Rounsaville, B. (1992). Naltrexone and coping skills therapy for alcohol dependence. *Archives of General Psychiatry, 49*, 881–887.

Peroutka, S. J. (1994). 5-Hydroxytryptamine receptor interactions of d-lysergic acid diethylamide. In A. Pletscher & D. Ladewig (Eds.), *50 years of LSD* (pp. 19–26). New York: Parthenon.

Raynor, K., Kong, H., Chen, Y., Yasuda, K., Yu, L., Bell, G. I., & Reisine, T. (1994). Pharmacological characterization of the cloned κ-, δ-, and μ-opioid receptors. *Molecular Pharmacology, 45*, 330–334.

Ricuarte, G., Byran, G., Strauss, L., Seiden, L., & Schuster, C. R. (1985). Hallucinogenic amphetamine selectively destroys brain serotonin nerve terminals. *Science, 229*, 986–988.

Ritz, M. C., Lamb, R. J., Goldberg, S. R., & Kuhar, M. H. (1987). Cocaine receptors on dopamine transporters are related to self-administration of cocaine. *Science, 237*, 1219–1223.

Rose, J. E., Behm, F. M., Westman, E. C., Levin, E. D., Stein, R. M., Ripka, G. V. (1994). Mecamylamine combined with nicotine skin patch facilitates smoking cessation beyond nicotine patch treatment alone. *Clinical Pharmacology and Therapeutics, 56*, 86–99.

Russell, M. A. H. (1987). Nicotine intake and its regulation by smokers. In W. D. Martin, G. R. Van Loon, E. T. Iwamoto, & L. Davis (Eds.), *Tobacco smoking and nicotine* (p. 25). New York: Plenum Press.

Satel, S. L., Price, L. H., Palumbo, J., McDougle, C. J., Krystal, J. H., Gawin, F. H., Charney, D. S., Heninger, G. R., & Klever, H. D. (1991a). Clinical phenomenology and neurobiology of cocaine abstinence: A prospective inpatient study. *American Journal of Psychiatry, 148*, 1712–1716.

Satel, S. L., Southwick, S. M., & Gawin, F. H. (1991b). Clinical features of cocaine induced paranoia. *American Journal of Psychiatry, 148*, 495–598.

Substance Abuse and Mental Health Administration. (1995). *Preliminary estimates from the 1994 National Household Survey on Drug Abuse.* Washington, DC: U.S. Government Printing Office.

Tilly, J., O'Brien, C. P., McLellan, A. T., Woody, G. E., Metzger, D. S., & Cornish, J. (1992). Naltrexone in the treatment of federal probationers. In L. Harris (Ed.), *NIDA Research Monograph* 119 (Publication no. ADM-92-188): 458. Washington, DC: U.S. Government Printing Office.

Titeler, M., Lyon, R. A., & Glennon, R. A. (1988). Radioligand binding evidence implicates the brain 5-HT$_2$ receptor as a site of action for LSD and phenylisopropylamine hallucinogens. *Psychopharmacology, 94*, 213–215.

Volkow, N. D., Fowler, J. S., & Wolf, A. P. (1991). Use of PET to study cocaine in the human brain. In R. Rapaka & M. Kuhar (Eds.), *Emerging techniques for drug abuse research* (NIDA Monograph Series, pp. 168–179). Rockville, MD: National Institutes of Health.

Volpicelli, J., Alterman, A., Hayashida, M., Muentz, L., & O'Brien, C. P. (1990). Naltrexone and the treatment of alcohol dependence. In L. D. Reid (Ed.), *Opioids, bulimia and alcoholism* (pp. 195–214). New York: Springer-Verlag.

Volpicelli, J. R., Alterman, A. I., Hayashida, M., & O'Brien, C. P. (1992). Naltrexone in the treatment of alcohol dependence. *Archives of General Psychiatry, 49*, 876–880.

Walsh, D. C., Hingson, R. W., Merrigan, D. M., Levenson, S. M., Cupples, L. A., Heeren, T., Coffman, G. A., Becker, C. A., Barker, T. A., Hamilton, S. K., McGuire, T. G., & Kelly, C. E. (1991). A randomized trial of treatment options for alcohol-abusing workers. *New England Journal of Medicine, 325*, 775–782.

Weiss, S. R. B., Post, R. M., Szele, F., Woodward, R., & Nierenberg, J. (1989). Chronic carbamazepine inhibits the development of local anesthetic seizures kindled by cocaine and lidocaine. *Brain Research, 497*, 72–79.

Woody, G. E., O'Brien, C. P., McLellan, A. T., & Evans, B. D. (1982). Use of antidepressants along with methadone in maintenance patients. *Annals of the New York Academy of Sciences, 398,* 120–127.

Zacny, J. C. (1995). A review of the effects of opioids on psychomotor and cognitive functioning in humans. *Experimental and Clinical Psychopharmacology, 3,* 432–466.

APPENDIX A: POSTDETOXIFICATION MANAGEMENT

1. Drug free
2. Psychoactive medication for coexisting psychiatric disorders
   Mood disorder
   Anxiety disorder
   Schizophrenia
3. Brief maintenance
   Nicotine patch
   Methadone
   Naltrexone
4. Long-term maintenance (opiate dependence)
   Methadone
   LAAM
   Naltrexone
   Buprenorphine (not yet approved by Food and Drug Administration)

(*Note.* Psychosocial interventions must be included, but they are not discussed in this review.)

APPENDIX B: NICOTINE WITHDRAWAL SYNDROME

Anxiety
Unhappiness or depressed mood
Insomnia
Concentration difficulty
Impatience and irritability
Restlessness
Decreased heart rate
Increased appetite-weight gain

X

PLANNING AND MANAGING TREATMENT AND RECOVERY

26

IN SEARCH OF HOW PEOPLE CHANGE: APPLICATIONS TO ADDICTIVE BEHAVIORS

JAMES O. PROCHASKA, CARLO C. DICLEMENTE, AND
JOHN C. NORCROSS

Hundreds of psychotherapy outcome studies have demonstrated that people successfully change with the help of professional treatment (Lambert, Shapiro, & Bergin, 1986; Smith, Glass, & Miller, 1980). These outcome studies have taught us relatively little, however, about *how* people change with psychotherapy (Rice & Greenberg, 1984). Numerous studies also have demonstrated that many people can modify problem behaviors without the benefit of formal psychotherapy (Marlatt, Baer, Donovan, & Divlahan, 1988; Schachter, 1982; Shapiro et al., 1984; Veroff, Douvan, & Kulka, 1981a, 1981b). These studies have taught us relatively little, however, about *how* people change on their own.

Similar results are found in the literature on addictive behaviors. Cer-

Reprinted from the *American Psychologist, 47,* 1102–1114. (1992). Copyright © 1992 by the American Psychological Association. Used with permission of the author.

Bernadette Gray-Little served as action editor for this article.

This research was supported in part by Grants CA27821 and CA50087 from the National Cancer Institute.

tain treatment methods consistently demonstrate successful outcomes for alcoholism and other addictive behaviors (Miller & Hester, 1980, 1986). Self-change has been documented to occur with alcohol abuse, smoking, obesity, and opiate use (Cohen et al., 1989; Orford, 1985; Roizen, Cahaland, & Shanks, 1978; Schachter, 1982; Tuchfeld, 1981). Self-change of addictive behaviors is often misnamed "spontaneous remission," but such change involves external influence and individual commitment (Orford, 1985; Tuchfeld, 1981). These studies demonstrate that intentional modification of addictive behaviors occurs both with and without expert assistance. Moreover, these changes involve a process that is not well understood.

Over the past 12 years, our research program has been dedicated to solving the puzzle of how people intentionally change their behavior with and without psychotherapy. We have been searching for the structure of change that underlies both self-mediated and treatment-facilitated modification of addictive and other problem behaviors. We have concentrated on the phenomenon of intentional change as opposed to societal, developmental, or imposed change. Our basic question can be framed as follows: Because successful change of complex addictions can be demonstrated in both psychotherapy and self-change, are there basic, common principles that can reveal the structure of change occurring with and without psychotherapy?

This article provides a comprehensive summary of the research on the basic constructs of a model that helps us understand self-initiated and professionally assisted changes of addictive behaviors. The key transtheoretical concepts of the stages and processes of change are examined, and their applications to a variety of addictive behaviors and populations are reviewed. This transtheoretical model offers an integrative perspective on the structure of intentional change.

STAGES OF CHANGE

One objective of treatment outcome research in the addictions is to establish the efficacy of interventions. However, study after study demonstrates that not all clients suffering from an addictive disorder improve: Some drop out of treatment, and others relapse following brief improvement (Kanfer, 1986; Marlatt & Gordon, 1985). Inadequate motivation, resistance to therapy, defensiveness, and inability to relate are client variables frequently invoked to account for the imperfect outcomes of the change enterprise. Inadequate techniques, theory, and relationship skills on the part of the therapist are intervention variables frequently blamed for lack of therapeutic success.

In our earliest research we found it necessary to ask *when* changes

ve contributions of client and inter-
the underlying structure of behavior
'82; Prochaska & DiClemente, 1983).
viors move through a series of stages
:e. A linear schema of the stages was
attempting to quit on their own and
ent programs (DiClemente & Pro-
as progressing linearly from precon-
om preparation to action, and finally
tage model can be found in the writ-
Cashdan (1973), and Egan (1975).
stage model can be found in more
Brownell, Marlatt, Lichtenstein, and
Marlatt and Gordon (1985).
the stages of change construct (Proof change have been assessed in out-
f-changers (DiClemente & Hughes,
1985; DiClemente, Prochaska, &
Priddy, & Gehred-Schultz, 1988;
ka, & Velicer, 1989). Clusters of in-
f the stages of change, whether the
otherapy or attempting to change on
en ascertained by two different self-
l measure, which assesses the stage
uestions (DiClemente et al., 1991),
lds separate scales for precontempla-
tenance (McConnaughy et al., 1989;
McConnaughy, Prochaska, & Velicer, 1983).

In our original research we had identified five stages (Prochaska &
DiClemente, 1982). But in principal component analyses of the continuous
measure of stages, we consistently found only four scales (McConnaughy
et al., 1983, 1989). We misinterpreted these data to mean that there were
only four stages. For seven years we worked with a four-stage model, omitting the stage between contemplation and action (Prochaska & Di-
Clemente, 1983, 1985, 1986). We now realize that in the same studies on
the continuous measures, cluster analyses had identified groups of individuals who were in the preparation stage (McConnaughy et al., 1983, 1989).
They scored high on both the contemplation and action scales. Unfortunately we paid more attention to principle component analyses rather than
the cluster analyses and ignored the preparation stage. Recent research has
supported the importance of assessing preparation as a fifth stage of change
(DiClemente et al., 1991; Prochaska & DiClemente, 1992). Following are
brief descriptions of each of the five stages.

Precontemplation is the stage at which there is no intention to change behavior in the foreseeable future. Many individuals in this stage are unaware or underaware of their problems. As G. K. Chesterton once said, "It isn't that they can't see the solution. It is that they can't see the problem." Families, friends, neighbors, or employees, however, are often well aware that the precontemplators have problems. When precontemplators present for psychotherapy, they often do so because of pressure from others. Usually they feel coerced into changing the addictive behavior by a spouse who threatens to leave, an employer who threatens to dismiss them, parents who threaten to disown them, or courts who threaten to punish them. They may even demonstrate change as long as the pressure is on. Once the pressure is off, however, they often quickly return to their old ways.

In our studies using the discrete categorization measurement of stages of change, we ask whether the individual is seriously intending to change the problem behavior in the near future, typically within the next six months. If not, he or she is classified as a precontemplator. Even precontemplators can *wish* to change, but this seems to be quite different from intending or seriously considering change in the next six months. Items that are used to identify precontemplation on the continuous stage of change measure include "As far as I'm concerned, I don't have any problems that need changing" and "I guess I have faults, but there's nothing that I really need to change." Resistance to recognizing or modifying a problem is the hallmark of precontemplation.

Contemplation is the stage in which people are aware that a problem exists and are seriously thinking about overcoming it but have not yet made a commitment to take action. People can remain stuck in the contemplation stage for long periods. In one study of self-changers, we followed a group of 200 smokers in the contemplation stage for two years. The modal response of this group was to remain in the contemplation stage for the entire two years of the project without ever moving to significant action (DiClemente & Prochaska, 1985; Prochaska & DiClemente, 1984).

The essence of the contemplation stage is communicated in an incident related by Benjamin (1987). He was walking home one evening when a stranger approached him and inquired about the whereabouts of a certain street. Benjamin pointed it out to the stranger and provided specific instructions. After readily understanding and accepting the instructions, the stranger began to walk in the opposite direction. Benjamin said, "You are headed in the wrong direction." The stranger replied, "Yes, I know. I am not quite ready yet." This is contemplation: knowing where you want to go but not quite ready yet.

Another important aspect of the contemplation stage is the weighing of the pros and cons of the problem and the solution to the problem. Contemplators appear to struggle with their positive evaluations of the addictive behavior and the amount of effort, energy, and loss it will cost to overcome the problem (DiClemente, 1991; Prochaska & DiClemente,

1992; Velicer, DiClemente, Prochaska, & Brandenburg, 1985). On discrete measures, individuals who state that they are seriously considering changing the addictive behavior in the next six months are classified as contemplators. On the continuous measure these individuals would be endorsing such items as "I have a problem and I really think I should work on it" and "I've been thinking that I might want to change something about myself." Serious consideration of problem resolution is the central element of contemplation.

Preparation is a stage that combines intention and behavioral criteria. Individuals in this stage are intending to take action in the next month and have unsuccessfully taken action in the past year. As a group, individuals who are prepared for action report some small behavioral changes, such as smoking five cigarettes less or delaying their first cigarette of the day for 30 minutes longer than precontemplators or contemplators (DiClemente et al., 1991). Although they have made some reductions in their problem behaviors, individuals in the preparation stage have not yet reached a criterion for effective action, such as abstinence from smoking, alcohol abuse, or heroin use. They are intending, however, to take such action in the very near future. On the continuous measure they score high on both the contemplation and action scales. Some investigators prefer to conceptualize the preparation stage as the early stirrings of the action stage. We originally called it *decision making*.

Action is the stage in which individuals modify their behavior, experiences, or environment in order to overcome their problems. Action involves the most overt behavioral changes and requires considerable commitment of time and energy. Modifications of the addictive behavior made in the action stage tend to be most visible and receive the greatest external recognition. People, including professionals, often erroneously equate action with change. As a consequence, they overlook the requisite work that prepares changers for action and the important efforts necessary to maintain the changes following action.

Individuals are classified in the action stage if they have successfully altered the addictive behavior for a period of from one day to six months. Successfully altering the addictive behavior means reaching a particular criterion, such as abstinence. With smoking, for example, cutting down by 50% and changing to lower tar and nicotine cigarettes are behavior changes that can better prepare people for action but do not satisfy the field's criteria for successful action. On the continuous measure, individuals in the action stage endorse statements such as "I am really working hard to change" and "Anyone can talk about changing; I am actually doing something about it." They score high on the action scale and lower on the other scales. Modification of the target behavior to an acceptable criterion and significant overt efforts to change are the hallmarks of action.

Maintenance is the stage in which people work to prevent relapse and consolidate the gains attained during action. Traditionally, maintenance was viewed as a static stage. However, maintenance is a continuation, not an absence, of change. For addictive behaviors this stage extends from six months to an indeterminate period past the initial action. For some be-haviors maintenance can be considered to last a lifetime. Being able to remain free of the addictive behavior and being able to consistently engage in a new incompatible behavior for more than six months are the criteria for considering someone to be in the maintenance stage. On the contin-uous measure, representative maintenance items are "I may need a boost right now to help me maintain the changes I've already made" and "I'm here to prevent myself from having a relapse of my problem." Stabilizing behavior change and avoiding relapse are the hallmarks of maintenance.

Spiral Pattern of Change

As is now well-known, most people taking action to modify addic-tions do not successfully maintain their gains on their first attempt. With smoking, for example, successful self-changers make an average of from three to four action attempts before they become long-term maintainers (Schachter, 1982). Many New Year's resolvers report five or more years of consecutive pledges before maintaining the behavioral goal for at least six months (Norcross & Vangarelli, 1989). Relapse and recycling through the stages occur quite frequently as individuals attempt to modify or cease addictive behaviors. Variations of the stage model are being used increas-ingly by behavior change specialists to investigate the dynamics of relapse (e.g., Brownell et al., 1986; Donovan & Marlatt, 1988).

Because relapse is the rule rather than the exception with addictions, we found that we needed to modify our original stage model. Initially we conceptualized change as a linear progression through the stages; people were supposed to progress simply and discretely through each step. Linear progression is a possible but relatively rare phenomenon with addictive behaviors.

Figure 1 presents a spiral pattern that illustrates how most people actually move through the stages of change. In this spiral pattern, people can progress from contemplation to preparation to action to maintenance, but most individuals will relapse. During relapse, individuals regress to an earlier stage. Some relapsers feel like failures—embarrassed, ashamed, and guilty. These individuals become demoralized and resist thinking about be-havior change. As a result, they return to the precontemplation stage and can remain there for various periods of time. Approximately 15% of smok-ers who relapsed in our self-change research regressed back to the precon-templation stage (Prochaska & DiClemente, 1986).

Fortunately, this research indicates that the vast majority of re-lapsers—85% of smokers, for example—recycle back to the contemplation

676   PROCHASKA, DICLEMENTE, AND NORCROSS

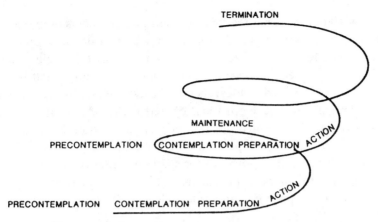

Figure 1. A Spiral Model of the Stages of Change.

or preparation stages (Prochaska & DiClemente, 1984). They begin to consider plans for their next action attempt while trying to learn from their recent efforts. To take another example, fully 60% of unsuccessful New Year's resolvers make the same pledge the next year (Norcross, Ratzin, & Payne, 1989; Norcross & Vangarelli, 1989). The spiral model suggests that most relapsers do not revolve endlessly in circles and that they do not regress all the way back to where they began. Instead, each time relapsers recycle through the stages, they potentially learn from their mistakes and can try something different the next time around (DiClemente et al., 1991).

On any one trial, successful behavior change is limited in the absolute numbers of individuals who are able to achieve maintenance (Cohen et al., 1989; Schachter, 1982). Nevertheless, in a cohort of individuals, the number of successes continues to increase gradually over time. However, a large number of individuals remain in contemplation and precontemplation stages. Ordinarily, the more action taken, the better the prognosis. Much more research is needed to better distinguish those who benefit from recycling from those who end up spinning their wheels.

Additional investigations will also be required to explain the idiosyncratic patterns of movement through the stages of change. Although some transitions, such as from contemplation to preparation, are much more likely than others, some people may move from one stage to any other stage at any time. Each stage represents a period of time as well as a set of tasks needed for movement to the next stage. Although the time an individual spends in each stage may vary, the tasks to be accomplished are assumed to be invariant.

Treatment Implications

Professionals frequently design excellent action-oriented treatment and self-help programs but then are disappointed when only a small percentage of addicted people register, or when large numbers drop out of the program after registering. To illustrate, in a major health maintenance organization (HMO) on the West Coast, over 70% of the eligible smokers said they would take advantage of a professionally developed self-help program if one was offered (Orleans et al., 1988). A sophisticated action-oriented program was developed and offered with great publicity. A total of 4% of the smokers signed up. As another illustration, Schmid, Jeffrey, and Hellerstedt (1989) compared four different recruitment strategies for home-based intervention programs for smoking cessation and weight control. The recruitment rates ranged from 1% to 5% of those eligible for smoking cessation programs and from 3% to 12% for those eligible for weight control programs.

The vast majority of addicted people are *not* in the action stage. Aggregating across studies and populations (Abrams, Follick, & Biener, 1988; Gottlieb, Galavotti, McCuan, & McAlister, 1990; Pallonen, Fava, Salonen, & Prochaska, in press), 10%–15% of smokers are prepared for action, approximately 30%–40% are in the contemplation stage, and 50%–60% are in the precontemplation stage. If these data hold for other populations and problems, then professionals approaching communities and worksites with only action-oriented programs are likely to underserve, misserve, or not serve the majority of their target population.

Moving from recruitment rates to treatment outcomes, we have found that the amount of progress clients make following intervention tends to be a function of their pretreatment stage of change (e.g., Prochaska & DiClemente, 1992; Prochaska, Norcross, Fowler, Follick, & Abrams, 1992). Figure 2 presents the percentage of 570 smokers who were not smoking at four follow-ups over an 18-month period as a function of the stage of change before random assignment to four home-based self-help programs. Figure 2 indicates that the amount of success smokers reported after treatment was directly related to the stage they were in before treatment (Prochaska & DiClemente, 1992). To treat all of these smokers as if they were the same would be naive. And yet, that is what we traditionally have done in many of our treatment programs.

If clients progress from one stage to the next during the first month of treatment, they can double their chances of taking action during the initial six months of the program. Of the precontemplators who were still in precontemplation at one month follow-up, only 3% took action by six months. For the precontemplators who progressed to contemplation at one month, 7% took action by six months. Similarly, of the contemplators who remained in contemplation at one month, only 20% took action by six months. At one month, 41% of the contemplators who progressed to the preparation stage attempted to quit by six months. These data demonstrate that treatment programs designed to help people progress just one stage in

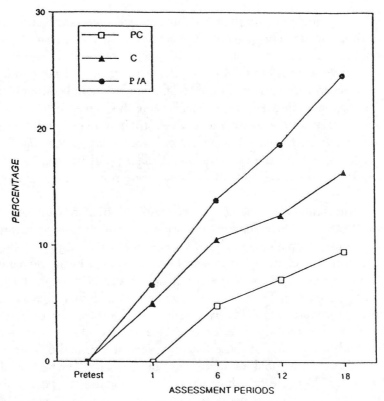

Figure 2. Percentage Abstinent Over 18 Months for Smokers in Precontemplation (PC), Contemplation (C), and Preparation (P/A) Stages Before Treatment (*N* = 570).

a month can double the chances of participants taking action on their own in the near future (Prochaska & DiClemente, 1992).

Mismatching Stage and Treatment

A person's stage of change provides proscriptive as well as prescriptive information on treatments of choice. Action-oriented therapies may be quite effective with individuals who are in the preparation or action stages. These same programs may be ineffective or detrimental, however, with individuals in precontemplation or contemplation stages.

An intensive action- and maintenance-oriented smoking cessation program for cardiac patients was highly successful for those patients in action and ready for action. This same program failed, however, with smokers in the precontemplation and contemplation stages (Ockene, Ockene, & Kristellar, 1988). Patients in this special care program received personal counseling in the hospital and monthly telephone counseling calls for six months following hospitalization. Of the patients who began the program in action or preparation stages, an impressive 94% were not smoking at six-month follow-up. This percentage is significantly higher than the 66% nonsmoking rate of the patients in similar stages who received regular care for their smoking problem. The special care program had no significant effects, however, with patients in the precontemplation and contemplation stages. For patients in these stages, regular care did as well or better.

Independent of the treatment received, there were clear relationships between pretreatment stage and outcome. Twenty-two percent of all precontemplators, 43% of the contemplators, and 76% of those in action or prepared for action at the start of the study were not smoking six months later.

A mismatched stage effect occurred with another smoking program. An HMO-based self-help smoking cessation program for pregnant women was successful with patients prepared for action but had negligible impact on those in the precontemplation stage. Of the women in the preparation stage who received a series of seven self-help booklets through the mail, 38% were not smoking at the end of pregnancy (which was approximately 6 months posttreatment). This was triple the 12% success rate obtained for those who received regular care of advice and fact sheets. For precontemplators, however, 6% of those receiving special care and 6% receiving regular care were not smoking at the end of pregnancy (Ershoff, Mullen, & Quinn, 1987). These two illustrative studies portend the potential importance of matching treatments to the client's stage of change (DiClemente, 1991; Prochaska, 1991).

Stage Movements During Treatment

What progress do patients in formal treatment evidence on the stages of change? In a cross-sectional study we compared the stages of change scores of 365 individuals presenting for psychotherapy with 166 clients currently engaged in therapy (Prochaska & Costa, 1989). Patients entering therapy could usually be characterized as prepared for action because their highest score was on the contemplation scale and second highest was on the action scale. The contemplation and action scores crossed over for patients in the midst of treatment. Patients in the middle of therapy could be characterized as being in the action stage because their highest score was on the action scale. Compared with patients beginning treatment, those in the middle of therapy were significantly higher on the action scale and significantly lower on the contemplation and precontemplation scales.

We interpreted these cross-sectional data as indicating that, over time, patients who remained in treatment progressed from being prepared for action into taking action. That is, they shifted from thinking about their problems to doing things to overcome them. Lowered precontempla-

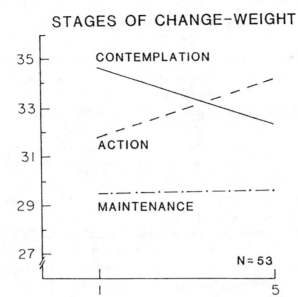

STAGES OF CHANGE-WEIGHT

Figure 3. A Longitudinal Comparison of Stages of Change Scores for Clients Before (Week 1) and Midway Through (Week 5) a Behavioral Program for Weight Reduction.

tion scores also indicated that, as engagement in therapy increased, patients reduced their defensiveness and resistance. The vast majority of the 166 patients who were in the action stage were participating in more traditional insight-oriented psychotherapies. The progression from contemplation to action is postulated to be essential for beneficial outcome, regardless of whether the treatment is action oriented or insight oriented (also see Wachtel, 1977, 1987).

This crossover pattern from contemplation to action was also found in a longitudinal study of a behavior therapy program for weight control (Prochaska, Norcross, et al., 1992). Figure 3 presents the stages of change scores at pre- and midtreatment. As a group, these subjects entering treatment could be characterized as prepared for action. During the first half of treatment, members of this contingent progressed into the action stage, with their contemplation scores decreasing significantly and their action scores increasing significantly.

The more clients progressed into action early in therapy, the more successful they were in losing weight by the end of treatment. The stages of change scores were the second best predictors of outcome; they were better predictors than age, socioeconomic status, problem severity and duration, goals and expectations, self-efficacy, and social support. The only variables that outperformed the stages of change as outcome predictors were the processes of change the clients used early in therapy.

The stages of change represent a temporal dimension that allows us to understand *when* particular shifts in attitudes, intentions, and behaviors occur. The processes of change are a second major dimension of the transtheoretical model that enable us to understand *how* these shifts occur. Change processes are covert and overt activities and experiences that individuals engage in when they attempt to modify problem behaviors. Each process is a broad category encompassing multiple techniques, methods, and interventions traditionally associated with disparate theoretical orientations. These change processes can be used within therapy sessions, between therapy sessions, or without therapy sessions.

The change processes were first identified theoretically in a comparative analysis of the leading systems of psychotherapy (Prochaska, 1979). The processes were selected by examining recommended change techniques across different theories, which explains the term *transtheoretical*. At least 10 subsequent principal component analyses on the processes of change items, conducted on various response formats and diverse samples, have yielded similar patterns (Norcross & Prochaska, 1986; Prochaska & DiClemente, 1983; Prochaska & Norcross, 1983; Prochaska, Velicer, DiClemente, & Fava, 1988). Extensive validity and reliability data on the processes have been reported elsewhere (Prochaska et al., 1988). The processes are typically assessed by means of a self-report instrument but have also been reliably identified in transcriptions of psychotherapy sessions (O'Connell, 1989).

Our research discovered that naive self-changers used the same change processes that have been at the core of psychotherapy systems (DiClemente & Prochaska, 1982, 1985; Prochaska & DiClemente, 1984). Although disparate theories will emphasize certain change processes, the breadth of processes we have identified appear to capture basic change activities used by self-changers, psychotherapy clients, and mental health professionals.

The processes of change represent an intermediate level of abstraction between metatheoretical assumptions and specific techniques spawned by those theories. Goldfried (1980, 1982), in his influential call for a rapprochement among the therapies, independently recommended change principles or processes as the most fruitful level for psychotherapy integration. Subsequent research on proposed therapeutic commonalities (Grencavage & Norcross, 1990) and agreement on treatment recommendations (Giunta, Saltzman, & Norcross, 1991) has supported Goldfried's view of change processes as the content area or level of abstraction most amenable to theoretical convergence. Although there are 250–400 different psychological therapies (Herink, 1980; Karasu, 1986) based on divergent theoretical assumptions, we have been able to identify only 12 different processes of change based on principal components analysis. Similarly, although self-changers use over 130 techniques to quit smoking, these techniques can be summarized by a much smaller set of change processes (Prochaska et al., 1988).

Table 1 presents the 10 processes receiving the most theoretical and empirical support in our work, along with their definitions and representative examples of specific interventions. A common and finite set of change processes has been repeatedly identified across such diverse problem areas as smoking, psychological distress, and obesity (Prochaska & DiClemente, 1985). There are striking similarities in the frequency with which the change processes were used across these problems. When pro-

TABLE 1
Titles, Definitions, and Representative Interventions
of the Processes of Change

Process	Definitions: Interventions
Consciousness raising	Increasing information about self and problem: observations, confrontations, interpretations, bibliotherapy
Self-reevaluation	Assessing how one feels and thinks about oneself with respect to a problem: value clarification, imagery, corrective emotional experience
Self-liberation	Choosing and commitment to act or belief in ability to change: decision-making therapy, New Year's resolutions, logotherapy techniques, commitment enhancing techniques
Counterconditioning	Substituting alternatives for problem behaviors: relaxation, desensitization, assertion, positive self-statements
Stimulus control	Avoiding or countering stimuli that elicit problem behaviors: restructuring one's environment (e.g., removing alcohol or fattening foods), avoiding high risk cues, fading techniques
Reinforcement management	Rewarding one's self or being rewarded by others for making changes: contingency contracts, overt and covert reinforcement, self-reward
Helping relationships	Being open and trusting about problems with someone who cares: therapeutic alliance, social support, self-help groups
Dramatic relief	Experiencing and expressing feelings about one's problems and solutions: psychodrama, grieving losses, role playing
Environmental reevaluation	Assessing how one's problem affects physical environment: empathy training, documentaries
Social liberation	Increasing alternatives for nonproblem behaviors available in society: advocating for rights of repressed, empowering, policy interventions

cesses were ranked in terms of how frequently they were used for each of these three problem behaviors, the rankings were nearly identical. Helping relationships, consciousness raising, and self-liberation, for example, were the top three ranked processes across problems, whereas contingency management and stimulus control were the lowest ranked processes.

Significant differences occurred, however, in the absolute frequency of the use of change processes across problems. Individuals relied more on helping relationships and consciousness raising for overcoming psychological distress than they did for weight control and smoking cessation. Overweight individuals relied more on self-liberation and stimulus control than did distressed individuals (Prochaska & DiClemente, 1985).

Processes as Predictors of Change

The processes have been potent predictors of change for both therapy changers and self-changers. As indicated earlier, in a behavioral weight control program, the processes used early in treatment were the single best predictors of outcome (Prochaska, Norcross, et al., 1992). For self-changers with smoking, the change processes were better predictors of progress across the stages of change than were a set of 17 predictor variables, including demographics, problem history and severity, health history, withdrawal symptoms, and reasons for smoking (Prochaska, DiClemente, Velicer, Ginpil, & Norcross, 1985; Wilcox, Prochaska, Velicer, & DiClemente, 1985).

The stages and processes of change combined with a decisional balance measure were able to predict with 93% accuracy which patients would drop out prematurely from psychotherapy. At the beginning of therapy, premature terminators were much more likely to be in the precontemplation stage. They rated the cons of therapy as higher than the pros, and they relied more on willpower and stimulus control than did clients who continued in therapy or terminated appropriately (Medieros & Prochaska, 1992).

INTEGRATING THE PROCESSES AND STAGES OF CHANGE

The prevailing zeitgeist in psychotherapy is the integration of leading systems of psychotherapy (Norcross & Goldfried, 1992; Norcross, Alford, & DeMichele, 1992). Psychotherapy could be enhanced by the integration of the profound insights of psychoanalysis, the powerful techniques of behaviorism, the experiential methods of cognitive therapies, and the liberating philosophy of existentialism. Although some psychotherapists insist that such theoretical integration is philosophically impossible, ordinary people in the natural environment can be remarkably effective in finding practical means of synthesizing powerful change processes.

The same is true in addiction treatment and research. There are multiple interventions but little integration across theories (Miller & Hester, 1980). One promising approach to integration is to begin to match particular interventions to key client characteristics. The Institute of Medicine's (1989) report on prevention and treatment of alcohol problems identifies the stages of change as a key matching variable. A National Cancer Institute report of self-help interventions for smokers also used the stages as a framework for integrating a variety of interventions (Glynn, Boyd, & Gruman, 1990). The transtheoretical model offers a promising approach to integration by combining the stages and processes of change.

A Cross-Sectional Perspective

One of the most important findings to emerge from our self-change research is an integration between the processes and stages of change (DiClemente et al., 1991; Norcross, Prochaska, & DiClemente, 1991; Prochaska & DiClemente, 1983, 1984). Table 2 demonstrates this integration from cross-sectional research involving thousands of self-changers representing each of the stages of change for smoking cessation and weight loss. Using the data as a point of departure, we have interpreted how particular processes can be applied or avoided at each stage of change. During the precontemplation stage, individuals used eight of the change processes significantly less than people in any of the other stages. Precontemplators processed less information about their problems, devoted less time and energy to reevaluating themselves, and experienced fewer emotional reactions to the negative aspects of their problems. Furthermore, they were less open with significant others about their problems, and they did little to shift their attention or their environment in the direction of overcoming problems. In therapy, these would be the most resistant or the least active clients.

TABLE 2
Stages of Change in Which Particular Processes
of Change Are Emphasized

Precontemplation	Contemplation	Preparation	Action	Maintenance
Consciousness raising				
Dramatic relief				
Environmental reevaluation				
	Self-reevaluation			
		Self-liberation		
			Reinforcement management	
			Helping relationships	
			Counterconditioning	
			Stimulus control	

Individuals in the contemplation stage were most open to consciousness-raising techniques, such as observations, confrontations, and interpretations, and they were much more likely to use bibliotherapy and other educational techniques (Prochaska & DiClemente, 1984). Contemplators were also open to dramatic relief experiences, which raise emotions and lead to a lowering of negative affect if the person changes. As individuals became more conscious of themselves and the nature of their problems, they were more likely to reevaluate their values, problems, and themselves both affectively and cognitively. The more central their problems were to their self-identity, the more their reevaluation involved altering their sense of self. Contemplators also reevaluated the effects their addictive behaviors had on their environments, especially the people with whom they were closest. They struggled with questions such as "How do I think and feel about living in a deteriorating environment that places my family or friends at increasing risk for disease, poverty, or imprisonment?"

Movement from precontemplation to contemplation and movement through the contemplation stage entailed increased use of cognitive, affective, and evaluative processes of change. Some of these changes continued during the preparation stage. In addition, individuals in preparation began to take small steps toward action. They used counterconditioning and stimulus control to begin reducing their use of addictive substances or to control the situations in which they relied on such substances (DiClemente et al., 1991).

During the action stage, people endorsed higher levels of self-liberation or willpower. They increasingly believed that they had the autonomy to change their lives in key ways. Successful action also entailed effective use of behavioral processes, such as counterconditioning and stimulus control, in order to modify the conditional stimuli that frequently prompt relapse. Insofar as action was a particularly stressful stage, individuals relied increasingly on support and understanding from helping relationships.

Just as preparation for action was essential for success, so too was preparation for maintenance. Successful maintenance builds on each of the processes that came before. Specific preparation for maintenance entailed an assessment of the conditions under which a person was likely to relapse and development of alternative responses for coping with such conditions without resorting to self-defeating defenses and pathological responses. Perhaps most important was the sense that one was becoming the kind of person one wanted to be. Continuing to apply counterconditioning and stimulus control was most effective when it was based on the conviction that maintaining change supports a sense of self that was highly valued by oneself and at least one significant other.

A Longitudinal Perspective

Cross-sectional studies have inherent limitations for assessing behavior change, and we, therefore, undertook research on longitudinal patterns of change. Four major patterns of behavior change were identified in a two-year longitudinal study of smokers (Prochaska, DiClemente, Velicer, Rossi, & Guadagnoli, 1992): (a) *Stable* patterns involved subjects who remained in the same stage for the entire two years; (b) *progressive* patterns involved linear movement from one stage to the next; (c) *regressive* patterns involved movement to an earlier stage of change; and (d) *recycling* patterns involved two or more revolutions through the stages of change over the two-year period.

The stable pattern can be illustrated by the 27 smokers who remained in the precontemplation stage at all five rounds of data collection. Figure 4 presents these precontemplators' standardized scores ($M = 50$, $SD = 10$) for the 10 change processes being used at six-month intervals over the two-year period. All 10 processes remained remarkably stable over the two-year period, demonstrating little increase or decrease over time.

This figure graphically illustrates what individuals resistant to change were likely to be experiencing and doing. Eight of 10 change processes, like self-reevaluation and self-liberation, were between 0.4 and 1.4 standard deviations below the mean (i.e., 50). In brief, these subjects were doing very little to control or modify themselves or their problem behavior.

This static pattern was in marked contrast to the pattern representing people who progressed from contemplation to maintenance over the two-year study. Significantly, many of the change processes did not simply increase linearly as individuals progressed from contemplation to maintenance. Self-reevaluation, consciousness raising, and dramatic relief—processes most associated with the contemplation stage—demonstrated significant decreases as self-changers moved through the action stage into maintenance. Conversely, self-liberation, stimulus control, contingency control, and counterconditioning—processes most associated with the action stage—evidenced dramatic increases as self-changers moved from contemplation to action. These change processes then leveled off or decreased when maintenance was reached (Prochaska, DiClemente, et al., 1992).

Progressive self-changers demonstrated an almost ideal pattern of how change processes can be used most effectively over time. They seemed to increase the particular cognitive processes most important for the contemplation stage and then to increase more behavioral processes in the action and maintenance stages. Before over-idealizing the wisdom of self-changers, note that only 9 of 180 contemplators found their way through this progressive pattern without relapsing at least once.

The longitudinal results of the 53 clients completing a behavior therapy program for weight control provide additional support for an integra-

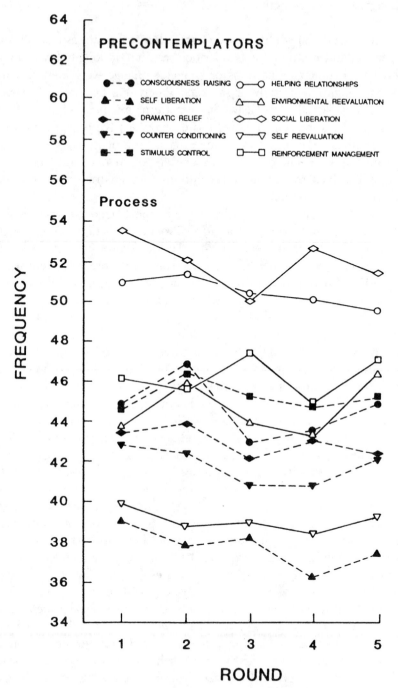

Figure 4. Use of Change Processes (T scores) for 23 Smokers Who Remained in the Precontemplation Stage at Each of Five Assessment Points Over Two Years.

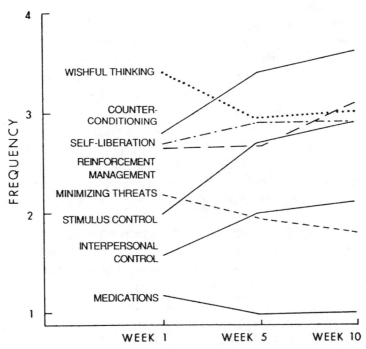

Figure 5. Change Processes That Significantly Increased or Decreased During a 10-Week Behavioral Program for Weight Reduction on a Likert Scale Ranging From 1 (Never Use) to 5 (Almost Always Use) (*N* = 53).

tion of the processes and stages of change (Prochaska, Norcross, et al., 1992). As mentioned earlier, this group progressed from contemplation to action during the 10-week therapy program. Figure 5 presents the six change processes that evidenced significant differences over the course of treatment. As predicted by the transtheoretical model, clients reported significantly greater use of four action-related change processes: counterconditioning, stimulus control, interpersonal control, and contingency management. They also increased their reliance on social liberation and decreased their reliance on medications, wishful thinking, and minimizing threats. In other words, these clients were substituting alternative responses for overeating; they were restructuring their environments to include more stimuli that evoked moderate eating; they reduced stimuli that prompted overeating; they modified relationships to encourage healthful eating; and they paid more attention to social alternatives that allow greater freedom to keep from overeating.

INTEGRATIVE CONCLUSIONS

Our search for how people intentionally modify addictive behaviors encompassed thousands of research participants attempting to alter, with and without psychotherapy, a myriad of addictive behaviors, including cigarette smoking, alcohol abuse, and obesity. From this and related research, we have discovered robust commonalities in how people modify their behavior. From our perspective the underlying structure of change is neither technique-oriented nor problem specific. The evidence supports a transtheoretical model entailing (a) a cyclical pattern of movement through specific stages of change, (b) a common set of processes of change, and (c) a systematic integration of the stages and processes of change.

Probably the most obvious and direct implication of our research is the need to assess the stage of a client's readiness for change and to tailor interventions accordingly. Although this step may be intuitively taken by many experienced clinicians, we have found few references to such tailoring before our research (Beutler & Clarkin, 1990; Norcross, 1991). A more explicit model would enhance efficient, integrative, and prescriptive treatment plans. Furthermore, this step of assessing stage and tailoring processes is rarely taken in a conscious and meaningful manner by self-changers in the natural environment. Vague notions of willpower, mysticism, and biotechnological revolutions dominate their perspectives on self-change (Mahoney & Thoreson, 1972).

We have determined that efficient self-change depends on doing the right things (processes) at the right time (stages). We have observed two frequent mismatches. First, some self-changers appear to rely primarily on change processes most indicated for the contemplation stage—consciousness raising, self-reevaluation—while they are moving into the action stage. They try to modify behaviors by becoming more aware, a common criticism of classical psychoanalysis: Insight alone does not necessarily bring about behavior change. Second, other self-changers rely primarily on change processes most indicated for the action stage—reinforcement management, stimulus control, counterconditioning—without the requisite awareness, decision making, and readiness provided in the contemplation and preparation stages. They try to modify behavior without awareness, a common criticism of radical behaviorism: Overt action without insight is likely to lead to temporary change.

We have generated a number of tentative conclusions from our research that require empirical confirmation. Successful change of the addictions involves a progression through a series of stages. Most self-changers and psychotherapy patients will recycle several times through the stages before achieving long-term maintenance. Accordingly, intervention programs and personnel expecting people to progress linearly through the stages are likely to gather disappointing and discouraging results.

With regard to the processes of change, we have tentatively concluded that they are distinct and measurable both for self- and therapy changers. Similar processes appear to be used to modify diverse problems, and similar processes are used within, between, and without psychotherapy sessions. Dynamic measures of the processes and stages of change outperform static variables, like demographics and problem history, in predicting outcome.

Competing systems of psychotherapy have promulgated apparently rival processes of change. However, ostensibly contradictory processes can become complementary when embedded in the stages of change. Specifically, change processes traditionally associated with the experiential, cognitive, and psychoanalytic persuasions are most useful during the precontemplation and contemplation stages. Change processes traditionally associated with the existential and behavioral traditions, by contrast, are most useful during action and maintenance. People changing addictive behaviors with and without therapy can be remarkably resourceful in finding practical means of integrating the change processes, even if psychotherapy theorists have been historically unwilling or unable to do so. Attending to effective self-changers in the natural environment and integrating effective change processes in the consulting room may be two keys to unlocking the elusive structure of how people change.

REFERENCES

Abrams, D. B., Follick, M. J., & Biener, L. (1988, November). Individual versus group self-help smoking cessation at the workplace: Initial impact and 12-month outcomes. In T. Glynn (Chair), *Four National Cancer Institute-funded self-help smoking cessation trials: Interim results and emerging patterns.* Symposium conducted at the annual meeting of the Association for the Advancement of Behavior Therapy, New York.

Beitman, B. D. (1986). *The structure of individual psychotherapy.* New York: Guilford Press.

Benjamin, A. (1987). *The helping interview.* Boston: Houghton Mifflin.

Beutler, L. E., & Clarkin, J. F. (1990). *Systematic treatment selection.* New York: Brunner/Mazel.

Brownell, K. D., Marlatt, G. A., Lichtenstein, E., & Wilson, G. T. (1986). Understanding and preventing relapse. *American Psychologist, 41,* 765–782.

Cashdan, S. (1973). *Interactional psychotherapy: Stages and strategies in behavioral change.* New York: Grune & Stratton.

Cohen, S., Lichtenstein, E., Prochaska, J. O., Rossi, J. S., Gritz, E. R., Carr, C. R., Orleans, C. T., Schoenbach, V. J., Biener, L., Abrams, D., DiClemente, C. C., Curry, S., Marlatt, G. A., Cummings, K. M., Emont, S. L., Giovino, G., & Ossip-Klein, D. (1989). Debunking myths about self-quitting: Evidence from 10 prospective studies of persons quitting smoking by themselves. *American Psychologist, 44,* 1355–1365.

DiClemente, C. C. (1991). Motivational interviewing and the stages of change.

In W. R. Miller & S. Rollnick (Eds.), *Motivational interviewing: Preparing people for change* (pp. 191–202). New York: Guilford Press.

DiClemente, C. C., & Hughes, S. L. (1990). Stages of change profiles in alcoholism treatment. *Journal of Substance Abuse, 2,* 217–235.

DiClemente, C. C., & Prochaska, J. O. (1982). Self-change and therapy change of smoking behavior: A comparison of processes of change in cessation and maintenance. *Addictive Behaviors, 7,* 133–142.

DiClemente, C. C., & Prochaska, J. O. (1985). Processes and stages of change: Coping and competence in smoking behavior change. In S. Shiffman & T. A. Wills (Eds.), *Coping and substance abuse* (pp. 319–343). San Diego, CA: Academic Press.

DiClemente, C. C., Prochaska, J. O., Fairhurst, S. K., Velicer, W. F., Velasquez, M. M., & Rossi, J. S. (1991). The process of smoking cessation: An analysis of precontemplation, contemplation, and preparation stages of change. *Journal of Consulting and Clinical Psychology, 59,* 295–304.

DiClemente, C. C., Prochaska, J. O., & Gilbertini, M. (1985). Self-efficacy and the stages of self-change of smoking. *Cognitive Therapy and Research, 9,* 181–200.

Donovan, D. M., & Marlatt, G. A. (Eds.). (1988). *Assessment of addictive behaviors: Behavioral, cognitive, and physiological procedures.* New York: Guilford Press.

Dryden, W. (1986). Eclectic psychotherapies: A critique of leading approaches. In J. C. Norcross (Ed.), *Handbook of eclectic psychotherapy.* New York: Brunner/Mazel.

Egan, G. (1975). *The skilled helper: A model for systematic helping and interpersonal relating.* Monterey, CA: Brooks/Cole.

Ershoff, D. H., Mullen, P. D., & Quinn, V. (1987, December). *Self-help interventions for smoking cessation with pregnant women.* Paper presented at the Self-Help Intervention Workshop of the National Cancer Institute, Rockville, MD.

Giunta, L. C., Saltzman, N., & Norcross, J. C. (1991). Whither integration? An exploratory study of contention and convergence in the Clinical Exchange. *Journal of Integrative and Eclectic Psychotherapy, 10,* 117–129.

Glynn, T. J., Boyd, G. M., & Gruman, J. C. (1990). Essential elements of self-help/minimal intervention strategies for smoking cessation. *Health Education Quarterly, 17,* 329–345.

Goldfried, M. R. (1980). Toward the delineation of therapeutic change principles. *American Psychologist, 35,* 991–999.

Goldfried, M. R. (1982). *Converging themes in psychotherapy.* New York: Springer.

Gottlieb, N. H., Galavotti, C., McCuan, R. S., & McAlister, A. L. (1990). Specification of a social cognitive model predicting smoking cessation in a Mexican-American population: A prospective study. *Cognitive Therapy and Research, 14,* 529–542.

Grencavage, L. M., & Norcross, J. C. (1990). Where are the commonalities among the therapeutic common factors? *Professional Psychology: Research and Practice, 21,* 372–378.

Herink, R. (Ed.). (1980). *The psychotherapy handbook*. New York: Meridian.

Horn, D., & Waingrow, S. (1966). Some dimensions of a model for smoking behavior change. *American Journal of Public Health, 56*, 21–26.

Institute of Medicine. (1989). *Prevention and treatment of alcohol problems: Research opportunities*. Washington, DC: National Academy Press.

Kanfer, F. H. (1986). Implications of a self-regulation model of therapy for treatment of addictive behaviors. In W. R. Miller & N. Heather (Eds.), *Treating addictive behaviors: Processes of change* (pp. 29–50). New York: Plenum Press.

Karasu, T. B. (1986). The specificity versus nonspecificity dilemma: Toward identifying therapeutic change agents. *American Journal of Psychiatry, 143*, 687–695.

Lam, C. S., McMahon, B. T., Priddy, D. A., & Gehred-Schutlz, A. (1988). Deficit awareness and treatment performance among traumatic head injury adults. *Brain Injury, 2*, 235–242.

Lambert, M. J., Shapiro, D. A., & Bergin, A. E. (1986). The effectiveness of psychotherapy. In S. L. Garfield & A. E. Bergin (Eds.), *Handbook of psychotherapy and behavior change* (3rd ed.). New York: Wiley.

Mahoney, M. J., & Thoreson, C. E. (1972). Behavioral self-control: Power to the person. *Educational Researcher, 1*, 5–7.

Marlatt, G. A., Baer, J. S., Donovan, D. M., & Divlahan, D. R. (1988). Addictive behavior: Etiology and treatment. *Annual Review of Psychology, 39*, 223–252.

Marlatt, G. A., & Gordon, J. R. (1985). *Relapse prevention: A self-control strategy for the maintenance of behavior change*. New York: Guilford Press.

McConnaughy, E. A., DiClemente, C. C., Prochaska, J. O., & Velicer, W. F. (1989). Stages of change in psychotherapy: A follow-up report. *Psychotherapy, 26*, 494–503.

McConnaughy, E. A., Prochaska, J. O., & Velicer, W. F. (1983). Stages of change in psychotherapy: Measurement and sample profiles. *Psychotherapy, 20*, 368–375.

Medieros, M., & Prochaska, J. O. (1992). *Predicting premature termination from psychotherapy*. Manuscript submitted for publication.

Miller, W. R., & Hester, R. R. (1980). Treating the problem drinker: Modern approaches. In W. R. Miller (Ed.), *The addictive behaviors: Treatment of alcoholism, drug abuse, smoking and obesity* (pp. 11–141). Oxford, England: Pergamon Press.

Miller, W. R., & Hester, R. R. (1986). The effectiveness of alcoholism treatment. In W. R. Miller & N. Heather (Eds.), *Treating addictive behaviors: Processes of change* (pp. 121–174). New York: Plenum Press.

Norcross, J. C. (1991). Prescriptive matching in psychotherapy: Psychoanalysis for simple phobias? *Psychotherapy, 28*, 439–443.

Norcross, J. C., Alford, B. A., & DeMichele, J. T. (1992). The future of psychotherapy: Delphi data and concluding observations. *Psychotherapy, 29*, 150–158.

Norcross, J. C., & Goldfried, M. R. (Eds.). (1992). *Handbook of psychotherapy integration*. New York: Basic Books.

Norcross, J. C., & Prochaska, J. O. (1986). Psychotherapist heal thyself: 1. The psychological distress and self-change of psychologists, counselors, and lay-persons. *Psychotherapy, 23,* 102–114.

Norcross, J. C., Prochaska, J. O., & DiClemente, C. C. (1991). *The stages and processes of behavior change: Two replications with weight control.* Manuscript submitted for publication.

Norcross, J. C., Ratzin, A. C., & Payne, D. (1989). Ringing in the New Year: The change processes and reported outcomes of resolutions. *Addictive Behaviors, 14,* 205–212.

Norcross, J. C., & Vangarelli, D. J. (1989). The resolution solution: Longitudinal examination of New Year's change attempts. *Journal of Substance Abuse, 1,* 127–134.

Ockene, J., Ockene, I., & Kristellar, J. (1988). *The coronary artery smoking intervention study.* Worcester, MA: National Heart Lung Blood Institute.

O'Connell, D. (1989). *An observational coding scheme for therapists' processes of change.* Unpublished doctoral dissertation, University of Rhode Island, Kingston.

Orford, J. (1985). *Excessive appetites: A psychological view of addictions.* New York: Wiley.

Orleans, C. T., Schoenback, V. J., Salmon, M. A., Wagner, E. A., Pearson, D. C., Fiedler, J., Quade, D., Porter, C. Q., & Kaplan, B. A. (1988, November). Effectiveness of self-help quit smoking strategies. In T. Glynn (Chair), *Four National Cancer Institute-funded self-help smoking cessation trials: Interim results and emerging patterns.* Symposium presented at the annual meeting of the Association for the Advancement of Behavior Therapy, New York.

Pallonen, U. E., Fava, J. L., Salonen, J. T., & Prochaska, J. O. (1992). Readiness for smoking change among middle-aged Finnish men: The KUOPIO CVD risk factor trial. *Addictive Behaviors, 17,* 415–423.

Prochaska, J. O. (1979). *Systems of psychotherapy: A transtheoretical analysis.* Homewood, IL: Dorsey Press.

Prochaska, J. O. (1991). Prescribing to the stages and levels of change. *Psychotherapy, 28,* 463–468.

Prochaska, J. O., & Costa, A. (1989). *A cross-sectional comparision of stages of change for pre-therapy and within-therapy clients.* Unpublished manuscript, University of Rhode Island, Kingston.

Prochaska, J. O., & DiClemente, C. C. (1982). Transtheoretical therapy: Toward a more integrative model of change. *Psychotherapy: Theory, Research and Practice, 20,* 161–173.

Prochaska, J. O., & DiClemente, C. C. (1983). Stages and processes of self-change in smoking: Toward an integrative model of change. *Journal of Consulting and Clinical Psychology, 5,* 390–395.

Prochaska, J. O., & DiClemente, C. C. (1984). *The transtheoretical approach: Crossing traditional boundaries of change.* Homewood, IL: Dorsey Press.

Prochaska, J. O., & DiClemente, C. C. (1985). Common processes of change in smoking, weight control, and psychological distress. In S. Shiffman & T. Wills (Eds.), *Coping and substance abuse* (pp. 345–363). San Diego, CA: Academic Press.

Prochaska, J. O., & DiClemente, C. C. (1986). Toward a comprehensive model of change. In W. R. Miller & N. Heather (Eds.), *Treating addictive behaviors: Processes of change* (pp. 3–27). New York: Plenum Press.

Prochaska, J. O., & DiClemente, C. C. (1992). Stages of change in the modification of problem behaviors. In M. Hersen, R. M. Eisler, & P. M. Miller (Eds.), *Progress in behavior modification* (pp. 184–214). Sycamore, IL: Sycamore Press.

Prochaska, J. O., DiClemente, C. C., Velicer, W. F., Ginpil, S., & Norcross, J. C. (1985). Predicting change in smoking status for self-changers. *Addictive Behaviors, 10,* 395–406.

Prochaska, J. O., DiClemente, C. C., Velicer, W. F., Rossi, J. S., & Guadagnoli, E. (1992). *Patterns of change in smoking cessation: Between variable comparisons.* Manuscript submitted for publication.

Prochaska, J. O., & Norcross, J. C. (1983). Psychotherapists' perspectives on treating themselves and their clients for psychic distress. *Professional Psychology: Research and Practice, 14,* 642–655.

Prochaska, J. O., Norcross, J. C., Fowler, J. L., Follick, M. J., & Abrams, D. B. (1992). Attendance and outcome in a work-site weight control program: Processes and stages of change as process and predictor variables. *Addictive Behaviors, 17,* 35–45.

Prochaska, J. O., Velicer, W. F., DiClemente, C. C., & Fava, J. S. (1988). Measuring processes of change: Applications to the cessation of smoking. *Journal of Consulting and Clinical Psychology, 56,* 520–528.

Rice, L. N., & Greenberg, L. (Eds.). (1984). *Patterns of change.* New York: Guilford Press.

Roizen, R., Cahaland, D., & Shanks, R. (1978). Spontaneous remission among untreated problem drinkers. In D. Randell (Ed.), *Longitudinal research on drug use: Empirical findings and methodological issues.* Washington, DC: Hemisphere.

Schachter, S. (1982). Recidivism and self-cure of smoking and obesity. *American Psychologist, 37,* 436–444.

Schmid, T. L., Jeffrey, R. W., & Hellerstedt, W. L. (1989). Direct mail recruitment to home-based smoking and weight control programs: A comparison of strengths. *Preventive Medicine, 18,* 503–517.

Shapiro, S., Skinner, E., Kessler, L., Van Korff, M., German, P., Tischler, G., Leon, P., Bendham, L., Cottler, L., & Regier, D. (1984). Utilization of health and mental health services. *Archives of General Psychiatry, 41,* 971–978.

Smith, M. L., Glass, G. V., & Miller, T. I. (1980). *The benefits of psychotherapy.* Baltimore: John Hopkins University.

Tuchfeld, B. (1981). Spontaneous remission in alcoholics: Empirical observations and theoretical implications. *Journal of Studies on Alcohol, 42,* 626–641.

Velicer, W. F., DiClemente, C. C., Prochaska, J. O., & Brandenburg, N. (1985). A decisional balance measure for assessing and predicting smoking status. *Journal of Personality and Social Psychology, 48,* 1279–1289.

Veroff, J., Douvan, E., & Kulka, R. A. (1981a). *The inner America.* New York: Basic Books.

Veroff, J., Douvan, E., & Kulka, R. A. (1981b). *Mental health in America.* New York: Basic Books.

Wachtel, P. L. (1977). *Psychoanalysis and behavior therapy: Toward an integration.* New York: Basic Books.

Wachtel, P. L. (1987). *Action and insight.* New York: Guilford Press.

Wilcox, N., Prochaska, J. O., Velicer, W. F., & DiClemente, C. C. (1985). Client characteristics as predictors of self-change in smoking cessation. *Addictive Behaviors, 40,* 407–412.

27

RELAPSE PREVENTION AS A PSYCHOSOCIAL TREATMENT: A REVIEW OF CONTROLLED CLINICAL TRIALS

KATHLEEN M. CARROLL

Increasing attention to the issue of relapse in substance use disorders has led to increasing sophistication in our understanding of the determinants, precipitants, and correlates of relapse as well as similarities in the relapse process across substances of abuse (Hunt, Barnett, & Branch, 1971; Marlatt & Gordon, 1985). Greater understanding of relapse is intended to prevent relapse and thereby increase the effectiveness of substance abuse treatment. More focus in this area has led to the development of treatment strategies explicitly intended to foster the maintenance of behavior change. Significant contributions to this area have been made by the work of Marlatt and colleagues (e.g., Brownell, Marlatt, Lichtenstein, & Wilson, 1986; Marlatt, 1979; Marlatt & George, 1984; Marlatt & Gordon, 1980, 1985),

Reprinted from *Experimental and Clinical Psychopharmacology, 4*, 46–54. (1996). Copyright © 1996 by the American Psychological Association. Used with permission of the author.

Support was provided by National Institute on Drug Abuse Grants R18-DA06963, P50-09241, and K02-DA00248 and by National Institute on Alcohol Abuse and Alcoholism U10-AA08430.

who articulated a treatment approach grounded in a cognitive–behavioral framework. Techniques that characterize this approach include the identification of high-risk situations for relapse, instruction and rehearsal of strategies for coping with those situations, self-monitoring and behavioral analysis of substance use, strategies for recognizing and coping with craving and thoughts about substance use, planning for emergencies and coping with lapses, instruction in problem-solving strategies, and focus on lifestyle balance. Consistent with other cognitive–behavioral approaches, relapse prevention emphasizes exposure to, practice, and mastery of skills through rehearsal, role-playing, and extrasession homework tasks. This approach has an abundance of intuitive appeal, has been eagerly accepted by the treatment community, and advocated as an approach for the treatment of all psychoactive substance use disorders. Books, manuals, and articles describing variations and adaptations of relapse prevention for a variety of disorders, populations, and settings, have proliferated.

How effective is relapse prevention in actually preventing relapse? In this article, I review available controlled trials that have evaluated the effectiveness of relapse prevention as a psychosocial treatment for substance use disorders, including smoking, alcohol, marijuana, opioid, and cocaine dependence. Only those randomized controlled trials that evaluated a treatment approach defined as *relapse prevention* or evaluated a coping skills approach that explicitly invoked the work of Marlatt are included (i.e., not general cognitive–behavioral or broad social skills training approaches that did not include an explicit relapse prevention component, nor studies that included a relapse prevention component within a multimodal treatment approach but did not evaluate the effectiveness of the relapse prevention component itself). Also, only those studies that evaluated and reported on substance use as a primary outcome variable (rates of abstinence, percentage days of substance use) are included (i.e., not studies for which the primary dependent variable was coping skills, self-efficacy, or job-seeking skills). The reader should note that although this group of studies is comparatively methodologically sophisticated (patients were randomized to treatments, treatments were defined in manuals, participant samples were defined through use of standardized diagnostic criteria), the studies vary widely with respect to sample size (and hence power), the possibility of ceiling or floor effects, assessment of treatment integrity, sensitivity of primary outcome measures, as well as broad differences in choice of control and comparison conditions. Following a brief general review within each substance class, I summarize major topics across classes, including the evidence for the effectiveness of relapse prevention relative to other treatments, durability of effects, methodological issues, and areas worthy of greater attention in research.

Twelve studies have evaluated relapse prevention as treatment for smoking. In an early report, Brown, Lichtenstein, McIntyre, and Harrington-Kostur (1984) compared relapse prevention in combination with nicotine fading to relapse prevention alone to nicotine fading alone for 30 smokers. Written treatment outlines rather than formal treatment manuals were used. Treatments were delivered in a group format over 7 weeks by 2 undergraduate and 2 graduate student therapists. All participants received self-management training as well. No significant differences in rates of abstinence or prevention of relapse were seen at posttreatment or 6- and 12-month follow-up, but the combined relapse prevention–nicotine fading group tended to have better outcome than either treatment alone (e.g., at 6 months, abstinence rates for the relapse prevention, nicotine fading, and combination groups were 13.3%, 6.7%, and 25.0%, respectively; at 1 year, rates were 0.0%, 6.7%, and 18.7%, respectively).

Killen, Maccoby, and Taylor (1984) compared relapse prevention skills training versus skills training plus nicotine gum and nicotine gum alone as maintenance treatments for 64 smokers who had received aversion and skills training in an intensive 4-day program. Thus, all participants, including those in the nicotine gum only condition, had significant exposure to the skills approach. Therapists were clinical psychologists or social workers. Use of treatment manuals was not mentioned. Treatments were delivered in weekly groups over 7 weeks. At 6 weeks posttreatment, abstinence rates for the combined condition (86%) were significantly higher than the skills training only condition (55%), but not significantly different from the gum alone condition (64%). At 15-week and 10.5-month follow-up, the combined treatment continued to have the best outcome, but differences were not statistically significant.

Hall, Rugg, Tunstall, and Jones (1984) evaluated behavioral skills training versus discussion control and two levels of aversive smoking (6- vs. 30-s inhalations) in a 2 × 2 design for 135 smokers. Treatments were delivered in 14 sessions (8 aversive smoking sessions followed by 6 skills training or discussion control sessions) over 6 weeks by graduate student therapists. Manuals were used, but there was no report of an adherence check or treatment discriminability evaluation. Dropouts were excluded from the analyses. Significant differences in abstinence rates and number of cigarettes smoked, favoring the skills training condition, were seen posttreatment (abstinence rates were 80.7% for the skills training and 66.7% for the discussion groups) and at 1-year follow-up (45.6% vs. 30.3%) but not the 6-month follow-up (52.6% vs. 40.9%). A significant Patient × Treatment interaction was found, in which participants who smoked less at pretreatment had better response in the skills training condition. Finally, abstinence during follow-up was associated with greater use of skills, even in the absence of group differences in smoking (e.g., at the 6-month follow-up).

In a unique study in this area, Supnick and Colletti (1984) specifically evaluated the effectiveness of two important components of relapse prevention treatment: (a) a recommendation of total abstinence versus the message that smokers could learn to cope with lapses, and (b) specific training in problem-solving strategies. Following a 7-week smoking cessation program, 33 smokers were randomly assigned to one of four manual-specified conditions in a 2 × 2 factorial design: relapse coping (discussion of the abstinence violation effect and alternate interpretations of a slip to avoid intense negative feelings) versus an absolute abstinence message (reinforcing participants' beliefs that one slip would lead to a full-blown relapse), crossed with problem solving (learning to identify and cope with high-risk situations for relapse) versus attention placebo. Maintenance sessions were delivered in three 45-min sessions by graduate students. Thus, the sample size was small and participants received comparatively little study treatment relative to the initial 7-week smoking cessation program. At posttreatment and 5-month follow-up, relapse-coping participants showed significantly greater increases in smoking than those who received the abstinence message. No effect of the problem-solving condition was seen at posttreatment or follow-up for the full sample, but among participants who became abstinent before the delivery of the maintenance treatments, significantly fewer relapses occurred for those assigned to the problem-solving condition. Abstinence rates were not reported by treatment group.

Davis and Glaros (1986) compared manual-guided multicomponent relapse prevention versus an enhanced program (which included discussion of problem situations but not skills training) versus a standard broad spectrum smoking cessation package based on Pomerleau and Pomerleau (1977) for 45 smokers. Treatments were delivered in groups over 6 weeks by advanced graduate students who did not have prior experience. No significant effects for treatment condition were seen on most smoking outcomes at posttreatment (abstinence rates for the multicomponent, enhanced, and standard treatment programs were 73%, 21%, and 56%, respectively) or through 1-year follow-up (abstinence rates were 13%, 21%, and 12%, respectively). An effect for skills acquisition (increased competence in coping skills) favoring the relapse prevention group was seen, but this effect degraded during follow-up. The relapse prevention condition was also associated with fewer cigarettes smoked when participants did relapse, as well as slightly longer periods to relapse (21.4, 11.6, and 16.2 days, respectively).

Goldstein, Niaura, Follick, and Abrahms (1989) compared behavioral skills training, which included relapse prevention to an educational support condition crossed with fixed- versus ad-lib schedules of nicotine gum administration in a 2 × 2 factorial design for 89 smokers. Treatments were manual guided and delivered in 10 group sessions over 11 weeks by doctoral level therapists, but therapist adherence checks were not described. No treatment main effects or interactions with severity of smoking (as measured by the Fagerström Tolerance Questionnaire) were seen at posttreatment (abstinence rates for the skills training vs. the supportive conditions were 55% vs. 45%). However, at 6-month follow-up, a significant effect favoring the behavioral skills training was seen, with double the rate of abstinence in the relapse prevention compared with the educational support condition (36.7% vs. 17.5%).

In a study involving a large sample of smokers (n = 744) Stevens and Hollis (1989) randomly assigned abstinent participants completing an intensive cognitive–behavioral smoking cessation program to either (a) relapse prevention skills training, (b) discussion control, or (c) no-treatment control. Treatments were delivered in three sessions over 3 weeks by "experienced smoking counselors," but adherence and treatment discriminability checks were not reported. Rates of abstinence were significantly higher for the relapse prevention condition compared with the control conditions at 1 month (for the relapse prevention, discussion, and no-treatment conditions rates were 83.6%, 77.4%, and 65.4%, respectively) and 1-year follow-up (41.3%, 34.1%, and 33.3%, respectively).

In a 2 × 2 factorial design, Zelman, Brandon, Jorenby, and Baker (1992) compared two counseling strategies (coping skills vs. supportive counseling) crossed with two nicotine exposure strategies (rapid smoking vs. nicotine gum) for 126 smokers. Treatments were delivered in six sessions over 2 weeks by the investigators and advanced graduate students. A syllabus for discussion topics was used and transcript analysis of session tapes indicated greater use of coping skills interventions in the coping skills condition. Skills training was associated with significantly fewer smoking days during treatment (0.47 vs. 1.08) and significantly higher initial rates of abstinence (98% vs. 88%) compared with supportive counseling. Significantly greater acquisition of coping skills was seen in the coping skills condition, and higher coping response scores were associated with greater abstinence. Finally, Patient × Treatment interactions with counseling condition were seen: Participants lower in negative affect had better outcome in the skills training condition, but participants higher in baseline negative affect had better outcome in supportive counseling. No treatment main effects or interactions were seen at 1-year follow-up.

Hill, Rigdon, and Johnson (1993) compared behavioral skills training (which included relapse prevention), skills training plus nicotine gum, skills training plus an exercise program, and the exercise program alone as treatment for 82 smokers aged 50 years and older. Treatment was delivered in 12 90-min groups over 3 months. Therapists and level of training were not described, nor were adherence checks. No differences in rates of quitting were seen at the end of treatment (abstinence rates were 45.5%,

45.5%, 33.3%, and 25.0%, respectively). At 1-year follow-up, there were no significant differences in abstinence among the three groups that included the behavioral skills training, but all three behavioral groups combined had significantly higher abstinence rates than the group that received the exercise program only (32.3% for the combined behavioral groups vs. 10% for exercise alone).

In another large-scale program, Stevens, Glasgow, Hollis, Lichtenstein, and Vogt (1993) evaluated a single-session, in-hospital based relapse prevention intervention (which included a videotape followed by 20 min of individual counseling in smoking cessation methods, discussion of high-risk situations, and coping plans) relative to no intervention for 1,119 hospitalized smokers, regardless of their interest in quitting smoking. Treatments were not manual guided and were delivered by two master's-level therapists. Treatment assignment was not random because of the nature of the hospital-based intervention (e.g., possible contamination between roommates), and so delivery of treatments alternated between participating hospitals. At both 3-month and 1-year follow-up, there were significant effects on abstinence rates favoring the relapse prevention intervention (at 3 months, abstinence rates were 20.5% vs. 13.7%; at 1 year, abstinence rates were 13.5% vs. 9.2%).

Cinciripini et al. (1994) evaluated a combination of relapse prevention plus scheduled smoking (instructing participants to follow a fixed, decreasing schedule of smoking over 5 weeks) versus a minimal treatment group consisting of distribution of the American Cancer Society "I Quit Kit" for 34 smokers. The experimental treatment was delivered in nine weekly groups. A manual was used, but therapists and adherence checks were not described. Patients were alternately, rather than randomly, assigned to groups. Significant differences in abstinence rates at posttreatment and 1-year follow-up were seen, which favored the combined relapse prevention-scheduled smoking condition over the control condition (at posttreatment, 59% vs. 18%; at 1 year, 41% vs. 6%).

Hall, Muñoz, and Reus (1994) compared the addition of a cognitive–behavioral intervention, which emphasized strategies for mood management to reduce dysphoria-related smoking, with standard treatment for 149 smokers. The cognitive–behavioral intervention was delivered in 10 sessions and the standard treatment in 5 sessions, so there was a confound between amount and content of treatment. Treatments were manual guided and delivered by doctoral-level therapists, but an adherence check was not described. There were no main effects of treatment type for the full sample or for patients without a history of depressive illness (for patients without depressive illness, posttreatment abstinence rates were 60% vs. 59%). However, patients with a history of major depressive disorder had significantly higher abstinence rates when assigned to the cognitive–behavioral condition compared with standard treatment both at posttreatment (72% vs. 47%) and 1-year follow-up (34% vs. 18%).

ALCOHOL

Relative to the smoking studies that unanimously report rates of continuous abstinence as the primary outcome measure, the alcohol and drug treatment studies reviewed in the next sections tend to report on a broader range of outcomes (e.g., reductions in both alcohol and drug use, improvements in psychosocial functioning), as well as continuous outcomes (e.g., days of substance use, time to relapse). This may reflect greater emphasis on the multidimensional nature of alcohol and drug abusers' problems, as well as greater variability in outcome for these groups.

Chaney, O'Leary, and Marlatt (1978) evaluated a relapse prevention skills training approach compared with a discussion control and no-treatment condition for 40 alcoholic inpatients. Treatments were delivered in 8 semiweekly 90-min groups. Manuals were used for the experimental but not for the control conditions. Therapists were graduate students and rehabilitation technicians. The skill-training approach was associated with significant treatment effects for several, but not all, alcohol outcomes evaluated (significant effects were found for days drunk, 11 vs. 64 days; total number of drinks, 400 vs. 1,593; and length of drinking period, 5 vs. 44 days) at 1-year follow-up. There were no significant differences in percentage of participants relapsed. Significant differences in acquisition of coping skills was seen for the experimental versus the control and no-treatment groups at posttreatment, with some degradation of skills seen at follow-up.

Ito, Donovan, and Hall (1988) compared relapse prevention versus interpersonal process aftercare groups for 39 alcoholic men. Doctoral-level therapists in teams with hospital staff delivered treatments in 8 weekly aftercare sessions. A manual was used for the relapse prevention condition. No difference in alcohol outcomes, including rates of abstinence, alcohol consumption, or aftercare attendance were seen by treatment group either at posttreatment (abstinence rates were 76.5% for relapse prevention vs. 73.3% for the interpersonal group) or 6-month follow-up (50% vs. 42.1%, respectively).

Annis and colleagues (e.g., Annis & Davis, 1989; Annis, Davis, Graham, & Levinson, 1989) compared relapse prevention versus counseling for 83 alcoholic individuals completing a 3-week inpatient program. Treatments were delivered in eight sessions over 3 months. At the end of a 6-month follow-up, no main effects for treatment type were found for the full sample. However, an effect favoring relapse prevention for those patients who had specific deficits in coping skills (e.g., a differentiated vs. uniform profile for specific high-risk situations) was reported.

Kadden, Cooney, Getter, and Litt (1989) compared a cognitive–behavioral coping skills approach with interactional groups for 96 alcohol aftercare patients. Treatments were delivered in 26 weekly group sessions by postdoctoral, predoctoral, and master's-level clinicians. Therapist effects on primary outcomes were not found. This was explicitly a matching study rather than a main effects "horse race" study. Thus, no main effects of study treatments were seen, but several of the investigators' a priori matching hypotheses were confirmed: Patients higher in sociopathy had better outcome (as measured by abstinent days or heavy drinking days) when treated with cognitive behavioral therapy, and patients lower in sociopathy had better outcome when treated with the interactional approach. For patients higher in psychopathology, the coping skills treatment was superior. For patients higher in neuropsychological impairment, the interactional therapy was superior. A 2-year follow-up showed the matching effects were durable (Cooney, Kadden, Litt, & Getter, 1991).

O'Farrell, Choquette, Cutter, Brown, and McCourt (1993) evaluated the effectiveness of adding a 15-session conjoint relapse prevention component to behavioral marital therapy for 59 alcoholic men and their wives. All treatments were manual guided and delivered by study investigators and advanced graduate students. Although treatment assignment was random, some replacement of couples who refused to participate in the study was done. At posttreatment, patients who had received the additional relapse prevention treatment with their wives had significantly more days of abstinence (94 days vs. 82 days) and significantly better marital adjustment. Contrary to the investigators' hypotheses, no significant Patient × Treatment interactions were found for baseline characteristics such as severity of alcoholism or marital instability.

O'Malley et al. (1992) compared coping skills therapy, which included relapse prevention, with supportive therapy in a 2 × 2 factorial design that also evaluated naltrexone versus placebo for 97 alcohol-dependent patients. Treatments were manual guided and delivered over 12 weeks by doctoral-level therapists. Naltrexone was found to be superior to placebo on several drinking related outcomes, but significant main effects for psychotherapy condition were not seen. However, there were significant Psychotherapy × Pharmacotherapy interactions, with highest rates of complete abstinence for participants who received the naltrexone–supportive therapy condition (61% vs. 28% for naltrexone–coping skills, 21% for placebo coping skills, and 19% for placebo–supportive). However, significantly fewer drinks per day and fewer drinks per drinking occasion were reported for participants who received the naltrexone–coping skills condition. The investigators pointed out this suggests that the clear abstinence message of the supportive therapy condition may have made it less likely for patients to initiate drinking, whereas the skills training approach, which taught about the abstinence violation effect as well as strategies for coping with a lapse, may have increased the likelihood that patients would initiate drinking but prevented heavier drinking or relapse when patients did drink (O'Malley et al., 1992). A 6-month follow-up also indicated participants who had received the naltrexone–coping skills treatment were least likely to relapse (O'Malley et al., 1994).

MARIJUANA

One study has evaluated the effectiveness of relapse prevention as treatment for marijuana use. Stephens, Roffman, and Simpson (1994) evaluated manual guided relapse prevention versus a social support group intervention for 212 individuals seeking treatment for marijuana use. Therapists were doctoral and master's level, and independent ratings of session tapes indicated the treatments were discriminable. No significant treatment effects for days of marijuana use or abstinence rates were found posttreatment (12 weeks) or through the 1-year follow-up (abstinence rates were 15.2% for relapse prevention and 18.1% for the social support condition).

COCAINE

Three studies have evaluated relapse prevention as treatment for cocaine abusers. Carroll, Rounsaville, and Gawin (1991) evaluated relapse prevention versus interpersonal psychotherapy (IPT) for 42 outpatient cocaine abusers. Both treatments were manual guided and delivered by advanced graduate students in individual sessions over 12 weeks. Significant main effects for treatment were not found. However, significant Patient × Treatment interactions did emerge when participants were stratified by severity of substance use: For the more severe cocaine users (defined by median splits on the Addiction Severity Index), participants who received relapse prevention were significantly more likely to achieve at least 3 weeks of continuous abstinence compared with high severity patients who received IPT (54% vs. 9%). No significant differences were found for the less severe users.

In a subsequent study, Carroll, Rounsaville, Gordon, et al. (1994) evaluated psychotherapy (either relapse prevention or supportive clinical management) and pharmacotherapy (either desipramine or placebo) in a 2 × 2 factorial design for 139 cocaine abusers in a 12-week abstinence initiation trial. This study used random assignment, treatment manuals for all conditions, delivery of treatment by experienced doctoral-level therapists, monitoring the delivery of pharmacotherapy through medication plasma levels and delivery of psychotherapy through process assessment of session videotapes that showed that study treatments were discriminable, and assessment of outcome by independent evaluators unaware of both psychotherapy and pharmacotherapy condition (Carroll, Rounsaville, & Nich, 1994). After 12 weeks of treatment, all groups showed significant improvement, but significant main effects for medication or psychotherapy type were not found for treatment retention, reduction in cocaine use, or other outcomes. However, exploratory analyses suggested a disordinal interaction of baseline severity with psychotherapy, which was consistent with that found in the earlier (Carroll et al., 1991) study: Higher severity patients had significantly better outcomes including fewer urine toxicology screens positive for cocaine (28% vs. 47%) when treated with relapse prevention compared with supportive clinical management. Subsequent exploratory analyses also suggested better retention and cocaine outcomes for depressed patients treated with relapse prevention over clinical management (Carroll, Nich, & Rounsaville, 1995). Finally, 1 year follow-up indicated delayed emergence of significant effects for relapse prevention (Carroll, Rounsaville, Nich et al., 1994). That is, although all groups sustained gains they made in treatment, significant continuing improvement across time in continuous cocaine outcomes (days of use, Addiction Severity Index scores) was seen for patients who had received relapse prevention compared with clinical management.

Wells, Peterson, Gainey, Hawkins, and Catalano (1994) compared relapse prevention group approach with a twelve-step recovery support group for 110 treatment-seeking cocaine abusers in a 12-week treatment program with a 6-month follow-up. Although participants in both groups reduced their cocaine and marijuana use, differential treatment effects on cocaine outcomes or retention were not seen (at posttreatment, participants in the relapse prevention group reported 2.3 days of cocaine use in the past 30 days, whereas participants in the twelve-step group reported 1.3 days of cocaine use). This study included a manipulation check to assess acquisition of coping skills, but although both groups did indicate significant increases in skill level, this measure did not indicate differences in skill acquisition between the two treatment groups. However, as participants were assigned to their study treatment after a mean of 4 weeks (while groups were being formed) some patients may have been exposed to other forms of treatment while waiting assignment to their study group.

OTHER DRUG USE

Hawkins and colleagues (e.g., Hawkins, Catalano, Gillmore, & Wells, 1989; Hawkins, Catalano, & Wells, 1986) evaluated the effectiveness of adding a 10-week skills training component (which included relapse prevention interventions) to the reentry phase of treatment for 130 drug abus-ers in residential treatment programs (type of substance was not specified). Manuals were not used in this study, and neither the study therapists (who included community volunteers) nor the existing program of the therapeu-tic communities was described. At 6- and 12-month follow-up, no differ-ence in drug use was seen between treatment groups (Hawkins et al., 1989). Also, although skill levels showed some reduction from posttreatment to follow-up, skill levels remained significantly higher for the skills training group at 1 year.

McAuliffe, Ch'ien, Launer, Friedman, and Feldman (1985) compared recovery training (similar to relapse prevention) combined with self-help aftercare to no aftercare for 144 opiate addicts in Hong Kong and the United States. Treatments were delivered in weekly groups over 6 months by master's level and ex-addict counselors. A treatment manual was used, but therapist adherence measures were not reported. The combination of recovery training and self-help was associated with significant effects for abstinence at 12-month follow-up.

SUMMARY

The Effectiveness of Relapse Prevention Across Substances of Abuse

Research and clinical conceptions of substance use have increasingly moved toward recognizing broad similarities in pathological patterns of use across various psychoactive substances (Edwards, Arif, & Hodgson, 1981; Edwards & Gross, 1976; Kosten, Rounsaville, Babor, Spitzer, & Williams, 1987), codified by the adoption of a uniform set of dependence criteria across substances in the development process of both the revised third edition of the *Diagnostic and Statistical Manual of Mental Disorders* (DSM; Rounsaville, Spitzer, & Williams, 1986) and the fourth edition of the DSM (Nathan, 1991). Moreover, this broader conception of substance use dis-orders is reinforced by recent research that has pointed to consistencies in the nature, timing, and correlates of the relapse process across substances (Brownell et al., 1986; Cummings, Gordon, & Marlatt, 1980; Hunt et al., 1971; Marlatt & Gordon, 1985). As mentioned earlier, Marlatt and Gor-don (1985) articulated relapse prevention as a treatment approach that could be applied across a variety of addictive behaviors to address the common problems of relapse.

The remainder of this review considers the evidence for the effec-tiveness of relapse prevention combining the various studies that have eval-uated different classes of substance use. First, however, is there any evi-dence for varying effectiveness of relapse prevention across the different types of substance use? Of the 24 studies that met selection criteria for review here, 12 evaluated relapse prevention as treatment for smoking, with 9 of these 12 reporting significant main effects at either posttreatment or follow-up. Given the inception of relapse prevention within the area of alcohol treatment, few studies have evaluated a specific relapse prevention as treatment for alcohol dependence (6 studies, with 3 reporting significant main effects at either posttreatment or follow-up). Far fewer have evaluated relapse prevention as a treatment for marijuana (1 study with no main effects), cocaine (3 studies with no main effects, some interaction effects, and 1 showing delayed emergence of effects at follow-up), or other drug use (2 studies, 1 with main effects for relapse prevention and 1 without). However, comparison of results of studies that evaluated licit (smoking and alcohol) versus illicit substances, although confounded with the number of studies conducted in each area, suggest more promise for relapse as a treatment for licit substance dependence.

Thus, although the small number of studies within each drug class makes comparison across drug classes tenuous, it appears there is little strong evidence for differential effectiveness of relapse prevention treatment across particular classes of substance abuse. Furthermore, the time is approaching for meta-analysis of this literature, which can address some of the questions taken up below quantitatively.

The Effectiveness of Relapse Prevention: Compared With What?

Rather than address the undifferentiated question "Is relapse prevention treatment effective?" findings from the studies reviewed above are discussed in terms of what they suggest about the effectiveness of relapse prevention relative to the control conditions or alternate treatments to which it has been compared. That is, different choices of control conditions lead to different research questions and varying difficulty of the test of the treatment evaluated. For example, a comparison of a relapse prevention approach relative to a no-treatment control is more likely to show significant differences than a comparison of relapse prevention to a standard treatment. However, a no-treatment comparison design cannot address the question of whether differences, if found, were due to the specific "active ingredients" of the relapse prevention approach or to nonspecific aspects of treatment. Conversely, a design in which a relapse prevention approach is evaluated relative to another, active treatment is a more rigorous test of relapse prevention (as it evaluates whether relapse prevention is superior to standard treatment for this disorder). A comparative design may address some questions regarding relapse prevention's active ingredients and mechanisms of action but also may be less likely to result in significant main effects.

Compared With No Treatment

Six of the studies reviewed (four smoking, one alcohol, and one drug) compared relapse prevention with no treatment or very minimal control treatments. Four of the five studies that reported posttreatment effects indicated significant effects for relapse prevention (Cinciripini et al., 1994; Hall et al., 1994; O'Farrell et al., 1993; Stevens et al., 1993). The Hill et al. (1993) study, which did not find significant effects posttreatment favoring relapse prevention training alone or with nicotine gum and exercise at posttreatment, did find significant effects favoring relapse prevention at follow-up. Similarly, all four studies that included a follow-up (Cinciripini et al., 1994; Hill et al., 1993; McAuliffe et al., 1985; Stevens et al., 1993) reported significant effects favoring relapse prevention up to 1 year posttreatment. Thus, the majority of studies suggest relapse prevention is effective relative to no treatment, with fairly durable results. The evidence is strongest for smoking; however, the number of studies is small for all classes of substances.

Compared With Discussion and Attention Controls

Twelve studies compared relapse prevention to attention controls or standard treatment (6 smoking, 3 alcohol, 1 cocaine, 1 marijuana, and 1 drug). Of these, only 4 out of 10 reported significant main effects at posttreatment favoring the relapse prevention condition (Chaney, O'Leary, & Marlatt, 1978; Hall et al., 1984; Stevens & Hollis, 1989; Zelman et al., 1992). The others reported no differences between the relapse prevention and control treatments, but some of these (Annis et al., 1989; Carroll, Rounsaville, Gordon, et al., 1994) found Patient × Treatment interactions effects. Thus, relapse prevention was significantly more effective than attention and discussion control treatments in only about one-half of the studies. However, follow-up findings were somewhat more positive, with 7 of 11 studies indicating sustained effects, continuing improvement, or less relapse associated with relapse prevention (Carroll, Rounsaville, Nich, Gordon, et al., 1994; Chaney et al., 1978; Goldstein et al., 1989; Hall et al., 1984; O'Malley et al., 1994; Stevens & Hollis, 1989; Supnick & Colletti, 1984), and only 1 study (Zelman et al., 1992) reporting significant effects favoring relapse prevention at posttreatment but not at follow-up.

Compared With Alternate Treatments

Four studies (two cocaine and two alcohol) have compared relapse prevention to alternate psychotherapeutic treatments. All of these studies found relapse prevention treatment to be comparable to, but not significantly better than, alternate treatments both at posttreatment and follow-up (Carroll et al., 1991; Ito et al., 1988; Kadden et al., 1989; Wells et al., 1994). Two of these studies reported Patient × Treatment interactions

(Carroll et al., 1991; Kadden et al., 1989), with relapse prevention associated with significantly better outcome than alternate approaches for participants with greater impairment along several dimensions (psychopathology, sociopathy, and substance use severity) and better outcome or no difference for participants at the lower end of impairment along these dimensions. In addition, two smoking studies (Brown et al., 1984; Killen et al., 1984) evaluated relapse prevention treatment alone or in combination with a pharmacologic treatment (nicotine gum or nicotine fading, respectively). Results for both studies were mixed, with effects for the relapse prevention comparable to the pharmacologic treatment, but with trends favoring the combination treatment over either approach alone.

Summary

Across the different substances of abuse, there is evidence for the effectiveness on substance use outcomes for relapse prevention over no-treatment control conditions, mixed findings when compared with attention and discussion control conditions, and findings that relapse prevention appears comparable to but not better than other active treatments. These findings appear consistent, then, with the bulk of the general psychotherapy outcome literature, which has been fairly consistent in pointing to the effectiveness of active psychotherapy relative to no-treatment controls, but direct contrasts of different forms of psychotherapy, or comparisons of psychotherapy relative to attention–placebo control treatments, have yielded less consistent findings (Garfield, 1990; Parloff, 1982; Smith, Glass, & Miller, 1980).

However, although relapse prevention does not appear superior to other forms of treatment based on the trials conducted thus far, three areas have emerged where relapse prevention may have particular promise. First, there is some evidence that although relapse prevention may not differentially prevent relapse compared with other approaches (and some studies suggesting that preparing participants for relapse may increase the likelihood of relapse occurring), several studies have suggested relapse prevention may reduce the intensity of relapse episodes if they do occur (Davis & Glaros, 1986; O'Malley et al., 1992; Supnick & Colletti, 1984). Second, several studies, primarily those comparing relapse prevention to psychotherapy control conditions, have found sustained main effects or delayed emergence of effects for relapse prevention. This may suggest that even though minimal treatments may be sufficient over short periods of time, sustained or continuing improvement may be associated with the implementation of generalizable coping skills conferred through relapse prevention treatment. Third, across substances of abuse, patient–treatment matching effects have emerged, that, though preliminary and not supported in all studies (e.g., Hall et al., 1984; Zelman et al., 1992), tend to support the effectiveness of relapse prevention for more impaired substance abusers, including those with more severe levels of substance use, greater levels of negative affect, and greater perceived deficits in coping skills (Carroll, Nich, & Rounsaville, 1995; Carroll et al., 1991; Cooney et al., 1991; Hall et al., 1994; Kadden et al., 1989). However, only two of these studies tested a priori matching hypotheses (Hall et al., 1994; Kadden et al., 1989). The rest of the matching effects were identified through exploratory analyses and thus require replication through prospective studies. Finally, it should be noted that some studies that have hypothesized matching effects have failed to find evidence supporting them (Goldstein et al., 1989; O'Farrell et al., 1993). Nevertheless, the notion that relapse prevention treatment may be differentially effective for different types of patients, particularly those with more impairment, has considerable appeal and is the subject of several ongoing trials, including Project MATCH (Project MATCH Research Group, 1993).

Relapse Prevention as an Abstinence Initiation Versus Maintenance Treatment

The studies reviewed above can also be categorized in terms of treatment goals and stage of treatment, that is, abstinence initiation or maintenance. Relapse prevention was originally conceptualized as a maintenance strategy and thus might be more effective for more highly motivated patients who have completed treatment, initiated a period of abstinence, or both. The use of relapse prevention to foster initial abstinence in individuals currently dependent as they came in to treatment and were not necessarily committed to abstinence might be a less optimal fit.

Fourteen of the studies evaluated relapse prevention as a treatment intended to facilitate initial abstinence (Brown et al., 1984; Carroll et al., 1991; Carroll, Rounsaville, Gordon, et al., 1994; Chaney et al., 1978; Cinciripini et al., 1994; Davis & Glaros, 1986; Hall et al., 1984, 1994; Hill et al., 1993; O'Malley et al., 1992; Stephens et al., 1994; Stevens et al., 1993; Wells et al., 1994; Zelman et al., 1992). The remaining 10 studies were maintenance studies evaluating the effectiveness of relapse prevention in preventing relapse in participants who were abstinent when they began the study (Annis et al., 1989; Goldstein et al., 1989; Hawkins et al., 1986, 1989; Ito et al., 1988; Kadden et al., 1989; Killen et al., 1984; McAuliffe et al., 1985; O'Farrell et al., 1993; Stevens & Hollis, 1989; Supnick & Colletti, 1984). Nine of the 14 abstinence initiation studies found significant effects for relapse prevention treatment at posttreatment or follow-up; 5 of 10 maintenance studies found effects favoring relapse prevention. Thus, although no single study has directly contrasted the effectiveness of relapse prevention as a maintenance versus abstinence initiation treatment, taken together the studies reviewed here suggest the effectiveness of relapse prevention in both formats appears roughly comparable.

Methodological Issues

As mentioned previously, most of the studies evaluating relapse prevention have been conducted during the past 10 years and thus have used and benefited from the increasingly rigorous methodology and technological developments that have become available during this period. For example, most (20 of the 24) used manuals or formal written protocols to specify the treatments delivered. Nearly all of the studies also used random assignment to treatments, standardized diagnostic criteria for substance dependence disorders, well-defined outcome measures, and some means of validating participants' self-reports of outcome through biochemical measures or collateral reports. Moreover, the majority of the studies reviewed here included a follow-up.

Some methodological limitations characterize this body of literature as well. First, few studies included manipulation checks intended to ascertain the extent to which patients in the coping skills condition acquired coping skills over control conditions (e.g., Chaney et al., 1978; Davis & Glaros, 1986; Hall et al., 1984; Hawkins et al., 1986; Ito et al., 1988; Wells et al., 1994; Zelman et al., 1992). Second, there appeared to be a great deal of variability across the studies in terms of what relapse prevention actually consisted of. Many of the studies evaluated a package relapse prevention approach that may have included a variety of techniques and interventions adopted from other types of treatment. Only one study (Supnick & Colletti, 1984) has conducted a careful component analysis of specific relapse prevention interventions and their impact on outcome. Third, with the exception of the two large-scale studies included here (Stevens et al., 1993; Stevens & Hollis, 1989), the sample size in most of the studies was small (with as few as 8 participants per cell) and thus limited statistical power to detect differences between conditions. Fourth, although there was consistency across the smoking studies regarding choice of a primary outcome measure, primary outcome measures for the studies evaluating other types of substance use was quite variable. Greater consistency in selection of assessments and outcome measures would greatly facilitate comparisons across studies. Similarly, greater evaluation of sensitivity of outcome measures selected is needed to evaluate the possibility of ceiling or floor effects, which may have precluded detection of differences between groups in some of the studies reviewed here. Finally, duration and intensity of treatment in the studies reviewed also varied widely, from 20 min (Stevens et al., 1993) to 24 weeks (e.g., Kadden et al., 1989; Wells et al., 1994). Thus, the optimal dose of relapse prevention treatment and extent to which dose of relapse prevention treatment may be associated with robustness or durability of effects has not yet been evaluated empirically.

Regarding implementation of the treatments, few of the studies reported on independent assessment of therapist adherence to treatment manuals or treatment discriminability (those that did include Carroll, Rounsaville, Gordon, et al., 1994; Kadden et al., 1989; Stephens et al., 1994; Zelman et al., 1992). Thus, few of the studies reviewed here could document that study treatments were implemented as intended or that significant overlap between conditions did not occur. Very few of the studies reported that therapist effects on primary outcomes were evaluated (those that did include Carroll, Rounsaville, Gordon, et al., 1994; Kadden et al., 1989; Zelman et al., 1992). No study reported on therapist competence or the effect of therapist skill on outcome. Furthermore, although most studies included detailed therapist training procedures and ongoing supervision sessions, which were intended to limit variability and prevent drift in the implementation of study treatments, therapists' level of experience and training varied widely, and many studies included therapists at the predoctoral trainee level. Greater consideration to these issues in future research is needed.

CONCLUSIONS

Ten years of research on relapse prevention as a psychosocial treatment for adult substance abusers has produced mixed results regarding its effectiveness. The literature suggests that, across substances of abuse but most strongly for smoking, there is good evidence for relapse prevention approaches compared with no-treatment controls, but less consistent evidence regarding its superiority relative to discussion control conditions or other active treatments. Outcomes where relapse prevention may hold greater promise include reducing severity of relapses when they occur, durability of effects after cessation of acute treatment, and patient–treatment matching, but these require further study. Particular areas warranting additional research include analysis of the effects of specific components of relapse prevention treatment as well as more prospective matching studies to define the types of patients who are best suited for this approach.

REFERENCES

Annis, H. M., & Davis, C. S. (1989). Relapse prevention. In R. K. Hester & W. R. Miller (Eds.), *Handbook of alcoholism treatment approaches* (pp. 170–182). Elmsford, NY: Pergamon Press.

Annis, H. M., Davis, C. S., Graham, M., & Levinson, T. (1989). *A controlled trial of relapse prevention procedures based on self-efficacy theory.* Unpublished manuscript.

Brown, R. A., Lichtenstein, E., McIntyre, K. O., & Harrington-Kostur, J. (1984). Effects of nicotine fading and relapse prevention on smoking cessation. *Journal of Consulting and Clinical Psychology, 52,* 307–308.

Brownell, K. D., Marlatt, G. A., Lichtenstein, E., & Wilson, G. T. (1986). Understanding and preventing relapse. *American Psychologist, 41,* 765–782.

Carroll, K. M., Nich, C., & Rounsaville, B. J. (1995). Differential symptom reduction in depressed cocaine abusers treated with psychotherapy and pharmacotherapy. *Journal of Nervous and Mental Disease, 183,* 251–259.

Carroll, K. M., Rounsaville, B. J., & Gawin, F. H. (1991). A comparative trial of psychotherapies for ambulatory cocaine abusers: Relapse prevention and interpersonal psychotherapy. *American Journal of Drug and Alcohol Abuse, 17,* 229–247.

Carroll, K. M., Rounsaville, B. J., Gordon, L. T., Nich, C., Jatlow, P. M., Bisighini, R. M., & Gawin, F. H. (1994). Psychotherapy and pharmacotherapy for ambulatory cocaine abusers. *Archives of General Psychiatry, 51,* 177–187.

Carroll, K. M., Rounsaville, B. J., & Nich, C. (1994). Blind man's bluff? Effectiveness and significance of psychotherapy and pharmacotherapy blinding procedures in a clinical trial. *Journal of Consulting and Clinical Psychology, 62,* 276–280.

Carroll, K. M., Rounsaville, B. J., Nich, C., Gordon, L. T., Wirtz, P. W., & Gawin, F. H. (1994). One year follow-up of psychotherapy and pharmacotherapy for cocaine dependence: Delayed emergence of psychotherapy effects. *Archives of General Psychiatry, 51,* 989–997.

Chaney, E. F., O'Leary, M. R., & Marlatt, G. A. (1978). Skill training with problem drinkers. *Journal of Consulting and Clinical Psychology, 46,* 1092–1104.

Cinciripini, P. M., Lapitsky, L. G., Wallfisch, A., Mace, R., Nezami, E., & Van Vunakis, H. (1994). An evaluation of a multicomponent treatment program involving scheduled smoking and relapse prevention procedures: Initial findings. *Addictive Behaviors, 19,* 13–22.

Cooney, N. L., Kadden, R. M., Litt, M. D., & Getter, H. (1991). Matching alcoholics to coping skills or interactional therapies: Two-year follow-up results. *Journal of Consulting and Clinical Psychology, 59,* 598–601.

Cummings, C., Gordon, J. R., & Marlatt, G. A. (1980). Relapse: Prevention and prediction. In W. R. Miller (Ed.), *The addictive behaviors* (pp. 291–321). New York: Pergamon.

Davis, J. R., & Glaros, A. G. (1986). Relapse prevention and smoking cessation. *Addictive Behaviors, 11,* 105–114.

Edwards, G., Arif, A., & Hodgson, R. (1981). Nomenclature and classification of drug- and alcohol-related problems: A WHO memorandum. *Bulletin of the World Health Organization, 59,* 225–242.

Edwards, G., & Gross, M. M. (1976). Alcohol dependence: Provisional description of a clinical syndrome. *British Medical Journal, 1,* 1058–1061.

Garfield, S. L. (1990). Issues and methods in psychotherapy process research. *Journal of Consulting and Clinical Psychology, 58*, 273–280.

Goldstein, M. G., Niaura, R., Follick, M. J., & Abrams, D. B. (1989). Effects of behavioral skills training and schedule of nicotine gum administration on smoking cessation. *American Journal of Psychiatry, 146*, 56–60.

Hall, S. M., Muñoz, R. F., & Reus, V. I. (1994). Cognitive-behavioral intervention increases abstinence rates for depressive-history smokers. *Journal of Consulting and Clinical Psychology, 62*, 141–146.

Hall, S. M., Rugg, D., Tunstall, C., & Jones, R. T. (1984). Preventing relapse to cigarette smoking by behavioral skills training. *Journal of Consulting and Clinical Psychology, 52*, 372–382.

Hawkins, J. D., Catalano, R. F., Gillmore, M. R., & Wells, E. A. (1989). Skills training for drug abusers: Generalization, maintenance, and effects on drug use. *Journal of Consulting and Clinical Psychology, 57*, 559–563.

Hawkins, J. D., Catalano, R. F., & Wells, E. A. (1986). Measuring effects of a skills training intervention for drug abusers. *Journal of Consulting and Clinical Psychology, 54*, 661–664.

Hill, R. D., Rigdon, M., & Johnson, S. (1993). Behavioral smoking cessation treatment for older chronic smokers. *Behavior Therapy, 24*, 321–329.

Hunt, W. A., Barnett, L. W., & Branch, L. G. (1971). Relapse rates in addiction programs. *Journal of Clinical Psychology, 27*, 455–456.

Ito, J. R., Donovan, D. M., & Hall, J. J. (1988). Relapse prevention in alcohol aftercare: Effects on drinking outcome, change process, and aftercare attendance. *British Journal of Addiction, 83*, 171–181.

Kadden, R. M., Cooney, N. L., Getter, H., & Litt, M. D. (1989). Matching alcoholics to coping skills or interactional therapies: Posttreatment results. *Journal of Consulting and Clinical Psychology, 57*, 698–704.

Killen, J. D., Maccoby, N., & Taylor, C. B. (1984). Nicotine gum and self-regulation training in smoking relapse prevention. *Behavior Therapy, 15*, 234–248.

Kosten, T. R., Rounsaville, B. J., Babor, T. F., Spitzer, R. L., & Williams, J. B. W. (1987). Substance use disorders in DSM-III-R: Evidence for the dependence syndrome across different psychoactive substances. *British Journal of Psychiatry, 151*, 834–843.

Marlatt, G. A. (1979). Alcohol use and problem drinking: A cognitive-behavioral analysis. In P. C. Kendall & S. D. Hollon (Eds.), *Cognitive-behavioral interventions: Theory, research, and procedures* (pp. 319–355). New York: Academic Press.

Marlatt, G. A., & George, W. H. (1984). Relapse prevention: Introduction and overview of the model. *British Journal of Addiction, 79*, 261–273.

Marlatt, G. A., & Gordon, J. R. (1980). Determinants of relapse: Implications for the maintenance of behavior change. In P. O. Davidson & S. M. Davidson (Eds.), *Behavioral medicine: Changing health lifestyles* (pp. 410–452). New York: Brunner/Mazel.

Marlatt, G. A., & Gordon, J. R., (Eds.). (1985). *Relapse prevention: Maintenance strategies in the treatment of addictive behaviors*. New York: Guilford.

McAuliffe, W. E., Ch'ien, J. M. N., Launer, E., Friedman, R., & Feldman, B. (1985). The Harvard group aftercare program: Preliminary evaluation results and implementation issues. In R. S. Ashery (Ed.), *Progress in the development of cost-effective treatment for drug abusers* (NIDA Research Monograph Series No. 58, pp. 147–156). Rockville, MD: National Institute on Drug Abuse.

Nathan, P. E. (1991). Substance use disorders in the DSM-IV. *Journal of Abnormal Psychology, 100,* 356–361.

O'Farrell, T. J., Choquette, K. A., Cutter, H. S. G., Brown, E. D., & McCourt, W. F. (1993). Behavioral marital therapy with and without additional couples relapse prevention sessions for alcoholics and their wives. *Journal of Studies on Alcohol, 54,* 652–666.

O'Malley, S. S., Jaffe, A. J., Chang, G., Rode, S., Schottenfeld, R. S., Meyer, R. E., & Rounsaville, B. J. (1994). Six month follow-up of naltrexone and coping skills therapy for alcohol dependence. Manuscript submitted for publication.

O'Malley, S. S., Jaffe, A. J., Chang, G., Schottenfeld, R. S., Meyer, R. E., & Rounsaville, B. J. (1992). Naltrexone and coping skills therapy for alcohol dependence: A controlled study. *Archives of General Psychiatry, 49,* 881–887.

Parloff, M. D. (1982). Psychotherapy research evidence and reimbursement decisions: Bambi meets Godzilla. *American Journal of Psychiatry, 139,* 718–727.

Pomerleau, O. F., & Pomerleau, C. S. (1977). *Break the smoking habit: A behavioral program for giving up cigarettes*. Champaign, IL: Research Press.

Project MATCH Research Group. (1993). Project MATCH: Rationale and methods for a multisite clinical trial matching alcoholism patients to treatment. *Alcoholism: Clinical and Experimental Research, 17,* 1130–1145.

Rounsaville, B. J., Spitzer, R. L., & Williams, J. B. W. (1986). Proposed changes in DSM-III substance use disorders: Description and rationale. *American Journal of Psychiatry, 143,* 463–468.

Smith, M. L., Glass, G. V., & Miller, T. I. (1980). *The benefits of psychotherapy*. Baltimore, MD: Johns Hopkins University Press.

Stephens, R. S., Roffman, R. A., & Simpson, E. E. (1994). Treating adult marijuana dependence: A test of the relapse prevention model. *Journal of Consulting and Clinical Psychology, 62,* 92–99.

Stevens, V. J., Glasgow, R. E., Hollis, J. F., Lichtenstein, E., & Vogt, T. M. (1993). A smoking cessation intervention for hospital patients. *Medical Care, 31,* 65–72.

Stevens, V. J., & Hollis, J. F. (1989). Preventing smoking relapse using an individually tailored skills-training technique. *Journal of Consulting and Clinical Psychology, 57,* 420–424.

Supnick, J. A., & Colletti, G. (1984). Relapse coping and problem solving training following treatment for smoking. *Addictive Behaviors, 9,* 401–404.

Wells, E. A., Peterson, P. L., Gainey, R. R., Hawkins, J. D., & Catalano, R. F.

(1994). Outpatient treatment for cocaine abuse: A controlled comparison of relapse prevention and twelve-step approaches. *American Journal of Drug and Alcohol Abuse, 20,* 1–17.

Zelman, D. C., Brandon, T. H., Jorenby, D. E., & Baker, T. B. (1992). Measures of affect and nicotine dependence predict differential response to smoking cessation treatments. *Journal of Consulting and Clinical Psychology, 60,* 943–952.

28

SIMILARITY OF OUTCOME PREDICTORS ACROSS OPIATE, COCAINE, AND ALCOHOL TREATMENTS: ROLE OF TREATMENT SERVICES

A. THOMAS McLELLAN, ARTHUR I. ALTERMAN, DAVID S. METZGER, GRANT R. GRISSOM, GEORGE E. WOODY, LESTER LUBORSKY, AND CHARLES P. O'BRIEN

There is now substantial evidence suggesting that substance abuse treatments can be effective in reducing substance use and in bringing about improvements in the areas of employment, criminal activity, social adjustment and use of health care resources (Anglin & Hser, 1990; Ball & Ross, 1991; DeLeon, 1984; Gerstein & Harwood, 1990; Hubbard et al., 1986; Institute of Medicine, 1990; McLellan, Luborsky, Woody, & O'Brien, 1982; Miller & Hester, 1986; Saxe, 1983; Simpson & Savage, 1980). Although

Reprinted from the *Journal of Consulting and Clinical Psychology, 62*, 1141–1158. (1994). Copyright © 1994 by the American Psychological Association. Used with permission of the author.

This work was supported by grants from the National Institute on Drug Abuse, the National Institute on Alcoholism and Alcohol Abuse, and the Department of Veterans Affairs.

this has been gratifying, it is clear that the effects of treatment are not uniform and that there is typically substantial variability in the posttreatment outcomes of the patients sampled. For example, a large national field study of drug-dependent patients entering inpatient and outpatient public treatment programs (Hubbard & Marsden, 1986) showed that at 12-month follow-up, approximately 12% of patients reported complete abstinence, employment, no crime, and no psychiatric or family problems. In contrast to these "complete successes," approximately 18% were in jail, 29% had resumed significant substance use, and 13% had been readmitted to additional care since the initial treatment episode. In a national study of alcohol treatment outcome, the RAND group (Armor, Polich, & Stambul, 1976) found that 31% reported complete abstinence and no significant social problems at the 12-month follow-up, whereas 41% had returned to alcohol use and 19% had required additional treatment. Even controlled trials of single treatments in well-specified samples of patients have reported similar levels of variability in outcome (see, e.g., Chapman-Walsh, Hingson, Merrigan, 1991; Edwards et al., 1977; Hayashida et al., 1989; Rounsaville, Glaser, Wilber, & Kleber, 1983; Woody, McLellan, & Luborsky, 1984).

Two points are important here. First, as indicated, there has been substantial variability in the outcomes of substance abuse treatments, regardless of how these outcomes have been measured or the types of patients and treatments studied. Second, "outcome" has rarely been defined merely as elimination or improvement in substance use only. Instead an evaluation of patient outcome has generally included measures of adjustment in the areas of employment and crime, and often, medical psychological and family status measures in the overall determination of "success" (McLellan et al., 1982; McLellan, Grissom, Alterman, Brill, & O'Brien, 1993; Rounsaville et al., 1983; Simpson & Savage, 1980; Woody, Luborsky, McLellan, & O'Brien, 1983; Woody et al., 1984). The "psychosocial adjustment" of substance-dependent patients has been considered by some to be an appropriate evaluation domain because of its effect on the severity of substance dependence and its relation to posttreatment relapse (Gerstein & Harwood, 1990; McLellan, Metzger, et al., 1992). At the same time, others have argued that these aspects of patient status are conceptually distinct from the primary goal of reduction in substance use and, from a treatment perspective, well beyond the scope of substance dependence treatment capabilities.

Given the often extreme variability in outcome status after treatment for substance abuse, researchers have attempted to identify and study those factors that may account for this variability. Several of the most prominent and widely studied factors are discussed briefly.

The majority of studies attempting to predict outcome have focused on patient variables at the start of treatment because these have been considered the most important predictors of patient status after treatment. In this regard, factors such as severity of dependence (Babor, Dolinsky, Rounsaville, & Jaffe, 1988), presence of family and social supports (Havassy, Hall, & Wasserman, 1989), severity of psychiatric symptoms (McLellan, Luborsky, Woody, Druley, & O'Brien, 1983; McLellan, Luborsky, Woody, O'Brien, & Druley, 1983; Rounsaville, Dolinsky, Babor, & Meyer, 1987), and presence of an antisocial personality diagnosis (Alterman & Cacciola, 1991; Hesselbrock, Meyer, & Keener, 1985; Schuckit, 1985) have been among the more salient and well-replicated patient variables associated with posttreatment outcome. At the same time, it has been difficult to evaluate the strength of these and other predictors in more than one type of patient (i.e., alcohol, opiate, or cocaine dependent; male or female; etc.) or treatment (e.g., inpatient or outpatient) because different studies have typically used different patient and treatment measures and different follow-up intervals.

More recently, there have been improvements and innovations in the measurement of the treatment environment and the treatment processes that occur during rehabilitation (Allison & Hubbard, 1982; Ball & Ross, 1991; Finney, Moos, & Chan, 1981; Joe, Simpson, & Sells, 1992; McLellan, Cacciola, Kushner, Peters, Smith, & Pettinati, 1992). For example, Moos et al. have developed and tested measures of the treatment environment for both inpatient and outpatient settings (Moos, 1974; Moos, Finney, & Cronkite, 1990). Similarly, Ball and his colleagues have demonstrated that it is possible to reliably and validly characterize the leadership, environment, number and types of services provided, and other aspects of a treatment environment (Ball & Ross, 1991).

With these additional measures, it is now possible to assess potentially relevant dimensions of the treatment as it is delivered. In turn, it becomes possible and pertinent to determine which of these treatment dimensions are related to outcome. Although this type of investigation is still relatively new, there is practical clinical value to this type of research. The identification of treatment process and management dimensions that are reliably associated with outcome may enable refinement and enhancement of these "active ingredients" of care. Unfortunately, it has not yet been possible to compare different types of treatments as a means of determining the generalizability of findings regarding treatment milieu and process.

Given these considerations, the present article represents an attempt to continue and expand the study of outcome prediction in the field of substance dependence treatment through the use of standardized measures of the patient at the start of treatment and at follow-up and of the treatment services provided during rehabilitation. These measures were used in a uniform and systematic way across large samples of substance-dependent patients treated for primary problems of alcohol, opiate, or cocaine dependence during 1990 to 1992. These patients were drawn from methadone maintenance and inpatient or outpatient abstinence-oriented programs and from both private and public funding sources.

Thus, this report explores the patient and treatment factors that are associated with substance use and social adjustment at 6 months after substance abuse treatment. We were interested in three specific research questions. (a) Are the factors that predict posttreatment substance use similar to or different from the factors that predict posttreatment "social adjustment?" (b) Are the factors that predict posttreatment substance use and social adjustment similar to or different among three primary drug use samples (e.g., alcohol, cocaine, opiate)? (c) Are the factors that predict posttreatment substance use and social adjustment similar to or different among various types of treatment (e.g., inpatient and outpatient; public and private)?

It should be clear at the outset that the analytic strategy here is not designed as a comparison of treatment efficacy among the different forms of treatment or the three drug use groups. Such an approach would be logically flawed. The patient groups selected differ substantially in the nature, number, and severity of the treatment problems they present at treatment admission. Furthermore, the underlying assumptions and treatment goals are quite different among the selected treatment types. Instead, the present strategy is designed to examine the ways in which patient and treatment factors affect outcomes among these very different groups. A finding of substantial differences in these relationships among different patient and treatment samples would provide evidence for the unique needs of some of the patient groups and may suggest specific mechanisms of action associated with particular treatments. On the other hand, a finding of general similarity of predictive relationships across these groups would suggest common mechanisms associated with the rehabilitation process across these different groups.

METHOD

Treatment Programs

Data from 22 treatment programs were used in the present study. All were standard programs in the Philadelphia area that had participated in one of the alcohol and drug rehabilitation outcome research studies performed by our center over the past 3 years. Twelve of the 22 programs were based within the city, and the remainder were based in suburban settings. These studies involved systematic evaluations of various different forms of standard care in various settings. For example, methadone maintenance data were drawn from a large-scale study of four public and three private methadone programs. Nine private treatment programs (four inpatient, five outpatient) focusing primarily on alcohol and cocaine dependence participated in a study of patient–treatment matching. Six public programs (three inpatient, three outpatient) participated in comparative studies of inpatient and outpatient alcohol and cocaine treatment.

The treatment studies for which these patients volunteered consisted primarily of comparisons of "treatment-as-usual" groups and enhanced treatments such as additional counseling, medical care, family therapy, and psychiatric services. We excluded all patients who participated in any type of experimental drug treatment or any nonstandard therapeutic intervention (e.g., cue exposure, acupuncture, etc.), because these may not generalize to the majority of substance abuse programs. Thus, the present results represent a reasonable "treatment-as-usual" sample in each of these programs.

For the majority of publicly funded programs, referral and admission were based on patient request (in turn, this was often based on geography, previous experience, or hearsay) and bed–treatment slot availability. This was generally similar for the private program patients as well, except that managed care and employee assistance organizations were also part of the admission decision. Approximately 22% of patients reported that they were under some legal or work-related order to attend treatment. This proportion was not significantly different ($p > .10$) across all the patient types and treatment programs included in the analyses.

The 22 treatment programs included in the analyses are described briefly here by category:

1. In methadone maintenance (seven programs, all outpatient; four publicly funded), 195 patients were sampled. Three programs were hospital affiliated, and the other four were free-standing and community based. All programs would be considered medium- to high-dose programs, with modal doses ranging from 50 to 80 mg/day. All programs relied on individual counseling as the main therapeutic intervention. All included AIDS risk awareness training and pre- and post-HIV test counseling as part of their programs. Four programs also included regular group education and therapy sessions. All programs required regular, random urine testing for drug use (range once per month to twice per week), and all permitted take-home doses after some period of stabilization, although exact criteria for eligibility varied.

2. In the inpatient alcohol–cocaine programs (seven programs, three publicly funded), 209 patients were sampled. Planned duration of stay ranged from 18 to 40 days. Four programs (two public, two private) were hospital based, whereas the three others were free-standing residential programs. All were

abstinence oriented, and all relied heavily on group therapy, individual counseling, alcohol–drug education sessions, relapse prevention groups, and referral to Alcoholics Anonymous, Cocaine Anonymous, or Narcotics Anonymous (AA–CA–NA).

3. In the outpatient alcohol–cocaine programs (eight programs, three publicly funded), 245 patients were sampled. Planned duration of stay ranged from 4 to 10 weeks. Hours of treatment per week ranged from 8 (two 4-hour days) to 30 (five 6-hour days). Three programs (one public, two private) were hospital affiliated, the remainder were freestanding community-based programs. Again, all were abstinence oriented and all relied heavily on group therapy, individual counseling, alcohol–drug education sessions, relapse prevention groups, and referral to AA–CA–NA.

Subjects

Subjects were 649 adults admitted to substance abuse treatment in these programs. All patients except those in methadone maintenance treatment were admitted after completion of detoxification or self-induced sobriety.

Participation Rates

All patients were voluntary participants in one of our treatment research studies. The proportion of patients who agreed to participate varied with the population and the treatment site. In no case did we recruit fewer than 75% of those admissions who were asked to participate. It was not possible to evaluate whether those who declined to participate were systematically different from those who ultimately participated. At the same time, we saw no obvious differences at any site or in any project. Some patients simply did not want to be bothered by the additional information collection. Some did not wish any additional treatment that may have been provided during one of the studies, whereas others did not want to risk being randomly assigned to a type of care that they had not intended.

Treatment Dropout

All patients who completed at least 5 days of inpatient care or day-hospital treatment or attended at least two consecutive outpatient treatment sessions were followed up at 6 months and included in the analyses. We have used this criterion in previous studies (McLellan, Luborsky, Woody, Druley, & O'Brien, 1983; McLellan, Luborsky, Woody, O'Brien, & Druley, 1983) to exclude those who received less than 25% of the intended duration of treatment. There were differential rates of dropout from treatment (as defined earlier) across the multiple types of treatments and patient samples presented. For example, methadone maintenance patients were encouraged to remain in treatment for at least 1 year, and these patients were evaluated at follow-up while they were still maintained on methadone. Early dropout from methadone maintenance (less than 6 months) ranged from 2% to 23% across the seven programs sampled. Dropout from cocaine treatment, alcohol treatment, or both ranged from 0% to 19% across the seven inpatient programs and from 11% to 38% across the eight abstinence-oriented outpatient programs. There were significant differences in dropout rates ($p < .05$ or less) between the inpatient and outpatient treatment categories and among programs within each of these categories. Of course, we collected baseline information on all dropouts and attempted to examine for systematic differences. There were no overall differences in demographic or severity differences for the total group of dropouts, compared with the total number of participants included here. At the same time, it was not possible (because of power constraints) to examine differences at the individual program level, and therefore, it remains possible and even likely that specific programs had particular patterns of patient dropout. This produces unwanted and unmeasured variability in the outcome data, and it must be admitted that there is no perfectly satisfactory method for dealing with this in the analyses. In fact, we have simply collapsed data across the categories, and we have tried to present the results with this in mind.

Demographic and Background Descriptors

Table 1 provides a description of the demographic characteristics, background variables, and problem severity measures on all patients at the start of treatment. This total population has been divided into the three major drug preference subgroups. In the many cases in which there were multiple drug problems, this designation was based on the reported duration, the recent severity of the problems, and the patient report of the primary problem. Again, although multiple substance use was the rule (see Table 1), in the majority of cases the drug preference decision was quite clear. Cases in which no clear designation could be made (approximately 5% of all patients) were not included.

As can be seen, these patients presented for treatment with significant and long lasting problems of alcohol and other drug use but all groups also showed major problems in the areas of family and social relations and in medical and psychiatric symptomatology. Between-group comparisons are not presented, because this is outside the focus of this article. At the same time, it is clear from Table 1 that there were some demographic differences among the groups as well as severity differences in almost all variables measured. In general, the opiate-dependent patients showed more severe

TABLE 1
Background Characteristics at Admission

Demographic and background factors	Total (n = 649)	Opiate (n = 195)	Cocaine (n = 212)	Alcohol (n = 242)
Demographic factors				
Age	40 ± 7	42 ± 6	34 ± 8	43 ± 7
% Male	89	77	95	95
% White	28	40	20	41
% Black	65	58	78	58
Education (no. of years)	12 ± 2	12 ± 2	12 ± 2	13 ± 3
Medical problems				
% with chronic medical problems	31	42	18	32
Medical hospitalizations	3 ± 2	5 ± 3	2 ± 2	3 ± 2
Employment problems				
% with skill or trade	80	80	78	83
Longest period of employment (years)	7 ± 3	5 ± 3	6 ± 3	9 ± 2
% employed	79	66	91	81
Substance abuse				
No. of years of:				
Problematic alcohol use	12 ± 4	8 ± 4	8 ± 4	19 ± 3
Problematic opiate use	5 ± 3	14 ± 2	1 ± 3	1 ± 2
Problematic cocaine use	2 ± 2	3 ± 2	3 ± 2	1 ± 3
Problematic barbiturate and tranquilizer use	2 ± 2	4 ± 2	1 ± 2	1 ± 3
No. of previous alcohol treatments	1 ± 2	1 ± 2	1 ± 2	2 ± 2
No. of previous drug treatments	2 ± 3	4 ± 5	1 ± 2	1 ± 1
Longest period of abstinence (months)	9 ± 6	15 ± 7	3 ± 3	9 ± 6
Legal problems				
% awaiting charges	7	7	6	8
% on probation or parole	11	13	10	10
% ever incarcerated	24	47	10	15
Family or social problems				
% married	25	22	23	30
% separated	25	19	25	18
% divorced	22	28	14	23
% living alone	16	17	17	15
% unstable living arrangement	3	3	4	1
Psychological problems				
% having had previous psychiatric treatment	30	44	19	28
% attempted suicide	13	22	9	9
% reporting lifetime depression	61	68	56	58
% with violence control problem	30	29	32	30

Note. All numbers are means plus or minus standard deviations or percentages, as indicated, from the baseline Addiction Severity Index interview.

problems than either of the other two groups. Because of space constraints, we have not presented these background data divided by inpatient and outpatient or public and private treatment groups. More than half of the opiate-dependent and alcohol-dependent populations and 78% of the cocaine-dependent group were African American. This is the only demographic variable that was systematically different between public and private treatment programs, with many of the private programs treating a majority of White patients and most of the inner-city public programs treating almost entirely African American populations of primarily cocaine (crack)-dependent patients. Fewer than 3% of any of our samples was Hispanic, and this was proportionate with the actual numbers of patients from this ethnic group who were in treatment. In summary, these comparisons showed significant differences in almost all of the areas shown in Table 1. In each case, the inpatients and the public treatment group showed the most severe problems in almost all areas.

Data Collection Methods

The same core battery of evaluation instruments and research procedures was used in each of the treatment programs and for all participants. Although there were specific types of additional information collected for the particular needs of each of the studies, this additional information did not affect the collection of the common core that is discussed here.

Admission Information

We interviewed all participants at admission to treatment using the Addiction Severity Index (ASI; McLellan, Luborsky, Cacciola, & Griffith, 1985; McLellan, Luborsky, O'Brien, & Woody, 1980; McLellan, Metzger, et al., 1992) administered by a trained technician who was independent of the treatment program. The ASI is a 45- to 60-min structured interview that measures the lifetime and recent (past 30 days) severity of problems in seven areas commonly affected among alcohol- and drug-dependent individuals. These include medical status, employment, alcohol use, drug use, crime, family–social relationships and psychiatric symptoms.

In each of these areas, items measuring the severity of the problem during the previous 30 days are combined into a composite or factor score. These composites are computer scored with values ranging from 0 (*no significant problem*) to 1.0 (*extreme problem*). Examples of these items are presented in Table 1 and also later in Table 3. The ASI has been in use since 1980 and has been repeatedly found to offer reliable and valid measures of patient status in each of the problem areas (see McLellan, Metzger, et al., 1992). In particular, the ASI composite scores have shown acceptable internal consistency (Cronbach's alphas ranged from .68 to .87) and test-retest reliability over a two-day interval (kappas ranged from .88 to .99) in opiate-, alcohol-, and cocaine-dependent populations (McLellan, Metzger, et al., 1992).

At the time of admission, all patients were asked to participate in the during-treatment and posttreatment follow-up phases of evaluation. All participants were assured that information collected at any point in the study would be kept in strictest confidence and would not be released to any individual or agency, including their own treatment program. Consenting patients were asked to provide the names, addresses, and phone numbers of 3 persons who would know where to contact them for follow-up. Participants were assured that these individuals would not be told anything about the nature of the follow-up contact, nor would we discuss their progress or any aspect of their condition with these sources. They were only used to provide access to the patients themselves. The phone numbers and addresses were all checked for accuracy during the following week and, when inaccuracy was found, the participant was reassured and was asked again to participate. No patient was paid to complete the baseline ASI.

During-Treatment Measures

Although the ASI measures the nature and severity of treatment problems presented by the patient at the start of treatment and later at follow-up, we have developed a new measure of the nature and number of treatment services actually received by patients for those problems during the course of their rehabilitation. This instrument, the Treatment Services Review (TSR; McLellan, Alterman, et al., 1992) is also a technician-administered interview that requires 5 min to complete and is administered to each patient on a weekly basis (usually each Friday) during the course of treatment. This interview was done either in person or over the phone by a trained independent technician. The TSR provides a simple weekly record of the number of professional services (specialized therapy or treatment sessions, medications, etc.) and discussion sessions (group or individual counseling) that each patient received in each of the same seven problem areas covered by the ASI. For example, in the medical section, patients were asked to report the number of times in the previous week they had seen a doctor, seen a nurse, received a prescription for a medication, received any type of medical testing, or had a significant discussion related to their medical problems with a counselor or other member of the program staff. The TSR measures both the services that are provided within the program and through referral.

As in the ASI, the total amount of treatment activity received by the patient in each problem area is summarized into a composite score. Weekly TSRs were collected on all consenting patients throughout their treatment. Patients were paid $2 per week for the time required to complete these during-treatment interviews. Reimbursement checks were sent to each patient's address, and this provided additional opportunity to verify addresses and to build trust with the patient, thereby increasing the likelihood of successful follow-up contact at the 6-month point.

Because measures from the TSR were used as predictor variables in the present analyses and because the TSR is still a relatively new instrument, we have presented some TSR items from each of the problem areas in Table 2, for the same drug preference groups shown in Table 1. It should

TABLE 2
Percentage of Patients Receiving Services During Week 2
of Treatment

TSR section and variable	Total (n = 592)	Opiate (n = 178)	Cocaine (n = 191)	Alcohol (n = 223)
Medical section				
Saw a physician	32	12	36	49
Saw a nurse[a]	14	8	18	16
Had a group or individual discussion about medical problems	22	16	21	29
Employment section				
Saw an employment specialist	7	2	11	9
Had a group or individual discussion about employment problems	24	33	25	14
Alcohol section				
Received medications for detoxification	9	0	2	24
Had a Breathalyzer screen	26	12	27	39
Attended alcohol education session	57	0	80	91
Attended Alcoholics Anonymous	32	9	39	49
Had an alcohol relapse prevention session	31	0	51	43
Had a group or individual discussion about alcohol problems	49	6	49	91
Drug section				
Received medications for detoxification or maintenance	35	97	5	2
Had a urine screen	51	64	78	12
Attended drug education session	40	3	72	44
Attended Narcotics Anonymous or Cocaine Anonymous	39	9	71	37
Had a drug relapse prevention session	19	1	32	25
Had a group or individual discussion about drug problems	54	48	87	28
Legal section				
Had justice system contacted	2	4	1	2
Had a group or individual discussion about legal problems	6	6	4	9
Family section				
Saw a family specialist	10	7	8	15
Saw a counselor or social worker about family problems	18	7	24	24
Psychiatric section				
Received psychiatric medication	4	3	0	8
Had psychiatric testing	3	0	4	6
Had relaxation training	25	3	31	41
Saw a psychiatric specialist	3	0	5	5
Saw a counselor or social worker about psychiatric problems	23	10	23	35

Note. Data were derived from weekly Treatment Services Review (TSR) interviews. Frequencies of services provided varied substantially across settings and programs sampled.
[a]This includes having seen a nurse practitioner or a physician's assistant.

be noted that the data that were used in the predictive analyses were the frequencies of each of these services for each patient across their entire treatment period. We felt that the proportion of patients receiving each of these services would provide a more informative functional description of the activities that go on during substance abuse treatments. We have shown TSR data from Week 2 of treatment. We have found that, in most programs, the first week of treatment is atypical with regard to the number and types of services provided to patients. However, the succeeding weeks up to the point of discharge are usually quite similar in terms of the nature and amount of services provided. Thus, the Week 2 data presented here are reasonably representative of the nature of services offered and the proportion of patients receiving them in a "typical" week of treatment in these samples. Again, we have not performed comparative analyses among the three groups because it was not pertinent to the aims of the article. However, it is clear that there were major differences among these groups in terms of the pattern of services provided among these primary drug use groups. Indeed, there were major differences in almost all categories of treatment services among the various programs sampled in this analysis.

Follow-Up Information

As indicated, patients were told at admission that they would be contacted 6 months after treatment and they were reminded of this throughout the course of their care and at discharge, regardless of whether they completed or dropped out. Patients in inpatient programs were contacted 6 months from their program discharge date. Because inpatient treatment typically ranged from 14 to 40 days, to make the data from the inpatient and outpatient abstinence-oriented programs reasonably comparable we elected to contact the outpatients 7 months from admission to treatment. Patients in methadone maintenance programs were expected to remain in treatment for at least 1 year and so follow-up evaluations were performed on these subjects 7 months postadmission.

Only patients who had signed a consent to participate at admission were followed. Follow-up efforts were begun 2 weeks before the exact anniversary date and were extended 2 weeks after that point in the event that a patient was not able to be located. Ninety-two percent of patients across all studies were successfully contacted during this "follow-up window" using these techniques and that ranged from a high of 98% in one of the methadone maintenance programs to a low of 89% in one of the private treatment programs. There were no significant differences in proportion of successful contacts across types of patients or types of treatment.

It is important to note that in the interests of maintaining the confidentiality agreement, no information was requested from the relatives or collateral sources of these patients. Relatives were merely told to tell the patient that we had called and to please call us back. A 24-hr, toll-free number was available for them. In addition, patients were assured that no information would be released either to the treatment program they had attended or to their employers or families. We have used these procedures in our studies because they provide the maximum in patient confidentiality.

The follow-up ASI required approximately 20 min and was again administered by a trained research technician who was not part of the treatment process. Patients were paid $15 to $25 (depending on the study) for their time required to complete the follow-up interview. There were several methods for insuring information validity built into the follow-up interview. First, patients were repeatedly reassured that their information would not be communicated to any individual or agency. Second, patients were told that they did not have to answer a question with which they were uncomfortable or provide information that they wished to keep private. These two aspects of the interview procedure provided confidentiality reassurance as well as an additional option for the subject (in lieu of falsification). Third, there are several information cross-checks in the interview, and technicians are trained to notice and respond to inconsistencies. Sections of the ASI that the interviewer felt were compromised by failure to understand or by purposeful distortion were not used in the data analyses. Where three or more sections were compromised, the entire interview was eliminated. We discarded 21 follow-up interviews because of three or more invalid sections, and these were spread approximately evenly across all the programs and populations represented.

As a final check on the validity of the information collected, patients were asked to come in to pick up their reimbursement for the interview and, at that time, they were asked to provide urine and breath samples for testing. We had excellent compliance with this request. Only nine patients refused to submit samples (three from one program and the rest randomly distributed across studies and programs), and their data were also eliminated from consideration. The accuracy of the self-report drug and alcohol use was partially tested by comparing the patient reports of use with the results of unannounced urine and breath tests. Overall, 76% of the urinalyses were consistent with the self-reports, 21 urine tests (17%) were negative although the patient had reported recent use, and the remaining 7% of interviews were eliminated.

Data Analysis Methods

Data Entry and Verification

All data were double entered by professional data entry technicians that were part of our data management unit. This unit receives and processes all collected data after they have been checked for accuracy by the interviewer supervisors.

Predictive Analyses: The Outcome Criteria

The outcome variables used were the composite scores derived from the 6-month ASI interview. This has been a standard procedure since its introduction in 1980 (McLellan, Cacciola, et al., 1993; McLellan, Grissom, et al., 1993; McLellan, Luborsky, Woody, Druley, & O'Brien, 1983; McLellan et al., 1982; McLellan, Luborsky, Woody, O'Brien, & Druley, 1983; Rounsaville et al., 1983; Woody et al., 1983).

Predictive Analysis: Rationale for the Use of Multiple Outcome Measures

Although it is clear that the most visible and immediate problems of substance abusers who apply for treatment are usually (not always) the alcohol and drug use itself, there are usually additional and often equally serious problems of criminal activity, unemployment, excessive use of health and social services, as well as significant psychiatric, medical and family problems. We have argued that the public, the payers, and the patients themselves have come to expect improvements in these adjunctive problems as well as reduction or elimination of the substance abuse (McLellan, Metzger, et al., 1992). For these reasons, we felt that it would be inappropriate and inadequate to focus solely on the substance use outcomes of these patients in the predictive analyses presented here. Thus, in the work presented, we have evaluated patient status and attempted to predict 6-month outcome in each of the seven problem areas covered by the ASI.

The Predictive Analyses Used

We report the results of the hierarchical stepwise multiple regression analysis as discussed by Cohen and Cohen (1975) for each of the outcome measures. This stepwise procedure performs two functions that are important for the present exploration. First, the procedure sequentially tests independent (predictor) variables for their contribution to explaining variation (expressed as R^2) in the dependent (criterion) variable. The predictor that accounts for the largest proportion of variance is entered into the equation at that point. Second, the variance accounted for by that variable is removed from the equation, thereby providing an opportunity to test remaining variables for their independent contribution to explaining the remaining variance. This is important in that it provides a test of the individual contribution of subsequent variables, adjusting for the contribution of all previous variables. These subsequent predictors are then tested and entered in order of their contribution to the explanation of variance in the particular outcome criterion.

In the general analytic strategy used here, three sets of variables were tested sequentially as predictors. These were background variables, problem severity composite scores from the admission ASI and finally, treatment service composite scores summed from the weekly TSRs. Any variable from the first set of predictors that made a significant contribution to the explanation of variance was entered before any other variable from the second or third set of predictors. This strategy was used since we were specifically interested in assessing the contribution of all patient background factors prior to testing the predictive value of patients' pre-treatment problem severity. In like fashion, we wanted to test for the predictive value of treatment services provided, only after the effects of background and patient pretreatment variables had been partialed out. We believe that this strategy provides the most conservative, nonexperimental assessment of the contribution of these individual measures in accounting for treatment outcome and the strategy has been used in our earlier outcome prediction studies (McLellan, Luborsky, Woody, Druley, & O'Brien, 1983; McLellan, Luborsky, Woody, O'Brien, & Druley, 1983; McLellan, Luborsky, & O'Brien, 1986).

Confirmatory Analyses

Because no single analytic strategy is clearly superior to any other and because each type of analysis is subject to particular challenges to its validity, we thought it best to subject the data to additional methods as an additional reliability check. To this end, we performed all analyses a second time using a backward stepwise deletion procedure (Cohen & Cohen, 1975). The backward stepwise deletion procedure enters all variables into the predictive equation initially (thus serving as an overall test of significance of all predictors) and then sequentially eliminates those variables that do not contribute to the predictive equation.

An additional set of analyses were computed using the same stepwise multiple regression procedures (both forward and backward versions) to predict patient change from admission to follow-up in each of the seven ASI composite scores. Finally, as a check on the validity of the ASI composite scores, we constructed three dichotomous outcome measures from the follow-up ASI data. These were "abstinent from all drugs," "abstinent from alcohol," and "employed." Each measure was coded 0 for no and 1 for yes, and stepwise multiple discriminant analyses were performed on each of these measures using the same sets of predictive variables. Although there were, of course, some differences in the results of these different procedures, there was substantial similarity across all methods used, thereby increasing our confidence in the results reported. We have chosen to present the results of the forward stepwise multiple regression analyses in the tables included.

Treatment of Missing Data

There were, of course, some missing data from these measures, and the following procedures were developed to account for the effects of missing data on the conclusions. First, no variable was used in the analyses that had more than 10% missing values. We felt that there could be systematic causes for missing data at frequencies above this level. Because all data were collected by research technicians as part of our ongoing studies, only 6 of the 198 variables were eliminated in this way. We analyzed the data using two strategies. In the first set of analyses, we did not use any of the various forms of replacement techniques for handling missing values but instead left the missing values as part of the data set. This had the effect of excluding any patient with any missing value from the analyses. Typically, this produced a 5% to 15% reduction in sample size depending on the particular groups and outcome measures.

In the second set of analyses, we used mean replacement techniques to substitute the group mean for any variable for the actual missing value on any single case. Comparison of these two strategies showed no differences in outcome results of any type, and the data reported here reflect the results without the mean substitution procedure.

Summarizing the Results of the Predictive Analyses

The predictive analyses were completed for each of the seven outcome measures separately in each of the subgroups. For the sake of presentation of all these complex relationships, we decided to divide the seven outcome areas into two domains: substance use (combining the results of the alcohol and drug analyses) and "social adjustment" (combining the results of the medical, employment, legal, family, and psychiatric analyses). Thus, it should be clear that, although the analyses were completed individually for each of the seven outcome measures, in the tables that follow the results have been summarized in the manner discussed later.

What Is Considered a "Significant Predictor of Outcome"?

We developed an a priori set of conventions to designate "significant" predictors. Although any such strategy can legitimately be argued as arbitrary, we feel that these conventions are quite conservative and serve as an aid to summarizing the complex sets of relationships between multiple predictors of multiple outcomes in multiple samples. A variable was considered a significant predictor of substance use at follow-up if it was a significant contributor to (a) the explanation of variance on either of the two substance abuse outcome variables at $p < .01$, or to (b) explaining variance on both alcohol and drug use measures at $p < .05$ or less. An independent variable was considered to be a significant predictor of social adjustment at follow-up if it was selected at $p < .05$ on three or more of the five analyses of the social adjustment ASI problem domains. Finally, only variables that met the a priori significance conventions described earlier on both the forward and backward analyses are reported as being significant predictors of outcome in any of the results (see Table 3, Table 4, and Table 5).

In the tables presented, we have averaged the proportion of outcome variance (R^2) uniquely accounted for by each of those variables that met the aforementioned conventions as significant outcome predictors. Again, we feel that these conventions provide a conservative estimate of the most important variables associated with patient adjustment in these two general domains.

RESULTS

Improvements Following Treatment

As a first step in these analyses, we wanted to examine the nature and extent of the improvements that had occurred in these groups following treatment. Although it is, of course, not possible from these data to claim that any improvements shown were directly due to the effects of treatment, we began nonetheless with an examination of the amounts, types, and variability of improvements shown by these patients following treatment. Admission to 6-month comparisons of the ASI data are shown for the three primary drug use groups in Table 3. A within-subjects multiple analysis of variance (MANOVA) was calculated for each of the three drug preference groups using the seven ASI composite scores collected at admission and follow-up. Each of these analyses showed an overall difference from admission to follow-up ($p < .05$ or less) and therefore we were justified in performing individual paired t tests on all the ASI variables selected. As can be seen, all groups showed significant pre- to posttreatment changes in the areas of drug and alcohol use, family relations, and psychiatric condition. Only the cocaine group showed significant change in medical and employment status.

These data indicate two important points. First, although it is not possible to conclude that treatment caused the observed changes, there were nonetheless significant and pervasive improvements shown by all groups from admission to follow-up. Thus, these substance-dependent patients—as a group—were in much better condition 6 months following treatment than they were before treatment. Second, although these group improvements were generally significant, an examination of the standard deviations on the ASI follow-up scores reveals very substantial variability among all groups and all measures, indicating that these generally positive changes were by no means uniform across patients and outcome measures. It was this variability that was the focus of the subsequent prediction analyses.

734   McLELLAN ET AL.

TABLE 3
Change From Admission to 6-Month Follow-Up in Treated Opiate-, Cocaine-, and Alcohol-Dependent Patients

Problem measure	Opiate (n = 195)			Cocaine (n = 212)			Alcohol (n = 242)		
	Baseline	6 months	p	Baseline	6 months	p	Baseline	6 months	p
Medical factor	.349	.311	—	.230	.168	<.05	.229	.223	—
Medical problems (no. of days)	8	8	—	6	4	.08+	7	6	—
Employment factor	.675	.641	—	.621	.571	<.05	.552	.487	—
No. of days worked in the past 30	8	10	—	12	14	<.05	11	14	<.01
Employment income ($)	417	537	<.05	613	783	<.05	697	841	<.05
Drug factor	.336	.256	<.001	.228	.081	<.001	.022	.011	<.01
No. of days of:									
Opiate use	11	6	<.001	1	2	<.05	1	1	—
Stimulant use	5	3	<.001	11	2	<.001	1	1	—
Depressant use	6	6	—	1	1	—	2	1	<.05
Alcohol factor	.109	.093	—	.209	.080	<.001	.642	.158	<.001
Alcohol use (no. of days)	6	5	<.05	8	3	<.001	17	4	<.001
Drank to intoxication (no. of days)	3	2	<.05	6	2	<.001	16	3	<.001
Legal factor	.133	.102	—	.064	.024	<.01	.051	.006	<.001
Illegal activity (no. of days)	4	2	<.05	2	1	<.01	1	1	—
Illegal income ($)	289	109	<.01	105	83	—	26	1	—
Family factor	.268	.225	<.05	.250	.136	<.001	.198	.094	<.001
Family conflicts (no. of days)	4	3	—	3	2	—	2	1	<.01
Social conflicts (no. of days)	2	2	—	2	1	<.05	2	1	<.05
Psychiatric factor	.309	.268	<.05	.222	.089	<.001	.220	.115	<.001
Psychological problems (no. of days)	12	8	<.001	9	3	<.001	9	4	<.001

Note. All measures were derived from Addiction Severity Index interviews covering the 30-day periods before baseline and 6-month follow-up. *p*s are by paired *t* test. Dashes indicate that data were not significant.

Prediction of Outcome by Outcome Measure

The first question regarding outcome prediction was which of our independent variables would be most associated with posttreatment alcohol and drug use; and whether the same variables would also be predictive of posttreatment social adjustment. To operationalize this question, we performed the stepwise multiple regression analyses on the entire sample for each of the seven follow-up ASI composite scores and summarized in the manner described previously. Table 4 presents the average proportion of outcome variance accounted for by each predictor. In the interests of summarization, only variables that were significant predictors (see Data Analysis Procedure section given earlier) have been presented.

TABLE 4
Prediction of Outcome by Outcome Domain

Demographic and background factors	% variance explained from	
	Substance use[a]	Social adjustment[b]
Demographics		
Age	—	—
Race	—	—
Gender	—	—
Marital status	—	—
Years of education	—	—
Previous substance abuse treatment	4	—
Forced into treatment	—	—
Years of alcohol use	—	—
Years of opiate use	—	—
Years of stimulant use	2	—
Severity of admission problems[c]		
Medical	2	—
Employment	—	9
Alcohol	4	—
Drug	4	—
Legal	—	—
Family	—	4
Psychiatric	2	5
Treatment services provided[d]		
Medical	—	2
Employment	—	2
Alcohol	—	—
Drug	—	—
Legal	—	
Family	—	2
Psychiatric	—	5

Note. $N = 649$. Dashes indicate that variables did not account for at least 1% outcome variance.
[a]Average outcome variance explained across the alcohol and drug use criteria from the 6-month follow-up Addiction Severity Index (ASI). [b]Average outcome variance explained across the medical, employment, legal, family, and psychiatric criteria from the 6-month follow-up ASI. [c]Predictor variables were composite scores from the seven scales of the admission ASI. [d]Predictor variables were composite scores from the seven scales from the Treatment Services Review.

As can be seen, the results from the two sets of regression analyses were different. Perhaps the area of greatest similarity was the contribution of patient demographic and background variables. In both cases, these background variables accounted for very little outcome variance (6% substance use, 0% social adjustment). One minor difference between the two predictive equations was the contribution of the number of previous alcohol and drug treatments. Having had more previous treatments was associated with more substance use at follow-up and accounted for 4% of variance in that criterion. However, it was not well related to posttreatment social adjustment, accounting for less than 1% of variance in that outcome domain.

The severity of patient problems at treatment admission, measured by the ASI composite scores, were generally more predictive of outcome than the background variables but were again, somewhat different for each of the outcome measures (12% substance use, 18% social adjustment). The severity of patients' alcohol and drug use at admission were the major predictors of posttreatment substance use (4% each variable). However, neither of these was related to posttreatment social adjustment (less than 1% variance accounted for). Instead, the severity of patients' employment (9%), psychiatric (5%), and family (4%) problems were the variables that accounted for significant proportions of variance in this measure.

We were particularly interested to see whether the nature and quantity of treatment services, as summarized by the TSR composite measures offered any additional predictive information after patient demographic, background, and problem severity factors had been accounted for. As can be seen in Table 4, none of the treatment service variables was related to the substance use outcome variable (each accounted for less than 1% variance), not even the composite measures of alcohol and drug-related sessions and services. In contrast, the number of services received in the areas of medical, employment, family, and particularly psychiatric care were significantly and positively related to posttreatment social adjustment, jointly accounting for an additional 11% of outcome variance in that criterion.

In summary, the data indicate that the different outcome measures of substance use and social adjustment were predicted by different independent variables. Neither the substance use outcome nor the social adjustment outcome was very well predicted by patient demographic or background status variables. The posttreatment substance use of these patients was best predicted by the severity of their pretreatment use of alcohol and other drugs and, to a lesser extent, the severity of their employment and psychiatric problems at admission. None of the treatment service variables was significantly related to posttreatment substance use. A total of 18% of outcome variance in the substance use criterion was accounted for with the full combination of these variables. In contrast, the social adjustment composite outcome measure was best predicted by measures of patients' pretreatment problem severity in the areas of employment, psychiatric adjustment, and family relations. Furthermore, receiving greater numbers of services during treatment in these same areas was independently, significantly, and positively related to better social adjustment outcome. The combination of these variables accounted for 31% of the variance in this criterion.

Prediction of Outcome by Primary Drug Use Group

The initial findings from the first set of analyses came from an extremely large and diverse population of patients. The same predictive analyses could offer quite different results for different subgroups within that total sample. Thus, in the next set of analyses, we examined the same issues for three primary drug use groups: opiate-dependent patients (all in methadone maintenance), cocaine-dependent patients, and alcohol-dependent patients. Given the results of the first set of predictive analyses, we felt that it would be necessary to consider both the substance use and the social adjustment outcomes separately in the remaining predictive analyses. Thus, in the second set of analyses, we examined the extent to which predictive factors in one drug use group are similar to those from each of the other groups.

Table 5 presents the results of the predictive analyses for the two outcome criteria and for each of the three drug use groups. As can be seen, there were general similarities but also some differences in the results among the three groups. For example, the number of previous substance abuse treatments was again significantly and negatively related to substance use (but not social adjustment) outcome in all three groups. None of the other patient demographic and background variables were particularly well related to either outcome measure across the groups. Greater age was positively related to better outcome in both substance use and social adjustment for the opiate group but not for either of the other two groups. In summary, the total set of demographic and background variables accounted for less than 10% of outcome variance in the substance use criterion across all three groups and even less in the social adjustment measure (6% opiate, 2% alcohol, 1% cocaine).

The contribution of the admission problem severity measures was quite similar between the alcohol and cocaine groups but somewhat different for the opiate sample. For example, the severity of the methadone patients' alcohol and drug use problems at admission were the major variables accounting for their posttreatment alcohol and drug use (14% and 15% respectively). Greater severity of the drug problem (usually cocaine and marijuana) at admission was also a significant predictor of more posttreatment substance use in the alcohol group (6%), and greater alcohol problem severity at admission was a significant predictor of posttreatment substance use in the cocaine group (2%). It is interesting that the two substance use problem measures at admission were not significant predictors of social adjustment in any of the three groups and that very few other problem severity measures were significant predictors of posttreatment substance use. Instead, the employment and psychiatric problem measures at admission were significant negative predictors of social adjustment in all three groups. Greater severity of medical problems at admission was also a significant negative predictor of outcome in both the opiate and alcohol groups (2%). The severity of the legal and family problems of the methadone patients at admission was also a significant negative predictor of their 6-month social adjustment (10%), but this was not seen in either the alcohol or cocaine groups. These admission problem severity measures accounted for 31% and 28% of the substance use and social adjustment measures, respectively, in the opiate group but much less in the alcohol (9% and 17%, respectively) and cocaine (2% and 16%, respectively) groups.

With regard to the contribution of the treatment services variables, Table 5 indicates that medical, drug, and psychiatric services were significantly and positively associated with less substance use at follow-up in the opiate group (7% total), but no treatment service measures were predictive of this outcome measure in either of the other two groups (each accounted for less than 1% variance). Better social adjustment following treatment was significantly predicted in all groups by more psychiatric services during treatment. In addition, more employment services was predictive of better social adjustment in the methadone and cocaine groups and the variable more medical services was significantly associated with better social adjustment in the alcohol group. The total of all the treatment service variables accounted for 11% of outcome variance in the social adjustment measure in the opiate group and 9% in both the alcohol and cocaine groups.

It is interesting that the provision of more legal services was significantly associated with better social adjustment in the opiate group but worse social adjustment in the two other groups. We believe that legal services may have actually played a part in reducing the generally higher levels of legal problems seen in the methadone maintenance patients but that the receipt of legal services in the two other groups (whose patients each had much lower levels of legal problems at admission) was merely a marker for a more severely impaired, poor prognosis patient.

In summary, substance use at follow-up was generally poorly predicted by the available independent variables in the alcohol and cocaine groups (15% and 8% variance accounted for respectively), but relatively well in the opiate group (45%). The number of previous treatments and the severity of the substance use problems at admission were the most significant predictors. As in the earlier analyses, the number of sessions and services specifically focused on the substance abuse problem during treatment was

TABLE 5
Prediction of Outcome by Primary Drug Use Group

| | % variance explained from: | | | | | |
| Demographic and background factors | Methadone maintenance (n = 195)[a] | | Alcohol rehabilitation (n = 242) | | Cocaine rehabilitation (n = 212) | |
	Substance use	Social adjustment	Substance use	Social adjustment	Substance use	Social adjustment
Demographics						
Age	3	4	—	—	—	—
Race	—	2	—	—	—	—
Gender	—	—	—	—	—	—
Marital status	—	—	—	—	—	—
No. of years of education	—	—	—	—	—	—
Forced into treatment	—	—	—	—	—	—
Previous substance abuse treatments	2	—	5	—	6	—
No. of years of:						
Alcohol use	—	—	2	—	—	—
Opiate use	—	—	—	—	—	—
Stimulant use	2	—	—	—	—	—
Severity of admission problems[b]						
Medical	2	2	—	2	—	—
Employment	—	10	2	9	—	9
Alcohol	14	—	—	—	2	—
Drug	15	—	6	—	—	—
Legal	—	2	—	—	—	—
Family	—	11	—	—	—	—
Psychiatric	—	3	—	4	—	2

Treatment services provided[c]

Medical	3	—	—	2	2
Employment	—	2	—	—	—
Alcohol	—	—	—	—	—
Drug	2	2	—	—	3
Legal	—	—	—	—	—
Family	—	—	—	—	—
Psychiatric	2	6	—	7	3
Total	45	44	15	24	19

Note. Dashes indicate that variables did not account for at least 1% outcome variance.

[a] All measures were derived from Addiction Severity Index (ASI) interviews covering the 30-day period before the 6-month follow-up. [b] Predictor variables were composite scores on the seven scales of the admission ASI. [c] Predictor variables were composite scores on the seven scales from the Treatment Services Review.

poorly related to substance use at follow-up in all of the three drug use groups. More outcome variance in the substance use criterion was accounted for in the opiate group than in either of the other two groups, but this was due to a greater contribution by the same predictors rather than the effects of different independent variables.

The employment, psychiatric, and medical problems at admission were among the major patient variables predictive of social adjustment for all three groups, and more psychiatric, employment, and legal services were the major treatment variables predictive of better social adjustment for these groups. Again, these variables accounted for substantially more variance in the methadone maintenance group (totals = 38%) than for the alcohol group (24%) or cocaine group (19%). In addition, the provision of legal services was positively related to outcome for the methadone patients, whereas it was negatively related to outcome in the other two groups.

Prediction of Outcome by Treatment Setting

One of the long-standing debates within the substance abuse treatment field is the relative efficacy and worth of inpatient versus outpatient treatment. Although much has been written about the concept and methods associated with various tests of the efficacy of each, it remains a question whether outcome from the two forms of treatment is governed by similar or different patient and treatment factors. To this end, in our third set of analyses we explored the relationships between the three sets of predictive variables and the two outcome criteria among substance abuse patients treated in inpatient and outpatient settings. Because of the major conceptual and methodological differences between methadone and the other forms of abstinence-oriented treatments, because our earlier findings suggested that the factors associated with outcome from methadone maintenance were somewhat different from those associated with alcohol and cocaine treatment, and because of the relatively greater number of individuals affected by alcohol and or cocaine, we elected to restrict the inpatient–outpatient predictive analyses to just the alcohol- and cocaine-dependent samples.

Table 6 presents the results of the same multiple regression analyses for the two treatment setting conditions. Again, as can be seen, patient demographic and background factors were generally poorly related to either of the two outcome criteria and this was true in both treatment setting groups. The only exception was that a greater number of previous substance abuse treatments was significantly related to more posttreatment substance use in both groups and to worse posttreatment social adjustment in the outpatient group.

TABLE 6
Prediction of Outcome by Treatment Setting

| Demographic and background factors | % variance explained from: | | | |
| | All inpatient rehabilitation (n = 205)[a] | | All outpatient rehabilitation (n = 249) | |
	Substance use	Social adjustment	Substance use	Social adjustment
Demographic factors				
Age	—	—	—	—
Race	—	—	—	—
Gender	—	—	—	—
Marital status	—	—	—	—
No. of years of education	—	—	—	—
Forced into treatment	—	—	—	—
Previous substance abuse treatments	3	—	7	3
No. of years of:				
Alcohol use	—	—	—	—
Opiate use	—	—	—	—
Stimulant use	—	2	2	—
Severity of admission problems[b]				
Medical	3	3	—	3
Employment	2	10	—	10
Alcohol	2	—	2	3
Drug	6	—	8	—
Legal	2	—	3	—
Family	—	3	—	2
Psychiatric	—	3	—	3
Treatment services provided[c]				
Medical	2	3	—	2
Employment	—	2	—	—
Alcohol	—	—	—	—
Drug	—	—	—	—
Legal	2	—	—	—
Family	—	2	—	—
Psychiatric	—	2	3	4
Total	22	30	25	30

Note. Dashes indicate that variables did not account for at least 1% outcome variance.
[a]All measures were derived from Addiction Severity Index (ASI) interviews covering the 30-day period before the 6-month follow-up. [b]Predictor variables were composite scores on the seven scales of the admission ASI. [c]Predictor variables were composite scores on the seven scales from the Treatment Services Review.

As in previous analyses, patients' problem severity at admission was generally predictive of both outcome domains and the two treatment setting groups showed substantial similarity in both the nature and extent of relationships shown. As can be seen, drug use severity was the most significant predictor of substance use at outcome in both groups, accounting for 6% of variance in the inpatient group and 8% in the outpatient group. In addition, the severity of the alcohol and legal problems at admission were significant predictors of substance use in both groups, although medical and employment problem severity at admission made additional contributions to accounting for variance in the substance use outcome in the inpatient group. Again, with regard to prediction of the social adjustment outcome, both groups showed very similar results. The admission severity of patients' employment, psychiatric, medical, and family problems were the best predictors in both groups.

The treatment services variables also showed generally similar relationships to the outcome criteria in the two groups. Again, treatment services received were poorly related to substance use outcomes in both groups. In the inpatient group, medical service provision was associated with less posttreatment substance use but legal service provision was associated with more posttreatment use. In the outpatient sample, the provision of more psychiatric services was the only treatment service variable significantly associated with lower posttreatment substance use. Again, as in the earlier analyses, there was no significant relationship between the amount of alcohol- and drug-related services received during treatment and posttreatment substance use or social adjustment. Better posttreatment social adjustment was significantly predicted by more medical and psychiatric services in both samples and by more employment and family services in the inpatient sample.

Thus, the results of these predictive analyses indicated that similar types of patient and treatment variables affected outcomes in both treatment settings. The variance subtotals for each category of predictor variables were quite similar for both groups on each of the outcome criteria assessed. As in previous analyses, demographic and background characteristics were generally poorly associated with either outcome measure. The severity of patients' alcohol and drug problems at admission were the most significant predictors of posttreatment substance use in both treatment settings, whereas the contribution of treatment services was minimal. Patients' employment, psychiatric, medical, and family problems at treatment admission were the most significant patient variables associated with posttreatment social adjustment. In addition, the treatment services provided in the medical and psychiatric areas, but not the substance abuse area, were also significant predictors of positive social adjustment in both groups.

Prediction of Outcome by Treatment Funding Source

With the marked increase in the number of private drug abuse treatment programs over the past several years and the widely observed differences in background and socioeconomic variables between the patient populations in publicly funded and private treatment sectors, we felt that it would be worthwhile to examine these same predictive factors for these two forms of treatment funding. Again, we restricted these analyses to just the alcohol- and cocaine-dependent patients treated in inpatient or outpatient settings.

In the interests of space conservation and because the results were so similar to those seen in Table 6, we only summarize the results here. As in the previous analyses, there was only a minor contribution to outcome prediction for any of the patient demographic or background variables, accounting for 6% and 4% of criterion variance, respectively, in the public and private sectors with the number of previous substance abuse treatments being the only significant predictor. No background variable accounted for a significant proportion of social adjustment outcome variance in either of the two funding source subgroups.

The contribution of the patients' admission problems in this analysis was also similar to the results seen in Table 6. Again, for both groups, greater severity of alcohol and drug use at treatment admission was associated with greater posttreatment substance use, although the severity of patients' employment and psychiatric problems also made a significant predictive contribution to this outcome domain in the private sector. All patient problem measures at admission accounted for 6% of outcome variance on the substance abuse criterion for patients in the public sector and 13% for patients in the private sector. The severity of patients' employment, psychiatric, and family problems was the major predictor of follow-up social adjustment in both groups, accounting for 13% of outcome variance on this criterion for patients in the public sector and 15% for the private sector.

No treatment service variable made a significant contribution to the prediction of posttreatment substance use in either group. In contrast, a greater number of services provided for employment, psychiatric, and medical problems were major contributors to prediction of social adjustment in both groups. These variables accounted for approximately 11% of social adjustment outcome variance in the public group and 10% of variance on this measure in the private group. In total, 12% and 17% of variance in the substance use measure was explained by these predictive variables in the public and private groups, respectively. Twenty-four percent and 25% of social adjustment outcome variance were accounted for by all variables in the public and private groups, respectively.

DISCUSSION

The present article has examined the patient and treatment factors that predicted 6-month outcome from treatment for substance dependence. Using the Addiction Severity Index (ASI; McLellan, Luborsky, O'Brien, & Woody, 1980; McLellan, Luborsky, Woody, & O'Brien, 1982; McLellan, Luborsky, Cacciola, & Griffith, 1985; McLellan, Metzger, et al., 1992) we interviewed patients who had been admitted to substance abuse treatments with regard to their background characteristics and the severity of their problems in the areas of medical status, employment, alcohol use, drug use, crime, family and social relations, and psychiatric status. All patients were then interviewed weekly during their treatments using a new, quantitative measure of treatment services received, the TSR (McLellan et al., 1991). Ninety-two percent of patients were successfully recontacted at 6-month follow-up and re-interviewed with the ASI. Record checks of employment status and arrests as well as urine and breath samples were used for verification of self-reported employment, criminal activity, and substance use at follow-up.

Separate predictive analyses were conducted in samples of opiate-, alcohol-, and cocaine-dependent adults. Subsequent analyses divided the total sample into those treated in inpatient and outpatient settings and in publicly and privately funded programs. Outcome criteria included composite measures of substance use (alcohol and all other drugs) and social adjustment (employment, crime, family and social relations, medical status, and psychiatric status) during the month before the 6-month follow-up point. Hierarchical, stepwise multiple regression procedures were used to test sequentially the predictive value of patient and background variables and then to test their ASI problem severity composite scores at admission, followed by composite measures from the TSR as a quantitative estimate of the number and types of services received by the patients during treatment.

Summary of Findings

There were four questions addressed by this research and the results of the analyses pertaining to each of these are summarized as follows.

1. What is the relative contribution of patient background variables, severity of patient problems at admission, and services received during treatment in predicting posttreatment outcome? In general, the results of the analyses across all the groups examined showed that demographic characteristics (e.g., age, race, gender, education, etc.) were the least related to treatment outcome regardless of the outcome criterion evaluated. This category of predictors accounted for an average of 5% of the outcome variance in the substance use measure and only 3% in the social adjustment mea-

sure. The only variable from this category that was found to be significantly related to outcome was the number of previous substance abuse treatments, which was modestly (average, 4% variance) and negatively related to posttreatment substance use.

It was clear in all analyses that the severity of patients' problems at admission was the most significant and general predictor of posttreatment outcome. The severity of the alcohol and drug problems at admission was the most significant predictor of posttreatment substance use but was not well related to posttreatment social adjustment. The severity of patients' psychiatric, employment, and family problems was the most significant predictor of social adjustment but, for each problem, was also often associated with posttreatment substance use. The severity of patients' problems at the time of admission accounted for an average of 12% of the outcome variance in the substance use domain and 18% of the variance in the social adjustment domain. In general, greater problem severity at treatment admission was associated with poorer outcomes at follow-up.

Even after the variance associated with the severity of the admission problems was accounted for, the analyses indicated that the quantity of services received during treatment was independently and positively associated with posttreatment social adjustment and, to a much lesser extent, posttreatment substance use. Treatment services accounted for an average of 11% of the variance in the social adjustment domain but only 2% to 5% of the variance in the substance use outcome domain. A greater number of psychiatric, medical, employment, and family services received during treatment was significantly associated with better social adjustment at follow-up. Similarly, a greater number of psychiatric and medical services during treatment was positively but weakly associated with less substance use at follow-up. It is interesting (discussed later) that the number of substance abuse services provided during treatment (e.g., drug counseling sessions, 12-step meetings, alcohol education classes, etc.) was poorly related to both outcome measures, accounting for less than 1% of the variance in each.

2. Are the factors that predict posttreatment substance use similar to or different from the factors that predict posttreatment social adjustment? Greater posttreatment substance use was positively predicted by the severity of the substance use problem at admission, the number of previous substance abuse treatments, and positively but to a far lesser extent, by the number of medical and psychiatric services received during treatment (see tables 4 through 6). A total of only 15% to 20% of the variance in this measure was accounted for by these factors. In contrast, an average of 28% to 40% of the variance in the social adjustment outcome domain was accounted for primarily and negatively by the severity of patients' psychiatric, employment, and family problems at admission and positively by the

number of psychiatric, medical, employment, and family services received during the course of treatment.

3. Are the factors that predict posttreatment substance use and social adjustment similar or different among three primary drug use samples (e.g., alcohol, cocaine, and opiate)? The factors that predicted outcome among opiate abusers in methadone maintenance were somewhat different from those that predicted outcome among alcohol- and cocaine-dependent patients. The predictive contribution of the demographic variables was quite similar and minor across all drug use groups (see Table 5). The severity of the patients' problems at admission was the major predictor of outcome for all groups, but this category of variables made a much greater contribution to the prediction of outcome (both substance use and social adjustment) in opiate patients than in either of the alcohol or cocaine samples, in which the contributions were very similar. The predictive contribution of the treatment services was very similar across all three drug preference groups with regard to posttreatment social adjustment. However, with regard to the substance use outcome domain, the number of services received during treatment made a somewhat larger predictive contribution in the methadone maintenance patients than in the alcohol or cocaine samples, in which again, the contribution was very similar.

4. Are the factors that predict posttreatment substance use and social adjustment similar to or different among various "types" of treatment (e.g., inpatient and outpatient; public and private)? There was great similarity among the factors that predicted both outcome measures across both the inpatient and outpatient treatment settings examined and both the publicly and privately funded treatment programs evaluated. Again, demographic variables were poorly related to both outcome measures for all these groups despite the fact that there were substantial demographic differences among public and private treatment samples and, to a lesser extent, between inpatient and outpatient treatment settings. In all cases, the severity of treatment problems at admission was a major and negative predictor of both outcomes for all these groups, whereas the number of treatment services received was a secondary but positive predictor of better social adjustment outcomes for all groups. The similarity of these predictive factors across a rather widely divergent set of patient populations and treatment programs suggests that there may be general principles associated with rehabilitation from substance dependence, regardless of the primary substance abused or the type of treatment. The implications of this suggestion for both treatment and research are discussed later.

Limitations of the Present Approach

Before discussing the implications of these findings, it is important to delineate the limitations on the available data. For example, patients in the present research were not randomly assigned to their treatment programs. This was not possible from either an ethical or practical perspective. Instead, the data result from a collection of patient and treatment samples during the past 3 years of treatment evaluation studies that have been conducted through the Pennsylvania–Veterans Affairs Center for Studies of Addiction. In addition, although we have provided data on a reasonably wide range of treatment types, this cannot be considered a full representation of either the variety of inpatient and outpatient programs or the range of public and private treatment funding sources. Furthermore, it should be repeated that we did not design this study as a comparison of the efficacy of inpatient versus outpatient or public versus private substance abuse treatments.

There are also some important limitations with regard to patient representation in the analyses. For example, although women and virtually every ethnic group are represented to some extent in the patient samples, we have not examined the factors associated with treatment outcome among samples composed exclusively of women, adolescents, or particular ethnic groups. These samples have simply not been available to us in sufficient quantity for this type of analysis. Furthermore, given the magnitude of the social and cultural differences between these groups and the predominantly adult male samples evaluated here, we do not feel it is safe to assume that the outcome predictors found for the present samples would be similar in these groups. Additional studies to address the factors governing treatment outcome among these and other subgroups are particularly important given the suggestion of unique treatment needs among gender, racial, and cultural subgroups and the widespread development of specialty treatment programs to address those needs. We urge other researchers with access to these populations to pursue a similar line of investigation.

Although we have used a reasonably wide range of patient background and treatment status variables as predictors of outcome, it would have been reasonable to include several others. Diagnostic measures of depression and personality disorders; measures of the patients' "stage of change" as has been characterized by Prochaska and his colleagues (Prochaska & DiClemente, 1983); and family history of alcohol, drug, or psychiatric problems would all have been very desirable given the growing body of research investigating each (Cloninger, 1987). Similarly, although we measured treatment services (albeit only quantitatively), we did not include (a) measures of program environment, administration, or leadership as have been studied by Moos and his colleagues (1974; Moos, Finney, & Cronkite, 1990) and more recently by Ball (Ball & Ross, 1991), (b) therapist characteristics (Luborsky, McLellan, Woody, & O'Brien, 1985), or (c) the posttreatment environment to which patients returned (Havassy et al., 1989). These are significant omissions in any truly comprehensive evaluation of the full range of factors that could be predictive of treatment outcome, and it is likely that additional outcome variance could have been accounted for had these and other variables been included. The main purpose of the present evaluation was to study the same sets of predictive factors across multiple patient and treatment samples, thus permitting a test for the degree of comparability. Although we would have liked to include more variables in our predictive equations, we simply did not have comparability across all the patient samples. This will be an important goal of future research.

There has also been discussion regarding the appropriate or optimal point at which to evaluate treatment effects, with previous workers using intervals ranging from 1 to 24 months. Our choice of 6 months was in part based on our earlier work over the past 15 years, suggesting that approximately 60% to 80% of those patients who relapse following treatment do so within 3 to 4 months after discharge (McLellan, Metzger, et al., 1992). Finally, because many of the patients who do relapse return to treatment, later follow-up evaluations of a single treatment episode may become contaminated by the effects of subsequent treatments. To our knowledge, there is no optimum point at which to evaluate treatment effects, and multiple evaluations are therefore preferable. Thus, we suggest that, although earlier or later follow-up assessments are important and appropriate, the 6-month evaluations provided here also offer one appropriate indication of treatment effects.

A related question is the use of the ASI's 30-day "window" to sample patient status at a follow-up point and whether this window is comparable to other, perhaps more common, methods of characterizing the full period of time from treatment discharge to follow-up. In fact, these are different methods of measurement with different strengths and weaknesses. Retrospective reports for the full period of time since treatment discharge are particularly useful for characterizing the full spectrum of changes in individual behavior throughout the entire period. At the same time, this complete characterization of behavior across a significant period of time is often done at the expense of detail on specific behaviors or symptoms (e.g., frequency of particular drug use, or specific medical, psychiatric, and family problems). In contrast, we have found that the behaviors represented by the 30-day period preceding a 6- or 12-month follow-up point are not necessarily representative of those behaviors throughout the follow-up interval. Thus, it is not possible to assume that the behaviors observed in any single subject during any 30-day period will be representative of that individual's behavior for preceding or succeeding months. We have not represented this measure in this way. At the same time, we have found that the frequency of rather specific behaviors can be recalled reliably and validly for a 30-day period and that these frequency samples are quite sensitive to change over time. Thus, just as we have sampled subjects in treatment to represent the population of patients in treatment at a point in time, we have sampled relatively specific and distinct measures of their behaviors during fixed periods of their lives to represent the behavioral status of the total group at that time.

Because we have focused on the contribution of treatment services to the prediction of outcome and because the instrument used (the TSR) is still relatively new, it is important to discuss the limitations in this area of measurement. First, although the TSR has been shown to be a reliable and valid quantitative measure of services received during treatment (McLellan, Alterman, et al., 1992), it is not designed to measure the undoubtedly important domain of treatment quality. For these reasons, the finding of a relationship between the quantity of services received during treatment and posttreatment outcome must be taken cautiously. Clearly, such a finding is not proof that these treatment services were the causal agent in the improved outcomes observed. For example, it is possible that those patients who received the most treatment services were merely the most motivated patients and that this greater level of motivation is truly responsible for the improved social adjustment that was observed.

Although such a possibility cannot be completely ruled out by this study, there are reasons why we do not believe that receiving more services is merely a marker for increased patient motivation. First, the other measure of motivation included in the predictors (e.g., forced into treatment by work or legal pressure) was not significantly related to either outcome criterion in any sample, and this variable was not significantly related to any of the TSR composite measures. In addition, there was little relation among the seven TSR composite measures; that is, those patients who received the most sessions and services in one particular problem area did not necessarily receive more services in other areas. Such a finding would not be expected if these TSR scores were merely markers for greater general motivation. Finally, as was pointed out earlier, the significant relationships seen were generally specific between a particular outcome measure and the corresponding TSR measure of services specifically provided for that problem. This correspondence between type of problem and type of service prompts us to suggest that these measures offer more than just global indications of patient motivation, and we continue to operate under the view that these services may have specific effects. Clearly more research is warranted in this important area before this view can be fully accepted.

Given these important caveats, it is reasonable to question whether and in what way the data can contribute to the understanding of the factors that are most related to outcomes from substance abuse treatments. In this regard, there were a number of positive aspects of the study that give us confidence in the results. For example, all admission and follow-up data were obtained by trained and supervised research technicians who were independent of all treatment programs. In addition, follow-up data were collected on an average of 92% (range, 89% to 98%) of the patients sampled, thus ensuring a full representation of the treatment effects.

A major consideration in all studies using self-report data is the reliability and validity of the information collected. Several points are relevant here. First, the data collected were based on confidential interviews at admission and follow-up with instruments and procedures that have been validated in many similar studies (McLellan, Cacciola, et al., 1992). Within the ASI that was used at both admission and follow-up, there are built in consistency checks to monitor the accuracy of reporting on sensitive issues such as drug use and crime. The self-reported data on drug and alcohol use were supported by the results of concurrent, independent urinalysis and Breathalyzer readings and the results of employment were spot checked for validity by requiring pay stubs.

Finally, the data were analyzed using well-established, stepwise multiple regression techniques. Both forward and backward stepwise procedures were used, and although there were, of course, some quantitative differences in the amounts of criterion variance accounted for by a particular predictor, these procedures produced very similar overall results, thus increasing our confidence that the findings are not merely an artifact of a particular analytic procedure.

Issues Regarding the Contribution of Treatment Services to Outcome

Relationship Between Substance-Abuse-Focused Treatment Services and Outcome

It must be admitted at the outset that we are not sure why there was not a more robust relationship between the number of treatment services targeted directly to the substance abuse problems of these patients (e.g., drug counseling sessions, alcohol education sessions, etc.) and the two outcome measures studied. However, on the basis of the available data as well as a number of previous studies examining these factors, we offer the following post hoc explanation. First, we emphasize that all patient samples in all treatment environments showed significant levels of improvement in substance use (see Table 2). Indeed, it was among the most improved areas in virtually all samples. Second, because the treatments under study were all substance abuse programs, it follows that all patients received substantial amounts of treatment services directed at their presenting problems of alcohol and drug use. We considered the possibility that there was not sufficient range in the quantitative measure to properly test for relationships between these services and outcome. In fact, this was not the case. The cumulative measure of treatment services directed at alcohol and drug abuse problems ranged from a low of five sessions per week to a high of 38 sessions per week. On the basis of these cumulative findings, we have come to believe that all treatment programs examined in this study may have provided more than the minimum number of alcohol- and drug-related services necessary to effect significant positive change in substance use at the 6-month point and that the additional alcohol- and drug-related services provided by some programs had little additional effect beyond that.

With regard to the relationship between substance-abuse-related services and psychosocial outcome, the data from all analyses indicate that there is virtually no relationship here, and we find no reason to qualify or modify this result; it appears that alcohol- and drug-focused services (e.g., group therapy for denial, alcohol and drug education, 12-step meetings, etc.) may have rehabilitative effects that are specific to drug and alcohol problems but that there is a point of diminishing returns with regard to the provision of these services on the expected outcomes of reduction in alcohol and drug use.

Relationship Between Psychosocially Focused Treatment Services and Outcome

The present data suggest that the employment counseling, family therapy and particularly the psychiatric sessions provided by the treatment programs studied, were not consistently related to change in the substance abuse problems of these patients but were significantly related to improved psychosocial function across a wide range of patient and treatment types. There are at least three ways in which treatment services could have exerted a positive effect upon post treatment social adjustment. First and most directly, treatment services such as family therapy, individual psychotherapy, employment counseling etc. could function in much the same way as "medicines," to reduce the severity of the particular problem symptoms to which they are directed. If this is true, it suggests that more parametric studies of these services are needed to investigate the dose–response and potency–purity dimensions of these services. A second possibility is that these treatment service variables serve as markers for those patients who had the most motivation for change and rehabilitation (see Limitations section above). A third way in which treatment services could affect outcome is through an indirect but continuing influence on the post treatment environment of the patients. As has been clearly documented by workers such as Moos and Finney (Moos, 1974; Moos, Finney, et al., 1990) and more recently by Havassy (Havassy et al., 1989), the level of environmental support that is available to a patient for the maintenance of gains achieved during rehabilitation is an understandably powerful predictor of continued positive outcome following treatment for substance abuse problems. In this regard, it is possible and even likely that the provision of effective treatment for the psychosocial problems of patients during treatment could have a continuing positive effect on their posttreatment environment. For example, the provision of family therapy during treatment or referral of a family member who also has a substance abuse problem into treatment (or both) can alter the environment to which the patient returns after treatment. Consistent with this possibility are the growing number of studies within the substance abuse field showing the significant effects of supplemental psychotherapy (Kadden, Cooney, Getter, & Litt, 1990; Woody et al., 1983, 1984), family therapy (McCrady et al., 1986; Stanton & Todd, 1982), employment counseling (Azrin et al., 1982; Higgins et al., 1991), and social skills training (Hall, Loeb, LeVois, & Cooper, 1981) on posttreatment function. If this suggestion is true, and it should be examined parametrically in subsequent studies, it has implications for the planning and conduct of substance abuse rehabilitation. It may be that the most efficient and effective treatments for substance dependence will require an as-yet-unspecified mix of services directed at both the alcohol and drug problems as well as the psychosocial problems of substance abuse patients.

CONCLUSION

In summary, these data suggest that, regardless of whether substance abuse treatment is directed at primary problems of opiate, alcohol, or cocaine dependence and whether the treatment is delivered in an inpatient or outpatient setting in a publicly or privately funded program, the outcomes of those treatments are apparently governed by the same patient and treatment factors. As has been shown in many previous studies, the severity of patients' problems at treatment admission were significant predictors of 6-month outcome. In addition, the present results indicate that the quantity of services received during the rehabilitation process are also significantly related to outcome. In particular, substance abuse services (e.g., group therapy for denial, alcohol and drug education, 12-step meetings, etc.) may effect change in substance use but apparently have little effect on the psychosocial problems of substance abuse patients. The number of psychosocial services (e.g., employment counseling, psychotherapy, family therapy, etc.) provided during treatment was not well related to posttreatment alcohol and drug use but was significantly related to posttreatment psychosocial adjustment. It may be that, although alcohol- and drug-focused services function to produce patient acceptance of the severity of a substance abuse problem and to engender the motivation and specific behaviors necessary to initiate abstinence, psychosocial sessions and services may be essential to the reduction of the psychosocial problems that are so important in the posttreatment environment of a patient and that have such profound effects on sustained recovery. The fact that these relationships have been shown across a wide range of patient types and treatment conditions suggests that these may be general guiding principles in the treatment and rehabilitation of substance abuse disorders regardless of the philosophy, setting, or funding of the treatment. It is important to extend this retrospective evaluation with more controlled, clinical trials of various doses of both psychosocial and substance-abuse-focused services to ultimately develop the most effective and enduring forms of rehabilitation for these pervasive and debilitating disorders.

REFERENCES

Allison, M., & Hubbard, R. L. (1982). Drug abuse treatment process: A review of the literature. *TOPS Research Monograph*. Raleigh, NC: Research Triangle Press.

Alterman, A. I., & Cacciola, J. S. (1991). The antisocial personality disorder diagnosis in substance abusers: Problems and issues. *Journal of Nervous and Mental Diseases, 179*, 401–409.

Anglin, M. D., & Hser, Y. (1990). Legal coercion and drug abuse treatment. In J. Inciardi (Ed.), *Handbook on drug control in the United States* (pp. 235–247). Westport, CT: Greenwood Press.

Armor, D. J., Polich, J. M., & Stambul, H. B. (1976). *Alcoholism and treatment*. Santa Monica, CA: RAND Corporation Press.

Azrin, N. H., Sisson, R. W., Meyers, R. W., & Godley, M. (1982). Alcoholism treatment by disulfiram and community reinforcement therapy. *Journal of Behavior Therapy and Experimental Psychiatry, 13*, 105–112.

Babor, T., Dolinsky, Z., Rounsaville, B. J., & Jaffe, J. (1988). Unitary versus multidimensional models of alcoholism treatment outcome: An empirical study. *Journal of Studies on Alcohol, 49*, 167–177.

Ball, J. C., & Ross, A. (1991). *The effectiveness of methadone maintenance treatment*. New York: Springer-Verlag.

Chapman-Walsh, D. C., Hingson, R., & Merrigan, D. (1991). A randomized trial of treatment options for alcohol-abusing workers. *New England Journal of Medicine, 325*, 775–782.

Cloninger, C. R. (1987). Neurogenetic adaptive mechanisms in alcoholism. *Science, 236*, 410–416.

Cohen, J., & Cohen, P. (1975). *Applied multiple regression/correlation analysis for the behavioral sciences*. New York: Wiley.

DeLeon, G. (1984). *The therapeutic community: Study of effectiveness* (NIDA Treatment Research Monograph 84-1286). Rockville, MD: U.S. Government Printing Office.

Edwards, G., Orford, J., Egert, S., Guthrie, A., Hawker, C., Hensman, M., Mitcheson, M., Oppenheimer, E., & Taylor, C. (1977). Alcoholism: A controlled trial of treatment and advice. *Journal of Studies on Alcohol, 38*, 1004–1031.

Finney, J. W., Moos, R. H., & Chan, D. A. (1981). Length of stay and program component effects in the treatment of alcoholism: A comparison of two techniques for process analyses. *Journal of Consulting and Clinical Psychology, 49*, 120–131.

Gerstein, D., & Harwood, H. (Eds.). (1990). *Treating drug problems* (Vol. 1). Washington, DC: National Academy Press.

Hall, S. M., Loeb, P., LeVois, P., & Cooper, J. (1981). Increasing employment in ex-heroin addicts II: Methadone maintenance sample. *Behavioral Medicine, 12*, 453–460.

Havassy, B. E., Hall, S. M., & Wasserman, D. A. (1989). Social support and relapse: Commonalities among alcoholics, opiate users and cigarette smokers. *Addictive Behaviors, 16*, 235–246.

Hayashida, M., Alterman, A. I., McLellan, A. T., O'Brien, C. P., Purtill, J., & Volpicelli, J. (1989). Comparative effectiveness and costs of inpatient and outpatient medical alcohol detoxification. *New England Journal of Medicine, 678*, 1234–136.

Hesselbrock, V., Meyer, R., & Keener, J. (1985). Psychopathology in hospitalized alcoholics. *Archives of General Psychiatry, 42*, 1050–1055.

Higgins, S. T., Delaney, D. D., Budney, A. J., Bickel, W. K., Hughes, J. R., Foerg, F., & Fenwick, J. W. (1991). A behavioral approach to achieving initial cocaine abstinence. *American Journal of Psychiatry, 148*, 1218–1224.

Hubbard, R. L., & Marsden, M. E. (1986). Relapse to use of heroin, cocaine and other drugs in the first year after treatment. *Relapse and recovery in drug abuse* (NIDA Research Monograph 72, pp. 247–253). Rockville, MD: U.S. Government Printing Office.

Hubbard, R. L., Marsden, M. E., Rachal, J. V., Harwood, H. J., Cavanaugh, E. R., & Ginzburg, H. M. (1989). *Drug abuse treatment: A national study of effectiveness.* Chapel Hill: University of North Carolina Press.

Institute of Medicine. (1990). *Broadening the base of treatment for alcohol problems.* Washington, DC: National Academy Press.

Joe, G. W., Simpson, D. D., & Sells, S. B. (1992). Treatment process and relapse to opioid use during methadone maintenance. *American Journal of Drug and Alcohol Abuse, 19*, 124–130.

Kadden, R. M., Cooney, N. L., Getter, H., & Litt, M. D. (1990). Matching alcoholics to coping skills or interactional therapies: Posttreatment results. *Journal of Consulting and Clinical Psychology, 57*, 698–704.

Luborsky, L., McLellan, A. T., Woody, G. E., & O'Brien, C. P. (1985). Therapist success and its determinants. *Archives of General Psychiatry, 42*, 602–611.

McCrady, B. S., Noel, N. E., Abrams, D. B., Stout, R. L., Nelson, H. F., & Hay, W. M. (1986). Comparative effectiveness of three types of spouse involvement in outpatient behavioral alcoholism treatment. *Journal of Studies on Alcohol, 47*, 459–467.

McLellan, A. T., Alterman, A. I., Woody, G. E., & Metzger, D. (1992). A quantitative measure of substance abuse treatments: The Treatment Services Review. *Journal of Nervous and Mental Diseases, 180*, 101–110.

McLellan, A. T., Cacciola, J., Kushner, H., Peters, F., Smith, I., & Pettinati, H.

(1992). The fifth edition of the Addiction Severity Index: Cautions, additions and normative data. *Journal of Substance Abuse Treatment, 9,* 199–213.

McLellan, A. T., Grissom, G., Alterman, A. I., Brill, P., & O'Brien, C. P. (1993). Substance abuse treatment in the private setting: Are some programs more effective than others? *Journal of Substance Abuse Treatment, 27,* 561–570.

McLellan, A. T., Luborsky, L., Cacciola, J., & Griffith, J. E. (1985). New data from the Addiction Severity Index: Reliability and validity in three centers. *Journal of Nervous and Mental Diseases, 173,* 412–423.

McLellan, A. T., Luborsky, L., & O'Brien, C. P. (1986). Alcohol and drug abuse in three different populations: Is there improvement and is it predictable? *American Journal of Drug and Alcohol Abuse, 12,* 101–120.

McLellan, A. T., Luborsky, L., O'Brien, C. P., & Woody, G. E. (1980). An improved evaluation instrument for substance abuse patients: The Addiction Severity Index. *Journal of Nervous and Mental Diseases, 168,* 26–33.

McLellan, A. T., Luborsky, L., Woody, G. E., Druley, K. A., & O'Brien, C. P. (1983). Predicting response to alcohol and drug abuse treatments: Role of psychiatric severity. *Archives of General Psychiatry, 40,* 620–625.

McLellan, A. T., Luborsky, L., Woody, G. E., & O'Brien, C. P. (1982). Is treatment for substance abuse effective? *Journal of the American Medical Association, 247,* 1423–1427.

McLellan, A. T., Luborsky, L., Woody, G. E., O'Brien, C. P., & Druley, K. A. (1983). Increased effectiveness of substance abuse treatment: A prospective study of patient–treatment "matching." *Journal of Nervous and Mental Diseases, 171,* 597–605.

McLellan, A. T., Metzger, D., Alterman, A. I., Cornish, J., & Urschel, H. (1992). How effective is substance abuse treatment—Compared to what? In C. P. O'Brien & J. Jaffe (Eds.), *Advances in understanding the addictive states* (pp. 312–327). New York: Association for Research in Nervous and Mental Disorders Press.

Miller, W. R., & Hester, R. K. (1986). Inpatient alcoholism treatment: Who benefits? *American Psychologist, 41,* 794–805.

Moos, R. H. (1974). *Evaluating treatment environments.* New York: Wiley.

Moos, R. H., Finney, J. W., & Cronkite, R. C. (1990). *Alcoholism treatment: Context, process and outcome.* Oxford, England: New York, Oxford University Press.

Prochaska, J. O., & DiClemente, C. C. (1983). Stages and processes of self-change of smoking: Toward an integrative model of change. *Journal of Consulting and Clinical Psychology, 51,* 390–395.

Rounsaville, B. J., Dolinsky, Z. S., Babor, T. F., & Meyer, R. E. (1987). Psychopathology as a predictor of treatment outcome in alcoholics. *Archives of General Psychiatry, 44,* 505–513.

Rounsaville, B. J., Glaser, W., Wilber, C. H., & Kleber, H. (1983). Short-term interpersonal psychotherapy in methadone-maintained opiate addicts. *Archives of General Psychiatry, 40,* 619–626.

Saxe, L. D. (1983). *The effectiveness and costs of alcoholism treatment: Health Technology Case Study 22.* Washington, DC: United States Government Printing Office.

Schuckit, M. A. (1985). The clinical implications of primary diagnostic groups among alcoholics. *Archives of General Psychiatry, 42,* 1043–1049.

Simpson, D., & Savage, L. (1980). Drug abuse treatment readmissions and outcomes. *Archives of General Psychiatry, 37,* 896–901.

Stanton, M. D., & Todd, T. (1982). *The family therapy of drug abuse and addiction.* New York: Guilford Press.

Woody, G. E., Luborsky, L., McLellan, A. T., & O'Brien, C. P. (1983). Psychotherapy for opiate addicts: Does it help? *Archives of General Psychiatry, 40,* 639–645.

Woody, G. E., McLellan, A. T., & Luborsky, L. (1984). Psychiatric severity as a predictor of benefits from psychotherapy. *American Journal of Psychiatry, 141,* 1171–1177.

29

VOCATIONAL REHABILITATION OF DRUG ABUSERS

The purpose of this review is to examine the existing literature on employment, drug use, and addiction over approximately the past 20 years to clarify the role that has been played by employment in the onset of, maintenance of, and recovery from addiction. In addition, interventions designed to improve employment are reviewed in an attempt to identify those variables that may be useful in increasing employment in the addict population. The conclusions to be drawn from the existing literature reflect an increasing awareness of the important role employment and employment-related interventions play in the treatment of and recovery from drug abuse. Recommendations are made with respect to (a) areas in which additional research is needed regarding the relationship between employment and addiction and (b) those elements that require inclusion

Reprinted from *Psychological Bulletin*, *117*, 416–433. (1995). Copyright © 1995 by the American Psychological Association. Used with permission of the author.

I would like to gratefully acknowledge the support provided by the National Institute on Drug Abuse for this review. I am particularly indebted to Frank M. Tims and Mindy Widman for their significant contributions to the preparation of this article.

This article reviews publications appearing in the literature since 1972. Because of cultural differences affecting employment, the review is limited to research conducted in the United States.

in any model of employment rehabilitation for drug abusers. The literature chosen has been limited to the nonprison population. The articles chosen for the review are among the most regularly cited in the field and can thus be viewed as prototypical.

This review focuses on opiate (almost always heroin) addicts, because this group has been the primary concern of employment-related studies, many of which have taken place within the context of methadone maintenance treatment; the extent to which these findings are generalizable to other populations of drug users (e.g., cocaine addicts) is not known. Also, the term *ex-addict*, when used, is reflective of the descriptions applied by the authors of specific studies, and thus its use may not be consistent across all studies. Considering the predominant conception of addiction as a chronic relapsing disease (e.g., Kleber, 1989; Platt, 1995a), the term may have different meanings, depending on the client's position in the frequently repetitive cycle of addiction, recovery, and readdiction at the time of study.

There are long-standing and convincing arguments for the importance of employment in addiction treatment. Although a number of models can be suggested that would anchor these studies (e.g., the addict as disabled, the addict as morally flawed, or, as currently held, the addict as criminal), there is a startling lack of stated theoretical underpinnings for the research reviewed here. Changes in the definition of the addict have been evident in a shift to social control measures, as reflected by changes in funding emphasis over time (Humphreys & Rappaport, 1993). Most of the research reviewed here, however, has tended to speak of treatment and intervention reflecting a more medicalized model of addiction. Because no specific statement of the views of the researchers about addicts is available from the literature reviewed, however, evidence of theory shift toward (or away from) social control of addicts is not present.

This lack of theory does not, however, diminish the importance of the role of employment. In addiction treatment evaluation research, employment is viewed as both a desired outcome and an element of treatment. The acknowledgment by the drug treatment community of employment as a criterion for treatment outcome is reflected in the use of such a criterion by a number of researchers in the field of drug abuse treatment evaluation (e.g., DeLeon, 1984; Hall, 1984; Hubbard, Rachal, Craddock, & Cavanaugh, 1984; Simpson, 1984). In addition, employment may be an essential ingredient not only for a successful outcome to addiction treatment (e.g., National Institute on Drug Abuse [NIDA], 1979; Preble & Casey, 1976; see also Platt, 1986, pp. 287–291, for a discussion of this issue) but also for retention in treatment, a variable closely related to treatment outcome (e.g., DeLeon, 1984). In this regard, after comprehensively reviewing studies of the relationship between client characteristics and the impact of treatment, McLellan (1983) reported that 26 of 31 studies that included employment status as a variable found significant and positive correlations between employment status and retention in treatment. By holding a job, the client not only establishes a legal source of income but improves his or her self-esteem, which in turn may reduce use of illicit drugs and thus allow him or her to refrain from criminal activity (Joe, Chastain, & Simpson, 1990). Employment may also serve as a means of (re)socialization, allowing for integration into the "straight world." Thus, employment assumes a number of important roles in addiction treatment.

RATES AND CORRELATES OF EMPLOYMENT AMONG ADDICTED POPULATIONS

Rates of Pretreatment Employment in Addicted Populations

Employment is not usual for heroin addicts. Vaillant (1966, 1988) noted that, by age 40, New York heroin addicts had spent some 80% of their lives unemployed. He observed that "in someone whose daily life is unpatterned by a job, addiction poses a very definite and gratifying, if rather stereotyped, pattern of behaviour" (Vaillant, 1988, p. 1150).

The employment rate in the addict population before admission or at admission to drug treatment has remained, for the most part, relatively (and stably) low since 1970, ranging from approximately 15% to 35%. This range is found across different treatment modalities. Maddux and McDonald (1973), for example, found an employment rate of 21% among 100 chronic heroin users entering methadone treatment in Texas. Of those enrolled in the New York State Drug Abuse Control Commission methadone program, 14% were employed at the time of their admission in 1971 (Bloch, Ellis, & Spielman, 1977). Newman, Bashkow, and Cates (1974) found an employment rate of 14.8% for the 11,365 individuals applying for admission to the New York City Methadone Maintenance Program from July through December 1972. At about the same time, Dale and Dale (1973) found employment rates of 16% for female clients and 20% for male clients entering another New York methadone program.

In 1974, Suffet and Brotman (1976) found an employment rate of 29% at admission into an abstinence program; the same rate was found in the early 1980s in a sample of addicts maintained on methadone or in outpatient drug-free treatment (Aiken, LoSciuto, Ausetts, & Brown, 1984). McLellan, Luborsky, O'Brien, Barr, and Evans (1986) found that 34% of those addicted to alcohol or drugs were employed at the time of admission to three settings offering several treatment modalities. In a review article, Wolkstein and Hastings-Black (1979) noted that 73% of clients leaving treatment in 1976 were unemployed. Singh and his colleagues (Singh, Joe, Lehman, Garland, & Sells, 1982), reporting on the characteristics of more than 12,000 admissions to 211 methadone programs in 1977, found the mean rate of unemployment to be 63% at treatment entry; the median unemployment rate among the programs was 66%, a figure matched by the 65.5% rate found by Tims (1981) in 1980. Metzger and Platt (1987) reported an almost 26% employment rate in a sample of clients in four methadone clinics located in the greater Philadelphia/southern New Jersey geographic area for the period 1979 to 1981, a figure that, on reexamination, remained remarkably stable from 1981 through 1985 (Metzger, 1987). In 1989, Miranda, Frank, Marel, and Schmeidler reported unemployment rates among clients in outpatient treatment to be 70% after 9 to 12 months in treatment. In 1990, Livingston, Randall, and Wolkstein reported that, for clients under the auspices of the New York State Division of Substance Abuse Services, there was an employment rate of 37%, noting this to be a decline of some 10% since 1980.

Thus, employment rates seem not to have dramatically changed over the last 20 years, despite several cycles of significant change in the economic environment. There is, however, at least one major exception to this pattern. Anglin, Booth, Ryan, and Hser (1988) found that more than 80% of Anglo and Chicano participants were employed in the period between the onset of their addiction and their entry into treatment. When the percentage of time these individuals were employed was factored in, however, their full-time employment rate was approximately 40%.

Thus, employment rates (and patterns) for the nonaddicted segment of the population are substantially above those for populations of drug abusers. For example, 72.3% of the civilian population between 25 and 64 years of age were employed in 1980, and 76.8% were employed in 1991 (U.S. Bureau of the Census, 1993). Even when the lack of a high school diploma is factored in, only 8.4% and 11.0% of the population between 25 and 64 years of age were unemployed in 1980 and 1991, respectively (U.S. Bureau of the Census, 1993). These data clearly indicate the need for interventions to increase employment among drug abusers.

Although drug addicts are defined as disabled by the Americans With Disabilities Act of 1990, their description would make them appear less so. Many studies have assessed the characteristics of addicts that might place them at higher risk for unemployment. In general, drug addicts can be described as more likely to be members of a minority group than the general population (Hser, Anglin, & Liu, 1990–1991; Kosten, Rounsaville, & Kleber, 1987b; Mathis, Navaline, Metzger, & Platt, 1994; McLellan, Ball, Rosen, & O'Brien, 1981; Simpson & Friend, 1988; U.S. Bureau of the Census, 1993). Their mean education level (highest year completed) ranges from 9.4 years (Hser et al., 1990–1991) to 11.8 years (Kosten et al., 1987b). This is comparable to the median education levels of the general population of 9.8 to 12.1 years (age 25+ and ages 25–29, respectively) in 1970, 12.0 to 12.5 years in 1980, and 12.4 to 12.7 years in 1990 (U.S. Bureau of the Census, 1993). Between 40% and 74% have completed high school (Marsh & Simpson, 1986; Mathis et al., 1994), a range slightly lower than the 51% to 79% found in the general population in 1990 (U.S. Bureau of the Census, 1993).

Definition of Employment

The results of the Anglin et al. (1988) study raise an important issue in any examination of employment among addicts: What definition of employment should be used? Different authors have reported employment at a given point in time, the number of days employed over a given period of time, the percentage of time worked, and the percentage of income derived from work.

Bloch et al. (1977) reviewed the literature on employment and identified three measures (time frames) commonly used in evaluation of treatment effectiveness (and assessed the value of each through comparisons): (a) employment at program admission as compared with employment at the point of evaluation (point in time vs. point in time; 56% difference noted), (b) employment between the onset of addiction and program admission as compared with employment at the point of evaluation (period of time vs. point in time; 27% difference noted), and (c) employment between the onset of addiction and program admission as compared with employment during a minimum of 2 years of methadone treatment (period of time vs. period of time; 17% difference noted). The variability of each measurement type was attributed to the use of point in time or period of time measures. Treatment admission point in time data predispose findings of later success because functioning is lowest immediately before admission. The period of time between addiction onset and treatment entry provides a more stable baseline, but comparisons with a point of evaluation measure do not consider the extent of employment during treatment. Only period of time measures (both baseline and outcome) consider each of the failings of point in time measures.

Examination of later studies reveals similar patterns of difference resulting from the selection of baseline and outcome measurements. Kosten, Rounsaville, and Kleber (1987a) reported the mean number of days worked in the month before entrance into treatment and the average dollars earned during that time, whereas Anglin et al. (1988) reported the percentage of people employed and the average percentage of time they were employed for a defined period. Mathis et al. (1994) defined employment as currently having a job and examined the percentage of income derived from work by race and sex.

The variability of baseline and outcome measures chosen by researchers and discussed earlier makes comparison of the results of research very difficult at the least. In addition, the lack of distinction between full-time and part-time work in most studies makes results difficult to evaluate and comparisons with the population as a whole speculative.

Employment Patterns

In addition to discussions of the rate of employment, some researchers have developed typologies to categorize the work patterns of addicts. Platt and Metzger (1987) used a five-category classification for consistency of employment, and current employment at each of four data collection points was assessed. Addicts were described as "consistently unemployed" if they were unemployed at all four data collection points, "typically unemployed" if they were employed at only one point, "inconsistently employed" if they were employed twice during data collection, "typically employed" if they were employed at three data points, and "consistently employed" if they were employed at all four data collection points. As noted earlier, more than 26% of addicts were found to be typically or consistently employed (Platt & Metzger, 1987). Variability by race and gender was found in the data just described (Mathis et al., 1994) in that female clients had worked significantly less than had male clients, had received significantly less monthly income than their male counterparts, and had significantly more income from public assistance. In addition, female clients were less likely than male clients to be looking for work, and they reported more frequently that they did not want employment. These findings are consistent with those reported elsewhere (e.g., Anglin, Hser, & McGlothlin, 1987) and should not be surprising, given the child-care responsibilities of women as well as the smaller workforce participation of women in the general population.[1] A typology of the employment activity of narcotic addicts similar to that developed by Platt and Metzger (1987) was developed by Shaffer, Wegner, Kinlock, and Nurco (1983). Regular full- or part-time work characterized the "successful straddler," "unsuccessful working addict," "solitary working addict," and "sociable, semiconventional addict" types, whereas antipathy toward work, often long-standing, characterized the "nonworking addict" and the "solitary, successful criminal addict." Irregular work attendance characterized "deviant associates" and the "marginally subsisting addict."

Drawing on the same database used by Platt and Metzger (1987), Metzger (1987) was able to identify a number of variables that discriminated methadone clients with more or less stable patterns of employment (i.e., mostly unemployed, mostly employed, or stable employment). For all

---

[1] It should be noted that women have been at a particular disadvantage in receiving drug abuse treatment in general; few programs have been developed to either identify or meet their specific needs (e.g., see Anglin, Hser, & Booth, 1987; Cuskey, Berger, & Densen-Gerber, 1977; Marsh & Simpson, 1986). It is interesting to note, however, that the employment of women in treatment is reflective of the employment of all women in the general population.

clients, three variables were found to significantly discriminate employment groups: parental employment, marital status, and race. In addition, for Black clients, two program involvement variables (length of time in the clinic and receiving take-home privileges) were found most strongly to discriminate between employment patterns, whereas four other variables also contributed to the prediction of stable employment (self-esteem, current drug use, parental employment, and marital stability). For White methadone clients, however, the factor scores representing work-related variables (i.e., not having problems at work, motivation to work, not seeking work, no work terminations, and relevant search for work) were related significantly to employment patterns. Interestingly, whereas the variables that best predicted employment patterns differed for Blacks and Whites, the pattern of parental work (type and frequency of parental employment during the client's childhood) was found to contribute most strongly to the function that predicted stable employment in both Black and White clients.

Race also plays a role in relationships between employment and other treatment variables. For example, Metzger and Platt (1983) reported a relationship between race and methadone dose, with Whites receiving higher doses of methadone than Blacks, and Blacks receiving higher doses than Hispanics. In the Metzger (1987) study, Blacks who received higher daily doses of methadone were more likely to acquire work within the study period that followed. Furthermore, when all other variables were held constant, race was found to be the most powerful explanatory variable for the employment characteristics of the study clients, which Metzger (1987) interpreted as suggesting a limiting effect of the environment on the rate of employment for Blacks. This result is consistent with an earlier one by Linn, Shane, Webb, and Pratt (1979), who found that perceptions of the social climate of the ward environment were instrumental in whether or not Black addicts remained in treatment. Ward environment did not play a role in the retention of White patients, whose retention was influenced by intrapsychic factors.

Blacks also appeared to be helped more from the employment readiness intervention developed by Metzger and Platt (Metzger, Platt, Zanis, & Fureman, 1992). Black clients in this study (Platt, Husband, Hermalin, Cater, & Metzger, 1993; see later discussion) benefited more from the intervention than did White clients (19.7% employment in the experimental group and 8.1% in the control group for Blacks vs. 15.0% and 22.2%, respectively, for Whites), a finding that may be a function of the greater psychopathology often seen in White addicts (Platt, Steer, Ranieri, & Metzger, 1989). Furthermore, the results of the evaluation of the employment readiness intervention suggested that the effects of the intervention may have been more long lasting among Black than among White participants. At 12 months postintervention, the employment rate of Black participants was double the rate immediately after the intervention (20% and 10%, respectively). For White participants, employment decreased from 13% to 4% over the same period.

ROLE OF EMPLOYMENT IN THE DEVELOPMENT OF ADDICTION

Anglin et al. (1988) defined the stages of an addiction career as the *preexperimentation phase*, the 12 months before the first use of narcotics; the *experimentation phase*, the first use of narcotics to the first daily use of narcotics; the *addiction phase*, daily narcotics use to first entry into treatment; and the *first treatment phase*, first entry into treatment to first discharge from treatment. Aside from the recognition of the multiple treatment episodes most addicts require, this model also acknowledges that, even before experimentation with narcotics, the future addict has begun his or her addiction career. In a study of more than 500 addicts enrolled in methadone maintenance in 1978, Anglin et al. (1988) found that 17% of Anglo women, 32% of Hispanic women, 34% of Anglo men, and 28% of Hispanic men reported that they had committed a property crime in the preexperimentation phase (before the age of first use [i.e., 15 to 30 years of age]). Between 17% and 45% were dealing, and between 19% and 47% had been arrested before any narcotic use. Nonnarcotic drugs were used by between one fifth and one half of the respondents in treatment. By contrast, the rate of nonmedical, nonnarcotic drug (excluding alcohol) use in the same age group in the general population ranged from 17% to 68% in 1979 (U.S. Bureau of the Census, 1993). These measures of delinquent behavior appear to be inversely related to the positive measure of employment. Employment rates were fairly high, ranging from 46% for Hispanic women to 63% for Hispanic men, and were comparable with the rates of the female and Hispanic populations as a whole in 1980 (U.S. Bureau of the Census, 1993). However, the employment involved was usually part time.

Helzer, Robins, and Davis (1976) studied addicted Vietnam veterans as to their preinduction employment status. Those who had had no full-time employment before induction were the most likely to become addicts after induction, those with more than 3 months of full-time employment were least likely to become addicted, and those with less than 3 months of full-time employment fell between the other two groups (Helzer et al., 1976).

EMPLOYMENT AND CRIMINAL ACTIVITY

There is a clear relationship between higher unemployment and higher levels of criminal activity among addicts (e.g., Faupel, 1988; Platt,

1986). Not surprisingly, it has been concluded that addicts appear to rely less on legitimate work than on criminal or quasi-criminal activity as a source of income to maintain their habits (Flaherty, Kotranski, & Fox, 1984; Kozel, DuPont, & Brown, 1972; Nurco, Cisin, & Balter, 1981). Marsh and Simpson (1986) found dramatic decreases in criminal involvement clearly evident after treatment admission.

The relationship between crime and the maintenance of addiction has also been found among those involved in vocational rehabilitation programs (Brewington, Deren, Arella, & Randell, 1990). The most detailed study of this relationship was probably that of Faupel (1988); for this reason, it is reviewed here in some detail. Faupel (1988) hypothesized that when a person is legally employed, he or she has neither the time nor the need to obtain money through illicit sources, and that employment represents the shift of the addict from the drug subculture to mainstream culture. This relationship may be more complex, however. In a study conducted by Anglin et al. (1988), the percentage of addicts who were employed remained fairly stable across the addiction career. However, as the percentage of time spent working decreased, the percentage of persons reported committing property crimes increased, and vice versa. This finding suggests that legal employment itself may not be as significant as the amount of money earned through employment. The percentage of individuals arrested for drug-related offenses also follows this same pattern, thus explaining the need for more money. Faupel (1988) further illuminated the complexity of the relationship between crime and addiction in a careful analysis of the employment–criminality relationship in addicts. He examined addict criminality across legal employment levels (full time, part time, unemployed, or not in labor force), occupational categories (white collar, skilled–semiskilled, or unskilled), and crime types (personal, property, drug sale, or public order offenses) to test the hypothesis that occupational status and increased employment levels inhibited criminal involvement.

Using data from interviews with 544 daily heroin users in five cities, Faupel (1988) found only partial support for his hypothesis in that the average number of crimes in which his respondents were involved was greatest at the two extreme ends of his level of employment scale. Unemployed respondents (i.e., those not legally employed) had the highest levels of criminal activity, followed, in descending order, by full-time workers, part-time workers, and those not in the labor force (students, homemakers, etc.). When Faupel examined occupational status, however, he found that skilled and semiskilled workers reported the highest levels of criminal involvement, followed by white-collar employees and unskilled workers. Among women, the pattern was different, with the highest level of criminal involvement among unskilled workers, followed by white-collar, skilled, and semiskilled workers. When Faupel examined type of criminal activity, different patterns emerged. Women not in the labor force tended to commit the most property crimes, and both men and women who were employed full time tended to commit the most drug sale offenses (Faupel, 1988). For all crimes except public order offenses (i.e., prostitution, procuring, gambling, and alcohol offenses), full-time workers reported higher averages than part-time workers. Furthermore, with the exception of property crimes committed by women, full-time employees reported more criminal activities than did those not in the labor force. These findings appear to fly in the face of the belief that increased employment will result in decreased criminal activity, as well as the conclusions of Anglin et al. (1988) that hours worked and money earned are more significant than employment alone.

The study by Metzger (1987) similarly found criminal involvement to play only a minor role in explaining the current employment status of methadone clients. Criminal involvement was found to be related strongly to the acquisition of employment for Blacks but not to be related to acquisition of employment for Whites. Criminal involvement was found not to be related to the pattern of employment for either Blacks or Whites.

EMPLOYMENT AND DRUG ABUSE TREATMENT

Entry into treatment and retention in treatment may have varying effects on employment. These effects are examined here from several perspectives. In considering the results of these studies, however, it should be kept in mind that vocational or employment services, or both, do not generally appear to be readily available to clients of addiction treatment programs. Hubbard (1981), for example, in his 1977 survey of 162 drug abuse treatment programs, found that only 9% of programs had funds specifically devoted to vocational services. Similarly, Senay, Dorus, and Joseph (1981) found that more than half the clients they studied reported that no employment-related services were available in their treatment programs. Joe, Simpson, and Hubbard (1991) reported that although 39.8% of the clients in their study of methadone maintenance programs were in need of employment services, only 8.8% actually received such services. These findings are perhaps explained by the fact that client vocational and employment needs, in contrast to other service needs, are typically given a low priority by programs (Arella, Deren, Randell, & Brewington, 1990a).

Pretreatment Employment and Treatment Outcome

Vaillant (1988), after examining admission variables predicting outcome at 12 years in a sample of treated heroin addicts, found that 63% of his stably abstinent group (n = 30), in contrast to 0% of his sustained addiction group (n = 30), had been employed for half of their adult lives before admission. Marsh and Simpson (1986) examined the posttreatment addiction careers of 84 female and 91 male addicts enrolled in methadone maintenance programs between 1969 and 1972. These addicts were interviewed at 6-year and 12-year intervals after admission to treatment. Employment was found to have improved over that time but was directly related to the employment that had occurred before treatment enrollment. The percentage of female addicts employed for 1 month or more increased from 49% in the year before enrollment to 54% at the 12th year posttreatment, a change that is consistent with the employment status of women in the general population between 1970 and 1980 (U.S. Bureau of the Census, 1993). The percentage of those with 6 or more months of employment increased from 25% to 34%. For men, the percentage with 1 or more months of employment increased from 65% to 68%, both rates being lower than those of the general population in 1970 and 1980 (79.7% and 77.4%, respectively; U.S. Bureau of the Census, 1993). Unlike in the general population, however, increased employment was reported at intake and at 12-year follow-up. For those employed for 6 or more months in the previous year, an increase of 14% to 52% was reported. Marsh and Simpson (1986) concluded that posttreatment differences in employment were more closely related to pretreatment differences (i.e., employment history) than to differential treatment effects. Elsewhere, Simpson (1984) summarized the results of several studies that found that a poor employment history *before* and *during* treatment was predictive of unemployment *after* treatment.

A retrospective examination of the employment patterns of 342 methadone clients in New York City conducted by Rothenberg (1978) revealed that, for clients remaining in treatment for a full year, the best predictor of employment during treatment was a history of work before treatment entry. Similarly, Hall, Loeb, LeVois, and Cooper (1981) found that lack of a recent history of employment before treatment was a powerful predictor of failure to obtain employment. When treatment outcome was examined as a function of client source of income before treatment, McLellan et al. (1981) found substantial treatment improvement among clients who had received their pretreatment income from jobs and illegal activities in contrast to those clients who had received their income from public assistance, despite general equivalence among clients in terms of demography, educational levels, and treatment histories.

Pretreatment employment has also been found to be related to remaining in naltrexone treatment (Capone et al., 1986). Of those in Capone et al.'s study who remained on medication for more than 60 days, more than 60% were employed; only 48% of those who did not remain in treatment were employed. At termination, 61% of those who remained more than 60 days were employed, with only 33% of those terminated at fewer than 60 days employed. Not all of those who were terminated had completed treatment, but the authors assumed that longer treatment leads to improvement (Capone et al., 1986). Employment before treatment entry has also been found to be associated with retention in methadone maintenance treatment (Ruiz, Langrod, Lowinson, & Marcus, 1977).

Craig (1980) reported a similar finding, namely a 31% employment rate among 322 methadone clients on entry into treatment, but an employment rate at entry of 61% for those clients who remained in treatment for 12 months. Not surprisingly, it should be noted that these results are similar to those obtained in outcome studies of alcohol dependence treatment, in which the best predictor of employment at follow-up after treatment has been found to be work history before treatment (Walker, Sanchez-Craig, & Bornet, 1982). Similarly, greater employment, either alone (Sullivan, Targum, & Avani, 1982) or together with age and being married, has been found to characterize those individuals most likely to succeed in treatment for alcohol dependence (Ornstein & Cherepon, 1985).

A relationship between pretreatment primary source of income from employment and improvement in drug use, legal status, and psychological functioning for a group of addicts in methadone treatment was found by McLellan et al. (1981). However, those whose primary source of income had been criminal activity appeared to have had the greatest gains on the three outcome variables. Changes in source of income from illegal to legal were noted for this subpopulation (McLellan et al., 1981). Those individuals whose primary income source was public assistance fared poorest. A later study conducted by Kosten, Rounsaville, and Kleber (1987b) produced different findings, however, and reported improvement among all three groups, with the most consistent gains made by those whose primary source of income was public assistance.

Treatment and Employment: Posttreatment Measurement Only

Given that social adjustment through employment is a major goal of drug treatment, it is not surprising that most intervention studies for addicts, even when not focusing on interventions targeted on employment, include data on employment status after treatment as a measure of success. One such study found that 56.5% of clients successfully completing a detoxification program or attaining abstinence were employed or in school, in comparison with 43.5% of completers who were unemployed (Swartz & Jabara, 1974).

Treatment and Obtaining Employment: Premeasurement and Postmeasurement

In studies comparing employment at the time of enrollment and employment at discharge, improvement in the employment rate is usually found, with a wide variation in the magnitude of that change. Harlow and Anglin (1984), for example, found an increase of almost 18% in regular employment (from approximately 60% to approximately 70%) for heroin addicts in methadone maintenance. The increase was approximately concurrent with enrollment. This study also showed a downward curve in employment in the 10 years before enrollment in methadone treatment and fairly steady maintenance of employment for the 6 years after treatment entry (Harlow & Anglin, 1984).

An increase in employment from approximately 29% to almost 47% was found in a sample of clients in methadone maintenance and drug-free outpatient treatment from 30 days before the point of entry to 4-month follow-up (Aiken et al., 1984). There was, however, a great deal of variation in these increases by type of counselor. Employment increased from 29% to 48% for those clients who had been seen by professional counselors, from 30% to 55% for those who had been seen by paraprofessionals who were not ex-addicts, and from 28% to 40% for those who had been seen by paraprofessionals who were ex-addicts (Aiken et al., 1984). None of these increases were found to be significant, but significant differences were found between the time of first client interview and follow-up for all three counselor groups (Aiken et al., 1984).

McLellan, Childress, Griffith, and Woody (1984) evaluated employment in the month before admission and in the month before a 6-month evaluation for drug abuse clients enrolled in methadone maintenance or a therapeutic community. They also ranked the clients by psychiatric severity (low, moderate, and high severity). The number of days worked increased for each of the six groups. For methadone clients, the increases were from 12 to 16 days among those with low psychiatric severity, from 15 to 18 days among those with moderate severity, and from 8 to 10 days among those with high severity. For therapeutic community patients, the increases were from 8 to 16 days among those with low severity, from 10 to 19 days among those with moderate severity, and from 6 to 9 days among those with high severity. Only the increases for therapeutic community patients with low and moderate severity levels were statistically significant.

A second study examining pretreatment and posttreatment employment, measured by the number of days worked during the month before intake and during the month before a 6-month, posttreatment follow-up, found significant increases (Arndt, McLellan, & O'Brien, 1984). The increases were significant both for those enrolled in a therapeutic community and those receiving naltrexone. When the two interventions were compared, however, the relationship was stronger for the first group, although not significantly so (Arndt, McLellan, & O'Brien, 1984).

A third study of this type reported the employment rates of alcohol abusers and drug abusers treated at three facilities (McLellan et al., 1986). The facilities differed by sponsorship and treatment offered. The first was a private treatment center outside Philadelphia offering inpatient, abstinence-oriented, therapeutic community treatment. The second was a private psychiatric hospital in New Jersey at which inpatient treatment averaging 28 days' duration was offered to a predominantly middle-class clientele. The third was an urban Veterans Administration (VA) clinic in Philadelphia offering methadone maintenance, narcotic antagonist, drug-free outpatient, and abstinence-oriented therapeutic community treatment. Overall, the number of days worked by alcohol abusers in the month before treatment and at 6 months increased significantly. However, when the treatment facility was considered, only those receiving treatment at the private center improved significantly. Drug abusers also showed overall improvement in the number of days worked, with the VA hospital and the private treatment center showing significant results (McLellan et al., 1986).

Joe and Simpson (1983) examined employment among opiate addicts over a 6-year period from 1972–1973 through 1978–1979. These addicts were divided into five types: those who became abstinent before entry into treatment, those whose abstinence followed entry into treatment or incarceration, those whose abstinence was delayed but who did not enter treatment or jail, those who continued their use of opiates, and those who substituted other nonopioid drugs (including alcohol) for their opiate use. Improvements in employment (measured as percentage of months employed) were found. Increases in percentage of months employed ranged from 53.92% to 55.14% for immediate abstainers (2.3% improvement) and from 38.05% to 52.94% for those abstaining after treatment or incarceration (a 39.1% improvement). For those who continued their drug use, a decrease in employment of more than 13% (from 35.89% to 31.19%) was also found.

A 1-year and 6-year follow-up study conducted by Simpson and Friend (1988) discussed the changes in employment for opiate addicts in four treatment modalities: methadone maintenance, therapeutic community, drug-free treatment, and detoxification. Simpson and Friend also divided the sample by judicial status. Employment rates of between 53% and 64% were found in the 1st year after admission to treatment both for the methadone and therapeutic community clients and for the drug-free treatment clients with judicial involvement. Improvements of between 8.8% and 15.8% were found after 6 years for these groups. Greater increases in employment were found for the drug-free treatment (50% to 63%, an increase of 26%) and detoxification (41% to 56%, an increase of 36.6%) clients with no judicial involvement. The greatest improvement was for the detoxification clients with judicial involvement, whose employment rate increased from 43% to 74%.

A series of studies examined the addiction careers of Anglo and Hispanic substance abusers in southern California (Anglin, Booth, Kao, Harlow, & Peters, 1987; Anglin et al., 1988; Anglin, Hser, & Booth, 1987).

These studies compared the period of time from entry into treatment to discharge from treatment (Period 1) with the period from discharge from treatment to time of interview (Period 2). Little change in employment rates for Anglo men from Period 1 (85%, n = 193) to Period 2 (87%, n = 171) was found (Anglin et al., 1988). Employment for Hispanic men did increase from 72% (n = 89) to 83% (n = 81%) between the two periods. An interesting result was that the mean percentage of time spent working decreased between the two periods by almost 13% for Anglo males and more than 15% for Hispanic males (Anglin et al., 1988). Large increases in the percentage of women who worked were also found, particularly among Anglo women, whose employment increased 58.6% (from 46% to 73% between Period 1 and Period 2; Anglin, Hser, & Booth, 1987). The magnitude of the increase for Hispanic women was almost as large (43.3%), but the actual increase was substantially smaller (from 30% to 43%; Anglin, Hser, & Booth, 1987). Similar increases in the percentage of non-incarcerated time spent working were found for men in "real couples" (defined as having been in a relationship for at least 1 year) and for both men and women in "pseudocouples" (participants selected by the researchers to match as closely as possible the real couples; Anglin, Booth, et al., 1987). For women in real couples, the percentage of time spent working dropped 35% from 27% to 20% (Anglin, Booth, et al., 1987).

Some studies have shown no relationship between employment and success in treatment. Each of these studies has used a single measure of success: abstinence or retention in treatment. Dolan, Black, Penk, Robinowitz, and DeFord (1986) found that employment was not different for those who were abstinent or nonabstinent. No discernible difference was found in the employment rates of opiate addicts in four treatment conditions at entry and 2.5 years after initial evaluation (Kosten, Rounsaville, & Kleber, 1987b).

TREATMENT MODALITIES AND VOCATIONAL SERVICES

In methadone maintenance, Dole and Nyswander (1965) envisioned supportive services, such as vocational training, as important to the successful treatment of addicts. Hubbard et al. (1989) suggested that although service intensity (in terms of number of supportive services received by clients) seemed to be increasing during 1979–1981, the availability of services across programs varied. Hubbard et al. (1989) also examined receipt of services in drug-free outpatient treatment, finding only 13% of Treatment Outcome Prospective Study (TOPS) clients reporting receiving job or financial services. Among the drug-free outpatient programs studied in the TOPS, only one reported that it specialized in vocational rehabilitation (Hubbard et al., 1989).

In a national study of outpatient drug abuse treatment, Price et al. (1991) reported that 35.9% of programs provided employment counseling. On the whole, employment counseling was more prevalent in methadone maintenance than drug-free programs, with 35.1% of methadone programs in community mental health centers, 59.4% of hospital-based methadone programs, and 47.3% of other methadone programs providing this service. In addition, referral to vocational rehabilitation programs outside the treatment setting was infrequently reported, with 2.8% of all programs indicating that such referrals were provided.

For those in residential treatment, Hubbard et al. (1989) found that employment history was important but that other factors (e.g., gender) played a significant role in predicting posttreatment employment. They observed that although male clients in outpatient treatment were more likely than female clients to hold full-time employment, female clients who participated in residential treatment were more likely than male clients to be employed full time. They suggested that the stronger emphasis on vocational services in residential treatment "may help residential clients surmount obstacles to employment, such as sex bias and a history of drug abuse treatment" (Hubbard et al., 1989, p. 137).

EMPLOYMENT AND RELAPSE TO ADDICTION

It is a commonly held belief that addicts require repeated episodes of treatment to attain what is commonly thought of as a "cure" (e.g., Platt, 1986). The extent to which relapse and the "revolving door" to treatment are inevitable receives a great deal of attention (e.g., Marlatt & Gordon, 1985; Vaillant, 1988).

An absence of adequate problem-solving skills exacerbates the stress and anxiety experienced by the addict. In the workplace, this lack of skills and emotional stress may result in work failure for the ex-addict (e.g., Hermalin, Husband, & Platt, 1990; Platt & Metzger, 1987). The loss of a job is clearly associated with relapse (Fisher & Anglin, 1987). Examining associations between postrelease circumstances and the behavior of youthful heroin offenders on parole, Platt and Labate (1976) found steady employment and absence of drug use to be related to parole success and to each other.

Anglin and Fisher (1987) identified a sequence of events in the treated addict's life that leads not only to relapse but to incarceration. Data were obtained from almost 300 admissions to methadone programs in California and analyzed for rates of retention, incarceration, addiction, crime, dealing, and loss of employment. In Anglin and Fisher's schema, the onset of any drug use by a recovering addict was followed (in order) by the loss of a job, the start of dealing in illicit drugs, discharge from the treatment program, readdiction to the primary drug of abuse, participation in criminal behavior, and incarceration.

Vaillant (1966), examining factors associated with absence of relapse, concluded that a year of parole was much more effective in preventing relapse than either a short period of imprisonment or voluntary hospitalization. He related this to the fact that parole officers required proof, on a weekly basis, of employment in individuals who had previously believed that they could never hold a job. Citing similar findings for addicts who performed well in the highly structured setting of the armed forces, Vaillant (1988) concluded that "work provides structure to the addict's life and structure interferes with addiction" (p. 1154).

VOCATIONAL REHABILITATION PROGRAMS FOR DRUG ABUSERS

Vocational rehabilitation is generally viewed as the most effective means of refocusing drug abusers toward the world of work and, subsequently, mainstream society (M. P. Deren & Randell, 1990). Rehabilitation typically includes assessment of individual vocational needs, counseling, skills training, and job placement. A number of vocational rehabilitation programs for addicted populations have been attempted. These programs, providing one or more of a range of interventions including supported employment, job placement, training in job-seeking skills, and employment readiness training, have met with varying success.

Supported Work Programs

Supported work refers to subsidized employment characterized by intensive, ongoing support for clients with severe disabilities (Kreutzer & Morton, 1988). Supported employment involves job-site training, ongoing assessment, and, frequently, job-site intervention. It can be used with individuals whose background would indicate difficulties in obtaining or maintaining employment and is often recommended for drug abusers as a likely solution to employment problems. It generally involves on-site rather than classroom or other preparatory training and takes place in a real work setting, with wages and benefits comparable to those of other workers of similar experience (Groah, Goodall, Kreutzer, Sherron, & Wehman, 1990). Three types of supported work projects (described in the sections to follow) have been conducted with drug abusers.

The Wildcat Experiment

This program was the first large-scale, random-assignment, controlled study of vocational rehabilitation in drug treatment. It was initiated by the

VERA Institute of Justice and targeted ex–drug addicts (most of whom were methadone clients) and ex-offenders in New York City (Friedman, 1978). Over the 4 years of its existence, this demonstration project provided employment to more than 4,000 individuals, including 604 drug treatment clients, 80% of whom were involved in methadone programs. The project's approach was unique. Rather than using the traditional approach of providing job training and placement, it sought to restructure jobs so that these chronically unemployed people's chances of maintaining employment could be maximized. Participants were randomly assigned to an experimental group, in which jobs would be made available, or to a control group, in which members would receive only those services offered by the referring treatment agencies.

Those in the experimental group were assigned to jobs in groups of 3 to 7 under a crew chief, who was also a participant. The supervisors placed equal emphasis on the rehabilitative needs of the participants and the production goals of the job. Forty percent of these jobs were classified as clerical or paraprofessional, 30% as maintenance, 14% as social or public service, 8% as construction related, and the remaining 8% as messenger positions.

It was hypothesized, in this project, that chronically unemployed people would work if they could obtain jobs, that they would keep the jobs for an extended period if the jobs were structured properly, that they would be productive in a supported work environment, and that the program would prepare the participants for jobs in the nonsubsidized labor market. At the conclusion of the period of supported work, efforts were made to place participants in nonsupported jobs.

Data were collected at intake and at follow-ups during the next 3 years. The findings provided support for all four hypotheses. Of the 302 participants offered jobs under the Wildcat program, all but 30 showed up for work. More than half of those who started work stayed on the job for at least a year. The typical supported work participant was absent 1 day in 10. About one third of Wildcat workers "graduated" to nonsubsidized jobs, and most kept these jobs for at least 6 months. The longer an employee was involved in the program, the more likely the employee was to find subsequent employment. The cost–benefit ratio was found to be 1:1.12, with $15,405 produced for each $13,127 spent. No differences were found with respect to drug use (Friedman, 1978).

Several problems complicated the interpretation of the Wildcat findings. For instance, the intervention itself was diffuse and insufficiently articulated, thus limiting the possibility of replication. Also, one third of the original sample dropped out, including the 30 participants from the experimental group who failed to take jobs assigned to them. Hall (1984), in the only comprehensive critique of the Wildcat experiment, correctly pointed out that these 30 clients probably were least motivated and that their exclusion probably increased the difference in outcomes.

National Supported Work Demonstration Project

Like the Wildcat experiment, this project provided supported work for people commonly faced with severe employment problems (in this case, approximately 8,696 individuals; Dickinson & Maynard, 1981). Targeted to chronically unemployed individuals, the study included ex-addicts ($n = 1,124$), former psychiatric patients and alcoholics ($n = 554$), ex-offenders ($n = 3,384$), recipients of Aid to Families with Dependent Children ($n = 1,766$), and youths ($n = 1,867$). Participants were recruited from 15 cities throughout the United States and were randomly assigned to an experimental or a control condition.

The experimental condition placed workers in jobs within a supportive environment for a period of up to 18 months. Work expectations were increased over this period, with the intent of developing job skills and appropriate work habits, to prepare participants to enter the job market on completion of the project. Those in the control condition were placed in regular employment settings.

At the initial follow-up, few differences were found between the group of ex-addict experimentals and the controls on the variables of employment status, hours worked, or earnings. Follow-up at 36 months, however, showed moderately strong differences, with 48% of the experimental group employed and 31.6% of the controls employed.

Manpower Demonstration Supported Work Project

This study (Board of Directors, Manpower Demonstration Research Corporation, 1980) involved 10,043 participants, of whom approximately 1,200 were primarily ex-addicts in methadone maintenance programs, although some were drawn from drug-free programs. A 12-month supported work period was used, following which assistance was provided in finding employment. A 1-year follow-up yielded data on 974 ex-addict participants.

The results indicated that participants in the experimental group had worked more hours than controls and had higher employment rates; however, differences were much greater (and, thus, statistically significant) only for earlier, in contrast to later, entrants, apparently because of lower employment rates among early controls. The other findings were that arrest rates for the control group were lower, most noticeably during the period immediately after supported work; that methadone clients profited more from the program than did other drug treatment clients; and that drug and alcohol use did not differ as a function of participation in the supported work condition.

Again, problems such as the precise specification of the intervention and control over its delivery, particularly given the multisite nature of the experiment, attenuate the findings. Other problems noted by Hall (1984) involved lack of attention controls and handling of dropouts.

Job-Seeking and Placement Programs

Training, Rehabilitation, and Employment for Addicts in Treatment (TREAT) Program

The report on this major vocational program is out of print and currently unavailable. It has been discussed and evaluated, however, in a secondary source. As a major program in the field of job seeking and placement, it must be discussed despite the inability to independently analyze the data. TREAT (Bass & Woodward, 1978, cited in Hall, 1984) recruited clients from a large multimodality program and randomly assigned them to either vocational training or a control condition. Training was provided under the Comprehensive Employment and Training Act (1973). Clients assigned to vocational training showed a decrease in drug use and better treatment outcome but did not differ from controls with respect to retention in treatment or criminal behavior. With respect to employment, clients in the experimental group worked full time more often and earned higher salaries but did not differ from controls in terms of the number of weeks worked.

Hall (1984) critiqued the TREAT program evaluation findings, noting that bias may have existed in favor of the experimental condition because of a difference in employment rate between the experimental and control participants: 21% of the experimental participants and 35% of the controls had not worked in the 2 years before the study. Also, bias may have resulted from the practice of replacing early, but not later, dropouts from the experimental condition during the course of the study.

Employment Specialist Programs

Employment specialists were assigned to work with methadone, residential drug-free, or outpatient programs in New Jersey, Detroit, and Chicago in a study conducted by NIDA (1982). Control clinics were matched to those receiving the assistance of the specialists. The specialists worked either directly with clients or as staff consultants. Outcome was measured by global changes in clinic employment rates. No significant differences in employment were found, although significant improvements in treatment retention and reduction in illicit drug use were found in the experimental groups. It was also found that, of the 407 clients who did not see a specialist, 13% of those unemployed at admission became employed and 78% of those employed at admission remained employed. In a more recent study,

McLellan, Arndt, Metzger, Woody, and O'Brien (1993) compared outcomes (medical, employment, drug, legal, and psychiatric) for 92 methadone patients randomly assigned to receive standard methadone service, enhanced methadone services, or minimum methadone services. As part of the enhanced condition, a half-time employment counselor was employed. The counselor "conducted a series of workshops and group sessions designed to teach reading and prepare for a general equivalency diploma, as well as job-seeking and job-holding skills" (McLellan et al., 1993, p. 1955). Those in the enhanced condition had significant improvements from baseline to 6 months in number of days worked, percentage of patients working, and income from public assistance, with close to significant improvement in income from employment.

JOBS for Rehabilitated Drug Abusers

This project was implemented in Boston, Detroit, Chicago, and Philadelphia by NIDA and the Special Action Office for Drug Abuse Prevention (Double & Koenigsberg, 1977). It was designed as a demonstration project to obtain jobs for ex–drug abusers, provide screening and counseling to facilitate appropriate placement within these jobs, and furnish follow-up to employers and workers in terms of problems encountered.

The jobs ranged from professional to service positions, with most placements in clerical and laborer positions. Four hundred twenty-two clients were placed in jobs in the four cities. Almost 79% of the employers rated the performance of employees who were ex–drug abusers as the same as or better than that of their other employees. Their attitudes toward the job, ability to relate to co-workers, and desire to succeed were rated very high in comparison with other employees. Only in the areas of punctuality (20.7%) and absenteeism (34.5%) were the negative ratings for ex-abusers greater than 20%.

Personal Competency/Skill-Building Programs

Job Seekers' Workshop

This project (Hall, Loeb, LeVois, & Cooper, 1981) was designed to increase success in obtaining employment by improving the job-seeking and interviewing skills of a sample of methadone maintenance clients seeking employment in San Francisco. It is included in this section because it was a *behaviorally based, skill training* program.

In the initial study (Hall, Loeb, Norton, & Yang, 1977), 49 methadone maintenance clients were randomly assigned to the treatment condition ("the workshop"), a 12-hr manual-based program specifically designed to address the "particular behavioral difficulties which urban drug addicts show in job-seeking situations" (Hall et al., 1977, p. 227), or to a

1-hr orientation to available employment resources in the area. After the workshop, a rater unaware of client assignments evaluated clients on their "employability/acceptability" as trainees. Three months later, participants were contacted about whether they had found a job. Fifty percent of those in the experimental group, versus 14% of the controls, had found employment or placement in a training program. In addition, higher ratings were attained by the workshop participants for both interview skills and completed application forms.

The second study (Hall, Loeb, LeVois, & Cooper, 1981) assigned 60 job-seeking methadone maintenance clients to either the workshop (presented in 11 hr over 4 days) or the minimal contact (information only) condition. After the intervention, ratings (made by a rater unaware of condition assignments) on a scale tapping specific interview behaviors were more favorable for the experimental participants. By the end of the 3-month follow-up study, 15 of the 30 experimental participants had found employment, as opposed to 9 of the 30 participants in the control group. The differences between the two groups, however, were not statistically significant. (Interestingly, it was found that a work history within the previous 5 years was significantly related to finding a job, regardless of the condition to which the individual had been exposed.)

When a sample of 55 probationers and parolees with heroin abuse histories participated in a modified form of the Job Seekers' Workshop, the results were stronger (Hall, Loeb, Coyne, & Cooper, 1981). As before, the two groups were rated differently on scales measuring interview skills and rates of employment immediately after the intervention. Three months after the workshop ended, however, 86% of the experimental group had found employment, as opposed to 54% of the controls.

Hall (1984) herself pointed out some of the weaknesses of her studies in that there was no control for either time in treatment or client expectations and that group leader characteristics were only partly examined in one of the three studies (Hall, Loeb, Coyne, & Cooper, 1981). Nonetheless, Hall's studies represent an important step in research in this field: the application of principles of behavioral analysis to the problem of increasing employment among drug abusers.

One important aspect of the Job Seekers' Workshop studies was the evaluation by Sorensen et al. (1988) of the effectiveness of three methods of disseminating information (technology transfer) about the workshop to drug treatment programs in six states. Sorensen et al.'s study provides important information regarding the dissemination of any successful program in this area. Sorensen and his colleagues (1988) attempted to target individual treatment programs rather than high-level decision makers or system planners who control organizational resources or policy. One hundred seventy-two drug treatment programs were randomly assigned to receive printed materials only, printed materials plus on-site technical assistance, printed materials plus training at a conference, or no intervention. These dissemination methods reflect the techniques used since the late 1960s (Hall, Sorensen, & Loeb, 1988). At follow-up 3 months later, the highest adoption rate was for those programs that had involved site visits (28%), followed by those in the conference (19%), printed material (4%), and control (0%) conditions. Residential treatment facilities were more likely to adopt the program than were outpatient drug-free or methadone maintenance programs.

When another criterion defining adoption (implementing the workshop or adopting elements of it) was used, adoption rates increased 31.3% for the programs involving site visits and 25.8% and 5.6%, respectively, for programs in the conference and printed materials only conditions (the adoption rate did not increase in the control condition; Hall et al., 1988). Increased rates were also found for a subsample of clinics followed through 9 months after dissemination (Hall et al., 1988).

Because random assignment to the dissemination methods was important to the conduct of the study, little effort was made to assess which programs were unmotivated to adopt or which programs had characteristics making them conducive to adoption (Sorensen et al., 1988). When programs were queried as to why they did not adopt the workshop, concerns included time, staff, and funding limitations, as well as lack of involvement of those higher in the drug treatment system (Hall et al., 1988).

Sorensen et al. (1988) and Hall et al. (1988) concluded that those dissemination methods that involved personal contact (site visits and conferences) produced more adoption than did the use of printed materials alone and that residential treatment programs, in comparison with outpatient drug-free or methadone programs, were more likely to adopt the workshop. These findings clearly indicate the superiority of planned dissemination over dissemination through traditional academic channels (i.e., paper presentation and publication) alone. The authors noted that the finding that residential programs adopted the workshop at a higher rate was not surprising given these programs' greater likelihood of including employment as a particular focus in later stages of treatment. Perhaps the most important finding was that in-person contact with programs appeared to have been absolutely essential for adoption to have taken place.

Employment Readiness Skill Intervention

The objectives of this project (Platt et al., 1993) were to document patterns of employment among methadone clients and to develop and implement a program, based on interpersonal cognitive problem-solving training (i.e., Platt, Prout, & Metzger, 1986; Platt, Taube, Duome, & Metzger, 1988), designed to assist these clients to identify and respond to their personal employment barriers, thus readying them for work (Platt & Metzger, 1987). The theoretical basis of the project was that effective coping with employment barriers would lead to higher employment rates.

Participants were recruited from methadone clinics in Philadelphia and southern New Jersey. Participants were randomly assigned either to an experimental group that received a series of 10 small-group workshop sessions in addition to regular methadone treatment or to a control group that received methadone treatment only. The 10 sessions addressed the following issues: the value of work, barriers to employment, assessing resources to overcome barriers, identifying personal skills and strengths, projecting positive images, developing networks, setting realistic goals, assessing alternative employment-seeking strategies and the consequences of these strategies, defining success and failure, and taking responsibility for one's own behavior. Training on overcoming the barriers to employment included discussions of motivation, education, experience, the job market, job-seeking skills, personal issues, transportation, and child care.

Six months after the training, employment was found to be significantly higher for those participating in the experimental condition (26.9% at 6-month follow-up vs. 13.4% at baseline) than for those involved in the control condition (9.5% at 6-month follow-up vs. 11.1% at baseline). Client sex, source of financial support, previous job training, past history of unemployment compensation, perceived job problems related to work history, level of schooling completed, and perception of job availability were found to be unrelated to employment at outcome. Only race was significantly related to employment at follow-up, with Black participants demonstrating greater benefits (i.e., rate of employment) after the intervention than Whites.

The gains in this study were, however, limited to the 6-month follow-up point. At a 12-month follow-up, the experimental and control groups did not differ, with the experimental group losing gained ground. Also, this study, as has been the case with other employment interventions, suffered from a significant loss of the original sample (Platt et al., 1993).

INTERVENTIONS FROM OTHER FIELDS AND POPULATIONS

The Job Club

The Job Club (Azrin & Besalel, 1982; Azrin, Flores, & Kaplan, 1975) is aimed at helping clients identify and obtain jobs that will promote their mental health. Although the Job Club is not directed specifically at drug abusers, such clients have been included in samples of primarily nonaddicts. This program, which involves a standardized, manual-driven intervention (Azrin & Besalel, 1982), is based on a conception of job seeking as a social interaction in which obtaining job leads is the initial response of a chain of behaviors (Jones & Azrin, 1973).

One study (Azrin & Philip, 1979) used the intervention with people with severe handicaps, including alcohol or drug problems, that limited job seeking. One hundred fifty-four clients were randomly assigned to either the Job Club condition or a standard counseling condition. At 6 months postintervention, 95% of the clients had obtained jobs, in comparison with 28% of the controls. In addition, the Job Club participants obtained jobs with a higher median salary and obtained jobs earlier (10 days vs. 30 days) than control subjects. Similar findings were obtained in a later evaluation of the Job Club program with welfare recipients (Azrin, Philip, Thienes-Hontos, & Besalel, 1980).

The approach was specifically recommended for use with alcoholics by its developers (Sisson & Azrin, 1989), who noted that jobs requiring long work hours followed by long periods of unemployment encourage the use of alcohol during times of hiatus to relieve boredom. They stated that the Job Club would help clients to identify the link between the jobs they choose and their drinking behavior and to seek other kinds of work in appropriate instances. Clients would then be trained on approaches designed to obtain such a job (e.g., discovery of initial job lead, first contact with potential employers, and interview techniques).

Improving Interview Skills

Among the most commonly used techniques to improve chances of employment has been instruction to improve interviewing skills (Hall, Loeb, Norton, & Yang, 1977; Hollandsworth, Dressel, & Stevens, 1977; Kelly, Laughlin, Claiborne, & Patterson, 1979; Venardos & Harris, 1973). Such programs have been both self-contained (Hollandsworth et al., 1977; Kelly et al., 1979; Venardos & Harris, 1973) and part of larger rehabilitation programs (e.g., methadone maintenance; Hall, Loeb, Norton, & Yang, 1977). This approach has been applied to college students as well as to mentally ill clients and other rehabilitation clients. Although employment has not necessarily been the outcome measured in these studies, all have found improvement in skills deemed important for successful job interviewing.

Various techniques of teaching interviewing skills, including discussion only, approaches to modify behavior, videotaping, and role-playing (Hall, Loeb, Norton, & Yang, 1977; Hollandsworth et al., 1977; Venardos & Harris, 1973), have been used. When the techniques have been compared, behavioral interventions have been found to be more effective than discussion (Hollandsworth et al., 1977).

BARRIERS TO VOCATIONAL REHABILITATION
AND EMPLOYMENT

Even an optimal rehabilitation program cannot overcome all of the structural or societal barriers to employment that may be faced by recovering addicts (Arella, Deren, Randell, & Brewington, 1990a). Not surprisingly, employment has been found to be inversely proportional to the number of social disadvantages for each addict (Hermalin, Steer, Platt, & Metzger, 1990; Suffet & Brotman, 1976). Social disadvantages, defined as the absence of a high school diploma, the presence of a criminal record, and minority group status, have been found to decrease the likelihood of employment (Suffet & Brotman, 1976).

Brewington, Arella, Deren, and Randell (1987) categorized the obstacles faced by drug abusers in their use of vocational services under the classifications *client level* (financial disincentives and psychological factors), *program level* (treatment philosophy and program priorities, staff development and coordination, choice of strategy, criminal justice issues, and strategy information dissemination), *client–program interactions* (client–counselor relationship, discrepant perceptions of vocational issues, and joint commitment to goals of treatment), and *external–societal* (special needs of women and employer issues).[2] Evaulation of clients in four methadone programs (one each in Buffalo, Pittsburgh, Milwaukee, and San Jose) before assignment to training and employment programs indicated that the following types of barriers mediated against client employment: family and societal barriers (including lack of social skills, inadequate clothing, and disincentives from public financial support), job-related barriers (including lack of education and training, minimal work experience, employment gaps, and lack of needed equipment), medical and emotional barriers (including continued drug use, current methadone use, unrealistic goals, low self-esteem, and lack of motivation), program-level barriers (including poor staff training regarding vocational services, lack of referrals, and lack of integration of vocational rehabilitation programs), and structural barriers (including employer bias, trainer bias, tight job market, bureaucracy, and red tape; French, Dennis, McDougal, Karuntzos, & Hubbard, 1992).

A survey of employers and personnel managers conducted in the early 1970s revealed a decreasing order of acceptance for employment by ethnic background, physical disability, criminal record, and mental instability (Colbert, Kalish, & Chang, 1973). A more recent study of barriers to employment for homeless people found that 31% were prevented from obtaining employment as a result of their drug use, the second most-cited reason after lack of a high school education (Hagen, 1989). Given that

---

[2]The reader is referred to Brewington, Arella, Deren, and Randell (1987) for a more detailed discussion of obstacles to the use of vocational services than is possible here.

employers cannot legally terminate an employee simply because the employee is addicted and that employers are also responsible for the negligence of their employees, reluctance to hire addicted or formerly addicted individuals may be understandable, even if deplorable (Howard, 1990).

Even among those working in the field of addiction treatment or those whose interest in addicted individuals led them to attend a drug symposium, concern about hiring ex-addicts can be seen (Morton, 1976). Morton found that more than 30% of such individuals believed that poor attendance or performance worked against their hiring ex-addicts, whereas 13% feared thefts or violent crime. Responses to a 1-year demonstration project conducted by the Pennsylvania State Employment Service to provide support services to soon-to-be-released offenders (62% of whom were ex-addicts) confirmed the existence of this fear. Regardless of the occupational level at which the ex-addict–ex-offender found work, placement was difficult not only because of the individual's lack of skills and knowledge but because of employer attitudes. Some employers feared the ex-addict would resume his or her habit "and steal me blind" (Snyderman, 1974, p. 713).

The Venus Project

This project (M. P. Deren & Randell, 1988) was designed to identify the major obstacles to the provision and use of vocational services in drug treatment, as well as to implement and evaluate strategies to overcome these obstacles. Obstacles to vocational service use by drug abuse clients were identified through a literature review and a field study in four methadone clinics in New York City. Obstacles identified included public assistance disincentives to work, the client's fear of work, a lack of sufficiently trained professionals, the lower priority given to vocational services by clinics, understaffing, gender stereotyping, employer biases, and unrealistic or nonexistent client goals.

An expert panel recommended remedies to these problems, including the removal of welfare disincentives and the hiring of "vocational integrators" to work with clinic staff. The presence of such integrators was found to increase client participation in vocational programs. Changes in welfare disincentives were found to have resulted in only a small decline in the use of services. The strategy phase of the project lasted only 1 year, however, and a longer assessment period may have been needed to determine the full effect of the project.

In addition to structural and societal barriers, factors specific to the addict and to the availability of drug treatment services interfere with successful vocational rehabilitation. For the client, unrealistic expectations may severely hamper his or her ability to find work. In a study of 40 clients in four methadone maintenance clinics, only those individuals involved in rehabilitation programs were seen as having realistic vocational aspirations (i.e., those consonant with training or experience; Brewington et al., 1990). Even among those who were employed at that time, 25% had unrealistic vocational expectations (Brewington et al., 1990). The importance of cognitions (e.g., perceptions, set, and expectations) on the part of the addict appears to be particularly relevant. In the study by Metzger (1987), the absence of self-perceived work problems, together with the frequency of job-seeking behaviors, was most strongly associated with work status and pattern and job acquisition.

The psychiatric status of clients can also prevent their participation in either vocational rehabilitation or work (Arella, Deren, Randell, & Brewington, 1990b; Brewington et al., 1987; M. P. Deren & Randell, 1990), although some findings suggest that psychological symptomatology in methadone clients is more likely a consequence than a cause of unemployment (Metzger, 1987). Outside responsibilities (e.g., caretaking) that compete with participation in rehabilitation, income and type of insurance, and current criminal justice involvement have all been found to be related to participation (Arella et al., 1990a, 1990b; Brewington et al., 1987; M. P. Deren & Randell, 1990). Clients have also cited lack of motivation, fear of work, lack of child-care services, poor education, language barriers, and other factors as interfering with their participation (Brewington et al., 1990).

Elements specific to the treatment site can also interfere with the use of vocational rehabilitation services or employment of clients. Rehabilitation programs have been historically underfunded for such services, reflecting either a lower priority having been given to these services or the frequent medical–psychiatric orientation of drug treatment (Arella et al., 1990a; Brewington et al., 1987). The background of the counseling staff has also been found to be related to employment. Brown and Thompson (1975–1976) found employment rates of 58.1% for clients treated by ex-addict counselors and 70.0% for those treated by nonaddict counselors. Livingston et al. (1990) were undoubtedly correct when they stated that the development and implementation of effective vocational services in drug abuse treatment settings require well-trained staff who are both knowledgeable about the problems of clients with disabilities and skilled in developing appropriate interventions.

GENERAL DISCUSSION

Limitations

Several overall conclusions can be drawn from this review of the literature. One is that, over the last 20 years, there has been an increasing awareness of the importance of employment and employment-related issues in drug abuse treatment, together with a number of efforts to develop interventions for the purpose of increasing employment.

Relatively few interventions exist, however, and there are none without shortcomings that either limit their generalizability or raise questions about the worth of investing scarce program funds in applying them on a large scale. In instances in which an intervention appears to be powerful in other populations, such as in the case of Azrin's Job Club, further evidence supporting the applicability of the intervention to drug addicts is needed. Perhaps the most glaring absence in the employment literature, however, is that of *a comprehensive theory that can drive research*. Some of the existing interventions do derive from theories (e.g., behavior therapy, behavioral analysis, and interpersonal cognitive problem-solving theory), but *there are no theoretical schemas specific to employment and related issues.* Given the multiplicity of the variables affecting employment and the complexity of employment behavior itself, organizing theories are sorely needed. Merely changing the behavior or improving the skills of the addict will not sufficiently address societal attitudes, the job market, and other factors that complicate the training and employment of this population.

Another limitation of the present body of knowledge on the vocational rehabilitation of drug abusers is its extensive reliance on publicly funded clinics that tend to serve lower socioeconomic groups as sites for the conduct of the research on which it is derived. Even when research is sited in nonpublic clinics (i.e., proprietary programs), such clinics typically serve clients similar to those in public programs. It is highly likely that such programs typically attract a higher percentage of nonworking clients than do fully private programs that do not welcome research. Thus it is not possible to develop a completely accurate understanding of employment rates among all drug abusers. This criticism applies equally to almost all drug abuse research on users of "hard" drugs. Those clients treated in private residential treatment settings, for example, are rarely if ever included in treatment evaluation studies (Platt, 1995a, 1995b). Such settings are largely oriented toward treating employed individuals and their families (Gerstein & Harwood, 1990). Thus, the paucity of data on the clients of such programs represents a serious deficiency in current knowledge.

Issues for Future Research

Even after acknowledging the concerns just mentioned, however, there is a good deal to glean from the current literature, and a number of recommendations for future research can be made on the basis of the existing findings. These recommendations can be conceptualized as a preliminary agenda for a third generation of employment research. In the first generation, the work histories and habits of addicts were assessed. In the second generation, attempts to provide vocational rehabilitation leading to employment were instituted. The third generation would attempt to create and evaluate programs resulting from a synthesis of successful elements found in earlier studies. Such studies would enable researchers to determine which elements work for which clients and the configuration of elements needed to ensure successful outcomes.

It is critical that future research learn from the successes of the past and seek to answer the questions raised by previous research. For this reason, a presentation of some of the issues that should be addressed echoes the format of the previous discussion of employment research. Recommendations for future research studies and for program modification are also made.

Definition of Employment

The questions raised by the varying definitions of employment (e.g., income earned, days worked, weeks worked, and full time or part time) must be addressed, as must the time frame within which employment factors are examined (point in time or period of time). Consistent measurement tools must be adopted if comparisons across research studies are to be made. The *Documentation Standards 2 for the Treatment of Addictions* (Deutsche Gesselschaft für Suchtfroschund und Suchttherapie e. V. [Hrsg.], 1992), developed in Germany, may serve as a model for the development of measurement tools (Platt, Bühringer, Widman, Künzel, & Lidz, 1994).

Employment Patterns

Studies examining the variables unerlying the important role played by parents and significant others in modeling employment behaviors should be conducted. The study by Metzger (1987), for example, suggests that a salient family characteristic consistently associated with methadone clients' pattern of employment is the type and frequency of parental employment during the addict's childhood. Another issue here is that fewer job opportunities are available to those in poor neighborhoods, thus continuing the discouraging cycle of intergenerational unemployment (Tienda & Stier, 1991). Such findings indicating the importance of parental models and the familial route to influencing employment suggest that programs such as supported work be explored. Supported work could begin to act as a means of counteracting intergenerational patterns of unemployment in two ways: by replacing the example of an unemployed parent with an employed one and through prevention efforts directed at the children of addicted parents.

Further evaluation is needed regarding the special employment-related needs associated with membership in ethnic minority groups. Distinct differences appear to exist between Black and White methadone clients with respect to variables explaining employment (e.g., Metzger, 1987;

Metzger & Platt, 1983) and with respect to the outcome of the employment readiness intervention described earlier (Platt et al., 1993). This issue requires additional study.

Because many studies are limited to male clients, there is a lack of information on employment for female clients. For example, although the Drug Abuse Reporting Program research sample included women, the comparative analyses involved only men, because women were not available in sufficient numbers across modalities (i.e., methadone and drug-free outpatient treatment). Studies that oversample female populations or that are devoted solely to women should be initiated to examine gender differences.

Employment-related needs of women present a range of special problems, including the fact that women usually have more demands placed on them for child care than do men. As noted elsewhere (Mathis et al., 1994; Platt, 1995b), child-care services are needed that would provide female drug abusers with the time needed to acquire employment-related skills and to seek, gain, and maintain employment. There may, however, be other issues operative with respect to women entering employment in that women in the Mathis et al. (1994) study also were less likely than men to want or to be looking for work. For example, many women enter into drug use through their male partner and develop a dependent relationship during the addiction, relying on the man for the continuation of the habit. They may remain more dependent on men during and after treatment, thus necessitating preemployment interventions designed to socialize them into the workforce. On the other hand, research designed to examine female addicts in the workforce has noted a participation rate rather similar to that for all women. Further research on the special situations facing women and on their unique needs is called for.

Studies examining the predictive formulas of age, length of addiction, work history, treatment history, and employment outcomes need to be conducted. Finally, attention must be paid to the individuals for whom vocational rehabilitation is appropriate and those for whom physical or emotional disability makes employment unrealistic.

Role of Employment in the Development of Addiction

The evidence strongly suggests that preaddiction employment status is associated with the start of addiction, with unemployed people more likely to become addicts than employed people. More intensive qualitative studies leading to a greater understanding of the behaviors and attitudes underlying preaddiction employment need to be conducted. Such studies would allow the assessment of the possibility of the prevention of addiction through early identification and intervention in high-risk groups.

Treatment Modalities and Vocational Services

Drug treatment programs need to make a serious effort to provide vocational/employment services, particularly in light of the importance of employment in the social (re)adjustment of addicts. As noted earlier (e.g., Hubbard, 1981; Senay et al., 1981), such services tend to be relatively nonexistent in drug abuse clinics, and the situation has become worse, if anything, during the past 10 years. Furthermore, staff members engaged in providing such services should have specific training in "what works" and should ideally provide services in accord with a predetermined protocol that allows for identification of personal barriers to employment and provides for their remediation. In addition, the appropriateness of specific vocational rehabilitation programs in different treatment modalities must be assessed; for example, the suitable programs for a 28-day inpatient treatment or detoxification program might differ from those used in long-term treatment.

Employment and Relapse to Addiction

Studies concerned with determining the role played by cognitions (e.g., sets, attitudes, perceptions, and expectations) in obtaining and maintaining employment are needed. Such studies would address the way in which cognitions influence motivation for work, job seeking, and use of vocational services. For instance, Hermalin, Steer, et al. (1990) found that clients who did "not know how to look for work," who "believed that no jobs were available," or who "lacked the desire to work" were approximately 3 times more likely than those not citing these and similar work-related problems to be unemployed.

General Vocational Rehabilitation Programs for Drug Abusers

Any model program needs to be carefully designed, implemented, and evaluated. As Hall (1984) has correctly pointed out, several studies using random assignment and control groups have suffered from ambiguities in interpretation because of such problems as poor definition of the intervention and failure to adhere to the experimental design, among others. The use of treatment manuals that would guide the intervention, allow for evaluation and revision of modular units requiring "adjustment," and permit replication of the intervention is essential to careful program design. Such manuals have been used in several studies with successful outcomes (e.g., Azrin et al., 1980; Hall et al., 1977; Platt et al., 1993). Other means of technology transfer must also be used and assessed so that the knowledge gained can be transmitted successfully (Sorensen et al., 1988). The provision of "booster sessions" to consolidate and maintain gains made in rehabilitative programs, thus minimizing relapse, may also be necessary.

Supported Work Programs

As a means of addressing criticisms of the rigor of the work required by supported work programs, procedures should be instituted that would involve gradual increases in the expectations placed on workers to ensure their ability to maintain jobs in the workplace. Furthermore, the impact of such procedures should be measured (e.g., Dickinson & Maynard, 1981).

Personal Competency and Skill Building

Clients need to be assisted in the identification of personal barriers to employment, development of personal skills and competencies needed to overcome such barriers, and maintenance of effective employment-related behaviors (Azrin & Besalel, 1982; Platt & Metzger, 1987). There is also a need for ongoing encouragement and support for attendance at vocational rehabilitation programs designed to assess individual vocational needs and to provide the counseling and skills training necessary to meet those needs (e.g., see S. Deren & Randell, 1988). In addition, attention to an evaluation of the most effective methods for increasing interviewing and job-seeking skills of addicts are necessary (e.g., see Hall, Loeb, Coyne, & Cooper, 1981; Hall, Loeb, LeVois, & Cooper, 1981; Hall et al., 1977; Hollandsworth et al., 1977). Clients who have never been a regular part of the workforce will need special attention in terms of identification of their personal strengths and weaknesses. There will also need to be a careful assessment of those client and workplace attributes that relate to success and identification of the most salient ones so that a proper "match" that maximizes positive outcomes can be attained.

Barriers to Vocational Rehabilitation and Employment

Attention should be paid to the significance of psychopathology and vocational participation in obtaining and maintaining employment. Given the importance of social participation to mental health and the high prevalence of personality disorders (especially antisocial personality), affective disorders (especially depressive disorders), and anxiety disorders (Havassy & Wasserman, 1992; Rounsaville, Weissman, Kleber, & Wilber, 1983) among drug abuse clients, two or three strategies might be followed. For example, strategies for combining mental health services—medications with vocational rehabilitation or habilitation programs, during both formal treatment and aftercare, should be developed. Also, research is needed to better understand the obstacles presented to vocational functioning by psychopathology (e.g., How is "fear of work" operationalized by the client? What are its roots?). These strategies and research should lead to the identification of a spectrum of interventions for drug abuse clients with psychiatric disorders and differing levels of impairment.

Further understanding is required concerning the relationship between the economic climate, particularly that at the local (and even neighborhood) level, and the employment of addicts. It should be determined whether attempts to provide employment to drug abusers are likely to be fruitless in an economic climate that undermines these attempts at rehabilitation. On the other hand, economic downturns do not last forever, and drug abusers need to be prepared to reenter the workforce when opportunities become available.

In addition, structural factors related to the willingness of employers to hire and train drug abuse clients must be considered to address the interplay of labor market and employer attitudes and to identify strategies that would increase the labor force participation of drug abuse clients. Appropriate provision of worker support services in the workplace would allow attention to be paid to the rehabilitative needs of clients "in the field" (e.g., Friedman, 1978). "Employer support services" would provide employers with guidance in terms of worker problems such as maintaining discipline, following work rules, and coping with relapse.

For an evaluation of the worth of such a program in the real world, it is perhaps important that it not only offer, for example, supported employment in its early stages, but that success be measured through the attainment and maintenance of employment outside of a sheltered or supported setting. Finally, studies assessing the maintenance of employment gains made by clients immediately after treatment should be conducted, and methods to encourage or increase employment later in the posttreatment career should be developed.

CONCLUSIONS

The literature reviewed in this article clearly demonstrates the validity of the long-held belief that employment is essential to the social rehabilitation of addicts and establishes employment as one reasonable measure of treatment success. The extent of employment after what was otherwise seen as successful treatment is less clearly delineated. A range of innovative interventions designed to increase the employability and employment of addicts has been presented here. Each of these programs has had some success, but none has provided the sole answer to meeting the vocational needs of this vulnerable population. What has also been demonstrated, however, is the need for future research and imaginative programs to continue the processes described.

One caveat should, however, be noted. As Brown et al. (1972) stated,

> A client's employability depends not only on his nonuse of illicit drugs,
> it depends as well on diverse factors such as the state of the economy,
> the attitudes of employers, the vocational and academic skills of the
> client, municipal and state law, and so on. (p. 395)

Failure to take into account these important environmental variables will result in an incomplete understanding of programs designed to reduce drug use, increase employment, or both. For employment to occur and be maintained, a complex interaction among client, intervention, and environment is required. Each must provide the appropriate set of circumstances but must not ignore the realities of the other factors involved.

REFERENCES

Aiken, L. S., LoSciuto, L. A., Ausetts, M. A., & Brown, B. S. (1984). Paraprofessional versus professional drug counselors: The progress of clients in treatment. *International Journal of the Addictions, 19*, 383–401.

Americans With Disabilities Act of 1990, 42 U.S.C.A. § 12101 *et seq.* (West 1993).

Anglin, M. D., Booth, M. W., Kao, C., Harlow, L. L., & Peters, K. (1987). Similarity of behavior within addict couples: II. Addiction related variables. *International Journal of the Addictions, 22*, 583–607.

Anglin, M. D., Booth, M. W., Ryan, T. M., & Hser, Y. (1988). Ethnic differences in narcotics addiction: II: Chicano and Anglo addiction career patterns. *International Journal of the Addictions, 23*, 1011–1027.

Anglin, M. D., & Fisher, D. G. (1987). Survival analysis in drug program evaluation: II. Partitioning treatment effects. *International Journal of the Addictions, 22*, 377–387.

Anglin, M. D., Hser, Y., & Booth, M. W. (1987). Sex differences in addict careers: IV. Treatment. *American Journal of Drug and Alcohol Abuse, 13*, 253–280.

Anglin, M. D., Hser, Y., & McGlothlin, W. H. (1987). Sex differences in addicts' careers. 2. Becoming addicted. *American Journal of Drug and Alcohol Abuse, 13*, 59–71.

Arella, L. R., Deren, S., Randell, J., & Brewington, V. (1990a). Structural factors that affect provision of vocational/educational services in methadone maintenance treatment programs. *Journal of Applied Rehabilitation Counseling, 21*, 19–26.

Arella, L. R., Deren, S., Randell, J., & Brewington, V. (1990b). Vocational functioning of clients in drug treatment: Exploring some myths and realities. *Journal of Applied Rehabilitation Counseling, 21*, 7–18.

Arndt, I., McLellan, A. T., & O'Brien, C. P. (1984). Abstinence treatments for opiate addicts: Therapeutic community or naltrexone? *National Institute on Drug Abuse Research Monographs, 49*, 275–281.

Azrin, N. H., & Besalel, V. B. (1982). *Finding a job.* Berkeley, CA: Ten Speed Press.

Azrin, N. H., Flores, T., & Kaplan, S. J. (1975). Job-finding club: A group assisted program for obtaining employment. *Behaviour Research and Therapy, 13*, 17–27.

Azrin, N. H., & Philip, R. A. (1979). The job club method for the job-handicapped: A comparative outcome study. *Rehabilitation Counseling Bulletin, 23*, 144–155.

Azrin, N. H., Philip, R. A., Thienes-Hontos, P., & Besalel, V. B. (1980). Comparative evaluation of the Job Club Program with welfare recipients. *Journal of Vocational Behavior, 16*, 133–145.

Bloch, H. I., Ellis, R. D., & Spielman, C. R. (1977). Use of employment criteria for measuring the effectiveness of methadone maintenance programs. *International Journal of the Addictions, 12*, 161–172.

Board of Directors, Manpower Demonstration Research Corporation. (1980). *Summary and findings of the National Supported Work Demonstration*. Cambridge, MA: Ballinger.

Brewington, V., Arella, L., Deren, S., & Randell, J. (1987). Obstacles to the utilization of vocational services: An analysis of the literature. *International Journal of the Addictions, 22*, 1091–1118.

Brewington, V., Deren, S., Arella, L., & Randell, J. (1990). Obstacles to vocational rehabilitation: The clients' perspectives. *Journal of Applied Rehabilitation Counseling, 21*, 27–37.

Brown, B. S., Dupont, R. L., Bass, U. F. III, Glendinning, S. T., Kozel, N. J., & Meyers, M. B. (1972). Impact of a multimodality treatment program for heroin addicts. *Comprehensive Psychiatry, 13*, 391–397.

Brown, B. S., & Thompson, R. E. (1975–1976). The effectiveness of formerly addicted and nonaddicted counselors on client functioning. *Drug Forum, 5*, 123–129.

Capone, T., Brahen, L., Condren, R., Kordal, N., Melchionda, R., & Peterson, M. (1986). Retention and outcome in a narcotic antagonist treatment program. *Journal of Clinical Psychology, 42*, 825–833.

Colbert, J. N., Kalish, R. A., & Chang, P. (1973). Two psychological portals of entry for disadvantaged groups. *Rehabilitation Literature, 34*, 194–202.

Comprehensive Employment and Training Act (CETA) of 1973. Title 29 U.S.C. § 801 *et seq.*

Craig, R. J. (1980). Effectiveness of low dose methadone maintenance for the treatment of inner-city heroin addicts. *International Journal of the Addictions, 15*, 701–710.

Cuskey, W. R., Berger, L. H., & Densen-Gerber, J. (1977). Issues in the treatment of female addiction: A review and critique of the literature. *Contemporary Drug Problems, 6*, 307–371.

Dale, R. T., & Dale, F. R. (1973). The use of methadone in a representative group of heroin addicts. *International Journal of the Addictions, 8*, 293–308.

DeLeon, G. (1984). Program-based evaluation research in therapeutic communities. In F. M. Timms & J. P. Ludford (Eds.), *Drug abuse treatment evaluation: Strategies, progress, and prospects* (NIDA Research Monograph 51, pp. 69–87). Rockville, MD: National Institute on Drug Abuse.

Deren, M. P., & Randell, J. (1990). The vocational rehabilitation of substance abusers. *Journal of Applied Rehabilitation Counseling, 21,* 3–6.

Deren, S., & Randell, J. (1988). *The results of the Venus Project: Increasing programs' utilization of vocational services* (Treatment issues report No. 68). New York: New York State Division of Substance Abuse Services.

Deutsche Gessellschaft für Suchtfroschund und Suchttherapie e. V. (Hrsg.). (1992). *Documentation standards 2 for the treatment of addictions.* Freiburg im Breisgau, Germany: Lambertus.

Dickinson, K., & Maynard, E. S. (1981). The impact of supported work on ex-addicts. *Financial report on the Supported Work Evaluation* (Vol. 4). New York: Manpower Demonstration Research Corporation.

Dolan, M. P., Black, J. L., Penk, W. F., Robinowitz, R., & DeFord, H. A. (1986). Predicting the outcome of contingency contracting for drug abuse. *Behavior Therapy, 17,* 470–474.

Dole, V. P., & Nyswander, M. E. (1965). A medical treatment for diacetyl-morphine (heroin) addiction. *Journal of the American Medical Association, 193,* 80–84.

Double, W. G., & Koenigsberg, L. (1977). Private employment and the ex-drug abuser: A practical approach. *Journal of Psychedelic Drugs, 9,* 51–58.

Faupel, C. E. (1988). Heroin use, crime and employment status. *Journal of Drug Issues, 18,* 467–479.

Fisher, D. G., & Anglin, M. D. (1987). Survival analysis in drug program evaluation: I. Overall program effectiveness. *International Journal of the Addictions, 22,* 115–134.

Flaherty, E. W., Kotranski, L., & Fox, E. (1984). Frequency of heroin use and drug users' life-style. *American Journal of Drug and Alcohol Abuse, 10,* 285–314.

French, M. T., Dennis, M. L., McDougal, G. L., Karuntzos, G. T., & Hubbard, R. L. (1992). Training and employment programs in methadone treatment: Client needs and desires. *Journal of Substance Abuse Treatment, 9,* 293–303.

Friedman, L. N. (1978). *The Wildcat experiment: An early test of supported work in drug abuse rehabilitation* (DHHS Publication No. CADM 82-728). Washington, DC: U.S. Government Printing Office.

Gerstein, D. R., & Harwood, H. J. (Eds.). (1990). *Treating drug problems: Vol. 1. A study of the evaluation, effectiveness, and financing of public and private treatment problems.* Washington, DC: National Academy Press.

Groah, C., Goodall, P., Kreutzer, J. S., Sherron, P., & Wehman, P. (1990). Addressing substance abuse issues in the content of a supported employment program. *Cognitive Rehabilitation, 8,* 8–12.

Hagen, J. L. (1989). Participants in a day program for the homeless: A survey of characteristics and service needs. *Psychosocial Rehabilitation Journal, 12,* 29–37.

Hall, S. M. (1984). Clinical trials in drug treatment: Methodology. In F. M. Tims & J. P. Ludford (Eds.), *Drug abuse treatment evaluation: Strategies, progress, and prospects* (NIDA Research Monograph 51, pp. 88–105). Rockville, MD: National Institute on Drug Abuse.

Hall, S. M., Loeb, P., Coyne, K., & Cooper, J. (1981). Increasing employment in ex-heroin addicts: I. Criminal justice sample. *Behavior Therapy, 12,* 443–452.

Hall, S. M., Loeb, P., LeVois, M., & Cooper, J. (1981). Increasing employment in ex-heroin addicts: II. Methadone maintenance sample. *Behavior Therapy, 12,* 453–460.

Hall, S. M., Loeb, P., Norton, J. W., & Yang, R. (1977). Improving vocational placement in drug treatment clients: A pilot study. *Addictive Behaviors, 15,* 438–441.

Hall, S. M., Sorensen, J. L., & Loeb, P. C. (1988). Development and diffusion of a skills-training intervention. In T. B. Baker & D. S. Cannon (Eds.), *Assessment and treatment of addictive disorders* (pp. 180–204). New York: Praeger.

Harlow, L. L., & Anglin, M. D. (1984). Time series design to evaluate effectiveness of methadone maintenance intervention. *Journal of Drug Education, 14,* 53–72.

Havassy, B. E., & Wasserman, D. A. (1992). Prevalence of comorbidity among cocaine users in treatment. In L. Harris (Ed.), *Problems of drug dependence, 1991* (p. 227). Washington, DC: U.S. Government Printing Office.

Helzer, J. E., Robins, L. N., & Davis, D. H. (1976). Antecedents of narcotic use and addiction: A study of 898 Vietnam veterans. *Drug and Alcohol Dependence, 1,* 183–190.

Hermalin, J., Husband, S. D., & Platt, J. J. (1990). Reducing costs of employee alcohol and drug abuse: Problem-solving and social skills training for relapse preventions. *Employee Assistance Quarterly, 6,* 11–25.

Hermalin, J., Steer, R. A., Platt, J. J., & Metzger, D. S. (1990). Risk characteristics associated with chronic unemployment in methadone clients. *Drug and Alcohol Dependence, 26,* 117–125.

Hollandsworth, J. G., Dressel, M. E., & Stevens, J. (1977). Use of behavioral versus traditional procedures for increasing job interviewing skills. *Journal of Counseling Psychology, 24,* 503–510.

Howard, G. (1990). Alcoholism and drug abuse: Some legal issues for employers. *British Journal of Addiction, 85,* 593–603.

Hser, Y. I., Anglin, M. D., & Liu, Y. (1990–1991). A survival analysis of gender and ethnic differences in responsiveness to methadone maintenance treatment. *International Journal of the Addictions, 25,* 1295–1315.

Hubbard, R. (1981). *Employment related services in drug treatment programs* (DHHS Publication No. ADM 81-1144). Washington, DC: U.S. Government Printing Office.

Hubbard, R. L., Marsden, M. E., Rachal, J. V., Harwood, H. J., Cavanaugh, E. R., & Ginzburg, H. M. (1989). *Drug abuse treatment: A national study of effectiveness.* Chapel Hill: University of North Carolina Press.

Hubbard, R. L., Rachal, J. V., Craddock, S. G., & Cavanaugh, E. R. (1984). Treatment Outcome Prospective Study (TOPS): Client characteristics and behaviors before, during, and after treatment. In F. M. Tims & J. P. Ludford (Eds.), *Drug abuse treatment evaluation: Strategies, progress, and prospects* (NIDA Research Monograph 51, pp. 42–68). Rockville, MD: National Institute on Drug Abuse.

Humphreys, D., & Rappaport, J. (1993). From the community mental health movement to the war on drugs: A study of the definition of social problems. *American Psychologist, 48,* 892–901.

Joe, G. W., Chastain, R. L., & Simpson, D. W. (1990). Relapse. In D. D. Simpson & S. B. Sells (Eds.), *Opioid addiction and treatment: A 12-year follow-up* (pp. 121–136). Malabar, FL: Krieger.

Joe, G. W., & Simpson, D. D. (1983). Social factors related to the follow-up status of opioid addicts. *Journal of Psychoactive Drugs, 15,* 207–217.

Joe, G. W., Simpson, D. D., & Hubbard, R. (1991). Unmet service needs in methadone maintenance. *International Journal of the Addictions, 26,* 1–22.

Jones, R. J., & Azrin, N. H. (1973). An experimental application of social reinforcement approach to the problem of job-finding. *Journal of Applied Behavior Analysis, 6,* 345–353.

Kelly, J. A., Laughlin, C., Claiborne, M., & Patterson, J. (1979). A group procedure for teaching job interviewing skills to formerly hospitalized psychiatric patients. *Behavior Therapy, 10,* 299–310.

Kleber, H. D. (1989). Treatment of drug dependence: What works. *International Review of Psychiatry, 1,* 81–100.

Kosten, T. R., Rounsaville, B. J., & Kleber, H. D. (1987a). Multidimensionality and prediction and treatment outcome in opioid addicts: 2.5 year follow-up. *Comprehensive Psychiatry, 28,* 3–13.

Kosten, T. R., Rounsaville, B. J., & Kleber, H. D. (1987b). Predictors of 2.5 year outcome in opioid addicts: Pretreatment source of income. *American Journal of Drug and Alcohol Abuse, 13,* 19–32.

Kozel, N. J., DuPont, R. L., & Brown, B. S. (1972). Narcotics and crime: A study of narcotic involvement in an offender population. *International Journal of the Addictions, 7,* 443–450.

Kreutzer, J., & Morton, M. V. (1988). An overview of traumatic brain injury: Outcome and techniques for enhancement of vocational potential. In P. Wehman & S. Moon (Eds.), *Vocational rehabilitation and supported employment.* Baltimore: Paul Brookes.

Linn, M., Shane, R., Webb, N. L., & Pratt, T. C. (1979). Cultural factors and attribution in drug abuse treatment. *International Journal of the Addictions, 14,* 259–280.

Livingston, P., Randall, J., & Wolkstein, E. (1990). A work-study model for rehabilitation counselor education in substance abuse. *Journal of Applied Rehabilitation Counseling, 21,* 16–20.

Maddux, J. F., & McDonald, L. K. (1973). Status of 100 San Antonio addicts one year after admission to methadone maintenance. *Drug Forum, 2,* 239–252.

Marlatt, G. A., & Gordon, J. R. (Eds.). (1985). *Relapse prevention: Maintenance strategies in the treatment of addictive disorders*. New York: Guilford Press.

Marsh, K. L., & Simpson, D. D. (1986). Sex differences in opioid addiction careers. *American Journal of Drug and Alcohol Abuse, 12*, 309–329.

Mathis, D. A., Navaline, H. A., Metzger, D. S., & Platt, J. J. (1994). Service needs of injection drug users: Gender and racial differences. In R. R. Watson (Ed.), *Alcohol and drug abuse reviews* (Vol. 14, pp. 329–358). Clifton, NJ: Humana.

McLellan, A. T. (1983). Patient characteristics associated with outcome. In J. R. Cooper, F. Altman, B. S. Brown, & D. Czechowicz (Eds.), *Research on the treatment of narcotic addiction: State of the art* (DHHS Publication No. ADM 87-1281, pp. 500–529). Washington, DC: U.S. Government Printing Office.

McLellan, A. T., Arndt, I. O., Metzger, D. S., Woody, G. E., & O'Brien, C. P. (1993). The effects of psychosocial services in substance abuse treatment. *Journal of the American Medical Association, 269*, 1953–1959.

McLellan, A. T., Ball, J. C., Rosen, L., & O'Brien, C. P. (1981). Pretreatment source of income and response to methadone maintenance: A follow-up study. *American Journal of Psychiatry, 138*, 785–789.

McLellan, A. T., Childress, A. R., Griffith, J., & Woody, G. E. (1984). The psychiatrically severe drug abuse patient: Methadone maintenance or therapeutic community? *American Journal of Drug and Alcohol Abuse, 10*, 77–95.

McLellan, A. T., Luborsky, L., O'Brien, C. P., Barr, H. L., & Evans, F. (1986). Alcohol and drug abuse treatment in three different populations: Is there improvement and is it predictable? *American Journal of Drug and Alcohol Abuse, 12*, 101–120.

Metzger, D. S. (1987). *Factors predicting employment status of methadone maintained clients*. Unpublished doctoral dissertation, Rutgers University, New Brunswick, NJ.

Metzger, D. S., & Platt, J. J. (1983, August). *Correlates of methadone dose levels in heroin addicts*. Paper presented at the 91st Annual Convention of the American Psychological Association, Anaheim, CA.

Metzger, D. S., & Platt, J. J. (1987). Methadone dose levels and client characteristics in heroin addicts. *International Journal of the Addictions, 22*, 187–194.

Metzger, D. S., Platt, J. J., Zanis, D., & Fureman, I. (1992). *Vocational problem solving: A structured intervention for unemployed substance abuse treatment clients*. Philadelphia: University of Pennsylvania/Hahnemann University School of Medicine.

Miranda, M., Frank, B., Marel, R., & Schmeidler, J. (1989). *Illicit drug use among New York State residents in the labor force*. Paper presented at the National Institute on Drug Abuse Conference on Drugs in the Workforce: Research and Evaluation Data, Rockville, MD.

Morton, F. L. (1976). Employing ex-addicts: Determinants of support and opposition. *International Journal of the Addictions, 11*, 681–694.

National Institute on Drug Abuse. (1979). *Developing an occupational drug abuse program: Considerations and approaches* (DHEW Publication No. ADM 79-692). Washington, DC: U.S. Government Printing Office.

National Institute on Drug Abuse. (1982). *An evaluation of the impact of employment specialists in drug treatment* (DHHS Publication No. ADM 82-1230). Washington, DC: U.S. Department of Health and Human Services.

Newman, R. G., Bashkow, S., & Cates, M. (1974). Applications received by the New York City Methadone Maintenance Treatment Program during its first two years of operation. *Drug Forum, 3*, 183–191.

Nurco, D. N., Cisin, I. H., & Balter, M. B. (1981). Addict careers. II. The first ten years. *International Journal of the Addictions, 16*, 327–356.

Ornstein, P., & Cherepon, J. (1985). Demographic variables as predictors of alcoholism treatment outcome. *Journal of Studies on Alcohol, 46*, 425–432.

Platt, J. J. (1986). *Heroin addiction: Theory, research and treatment* (Vol. 1, 2nd ed.). Melbourne, FL: Krieger.

Platt, J. J. (1995a). *Heroin addiction: Theory, research and treatment: Vol. 2. The addict, the treatment process, and social control.* Melbourne, FL: Krieger.

Platt, J. J. (1995b). *Heroin addiction: Theory, research and treatment: Vol. 3. Treatment advances and AIDS.* Melbourne, FL: Krieger.

Platt, J. J., Bühringer, G., Widman, M., Künzel, J., & Lidz, V. (1994). *Uniform standards for drug treatment research: An example from Germany for the United States.* Unpublished manuscript, Medical College of Pennsylvania and Hahnemann University, Division of Addiction Research and Treatment, Philadelphia.

Platt, J. J., Husband, S. D., Hermalin, J., Cater, J., & Metzger, D. S. (1993). Cognitive problem-solving employment readiness intervention for methadone clients. *Journal of Cognitive Psychotherapy, 7*, 21–33.

Platt, J. J., & Labate, C. (1976). Recidivism in youthful heroin offenders and characteristics of parole behavior and environment. *International Journal of the Addictions, 11*, 651–657.

Platt, J. J., & Metzger, D. S. (1987). *Final report, role of work in the rehabilitation of methadone clients.* Rockville, MD: National Institute on Drug Abuse.

Platt, J. J., Prout, M. F., & Metzger, D. S. (1986). Interpersonal cognitive problem-solving therapy. In W. Dryden & W. Golden (Eds.), *Cognitive-behavioral approaches to psychotherapy* (pp. 261–289). London: Pergamon Press.

Platt, J. J., Steer, R. A., Ranieri, W. F., & Metzger, D. S. (1989). Differences in the Symptom Checklist-90 profiles of Black and White methadone patients. *Journal of Clinical Psychology, 45*, 342–345.

Platt, J. J., Taube, D. O., Duome, M. A., & Metzger, D. S. (1988). Training in interpersonal problem-solving (TIPS). *Journal of Cognitive Psychotherapy, 2*, 1–30.

Preble, E., & Casey, J. J. (1976). Taking care of business—The heroin user's life on the street. In P. H. Coombs, L. J. Fry, & P. G. Lewis (Eds.), *Socialization in drug abuse* (pp. 309–331). Cambridge, MA: Schenkman.

Price, R. H., Burke, A. C., D'Aunno, T. A., Klingel, D. M., McCaughrin, W. C.,

Rafferty, J. A., & Vaughn, T. E. (1991). Outpatient drug abuse treatment services, 1988: Results of a national survey. In R. W. Pickens, C. G. Leukefeld, & C. R. Schuster (Eds.), *Improving drug abuse treatment* (NIDA Research Monograph 106, pp. 63–92). Washington, DC: U.S. Government Printing Office.

Rothenberg, P. B. (1978). Employment patterns of male methadone maintenance patients. *American Journal of Drug and Alcohol Abuse, 5,* 425–439.

Rounsaville, B. J., Weissman, M. M., Kleber, H. D., & Wilber, C. H. (1983). Heterogeneity of psychiatric disorders in treated opiate addicts. *Archives of General Psychiatry, 40,* 629–638.

Ruiz, P., Langrod, J., Lowinson, J., & Marcus, N. J. (1977). Social rehabilitation of addicts: A two year evaluation. *International Journal of the Addictions, 12,* 173–181.

Senay, E. C., Dorus, W., & Joseph, M. L. (1981). Evaluating service needs in drug abusing clients. *International Journal of the Addictions, 16,* 709–722.

Shaffer, J. W., Wegner, N., Kinlock, T. W., & Nurco, D. N. (1983). An empirical typology of narcotic addicts. *International Journal of the Addictions, 18,* 183–194.

Simpson, D. D. (1984). National treatment system evaluation based on the Drug Abuse Reporting Program (DARP) follow-up research. In F. M. Tims & J. P. Ludford (Eds.), *Drug abuse treatment evaluation: Strategies, progress, and prospects* (NIDA Research Monograph 51, pp. 29–41). Rockville, MD: National Institute on Drug Abuse.

Simpson, D. D., & Friend, H. J. (1988). Legal status and long-term outcomes for addicts in the DARP follow up project. In C. G. Leukefeld & F. M. Tims (Eds.), *Compulsory treatment of drug abuse: Research and clinical practice* (NIDA Research Monograph 86, pp. 81–98). Rockville, MD: National Institute on Drug Abuse.

Singh, B. K., Joe, G. W., Lehman, W., Garland, J., & Sells, S. B. (1982). A descriptive overview of treatment modalities in federally funded drug abuse treatment programs. *International Journal of the Addictions, 17,* 977–1000.

Sisson, R. W., & Azrin, N. H. (1989). The community reinforcement approach. In R. K. Hester & W. R. Miller (Eds.), *Handbook of alcoholism treatment approaches: Effective alternatives* (pp. 242–258). New York: Pergamon Press.

Snyderman, G. S. (1974). Rehabilitating the ex-offender, ex-addict. *International Journal of the Addictions, 9,* 701–717.

Sorensen, J. L., Hall, S. M., Loeb, P., Allen, T., Glaser, E. M., & Greenberg, P. D. (1988). Dissemination of a job seeker's workshop to drug treatment programs. *Behavior Therapy, 19,* 143–155.

Suffet, F., & Brotman, R. (1976). Employment and social disability among opiate addicts. *American Journal of Drug and Alcohol Abuse, 3,* 387–395.

Sullivan, A. C., Targum, S., & Avani, M. (1982). Variables related to the outcome of treatment for inpatient alcoholics. *Alcohol Health and Research World, 6,* 58–60.

Swartz, J., & Jabara, R. (1974). Short-term follow-up of narcotic addicts. *Rehabilitation Counseling Bulletin, 17,* 158–165.

Tienda, M., & Stier, H. (1991). Joblessness and shiftlessness: Labor force activity in Chicago's inner city. In C. Jencks & P. E. Peterson (Eds.), *The urban underclass* (pp. 135–154). Washington, DC: Brookings Institute.

Tims, F. M. (1981). *Effectiveness of drug abuse treatment programs* (DHHS Publication No. ADM 84-1143). Washington, DC: U.S. Government Printing Office.

U.S. Bureau of the Census. (1993). *Statistical abstract of the United States: 1993* (113th ed.). Washington, DC: U.S. Government Printing Office.

Vaillant, G. E. (1966). A 12-year follow-up of New York narcotic addicts: IV. Some characteristics and determinants of abstinence. *American Journal of Psychiatry, 123,* 573–584.

Vaillant, G. E. (1988). What can long-term follow-up teach us about relapse and prevention of relapse in addiction? *British Journal of Addiction, 83,* 1147–1157.

Venardos, M. G., & Harris, M. B. (1973). Job interview training with rehabilitation clients: A comparison of videotape and role-playing procedures. *Journal of Applied Psychology, 58,* 365–367.

Walker, K., Sanchez-Craig, M., & Bornet, A. (1982). Teaching coping skills to chronic alcoholics in a coeducational halfway house: II. Assessment of outcome and identification of outcome predictors. *British Journal of Addiction, 77,* 185–196.

Wolkstein, E., & Hastings-Black, D. (1979). Vocational rehabilitation. In R. I. DuPont, A. Goldstein, & J. O'Donnell (Eds.), *Handbook on drug abuse* (pp. 159–164). Washington, DC: U.S. Government Printing Office.

XI

ISSUES IN SPECIFIC POPULATIONS

30

LIFE STRESSORS, SOCIAL RESOURCES, AND LATE-LIFE PROBLEM DRINKING

PENNY L. BRENNAN AND RUDOLF H. MOOS

There is widespread speculation that life stressors prompt drinking problems in later life (e.g., Dupree, Broskowski, & Schonfeld, 1984; Glatt, Rosin, & Jauhar, 1978; Nowak, 1985). Two lines of indirect evidence support this view. First, studies with late-middle-aged and older populations show that undesirable life events and chronic stressors are associated with various negative health outcomes, including physical illness and depression (e.g., Arling, 1987; Holahan, Holahan, & Belk, 1984; Krause, 1987; Murrell & Norris, 1984). Second, research on young and middle-aged adults shows a relationship between life stressors and alcohol abuse. Chronic

Reprinted from *Psychology and Aging*, 5, 491–501. (1990). Copyright © 1990 by the American Psychological Association. Used with permission of the author.

This work was supported by National Institute on Alcohol Abuse and Alcoholism Grants AA06699 and AA02863, National Institute of Mental Health Grant MH16744, and Department of Veterans Affairs Medical and Health Services Research and Development Service research funds.

We thank John Finney for assistance in project development; Bernice Moos for help in organizing the data files; and Nancy Andrus, Phil Granof, John Kurtz, Colleen Moore, Erica Sharkansky, and Cathy Wocasek for help in data collection and analysis; Virginia Junk assisted with data reanalyses. John Finney and Christine Timko made valuable comments on drafts of the manuscript, and Adrienne Juliano assisted with manuscript preparation.

stressors such as serious physical illness, financial problems, work demands, and ongoing personal problems have been linked to fluctuations in alcohol use and drinking problems (Linsky, Straus, & Colby, 1985; Marlatt & Gordon, 1985; Parker & Brody, 1982). Chronic strains and stressful life events are also associated with poorer treatment outcome among alcoholic patients (Moos, Finney, & Cronkite, 1990; Vannicelli, Gingerich, & Ryback, 1983).

LIFE STRESSORS AND LATE-LIFE PROBLEM DRINKING

Very few studies have directly examined the relationship between life stressors and late-life problem drinking. Wells-Parker, Miles, and Spencer (1983) found that adults aged 60 and older who were arrested for driving while intoxicated reported more stressful events during the past year than did control respondents. Hermes, LoCastro, Bouchard, and Glynn (1984) showed that physical health stressors (i.e., hypertension and ischemic heart disease) may lead to reduced alcohol consumption among late-middle-aged men.

However, most prior studies have found no association between life stressors and late-life problem drinking, possibly because of the limited range of stressors assessed. Some investigators have indexed life stressors by a single event, such as widowhood, retirement, or relocation (e.g., Barnes, 1979; Kivela et al., 1988), but such events represent a very limited sampling of stressors reported by middle-aged and older adults (Chiriboga & Cutler, 1980). Another approach is to use life-event checklists to assess stressors (e.g., LaGreca, Akers, & Dwyer, 1988). However, it is important to assess chronic stressors as well as negative life events and to separately examine the relationship of each of these types of stressors to health outcomes. Whereas negative life events are discrete, relatively short-term experiences, chronic stressors represent enduring adverse circumstances in people's lives. These ongoing stressors are often more closely associated with negative health outcomes than are acute life events (Avison & Turner, 1988; Moos, Fenn, Billings, & Moos, 1989). In this study, we examine the relationship of negative life events and several different domains of chronic stressors to alcohol consumption and drinking problems among late-middle-aged adults.

SOCIAL RESOURCES AND LATE-LIFE PROBLEM DRINKING

Social support helps late-middle-aged and older adults avoid negative health outcomes (Holahan & Holahan, 1987; Krause, 1986). However, most studies of late-life problem drinking overlook the potential role of social resources in alcohol misuse. Some social subcultures seem to promote problem drinking, whereas others have protective social processes that help individuals avoid stressor-induced alcohol problems (Seeman & Anderson, 1983; Whitehead & Simpkins, 1983). Late-middle-aged adults who can draw on sustained, supportive relationships may be less likely to rely on excessive alcohol use as a means of managing stressors. Consistent with this idea, Moos, Finney, and Cronkite (1990) found that lack of family support is associated with relapse among individuals who have undergone treatment for alcohol problems. In this article, we examine the association between late-middle-aged adults' social resources and drinking behavior, independent of negative life events and chronic stressors.

COMPARING LATE-LIFE PROBLEM AND NONPROBLEM DRINKERS

We address several issues related to life stressors, social resources, and late-life problem drinking. We first compare the life stressors and social resources reported by late-life problem drinkers with those of nonproblem drinkers. Prior research shows that young and middle-aged alcohol abusers tend to report more stressors and fewer personal and social resources than do community-dwelling control respondents (Moos et al., 1989; Timmer, Veroff, & Colten, 1985). We expect that late-middle-aged adults who have drinking problems will also report more stressors and social resource deficits than will their counterparts who do not have drinking problems.

COMPARING MALE AND FEMALE PROBLEM DRINKERS

We also examine differences in the stressors and social resources reported by men and women who have late-life drinking problems. In general, women report more interpersonal stressors than do men (Kessler, Price, & Wortman, 1985). Women with drinking problems may be even more likely than men to report stressors involving spouses, children, and extended-family members. Many alcoholic women identify family problems as the reason for their problem drinking (Gomberg & Lisansky, 1984). Women who abuse alcohol violate sex role norms by failing to meet socially prescribed obligations, such as completion of domestic tasks and care of family members. This failure may contribute to conflicts with husbands, children, and extended-family members.

Sex role norms may also influence the pattern of stressors reported by men with drinking problems. Pressures to attain career and financial goals may be involved in the development of men's drinking problems; in turn, drinking problems may interfere with how men function in the work-place. Consistent with this view, men tend to cite work rather than family problems as the source of their alcohol-related difficulties (Gomberg & Lisansky, 1984). Thus, stressors involving work and finances may be es-pecially pronounced among men with drinking problems.

Men and women with drinking problems may also report different patterns of social resources. We expect that women with drinking problems will report less support from family members and friends than will men. In this regard, Clausen (1986) found that among former psychiatric patients, women received less support and sympathy from their spouses than did men. Female problem drinkers may have little support from their spouses because women are more likely than men to have a spouse with drinking problems (Braiker, 1984; Wilsnack, Wilsnack, & Klassen, 1984). A hus-band's own alcohol abuse may prevent him from providing support to his problem-drinking wife.

RELATIONSHIP BETWEEN LIFE STRESSORS AND SOCIAL RESOURCES

To our knowledge, no one has examined the relationship between stressors and social resources among late-life problem drinkers. Some re-searchers have argued that the concepts of life stressors and social resources are largely overlapping (Cohen & Wills, 1985; Thoits, 1982). For example, death of a spouse is not only stressful in its own right, it also removes a potential source of social support. In fact, several studies have identified a modest relationship between global measures of stressful life events and lack of social support (Barrera, 1986). Longitudinal research suggests that this relationship exists because ongoing stressors diminish the perceived availability of help from others (Lin & Ensel, 1984; Mitchell & Moos, 1984).

We assess the associations between individual domains of life stressors and social resources to address the following questions. First, to what extent are life stressors associated with lack of social resources in the same life domain? Second, do negative life events and chronic stressors have similar relationships to social resources? Acute life events may elicit helping ef-forts, but ongoing stressors may tax and eventually overburden help pro-viders. Thus, whereas more negative life events may be correlated with more social resources, more chronic stressors may be associated with less social support. Third, does the relationship between stressors and social resources differ in problem drinkers and nonproblem drinkers? Social re-source deficits may be especially likely among problem drinkers, who place a heavier burden on their sources of social support than do nonproblem drinkers. The association between life stressors and social resources may therefore be stronger in the group of problem drinkers.

STRESSORS, RESOURCES, AND LATE-LIFE PROBLEM DRINKERS' FUNCTIONING

We also examine the relationship of life stressors and social resources to four indexes of functioning: alcohol consumption, drinking problems, depression, and self-confidence. The relationship between life context and functioning is probably reciprocal; stressors and social resource deficits both influence and are shaped by drinking behavior, depression, and self-confidence. The data we present are cross-sectional, so we cannot draw conclusions about the direction of causality in associations between life-context factors and late-life functioning outcomes.

Previous studies of late-life problem drinking have focused on a possible link between acute stressors and drinking behavior. We examine this relationship, then focus on whether chronic stressors are associated with drinking behavior independent of negative life events. We also examine whether deficits in social support are associated with drinking behavior even after negative life events and chronic stressors have been considered. In addition, we examine whether individual domains of life stressors and social resources are differentially associated with alcohol consumption and drinking problems.

Assessing multiple outcome criteria presents a more complete picture of the functioning of people with alcohol problems (Moos, Finney, & Cronkite, 1990). Increased depression and lower self-confidence may foreshadow renewed and continued drinking problems (Beck, Steer, & McElroy, 1982; Hatsukami & Pickens, 1982). Therefore, in addition to examining how life stressors and social resource deficits are related to drinking behavior, we focus on their associations with depression and self-confidence.

Compared with nonproblem drinkers, problem drinkers may be more susceptible to excessive drinking, depression, and lower self-confidence as a result of stressors and social resource deficits. Thus, the magnitude of the relationship of stressors and social resources to outcomes may be larger among problem drinkers than among nonproblem drinkers. Moreover, different domains of stressors and social resource deficits may be linked to negative outcomes in the two groups. For example, problem drinkers often have difficulties with interpersonal relationships; they may be more likely than nonproblem drinkers to drink excessively in response to stressors and to a lack of support from spouses. We therefore examine the relationship of stressors and social resources to functioning outcomes in problem drinkers and nonproblem drinkers.

METHOD

Identifying Late-Life Problem and Nonproblem Drinkers

Our sampling strategy was guided by two main goals: to obtain a sample of late-middle-aged men and women with a range of drinking problems and to identify a suitable comparison group of nonproblem drinkers. The prevalence of drinking problems is relatively low (between 2% and 10%) among late-middle-aged respondents in community surveys of drinking behavior (Fillmore, 1987a, 1987b; Hilton, 1987a, 1987b). In contrast, the prevalence of drinking problems is estimated to be between 5% and 30% among people who use general medical services (Atkinson & Schuckit, 1983; Curtis, Geller, Stokes, Levine, & Moore, 1989). Therefore, we used a screening survey to obtain initial information on drinking problems and health from men and women between the ages of 55 and 65 who had had recent contact with one of two large medical centers. Because we wanted to obtain a varied group of problem drinkers and to include untreated individuals, we did not recruit patients from alcohol treatment programs.

We obtained screening surveys from 5,125 persons; 4,308 of the surveys were adequately completed. We developed screening criteria to identify individuals who reported that they (a) had current or past drinking problems or both or (b) consumed alcohol at least once a week but had never had a drinking problem. We did not select persons who abstained from alcohol or who consumed alcohol less than once a week for the sample of nonproblem drinkers because their personal and social characteristics were likely to make them an inappropriate comparison group (Cahalan, Cisin, & Crossley, 1969; Hilton, 1986). We eliminated 1,914 persons as potential respondents because they failed to meet the screening criteria (e.g., abstained from alcohol or drank too infrequently). An additional 76 persons were eliminated as we filled sampling quotas.

We tried to contact potential respondents (N = 2,318) by telephone and were able to reach 2,217 (96%) of them; 2,125 (96%) of these respondents agreed to participate. Overall, 1,884 (89%) of the people who agreed to participate completed the data collection procedures. We conducted intensive follow-ups by telephone and mail to maximize the response rate and to obtain complete data.

Because we selected respondents who had sought health services and because we excluded abstainers and very light drinkers, this is not a representative sample and cannot provide general prevalence rates of late-life problem drinking. However, the sample does not differ widely from community samples with respect to health characteristics. For example, in the National Health Survey, 17.5% of respondents between the ages of 45 and 64 years were hospitalized in the past year, with an average stay of 11.8

days. In our sample of 55- to 65-year-olds, 24.5% of respondents were hospitalized; their average stay was 13.8 days. Arthritis and high blood pressure were reported by about 25% of the National Health Survey respondents; these conditions were reported by about 30% of the respondents in our sample (Vital and Health Statistics, 1981, 1985).

Classification into problem-drinker and non-problem-drinker groups was based on responses to alcohol-related items in the screening survey and to a 17-item Drinking Problems Index (α = .92). This index includes items specifically appropriate for middle-aged and older adults and covers (a) general problems caused by drinking, such as being intoxicated or drunk, and feeling confused after drinking; (b) alcohol dependence or withdrawal symptoms; and (c) adverse consequences or life problems that result from excessive drinking.

To be classified as a problem drinker, a person had to respond positively to two or more of the Drinking Problem Index items. We chose this criterion to link our definition of problem drinking to *DSM-III-R* (American Psychiatric Association, 1987) criteria for alcohol abuse, which include continued alcohol use despite an associated social, psychological, or physical alcohol-related problem. The presence of two problems indicates that a diagnosis of alcohol abuse probably is warranted; however, we did not conduct diagnostic interviews and do not know whether such a diagnosis would be made in a clinical interview. Participants who drank alcohol at least once a week and who reported no current or past problems were classified as nonproblem drinkers.

These criteria resulted in groups of 501 current problem drinkers (387 men and 114 women) and 609 nonproblem drinkers (299 men and 310 women). Participants who reported only one current drinking problem (n = 203) or who were remitted problem drinkers (n = 571) were not included in the analyses reported in this article.

Analyses of variance and Duncan's multiple-range tests showed that men and women with drinking problems were less likely to be married than were non-problem-drinking men and women (Table 1). By definition, nonproblem drinkers reported no current drinking problems; male and female problem drinkers reported an average of 5.50 and 4.20 drinking problems, respectively. In general, problem drinkers consumed about twice as much ethanol as did nonproblem drinkers.

Life Stressors and Social Resources Inventory

The Life Stressors and Social Resources Inventory is composed of nine indexes of life stressors and seven indexes of social resources. Information about the development of the inventory and its psychometric and normative properties is presented elsewhere (Moos et al., 1989; Moos & Moos, 1988). Briefly, the indices have moderate to high internal consistency (av-

TABLE 1
Demographic and Drinking Characteristics of Problem and
Nonproblem Drinkers

Characteristic	Problem drinkers		Nonproblem drinkers		F
	Men ($n = 387$)	Women ($n = 114$)	Men ($n = 299$)	Women ($n = 310$)	
Age (years)	61.3	61.4	62.0	61.4	3.68
Education (% completed high school)	70.5	70.2	70.2	76.1	1.22
Married (%)	63.8[a]	59.7[b]	85.0[a]	69.4[b]	15.60*
Caucasian (%)	89.2	90.4	90.6	95.2	2.82
Protestant (%)	47.6	61.4	47.7	53.7	3.01
Number of current drinking problems	5.50[a, c]	4.20[b, c]	0.0[a]	0.0[b]	425.17*
Ounces ethanol (QF index)	1.74[a]	1.23[b]	0.66[a]	0.53[b]	77.26*
Ounces of ethanol on typical drinking day	3.61[a, c]	2.59[b, c]	1.83[a]	1.43[b]	88.19*
Largest quantity ethanol per day (ounces)	6.03[a, c]	4.46[b, c]	2.91[a]	2.18[b]	112.52*

Note. Sample sizes varied from 1,108 to 1,110. Duncan's multiple-range tests were used to compare (a) problem- and non-problem-drinking men, (b) problem- and non-problem-drinking women, and (c) problem-drinking men and problem-drinking women. Group means that share superscripts differ significantly ($p < .05$) by Duncan's multiple-range test. QF = quantity–frequency.
*$p < .01$.

erage α = .81 for the stressors and .79 for the resources), are only moderately intercorrelated (average rs = .20 for both stressors and resources), and discriminate as expected between groups of healthy and ill respondents (Moos & Moos, 1988).

Life Stressors Indexes

These subscales measure the overall number of acute life events that occurred in the past year and chronic stressors within each of eight life domains. The Negative Life Events subscale is a count of 86 possible acute life events (e.g., having a car or home burglarized, being laid off or demoted at work, and death of a spouse) that occurred in the past year. The Physical Health Stressors subscale is a count of 13 possible medical conditions (e.g., cancer, diabetes, or high blood pressure) and 13 serious physical ailments (e.g., trouble breathing or back pain) that began more than 1 year ago. The Home and Neighborhood Stressors subscale is composed of 10 items rated on 4-point scales that assess the physical condition of home and neighborhood, such as lack of comfort and safety. The Financial Stressors subscale is composed of 6 items rated on 4-point scales that measure problems such as inability to afford necessities and pay bills. The Work Stressors subscale is the sum of 6 items rated on 5-point scales that index difficulties such as problems with a supervisor or coworkers, pressure at work, or unpleasant physical conditions at work. Indexes of spouse, children, extended-family, and friends stressors assess stressful aspects of interpersonal relationships (for scoring details, see Moos & Moos, 1988).

Social Resources Indexes

These subscales assess ongoing resources for six of the domains in which life stressors are measured. The Financial Resources subscale is total annual family income. The Work Resources subscale is the sum of scores on six items rated on 5-point scales that assess the extent of challenge, independence, and support at work. The spouse, child, extended-family, and friend resources subscales tap the degree of support and empathy available from these sources (for scoring details, see Moos & Moos, 1988).

Indexes of Functioning

In addition to the Drinking Problems Index, several measures of individual functioning were used. These indexes were drawn from the Health and Daily Living Form (Moos, Cronkite, Billings, & Finney, 1984). They have been used in several studies and show high reliability and construct and concurrent validity (Billings, Cronkite, & Moos, 1983; Billings & Moos, 1985). Alcohol Consumption, a quantity index, measures the amount of alcohol consumed in ounces of ethanol on a typical drinking day. The Depression index (α = .93) is the sum of 18 symptoms derived from the Research Diagnostic Criteria (Spitzer, Endicott, & Robins, 1978) rated on 5-point scales ranging from *never* to *often*. The Self-Confidence index (α = .79) is the sum of the ratings of six adjectives, such as *confident*, *assertive*, and *ambitious*, rated on 5-point scales ranging from *not at all* to *quite accurate*.

RESULTS

We first compared the life stressors and social resources reported by problem drinkers with those of nonproblem drinkers. Next, we identified differences in the stressors and social resources reported by men and women who have late-life drinking problems. We then examined the association between individual domains of life stressors and individual domains of social resources. Finally, we looked at the relationship of stressors and social resources to drinking behavior, depression, and self-confidence in the problem- and non-problem-drinking groups.

TABLE 2
Differences Between Problem Drinkers' and Nonproblem Drinkers' Stressors and Social Resources, With Marital Status Controlled

Measure	Problem drinking		Nonproblem drinking		F
	Men ($n = 387$)	Women ($n = 114$)	Men ($n = 299$)	Women ($n = 310$)	
Life stressor					
Negative events	3.9[a, c]	4.7[b, c]	3.1[a]	3.5[b]	7.40*
Physical health	4.1	3.9	3.5	3.5	2.40
Home & neighborhood	4.8[a]	5.4[b]	3.7[a]	3.8[b]	6.81*
Finances	5.5[a, c]	4.1[b, c]	3.7[a]	2.9[b]	19.60*
Work	8.5	8.3	7.6	7.9	0.93
Spouse	10.8[a, c]	14.8[b, c]	9.3[a]	10.7[b]	15.35*
Children	9.9[a]	10.3	7.4[a]	9.7	5.66*
Extended family	8.1[c]	11.2[b, c]	7.6	9.2[b]	10.01*
Friends	5.1[a, c]	4.3[b, c]	4.0[a]	3.7[b]	15.96*
Social resource					
Finances	35.2[a]	37.0[b]	43.3[a]	44.0[b]	7.36*
Work	17.7	17.6	18.3	17.9	0.70
Spouse	19.3[a, c]	17.6[b, c]	20.2[a]	19.1[b]	6.89*
Children	16.1[a, c]	18.0[b, c]	18.4[a]	19.1[b]	19.47*
Extended family	13.6[a, c]	14.9[b, c]	14.6[a]	16.1[b]	12.94*
Friends	22.6[a, c]	27.2[c]	24.2[a]	27.9	36.71*

Note. Sample sizes ranged from 906 to 1,110, except for spouse and work stressors ($ns = 888$ and 467, respectively) and spouse and work resources ($ns = 893$ and 468, respectively). Group comparisons were made between (a) problem- and non-problem-drinking men, (b) problem- and non-problem-drinking women, and (c) problem-drinking men and problem-drinking women. Group means that share superscripts differ significantly ($p < .05$) by Duncan's multiple-range test.
*$p < .01$.

Differences Between Problem Drinkers and Nonproblem Drinkers

Negative Life Events and Chronic Stressors

As expected, problem drinkers experienced more stressors than did nonproblem drinkers (Table 2). Compared with nonproblem drinkers, problem-drinking men and women reported more overall negative life events and more chronic stressors in the domains of home and neighborhood, finances, spouse, and friends. Problem-drinking men reported more stressors related to children than did non-problem-drinking men. Women with drinking problems reported more extended-family stressors than did women without drinking problems. These group differences remained when we controlled for marital status.

Social Resources

Problem drinkers also reported fewer social resources than did nonproblem drinkers. Compared with nonproblem drinkers, problem-drinking men and women reported fewer financial, spouse, children, and extended-family resources. Problem-drinking men reported fewer friend resources than did non-problem-drinking men. These group differences remained when we controlled for marital status.

Problem-Drinking Men and Women

Compared with problem-drinking women, problem-drinking men reported more ongoing financial problems and difficulties with friends. They were also more likely than were problem-drinking women to lack support from children, extended-family members, and friends. In contrast, problem-drinking women reported more negative life events, more ongoing stressors in the domains of spouse and extended family, and fewer spouse resources.

Associations Between Life Stressors and Social Resources

To examine the relationship between negative life events and social resources, we calculated the association between all pairs of negative life-event and social resource domains in the problem-drinking group. We found almost no association between individual domains of negative life events and individual domains of social resources (48 pairs; average $r = -.06$). The only significant within-domain correlations were between negative spouse events and spouse resources ($r = -.13$) and between negative friend events and friend resources ($r = .13$).

Next, we calculated the correlation between all pairs of chronic stressor and social resource domains. Of 48 pairs of chronic stressor and social resource subscales, the average correlation was $-.12$. Ongoing stressors and social resources in the same domain were significantly correlated in only three cases: Ongoing financial, spouse, and child-related stressors were associated with a lack of social resources in the same areas ($rs = -.65$, $-.47$, and $-.24$, respectively). We found basically the same pattern of correlations in the non-problem-drinker group.

Life Stressors, Social Resources, and Functioning Outcomes

Using data from the problem-drinker group, we first calculated simple correlations between sex and marital status and the four functioning criteria (Table 3). Women drank less and had fewer drinking problems than did men, but women were also more depressed. Married respondents had fewer drinking problems, were less depressed, and were more self-confident than were unmarried respondents.

Because sex and marital status were associated with the criteria, we next calculated the associations between each domain of stressors and social resources and the functioning outcomes, controlling for sex and marital status. In general, people who experienced more stressors were functioning more poorly. Respondents who experienced more negative life events re-

TABLE 3
Associations Between Demographic Characteristics, Stressors and Social Resources, and Functioning Outcomes (Problem-Drinker Group)

Measure	Correlations				β and R^2			
	Alcohol consumption	Drinking problems	Depression	Self-confidence	Alcohol consumption	Drinking problems	Depression	Self-confidence
Demographic characteristic								
Sex	-.17**	-.15**	.12**	-.01	-.17**	-.16**	.11**	-.01
Marital status	-.06	-.24**	-.17**	.11**	-.06	-.24**	-.16**	.11**
R^2 change	—	—	—	—	.03**	.08**	.04**	.01*
Negative life events	-.06	.11**	.28**	.06	-.06	.11**	.28**	.06
R^2 change	—	—	—	—	.00	.01**	.08**	.00
Chronic stressor								
Physical health	.00	.09*	.38**	-.16**	-.06	.01	.28**	-.10*
Home & neighborhood	.01	.11**	.30**	-.25**	-.01	.01	.15**	-.21**
Finances	.03	.21**	.28**	-.22**	.03	.16**	.09*	-.16**
Spouse	.16**	.18**	.32**	-.06	.19**	.12*	.13**	.02
Extended family	.01	.09*	.24**	.00	.01	-.01	.04	.06
Friends	-.01	.17**	.22**	-.05	-.02	.12**	.09*	-.04
R^2 change	—	—	—	—	.03**	.06**	.22**	.10**
Social resource								
Finances	-.03	-.19**	-.18**	.25**	.09	-.10	.02	.18**
Spouse	-.20**	-.25**	-.29**	.22**	-.19**	-.13**	-.06	.09
Extended family	-.04	-.12**	-.17**	.21**	-.02	-.03	-.06	.08
Friends	-.03	-.19**	-.26**	.37**	.03	-.12**	-.15**	.28**
R^2 change	—	—	—	—	.03**	.04**	.04**	.12**
Overall R^2	—	—	—	—	.10**	.20**	.37**	.24**

Note. The sample sizes varied between 476 and 501, except for spouse stressors ($n = 385$) and spouse resources ($n = 386$). In the four left-hand columns, the associations between sex and marital status and the criteria are simple correlations; the remaining associations in these columns are partial correlations, with sex and marital status controlled. Dashes indicate data are inapplicable.
*$p < .05.$ **$p < .01.$

ported more drinking problems and depression. Those who reported more ongoing spouse stressors consumed more alcohol. Across life domains, more chronic stressors were associated with more drinking problems and depression. Respondents who reported more physical health, home and neighborhood, and financial stressors had less self-confidence.

Respondents with fewer social resources also functioned more poorly. Those who reported less support from their spouses consumed more alcohol. Across life domains, fewer social resources were associated with more drinking problems, more symptoms of depression, and less self-confidence.

Next, we conducted hierarchical multiple regression analyses to fulfill two purposes: (a) to examine the successive contributions of sex and marital status, negative life events, chronic stressors, and social resources to the functioning criteria and (b) to identify the independent contributions of negative life events and individual domains of chronic stressors and ongoing social resources to the criteria (Table 3). Because preliminary analyses showed that sex and marital status were associated with the criteria, we entered these characteristics first in the multiple regression equation. We entered negative life events next, followed by chronic stressors, and social resources were entered last. Each R^2 change in Table 3 indicates the amount of additional variance accounted for by entering the preceding group of variables in the regression equation. Overall R^2 values indicate the total variance in the criteria accounted for by the predictors. The beta values in Table 3 show the contribution of each variable to the criterion, controlling for all other variables in the same and preceding set or sets of variables.

We did not examine the effects of stressors and social resources involving work and children because a relatively large proportion of the problem drinkers were not employed or did not have children. When specific dimensions of stressors and social resources were not applicable for a respondent (e.g., spouse stressors and resources for individuals who were widowed), they were treated as missing data.

Negative Life Events

After controlling for sex and marital status, negative life events accounted for a small but significant increment in variance in drinking problems and depression. More negative life events were associated with more drinking problems and depression, but not with alcohol consumption or self-confidence.

Chronic Stressors

Chronic stressors as a set added significantly to the explanation of variance in all four of the criteria. Several individual domains of chronic stressors were independently related to the functioning outcomes. Problem drinkers who experienced more ongoing stressors involving spouses consumed more alcohol. Those who had more financial, spouse, and friend-related stressors reported more drinking problems. Except in the extended-family domain, more chronic stressors were associated with more depression. Problem drinkers who experienced more physical health, home and neighborhood, and financial stressors were less self-confident.

Social Resources

Even after sex, marital status, and stressors were considered, social resources as a set added significantly to the explanation of variance in all four indexes of functioning. Several individual indexes of social resources were independently related to the functioning criteria. Problem drinkers who reported fewer spouse resources drank more alcohol. Those with fewer resources from spouses and friends reported more drinking problems. Respondents with fewer resources from friends reported more depression; those with fewer financial and friend resources reported less self-confidence. Taken together, sex and marital status, negative life events, chronic stressors, and social resources explained 10% of the variance in alcohol consumption, 20% in drinking problems, 37% in depression, and 24% in self-confidence.

Stressors, Resources, and Functioning Among Nonproblem Drinkers

We conducted comparable correlational and multiple regression analyses in the non-problem-drinking group (Table 4). The pattern of results was quite similar. Correlational analyses showed that non-problem-drinking women consumed less alcohol but reported more depression than did non-problem-drinking men. Nonproblem drinkers who were married consumed more alcohol and reported less depression and more self-confidence than did those who were unmarried. More negative life events were associated with more depression. In general, nonproblem drinkers who reported more chronic stressors and social resource deficits were functioning more poorly.

The multiple regression analyses showed that more negative life events were associated with more depression but not with alcohol consumption or self-confidence. Chronic stressors as a group added significantly to negative events in predicting all three criteria. Nonproblem drinkers who reported more chronic stressors involving home and neighborhood and finances drank less alcohol; however, those who had more difficulties with friends drank more. Those with more ongoing stressors involving physical health, home and neighborhood, spouses, and extended family reported more depression. Nonproblem drinkers with more home and neighborhood stressors were less self-confident.

Social resources as a set accounted for an additional significant in-

TABLE 4
Associations Between Demographic Characteristics, Stressors and Social Resources, and Functioning Outcomes (Nonproblem-Drinker Group)

Measure	Correlations			β and R^2		
	Alcohol consumption	Depression	Self-confidence	Alcohol consumption	Depression	Self-confidence
Demographic characteristic						
Sex	-.18**	.11**	-.10**	-.16**	.09*	-.08
Marital status	.12**	-.13**	.15**	.09*	-.11**	.13**
R^2 change	—	—	—	.03**	.02**	.03**
Negative life events	-.06	.37**	-.04	-.06	.36**	-.04
R^2 change	—	—	—	.00	.13**	.00
Chronic stressor						
Physical health	-.07*	.32**	-.09*	-.03	.19**	-.03
Home & neighborhood	-.14**	.23**	-.24**	-.10*	.11**	-.20**
Finances	-.14**	.25**	-.15**	-.11*	.05	-.07
Spouse	-.01	.30**	-.12**	.03	.12**	-.07
Extended family	-.02	.29**	-.03	-.01	.14**	.02
Friends	.09*	.19**	-.01	.10**	.06	.02
R^2 change	—	—	—	.04**	.14**	.06**
Social resource						
Finances	.13**	-.16**	.23**	.07	-.03	.25**
Spouse	.04	-.32**	.17**	.02	-.14**	.05
Extended family	.06	-.21**	.18**	.02	-.08*	.04
Friends	.07	-.23**	.39**	.03	-.15**	.35**
R^2 change	—	—	—	.00	.05**	.15**
Overall R^2	—	—	—	.08**	.35**	.24**

Note. The sample sizes varied between 580 and 609, except for spouse stressors ($n = 503$) and spouse resources ($n = 507$). In the three left-hand columns, the associations between sex and marital status and the criteria are simple correlations; the remaining associations in these columns are partial correlations, with sex and marital status controlled. Dashes indicate data are inapplicable.
*$p < .05$. **$p < .01$.

crement in the explained variance in depression and self-confidence. Non-problem drinkers who reported fewer resources from spouses, extended family, and friends reported more depression. Those with fewer financial and friend-related resources reported less self-confidence. Taken together, background characteristics, life events, ongoing stressors, and social resources accounted for 8% of the variance in alcohol consumption, 35% of the variance in depression, and 24% of the variance in self-confidence.

DISCUSSION

We examined four issues concerning life stressors, social resources, and problem drinking during later life: (a) differences in life stressors and social resources reported by late-life problem and nonproblem drinkers, (b) stressors and social resources that distinguish men with late-life drinking problems from women with late-life drinking problems, (c) the association between stressors and social resources, and (d) the relationship of stressors and resources to drinking behavior and functioning in both the problem- and non-problem-drinking groups.

Differences Between Problem Drinkers and Nonproblem Drinkers

The life contexts of late-middle-aged adults who have drinking problems are different from those of individuals who do not have drinking problems. Late-life problem drinkers experience more stressors than do nonproblem drinkers—more ongoing adverse circumstances across a range of life domains, as well as more acute negative events. Across most life domains, late-life problem drinkers also have fewer social resources than do non-problem drinkers. These group differences suggest that negative life events, ongoing stressors, and a lack of social support may all play a role in the maintenance of late-life drinking problems. Conversely, drinking problems may contribute to stressful circumstances and diminished social support.

Differences Between Problem-Drinking Men and Women

We found that women reported more negative life events than did men. Moreover, consistent with prior studies (Kessler et al., 1985), women also reported fewer financial but more family-related stressors than did men. These differences were especially pronounced among problem drinkers. Compared with problem-drinking men, problem-drinking women reported more chronic stressors involving spouses and extended-family members. This finding is consistent with studies showing that alcoholic women frequently identify difficulties with husbands and other family members as the reason for their substance abuse (Gomberg & Lisansky, 1984). In addition, women with drinking problems may not fulfill socially prescribed domestic obligations, which may contribute to conflicts with spouses and extended-family members.

In contrast, men with drinking problems were more likely than problem-drinking women to report chronic financial difficulties and problems with friends. In part because of sex role norms, financial problems may be a more focal determinant and consequence of drinking problems among men than among women. Whereas women with alcohol problems tend to drink alone or at home, men with drinking problems are likely to drink in groups (Cronkite & Moos, 1984). Drinking companions may be important friendships for late-middle-aged men with alcohol-related problems. However, because alcohol consumption is so central in these friendships, they may become an arena for interpersonal conflict.

Overall, women reported having more social resources than did men. Specifically, compared with problem-drinking men, problem-drinking women reported having more resources from children, extended-family members, and friends. However, consistent with Clausen's (1986) findings concerning spouses of former psychiatric patients, problem-drinking women reported receiving less support from their husbands than problem-drinking men reported receiving from their wives. One reason for this may be the greater likelihood for problem-drinking women to be married to someone with drinking problems (Braiker, 1984; Wilsnack et al., 1984). A husband's own alcohol abuse may prevent him from providing support to his problem-drinking wife. Women may also be more likely than men to view nurturing a spouse with drinking problems as part of their role.

These findings support the idea that prevention and treatment efforts may need to be tailored more closely to the life situations of men and women who have drinking problems (Cronkite & Moos, 1984; Moos, Finney, & Cronkite, 1990). For example, spouses are clearly a source of ongoing stressors and low social resources for many late-middle-aged women who have drinking problems. Prevention and treatment efforts for these women might focus more closely on this life domain. Unlike men who abuse alcohol, women who do so may continue to receive considerable support from children, extended-family members, and friends, despite their drinking problems and family-related conflicts. These social resources may be especially important to cultivate during treatment.

Association Between Stressors and Social Resources

To our knowledge, no one has examined the relationship between problem drinkers' stressors and their social resources. Our findings indicate that stressors and social resources are associated only within certain life domains. More negative events involving friends are correlated with more support from friends, but more acute spouse events are associated with less spouse support. Similarly, ongoing difficulties involving finances, spouses, and children are associated with fewer resources in these domains.

These findings help reconcile the view that stressors and lack of social support may be largely overlapping concepts (Cohen & Wills, 1985; Thoits, 1982), with empirical results showing that there is at best only a moderate correlation between more stressors and less social support (Barrera, 1986). In domains where there is a single source of both stressors and support (e.g., the spouse domain), stressors and lack of support may often be closely connected. In contrast, in domains where there are multiple sources of problems and assistance (e.g., work, extended family, and friends), stressors and social resources may be more independent. The moderate correlation usually found between global stressors and overall lack of support may reflect the fact that although there are a few strong, domain-specific correlations between more stressors and fewer social resources, within most life domains social resources are relatively independent of stressors.

On average, chronic stressors are more closely associated with social resources than are negative life events. This result is consistent with the idea that the effects of chronic stressors are more enduring than the effects of negative life events (Avison & Turner, 1988). However, we found no evidence that compared with the social resources of nonproblem drinkers, those of problem drinkers are more likely to be diminished by chronic stressors.

Life Stressors, Social Resources, and Functioning

Problem drinkers who experience more stressors and social resource deficits function more poorly than do those who live in more benign contexts. Partial correlations showed that problem drinkers who experienced more negative life events and chronic stressors drank more alcohol and reported more drinking problems, more symptoms of depression, and less self-confidence. Those with fewer social resources also functioned more poorly according to these indicators.

Negative Life Events, Chronic Stressors, and Functioning Outcomes

Independent of sex and marital status, negative life events were associated with more drinking problems and depression. After demographic characteristics and negative life events were considered, ongoing stressors added significantly to the explanation of drinking behavior. In fact, across functioning criteria, chronic stressors as a set accounted for a larger increment in variance than did negative life events. This finding highlights the importance of separately assessing negative life events and chronic stressors

(Avison & Turner, 1988; Moos et al., 1989). Studies that use a single transitional event or a count of negative life events to index stressors have typically shown no association between stressful circumstances and late-life drinking problems. Our broader assessment procedure may increase the likelihood of identifying a relationship between stressors and drinking behavior.

Moreover, chronic stressors may have a different relationship with health outcomes than negative life events have. The effects of negative life events tend to be more short-lived than those of chronic stressors (Avison & Turner, 1988). Compared with negative life events, ongoing adverse circumstances may have more cumulative effects that contribute to the likelihood of negative health outcomes (Rutter, 1986), including excessive alcohol consumption.

These results also underscore the importance of assessing individual domains of stressors and their relationship to functioning outcomes. For instance, independent of other variables, marital stressors were associated with more alcohol consumption and drinking problems; more stressors involving friends were also associated with more drinking problems. This finding suggests that for problem drinkers, conflicts within close personal relationships may be especially likely to prompt alcohol abuse; conversely, these relationships may be vulnerable to damage as a result of alcohol-related problems. Domain-specific associations such as these indicate areas in which it may be beneficial to intervene to change the relationship between ongoing stressors and drinking behavior.

Social Resources and Functioning Outcomes

Even when sex, marital status, and stressors were considered, social resources as a set added significantly to the prediction of all four of the criteria. Thus, to understand the drinking behavior and functioning of late-life problem drinkers, consideration must be given to the social resources available to them, as well as the stressors they experience.

Independent of other variables, more spouse support was associated with less alcohol consumption and fewer drinking problems. More support from friends was associated with fewer drinking problems, less depression, and more self-confidence. These findings reinforce the importance of problem drinkers' marriages and friendships: Interventions that enhance the support available from spouses and friends may help prevent alcohol abuse and improve psychological functioning among problem drinkers; in turn, improved drinking behavior and functioning can positively affect the quality of these relationships.

Differences Between Problem and Nonproblem Drinkers

The relationship of life stressors and social resources to functioning outcomes was quite similar among problem and nonproblem drinkers. However, there were a few areas in which the groups differed. Among non-problem drinkers, married people tended to consume more alcohol than did unmarried people; nonproblem drinkers who reported more home and neighborhood and financial stressors tended to consume less alcohol. We did not find these associations among problem drinkers. This difference may reflect the fact that nonproblem drinkers tend to use alcohol primarily in social contexts. Married individuals may be more likely to consume alcohol during meals and to attend more social occasions at which alcohol is served. Financial adversity may prompt nonproblem drinkers to cut back on the purchase of alcohol and to limit their participation in situations where alcohol consumption is more likely (e.g., parties and vacations).

Among nonproblem drinkers, spouse stressors and resources were not associated with alcohol consumption; in contrast, problem drinkers who reported more conflicts and lack of support from their spouses drank more alcohol. This result points once more to the centrality of the marital relationship among individuals who drink excessively. Nonproblem drinkers who consumed more alcohol reported more friend-related stressors, but this was not the case among problem drinkers. This finding suggests that compared with problem drinkers, nonproblem drinkers may be more likely to have friends who object to excessive drinking.

Prospective longitudinal studies are needed to clarify the relationship between life stressors and social resources and to show how these together influence late-life drinking behavior. More research is needed to determine how the results of this study generalize to other groups of late-middle-aged adults (e.g., less educated samples) and to elderly individuals. Moreover, stressors and social resources together still explain only a modest part of the variance in alcohol consumption and drinking problems. Further consideration of people's personal characteristics and resources may help to explain the association between life context and late-life drinking problems. For instance, the duration and course of a person's difficulties with alcohol may mediate the relationship between stressors and current drinking problems. Coping responses may also be important: The type and severity of stressors experienced by late-life problem drinkers influence their coping responses; in turn, these coping responses are associated with functioning outcomes (Moos, Brennan, Fondacaro, & Moos, 1990). Despite its limitations, this study demonstrates the value of assessing life context and its connections with the alcohol-related problems of late-middle-aged adults. Further investigation of these connections may help inform efforts to prevent and change the course of late-life drinking problems.

REFERENCES

American Psychiatric Association. (1987). *Diagnostic and statistical manual of mental disorders* (3rd ed., rev.). Washington, DC: Author.

Arling, G. (1987). Strain, social support and distress in old age. *Journal of Gerontology, 42,* 107–113.

Atkinson, J. H., & Schuckit, M. A. (1983). Geriatric alcohol and drug misuse and abuse. *Advances in substance abuse* (Vol. 3, pp. 195–237). Greenwich, CT: JAI Press.

Avison, W. R., & Turner, R. J. (1988). Stressful life events and depressive symptoms: Disaggregating the effects of acute stressors and chronic strains. *Journal of Health and Social Behavior, 29,* 253–264.

Barnes, G. M. (1979). Alcohol use among older persons: Findings from a Western New York general population survey. *Journal of the American Geriatrics Society, 27,* 244–250.

Barrera, M. (1986). Distinctions between social support concepts, measures, and models. *American Journal of Community Psychology, 14,* 413–445.

Beck, A. T., Steer, R. A., & McElroy, M. G. (1982). Self-reported precedence of depression in alcoholism. *Drug and Alcohol Dependence, 10,* 185–195.

Billings, A., Cronkite, R., & Moos, R. (1983). Social environmental factors in unipolar depression: Comparisons of depressed patients and nondepressed controls. *Journal of Abnormal Psychology, 92,* 119–133.

Billings, A., & Moos, R. (1985). Psychosocial processes of remission in unipolar depression: Comparing depressed patients with matched community controls. *Journal of Consulting and Clinical Psychology, 53,* 314–325.

Braiker, H. B. (1984). Therapeutic issues in the treatment of alcoholic women. In S. C. Wilsnack & L. J. Beckman (Eds.), *Alcohol problems in women* (pp. 349–368). New York: Guilford Press.

Cahalan, D., Cisin, I. H., & Crossley, H. M. (1969). *American drinking practices: A national study of drinking behavior and attitudes.* New Brunswick, NJ: Rutgers Center of Alcohol Studies.

Chiriboga, D. A., & Cutler, L. (1980). Stress and adaptation: Life span perspectives. In L. W. Poon (Ed.), *Aging in the 1980s: Psychological issues* (pp. 347–362). Washington, DC: American Psychological Association.

Clausen, J. A. (1986). A 15- to 20-year follow-up of married adult psychiatric patients. In L. Erlenmeyer-Kimling & N. E. Miller (Eds.), *Life-span research on the prediction of psychopathology* (pp. 175–194). Hillsdale, NJ: Erlbaum.

Cohen, S., & Wills, T. A. (1985). Stress, social support, and the buffering hypothesis. *Psychological Bulletin, 98,* 310–357.

Cronkite, R., & Moos, R. (1984). The role of predisposing and moderating factors in the stress–illness relationship. *Journal of Health and Social Behavior, 25,* 372–393.

Curtis, J. R., Geller, G., Stokes, E. J., Levine, D. M., & Moore, R. D. (1989). Characteristics, diagnosis, and treatment of alcoholism in elderly patients. *Journal of the American Geriatrics Society, 37,* 310–316.

Dupree, L. W., Broskowski, H., & Schonfeld, L. (1984). The Gerontology Alcohol Project: A behavioral treatment program for elderly alcohol abusers. *The Gerontologist, 24,* 510–516.

Fillmore, K. M. (1987a). Prevalence, incidence and chronicity of drinking patterns and problems among men as a function of age: A longitudinal and cohort analysis. *British Journal of Addiction, 82,* 77–83.

Fillmore, K. M. (1987b). Women's drinking across the adult life course as compared to men's. *British Journal of Addiction, 82,* 801–811.

Glatt, M. M., Rosin, A. J., & Jauhar, P. (1978). Alcoholic problems in the elderly. *The Lancet, 2,* 472–473.

Gomberg, E. S., & Lisansky, J. M. (1984). Antecedents of alcohol problems in women. In S. C. Wilsnack & L. J. Beckman (Eds.), *Alcohol problems in women* (pp. 233–255). New York: Guilford Press.

Hatsukami, D., & Pickens, R. W. (1982). Posttreatment depression in an alcohol and drug abuse population. *American Journal of Psychiatry, 139,* 1563–1566.

Hermos, J. A., LoCastro, J. S., Bouchard, G. R., & Glynn, R. J. (1984). Influence of cardiovascular disease on alcohol consumption among men in the Normative Aging Study. In G. Maddox, L. N. Robins, & N. Rosenberg (Eds.), *The nature and extent of alcohol problems among the elderly* (pp. 117–132). New York: Springer.

Hilton, M. E. (1986). Abstention in the general population of the U.S.A. *British Journal of Addiction, 81,* 95–112.

Hilton, M. E. (1987a). Demographic characteristics and the frequency of heavy drinking as predictors of self-reported drinking problems. *British Journal of Addiction, 82,* 913–925.

Hilton, M. E. (1987b). Drinking patterns and drinking problems in 1984: Results from a general population survey. *Alcoholism: Clinical and Experimental Research, 11,* 167–175.

Holahan, C. K., & Holahan, C. J. (1987). Self-efficacy, social support, and depression in aging: A longitudinal analysis. *Journal of Gerontology, 42,* 65–68.

Holahan, C. K., Holahan, C. J., & Belk, S. S. (1984). Adjustment in aging: The roles of life stress, hassles, and self-efficacy. *Health Psychology, 3,* 315–328.

Kessler, R. C., Price, R. H., & Wortman, C. B. (1985). Social factors in psychopathology: Stress, social support, and coping processes. *Annual Review of Psychology, 36,* 531–572.

Kivela, S., Nissinen, A., Ketola, A., Punsar, S., Puska, P., & Karvonen, M. (1988). Changes in alcohol consumption during a ten-year follow-up among Finnish men aged 55–74 years. *Functional Neurology, 3,* 167–178.

Krause, N. (1986). Social support, stress, and well-being among older adults. *Journal of Gerontology, 41,* 512–519.

Krause, N. (1987). Chronic financial strain, social support, and depressive symptoms among older adults. *Psychology and Aging, 2,* 185–192.

LaGreca, A. J., Akers, D. L., & Dwyer, J. W. (1988). Life events and alcohol behavior among older adults. *The Gerontologist, 28,* 552–558.

Lin, N., & Ensel, W. M. (1984). Depression-mobility and its social etiology: The role of life events and social support. *Journal of Health and Social Behavior, 25,* 176–188.

Linsky, A. S., Straus, M. A., & Colby, J. P. (1985). Stressful events, stressful conditions and alcohol problems in the United States: A partial test of Bales's theory. *Journal of Studies on Alcohol, 46,* 72–80.

Marlatt, G. A., & Gordon, J. R. (Eds.). (1985). *Relapse prevention: Maintenance strategies in addictive behavior change.* New York: Guilford Press.

Mitchell, R. E., & Moos, R. H. (1984). Deficiencies in support among depressed patients: Antecedents or consequences of stress? *Journal of Health and Social Behavior, 25,* 438–452.

Moos, R. H., Brennan, P. L., Fondacaro, M. R., & Moos, B. S. (1990). Approach and avoidance coping responses among older problem and nonproblem drinkers. *Psychology and Aging, 5,* 31–40.

Moos, R. H., Cronkite, R., Billings, A., & Finney, J. (1984). *Health and Daily Living Form manual.* Palo Alto, CA: Social Ecology Laboratory, Stanford University and Department of Veterans Affairs Medical Centers.

Moos, R. H., Fenn, C. B., Billings, A. G., & Moos, B. S. (1989). Assessing life stressors and social resources: Applications to alcoholic patients. *Journal of Substance Abuse, 1,* 135–152.

Moos, R. H., Finney, J. W., & Cronkite, R. C. (1990). *Alcoholism treatment: Context, process, and outcome.* New York: Oxford University Press.

Moos, R., & Moos, B. (1988). *Life Stressors and Social Resources Inventory preliminary manual.* Palo Alto, CA: Social Ecology Laboratory, Stanford University and Department of Veterans Affairs Medical Centers.

Murrell, S. A., & Norris, F. H. (1984). Resources, life events, and changes in positive affect and depression in older adults. *American Journal of Community Psychology, 12,* 445–465.

Nowak, C. A. (1985). Life events and drinking behavior in later years. In E. Gottheil, K. A. Druley, T. E. Skolada, & H. M. Waxman (Eds.), *The combined problems of alcoholism, drug addiction, and aging* (pp. 36–50). Springfield, IL: Charles C Thomas.

Parker, D., & Brody, J. (1982). Risk factors for alcoholism and alcohol problems among employed women and men. In *Occupational alcoholism: A review of research* (National Institute on Alcohol Abuse and Alcoholism Research Monograph No. 8, pp. 99–127). Washington, DC: U.S. Government Printing Office.

Rutter, M. (1986). Meyerian psychobiology, personality development, and the role of life experiences. *American Journal of Psychiatry, 143,* 1077–1087.

Seeman, M., & Anderson, C. S. (1983). Alienation and alcohol: The role of work, mastery, and community in drinking behavior. *American Sociological Review, 48,* 60–77.

Spitzer, R. L., Endicott, J., & Robins, E. (1978). Research Diagnostic Criteria: Rationale and reliability. *Archives of General Psychiatry, 35,* 773–782.

Thoits, P. A. (1982). Conceptual, methodological, and theoretical problems in studying social support as a buffer against life stress. *Journal of Health and Social Behavior, 23,* 145–159.

Timmer, S. G., Veroff, J., & Colten, M. E. (1985). Life stress, helplessness, and the use of alcohol and drugs to cope. In S. Shiffman & T. A. Wills (Eds.), *Coping and substance use* (pp. 171–198). New York: Academic Press.

Vannicelli, M., Gingerich, S., & Ryback, R. (1983). Family problems related to the treatment and outcome of alcoholic patients. *British Journal of Addiction, 78,* 193–204.

Wells-Parker, E., Miles, S., & Spencer, B. (1983). Stress experiences and drinking histories of elderly drunken-driving offenders. *Journal of Studies on Alcohol, 44,* 429–437.

Whitehead, P. C., & Simpkins, J. (1983). Occupational factors in alcoholism. In B. Kissin & H. Regleiter (Eds.), *The pathogenesis of alcoholism: Psychosocial factors* (Vol. 6, pp. 405–496). New York: Plenum Press.

Wilsnack, R. W., Wilsnack, S. C., & Klassen, A. D. (1984). Women's drinking and drinking problems: Patterns from a 1981 national survey. *American Journal of Public Health, 74,* 1231–1238.

Vital and Health Statistics. (1981). *Current estimates from the National Health Survey: United States, 1981* (DHHS Publication No. 82-1569). Washington, DC: U.S. Government Printing Office.

Vital and Health Statistics. (1985). *Current estimates from the National Health Survey: United States, 1985* (DHHS Publication No. 86-1588). Washington, DC: U.S. Government Printing Office.

31

COMPARISON OF AFRICAN-AMERICAN ADOLESCENT CRACK COCAINE USERS AND NONUSERS: BACKGROUND FACTORS IN DRUG USE AND HIV SEXUAL RISK BEHAVIORS

BENJAMIN P. BOWSER AND CARL O. WORD

Crack cocaine use is associated with extraordinarily high human immunodeficiency virus (HIV) sexual risks. Although the chemical properties of crack do not directly stimulate sexual activity, the user subculture and marketing of crack are sexually exploitative despite the growing risk of HIV infection amid an acquired immunodeficiency syndrome (AIDS) crisis (Bowser, Fullilove, & Fullilove, 1990). Specifically, "sex for drugs" behavior places crack users, especially female users, at extraordinarily high risk of becoming HIV infected. In areas where crack use has spread among African-American teens and young adults, the rate of sexually transmitted

Reprinted from *Psychology of Addictive Behaviors*, 7, 155–161. (1993). Copyright © 1993 by the Educational Publishing Foundation. Used with permission of the author.

This work was supported by the California University-Wide AIDS Research Program.

diseases has increased dramatically after years of decline (Edlin et al., 1992). In addition, there have been increasing rates of newborns who are chemically addicted (Centers for Disease Control, 1991), and sex for drugs is putting crack-addicted men and women into sexual contact with inject- ing drug–using clients, many of whom are HIV infected (Watters & Cuth- bert, 1992).

The crack epidemic, through sex for drugs behaviors, has opened the possibility of a third wave of HIV infection among African-American young people. The first wave of HIV infection involved gay and bisexual men; the second wave is claiming injecting drug users. The spread of HIV through crack-induced sex for drugs behaviors is particularly critical be- cause the sexual networks of crack users are usually more extensive than the networks of older injecting drug users. Also, they are less likely to be separate from those of other sexually active teens and young adults.

A puzzling observation is that African-American young people who elect to use crack appear indistinguishable from their peers who do not use the drug. They live in the same communities, experience the same poverty, attend the same schools, and are even in the same families. However, it is appropriate to think of users and nonusers as distinct groups because they do socially self-select according to use and nonuse. The crucial question is, given their apparent similarities, how do users differ from nonusers? This critical question can be approached from any theoretical perspective. Both practical and theoretical answers are important to early prevention of fur- ther crack use and the development of effective psychosocial treatments. We conducted a study to gain insight that might lead to an answer to the question of how crack users are distinct from nonusers and what theoretical approach might be most useful for further study.

BACKGROUND

Prior research has established the statistically significant associations among crack use, HIV sexual high-risk behaviors, and having had a sex- ually transmitted disease for African-American adolescents (Fullilove, Ful- lilove, Bowser, & Gross, 1990). In comparison with their non–crack-using peers, crack users have unprotected sex more frequently, have more sexual partners, are more likely to trade sex for drugs, and are more likely to have had a sexually transmitted disease. In a comparable follow-up study of African-American crack-using and nonusing young adults, trading sex for drugs was a significant risk factor for sexually transmitted disease infections (Edlin et al., 1992). This finding was consistent across samples of young adults in San Francisco, Miami, and New York City.

Similarly, street-recruited adults in San Francisco, Miami, and Denver were interviewed regarding HIV risk behavior and drug use. More than

62% of crack smokers had tested positive for gonorrhea. The authors concluded that sexual transmission among crack users may become as high a risk as is sharing contaminated drug paraphernalia (Booth, Watters, & Chitwood, 1992). Seropositivity has been linked to crack cocaine use among adults attending a sexually transmitted disease clinic in New York City. Among those who denied intravenous drug use or homosexual sex, men were 2.8 times and women 4.7 times more likely to have the disease if they used crack (Chiasson et al., 1991). At another municipal, hospital-based sexually transmitted disease clinic in central Brooklyn, crack cocaine use was independently associated with genital ulcer disease and HIV infection in 194 clients tested for HIV (Chirgwin, De Havitz, Dillon, & McCormick, 1991).

At an inner-city hospital in New York City, cocaine use was positively associated with both HIV and syphilis (Minkoff, McCalla, Delke, Stevens, & Feldman, 1990). Intravenous-drug-using women in San Francisco were found to be at increasing risk of HIV as a result of trading sex for drugs when they also smoked crack cocaine (Watters & Cuthbert, 1992). Prostitutes in New Jersey who used intravenous drugs were also found to be as much at risk for HIV when they smoked crack as when they injected heroin (Sterk, 1988). Finally, a survey of indigent African-American men in New York City found that those who used crack were significantly less likely to use condoms (El-Bassel & Schilling, 1991).

The evidence to date appears very clear. Crack users are more at risk for HIV than are nonusers as a result of more frequent and unprotected sex. These background findings lead one back to the initial question: How are crack users different from nonusers? Key dimensions were taken from a broad range of theoretical explanations, and the differences between crack users and nonusers were explored (Lettieri, Sayers, & Pearson, 1980).

METHOD

Two groups of equal numbers of African-American male and female adolescents between 13 and 18 years of age were recruited by street outreach workers in San Francisco's Bayview Hunter's Point. The first group was a pilot sample used to identify the most promising research questions. Once these questions had been isolated, we interviewed a second group from which our data and inferences were drawn. Because crack use is a clandestine behavior, users represent a hidden population that is inaccessible by random household or street enumeration. Thus, both groups of respondents were recruited by experienced youth outreach workers who were knowledgeable of individuals and groups in the community who did and did not use crack. We estimated that more than 90% of those approached agreed to participate in the interview, probably because (a) they knew and trusted the outreach workers, and (b) they were compensated $15 for their time.

Pilot Sample

By self-report, two thirds of the pilot sample ($n = 50$) had used crack cocaine more than once, and one third had not used crack. Each respondent was interviewed by a youth counselor trained to use our protocol. Each private, one-on-one interview lasted approximately an hour and was tape recorded and transcribed. Interviewers were of the same sex as respondents. The interview questions were open ended and derived from social environmental influences (Johnson, 1980), family influences (Stanton, 1979), health beliefs, social peer influences (Jessor & Jessor, 1973), and social cognitive theories (Bandura, 1986). Instead of selecting which factors were most salient in determining the difference between crack users and nonusers, we allowed respondents to react to a range of factors drawn from each theoretical framework. Each interview explored the following topics in depth: (a) family circumstances before the initiation of drug use; (b) timing of initial drug use and sexual intercourse; (c) quality of respondents' relationships with family members, friends, and sexual partners; (d) attitudes toward school and teachers; and (e) respondents' own and their parents' work histories.

The completed transcripts were read for consistent themes, insights, and patterns of response. Respondents' answers and comments appeared to support continuing questions based on all of the theoretical frames except peer influences and health beliefs. On the basis of these critical readings, a series of more specific and focused questions was developed for further analysis with a second sample.

Analytic Sample

A second group of adolescents between 13 and 18 years of age was recruited a year after the first group. Participants in the pilot sample were not included. There were an equal number of male and female adolescents ($n = 58$), among whom 22 were crack users and 36 were nonusers. They, too, were interviewed by youth counselors trained as interviewers. The second and more specific protocol was used, which asked respondents to discuss their relationships with their immediate family, extended family, and school officials and teachers and asked whether or not they had close friends. Respondents were also asked whether they were sexually active. If they were, they were asked whether they considered their relations to be long term or casual and whether they had multiple partners. Furthermore, respondents were asked about traumatic events in their lives, whether they could remember pleasant events as children, and their future aspirations.

Finally, they were asked about their work histories and drug use and frequency. These factors were either important to repeat or were missing in the pilot sample. Again, same-sex interviewers conducted private, one-to-one interviews that lasted approximately an hour and were tape recorded and transcribed.

Coding and Analysis

The wealth of information and insight generated from the interviews presented opportunities to extract both qualitative and quantitative data. For this analysis, all the protocol questions were coded as dichotomous variables. Then the open-ended discussions were used to assist in qualitatively interpreting and analyzing each variable and the relations between variables. The Statistical Package for the Social Sciences (SPSSX) was used to analyze the complete data set on an IBM 9730 computer with a VM/CMS environment.

RESULTS

Analysis focused on social relationships as major sources of motivation either to use or not to use crack cocaine. First, factors that were not significantly different between users and nonusers should be pointed out. The areas in which we were unable to find statistically significant differences are equally as telling as those in which differences were found. The quality of respondents' reported relations with their parents; whether the heads of their households were female, male, or both; and the basis of family financial support (welfare, jobs, and so forth) did not distinguish users from nonusers. School experiences and whether or not respondents had any teachers they liked were also insignificant. Neither one nor a number of specific traumatic experiences distinguished users from nonusers, nor did the unexpected deaths of close friends or relatives. A number of respondents reported that close friends had been killed in the community. Finally, work experience or nonexperience was also insignificant.

Table 1 presents distributions and key statistics for variables in which statistically significant differences were found between crack users and nonusers. Age was the only significant demographic variable. Sixty-eight percent of users began regular crack smoking soon after 16 years of age; 15.2% began using crack before they were 15 years old. The social significance of 15 and 16 years is contextualized by school grade: Most regular crack use started at the transition between junior and senior high school.

What respondents told us about the quality of their interactions with parents (guardians) and their family composition did not statistically distinguish between users and nonusers, but other indirect family relationship

TABLE 1

Comparison of African-American Adolescent Crack Cocaine Users and Nonusers by Social Relation Variables

Variable	Total	Users		Nonusers		X^2	p	Odds ratio	95% confidence interval
		%	N	%	N				
Age (years)						16.8	.000	0.20	0.095–0.520
13–15	33	15.2	5	84.8	28				
16–18	25	68.0	17	32.0	8				
Grade						9.4	.002	0.25	0.080–0.750
6–9	22	13.6	3	86.4	19				
10–12	35	54.3	19	45.7	16				
Good memories						4.18	.041	0.50	0.273–0.930
Yes	43	30.2	13	69.8	30				
No	15	60.0	9	40.0	6				
Celebrate holidays with						7.03	.008	0.37	0.230–0.590
Family	54	33.3	18	66.7	36				
Others	4	100.0	4	0.0	0				
Rules at home						6.98	.008	0.41	0.232–0.720
Yes	47	29.8	14	70.2	33				
No	11	72.7	8	27.3	3				
Use alcohol						8.88	.003	3.87	1.29–11.60
Yes	36	52.8	19	47.2	17				
No	22	13.6	3	86.4	19				
Use marijuana						16.7	.000	7.57	1.94–27.40
Yes	33	60.6	20	39.4	13				
No	25	8.0	2	92.0	23				
Ever had a sexually transmitted disease						9.56	.002	2.42	1.52–03.90
Yes	8	100.0	8	0.0	0				
No	31	38.7	12	61.3	19				

factors did distinguish users from nonusers. Most respondents could remember pleasant childhood memories; however, 60% of those who could not remember such moments were crack users, in comparison with only 30% of those who did not use. Clearly, long-term crack use could have affected users' ability to recall early memories. It is unlikely that they were "high" on crack at the time of the interview and had their responses immediately affected by an altered mood. If so, they could not have lasted as they did through an hour-long interview. Regardless, they either lost pleasant childhood memories or did not have them. In either case, their memories were distinct from those of nonusers.

Prior to drug use, most respondents spent holidays at home with their nuclear or extended family even when they were separated from their parents. However, all of those who spent holidays alone or with friends were crack users. Seventy-two percent of crack users had no rules governing their conduct at home prior to their drug use. Childhood memories, where respondents spent holidays, and developmental rules at home were indirect measures of the extent to which either nuclear or extended families were part of respondents' social influences, regardless of whether those relationships were positive or negative.

One of the more interesting findings is that earlier alcohol and marijuana use more clearly distinguished crack users from nonusers than did the indirect measures of family social relations. Almost 61% of those who used marijuana as their first drug moved on to crack, whereas only 8% of respondents who did not use marijuana before crack went directly to crack. The same was true for alcohol use. Drinking preceded crack use, and not drinking was strongly associated with not using crack. Finally, virtually all the respondents 15 years of age or older were sexually active, but all the crack users had at least one sexually transmitted disease, in comparison with 38.7% of nonusers.

Table 2 presents the results of a series of logistic regression analyses showing the interactions of significant variables as predictors of crack use. After intercorrelated significant variables had been separated, the logistic regression models produced the following results.

In Model 1, several independently significant variables associated with crack use and nonuse were tested in relation to each other. The only significant variable was smoking marijuana, which was a better predictor of crack use than any of the family quality or engagement variables. Model 2 is distinct from Model 1 by the inclusion of school grade. Because drinking alcohol and smoking marijuana before the initiation of crack use were highly intercorrelated, the marijuana variable was dropped from the equation. Again, however, the prior drug use variable, drinking alcohol, was a better predictor than were the family relation measures. The third model is distinct from the first two because having rules at home and drinking alcohol were included together. Again, the prior drug use variable, drinking

TABLE 2
Multiple Regression Models of Predictors of Crack Use for
African-American Adolescents

Variable	Coefficient	SE	p
Model 1 ($c = 47.1$, $df = 50$, $p = .589$)			
Pleasant memories	−1.033	0.806	.198
Ever had sexually transmitted disease	−0.089	0.452	.843
Smoking marijuana	2.118	0.921	.022
Drinking alcohol	0.692	0.864	.423
Rules at home	−1.266	0.957	.187
Holidays with family/others	−7.281	28.465	.798
Model 2 ($c = 53.1$, $df = 51$, $p = .392$)			
Holidays with family/others	−8.158	29.454	.782
Ever had sexually transmitted disease	−0.298	0.392	.447
Drinking alcohol	1.531	0.752	.042
School grades	0.039	0.143	.787
Pleasant memories	−1.105	29.508	.773
Model 3 ($c = 51.3$, $df = 51$, $p = .461$)			
Rules at home	−1.624	0.835	.052
Ever had sexually transmitted disease	−0.306	0.396	.440
Drinking alcohol	1.621	0.761	.033
School grades	0.042	0.154	.788
Pleasant memories	−1.152	0.719	.109
Model 4 ($c = 51.2$, $df = 53$, $p = .544$)			
Drinking alcohol	1.603	0.741	.031
Pleasant memories	−1.167	0.732	.111
Holidays with family/others	−7.692	27.904	.783
Rules at home	−1.416	0.891	.112

Note. c is goodness-of-fit statistic.

alcohol, was a significant predictor, along with having rules at home. In the final model, drinking was again a significant predictor, and the variable where one spends holidays appeared to have surpassed the significance of having rules at home.

DISCUSSION

One can conclude that there is a "gateway" process at work (Kandel, 1980). Marijuana and alcohol use appear to be important gateways to crack use. We had no way of knowing the extent to which the chemical effects of marijuana and alcohol were habituated with our respondents. However, the social role that these drugs play in the lives of our crack-using respondents is associated with the transition from junior or middle school to high school. For most respondents, drug use and sexual intercourse began at this transition point. Fortunately, in this research project we had ample respondent comments to help us interpret the statistical findings. We were impressed by the importance of the transition from junior to senior high school in the respondents who were 15 and 16 years old. Their parents, extended families, and friends view this transition as an entry into adulthood. Adolescents are expected to obtain part-time jobs and to be more responsible for themselves. Alcohol and marijuana use, viewed as "adult behavior," ritualize this transition; adventure and excitement are attached to these behaviors because they are new and involve risk. Once these adolescents begin using alcohol and marijuana, they begin to question the fear of addiction and the social warnings about negative effects. They believe that their functioning is not impaired and they are no worse for using. This social context for initiating and using marijuana or alcohol is probably no different for this generation of adolescents than for any that have preceded them. What is distinct for this generation is the next step.

It is a long jump from marijuana and alcohol use to injecting drugs because of needle phobia and all that is involved in preparing injectable drugs. For those who already smoke marijuana, drink, and engage in sex, however, moving to crack is an easy step. Crack, which is smoked just like marijuana, is a more powerful and equally inexpensive drug that is exciting and clearly more attractive. Using crack and not getting hooked is a challenge. Because what "they" said about marijuana was not true, potential users are less inclined to believe the warnings about crack. It is in this specific and very casual context that crack use begins. From what we can determine from the interview transcripts, initial use almost always occurs in small groups with peers and begins with "chipping" (mixing crack with marijuana).

We were impressed by how the adolescents' curiosity, risk taking, and need to challenge and initiate adult behaviors were the motives for beginning crack use. Given the social context of initiating crack use, nonuse is all the more interesting. This research suggests that family relations act as a barrier to early gateway drug use and to subsequent crack use. Surprisingly, it made no difference whether the respondent reported having good or poor interactions with parents or other extended family members. The significant distinction was whether or not there were parents and extended family with whom to interact in the first place, as indicated by the presence of rules at home and where holidays were spent. It appears that young people who are left on their own to make the transition to adult status and behaviors are more likely to use marijuana and alcohol and to move on to crack.

The theoretical frameworks suggested by these findings are sensitive to subtle family social distance dynamics, gateway progressions, and alienation from mainstream advice and messages. If peer influences were strong enough to dispose our respondents to use crack, they were not statistically detectable from this sample. We recommend that further research focus on the influences of social environments (Johnson, 1980) and family dynamics (Stanton, 1979) and on drug use among African-American adolescents rather than on more individual-focused theories.

We may not have isolated the initial distinction between crack users and nonusers. Crack use and the subsequent superexploitative behaviors that come with it may have wiped out respondents' memories of any pleasant childhood experiences. Crack users' families may have distanced themselves from these adolescents after they began using the drug. In this case, what users reported about their families prior to initiating use may be biased by their present experiences as users. Finally, we were totally dependent on the truthfulness of the self-reports from users and nonusers alike. Given the culturally appropriate relationships between our recruiters and interviewers and the respondents, we are inclined to trust the validity of our respondents' self-reports. Clearly, additional research is needed to assess the validity of this self-report analysis.

IMPLICATIONS FOR PREVENTION

Education about drugs clearly must address the conflict between the experience of marijuana–alcohol use and crack use. First, because their experiences with marijuana and alcohol do not match public warnings, young people must be convinced that crack cocaine is, indeed, a far more dangerous drug. Second, prevention of crack use begins with prevention of marijuana and alcohol use. The entire community, including parents, must step up to this issue. Drinking cannot be socially accepted, heavily advertised, and associated with success, and cannot be a marker of adult status separate from crack cocaine. For adolescents, the motivations for using crack are the same as adults' motivation for drinking. Third, the specific focus of prevention should be the transition between middle school and high school, the point at which most of our respondents began alcohol and marijuana use and regular sexual activity. Fourth, there is a desperate need for the African-American community to define and to take control of what constitutes an appropriate transition from adolescence to adulthood and what rituals are indicative of this transition. Fifth, nuclear and extended families are underestimated barriers to drug use that need assistance in their efforts to contextualize the transition of young people from adolescence to adulthood.

Finally, the presence or absence of either nuclear or extended families is not a primary causal factor in distinguishing crack users from nonusers. A reading of crack users' descriptions of family circumstances clearly suggests that their family's expectations of early transitions to adulthood and independence are economically driven. Users' families appear less able than nonusers' families to provide support to teens whose emotional and financial needs are growing in their transition to adulthood. Subsequent research must address this point more directly.

REFERENCES

Bandura, A. (1986). *Social foundations of thought and action: A social cognitive theory.* Englewood Cliffs, NJ: Prentice Hall.

Booth, R., Watters, J., & Chitwood, D. (1992, July). *HIV sexual risk factors among crack cocaine smokers.* Paper presented at the VIII International Conference on AIDS, Amsterdam, The Netherlands.

Bowser, B., Fullilove, M. T., & Fullilove, R. E. (1990). African-American youth and AIDS high risk behavior: The social context and barriers to prevention. *Youth and Society, 22,* 54–66.

Centers for Disease Control. (1991). *HIV/AIDS surveillance report.* Atlanta, GA: Author.

Chiasson, M., Stoneburger, R. L., Hildebrandt, D. S., Ewing, W. E., Telzak, E. E., & Jaffe, H. W. (1991). Heterosexual transmission of HIV-1 associated with the use of smokeable free-base cocaine (crack). *AIDS, 5,* 1121–1126.

Chirgwin, K., De Havitz, J., Dillon, S., & McCormick, W. (1991). HIV infection, genital ulcer disease and crack cocaine use among patients attending a clinic for sexually transmitted diseases. *American Journal of Public Health, 81,* 1576–1579.

Edlin, B., Irwin, K., Ludwig, D., Serrano, Y., Word, C., McCoy, C., Byers, R., & Holberg, S. (1992, July). *HIV infection and crack cocaine smoking in street recruited urban youth, U.S.* Paper presented at the VIII International Conference on AIDS, Amsterdam, The Netherlands.

El-Bassel, N., & Schilling, R. (1991). Drug use and sexual behavior of indigent African-American men. *Public Health Reports, 106,* 586–590.

Fullilove, R., Fullilove, M. T., Bowser, B. P., & Gross, S. A. (1990). Risk of sexually transmitted disease among Black adolescent crack users in Oakland and San Francisco, Calif. *Journal of the American Medical Association, 263,* 851–855.

Jessor, R., & Jessor, S. (1973). A social psychology of marijuana use. *Journal of Personality and Social Psychology, 26,* 1–15.

Johnson, B. (1980). Toward a theory of drug subcultures. In D. Lettieri, et al. (Eds.), *Theories of drug abuse* (NIDA Research Monograph 30, pp. 110–119). Washington, DC: U.S. Government Printing Office.

Kandel, D. (1980). Developmental stages in adolescent drug involvement. In D. Lettieri et al. (Eds.), *Theories on drug abuse* (NIDA Research Monograph 30, pp. 120–127). Washington, DC: U.S. Government Printing Office.

Lettieri, D., Sayers, M., & Pearson, H. W. (Eds.). (1980). *Theories on drug abuse* (NIDA Research Monograph 30). Washington, DC: U.S. Government Printing Office.

Minkoff, H., McCalla, S., Delke, I., Stevens, R., and Feldman, J. (1990). The relationship of cocaine use to syphilis and HIV infection among inner city parturient women. *American Journal of Obstetrics-Gynecology, 163,* 521–526.

Stanton, M. (1979). Drugs and the family. *Marriage and Family Review, 2,* 1–10.

Sterk, C. (1988). Cocaine and HIV positivity [letter]. *Lancet, 1,* 1052–1053.

Watters, J., & Cuthbert, M. (1992, July). *Does smoking crack cocaine increase risk in drug injecting women?* Paper presented at the VIII International Conference on AIDS, Amsterdam, The Netherlands.

32

SUBSTANCE ABUSE AMONG NATIVE-AMERICAN YOUTH

MICHAEL S. MONCHER, GARY W. HOLDEN, AND JOSEPH E. TRIMBLE

Nonmedical drug use, including tobacco and alcohol use, threatens the health, development, and future well-being of many American-Indian adolescents. Compared with members of other American ethnic–racial populations, Indian adolescents use drugs and alcohol earlier, more heavily, and with dire consequences (Austin, 1988; Beauvais & LaBoueff, 1985; Hall & Dexter, 1988; Oetting et al., 1983; Okwumabua & Duryea, 1987; Red Horse, 1982).

BACKGROUND

The United States today has 505 federally recognized Native-American tribes and 304 federal Native-American reservations. Between 1950 and 1980 there was a 282% increase in the number of Native Amer-

Reprinted from the *Journal of Consulting and Clinical Psychology, 58*, 408–415. (1990). Copyright © 1990 by the American Psychological Association. Used with permission of the author.

Preparation of this article was supported by National Institute on Drug Abuse Grant DA 03277 and National Cancer Institute Grant CA 44903. Gary W. Holden is now at Mt. Sinai School of Medicine.

icans recorded by the Census Bureau. Although methodological changes in census procedures and other factors may have inflated these figures, it seems clear that the Native-American population is growing and currently is at least as large the 1980 Census estimate of 1.4 million (U.S. Department of Health and Human Services, 1988; U.S. Department of Commerce, 1983).

Native-American birth rates were 28.8 per 1,000 population in 1982–1984 as compared with 15.5 per 1,000 for all races in 1983. The life expectancy for Native Americans in 1979–1981 was 67.1 years for men and 75.1 years for women. Native Americans have a lower death rate for diseases of the heart (137 vs. 183.6 per 100,000), but a higher rate for accidental deaths (81.3 vs. 35 per 100,000) than the rest of the population.

Native-American suicide rates are higher than for the general population of the United States. Among children of school age, suicide rates have been reported up to three times higher than those of majority youth (LaFromboise, 1988; U.S. Congress, Office of Technology Assessment, 1986). In 1979, the median income for Native Americans living on reservations was $9,920. Approximately 45% of the reservation population was below the poverty line (U.S. Department of Health and Human Services, 1988; U.S. Department of Commerce, Bureau of the Census, 1983).

Unhealthy for all Americans, substance abuse is inordinately harmful for American-Indian and Alaskan-Native people. They lead the nation in rates of alcohol-related cirrhoses, diabetes, fetal abnormalities, accident fatalities, and homicide (Pedigo, 1983; Travis, 1983; Ward, 1984). Alone, the use of smoked and smokeless tobacco causes several types of cancers, coronary damage, and cardiovascular disease. A 1985 Congressional hearing on Indian youth substance use found that over 50% of nonreservation and 80% of reservation Indian adolescents were at least moderately involved with alcohol, compared with 23% of urban, non-Indian youth (LaFromboise, 1988; U.S. Senate Select Committee on Indian Affairs, 1985). Combined use of alcohol and tobacco places Indian and Native people at risk for throat cancer and for fire injuries (Bobo & Gilchrist, 1983; Bobo, Gilchrist, Schilling, Noach & Schinke, 1987).

Indian and Native people are also highly susceptible to the harmful effects of marijuana, inhalant, and other illicit drugs (Query, 1985; Red Horse, 1982). Among American-Indian groups, substance use is implicated in educational setbacks for children (see LaFromboise, 1988), criminal acts for adults, and economic disadvantages for families (Beiser, 1984; Trimble, 1984). LaFromboise reports that "American Indians in urban areas are taken into police custody for violations committed under the influence of drugs or alcohol four times as often as Blacks and ten times as often as Whites (LaFromboise, 1988, p. 388).

These consequences are all the more serious because they manifest themselves immediately during the adolescent years by academic failure and delinquent behavior and later during adulthood by unemployment and violent crimes (Oetting et al., 1983; Pedigo, 1983; Travis, 1983; Ward, 1984).

PREVALENCE RATES OF SUBSTANCE USE

Recent findings (Beauvais, Oetting, Wolf, & Edwards, 1989) highlighting the severity of American-Indian adolescent drug and alcohol involvement validate the results of earlier studies on this population (Cockerham, 1977; Oetting et al., 1983; Weibel-Orlando, 1983). Samples of 7th- to 12th-grade American-Indian youth obtained from diverse tribal groups between 1975 and 1987 indicate that across the majority of substances, reported lifetime prevalence of use has increased. The following proportions of Native-American high school seniors in a 1986–1987 sample reported use in the past month: alcohol (58.5%); marijuana (36.5%); inhalants (1.8%); cocaine (3.7%); stimulants (9.1%); cigarettes (38.3%); and smokeless tobacco (31.4%) according to Johnston, Bachman, and O'Malley (1988). In terms of younger Native Americans, Beauvais et al. (1989) have stated that "by the time they are in the 7th grade, 28 per cent of Indian youth report at least one episode of getting drunk, 44 per cent have tried marijuana, 22 per cent inhalants, 12 per cent stimulants, and 72 per cent cigarettes" (p. 635).

In a recent study using derived risk factors to assess the predictability of substance use rates among 4th- and 5th-grade American-Indian youth in the Pacific Northwest and Oklahoma (mean age = 10.27, % female = 48.1), we obtained data indicating similarly disquieting rates. Table 1 presents lifetime and more recent rates of use for selected substances.

Alcohol was the most prevalent substance used by the sample, with 44% indicating use. Smokeless and smoked tobacco each have been used by over one third of subjects reporting. Marijuana has been tried by over 10% of the sample, and inhalants and cocaine by 7% and 3%, respectively.

TABLE 1
Percentages of Lifetime and Past Month Use of
Substances Within a Sample of Native-American Youth

Substance	Lifetime use (%)	Use in past week (%)
Cigarettes	33.6	11.6
Smokeless tobacco	36.6	25.5
Alcohol	43.6	6.8
Inhalants	6.6	3.5
Cannabis	10.2	3.8
Cocaine/crack	2.6	1.6

Use in the last week was almost 26% for smokeless tobacco and 12% for smoked tobacco products. Past weekly use of alcohol and marijuana was reported by 7% and 4% of the sample, respectively.

ISSUES IN PREVENTION

Of all the means for remediating the problems of drug use among American-Indian adolescents, none offer more hope than prevention. Preventive interventions hold the promise of not only reducing the lifetime incidence of drug use problems among Indian people, but also of helping Indian adolescents promote their health and social functioning in positive and lasting ways.

Yet prevention efforts for American-Indian youth continue to suffer in several areas. First, although a number of etiological constructs have been advanced as explicative of empirically derived findings that describe disparate rates of substance use, only recently have researchers begun to develop and test theoretical models taking advantage of these constructs (Gilchrist, Schinke, Trimble, & Cvetkovich, 1987; Schinke, Botvin, et al., 1988).

Second, we have yet to develop a strong theoretically based risk assessment model for targeting youth in particular jeopardy for substance use. Even less is known about protective factors, "about why some youths from high-risk environments fail to develop a substance abuse problem" (Austin, 1988, p. 1; see also McIntyre & White, 1988). Synergistically, how protective and high-risk factors work together on an individual level toward risk for substance use is sorely underresearched. Bell (1988) and Tarter (1988) have both proposed multivariate models that may be useful in explaining variance for at-risk substance abusing behaviors. Our current research continues this work.

Third, issues of bicultural competence require that interventions work toward helping American-Indian youth achieve a level of comfort in both worlds within which they must reside (LaFromboise & Rowe, 1983; Schinke, Botvin, et al., 1988). Preventive interventions must more sensitively address acculturation issues if they are to be successful within this population.

CORRELATES OF SUBSTANCE USE AND ASSESSMENT OF RISK

Correlates of Use

Numerous psychosocial models have been derived to explain substance use among American Indian youth. Although not culturally specific, many of them provide insight regarding the problems of this population (see Donovan & Jessor, 1985; Oetting & Beauvais, 1986, 1987; Yamaguchi & Kandel, 1984; Newcomb & Bentler, 1986, 1988; Newcomb, Maddahian & Bentler, 1986; Carpenter, Lyons, & Miller, 1985). Modeling variables, peer pressure, experimental substance use as an expression of stage-related rebelliousness, tension reduction and coping, and a sense of alienation very likely combine to partially explain the generally high rates of use among Indian youth.

Given that Indian youth tend toward earlier experimentation with a number of substances than does the general population (Oetting, Edwards, Goldstein, & Garcia-Mason, 1980; Okwumabua & Duryea, 1987), examination of culturally specific correlates is needed to explain additional variance. Recent reviews have focused primarily on acculturation theory and ethnography (LaFromboise, 1988; LaFromboise & Rowe, 1983; Schinke, Botvin et al., 1988; Schinke et al., 1990). Acculturation theory has been applied to explain deviant behavior among youth from other minority cultures as well as American-Indian youth (Schinke, Moncher, Palleja, Zayas, & Schilling, 1988; Szapozcnik, Scopetta, & King, 1978; Szapozcnik, Scopetta, & Tillman, 1978).

Acculturation theory suggests that youth from minority cultural backgrounds will experience greater amounts of stress to the extent that they will not develop the necessary skills to comfortably interact within both minority and majority cultures. Skills deficiencies often lead to stress among youth, and substance use has been noted as a coping response to both environmental and interpersonal stressors. Consequently, development of a bicultural competence skills repertoire is an important goal in prevention intervention development.

LaFromboise (1982) noted that bicultural competence skills allow youth to "blend the adaptive values and roles of both the culture in which they were raised and the culture by which they are surrounded" (p. 12). LaFromboise and Rowe (1983) elaborated: "A socially competent, bicultural assertive lifestyle involves being benevolently interested in the needs of the group, socially responsible to perpetuate a belief system that highly values personal rights and the rights of others, self-confident . . . , and decisive" (p. 592).

The Continuum of Risk

The multivariate nature of substance use correlates as they relate to the determination of risk proneness has long been recognized. A review of the literature documents the illusive nature of causation in that generally small amounts of variance are explained. Multicollinearity issues, the constant emergence of new potential variables, differential sampling techniques, and the general complexity of this type of behavioral assessment have led to a multiplicity of assessment batteries and competing viewpoints.

Thus it becomes difficult to develop a strong theoretical basis for establishing a fixed developmental chain leading to substance use initiation, experimentation, and finally habituation. In approaching our work, we have chosen to use a risk factor strategy that has been employed by others (Bry, McKeon, & Pandina, 1982; Newcomb, Maddahian, & Bentler, 1986; Newcomb, Maddahian, Skager, & Bentler, 1987).

This approach maintains that if a multitude of personal and environmental variables account for some unique variance explaining youth substance use, then a subject possessing or exposed to multiple factors should be at higher risk for use. For example, Newcomb et al. (1987) reported that 12% of their overall sample reported daily smoking. This percentage was reduced to 1% for those subjects reporting no risk factors; by contrast, the percentage increased to 56% for those subjects reporting seven or more risk factors.

Increasing complexity of analyses has resulted in an increasing number of risk factors, ranging from 6 (Bry et al., 1982) to 12 (Newcomb, Maddahian, Skager, & Bentler, 1987). On the basis of our assessment battery pretesting results, we have continued this trend as we focus on substance use behaviors among Native-American youth. Although use of smoked and smokeless tobacco appears to be more accepted among Northwest Native-American youth, we have included these behaviors as likely predictors of future substance use behaviors (see Yamaguchi & Kandel, 1984).

We have developed 16 categories of risk, assessed by a composite battery of self-report items. The categories include use of smoked tobacco; use of smokeless tobacco; family smoking; peer smoking; family smokeless tobacco use; peer smokeless tobacco use; experimentation, intentions to use, and peer use of alcohol, inhalants, marijuana, and cocaine/crack; quality of family relationship; school adjustment; non-substance-related deviant behaviors; perceived deviance in school environment; cultural identification; and religiosity.

Our pilot data indicate good internal interitem consistency (Cronbach α = .73). The categories express substance use modeling by significant others, intentions to use substances in the future, prior and current experimentation with substances, and a number of variables more distally related to substance use.

For example, perceived deviant school environment was operationalized using a 5-point Likert scale by asking subjects how often the following activities were observed at their schools: students using drugs; students destroying property; students drinking beer, wine, or hard liquor; students getting into fights; students stealing things; and students using inhalants.

We believe that by extension of risk categories to include parent and peer modeling of tobacco and other substance use as well as behavioral intentions, we may increase the accuracy of classification of subjects at high risk for future substance use and abuse.

We have redefined several of the traditional risk factors. For example, Newcomb et al., 1986, utilized three variables to represent three separate risk categories: absenteeism, low academic achievement, and low educational aspirations. We have combined our educationally related variables into a single category, school adjustment. We have attempted to increase explained variance in this category by using six items to assess risk, thus offering the possibility of greater accuracy of classification.

Furthermore, we have attempted incorporation of a weighting scheme into our assessment battery to target more sensitively the most vulnerable youth. In the work of the Newcomb group (1986), a subject exceeding the cutoff in a given risk category received one risk factor toward the total computation of the risk score. We would suggest that such equal weighting of risk factors may not accurately reflect high risk.

Because our review did not disclose previous empirical work, weightings have been derived using more general empirical data that indicate the presence of the strongest relations between substance use and modeling variables, attitudes and intentions regarding smoking and other substance use, and prior experimentation. Several studies have shown that these variables explain two or more times the variance of other variables included in risk assessment (see Kleinman, Wish, Deren, Rainone, & Morehouse, 1988; Kline, Canter, & Robin, 1987; Oetting, Beauvais, & Edwards, 1988; Reid, Martinson, & Weaver, 1987). Over the course of our study we have evaluated the salience of our risk factors, whether a weighting scheme will add sensitivity to the identification of youth at greatest risk, and what combination of weights will be most effective.

Although some might suggest that a risk factor approach may confuse the consequences of substance use with its antecedents, we believe that the majority of the risk factors we have identified have been shown to temporally precede use. In cases where there is no clearcut temporal ordering, the youthful age of our sample offers at least theoretical protection against confounds. This may be problematic in the areas of smoked and smokeless tobacco given the normative use of these substances by the subject population.

Our study attempts to assess the utility of our risk factor scheme as well as the hypothesis that weighting risks may provide more accurate assessment of current and future substance use. Due to the overall high-risk nature of the sample, we have chosen cut scores allowing assignment of one risk factor to all subjects who score above the mean in a given risk category. As more data become available over the course of our work, we will refine this scheme on the basis of use rates over time.

METHOD

The data reported here are taken from a sample of Native-American youth located in the Western United States ($n = 1,147$; mean age = 10.27; percentage female = 48.1; percentage Indian = 93.0). (The balance of the sample were White.) Fourth- and fifth-grade youth from reservation sites and tribal communities throughout the Northwest were recruited through schools, tribal councils, and community organizations. Local community advisory boards were formed to provide direction regarding collaborative contacts and instrument development. Study design and assessment were further shaped by an earlier pilot study of a similar population (Gilchrist et al., 1987).

Refusal rates did not differ by site and averaged 2% across the sample. Survey items included measures of knowledge and attitudes regarding substance use, self-reported use rates, and intentions to use substances in the future. Other questions assessed subjects' acculturation, propensity for engaging in risk-taking behaviors, school adjustment, and self-concept. Measures included items adapted from Oetting, Beauvais, Edwards, & Waters (1984); Trimble (in press); and Gilchrist, Schinke, Trimble, & Cvetkovich (1987). Mean test–retest reliability for the battery was .78.

Biochemical validation was obtained for cotinine and thiocyanate. Correlations with self-report data are not yet available. No procedures were used to assess self-report accuracy concerning other substances, however the "bogus pipeline" effect should serve to enhance data reliability.

RESULTS

T tests and correlations were performed to examine the predictive utility of the authors' assessment battery in terms of identifying subjects at highest risk for substance use. Our weighted risk scheme did not provide additional discrimination, and we have thus chosen to present only unweighted results. Tables 2 and 3 report these data. Because nonindependent tests were performed, the Bonferroni correction was applied, reducing the analysiswise significance level from 0.5 to .004.

Table 2 reports subjects' risk scores correlated with the most current available measure of use for smoked and smokeless tobacco, alcohol, marijuana, inhalants, and cocaine/crack. In all cases, there was a significant correlation ($p < .001$) between the total risk score and reported use of these substances. Correlations were highest between risk factor totals and lifetime use of smokeless tobacco, $r(1129) = .58$; reported lifetime use of smoked tobacco, $r(1141) = .54$; and reported lifetime use of alcohol, $r(1117) = .54$.

Associations were weaker, yet still highly significant, for lifetime use

TABLE 2
Correlation of Risk Factors and Lifetime Use of Selected Substances

Substance	r	df
Smoked tobacco	.54	1141
Smokeless tobacco	.58	1129
Alcohol	.54	1117
Inhalants	.38	1120
Marijuana	.45	1118
Cocaine/crack	.28	1116

Note. p < .001.

of marijuana, $r(1118) = .45$; lifetime inhalant use, $r(1120) = .38$; and lifetime use of cocaine/crack, $r(1116) = .28$. Given the low rates of use noted in the sample for inhalants and cocaine/crack, these results are not surprising.

Table 3 reports t tests derived by obtaining overall mean risk factor scores from the 16 individual risk factor scores, then dichotomizing these overall scores at their means into high and low risk groups. As before, in the case of each substance examined, the high-risk group used at significantly higher rates ($p < .001$) than did the low-risk group. Again, t values were highest for alcohol, $t(657) = -13.65$; smokeless tobacco, $t(647) = -13.07$; and marijuana, $t(586) = -9.31$. Lower t values were obtained for smoked tobacco, inhalant, and cocaine/crack use.

Figure 1 illustrates the linear relationship observed by Newcomb, Maddahian, Skager, and Bentler (1987) between the cumulative number of obtained risk factors and subjects' use of various substances.

Figure 1 shows that with very few exceptions, higher numbers of risk factors indicate higher percentages of use during the past year across all substances. Of those youth with 10 or more of a possible 16 risk factors, over 90% were currently using beer or wine, and nearly 80% were currently using marijuana. During the past year, almost 50% of subjects reported inhalant use, and nearly 30% had used cocaine/crack.

TABLE 3
Comparison of High and Low Risk Groups on Selected Substances

Substance	Low-risk mean	High-risk mean	t	df
Smoked tobacco[a]	0.02	0.73	-5.79	503
Smokeless tobacco[a]	1.10	1.85	-13.07	647
Alcohol[a]	1.10	1.69	-13.65	657
Inhalants[ab]	1.00	1.26	-7.79	565
Marijuana[ab]	1.01	1.34	-9.31	586
Cocaine/crack[ab]	1.00	1.11	-5.05	560

[a]p < .001. [b]Lifetime prevalence rates reported for these substances.

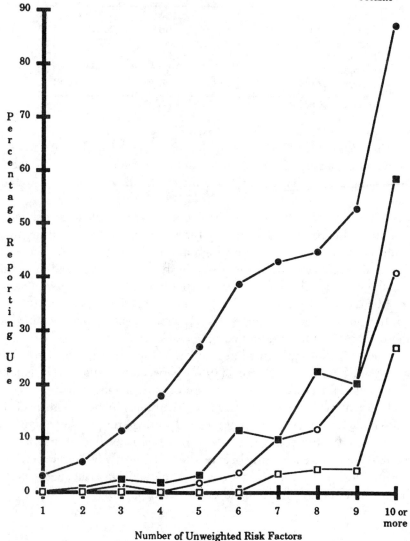

Figure 1. Percentage of subjects using selected substances during past year by cumulative risk factors.

DISCUSSION

These data provide some evidence of the utility of the risk-factor approach in identifying youth at high risk for substance use or abuse. Risk scale scores were strongly correlated with reported use across a range of substances. Further, dichotomization of scores into high and low risk groups provided significantly different mean rates of use for all substances reported.

The highest correlations with total risk scores were obtained with reported lifetime smokeless tobacco use, followed by lifetime smoked tobacco use and lifetime alcohol use. The smallest correlation was obtained for lifetime cocaine/crack use. This is consistent with the high frequency of tobacco use in this young sample compared with the more limited use of harder substances including inhalants and cocaine/crack.

Given the lack of additional predictive utility obtained with our weighted risk factor approach, we are currently experimenting with other weighting schemes. Longitudinal data may allow empirical testing of the predictive utility of risk factor strategies generally and may provide additional information regarding the value of weights.

These results may have implications for future risk assessment models specific to this population, given its disproportionately high early use of tobacco products. Future studies might longitudinally assess American Indian youth with differential early rates of tobacco use to ascertain whether those using with greater frequency do go on to use other substances at higher rates than those youth not involved with tobacco. Further, gender differences may be significant in this progression as explored by Kandel and her colleagues (Yamaguchi & Kandel, 1984; Kandel & Logan, 1984).

These data reaffirm the uncharacteristically high rates of substance use among Native-American youth. We compared a demographically representative, older, high-risk, school-based population in the Western United States (n = 2,005, mean age = 10.95) on variables related to tobacco. American-Indian youngsters exhibited substantially higher rates across all categories examined. These data, collected concurrently, are disquieting if tobacco use is a significant correlate in predicting future other substance use (Yamaguchi & Kandel, 1984).

As an example, more than 28% of the Indian sample indicated an intention to smoke in high school, and 36.4% said they might smoke as adults. The more "generic" school-based sample reported intentions of 1.5% and 2.0%, respectively. Intentions to use smokeless tobacco in high school and as adults were 20.6% and 19.4%, respectively, in the Indian sample. Almost 20% of that sample reported intentions to smoke or use smokeless tobacco in the next 12 months.

These data indicate substantially higher sibling tobacco use rates than were reported by the more demographically representative school-based sample. More than 14% of the Indian sample reported brothers who smoked in contrast with only 5.2% of the generic sample, and almost 25% had brothers who used smokeless tobacco. Over 16% of the Indian subjects reported sisters who smoked, three times the number in the non-Indian school-based sample (5.5%). Almost 10% reported sisters who had used smokeless tobacco at time of administration of the test.

Regarding parental rates, over 40% of fathers, mothers, and other relatives smoked cigarettes. Smokeless tobacco rates were considerably lower, consonant with the literatures indicating a drop in smokeless tobacco use and a corresponding increase in smoked tobacco use in adulthood. Also alarming and perhaps reflective of the need for community intervention are the rates at which both smoked and smokeless tobacco products are provided to youth by parents and siblings. Almost 16% of the subjects reported having been given smokeless tobacco by their parents or primary caretakers. This figure increased to 17% by their siblings, and 23% by other relatives and family friends. Cigarettes were given to almost 7% of the sample by their parents, 12% by their friends, and 16% by other relatives and family friends.

On our scales of knowledge and deviance, the Indian sample did not report significantly differently from the non-Indian school-based sample. This strengthens the inference that behaviors regarding use of tobacco products are normative and pervasive in the Indian sample, related neither to lack of knowledge concerning their detrimental health effects, nor, as is traditionally believed to be the case in majority cultures, to propensity for involvement in deviant or risk-taking behaviors.

CONCLUSION

In any discussion of substance use rates among American-Indian youth, it is important to avoid stereotyping. Trimble (1977), discussing research on American Indian personality, wrote,

> results did little to provide a base for program development or problem solving, findings were typically cast into non-native theoretical frameworks and did not include native interpretation of outcomes; and . . . methodology and procedures approached research questions from perspectives foreign to respondents, tending to restrict elaboration within the native view . . . most of the findings focused on negative outcomes (e.g., drug addiction, alcoholism, suicide, dropouts, etc.). Few studies addressed the positive competent Indian adolescent. . . . If research on American Indians is to continue, accuracy of content from a native viewpoint should guide efforts. (pp. 161–162)

While correlates of use among Native-American early adolescents almost certainly include issues of acculturation, isolation, family and peer modeling, and normative behavior patterns regarding certain substances considered by some as precursors to more serious substance use (Yamaguchi & Kandel, 1984), there is still much to be done toward development of a more thorough model of the etiology of substance use, abuse, and habituation among this population.

As noted, our attempt to construct a weighted risk factor model that is based on the theoretical and empirical literature has not to date proven fruitful. A longitudinal study might yield more sensitive data both in terms of predictive risk categorization and the assignment of more appropriate weights.

Ethical issues involved in the use of assessment tools to identify youth at high risk for substance use and abuse remain to be addressed. Certainly negative labeling may result to the extent that youth are selected for differential intervention solely on the basis of a predictive instrument. This is especially important among Native-American youth, many of whom must deal with issues of cultural scapegoating at an early age. Furthermore, these data are not representative of all American-Indian youth. Vast intertribal and geographic differences exist within this population, and these must be accurately assessed. The reliability and validity of any risk assessment battery must therefore be very high. If, however, strong and predictive information becomes available on the basis of empirical testing of assessment models that explain greater amounts of variance, curricula developers will have a stronger arsenal of tools available for sensitive use. This will facilitate the possibility of crafting prevention programs more likely to be effective with American-Indian youth at high risk for substance use, without the need to isolate them from their lower risk peers.

REFERENCES

Austin, G. (1988). *Substance abuse among minority youth: 1. Native Americans* (Prevention Research Update No. 2). Western Center for Drug-Free Schools.

Beauvais, F. B., & LaBoueff, S. (1985). Drug and alcohol abuse intervention in American Indian communities. *International Journal of the Addictions, 20,* 139–171.

Beauvais, F. B., Oetting, E. R., Wolf, W., & Edwards, R. W. (1989). American Indian youth and drugs, 1976–87: A continuing problem. *American Journal of Public Health, 79,* 634–636.

Beiser, M. (1984). Flower of the two soils: Emotional health and academic performance of Native North American Indian children. *Journal of Preventive Psychiatry, 2,* 365–369.

Bell, R. (1988). Using the concept of risk to plan drug use intervention programs. *Journal of Drug Education, 18,* 135–142.

Bobo, J. K., & Gilchrist, L. D. (1983). Urging the alcoholic client to quit smoking cigarettes. *Addictive Behaviors, 8,* 297–305.

Bobo, J. K., Gilchrist, L. D., Schilling, R. F., Noach, B., & Schinke, S. P. (1987). Cigarette smoking attempts by recovering alcoholics. *Addictive Behaviors, 12,* 209–215.

Bry, B. H., McKeon, P., & Pandina, R. J. (1982). Extent of drug use as a function of number of risk factors. *Journal of Abnormal Psychology, 91,* 273–279.

Carpenter, R. A., Lyons, C. A., & Miller, W. R. (1985). Peer managed self-control program for prevention of alcohol abuse in American Indian high school students: A pilot evaluation study. *International Journal of the Addictions, 20,* 299–310.

Cockerham, W. C. (1977). Patterns of alcohol and multiple drug use among rural White and American Indian adolescents. *International Journal of the Addictions, 11,* 271–285.

Donovan, J. E., & Jessor, R. (1985). Structure of problem behavior in adolescence and young adulthood. *Journal of Consulting and Clinical Psychology, 53,* 890–904.

Gilchrist, L. D., Schinke, S. P., Trimble, J. E., & Cvetkovich, G. T. (1987). Skills enhancement to prevent substance abuse among American Indian Adolescents. *International Journal of the Addictions, 22,* 869–879.

Hall, R. L., & Dexter, D. (1988). Smokeless tobacco use and attitudes toward smokeless tobacco among Native Americans and other adolescents in the Northwest. *American Journal of Public Health, 78,* 1586–1588.

Johnston, L. D., Bachman, J. G., & O'Malley, P. M. (1988). *Summary of 1987 drug study results.* University of Michigan News and Information Service Press Release.

Kandel, D., & Logan, J. (1984). Patterns of drug use from adolescence to young adulthood: Periods of risk for initiation, continued use and discontinuation. *American Journal of Public Health, 74,* 660–666.

Kleinman, P. H., Wish, E. D., Deren, S., Rainone, G., & Morehouse, E. (1988). Daily marijuana use and problem behaviors among adolescents. *International Journal of the Addictions, 23,* 87–107.

Kline, R. B., Canter, W. A., & Robin, A. (1987). Parameters of teenage alcohol use: A path analytic conceptual model. *Journal of Consulting and Clinical Psychology, 55,* 521–528.

LaFromboise, T. D. (1982). *Assertion training with American Indians: Cultural/ behavioral issues for trainers.* Las Cruces: New Mexico State University.

LaFromboise, T. D. (1988). American Indian mental health policy. *American Psychologist, 43,* 388–397.

LaFromboise, T. D., & Rowe, W. (1983). Skills training for bicultural competence: Rationale and application. *Journal of Counseling Psychology, 30,* 589–595.

McIntyre, K., & White, D. (1988, October 17–20). *Building an information network on high risk youth.* Paper presented at the 10th Annual Conference of Substance Abuse Librarians and Information Specialists, Seattle, WA.

Newcomb, M. D., & Bentler, P. M. (1986). Frequency and sequence of drug use: A longitudinal study from early adolescence to young adulthood. *Journal of Drug Education, 16,* 101–120.

Newcomb, M. D., & Bentler, P. M. (1988). Impact of adolescent drug use and social support on problems of young adults: A longitudinal survey. *Journal of Abnormal Psychology, 97,* 64–75.

Newcomb, M. D., Maddahian, E., & Bentler, P. M. (1986). Risk factors for drug use among adolescents: Concurrent and longitudinal analyses. *American Journal of Public Health, 76,* 525–531.

Newcomb, M. D., Maddahian, E., Skager, R., & Bentler, P. M. (1987). Substance abuse and psychosocial risk factors among teenagers: Associations with sex, age, ethnicity and type of school. *American Journal of Drug and Alcohol Abuse, 13,* 413–433.

Oetting, E. R., & Beauvais, F. (1986). Peer cluster theory: drugs and the adolescent. *Journal of Counseling and Development, 65,* 17–22.

Oetting, E. R., & Beauvais, F. (1987). Peer cluster theory, socialization characteristics, and adolescent drug use: A path analysis. *Journal of Counseling Psychology, 34,* 205–213.

Oetting, E. R., Beauvais, F., & Edwards, R. (1988). Alcohol and Indian youth: Social and psychological correlates and prevention. *Journal of Drug Issues, 18,* 87–101.

Oetting, E. R., Beauvais, F., Edwards, R., & Waters, M. (1984). *The Clinical Drug Abuse Scale: Book II. Instrument development, reliability and validity.* Fort Collins, CO: Rocky Mountain Behavioral Science Institute.

Oetting, E. R., Beauvais, F., Edwards, R., Waters, M. R., Velarde, J., & Goldstein, G. (1983). *Drug use among Native American youth.* Fort Collins: Colorado State University.

Oetting, E. R., Edwards, B. A., Goldstein, G. S., & Garcia-Mason, V. (1980). Drug use among adolescents of five Southwestern Native American tribes. *International Journal of the Addictions, 15,* 439–445.

Okwumabua, J. O., & Duryea, E. J. (1987). Age of onset, periods of risk, and patterns of progression in drug use among American Indian high school students. *International Journal of the Addictions, 22,* 1269–1276.

Pedigo, J. (1983). Finding the "meaning" of Native American substance use: Implications for community prevention. *Personnel and Guidance Journal, 61,* 273–277.

Query, M. N. (1985). Comparative admission and follow-up study of American Indians and whites in the youth chemical dependency unit on the North Central Plains. *International Journal of the Addictions, 20,* 489–502.

Red Horse, Y. (1982). A cultural network model: Perspectives for adolescent services and para-professional training. In S. M. Manson (Ed.), *New directions in prevention among American Indian and Alaska Native communities* (pp. 175–190). Portland: Oregon Health Sciences University.

Reid, L., Martinson, O., & Weaver, L. (1987). Factors associated with the drug use of fifth through eighth grade students. *Journal of Drug Education, 17,* 149–161.

Schinke, S. P., Botvin, G. J., Trimble, J. E., Orlandi, M. A., Gilchrist, L. D., & Locklear, V. S. (1988). Preventing substance abuse among American-Indian adolescents: A bicultural competence skills approach. *Journal of Counseling Psychology, 35,* 87–90.

Schinke, S. P., Moncher, M. S., Palleja, J., Zayas, L. H., & Schilling, R. F. (1988).

Hispanic youth, substance abuse, and stress: Implications for prevention research. *The International Journal of Addictions, 23,* 809–826.

Schinke, S. P., Orlandi, M. A., Schilling, R. F., Botvin, G. J., Gilchrist, L. D., & Landers, C. (1990). Tobacco use by American Indian and Alaska Native people: Risks, psychosocial factors, and preventive intervention. *Journal of Drug Education, 35*(2), 1–12.

Szapocznik, J., Scopetta, M., & King, O. (1978). Theory and practice in matching treatment to the special characteristics and problems of Cuban immigrants. *Journal of Community Psychology, 6,* 112–122.

Szapocznik, J., Scopetta, M., & Tillman, W. (1978). What changes, what remains the same, and what affects acculturative change in Cuban immigrant families. In J. Szapocznik & M. C. Herra (Eds.), *Cuban Americans: Acculturation, adjustment and the family.* Miami: University Press.

Tarter, R. E. (1988). The high-risk paradigm in alcohol and drug abuse research. In R. W. Pickens & D. S. Svikis (Eds.), *Biological vulnerability to drug abuse.* (NIDA Research Monograph No. 88, DHHS Publication No. ADM 88-1590). Washington, DC: U.S. Government Printing Office.

Travis, R. (1983). Suicide in northwest Alaska. *White Cloud Journal, 3,* 23–30.

Trimble, J. E. (1977). The sojourner in the American Indian community: Methodological issues and concerns. *Journal of Social Issues, 33,* 159–174.

Trimble, J. E. (1984). Drug abuse prevention research needs among American Indians and Alaska Natives. *White Cloud Journal, 3,* 22–24.

Trimble, J. E. (in press). *Self-Perception and the American Indian.* New York: Praeger.

U.S. Congress, Office of Technology Assessment. (1986). *Indian health care* (OTA-H-290). Washington, DC: U.S. Government Printing Office.

U.S. Department of Commerce, Bureau of the Census. (1983). *We, the first Americans.* Washington, DC: U.S. Government Printing Office.

U.S. Department of Health and Human Services. (1988). *Indian Health Service: Chart series book* (0-218-547:QL3). Washington, DC: U.S. Government Printing Office.

U.S. Senate Select Committee on Indian Affairs. (1985). *Indian juvenile alcoholism and eligibility for BIA schools* (Senate Hearing 99-286). Washington, DC: U.S. Government Printing Office.

Ward, J. A. (1984). Preventive implications of a Native Indian mental health program: Focus on suicide and violent death. *Journal of Preventive Psychiatry, 2,* 371–385.

Weibel-Orlando, J. (1983). *Substance abuse among American Indian Youth: A continuing crisis.* Unpublished manuscript.

Yamaguchi, K., & Kandel, D. B. (1984). Patterns of drug use from adolescence to young adulthood: 3. Predictors of progression. *American Journal of Public Health, 74,* 673–681.

33

USING RESEARCH TO GUIDE
CULTURALLY APPROPRIATE DRUG
ABUSE PREVENTION

RICHARD F. CATALANO, J. DAVID HAWKINS, CLAUDIA KRENZ,
MARY GILLMORE, DIANE MORRISON, ELIZABETH WELLS,
AND ROBERT ABBOTT

Until recently, little research has focused on drug use among people of color, although it has long been asserted that responses to drug problems should be sensitive to cultural diversity (Artz, 1976; National Association of Black Social Workers and Association of Black Psychologists, 1973; Brown, Joe, & Thompson, 1985; Martinez, 1976; Tucker, 1985). One author (Tucker, 1985) concluded that

> There are no substantive comprehensive reviews of either empirical or clinical literature on ethnic minority drug abuse . . . , etiological studies that attempt to account for ethnic variations in drug use patterns are virtually nonexistent . . . , and there is no body of empirical literature

Reprinted from the *Journal of Consulting and Clinical Psychology*, 61, 804–811. (1993). Copyright ©
1993 by the American Psychological Association. Used with permission of the author.
    This article was supported by Grant No. 1-R01-DA04506-01 from the National Institute on
Drug Abuse and the Office of Juvenile Justice and Delinquency Prevention and Grant No.
2-R01-DA03721-09 from the National Institute on Drug Abuse.

857

to guide the design and selection of drug treatment and prevention procedures specific to ethnic minorities. (p. 1038)

Past research has investigated questions of risk and etiology (e.g., see Catalano et al., 1992; Maddahian, Newcomb, & Bentler, 1988a, 1988b) and prevention (e.g., see Beaulieu & Jason, 1988; Botvin et al., 1989; Hawkins, Von Cleve, & Catalano, 1991; Rotheram-Borus & Tsemberis, 1989; Schinke, Moncher, Palleja, Zayas, & Schilling, 1988) as they vary with ethnicity. However, these studies have not provided clear guidance for using research to ensure the cultural appropriateness of drug abuse prevention efforts. This article suggests several ways in which research can inform the design and implementation of prevention interventions and then illustrates these points with results from a study comparing European-American and African-American fifth-grade children who are part of a multiethnic urban sample.

First, studies of the prevalence and incidence of drug use within ethnic groups can provide important information on developmental points at which initiation occurs and patterns of use change (Gary & Berry, 1985). With few exceptions (Dembo, Blount, Schmeidler, & Burgos, 1986; Kandel, Single, & Kessler, 1976), studies have found that the early initiation of alcohol and other drug use is more prevalent among European-American youth than among Hispanic-, African-, or Asian-American youth (Barnes & Welte, 1986; Gillmore et al., 1990; Johnston, O'Malley, & Bachman, 1987; Maddahian et al., 1988b). Yet research indicates that African Americans and Hispanic Americans are overrepresented in statistics indicating addiction or drug-related problems (Adalf, Smart, & Tan, 1989; Johnson & Nishi, 1976).

If well understood, prevalence and incidence data can provide useful information on the developmental appropriateness and timing of prevention interventions. For instance, as a group, African-American youth appear to initiate drug use later than European-American youth. This later initiation may indicate that early experiences of African Americans help to protect them from the risk of early initiation when compared with European Americans. Although a complete review of the family and community strengths among African Americans is beyond the scope of this article, there is some evidence that (a) African-American adolescents report less access to alcohol (Harford, 1985) and marijuana (Maddahian et al., 1988b) than European-American adolescents and (b) African-American parents are more proactive in setting rules and monitoring their children's behavior (Catalano et al., 1992). Thus there appear to be early protective processes operating for African-American children, suggesting that prevention programming for them may be particularly important later developmentally, when initiation rates accelerate.

Second, research can inform culturally appropriate risk-focused prevention by exploring whether risk factors for drug abuse (see Hawkins, Catalano, & Miller, 1992; Kandel, Simcha-Fagan, & Davies, 1986; Maddahian et al., 1988b) differ across ethnic groups. With sound empirical knowledge regarding culturally specific risk factors, prevention efforts in specific communities can concentrate on reducing culturally salient risks. However, few etiological studies have provided specific information about risk factors for different ethnic groups. Rather, "some risk factors that have been identified are based on predominantly white samples, some are derived from predominantly black samples, and some are based on stratified samples which presumably give greater weight to those factors important for white subjects" (Wells et al., 1992, p. 116).

Third, when different cultural groups share common risk factors, research can investigate questions of differential exposure and help to establish intervention priorities. Maddahian, Newcomb, and Bentler (1988a, 1988b, 1988c) found that European-American and Hispanic-American youth were exposed to greater numbers of risk factors than African- and Asian-American youths. In their sample of 10th-, 11th-, and 12th-grade students, 31% of Hispanic-American, 30% of European-American, 25% of Asian-American, and 10% of African-American students were exposed to five or more risk factors. For example, although religiosity was a common predictor across racial groups, Asian- and European-American students had lower religiosity compared with African- and Hispanic-American students.

Fourth, research can also inform culturally effective communication of prevention activities. Szapocznik and his colleagues (Szapocznik & Kurtines, 1980; Szapocznik, Ladner, & Scopetta, 1979) suggested that the discrepancy between the acculturation rate of Cuban parents and children at their clinic had generated family conflict and led the children to be more influenced by antisocial and drug-using peers. The investigators designed their intervention to address directly both the Cuban and the American cultural values of these families and the tension created by the different cultural identities of the parents and their children. The Szapocznik study underscores the importance of recognizing, when designing prevention programs, the diversity in values, norms, socioeconomic status (SES), behavior, and even cultural identity that is likely to characterize all broad cultural groupings.

Finally, research on the relative effectiveness of methods for gaining access to various cultural groups should also enhance program effectiveness. Suggestions have ranged from employing therapists who live in the same community (Coleman, 1981) to involving African-American churches in the delivery of prevention services (Gary & Berry, 1985).

To illustrate the uses of research for culturally appropriate prevention, we draw on a continuing longitudinal study guided by the social development model (Hawkins et al., 1992; Hawkins & Weis, 1985). This study's goals are to identify the relative contributions of childhood risk factors to the etiology of adolescent drug initiation, regular use, and delinquency and to test the effects of preventive interventions. In our research we are particularly interested in early drug use initiation, because it has been shown to be a predictor of later drug problems (Kandel, 1978; Robins & Przybeck, 1985). The research analysis presented here is the fourth in a series examining cultural differences in the degree to which specific factors predict the variety of substances initiated by a sample of urban children 10 to 11 years old. Previous analyses in this series (Catalano et al., 1992; Gillmore et al., 1990; Wells et al., 1992) explored the differences across European-, African-, and Asian-American subjects in predictors of drug use initiation grouped by specific social interaction domain (i.e., family, school, and community). These previous studies completed within-ethnic-group regressions to estimate the predictive strength of the set of risk factors and to identify the risk factors that were salient for any of the groups.

The present analysis takes a more comprehensive approach to examine group differences explicitly. To look comprehensively at risk across ethnic groups, the analysis simultaneously examines four categories of risk factors that were significant for any of the ethnic groups: (a) availability of drugs and acceptability of drug use, (b) family factors, (c) other antisocial behavior, and (d) school factors. We also directly examine the contribution of ethnic group differences by including African- and European-American subjects in a single regression and testing the main and interaction effects of ethnic group membership on drug use initiation, while controlling for the effects of other drug abuse predictors.

METHOD

Data collection began in 1981 with a panel of 568 first-grade students in 8 Seattle, Washington, schools. In 1985, when the initial subjects entered fifth grade, the panel was expanded to include all fifth-grade students in 18 Seattle elementary schools. Subjects for the present study are from the expanded population (N = 1,053).

Data from students were collected during the fall of 1985 and the spring of 1986. Questionnaires were administered in classrooms. Students were given copies of the questionnaire, and project personnel read each question and its associated response categories aloud. Of the 1,053 eligible fifth graders, 919 (87%) completed usable fall surveys and 778 (74%) usable spring surveys. These completion rates compare favorably with those reported by others (Kaplan, Martin, & Robbins, 1984; Newcomb & Bentler, 1986). Data from teachers were collected during the spring of 1986. Teachers completed the Child Behavior Checklist (CBCL; Achenbach & Edelbrook, 1983) for 790 of the 919 students completing usable fall surveys.

The fall fifth-grade sample (N = 919) was 46% European American,

25% African American, and 21% Asian American. Forty-eight percent of this sample were female, and 93% were between 10 and 11 years old at the time of the survey. Thirty-eight percent of these students qualified for the federally funded free-lunch program. No significant differences were found on race, sex, and free-lunch eligibility between those who completed the spring survey and those who did not (Gillmore et al., 1990).

The two criteria for inclusion in the present analysis were ethnicity (African American and European American, $N = 649$) and completion of both the fall and the spring surveys ($N = 541$). This sample was further reduced ($N = 316$) when we deleted cases that had missing values on the relevant variables. The analyzed sample—218 European-American and 98 African-American subjects—was 50% female, 95% between the ages of 10 and 11, and 32% eligible for the free-lunch program. In summary, this sample consisted of students staying in the same schools for their fifth-grade year for whom complete data were available for these analyses. This sample included fewer children from poverty (eligible for the free-lunch program) than the original fifth-grade sample.

All student predictor indicators were taken from the fall student survey. The completed CBCL predictor measures were gathered in the spring, and the dependent measures were taken from the spring student data. The free-lunch and ethnicity variables were taken from official district records.

The dependent measure, substance initiation, is based on three dichotomously scored items in which students were asked about their use of each of three substances: alcohol, tobacco, and marijuana. A score was created for each substance (0 = *no initiation*; 1 = *initiation*). The dependent measure was formed by adding the number of substances initiated and dividing the sum by 3. The resulting proportions range from 0 (*initiated none*) to 1 (*initiated all three*), with intermediate values of .33 (*one substance initiated*) and .67 (*two initiated*).

We controlled SES in the analyses because racial and ethnic minority groups are often disproportionately represented in lower income groups. Failure to control for this variable can lead to spurious results, because income differences are confounded with racial and ethnic differences. Free-lunch eligibility status, which incorporates family income and family size, was chosen to tap SES.

Predictors

In prior analyses, the dependent measure has been regressed separately on the variables within each of four different predictor groups: family (Catalano et al., 1992), antisocial behavior and attitudes (Wells et al., 1992), acceptability and availability of drugs (Gillmore et al., 1990), and school predictors. In these analyses, the free-lunch variable was entered first, followed by the simultaneous entry of other predictors. Risk indicators that had slopes significantly different from zero at the $p < .10$ level in any of these four regressions were included in the model examined here. Predictors were developed from student responses to 4-point Likert items (YES!, yes, no, NO!; Slavin & Karweit, 1984) unless otherwise specified.

Family Factors

The predictors included two measures of family-management practices, a measure of family bonding, and one of sibling deviance. The family-management predictors included a single item asking whether parents revoked privileges for misbehavior, with higher scores indicating less tendency to revoke; a scale of proactive family management practices was constructed from six items. Example items include "Do your parents make family rules clear" and "Do they praise you for school achievements?" This measure ($\alpha = .66$) is scaled so that higher scores indicate greater proactive management.

The measure of family bonding is an average of five items tapping how well family members get along, share intimacies, and identify with each parent. In single-parent families, the index consists of an average of responses to how well family members get along and the two items referring to the present parent. This measure ($\alpha = .62$) is scaled so that higher values indicate greater family attachment.

The measure of sibling deviance is a dichotomy differentiating between those having and those not having a sibling who has used marijuana, been suspended from school, or been arrested.

Antisocial Behavior and Attitudes

The selected predictors include a measure of aggressiveness and one of delinquent behavior. Two reports of antisocial behavior were chosen: teacher and self-reported ratings. Self-reports were used because only the children know their own behavior across settings. Teacher reports were used as a check against underreporting. We chose teachers rather than parents or friends because data were not collected from friends and we had more complete reports from teachers than parents. Aggressiveness was developed from teacher ratings of student behavior on 10 items from the CBCL. Examples include "defiant, talks back"; "cruelty, bullying, meanness to others"; and "gets in many fights." This measure ($\alpha = .94$) is scaled so that higher scores indicate more aggressive behavior.

Delinquent behavior is an additive scale composed of six items reflecting the delinquency of subjects during the previous calendar year, reported in the following categories: *never, once or twice, three or four times,* and *more than four times.* Examples of items are "throwing objects at cars or people" and "picking a fight with someone." This measure ($\alpha = .67$) is scaled so that higher scores indicate more delinquent acts.

Acceptability and Availability

The selected predictors include measures of marijuana availability, peer use of alcohol, certainty of punishment for drug use, and intentions to use as an adult. Access to marijuana was based on student responses to three items, two of which are dichotomous. We transformed scores on these items to z scores before averaging to account for different response coding. This measure (α = .56) is scaled so that higher scores indicate greater access to marijuana.

For the peer-use measure, students were asked to indicate whether any of their four best friends used alcohol without parental knowledge. This measure is a dichotomy differentiating between those reporting at least one friend who drinks without parental knowledge and those reporting no such friends.

Certainty of punishment (α = .73) is an average of two items asking whether respondents expected to be caught and punished if they drank alcohol or used marijuana. Intention to use as an adult (α = .51) is an average of two items: intentions to use cigarettes and marijuana.

School Risk

The selected predictor was a measure of opportunity for involvement in school activities drawn from earlier regressions on school risk factors. Higher values indicate greater opportunity.

Nunnally (1978) suggested that reliabilities in the .70 range are acceptable for etiological analyses. However, several of these scales fall below this level. This may differentially affect the power of the scales with lower reliability to predict the number of substances initiated. As will be seen, however, several of these scales are significant predictors.

Analysis

Because the design was not orthogonal, we used effect coding for all dichotomous terms (Pedhazur, 1982). We then computed interactions to provide an unweighted means solution, with each cell mean being given equal weight regardless of the number of subjects in the cell.

Two types of analysis are presented. The first consists of comparisons, by ethnicity and sex, of risk factors related to early initiation of drug use. These analyses address the question of whether there are ethnic and sex differences in the risk factors. The second type of analysis consists of longitudinal regressions of self-reported number of substances initiated on these selected risk factors to answer two questions: (a) Are the selected risk factors, as well as ethnicity, related to substance initiation by European-American and African-American fifth graders? and (b) Are there differences in the relationship between risk factors and substance initiation for European-American and African-American students?

RESULTS

As reported in Gillmore et al. (1990) and briefly summarized here, drug use initiation among fifth-grade students varied by ethnic group, sex, and drug type after free-lunch eligibility was controlled. Tobacco use initiation was most prevalent among European-American youth (22.7%) and least prevalent among African-American youth (18.6%). European-American boys were significantly more likely than girls to have initiated tobacco use by fifth grade (27% vs. 18%), whereas the difference in tobacco use initiation rates between African-American boys and girls was not significant. European-American students led in the initiation of alcohol use; almost half (49.4%) had tried alcohol by the fifth grade. Fewer African Americans in the sample (37.8%) had ever consumed alcohol. Among European Americans, more boys (57%) than girls (41%) had used alcohol, whereas among African Americans, girls' and boys' initiation rates were not significantly different. The prevalence of initiation of marijuana use was low among fifth-grade students (5.7%), and no significant differences by ethnic group or sex were found.

To check for attrition bias, we compared means and standard deviations on the dependent measure, both for the analyzed sample with complete data on all variables (N = 316) and for African-American and European-American students who completed the fall and spring surveys (N = 581). These data were strikingly similar, with only marginally higher means and standard deviations in the analyzed sample compared with the panel. These analyses suggested that the 42% attrition rate did not result in a loss of cases with extreme values on the dependent measure.[1]

Patterns of Risk Factors by Ethnicity and Sex

The results of the cross-sectional analyses are presented in Table 1. This table shows means (adjusted for SES) broken down by ethnicity and sex and indicates which differences were significant. There were significant ethnic differences on four risk factors and marginally significant differences on a fifth. Compared with African-American students, fewer European-American students either reported having a deviant sibling or were rated by teachers as being aggressive. European-American students on average reported less involvement in delinquent behavior but greater intentions of using cigarettes and marijuana as adults. Finally, European-American stu-

---

[1]Attrition analyses are available on request from Richard F. Catalano.

TABLE 1

Analysis of Covariance for Selected Risk Factors by Ethnic Group and Sex

	Adjusted M^a				F ratios		
	European American		African American				
Variable	Boy	Girl	Boy	Girl	Ethnicity	Sex	Ethnicity × Sex
Availability–accessibility							
Access to marijuana	1.15	1.00	1.01	1.01	<1	<1	1.15
Intention to use as an adult	1.52	1.30	1.36	1.21	5.14**	3.40*	<1
Certainty of punishment for drug use	1.31	1.23	1.24	1.25	<1	<1	<1
Friends drink	0.24	0.16	0.19	0.16	<1	<1	<1
Family factors							
Parents take away privileges for misbehavior	2.45	2.46	2.37	2.44	<1	<1	<1
Family bonding	2.95	2.97	2.90	2.95	<1	<1	<1
Deviant siblings	0.17	0.19	0.26	0.38	13.24***	3.87**	1.77
Proactive family management	3.38	3.50	3.47	3.56	2.84*	1.68	<1
Antisocial behavior							
Teacher-reported aggressiveness	1.29	1.12	1.52	1.45	46.21***	1.51	1.19
Self-reported delinquency	7.68	6.69	7.89	7.55	5.78**	1.05	2.62
School factor							
Opportunities for involvement in school activities	3.17	3.29	3.31	3.30	<1	<1	<1

^{a}Measure adjusted to free-lunch status of subject.
*$p \leq .10$. **$p \leq .05$. ***$p \leq .001$.

dents reported less use of proactive family management practices by their parents than did African-American students.

There were significant sex differences on one risk factor and marginally significant differences on another. Fewer boys reported having a deviant sibling than girls, but they tended to be more likely to express intentions of using cigarettes and marijuana as adults. None of the Ethnicity × Sex interactions were significant.

Longitudinal Regression Analyses of Initiation

Table 2 provides the correlations among the predictor variables and the variety of substances initiated by the end of Grade 5. The ethnicity and SES indicators were significantly moderately correlated ($-.36$); however, ethnicity was only correlated over .15 with two other variables: having a deviant sibling and teacher-rated aggressiveness. All except two (having deviant siblings and involvement in activities outside of the classroom) of the other predictors were correlated above .15 with the variety of substances initiated. The predictors themselves were relatively independent with only four correlated over .30. Family bonding and proactive family management had the highest correlation (.54), and having friends who drink, access to marijuana, and the number of delinquent acts in the past year were all intercorrelated at the .31 to .33 range. None of the correlations of the interaction terms with the dependent variable was over .15. The ethnic predictor main and interaction terms were mostly moderately correlated, with only three over .25.

The results of the regression analyses previously outlined are presented in Table 3, which shows unstandardized slopes and associated F ratios for the variables included in the two models. As in our previous studies, the covariate—free-lunch eligibility—was insignificant. The ethnicity variable was also insignificant. The first model indicates that, of the four selected family predictors, only taking away privileges for misbehavior was significant; of the two antisocial behavior and attitude predictors, aggressiveness was significant and self-reported delinquency was marginally significant; of the four selected acceptability and availability predictors, only certainty of punishment was not significant, and the selected school predictor was significant. The adjusted R^2 for this model, .34, indicates greater total explained variance than in regressions of substance initiation on single groups of predictors reported in our earlier studies.

Three of these predictors were also significant when African-American and European-American students were considered separately (Gillmore et al., 1990; Wells et al., 1992). Four of them, however, were significant only for European Americans in the earlier separate regressions. Although in each case the results were in the same direction in the African-American-only regressions, they did not reach significance. Inves-

TABLE 2
Correlation Coefficients Among Predictors and the Variety of Substances Initiated

Variable	1	2	3	4	5	6	7	8	9	10	11	12	13
1. Free lunch eligibility	-.014												
2. Ethnicity	.024	-.362											
3. Proactive family management	-.243	-.033	-.085										
4. Parents take away privileges for misbehavior	.183	-.028	.040	-.026									
5. Family bonding	-.120	.036	.032	.538	-.069								
6. Deviant siblings	.132	.149	-.160	-.040	.003	-.071							
7. Self-reported delinquency	.321	.047	-.122	-.235	-.021	-.195	.246						
8. Teacher-reported aggressiveness	.152	.215	-.239	.012	.006	.031	.289	.211					
9. Opportunities for involvement in school activities	-.132	.072	-.018	.103	-.017	.115	.009	-.047	-.068				
10. Certainty of punishment for drug use	.243	-.135	.039	-.141	.135	-.085	-.021	.205	-.003	-.109			
11. Intention to use as an adult	.382	-.079	.109	-.117	.161	-.126	.047	.167	-.019	-.038	.208		
12. Friends drink	.352	-.075	.049	-.175	.040	-.151	.070	.309	.063	-.109	.187	.282	
13. Access to marijuana	.425	-.013	.045	-.174	.009	-.157	.198	.326	.022	.083	.256	.218	.332

TABLE 3
Regressions of Substance Initiation on Selected Risk Factors for
European-American and African-American Students ($N = 316$)

Variable	Main effects only (13 predictors)		Main effects and interactions (24 predictors)	
	b^a	$F(13, 302)$	b^a	$F(24, 291)$
Free-lunch eligibility	.001	<1	.005	<1
Ethnicity	.002	<1	.032	<1
Availability–accessibility				
Access to marijuana	.109	27.54****	.113	21.49****
Friends drink	.042	5.00**	.046	4.71**
Certainty of punishment for drug use	.022	<1	.038	1.45
Intention to use as an adult	.118	21.21****	.095	8.66***
Family factors				
Parents take privileges away for misbehavior	.037	7.58***	.039	7.32***
Proactive family management	−.066	2.69	−.040	<1
Family bonding	−.010	<1	−.029	<1
Deviant siblings	.007	<1	.010	<1
Antisocial behavior				
Teacher-reported aggressiveness	.077	4.91**	.073	4.14**
Self-reported delinquency	.014	3.05*	.015	2.83*
School factor				
Opportunities for involvement in school activities	−.034	4.77**	−.031	3.16*
Interactions with ethnicity				
Access to marijuana			−.012	<1
Friends drink			−.004	<1
Certainty of punishment for drug use			−.026	<1
Intention to use as an adult			.032	<1
Parents take away privileges for misbehavior			−.007	<1
Proactive family management			−.031	<1
Family bonding			.033	1.08
Deviant siblings			−.002	<1
Teacher-reported aggressiveness			.019	<1
Self-reported delinquency			−.000	<1
Opportunities for involvement in school activities			−.006	<1
R^2	.368		.375	
Adjusted R^2 [b]	.341		.324	

[a]Unstandardized regression coefficients. [b]Adjusted for the number of variables in the equation.
*$p \leq .10$. **$p \leq .05$. ***$p \leq .01$. ****$p \leq .001$.

tigation revealed that these differences were due to decreased power stemming from the relatively smaller sample size resulting when groups were examined separately. Taking away privileges, for example, was significant at the .10 level in the African-American-only regression (Catalano et al., 1992). Post hoc analysis also supported this conclusion. No significant deviation was found from parallelism of the African-American and European-American slopes on the other three predictors, indicating that the groups had similar regression coefficients.

The second model indicates the same pattern of significant predictors as the first: Although these F ratios are typically attenuated, with one variable becoming only marginally significant at the .10 level, the pattern of significance of the regression is otherwise the same, and none of the Predictor $\times$ Ethnicity interaction terms are significant. The adjusted R^2 for this model is slightly less than that for the first model.

In summary, results from the first model suggest that 7 of the 11 predictors, but not ethnicity per se, are related to substance initiation in fifth-grade students. Results from the second model suggest that the relationship between risk factors and initiation does not vary with ethnicity. Finally, the ethnic differences in risk factors reported in earlier analyses could be due to relative differences in power stemming from differences in sample size.

DISCUSSION

The results of analysis of these data have shown that European-American fifth-grade students, particularly boys, have higher rates of tobacco and alcohol initiation, whereas there are no significant differences on marijuana initiation. Approximately 34% of the variance in the variety of substances initiated by the end of fifth grade was accounted for by seven risk factors, including indicators of family management, early antisocial behavior, accessibility and availability of drugs, and school risk factors. There were no differences between African-American and European-American students in the significance of any of the risk factors in predicting substance initiation. This suggests that the predictive structure of risk factors is the same for both groups.

However, several differences between African-American and European-American students were evident in level of exposure to risk factors. African-American students were rated by their teachers as more aggressive and by themselves as more delinquent, and they reported the presence of more deviant siblings in their families. European-American students reported being more likely to intend to use substances as adults and reported that their families used less proactive family management practices.

Although far from definitive, this study suggests the promise of research in contributing to developmental appropriateness and timing of drug prevention programs for different groups. For example, the higher early initiation rates of alcohol and tobacco for European-American students suggests that they be targeted earlier by prevention programs to reduce this early onset. Although early prevention efforts are perhaps to be preferred for all groups (Hawkins et al., 1992), it may be particularly important for European Americans, to reduce their higher levels of early initiation. Also, the lower early initiation rates for African Americans suggest that the experiences of these children are protecting some of them from drug initiation in spite of early exposure to other risk factors. For example, data reported here suggest that African-American fifth-grade students engage in more early antisocial behavior (whether reported by themselves or teachers) and have more deviant siblings. However, they are more likely to report that their parents use proactive family management practices such as monitoring, praising them, making clear rules, and refraining from putting them down, and they report less intention to use drugs as adults. This suggests that these latter two factors may be inhibiting early drug use initiation in the African-American sample. This information should be of use to programs in engaging the family and peer group to act as protective agents in preventing substance initiation among African-American children. Again, although the results of the regression analysis suggest that these factors behave similarly for European- and African-American children, differential exposure to them in each group suggests their culture-specific value as points of intervention.

Perhaps of most interest for those developing culturally appropriate prevention interventions are the similarities and differences between groups in significant predictors of the variety of substance initiation. African-American and European-American fifth-grade students were equally exposed to four significant predictors of substance initiation: access to marijuana, friends who drink, parents taking away privileges when students misbehaved, and opportunities for involvement in activities outside of the classroom. Prevention programs for both African-American and European-American fifth-grade students could therefore equally emphasize attention to these four factors in risk reduction programming for both groups. In contrast, two of the significant predictors of substance initiation showed differential exposure by ethnic group. These were aggressiveness (measured by teacher and student reports) among African-American students and intentions to use substances as an adult among European-American students. Depending on the source of the aggressive behaviors, programs that help teachers manage their diverse classrooms proactively or help students meet their goals in nonaggressive ways may be more relevant for the African-American students, whereas programs that address norms and intentions to use substances as adults may be more important for European-

American students in elementary grades. Targeting families, peer groups, or individuals so as to understand the consequences of drug use may be alternative or complementary ways to address these intentions.

Several cautions are suggested, however. First, despite differences in exposure to these latter two risk factors, the factors themselves are significant predictors for both groups. Second, before forming the basis for intervention design, one must demonstrate the consistency of these findings in multiple studies. Third, although the variety of substance initiation was measured at a later point in time, the length of time between measurement points is not great. These findings should be confirmed in longitudinal data of greater duration. Fourth, because early initiation is a predictor of later substance abuse, these findings are important in themselves. However, studies show that the rate of early drug use initiation is greater for European-American than African-American students in elementary grades, but rates of drug-related problems are greater for African Americans later in development. It will be of interest to watch how these early risk factors predict frequent drug use and problems associated with drug use as the students mature. Fifth, the findings of nonsignificance for several of the measured risk factors should be examined with caution. Only direct effects of these predictors have been examined here. More detailed analysis may reveal indirect or interactive effects of these factors on drug use behaviors.

REFERENCES

Achenbach, T. M., & Edelbrook, C. (1983). *Manual for the child behavior checklist and revised child behavior profile*. Burlington: University of Vermont Press.

Adalf, E. M., Smart, R. G., & Tan, S. R. (1989). Ethnicity and drug use: A critical look. *International Journal of the Addictions, 24,* 1–18.

Artz, J. (1976). Can minorities be invisible: If not, why not? *American Journal of Drug and Alcohol Abuse, 3,* 181–183.

Barnes, G. M., & Welte, J. W. (1986). Patterns and predictors of alcohol use among 7–12th grade students in New York State. *Journal of Studies on Alcohol, 47,* 53–62.

Beaulieu, M. A., & Jason, L. A. (1988). A drug abuse prevention program aimed at teaching seventh grade students problem-solving strategies. *Children and Youth Services Review, 10,* 131–149.

Botvin, G. J., Batson, H. W., Witts-Vitale, S., Bess, V., Baker, E., & Dusenbury, L. (1989). A psychosocial approach to smoking prevention for urban black youth. *Public Health Reports, 104,* 573–582.

Brown, B. S., Joe, G. W., & Thompson, P. (1985). Minority group status and treatment retention. *The International Journal of the Addictions, 20,* 319–335.

Catalano, R. F., Morrison. D. M., Wells, E. A., Gillmore, M. R., Iritani, B., & Hawkins, J. D. (1992). Ethnic differences in family factors related to early drug initiation. *Journal of Studies on Alcohol, 53*, 208–217.

Coleman, S. B. (1981). Cross cultural approaches to working with addict families. In A. J. Schecter (Ed.), *Drug dependence and alcoholism: Vol. 2. Social and behavioral issues* (pp. 941–948). New York: Plenum Press.

Dembo, R., Blount, W. R., Schmeidler, J., & Burgos, W. (1986). Perceived environmental drug use risk and the correlates of early drug use or nonuse among inner-city youths: The motivated actor. *The International Journal of the Addictions, 21*, 977–1000.

Gary, L. E., & Berry, G. L. (1985). Predicting attitudes toward substance use in a black community: Implications for prevention. *Community Mental Health Journal, 21*, 42–51.

Gillmore, M. R., Catalano, R. F., Morrison, D. M., Wells, E. A., Iritani, B., & Hawkins, J. D. (1990). Racial differences in acceptability and availability of drugs and early initiation of substance abuse. *The American Journal of Drug and Alcohol Abuse, 16*, 185–206.

Harford, T. C. (1985). Drinking patterns among Black and non-Black adolescents: Results of a national survey. In R. Wright & T. D. Watts (Eds.), *Prevalence of Black alcoholism: Issues and strategies* (pp. 122–139). Springfield, IL: Charles C Thomas.

Hawkins, J. D., Catalano, R. F., & Miller, J. L. (1992). Risk and protective factors for alcohol and other drug problems in adolescence and early adulthood: Implications for substance abuse prevention. *Psychological Bulletin, 112*, 64–105.

Hawkins, J. D., Von Cleve, E., & Catalano, R. F. (1991). Reducing early childhood aggression: Results of a primary prevention program. *Journal of the American Academy of Child and Adolescent Psychiatry, 30*, 208–217.

Hawkins, J. D., & Weis, J. G. (1985). The social development model: An integrated approach to delinquency prevention. *Journal of Primary Prevention, 6*, 73–97.

Johnson, B., & Nishi, M. S. (1976). Myths and realities of drug use by minorities. In P. Iiyama, M. S. Nishi, & B. Johnson (Eds.), *Drug use and abuse among U.S. minorities* (pp. 3–68). New York: Praeger.

Johnston, L. D., O'Malley, P. M., & Bachman, J. G. (1987). *National trends in drug use and related factors among American high school students and young adults, 1975–1986* (DHHS Publication No. ADM 87-1535). Washington, DC: U.S. Government Printing Office.

Kandel, D. B. (1978). Convergences in prospective longitudinal surveys of drug use in normal populations. In D. B. Kandel (Ed.), *Longitudinal research on drug use: Empirical findings and methodological issues* (pp. 3–38). Washington, DC: Hemisphere.

Kandel, D., Single, E., & Kessler, R. C. (1976). The epidemiology of drug use among New York State high school students: Distribution, trends, and change in rates of use. *American Journal of Public Health, 66*, 43–53.

Kandel, D. B., Simcha-Fagan, O., & Davies, M. (1986). Risk factors for delinquency and illicit drug use from adolescence to young adulthood. *Journal of Drug Issues, 16,* 29–66.

Kaplan, H. B., Martin, S. S., & Robbins, C. A. (1984). Pathways to adolescent drug use: Self-derogation, peer influence, weakening of social controls, and early substance use. *Journal of Health and Social Behavior, 25,* 270–289.

Maddahian, E., Newcomb, M. D., & Bentler, P. M. (1988a). Adolescent drug use and intention to use drugs: Concurrent and longitudinal analyses of four ethnic groups. *Addictive Behaviors, 13,* 191–195.

Maddahian, E., Newcomb, M. D., & Bentler, P. M. (1988b). Risk factors for substance use: Ethnic differences among adolescents. *Journal of Substance Abuse, 1,* 11–23.

Maddahian, E., Newcomb, M. D., & Bentler, P. M. (1988c). Single and multiple patterns of adolescent substance use: Longitudinal comparisons of four ethnic groups. *Journal of Drug Education, 15,* 311–326.

Martinez, J. (1976). Minorities and alcohol/drug abuse. *American Journal of Drug and Alcohol Abuse, 3,* 185–187.

National Association of Black Social Workers and Association of Black Psychologists. (1973, November). *The psychodynamics of addiction from a Black perspective: Strengths and pitfalls: Conference Proceedings, November 9–10, 1973, Washington, DC.* Detroit, MI: Author.

Newcomb, M. D., & Bentler, P. M. (1986). Substance abuse and ethnicity: Differential impact of peer and adult models. *Journal of Psychology, 120,* 83–95.

Nunnally, J. C. (1978). *Psychometric theory.* New York: McGraw-Hill.

Pedhazur, E. J. (1982). *Multiple regression in behavioral research: Explanation and prediction* (2nd ed.). New York: Holt, Rinehart & Winston.

Robins, L. N., & Przybeck, T. R. (1985). *Age of onset of drug use as a factor in drug use and other disorders* (NIDA Research Monograph No. 56, DHHS Publication No. 1415). Washington, DC: U.S. Government Printing Office.

Rotheram-Borus, M. J., & Tsemberis, S. J. (1989). Social competency training programs in ethnically diverse communities. In L. Bond & C. Swift (Eds.), *Primary prevention and promotion in the schools* (pp. 297–318). Newbury Park, CA: Sage.

Schinke, S. P., Moncher, M. S., Palleja, J., Zayas, L. H., & Schilling, R. F. (1988). Hispanic youth, substance abuse, and stress: Implications for prevention research. *The International Journal of the Addictions, 23,* 809–826.

Slavin, R. E., & Karweit, N. (1984). Mastery learning and student teams: A factorial experiment in urban general mathematics classes. *American Educational Research Journal, 21,* 725–736.

Szapocznik, J., & Kurtines, W. (1980). Acculturation, biculturalism, and adjustment among Cuban Americans. In A. M. Padilla (Ed.), *Acculturation: Theory, models, and some new findings* (pp. 139–158). Boulder, CO: American Association for Advancement of Science.

Szapocznik, J., Ladner, R. A., & Scopetta, M. (1979). Youth drug abuse and subjective distress in a Hispanic population. In G. M. Beschner & A. S. Friedman

(Eds.), *Youth drug abuse: Problems, issues, and treatment* (pp. 493–511). Lexington, MA: Lexington Books.

Tucker, M. B. (1985). U.S. ethnic minorities and drug abuse: An assessment of the science and practice. *The International Journal of the Addictions, 20,* 1021–1047.

Wells, E. A., Morrison, D. M., Gillmore, M. R., Catalano, R. F., Iritani, B., & Hawkins, J. D. (1992). Race differences in antisocial behaviors and attitudes and early initiation of substance abuse. *Journal of Drug Education, 22,* 115–130.

AUTHOR INDEX

Numbers in italics refer to listings in the reference sections.

Argeriou, M., 338
Arif, A., 428, 707, 714
Arling, G., 805, 825
Armor, D., 266, 287, 581, 582, 598, 599,
    605, 625, 719, 755
Arndt, I., 771, 793
Arndt, I. O., 779, 798
Arndt, J., 652, 665
Arndt, S., 409
Aronson, M. D., 386
Arria, A., 53, 54, 66, 67
Artz, J., 857, 871
Ary, D., 232, 235
Asarnow, J. R., 235
Asberg, M., 85
Asberg, S., 84
Aseltine, R. H., Jr., 130, 158
Askenasy, A. R., 586, 598
Atkeson, B., 57, 65
Atkinson, J. H., 810, 825
Attewell, P. A., 573
Aubuchon, P., 158
August, D. S., 644, 663
Ausetts, M. A., 761, 793
Austin, G., 393, 409, 841, 844, 853
Avani, M., 770, 800
Averill, J. R., 436, 469
Avison, W. R., 806, 822, 823, 825
Awouters, F., 72, 90
Axelrod, R., 437, 469
Azrin, N. H., 632, 645, 754, 755, 782,
    783, 790, 791, 793, 794, 797,
    800

Babor, T., 26, 38, 78, 80, 85, 86, 90, 374,
    385, 386, 387, 419, 422, 423,
    427, 429, 568, 572, 612, 625,
    625, 707, 715, 720, 755, 757
Baca, L. M., 267, 271, 282, 286
Bachman, J., 4, 37, 98, 124, 131, 134,
    135, 136, 147, 152, 156, 158,
    160, 161, 162, 163, 203, 207,
    531, 843, 854, 858, 872
Bachorowski, J., 442, 476, 478, 479, 480
Bachrach, L. L., 403, 409
Bacon, S., 153, 156, 161, 163
Badger, G. J., 644, 664
Baer, J. S., 131, 158, 172, 208, 671, 693
Baer, R. A., 353, 490, 505
Bailey, C. A., 201, 207
Bailey, D. S., 469, 478, 481
Baker, E., 217, 238, 871

Baker, M. B., 767, 799
Baker, T. B., 648, 664, 701, 717
Baldwin, A., 242, 264
Baldwin, C., 242, 264
Ball, J. C., 649, 663, 718, 720, 749, 755,
    762, 798
Balla, J. R., 181, 208
Ballenger, J., 69, 70, 85, 86
Balogh, M., 410
Balter, M. B., 180, 210
Bandura, A., 220, 234, 832, 839
Bangert-Drowns, R. L., 216, 234
Banki, C. J., 85
Barbaccia, M., 77, 92
Barbee, J. G., 393, 398, 399, 409
Barboriak, J. J., 374, 386
Barker, T. A., 666
Barnes, G., 52, 63
Barnes, G. M., 133, 134, 163, 489, 504,
    806, 825, 858, 871
Barnett, L. W., 697, 715
Barocas, R., 242, 264
Baron, R. A., 460, 469
Baron, R. M., 249, 262
Barr, H. L., 645, 761, 798
Barrera, M., 47, 50, 63, 99, 103, 123,
    509, 510, 514, 530, 531, 808,
    822, 825
Barrett, J. D., 73, 88
Barrett, R. J., 172, 204
Barrio, J. R., 494, 507
Bartsch, T. W., 178, 208
Bartusch, D. J., 533
Bashkow, S., 761, 799
Bass, U. F. III, 794
Bathija, J., 410
Batki, S. L., 658, 663
Batson, H. W., 871
Baughman, T., 51, 63
Baum-Baicker, C., 171, 204
Bauman, K. E., 526, 531
Baumeister, R. F., 472
Baumgarten, R., 86
Baumrind, D., 131, 158, 197, 204
Baydar, N., 64
Bayog, R., 401, 409
Beals, J., 516, 532
Beaman, C. M., 88
Beattie, M. C., 604, 609, 613, 620, 623,
    626, 627, 628
Beaulieu, M. A., 858, 871

Bloom, F. E., 73, 93, 432, *474*
Blount, J. P., *367*
Blount, W. R., 858, 872
Blum, K., 74, 75, 83, 85, 86, 92
Board of Directors, Manpower Demonstration Research Corporation, 777, 794
Bobo, J. K., 842, 853
Bocchi, R., 87
Boggan, W. O., 75, 90
Bohman, M., 46, 63, 78, 86, 425, 426, *427, 429, 538, 572*
Bohn, M. J., 68, 86, 89
Bolanos, F., 88
Bollen, K. A., 516, *530*
Bolos, A. M., 83, 86, 88
Bond, A., 442, *470*
Bond, C. F., 432, 473, 560, *573*
Bond, G. R., 405, *409*
Bonett, D. G., 185, *205*
Boni, C., 88
Bonner, W. I., 661, *665*
Booth, M. W., 762, 764, 772, 773, 793
Booth, P. G., 282, *284*
Booth, R., 831, *839*
Borg, S., 75, 90
Borison, R., 86
Bornet, A., 770, *801*
Bornet, A. R., 267, *287*
Bortveit, T., 362, *369*
Borus, J., 339, 374, *386*
Botvin, G. J., 216, 217, 235, 238, 844, 845, 855, 856, 858, 871
Bouchard, G. R., 419, *428*, 806, *826*
Boutin, P., 65
Bowen, W. T., 200, 266, *287*
Bowers, M. B., 391, *409*
Bowser, B., 829, 830, *839*
Bowser, B. P., 664, *839*
Boyatzis, R. E., 450, 451, 452, 470, *479*
Boyd, G., 132, *163*
Boyd, G. M., 685, *692*
Boyd, J. L., 406, *410*
Bozevich, C., *572*
Bradley, B. P., 298, 299, *304*
Brady, J. V., 32, 36
Brady, K., 90
Brady, R., *429*
Braff, D. L., 400, *409*
Brahen, L., *794*
Brahen, L. S., 655, *663*

Braiker, H. B., 266, 287, 581, 599, 808, 821, 825
Branch, L. G., 697, *715*
Branchey, L., 419
Branchey, M. H., 81, 86, *427*
Branden, L., 7, 38
Brandenburg, N., 675, 696
Brandon, T. H., 701, *717*
Brandt, D. L., *409*
Brandt, J., 401
Brase, D. A., 653, *665*
Braun, A. R., 502, *507*
Bravo, M., 36
Breakey, W. R., 399, *409*
Bree, M. P., 658, *665*
Brennan, A. F., 134, *158*
Brennan, P. L., 824, *827*
Brenner-Liss, D., 298, *305*
Brent, D. A., 169, *205*
Brent, E., 50, 66
Brent, E. E., 99, 126, 512, *533*
Breslau, N., 27, 36
Breuer, A., 663
Brewin, C. R., 298, *304*
Brewington, V., 767, 768, 784, 786, 793, 794
Briggs, A. H., 85
Brill, P., 719, *757*
Brinson, M., 605, *627*
Brochu, S., 267, *284*
Brodsky, A., 408
Brody, D., 389
Brody, J., 806, *827*
Bromet, E. J., *284*
Brook, A., 197, *205*
Brook, D. W., 100, *123*, 197, *205*
Brook, J., 98
Brook, J. S., 100, *123*, 132, 134, 142, *158*, 197, *205*, 239, *262*
Brooks-Gunn, J., 156, 157, *158*
Brooner, R. K., 645
Broskowski, H., 805, *825*
Brotman, R., 761, 784, 800
Brown, B. B., 122, *126*
Brown, B. S., 761, 767, 792, 793, 794, 797, 857, 871
Brown, D., 284, 288
Brown, E. D., 595, 599, 704, *716*
Brown, E. F., 388
Brown, G., 86
Brown, G. L., 69, 70, 85, 86, 88
Brown, G. M., *410*

Brown, J., 84, 86, 89
Brown, J. M., 121, *125*, 356, 367, 368
Brown, K., 288
Brown, L. S., *337*
Brown, R. A., 699, 710, 711, *714*
Brown, R. L., 400, *410*
Brown, S. A., 133, *159*, 432, *470*
Brown, Z., 85
Brownell, K. D., 673, 676, 691, 697, 707, *714*
Brownlee, M., *416*
Brownstein, M. J., 75, 86, 661, 665
Bruno, F., 72, 86
Bruun, K., 537, *575*
Bruvold, W. H., 216, *238*
Bry, B. H., 46, *63*, 242, 260, 263, 846, *853*
Bryan, G., 662, 665
Bryant, K., 642, *644*
Bryk, A., 225, *235*, 614, *627*
Buchan, I. C., 384, *386*
Buchanan, R. G., 374, *386*
Bucholz, K. K., 34, 36
Buchsbaum, D. G., 374, *386*
Buckley, E. G., *386*
Budney, A. J., 629, 630, 632, 633, 639, 641, *644, 645*, 664, 756
Bühringer, G., 788, *799*
Bukstein, O., 50, *65*
Bukstein, O. G., 169, *205*
Bunt, G., 396, *409*
Buonpane, N., 49, 67
Burgess, P. M., 422, *429*
Burgos, W., 858, *872*
Burke, A. C., *799*
Burke, J., 36, *38*
Burke, J. D., 389, *575*
Burkhart, B. R., 134, *162*
Burleson, J. A., 89
Burling, T. A., 298, *305*
Burman, A., 46, *64*
Burnam, A., *389*
Burnam, M. A., 374, 377, 387, 388, *389*
Burns, B., *389*
Burns, B. J., 374, *388*
Burton, D., 240, *264*
Bush, B. T., *386*
Bushman, B. J., 431, 442, 446, 469, *470*, 479
Bushnell, J. A., 28, *39*
Buss, A., 49, 60, *63*

Buss, A. H., 439–440, 469, *470*, 476, 517, *530, 531*
Butchart, A. T., 217, *238*
Butcher, J. N., 340, 341, 351, *353*
Butters, N., *320, 321*, 401, 409, *412, 415*
Buydens-Branchey, L., 81, 86, 419, *427*
Byck, R., 664
Byers, R., *839*

Caccavari, R., 87
Cacciola, J., 324, *339*, 720, 726, 731, 746, 752, *756, 757*
Cacciola, J. S., 720, *755*
Caces, M., 7, *38*
Cadoret, R., 400, *416*, 528, 530, 542, 543, 554, 557, *572, 577*
Cahalan, D., 419, *427, 429*, 584, *598*, 810, *825*
Cahalan, V., 314, *320*
Cahaland, D., 672, *695*
Cairns, E., 491, *504*
Cairns, R. B., 135, *158*
Calcagnetti, D., 75, 92
Calinski, R. B., *353*
Cammock, T., 491, *504*
Campanelli, P. C., 217, *238*
Campion, S. L., *388*
Cancilla, A., 601
Canino, G. J., 28, 36
Canter, W. A., 847, *854*
Cantwell, D., 49, *63*
Capasso, D. R., 477
Capone, T., 769, 770, *794*
Cappo, L., 516, *532*
Carboni, E., 73, 86
Carey, G., 488, *505*
Carey, K., 285, 405, *410*, 559, *575*
Carey, M. P., 405, *410*
Carlin, A. S., *411*
Carlson, M., 439, 443, 464, 470, 474
Caron, C., 65
Carpenter, J. A., 469, 542, 548, *574*
Carpenter, R. A., 845, *854*
Carr, C. R., 598, 690
Carroll, D., *505*
Carroll, K. M., 642, 643, *644*, 705, 706, 710, 711, 713, *714*
Carroll, W. K., 489, *504*
Carrolli, K. M., 709
Carter-Menendez, N., 133, *159*
Caruso, K. A., *211*
Carver, C. S., 105, *123*, 439, *470*

Cohen, R. J., 327, *337*
Cohen, S., 179, *205*, 597, 598, 672, 677, 695, 808, 822, 825
Cohn, J. B., *85*
Coie, J. D., 216, *235*
Colbert, J. N., 784, *794*
Colby, J. P., 806, *827*
Cole, D. A., 100, 103, *123*
Coleman, S. B., 859, *872*
Colletti, G., 700, 709, 710, 711, 712, 716
Collins, C., 132, *161*, 171, *209*
Collins, D. M., 71, *86*
Collins, L. M., 220, 233, *236*, *237*
Collins, N. L., 232, *236*
Collins, R. L., 291, 293, 295, 301, 303, *304*
Colombo, G., 72, *87*
Colten, M. E., 807, *828*
Combs-Orme, T., *285*
Comings, B. G., *86*
Comings, D. E., 83, *86*
Comprehensive Employment and Training Act (CETA) of 1973, 778, *794*
Compton, J. V., 275, *288*
Compton, W. M., 28, *36*
Comrey, A. L., 336, *337*
Condren, R., *794*
Conger, B., *387*
Conger, K. J., *123*
Conger, R. D., 121, *123*
Conners, C. K., 492, *506*
Conovan, J. E., *160*, *854*
Conte, H. R., *410*
Cooney, N., 80, 89, 90, 407, *413*, 422, 423, *427*, 607, *626*, 704, 711, *714*, *715*, 754, 756
Cooper, A. M., 605, *627*
Cooper, H. M., 431, 442, 446, 469, *470*, 479
Cooper, J., 754, 756, 769, 779, 780, 791, 796
Cooper, M. C., 107, *125*, 354
Cooper, M. L., 100, 114, *123*
Copone, T., *663*
Coquette, K. A., *599*
Cornish, J., 644, 658, 663, 666, 757
Corrigan, G. V., *387*
Corrigan, P. W., 406, *413*
Corty, E., 98, *123*, 395, *412*
Coryell, W., *408*

Costa, A., 680, *694*
Costa, F., 47, *64*
Costa, F. M., *160*, 242, *263*
Costall, B., 73, *87*
Costanzo, P. R., 178, *211*
Cote, R., *65*
Cottler, L., 6, *36*, *695*
Cotton, N. S., 535, 537, *572*
Coulehan, J. L., 374, *387*
Cox, W. M., *367*
Coyne, K., 780, 791, 796
Crabbe, J., 60, *65*
Crabtree, B. L., 75, *87*
Craddock, S. G., 760, *796*
Craig, R. J., 770, *794*
Craik, F. I. M., 433, *470*
Cranston, J. W., 469, *477*
Crapanzano, M. S., 393, *409*
Critcher, E., 75, *90*
Critchlow, B., 432, *470*
Criteria Committee, National Council on Alcoholism, 312, *320*
Cronbach, L. J., 178, *205*, 328, *338*, 603, *627*
Cronkite, R., 581, 599, 603, *627*, 720, *749*, *757*, 806, 807, 809, 813, 821, 825, *827*
Croot, K., 548, *577*
Crossley, H. M., 314, *320*, 810, *825*
Croughan, J., 8, *38*, 515, *532*, 605, *627*
Crum, R. M., 34, *36*
Crumbaugh, J. C., *205*
Csernansky, J. G., 393, *413*
Cuesta, M. J., 394, *414*
Culbert, A., 582, *598*
Cullum, M., *409*
Cummings, C., 707, *714*
Cummings, K. M., *691*
Cummings, M. K., *598*
Cupples, L. A., *666*
Curran, P., 47, 63, 103, *123*, 510, *530*
Curry, S., 292, 293, 294, 295, 298, 299, 303, *304*, 598, *691*
Curtin, L., *367*
Curtis, J. R., 810, *825*
Cuskey, W. R., 764, *794*
Cuthbert, M., 830, 831, *840*
Cutler, L., 806, *825*
Cutter, H. S. G., 595, *599*, 704, *716*
Cvetkovich, G. T., 844, 848, *854*
Cyphers, L., 49, *63*
Cyr, M. G., 374, 385, *387*

Czirr, S., 88

Dackis, C. A., 171, 172, *205, 206*
Dahlmann, T., *85*
Daily, J., 548, *574*
Dale, B., *284*
Dale, F. R., 761, *794*
Dale, R. T., 761, *794*
Dance, K. A., 602, *626*
Daniels, M., 377, *387*
Danish, S. J., 527, *531*
D'Aunno, T. A., *799*
Dauphinais, D., *411*
Davidson, S. T., 197, *208*
Davies, D. L., *284*
Davies, M., 64, 99, 100, 119, *124, 132,*
160, 170, 207, 339, 859, 872
Davieson, L. A., *317*
Davis, C. S., 703, *713*
Davis, D. H., 766, *796*
Davis, J. M., 395, *416*
Davis, J. R., 700, 710, 711, 712, *714*
Davis, P. E., 298, *304*
Davison, L. A., *321*
Dawis, R. V., 336, *338*
Dawson, D. A., 488, *505*
Dawson, M. E., 391, 400, *414, 505*
Day, N., 582, *598*
De Havitz, J., 831, *839*
De Labry, L. O., 419, *428*
De Soto, C. B., 310, 311, 318, *320, 321*
De Witte, P., 75, *87*
Deacon, G. L. S., *386*
Dean, M., 86, *88*
Dean, S. I., 355, *368*
DeBaryshe, B., 56, 65, 99, *125*
DeCicco, L., 355, *368*
DeDonato, N., *267*
DeFord, H. A., 773, *795*
DeFries, J. C., 49, *65*
deGruy, F., *389*
Del Arbol, J. L., 74, *85*
Del Boca, F., 80, 85, 89, 90, *368*
Delaney, D. D., 645, *756*
Delaney, H., 270, 286, *368, 369*
Delbanco, T. L., *386*
DeLeon, G., 718, 755, 760, *794*
DeLisi, L. E., *411*
Delke, I., 831, *840*
Delsignore, R., *87*
DeMaris, A., 147, *159*
Dembo, R., 858, *872*

DeMichelle, J. T., 684, *693*
Dengerink, H. A., 437, *471*
Dennis, M. L., 784, *795*
Denny, J. P., 319, *321*
Densen-Gerber, J., 764, *794*
Dent, C. W., 240, *264*
Depalma, N., 543, 548, *573*
DePhilippis, D., *665*
DePry, D., 433, *474*
Deren, M. P., 775, 785, 786, *795*
Deren, S., 767, 768, 784, 791, 793, *794,*
795, 847, 854
Descutner, C., 559, *577*
Deutsche Gesselschaft für Suchtfroschund
und Suchttherapie e. V., 788,
795
Devane, W. A., 661, *663*
DeVaul, R., 394, *411*
Devins, N. P., 374, *386*
Devor, E. J., *91*
Dewey, M. E., 271, *284*
Dewey, W. L., 653, *665*
Dexter, D., 841, *854*
Di Chiara, G., 73, 76, 81, 86, *87*
Diamond, I., 401, *411*
Dickinson, K., 777, 791, *795*
DiClemente, C., 356, 357, 366, 368, *369,*
582, 598, 599, 624, 627, 673,
674, 675, 676, 677, 678, 679,
680, 682, 683, 684, 685, 686,
687, 691, 692, 693, 694, 695,
696, 749, 757
DiDario, B., 401, *415*
DiDonato, N., *287*
Dielman, T., 217, 230, *235, 238*
Diener, E., 440, *471*
Dietz, G., *86*
DiLalla, D. L., 488, *505*
Dillon, S., 831, *839*
DiMatteo, M. R., 106, *124, 202, 210*
Dingman, C. W., II, *411*
Dishion, R. J., 134, *159*
Dishion, T. J., 527, *531*
DiTraglia, G., *412*
Divlahan, D. R., 671, *693*
Dixon, L., 398, 399, *410*
Dixon, W. J., 114, *123, 634, 644*
Doherty, W. J., 109, *125*
Dohrenwend, B. P., 201, *205, 586, 598*
Dohrenwend, B. S., 586, *598*
Dolan, M. P., 773, *795*
Dole, V. P., 773, *795*

Dolinsky, Z., 78, 85, 419, 429, 720, 755, 757
Dollard, J., 438, 471
Domeney, A. M., 73, 87
Donaldson, S. I., 217, 218, 224, 225, 230, 231, 232, 233, 234, 235, 236
Donham, R., 644
Donovan, D. M., 172, 208, 395, 410, 603, 626, 671, 676, 692, 693, 703, 715
Donovan, J., 47, 64, 101, 124, 132, 134, 135, 152, 153, 156, 159, 160, 242, 263, 845
Doob, L., 438, 471
Dornbusch, S. M., 122, 126
Dorus, W., 170, 206, 768, 800
Double, W. G., 779, 795
Douglas, D. E., 398, 414
Douglas, M. S., 403, 413
Douglas, R., 387
Douvan, E., 671, 696
Drake, R. E., 391, 393, 396, 399, 403, 404–405, 406, 407, 410
Dressel, M. E., 783, 796
Drew, L. R. H., 276, 284
Drews, V., 542, 543, 554, 577
Droba, M., 644, 663
Droungas, A., 660, 663
Druley, K. A., 404, 413, 720, 723, 731, 732, 757
Druley, P., 665
Drummond, D. C., 422, 427
Dryden, W., 673, 692
Dryfoos, J. G., 216, 235
Duams, M., 88
Duby, J., 540, 541, 542, 544, 545, 552, 576, 577
Duckitt, A., 284, 288
Duda, R. O., 353
Duffy, P., 77, 89
DuHamel, K., 120, 121, 122, 127, 512, 533
Duncan, E. M., 198, 207
Duome, M. A., 781, 799
DuPont, R. L., 767, 794, 797
Dupree, L. W., 805, 825
Duryea, E. J., 841, 845, 855
Dusenbury, L., 871
Duval, S., 439, 471, 475
Duval, V. H., 439, 471
Dwyer, J. H., 206, 237

Dwyer, J. W., 806, 826
Dysarz, F. A., 661, 663

Eagly, A. H., 443, 466, 471
Earleywine, M., 531
Eaves, L., 45, 64, 554, 555, 572
Eckardt, M. J., 374, 387
Eckblad, M., 180, 206
Edelbrook, C., 516, 530, 860, 871
Edelmann, R. J., 298, 304
Edgerton, R. B., 432, 474
Edlin, B., 656, 663, 830, 839
Edwards, B. A., 845, 855
Edwards, D. A., 122, 123, 132, 159
Edwards, G., 8, 36, 268, 276, 277, 278, 282, 284, 288, 428, 429, 707, 714, 719, 755
Edwards, K., 43, 54, 66
Edwards, K. L., 401, 416, 533
Edwards, R., 511, 533, 847, 848, 855
Edwards, R. W., 843, 853
Egan, G., 673, 692
Egert, S., 755
Egri, G., 201, 205
Ehrhardt, J. C., 402, 408
Ehrman, R., 660, 663, 665
Eison, A. S., 73, 87
El-Bassel, N., 831, 839
el-Guebaly, N., 325, 338
El Mestikawy, S., 88
Elal-Lawrence, G., 271, 273, 276, 278, 279, 282, 284
Elder, G. H., Jr., 132, 156, 158, 159
Elder, G. J., Jr., 123
Eldridge, K. L., 305
Elingboe, J., 568, 572
Ellickson, P. L., 133, 142, 154, 159, 216, 217, 235, 237
Elliott, D. S., 99, 101, 123, 135, 159
Elliott, G., 625
Ellis, R. D., 761, 794
Elmasian, R., 548, 565, 575
Emmerson, R. Y., 298, 305
Emont, S. L., 598, 691
Emory, E. K., 565, 575
Endicott, J., 48, 64, 385, 387, 408, 422, 428, 488, 505, 514, 530, 813, 827
Engel, J. A., 71, 87, 92
Engstrom, D., 542, 552, 565, 576

Fleming, J. S., 106, *123*
Flewelling, R. L., 217, *235*
Flores, T., 782, *793*
Foerg, F., 629, 630, 634, 639, 641, *644,*
  645, 664, 756
Follick, M. J., 678, *691, 695, 700, 715*
Folstein, M., 310, *320*
Folstein, S., 310, *320*
Fondacaro, M. R., 824, *827*
Ford, J., 169, 202, 203, *206*
Forsythe, R., 172, *210*
Forth, A. E., *338*
Foster, F. M., 343, *353, 368*
Fountain, D., *664*
Fowler, D. R., 605, *626, 627*
Fowler, J. L., 678, *695*
Fowler, J. S., 658, *666*
Fowler, R. C., 400, *410*
Fowles, D. C., *505*
Fox, E., 767, *795*
Foy, D. W., 269, 277, 282, *285, 287*
Frackowiak, R. S. J., 491, *505*
Frances, A. J., 398, *410*
Franco, S., *410*
Frank, B., 762, *798*
Frankel, M. R., 12, *37*
Frankenhaeuser, M., 465, *475*
Franzen, M., *320*
Frasano-Dube, B., *415*
Frau, R., 73, *86*
Frechen, K., *415*
Freed, E. X., 398, *410*
French, M. T., 784, *795*
Friedman, L. N., 776, 792, *795*
Friedman, R., 707, *716*
Friend, H. J., 762, 772, *800*
Friston, K. J., 491, *505*
Frith, C. D., 491, *505*
Froehlich, J. C., 75, 76, 77, *87*
Frost, R. O., 295, *304*
Fudala, P. J., *663*
Fulker, D., 49, *63*
Fuller, F., *626*
Fullilove, M. T., 829, 830, *839*
Fullilove, R. E., 829, 830, *839*
Furby, L., 178, *205*
Fureman, I., 765, *798*
Furnham, A., 335, *338*
Fuster, J. M., 487, *505*
Futterman, S., 75, *85*

Gabrielli, W. F., *575*

Gainey, R. R., 706, *716*
Galanter, M., 391, 396, *409, 411*
Galavotti, C., 678, *692*
Gallant, D., 71, *87*
Gallison, C., 232, *235*
Gamal, R., *408*
Gammon, C. B., 437, *477, 478*
Gammon, D., *211*
Gandour, M., 55, 56, 64, *67*
Ganter, A. B., *471, 479*
Garau, B., 72, *87*
Garber, J., 197, *206*
Garcia-Mason, V., 845, *855*
Garfield, S. L., 710, *715*
Garland, J., 761, *800*
Garmezy, N., 239, 242, *263*
Gary, L. E., 858, 859, *872*
Gatto, G. J., 570, *573*
Gaudry, E., 327, *338*
Gawin, F. H., 171, 172, 206, 207, 401,
  414, 644, 657, 658, 664, 666,
  705, 714
Gee, M., 217, *236*
Geen, R. G., 460, 462, 464, *471*
Gehred-Schultz, A., 673, *693*
Gehring, M., 516, *532*
Geisler, S., *413*
Gelernter, J., 83, *87*
Geller, G., 810, *825*
Genazzani, A., 74, *87*
George, D. T., *85*
George, W. H., 100, 114, *123, 291, 304,*
  697, 715
Gephart, D., *387*
Gerard, D. L., 266, *285*
German, P., 389, *695*
Germanson, T., 169, 209, 375, *388*
Gerra, G., 80, *87*
Gershon, E. S., 399, *411*
Gerstein, D., 649, 664, 718, 719, *756,*
  787, 795
Gessa, G., 72, *87*
Getter, H., 80, 89, 608, 627, 704, *714,*
  715, 754, 756
Geweke, J. F., 330, *338*
Gfroerer, J. C., 29, *35*
Giancola, P. R., 464, *477*
Gianoulakis, C., 74, 88, 431, 471, 656,
  664
Gibbon, M., 326, 339, 389, 397, *416*
Gibbons, F. X., 439, *471*
Gibbs, L. E., 603, *626*

Hirschman, R. S., 100, *124*
Hodge, J. E., 267, *287*
Hodgins, D. C., 325, *338*
Hodgson, R., 266, 288, 374, 386, 428, 707, *714*
Hoebel, B. G., 77, *91*
Hoefer, M. A., 378, *388*
Hofer, S. M., 233, *236*
Hoffman, P. L., 431, *473*
Hoffmann, E. J., 494, *507*
Hofmann, M., *85*
Holahan, C., 805, 806, *826*
Holberg, S., *839*
Hollandsworth, J. G., 783, 791, *796*
Hollis, J. F., 701, 702, 709, 711, 712, *716*
Hollister, L., 393, 394, *412, 413*
Hollon, S. D., 197, *206*
Holman, C. P., 422, *429*
Holmberg, S. D., *664*
Holmes, T. H., 586, *599*
Hood, B., 374, *387*
Hoodecheck, E., *288*
Hooley, J., 403, *412*
Hope, B. T., 647, *665*
Hope, J. M., 394, *416*
Hore, B. D., 582, *598*
Horn, D., 673, *693*
Horn, J. L., 343, 346, 353, 368, 584, *600*
Hornblow, A. R., 28, *39*
Hornsby, R. I., 71, *91*
Hotujac, L., 394, *412*
Howanitz, E., *410*
Howard, G., 785, *796*
Howard, J., 132, *163*
Howes, M. J., 339, 374, *386*
Howlett, A. C., 661, *663*
Hoyer, D., 70, *88*
Hrubec, Z., 537, 538, *573*
Hser, Y., 718, *755*, 762, 764, 772, 773, *793*
Hser, Y. I., *796*
Hsieh, Y., 57, *65*
Huang, S. C., 494, *507*
Huba, G., 169, 179, 207, 209, *210*
Hubbard, R., 768, 795, 796, *797*
Hubbard, R. B., *573*
Hubbard, R. L., 649, 664, 718, 719, 720, 755, 756, 760, 768, 773, 774, 784, *790*
Hubbell, C., 75, 88, *89*

Huck, S., *123*
Huey, L. Y., *573*
Hughes, J. R., 644, 645, *756*
Hughes, M., *37*
Hughes, S. L., 673, *692*
Hughes, S. O., 357, *368*
Huizinga, D., 99, *123*, 135, *159*
Hull, J. G., 432, 440, 442, 465, 473, 560, *573*
Hulten-Nosslin, B., 374, *387*
Humphreys, D., 760, *797*
Hunt, W. A., 431, *473*, 697, 707, *715*
Hunter, G., *88*
Huntley, M. J., 433, *473*
Hurrelmann, K., 130, *160, 162*
Hurt, R. D., 374, *387*
Husband, S. D., 765, 774, 796, *799*
Hussong, A., 528, *531*
Hwu, H. G., 28, 36, *37*
Hyman, M. M., 267, 275, *285*
Hynd, G. W., 494, *504*

Imperato, A., 73, 76, 81, *87*
Inciardi, J. A., *664*
Inn, A., 432, *470*
Institute of Medicine, 285, 685, 693, 718, *756*
Institute of Medicine Report, 653, *664*
Ionescu-Pioggia, M., 398, *414*
Iritani, B., 871, 872, *873*
Irles, J. R., 74, *85*
Irvine, R., *386*
Irwin, K., 663, *839*
Irwin, M., 92, 385, 388, 396, 411, *412*
Isaac, N., 133, 134, 137, 142, 152, 153, *163*
Isaac, W., 494, *504*
Isenhart, C. E., 342, 343, 353, 354, 362, *368*
Ishikawa, R., 543, *573*
Ito, J. R., 703, 709, 711, 712, *715*
Iyenger, S., 77, *89*
Izzo, C. V., 301, *304*

Jabara, R., 770, *801*
Jablenski, A., *38*
Jackson, J. S., 157, *160*
Jacob, P. III, 658, *663*
Jacob, T., 50, *66*
Jacobs, L., *288*

Jacobson, G. R., 78, 89
Jaffe, A. J., *91*, *716*
Jaffe, H. W., *839*
Jaffe, J., 68, 78, *85*, 89, 401, *411*, 665, 720, *755*
Jagadeeswaran, P., *85*
Jaggi, J., *663*
Janca, A., *36*
Janer, K. W., 502, *506*
Janis, I. L., 356, *368*
Janowsky, D. S., *573*
Janssen, P. A. J., 72, *90*
Jardine, R., 54, *64*
Jasinski, D., 653, *664*
Jason, L. A., 858, *871*
Jatlow, P., 664, *714*
Jauhar, P., 805, *826*
Javitt, D. C., 394, *412*
Jeavons, C., 460, *473*, 478
Jeffrey, R. W., 678, *695*
Jellinek, E. M., *285*
Jernigan, T. L., 402, *412*
Jessor, R., 47, *64*, 99, 100, 101, 105, 109, *124*, 132, 133, 134, 142, 153, 154, *159*, *160*, 207, 237, 239, 240, 242, 263, 605, 626, 832, 839, 845, 854
Jessor, S. L., 99, 100, 101, 105, *124*, 132, 133, 134, 142, *159*, *160*, 237, 242, 263, 605, 626, 832, 839
Jody, D., *413*
Joe, G. W., 720, *756*, 761, 768, 772, 797, 800, 857, *871*
Johannessen, K., *87*
Johnson, B., 832, 838, 839, 858, 872
Johnson, B. T., 445, *473*
Johnson, C. A., 217, 220, 232, 233, 236, 237, 238
Johnson, H. J., 586, *599*
Johnson, J. G., *389*
Johnson, K., *387*
Johnson, M. K., 433, 469
Johnson, M. R., 661, *663*
Johnson, R. A., *664*
Johnson, R. J., 98, 99, 100, *124*, 201, 207
Johnson, S., 701, *715*
Johnson, V., 46, *64*, *125*, 131, 135, *160*, 161
Johnston, A., *90*
Johnston, L., *531*
Johnston, L. D., 4, 29, *37*, 98, *124*, 131,

133, 134, 135, 136, 137, 152, 153, 156, *158*, *160*, 161, *162*, *163*, 203, 207, 843, 854, 858, 872
Johnstone, B. M., *206*
Jones, B., 568, *574*
Jones, B. M., 433, *473*, *477*, 560, *573*
Jones, M., 49, *64*
Jones, M. K., 433, *473*
Jones, R. J., 783, *797*
Jones, R. T., 658, 661, 663, 664, 699, 715
Jones, S. L., *320*
Jorenby, D. E., 648, *664*, 701, *717*
Joreskog, K. G., 224, *237*
Joseph, H., 654, *665*
Joseph, M. L., 768, *800*
Josephs, R. A., 435, 457, 458, *476*
Jou, S. C., 202, *208*
Jouriles, E., 440, *473*
Joyce, M. A., 271, 276, 282, *286*
Joyce, P. R., 28, *39*
Judd, C. M., *263*
Judd, L. L., 209, 388, 401, *411*, *415*, 547, 561, *573*

Kabene, M., 50, *66*
Kadden, R., 80, 89, 90, 407, *413*, 607, 626, 704, 709, 710, 711, 712, 713, *714*, *715*, 754, *756*
Kadlec, K. E., 71, *91*
Kaelber, C. T., *387*
Kagan, J., 52, *64*
Kaij, L., 537, *573*
Kalish, R. A., 784, *794*
Kalivas, P. W., 77, *89*
Kallmen, H., 465, *472*
Kamal, M., *408*
Kamerow, D. B., 374, *387*
Kaminer, Y., 169, *205*
Kandel, D., *64*, 153, 156, *160*, 836, 839, 854, 858, 872
Kandel, D. B., 5, 29, 30, *37*, 97, 98, 99, 100, 109, 119, *124*, 132, 134, *160*, 170, 171, 173, 198, 199, 207, 511, 526, *531*, *532*, 845, 846, 851, 852, 856, 859, 860, 872
Kane, J., 339, *415*
Kanel, J. S., 74, *87*
Kanfer, F. H., 672, *693*
Kanter, S. L., 393, *413*

Lyons, C. A., 845, 854

Maany, I., 663
MacAndrew, C., 432, 474
Macari, M. A., 393, 409
MacCallum,, 188
Maccoby, N., 699, 715
Macdonald, D. I., 374, 387
MacDonald, K. R., 267, 287
Mace, R., 714
Mack, D., 290, 305
Mack, J. E., 355, 368
MacKinnon, D. P., 218, 237
MacMurray, J., 86
Maddahian, E., 119, 125, 242, 264, 845,
    846, 849, 854, 855, 858, 859,
    872, 873
Maddock, J. M., 541, 543, 546, 574
Maddux, J. F., 761, 797
Maggs, J., 130, 162
Magliozzi, J. R., 393, 413
Magnusson, D., 130, 135, 161
Mahler, H. M., 92
Maholick, L. J., 205
Mahoney, M. J., 690, 693
Maisto, S. A., 271, 276, 281, 282, 285,
    286, 540, 542, 551, 559, 567,
    575, 596, 598, 605, 622, 627
Major, L. F., 69, 70, 85, 86
Malcolm, R., 90
Malitz, F. E., 374, 387
Malloy, K., 664
Malloy, P., 603, 626, 627
Malotte, C. K., 233, 237
Malow, R. M., 172, 208
Mandelbaum, A., 663
Mandeli, J., 415
Manfredi, L., 658, 663
Manheimer, D. I., 197, 208
Mann, L., 356, 368
Manno, B. R., 464, 470
Marchel, F., 72, 87
Marcus, N. J., 770, 800
Marder, S., 396, 411
Marel, R., 762, 798
Marglin, S. H., 89
Margulies, R. S., 132, 160
Margulies, R. Z., 109, 124, 526, 531
Marien, M., 77, 89
Mark, G. P., 77, 91
Markkanen, T., 537, 575
Markman, H. J., 235

Marks, G. S., 218, 236
Marlatt, A., 432, 476
Marlatt, A. G., 559, 560, 575, 676, 691,
    692
Marlatt, D. A., 395, 410
Marlatt, G. A., 71, 90, 172, 208, 266,
    285, 290, 297, 298, 299, 301,
    304, 305, 354, 356, 368, 405,
    407, 413, 474, 582, 595, 596,
    598, 599, 671, 672, 673, 691,
    693, 697, 703, 707, 709, 714,
    715, 716, 774, 798, 806, 827
Marlatt, G. R., 464, 474
Marsden, M. E., 664, 719, 756, 796
Marsh, H. W., 181, 208
Marsh, K. L., 763, 764, 767, 769, 798
Marshall, T., 572
Martin, C., 47, 50, 54, 57, 58, 63, 65, 66
Martin, C. S., 512, 531
Martin, J. B., 561, 574
Martin, N., 64
Martin, S. S., 124, 860, 873
Martin, W. R., 653, 664
Martinez, J., 857, 873
Martinez, R., 36
Martinson, O., 847, 855
Maslow, H., 319, 321
Masten, A. S., 239, 263
Mathis, D. A., 762, 763, 764, 789, 798
Matsuda, L. A., 661, 665
Matthews, C. G., 311, 320
Mattson, M. E., 603, 626
Maude-Griffin, P. M., 344, 354
Maurer, H. S., 267, 287
Mavis, B. E., 339
Maxwell, M. E., 411
Mayer, F. A., 439, 475
Maynard, E. S., 777, 791, 795
Maziade, M., 58, 65
Mazzella, G. L., 87
McAlister, A. L., 678, 692
McArdle, J., 518, 532
McArdle, J. J., 328, 339
McAuliffe, W. E., 707, 709, 711, 716
McBride, H., 49, 67
McBride, W. J., 77, 90, 570, 573
McCabe, R. J. R., 267, 282, 286
McCall, R., 531
McCalla, S., 831, 840
McCallum, R., 208
McCaughrin, W. C., 799
McChesney, C., 409

McClearn, G., 65
McClelland, G. H., 263
McClelland, M., 374, 387
McConnaughy, E. A., 357, 368, 673, 693
McCord, J., 49, 52, 65
McCord, W., 49, 65
McCormick, W., 831, 839
McCourt, W. F., 595, 599, 704, 716
McCoy, C., 663, 839
McCrady, B. S., 266, 286, 362, 369, 607,
    627, 754, 756
McCuan, R. S., 678, 692
McDermott, P. A., 329, 338
McDonald, L. K., 761, 797
McDonald, R. P., 181, 208
McDonel, E. C., 405, 409
McDougal, G. L., 784, 795
McDougle, C. J., 666
McElroy, M. G., 809, 825
McEvoy, L., 36, 46, 64, 532
McGahan, P., 324, 336, 338, 339
McGee, C. R., 131, 132, 160
McGee, L., 179, 208
McGill, C. W., 406, 410
McGlothlin, W. H., 764, 793
McGlynn, E. A., 389
McGonagle, K. A., 37
McGree, S. T., 295, 305
McGue, M., 46, 65, 156, 161
McGuire, T. G., 666
McHugh, D., 77, 89
McHugh, P., 310, 320
McHugh, P. R., 399, 409
McIntyre, K., 699, 714, 844, 854
McKay, J., 337, 623, 628
McKeon, P., 46, 846, 853
McKinley, J. C., 353
McKirnan, D. J., 294, 296, 306
McLaughlin, P., 405, 406, 410
Mclearn, G., 60
McLellan, A. T., 323, 324, 326, 336,
    338, 339, 404, 413, 632, 644,
    645, 648, 650, 652, 663, 665,
    666, 667, 718, 719, 720, 723,
    726, 727, 731, 732, 746, 749,
    750, 751, 752, 756, 757, 758,
    760, 761, 762, 769, 770, 771,
    772, 779, 793, 798
McLellan, T., 665
McMahon, B. T., 673, 693
McNamara, G., 100, 112, 119, 120, 121,
    127, 240, 264

Meaney, M., 88
Mechoulam, R., 663
Medieros, M., 684, 693
Medline, 474
Mednick, S. A., 575
Meehl, P. E., 340, 354
Meek, P. S., 543, 553, 574
Meert, T. F., 72, 90
Meiller, R. M., 414
Meisler, A. W., 405, 410
Melby, J. N., 123
Melchionda, R., 794
Melchior, C., 75, 91, 431, 475
Mellinger, G. D., 180, 197, 208, 210
Mello, N. K., 374, 658, 665
Meltzer, H. Y., 89
Melville, J., 267, 287
Melvin, L. S., 661, 663
Menard, S., 135, 159
Mendelsen, J. H., 658, 665
Mendelsohn, F. S., 201, 205
Mendelson, J. H., 374, 375, 384, 387,
    540, 541, 542, 543, 568, 572,
    574
Mendelson, M., 313, 320
Meredith, L. S., 388
Meredith, W., 518, 532
Merikangas, K., 87
Merikangas, K. R., 211
Merrette, C., 65
Merrigan, D., 666, 719, 755
Merskey, H., 400, 412
Merydith, S. P., 340, 354
Meshkoff, J. E., 582, 598
Messick, S., 295, 306, 336, 339
Metzger, D., 338, 652, 665, 666, 719,
    726, 731, 746, 750, 756, 757
Metzger, D. S., 652, 665, 762, 764, 765,
    768, 774, 779, 781, 784, 786,
    788, 789, 791, 796, 798, 799
Mewcomb, M. D., 100, 103, 104
Meyer, E., 502, 506
Meyer, J., 54, 64
Meyer, R., 720, 756
Meyer, R. E., 72, 85, 90, 170, 201, 207,
    208, 400, 412, 419, 420, 428,
    429, 665, 716, 720, 757
Meyers, M. B., 794
Meyers, R. J., 368
Meyers, R. W., 755

Schulsinger, F., 49, *64*, 538, 540, 541, *573, 577*
Schultz, C., 554, *572*
Schultz, J. M., 374, 388
Schuster, C. R., 30, 32, *38*, *645*, 662, 665
Schwartz, M., *321*
Schwei, M. G., 419, *429*
Schwertner, H., 75, 85
Scopetta, M., 845, 856, 859, *873*
Scotch, N., 582, 598
Scott, E., 374, 385, 386
Scott, T., 269, *287*
Searles, J. R., *287*
Searles, J. S., 537, *577*
Sears, J. D., 437, 477, 478
Sears, R., 438, *471*
Sechrest, L., 603, *627*
Seeley, J. R., 100, *125*
Seeman, M., 807, *827*
Segvardsson, S., 425
Seiden, L., 662, *665*
Seifer, R., 242, *264*
Seilhamer, R., 47, 57, 58, 66
Sellers, E. M., 71, *91*, 92
Sellew, A. P., *415*
Sells, S. B., 720, *756*, 761, 800
Seltzer, M. L., 584, *599*
Selvaggi, N., 85
Selzer, M. L., *287*, 297, 306, 343, 397, *415*, 559, *577*
Senay, E. C., 170, 206, 768, 790, 800
Serizawa, K., *91*
Serrano, Y., 663, 839
Sesman, M., *36*
Sevy, S., 398, *415*
Shacham, S., 301, 306
Shaffer, J. W., 764, 800
Shahbahrami, B., 86
Shallice, T., 487, *507*
Shane, R., 765, *797*
Shanks, P., 419, *429*
Shanks, R., 672, *695*
Shapiro, S., *389*, 671, 693, *695*
Shaskan, E., 541, 545, *577*
Shedler, J., *126*, 181, 200, *210*
Sheehan, M., *284, 288*
Sheffield, D., 85
Shelly, C., 51, 66, 571, *577*
Shelton, M. D., 310, 319, *321*
Sher, K., 50, 51, 52, 66, 99, 121, *126*, 172, *210*, 398, *412*, 440, 473,

485, 487, 501, *507*, 510, 512, 526, 528, 529, 532, 533, 553, 554, 555, 559, 574, 577
Sherbourne, C. D., 389
Sherer, M. A., 568, *574*
Sheridan, P. J., 85
Sherman, S. J., 98, 122, *123*, *159*
Sherrod, L. R., 130, *162*
Sherron, P., 775, 795
Shiffman, S., 100, *127*, 282, *287*
Shilling, P., 92
Shipley, T. C., 172, *210*
Shipley, W. C., *321*
Shoham-Salomon, V., 603, *627*
Shope, J. T., 217, 230, 235, 238
Shrout, P. E., 36, 201, *205*
Shuntich, R. J., 437, *476*
Shure, M. B., *235*
Sibereisen, R. K., *162*
Sibrel, P. A., 432, *474*
Siegel, J. M., 586, *599*
Sigvardssen, S., *63*
Sigvardssin, S., *46*
Sigvardsson, S., 78, *86*, 427, *429*, 538, *572*
Silbereisen, R. K., *162*
Silva, P. A., 133, *159*
Silverman, K., 629, *645*
Simcha-Fagan, O., 132, *160*, 859, *872*
Simon, E. J., 75, 88
Simon, M., 52, *64*, 133
Simon, M. B., *160*
Simons, R. L., *123*
Simpkins, J., 807, *828*
Simpson, C. D., *477*
Simpson, D., 718, 719, *758*
Simpson, D. D., 720, *756*, 760, 762, 763, 764, 767, 768, 769, 772, 798, 800
Simpson, D. W., 761, *797*
Simpson, E. E., 705, *716*
Simpson, J. C., 399, *416*
Sinforiani, E., 87
Singh, B. K., 761, 800
Singh, H., *413*
Single, E., 858, *872*
Singleton, K. I., 330, *338*
Siris, S. G., 398, *415*
Sisson, R. W., 632, *645*, 755, 783, 800
Siviy, S., 75, 92
Skager, R., 846, 849, 855
Skeu, W., 586, 600

Vanderveen, E., 387
Vandewater, S., 408
Vangarelli, D. J., 676, 677, 694
Vannicelli, M., 806, 828
Vanyukov, M., 59, 66, 67, 122, 126, 531
Varma, D. K., 398, 414
Vaughn, T. E., 800
Vega, A., 433, 477
Vega, R., 540, 541, 545, 577
Velarde, J., 855
Velasquez, M. M., 692
Velicer, W. F., 336, 338, 357, 368, 673,
       675, 682, 684, 687, 692, 693,
       695, 696
Venardos, M. G., 783, 801
Veroff, J., 671, 696, 807, 828
Vicary, J., 58, 65
Victor, M., 394, 416
Vilmar, T., 400, 412
Vinokur, A., 297, 306, 559, 577
Virkkunen, M., 69, 70, 84, 88, 89, 91, 92
Vital and Health Statistics, 811, 828
Vital-Herne, J., 413
Vogel-Spratt, M., 543, 551, 552, 578
Vogele, C., 503, 507
Vogler, R. E., 275, 288
Vogt, T. M., 702, 716
Volavka, J., 575
Volkow, N. D., 658, 666
Volpicelli, J., 75, 92, 655, 663, 666, 756
Von Cleve, E., 872
Von Korff, M., 28, 38, 374, 389
von Zerssen, D., 28, 39
VonKnorring, A., 425, 427
Vuchinich, R. E., 582, 586, 587, 595,
       598, 600, 601

Wachs, T., 55, 67
Wachtel, P. L., 681, 696
Wachter, K. W., 477
Wade, J., 403, 404, 409, 413
Wadsworth, K., 135, 156, 162, 163
Wagner, E. A., 694
Wainer, H., 328, 329, 339
Waingrow, S., 673, 693
Walfish, S., 158
Walitzer, K., 50, 66, 99, 126, 512, 533
Walker, K., 267, 287, 770, 801
Wallace, J., 75, 85
Wallach, M. A., 393, 403, 404–405,
       407, 410
Wallbom, M., 440, 471

Wallbrown, F. H., 340, 354
Waller, M. B., 570, 573
Wallfisch, A., 714
Wallisch, L. S., 398, 416
Walsh, D. C., 648, 666
Walsleben, J., 413
Wanberg, K. W., 343, 353, 368
Wang, E. Y., 237
Wang, M. W., 328, 339
Warburg, M. M., 386
Ward, C. H., 313, 320
Ward, J. A., 842, 843, 856
Ward, N. G., 211
Wardle, J., 298, 299, 305
Ware, J. E., 377, 389
Warren, K. R., 387
Wartman, S. A., 374, 385, 387
Washburne, C., 434, 440, 477
Washton, A. M., 172, 206, 211
Wasserman, D. A., 305, 405, 411, 720,
       756, 791, 796
Wasson, J., 387
Waters, M., 848, 855
Watson, C. G., 267, 277, 279, 280, 288
Watson, D., 512, 533
Watt, L. F., 235
Watters, J., 830, 831, 839, 840
Watts, D., 353
Watts, W. A., 106, 123
Weaver, L., 847, 855
Webb, G. R., 374, 388
Webb, M. G. T., 387
Webb, N. L., 765, 797
Webster-Stratton, C., 57, 67
Wechsler, D., 322, 490, 491, 508
Wechsler, H., 133, 134, 137, 142, 152,
       153, 163
Wedding, D., 320
Weddington, W., 401, 411
Wegner, N., 764, 800
Wehman, P., 775, 795
Wei, L. J., 607, 628
Weibel-Orlando, J., 843, 856
Weiden, P. J., 398, 410
Weidenman, M. A., 420, 428
Weiland, S., 70
Weinstein, M., 133, 159
Weintraub, J. K., 105, 123
Weis, J. G., 859, 872
Weisman, A. M., 477
Weisner, C., 597, 602
Weiss, D. J., 329, 339

Weiss, F., 73, 93
Weiss, R. D., 201, *211*
Weiss, S. R. B., 657, 666
Weissbach, T. A., 275, 288
Weissman, M. M., 169, 173, 210, 211, *575*, 791, 800
Weixel, L. J., 560, *574*
Wells, E. A., 706, 709, 711, 712, *715*, *716*, 859, 860, 861, 866, *871*, *872*, *974*
Wells, J. E., 28, 39, 172
Wells, K. B., 374, 377, 384, 385, 387, 388, 389
Wells, V., 207
Wells-Parker, E., *354*, 806, 828
Welsh, M. C., 494, *508*
Welte, J. W., 489, *504*, 858, *871*
Welti, C. V., 394, *416*
Wender, P., 50, 67
Weng, L.-J., 201, *211*
Werner, E. E., 133, *163*, 239, *242*, *264*
West, J. A., 172, 208
West, M. O., 486, 508, 510, *533*
West, S. G., 235, *262*
Westenhoefer, J., 295, *306*
Westermeyer, J., 394, *416*
Westman, E. C., 666
Wetter, M. W., *353*
Whitbeck, L. B., *123*
White, D., 844, *854*
White, H., 528
White, H. R., 131, *161*
White, J. L., 512, *533*
Whitehead, P. C., 807, 828
Whiteman, M., 98, 100, *123*, 132, *158*, 239, *262*
Whitters, A. C., 400, *416*
Wicklund, R. A., 439, *471*
Wickramaratne, P., *211*
Widaman, K. F., 106, *124*, 202, *210*
Widman, M., 788, *799*
Widmer, R. B., 400, *416*
Widnell, K. L., 647, *665*
Wieland, S., 90
Wilber, C., 169, *210*
Wilber, C. H., 719, *757*, 791, 800
Wilcox, N., 684, 696
Wild, K. D., 89
Wilkinson, D. A., 267, 287, 402, *416*
Willenbring, M., 395, *415*
Williams, D. L., 465, *477*
Williams, D. R., 121, *126*

Williams, J. B., 26, 38, 429
Williams, J. B. W., 326, 327, 339, 389, 397, 416, 420, 429, 707, *715*, *716*
Williams, J. L., 172, 208
Williams, R. M., 465, *477*
Willis, G. L., 398, *411*
Willner, A. E., *322*
Wills, T., 47, 67, 98, 99, 100, 103, 104, 105, 112, 114, 119, 120, 121, 122, *122*, 126, *127*, 172, 179, 205, *211*, 217, 238, 240, 241, 264, 510, 512, *533*, 808, 822, 825
Wilsnack, R. W., 808, 821, 828
Wilsnack, S. C., 808, 828
Wilson, D. B., 216, 237
Wilson, G. T., 673, 691, 697, *714*
Wilson, J. R., 543, 551, 565, *575*
Windle, M., 67, 133, 134, *163*, 512, 526, 533
Wing, J., 38
Winkler, K., 540, 541, *577*
Winokur, G., 49, 64, 408, 514, 530, 538, 573, *577*
Winton, M., 271, *285*
Wirtz, P., 613, 625, 628, 644, *714*
Wise, R. A., 172, *211*
Wish, E. D., 847, *854*
Wittchen, H. U., 6, 28, 36, 37, 38, 39, 339
Witts-Vitale, S., *871*
Woerner, M. G., *413*
Wolf, A. P., 658, 666
Wolf, W., 843, 853
Wolff, P. H., 544, *578*
Wolkenstein, B. H., 220, 237
Wolkstein, E., 761, 762, 797, 801
Wood, D., 50, 51, 67
Wood, L. F., 606, 628
Wood, P., 50, 66
Wood, P. K., 99, *126*, 512, *533*
Wood, P. L., 77, 89
Woodley, D. V., *91*
Woodley-Remus, D., 71, *91*
Woodruff, R. A., *573*
Woodruff, R. S., 12, 39
Woods, D., 548, *575*
Woodward, R., 657, 666
Woodworth, G., 528, *530*
Woody, E. Z., 178, *211*
Woody, G., 652, 665, 666

908   *AUTHOR INDEX*

Woody, G. E., 323, 339, 404, *413*, 650, 665, 667, 718, 719, 720, 723, 726, 731, 732, 746, 749, 754, 756, *757*, *758*, 771, 779, 798
Word, C., 663, 839
Workman, D. E., *353*
World Health Organization, 420, 423, *429*
Wortman, C. B., 807, 826
Wozniak, K. M., 73, 93

Yadaam, K. G., *413*
Yamaguchi, K., 97, 98, *124*, 170, 207, 845, 846, 851, 852, 856
Yamamoto, J., 38
Yang, R., 779, 783, 796
Yao, J. K., 541, 543, 546, *574*
Yarnold, P. R., 398, *413*
Yasuda, K., 665
Yates, F. E., 267, 279, 280, 288
Yates, W. R., 409, 528, *530*
Yeh, E. K., 28, 36, 37
Yen, W. M., *337*
Yohman, J. R., 313, *322*
Young, A. C., 661, 665
Young, D., 400, *410*
Young, J. A., 465, 477
Young, R. D., 440, *473*
Yozawitz, A., 310, *322*

Yu, L., 665
Yuan, Z., 374, 386
Yuh, W. T. C., *408*

Zaballero, A., *337*
Zacchia, C., *475*, *478*, 478
Zacny, J. C., 653, 667
Zanis, D., 765, 798
Zatz, L. M., 402, *412*
Zaudig, M., 28, 39
Zax, M., 242, 264
Zayas, L. H., 845, 855, 858, 873
Zeichner, A., 431, 456, 464, *475*, 477, 478, 478, 479
Zeitouni, N., 51, 64
Zelman, D. C., 701, 709, 710, 711, 712, 713, *717*
Zettler-Segal, M., 374, *387*
Zevon, M. A., *127*
Zhao, S., 37
Zigler, E., 240, 263
Zimmerman, A. W., 653, 665
Zisook, S., 409, 420, *429*
Zubkoff, M., *387*
Zucker, R., 526, *533*
Zucker, R. A., *127*, 132, 133, 135, 153, 155, *163*
Zuckerman, M., 52, 56, 67, *127*
Zweben, A., 366, 369, 626
Zweifel, M., 75, 87

SUBJECT INDEX

Abstinence
 beliefs, as outcome predictor, 272–274
 in change process, 675–676
 initiation/maintenance, 597
 motivation, 281, 595
  abstainer's perception, 596
  preceding controlled drinking treatment, 279–280
 recovery of cognitive functioning, 401
 recovery patterns, 591–592
 relapse prevention for initiation of, 711–712
 social involvement and, 614, 617–625
 treatment for substance abuse in schizophrenia, 404, 406
Abstinence violation effect, 290–291
 clinical evidence for, 298–299
 concept, 297–298
 continuum of intensities, 299
 in restrained drinkers, 299–303
Academic attitudes/performance, 245, 255–256, 261
Access to drugs, 863
Acculturation theory, 845
Acetaldehyde metabolism, 544–545
1-α-Acetylmethadol, 654
Addiction. *See* Dependence
Addiction Severity Index, 726
 application, 323
 features, 323–324, 326
 problem areas assessed by, 323–324
 reliability/validity
  concerns about, 323, 324–325
  research findings, 329–337
  research method for evaluation of, 325–329
Adolescence
 coping processes, 105
 deviance proneness, 105
 psychosocial assessment, 179
 social support, 179
 transition to adulthood
  binge drinking during, 130–131
  drug use risk in, 836–837
  research methodology, 134–135
  significance of, 129–130

substance use effects, 200–201
Adolescent Alcohol Prevention Trial
 data analysis procedures, 223–225
 design, 220–221
 efficacy, 230–232
  evaluation methodology, 219–220
  prior findings, 218
 findings, 225–230
 limitations to evaluation, 232–233
 measures, 222–223
Adolescent alcohol use
 alcohol belief effects, 221
 assessment, 222–223
 binge drinking
  associated personality characteristics, 132–133, 139–142, 151–152
  associated social context, 134, 142
  changes over time, 146, 155
  during transition to adulthood, 130–131
  future research directions, 156
  gender differences, 134, 152–153
  generalizability of research, 155–156
  measures of, 137–139
  motivation and expectations, 133, 142
  pattern-centered analysis, 134–135, 147–151
  pattern-centered findings, 154–155
  research findings, 142–143, 151–152, 157
  research methodology, 136–142
  risk theory, 131–132
  variable-centered analysis, 134–135, 143–146
  variable-centered findings, 152–153
 etiology, 47
 measurement, 248
 perceptions of alcohol prevalence and, 218, 219, 223, 227–230
 preventive interventions
  design, 234
  efficacy, 216
  fifth grade intervention, 225–226
  public/Catholic school comparison, 224, 227–230, 231

crack cocaine use, 830
  research methodology, 831–833
culturally appropriate drug use prevention, 870–871
sex-for-drugs behavior, 829–830
substance use patterns, 858, 869
Age-related variables
  alcoholism treatment outcome predictor, 276
  crack cocaine use, 833
  dependence by drug group, 20
  dependence prevalence, 13, 15–16
    assessment methodology, 29–30
  onset of alcoholism, 46
  substance abuse in schizophrenia, 392
Aggression/aggressive behavior
  alcohol and, 52
    alcoholic subtypes, 78
  alcohol-induced, 430–431
    access to nonaggressive-response alternatives, 455
    affective, 460
    alcohol intake characteristics, 444, 456
    anxiolysis–disinhibition model, 434–435, 449, 456–459, 467
    appraisal-disruption model, 434
    cognitive theories, 433
    distraction effects, 455–456
    dose-moderated, 450–451, 452, 457
    drinking history and, 456
    expectancy effects, 432
    frustration as factor in, 431, 438–439, 452–453, 459–464, 467–468
    future research directions, 466–469
    gender differences, 456
    hostile, 460
    inhibition conflict model, 435–436, 449–451, 456–459, 467
    instrumental, 460
    limitations of research, 466
    measuring effect sizes, 445–446, 447–448, 459
    meta-analysis findings, 447–453, 455–456, 469
    meta-analysis methodology, 441–447, 478–481
    neuropsychological models, 431–432
    possibility of retaliation as moderator of, 455

provocation as factor in, 431, 436–438, 439, 451–452, 459–464, 467–468
    self-focused attention and, 439–441, 453, 464–466, 468
    situational moderators, 435–436
    theoretical models, 431–432
  as response to provocation, 436–437
  serotonergic abnormalities in, 69–70
AIDS/HIV, 829, 830–831
Alcohol challenges
  acetaldehyde levels, 544–545
  alcohol delivery method, 560–561
  alcoholism risk markers
    specificity, 537
    vs. alcoholism effects, 536
  blood concentration
    measurement, 540–544
    rising vs. falling effects, 567–569, 571
  cortisol response, 546, 547, 561
  differentiator model, 563, 567–568
  dose dependency effects, 562–563
  electroencephalography, 547–548
  follow-up studies, 558
  genetic research, 537
  methodological issues, 571
  mood effects, 568–569
  motor/muscle response, 552, 565–567
  multiple sessions, 562
  novelty factors in laboratory research, 561–562
  placebo controls, 559–560
  research goals, 535–536
  research significance, 540
  risk indicators for alcoholism, 535
    methodological issues, 554–563
  serum biochemistry, 545–547
  specificity of response, 557–558
  static ataxic response, 548–550, 551, 553
  stress-response dampening, 553–554, 559
  subject selection, 558–559
  subjective responses, 550–552, 560–561
    rising vs. falling blood levels, 568–569
  tolerance/sensitization effects, 552–553, 562, 569–571
Alcohol dependence
  activity level associated with, 49–50, 56–57

Alcohol dependence (*continued*)
affective functioning associated with, 50–51
age at onset, 46, 78, 80, 81, 135
assessment in primary care settings, 373–374
associated cognitive skills, 47
associated temperament phenotypes, 48–49, 53
attention-span persistence and, 51–52
comorbid presentation in primary care settings, 374–386
definitional issues, 266
developmental context, 46–48
diagnostic criteria, 45, 54
DSM–III–R conception, 421–422
epidemiology, 4
epigenetic model, 58–60
etiology, 48
obstacles to research, 534–535
genetic predisposition, 60, 277, 425–426, 535, 537–538
health and functional status, 380–383
molecular genetics, 82–84
opioidergic system in, 74–77
pharmacological disposition, 52
phenotype definition, 53–54
phenotype-environment interaction, 55–58
prevalence, 12–13
preventive interventions, 48, 60–62
problem drinking and, 266
risk markers, 485–486, 536–537, 556–557
cardiovascular function, 486, 498–499
cognitive functioning, 486–487
personality characteristics, 487–488
See also Adolescent alcohol use, risk among SOMMAS
serotonergic abnormalities in, 69–70, 81–82
severity
measurement, 54–55
as outcome predictor, 269–272
sociability and, 52–53
sociodemographic factors associated with, 13–16
subtypes, 78–81, 135, 538–539
DSM–IV conception, 425–426
Alcohol use

abstinence violation effect, 290–291, 297–303
adolescent. See Adolescent alcohol use
adult psychopathology and, 199
aggression and. See Aggression/aggressive behaviors
associated health problems, 215–216
autonomic hyperreactivity, 486
binge drinking. See also Adolescence, binge drinking
defined, 130
health risks, 131
cognitive impairments related to, 401, 433
late-life nonproblem drinkers, 818–820, 823–824
positive effects, 199
problem drinking, 266
response-mediated risk for alcoholism, 535
restraint. See Restraint, drinking
schizophrenia and, 396, 399–400
self-reported data, 281
subsequent crack cocaine use and, 835–837
See also Adolescence, binge drinking; Alcohol challenges; Alcohol dependence; Late-life problem drinking
Alcohol Use Inventory, 342, 343, 346–347, 351–352
Alcoholics Anonymous, 404, 584, 597
controlled drinking and, 273, 278
Alcoholism treatment
behavioral self-control training, 271
cognitive–behavioral interventions, 704
comorbid anxiety, 72
counseling interventions, 703–704
developmental behavior–genetic model, 62
dopaminergic system interactions, 73–74, 76–77
educational interventions in primary care settings, 385
extended cognitive–behavioral, 604, 607–608, 618, 621, 622
individualized approach, 54
interpersonal process aftercare groups, 703
motivation for change, 355–356

Change processes (*continued*)
stage models, 672–673
stage–process integration, 684–691
transtheoretical model, 682–684, 690
treatment implications, 677–681, 690–691
See also Motivation for change; Self-change
Child–caretaker interaction
dispositional mismatch, 57
father's substance abuse and, 59
Children
difficult temperament, developmental pathway to alcoholism, 58–60
high activity level, maladaption risk associated with, 56–57
m-Choloropheny lpiperazine, 81–82
Citalopram, 71
Cocaine use/dependence
addiction risk factors, 656
adolescent, adult psychopathology and, 198
associated psychopathology, 170–171
community reinforcement approach
design, 632, 644
follow-up assessments, 630–632, 638
outcomes, 629–630, 642–644
outcomes analysis, 633–634
vs. drug abuse counseling, 634–638
with and without vouchers, 638–641
comorbid depression, 650
drug abuse counseling
design, 633
vs. community reinforcement approach, 634–638
epidemiology, 4, 656
interpersonal therapy, 705
limbic system activation, 657
outcome studies, 705–706
paranoia induced by, 657
pharmacotherapy, 705–706
physiologic effects, 656–657
relapse prevention, 705–706
sensitization, 657
treatment outcome predictors, 722–723, 738–742
treatment strategies, 658–659
treatment success, 648, 649
twelve-step interventions, 706
withdrawal effects, 657–658
See also Crack cocaine

Cognitive functioning
alcoholism risk, 47
rationale, 487
SOMMA assessment, 490–492, 495–498, 501–503
alcoholism risk markers
rationale, 486–487
alcoholism treatment outcome predictor, 275–276
boundary model of regulation, 289–290
conduct disorder and, 502–503
in drinking restraint, 290–291, 296–297
frontal lobe domain, 487
mental arithmetic protocol, 493–494
neuropsychological screening, 310, 311–312
preoccupation with control of drinking, 290–291, 296–297
stages of change, 673–676
substance abuse in schizophrenia and, 400–403
theories of alcohol–aggression linkage, 433–436
Community reinforcement
cocaine outpatient therapy
evaluation methodology, 629–634
outcomes, 642–644
vs. drug abuse counseling, 634–638
with and without vouchers, 638–641
Comorbid disorders
assessment in primary care settings, 374–378
patterns in primary care settings, 378–386
pharmacotherapies, 649–650
severity of alcohol use as factor in, 384–385
trends, 390
See also Mental illness/dysfunction, substance use in; Schizophrenia, substance abuse in
Competence, adolescent self-assessment, 104
Composite International Diagnostic Interview, 6, 8
Conduct disorders
alcoholism risk indicator, 488
findings among SOMMAs, 502–503
cognitive function and, 502–503

in developmental pathway to alcoholism, 57–58

See also Adolescent problem behavior

Conformity/conventionality, adolescent
adult psychopathology and, 200
assessment, 179
drinking patterns and, 132–133, 153, 154
protective factors, 245, 246

Conners Parent Rating Scale, 492, 499

Control orientation
adolescent assessment, 106
adolescent binge drinking risk, 133, 151, 154, 157
adolescent protective factors, 260
drinking restraint, 290–293, 296

Controlled drinking
AA participation and, 273–274, 278
abstinence preceding, 279–280
clinical conceptualizations, 266–268
clinical issues, 265
definitional issues, 265–266, 280
demographic moderators, 276–277
frequency of treatment and, 275
methodological issues in research, 280–282, 283–284
outcome predictors, 268–284
abstinence beliefs, 272–274
family history of drinking, 277–278
posttreatment, 278–280
referral source, 278
severity of dependence, 269–272
patient characteristics, 268, 283
pretreatment drinking style and, 275
psychosocial functioning and, 275–276, 279, 281
sustainability, 267
treatment design, 267, 282–283

Coping
adolescent alcohol use, 133
adolescent assessment, 105

Cortisol, 546, 547, 561

Cost effectiveness of treatment, 648–649

Crack cocaine
among African-American adolescents, 831–833
demographic characteristics of users, 833
family structure and functioning as factor in, 833–835
initiation patterns, 837
preventive interventions, 838–839

prior alcohol/marijuana use, 835–837
risk factors, 838
sexually transmitted disease risk and, 829–831
social relationships as motivation to use, 833

Criminal activity, unemployment among addicts and, 766–768

Cultural factors
bicultural competence, 845
drug use risk, 859, 860–869
in minority substance use, 845
preventive intervention considerations, 858, 859–860, 870–871

Delay of gratification, 292

Delinquent/deviant behavior
intolerance of, as protective factor, 245, 255–256, 260
moderators of, 254

Dependence
age group assessments, mortality and, 29–30
biphasic mechanism, 172
clinical conceptualization, 662
comparative epidemiology, 28–30
by drug group
age-related variation in, 20
gender-related variation in, 20–22
similarities across substances, 707–708

DSM conceptualizations, 646–647
current edition, 421–423
DSM–III–R criteria, 8, 395
future prospects, 423–427
historical development, 418–421
educational achievement and, 16–17
employment status and, 16, 766
Epidemiologic Catchment Area assessments, 9
epidemiology, 4
household composition and, 17
international comparison, 28
location of residence as factor in, 18
marijuana, 661
marital status and, 17–18
National Comorbidity Survey diagnostic assessments, 8–9
nicotine, 659
prevalence, 12–13, 25–27
compared to mood disorders, 26–27
religiosity/spirituality and, 18

neurochemical activity, 661
pharmacology, 661
relapse prevention, 705
subsequent crack cocaine use and, 835–837
Marital status, 17–18
Matching Familiar Figures Test, 491–492
MDA, 661, 662
MDMA, 662
Mecamylamine, 660–661
Medical Outcomes Study Short Form General Health Survey, 377–378
Memory
  childhood memories of crack users, 835
  long-term alcohol effects, 401
Mental dysfunction/illness
  adolescent assessment, 179
  adult assessment, 179–180
  cocaine use and, 170–171
  diagnostic limitations, 203
  drift theory, 201
  substance use and
    DSM–IV conception, 425
    limitations of longitudinal research, 173–174
    research findings, 169–171
    theoretical models, 171–173
    See also Adolescent substance use, adult psychopathology and;
    See also Comorbid disorders
  as treatment outcome factor, 739, 742
Mescaline, 661
Methadone programs, 649, 650
  alternative pharmacotherapies, 654
  employment patterns among addicts, 761–762, 764–766
    changes during course of treatment, 770–773
    as outcome factors, 768–770
  enrollment, 652
  features, 651
  length of treatment, 652–653
  outcome predictors, 722, 738–742
  physiological effects, 652
  public policy, 652–653
  recovery patterns, 651–652, 653
  vocational rehabilitation programs, 773–782
Methylenedioxyamphetamine, 661, 662
Methylenedioxymethamphetamine, 662
Minnesota Multiphasic Personality Inventory, 310

defensive profile, 342
generalizability to alcohol assessment instruments, 351–353
validity scales
  goals, 340–341
  methodology for evaluation of, 342–345
  research findings, 345–348, 351–353
MK-212, 82
Monoamine oxidase metabolism, 545
Mood disorders
  nicotine dependence-associated, 659
  prevalence compared to substance dependence, 26–27
Mortality, dependence and, 29–30
Mother–child interaction, father's substance abuse and, 59
Motivation
  adolescent binge drinking, 133, 153–154
  for alcohol abstinence, 595
  alcohol effects, 468–469
  alcohol recovery, 593–595, 597–598
  alcoholism risk factor, 535–536
  for change
    alcohol abstinence, 281
    assessment, 356–357
    clinical conceptualizations, 355–356
    SOCRATES assessment instrument, 357–367
    substance abuse in schizophrenia and, 406
    theoretical model, 356
    vs. motivation for maintenance of change, 596
    See also Change processes
  heroin recovery, 651
  negative affect, 352
  to quit, 677–678
  for substance abuse in schizophrenia, 396–399
Motivational Structure Questionnaire, 356

Nalmefene, 77
Naloxone, 75, 77, 655
Naltrexone, 75, 76, 654–655, 769
  alcoholism intervention, 704–705
National Comorbidity Survey, 3, 5–6
  analysis procedures, 10–12
  applications, 5

indications, 710–711, 713
initiating vs. maintaining change, 596
marijuana interventions, 705
outcome studies, 698–707, 712–713
smoking interventions, 699–703
for substance abuse in schizophrenia,
405, 407
techniques, 698
therapeutic goals, 698
vs. attention controls, 709
vs. other therapies, 708–710
Religiosity/spirituality, 18
Resistance-skills training
in Adolescent Alcohol Prevention
Trial, 221
alcohol use prevention, 217–218,
233–234
efficacy, 230
potentially harmful effects, 230
Restrained Drinking Scale, 294, 295,
296
Restraint, drinking
abstinence violation effect, 290–291,
299–303
as alcohol abuse risk factor, 292
clinical conceptualizations, 289–290,
303
as cognitive preoccupation with control, 290–291, 296–297
delay of gratification and, 292
disinhibition and, 295
future research, 303
limit violation effect, 298
measurement, 293–297
other consummatory behaviors and,
292–293
as response conflict, 291–293
self-control style and, 292–293
taste motivation, 292
Restraint Scale, 295
Ritanserin, 73

Schizophrenia, substance abuse in
assessment, 394–396, 405
clinical effects, 399–400
cognitive effects, 400–403
epidemiology, 391–394, 403
genetic predisposition, 399
outcomes, 390–391, 400
public health policy issues, 407
reasons for, 396–399
research needs, 408

self-reports, 395–396
situational context, 398–399
suicidal behavior/ideation, 400
treatment, 391, 402–407
School, as risk factor, 863
Self-change, 671
contemplation stage, 674–675
current understanding, 672
longitudinal patterns, 687
precontemplation stage, 673–674
process–stage integration, 685–686,
690
processes, 682
relapse patterns, 676
stage models, 673
See also Natural recovery
Self-concept
in stages of change, 686
treatment outcomes related to, 273
Self-confidence, late-life problem drinking and, 809, 818–820
Self-control training, 271
Self-esteem
adolescent assessment, 106
adolescent binge drinking and, 133
adolescent risk factors, 246–247, 255–
256
adolescent substance use risk model,
511
Self-focused attention, in intoxicated aggression, 439–441, 453, 464–
466, 468
Self-medication theory, 172
of substance abuse in schizophrenia,
396–398
Self-ordered Pointing, 490–491
Sensation seeking, 52
Serotonergic system
in alcoholism, 68–69, 432
agonist effects, 70–73
dopaminergic system interactions,
73–74
future research directions, 84
molecular genetics, 83–84
neural mechanism, 69–70
subtype-specific effects, 81–82
associated impulsive behaviors, 69–70
cocaine effects, 657
psychedelic drug activity, 662
receptor subtypes, 70, 71–73
Set-point theory, 289
Sexuality/sexual behavior

ABOUT THE EDITORS

G. Alan Marlatt, PhD, is currently professor of psychology and director of the Addictive Behaviors Research Center at the University of Washington. He received his doctorate in clinical psychology from Indiana University in 1968 and served a clinical internship at Napa State Hospital in California (1967–1968). After serving on the faculties of the University of British Columbia (1968–1969) and the University of Wisconsin (1969–1972), he joined the University of Washington faculty in the fall of 1972. His major focus in both research and clinical work is the field of addictive behaviors. He has been licensed as a clinical psychologist and has maintained a small private practice in Washington state since 1973.

In addition to writing many published journal articles and book chapters, Dr. Marlatt has coedited several books in the addictions field, including *Alcoholism: New Directions in Behavior Research and Treatment* (1978), *Relapse Prevention: Maintenance Strategies in the Treatment of Addictive Behaviors* (1985), *Assessment of Addictive Behaviors* (1988), and *Addictive Behaviors Across the Lifespan* (1993). He is a consultant with the Veterans Administration, the National Institute on Alcohol Abuse and Alcoholism, and the Institute of Medicine (National Academy of Sciences). In 1996, Dr. Marlatt was appointed as a member of the National Advisory Council on Drug Abuse for the National Institute on Drug Abuse, National Institutes of Health. His present academic appointment is supported by a Research Scientist Award (1987–1997) from the National Institute on Alcohol Abuse and Alcoholism. In 1990, Dr. Marlatt was awarded the Jellinek Memorial Award for outstanding contributions to knowledge in the field of alcohol studies.

Gary R. VandenBos, PhD, received his doctorate in clinical psychology from the University of Detroit. He is the Executive Director of the Office

929

of Publications and Communications of the American Psychological Association. As a practicing clinical psychologist, he directed or served as consultant to various professional organizations, such as projects on crisis intervention, child abuse, and family stress. He was an Executive Board member of the Michigan Jail Rehabilitation Service Association, and a psychological consultant to the Drug Education Center in East Lansing and other drug and alcohol intervention projects in Michigan; to several police departments; and to courts in four states. He is a diplomate in forensic psychology. He co-authored, with Bertram Karon, *Psychotherapy of Schizophrenia: The Treatment of Choice* (1981); *Violence on the Job: Identifying Risks and Developing Solutions* (with E. Q. Bulatao, 1996); and "Professionals in distress" (with R. R. Kilburg and F. W. Kaslow in *Hospital & Community Psychiatry*, 1988). He received the Early Career Award for Contribution to Psychotherapy from Division 29. Dr. VandenBos is interested in facilitating the application and dissemination of psychological research knowledge into clinical practice and policy formulation, whether that be in training, clinical practice, the shaping of public policy, or in the dissemination of scholarly information to the professional community and the public.